Now I Am Here

CANCELLED

Chidi Ebere

Now I Am Here

PICADOR

First published 2023 by Picador
an imprint of Pan Macmillan
The Smithson, 6 Briset Street, London EC1M 5NR
EU representative: Macmillan Publishers Ireland Ltd, 1st Floor,
The Liffey Trust Centre, 117–126 Sheriff Street Upper,
Dublin 1, D01 YC43
Associated companies throughout the world
www.panmacmillan.com

ISBN 978-1-0350-0401-0

Copyright © Chidi Ebere 2023

The right of Chidi Ebere to be identified as the author of this work has been asserted by him in accordance with the Copyright, Designs and Patents Act 1988.

The epigraph is from Hannah Arendt, *The Life of the Mind* (London: Secker and Warburg, 1978).

All rights reserved. No part of this publication may be reproduced, stored in a retrieval system, or transmitted, in any form, or by any means (electronic, mechanical, photocopying, recording or otherwise) without the prior written permission of the publisher.

Pan Macmillan does not have any control over, or any responsibility for, any author or third-party websites referred to in or on this book.

1 3 5 7 9 8 6 4 2

A CIP catalogue record for this book is available from the British Library.

Typeset in Janson Text by Jouve (UK), Milton Keynes
Printed and bound by CPI Group (UK) Ltd, Croydon, CR0 4YY

This book is sold subject to the condition that it shall not, by way of trade or otherwise, be lent, hired out, or otherwise circulated without the publisher's prior consent in any form of binding or cover other than that in which it is published and without a similar condition including this condition being imposed on the subsequent purchaser.

Visit **www.picador.com** to read more about all our books and to buy them. You will also find features, author interviews and news of any author events, and you can sign up for e-newsletters so that you're always first to hear about our new releases.

My heartfelt thanks to Ingrid, a constant source of inspiration and strength; to Eleanor, who believed in me, and for her calming guidance; to Ansa, for saying yes, and smoothing out the narrative wrinkles; to the exceptional team at Picador who took a chance and gave this work a welcome abode; and to you, the reader, for honouring these pages with your attention.

Falkirk Council	
30124 03180353 1	
Askews & Holts	
AF	£16.99
MK	

The sad truth is that most evil is done by people who never make up their minds to be good or evil.

Hannah Arendt, *The Life of the Mind*

1

My love, it is finished and we are done. Here is a sad truth: your eyes will never read these words, though each one is addressed to you. At least your mind shall have no need to worry about the truths contained herein. Three days ago, we received a message: 'Due to adverse conditions and events on the ground, planned reinforcement and/or resupply cancelled.' Today, our once great army lies in tatters, scattered across the fields and forests of the East. The enemy we thought vanquished, whose bones we trampled over, has performed a certain magic and risen from the dead. The Easterners have put an end to our forward march and tear through us as if we are sheets of cheap paper. It turns out that we, the invincible forces of the NDM, are not supermen, but ordinary beings of flesh, blood and bone.

You knew this would be our ruin. You warned me. I did not listen, and now the end rushes towards us at increasing speed. Moments are now so precious. This understanding has freed me from a prison of sorts. I was locked into a state of mind. An acceptable 'lodging' within which I hid my feelings and conscience. Such an arrangement allowed me to travel through this war: carrying out my duties to the letter, fully committed, always deeply involved. Such a hiding place is of no use under current circumstances. There is also a new, last-minute clarity. From this position I see how (though do not understand why) the collective madness we welcomed as a nation of blind souls led us into an abyss. At the moment of writing, I have no idea about the news and mood back home. Has the truth arrived? Have you woken from the dream and entered the nightmare? Give it time. Those of us in receipt of our just rewards watch as this episode approaches its finale. We are falling, and there is nothing to slow our descent. Many of us tremble and worry on the inside, though not in panic. We understand and accept these circumstances. Our apprehension exists because we have seen and know what ugliness comes your way. Reports trickle in from those fortunate enough to escape the approaching beast: the Easterners feast on blood and see no need for prisoners.

*

Hunger for vengeance, which the Easterners have in abundance, is a potent fuel for any killing machine. The Eastern enemy behaves as nothing we have seen before. I tell you, at our absolute worst, during our darkest moments, we never slaughtered in this manner. When circumstances necessitated our taking of life, there was always a reason, a logic to our actions. No matter how distorted our justifications, the existence of such reasoning gave us licence to function as we did. The enemy we face today is worse than a barbarian and wilder than any animal I know: they kill without hesitation. They kill with joy, and kill without rules.

We spent yesterday morning and most of the afternoon fleeing from these wild hordes. Placing as much space between our backs and their claws as possible, we retreated west, towards home, until a wall of Eastern armour said 'No further!' and sent the survivors scurrying back to our current position. Then, at 1723, the fighting stopped. Bullets remained in their magazines. Shells let us be. The enemy found other things to do. A silence fell over our part of the world. No wind, no birds. The groans of our wounded faded. A strangely comforting fear sang along every nerve in my body. My eyes noticed colours I had never seen before. I could read the clouds up ahead as if they were tomorrow's papers: column after column announcing our defeat. Glory was not ours.

The remnants of our battalion gathered together and made the necessary preparations. The arrangement of defences was completed without fuss. We ignored the futility of our actions. We are the mice, the enemy a vindictive cat playing a waiting game. The moment boredom sets in, it will crush us. No matter how great our bravery, honour and determination, there is no defence against what we face. Setting aside the fact that we are outnumbered by a truly hopeless ratio, we also have a finite supply of ammunition. How many more assaults can our bullets repel?

This camp at the forest's edge will be our resting ground, and we have no choice in the matter. Not in the when, and minimal influence in the how. This realization sent me into a thoughtful loop as I stared at all around me: a last opportunity to inspect the world. A jagged shadow. A card game. An automatic rifle at rest. Tent flaps conversing with the breeze. Two men engage in a chessboard battle, backs hunched forward, heads leaning in. A water can. An abandoned bandage, twisted and clotted with blood. Who owns those boots? A holy book calls out for a believer. Some find energy to talk and laugh. A few suppress curses and rue their misfortune. Here and there, solo characters read or focus on faraway points. The shapes and smells, the colours and other components of my immediate surroundings wait patiently to be registered by my senses, while there is still a chance.

These current circumstances bend our courage and test its strength. We camouflage all awareness of the fast-approaching conclusion. In this we almost succeed, but the truth is there to see in our eyes and general demeanour. At this moment, we thank heavens for our training. It helps us remember how to act as brave men should: we grit our teeth and pretend. Defeat and death are just 'things' that happen from time to time. It is an interesting form of theatre.

A new today. It is now 0809. The Easterners continue to bless us with an uncanny silence. We sense them out there, in between the shadows and foliage. Waiting, watching, invisible. Our eagle-eyed lookouts stare at the camp perimeters and beyond, yet remain blind. This is our enemy's land. They know it, and we do not. We wait in our holding position, surrounded on every side by bloody retribution. The waiting makes us anxious: it gives us too much time to think.

In order to burn off nervous energy, I begin an inventory of personal belongings. Among the items to be catalogued is this journal. A gift from another life. The cover has taken a light bruising (it has lived at the bottom of my bag all this while), but the paper within remains clean and uncreased. I stare at it and remember.

You were sad, frightened, and constantly fussed at invisible flecks of lint on my uniform. You cried, and apologized for your tears. 'Tears keep you human,' I said. You tried to laugh. You managed a smile, and then handed me a blue paper package tied with string. I fumbled with the knot. Your fingers, cool and dry and strong, took hold of mine and guided them through the unwrapping process. You whispered, 'Fill these pages with your adventures!' You mentioned the journal again, a quiet reminder, at the end of my last visit home. A solemn affair. Seasonal winds moaned and spread dust along the station platform. You asked why the faces of soldiers boarding the train were either sad, tired or terrified. There was no need to solicit your thoughts on my face. We had spent most of my leave wrestling with the matter of our business in the East. You asked what had I done to change as I had. I said nothing. You asked whether the rumours, reported in the foreign media, about NDM behaviour in the East were true. I replied with a grumble about the need to keep work and family life separate. 'And what happens when work changes the family member?' you asked. I remained silent.

Later. The stationmaster's whistle. Those left behind sobbed, and tears filled the eyes of all departing. From you, a final expression of understanding: 'I know it is hard for you to talk. I do.' You said, 'Write down your thoughts. It will help.' The train began its journey east. You followed, blowing kisses. You ran, yet the space between us grew.

I had completely forgotten about the journal. For a while, I wonder how it could help me. An hour later, conversation with fellow soldiers and private thoughts about the East have pushed the journal out of mind. The truth is, until now, I have been too busy adventuring and fighting for Our Dear Leader and the Greater Glory to write. There was only enough time to scratch down a date on the first page. The date is two and a half years old.

Perhaps the sudden appearance of the journal, at this late stage, is no coincidence. It calls out for my attention.

I hear its voice. Or is that simply the imagination running scared? Our situation has infected my thinking with mild superstition. By the way, these are not the words of a man attempting to make last-minute contact with a supreme being. There is no need to converse with any God who saw this bloody business and refused to intervene. The journal's reappearance also coincides with my new-found conviction (but a few hours old) that there is a correct manner for me to step away from the living: stripped naked by the truth.

Last night I had a dream. The first in many months. In the middle of a twitchy sleep, my mind transformed into a private cinema. 'Now Showing: Re-runs of Recent History!' Endless reels of full-colour action, starring me. The content was grim and shameful. These were not films I cared to see. Yet, no matter how I struggled and twisted, it was impossible to avert my eyes or turn my head. I could not leave my viewing position in order to switch off the projector. Within the dream I believed an external force (with a mighty grudge) held me captive, brainwashing me with mad images. Common sense returned the moment my eyes jumped open, and saw the films for what they were: honest recordings of my own deeds, shot from a frighteningly revealing perspective. Perhaps circumstances have chased these terrible memories from their hiding places. As an aggressive cleansing caustic, they eat away at my nerves.

It would be impossible to live and function well in civilian society with what I carry inside. Time is short and these vivid recollections make me restless. Like the air in a distended balloon, the memories need to get out. A disquiet fills my heart, which has nothing to do with a fear of death. The worries about dying sooner than planned exist because of the cargo carried by my conscience: heavy, rotten and bitter. A by-product of my actions. Memories too ugly to travel with me to the other side.

Two hours ago, on the way back from a mission to empty my bladder, I experienced a sudden, violent rupture within my chest. A furious pain. I waited for a distant crack to confirm this was a sniper bullet's work. I heard nothing but the grind of my clenched teeth. I looked down, my breast was clean. Unscathed, unbloodied, yet the pain was such that I could barely stand, hardly breathe.

I leaned my back against a nearby tree. Panting. Trembling. I closed my eyes and watched a thousand shades of red and yellow burn a path across my mind. Like a bushfire, though much faster. Had I fallen into terminal madness? It was not a constant pain, rather a series of eruptions: here, then gone. Here, then gone. A pulse. For fragments of a second, and much confused, I wondered 'what?' and 'why?' and 'how?' Then it clicked. I understood. The source of pain was not external, the torment within came from my own heart. My heart, which I believed long since crumbled into dust, had returned! It announced its presence with a ravenous agony that chewed through my chest and consumed my soul. This may sound strange to you, but I suddenly filled with joy. Like a child who received every item on a list of birthday gifts, I became ecstatic. 'Everything all right, sir?' a passing soldier asked. I looked. I smiled and nodded. The reason for my happiness was the pain tearing through my system. The discomfort was proof I still had a beating heart. An important realization: it meant I was not yet one of the living dead. My heart: I feel it bleed. I hear it weep.

Sad cries. My heart remembers, and brings you here. My face against your neck. Warm. Just right. I breathed you in until it was impossible to know where one of us ended and the other began. Not once during this war had I imagined never seeing you again. Today, there is no longer any need to imagine. How I wish everything I see around me was a trick of the imagination, the unshakeable sense of doom an illusion.

We will never meet again. You will never hold me again. I will never touch you, never hear your laughter, or listen to you sing again. We will never quarrel over tiny matters, and then make everything good once more. We will never dance together again, or be drenched by a shower. No more sitting for coffee and cakes at our favourite corner café while commenting on the world passing by. There is not enough time to list all the busyness we will never get up to, and it hurts. For a moment, I am a child, wishing for some great and mysterious power to take pity and grant me a little more time with you . . .

There are other reasons for my weeping heart. All I am going to miss: the sounds, the tastes, smells, colours, the change of seasons. The sights, words, music and the food! Friends and family, those known only by sight. Hills, clouds, water, all of it. Such a shame. No more home for me. Multiples of unfinished conversations with cousins, aunts and uncles. Endless unanswered questions still float around my head. What am I supposed to do with them all?

In the meantime, as if our present circumstances are not sour enough, a question buzzes around my head: 'How did I get here?'

It is impossible to hold this journal and not think of you. 'It will help.' Yes, and I know you hear me. Perhaps not my words, but certainly you still feel my existence, out there. Listen. Then there is also the fact I know of no better listener, no one else with your strength and patience. And so, this is where we are: I, who never writes, have suddenly discovered the joy of penmanship. Your memory and this journal have saved me.

My plan is to retrace the final segment of my journey from <u>then</u> to <u>here</u>, and present the memories in a clear and logical fashion. Regarding the content: I have spent my time in the East wading through terror and blood. This has moulded my character into its present shape. All is twisted, especially my tongue. The funny-sweet radio transmissions that once tickled your ears are gone. Lost. As is my light. Today's words are heavy with blood, and death runs through them: such is the nature of my deeds. The acts I have committed will hurt and confuse you. They will challenge you to prove you knew nothing, saw <u>nothing</u> of this in me. I am sorry. Our elders say: 'Circumstances make the shrimp bend as it does.' Along the way, circumstances opened doors within me that had best been left shut. The pain you feel is the truth burning away your illusions. In time, it will fade.

2

We are here, and all is not well. It has been this way for some time. The first signs of difficulty appeared nine months ago when the Easterners discovered cracks and weaknesses in our war machine. Our onward march slowed to a crawl. We no longer captured territory with ease and speed. Every step forward came at a great price: materiel, blood and lives. Directives from NDM High Command, which had once been tethered to well-reasoned strategy, dissolved into nonsense. Only those well away from the slaughterhouse and detached from the truth of battle could think in this manner. However, our programming to carry out orders overrode our doubts. We employed the best of our skills and convinced the men to believe in fairy tales. For a while, our efforts paid off.

Six months ago, our air superiority evaporated. A mighty God (without doubt operating at the enemy's side) puffed her cheeks and blew the NDM Flying Forces out of the skies. The Easterners employed a new class of anti-aircraft weapon, lethal and agile. We could no longer move forward. We dug in and considered how to regain momentum. In the meantime, the Easterners, rather than attack our static army divisions, turned their attentions to our inadequately protected supply units, whose speciality was hauling and moving, not fighting. For every tonne of materiel that made it through, another seven were lost.

Attaining the Greater Glory had become a burdensome task. Our problem, the result of a self-inflicted wound: we lost focus. What purpose did our fighting, burning and terrorizing serve? We could no longer say. Our orders were to teach the Eastern natives the meaning of terror. This we did, until the Easterners decided enough was enough and turned events upside down. Our losses were such that national conscription was introduced. Back home, the NDM crowed: 'The nation calls on all able-bodied men to step forward as fighting heroes! Lead the nation on to victory and the Greater Glory!' Our ranks began to fill with average men chasing foolish dreams. They were swiftly consumed by the fighting. The 'below average' were then invited to enter the fray. The result was an acceleration of the appearance and disappearance of new faces. The quality of the recruits plunged until most of the soldiers joining the melee resembled children. Lost, frightened and teary-eyed. 'Where are we going?' 'What are we doing?' their faces ask. I suppress the urge to tell them to be calm, and accept their role as guinea pigs in an experiment to discover the depths to which a man can sink, if given the necessary clearance. The children do not need my cynical words.

Our enemy began to fight like people protecting their families, land, culture, stories . . . They abandoned fear. For two of the most brutal months I experienced in this war, we held our ground. We stood, we fought, we bled, we died, and watched as the Easterners, perhaps having inhaled the sweet perfume of blood and victory, developed an unquenchable thirst for slaughter. We pulled back westward. Metre after metre, fallen man after fallen man. Word from NDM High Command: under no circumstances should our rearward movement be viewed as a retreat. It was a 'necessary tactical adjustment'.

One especially beautiful evening, thirteen days ago, we learned the enemy had cut through our lines to the north. Three days later, the same happened to our south. Their aim was clear: encirclement. Wrap a giant noose around our army's neck and then choke us out of existence. We were ordered to increase the pace of our 'necessary tactical adjustments' to the west. We vacated territory by the kilometre. We abandoned everything that slowed us down: the munitionless heavier weapons, fuelless vehicles and the wounded. I am extremely proud of the men we left behind. Not one of them asked us to hasten their end. This would be an understandable choice, given the condition of many. Instead, all they requested were rifles, bullets and a few grenades. They were ready to do what was necessary.

A week ago, the fighting eased off. Sporadic sniper fire, that was all. A ceasefire. A chance to catch our breath while NDM High Command and the Eastern leadership began the process of discussing an end to the war. We received a new set of orders: hold position until further notice. Our response was to advise against. Local intelligence revealed the enemy had continued to close in from both north and south: our western exit narrowed by the hour. Were negotiations to fail and the fighting start up once more . . . our entrapment and defeat would be likely. We abandoned such thoughts. Of course that could never happen, once NDM High Command understood our true position. We requested permission to head twenty kilometres west, minimum, and regroup with the remains of other units in the area. Request denied. The peace negotiations were a game of bluff, and Our Dear Leader could not afford the appearance of weakness that further movement west would give. They reiterated our orders to hold position. Supplies and reinforcements were promised within twenty-four hours. The parts within us that wished to remain alive kicked up a fuss. We felt the noose tighten. Instinct screamed: 'Get out! Move now!' But our training prevailed: it suppressed common sense and knocked aside the truth. We obeyed. We waited.

It was a long twenty-four hours. Eventually we learned a 'technical matter' had delayed the reinforcement/resupply process for at least another day. Again, and this time with the greatest urgency, we made clear that our survival, in the event of a fresh outbreak of hostilities, depended on either immediate reinforcement, or moving our units west as swiftly as possible. NDM High Command thanked us for our input. They repeated their promise to fulfil all requests within a reasonable time frame. We also received a gentle 'reminder' that those with an overview of the situation saw what the rest of us could not. We resisted the temptation to scream and tell them they were too distant from the action to understand. Encirclement would mean defeat. NDM High Command claimed to know what they were doing, they asked us to have faith. We waited. Twenty-four hours came and went.

Three days ago our circumstances took a turn for the worse. At 0815 we received confirmation the enemy's encirclement was complete, our westward route home blocked. Later, at 0927, we learned ceasefire negotiations had ended without success. Hostilities would resume at noon. Unfortunately adverse conditions and events on the ground prevented the timely reinforcement and resupply of our units. NDM High Command praised everything we had done for the Greater Glory. They praised our courage and fighting spirit, said we were in the thoughts of 'every man, woman and child in the nation!' Finally, we were reminded of our duty to honour Our Dear Leader, the nation and our uniforms, by fighting to the last man. The communiqué's footnote encouraged us to take the opportunity provided by current circumstances and inspire the nation with the ferocity of our final stand. There has been no contact with NDM High Command since.

I spent a good half-hour thinking how best to share the news. As you can imagine, it was an unusual situation.

Usually our troops surrounded, outnumbered and outgunned others. Not this time. The expectation (during moments such as these) was that I deliver a composition of words with the power to light a fire in the men's guts. A speech to gather their spirits and make from each and every one a raging warrior: willing and ready to battle to the very end with such ferocity, our demise would become the substance of legend. As it is, expectation and reality are not always the best of friends. How should I tell the men our last hope had been crushed beneath the heels of circumstance? Half of my spirit felt tired and empty. It begged to lie down, sleep and not wake again. The other half reminded me that these men were my brothers and my sons. We had travelled here as one, and as one we had eaten, drunk, fought, burned, smashed and killed. As one, you know . . . I apologized to the men for my shortcomings, for my inability to shepherd them away from these killing grounds, and for leading them to defeat.

It was a sad, drawn-out moment as I explained our situation: we were truly beyond help and hope. The men listened. Some glared out at the world with anger. Others stared at the grass below. Some looked at me with relief.

Others remained indifferent. Many were tired. Some were so disturbed by the thought of our end at the enemy's hands, they suggested self-inflicted head shots as an easier way out. For a few seconds, morale threatened to crumble. After all, it is only the mad who welcome death without a shiver or a tear.

I remembered a scene towards the end of a popular war film. It was almost over for a group of fighting men (their situation, like ours, was hopeless). One after the other, the soldiers walked up to their CO and told him what an honour it had been to fight at his side. They were humbled and proud to stand with him one final time. It was a beautiful scene. Around me, the approach of death did not generate such packaged drama. The camp atmosphere became a sad, weighty grey. We knew running was pointless: there was nowhere to go. What to say? I looked around and took inspiration from the men's faces. 'We are soldiers,' I said. 'We do not run. No matter the circumstances. No matter the horror. Regardless of whether victory is ours, or belongs to the enemy, we are soldiers. Let us use the time we have left to make peace with ourselves.' The men understood. Tired souls creaked as they pulled together the remains of their warrior spirits. I watched backs straighten. A beautiful spark of defiance and courage appeared once again in their eyes. I listened to the coughs and sighs as the men looked within and made ready. In that moment I felt a great love for every one of them.

3

I now remember the start of my journey to this place. That hot, magical afternoon as you and I sat on the banks of Little River. The sun was especially bright. The blue above made us dizzy, as we pointed out creatures and shapes in the clouds. The air, sweet and warm, filled us with love. That was a happy moment. I remember it and smile. Our need to be together had become an addiction, surviving longer than an hour without the other was insufferable agony.

Now, however, we sat in silence, on the edge of uncomfortable. A few minutes earlier, you had concluded a lecture on the need for a life plan that looked further than the here and now. 'What are you going to do with yourself?' you had asked. I knew what you meant, yet tried to deflect your query with humorous commentary on various professions, complete with theatrical impersonations. My actions were blown off course by your impatient sigh. I froze, somewhat ashamed at having the truth presented in this way. You knew I had no idea about any of my future tomorrows, and I had no idea how to cope with you seeing this in me. To lose you, not to another, but due to my own aimlessness, was a terrifying thought. It dried my throat and locked my tongue. Then, with a touch and a laugh, you took the moment's gravity and placed it to one side.

We stood. We walked, fingers intertwined, talking, laughing . . . every so often we stopped for a kiss. Then, as if sent by great and mysterious forces, two butterflies, orange and brown, appeared out of the bushes and began to dance about our heads! You claimed they were a butterfly couple happy to share the company of lovers. You suggested we had been butterflies in previous lives. Our new orange and brown friends recognized this, and tried to communicate in a language we had long since forgotten. I remember how our attempts at psychic communication with the butterflies ended in nothing but static and laughter. Perhaps we should have tried harder, as you suggested. In the end, we agreed their presence was an omen. A beautiful omen.

I think about that day now. I had been about to write on another matter, when a sudden commotion interrupted my thoughts. Raised voices and laughter! The laughter was especially surprising, as I cannot remember the last time we heard such within our ranks. Laughter has become too afraid to visit our patch of earth.

I searched for the source of the fun, and saw a trio of men using shirts and other garments in a poorly coordinated attempt to guide something out through the main opening in the tent. My first thought was to believe the war had finally broken their minds. But mad they were not. They were simply happy to chase that 'something' around the tent. It took a few moments to discover the object of their attention. Into a slice of early morning sunlight flew a butterfly. Black with fluorescent blue dashes. It was beautiful.

Rather than leave through the available exit, the creature seemed to toy with its pursuers. The action was cyclical in nature: as the butterfly approached an opening lined with the glow of a sunny outside, the men's voices rose in an expectant cheer, reminiscent of the terrace crowds as the ball approaches the goal. The pitch of the voices reached a high-frequency peak, before collapsing into a groan of disappointment and more laughter. The butterfly had an independent streak. It performed a loop the loop that returned it to the middle of the tent, from where it continued its exploration. The message being, it would be with us a while longer. A brief pause, and then the pursuit began again.

The men made another five attempts to steer the creature towards the exit and, as always, at the last moment the butterfly changed its mind and headed to a location beyond the reach of the groaning, laughing soldiers. Such a wonderful sight. Simply and effectively, the butterfly transformed the grey mood inside the tent into one of joy. Perhaps that was its mission: provide a moment of light entertainment and distraction. A temporary respite from the gloom and weight of the inevitable.

Another (unsuccessful) attempt left the men gasping, perspiring and grinning. The butterfly made two more circuits of our space. These included trips around our heads, hops from one object to another, and a brief stop on this journal. Finally, perhaps because its work was done, the butterfly flew off on a dusty beam of sunlight. Its departure was met with a chorus of tender sighs. For a few moments we shared a collective joy at the butterfly's 'escape'. The idea that something we cared for could get away from this grim location filled us with light.

The men are presently involved in a noisy debate about the butterfly: was its presence an omen or not? An optimistic minority argue its appearance is a hopeful sign. 'Such beauty in these hopeless circumstances is no coincidence,' they say. 'When did we last notice an insect, let alone one as beautiful as that?' The practical majority swat these beliefs aside: 'We were too busy with war to notice Nature's minutiae. The butterfly is a butterfly, as simple as that.' I choose not to involve myself in the discussion. Instead, I marvel at how this war has shaped our minds. The butterfly's appearance becomes a key. A box of long-forgotten memories opens up. Here I sit, with nowhere to go but the end, and the thoughts in my mind are of happier days.

On that hot afternoon by the river, the butterflies escorted us to your front door (the better part of two kilometres away). Then, with you gone, I received their undivided attention on the walk home through Nation Park. Such was my preoccupation with the creatures, I failed to notice the private barbecue until my path was blocked by a large grill, filled with glowing embers and covered with sizzling, browning meat. The guests were young men of a similar age to myself. Their uniform dress (anthracite chinos, grey short-sleeved shirts, black belts, silver buckles, black ties, black sandals) was casual. They were not. These were NDM people!

You remember my view of the NDM at the time. By the late afternoon of this encounter, the National Defence Movement had ruled for three and a half years. The memories of their takeover are still clear. Endless hours of martial music on every radio station in the country. The telephone lines silent. Not even the hum of disconnection. I knew about military coups. Read news pieces about them taking place in faraway lands, listened to experts on the radio discuss such matters. But that did not prepare me for the thrill of one day finding myself in the middle of such a business. I dashed out into the city and began wandering around. Trucks, tanks, soldiers, blockades. The NDM troops went about their business without saying very much. Meanwhile, I was free to move around and look, though it was impossible to travel longer than five minutes without being stopped and asked to present papers. At 0943 two uniformed ladies approached me. They studied my documents for longer and with greater care than any of the other officials I had interacted with. I asked why the military were everywhere. Was this a coup d'état? Where were the heads of government? They ignored my queries, suggested I head home, listen to the eleven o'clock broadcast, and all would become clear.

The NDM wished to make a point. Their first 'grand' action was a public and brutal elimination of the previous government. At 1100, our new champion, the Dear Leader, addressed the nation from an unusual setting: a live radio broadcast on Nation Beach. The microphones picked up the squawks of seabirds passing comment in the background, and the faint sighs of the sea wind.

'Mothers, fathers, sisters and brothers . . .' The Dear Leader's voice was calm and warm. 'As a soldier, I took an oath to protect the health of our nation. As a soldier, I was taught to fend off external threats. As such, I never imagined the greatest threat to our well-being would come from within . . .' He then asked us to look around and see how the nation had been choked by incompetence, nepotism, daylight robbery and disdain for honest, hard work. A rotten gift from the previous leadership.

A first set of newspaper photographs showed twenty-nine members of the former government tied to stakes, arranged in a grid on Nation Beach. The sea appeared calm, as if it did not wish to stir up unnecessary trouble. The Dear Leader shared his vision of a way forward.

He gave us a clear path and attainable goals. He spoke of harnessing the nation's creative potential, of building greatness upon a foundation of dignity, honesty and transparency. I truly thought him mad at the time. What did he take us for, fools? We knew this song, had heard it a hundred times before.

His voice then changed in tone. We heard the fizz of suppressed rage, we heard disgust. The Dear Leader spat out a list of the former government's crimes and misdeeds. An eleven-minute-and-twenty-three-second inventory of criminal actions. The recital was followed by two minutes of quiet. We heard the gentle wind. The seabirds continued to deliver sporadic commentary, and we heard the sound of hard to distinguish metallic clicks and taps. We soon understood.

The Dear Leader picked up the executioner's cloak and wrapped it around his shoulders: twenty-nine shots, ten to fifteen seconds apart. Crack! A life gone. Crack! A life gone. It was terrible and sad. A second set of newspaper photographs showed the twenty-nine former members of our government: bloodied chests, heads bowed, bodies held upright by ropes. I remember sitting, frozen. I tried to leave my chair. I had to switch off the radio. My body refused to move. I sat and listened.

A majority of the nation's citizens applauded the Dear Leader's actions. I understood how years of political, social and economic abuse at the hands of the previous government could make one fed up enough to believe execution without trial was acceptable. At the same time, what was the point of having a National Law if we resolved such matters with bullets? By the way, I never managed to erase the memory of those twenty-nine gunshots.

Regardless of my horror at the public executions, I must admit the NDM were not the same familiar, arrogant, incompetent opportunists in a different guise. The Dear Leader and the NDM surprised us by keeping their promise to 'use our wealth and set us free'. The fortune generated by our considerable industrial capacities was channelled back into the nation. The sudden monetary abundance twisted the spirits and upset the mental balance of some who came to believe (encouraged by nefarious characters who watched from the sidelines) that wealth could be a salve for low self-esteem, or a filler for various spiritual cavities. The Dear Leader and the top echelons of the NDM stepped in when the infectious vulgarity that had entered our way of thinking threatened to become the norm.

Another, rarely discussed aspect to the NDM was the violence. Rumours. Whispers. Nothing overt. Within my circles and beyond, hushed voices spoke of someone who heard from somebody else who knew how the NDM dealt with those they did not like. 'Excessive!' 'Crossing the line!' 'Ugly!'

The NDM acts of violence were all grapevine stuff. My eyes had yet to witness any acts of brutality. But the rumours . . . If anything, their volume had increased in recent months. The whispers had built to a cacophony, and National Radio, the NDM mouthpiece, was forced to step in and dismiss claims of such incidents as fairy tales and fantastical gossip. They also informed us of the subversive and unpatriotic nature of these allegations. Rumours aside, I had no interest in experiencing 'fantastical gossip' first-hand. Yet, in spite of all the scheming and energy spent avoiding contact with NDM types, here I was.

At the barbecue, I looked around at the NDM officers. A voice within told me to be calm, to show no fear. I viewed matters of violence, fighting and the like as foolish, painful and unnecessary activities, at the time. That said, I never ran from a fight. Up until my late teens I was involved in a number of physical contests, in defence of one honour or another. Some fights were won and others lost. That afternoon, experience told me that if, as a result of my gatecrashing the NDM barbecue, a fight broke out, I would lose in a terrible manner.

From here, it is easy to see how my understanding of the NDM was shaped by gossip and macabre retellings of allegedly committed acts. Sometimes it is easier to believe what we imagine than to accept what we see. My war is punctuated with moments when I refused to view the person before me as a human, another being blessed with a unique blend of qualities. Rather, I saw what Our Dear Leader, our society and my training told me to see: an abomination. Beings whose attempts at mimicking human behaviour filled us with disgust, and made us hate them all the more. These . . . things had no worth. It embarrasses me to say, such was my thinking until recently. Today, the curtain has dropped and the rotten construction is there for all to see.

*

My general apprehension about taking a thumping at the hands of the NDM officers was greatly overblown. During the course of the evening, I discovered that not all members of the NDM were thuggish and crude. Life is filled with small lessons. This one being: second-hand knowledge is no match for what we see with our own eyes.

The men were newly inducted National Defence Movement officers, and the immense barbecue their way of celebration. My arrival added to the general good humour. The officers claimed to have instructed the butterflies to go out and find a suitable guest. By the way, these are the NDM officers' words, not mine! They delivered the information in such a serious tone, I was momentarily fooled, and the resulting confusion written across my face triggered an outburst of laughter. This was followed by a noisy invitation to join their celebrations. There was no escape from the warm clutches of their welcome. I could not deny that, but for their NDM membership, these men appeared as living facsimiles of similarly aged friends, relatives, colleagues and acquaintances. Given I had nothing else planned for the evening, I said, 'Yes, why not?'

Linen-covered tables and accompanying benches were placed around the barbecue in a large, squared-off U formation. It was quite a feast. There was an abundance of beer, wine and various liquors. There was enough meat, fruit and dessert to satisfy a city district's hunger. Did NDM officers have larger stomachs than other human beings?

Sometime later, with the sun long gone, I was deep into a debate about the merits of a film currently playing in the city's largest cinema. My debating partner, sitting to the left, disagreed and countered my praise with well-reasoned arguments. My brain was forced to think fast and push hard. In the middle of our back and forth, a voice from across the table moved our discussion to the side and asked: 'What do you have against the National Defence Movement?'

It is possible my mouth fell open as some part of me asked: What kind of question is that? Why here? Why now? Another part recalled how, during an awkward moment at a wedding reception, a distant aunt told me that every decent get-together has a 'serious intermission'. The classification was her own invention, and referred to the moment when light chatter stepped back and allowed 'the serious stuff' to take centre stage. The NDM officers' barbecue was a decent get-together. It had also grown very still. All was silent but for the sizzling meat, and the crickets.

I looked up and expected to see the kind of character who, in the hopes of being provocative, begins to harass other dinner guests with annoying questions. That was not the case. The man at the other side of the table had materialized out of the night air. He had not been there five minutes ago.

It took a few seconds. I recognized him. Back during university days, from time to time we literally crossed paths on campus. We never spoke: he was always over there, and I over here. When we passed, the greeting was usually a simple nod: a neutral acknowledgement of the other.

Bumping into him at the barbecue conjured up a couple of old memories about his permanent 'correctness'. Imagine someone who, whenever you see them, is always in the act of doing or saying the right thing. That is how I saw him back then. He was a fascinating person to watch. I once saw the man hold open a door for a pair of junior students. He did so with such style, as if he was honoured to make way for the others. In fact, I was so impressed with that move, it influenced the manner in which I allow others to pass before me. Another small thing you now know. Something else, and this happened on many occasions while on the way from A to B: a burst of laughter would ambush my thoughts. In reflex I looked up, and who would I see, surrounded by a flock of students? My man, glowing in the adoration that comes with saying the right thing. Now, five years later . . . here he is, asking what ill feelings I harbour towards the NDM!

He explained there was no right or wrong answer to the question. I should see it as an invitation to speak from the heart, and without fear. 'You are a guest at our table,' he said. 'Not an enemy. Here you are safe. Do you understand?' I nodded.

Perhaps the wine had some part to play in my uncharacteristic lack of caution. On the other hand, he did ask for the truth . . . I shared my experience of the twenty-nine gunshots on live radio. I expressed how the incident coloured my views of the NDM. I also mentioned the constant rumours about NDM members' violent behaviour.

He neither dismissed nor laughed at my words. My man nodded slowly, and then said: 'I understand. Truly. Such a violent, yet necessary, break with the old ways would horrify most. However, before shedding tears for those twenty-nine jackals, remember how many citizens died on unsafe roads, or in poorly equipped hospitals, or from hunger or depression. The result of those scoundrels' behaviour. Only gangsters treat their fellow countryfolk in this manner.' He then asked me to compare the nation today with life under the old guard. While doing so, I might also care to check how many times I had witnessed members of the National Defence Movement carrying out aggressive or violent acts. I did as asked . . .

There was no comparison between the old and the new. That was the truth. Most of us were much better off under the NDM. As for the rumoured acts of NDM thuggery, they remained but rumours. Whenever I spotted NDM members about town, they were either minding their own business or helping others. I had not witnessed a single act of brutality. This would happen in due course.

'All right,' I said. 'We are better off. And those rumours about violent deeds . . . Well, I have not personally witnessed any such actions.'

My man shrugged and said, 'That's all right.' His words had the effect of switching the power back on: we returned to the chatter and laughter of minutes earlier.

I never finished that film discussion. The rest of the

night was spent in conversation with my man across the table. The topics remained light, and ranged from sports to fashion to best beers and, believe it or not, our favourite fairy tales! We shared similar views on a number of matters, albeit from distinct perspectives.

At some point during our rambling conversation, he threw in the question, 'What do you know about the National Defence Movement?'

I thought for a bit, dug around for useful info. There was nothing but gossip. 'Not much,' I admitted.

He flashed an easy-going smile. 'Not a problem. If you truly wish to learn more about the National Defence Movement, I can arrange for a visit to HQ. What are you doing tomorrow?'

Tomorrow? Had my man invited me to an aircraft or pottery factory, a bank headquarters, a garment studio . . . instant acceptance would have been my response. But the National Defence Movement Headquarters . . . the Dear Leader . . . twenty-nine gunshots . . . At the same time, I did not wish to come across as hesitant or timid. A matter of ego, perhaps. We agreed to meet in the morning. Eight o'clock. On the steps in front of NDM HQ.

*

As I write, my thoughts are thrown back to an interaction between my nine-and-a-half-year-old self and Father. I stood before a large, well-constructed desk: simple lines, all function. On the opposite side sat Father, watching me. Back then, being much younger and with less life experience, the effect of his gaze was mercilessly uncomfortable. His infinite patience added to the discomfort. Something I had done had received, in my view, an unnecessarily complicated response: I was expected to, one, explain the motivation behind my action, and two, let it be known whether I intended to do this sort of thing for the rest of my life. Could anyone, other than Father, honestly expect a child of my age to have such insight? Father then leaned back in his chair, all the while gazing right through my head. I considered running, but the consequences were too severe and would lead to even more of that withering gaze. 'What will you do tomorrow?' he asked.

Three times, and I remember this clearly, Father tried to extract an answer from me. 'I am not asking for the right answer. I just need an answer. Any kind is good enough!' he said. By this time, I had come to the understanding that answers were extremely dangerous.

4

NDM HQ building was located in the city's East-Central District. As far as I remembered, it had always been home to one government department or another. It was also the least friendly building in the city. No matter how warm and bright the sun, NDM HQ remained cold. The combination of a stern facade and the rows of rectangular windows always set my nerves on edge. I could never shake the feeling NDM HQ watched my every move. The building spooked me to the point where my imagination generated visions of gloomy scenarios involving myself and NDM HQ. None included me walking in through the heavy doors of my own volition. I was usually dragged in screaming. This is why, as you discovered, whenever in this part of town, great efforts were made to avoid NDM HQ and the surrounding area.

That day I arrived forty-five minutes early. My nerves were not in the best of shape. Too much wine, too little sleep. The previous night, accepting the invitation had seemed like an excellent idea, an opportunity to enter the unknown (NDM HQ) and discover what went on inside. That morning, I was reminded once again that the heart of the National Defence Movement lies here. The beating control centre of the machine that lifts the nation and moves us all in a direction of the NDM's choice. As I paced back and forth in front of the dark facade, a small voice within (my conscience perhaps) asked what I was doing there.

Around the time of the NDM officers' barbecue, I struggled with the 'Purpose-in-life Blues'. I was terrified by my choices: was this the right way to go or thing to do? Or what about that? Too many options got in the way. I could try my hand at just about anything, which I did. Though I never stuck at the various activities long enough for my actions to result in anything of value. My uncles saw fit to involve themselves in my business. Such had been their way since Father's death. Whenever I crossed paths with my uncles (by that time a suspiciously frequent occurrence), they began hammering my ears with a hundred and one versions of the same questions. What was I doing? Where was I heading? 'Just trying to help you get out of the rut you are in,' they claimed. If anything, their actions pushed me deeper into the trench.

Their mission, according to Mother, was to help take care of us as Father would have done. In recent years, however, rather than offer any useful wisdom, my uncles engaged in a campaign of personal harassment. There were times I believed my uncles' aim (on the matter of what I planned to do with my life) was to worry and complain harder than their deceased brother, Father, ever had. The previous night was no exception. Without so much as a greeting, they launched into a vicious, two-pronged verbal attack on my lifestyle. They even had the condescending audacity to bring up the young, hyperactive me, the one accused of either having ants in his pants, or some affliction of the nerves. The 'troublesome' one. The one who caused family members to sigh, shake their heads and wonder what would ever become of me. What they hoped to achieve by bringing that up is beyond my understanding. However, my uncles' unnecessary reminder of the past is not what kept me awake for much of the night. Rather, it was a question of theirs: 'Are you committed to anything other than yourself?' As a child I would engage in a game in which I repeated a word for minutes on end. Again and again, until the meaning of the word disappeared, and what remained was a new appreciation of the many noises made by my throat and mouth. The night of the barbecue, my uncles' question behaved in a similar fashion: I heard it again and again. Between the hours of four and five I experienced an unfortunate revelation: so far in this life, I had committed to nothing. The non-committed status had little to do with a principled neutrality. The truth as understood from this position was that I was simply too scared to be bothered. Too afraid to face the possibility of failure, and as a result, my achievements thus far had amounted to nothing. This insight followed me out of bed and accompanied me as I shaved. It was there through coffee and toast, and travelled with me to NDM HQ.

I stopped pacing at 0754, and turned my attention to the stream of uniformed women and men moving in and out through the grand entrance. I watched until patterns emerged. Those heading in greatly outnumbered those coming out. Of course it was morning, and the start of the working day for most. By observing the hundreds of NDM staff, I soon learned to apportion rank according to how much each person carried: the higher the rank, the emptier the hands. I counted five instances in which the level of importance was such that others were employed to do the carrying. I also noticed that everyone, no matter their age, shape or size, walked upright, proud and self-assured. They moved like people who knew how to achieve their life goals. The general appeal of this vibrant energy did not leave me untouched. I felt slow, to the point of moving backwards. My mind threw up two sentences and recited them twice: 'Those with plans move forward. Those without, step back.' My uncles again.

A light tap on my left shoulder. I turned and found my man standing with two colleagues, all smiling. We exchanged greetings. I was introduced, jokingly, as a 'non-believer with a curious soul'. His colleagues (childhood friends, by the way) said they were honoured by my presence, and hoped I would have an enlightening visit. They also gave me a brief summary of their work within the NDM. To tell the truth, these men could just as well have been discussing the frying of pancakes or the breeding of cattle. I heard nothing they said. My eyes and brain focused every gram of attention on their uniforms! Since the NDM takeover, I had become aware of the appearance and spread of uniformed characters across the city and country. However, my MO of avoiding NDM members meant I was never in close enough range to inspect an NDM officer's kit. The three men in their uniforms looked magnificent! Stunning.

Looking back with the benefit of time, I have the feeling my man (goodness knows what has become of him) noticed the effect their uniforms had on my impressionable self. He must have seen how I stared at the fabric, the cut, the colour, the buttons, the belt, boots, insignia, etc. The pride I usually had in my scruffy-casual-intellectual look vanished on the spot. I stood there and felt very much a raggedy soul, committed to nothing.

They say you never know until you look with care. My imagination, and the usually safe distance I kept from the NDM HQ building, had rendered its doors the spiritual boundary between light and darkness. As we walked towards the mighty entrance, the doors transformed into two giant canvases covered in multiple layers of exquisite ironwork. The resulting piece, called 'Forest of Life', was spectacular. Plants, creatures, people and structures, given a magical depth by the morning shadows, told the visual history of the nation. I could have spent an hour studying the work.

We passed through five pairs of double doors on our

way to the official entrance. Each door was significantly larger than the one before, and the effect on the viewer was a shrinking sensation. By the time we arrived at the fifth pair, I felt exceptionally small. The doors opened, and I expected to enter a gloomy hall through which NDM staff moved in dignified silence. Instead, the building delivered a wonderful surprise: I walked into a bright and finely landscaped courtyard garden .

The garden's surface was a series of gently rolling hills in miniature. The fresh green grass was criss-crossed with a network of paths along which NDM HQ staff moved one way and another. A few park benches were scattered around an oval pool at the centre of the garden. From just below the water's surface, a grid of nozzles fired random jets of water at the sky. The trees were arranged in five groups (of shared interests or similar disposition) across the garden. Trees <u>inside</u> a building? Incredible! For a few seconds, I fought a powerful urge to run through the landscape while letting out whoops of youthful joy. How I loved the new and unexpected. Naturally, I controlled myself, and chose the next best option, which was to stare about me with a wide-open mouth.

The surrounding facades (the vertical boundaries of

the garden) were constructed from glass and steel, using a technique I had not seen before. From my position, and because there was so much glass, I could peer deep inside most of the lower-floor offices and observe the goings-on within. NDM members, every one of them fully committed to the nation's glory, went about their business with confidence and efficiency. After what might have been minutes of gawking, we made our way to the official entrance at the opposite end of the garden.

My personal tour of the headquarters involved significant mileage on foot and an almost never-ending series of introductions. We began at my man's office, which handled the strategic analysis of national-security-relevant information. I gathered from the pride with which he spoke that it was one of the NDM's more important departments. We were out and off to other places before I had a chance to discover anything more about national-security-relevant matters.

We dashed in and out of meeting areas. We visited rooms filled with maps and charts. I saw scale model tanks in one workshop, and a collection of model aircraft in another: they were not toys. One section of the building, four or five rooms, was dedicated to formulating and disseminating the NDM's message. Two of the rooms had walls covered in posters: dramatic lines, NDM colours and catchy public-facing slogans. Over the next months, I spotted a number of these posters out and about in the city.

I shook hands with people usually seen in newsreels and newspaper photographs. I was too surprised to remember the expected deference. Thankfully my ill manners were forgiven. One of my visit's highlights was the NDM Library. How I loved the place: the light, the shelves, that familiar 'old book' smell. The one that always made me feel at home. Do you remember when we tried to discover if it was a perfume created and maintained by librarians around the world?

A complex as sophisticated as NDM HQ cannot run on empty stomachs. The kitchen ensured every member of staff (and any guests) received a choice of nourishment to keep the spirits up and the body strong. A variety of healthy and tasty food was served in the great cafeteria, which was another impressive room. Picture a large, triple-height space, marked out by a grid of columns. Suspended a little over halfway up from each of the columns was a circular balcony. My man informed me that these were the prime dining spots. I looked around and understood why: the view. An entire wall of the cafeteria, consisting of floor-to-ceiling glass-and-steel panels, opened onto the garden and blurred the boundary between inside and out. The food was so much better than usual canteen fare. I sat and ate and looked around. As far as I could see, there were only seven of us without uniform, six of whom were impeccably dressed. This probably bothered me more than anyone else. The NDM members taking lunch in the cafeteria radiated joy, camaraderie and confidence. They had more important matters on their minds than my clothing.

In between the trips from one corner of the building to another, I was bombarded with nuggets of information and flashes of opinion. Every word was employed in the explanation of an NDM position or choice. At times I was challenged and asked about my views. Once, quite unexpectedly, my man asked if I was one of those who preferred to let others do the heavy lifting, while watching from a position of comfort. Later on, he asked if I believed my opinions represented the full extent of reason on our globe. At another moment, he speculated whether such an excessively comfortable citizen as myself, insulated from the machinery of society, could ever understand what it meant for the baker to make bread, or how the city remained clean, or how the NDM kept the nation's citizens safe. He always moved on before I could think up an answer. My man also presented me with arguments regarding the necessity of national preparedness. Did I know that, as we spoke, the nation was in peril? Was I aware of the vast army amassed along our western border? Men and materiel of the Western forces, who were certainly not there for farming purposes! Did I not agree our nation had the right to develop the capacity for offensive defence as a deterrent, as would any other nation? I remained silent during such moments. What could I say?

We visited a room unofficially known as 'The Shrine'. A quiet, hallowed chamber, with space for no more than a dozen visitors at a time. A perfect cube, the walls and ceiling of which were covered in padded midnight-blue velvet. There was no natural light. An array of thoughtfully positioned spotlights illuminated a volume encased in glass at the centre of the room. It was the original, handwritten version of the Dear Leader's manifesto! I moved in for a closer look, and noted the man had exceptional penmanship. I read: 'When every member in every quarter of the nation comes together and pulls as one, we can lift ourselves from the stagnant swamp that has been our home for too long. A nation that functions as a single, committed unit can eliminate all obstacles, home-grown or external, that litter the path of progress.'

5

Time must have run at quadruple speed. Without an understanding of quite how, we suddenly found ourselves in the middle of the afternoon. The end of my visit approached. We stood in silence and waited for the lift. Half a day's worth of information had been poured into my eyes and ears. It made me dizzy, and the foundations supporting my understanding of the NDM began to crumble. These cracks developed out of an inability to match what I saw around me with the preconceptions in my head. Of course, it is impossible to learn the truth about anyone or any organization within the space of a few hours. However, as with the officers at the barbecue the day before, there was nothing menacing about NDM HQ. The simple fact was, during my visit I saw and heard nothing to confirm a single one of my suspicions or prejudices. The building spoke to me. There are no adequate words to describe the vibrations emanating from every body and every surface within it. I can say, at the risk of sounding peculiar, the place felt like a home, and it called out a welcome.

The lift stopped at the second floor, and we stepped out. We turned left, and then right, through a short passage that brought us to a vast atelier. It occupied half of the floor. This is where the National Defence Movement's aesthetic was designed and perfected. The atelier was run by NDM Messaging and Public Relations, the same department responsible for the posters I had seen earlier in the day.

We were received by a member of the design team responsible for the officer uniforms. The Head of Design and I did not share the same concept of personal space. She stood close enough for me to feel her body warmth, and hear the air flow in and out through her nostrils. It was a patient sound. She seemed to spend an eternity peering into my head. It was a near spiritual experience, and just before the designer's examination caused the invisible me to float, she asked: 'Who are you?' Eyes are funny and filled with all kinds of information. They are often the starting point for unusual events. Who was I? I gazed into the designer's round, brown eyes. A quiet flash.

*

The designer coughed gently. I smelled oranges or tangerines, and blinked myself back into the atelier. Had I been staring at her all the while? I looked at my man. A gentle smile, nothing more. I had drifted away. My man chimed in with the suggestion last night might have been rather heavy on the liver. The Head of Design sighed, and then said: 'Please try to pay attention.' I apologized, and then listened with a determined focus as she explained the atelier's workings. In order to stave off the onset of boredom, and to encourage a holistic understanding of the creative process, from sketched-out idea to finished product, staff were rotated from one section to another every three months.

I looked around the atelier. Everyone present was engaged in one of the component processes: sketching, cutting, pressing, sewing, etc. A good number of the activities were alien to my eyes. What struck me most of all was the focus and efficiency applied to the work. Every move and every action appeared deliberate and natural to the task at hand. Did those who designed and built machines draw their inspiration from places such as this? As the designer spoke, a young man with an off-white tape appeared and began measuring various sections of my structure. I was told not to worry. This happened swiftly and with minimal interference. Measurements done, the young man spun around and walked out of the room.

The Head of Design concluded her presentation with a brief lesson on the evolution and multiple functions of the uniform. One of which was to serve as an integral element in the 'Aesthetic of the Moment'. This was a concept developed by the Dear Leader. 'In a time where our actions are increasingly recorded through photography and motion film, the uniform plays a significant role in shaping the world's view of our nation.' The Head of Design, who had memorized every word, delivered the full three-minute manifesto. She quoted the Dear Leader with joy. Or was that love?

In conclusion, before leaving the room, the Head of Design thanked me for listening. I thanked her for an enlightening presentation. Seconds later, the man who measured me returned with a team of five assistants. They took up positions around me. One held a pair of grey socks and a set of blue and white underwear. Another carried in one hand a black cotton shirt and tie, the other hand cupping a small bowl, half-filled with brassy-looking bits and pieces. One assistant carried a jacket. Another, a pair of trousers and a wide canvas belt, the buckle of which was simple and functional, without engraving or other ornamentation. The last assistant gripped a rectangular tray, on which stood a pair of shiny black boots. I recognized these as the components of an NDM officer uniform. What did they have to do with me?

My man noted my confusion and assured me all was good and well. He did, however, have a confession to make. While it was true, our acquaintance was less than a day old, certainly not enough time to fully assess the character of another or begin to understand them, he had, during the hours of my tour and during last night's barbecue, picked up on a certain resonance. A particular honesty, openness and wit . . .

His compliments tickled my ego and my chest tingled with pride, especially when he said: 'You know . . . There is something in you. Underneath all this scruffy business . . .' An up-and-down wave of the hand made reference to my attire. 'I catch a glimpse of officer material.' My body received a compliment as well: my man claimed I had the perfect size and shape, almost as if I was born to carry an NDM officer's uniform! Furthermore, given my education, there would be no need to join the Movement at the lower ranks. Were I to choose the NDM, I could step in at officer level. 'And trust me,' he said, 'there are certain benefits that come with the NDM officer class.' My man stepped forward and began to tempt my ears with an impressive and irresistible list of all I stood to gain. As I listened, odd shifts occurred within me. It felt like preparation. The recital ended, leaving me in no doubt about how well the NDM looked after its own. 'The choice is entirely up to you,' he said. 'I think you should, at the very least, give the opportunity some consideration.' I learned that because he saw me as an open-minded fellow, and understood how such considerations might present a challenge, he had taken the liberty of requesting a uniform fitting. I should see it as a little 'thinking assistance'. It was a straightforward agreement. I was free to take the uniform and wear it about town for a week. There were no strings attached, other than the obligation to treat the uniform with care, make notes on my experiences while wearing it and, on return, share my observations with the design team.

I was then asked to remove my clothes. All of them. My first thought was that I had misheard. But, after a few seconds of disbelief, the request was repeated. That is correct, they expected me to strip naked in front of everyone! I took a few moments to consider. Perhaps it was my pride, or a strong desire not to come across as insecure. Usually such a demand would result in my telling someone to go and jump in a lake. Yet on that afternoon, meek as a lamb, I followed instructions. To my surprise, and deep gratitude, no one looked. It was a unique and slightly amusing experience. There I was, standing, birthday naked, in the middle of a room on the second floor of NDM HQ and no one cared!

You once asked what I believed were the three most important elements of clothing. 'A good piece of clothing,' I told you, 'contains, comfort, more comfort, and even more comfort.' Well, the NDM uniform was the most comfortable, best-fitting cloth to ever wrap itself around my skin. I turned one way and then the other, moved my arms around, stepped forwards, backwards . . . No matter how I contorted my body, the uniform's fabric moved with me, no resistance whatsoever. At the risk of sounding like one whose mind has run away, I clearly remember the uniform and my spirit taking an instant liking to one another. They fused together and formed a beautiful shell. There is no other way to describe the sensation: pure beauty!

The moment of joy was interrupted by a touch on my shoulder. I turned and found the man who had measured me beckoning with his left hand. 'This way,' he said. I was led to a mirrored wall where I received a simple set of instructions: 'Take your time, sir. Admire yourself.'

Thoughtless. Speechless. How do I describe that first impression? Speaking without exaggeration, were it possible to fall in love with oneself I would have done so then and there. I gazed at my reflection. The world around me vanished. Who was that man? He looked familiar. Picture a radiant version of myself who, though clad in black, gave off a light that bounced out of the mirror and reverberated in my stomach and chest. It glowed within my heart, at my fingertips, and along every nerve. Looking back, I now understand what happened in that moment. The old me stepped out from my static cocoon, the new me opened my wings and prepared to take flight.

I remember the energy released during that moment as phenomenal. It brought to mind an incident from many years ago. As I wandered through the spring meadows, just beyond the city's eastern boundaries, six or seven stampeding horses appeared out of nowhere and practically gave me a heart attack. The size. The noise. Their power! The lady who looked to be in charge said I had no reason to worry: the horses were simply happy to be out running for the first time in a while. Dressed in the NDM officer's uniform, I felt a thousand such horses run through me. I grew inside, though not as a balloon inflated with hot air: my new volume had substance. I stared at me in the mirror and saw glory. My flesh tingled and became hot. A result of the friction taking place within. My soul, it changed shape. Back then, of course, it all felt so wonderful. I was a beautiful sight. Near perfect. The one blemish, if we may call it that, was the shadow that flickered in the eyes of my reflection.

Once, long ago, I heard one of Mother's friends claim to have become afraid of herself. They were involved in what I called 'grown-up' talk. However, the concept of being afraid of oneself fascinated my young mind, and I spent a few weeks, without success, thinking how best to achieve such a condition. Had this memory come to mind as I stared in the mirror, would I have recognized the true darkness of the shadows in my eyes, and become afraid? As it was, I did not. Instead, I gazed and admired my glorious self. Oh how my spirit grinned. It felt reborn. You know, along the way, I sometimes wondered how a combination of colour, cloth, cut and shiny leather boots could bring about such transformation. Today, I believe the answer is because I am an ordinary man, filled with basic desires. I wished for a uniform, and now I am here.

I left NDM HQ clad in magnificent black. My 'test' uniform bore no official insignia other than the NDM emblems integral to its design. It gave me no rank and no particular position. However, as I meandered through the city, it did not take long for the uniform's effects to become apparent. A change, though not so much within myself (that metamorphosis had already taken place, back in the NDM atelier), but in the public's reaction to my presence. There was a new deference that took some getting used to. I received an automatic right of way, everywhere. For example, as I casually approached the doors of a department store, a man (a good twenty years my senior) grabbed his partner (also of similar age) as she entered the door. She was just as surprised as I, when her man scolded her for failing to notice my presence and let me through. I offered to wait for them to go through the door, but the gentle, polite style I borrowed from my man failed to work in that particular instance. The man kicked up such a fuss, the only way I could get the couple to walk in first was by invoking imaginary authority. Everywhere, people stood back to let me through. It was an unusual yet pleasant experience.

At one point I entered a park without knowing why I was there. To my right, a hive of primary school children were chaperoned by three ladies who oozed experience and self-control. I watched them pass, every one of them staring wide-eyed and open-mouthed. It was all too much for the second to last child, who broke ranks and ran up to me. His actions provoked an instant reaction from the rest of the class (minus the chaperones). Within seconds I was surrounded by a buzzing, cheerful crowd of children, filled with laughter and brimming with questions. Was I a soldier? Where was my rifle? Was I a general? Did I have a tank? The adoration and attention felt very good. My spirits received a much-needed shot of vitality.

I walked for hours, catching smiles and gracious nods from the citizens. Their attitude (and this memory could be distorted by time and circumstance) suggested I was a different kind of being. They gazed up, I looked down. Was it true, the uniform transformed me into a man of higher status? A better man? A greater man? It felt this way as I experienced the world on that first afternoon dressed in NDM officer kit.

Ah, I can still see the burst of surprise that lit up your face when I arrived the next morning. You were intrigued, claimed the uniform made me look 'interesting', and could not wait to ask your friends for their opinions. The rest of your family, on the other hand, were clear in their approval of my new attire. And my family . . . Father, long dead, was unable to comment and Mother was still too busy with grief. My younger sisters looked, shrugged and then asked how I could possibly be a soldier without a gun.

The uniform allowed me to feel a new range of sensations. Previously dormant parts of my being awoke and prepared for action. Potent and powerful. From where I sit now, it is easy to think of the old tales where adorning oneself with a particular attire, or using a specific tool, led to the capture (or destruction) of the soul. There are truths in those ancient myths. Two days after my trip to NDM HQ, I signed up for officer training. You supported my new and unexpected allegiance to the NDM, and my need to explore what it meant to commit to a belief. Though you also warned me to remain wary of the power of collective thought. I laughed at that and professed to know what I was doing. Your questions and occasional comments made it clear you never fully accepted my reasons for joining up. You were right. The reasons I gave were feeble and built upon shaky foundations and big talk. I lied because I feared your reaction. I was too ashamed to admit my move in this direction was not driven by philosophical insight or the need to commit. The motivation to join the NDM was driven by nothing more than a desire to keep hold of what the uniform gave me: love, respect and authority. That was all it took to turn my head and send me along this disastrous path.

On the matter of our training, there was one class called 'Self-Identification'. I never discussed it before because we were explicitly forbidden from doing so. The lessons in this class were for the elite and no one else. In truth, it was, and still is, difficult to view the happenings in Self-Identification as lessons. Our sole activity was to chant a number of carefully selected mantras for various lengths of time. I honestly planned to tell you about this class one day, when circumstances allowed. Well, here we are . . .

On the day of our final class, two hundred and twenty-five of us stood erect, arranged in a fifteen-by-fifteen grid, three paces apart. Our location was a large aircraft hangar. At the far end of the space, the hands of a large clock mounted on a white panel indicated thirteen minutes past five in the morning. Before us a stocky sergeant, more bear than man, stood legs apart in the manner of a conqueror. He barked out a question: 'What are you?' We officer cadets replied with a resounding: 'I am a God!' 'What are you?' he roared. 'I am a God!' we thundered. 'What are you?' 'I am a God!' Initially the timing of our replies was a bit rough. Some of the men shouted out a touch too early, or a shade too late. Though by 0600 our voices had fused into a synchronized rhythm.

> *'What are you?' 'I am a God!' 'What are you?' 'I am a God!' 'What are you?' 'I am a God!' 'What are you?' 'I am a God!' 'What are you?' 'I am a God!' 'What are you?' 'I am a God!' 'What are you?' 'I am a God!' 'What are you?' 'I am a God!' 'What are you?' 'I am a God!' 'What are you?' 'I am a God!' 'What are you?' 'I am a God!' 'What are you?' 'I am a God!' 'What are you?' 'I am a God!'*

I repeat these words in the hope you can understand the madness of our situation. 'What are you?' 'I am a God!'

Again and again and again. The sergeant barked, and we screamed in reply. Our longest chanting session in the Self-Identification class had been three hours. On the final day of class we roared through that record with ease. 'What are you?' 'I am a God!' 'What are you?' 'I am a God!'

1100. A man on the left, close to where I stood, collapsed. He fell to the ground and was quietly removed. The muscles in our necks and throats were on fire, and had been so for a while. Our lungs begged for mercy. Our bones were shaken by the roar of our own thunder. 'What are you?' 'I am a God!' Whatever kept us going came from somewhere beyond ourselves.

1230. Agony and a deep, deep hatred of the sergeant. A few more men were removed. We found strength and perseverance in oneness. Meanwhile, my mind was not happy and threatened to climb out of my body. My ears heard what was not there. Donkeys! Mad donkeys. Thousands of screaming donkeys. But there were no donkeys in this space, only screeching officers-to-be. 'What are you?' 'I am a God!'

1310. I spent the last quarter of an hour wishing for sleep or death. Anything but the chanting. My body despised me for putting it through such torment. It was not my fault. Something else was in control. Our shouts were now driven by force of habit, and none of us could stop the noise erupting from our throats. 'What are you?' roared the bear. 'I am a God!' we screamed.

They say, just before the moment of death, a film of our lives plays out in the theatres of our minds. Obviously no one living can say whether or not this is true. I can, however, tell you (based on personal experience) that being trapped in the prison of one's final hours adds a vibrancy to the memories. As I now remember, at 1335, as our vocal cords prepared to die and our bodies collapse, we felt a light.

The sun threw down a beam. It erased our pain, removed our suffering, and replaced them with a sense of supremacy over every other being. We felt the change of status in our flesh, in our bones, our hearts and minds. The agony and fatigue were gone. With our feet planted firmly on the ground, our spirits rose metres into the air as our chanting elevated us into a state of collective ecstasy. There was no longer any need for the sergeant's question. The chant 'I am a God! I am a God! I am a God!' thundered around the aircraft hangar for another hour and thirty minutes.

Meanwhile, in the world around us, the armies massing along our western borders built up an aggressive momentum. There was nothing friendly about their presence. A radio reporter described the Western Armoured Divisions as 'fields of cats, waiting to pounce'. The language employed in communications between the Dear Leader and the Head of the West sharpened in tone. Unfortunately, neither man was able to hear the other. Pride is a stubborn and meddlesome force. Vicious polemics flew back and forth between our capitals. The angry poison trickled down and spread across the fields and streets. It touched us all. We no longer asked if war was coming. We wondered when.

Ah! A last-minute intervention at the behest of our bordering nations. The two leaders flew off to neutral territory and engaged in urgent talks aimed at defusing an explosive situation. The radio and the papers inserted words such as 'De-escalation' and 'Compromise' and 'Reason' into their headlines. For seven tense and infinitely long days, the Dear Leader 'negotiated'. The nation waited, breathless. A few of us noticed Hope pack its bags and head for safety.

6

War arrived during the second month of officer training. Early in the afternoon on the eighth day of peace talks, a flood of noisy chatter from the West claimed one of our units had broken through the border and attacked their troops. There were no NDM units in the vicinity of the alleged assault. We relayed this knowledge to the West, together with an urgent request for them to check their information again. In reply: disconnected lines of communication and white noise. Hours later we learned that a truckload of our well-known situational artists, in a bout of drunken foolishness, had crossed the border and hurled paint at Western army tanks. Apparently they wanted to make a statement of sorts. The unfortunate artists did not leave behind a note, and the deeper thinking contained within their statement was never known. The artists never discovered the wider repercussions of their actions. The Western delegation viewed the tossed paint as an insult to their armed forces and their nation. Such a deliberate and violent provocation could not be tolerated.

They swore our attack would be avenged. The Western negotiating delegation's response was needlessly dramatic: they stormed out of the talks and flew back to their capital. Our people were stunned, describing the Westerners as 'crying like a nursery of spoiled infants over a few splashes of paint'.

The Western leader was a weak man with a rotten spirit. He also had an ability to find personal insult and mischief lurking in every shadow on the ground, every cloud floating above, and certainly in a spot of paint. He was noisy, and we joked that his bark could be heard on the other side of the globe. He loved attention, and appeared happiest when showing off his latest excessive vanity project to adoring crowds. It is on record that their leader had paid followers! They went everywhere with him, cheering his every word and action. In the meantime, he, together with a select group of friends, plundered and squandered their land's wealth as if it were a personal cache of gold.

The Western leadership were a malfunctioning bunch, with nothing but corruption and a large, angry army to show for decades of rule. The rapid and enthusiastic embrace of war served as a convenient distraction: a well-known, often-used move. We saw through our neighbour's flimsy excuse for a declaration of war. The Western attack was driven by a case of sour grapes. The NDM's rise to power, together with its anti-corruption practices, put an end to the multiple kickback schemes established between the Western leadership and our since dispatched government. We hurt their wallets, and so they attacked. However, far more damaging than the bullets, bombs and shells was the West's treachery. We had once been such happy neighbours.

The result of our not-quite-ready military status was a series of heavy defeats. Worried voices asked why the NDM leadership had not tried harder to achieve a peaceful resolution. Those voices were few, and quickly shut down with a reminder that 'you cannot make peace with treacherous souls'. In the meantime, our neighbours to the north and east, perhaps sensing blood or an opportunity for profit, introduced irrational trade tariffs and other border-related hindrances. International shipping declared our southern ports 'unsafe' and rerouted their vessels to less volatile locations. Uncertainty and manic hoarding became the order of the day.

In addition to the slow strangulation of the nation and steady loss of our westernmost lands, we received a new gift from our enemy: fear. The confusion of war let the truth about our defeats evolve into a series of increasingly exaggerated tales and rumours. The Western forces were transformed into an invincible monster. One that was heading our way. A monster that, on closer inspection, was no more than the brutal and deadly combination of men and their machines. Unfortunately fear blocked much of our thinking. We used rumours and lies to build a terrifying version of the truth. Fear also gnawed at the bonds holding the nation together. We began to fall apart. The pillars of rationality, common sense and organization crumbled. Have you ever watched a herd of sheep panic? Some dash this way, others run that way, some become locked in a paralysis of indecision that keeps them planted to the spot. The initial phase of the war with the West was marked by nationwide chaos, which brought out the darker side of our survival instinct. Civility and compassion were kicked into the bushes. Even Nature seemed affected by the conflict: the wind hissed with increased aggression, birdsong became angry and shrill. Meanness and mistrust ran free. The idea of 'us' fell out of fashion. In its place appeared an obsessive focus on the 'me'.

*

Not all of us had the courage to remain. Those with the inclination, and means, packed what they could and fled. I understood their reasons for running (we all wish to live), but still found it unfair. We were taught that survival is a reward for the fittest. During those days, it appeared fitness was determined by the size of one's cash reserves. I watched one family after another scurry off until, one day, time ran out for all attempting to flee. I remember that moment well . . .

I had a few free days, and opted to spend them with Mother and my sisters. Mother was her familiar introverted self, and left me unsure whether she was happy to see me or not. My sisters, on the other hand, radiated joy and enthusiasm at my presence. They attacked me with a full battalion of queries about officer training, questions that had clearly been gathered in preparation for my appearance.

At 0420, the sound of excited voices in the street woke me up. I climbed out of bed, walked to the window . . . it was the family opposite. They had piled an impossible amount of luggage into their car. I watched them hug everyone in the small crowd that had gathered, before climbing in (three children in the rear, mother and father in front) and driving off. That the vehicle agreed to move was a miracle in itself! Two hours later, while enjoying my morning mug of coffee, those same neighbours reappeared, luggage and all. Their faces were so sad, and scared. At the behest of the Western leadership, the surrounding nations had sealed their borders, and also denied us access to their airspace. All routes and passages out of the country were closed. I heard months later, by way of my sisters, that the family had missed the border cut-off by fifteen minutes. En route to the airport, they were forced to make three stops because the terrified father's driving gave the children the most awful motion sickness. Wartime and tales of misfortune are very good friends.

The nation was trapped and alone. The worried voices grew louder, and this time no one shut them down. There was no hiding the daily funerals. Men too young to die, but dead nevertheless. Rumour had it, many of the sealed coffins were filled with ballast, as the battlefield had eaten the bodies. The nation trembled. The nation prayed for miracles. The Dear Leader responded. He spoke to us with the voice of a lion. Here, on the edge of ruin and death, I still hear those words. I remember how they straightened our backs, and filled every heart in the land with courage . . .

'The West, once a trusted friend, has shown its true self. They are not brothers and sisters, but a pack of mad dogs who run wild over our beautiful lands. I hear your voices ask: Why have we died at their hands? Why do they consume our territory with such abandon? Why do we absorb blow after blow after blow? The answer, my people, is as simple as it is unfortunate: we were not prepared.' Nothing the Dear Leader said was news to our ears. But we listened all the same. We were calmed by his simple honesty, and the fact he did not treat us as fools.

'Today, I come with good news.' The Dear Leader paused for a few seconds. 'Our forces are now able and ready to remind these gangsters from the West who we are!' The Dear Leader spoke to the nation of our warrior ancestry: 'Deep within every man, woman and child in the land is a warrior. A fighter!' The Dear Leader then commanded us to seek out this fighting spirit within ourselves, and set it free. 'Let it become the wind that blows the enemy dirt back from whence it came.' I have a recollection of listening and feeling a tingling sensation spread over my skin. Whether this was a mere coincidence, or the symptoms of the effect of the Dear Leader's words, I cannot say.

'A family is stronger than one who stands alone,' he said. 'As a nation, as a family, our strength has no bounds. There are no limits to what we can achieve. Citizens of the hamlets, villages, towns and cities in our beautiful nation, bound together by geography, language, culture and our collective histories, let us be one! As one single united family, we shall stop the enemy. We will drive those dogs from our lands and remove every last trace of their existence from our soil! My mothers, my fathers, sisters, brothers, my daughters and sons, it is time to fight!' The Dear Leader spent the next quarter of an hour setting out his vision for our path to victory. His love for the nation moved every one of us. The hollows in our chests filled with a determined fire.

The inspirational effects of the Dear Leader's speech were reflected in the radio and paper headlines, and also in the general demeanour of the nation's citizens. Across the country, here in the city, we began to hear stories about quarters of society coming together and unexpectedly rediscovering cooperation, sharing and mutual protection. During this period there was also an increase in the number of new faces on the city's streets. The newcomers were easy to spot. It was in their eyes and facial expressions: an unsettled, haunted shock. It was there to see in the peculiar way many had of moving from A to B, as if trying to evade invisible hunters. We welcomed them and provided comfort where possible. In those days, I had to try to imagine what events could paint such horror onto a face. Back then.

In the meantime, the officer training programme intensified. Leisure became ancient history. Ever-increasing portions of our time were devoted to studying battlefield tactics and the like. Increased emphasis was placed on flexibility and improvisation.

Two weeks after the Dear Leader's rousing speech, the enemy's march into our land came to a halt. The Westerners were taken aback by our new-found will to resist at all costs. Our armies remained frozen for a month. We made good use of the time afforded by the stalemate to manoeuvre ourselves into an advantageous position. Once NDM High Command determined all was ready, we struck. Our forces, supported by the nation's courage, began to move west. Buds of cautious optimism bloomed.

There was pride and joy as our unconventional battle methods terrified and scattered the Western troops. We reduced them to a broken, frightened mob. Decimated and humiliated on the battlefield, the enemy began a retreat. It quickly evolved into a rout.

My position and circumstances during officer training gave me access to a stream of insider information. This was primarily due to my trainee posting to NDM High Command, which occupied the whole of the top floor of the once feared NDM HQ. I was now one of them, and the building had become a second home.

I was tasked with clerical matters that mostly consisted of map preparation. Not cartography, rather the preparation of the maps employed during various strategic meetings. When performed as expected, mine was an invisible function. This transparency allowed me to listen in on the sounds of military success. Those sounds increased in volume as it became clear the Western armies had no response to our renewed fighting spirit. We thought faster, and fought harder. The strong erased the weak.

A side note about my time with the maps. There was a particular trio of senior officers at NDM High Command who were nowhere near as competent as their rank implied. Areas within their brains usually reserved for reason and common sense had quite probably been displaced by ego. The senior men could not understand what they saw on the maps, and rather than admit this in front of their colleagues, they used me as a vent for the fury ignited by embarrassment caused by their ignorance. In response to this frequent harassment, I developed a map data coding system comprising coloured dots and blocks. It allowed the trio to understand what they saw on the maps, and do so in a manner that made them look smart. It also kept them off my back.

The latter phase of my posting, as we approached the moment of victory, was especially interesting. I was present during five heated discussions (perhaps shouting contests is a better description). The NDM High Command debated the pros and cons of halting our advance at the border, or pushing on to capture Western territory. A small clique desperately wished to teach the Westerners a lesson. One to be remembered for centuries. They believed this could be achieved by continuing our forward momentum and destroying everything between our border and their capital city. A larger group cautioned against a loss of focus, and reminded all present that our military goal was the removal of Western forces. The Dear Leader was present during the fifth and final such meeting. I got to see him in the flesh for longer than a passing moment. Photographs and film could not capture the aura of this man. He had an air about him you needed to experience in order to understand.

I watched in awe as the Dear Leader listened carefully to both points of view. With arguments made, he sat in silence, palms together (as if in prayer), head raised, and eyes focused on some point far beyond the ceiling. Eventually, after an exceptionally long two minutes, the Dear Leader took a sip from his glass of water and said: 'War is an unfortunate but necessary horror. Victories are covered in blood and scarred with lost souls. We stop at our borders.' The Dear Leader believed the manner in which we drove the Western forces from our lands was lesson enough. 'Let them surrender,' he said, and received a round of applause from the majority in the room. Those who argued in favour of further conquest struggled to hide their disappointment. One high-ranking officer, in charge of the National Defence Appliance Programme, was so infuriated he lost his composure and began a bulging-eyed song and dance about the need to battle-test certain new weapons systems. The man complained at length about the time and effort and funding spent on the weapons. The Dear Leader nodded patiently, as a parent listens to a rambling child, and then thanked the man for his outstanding efforts. Of course he recognized, and was excited by, the potential of such weaponry. However, with the war as good as won, he saw little benefit in revealing the extent of our military capabilities to others. The new weapons would remain out of sight for the time being. The high-ranking officer had little choice but to sigh and accept defeat.

Annihilation is an ugly word, though it is an honest description of the Western army's fate. An obstinate pride infected the minds of the Western leadership and blinded them to the truth. On four occasions we offered surrender proposals that provided safe passage home for the Western troops still within our borders. Their leaders remained stubborn and did not believe we would punish their forces as we did, until we did just that. The battlefield slaughter cleared the Western leadership's minds, and our fifth proposal was accepted unconditionally. The surrender terms, given what the Westerners had done to us, were generous and fair, an exercise in restraint.

7

Peacetime. The Dear Leader's compassion towards the Westerners, in which he made clear our quarrel was with their leaders, and not with the citizens, had the additional effect of shaming the Western leadership and turning their people against them. Constitutional shifts and impeachment proceedings soon removed the old guard. Thankfully, the transfer of power occurred without the live radio horror our nation had experienced. The guilty received lengthy prison sentences during which they were free to reflect upon their deeds.

The new Western leadership, the polar opposite of the previous overlords, believed in progress and prosperity through mutual cooperation. A renewed emphasis was placed on our nations' common interests. New channels of communication opened wide, and reciprocal agreements were signed: our nations declared they would do everything in their power to prevent a repeat of the recent past. The devastating results of a communication breakdown were only too visible in every town between our midwest and the Western border. The rubble, the shattered spirits, the haunted eyes. Too much sorrow.

As for the lands to our north . . . a state of excellent relations was restored. We signed similar trade and diplomatic agreements to those made with the Westerners. All would have been good and well, were it not for the Easterners' brooding, unforthcoming stance. Communication, when it occurred, was strained and prickly. The relationship between our two nations soon devolved into one of 'necessary accommodation'. International trade did resume, and the border regions regained their natural hustling, bustling way of life. As before, we purchased essential raw materials from our neighbours and fed these to our many industries. The resulting variety of finished products were exported to the lands around us, including the East. All was just as before, but for that cloud.

As the wise often say: 'Silence carries its own message'. The Eastern reticence had us pondering their true intentions. Theirs was not the behaviour of a happy neighbour. What were they thinking? What were their plans? It was impossible to know as we barely spoke. The only information we had regarding the Easterners' position was their persistent and polite refusal to engage in high-level communication: they claimed all was fine between our nations, and further discussions unnecessary. Our response to Eastern behaviour, led by the Dear Leader, was to order all relevant officials to develop a contingency plan. One part of the plan included instructions to quietly build up a stockpile of essential raw materials. Another part of the plan asked for the nation's top strategists to come together to map out a route that would afford us maximum protection.

A lesson learned from the recent conflict was the importance of understanding what the world around us thought at any given moment. With this in mind, the NDM created the Ministry of Data and Security, and blessed it with an instruction guide filled with empty pages. The rules governing what was deemed acceptable practice within the Ministry of Data and Security were viewed as a work in progress. The blank pages would eventually be filled with a compilation of 'field observations'. Since there were no financial reference points for such an undertaking, the new ministry was given an ample and flexible budget.

The Ministry of Data and Security took form and quickly evolved into two divisions, one being External

Data and Security, known as the EDS. Their task was to collect all available information regarding conditions in our neighbours' systems (political, economic, military), and then translate the data into useful intelligence. The EDS were extremely adept at digging up information, no matter how well hidden, and during their first three months of operation brought to light a number of interesting matters. For instance, they discovered one of the primary reasons for our Eastern neighbour's behaviour: disappointment and a festering bitterness with regard to our victory over the Westerners. This, in turn, was connected to the contents of a secret, and quite despicable, agreement signed between the Easterners and the previous Western government. Following our expected defeat, the West and East planned to take joint control of our nation's industries and natural resources. Our victory put an end to such hopes. Exactly how the EDS managed to unearth these documents remains a mystery.

Another interesting and related matter: the Eastern economy was in terrible shape. Their public-facing, theatrical extravagance was all a sham, built upon lies and vague promises. Generations of corrupt and thoroughly incompetent officials, behaving in a manner similar to the former Western leaders, had emptied the nation's accounts, thus limiting its ability to progress. The EDS noted ripples of social discontent spreading through the usually calm Eastern society, as the citizens' patience wore thin. Protests against raised fuel and food prices increased in number and size. There was a worrying multiplication in the number of recorded disorderly and seditious acts. The EDS detected whispers that the Eastern leadership's nerves were on edge, and the search was on for an event, a ploy of sorts, to deflect attention away from the effects of internal rot. The memories of the faux attack used as a pretext by the West to declare war were still fresh in our minds. The EDS kept watching.

The Dear Leader, and his deputies at the top of the NDM, used the knowledge gleaned by the EDS to formulate a proposal of financial assistance. It was in our national interest to have peace and calm in the East. Remember, a happy family sees no need to quarrel with their neighbours. Our envoy in the East, following an insulting five-hour wait, presented the proposal, with the very best of intentions. We offered to pay twenty-four months in advance for our projected raw material needs over the next five years. This would allow the Eastern leadership to free up funds for pressing internal matters. We also offered the Easterners a line of financial credit with favourable rates of interest, accompanied by a justifiable demand for exclusive access to their copper and aluminium deposits.

The verbal ferocity of the Eastern response surprised us. They screamed in our direction: What an insult! How dare we treat their nation as if it were a breadline candidate! Of course we meant nothing of the kind. The Dear Leader immediately apologized for any misunderstanding, and then invited the Eastern leadership to our capital for talks. The invitation was slapped aside. The Easterners, according to EDS reports, believed there was more to gain by playing the hapless victim to our domineering merchant of greed. That was not a good sign.

The second division in the Ministry of Data and Security dealt with matters closer to home. It was not unusual to find people from neighbouring nations resident within our borders. This had always been the way of our nation. We accepted the place of one's birth as coincidence, but saw where one lived as a choice. And so our policy towards strangers was one of generous hospitality. Any who chose to live within our borders were welcomed with open arms, treated as equals, and given the same rights as everyone else. The logic behind this approach being that outsiders brought with them a fresh perspective that challenged our own ideas. The difference in cultures, languages, cuisine, etc., forced us to look again at what made us who we were. The result of such continued self-reflection should benefit the nation. The one obligation for our guests was that they follow the 'house rules'. The foundations of this idea were noble, but in practice it fostered an existence closer to 'equal but apart'. There was little close interaction between the various nationalities (the majority of whom came from the East). Encounters were usually limited to trade, or picking up on the rhythm of another language while out and about.

Such openness had a downside. An enemy who spoke in a tongue we did not understand could sprout roots in unexpected places. From such positions they would spread undetected, and by the time their poisonous intentions came to fruition, it would be too late. The recent Western treachery was a case in point: without the assistance of certain Westerners living among us, our wounds might not have been so deep, and the initial stages of the enemy invasion less successful. Equally as important as the need to maintain a watch over our international neighbours, was the need to remain fully informed on the activities of our resident guests. How did they live? Where did they go? What were they thinking? National observation became the remit of the Division of Internal Data and Security, known as DIDS.

The EDS and DIDS came into being as I made plans to head back to civilian life. Boredom was grinding me into the floor. You had no idea that thoughts about leaving the NDM had moved to the forefront of my mind. Today, I wonder whether sharing them with you might have led to a change in direction. I said nothing, and found myself suffocating in a slow-twisting cloud of repetition. How could I work so hard, so diligently, and still get nowhere? I knew the cause: too much peace and no action. It became impossible to define the boundary between my work and mandatory occupational therapy. And my uncles . . . They had stopped harassing me the moment I joined the NDM. But when did a leopard ever change its spots? It did not take long before they began to grumble and moan about my lack of promotion. As if the two of them had nothing better to do with their lives! As I gathered the momentum to leave the NDM, I crossed paths with an old friend. At first glance, it was just another happy, coincidental meeting. Yet by the end of our conversation, I had begun to move in a new direction. Another route, a darker road. It brought me here.

Fate is not a myth. At some point between then and now I learned to believe in its existence. While reflecting on the journey to this point, I notice how my path was marked by a number of odd coincidences. The butterflies that led me to the NDM officers' barbecue, and now this one. On an afternoon, eight months after our victory over the West, I travelled to an out-of-the-way antiquarian in the south-west of the city in order to pick up a hard-to-come-by volume. The seventy-three-year-old book on 'Modern Thought' (you know the one). The owner and I both had a good laugh about its age and title.

With the book in hand, I wandered around, exploring the neighbourhood. Despite being born and raised in this city, I had not only never visited that part of town, I had no idea it existed! The architecture was stern and proper. I imagined the neighbours to be exceptionally well behaved. Though it is possible my perception of the neighbourhood was distorted by personal thoughts on how best to compose my discharge request. A heavy weight of guilt had attached itself to the idea of leaving the NDM. I could neither remove it nor fully understand the reason for its presence.

While meandering about and scratching my head, who should I bump into as I rounded a corner? No one other than my man from the NDM officers' barbecue, and my guided tour of NDM HQ! The last time we met he was heading out to fight the Westerners, and I was about to commence NDM officer training. He radiated the same satisfied glow I had seen on many of those returning from the front. What experiences caused his spirit to light up in this manner?

Growing up, we were taught to always ask about what we did not know or understand. I mentioned the 'glow' to my man. He laughed, and then spent the next two minutes sharing a summary of his battlefield adventures. Among other things, I learned his unit was present during the Western leadership's surrender. My man planned to remember that moment forever. As he spoke, I felt a slight annoyance at having experienced no action at all. While soldiers such as he were out fighting for the nation, I had spent my time playing with maps.

And there was one other matter . . . his uniform. Yes,

uniforms again! In defence, my goodness, I had never seen one cut in this fashion. The attire of an NDM officer is quite pleasing to the eye, but where our uniforms were black, my man's was a dark maroon, and cut from fabric with a high-quality sheen. As for the tailoring: ours was sharp, his was sharper, and complimented with bold brass fittings and a wide dark brown belt of a similar leather to that of his well-polished boots. The breast-pocket buttons were a touch larger than usual for this type of uniform, though not distracting. The centre of each button was engraved with a wide-open eye. Four eyes down the middle of the jacket, one on the left breast pocket and another on the right. Yes, of course, I know it was a trick of the imagination, but those eyes did look at me. They saw <u>into</u> me, and whispered: 'We are watching. We are!' The same eyes also appeared on the embroidered shoulder patches. The result was truly impressive, and I suffered an attack of envy.

My man expressed his surprise at our meeting in that part of the city. 'Believe it or not,' he said, 'I had it in mind to get in touch, and here you are!' He then asked if I had time to spare. I did, and was invited for a drink at a local establishment.

We sat in a quiet section of the bar, each with a mug of cool, frothy beer. My man was born and still lived in the neighbourhood, a few minutes away from his parents. He asked what I was doing in the area. I showed him the book, which was immediately snatched from my hands. He began reading. Two and a half pages later, my man closed the book and returned the volume. 'May I read this, when you are done?' I agreed. He never did get around to borrowing the book.

The next item on our agenda was what I had been up to since our last meeting. 'Nothing to challenge the spirit,' I said, and went on to explain how the suffocating effects of boredom and lack of action encouraged my return to civilian life. My man listened and nodded with understanding. Then he asked: 'Are the butterflies around?' It took me a few seconds to pick up on the reference to the two butterflies that had escorted me to their picnic. 'I am sure they are here in spirit,' he said. 'I believe Fate has intervened and crossed our paths once again.'

He began with the uniform, though not its style, rather what it represented: the Division of Internal Data and Security. In developing the DIDS uniform, NDM Messaging and Public Relations had arrived at new levels in the expression of the power aesthetic. The importance and difference in the mission, methods and attitude of DIDS were communicated through their attire. I wondered whether the Head of Design I met in the NDM HQ atelier had anything to do with this creation. My man had been recruited by DIDS and given a position (with excellent growth prospects) in the Data and Information Extraction section (DIE). As he explained the generalities of his task, I realized a good amount of his glow was due to pride in his work.

The novelty of the Ministry of Data and Security, as well as the build-while-flying nature of its assembly, led to the occasional discovery of problems in need of effective solutions. One such matter was how to make sense of the increasing volume of data streaming in from the EDS and DIDS. Earlier that same day, during an urgent inter-divisional meeting about tackling the information overload, a reference was made to the thinking behind the colour-coded map analysis tools developed during my posting at NDM High Command, created, as you recall, for entirely skin-saving reasons. When my man told those higher up he knew the officer responsible, they ordered him to get in touch with me first thing tomorrow morning. Fate obviously thought: Why wait?

When offered a position at the Data and Information Extraction department, in the Division of Internal Data and Security, of course I said yes. Such was the power and influence of DIDS, within twenty-four hours I had been plugged into the team tasked with developing a method to process, as efficiently as possible, the streams of incoming data.

During my younger years, friends and I often played a game in which we imagined the lives of the people we saw on the street. Where did they live? Who was their mother and father, brother, sister? Where did they buy their clothes and shoes? Where had they gone to school? What books did they read? Which team did they support? And so on. I took the ideas and thinking found in those childhood memories and used them to develop the framework upon which we built the National Registry. Everyone living within our borders had a name, date of birth, a place of residence, education, employment, family, friends, an ethnicity. They had patterns to their movement, consumption, literature, entertainment, health, leisure, politics, etc. The National Registry was devised as a cross-referential database of all the above. It allowed us to build an understanding of an individual or group by studying every facet of their lives.

The first four months in DIE disappeared in the blink of an eye. We spent endless hours pushing and pulling problems apart in search of solutions. Ideas were born, shredded, reborn, adjusted, redeveloped. Time vanished, and did not reappear until the day we presented the results of our efforts to the Dear Leader. He loved our thinking. The DIE team's efforts in the conception of the National Registry were rewarded with promotions for all. Within the DIDS system, I climbed another few steps, and certainly made good use of the increase in salary: an upgrade in lifestyle. You accepted the changes. I loved them. A new house, with room enough for both of us, and more. Yet you did not move in. You <u>were</u> there, sometimes in person, always in spirit. A number of your clothes, shoes and other accessories took up residence at my place. But you never made it your home. I took consolation in your acceptance of the house keys. And yes, I did ask your mother to give you a nudge in the 'moving in' direction. 'Give her time. She is a free spirit,' was her advice. Time . . .

*

The National Registry was set up in conjunction with the 'Health For All' programme. The Dear Leader believed a healthy society was a productive society. And, given the citizens' efforts were of benefit to the nation, it was only decent and fair that the nation took good care of those who made it run. Health For All was an extremely popular programme, as it lowered the barriers usually associated with medical matters. Citizens (nationals and guests) signed up with great enthusiasm, and in doing so, provided the bricks and mortar with which we built our great house of information.

We began cataloguing individuals: name, age, address, nationality, medical history. The 'intakers' were instructed to make the data collection as conversational as possible, to discuss likes, interests, etc. The aim was to avoid unnecessary distress, while gaining a better understanding of the individual. The collated data was drawn from multiple aspects of a citizen's life: records of education, legal and/or criminal matters, financial condition, club and/or union and/or organization membership. The snippets of information were assessed and given specific values. Further examination allowed us to discover predictable patterns and sequences of behaviour. Without going into detail, I can say that we human beings are a very peculiar lot.

The National Registry was an outstanding tool, and within a year was deemed a national treasure and source of pride. On one occasion, the editor of a popular lifestyle magazine, together with a photographic crew, visited the DIE team offices to interview us about our creation. We told her the National Registry was the 'result of a serendipitous coming together of creative, intelligent and analytical minds'.

That was a happy period. Time was shared between us, my work on the National Registry, and ten days of combat training each month. Other than the persistent moodiness of our Eastern neighbours, which was not in itself a cause for alarm, all appeared well.

Ah. Much as I would prefer to complete this train of thought, my presence and attention is required elsewhere. I will return as soon as I can.

8

Bad news, and worrisome too. Our scouts have returned. We sent them out, to the north, south and west, in search of viable passages through the surrounding Eastern forces. The enemy has given them back. All dead. The men were discovered piled on top of one another, in a clearing a little beyond our perimeter. Some of us were deeply shocked and saddened by the sight of our brothers. Others could not comprehend how we failed to spot an enemy crossing the open clearing. They were, after all, carrying dead men not rabbits.

It took us the best part of forty-five minutes to retrieve the bodies. This war has allowed barbarity to run free on all sides, and now, unfortunately, booby-trapping corpses is one of the tactics employed by our adversary. My first experience of this tactic came two months ago, as we retreated west, towards home.

The war had changed, and victory had forgotten about us. Out of the chaos at NDM High Command came orders for our battalion to halt its westward march and move south. Our outnumbered forces had lost control of an Easterner oil refinery in the south of the country. They were driven out with such ferocity and speed, there was not enough time to inflict terminal damage on the structure. 'Send in the Factory Boys' was the general strategic consensus. NDM High Command believed it possible for our Property and Population Control battalion to make tactical adjustments, head south and destroy the refinery. Such a move might have been possible at the start of the war, but not at that moment. Our courage was well placed, but our armies were damaged, and circumstances had turned against us. On the ground, with reality's stench burning the hair in our nostrils, we failed to see the strategic benefits of such action. 'Optics,' said NDM High Command. They brushed aside our point of view, and refused to explain precisely what they meant by optics. We had our orders. The PPC marched south and destroyed the refinery: it was one of many, and a minor one at that. We lost a fifth of our men.

Some hours before leaving the area of the (still intact) refinery, and while searching through the rubble for our dead and wounded, a series of explosions shook our positions. These were not the result of incoming enemy shells.

These detonations were almost gentle, and quite deadly. The enemy was nowhere in sight, yet the search for dead and wounded created more dead and wounded. It took a while before we discovered the Easterners' trick: they had hidden explosive devices in or around the bodies of our dead. This was not the behaviour of a civilized people. I felt disgusted. What manner of poison had infected the enemy's thinking? Allowed them to desecrate a fallen man's body in this manner? Hatred of Easterners flowed through our blood, in vain: we were powerless to avenge these atrocities. On reflection, I wonder how it was possible not to see the hypocrisy of my complaint. The record of my activities up to that point was not a compendium of kindly deeds. Quite the opposite.

In the clearing, we checked the scouts' bodies for hidden explosive devices. They were clean. A cloud, heavy and present in the chest and gut, has descended from the skies above. The death of our three brothers, and the manner of their return makes it clear: there is no way out. There is nowhere to go. There is nothing for us to do but wait. Somewhere out there, beyond the range of our vision, the end approaches.

There were no smiles as I walked around our small patch. Correction. There were a few upwardly curved lips, but the fear in the men's eyes rendered smiles into grimaces. Officer training prepared us for many eventualities. It had not made me ready for this. The best I could do was rest my hand on a trembling shoulder for a quiet moment. 'Make your peace, brother,' I whispered, and then moved on.

It was a short trip. An odd one too. I studied the men. Some appeared locked in reflective pose. I watched others pray: to each their own. There were shivering boys, still green, thrown into the middle of the meat-grinder without the necessary training, and with no useful experience. Their stares ask nervous questions: Is this true? Am I really here? Their faces cry out for Mummy and Daddy to come and rescue them. I encourage these children to accept circumstances as they are. We have no other choice. Some weep. Others are struck by flashes of strategic genius, and advise me on how best to extricate our necks from the enemy's noose. They tell me where to move the troops, and how best to do so. I ask them to look around at the truth: we are all that is left. We <u>are</u> the troops. They stare back at me as if I am the Devil, and then declare, with the certainty of madmen, that reinforcements are on the way. They can feel our saviours' arrival in their bones.

These are strange hours. Yesterday, I would, without hesitation, have berated these men for such expressions of weakness. Today, all I have for them are words of comfort. Whether the noises I make are of any use is anyone's guess.

Thankfully, the majority of the men have pushed their fears and worries to one side. There is meaning to this uniform of ours: honour and courage. We are duty-bound to act befittingly. With braces of steel stiffening their spines, and a final burst of valour flowing through their systems, the men prepare. Yes, our end will be a noisy affair.

I remember reading an article about the experiences of people who had narrowly escaped death. One gentleman claimed his sense of smell improved by a factor of five. A woman was said to have discovered new layers to any music she heard. Another man swore he saw more colours than before. At the time, I found the article amusing. I now stand corrected. The knowledge of a fast-approaching end can intensify one's perception. As I walked through our encampment I discovered an ability to instantly absorb every detail of every face. The curve of ears, the flare of nostrils, the intertwine of eyebrow hairs, a mole, a scar, a field of stubble, a tear, a furrowed brow, eyes focused on a faraway place, a tongue soothing parched lips . . . I do not recall ever looking at faces in this way. You see what circumstances can do to the mind?

But I was writing about my time at DIE . . .

Our development projections had been far too conservative. We put the National Registry together at lightning speed, a rate that exceeded everything we imagined. The NDM leadership expressed their continued satisfaction with our endeavours by increasing the budget, and giving us licence to do whatever it took in order to get the job done. Protecting the nation was a vital task, and all obstacles in our path were removed. The NDM leadership rewrote sections of the National Law in order to accommodate our methods. Exciting days indeed.

Infinitely more rewarding than the results of office work, and a source of great personal joy, was the public's reaction to my uniform as I walked through the city. I wore the uniform of a National Defence Movement officer in the Division of Internal Data and Security. It gave me almost magical powers, setting those of us who wore it above and apart from all other citizens. You saw how it transformed me into an elite human being. I was met with reverence and joy, and suspect the citizens' behaviour was driven by DIDS' reputation as the 'Guardian of the Nation'. You, on the other hand, asked whether their conduct was the result of collective delirium. 'It is just a uniform. It is cloth,' you said. I probably smiled and reminded you how our work helped establish an environment of watchful safety, one that allowed citizens to go about their daily business free from worries. Only a select few would ever wear this cloth, members of the public knew this and were not at all shy about expressing their appreciation.

You and I reacted to this in quite opposite ways. You found it uncomfortable, unnatural, theatrical, dishonest, dangerous and 'not normal behaviour'. I, on the other hand, swallowed the adoration as if it were sweet wine. The public's praise drowned out your worries, and silenced common sense.

There was an episode, in the south of the country. I had left you for a three-day congress on Data Analysis. The final morning, a few hours before returning home, I visited a local bakery called (and I do not joke) 'A Loaf of

Bread'! It had an outstanding reputation with the locals and was packed with citizens of every size, shape and age. My entry was met with a few gasps of excitement, followed by a shower of greetings and compliments from the customers within. There was praise for myself, for DIDS, the National Defence Movement and the Dear Leader. The citizens practically carried me to the front of the queue, where the baker begged to take my order before anyone else's! It was an overwhelming experience. Especially given that the totality of my life's achievements thus far did not warrant such levels of adoration. Regardless, the uninhibited love and respect expressed by these citizens gave me so much joy.

I stood at the counter, filled with a sense of greatness that raised me high above everyone else in the bakery. From such an elevated position it was clear, while I was <u>among</u> them, I was not <u>of</u> them. I was 'special'. Their joyous reaction to my presence was proof enough. So much noise! My memory now of that morning is coloured by hindsight. Had I only remembered Mother's warnings about noisy compliments. Perhaps I should have listened harder to your pleas to keep my feet on the ground. But back then, I was a hundred years younger, and my spirit so loved the praise.

Back at university, I was sometimes mocked (though more often loved) for my practice of never leaving the house without a supply of 'emergency funds'. This habit was instilled in me by Father's youngest brother. I remember him being the happiest of my three uncles. Always buzzing with energy, and always with bundles of cash that he flashed around in a manner that infuriated Father and made Mother gasp. We laughed. He lived fast and died in a cloud of scandal. Once, long ago, I asked about the banknotes. He walked over to where I stood and dropped to one knee, then he took my chin in his right hand, looked me straight in the eye, and said: 'Emergency funds. Because you never know.'

That morning, in A Loaf of Bread, I realized wearing the uniform gave me a superpower. No, I could not suddenly lift great rocks and hurl them about. But I could look at another human being and make them glow. I could enter a room and those within would become ecstatic. Officer training had instilled this in us: 'Your uniform is the voice of the NDM. Your actions tell a story to the people.' The discovery regarding the power of my uniform put me in a generous and eloquent mood. I reached into my satchel, extracted five high-denomination banknotes and placed them on the counter. The baker's confusion was amusing. I then turned to the crowd and asked them to settle down. My tongue was possessed by the spirit of the occasion.

'Mothers, fathers, brothers, sisters,' I began. 'I am honoured and humbled. The nation thrives because of citizens such as yourselves. This is an unchallengeable fact. Therefore, on behalf of the National Defence Movement, permit me to express our gratitude with a small gesture. The Division of Internal Data and Security will cover the orders of everyone here.' The citizens erupted into a joyous thunder of cheering, pats on the back, hugs, a few kisses. All so wonderful! The baker protested (mildly). She argued the money on the counter was too much, enough to pay the collective bill many times over. 'That is fine,' I said, and then declared it to be A Loaf of Bread's lucky day. Whatever amount remained after covering the bill should be seen as a tip, wrapped in the eternal appreciation of the NDM. The people were still cheering, weeping, hugging and clapping as I left. I wore a huge smile across my face and a cloak of great satisfaction over my shoulders. 'What are you?' I asked myself. 'I am a God!' Yes, I was happy with life. I felt good.

The same could not be said of our relationship with the East. Out of the blue, Eastern media began to toss around careless and aggressive allegations, claiming our people's 'shady business practices' were bleeding their country dry. This was a complete fabrication! Rather than focus on their leaders' activities, the Easterners listened to fables about our people's supposed 'natural greed and dishonesty' or about our alleged 'insufferable arrogance'. I am sorry to say, the majority of the Eastern population chose to believe this nonsense rather than think for themselves.

Their comments shocked and offended us as a nation. They rattled the Dear Leader. Why would the Easterners say this? Were any of the allegations true? The EDS was asked to look into the matter. Their conclusion: the root cause of the Eastern leadership's behaviour was the impending economic (and subsequent political) collapse. The East was in deep trouble. Their citizens' previously sporadic expressions of unrest had evolved into daily occurrences that spread rapidly through the country. A pandemic of dissatisfaction loomed, and the Eastern leadership, in a state of panic, played the easiest card: scapegoat the 'other'. In this instance, we became the other. Their methods were simple and extremely effective. A number of popular commentators from the radio and papers (those with a large audience) were asked by the Eastern leadership to emphasize 'messages' that contained attacks and insults directed towards our people. The Eastern public's dissatisfaction and rage were deflected away from their leaders and refocused elsewhere. It should have taken but a sprinkle of common sense for the people to see through this ploy. However, anger, frustration and common sense are rarely ever friends.

The most influential of the Eastern commentators was a man with an extremely popular Saturday evening radio show. One evening, he proclaimed, by way of colourful melodrama, our people to be worse than cockroaches. The commentator then shared an anecdote about 'driving the sneaky, filthy cockroaches' out of his grandmother's kitchen. The vermin ate everything and left his grandmother with nothing! Had he not acted as he did, when he did, the poor woman might have starved to death. A week later, every place of trade belonging to our people in the East was attacked. Stalls, shops, kiosks were all smashed, gutted and burned. We were horrified. I remember how you sobbed. You said it could not be true. It was.

The Eastern leadership refused to condemn these acts, or express any remorse for the terror and economic loss experienced by our people. Instead, they praised the hoodlums' 'restraint' and said our people should be thankful that only shops and stalls had been destroyed. After all, the remedy for infestations of dishonest parasites was usually much worse. It broke our hearts to hear these dangerous falsehoods repeated again and again. Through our envoy in the East, the Dear Leader relayed in the strongest possible terms his disapproval of Eastern behaviour towards our nationals. As a reward, our envoy received an earful of curses. Within days, barely coherent messages and harrowing reports began to trickle in. They told of our people being driven out of Eastern towns and cities. Entire households were given no more than a few minutes to pack what they could and leave. Up to that point, I could not recall ever despising anyone. However, as I read about what was happening in the East, a hot and angry animosity towards Easterners grew within me. For the time being, this hatred served no purpose other than keeping me awake deep into the early hours. You noticed, on some of the nights you stayed over. You asked. I confessed. You suggested I find compassion and understanding for the Eastern population. 'Do you not wonder what forces have driven them to behave in this way?' By then, NDM dogma had already subverted my thinking. There was no need to wonder, I knew: the Easterners' conduct was driven by natural violent instincts. We agreed to disagree, and in the interests of our relationship I parked my dark thoughts to one side and tried to forget about them. Meanwhile, a new kind of traffic appeared at our Eastern border crossings: terrorized souls. A flood of refugees, but no strangers. These were our people, and it pained me to note their expressions carried more horror than the faces of the victims of Western aggression.

At 0930 on the morning after the last of our citizens returned, we recalled our envoy to the East and began the process of full disengagement. The border was sealed, and all new trade cancelled, with the exception of transactions finalized prior to 0800.

A brief note on the cancellation of trade with the East. One of the strategic measures implemented as a reaction to our war with the West was the creation of national reserves of essential materials. Raw materials from the East, enough to permit full manufacturing capacity for another eighteen months, were stored in hundreds of underground depots. These were spread around the country, always in areas of low population. We believed the eighteen-month margin afforded by the stockpiled material would be time enough for either the Easterners to come to their senses, or our alternative trading partners to lower their prices. Once again, the Dear Leader's vision proved correct. The Easterners believed the trade embargo to be a bluff on our part. They were wrong. Manufacturing and production continued without interruption.

Such was the state of affairs between our nations, when I arrived at the office one morning to find, in addition to my usual colleagues, three high-ranking DIDS officials. They were waiting for me. Highly unusual. After assuring me that all was good and well, I was thanked for my work on the National Registry, and then informed my talents were needed elsewhere. The DIDS operation was an efficient one: there was barely enough time to clear my desk and bid farewell to my colleagues. An hour later I arrived at the new Office of Easterner Observation. The name says it all. Here, we dealt with matters concerning the Easterners resident within our borders. We understood and accepted the madness in the East was driven by the scoundrels and vagabonds at the top of Eastern society. Those were desperate men and women, rotten to the core. Conditions encouraged them to lash out and blame others for their nation's misery. Generally speaking, the Easterners living with us, nurtured by the good lives they led here, were of a gentler character than their hysterical leaders. As such we did not expect them to make mischief. Yet, we saw no real harm in keeping a watchful eye on that segment of the population.

9

I believe there are moments in this life when we sense the approach of change. As if usually dormant voices within, disturbed by atmospheric vibrations or charged elements in the air, are awoken. They speak, you hear them, you feel them, but their message remains unclear. Only later, once change has altered all in its path, will you understand. Well, on <u>that</u> morning as my eyes opened, ready to greet the day, the inner voices began to chatter nervously. Their din rode with me as I cycled to NDM HQ.

I experienced the rest of the morning as a slow movement through hours weighed down by an expectant silence. Productivity levels were low. Every time the office door opened, every time one of the two telephones rang, or a pencil dropped, a bell chimed . . . a shot of adrenaline burst through our veins. We jumped and twitched and coughed. Our glances, and we could barely hold the other's eye, asked 'Do you feel it?'

The waiting ended. High-pitched rumours . . . Contact lost with the aircraft carrying the Dear Leader and a delegation of top-ranking NDM officials . . . Last known position, midway over Eastern territory. The EDS intercepted radio chatter alluding to the downing of an aircraft. Shortly thereafter we received confirmation of a crash in a remote region of the East. Identification markings matched those on the plane carrying the NDM leadership. Survivors . . . unspecified.

Such explosive information warranted urgent investigation. We managed to open a communication channel with the East and offered to assist them with the search and rescue effort. They rejected our offer, citing national sovereignty and claiming to possess the necessary expertise for such matters.

This was an unacceptable response. The matter at hand involved the fate of the entire NDM leadership. Cooperation, regardless of our diplomatic status, should be a given. We demanded immediate access to the crash site. The Easterners ignored us. They treated us like fools, obfuscating and distracting until their words made us dizzy. When we confronted them with our perception of their behaviour, the Easterners sneered at our observations while claiming ignorance. Their words were wrapped in dark shadows and dripped with lies.

It took the better part of a month to repatriate the bodies and allow us to bury our leaders with dignity. The Easterners, as if to rub salt in an open wound, sent a low-level, ragtag delegation to the Dear Leader's funeral. How they fidgeted and chatted among themselves during the burial ceremony was a disgrace! We learned that 'other matters arising' prevented the Eastern leadership from paying their final respects in person.

Our traditional national reaction to the death of a leader, regardless of political affiliation, is to enter the Two Chapters of Mourning. (The leader of our previous government was a notable exception.) The first chapter is the Month of Pain, in which all citizens in the nation are given the freedom to express such a terrible loss. We give thanks to Mother Nature for blessing us all with the capacity to feel such wretchedness. The Month of Pain begins on the night of the first full moon after a leader's burial, and lasts for twenty-eight days. The weeks following the Dear Leader's death were heavy and grey. The plants and trees, the air and the raindrops joined our mourning. A section of the nation remained frozen in collective grief, while others burned with an impotent rage.

The second chapter is the Time of Reflection: a full-moon cycle in which we recall, once again, the many ways the departed (in this case the Dear Leader) changed our lives, for better or worse. We have long since forgotten why the ancients believed it took two full-moon cycles for the collective's emotional wounds to heal. Only then, they declared, were we ready for new leadership. The Two Chapters of Mourning, like many of the old ways passed down to us by our forebears, have not aged well. I suspect our world is very different to theirs. Today is faster and more complex. We react and react and react. There is little time to reflect. I look around our tent in this doomed camp and wonder, if we had thought just a bit harder, just a bit longer, would I be here today? Who knows.

While a fair percentage of the general population used the Time of Reflection as tradition demanded, what remained of the NDM began to lash about, like the body of a decapitated snake. Nature abhors a vacuum, as does power. Vicious factional infighting quickly spread through the organization. Faction A eliminated faction B, who were removed by faction C, only to be replaced by faction D, and so on. It was a brutal and embarrassing exhibition. The quest for power brings out such ugliness of the spirit. Together with many of my fellow officers, I cringed at what was said, at what was done. We watched the contenders claw and hack their way to the top. If only they could see themselves, we thought. Eventually, the fighting stopped and the dust settled. There, standing all powerful, atop the mound of bile and machinations, was a new leader. At one o'clock on a rainy afternoon, Our Dear Leader spoke to the nation. His words jumped out of the radio speakers and into our ears. We were introduced to a new leader with a new style.

Whenever our recently deceased leader addressed the nation, he usually left us in a mood of 'thoughtful determination'. His words echoed in our minds, and encouraged us to work harder, and care more for the other. Brutal ascension aside, the Dear Leader was a man who truly loved our nation. He was at his most joyful when things changed for the better: a new hospital wing, a new school, a new factory. I met him on numerous occasions at NDM HQ, and came to see him as a leader who ruled by way of inspiration. He was a teacher whose mission, at the head of the nation, was to facilitate the elevation of others. In contrast, Our Dear Leader had a different approach. He made up for a lack of inspirational eloquence with raw power, and a unique ability to tap into the nation's mood. Our Dear Leader touched us, reached deep into our hearts, and into the very centre of our minds. He spoke, and we believed without resistance. To describe the phenomenon as mass hypnosis would be no exaggeration. We believed him when he said 'I feel your torment. Your loss is mine. The tears you shed are just as bitter as those on my face.' We believed him when he claimed 'My anger is as fierce as yours, as is my sense of betrayal.' Only a man with our best will in his heart could utter such words. We believed it when Our Dear Leader told us 'There is no need for despair. We shall have justice. We shall have justice when those who have wronged us begin to fear us. We shall have justice, people. We shall have justice! We shall have justice!' For a good minute, Our Dear Leader bellowed 'We shall – have – justice!' Again and again . . . We knew he spoke the truth. We felt it.

There were nine of us in the office. Standing, sitting, listening to the speech. As Our Dear Leader began his mantra, the room filled with an energy similar to what I had experienced during Self-Identification class.

From here, today, it occurs to me, Our Dear Leader's ability to dazzle our minds with what he <u>planned</u> to do made us forget to ask how! The force of his words spread across the land and removed our sadness. We began to look forward. In the meantime, Our Dear Leader allowed the nation to regain its strength and spirit before taking the next step on the road to justice. An open letter in the national papers. A well-crafted piece accusing 'certain scoundrels' of assassinating the Dear Leader and then, in the manner of cowards, lying about their deeds. As a nation, we were willing to let bygones be bygones, no matter how painful, if we received honesty in exchange. We promised there would be no retaliation or repercussions of any sort. All we asked for was the truth. The letter mentioned no names and pointed at no one in particular. Yet it was impossible to read the contents and not look east.

The official response to the letter from a furious Eastern leadership was an explosion of thunder and bombast. They ranted and raged. They declared Our Dear Leader's letter an insult of 'national proportion' and one they would never forget. The Eastern leadership's noisy focus on hurt feelings, as well as the lack of an actual denial, revealed enough. Many of us wondered how people who screamed in this manner ever managed to lead a nation. Any human being with a gram of common sense knew screaming was not an effective leadership style as it frightened away the truth. The Eastern leadership was lost in a forest of lies, without truth to guide the way. They no longer knew their left from right, nor up from down, truth from fabrication. They were blind, and afraid. Well, as we say, the frightened cat jumps in unexpected directions . . . External Data and Security reported back on the Eastern leadership's nervous desperation and increasingly erratic behaviour towards their own people. In among the chatter and vague whispers coming out of the East, the EDS detected a new willingness by their leaders to apply extreme methods in their attempt to survive. We <u>knew</u> the Easterners were up to something, but were unable to discover what.

10

None of us expected the terror. Markets were civilian territory. While it's true, war has destroyed many marketplaces around the world, it was always collateral damage: a poorly aimed mortar shell or bomb, the unfortunate setting for intense ground combat, but never deliberate targeting. So imagine the shock of an attack during peacetime. It was <u>not</u> warfare, this behaviour of theirs. We had never heard of, nor experienced, anything like this synchronized mindless slaughter. The nation was stunned. What should we call this merciless destruction of innocents? Blameless citizens going about their business, in the middle of the afternoon.

The three simultaneous double explosions in three marketplaces, in three cities, left too many dead. There were many hundreds of wounded, and thousands more traumatized souls. These were gangster tactics. This was <u>not</u> how nations fought. The country's eyes turned towards the Division of Internal Data and Security: 'How could this happen? Is it not your duty to keep us safe?' they asked. A number of noisy and influential voices across the media questioned whether DIDS was truly deserving of its budget. How could such a well-funded organization fail to protect the citizens? How could such tragedy be allowed to take place within our borders?

The publicly voiced accusations of waste and incompetence were painful. Our diligence and hard work had brought us to an obvious conclusion: the more we learned, the greater our understanding of how much we had yet to discover. Of course there were holes in our mesh of information. We patched them as quickly and effectively as possible, but certain clues, hints and activities escaped our attention. We tried our best, and always learned from our errors. We were not fools. All the same, the ultimate responsibility for national security lay with DIDS, and the public's anger was insatiable. Our Dear Leader sensed this and acted accordingly. Heads rolled. Our division chief and his two deputies were asked to resign. We viewed this as an unnecessary and ill-considered move. Their replacements were a trio of outsiders. The new chief immediately demanded an explanation for our incompetence. He did so by way of the radio and newspapers, and not by visiting our offices and speaking directly to us. Within DIDS, the Office of Easterner Observation took the blame.

The powers that be made it perfectly clear: we at the OEO were responsible for these acts of terror. Rather than sitting around in our offices, we should have been out there, preventing such ideas from developing into plots and subsequent horror. We were a national disgrace. An embarrassment to the Division of Internal Data and Security, an embarrassment to the National Defence Movement, and currently unmentionable to Our Dear Leader. The list of our wrongs was enough to have the Office of Easterner Observation disbanded with immediate effect. Fortunately, the NDM was not a cruel organization, and the OEO was given two weeks to save itself by identifying and capturing those responsible. With this threat ringing in our ears, the OEO staff created new definitions for focus, analysis and overtime.

We had very little information to work with. The timing of the three market bombings suggested they were carefully planned acts. The culprits remained invisible, though we strongly suspected Eastern involvement. As if in harmony with our increasingly fraught relationship with the East, we noted increased agitation among certain groups of Easterners. However, a motive for the bombing, beyond careless destruction of life, remained unclear. Who had devised such a wicked plot? Where had the planning taken place? These were questions beyond the scope of our data. We had no idea where to begin, and therefore chose to begin with everything.

The OEO sent out urgent requests to all our eyes and ears on the ground for reports of any memorable activities noticed during the weeks and days leading up to the bombings. It need not be criminal behaviour. We asked for anything that had made someone look twice, or lingered in their minds longer than usual. Fate came to our rescue. An informant reported back. An hour before the bombings, she and a few friends were having lunch on the terrace of a popular establishment in the west of the city. I knew the place by name, though had never visited. It was run by a couple of Eastern descent, and our records had it down as a favourite watering hole for artists, musicians and literary types, of all ages and nationalities.

During a lull in the afternoon conversation, our informant overheard a child ask his mother if two men had a fever: why else would they wear heavy coats on such a hot afternoon? Our informant turned and recognized the subjects of the conversation. The two men, clad in oversized and heavily padded coats, had not been wearing those garments thirty minutes earlier, when they arrived at the establishment and walked inside. Our informant remembered the men's faces: 'As if they were in a trance,' she said. 'And their eyes, they were empty.' At the time, our informant believed the two men were simply another pair of oddly dressed Easterners.

Further analysis of informants' reports from the three affected cities revealed eleven unique references of men wearing unseasonably heavy coats and walking towards or in the vicinity of the markets, prior to the bomb attacks. Was there a relationship between the watering hole and the stricken market twenty minutes away? Given the urgency of the situation (remember, the OEO was fighting for its survival), we took risks where we had once acted with caution. At two thirty in the morning, thirteen hours after receiving the new information, I looked around at my tired colleagues. The strong coffee, rather than helping, had turned against us: it stimulated our ability not to think in a clear manner, and nothing else. We were desperate. Empty. Unable to decide how best to proceed. A wrong move, and those we sought might escape. Our paralysis was caused by an inability to understand the thinking of those behind the bombings. The office clock chimed the half-hour. The gleeful 'ding' was accompanied by a flash of memory from officer training: 'Defeat and indecision are the best of friends.' My penchant for dithering was gone by the time I completed officer training. I knew what to do. Rather than take time to observe the suspect establishment in the west of the city, we raided it the following evening.

I am amused at how often we miss what stands right in front of our noses. The art, music and poetry was a distraction. Behind a false wall in the basement, we discovered a workshop. Tools, maps, knives, guns, ammunition and a whole range of items that challenged the knowledge of our technical staff. Of great interest was an area dedicated to inserting explosives inside everyday objects: coats, children's dolls, radios. I saw this with my own eyes. Such behaviour was unheard of, and I firmly believed at the time the hidden workshop to be the Devil's domain.

Within a week, five of the market-bombing masterminds were in our custody. Utilizing the wide variety of data extraction tools and methods at our disposal, we soon discovered connections between our five captives and certain influential individuals in the East. We noted how our guests' minds were filled with an unfortunate and incomplete view of the world. In their version, the problems in the East were a direct result of Our Dear Leader's spiteful actions. No mention was made of the role played by the corrupt Eastern leadership. When we challenged their beliefs with facts, the five accused us of concocting lies and other conspiracies. Internally, I sneered at the inability of their minds to see the brightly illuminated truth, even when held up on a platter right before their eyes! I saw these people as wicked, ignorant souls, lacking the intelligence to separate right from wrong. After all, what in Heaven's name was right about blowing up market-going innocents? I now have a much better understanding of such behaviour. Those five were not stupid, they were simply too busy acting to think about their actions. At the time, we noted their attitude but found it of secondary importance to the fact we finally had information to work with.

During the creation of the EDS and DIDS, care was taken to accommodate the fact that where there are people, there are egos . . . The sense of competition was kept to a minimum, and the boundaries between our divisions were designed to mimic the nation's porous borders.

The free flow of data traffic was essential for complete national security coverage. The inter-divisional cooperation on the market bombings project was outstanding, and our five captive masterminds were exceptionally helpful. They provided a list of twenty-seven new candidates for investigation. Those twenty-seven, in turn, gave us access to another hundred and thirty-three. Those were days of long hours and night-time work: scouring, cross-checking, extracting.

Most of the Eastern candidates we brought in were more than happy to help with our inquiries. Some, perhaps inspired by popular literature and film, chose the path of dogged heroism. Yet they too eventually came to their senses and realized it was better for all when they cooperated. An unfortunate few, due to a stubborn refusal to assist in a positive manner, found themselves in a condition that was of no use to us, or anyone else.

With renewed dedication and intensified focus, we spent the next five weeks identifying and subsequently destroying every node on the subversive Eastern terror network that threatened our nation's well-being. The speed and efficiency of our endeavours impressed the top layers of the NDM, all the way up to Our Dear Leader.

The Office of Eastern Observation was safe for now. We also heard, though this was never confirmed, our work had some influence on the content and tone of his next speech.

Our Dear Leader's voice filled the radio waves as he addressed the Easterners living among us: 'We welcomed you into our home as mothers, fathers, brothers, sisters, daughters and sons.' We heard the flames of rage as they spat and crackled around his words. 'We welcomed you as new members of our family and, because it is our nature to do so, we trusted you as we trust ourselves. We granted your wishes to build the houses of worship your culture requires. We gave you the freedom to think as you please. For countless seasons you have lived with us, in harmony, in prosperity. Why this? Why mimic the barbarous antics of your country's leadership?' Our Dear Leader declared himself to be an understanding man, who knew most Easterners were just as horrified by the market bombings as any other right-thinking beings. However, the slaughter had been planned and carried out in the Easterners' name. They had stood by and watched as a poisonous few of their people brought the malevolent scheme to life. No voices were raised in disagreement, and no attempt was made to warn us, their hosts, of the impending chaos and bloodshed. 'Such a pity,' Our Dear Leader said. 'Such disregard for our kindness and accommodation. Well, we have a message for those of you who choose to repay our generous hospitality with murder . . . We will find you. Do you hear that, Easties? Run far, hide low, do whatever you like. We will track and hunt you, drag you out from your filthy lairs, and bring you to face the consequences of your actions!'

'Easties' was a term approved and inserted into Our Dear Leader's speech by a special team within NDM Messaging and Public Relations that was focused on Easterners. Not a day went by during my time with the OEO without a member of that team popping into our office to ask for the latest summary of Easterner-relevant information, or to seek further clarification of one or another Easterner trait. Within the OEO we referred to Easterners as 'Easties'. This was out of convenience (one less syllable) rather than malice. The team from Messaging and Public Relations who, by the way, could transform a fresh drop of rain into acid, picked up on 'Eastie'. They liked it and passed it on to Our Dear Leader, who used it in his speech. The term stuck. From that day on, the resident Easterners became Easties, the enemy within.

11

One of the new measures relating to control of the Easties living among us was the Oath. A straightforward Oath of Allegiance to the nation and Our Dear Leader. What Easties thought, or how they behaved outside of our borders, was their own business. However, due to the actions of their fellow countryfolk, we were left with no choice but to clarify what was expected of guests in our land. The Oath was an agreement to abide by a set list of what Easties were and were not permitted to do. It might help to remember, these reduced freedoms existed as a result of Eastie behaviour. We would rather have done without them, but circumstances . . .

We understood that, for many Easties, taking the Oath was a purely pragmatic act: it allowed them to get on with their lives, and as far as we were concerned, that was fine. Those who took the Oath usually had no interest in politics or conspiracies. We knew this because we, at the OEO, watched them. The secondary purpose of the Oath was to identify members of a category we called the

Potentially Disruptive Eastie (PDE). Refusal to take the Oath signalled a stubbornness of character, and with it an aptitude for causing trouble. Once identified and marked accordingly, those in the PDE category were placed on the Action Pending Register (APR).

I tell you, the NDM were masters of lyrical chicanery: Action Pending was nothing more than a sugar coating applied to 'marked for punishment'. Again the Easties brought trouble upon themselves. It would not reflect well on the nation, or Our Dear Leader, if those Easties who refused to pledge allegiance walked free and unsanctioned. It was tantamount to a slap in the face! Were Easties allowed to insult Our Dear Leader and go free, what would be next? Hurling rotten fruit and rocks at the man? Violence? The Action Pending punishment was savage in how it always struck the hapless Eastie where it hurt most.

Another of the available methods of Eastie control was through the issuance of residency permits. A mere formality for those who had taken the Oath, the residency permit allowed Easties to reside in, or own property within our borders, so long as they paid the respective charges and taxes in full and on time. Potentially Disruptive Easties on the APR were deemed too unstable for permanent residency. As such, their permit requests were denied. The law being as it was, any Eastie without a residency permit was naturally given Unlawful Resident (UR) status. The consequence of UR status was an official Declaration of Illegality (DI). The sanctions for a DI included immediate forfeiture of all assets (excepting personal items able to be carried without mechanical assistance) and deportation to the land of ancestral origin.

Running parallel to these adjustments was an Eastie 'derecognition' campaign, managed by NDM Messaging and Public Relations. The aim was to highlight the 'natural, cultural and moral differences' between ourselves and our Eastie guests. Recent exposure to the violent facets of Eastie behaviour helped it along. The campaign also coincided with a shift in the nation's mood. Our hearts and minds were filled with a growing euphoria, an ecstasy conjured up by Our Dear Leader's words. Goodness knows how many times we passed wild-eyed citizens in the streets chanting, out loud, Our Dear Leader's phrases. Quoting his words!

I remember the bizarre incident in the library on that wet afternoon. You and I, together with thirty or so others, had run inside to take shelter from an unexpected rainstorm. In the foyer was an exhibition of portraits of Our Dear Leader. The artists were children, and it was clear they viewed Our Dear Leader as a God-like being. The collection of youthful artistic expression and adoration dizzied our minds. But that was nothing compared to the spontaneous outburst from almost everyone in the space. One moment there was the semi-excited hubbub of those who have just escaped a downpour, the next, an explosion of wild chanting of praise for Our Dear Leader. I found it amusing, you found it worrisome.

Our Dear Leader was very good with words. He weighed, arranged and fed them to us. The nation swallowed without resistance. Although, through the filters of time and circumstance, I realize just how much of what came out of his mouth was no more than well-dressed nonsense. That said, the man's execution was sublime. The force with which he delivered his loud assertions allowed us to ignore their hollow ring. Back then, there was a belief, a highly charged nationwide state of mind, that we, led by Our Dear Leader, were on the verge of greatness. The majority of us sensed the time had come to write a new chapter into the history books.

Accompanying the euphoria was a growing darkness. It manifested in how we vocalized our mistrust and dislike of Easties. Commentary about Easties inserted itself into daily conversation, none of it complimentary. Radio and theatre comics made Easties the target of many a joke. Where wit and surprise had once been used to entertain us, the public now took delight in the vicious skewering of Eastie characteristics. Those comics were brutal, extremely funny, and every one of them was pushed forward and promoted by NDM Messaging and Public Relations. How many shows did I see? Three, four? I sit here and recall how I laughed. Belly in agony, cheek muscles aching, tears streaming. You fidgeted through the first show: not really your kind of entertainment . . .

The jokes that had the nation splitting its sides were just the beginning: our first steps down the path of derecognition, and, eventually, complete dehumanization of the Easties. Had we known, would we have laughed so hard, or stopped and changed direction? Who knows. As I recall, we, as a nation, thoroughly enjoyed the humiliation of the Easties. Why this bigoted vulgarity made so many of us feel so good, I cannot say.

The radio and newspapers were next to join in. Theirs

was a humourless contribution. An endless series of articles, news items and commentary focused on Eastie misbehaviour. Eastie misappropriations of funds, Eastie molestation of grandmothers, Eastie cartel forming, Eastie membership of criminal organizations, attempted subversion, violent beliefs. No actual evidence of Eastie wrongdoing was ever revealed, only exceptionally well-dressed innuendo and vague allegations presented as fact. Quack scientists passed comment in the broadsheets or on air. They told us Easties lacked the higher levels of morality found in other civilized beings. Easties had a non-complex culture. Easties had naturally limited intellectual capacity. Eastie language was too primitive to contain nuance. The majority of the nation, myself included, swallowed this 'science' as if it were nourishment.

The media enhanced their reporting of Eastie activities with sensational eyewitness accounts of those who had been insulted, double-crossed or scandalized. There were heartbreaking tales of our children trying to play in public parks, only to be terrified and chased away by rough-mannered Eastie offspring. Behind the noise, I heard the sound of NDM Messaging and Public Relations, and behind that, the voice of Our Dear Leader.

As the anti-Eastie sentiments spread across the land, my work at the OEO began to lose its shine. I spent most of my time as an NDM officer inside an office, performing a routine series of actions over and over again. The only escape from those walls, windows and perfectly arranged desks were a few mandatory combat courses. I loved them, even though they fed my annoyance at having missed action during our fight with the Westerners. I began to choke. I needed to breathe, to run and shout.

A few months prior to the Dear Leader's assassination, a thirteen-strong DIDS team was assigned to the NDM Ministry of Housing and Justice. The plan was to provide consultation and training for ministry officials on the matters of data extraction, collation and analysis. The DIDS team would depart once ministerial levels of information competence were attained. The ascension of Our Dear Leader adjusted these plans. The DIDS section was absorbed by the Ministry of Housing and Justice and transformed into the Property Integrity Office (PIO). The PIO's remit was the management of all state properties. Various units within the PIO were given specific areas of specialization: parks, bridges, public buildings, housing, inspection, renovation, etc.

During the development of the National Registry, I had liaised with and come to know a number of people in the Ministry of Housing and Justice who currently operated within the PIO. We remained in touch: a beer here, a coffee there. During an evening drink with my PIO friends, I received a tip about a recruitment drive for the new Data and Security action teams within the PIO. The creation of these teams was a natural consequence of the increasing need for DIDS to carry out practical field work. And the teams were <u>not</u> office bound. The thought of operating outside of a building was sweet music to my soul! I applied and was accepted immediately: those higher up fast-tracked my transfer to the PIO. My excellent service record being a major factor in their considerations. I received two months of intensive training, which involved absorbing huge chunks of National Law. On completion, I moved up a rank and was given command of an action team: a PIO Site Inspection Unit (SIU).

The minister in charge declared the action teams to be the Ministry of Data and Security's surgical instruments, and the Potentially Disruptive Easties, having resisted the prescribed ointment of the Oath, the diseased flesh in need of removal.

My SIU was tasked with the preparation of properties for renovation. It does not take complex science to understand it is impossible to renovate a property and return it to a suitable 'living' condition when inhabited by unlawful residents. Our task began with the extraction of occupants. The first stage in this process was an Appropriation Order (AO) for the property to be renovated. As the AO made its way through the chambers of the Ministry of Housing and Justice to my SIU, it was joined by Unlawful Residency Status documents and official Declaration(s) of Illegality. What eventually arrived was a package of documents filled with complicated texts.

The extraction process began when we arrived at the site in need of inspection and presented the occupants with the official DI. My approach was to do so while quoting from the sections of National Law governing low moral standards, antisocial, subversive, potentially anti-national behaviour, and the consequences thereof. By the way, the information gleaned from the National Registry allowed for extremely effective targeting of Potentially

Disruptive Easties. We encouraged the occupant representative receiving the official DI to sign where necessary on the papers and accept the transfer of assets (residential and otherwise) to the NDM Ministry of Housing and Justice. With that done, I then made clear to the former occupants their Unlawful Resident status required them to leave the country within forty-eight hours. The Unlawful Resident Transfer Squads, who accompanied our SIU, would provide further assistance. We shuttered the property and then set off to our next inspection.

Site Inspections were not always smooth, straightforward affairs. The Easties employed, understandably, a wide range of delaying tactics. Everything from chaining themselves to immovable items, to feigning ill health or encouraging friendly neighbours to create all manner of peripheral distractions. We accepted these delays as an unfortunate component of the business. Occasionally, our arrival for a Site Inspection motivated occupants to discover a new, sudden and dramatic enthusiasm to take the Oath. They offered to do so right then and there, and were always disappointed, at times shocked, to learn our SIU lacked the authority to grant such requests. We understood how such sudden changes in circumstance would challenge anyone's spirits, and so, without fail, we waited with great patience as the forlorn Easties vacated the property.

The effects of the change in national mood and direction eventually made their way down to the PIO Site Inspection Units. We received a directive announcing a number of adjustments to our inspection methods. A growing number of Easties living among us had begun renouncing their Oaths. These acts of renunciation were often public affairs that included the burning of Oath of Allegiance certificates and other examples of Eastie thuggery. They claimed their barbaric conduct was no more than an expression of solidarity with extracted family, friends, and so on. Recent studies by prominent NDM sociologists had revealed the Easties' lack of capacity for natural honesty. Evidence could be seen in the ease with which these people tossed aside sworn Oaths. Of course these Easties were placed on the APR.

The escalating Eastie agitation had been duly noted, and an adequate response formulated. The new directive increased the number of daily Site Inspections by a factor of three. At the same time it decreased our tolerance for delays. We were requested to keep logistical hold-ups to an absolute minimum by 'utilizing all available resources and methods in the removal of hindrances'.

As mentioned earlier, the Easties were a wonderfully creative lot when it came to inventing excuses not to leave illegally appropriated ministry property. For example, they would argue back and forth forever about what gave us the right to act as we did. They demanded proof that our official documents had actually come from the Ministry of Housing and Justice. Can you imagine? Some even challenged us to prove how not signing an Oath automatically signified disdain for Our Dear Leader. Others spoke at length about the grandfathers, great uncles and aunts who built the properties they illegally occupied, throwing in the occasional claims of barehanded construction. As if we would bother our heads with such information! Prior to the new directive, our approach to occupant extraction had been non-physical, respectful and one of gentle persuasion. It could take anything up to six hours to fully vacate a property. Most of that time was consumed by debate.

Our 'new style' began with a reduction in patience. Where we had once tutted and sighed, while drumming our fingers against thighs, we now pushed and dragged. Occasionally, though only ever when the situation demanded, there might be need for a motivational slap or a punch or kick. Had time not been of the essence, I would have instructed the men to exercise restraint. However, proceedings needed to keep moving at a reasonable pace.

Another request listed in the directive was for the Site Inspection Units to share their on-site experiences. These reports and anecdotes were compiled into a reference library of extraction techniques. We learned what methods worked best, and when and how to employ them.

I have learned there are mad beasts inside us all. Under normal circumstances, these inner monsters never get the chance to come out and play. Our behaviour is prevented from straying beyond acceptable moral boundaries by our National Laws. Well, you know how we men love to push and smash through our barriers? Those five words, 'all available resources and methods', freed the beasts within us. The pushing and slapping, the kicking and prodding, evolved into beating and bludgeoning. In our view, the Easties brought this treatment upon themselves with their unnecessary attachment to material goods (including property) and stubborn refusal to accept the letter of our laws. Every one of the Unlawful Residents extracted from the appropriated properties had been given ample opportunity to express their respect for Our Dear Leader and the nation. They refused, and chose instead to make trouble.

From my current position, I see events from a different perspective. To drag people out of their homes and expect no resistance was sheer madness. Imagine yourself in a similar situation. I would certainly not leave politely. Perhaps we wished for the Easties to kick up a fuss and make trouble. Such behaviour then gave us justification to act as we did.

12

One evening, with multiple units involved in a large-scale Site Inspection, I witnessed two extraction disputes resolved with a bullet. The location, a high-rise complex in Southside. The population was predominantly Eastie, and the area a known hotbed of radical thought and opinion. It was home to many Potentially Disruptive Easties. A huge, raging Eastie refused to accept his UR status, and would not leave the property. He bellowed and cursed and stretched the patience of the officer in charge until it snapped. I was close enough to see an expression of surprise light up the Eastie brute's face before he collapsed to the ground. The man had been given an opportunity to leave quietly, and refused. Two floors below, a grey-haired fellow, carrying too many kilos of flesh, charged an SIU soldier with a bread knife. There was no need for a warning. His wife howled, the family dog barked as if it had lost its mind. The officer in charge ordered one of the men to attend to the baying hound. In both instances, I noted the surrounding reactions, especially the faces of the officers in charge. They remained calm, and I thought of a laboratory assistant mounting an insect onto a card.

Of course these incidents rattled my nerves, nausea attacked my guts and throat, but I hid this from the world around me. It was the wise thing to do. Many questions ran through my head as I watched the killings. 'Is this the right way to act?' or 'Why do you pretend to feel nothing?' or 'What are you doing here?' were not among them. Instead, my primary queries were about the ability and speed with which I could push the horror to one side and gather myself together. It took but a matter of seconds. I recited the mantra 'What are you?' 'I am a God!', straightened my back, and then adjusted to our new way of doing business with ease. Click. Just like that. 'All available resources and methods . . .'

There is one Site Inspection, a sticky memory, I would very much like to forget. I cannot. It was morning, and I led eight men to a neighbourhood north-west of Little River. As a child, I had occasionally passed through the area and never ceased to be impressed by the magnificent, sprawling villas. The homes here were glorious. They exuded wealth, power and comfort. With no more than the family home and those of my friends and relatives as reference,

I imagined that the families living in the villas must have tens of children. Why else live in a house that size?

We travelled together with an Unlawful Resident Transfer Squad. This was standard for such trips. There was also a Process Inspector, who would spend the day with our unit, monitoring activities and making notes. Occasionally there was a disconnect between methods thought up in the office and what took place on the ground. Process Inspectors located these fissures and prescribed solutions for areas in need of improvement. The PI's comments were never judgemental. They were usually helpful. It was our fifth Site Inspection with a PI in attendance, we were now used to their presence and went about our business as usual. I hoped, by the end of the day, to show our PI outstanding examples of Site Inspection practices.

Thus far, I had never been directly involved in the violence. This had nothing to do with shirking responsibilities, discomfort or fear of dirtying my hands. It happened that the men under my command were a proactive and enthusiastic lot, who enjoyed their work. I saw no reason to get in the way. My style was to stand back, oversee proceedings, and issue guidance when necessary.

We had an official Declaration of Illegality for the residents of No. 17. Our records had them down as a powerful Eastie trading family. Half of their business was conducted in our land, the rest in the East. Our records also told us that three of their five primary trading partners had links to radical elements within the Eastern power structure. This alone was not enough to place them under suspicion. However, in addition to the family refusing to sign the Oath, we had recordings of both parents demeaning the policies of the NDM, and witnesses to them publicly criticizing the stewardship of Our Dear Leader. Given these facts, even the most lenient Ministry of Housing and Justice officials would have no choice but to see the family for what they were: Potentially Disruptive Easties. Immediate Unlawful Resident status!

The weather was exceptionally bright. No. 17 was partially hidden from the road by a tall, precision-trimmed hedge and rows of slender trees. The route from the gate to the property's front door was breathtaking. We passed through a beautifully landscaped garden, where armies of flowers guarded a series of rolling slopes. There was a large pond with five wooden benches of superior quality.

At its centre was a fountain where three intertwined frogs, frozen in mid-leap, spewed thin jets of water from their open mouths. The glistening, twisting stream rose a good few metres into the air before falling back into the pond with musical splashes.

The Eastie family opened the door when we rang the bell. This kept us in a good mood. You would not believe the number of times we arrived for inspection only to have occupants pretend not to be home. The results were always the same: broken front doors. The occupants of No. 17 were an Eastie mother and her four offspring aged, I would say, between seventeen and twenty-five years: three males and a female. The father was away on business, which was no bother. In the husband's absence, the Ministry of Housing and Justice granted the wife full authority to sign the necessary documents. The signature was of course optional. We understood how the nerve-jangling nature of our inspections might make an Eastie struggle to put pen to paper. We made allowances for such conditions and also accepted thumbprints.

I immediately sent four men off to look around the property, and then offered the mother a few minutes to make her decision to sign, or not. In truth, her choice had no effect on our business. The arrival of a Site Inspection Unit at a location was as clear an indication as any that the Ministry of Housing and Justice had issued the occupants with official Declarations of Illegality. Why else would we be there?

The family had a typical reaction: shock and disbelief, followed by plenty of fumbling and muttering. This eventually gave way to acceptance of the situation. The mother, the female offspring and the eldest male hastily, and commendably, steadied their nerves. The mother explained that the absent husband would clear up any misunderstandings the instant he returned. She asked if we could please wait another three days. I corrected the mother on the matter of misunderstandings: there were none. As for the requested delay, our unit lacked the authority to adjust procedural schedules at such short notice. The two youngest males did not react well to the news, and began to express a noisy, quite irritating panic. The younger of the two commenced a hysterical sobbing. It was a terrible sound, and fortunately for all of our ears, the mother took pity. She pulled him into her arms, gave comfort and calmed him down.

As for the property itself, I had only ever seen inside

such places in the cinema, and on the pages of Mother's magazines. Had I not been on official business, my mouth might have dropped open at the sight of the finery adorning the entrance hall. I had grown up with an awareness of Easties, though my interactions with them were rare, always distant but polite. A few lived in my neighbourhood, some attended my school, university. That said, I never had Eastie friends or found a reason to seek out their company. There was no animosity or ill feeling of any kind. We had no contact because we were fundamentally different kinds of human beings. I had no issues with difference and variety, as they brought colour and inspiration into our world. I did, however, like the rest of the nation, have difficulty when the behaviour and activities of our guests had a negative impact on the lives of the hosts. The lack of contact also meant I had never seen the interior of an Eastie house. It was a pleasantly surprising experience.

One of my first impressions was the height of the ceiling, and the ingenious use of wood to create frames supporting the walls and floors. The door handles, light switches, bannister adornments, etc. were patterned with intricate sequences of ovals and circles. They appeared to be in constant motion, and made me dizzy.

The architect's remit must have included bringing as much light as possible into the house. Sunbeams on this beautiful morning found their way into most rooms in the house. The rooms themselves were extraordinary and they too had a hypnotic effect on the senses. I was forced to station one of the men outside the front gate as it became impossible to convince him that the property was not possessed with Eastie magic. I understood the man's point of view: every room in the house was blessed with its own distinct identity. Crossing the threshold from one room to another was like moving between worlds.

One room in particular held my attention. On the second floor, on the north side of the house, was a library. The walls were covered in bookshelves, filled to an unsafe degree with books. There was little furniture in the room. At the south end stood a magnificently constructed wooden lectern. The antique edition resting on its adjustable top was a book I had read about, but never seen with my own eyes. Turning the pages was a humbling experience. At the north end of the library, a pair of chairs sat in conversation close to the large window. And the view! A magnificent garden park rolled gently downhill towards a lake. I saw a wooden pier, a red boathouse, a variety of trees, arrangements of perfectly trimmed hedges dancing with benches, statues . . . Beyond the lake was a forest, dense and mysterious. I could easily have spent the rest of the day sitting in one of the chairs, reading, gazing out of the window for a while, before reading some more. But duty called.

Another item of note: on entering the house, our nostrils were met by a delicious aroma. Not one I recognized, other than perhaps the faint echo of cinnamon. The sheer culinary goodness infused in that fragrance made it impossible for the men not to start blinking and licking their lips. I wondered what the Process Inspector made of it. I followed the sweet smell to the kitchen and discovered a stew simmering away in a huge pan. There was enough to feed a squad of hungry men. 'Expecting guests?' I asked the eldest male, who shadowed me during my ground-floor inspection. He replied with a sullen grunt that said nothing. There was a faint glint of defiance in his eyes.

I had never seen so much vegetation inside a home. While the landscaped interior garden at NDM HQ was impressive, the variety and arrangement of greenery at No. 17 left me speechless. Plants everywhere. They had colonized half the interior of the house! It had more in common with a botanical garden than with a residence. Perhaps turning the insides of one's home into a forest was an Eastie custom. If so, it was a fine tradition. There was a soothing quality to the ubiquitous flora.

The family had a fondness for portraits, though not of themselves. Every wall on the ground floor, with the exception of those in the kitchen, had at least two framed portraits. The faces looked out at the world without comment, leaving the impression of being stared at by ghosts. A few were painted in styles I recognized from museum visits, the rest were alien, though beautiful and hypnotically interesting. While I was inspecting one particular portrait, in an attempt to understand how it could affect my head as it did, the men returned with the preliminary 'reports' of their Site Inspections. We were ready.

Three minutes later, I addressed the family members in the entrance hall. I handed the mother the necessary papers and indicated where we required her signature, or thumbprint. She accepted the documents and then, to our surprise, began to sing out loud. I did not understand the words, yet I felt the great sadness they carried. Her voice was so beautiful I could not order her to stop. To do so felt criminal. At no point during her recital did the mother make eye contact with me or any of the men. The mother finished the song, and then signed. The young female's eyes spat fire.

I took the signed copies of the document from the mother, folded one copy, placed it in an official envelope, and then handed that to the young female. By this time, the mother had returned to comforting her youngest. His sniffling and quaking annoyed me intensely, as it compelled me to share in his fear. I needed him out of my sight.

Under the accelerated inspection programme, illegal occupants received fifteen minutes in which to vacate the premises with whatever they could carry. On the matter of carrying, I was surprised at how many Easties overestimated their strength, and to such a large degree. The afternoon before the inspection at No. 17, I witnessed a middle-aged man attempt to move his mother's grand piano single-handed! We tried our best not to laugh. We were, after all, in the middle of official business . . .

That morning at No. 17, rather than offer the usual fifteen minutes, I took into account the tasteful elegance of the property, and gave the family half an hour to remove themselves from the premises. I explained my reasoning to the Process Inspector. As expected, she neither agreed nor disagreed with me. In truth, there was another reason for the time extension: it provided an opportunity for another quick visit to the family's library.

Twenty-three minutes later, the family, minus the mother, stood in the entrance hall. In their hands, wrapped across shoulders, and strapped onto their backs were suitcases, bags and articles of clothing. The eldest male wore a lampshade on his head. Quite a sight. I remember the confusion written across the two younger males' faces.

My next move was to select a cigarette from the pack in my breast pocket and light up, all the while observing the young Easties with an affected air of total disinterest. I am sure you would laugh at this, but you knew, just as I did, my whole smoking business was nothing but show. I smoked when bored during parties. I stood and posed, cigarette in hand, with members of the public who asked (always with deference) to have a photograph taken standing next to me. Of course I smoked on the job. One segment of our Site Inspection training focused on the value of what they termed 'non-vocal' communication. Within this module was a lesson on 'Situational Attitude', where we were taught how best to express the three Ds: Disdain, Disgust and Disinterest. We learned which of the Ds worked best, and under what circumstances. I discovered the sight of me casually puffing away while those around me shivered in terror, anger and panic introduced a certain panache. Sad to say, the moment was soured by the mother's absence. I dispatched three men to discover the cause of the delay. They returned a minute later requesting my presence upstairs.

I found the mother in the first-floor master bedroom, kneeling beside a dresser. In this room-world, the ovals and circles found on the fittings around the house were given carte blanche. Lights, mirrors and wallpaper patterns were all oval in form, as was the bed, with an oval mattress to match. The mother's attachment to the dresser was understandable. It was a magnificent piece of furniture, and I truly hope whoever owns it today does so with appreciation.

The mother knelt and whispered. It might have been in prayer, or a goodbye to an old friend. Her lips moved, tears dripped from her cheeks onto the parquet floor. Touching. But we did not have the time for Eastie theatrics. I had two men carry her downstairs, while another took care of her luggage.

The young Easties turned their mother's arrival into a highly emotional moment. Moaning, wailing, plenty of tears. Excessive and unnecessary. The mother had been upstairs for only a few minutes longer than everyone else, not recently pardoned while on the way to meet the hangman's noose. At the time, I believed it was a display of the volatile emotions that distinguished a simpler, more primitive being. It was a very sad scene. By reflex, without thinking (perhaps you will have difficulty understanding such a gesture, given the circumstances), I stepped forward and laid my hand on the mother's right shoulder. It was meant as an act of comfort. The mother responded by spinning around and snarling like a wild creature. This was our first eye contact since the Site Inspection Unit's arrival, and I tell you, it took much of my resolve not to wither. Such was the force of her glare.

The mother's expression was frosty and laced with disgust. 'Let me tell you,' she began. 'This uniform cannot hide what you do. It cannot hide the fact that apart from being a thug and a thief, you are nothing!' She concluded her statement by stepping forward and spitting in my face. I heard the slow bubbling noises made by her saliva as it dripped down my right cheek.

13

Sometimes life is much too fast. We act, and cannot remember why. I have searched for a reason to explain my conduct at No. 17, but the riddle remains unsolved. There is only the drawn-out recollection of events.

The room fell silent, a mad ringing erupted between my ears. Was the tingle of embarrassment that moved from one patch of my skin to another visible to everyone else? Pride had just been punctured in public and so Ego stepped in and demanded revenge. As I wiped my face clean with a handkerchief, the youngest male tried to suppress a giggle. He failed. Was it the thoroughly annoying squeak, or the look on his face? I cannot say. Whatever the case, a fury rose up from my toes, through my legs, my torso, and entered my heart.

This memory business can be strange. The version of events at No. 17 that currently fills my mind is not quite as I once recalled it. The setting, the players, the actions remain the same. However, now my memories are awash with details I had either avoided, forgotten or missed.

Do our minds record everything but keep it locked away somewhere safe until the time is right? The approach of our end has freed these memories.

The hall was so quiet I heard the sound of my handkerchief landing on the floor. In my head, a chorus of 'What are you?' 'I am a God!' and the edict from NDM officer training: 'It is of vital importance that the officer of the National Defence Movement remains in control, and separates necessary action from the banality of emotion.'

Here today, those words ring hollow as the shiny suit worn by a charlatan while he impresses a gullible subject. What, in Heaven's name, is 'banality of emotion'? I tell you from personal experience, a life disconnected from feeling is a terrible form of existence.

In the bright silence at No. 17, I became acutely aware of the men: watching, waiting. The Process Inspector looked on and took notes. The mother's stare projected hate and disgust. The young female's eyes threw fire. The eldest male offspring twitched and appeared nervous. The second to youngest stared at his feet. The last, the little one, wore a smirk and a look in his eyes that did not rest kindly with me.

I suppressed an urge to rage and scream at the mother.

How I would have loved to shout at the top of my voice, as a God, and demand an explanation for such vulgarity. I would ask how spitting in my face would resolve her grievances with the Ministry of Housing and Justice. However, such an outburst would have been very low in dignity. I held my tongue.

I would much rather not tar a whole people with a single brush. However, my experience commanding an SIU had shown there were no limits to the aggression expressed by Easties as we extracted them from appropriated properties. Generally speaking, they were barbaric and lacked any form of self-control. No amount of finery or wealth could disguise an Eastie's true character. Case in point: the mother and her venomous spitting. Although her actions were driven by genetic composition and, on a certain level, no fault of her own, it would have been better for all if she had remained in control of these tendencies. On that sunny morning, I saw no connection between the Easties' aggression and our Site Inspection Units tossing them out of their homes. I saw in the mother nothing but another wild, uncivilized being.

The spittle itself, while unpleasant, was harmless enough. The problem lay in the contempt behind the mother's actions. Such behaviour was, as I believed at the time, an insult to myself and my uniform, to the nation, and to Our Dear Leader. My rank and position compelled me to make a point about this matter. My eyes came to rest on the youngest of the mother's offspring. The manner in which she comforted him earlier on marked him out as her favourite. My decision spanned an age. There was a voice. Front-left of mind. An earnest, whispered caution: 'He is just a boy!'

The youngest stood before me. Quivering lips blocked his words. There was a frightened animal noise, a sound that lived between a cry and a groan. 'He is just a boy!' Again that voice. Followed by a quiet moment, and then a response, a loud and righteous chorus from the opposite side of my mind: 'What are you?' My body answered . . .

My arm rose slowly until the barrel of the pistol, held in my hand, pointed towards the young one's nose. His eyes became wide-open pools, and unhindered dread rippled the surface. I watched the Eastie's expression transform into terrified understanding about his very near future. Tears began a slow, downward crawl over his cheeks.

'He is just a boy!' That voice again, though now far away and barely audible, shouted into submission by the mighty chorus. 'What are you?' 'I am the answer.' 'I am Authority. I will decide because I am a God.'

I heard the mother's intake of breath. A powerful, endless hiss. A decision made. The trigger accepted my finger's pull. A click. A flash. A young life reached the end of its journey. One last whisper. 'He was just a boy.'

There were screams. All members of the Eastie family screamed. The offspring, the mother. My eyes, and I know this cannot be so, watched the mother's screams create a thousand cracks across her skin. Her eyes begged me to tell her it was a lie. I remember thinking about my uniform, the nation, Our Dear Leader and the Greater Glory. The mother crumbled and collapsed in a heap over her young offspring's body. It was as if her insides and outsides had turned to salt. That was my doing. This was my work.

At that same instant, I was overcome by a terrible sickness. As if my gall bladder had released its bitter juices into my system from where they infiltrated my heart. That was only the beginning. Waves of revulsion, a terrible urge to empty my stomach and bowels then and there. Not in front of the men and the Process Inspector. Certainly not in front of the Easties! That shame would destroy me. I steadied myself by locking my gaze onto the eyes of the farmer portrayed in the large painting on the wall opposite. In her arms was a lamb, loved and protected. The farmer's eyes reached out and held me fast. 'What have you done?' they asked. 'What have you done?'

I distinctly remember leaving my body and rising up to one of the entrance hall chandeliers. From that lofty position I looked down and saw the men, the Process Inspector, the suitcases and bags, the offspring, the shattered mother, the body, the blood, and then, where I should have been, was a something. That version of myself might have passed as human had it not lacked a few vital elements. A being without empathy, stripped of love and understanding, is an ugly creature. We try hard never to see this side of ourselves.

Eventually the mother's screams evolved into a howl. Spine-tingling notes of pain and disbelief escaped from deep within her chest. The sound rattled the windows and worried my nerves. In the meantime, my airborne self, because it had nowhere else to go, returned to the ground. All present watched as I returned the pistol to its holster, and then lit up a cigarette. My hands were as steady and calm as a mountain. On the inside, the banalities of emotion ground my soul into dust. 'What are you?' 'I am a God!'

I felt sorry for the now youngest male. Events had caused him to spontaneously soil his garments. I suggested a change of clothing, and sent him off with two of the men to clean up and find something appropriate to wear. He moved in a sequence of slow-motion jerks, a fragile, rickety puppet.

A quarter of an hour later, I granted the family permission to take the carcass with them to their next destination. The men had since removed the remains from the property, dragged it across the front garden, out through the gate, and deposited it on the pavement. A few neighbours came to the family's aid. Terrified Easties scurried one way and the other, doing all in their power to avoid my gaze. Using a combination of curtains, bedsheets and native skills, the carcass was packaged up and hoisted onto one of the Unlawful Resident Transfer Squad's trucks.

I stood erect and proud, under the trees outside No. 17. I puffed on my cigarette and observed the comings and goings. The bits and pieces of the world around me appeared far away. Back then I felt powerful, today I feel unclean. What manner of being takes pride in acting this way?

The rest of the day's Site Inspections were, thankfully, uneventful. We got on with the business of dispensing official Declarations of Illegality, the recipients got on with the business of vacating Ministry of Housing and Justice property. My feet carried me from one inspection site to the next. My lips moved, my tongue wagged, orders left my mouth. I was simultaneously present and absent. The outside world saw an officer of the NDM, functioning in a truly professional manner. On the inside, I felt nauseous.

That night, I, who never went beyond slightly tipsy, returned home late and very drunk. I could barely stand. The next morning over breakfast, with my head still ringing like church bells, you shared the story of me staggering in, practically foaming at the mouth, and raging incessantly about a pan of stew. My obsession with the pan was such, you wondered if my work had given me a mental attack. 'What do you mean?' I challenged you. Your response was to recite a list of the ways in which I had changed. I recognized nothing. You talked of a night in ruins. Dinner cold, efforts wasted. I apologized for letting dinner slip my mind. 'Has the NDM banned anniversaries?' you asked. I dared not reveal the circumstances that led me to forget. Instead, I produced a vague fable about the Eastie rabble-rousers we caught harassing some of our women and children. That was a lie. Every word nonsense. But you knew, your laugh said it all.

From the moment we left No. 17, not only was I plagued with a growing sense that I had shrunk in the world, but also by the constant echo of the mother's howls. Her sorrow filled my head and would not leave. Equally disturbing, I heard a voice within my head, and one I could not recognize, ask over and over again: 'What have you done? What have you done?'

I replaced my blood with liquor, then grabbed that whiny voice by the throat and strangled it. You mentioned how that night I howled out like some wild creature. I claimed to have no knowledge of this. In truth, I was wide awake. The cry marked the moment I let go of most that was good in me. And then, miracle of miracles, I slept like a man with no worries, without a conscience as ballast. I now understand that not all doors remain open when you pass through: some close behind you forever.

I made my choices. There was no coercion, no

enforcement. The sad conclusion was that I, with my supposed broad world-view and education, was not immune to the effects of nationalist euphoria sweeping across our land. With practically everyone else doing the same, I learned to act without thinking, and remained happily blind to the greater consequences of my choices. Back then it was easy to believe my actions, no matter how abhorrent, had the blessing of the nation, the NDM and Our Dear Leader. I delegated my thinking to Our Dear Leader, the top echelons of the NDM and to DIDS. It was easy to do so.

The delivery of official Declarations of Illegality and extraction of illegal Eastie occupants, driven by our use of 'all available resources', became a blood sport. I played without resistance or hesitation. We were officers of the NDM and guardians of the land. The occasional dead Eastie was an acceptable price to pay for national security and survival.

Today, and far too late to be of much use to you, I understand how thoroughly miserable the two months following the incident at No. 17 must have been for you. I lost count of how many times you pleaded with me to explain what was wrong. How often did you, in tears, declare my behaviour to be cold and without love or mercy? I remember that terrible argument, when you challenged me to find some other work, something that would not consume every gram of joy. I listened, but could not hear. One by one, the strands binding us together frayed. Your visits became less frequent. Our conversations became hot with the friction of differences. 'How can you not see them as fellow human beings?' More command than question. 'How can you blame everyone for the behaviour of a few?' Your increasingly sympathetic views of the Easties clashed with my understanding of the species. You spouted radical dogma. You claimed a culture or language could be different to, but never greater than, another. I countered with a memorized list of established truths. Back and forth we argued. Ever louder until the moment, at our wits' end, we agreed to disagree, and lapsed into an uncomfortable silence. Volatile was a fair description of our relationship. And then Our Dear Leader issued the Final Ultimatum. It was a welcome move.

The tense and soured relationship between ourselves and the East worsened. Barbed, ugly and passive-aggressive insults were tossed back and forth, like sticky mud, between our capitals. The Easties called us robbers, snakes and oppressors of their people. We, in turn, referred to them as corrupt, barbaric fools. Such was the state of our coexistence until one day, Our Dear Leader, backed by the NDM, decided enough was enough. He looked East and spoke: 'Neighbours to our East, our patience has come to an end, and justice is on the way. It can visit the few, or affect the many. The choice is yours.' On behalf of the NDM and the nation, Our Dear Leader issued a Final Ultimatum to the Eastern leadership. They were given seventy-two hours to hand over those responsible for the Dear Leader's assassination. Failure to comply within the allotted time frame automatically gave us the right to act in a manner that protected our honour and national interests.

The distraction of the Final Ultimatum provided an escape route from the constant examination of our personal relationship. There was an ominous ring to Our Dear Leader's voice. One newspaper columnist described it as 'the song of tempered steel leaving its sheath'. The nation listened and prepared. The state of affairs between us and the East demanded most of my attention. You stepped back, gave me room. A gap appeared between us.

14

War was coming. We could feel it, we smelled it. As hot metal: angry and dangerous. War called out from radio speakers across the land, channelled through Our Dear Leader's speeches. Each transmission was twice as fiery as the one before. War attached itself to every other newspaper headline. War infiltrated the games of children playing in their neighbourhood streets and the city's parks. War attached itself to the lyrics of popular songs. War influenced the fashions of the day: even household items were not immune. War adjusted our way of thinking and looking at the world. War rumbled in the accelerating mobilization. It beckoned the nation's young men (I among them), and promised adventure filled with glory of historical proportions. Still smarting from having missed out on the action in the previous conflict, of course I leapt at the opportunity.

Military vehicles became a regular part of city traffic. Our national ensign fluttered from flagpoles that seemed to sprout out of every facade and half the city's rooftops.

NDM forces, in their thousands and thousands, marched towards our eastern border. The nation looked on at the tanks, the guns, the men in their uniforms, and wept with pride. We were so much more than a war machine. We were a statement of intent. We were magnificent. We were power! The nation sent us off with cheers and wishes for a speedy victory. I saw the flags and listened to the joyous bands. Everyone loved us, with the exception of the Easties among us. They too watched, powerless and afraid, as we headed off to destroy their land.

Behind the noise and exuberance, behind my upright, eyes-forward pose, was a sorrow. An aching heart. We had been apart for two and a half, three weeks. Seeing you again gave me such warmth. Were it not for my uniform, and the need to maintain standards, I might have cried. I had missed you, though not as painfully as I do now. I remember my sisters, who thought I did not know they had arranged for you to come to say goodbye, fidgeting and giggling in the background. I remember your fingers touching my uniform, here, here, there . . . I remember your eyes. They revealed your sadness at my leaving (we had yet to smooth out matters between us) and worry about the nature of my adventure. Finally came your parting gift: this journal, and a request that I make a record of my travels.

I headed east with the Property and Population Control Battalion, also known as the PPC. Our battalion flag was dark maroon with a large golden circle in the middle. The circle, which also served as our shoulder sleeve insignia, contained a graphic representation of a house with a family inside. As was expected of anything developed by NDM Messaging and Public Relations, the design had a certain visual clarity: almost friendly. We were also provided with 'complimentary' cards, one side of which carried our battalion flag while the other bore the simple text: 'Approved by NDM Property and Population Control'.

I fear the PPC's contribution to the history books will be written in red ink. Something happened as we crossed the Eastern border. We threw off the part of ourselves that recognized the 'other' as human, jettisoned our conscience as if it were excess baggage.

By the time our armies were unleashed on the East, the language used to describe Easties had become vicious and extremely ugly. Stories about Easties in our nation being spat upon, beaten and worse, had become too common to make the news. As we soldiers of the NDM moved into the East, every one of us did so in the understanding we had entered a land inhabited by savages, an inferior category of human being. This being the case, our moral codes did not apply in the East.

Our Dear Leader compelled us to go forward, to become legends, to write our glorious chapter in the history books! He commanded us to scorch the earth beneath our enemy's feet, and then drench the ashes with Eastie blood. As hungry demons, we swallowed these words and nourished ourselves with what they implied.

The Easties' large, lumbering forces were no match for our agility and brutality, or for our discipline and focus. The superior firepower of the NDM troops, combined with tactics developed during and after our war with the West, allowed us to roll over their legions with ease. In addition, all NDM soldiers believed we fought for a superior purpose: the Greater Glory. The heady essence of one victory after another turned our minds and rendered our every action correct. I am sure you know what it is to win and succeed, in school, at work, in life . . . You remember the accompanying glow, warm and magnificent. The sense of floating above all others. I assure you, the thrill of defeating an army and reducing it to a memory is a thousand times greater than any of that.

Our behaviour in this land, and the PPC's existence, can be understood in the context of Our Dear Leader's belief that the removal of everything worth fighting for would break the spirit, and a broken people would have no will to resist. Prior to his ascension, Our Dear Leader had run the Ministry of Data and Security's Office of Strategic Possibilities. We referred to them as the 'What Ifs'. They used analysis from EDS and DIDS data streams as input for the generation of a seemingly unlimited range of possible scenarios: What if this? What if that? It was as Head of Strategic Possibilities that Our Dear Leader had developed the scenario of 'Erasure'.

He viewed 'identity' as a complex cement that held a people together. Identity included language, traditions, music, art, industry, and so on. Any single one, or a combination of these elements could be employed as 'fuel' to encourage resistance to external forces. An example of this was the use of our own warrior ancestry to rally the nation, and ultimately defeat the Westerners, during the last war.

The complete erasure of such elements, in a wartime setting, would allow for swifter victories. Furthermore, over time erasure could 'disappear' a people from history.

At the time, our since-deceased head of state, the Dear Leader, declared it a scenario conjured up by the Devil, and reminded those concerned that the Office of Strategic Possibilities was not the place for such thinking. The NDM's purpose was to facilitate growth and improvement. In short: to build, and not destroy. Now the brain behind the Erasure Doctrine belonged to our new man at the top. He was the law and believed, in the context of their deeds, and supported by the demands of justice, that erasure was an appropriate fate for the Easties.

The PPC became my home, and still remains so, though our current numbers would barely fill a platoon. We are the militarized arm of the Property Integrity Office. We report to the Ministry of Data and Security, rather than the Ministry of Defence, and are one of the NDM's 'special units'. The special units were a natural evolution of the action teams set up within Data and Security to carry out hands-on, rather than administrative tasks. When the need arose, the PPC performed duties in conjunction with regular NDM Army or Flying Forces.

Most of the time, as was the case with all other special units, we operated alone.

Some of the great tales of our time contain references to structures and cities that have long since disappeared. One hoped for by-product of our conquering the East would be the total erasure of their culture. The task given to the PPC was to focus on objects and structures of interest. These included architectural highlights, industry, art, museum artefacts, etc. We methodically recorded every last detail of what we believed worthy during our Property and Population Inspections, and then destroyed them. Our documentation was sent, via messenger, back to the Ministry of Data and Security. The photographs and filmed footage were analysed, categorized, and then given a quiet home in the vast Data and Security archives. There were also reports. Some made their way back to the PPC in the form of advised adjustments to specific methods: increased efficiency the goal, as always.

The PPC earned the nickname 'The Factory Boys' because of the huge mobile processing units that accompanied us. Our stone grinders transformed even the most stubborn materials into gravel. Our furnaces dealt with all leftover metals. We could smelt anything, from structural iron down to the precious solids found in museum pieces. For more menial duties, such as glass collection, book, fabric and wood burning, we employed able-bodied members of the local population.

Strictly speaking, the PPC is not a fighting battalion. Though when challenged or harassed in any way, we strike back. In the early days of the invasion, we fought alongside the 13th Armoured Battalion. However, within a week, the PPC was busy going about what we were created to do: recording and then destroying any item an Eastie might be proud of. Erasure.

The PPC became notorious for its scorched rubble blessings. There is a hypnotic quality to demolition, and a spirituality to the dismantling of splendour. We carried out orders, distilled from the words of Our Dear Leader, with great fervour. By the time we had completed our eighth or ninth inspection, turning objects into ashes and/or rubble had become a near-religious experience for the soldiers of the PPC. Meanwhile, the wanton destruction fed the wild within us. The beauty of much that we smashed was breathtaking. We created ruin, and then laughed at the Easties as they watched what we did and wept. The rout of the Eastern armies gave us the room to operate as we pleased. We believed our actions were those of higher beings, dishing out civilization to inferior creatures. Clearing out the waste in preparation for a more enlightened infrastructure. I am no longer able to see our behaviour as anything other than violent thuggery, perpetrated by men in finely tailored uniforms.

The East surprised me in many ways, the most notable of which was the architecture. Here were structures and proportions I had never seen before. The Easties appeared to have invented new colours and materials for their buildings. It was fascinating. Primitive, of course, and yet something about their constructions always caught my eye. Such a shame you and I never managed to travel in the East, back when our countries were still at peace. Perhaps there is some twisted consolation in being one of the last people alive to see these buildings, paintings, sculptures, and so on, in their full glory.

I ordered destruction with the excitement of a child who has just learned the joy of knocking down building blocks. I remember once, on holiday, Mother scolding a child on the beach. The boy, a little older than I, had come along and smashed the sandcastle complex my friends and

I had spent the afternoon constructing. 'How can you be happy breaking up what others have made?' she asked. I cannot remember the boy's answer. What would Mother have to say about my work here in the East? We soldiers of the PPC certainly knew how to demolish with glee. Our battalion was home to some of our nation's finest engineering minds. With bittersweet pride, I tell you these men came up with the most ingenious methods of reducing buildings to dust. No structure could withstand their destructive creativity.

The NDM High Command believed we were doing an exemplary job and complimented us on our inspirational and outstanding work. Their words gave us a boost, confirmed our belief in the righteousness of our mission for the Greater Glory, and in our sense of invincibility. This state of mind prepared us for the next phase of our mission. We were truly unstoppable.

One problem that confronts armies in the case of rapid territorial gain is what to do with the civilians, the stragglers and others caught up in our bloody business. NDM High Command understood military efficiency was achieved through a combination of factors, one being the careful management of resources. The wretched hordes of Eastie prisoners were a problem. Initially, we fed and sheltered the captives in rudimentary compounds, as per the conventions of war. Meanwhile, NDM High Command, in consultation with Our Dear Leader, made the necessary decisions. Ever-increasing food consumption by an ever-multiplying number of prisoners was seen as an unnecessary drain. The Easties were hungry: they ate as if food would be declared illegal within the hour. There were even a number of jokes in circulation themed around the Eastie plan to defeat us by consuming all our provisions! NDM High Command provided a simple and effective solution: they declared the continued management of Eastie holding compounds a needless waste of valuable resources. Commanding officers of the special units were given freedom to resolve matters relating to overconsumption as they saw fit. Our rules of engagement were adjusted to reflect this new flexibility. Additionally, improved manufacturing technology back home, and an efficient logistics network, kept us well supplied with bullets. At the time I understood the logic behind these choices. However, I was less understanding of our battalion's diversion away from straightforward erasure to 'prisoner management' duties.

To call the endless killing of captives boring may sound callous, even mad to your ears.

Unfortunately, bored is how we felt, and killing is what we did.

Such work is never easy, in the beginning. But in time, because we are soldiers loyal to the NDM, we learned to remove our actions from the clutches of conscience and emotion. All for the Greater Glory.

I heard a rumour, we all did, that Our Dear Leader paid a visit to one such prisoner management enclosure to get a first-hand glimpse of Eastie erasure in action. They say he watched and immediately took ill when the first body hit the floor of the burial trench. They whisked him away and sent him home in a flash, so the rumour goes. Word came down from NDM HQ warning us to ignore any 'cowardly gossip' about Our Dear Leader as this was the creation of 'filthy Eastie tongues'. We listened, we shrugged our collective shoulders, and then got on with our work.

Were our activities ever to appear in a work of fiction, any readers with stomachs hardy enough to read through to the end might call it a vivid depiction of Lucifer's work. The reality is otherwise. The Devil had nothing to do with our business. Every one of us functioned as expected, as elite soldiers with a clear objective. We slaughtered and shed blood with a delirious pride. We developed new methods of killing. Our murderous experimentation, more often than not, had little to do with tactics or efficiency and a lot to do with keeping the men entertained.

I was present at all times. I questioned nothing, resisted nothing. I saw to it our orders were carried out to the letter, and often led by example. Whenever doubt or a hint of conscience threatened to raise its head, I chased it off with a reminder that 'I am a God' and that all our actions were for the Greater Glory. Our souls, meanwhile, began to rot. The stench of spiritual decay was always about us. On our skin, on our uniforms, in the air, and in the results of our endeavours. How glad we were when the battalion returned to our regular erasure business.

For long stretches of our journey, there was no enemy to fight, and nothing to destroy. The bored men often shot at passing birds, or anything else that lived and moved. Others succumbed to a melancholy and claimed to no longer understand what they were doing, or why we were there. A gentle chat, and a reminder to honour their uniforms and focus on the Greater Glory, was usually enough to snap them out of their gloom. Though I did see their point: we were trained for action. Unfortunately, our destruction of the Eastern army saw us capture territory without resistance. There was little glory in that.

As exciting as destruction can be, smashing and breaking and crushing, day after day, does become monotonous. I noticed an increase in the number of errors and delays during operations. The reasons for the slips were often related to lapses in focus. This I reported back up the chain of command. I was met with understanding. The men of the PPC were not alone in suffering the tedium brought on by the Easties' military weakness and cowardice. This condition afflicted most of the NDM forces in the East. Boredom aside, in the bigger scheme of the war, I had noticed (in the same manner we note the approach of spring) the appearance of the first shoots of total victory. Glory approached. I could feel it in my bones, and heard it in the tone of messages between ourselves and High Command. I shared this insight with the men: 'Have patience. It is just a matter of time.' These were good men. They heard me. We marched further east, crushing and ripping apart every object of beauty that lay in our path.

The sheer size of the country was awe-inspiring and,

at times, menacing. The distance between towns and cities of interest appeared infinite. Imagine travelling for days through a landscape that does not change. At first, the endless sameness is hypnotic, almost soothing. But it soon becomes maddening. Everything we saw appeared to constantly transform into what we had just seen! The unchanging scenery made us question whether we were moving at all. I will never forget the unvarying crunch and groan of tracks and wheels, the rumble of engines and thud of booted feet as we moved through kilometre after kilometre of sun-bleached land. Thankfully, there were occasions when the monotony of the landscape was temporarily interrupted by an unusual geographic feature.

One moment. Aircraft approaching! I need to go out. I shall return soon.

15

What can I tell you? I have spent the last three minutes or so waiting for my fingers to stop trembling. The aircraft have gone. Rather than soften us up with bombs, or pepper our positions with bullets, they showered us with sheets of paper. Questionnaires! The enemy plays with us. At the top of each sheet was a crude illustration: a caricature of Our Dear Leader engaged in an act too foul for these pages, his partner in this activity being a dog. Beneath the image was text written in our language. 'Dear Animals of the NDM, please choose your manner of death. Encircle one of the options below and present it to our troops as they arrive.' Below, a list of options, A to D, described various ways to butcher a human being. Each more vicious than the one before. All very slow. I had nothing to say to the men. I could not lie and pretend these were idle threats.

One of our sergeants offered a witty comment regarding our enemy's originality. As a result, some of the recently recruited boy-soldiers began to weep. I understood. We longer-serving men had willingly signed up for this adventure, these unfortunate children had not. Press-ganged by the NDM into military service, thrown into this misery. And to what end? Their short lives will never see victory. They cannot fight. They slow us down. We are soldiers, not mothers! Goodness knows what madness reigns in NDM High Command. How can they not understand, sending children into battle is mass murder? Do they not have children of their own, or younger brothers? I am thankful my sisters were not the brothers I always wished for. How would I have protected them from this horror? One boy-soldier was in such a state, I had to comfort him as I would a child lost in the city. Frail and terrified, his every muscle trembled, including the ones controlling his lips. He asked me to save him. What could I do, send a bullet through his skull once the enemy began its final assault? I kissed his forehead, and then whispered hollow encouragements in his ear.

On the way back to the tent, I considered how the boy was beyond my help, and realized the same applied to myself. I no longer have influence over anything except the attitude with which I accept the end. Death is coming soon. The questionnaires from the sky confirmed this. I sat down, tried to write, and fear attacked my fingers. The others in the tent were too wrapped up in their own business to notice.

It occurs to me that among the reverential tales of our ancestral warriors who gave their lives for this, that and the other, not one tells us what these heroes felt or thought just before death carried them off.

I was about to describe to you one incident that made quite an impression on us, as we trundled through the unchanging landscape. Believe it or not, here and there in this abattoir, there are a few gentler moments. The morning after we first began to worry about the effects of geographic monotony on the men's spirits, Fate blessed us with a change of scenery. Our joy was infectious and exuberant. Imagine a whole battalion of men jumping about and whooping as if they had stumbled across the pot of gold at the rainbow's end.

The first indication was the change in colour of the long grasses, from bleached gold-brown to a green so lush, it took a fair amount of self-control to keep from ordering the driver to stop. I wished to step out and run through the grass! The expressions on the faces of the men around me made it clear I was not alone in harbouring such thoughts. Many of the infantrymen were unable to control themselves. Like children, they ran through the grass and released their inner foolishness. The ground beneath our feet marked the beginning of a long, slow descent into a valley, the likes of which we had never seen.

In the stories about ancient times, they talk of mighty beings with fists the size of mountains. The valley around us could well be the work of one such giant. Imagine the giant, in a fit of boredom, scraping a finger along the Earth's crust, much as we once did with our own fingers through damp sand at the water's edge. True, our country is home to many areas of natural beauty: the Southern Forest, the Highland Caves, not to mention the countless botanical gardens throughout the land. Trust me, all of that is mud compared to the beauty of this valley.

The flowers and shrubs were of completely alien shades, shapes and sizes. The sight of this flora filled our eyes with tears and our hearts with a sense of triumph. Another item of note was the absence of any paths or tracks in the valley. We felt like pioneers conquering lands usually left well alone by humankind. The sight of our battalion snaking its way through the valley was impressive indeed. I knew the image of our efficient, deadly serpent of war against the surrounding glory would impress those back home. I asked the photographers and camera crew trucks to circle around and record the PPC crossing the valley.

The noise of an army on the move is an assault on the ears. Engines, motors, caterpillar tracks, all manner of wheels, shouted commands, radio chatter, laughter, crunching boots, mechanical clatter, all combine into a symphony of dread. Enough to set the most committed pacifist's heart aflutter. This was not the case in the valley. The clangour of our battle-thirsty machine was drowned out by Nature's song. Our noise fell away as the sound of the wind and birds and crickets filled the audible foreground. I assumed this was an illusory effect created by the gently swaying grasses and the height of the valley's walls.

We travelled for a day and a half through the valley. I had never imagined it possible to descend to such depths yet remain above ground. The increased distance between ourselves and the sky above gave it an extraordinary blue tint. The sun, while bright and intense as ever, did not scorch us. As we crossed the valley's lowest point, a twenty-odd-kilometre stretch, the size of the walls to our north and south made us shrink. I believed, though I did not share this idea with anyone else, Mother Nature was giving a gentle reminder: on this globe, we humans, with our toys and manners, are not that important. A humbling experience, if ever there was one.

The final ten kilometres of the valley were even more impressive. The ground began to rise, and as it did so, trees appeared. A few here, some there, and there . . . Soon we found ourselves moving through a seemingly endless forest. The trees were magnificent, great in size and varied in attitude: proud trees, angry trees, laughing trees, dancing trees, quiet trees, wise trees. The trees must have been there at humanity's birth, and would still be around long after our demise. Had circumstances been otherwise, we would have stopped and taken the time to examine the forest. The experience of standing close to one of those mighty trees would have been quite a thrill.

16

With great sadness and shame, I can safely conclude that no other creature on this globe has butchered and drenched the soil in blood as we have. Yes, every action we took was for the good of the nation, but there is a price to pay for this. In the belief we had no choice but to distance ourselves from all emotional distractions, we became men of rock and iron, charged with carrying out actions and performing duties that lay beyond the abilities of ordinary citizens.

'What are you?' 'I am a God!'

We were reacquainted with the more stubborn Easties midway through their country. Our contact began with the occasional pocket of brief resistance. A skirmish here, another there. Always quickly snuffed out. Always a few casualties on our side: unfortunate and unnecessary. We were told their stubborn behaviour was a telltale sign of a simple, frightened mind. One unable to grasp, and therefore see, the reality before it. The reality was our cultural, intellectual and, of course, military superiority. Swollen with victory's arrogance, we failed to see the method in the Easties' mosquito warfare. A bite here, another there. A minor loss. Another minor loss. At the time we believed the Easties were very good at hiding the bodies of their dead. We rarely discovered any. Did we fight with invisible men? We found the Eastie style irritating, of course, but ultimately considered it ineffective. Our progress was irresistible. We could never be stopped. So we believed.

Today, I can do nothing but laugh at our annoyance and complaints regarding Eastie tactics. We called them unscrupulous vandals. We believed no action was too low or underhand for an Eastie. Whatever they called that 'business' of theirs, it was not warfare. It was scandalous. Baited traps in buildings, in animals. Bodies of our fallen rigged with explosive. If ever proof was needed that Easties belonged at the more primitive end of humanity's scale, it was plain to see in their despicable conduct. As the Easties' devious attacks on NDM forces increased, so did our loathing of them as living creatures. This evolution in our thinking was reflected in the escalating vindictiveness of our reprisals. Our Dear Leader and the top rungs of the NDM believed revenge, when employed with planning and precision, was an effective means of communication. In the case of the Easties, the special units, such as the PPC, used revenge to make it clear there was no equality between us. We meted out vengeance as if only we had the right to do so. If, for example, they killed one of us, we replied by executing ten of their number, selected at random.

Now, I realize that revenge is heavy work. My eyes and ears have seen too much. The misery, the terror, the blood. The cries of mothers with screaming children, weeping sisters, terrified brothers, fathers, aunts, uncles, friends . . . Desperation. Everyone wants to survive. I watched Easties beg and humiliate themselves as if shame did not exist. Anything for an extra second of life.

The threat of death gives birth to the strangest actions. The Easties always found one or two of their number who spoke our language well enough to be understood. Some believed this ability gave them the right to extra privileges, such as not joining the others in burial trenches. Hopeful translators offered us jewellery, money, property . . . We always laughed at that. As if soldiers of the PPC had time for, or interest in such items. They offered their assistance on matters of communication. We declined. Our orders were clear. We allowed Easties to keep hold of their worldly goods as we sent them off to that other place.

As I write of who I was then (a champion of our bloody business, aiming my weapon and pulling the trigger), there are moments when I am forced to pause. I touch these pages, my chest, my face. I look about me. The tent, the men and our circumstances confirm the truth. My actions brought us here, and as for how I managed to carry out such deeds with ease and pleasure, I do not know. Perhaps my mind at the time was preoccupied with thoughts of process and efficiency. Today it is visited by a troubling observation: all Easties looked and sounded very human to me.

17

An afternoon during what became my final trip home springs to mind. It is already thirteen months in the past! I wandered around the city without a plan. We had parted that morning with more anger than love. The cause of our friction was the foreign media and their lies about our war with the East. You challenged me, as you had throughout my visit, about these news articles. How much of what they said was true? I gave you a lecture on politics and devious propaganda. You called me blind and a puppet: a cheap clone of Our Dear Leader. I had no time for such nonsense and stormed out.

While out walking, I found myself surprised by the number of never before seen buildings, pavements, lamp-posts, neighbourhood parks, etc. I, with my supposed eye for detail, born and raised in this town, saw everything in a brand-new, quite beautiful light. Stranger still, I remember my eyes drinking it in, as if they were afraid to forget. From this position, it is as if Fate already knew . . .

My wanderings were interrupted by two schoolboys,

aged around nine or ten. They accosted me, announced their plans to become future heroes of the NDM, and asked for tips on how to make this happen. I became stuck. Whatever I had become at this point, I was not so far gone as to encourage the boys to take the same path as myself. At the same time, I had no desire to throw cold water on their dreams. The indecision that had plagued me prior to joining the NDM made a brief return. The result: paralysis. I stared at the boys. They stared back.

Eventually, and thankfully, the boys quickly removed us from the slightly awkward situation. They asked, in unison (as if the question had been posed many times before): 'How did you become a hero?' The question caught me flat-footed. These children still believed war was all guns and glory. I chose not to share the truth, and claimed to have pressing business elsewhere. I wished the two boys a pleasant afternoon and went on my way. Were they to see me now!

It was not long after this final trip home that Fate intervened to set up a meeting between the PPC and the 2nd Armoured Division. Our operations were such that we required a certain distance and disconnection from regular

NDM forces. All were happy with this arrangement, so this coincidence was an unusual affair. It took place early afternoon, eleven months ago. Our battalion was headed in a south-by-east direction, en route to a Property and Population Inspection: a small town, population approximately eight and a half thousand, though of great spiritual importance to the Easties. National folklore had this town as the birthplace of all things Eastie. Every one of them, at some point in their lives, visited the town to pay their respects. Our mission, following the usual recordings for later analysis, was complete erasure.

In the relentless push for efficiency, the strategists upstairs believed employing the NDM Flying Forces during the initial erasure phase would save time and materiel. Needless to say, our engineers and demolition teams were none too pleased. 'How accurate are the bombers?' they asked. 'What about unexploded ordnance?' We sent these and many other questions to NDM High Command. In reply, we were reminded of Our Dear Leader's expectation that officers of the NDM set an example to others and follow orders to the letter, without exception. We relayed this to the men, though in a milder tone. They accepted with grumbles. One of the engineers likened the use of aerial bombardment to an attempt at rendering an oil landscape with a tree trunk instead of a natural hair brush. We all got a laugh out of that.

The situation was as follows: the 1st, 4th and 5th Companies of the PPC were two hours ahead. We had remained behind with 3rd Company while they dealt with broken tracks on a number of their tanks. Problems solved, we moved on.

The region was free from enemy forces, and due to our preference for invisibility, Comms had cleared all regular military traffic from the area. We expected unhindered and unobserved passage. Unfortunately, Comms had not taken into account our two-hour delay. We approached the second to last crossroads before our final destination and found it blocked by the 2nd Armoured Division, travelling in an adjacent direction. Our initial response, as we were in no great hurry, was to wait. Motors were turned off as the caravan of troops and tanks and whatnot passed by.

As we waited, not a single hand was raised in salute, and not once did we receive a nod of acknowledgement. This in spite of our own salutes. The soldiers of the 2nd Armoured either ignored us, or looked upon us with disgust. As if we in the PPC were in some way inferior to them. We knew the rumours about regular NDM forces' disapproval of our methods. There were some who believed our actions had nothing to do with war. To such men, I would give a simple reminder: war evolves together with its participants. Today's armies behave and fight in a very different manner to those of a thousand years past. Other members of the regular forces argued our methods would bring shame and darkness upon the nation. The weakness in character displayed by those harbouring such thoughts was evident in the fact not one of them ever came and presented such an argument to my face.

The disregard of our salutes and our presence made us feel quite foolish. This treatment meted out by the 2nd Armoured was a thorny insult, as they punctured and then deflated our pride. We knew the role played by the special units in this war for the Greater Glory was just as important, if not more so, than that of anyone else. Yet, as a reward, we received silence and scowls from our very own brothers in arms! Rejection by one's own is an uncomfortable experience.

I now understand that the source of our discomfort was the sight of what we had become reflected back at us in the expressions of the 2nd Armoured soldiers. Not one of us had the desire to ask why the disdain was there. No need. We knew. The PPC battalion killed the old and unarmed, the weak, the scared. Men, women, children, infants. Meanwhile, many, like the two curious lads on my last trip home, looked upon men like myself and saw glory! With its array of colour-coded ribbons, those boys saw in my uniform an action hero from their comic books. They did not see the rot inside. How could they?

I cannot tell you what brings greater sadness: the results of my deeds, or the fact I performed every act without the slightest hint of shame or glimmer of mercy. Charity, compassion and sanctity of life were not words found in the PPC lexicon. That afternoon, the meeting with 2nd Armoured put us all in a very dark mood.

En route to the crossroads, about thirty minutes to the rear, we had spotted an odd-looking hill to our west. It was covered with a patchwork of crop and grazing fields, connected by a series of paths leading up to the small village at its summit. That a village should exist out in this emptiness, far from any other population centres, stirred my interest. The distance between our position and the village made it impossible to pick out much of the detail.

Though we did notice how no two buildings shared the same colour. Given that our business was elsewhere, we decided the village was too remote, too small, too insignificant. Dropping by for a visit was out of the question.

After fifteen minutes of chewing dust, I realized the 2nd Armoured, travelling along a road such as this, would take hours to pass. There was also a growing restlessness among the men, as the sting of wounded pride made itself known. Not all questions have simple answers. I cannot tell you why I allowed my insulted ego to play a role in the choices I made. Neither can I say why it was necessary to whip up such blood-red enthusiasm for an impromptu Property and Population Inspection. But I did, and I did. We decided to about-turn, head north, and pay the funny little village a visit after all.

18

The village occupants spotted us long before we arrived. There was nothing unusual about this. It was, after all, their terrain. As we approached the hill's summit (we were on foot, having parked our equipment in a large circle around the hill's base), a curious herd of goats came to inspect us, and then, with much bleating and tinkling of bells, escorted us into the village. Surprisingly, our arrival was greeted with cheers and applause! I would say close to three hundred and fifty occupants lined the main path into the village.

The village occupants showered us with dry grass and fuchsia-coloured petals. I still remember the dusty, salty fragrance of the grass. As for the petals . . . I plucked a few from my sleeve and rubbed them between my fingertips. They left behind a lightly tinted and oily residue. I sniffed at my fingers, and a blast of sweet-perfumed gasoline made me dizzy. Powerful stuff! The scent of dry grass and the petals combined to produce a heady welcome.

Easties welcoming the PPC into their village as if we

were heroes was simply unheard of. Had the world turned itself upside down? Believe it or not, one of the village occupants held aloft a framed photograph of none other than Our Dear Leader! The photograph captured him midway through what appeared to be a rant. Such expressive portraits of Our Dear Leader never appeared in the media back home. For a few seconds I believed the war had torn my mind to shreds and created a whole new reality. One in which the local population recieved death with joy and open arms. However, as I stood and conversed with a committee of five elders, I noticed all was not quite what it seemed. There was a familiar tension in their eye and body movements.

Given our activities in the East, the PPC's reputation brought terror to even the bravest souls. Hidden behind our clinically bureaucratic appellation ('Property and Population Control' did have a certain officious neutrality to it) was the destructive rage of wild, conscienceless animals. NDM High Command strategists believed in the importance of the psychological impact of our actions, an effect amplified by the near absence of survivors. By this stage in the war, the end phase of our Property and Population Inspections involved targeting anything that lived or moved. The aim, beyond erasing everything of value, was to fill the hearts of the Easties with absolute dread.

When the PPC arrived at a village or town and rounded up those who had not managed to run away, the atmosphere was usually one of anguish and desperation. Unfortunate natives filled the air with sounds of suppressed panic. I believe their restraint in expressing honest emotion had much to do with the myth that refusal to show fear could keep one alive. Perhaps there had been a few circumstances in which this was the case, though never in any situation involving the PPC. On occasion, usually driven by wickedness or boredom, we did nothing but wait and see how long before those left behind lost their composure. The impending collapse in decorum would be announced by a few random whimpers, and then moans, followed by squeals, cries, pleading. There was always plenty of weeping, begging and self-humiliation. At times the situation got so out of hand, we ended up with hordes of blabbering Easties prostrating themselves on the ground before us. That was not the case on this particular afternoon.

*

Once the village occupants' cheering and noise had calmed down (the anxious background chatter never stopped), I engaged in further conversation with the village elders. The exchange was facilitated by one of their females, whose age I would place between twenty and twenty-five years. She surprised us with her fluency in our tongue. As she spoke, her words sang to us, and we remembered home. How the female learned our language will forever remain a mystery.

We usually had little to say to the natives, but on occasion, when the mood took us, we chatted for a while before commencing our business. These 'conversations' were primarily for aesthetic purposes. Our photographers clicked away and recorded the always helpful, always friendly PPC soldiers chatting merrily with the natives. The themes of our talks were usually light-hearted matters: weather, the cost of living, family . . . That afternoon, the bulk of our conversation was filled with an endless stream of compliments from the village elders. These were expressed through a series of hisses and sounds from the back of the throat. Theirs was a strange dialect, quite unlike the usual Eastie noises. It conjured up visions in my head of ancient and primitive times. We learned how happy the occupants were to see us. How proud they were that we chose to bless them with our presence. They believed we were great warriors and virtuous men, and in honour of this, the village had prepared a toast.

You remember my allergy to loud public compliments? This is Mother's doing. Never one for acclamation, her approval was expressed with a hug, a kiss, a touch, a glance. The louder the praise, she claimed, the less it had to do with the receiver, and the more it involved the giver's need for attention. I looked at the village elders and noted their strained jollity. They did not seek attention, they sought a way to remain alive.

I watched the elders: their eagerness to please us returned me to a moment in high school. One slow-moving afternoon, during the last term of the school year, I sat passing time with some of the school's rougher characters. Back then, as was my way, I had complete freedom of movement between the school's various tribes. The sun was hot and bright, and we sat in the shade under the trees at the north end of the school fields, where the grass was soft, fresh and summer green. I was tuned into an animated conversation about motorcycles, when a junior student appeared and put an end to the chatter. It must have been an unforgettable moment for the unfortunate pupil. In his right hand was a large bag of goodies. He clenched it tight. On his left side, gripped firmly between upper arm and chest, were three bottles of fizzy drinks. Given our senior positions in the school hierarchy, sitting up, adjusting our near-horizontal poses, or so much as opening our mouths to address the boy, was out of the question. We simply ignored him and waited.

My strongest recollection of that moment is the boy's face. He blinked incessantly while struggling to hold back tears. Suppressed panic is the only way to describe what I saw. His nostrils flared wide and sucked fresh oxygen in by the cubic litre. He had the jittery antelope posture I often saw in those who spent much of their time running away from others. His lips were caught in a wrestling match between a smile and a sob. It was a sad sight, the counterfeit cheer.

The terrified pupil had arrived for a scheduled shakedown. In exchange for the bag of goodies and fizzy drinks, the boy received 'protection', which meant he remained free from further harassment for the remainder of term. The food and drink he handed over were delicious. The ruffians found, as they always did, a new victim. School life went on. The expressions on the faces of the five village elders were variations of what I had seen on the junior student's face, back in school.

A Property and Population Inspection of a village this size should take two to three hours, at the most. However, a number of factors led us to remain longer than usual. There was the time of day: the afternoon approached its end, and no matter how swiftly we worked, it would be impossible to leave the hill before dark. Our best move was to complete the main phase of our business by early evening and remain in the village overnight (there were houses enough to accommodate the men). At dawn, we would complete the erasure, before heading off to rendezvous with 1st, 4th and 5th Companies. We radioed our intentions forward to the rest of the PPC. Another reason to stay was the village occupants' enthusiastic reception and the prepared toast. Here was an opportunity for a novel experience.

At the centre of the village was a large oval area, the major axis of which was aligned north-east to south-west. The houses were arranged in haphazard rows around the open ground. A network of vines stretched between the houses and supported a patchwork of brightly coloured sheets. These offered pleasant shade from the afternoon sun. Here and there, attached to the same vines, were humanoid effigies made from wood and straw. The dolls shared a single expression: serenity, by way of a smile. Bunches of fuchsia-coloured flowers were everywhere. Their placement appeared haphazard. Was this by design, or a by-product of haste and worry? The two rows of tables, while arranged less chaotically, could have done with some straightening. The same could be said for the chairs: on either side of the tables I counted at least seventeen unique styles of seating. I abandoned my counting endeavours when my head began to spin. Our photographers, on the other hand, were delighted. For those happy fellows, this village was an absolute bonanza.

The toast took place in the central oval, though not before a five-piece band and two singers delivered a fifteen-minute serenade. It was the most extraordinary music, and it took me back to many of our city's squares and parks where, in times past, Eastie minstrels often performed. Their music had a magnetic quality that held us in place while it danced in and out of our systems. The music played in this village was quite similar, and a good number of our men recognized and expressed their delight at these familiar sounds.

Given our numbers, it was impossible to seat all present. We selected a number of the men and asked them to join us at the tables, while the rest stood around the oval's periphery, together with the village occupants. Everyone received a drinking vessel (we must have used every cup, glass and mug in the village) and then we settled down. The five village elders, through the voice of their lyrical translator, made a toast to Our Dear Leader and to long and prosperous lives. The contents of my mug were peculiar, yet pleasant on the tongue. I could take a liking to this drink. Imagine a grapefruit, add a touch of smoke, a garnish of bitters, and you would have it. By the way, that potion was at least 70–80° proof, and with a kick to match.

With the toast done, we expected to set about our business. The village occupants, however, had other ideas: the following item on the agenda was a guided tour. Encouraged by the effects of the drink, and the fact there was no reason to make haste, I thought the tour an excellent idea. It would be helpful to our Recording and Documentation teams.

As we walked through the village, I noted the contradictions between how the messaging from above demanded we view Easties and what I saw, especially the architecture and infrastructure. We had been taught to perceive this nation and people as inferior to ourselves in every aspect, and it was true that a fair amount of what we destroyed in the East was in a neglected and run-down condition (proof of the wretched Eastie leadership). That said, the cracks, decay and faded paint could not hide the inherent beauty in much that we obliterated. I swatted away these inconsistencies by reminding myself of our mission for the Greater Glory.

There was nothing primitive about what we saw in the village. Almost all the Eastie-made objects were developed around mysterious compositions of circles, ovals and domes. All were constructed from wood, stone, grass, cloth in a manner that brought to mind the house at No. 17. The intricate forms were not all that amazed us. On five separate occasions I had engineers run up, panting as excited teenagers do, and express their appreciation and delight at the quality of construction achieved by the natives. I asked them to remain calm and carry on with their good work. Our continued surprise at the occupants' technical abilities was such that I even had a few of the men come up and ask whether we had stumbled into the remains of an ancient empire: they refused to accept everything around us was the work of the village occupants. I asked the men to look and think for themselves.

19

Our tour began with a trip to the well at the south-west end of the village, at the highest point of the hill. We learned that, according to stories passed down by the village occupants' ancestors, the well had constructed the hill to protect itself from the surrounding drought. Of course we knew this to be an unlikely tale, as there was a perfectly good geological justification for its existence. An explanation, I must admit, I did not know. Far more compelling than the tale of the well's origin was the irrigation network supplying water to the entire village, as well as to the crops and livestock lower down the hill. There was an interesting moment when I asked how the occupants processed the waste water for plant and animal use. They did not. I learned the water used for livestock consumption and crop irrigation was just as fresh as that drunk by the occupants. Their argument being, what they fed to the crops and animals, they fed to themselves. They were a truly fascinating people.

Our next destination was the largest building in the

village. Located at the opposite end of the oval to the well, it was an outstanding example of a well-crafted structure. The translator informed us the building was a ceremonial hall. Once every twenty-eight days, on the morning after a full moon, the entire village, together with some livestock, entered the space and thanked Nature for another moon cycle of life. The entrance was guarded by two immense wooden doors. Goodness knows what mechanical wizardry had been used to erect them (it was a puzzle our engineers were unable to solve). Their size was not all that impressed us: as they opened out to welcome in guests, the mighty doors turned on their hinges as if each weighed no more than a feather.

The interior snatched my breath away. The space was filled with light, though there was nothing inside that could truly be called a window. Cut into the top of the structure's dome was a series of twenty-one slits. Thin beams of sunlight shot in through the openings and bounced back and forth between the hundreds of mirrors that hung in the upper half of the space. The network of original and reflected sunbeams interacted with the dust particles inside and filled the interior with an otherworldly glow.

Six stone ventilation shafts, three on each side, were there to ensure adequate air circulation during ceremonies. The lower third of the interior walls was padded with a thick cushion of the same dried grass and fuchsia-coloured petals used by the occupants to welcome us to the village. The petals and grass were held in place with raffia netting. I silently applauded whoever had designed and erected such a structure.

The reaction of some of our cameramen to the building bordered on the unprofessional. Usually, such inability to control emotional expression would be met with a reprimand. However, their obvious excitement was an important factor in encouraging the villagers to let down their guard. Our sincere appreciation filled them with pride, a feeling I could relate to. Having such a magnificent building in one's community was indeed special. As we left the ceremonial hall and began the next stage of our tour, I sent a team downhill to ready our machinery, prepare two of our fuel trucks, and await further instructions.

Given the opportunity, the occupants would certainly have shown us the contents of every drawer, in every room, of every house in the village. Initially, I suspected all this to be no more than a delaying tactic. However, although I could not understand a word of what was said, the enthusiasm and pride they displayed suggested otherwise. Their lifestyle was based around various modular systems, each one dedicated to a specific function. For instance, all houses had equivalent ventilation systems. This simplified repair, because most of the village occupants understood how they worked and the standard design allowed for easy cannibalization of parts from old units. Given the waste in some of our own industries, I hoped our Recording and Documentation team's reports might work their way through the system and eventually inspire our national factory owners to think a bit harder, about the reuse of parts and materials.

The village occupants had modular systems for water, goats, crops, for everything. The system for selecting a house colour was also modular. While true, no two shades were alike, we learned they were all derived from combinations of a fixed set of colours mixed with a specific percentage of white. All colours were required to be present in the final shade, even if only a drop. This served as a reminder to the village occupants that they all came from the same source. I had never viewed our existence this way.

I found it quite touching, though not completely correct: their same was not our same.

Midway through the tour I was surprised by a gentle tug on my right index finger. Sticky and warm. I looked down and gazed into a pair of round, smiling eyes. The infant, perhaps driven by curiosity, had escaped her parent's clutches and come over for a closer look. She stood just below hip height and radiated an energetic joy that would have melted my heart, had a heart been present. As an officer of the PPC, I was obliged to maintain emotional distance and remind myself that young Easties grow into big Easties.

I allowed the infant to keep hold of my finger as we strolled through the village. She was happy to do so, and babbled away merrily. Occasionally, when in need of attention, she tugged at my trouser leg, and then tossed an excited stream of words at my ears. I nodded and made noises as if I understood her every word. The men had a laugh at my 'natural parenting' abilities. So did the village occupants, though their laughter did not come as easily as ours. The contrast in attitude between the self-confident infant holding onto my finger and her worried mother was as night is to day. The innocent fear nothing. The rest of us know better.

Well, all things come to an end. So did our visit. The Recording and Documentation teams let me know their work was done. It was time to 'complete' our inspection. Removing the infant's hand from my finger turned into a major struggle. Her protests began once she realized the walkabout was over. She gripped my finger as if holding on for dear life. I honestly worried about dislocation, or some other damage. Her strength and determination were surprising. She screeched and complained as the mother, assisted by two other village occupants, pried open her tiny fingers, and then led her away. The infant's teary eyes remained locked onto mine until they disappeared behind the wall of a nearby house. I did not see her again, though I still see her eyes from time to time: angry and disappointed. This war is an ugly business.

During our extensive tour of the village, a section of my mind had been absorbed with the search for a solution to a particular problem: how to encourage the occupants to assist or at least not kick up too much of a fuss during the final stages of our inspection. Were panic to break out, the topography of the hill with its thousand and one paths would have us chasing the occupants around for hours on end. I eventually based my plan on observations made in the ceremonial hall.

Our campaign in the East has taught me much about patterns of behaviour under particular circumstances, especially when the stakes are high. We are told Easties lack the natural qualities expected in 'modern human beings'. So far, I am yet to discover any forms of behaviour in the Easties that I have not also seen exhibited by our own people. True, their customs and language are strange to my eyes and ears, but these are no more than accessories. At their core, whether we like it or not, the Easties are mirror images of you and me. They too, when placed in life-or-death situations, become gullible souls. They find promise and hope in the tiniest gesture: in a smile, an act of politeness, in an empty promise. Desperation encourages most to believe there is a means to wish reality away and cancel the inevitable. The thinking behind my plan in the funny little village was based on this misapprehension.

The village occupants had by now become used to the sight of our recording teams going about their business. I asked the five village elders if they would be so kind as to arrange a mock ceremony. It would be for our cameras' benefit. At first, the elders appeared confused and said it was impossible to hold a ceremony, as it was neither morning nor the day after a full moon. I explained we did not wish for them to perform a real ceremony, rather an imitation. We had hoped to take a few extra photographs and some footage of them in ceremonial regalia before we left. I added that the sooner they prepared and posed for us, which we would appreciate deeply, the sooner we could be on our way. The idea of our departure lit fires of enthusiasm in the five village elders, and everyone else.

The village occupants dashed off to their houses and returned within half an hour, every one of them in their shiniest, ceremonial best. They looked magnificent. Spectacular! The sight was enough to make our photographers and camera crews very nearly lose their minds. One unfortunate soldier collapsed. I heard the medics sedated the man. Thankfully, he was back on his feet within hours.

The village occupants, together with numerous chickens and goats, took their positions inside the ceremonial hall. They began singing and chanting in a way that rang in my ears for weeks afterwards. The volume of their song drowned out the sound of everything outside, including the noise of our equipment making its way up the hill.

Midway through the mock ceremony, the last of our camera crews backed out of the hall. We then closed the mighty doors shut. The three bulldozers we had at our disposal were used to keep them that way. The occupants, on the inside, soon stopped their singing and began a noisy collective complaint, which over time, and up to a point, continued to increase in volume. The fuel trucks were moved into position. A team of agile men spent the next twenty-five minutes pouring kerosene into the six ventilation shafts. The occupants no longer complained. They screamed.

Evening approached. We sat at the tables on the village oval, which we arranged in three tidy rows. I issued the men extra rations of food and liquor, as well as commendations for their creative and efficient work. As we chatted, laughed, traded jokes and tales, the hall at the north-east end of the oval smouldered and crackled.

That night, when the fire in the ceremonial hall had become but a glow, we lay down to sleep on the beds, the furniture and on the floors of their houses. The sound of the wind, the night birds and the insects faded away, and for a quiet moment, there was nothing. The last I remember, before waking the next morning, was the black empty fog that descended upon me. There was no place for rest in that particular darkness.

In the morning, as we prepared to erase the village, the engineers arrived with an unusual request. Given the unconventional nature of the village buildings' construction, could I grant them permission to experiment with various demolition methods? I gave the teams an hour, and an order to leave the well alone. They turned the village to gravel within thirty-seven minutes.

Later, when our work was done and we prepared to leave, I noticed the framed portrait of Our Dear Leader lying on the ground. The explosion blasts had shattered the glass and twisted its frame. A splash of colour, revealed by the broken wood, caught my attention. I picked the frame up for a closer inspection. Those sneaky Easties . . . The photograph of Our Dear Leader had come from the front page of one of their newspapers. It was dated a month earlier, and had been folded to fit within the frame. The accompanying headline (translated by one of our men who was vaguely familiar with their language) compared Our Dear Leader to the Devil. The village occupants had placed it, for our benefit, over a colour group portrait of the Easties' leadership.

As we left the village I could not remove the image of Our Dear Leader from my mind. What made the photograph so discomforting to look at was the fact it clearly portrayed a man insane. With regard to our actions on that and many similar occasions . . . it was just another day at the office. This is the work that has finished me as a human being.

Yesterday I began to hear the village occupants' screams again. And worse, the screams and howls as I hear them today are not the sounds of beasts, but the cries of people like you and me, our sisters, mothers, fathers, sons, cousins, aunts, uncles, nieces, nephews, grandparents. These are who I destroyed. For the cause of the Greater Glory, in honour of Our Dear Leader, and in accordance with instructions, this sweet man, who spent sunny afternoons tickling your face with flowers, orchestrated the murder of every living creature in that funny little village.

I wish these memories formed part of a terrible dream

from which I could awake whenever the horror within becomes too much. Unfortunately, this is not the case. No magic in this world can extract me from the truth, or remove my spirit and replace it with a demon who I can accuse, blame and hold responsible for my choices. I was present all along: every day, every minute, every death.

As a child, I often tried to adjust the facts of a situation in order to get out of a bind. I was young and lacked the wisdom needed for such ploys to work. 'Let the truth be your friend,' Father would tell me. Today, while writing, I try and embrace truth as a friend, but tell me, what friend would bring such indescribable pain? The feeling I have is of a leaking heart, and what escapes is a bitter acid that consumes me again and again. I can do nothing. I feel myself becoming ever more hollow by the minute. It hurts, my love. And yes, I know this is the least I deserve. It still hurts that I can undo nothing.

~~Is it not sad~~

I hear detonations, four of them. I would say, going by their intensity, they landed approximately three kilometres south of our position.

My love, I could sit and share my sorrows with you for

another thousand hours. There is so much to say. However, at this late hour, I still have responsibilities. I need to attend to a few matters, and believe we still have some time before the enemy attacks. I shall return shortly, as soon as the situation permits.

20

It is hard to know what the enemy is up to. We waited an hour and a half for a sign, for movement. Nothing but heightened tension. We expected the four explosions to herald the start of their final assault, and our last battle. Instead they presented us with silence, and it is still quiet as I begin writing again.

Before the interruption, I was about to complain how now, when I need such a power most of all, I, Master of Erasure, am unable to wipe away the blood, death and destruction that stains my shadow. There is shame coming your way because of my work, and the only hope of avoiding it would be for the world to disappear in a flash. You will hear terrible stories about the activities of my brothers in arms and I: much worse than anything printed in the foreign news. Most of these tales will be true. During one of our last 'reasonable' exchanges with NDM High Command, we learned certain groups of our own people now ask uncomfortable questions regarding our wartime behaviour and methods. Our Dear Leader, quite naturally, was furious. The man truly believes himself and his actions to be above question. Apparently, due to these questions (and you will know more about this than those of us at the front), Our Dear Leader now alternates between calling the stories falsehoods conjured up by subversive elements, and declaring any who listen to be traitorous and mad. He has transformed National Radio, the NDM mouthpiece, into a laughing stock. If Our Dear Leader asked National Radio to claim that he single-handedly created the mountains, seas and all the lands on our planet, they would do so without hesitation. To you, and any others challenging this madness, I say: More speed!

Given time's current rate of evaporation, I feel a great pressure to write down as much as I can about my life in the PPC. This is my only worry: I scribble as fast as I can, yet have only scratched the surface of the truth of my work.

I beg you, do not waste your sympathy on me. If anything, feel sorrow for the ease with which I discovered and followed this path. Cry in anger at the encouragement and good wishes we received as we set off east, on our adventure for the Greater Glory. Tremble in horror at how one such as I can be so full of death and yet remain alive. Is that a life as it should be? As there is no understandable explanation for my actions, there can be no excuse. I chose to follow Our Dear Leader into this frenzy and now, with great embarrassment, I have a confession to make. When I strip away the bluster, the purposeless nationalism, what is left as a reason for me being here is my attraction to a smart uniform. That is it. No politics. No principles. Nothing more than fancy dress. What became of the man who was happy to live without direction? Where has that fellow gone? He was not there when I looked into the mirror this morning. That was someone else: a beast, a grand champion in the art of murder. I could not meet his eye.

A moment ago, one of the men called out: 'All right, sir? You have a funny look on your face.' I looked across the tent and held his gaze for a while. Will he be here tomorrow? Does he have a similar thought? I assured him all was fine. The man's eyes said he believed otherwise. It is always the eyes. The eyes say it all.

I must tell you, for the last three weeks I have seen eyes everywhere. I look at a bush and I see them. The leaves and shadows knit together and form pairs of eyes that look straight back at me. They read my thoughts. I feel them. I gaze at the clouds above, and in a matter of seconds I find myself staring back at someone up there who looks down on me. In the bark of a tree, the shadows across the floor, ripples in a nearby pool, on butterfly wings. Everywhere, I find eyes locking me into their gaze. They pierce my heart, they are in my head!

Most unnerving, though not unexpected, is the fact I know them all. I looked into every pair of those eyes as their bodies shut down and their souls left for other places. My relationship with their owners was always brief. Right up until their very last moment, they found the strength, courage, madness . . . to look out at the world, at me, with hope. I watched the eyes dart right and left as they urged Destiny to arrive and convince me to have a last-minute change of heart. I saw those eyes become cloudy with sad acceptance as it dawned on them . . . I was Destiny.

As I see them now, these eyes hold no bitter expressions, they have neither fury nor hunger for vengeance. All I can detect is a slight hint of pity and another expression that makes me shiver. Mother had the same look in her eyes when forgiving my mischief. I look at these eyes and understand my mind has broken. Why do I see them this way? Why do they look at me so? Why do they refuse to hate and despise me? There is no forgiveness for those engaged in my kind of business. Yet those eyes burn me with love, and I cannot escape them. What is their message?

I have a few ideas why the eyes have returned. During t

• • •

The long whistle of incoming guests. Shell after shell punctures the soil. There is no love in their actions. The guests announce themselves with earth-shaking thunder and bursts of explosive mutilation. Their greeting is as the fists of bloodthirsty gods, smashing into the ground again and again. They are here to deliver a reward. This is it! Murderous souls sigh their last, and bid farewell to this place en masse.

The bombardment ends, but silence does not fall. There is sobbing, wailing, moaning, screaming . . .

The shells, violent and merciless as they were, spared two of the tents. See them standing, quiet and lonely in the middle of slaughter's leftovers. One is untouched. Three diagonal gashes decorate the other.

*

A new thunder approaches. Much nearer to the ground, and closer by the second. There is shouting and cheering. The roar of righteous vengeance. There is blood in those cries. Leather boots, heavy soles smash and crush the grass. Makeshift paths are born. The breathing is heavy and fast and rough and wild. The ravenous warriors have but one simple task. If it lives, then it should not!

Hear the flash, crackle and spit of small-arms fire. Bullets escape and say 'Die!' as they pass through flesh and bone with minimal resistance. Today, Glory chooses to ride with the opposition.

In through the freshly sliced opening step five battle-frenzied soldiers. Eyes red and wild, and on the lookout for prey. There are men in the tent. Dead, and those about to die. The tent's contents, including the bodies, bear the brunt of the soldiers' fury: they are knocked, kicked about and treated with disdain.

Three of the men flip open jerrycan lids and pour the contents in every direction. Kerosene sloshes in abundance, and fumes fill the air.

*

A strip of sunlight cuts the tent in two. A corpse, face down on the floor, a fresh blood halo around the upper body. The soldier notices the makeshift table and chair built from wooden crates. The first drops of kerosene leave the can's mouth and splash onto one of the crates. The soldier stops. He looks. A frown ruffles his brows. His eyes, meanwhile, focus on an open journal. It looks lonely, and appears to be waiting. The soldier places the jerrycan on the floor next to the body, as a powerful curiosity urges him to take a closer look.

A black fountain pen rests in the gutter between the pages. The pages to the right of the pen are empty and ready to receive their share of what appears on the left: written in deep-blue ink, line after line of near perfect script. The soldier's eyes travel across the lines. A growing excitement fills his chest. It glows. During peaceful times, calligraphy had been his trade. It does not matter that the language of the journal is one he cannot understand. The form and precision of the handwriting sing out to him. Bloody soldier that he is, even this man does not believe all things deserve destruction. The pen and journal find a new home in his bag. The soldier then lifts the can from the floor and douses the table and chair and the bodies with kerosene. Happy cheers ring out as the tent and its contents begin to burn.

Time comes. Time goes.

A Glossary of terms and abbreviations

NDM (National Defence Movement)
Came to power by way of military coup. Initially dedicated to dismantling corruption and boosting the nation's welfare. Having achieved their initial aims, and following the untimely loss of the Dear Leader, the NDM turned its attention to expansion and war.

The Greater Glory
A disastrous and megalomanic venture to conquer and ethnically cleanse the lands of the East. Driven by the ego and arrogance of Our Dear Leader. The circumstances of the author are a direct result of this venture.

Banality of Emotion
A concept burned into the minds of NDM officers. 'When engaged in duties deemed beneficial to the Greater Glory of the nation, situations may arise that necessitate taking radical action. To the casual observer, and the morally fragile, such actions may appear brutal and lacking in mercy.

During such moments, it is of vital importance that the officer of the National Defence Movement remains in control, and separates necessary action from the banality of emotion.'

Self-Identification
An essential indoctrination class in NDM officer training. It comprised chanting a number of carefully selected mantras for various lengths of time. The most important mantra had a sergeant demanding to know what the elite trainees were. They answered with a chorus of 'I am a God!' This would go on for many hours.

EDS (External Data and Security)
The division of the Ministry of Data and Security tasked with scooping up all available information regarding the goings-on in our neighbours' systems (political, economic, military, etc.) and translating this into useful intelligence.

DIDS (Division of Internal Data and Security)
The second division of the Ministry of Data and Security. Its remit was national observation, as there was a need to remain up to date on all comings, goings and sayings of

interest within the nation's borders. With particular attention paid to non-indigenous citizens.

DIE (Data and Information Extraction)

A section of the Division of Internal Data and Security tasked with processing and analysing the data collected by the various EDS and DIDS teams.

The National Registry

A cross-referential database of all citizens living within the nation's borders. This included: name, date of birth, place of residence, education, employment, family, friends, ethnicity, patterns of individual (and group) movement, consumption, literature, entertainment, health, leisure and politics.

Health For All

An extremely popular programme founded on the belief that a healthy society was a productive one, and that it was logical for the nation to take care of those who allowed it to function.

OEO (Office of Easterner Observation)
A department within the Division of Internal Data and Security whose sole function was to keep a watchful eye on the Easterner population living within the nation's borders.

Eastie
A derogatory term for Easterners (especially those resident within the nation) introduced to the nation by Our Dear Leader. The occasion being his response to an act of terror. Originally used by the OEO as an abbreviation for 'Easterners' but overheard and transformed into an insult by the NDM Messaging and Public Relations team.

PDE (Potentially Disruptive Eastie)
A category of Eastie identified by the OEO (through analysis of collated data) as likely to become involved in, or support, activities against the national interest.

The Oath
An obligatory oath (to the nation and Our Dear Leader) to be taken by all Easties resident within the nation's borders. Its primary function was to identify Potentially Disruptive Easties (PDEs), who were then placed on the Action

Pending Register. Residency permits were provided to all Easties who took the Oath.

APR (Action Pending Register)

A database of Easties managed by the NDM Ministry of Housing and Justice (MHJ), in conjunction with DIDS. As the relationship with the East deteriorated, retaliatory sanctions were taken against resident Easties. The groups and individuals listed for targeting were selected from the APR. Easties listed in the APR were not given access to residency permits.

UR (Unlawful Resident) Status

Easties without residency permits were given 'Unlawful Resident' (UR) status.

DI (Declaration of Illegality)

A pronouncement given by the MHJ to any Eastie with Unlawful Resident (UR) status. The sanctions for a DI included immediate forfeiture of all property (and items unable to be carried without assistance), as well as deportation to the land of ancestral origin.

PIO (Property Integrity Office)
An enclave of the Division of Internal Data and Security within the Ministry of Housing and Justice. The PIO managed all state properties through various Site Inspection Units, which handled all on-the-ground activities.

SIU (Site Inspection Unit)
These units were paramilitary teams, each with an area of specialization, for example the preparation of properties for renovation. In such cases, preparation commenced with the extraction of all occupants with UR status. The properties selected for preparation were always associated with Easties listed in the APR.

AO (Appropriation Order)
An official document from the MHJ that permitted the relevant SIU to begin immediate preparations.

Unlawful Resident Transfer Squad
Worked in partnership with an SIU. They facilitated the transport of evicted Easties to the appropriate departure points.

PI (Process Inspector)
Trained individuals tasked with monitoring SIU activities. Occasionally gaps appeared between theory and practice. The PI prescribed solutions for areas in need of improvement.

Situational Attitude
A training method created to improve the operations of SIU commanders. It taught how best to express the three Ds: Disdain, Disgust and Disinterest.

Erasure
A concept developed by Our Dear Leader, during his time as head of the Ministry of Data and Security's Office of Strategic Possibilities. He believed the complete erasure of such elements as language, traditions, music, art and industry would, over time, allow for a people to disappear from history.

PPC (Property and Population Control Battalion)
Nicknamed 'The Factory Boys' because of their mobile processing units. They were an effective part of Our Dear Leader's erasure machine. Their remit included the

'preparation of land for further civilization through the removal of unnecessary artefacts'. This was done by way of Property and Population Inspections.

PPI (Property and Population Inspection)
The recording followed by total destruction of any object, no matter the size, that could bring joy or hope to the hearts of Easties. The PPC translated Our Dear Leader's wishes into actions.

PART ONE

The History of Manipulation

Preface

I graduated in 1932, and 15 years later (1947) became an industrial medical officer at a shipyard in Oslo. It did not take me long to realise that almost half of the disorders for which my advice was sought was trouble in the moving parts of the body. Such complaints, especially affecting the back and limbs, were responsible for a large part of all absence from work. I found that lesions of the musculo-skeletal system provided 17 per cent. of industrial absence, second only in frequency to diseases of the respiratory system. Wear and tear lesions dominated the scene; the true rheumatic diseases such as rheumatoid arthritis played only a very small part. In 1955, of days lost by males from lesions of a moving part, 41·4 per cent. were due to lumbago or sciatica. In this shipyard, with 1,500 male workers, 2,000 working days were lost in 1957 on account of these two conditions, excluding short absences of 1 to 3 days.

In the autumn of 1955, I met James Cyriax, head of the Department of Orthopaedic Medicine at St. Thomas's Hospital, London. He had been invited to Oslo to examine postgraduate physiotherapy students in manipulation. The intention was to compile a register of manipulating physiotherapists which doctors could consult when wanting such treatment for a patient. I became very interested, seeing in the methods he advocated a way to reduce industrial absenteeism. It was with this idea that I started to study manipulation. Very soon I realised that it was necessary for me—in order to break down my colleagues' "iron curtain" as regards this branch of medicine—to study, first, the history of this treatment during the ages (this had never been done before), and secondly, to put forward—if possible—a theory on *how* manipulation works acceptable to the medical profession.

Here are the results of my research up to 1958 when this essay was first published, together with further facts that have come to light since.

Ankerveien 34, Eiler H. Schiötz
Oslo 3
October 1974

I

Ancient Medicine

All medicine seems to stem from Hippocrates. Manipulation is no exception. According to historians, of his huge compilation "Corpus Hippocrateum"—written about 400 B.C.—only a part is written identifiably in his own hand but, in this part, there are two relevant chapters: "Peri arthron" (About Joints), and "Mochlikon" (The Lever). Hippocrates wrote that he did not agree with contemporary ideas on treatment of lumbar kyphosis or "hyboma" (an alternative name). He advises (Peri arthron, Chapter 47) a steam-bath, followed by lying on a board to which the patient is bound in the prone position with bands at head, pelvis, knees and ankles. Traction is first given by assistants pulling simultaneously on head and feet; the physician now presses sharply on the kyphosis, while the pull is maintained (see Fig. 4). The direction of the thrust depends on the condition present; it may be towards head or pelvis. This manner of readjustment, we are assured, is not dangerous. Nor is it dangerous, he says, to sit on the back during traction imparting a shaking movement by getting up and down again quickly (Fig. 1). The foot can also be applied to the prominence, with pressure carefully increased by bringing the body weight to bear (Fig. 2). However, the most effective method of all, according to Hippocrates, is to put the end of a stout board in a cleft in a wall and place it across the patient's back with a pad of cloth or leather intervening. While two assistants maintain traction, one or two other men push the free end of the beam downwards (Fig. 3). Traction may also be secured by windlass, which makes for ease of control. Even traction alone, without the local pressure, can achieve a satisfactory result. Again, a thrust without traction may prove satisfactory.

At the end of the 15th century a collection of parchment manuscripts was discovered in Crete, written by a physician called Niketas about the year 900. They deal with ancient surgical practice

Fig. 1. Combined traction by means of a windlass and sustained pressure on the lumbar spine by a person *sitting* on the back of the patient in prone position, to regain lordosis. (*Apollonius, after Hippocrates*)

and contain a commentary by Apollonius of Cyprus on Hippocrates's two chapters, written A.D. 60–80. Included are 30 full-page pen-and-ink drawings by an unknown illustrator. This collection of papers is now preserved in the Bibliotheca Laurenziana in Florence (Codex LXXIV, 7), and were copied and published by a German scholar, Herman Schöne, in 1896. Full-sized coloured replicas of nearly all Apollonius's pictures are to be found in a 16th century manuscript, now in the University of Bologna (Codex 3632), described by Olivieri.

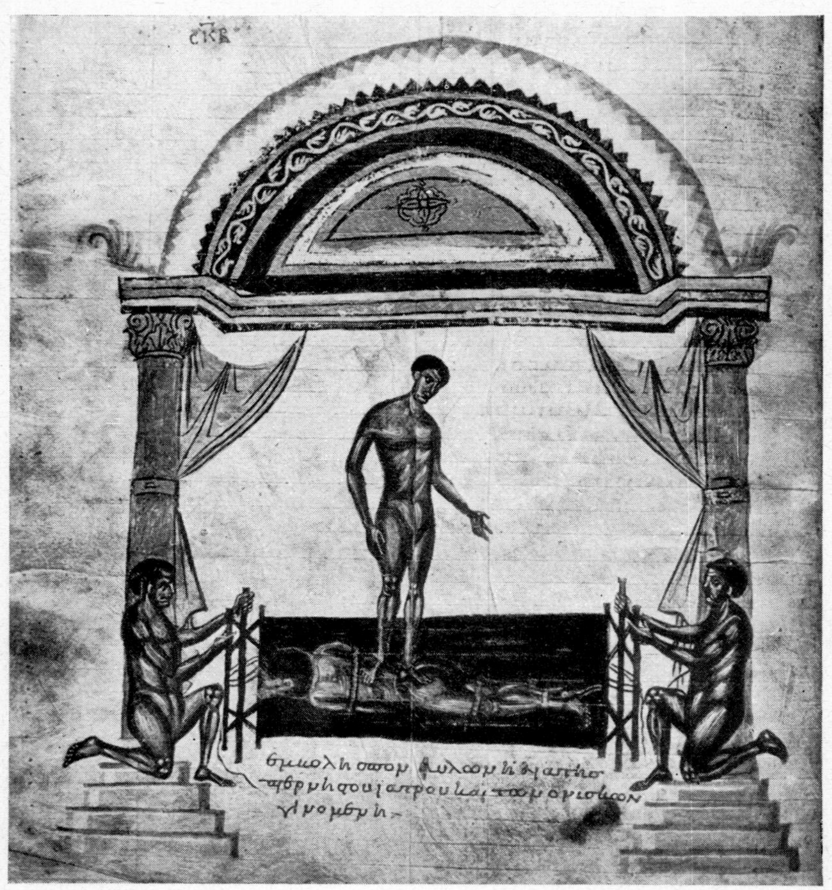

Fig. 2. Combined traction and sustained pressure by a person *standing* on the back of the patient. (*Apollonius, after Hippocrates*)

Ancient medical history starts with a great name and ends with another equally famous—Claudius Galenos, or Galen (A.D. 131–202). Eighteen of the 97 extant commentaries of his relate to Hippocrates's work, including that on joints. Galen mentions the case of a man who had fallen off a cart a month earlier and had developed pins and needles with numbness in the third, fourth and fifth fingers of his left hand. He localised the injury to the "spinal nerve below the seventh cervical vertebra" and cured the patient by treating his neck.

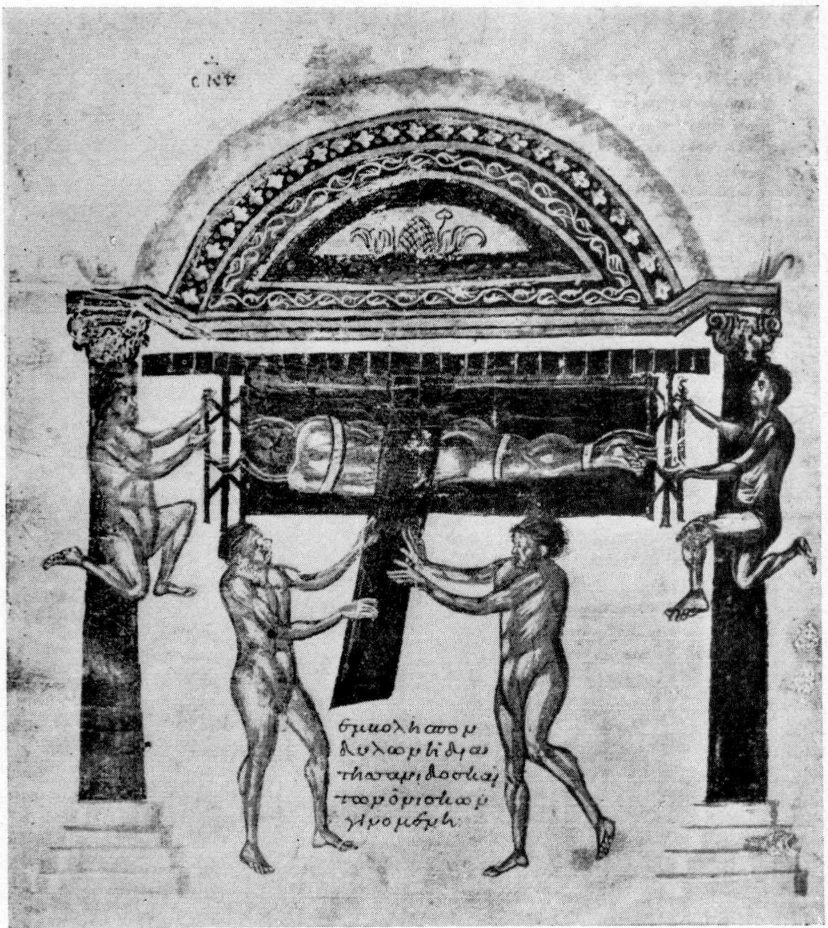

Fig. 3. Combined traction and sustained pressure by means of a board. (*Apollonius, after Hippocrates*)

Hippocrates's influence is also shown in two wood-cuts in an illustrated edition of Galen's Collected Works (Figs. 4 and 5).

Almost a thousand years ago, the Arabian doctor Abu'Ali ibn Sina (980–1037) was born. He was also known as Avicenna, was head of an important hospital in Bagdad and is best known for his "Qânun" (canon), a huge compilation in which he set out the whole amount of medical knowledge of his time. This was repeatedly

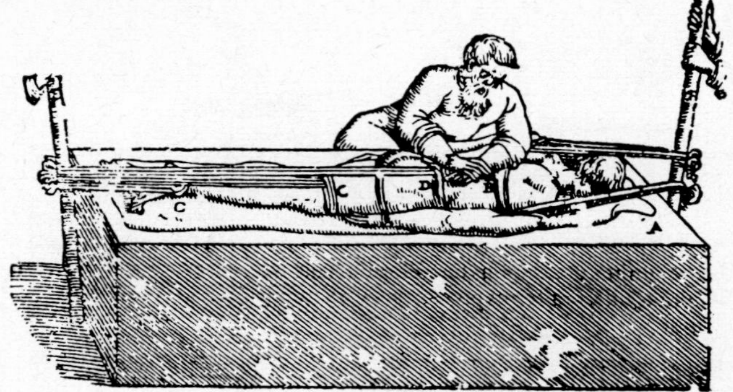

Fig. 4. A variant of the hippocratic methods for "dislocation outwards of a lumbar vertebra": Traction combined with a thrust or sustained pressure. (*Galen, after Hippocrates*)

reprinted in Latin between 1473 and 1608, and remained an authoritative textbook until the 17th century. The Giunta edition of "Canon Avicennae" in Latin (1595) contains illustrations showing that he practised Hippocrates's methods of treating backs. Avicenna is supposed to have ascribed love to mental disorder and is reported to have died at the age of 57 of a surfeit of wine, women and overwork (Bettmann).

A codex was recently discovered, probably written in Bologna in the early part of the 14th century. It is now housed at the library

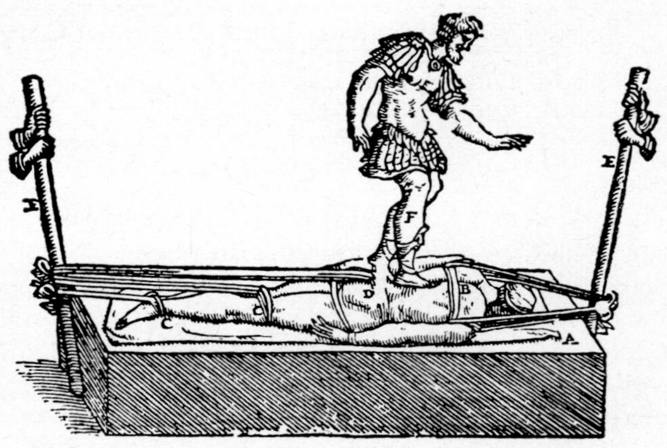

Fig. 5. The same process by means of a person standing on the patient's back. (*Galen, after Hippocrates*)

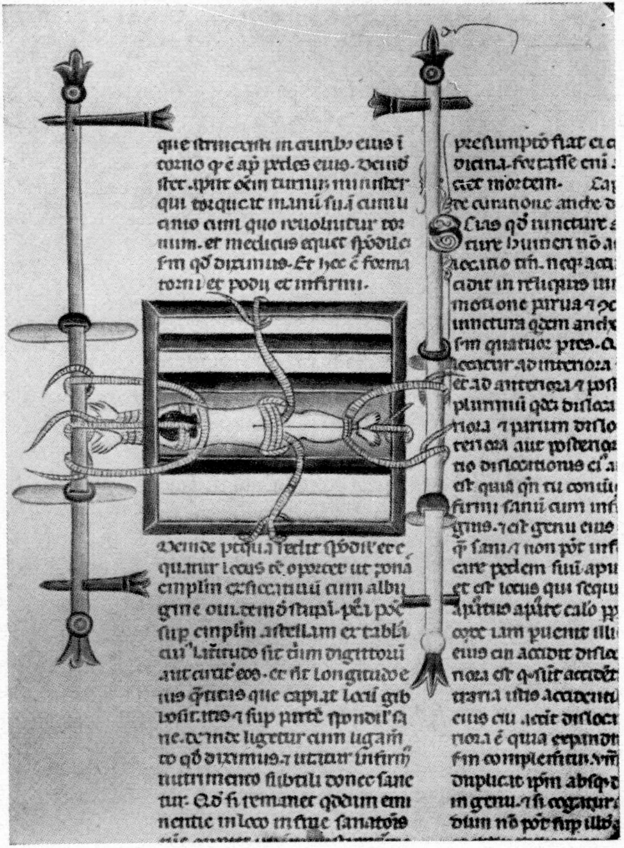

Fig. 6. Traction of the spine according to a treatise by the Arab physician Abû'L Qâsim. (*After F. A. Paneth*)

of medical history at Yale University. It contains six chapters on "Ars Medicinae" by the Spanish-Arabian physician Abû'L Qâsim (1013–1106) of Cordoba whose "Altasrif" remained a leading textbook on surgery for about 200 years. One drawing in this work (Fig. 6) illustrates spinal traction.

Fig. 7a depicts medieval Turkish manipulation during traction, as shown in a manuscript written by Charaf-Ed-Din in 1465 (Huard & Grmek, 1960).

In the 16th century, copies were made of Apollonius's pictures

Fig. 7a. Medieval Turkish traction: an illustration taken from "Le Premier Manuscrit Chirurgical Turc de Charaf-Ed-Din" (1465) (*Reproduced by permission of the Bibliothèque Nationale, Paris*)

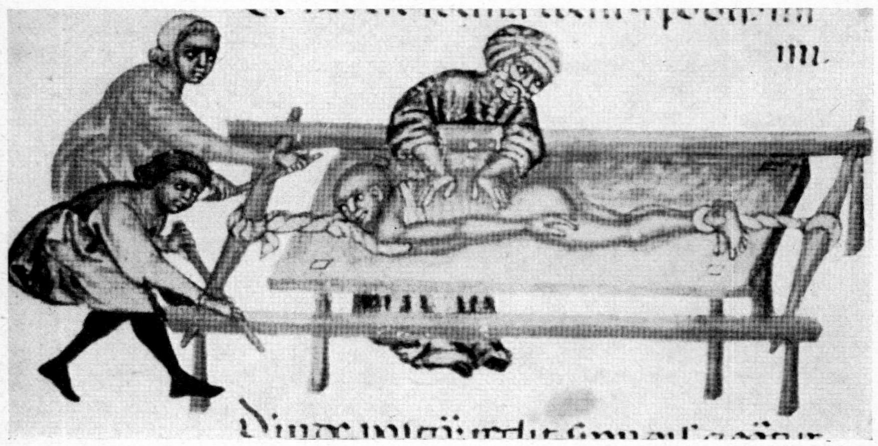

Fig. 7b. Manipulation during traction in Albucasis's Surgery. Latin translation. Vienna, fourteenth century. (*By courtesy of Wellcome Trustees*)

Fig. 8. Combined traction and sustained pressure treating a patient lying prone. (*Vidius Vidio*)

in the "Codex Laurentianus" by two renaissance artists for the Italian doctor Guido Guidi, also known as Vidius Vidio (about 1500–1569). He organised the medical faculty at the "Collège de France" and used the illustrations for his "Chirurgia è Graeco in Latinum conversa" (Figs. 8 and 9).

The greatest surgeon of renaissance times was Ambroise Paré (1510–1590), well-known especially as an obstetrician. His works contain a chapter on "vertebral dislocation". He states: "The external causes of dislocation are a fall, a severe blow or too much work with the trunk flexed, e.g. in the vineyards." How Hippocrates's influence had persisted for all but two thousand years is witnessed by Paré's description of treatment. His advice is:

"When the vertebrae are dislocated outwards forming a prominence, the patient should be tied down prone to a board

Fig. 9. Combined suspension and pressure on the lumbar spine by means of a board. The "scamnum Hippocratis". (*Vidius Vidio, after Brockbank & Griffiths*)

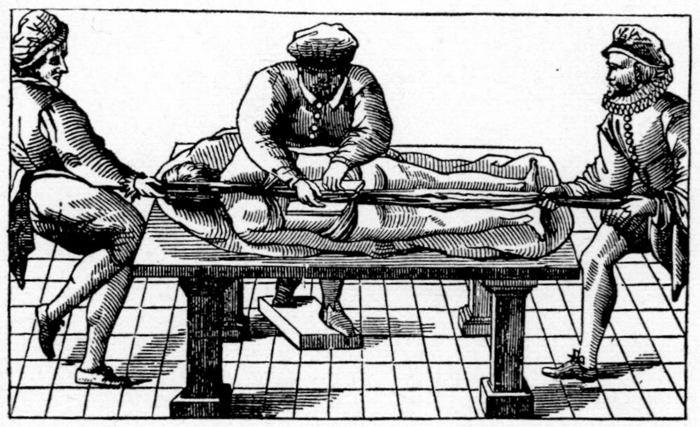

Fig. 10. "La manière de reduire l'épine luxée". (*Ambroise Paré*)

with ropes under the armpits, the waist and the thighs. He is then pulled and stretched as much as possible, from above and from below, but not violently. If traction is not applied, cure is not to be expected. The operator then places his hands on the kyphosis and presses the prominent vertebrae in" (Fig. 10).

Johan Schultes or Scultetus (1595–1645) was still advocating this method at the beginning of the 17th century. After that little is heard of such treatments until the bonesetters—and later on the osteopaths and chiropractors—once more popularised these measures toward the end of the 19th century.

II

Mechanical Treatment of Back Disorders in Folk Medicine

(Lord Horder, 1953): "The sun, the air, water, exercises and manipulation have been Medicine's handmaidens since earliest times."

From time immemorial it has certainly been recognised that lumbago (and even sciatica) or an acute stiff neck can be relieved as quickly as it came on by a sudden unintentional movement or a fall. This event has been described to doctors for centuries past, and I have myself encountered three instances.

> For example, a young man woke one morning with a severe crick in his neck (acute torticollis). I saw him the same day. In the evening he was knocked down by a car. He was not hurt; on the contrary, when he picked himself up he found he had regained a full painfree movement at his neck. He showed this to me next morning.

My colleague, Kjell Krüger of Bergen, recounted another instance to me (personal communication):

> In the spring of 1945, a teacher's wife developed pain in the back radiating along the course of the sciatic nerve to the foot. She received short-wave diathermy without benefit and lay in hospital for three weeks, having more physical treatment—again to no avail. Operation was mooted, but the patient was pregnant. She spent the last three months of pregnancy largely bedridden. After a normal confinement, the sciatica became still more severe and she could scarcely get about. In July 1946, she tripped over a doormat and twisted sideways to avoid falling. Her pain ceased

instantly, and had not recurred by eleven years later in spite of her carrying on with quite heavy household duties.

The German surgeon, Professor Zukschwerdt, has collected some similar cases and described the instance of a man in his practice who had been treated for a long time for sciatica by conservative means. He did not respond but one day fell down on his way to the hospital, felt a click in his back and got up fully relieved. He also refers to C. Mau's case of a young woman who was suddenly relieved of lumbago when she was twisted round by a huge wave while swimming.

It is thus hardly surprising that experiences like these have led to the emergence of jerks intended to "put the spine back in place". In Central Europe there have been gipsies who, one generation after another, have possessed the ability to cure "Hexenschuss" (shot of a witch), i.e. acute lumbago. Travellers returning from Tibet relate that some people there had developed a fine technique, and in Japan "distortion of the spinal column" resulting from jiu-jitsu and judo injuries to the neck are cured by special manipulations. Biedermann states that the Indians in Mexico used spinal treatments which he likens to manipulation; in due course, these methods were adopted by their white conquerors and are still employed today, e.g. "the shepherd's hug" or "the farmer's push".

There are different methods of manipulation in folk medicine. The most primitive cure for lumbago was named the "stamping" or "trampling" cure (Fig. 11). It has been practised in many countries from Hippocrates's time until today. A woman stood with both feet on the invalid's back and trampled up and down. Or she might walk across—or up and down—his back. These methods were first brought to my attention by a review in an Oslo newspaper of the fourth volume of Ingvald Reichborn-Kjennerud's great work on ancient witch medicine.

The earliest known description of the stamping cure as performed by laymen is that of Marcellus Burdigalensis, physician to the Emperor Theodosius I. About the year 400 he wrote: "A woman who has given birth to twins shall stamp on the painful kidneys and the person will be cured immediately." In 1211 the stamping-cure was put forward again, but now it had to be carried out by a woman whose twins were boys (Liebrecht). San Bernardino of Siena, who died in 1444, gave a penetential sermon advocating the same treatment.

Fig. 11. Trampling during traction. In Apollonius's "Dislocations". Greek. Bologna, fifteenth century. (*By courtesy of Wellcome Trustees*)

The first mention in Norway was in 1662. At a lawsuit about witchcraft in Skien, Ragnhild Joensdaughter gave evidence on the method she had been using for relieving backache. She averred that since the age of three she "had trodden on sufferers from rheumatism but now she could do it better with her hand". In Oslo, A.C. Bang has unearthed a magical formula for treating "blood-skudd" (old Danish for acute lumbago) from a Norwegian manuscript dated 1790:

The operator must be a first-born child who says: "I stamp on you." The patient replies: "Why do you stamp on me?" The answer comes: "For blood-shot, and in the name of F.S. and H.A." The operator now stamps three times with the right foot, walks on the patient's trunk and says: "Stand up and never get it again." [In Ireland, by contrast, it had to be a seventh child (Suilleabhain, 1942). In Northumberland (1860), the person was named a "stamp steener", one thrust from whom was enough to render the affected part painless. J.C.]

In his "Notes on the Folk-lore of the North-East of Scotland" Walter Gregor in 1881 described the remedy for treating backache in that district:

"Those who were born with their feet first possessed great power to heal all kinds of sprains, lumbago, and rheumatism, either by rubbing the affected part, or by trampling on it. The chief virtue lay in the feet. Those who came into the world in this fashion often exercised their power to their own profit." [Trampling was also considered a cure in Scotland (Gregory 1881) and in Cornwall (Black 1883), and there also the stamper had to be born foot-first. The situation was the same in the Ratnagiri district of India where Paranjpye states that foot-presentation was essential. J.C.]

Llewellyn Lloyd, an English hunter who spent nearly all his life in the Swedish forests, tells us:

"Lumbago is cured by a woman that has had twins trampling on the back of the sick man, who in the while lies with his face to the ground. Whilst in this position he enquires three several times of the woman 'Why dost thou tramp on me?' To which she replies, 'Because I am better than thou art.' The patient then asks, 'Why art thou better than myself?' 'For the reason', rejoins the woman, 'that I have borne under my breast two hearts, two pair of lungs, two livers, four ears, four hands, &c., and that thou hast not done.' "

Many other countries have the same tradition in their folklore. Stories abound: in Sweden by Eneström and others; Finland by Forsblom; Denmark by Ellekilde; England by Black and others; Germany by Wilke (Fig. 12); Poland; Ukraine by Kuzela; Hawaii and Tahiti by Handy and others; amongst Indians and Maoris by

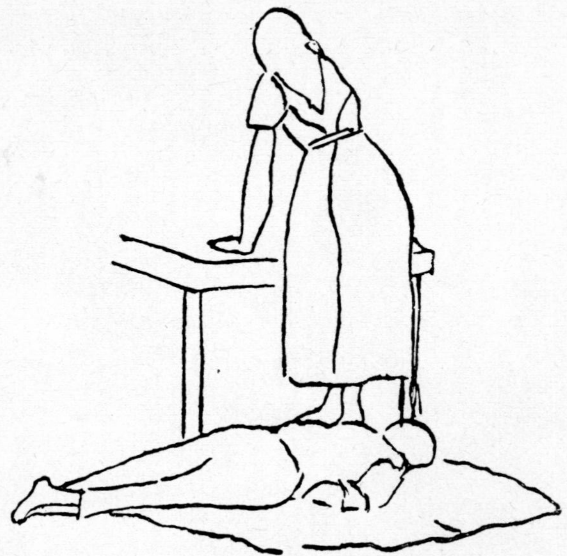

Fig. 12. The "trampling cure" as practised in German folk medicine. (*Georg Wilke*)

Turner, in China and Japan and in South Eastern Asia (Fig. 13). Here are a few excerpts:

Among the Huzuls in Austria, it was customary (Kaindl) for the priest to trample on the invalid's back during mass, or even let a tame bear do so (!). A similar practice was reported in Rumania. Kuzela tells from Ukraine that when his father was stricken by acute backache, the first-born child pressed on his back with hands or feet. In Finnish folklore, Forsblom states that "a woman who has given birth to twins stamps on the back with both feet and stays there for as long as it takes her to count backwards from 9 to 3 three times". From another part of Finland, the advice is to "stamp on the back without paying attention to the invalid's moans and groans". In Denmark, Hans Ellekilde reports: "When the men in the olden days got backache, they should be trampled by a young girl who must be a virgin; the one who was bad lay on the floor and the girl stamped on him properly."

I heard about a strange cure for many disorders, including lumbago, from a friend returned from Tahiti. I therefore wrote to

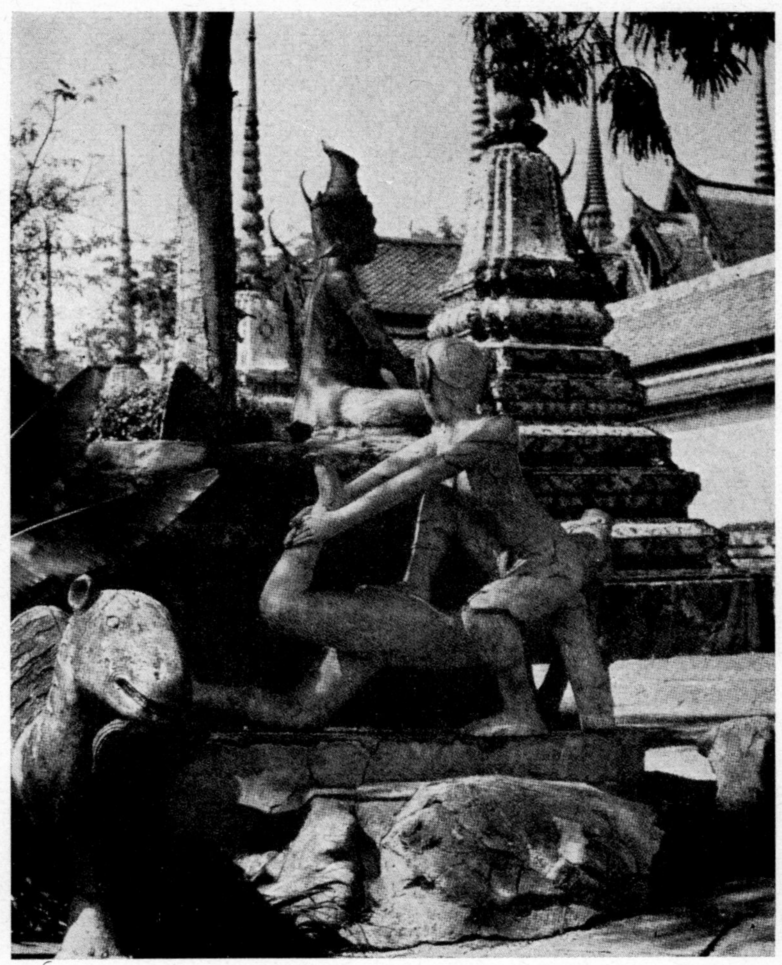

Fig. 13. Lumbar manipulation towards extension. Photograph taken by Dr. K. L. Mah at an ancient Buddhist temple at Bangkok, Thailand and regarded as 2,000 years old. (*By courtesy of Doctors Only*)

the Bernice P. Bishop Museum in Honolulu and was sent a photocopy of a paper by E. S. C. Handy et al. It runs:

"The most important and widely used form of physical therapy is massage, lomi-lomi . . . to serve mainly as a means of soothing pain and relaxing or limbering up tired and stiff muscles. The old

art as practised by experts . . . went much further than this . . . The exact procedure consists in both gentle and hard rubbing and stroking, in gentle and vigorous kneading, and in such heroic measures—when occasion demands—as *treading on the backbone of the prone patient with one or both feet* . . ." emphasised here.

Frederick O'Brien in his "Atolls of the Sun" (1922) tells us about the "omi-omi" on one of the Pacific islands:

"The *omi-omi* of these islands, and the *lomi-lomi* of the Hawaiians, all have a relation to the *momi-ryoji*, practised by the tens of thousands of whistling blind itinerants throughout Japan. I had a remarkable illustration of the curative merits of *omi-omi* when, having bruised my back in sliding down a rocky waterfall. [First he was given a steam-bath for about ten minutes in a tiny penthouse with a great wooden trencher of water in which white hot stones were dropped, viz. the Finnish *sauna*.] Then I submitted myself to the ministrations of (the young girls) Juno and Vanquished Often . . . They handled me as if they understood the location of each muscle and nerve. They pinched and pulled, pressed and hammered, and otherwise took hold of and struck me, but all with a most remarkable skill and seeming exact knowledge of their methods and its results . . . After a day I was as well as ever . . ."

A recent Associated Press report from Honolulu runs as follows:

"Lomi-lomi is an ancient Hawaiian version of massage. Its main feature is that the masseur walks on the patient's back, and while he walks, he kneads the flesh while regulating his weight by holding on a bar above the massage table . . . Jack Kaaua, 46, a graduate physical therapist in Honolulu, is one of the few remaining practitioners of the lomi-lomi . . . 'I didn't learn it in any school, but from my parents. It is an old Hawaiian practice that dates back more than 800 years,' he says."

I may say that I have used trampling when I got lumbago myself, with good result. I employed my little daughter as the stamper, since my wife, according to the Danish folklorist Ellekilde was not suitable, being neither a mother of twins nor a virgin. I have also used the method with good result in patients with a flattened lumbar curve presumably caused by a disc-protrusion.

Stories emanating from India, Egypt, the Aegean Islands, Bohemia and China all agree that by way of *prevention* farm workers

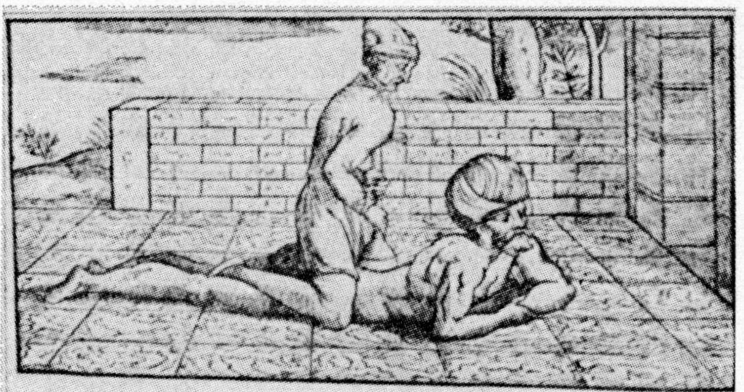

Fig. 14. "Reposition of a vertebral luxation" by means of a hammer. (*Avicenna*)

get their children to walk on their backs after a hard day's work stooping. The same applied to the Cossacks in Russia when they come home after a day on horseback. In "Notes and Queries", June 20, 1857, under the heading "Curious Parallelism of Customs", I have found the following note:

> "It is a custom in Berwickshire, among women-workers in the field, when their backs become very tired by stooping while hoeing turnips with short-handled hoes, to lie down their faces to the ground, and to allow others to step across the lower part of their backs, on the lumbar region, with one foot, several times, until the fatigue is removed. Burton, in his 'First Footsteps in East Africa', narrates a very similar custom amongst females who led the camels; who, on feeling fatigued, lie down at full length, face downward, and stand on each other's backs, trampling and kneading with their toes, until they rise like giants refreshed."

Other primitive methods. Peder Lunde recounts primitive manipulation in West-Agder county in Norway, called "wrestling the back". He says:

> "Nils in Syllskare stood out in the yard holding a dungfork. Then Per in Heia came forward: 'I have got such backache that I can scarcely walk', he said. Nils then ran to Per and twisted him round. Per declared his pain gone and went home."

There is also the "*lifting cure*" for lumbago; this was employed in Norway (the Sogn County) as described by S. Böyum. The patient leans against the projecting edge of a "stabbur" (a storehouse on

pillars), pressing his back against it, trying to "lift" the house. Similar accounts emanate from Sweden and Finland. This method and the stamp-cure both involve applying a lordotic strain to the lumbar joints.

Finally, Cramer quotes John Steinbeck who describes a negro tribe in which the medicine-man uses an instrument shaped like a hammer to "bring the vertebrae back into position", a method similar to one of those used by Avicenna one thousand years ago (Fig. 14).

Llewellyn Lloyd (quoted above) tells us from Sweden:

> "Lumbago is cured by someone, unobserved by the patient, giving him a smart blow with a broom on the part affected, whereby his back, consequent on the hurried movement the sudden shock causes him to make, comes all right again."

In some places in Norway, the back was struck with the weight of a steelyard.

In Swedish folk-medicine, there is an alternative cure for lumbar and thoracic pain called "*weighing salt*" (H. Aminson). A healthy person of the opposite sex stands back-to-back with the patient, takes hold of his arm, lifts him up and shakes him three times. According to Kuzela the same method is used in Eastern Galicia, there called "auf die Glocke nehmen". According to H.-D. Wolff's paper published in 1955 with the (translated) title "Precursors of Chiropractic Treatment", this measure is still practised; refugees from the Soviet occupied East Prussia gave him a demonstration (Fig. 15).

The Swedish clergyman Joh. Pontén published in 1841 (reprinted in a revised edition in 1851) a small handbook "on remedies for diseases in the country-side, if no doctor is available":

> "If a distortion has occurred in the back, the patient ought to hang by the hands from the rungs of a ladder . . . or, during summer time, sit clenching his ankles with his hands, tuck his head well down and roll down a steep but smooth edge to a field or a hill."

The Danish Dr. Arnold Larsen in 1887:

> "A lady of my acquaintance, while lifting a heavy object, suddenly got a severe pain in her lower back, and went to the 'rubbing woman' of the village. After having examined her, she diagnosed a distortion of the back. Then she put one of her knees

Fig. 15. The method of "weighing salt" practised amongst the refugees from East Prussia after the second world war. (*H.-D. Wolff*)

against the patient's back and pressed her shoulders and arms strongly backwards. The lady felt during this procedure a 'snap' in her back. 'Now it is in position again', declared the woman, and the lady was immediately relieved."

The following account was given me by a friend: When walking alone in the mountains, I developed an acute lumbago, leaving me absolutely fixed for a while. With great difficulty I got my heavy rucksack on my back and started to walk. After a while I noticed to my astonishment that my pain subsided. Ever since, if I get lumbago, I put on my rucksack loaded with 50 pounds of stones and walk until I am fully relieved. The cure may well have resulted in a "sucking back" of a protrusion consequent upon the compression force of the rucksack.

When James Cook reached Tahiti in 1777, "being much out of order", he tells:

"I returned on board with Otoo's mother, his three sisters and eight more women. At first I thought they came into my boat

with no other view than to get a passage . . . but when they got to the ship they told me they were come . . . to cure me of the disorder that I complained of, which was *a sort of rheumatic pain in one side from my hip to the foot.* This kind offer I excepted of . . . and submited my self to their direction, I was desired to lay down in the midst of them, then as many as could get round me began to squeeze me with both hands from head to foot, but more especially the parts where the pain was, *till they made my bones crack* and a perfect mummy of my flesh—in short after being under their hands about a quarter of an hour I was glad to get away from them. However I found immediate relief from the operation. They gave me another rubing down before I went to bed and I found my self pretty easy all the night after. They repeated the operation the next morning before they went ashore, and again in the evening when they came on board, after which I found the pains intirely removed . . . This they call *Romy*[1], an operation which in my opinion far exceeds the flesh brush, or any thing we make use of of the kind. It is universally practiced among them . . ."

In the Orient and the Pacific, manipulation has been used for centuries also for its *general stimulatory effect.*

In 1836, E. W. Lane, and in 1846, W. M. Thackeray, described the measure applied by Turkish bath attendants in Egypt. Lane tells:

"The bather soon starts to sweat profusely owing to the damp heat. He now sits down on the 'leewan'. The attendant starts to work, eliciting clicks from his neck and back. The limbs are then apparently violently twisted, but so dexterously that it never hurts and is without danger. He then goes on to massage the muscles" . . .

In 1836, J. S. Buckingham complained that in Persia bath attendants do not practise clicking the joints and twisting the limbs which deprived him of the Turkish bath's "high sensual pleasure".

According to David Urquhart, Sir John Fife (M.D.), in 1865, quotes his experiences in the Middle East:

---

1 *Rumi.* The reader of Hawkesworth may remember that among ailing sea-captains Wallis was also set upon in this way, shortly after his discovery of Tahiti, and benefited very much from the treatment.—Hawkesworth, I, p. 463. (The editor, John C. Beaglehole's commentary.)

"An Arab camel-driver in the desert is exhausted and unable to proceed. He rolls himself in the hot sand, one of his fellows comes up and tramples on him, or beats him. He jumps up ready to resume his journey . . .

"I come in exhausted—have pain accompanying that exhaustion . . . I go into the bath, wherein—in addition to heat—I have manipulations . . . I come forth again fit for my work . . .

"A Tartar, having an hour to rest, prefers a bath to sleep. He enters as if drugged with opium, and leaves it, his senses cleared and his strength restored . . . This is not attributed to the heat or moisture alone, but to the shampooing, which in such cases is of an extraordinary nature. The Tartar sits down and doubles himself up; the shampooer (and he selects the most powerful man) then springs with his feet on his shoulders, cracking the vertebrae; with all his force and weight he pummels the whole back, and then turning him on his back and face, aided by a second shampooer, tramples on his body and limbs; the Tartar then lays himself down for half an hour and perhaps sleeps."

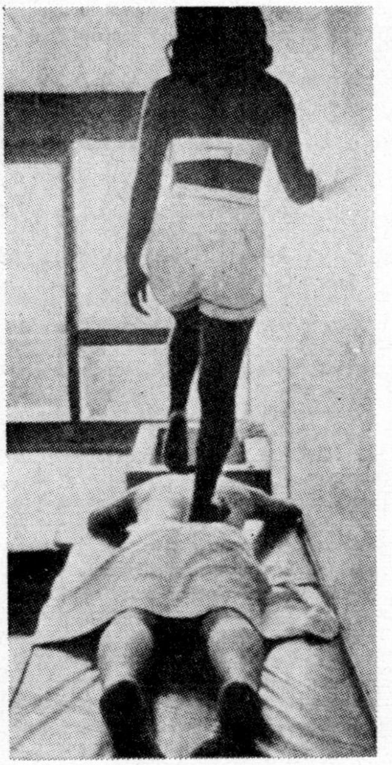

Fig. 16. In the modern Japanese bath the man receives female attention—she washes him, tramples the lumbago out of his back, and gives him massage. And the secret of the trampling massage (old as the hills in Japan) the newly married girl brings with her as a wedding gift from her mother". (*The weekly "Na", Oslo, 23 July* 1960)

This general stimulating effect is also known in Finnish folklore, according to Estlander (1872):

> "These rubbings have been developed into an art within certain families, being 'inherited' from one generation to another . . . The patients are exposed to a high temperature in a sauna . . . certain parts of the body are rubbed with ointments, whereupon each joint is passively moved in every direction . . . all fatigue is, as one would say, gone with the wind."

The Indians used this treatment on an exhausted individual (Little) as is mentioned in Kipling's "Kim".

Fig. 16 illustrates the physical methods offered at a modern Japanese bath.

Comment

It seems justified to infer that methods found effective by the natives of parts of the world as far apart as Norway, Mexico and the Pacific Islands over many, many centuries must be valid.

III

Professional Bone-setters

In Germany (Silesia, East Prussia, Erzgebirge, Northern Saxony) certain families have practised "Zieh-Methoden" (traction) and "Gliedersetzen" (bone-setting) for hundreds of years. There existed "les rebouteux" and "les bailleuls" in France, "algebristas" in Spain, "renunctores" in Italy and "ledd-setjarar" (joint-setters) and "kotknackare" (spine-knockers) in Scandinavia. And bone-setting has undoubtedly flourished in many other countries. Lady Stanhope, quoted by Bruce, wrote from Syria in 1813:

> "I saw also a man there, who let a weight slip off his back, and who could not walk upright afterwards, pulled right again by a Turk in a quarter of an hour, and many other instances I could name in the baths."

James M'Craith, working as a surgeon to the British Seamen's Hospital in Smyrna, records in 1880:

> "I have myself had very lately an attack of lumbago for the first time in my life. A patient, whom I could not go to see, came to see me . . . [and] said 'You cure me—I cure you'. He told me that he had cured very many people, almost instantly . . . He placed me on my face and hands on the sofa, kneaded the painful part very forcibly for some time, and then he told me, 'I don't hear the cric-cric which I hear when I cure my patients at once; so I fear I shall not succeed with you.'—I have also known cases of torticollis attended with great pain . . . get suddenly well on some violent movement being made, attended by a feeling as of something having given way or 'snapped' as it were . . ."

In Great Britain, practitioners of elementary manipulation have existed from time immemorial. Devoid of anatomical knowledge, they have treated injuries of the limbs and spine. Their methods

have been passed on from father to son as family secrets; some were rich farmers who treated their neighbours free of charge. In Cumberland, these men were often blacksmiths; in Wales, shepherds. Some of them moved to a town, settling there, and took on the name of a bone as their surname, and after getting themselves a skeleton, went in for bone-setting in a big way. In due course, they came also to use massage and plaster. The name "bone-setter" was adopted because they always insisted that a little bone lay out of place, and that relief ensued by its replacement. Some of these men became world famous, and in England one was even knighted for his ability (see p. 36). St. Bartholomew's Hospital appointed bone-setters to its staff in the 17th century, according to "Pertinax". But Richard Wiseman (1622–1676) grumbled about the bone-setters:

> "In several Observations in this Book ('Severall Chirurgicall Treatises'), I have had occasion to take notice of the inconvenience many people have fallen into, through the wickedness of those who pretend to the reducing luxated joints by the peculiar name of *Bone-setters*: who (that they may not want employment) do usually represent every bone dislocated they are called to look upon, though possibly it be but a Ganglion or other crude Tumour or preternatural Protuberance of some part of a Joint. In which cases their rash Extensions do frequently cause sad Accidents. But their more gainful way is, by extending and dressing up Joints rather wrencht than dislocated . . ."

The first of these bone-setters of whom details are extant was a woman called Sarah Mapp. She was very well-known and caricatures of her still exist, drawn by William Hogarth and G. Cruikshank (Fig. 17). Enormously fat and ugly, she was nicknamed "Crazy Sally" or "Cross-eyed Sally". "The London Magazine" for August 2, 1736, records in its column "The Monthly Chronologer":

> "The Town has been surpriz'd lately with the Fame of a young Woman at Epsom, who, tho' not very regular, it is said, in her Conduct, has wraught such Cures that seem miraculous in the Bone-setting way. The Concourse of People to Epsom on this Occasion is incredible, and 'tis reckon'd she gets near 20 Guineas a Day, she executing what she does in a very quick Manner . . . Her Strength makes the following Story the more credible. A Man came to her, sent, as 'tis supposed, by some Surgeons, on purpose to try her Skill, with his Hand bound up, and pretended his

Fig. 17. The famous bone-setter Mrs. Sarah Mapp ("Cross-eyed Sally") after a lithograph by G. Cruikshank in the British Museum (*after C. J. S. Thompson*)

Wrist was put out, which upon Examination she found to be false; but to be even with him for his Imposition, she gave him a Wrench, and really put it out, and bade him go to the Fools who sent him, and get it set again, or if he would come to her that Day Month, she would do it herself.

This remarkable Person is Daughter to one Wallin, a Bone-setter of Hindon, Wilts. Upon some Family Quarrel she left her Father, and wander'd up and down the Country in a very miserable Manner, calling herself *Crazy Salley*. Since she became famous, she married one Mr. Hill Mapp, late Servant to a Mercer or Ludgate-Hill; who, 'tis said, soon left her, and carried off £100 of her Money."

On August 19 the same year we read:

"Mrs. Mapp, the famous Bone-setter at Epsom, continues making extraordinary Cures: She has now set up an Equipage, and this Day came to Kensington and waited on her Majesty."

When she put right the niece of Sir Hans Sloane, a physician who had a large practice among the nobility, her reputation and fortune

were made. So popular she was that a play was written in her honour. The title "The Husband's Relief or The Female Bone-setter and the Worm Doctor" suggests that the medical man came off second best. There was also a song in her praise which went:

"You surgeons of London who puzzle your pates,
To ride in your coaches and purchase estates;
Give over for shame, for your pride has a fall,
The doctress of Epsom has outdone you all."

Once a week she drove up to London in a carriage drawn by four horses followed by footmen in gorgeous livery. On one occasion she was stopped by a mob, being thought to be one of the King's unpopular German mistresses. She put her head out of the window and shouted: "Damn your bloods, fools, don't you know me? I am Mrs. Mapp, the bone-setter." The crowd cheered her as she drove off. Later she moved her practice to Pall Mall, the most elegant part of London.

The famous English surgeon, Percivall Pott (1717–1788) wrote:

"We all remember that even the absurdities and impracticability of her own promises and engagement were by no means equal to the expectations and credulity of those who ran after her; that is of all ranks and degrees of people from the lowest laborer or mechanic up to those of the most exalted rank and station; several of whom not only did not hesitate to believe implicitly the most extravagant assertions of an ignorant, illiberal, drunken, female savage, but even solicited her company; at least seemed to enjoy her society." (Quot. Howard W. Haggard, 1929.)

Her decline was swift. She was forced to move to lodgings in the notorious Seven Dials district, and died in such poverty "that the parish was obliged to bury her", a demise that got four brief lines in the "London Daily Post". So are the mighty fallen when patronage is withdrawn! (Quot. R. Pearsall)

[Also in 1871, a female bone-setter was practising in Trieste. Regina dal Cin was, like Mrs. Mapp, the daughter of a bone-setter and not only ruptured adhesions but even reduced dislocations. In the end she received permission to practise in Vienna but this was later revoked. J.C.]

Only two hundred years ago, bone-setters occupied a respectable place in Society, and a friendly relationship was maintained with

doctors. Cheseldon (1688–1752), author of "The Anatomy of the Human Body", sent suitable patients to a bone-setter called Presgrove.

We owe the first description of the bone-setter's craft to Wharton Hood, a doctor who learnt manipulation in 1867. His father, a London physician, treated a bone-setter called Richard Hutton during a long and serious illness. He refused to charge a fee, and in return Hutton offered to teach the son his methods provided they were not published during his lifetime. This he did, and after Hutton's death Wharton Hood published an account of his own and Hutton's experiences. I gained knowledge, Hood said, that cannot be learnt from surgery, of the first importance in preventative and curative treatment if based on anatomy.

Hutton treated more than a thousand patients a year. It often happened, Hood would say, that people who had been treated for a long time by surgeons would come limping in on crutches with a stiff, painful and useless joint; they got the use back after one single treatment. When Hutton died in 1871, "The Lancet" obituary (1871 I, p. 63) stated that "successful he certainly was and it were folly to deny it, in some cases which had baffled the skill of the best surgeons". On April 1 the same year, a leading article on Dr. Wharton Hood and Mr. Hutton appeared. An extract is quoted:

> "The late Mr. Hutton, on whose practice Dr. Wharton Hood's papers are founded, was for many years a sort of bugbear to not a few of the most distinguished surgeons of London; and every few months some fresh case was heard of in which he had given immediate relief and speedy cure to a patient who seemed vainly to have exhausted the legitimate skill of the metropolis . . . It is quite manifest that quackery is only an expression of the extent to which legitimate practitioners fail to meet the desires of the sick. These desires may be either reasonable or unreasonable . . . They are sometimes perfectly reasonable; and then the medical practitioner who fails in fulfilling them, is the most effectual, indeed the only effectual, ally of the quack. If he does not know how to fulfil them, it is his duty to learn; and he in no way accomplishes this duty by railing at the quack for his failure, or for any mischief that he may do."

The English surgeon, Sir James Paget (1814–1899) set out similar views in his lecture at St. Bartholomew's Hospital in 1866. The title was "Cases that Bone-setters Cure", and he started by warning his

students: "Few of you are likely to practise without having a bone-setter for an enemy . . . Now, it would be of little use to us to estimate, even if it were possible, the quantity of mischief done by treatment such as this. It is more important to know and consider that it sometimes does good." After having explained how a bone-setter cured lumbago, he finishes, "Learn then to imitate what is good and avoid what is bad in the practice of bonesetting. *Fas est ab hoste doceri* (Wise it is to learn from your enemy)."

Bone-setting was the principal subject during the annual meeting of the British Medical Association in 1882. The first lecture in the section on Surgery was delivered by Howard Marsh, surgeon at St. Bartholomew's Hospital. He was followed by R. Dacre Fox, surgeon at the Southern Hospital in Manchester. During three years' assistantship he had learnt bone-setting from James Taylor, a doctor whose forebears had for over two centuries practised bone-setting at Witworth in Lancashire. He ascribed the success of bone-setters not only to their knowledge, but also to doctors' degree of ignorance amounting to neglect of how to treat joint disorders.

W. J. Penny in an article on bone-setting in 1888:

"Bone-setting has been little studied by the legitimate members of our profession . . . Many of these quacks . . . have acquired considerable skill . . . The public are perfectly within their right to get cured wherever they can. They do not care, and why should they, whether the cure is wrought by a Member of the College of Surgeons, or by the village blacksmith . . . we must recognise the fact that they often cure cases in which we have failed . . ."

Dr. David Rorie of Cardenden, Fife (Scotland) in 1902:

". . . A medical man can study anatomy and surgery for years, he may practise with success as a howdie or a pill-giver, but 'a body kens doctors ken naethin about bone' . . . Who are the patients of the bonesetters? There's the rub! Not only the *profanum vulgum*. The duchess elbows the dustman at the charlatan's door, the clergyman lends his pony-trap to the collier to drive past the house of the doctor and go to the smithy . . ."

In 1924, George Robertson, Honorary Surgeon at the Dunfermline and West of Fife Hospital, wrote:

". . . Bonesetters have lived and practised their art (for art it occasionally is) for generations, and they are with us today more publicly recognized than ever . . . With the doctor's knowledge and often consent, he [the patient] may travel hundreds of miles

Fig. 18. The most famous of all bone-setters, Sir Herbert Barker (1869–1950). A portrait in the Chenil Gallery, London, painted by Augustus John

to enter a bonesetter's clinic, where he may perchance rub shoulders with a famous actress, acrobat, or even a peer of the realm . . . A patient who reluctantly pays two or three guineas for a radiographic examination willingly hands to the bonesetter forty or fifty pounds . . . While we may rail against the bonesetter . . . we may be even more justified if we similarly criticise his 'professional brother' . . . Just as long as we have students improperly taught . . . so long will we have the bonesetter's 'professional brother' . . . The patients, who look to us as medical men for careful treatment . . . do not get fair play; one generation of doctors succeeds the former, no better instructed than their predecessors . . . and the vicious circle continues . . ."

The best known of all the bone-setters was Herbert Barker, who practised in London until 1927 (Fig. 18). He learnt from his cousin, a bone-setter called John Atkinson, working in Park Lane, who in turn had been taught by Robert Hutton, a nephew of Richard Hutton. They both came from a farming family in Northern England where their families had practised for over two centuries.

Barker's autobiography is entitled "Leaves from my Life" (1928). For many years he tried to get doctors to recognise his art, and invited them to visit him. He offered to give demonstrations at hospitals and asked medical associations to assemble a committee of orthopaedic experts to investigate his work. But all in vain. Both "The Lancet" and "The British Medical Journal" refused to publish the letters he submitted for publication in their correspondence columns—and those of his medical supporters. Self-satisfied and arrogant doctors refused at that time even to listen to him. He in his turn criticised them:

"Strong as the love of service to suffering is among many doctors as a whole, there existed some things much stronger and less worthy in prejudice and jealousy which have from time immemorial darkened the pages of surgical history and smirched its record of noble endeavours . . . I am certainly not prepared to be condemned by men who are culpably ignorant of what it is their business to know, and which they are too arrogant or too prejudiced to learn . . . It is still true [and it still is, in 1974! E.S.] that the Faculty has neglected the study of the methods, and are today incapable of relieving sufferers who resort to them. Yet they persist still in their refusal to accept the help of those who can instruct them in this beneficient branch of the healing art . . .

"I cannot afford the time and strength demanded for demonstrations for the benefit of individuals. What I desire is to bring the methods before the Faculty as a whole, secure them a place in the curricula of medical schools . . . obtain for the entire body of students a thorough and practical training in the work . . . I contend, unreservedly, that the methods of the manipulative art . . . are quite unknown to the general practitioner, and even to specialists in surgery . . . [they have] no real and effective knowledge even of its rudimentary principles . . ." (quoted from his autobiography).

He numbered amongst his patients royalty and the nobility, famous actors and athletes, members of parliament, Paderewski, H. G. Wells and John Galsworthy. Controversy raged in the newspapers about him for years:

". . . We here pass from the sphere of mere medical trade unionism . . . to that of medical priestcraft . . . assuming itself to be the sole depository of truth . . ." (the magazine "Truth", quoted by Mr. Barker in his autobiography).

As from 1910, consultants had begun to send him patients. In the June issue 1911 of the "English Review", there appeared an article by Dr. Whitebread entitled "Bone-setters and the Faculty", where he wrote:

> ". . . He succeeded when surgeons of repute and experience failed . . . I plead for this [investigation of Mr. Barker's methods] with all the more earnestness because I am convinced that the attitude adopted by the medical world towards the method of manipulative surgery is only adding another regrettable page to those chapters in its history which it recalls with profound shame . . ."

Finally, in 1916, the "Medical Press and Circular" opened their columns to him. At last his skill and honesty were openly recognised by important medical men: "If the testimony of beneficiaries is worth anything at all, then it is evident that Mr. Barker is possessed of knowledge and skill in a certain department of manipulative healing which is very much in advance of anything which is known to the profession" (leading article November 29, 1916). "Common knowledge has established that his art consists of procedures unknown to surgeons . . ." (Ibid., April 28, 1920). ". . . No living medical man within these islands has received such distinctions . . ." (Ibid., January 4, 1922).

A leading article in "The Lancet" appeared in 1925 and gave him his due: "The medical history of the future will have to record that our profession has greatly neglected this important subject . . . The fact must be faced that the bone-setters have been curing multitudes of cases by movement . . . and that by our faulty methods we are largely responsible for their very existence."

He was knighted in 1922, much to the chagrin of the majority of the medical men in Britain. In 1936, as an old man, years after he had retired from practice, his dream came true and he was invited by Mr. W. Rowley Bristow of St. Thomas's Hospital to give a demonstration at a meeting of the British Orthopaedic Association. Over a hundred members from all parts of the country attended. In their presence he manipulated about twenty of the hospital's patients—cases of tennis-elbow, ruptured meniscus, subluxation of the head of the ulna, lumbago, etc. [However, when Bristow and he together reviewed the same patients three months later, none of the cases with a ruptured cartilage at the knee had improved. J.C.] The report on the meeting in "The British Medical Journal"

(1938 II, 255) gave him great credit, stating: "He displayed in some cases remarkable dexterity . . . and the warm thanks of the meeting for a most interesting demonstration were conveyed by Mr. McMurray." A leading article in the same issue of the Journal (p. 233) was equally complimentary.

Still worth reading today is an article "On Bone-setting" by Thomas Marlin, Physician in Charge of the Massage, Light, and Electrotherapeutic Departments at the University College Hospital of London (1932). Here he tries to explain what happens in the joints of the extremities when these are treated successfully by bone-setters, emphasising the traction factor. About *spinal* manipulation he says: "Medical men seldom see any of this work, but I shall never forget the profound impression made on me when I first saw any of it done, and I have never given a first demonstration to any of my colleagues without noting their extreme amazement that such a thing can possibly be done".

In some instances, these bone-setter families have bred famous orthopaedic surgeons. The Welshman Hugh Owen Thomas, the son of a well-known bone-setter—Evan Thomas of Liverpool—became "the actual founder of modern orthopaedic surgery". His forebears had been bone-setters for several generations. He admitted that he had learnt a lot from his father and in one of his papers states: "That some of the bone-setters who practised in past time were in some few special matters *superior* to their qualified contemporaries, I know to be a fact." A reviewer of David Le Vay's biography of Thomas writes as follows: "In the intervening centuries many talented individuals without any formal qualifications have tried their hands at the revealing art of bone-setting, and sometimes with rather phenomenal success . . . Hugh Thomas deplores the persistent ignorance of his professional brethren in regard to the main principles involved in the proper management of pathological bones and joints."

Thomas's principles were furthered by his wife's nephew, the famous Sir Robert Jones. In 1878, when he was only twenty-one, he began helping his uncle in his huge practice in the Liverpool Docks. "He [Jones] was himself a master of manipulation", writes his biographer, Frederick Watson.

Bone-setters' Successes

The disorders in which bone-setters were especially successful fall into six groups:

1. Stiffness and pain in joints immobilised for a long time in the treatment of fractures, dislocations and sprains. In those days, the orthodox treatment of such conditions by prolonged rest produced endless stiff and painful joints for lay-manipulators to deal with—a situation which persisted well into the 20th century.

2. Stiffness and pain resulting from disuse. After an injury, or as the result of soft-tissue lesions (e.g. tendinitis, bursitis), the patient himself had avoided using the joint. This lack of mobility had allowed adhesions and shrinkage of the capsule to develop.

3. Internal derangement owing to rupture of a meniscus. Bone-setters had their greatest triumphs in reducing these displacements. They were known to perform miracles even in long-standing cases.

4. Arthrosis or subluxation at the joints of the hand and foot, especially at the trapezio-first-metacarpal and the mid-tarsal joints. Other common disorders successfully treated were subluxation of the acromio-clavicular joint, of the head of the radius in children, of the head of the ulna after Colles's fracture.

5. Ganglion about the wrist.

6. Lumbago and torticollis. Wharton Hood gives a detailed description of Richard Hutton's manipulations for neck trouble.

IV

Osteopathy

In his book "Pasienten og legen" ("The Patient and the Doctor"), published in 1952, a well-known Norwegian psychiatrist, Trygve Braatöy, relates that when he was in Kansas in 1949, he had a woman secretary who told him, when she returned his papers to him, that she had severe pain in her arm. When asked what she did about it, she answered that she went to an osteopath. "In America, this term includes a large group of highly educated healers who specialise in physical treatment. Many patients have learned that these osteopaths pay more attention to pains in muscles and similar complaints than does their regular doctor. Doctors are taught little of how to examine patients' musculature, how to assess posture and range of movement except in specific neurological disorders. Instead the doctor has X-ray photographs taken on which the muscles cannot show up. In consequence, patients with muscle trouble visit one doctor after another. Finally, they go to see an osteopath, who often helps them, with wrong theory but the correct hand grip."

The concept of osteopathy was introduced by Andrew T. Still (1828–1917), son of a methodist priest who was also a healer (Fig. 19). He called himself a doctor after attending a short course of lectures at the "Kansas City School of Physicians and Surgeons". He never took any examinations. As from 1853, he helped his father look after the simple Indian folk of the Middle West of the U.S.A. However, in 1864, after he had lost three of his children from cerebro-spinal meningitis, he started a campaign against doctors' "indiscriminate use of drugs". Like many of the healers in those days, he had much of the old-testament prophet about him. He had strong religious feelings with hallucinations. His textbook of osteopathy is dedicated to God: "Respectfully dedicated to the Grand Architect and Builder of the Universe".

His two main hypotheses were:

Fig. 19. Andrew T. Still (1828–1917), "the founder of osteopathy"

(1) The body has within itself the power to combat all disease.

(2) The cause of all disease is dislocated bones, abnormal ligaments or contracted muscles—especially in the back—with consequent mechanical pressure on blood-vessels and nerves, a pressure that in part produces ischaemia and necrosis, in part obstruction of the life-force travelling along the nerves.

This so-called "osteopathic lesion" was the cornerstone of his teaching; the alpha and omega of the cause of disease. On this basis, he worked out a system of manipulation for curing all diseases. It is not clear how he arrived at the conclusion that manipulation

provided a panacea. He himself states that God revealed this truth to him in 1874 and "asked him to fling to the breeze the banner of osteopathy". In fact, the idea could have emanated from immigrants from England who practised as bone-setters, like Robert Joy, who married one of the English bone-setter Evan Thomas's (d. 1814) daughters. He settled with a Welsh contingent in Wisconsin and practised there (according to David Le Vay). Alternatively, it could have been articles in the medical press: Wharton Hood (see p. 32) published his series of articles on "so-called bone-setting" in the Lancet in 1871 (and in book-form the same year); in other words, three years before Still had his "revelation". In this connection, it is also relevant that a French doctor called Cruveilhier had had a publication of his reviewed in detail in an American journal in 1837. Still's contemporaries regarded him partly as a miracle-man, partly as a quack and charlatan, and partly as a harmless but effective bone-setter. Some excerpts from Still's teaching are worth mentioning:

> "Dislocation of the hips is a frequent cause of diabetes. The use of nappies is the cause of dislocation of the hip in babies. Gall-stones result from displacement of the fifth, sixth or seventh rib. A very common cause of goitre is slipping of the first rib. In the treatment of constipation, I always start by correcting the atlas."

For diabetes, he advised, apart from manipulation, plenty of honey.

In 1892, he joined a doctor from Edinburgh named William Smith to found the first school of osteopathy in Kirksville, Missouri. There, successful candidates received the title of Doctor of Osteopathy (D.O.) after a two-year course. By the year 1900, the first osteopaths were granted full licence to practise medicine and surgery in some of the States of America! Fig. 20 reproduces an illustration dating from earliest days of osteopathy. It depicts mid-thoracic manipulation for dysentery or impotence (Home Study Course in Osteopathy, 1902). The book went into many editions.

Later, new schools were established, all of which clung religiously to Still's dogma; at one time there were thirty-seven of them. Later, the course was lengthened, the syllabus changed, and more medical subjects included. Doctors were introduced as lecturers. Today, highly respectable people are being trained and there is little difference now between doctors and osteopaths in the U.S.A.

For a detailed account of the history of osteopathy, the reader should consult Booth (1924), Reed (1932) and Keesecker (1957).

Fig. 20. Osteopathic treatment of dysentery in the early days of osteopathy. ("*Home Study Course in Osteopathy*", 1902)

Developments in England are given by Streeter (1932), and in the transcript of the Enquiry in the House of Lords in 1935. (The Osteopaths Bill. A Report of the Proceedings before a select Committee of the House of Lords). [At this enquiry, one well-known osteopath maintained that a child would not catch diphtheria if the cervical vertebrae were in proper position, and another alleged that he could cure deafness by dilating the Eustachian tube with his finger, quite unaware that the tube is too narrow to take anything thicker than a large needle. J.C.]

Two years later, Hill and Clegg (then Editor of the British Medical Journal) wrote: "What is Osteopathy?" Cyriax produced a popular account entitled "Osteopathy and Manipulation" in 1949

containing a chapter evaluating the evidence for the "osteopathic lesion". In 1953, Laycock brought out an illustrated book on osteopathic technique, and in 1962 appeared the first edition of Alan Stoddard's "Manual of Osteopathic Technique".

The situation in 1952 is best set out by reference to the findings of a committee of experts created by the American Medical Association "for the study of relations between osteopathy and medicine". Its inception was information tendered in 1951 to the Board of Trustees by doctors' associations on problems involving the relationship of medical men and osteopaths. Five doctors were appointed to make contact with the "American Osteopathic Association" and to decide whether osteopathy was still to be categorised as "cult healing". After a year's deliberation, the committee's findings were put before the Board of Trustees. Then there was a further meeting in New York in 1953 and another at Atlantic City in 1955. By now the committee had been strengthened by the cooption of university lecturers, experts in methods of teaching, and had visited six of the seven schools of osteopathy in the U.S.A. The two reports are summarised below:

All schools of osteopathy are "non-profit schools". The Government via the Health Department gives financial support for teaching and research. The pre-registration requirement for students is the same as at the medical faculties (high-school or three years at college) and the same standard is imposed as for medical students. The time involved in clinical study is the same as at the universities—four years. Purely medical subjects occupy 90–95 per cent. of students' time—again the same as at a university. Normal medical textbooks are used. Actual teaching time, calculated in hours, is just on 25 per cent. higher than in ordinary medical schools, owing to the extra time devoted to diseases of the musculo-skeletal system and their treatment by manipulation and the usual types of physical therapy. This tuition is an addition to that on basic medicine and the usual clinical subjects. All osteopathic schools possess separate clinics for musculo-skeletal disease.

Here lies the chief difference between tuition in medical and osteopathic schools. However, the Committee (1955) drew attention to the fact that, in orthopaedic departments, the use of manipulation had increased, whereas it had decreased at osteopathic schools. Furthermore, they pointed out that no real fact-finding research on manipulation had ever been organised by medical men, and assessment by trained objective researchers was overdue. The committee

found that the quality of training at the medical schools was on the whole higher than at the osteopathic establishments, but also stated that the best of the osteopathic schools was superior to the least satisfactory amongst the medical schools.

All osteopathic schools accepted the ordinary medical views on disease, and there was no instance of adherence to Still's notion of a panacea. They did, however, hold fast to the "osteopathic concept", by insisting that important syndromes were derived from musculo-skeletal lesions. However, they did not maintain that correction of such lesions could cure organic disease. There remained, they noted, practising osteopaths of the old school, who did treat systemic disorders by manipulation, but their number was rapidly diminishing. Tuition could, therefore, not be regarded as sectarian, according to the concept of cult healing as defined in the American Medical Association's "Principles of Medical Ethics".

Enquiry in eighteen States showed that the public did not distinguish between doctors and osteopaths. Complete integration between medicine and osteopathy was a future eventuality and they agreed that members of the A.M.A. could accept teaching-posts in osteopathic schools.

The council made the following recommendations (101 for, 81 against):

(1) The Committee's report should be put "ad acta" (accepted for orientation).

(2) If and when the American Osteopathic Association Central Board spontaneously abandons the osteopathic concept and omits this term from their teaching and then approaches the A.M.A.'s Board of Trustees for a fresh meeting on the relations between osteopaths and doctors, a new Select Committee will be brought into being to discuss the matter.

In 1958, there were 212,000 doctors in the U.S.A. and 13,000 osteopaths; the latter thus formed only 6 per cent. of the total. In 1956, students in training comprised 7,000 medical and 300 osteopathic (figures furnished by the A.M.A.). Keesecker found four hundred hospitals with medical and surgical departments where osteopaths were members of the staff. In a few cases they had doctors of medicine as colleagues (which entitled them to a government grant) in hospitals with up to 400–500 beds.

In December 1968 the A.M.A. discussed how to bring about the

eventual amalgamation of medicine and osteopathy. They decided to offer students and graduates in osteopathy education in medicine at undergraduate and graduate levels. They also proposed avenues for assimilating qualified osteopaths into medicine. Concern was voiced about the term "qualified" with reference to osteopaths. The delegates realised that the implementation of these ideas would be slow, but that opportunities for improvement would be created where none are available now. (*J. Louisiana State Med. Soc.,* Jan. 1969.)

Osteopaths now receive the full medical licence to practise in most American States. For insurance purposes, they are usually regarded as on a par with doctors in dealing with accidents, and they can treat patients privately insured; they can be Army doctors, general practitioners or school medical officers. Their health certificates are accepted by the important official institutions.

V

Chiropractic

Forty-five years ago, Professor Howard W. Haggard wrote: "America is still the happy hunting ground for all cults, as Europe was in the Middle Ages." From bone-setting and osteopathy, as the latter became more and more orientated towards orthodox medicine, a new and powerful sect developed—chiropractic.

In 1883, a group of men called "magnetisers" worked in Davenport, a small town in Iowa. A grocer and fishmonger there, one Daniel David Palmer (1845–1913, Fig. 21) became convinced that he possessed magnetic powers and started his own magnetism business, which he ran for ten years until 1895. Richard Cyriax, in an article of Chiropractic written in 1912 refers to the "Palmer School of Magnetic Healing". No record exists of how Palmer came in touch with manipulation, and it is often said that he made the system up himself, but we have his own story in his first textbook "The Chiropractor's Adjuster" (1910), which throws light on the origins of his craft. He stated that the art of replacing subluxated vertebrae had been practised for thousands of years. His first encounter was through a doctor, Jim Atkinson (see p. 60), who about fifty years previously (i.e. about 1860) practised in Davenport and "tried during his lifetime to promulgate the principles now known as chiropractic"—a name first suggested to him by the Reverend Samuel H. Weed. He states also:

> "Recently I had the honor and pleasure of entertaining my old friend W. J. Colville, the well known traveler, author and international speaker, who gave me the following typewritten information concerning the history of the principles which had been given me by Dr. Atkinson . . .: 'During my visit to Paris, in 1895, as the guest of Lady Gaithness . . . it was my privilege to meet many peculiar and distinguished persons, among whom and the

Fig. 21. The chiropractor D. D. Palmer and his son B. J. Palmer

most interesting of all, were some members of an occult society which made a speciality of healing ministrations. Among the methods employed by these extraordinary representatives of a very ancient Aesculapius sect was one closely resembling chiropractic' . . . I do claim, however, to be the first to replace displaced vertebrae by using the spinous and transverse processes as levers wherewith to rack subluxated vertebrae into normal position, and from this basic fact, to create a science which is destined to revolutionise the theory and practice of the healing art . . ."

From Palmer's own account it appears that he had heard of the 2,300-year-old Hippocratic method of treating backs—partly from a doctor, partly from a tourist returned from Paris—and that he revived these methods. Many maintain, however, that in the meanwhile he had worked in contact with the osteopaths, whose methods he adapted and elaborated. In his article on chiropractic, Ch. Turner (1931) writes that Dr. Charles Still, son of the founder of osteopathy, considers that Palmer got his knowledge from Stother, a student from Kirksville. The two of them had tried to operate an osteopathic school twenty years earlier, but without success.

In the British Medical Journal (1924, i, 964) chiropractic was described as a branch of osteopathy, first designed to maintain osteopathic dogma in its most primitive form, and secondly as maintaining its commercial character. "Chiropractic is the malignant tumour on the body of osteopathy," said Morris Fishbein in 1925.

There is such a scarcity of information in the literature that it is hard to assess to what extent chiropractic technique, as distinct from osteopathy, is original, and how much of the original methods is practicable. Palmer's first patient in September 1895 was a negro doorman who seventeen years earlier had become completely deaf after an injury to his neck. Palmer immediately discovered a large subluxation of a cervical vertebra. According to his son, B. J. Palmer's own words: "That bump was adjusted, and within ten minutes he had his hearing, and has had it ever since" (Maisel, 1946). This claim has always been regarded as nonsensical.

Together with a solicitor, Willard Carver, D. D. Palmer opened the first chiropractic school in Oklahoma City in 1897. All-comers were accepted if they paid $500 in cash for a fortnight's course. Later, the length of the course was increased and the fee diminished owing to competition from other schools. By 1910, the price was $150 for twelve months' tuition. In 1958, there still existed in the U.S.A. a few old chiropractors with the right to call themselves doctors on the strength of such education.

Chiropractic helps in all diseases. In one of the many lawsuits in which Palmer was involved, the following cross-examination was reported in the British Medical Journal (1924, i, 963).

Counsel: "And what particular vertebra did you teach them to adjust for lice in the head, if any?"

Palmer: "In the cervical region."

Counsel: "And suppose you had body lice in the groin, what vertebra would you adjust for those?"

Palmer: "In the lumbar region . . . from the 2nd to the 5th inclusive, it could be any one."

In 1922, according to a translation by a Norwegian chiropractor called H. Andersen, G. H. Patchen compiled a list of diseases permanently curable by chiropractic. It included anaemia, appendicitis, diabetes, goitre, hay fever, jaundice, poliomyelitis and rheumatic joints. It also appeared that the Spanish royal family's son, deaf and dumb since birth, was cured by a chiropractor in London.

In 1932, the leading chiropractor of Oslo, Arthur E. Lundh, wrote that a great part of all diseases results from abnormal pressure on one or more nerves. Chiropractic treatment achieves two ends: (1) to remove the cause which has facilitated the onset of disease and let it gain a foothold in the body; (2) to permit a

normal flow of life-energy from the brain to the tissues, thus preventing the disease from spreading further.

He further declared that, with the help of X-ray photographs taken before and after chiropractic treatment, it is easy to prove the existence of these displacements and show the change in position of the vertebra afterwards. "All older chiropractors have in their archives radiographs showing this alteration." Subluxation of the second cervical vertebra (as demonstrated by radiography) can cause disease in eyes or nose, pain in the face or head, and nervousness. Lumbar displacements can set up constipation, catarrh of the bowel, bladder and pelvic disease and sciatica, so it appears.

D. D. Palmer manipulated not only the spinal column but also the limbs. This system was continued by Carver when he took the school over alone. These chiropractors were named "mixers" and the system "The Carver Method of Chiropractic". In due course, this came to include normal methods of physical therapy, dietetics, etc. Chiropractors belonging to this category are now united in the "American Chiropractic Association", and there are eight approved chiropractic schools belonging to this category in the U.S.A. Most student chiropractors today are being trained there. The association had (1968) more than 7,000 members.

B. J. Palmer, the son (see Fig. 21), put up his own school in Davenport, which he still ran until about ten years ago. He manipulated only the spine and his supporters were therefore called "straights" and his system "The Palmer Method of Chiropractic". As time went on, the straights lost to the mixers. Chiropractors belonging to this category are united in the "International Chiropractors' Association", which has as its main base the Palmer College in Davenport, Iowa. This association approves only four chiropractic schools in the U.S.A., and only one of these is on the approved list of "American Chiropractic Association" (!):

> B. J. Palmer had a genius for business. He started one of the world's largest enterprises in bluff—namely, the production in 1924 of the "neuro-calometer". According to a statement put out by the Palmer School in 1957, they offered a proven scientific instrument for registering tiny variations in temperature of the skin along the vertebral column whereby to identify more accurately the places where the nerves were compressed and where the vital stream from the brain to the tissues was interrupted.

[Until then, a rough-and-ready method for deciding where the chiropractor should manipulate in visceral disease was for him to run his hand up and down the patient's back looking for a "hot-box". This was an area of skin along one or other side of the spine which was detectably warmer than at the segment immediately above or below. Such local warmth was held to indicate the level of the vertebra whose dislocation had caused the trouble. J.C.]

This instrument was not for sale, but was hired out on a yearly basis (Louis Reed, 1932) at a phenomenal rent which brought Palmer an enormous income. In 1935, a more advanced apparatus was introduced—the "neuro-calograph". This was the same instrument as before but with automatic registrations of skin-temperature on a graph. In 1953, this was replaced by a "chirometer"—an instrument giving (so it was said) utterly specific information on disturbance or interference in nerves, and whether this was or was not alterable by treatment. The use of these instruments forms an integral part of the teaching at the schools run by the International Chiropractors' Association, but not in the other chiropractic establishments in the U.S.A.

The "doctors" whom Palmer and others trained often found themselves better off teaching chiropractic than actually carrying it out, and large numbers of "colleges" sprang up. In 1930, there were 300 such places (Turner). The "British Medical Journal" (1925, i, 707) printed a comment: "The Editor of 'Truth' hardly exaggerated in saying that it seemed easier to establish a university in the United States than to open a pub in England. America is the land of freedom, freedom for faddists among others." Diploma-mills flowered in almost every large town, "releasing a horde of incompetents whose chief ambition was to get rich quickly . . . Numerous practitioners with only an original six-months' training eventually gained State credentials . . . Even today (1931), nearly one-half of the so-called members of the (chiropractic) profession are either unqualified to practise because of inadequate study or are justly included in the category of quacks . . . (but) gradually the correspondence courses and night-schools began to disappear . . ." (Turner). But as Stalvey pointed out in 1957: "The day of the mail-order and the short-term chiropractic course is not history yet."

In 1958, there were 25,000 chiropractors (i.e. 1 to each 7,000 inhabitants) who each year were visited by about 20 million new clients. One reason, according to Dewey Anderson's chiropractic

information bulletin (1956), is that American doctors charge too much—"all that the traffic will bear". Moreover, many patients seek from chiropractic a method of prophylaxis "a system that may add years of healthful, zestful living to their lives".

Eight schools hold (1956) the approval of the National (now American) Chiropractic Association as fulfilling the teaching standards laid down. These are: Entrance from high school (now often also two years' college)—at least 4,000 hours of teaching in the course of four periods of nine months. This can be reduced to three years by the student cutting out holidays, which is commonly done. Hours of tuition at evening-schools are accepted if a reasonable period is set aside. Such evening-classes could (1956) be taken at the "Chiropractic Institute of New York", one of the few States where chiropractice until recently was forbidden by law, but where in fact three thousand practised notwithstanding. Even before this law was repealed, about a third of them appeared under that heading in the classified telephone directory.

The syllabus in these "approved" institutions was in 1957: anatomy (740 hours), physiology (240 hours), biochemistry (180 hours), pathology and bacteriology (520 hours), public health and hygiene (220 hours), "diagnosis and treatment" (1960 hours). Pharmacology and surgery were (and still are) omitted. Dewey Anderson states that a well-equipped chiropractor in the U.S.A. possesses an X-ray apparatus, ophthalmoscope, otoscope, laryngoscope, proctoscope and electrocardiograph.

Except for Louisiana and Mississippi, all the States of the U.S.A. grant official licence to practise chiropractic, but each State holds to its own definition of chiropractic. No restriction is drawn on *what disease* a chiropractor can treat, only the *means* whereby he treats them. The statute regulating practice in each separate State is as confusing as is chiropractic education itself.

> The following figures relate to the year 1958: twenty-two States insist upon students passing the basic sciences examination (anatomy, physiology, chemistry, bacteriology, etc.) beforehand, like medical students. But chiropractic students avoid these States owing to their high rate of failure (Turner, Doyle). In thirty-three States, chiropractors are empowered to sign death certificates. In forty-two, they can call themselves "doctor" and can practise for Workmen's Compensation. In twenty-nine, they are allowed to give physical treatment. In thirty-six, their certifi-

cates for insurance benefit are valid. More than five hundred insurance companies recognise their certificates. The Social Security Act of 1950 allows patients on benefit their chiropractors' fees, as part of compensation defrayed from governmental funds. Many organisations and large film companies number a chiropractor on their staff. The American Olympic team at Helsinki had two with them.

The Governor of Illinois sent a letter of welcome to the National Chiropractic Association's annual congress in Chicago in 1956, which two thousand members attended: "Chicago is proud to be the host city for this great meeting of healers." The Vice-President of the "National Safety Council" gave a lecture giving reasons for chiropractors working together with his organisation.

The Association, with ample funds, ran a large advertisement campaign over the radio, with films, leaflets and so forth. A pamphlet on career guidance—"Chiropractic as a Career"—was handed to school-leavers "replete with chiropractic misstatements and half truths" (Stalvey). A little leaflet in colour was distributed to children in the lower and middle forms. This contained a picture of a row of happy children marching along singing:

Backbone, backbone
Key to health
Three cheers for Chiropractic
Get hep,
Keep in step
Rhythm and pep
Three cheers for Chiropractic.

Every month the Association sent round five copies of its magazine "Healthway" to each member, with the suggestion that these should be forwarded to prominent people in the district. A sound-film in colour was produced at great cost and shown all over the country. A brochure was published called "How Hollywood's stars regain and maintain their health and beauty" with photographs and testimonials from well-known cinema actors.

[This policy is continued now. In 1970 in Australia, two advertising broadsheets, extolling the virtues of chiropractic and giving a remarkable list of diseases alleged to be thus curable, was printed in the format of a newspaper and delivered to householders all over Sydney and Melbourne. J.C.]

It can well be regarded as unfair to bring up chiropractic events from 25 to 50 years ago, instead of dealing with its present state. After all, many doctors might not care to be confronted with what they believed and wrote so long ago. It is thus relevant to ask about chiropractic dogma as it stands in recent times. Great variations exist between one school and another. Chiropractic textbooks are not on sale in bookshops, one has to turn to the schools themselves, and even then it is far from certain that one is allowed to buy them. There is Janse, Houser and Well's textbook on chiropractic (second edition, 1947). The authors were "mixers". Their definition of chiropractic is "the science of treating human ailments, by manipulation and adjustment of the spine and other structures of the human body, and the use of such other mechanical, physio-therapeutic, dietetic and sanitary measures, except drugs and major surgery, as are incident to the care of the human body" (p. 3). Further: "The theory, or philosophy, underlying spinal adjustment may be summed up in five principles:

"(1) That a vertebra may become subluxated.

"(2) That this subluxation tends to impingement of the structures (nerves, blood vessels, and lymphatics) passing through the inter-vertebral foramen.

"(3) That, as a result of such impingement, the function of the corresponding segment of the spinal cord and its connecting spinal and autonomic nerves is interfered with and the conduction of the nerve impulses impaired.

"(4) That, as a result thereof, the nervous tone in certain parts of the organism is abnormally altered and such parts become functionally or organically diseased or predisposed to disease.

"(5) That adjustment of a subluxated vertebra removes the impingement on the structures passing through the inter-vertebral foramen, thereby restoring to diseased parts their normal nervous stimuli and rehabilitating them functionally and organically" (p. 7).

But there are many weird definitions and explanations, in part written in (for doctors) wholly incomprehensible language. One asks what the following phrase taken from the syllabus of the Institute of Chiropractic in New York, giving information about chiropractic technique, is supposed to mean: "This training in the

A.P. (Arm Place)	*7th Cervical Vertebra*
H.P. (Heart Place)	2ND DORSAL VERTEBRA
	3rd Dorsal Vertebra
Lu. P. (Lung Place)	3RD DORSAL VERTEBRA
	4th Dorsal Vertebra
Li. P. (Liver Place)	4TH DORSAL VERTEBRA
	5th Dorsal Vertebra
C. P. (Centre Place)	5TH DORSAL VERTEBRA
	4th Dorsal Vertebra
S. P. (Stomach Place)	*6th Dorsal Vertebra*
	7th Dorsal Vertebra
	8th Dorsal Vertebra
Spl. P. (Spleen Place)	9TH DORSAL VERTEBRA
K. P. (Kidney Place)	*10th Dorsal Vertebra*
	11th Dorsal Vertebra
	12th Dorsal Vertebra

Fig. 22. "Key to Spinal Analysis". (*W. Garsia,* 1952)

art of chiropractic is the tracto-thrust method of re-relating dis-related anatomical structures."

A couple of other quotations from Janse and his co-authors' textbook:

"Chiropractic science, through the past half century of its enlightened existence, has continued to hold to its original premise that disturbed nerve function is responsible for a major portion [sic] of man's ills, and that efforts to normalize nerve function through structural adjustment, is the greatest single agent in restoring and maintaining health . . . As a means of restoring and maintaining health chiropractic has been perhaps the greatest phenomenon in all the history of healing effort . . ." (p. v).

"That subluxations in certain segments of the spine produce certain diseases is attested by the fact that upon accurate determination of a subluxation in a certain section of the vertebral column an exact knowledge is gained as to what particular system or organ of the body is diseased. Naturally, the exact nature of the disease cannot be determined by examinations of the spine. For example, when the liver is affected, it may be accurately determined that there is an abnormal condition of that organ

[ADVERTISEMENT]

"I QUIT 160 UNITS INSULIN DAILY," SAYS

J. Jay Elston of 211 E. Carlson Blvd. "I was diabetic for 5 years and took 160 units of insulin daily. I took Dr. ▬▬ treatments for 8 weeks and was able to stop insulin altogether. In 3 months I was discharged."

"It has been over a year that I have not taken insulin or medicines. I am eating all I want anytime I want and am feeling fine. Anyone who wishes to see how well I am is welcome to drop in at my rabbit farm for a chat." (Signed) J. Jay Elston. ▬▬, D.C. Los Angeles office open only Tues., Thurs. 10-12 & 2-6. Sat. 10-1.

Fig. 23. An advertisement in a Los Angeles newspaper 1957. ("D.C." = "Doctor of Chiropractic")

by finding the fourth and eight dorsal vertebra subluxated, but whether this abnormality is cancer or congestion of the liver requires a direct examination of the organ itself . . . [Chiropractic] recognizes the true and primary cause of the disease and relieves the cause . . . Its action is specific and scientific, its results outstandingly successful" (pp. 16–17).

A full-page advertisement in the Sunday edition of the "New York Journal-American", published a "partial list" of diseases that chiropractors allege to cure. Amongst others, there were listed sinusitis, "female diseases", poliomyelitis, deafness, nephritis, tuberculosis, children mentally or physically retarded for their age, all types of skin disease, high blood pressure and prostatic trouble. (Doyle 1953).

That some of them—as late as in 1957—still treated diabetes is made clear from an advertisement which the Norwegian journal "Diabetikeren" ("The Diabetic") discovered in an American paper (see Fig. 23). Note that the letters D.C. (Doctor of Chiropractic) follow the quack's name.

A Danish chiropractor, H. A. Simonsen, lies not far behind. He wrote in 1949;

> "When patients with bronchial or nervous asthma are X-rayed, one always sees vertebral subluxations at the level where the nerves to the respiratory system emerge from the backbone. Chiropractic correction of these subluxations often greatly helps the asthmatic patient. Taken in time, goitre offers excellent opportunities for the chiropractor. Colic, whether coming from the stomach or the intestine, together with renal and gallstone colic, can be treated in the chiropractic way, often with nearly instant relief.
>
> "Displacement of an upper cervical vertebra may be the reason for a child's being cowardly, prone to illness, pale, restless when asleep, apt to get cramp, voiding urine involuntarily or being breathless. One, or just a few, chiropractic treatments will as a rule change this picture to one of happiness and gaiety. Eczema and pyloric stenosis can be cured by one simple chiropractic adjustment."

Members of the Danish "Kiropraktisk Landsforening" (an association of patients with 23,000 members) use the stamp illustrated in Fig. 24. Its text is "Chiropractic, a Path to Health".

Fig. 24. A stamp used on letters by chiropractors and lay members of the Danish "Kiropraktisk Landsforening". ("*Chiropractic, a Path to Health*")

Chiropractors with a Swedish "diploma" run a journal that makes fantastic reading whereas the Danish equivalent is not so bad.

However, there are also more sensible people in the group. In the spring of 1957, I travelled to Copenhagen to listen to a lecture given to medical students by Dr. Ove Böje (later Professor of physiatry) on treatment by manipulation. A chiropractor (Bruun-Hansen) demonstrated his cervical manual technique on the lecturer himself. Permission was given for students' remarks, and the chiropractor replied soberly and humorously. I noted amongst others the following questions and answers:

How many of the two hundred techniques do you yourself use?

Ten or twelve at most.

Can a chiropractor treat appendicitis?

No, but abdominal pain similar to appendicitis can be treated by manipulation if it stems from a vertebral disorder.

What about diabetes?

Diabetes is not included.

It has been suggested that chiropractic cures stomach ulcer.

A chiropractor may cure such a patient but not by chiropractic techniques.

Dr. Böje mentioned the euphoria that can follow treatment by manipulation, but also that a patient may start crying without apparent reason; is that your experience?

No, that is only after manipulation by doctors. (Cheers from the students.)

Doctors have seldom tried to find out if there is *anything* in chiropractic which we should add to our therapeutic armamentarium.

In 1939, the following questions and answers took place between Magne Schjödt (counsel for chiropractic Ohman, the defendant) and a distinguished Consultant in Oslo:

Do you know what chiropractic technique consists of?

No.

Do you know any doctor who has gone into the subject?

No.

From newspaper articles about the case, it appears that a well-known rheumatologist Dr. A. Tanberg considered that in some cases of lumbago and sciatica chiropractic could help. It had happened that patients had sought his advice on visiting a chiropractor, and in those cases where there was no contra-indication, he was always quite willing. Dr. Inga Saeves had advised patients to go to a chiropractor as she considered in some cases the treatment was effective. Indeed, she had herself consulted a chiropractor. In several cases Dr. Alex Brinchmann likewise had had no doubt of its advisability when the patient put the question to him.

According to the American H.E.W. report of 1968, students from a chiropractic school must undergo a "State Board Examination" before getting a licence to practise in the State concerned. This examination is done *in writing* in most cases. In 1968, thirty-eight States had examination boards on which only chiropractors sat; four others had a majority of chiropractors, and six a minority. Three States were satisfied with a testimonial only—from the "National Board of Chiropractic Examiners"—instead of an examination. No chiropractic school is approved by the "U.S. Office of Education" or "The National Commission on Accrediting".

Naprapathy

Naprapathy is an offshoot from chiropractic dating from 1908. It originated in Chicago but a School of Naprapathy has recently been opened in Stockholm. Ligamentous contracture, so its adherents maintain, draw the vertebrae too close together and cause disease (gallstones are mentioned) by obstructing nerves and blood-vessels (Richard Cyriax, 1912). The cure is a quick manual thrust, stretching the ligament out.

* * *

Until now I have exclusively dealt with *lay* (i.e. non-medical) manipulators past and present. It is then natural to ask: Did *medical* men manipulate before the osteopaths and chiropractors began? Yes, they did, but to a very limited extent.

VI

Manipulative Treatment in the Medical Literature of the 18th, the 19th and early 20th Century

As from the 17th century when the use of forcible Hippocratic methods came to an end (with Scultetus, see p. 14), and up to the "osteopathic era" starting in the 1870s, it seems that manipulative treatment was very little used by the medical profession. However, there may well be much more to be found on this subject than I have been able to trace.

The French doctor Lieutaud (1703–1789) wrote a textbook "Précis de la médecine pratique", whose second edition was published in 1761 (and third and fourth editions in 1765 and 1776). In the chapter on acute backache (or "fausse néphrésie" as it was called then) he writes: "This is a true sprain ('une vraie entorse') which can be cured on the spot by replacing the displaced part . . . I don't know why the doctors usually are not very lucky with these cases; they leave them to 'les rebouteux' (the bone-setters) . . . I have practised it myself in some cases, on patients consulting me first, and almost in every case successfully." But he admitted that the technique of the bone-setters was superior.

In 1835, the Scotsman John Torbet wrote: "The boasted cures and frequent occurrence of extraordinary cases in hands of professed 'spine doctors', by exciting the jealousy, or the incredulity of their brethren have alike operated in preventing this class of diseases

being considered as fallen within the ordinary range of professional study."

In 1837, Dr. Martin senior (Chirurgien en chef de l'Hospice de la Charité de Lyon) described cases of lumbago treated by manipulation with "almost immediate cure". During the discussion afterwards, Dr. Martin junior laid several other case notes on the table.—In his textbook "Traité de thérapeutique des maladies articulaires", Paris 1853, A. Bonnet quoted both Lieutaud and Martin the elder, and tells us how the last one claimed to be able to 'escamoter' (conjure) an acute lumbago.

The following year both Recamier and Seguin described cases of cervical brachialgia and torticollis cured by manual traction and "percussion cadencée" (rhythmic thrusts).

In 1842, J. Evans Riadore, Fellow of the Royal College of Surgeons, published a book on irritation of the spinal nerves which probably provided the inspiration for the first osteopath. One of the leading chiropractors of U.S.A., C. W. Weiant, says (1959) that he (Riadore) speaks the same language as a chiropractor, and that it was astonishing to see that a medical man as early as 1842 "recognized subluxation of the vertebrae as the cause of organic diseases" (!). But it must be said that Riadore did not use manipulative technique much; he just mentions it here and there in his book.

"*Ehrlich* has recorded [before 1842] a remarkable case of dislocation of the atlas . . .; he reduced [this] by extension of the head, while he forced back the atlas . . . thus he affected the replacement with a snap, thus the patient recovered immediately" (Riadore).

As already quoted (p. 46) the "founder" of chiropractic, D. D. Palmer, claimed to have been taught the principles of chiropractic about 1860 by a doctor named Jim Atkinson in Davenport, Iowa. (No man by that name exists in the archives of the American Medical Association.)

We have already mentioned (p. 32 that Sir James Paget (1814–1899) read a paper at St. Bartholomew's Hospital on "Cases that bone-setters cure".

The Dutch doctor Johann Mezger definitely used manipulative treatment in the 1860s and 1870s. He received patients from all over Europe, but did no writing himself on this subject. We have reports only from visiting colleagues, for instance, the Swedes Rossander and Curmann (both in 1872) and Berghman & Helleday (1873), all of whom were very impressed by Mezger's techniques and cures.

We have already mentioned (p. 32) Dr. Wharton Hood's series

of articles on bone-setting in "The Lancet" 1871, collected in book form the same year (surely a gold-mine for the first osteopaths); also Howard March and R. Dacre Fox, both in 1882; and Hugh Owen Thomas and Sir Robert Jones.

George L. Walton, neurologist at Harvard University, mentioned manipulative treatment of the cervical spine in several articles during the years 1889–1893.

Amongst medical men using manipulation in the last part of the 19th century, we must include the Swiss doctor Otto Naegeli (father of the famous haematologist) and his book "Therapie von Neuralgien und Neurosen durch Handgriffe" (The treatment of neuralgia and neuroses by means of hand-grips), 1894, in which he advocates manipulating the cervical spine. Manipulation (or rather "articulation") based on this foundation was taught at Klapp's so-called massage-courses in Germany at least as late as 1910.

Lannelongue (1904) and E. M. Corner (1907) both employed manipulation, and in his article "Mechano-therapy in Disease" Alex. Bryce (1910) writes:

> "It is very remarkable that the medical profession should so long have neglected such a wide field of therapeutics . . . The practitioner who dabbles in it, has too often been looked at askance by his medical brethren . . . Great benefits are likely to accrue from the admission of this mode of treatment into our therapeutical armamentarium . . ."

In 1911, the second English book on manipulation was published by Frank Romer and L. E. Creasy, "Bonesetting and the Treatment of Painful Joints". In it were collected several articles from "The Lancet" and "British Medical Journal". The famous bone-setter Herbert Barker (see p. 34) said in 1913 about this book that *one* of the authors (he presumably meant Romer) "is supposed to know more about the methods of the bone-setter than any other living surgeon". A new and revised edition was published in 1915 by Romer only, "Modern Bonesetting for the Medical Profession".

At the beginning of this century, Edgar F. Cyriax came into prominence. He was a prolific author of articles (mostly with an osteopathic bias) in different medical journals, both British and foreign. These were collected in book form in 1924 as "Collected Papers on Mechano-therapeutics". Fifteen years before Mixter & Barr revolutionised the concept on the pathogenesis of sciatica, Edgar F. Cyriax maintained (as the first, so far as I have been able to

discover) that displacement of the intervertebral disc could cause clinical symptoms. In "The Practitioner" 1919, he wrote: "The pathology of the vertebral cartilages has received but little attention . . . In the vertebral column symptoms are sometimes found which so exactly resemble those induced by cartilaginous displacements elsewhere, that it can with safety be assumed that these can occur in the spine . . ."

And in the "Journal de Chirurgie" (the same year), he describes symptoms regarded by him as due to disc-"luxations" in the cervical spine. These, he maintained, were capable of reposition either spontaneously or by passive movements. He further maintained that similar conditions were to be found both at thoracic and lumbar levels, and that they could affect the nerve roots by congestion at the foramen.

No wonder that David Le Vay writes (1971): "Great medical families, such as the Cyriaxes, arose to occupy themselves in successive generations chiefly with the advance of mechanotherapeutics. For the first time these techniques were properly related to a sound knowledge of anatomy and pathology. The bone-setters, their clothes stolen, could only impugn the accuracy with which their very personal tradition had been translated into medical jargon."

On the whole, one must admit that from the medico-historical point of view, the attitude of the medical profession generally—up to the very latest time—has been (at best) reserved or (more often) one of unmitigated scepticism or complete opposition, manipulative therapy regards.

CONCLUSION

For hundreds, even thousands, of years manipulative treatment of low back pain has been common practice—by very different methods and with entirely different theoretical aims: Hippocrates straightened a kyphosis, Galen replaced outward dislocated vertebrae and Ambroise Paré wrote about luxations of the spine. Patients have been trampled upon by women chosen on sexual grounds (virgins, mothers of seven children, etc.); birth by presentation of the foot has been regarded as giving magical powers to the stamper. Sufferers have been given blows on the back with different tools (from hammers to brooms and steelyards), they have been lifted back-to-back and shaken. Bone-setters have replaced small bones out of place, osteopaths have treated the mysterious "osteopathic lesion", chiropractors have replaced subluxated vertebrae, orthopaedic surgeons have manipulated "subluxations of the sacro-iliac joint", and the neurologists have "stretched the sciatic nerve". Curiously enough, all concepts and methods have met with some degree of success. Clearly, the mechanism has been a fragment of disc which had become dislocated and was put back in position, or when a protrusion of the disc was "sucked back", or (perhaps) when a jammed or blocked facet joint was "unlocked", or (perhaps) when a nerve root was shifted off the apex of a prolapsed disc.

PART TWO

Manipulation: Present Day

Preface

The question of manipulation is vexed. Strong opposing views are held, not least by those with no experience of it. As a result a perfectly straightforward medical remedy lies under a cloud, and doctors, so far from taking pains to manipulate better than laymen, have abandoned this method to them by default. The cloud is rendered more dense by the emotional attitudes taken up by advocates and detractors towards a treatment perfectly susceptible to a logical approach.

The position of manipulation in Medicine is bedevilled by its being no one person's business, being carried out as a side-line by various exponents. It hovers between orthopaedic surgery, rheumatology and neurology. The no-man's land enclosed within this triangle is invaded by various types of lay-manipulator, blithely stepping on to ground where medical men neglect to tread. It is performed by the best men (by which I mean orthopaedic surgeons) in circumstances that militate against success, and by the worst men (different sects of bone-setter) in a most haphazard fashion, and is largely avoided—with honourable exceptions—by the very men best placed for its performance under favourable conditions (family doctors). This is not their fault; for they were never shown or taught these methods as students. The omission lies with their teachers.

Obscurity and prejudice are deepened by osteopaths' and chiropractors' claims to cure diseases on which manipulation has in fact no influence. These far-fetched assertions have naturally turned scientific opinion against them (as is reasonable enough) but have led doctors to condemn manipulation as well, especially of the spinal joints: an entirely illogical projection. Though they complain of lack of recognition, lay-manipulators deserve their obscurity; for no-one has been at more pains to bring discredit on their calling than these laymen themselves. Such discredit is apt to extend even to the medical man who practises manipulation; for he tends

to become associated in his colleagues' minds with all sorts of dubious laymen.

On what grounds is manipulation condemned by doctors and withheld from those who need it? It is held in great esteem by patients. No-one thinks the worse of an orthopaedic surgeon for reducing a displaced cartilage in a man's knee; why then disparage the orthopaedic physician who reduces a displaced fragment of cartilaginous disc at a spinal joint?

Naturally, any method of treatment carried out by a heterogeneous set of people for reasons that are often demonstrably unsound is sure to be regarded with a jaundiced eye by doctors. Yet every medical man knows of patients cured, after other methods had failed, by manipulation, usually, alas, performed by some irregular practitioner. It is thus no help for doctors—however correctly—to dismiss his theories as pure fancy. Such a negative attitude carries no conviction to patients, since they find the practice effective. Now that the way manipulation achieves good results is known, and the indications for and against have been worked out, there remains the dissemination of this knowledge amongst those on whom the health of the nation depends—the medical profession. Time and patience will thus be needed to remove the slur that has descended on manipulation as the consequence of relegation to the hands of laymen for so many decades. The proper practice of medicine calls for this reappraisal, since the basic research has been done; the essential knowledge is there; the papers and books have been published—all with so slight an effect on contemporary medical thought that the provision of physicians and physiotherapists trained in this work remains entirely inadequate. This is an important problem: for lesions of the moving parts amenable to such treatment provide the commonest cause of avoidable disablement and unnecessary absence from work or athletics.

Neglect of manipulation as a normal therapeutic measure not only condemns numberless patients to unnecessary pain and loss of earnings, but it plays the medical profession straight into the hands of the very laymen whose existence they deplore. Who created the lay manipulator? Alas, the doctors themselves, whose neglect of a simple method of treatment, practised with good results throughout the world for centuries, has forced sufferers to look outside the profession for simple manual measures. The patient cannot be blamed if, told that he has a spinal displacement, he seeks help from a manipulating layman when neither his own physician, nor the

physiotherapist, nor the hospital consultant makes any move to put it back. Every family doctor, every medical officer in industry or in the Services, knows of this constant trickle to the layman. Yet a century of such awareness has not led to any visible steps to close such a conspicuous hiatus in the medical facilities available to the nation. Of all the maladies to which man is heir, it is only those amenable to medical manipulation for which our Health Service makes no appreciable provision.

Ignorance is responsible for the prejudice against manipulation. Education is thus the remedy. During my time at St. Thomas's Hospital, our medical and physiotherapy students were brought up to regard manipulation as an integral part of everyday medical treatment, called for in a few common conditions and to be performed without further ado whenever required. This matter-of-fact attitude brought manipulation out of its cloud back to where it belongs—within the medical field. When such simple teaching comes to be incorporated as a matter of course in all medical and physiotherapy students' curriculum, the manipulating layman will be superseded by the skilled doctor and the trained physiotherapist.

It is curious to reflect that the three main treatments for back troubles that I have employed over the last thirty years—manipulation, traction and epidural local anaesthesia—were first described 2,300, 500 and 73 years ago respectively. Yet they are still regarded as untried novelties and many label their use unorthodox. There must be a few cases of parallel delay in the history of Medicine.

This little book is not a treatise on when and how to manipulate; this subject is dealt with in my "Textbook of Orthopaedic Medicine". My contribution here comprises an account of the present position of manipulation, and follows Schiötz's erudite account of the historical aspect of the subject. It is my wish to engender objective re-assessment of outworn attitudes on a basis of historical perspective and a grasp of today's problems. On the positive side, the opinions set out here should dispel prejudice and render possible a balanced evaluation of a simple remedy. Agreement will then be possible on what can and what cannot be expected of it. On the negative side, it should help to mitigate the two outstanding evils of unqualified manipulation—namely, inaccurate diagnosis and poor technique leading to avoidable failure; alternatively, to endless vain expensive treatment in disorders that manipulation cannot benefit.

A hundred years ago, Paget enjoined the practice of manipulation on the medical profession, deploring bone-setters' cures. This has

been my message too for the past thirty years. The time is ripe; the urgency undisputed. It is my hope that, unlike Paget, I shall live to see this policy accepted.

London, October 1974 JAMES CYRIAX

I

History of Manipulation

Manipulation has a respectable history, having been practised by many of the most famous physicians of olden time. As Schiötz's contribution makes quite clear, there is nothing new about bone-setting, well-proven over the centuries. It is thus barely credible that anyone should look askance at an art that has been, and is, practised in all parts of the world with results that for millenia sufferers have combined to acclaim. Manipulation as the chief remedy for lumbago, for example, has been universally accepted from time immemorial by patients, but oddly enough not by doctors. Certainly this remedy has for the last two hundred years been rejected by doctors, only to be seized upon by laymen, quick to grasp a golden opportunity. This situation persists, whereby even today manipulation is relegated by silent default to laymen as an extra-medical treatment.

The book that provided the inspiration for lay manipulation was in fact written by a doctor. Riadore was a London physician who published a treatise on irritation of the spinal nerves in 1843; he attributed many diseases to such compression. He states (p. 4): ". . . if any organ is deficiently supplied with nervous energy or blood, its function is immediately, and sooner or later its structure become deranged". He sets out exactly what chiropractors echo today (p. 7): "When we reflect that every organ and muscle in the body is connected and dependent more or less upon the spinal nerves for the perfect performance of their individual functions—we cannot be otherwise than prepared to hear of a lengthened catalogue of maladies that are either engendered, continued or the consequence of spinal irritation." He continues (p. 101): "If the digestive organs become functionally or organically deranged from such a cause [i.e. spinal irritation] the nerve-roots emerging from the sixth to eighth dorsal ganglia recumbency in addition to manipulatia [sic] is often necessary." Again (p. 101): "Various branches that arise

from the sixth, seventh and eighth dorsal ganglia . . . become irritated by contact, or sympathy with disease, in the notches through which the nerves pass out of the vertebrae."

This must be the first account of root-pain emanating from "contact" at the intervertebral foramen. He recognised disc-degeneration (p. 115): "Disorganisation of the bones of the spine and their intervertebral cartilages . . ." and anticipated Hackett's work (p. 116): ". . . the intervertebral cartilage and ligaments become morbidly relaxed and elongated". In an account of a case he treated he stated that he "replaced the sixth dorsal vertebra". This concept had already been put forward by Harrison in 1821 who, discussing the spinal ligaments, stated that "these get relaxed and suffer a single vertebra to become slightly displaced".

Manipulation became unethical in 1858, with the passage of the Medical Act. Until then, doctors had cheerfully sent patients to bonesetters for manipulation. Now, they were recognised and registered; the bonesetters were not. Recommending resort to unqualified persons could now be regarded as "covering", and the practice ceased. The situation thus created legally led Sir James Paget to deliver a lecture in 1868 entitled "Cases that Bonesetters Cure". He pointed out how neglectful doctors were of manipulation, thereby leaving patients with no alternative but to frequent laymen. His homily applies equally today. In 1871, the first English book on manipulation appeared, written by Dr. Hood about the work of Hutton, a well-known bone-setter. In 1874 Still, in the U.S.A., founded osteopathy. He declared that all diseases were caused by vertebral displacements compressing arteries and depriving organs of blood. When he was shown that a spinal dislocation would cause paraplegia long before it has this effect, he changed his hypothesis to pressure on a nerve. Here he came very close to the truth; for this is just what the disc between the vertebrae can do, though such pressure is not of course the cause of more than a tiny fraction of *all* disease. Yet this dogma was still put forward at the enquiry at the House of Lords in 1935, when leading osteopaths maintained that all diseases had a spinal origin. After several days' hearing, the osteopaths asked leave to withdraw their plea. They were advised to reorganise their school which was found inefficient and dishonestly run.

Manipulation as a panacea still lives on; it is no mere historical survival. As lately as 1952, a chiropractor working in London published a book claiming that the second thoracic vertebra was the

heart place, the third the lung place, the fourth the liver place, and so on, thus bringing disorders of all these organs within the sphere of his brand of manipulation. Some years ago, it was "discovered" at the American School of Osteopathy at Kirksville that "splenic treatment" was called for in infectious disease. There they maintained that, since the spleen contains a hundred times as much antibody as serum, manipulation of the thoracic spine and of the spleen was a suitable treatment for influenza and pneumonia. At Osteopathic Congresses, lectures are still given on "osteopathic gynaecology" and on "osteopathy in cardiovascular disease". Osteopathy in respiratory disease, alimentary trouble and genito-urinary disorders figures prominently at these meetings. I have in my possession broadsheets sent round to householders in Australia (1970) extolling the virtues of chiropractice in every sort of visceral disease. I have also a pamphlet, printed for chiropractors in England, warmly recommending manipulation in acne; it is a mine of pseudo-scientific misinformation. No wonder doctors look askance at these laymen. But justice demands that the stigma should fall on those who profess that manipulation is a panacea; it should not be extended to the reasoned use of the method of treatment itself. After all, the fact that nature-curers prescribe all sorts of herbs is not allowed to prejudice doctors against the proper use of vegetable remedies.

II

Past Errors: Fibrositis

As it happens, the error of an authoritative physician misled the medical profession for over half a century. In 1904, Sir William Gower published an article stating that lumbago was caused by inflammation of the fibrous tissue in the sacrospinalis muscles. This view was accepted all over the world and kept doctors on the wrong track for decades. He coined the word "fibrositis". As a result, minor displacements of disc-substance at an intervertebral joint became known by this name, which persists as a common diagnosis even to this day, particularly in cervical disc-lesions. Gower's work remained unchallenged for forty-one years, until, twenty-eight years ago, an article appeared (Cyriax, 1945) pointing out that lumbago resulted from a low lumbar disc-lesion. The cause of pain was shown to be a sudden backward protrusion occurring centrally, which bulged out the posterior longitudinal ligament and compressed the dura mater. Fibrositis was debunked three years later (Cyriax, 1948). (The previous landmark in the history of disc-lesions was Mixter and Barr's paper in 1934 showing that sciatica could result from postero-lateral protrusion of disc-substance.)

The consequences of Gower's attribution of pain felt in a muscle to a muscle lesion, when its source was actually articular, was disastrous. Doctors' scientific training stood them in bad stead and they refused to manipulate the spinal joint when they were convinced—wrongly as it turned out—that the muscles were at fault. Gower's error was, therefore, important and far-reaching; it was also a great piece of good fortune for lay manipulators. They had no theoretical misgivings to worry them; they merely manipulated joints in the neighbourhood of people's pain and were thus able to effect a series of spectacular cures on a small proportion of their clients. Doctors learnt of these successes but ignored them as inexplicable and

scientifically suspect, so strongly was the tradition of fibrositis ingrained.

It has now become evident that, by a curious paradox, the correct treatment for a minor displacement at an intervertebral joint causing pain felt in the trunk (i.e. "fibrositis") has been given during the whole of this century by all sorts of irregular practitioners. By contrast, for the last fifty years, entirely worthless measures for "fibrositis", directed at the muscles, have been given by physiotherapists acting under the best medical auspices. Unhappily, this legacy from decades ago still retains its force, and I doubt if there is a physiotherapy department in Europe where patients with easily reducible disc-lesions are not wasting their own and the physiotherapists' time receiving heat to their normal muscles, massage to their normal muscles, and exercises for their strong muscles. Excessive respect for tradition keeps such patients' displacements in being; in consequence, a steady supply of potential dramatic cures is maintained for the bone-setter. Their successes, especially after the medical profession and its ancillary services have done their best in vain, naturally keep lay manipulators in high esteem by the public—to our recurrent discomfiture.

"Fibrositis" has a factual basis which is not generally understood. This is set out below.

DURAL PAIN

The only tissue connected with the moving parts of the body that does not refer pain on a segmental basis is the dura mater (Cyriax, 1947).

The dura mater is thought of as static and insensitive, but in fact it is neither. A frequent sign in lumbago is pain in the lower back increased by neck-flexion, and O'Connell (1956) has shown that the length of the neck, measured at the mid-part of the neural foramen, increases by 5 cm. between full extension and full flexion. Hence, transmitted dural pull accentuates the pain in the back, provided that the mobility of the dural tube is impaired, even when the cause is as far distant as a low lumbar disc-protrusion (Cyriax, 1945). Straight-leg raising too is often bilaterally painful and limited in lumbago—a sign that the dura mater resents stretching from below no less than from above. Though the dural range of movement is small, only a few millimetres, local pressure often gives rise to these clear signs of impaired mobility.

These clinical findings also show that the dura mater is not wholly insensitive, though the prick of a lumbar puncture needle is not felt. The reason was discovered in 1966 by Edgar and Nundy who investigated the innervation of the dura mater in humans. They found the anterior aspect of the membrane richly supplied by nerves from three different sources. but an entire lack of nervous supply posteriorly. Hence, the anterior aspect against which a disc protrudes is sensitive, but the posterior punctured by the needle is not. Final proof rests with the induction of epidural local anaesthesia. If 1 : 200 procaine solution is used, the external surface of the dural tube becomes insensitive and the signs and symptoms of lumbago cease for the time being. Conduction along the nerve-roots remains normal and the solution cannot get inside a lumbar facet or intervertebral joint. Moreover, contrast radiography shows that it does not; it merely flows further and further up the neural canal. It follows that the two dural signs in lumbago, painful neck-flexion and bilateral limitation of straight-leg raising, stem from the fact that the dura mater is sensitive anteriorly. The same sensitivity is doubtless the cause of neck-retraction and Kernig's sign in meningism.

When patients with lesions that impinge via the posterior ligament against the dura mater are questioned about their pain, extra-segmental reference is often described. The pain of a lower cervical disc-lesion is most often felt in the mid-scapular area, i.e. at the area of the third to sixth thoracic dermatomes. The pain of lumbago is often felt to spread from a low lumbar level to the lower posterior thorax, to any part of the abdomen, along any aspect of the thighs or to the coccyx. Such extra-segmental reference does not deceive as long as the main pain is lumbar, but when a patient with a low lumbar disc-lesion gets pain, for example, in one iliac fossa without backache, his symptoms may well be ascribed to chronic appendicitis. The possibility of a low lumbar disc-lesion is not even considered, since the doctor regards it as anatomically impossible for such a pain to arise from such a level. Were it not for extra-segmental reference of pain from the dura mater, he would be right. Many diagnostic errors arise from this every-day, but unregarded, phenomenon (Cyriax, 1947).

Tenderness in Dural Compression

A further misleading phenomenon makes the position more complicated yet: localised referred tenderness. Lewis (1942) described generalised tenderness, but that of dural provenance uniquely takes

the shape of an extremely localised spot within the painful area, quite unlike the more diffuse tenderness that he described all over any painful region. This area of localised tenderness is the direct result of the pressure exerted on the dura mater, nearly always from a disc-lesion, and the pain and tenderness change position as the protrusion shifts. For example, during manipulative reduction of a lower cervical disc-protrusion, the area of pain and the tender spot, first felt perhaps at the belly of the infraspinatus muscle, may be moved upwards and inwards to reappear at the supraspinatus or rhomboid muscle, and the patient has to search for the new spot. Further manipulation shifts it to the trapezius or levator scapulae and, finally, when a full and painless range has been restored to the cervical joint, the pain and tender spot are abolished. Extra-segmental referred pain and tenderness have been misunderstood for years and have given rise to endless diagnostic errors; for these areas of "fibrositis", these "trigger points" or "myalgic spots" have been regarded as the primary lesion, not the result of pressure on the dura mater at a level inconsistent with the segmentation of the body. The formation of metabolites at the muscle has been brought in to explain the tenderness, and fatty lobules had a vogue for a time. The simple experiment, whereby the tender spot can be made to move from place to place within a few seconds, is confirmable by any physician who cares to manipulate the neck of a sufferer from alleged "scapular fibrositis". Nevertheless, fibrositis has proved a most obstinately tenacious concept, for it endured without question for forty-four years. Though it was debunked twenty-seven years ago (Cyriax, 1948), the word remains semi-respectable.

This is a pity, since the treatment of a small cervical disc lesion is obviously immediate manipulative reduction, whereas ascription of symptoms to "fibrositis" leads to the waste of time and effort involved in giving endless heat, massage and injections (originally of procaine, more lately of hydrocortisone) at the site of a referred symptom. During this time many patients get better or worse as fortune dictates; some get well spontaneously during "treatment", but others get worse and progress to root pain—what used to be called "brachial neuritis"—and may suffer from severe symptoms and muscle weakness in the upper limb for months. Yet this sequence is usually avoidable, if the patient is seen early and manipulative reduction carried out before the protrusion has become too large. In other cases, a central protrusion may advance insidiously to pressure on the spinal cord and, finally, on the anterior spinal

artery. Various types of paralysis due to myelopathy result. Clearly, the only hope of preventing this serious later development is to reduce, and keep reduced, the displacement many years before pressure on the spinal cord begins. It may thus make all the difference between health and eventual crippledom, whether a scapular pain is regarded as extra-segmental reference from the dura mater as the result of a minor disc displacement and treated logically, or as "fibrositis".

III

Passive Movement

Manipulation and passive movement are not synonymous. The types of passive movement other than manipulative are dealt with in this chapter.

MECHANICAL FACTORS

How best to use the levers that the human body offers is an important study. The longer the lever, the less force is necessary to achieve a given result and the more finesse the manipulator can use. For example, the further down the tibia the manipulator's hand rests, the more easily he can flex the patient's knee. But he must not grasp the foot; for he then allows the tarsal joints to intervene between his hand and the tibia. This entails loss of control and exactitude. Hence, another joint must never be allowed to intervene unnecessarily between the manipulator's hand and the bones that constitute the joint under treatment.

At some sites, however, the advantage of using a lever at a distance outweighs the loss of accuracy. For example, when the pelvis is to be rotated on the thorax, the femur may be used as a lever. Since the pelvic lever then becomes two or three times the length of the thoracic, this entails a re-arrangement of the manipulator's body weight. To obtain the maximum torsion strain he must distribute most of his weight on the shorter thoracic lever and use the remainder of his strength on the femur. Leverage is employed in many spinal techniques, but by no means in all. For example, when an extension thrust is given at a lumbar or a thoracic joint, no leverage is involved.

Before attempting any manipulation, the practitioner must know the normal range of movement at the affected joint and be aware of the other movements of which the joint is passively capable. He must also know which movements have therapeutic value and what their end-point feels like. Extension at the elbow, for example, ceases when bone hits bone; forcing can be *felt* to be futile. He must learn to appreciate the tough and slightly elastic feel which appears at the extreme of elevation and rotation at the shoulder. A similar sensation is imparted to the manipulator's hand when rotation is forced to its extreme at the hip or the thoracic spinal joints. The moment when this tension reaches its maximum must be recognised; for its appearance signals to the manipulator when to apply his final pressure. Flexion at a normal elbow, hip or knee stops when extra-articular soft tissues meet; there is no exact point at which movement ceases. The sudden vibrant bar to further movement produced by intense muscle spasm springing into being to protect a joint must be recognised; for it signals disease more serious than those within the scope of manipulation. A springy block indicates internal derangement.

The manipulator must also be aware of those passive movements that possess a therapeutic value, though they cannot be performed actively. For example, when reduction is attempted at the wrist by gliding the proximal on the distal row of carpal bones, a movement incapable of active performance is carried out. Distracting the humeral head from the glenoid, rocking the tibia and rotating two adjacent thoracic vertebrae simultaneously in opposite directions are other examples of manoeuvres that fall outside the idea of applying overpressure at the extreme of range.

TYPES OF PASSIVE MOVEMENT

No controversy exists about manipulation for reduction in such conditions as fracture, dislocation, a displaced meniscus at knee or jaw, a strangulated hernia, a breech presentation, or a retroverted uterus. The manœuvres required, together with their indications, are set out in standard textbooks. In fact, the word "manipulation" is often omitted in these connections. A fracture or dislocation is "reduced"; hernia is treated by "taxis" and the position of the uterus or foetal malpresentation is "corrected".

The different types are set out below:

Passive Movement in Clinical Examination

This is required when the range of movement at a joint has to be ascertained, or how far a ligament or a muscle or a nerve-root will stretch; in either case, it is important to note if pain is provoked at the extreme of the possible range—limited, normal or excessive. During the movement, abnormal sensations of diagnostic importance may be imparted to the examiner's hand, e.g. crepitus. How the extreme of range makes itself apparent, in degrees of softness and hardness, with or without the provocation of muscle spasm, whether pain and limitation of movement come on together or separately—i.e. the "end-feel"—is often most informative. The examining hand is constantly alert to receive information from the tissues it is handling and, during manipulation, as the extreme of range is approached. The hand applying pressure is not only motor but sensory. The degree and type of final thrust that is delivered is in part determined by what is felt as the extreme of range is reached. The appropriate manœuvre may be discerned only a split second before it is performed.

Passive Movement Without Forcing

The purpose is the maintenance of a mobility already in existence. In a recent ligamentous sprain at, for example, the ankle, full range must be maintained at the other unaffected joints. This is most easily and effectively ensured by gentle passive movement. The same applies to a recent hemiplegic's shoulder or the joints other than the wrist after a Colles's fracture.

Sudden Thrust

Minor adhesions can be ruptured by a sharp jerk carried out at the extreme of the possible range. The position that best stretches the adhesion is ascertained and it is snapped by sudden overpressure exerted further in the same direction. Anaesthesia is sometimes required; it is never a disadvantage. Orthopaedic surgeons often refer to this type of forced movement as "mobilisation" (which is really a description of the result), but it is also common to speak of the manipulative rupture of an adhesion. Major adhesions, usually consequent upon prolonged immobilisation in plaster, have to be broken down by a strong sustained force. General anaesthesia is then necessary.

Slow Stretch

A contracture, congenital or acquired, can often be overcome by a series of strong maintained stretchings. The joint is moved as far as possible in the direction of limitation, then pressed on further and held there as long as is reasonable. Release is equally gradual. This is the type of forcing required in congenital torticollis, talipes equinovarus or osteo-arthrosis at hip or shoulder.

Another type of slow forcing also exists, i.e. slow distraction of joint surfaces. For example, one quite effective way of treating arthritis at the shoulder is gradual intermittent manual distraction of the head of the humerus from the glenoid surface.

This sort of stretching is not, in contemporary medical usage, called mobilisation or manipulation.

Manipulation

The indication is internal derangement. The essential difference between manipulation for this purpose and the other sorts of passive movement is the indirect manner of attaining a stated intention. In manipulation, an increased range of movement and diminution in pain are achieved, not by forcing movement in the direction in which it is restricted, but by a series of far more subtle manoeuvres that experience has taught afford benefit in this type of disorder. The reduction of an intra-articular displacement is attempted purely on a basis of what has been found effective in similar cases in the past. The likelihood of such reduction is, of course, enhanced if the loose fragment is given room to move; hence, manipulation with this intention is usually performed during distraction of the articulating surfaces. One passive movement—traction—is then the adjuvant to another type of passive movement.

This is such an important aspect of passive movement and so often required that it is considered in the next chapter.

Empirical Manipulation

Manipulation is regarded as an empirical method of treatment and is often advocated on purely negative grounds—viz.: the absence of contra-indications. Some unclear lesion of the moving parts is found present; movement at a joint is not wholly free; the radiograph and various laboratory tests reveal nothing relevant; no other treatment

comes to mind. Manipulation is now put forward for lack of a better alternative, and those surgeons who take a good view of manipulation then manipulate, while those who dislike it do not. The patient's treatment is thus determined, not by the nature of the lesion present, but by the predilections of the particular surgeon that he happens to see.

Manipulation carried out for lack of reasons against it is insecurely based; moreover, no indication of what purpose the manipulation is expected to serve has emerged, with the result that its type and technique remain uncertain. Naturally, when a treatment is usually selected on such vague grounds, there is room for many conflicting opinions. But this attitude is out of date. Nowadays, it is possible, by careful clinical examination, to single out those lesions suited to manipulation. The function of the radio-translucent tissues, lesions of which so often benefit from manipulation, can be examined by the method of selective tension on which orthopaedic medicine rests. If this system is employed, the doctor knows what he is dealing with, whereas reliance on the radiograph and on laboratory tests can lead to grave mistakes.

Many of the adverse opinions on the effects of manipulation are correctly founded on the results of manœuvres carried out in unsuitable cases, or when the joint is handled while subject to centrifugal instead of centripetal force. The opinions are justified, so far as they go, but should not be extended to include a type of manipulation that has the opposite effect to that correctly held to be dangerous. Technique is dictated by the type of lesion present; diagnosis determines technique.

TRACTION

Distraction of the bone ends is used in two distinct ways—traction as an adjuvant to manipulation, and traction alone.

(1) Traction is a most useful adjunct to manipulation for internal derangement. When the articular surfaces are pulled apart, pain is much lessened, whereupon the patient can relax his muscles. The loose fragment is given room to move. The ligaments about the joint, lax at mid-range, are tautened and exert centripetal force. This is aided by the negative pressure that distraction creates within the joint. Centripetal stress acting on the displacement is particularly desirable when protrusion beyond the articular edge is present at an

intervertebral joint, and a great safeguard against the increased displacement that manipulation without traction can effect.

(2) Traction can also be used alone, to create a negative pressure within a joint. In nuclear protrusion at an intervertebral joint, especially common in the lumbar region, the protrusion consists of soft material insusceptible to manipulation. Sustained traction results in suction, distraction of the bone ends and tautening of the posterior longitudinal ligament—all effects that encourage the bulge to recede.

IV

Manipulation

Manipulation is a method of treatment. It consists of different sorts of passive movement performed by the hands in a definite manner for a prescribed purpose. Its use does not involve the operator in any particular belief in the causes and treatment of *all* diseases; he is merely treating the patient with a mechanical disorder in what he believes is the best way. Fractures and dislocations often require manipulation for the reduction of the displacement, and the same applies when a loose fragment of cartilage has become displaced within a joint, blocking movement.

DEFINITION

In the past, definitions of manipulation have been framed too much with osteopathy in view. Definitions suited to a healing system confining itself to the spine and based on the idea of replacing a subluxated vertebra are too narrow. The osteopath points out quite correctly that the spinal joints possess an active range of movement of so much, a passive range of slightly more, and are capable of being forced a little further still by manipulative over-pressure. Hence, as far as osteopathy goes, manipulation consists merely in applying such overpressure to a spinal joint. Unfortunately, a definition based on this fact excludes a great many orthopaedic manœuvres. When, for example, manipulative reduction during traction is carried out at the neck or knee, the loose fragment often shifts before the extreme of even the active range is reached. In central posterior cervical protrusion, reduction is often secured by strong traction alone or with at most a few degrees of rotation added. Strictly speaking, in such a case no movement at all is forced

at the joint. Nor is it a case of forcing a movement found to be painful, since many manœuvres performed during traction succeed when a movement already found to be painless is carried to its extreme. Nor is it necessarily a question of restoring full range to a joint at which limitation exists; it is often directed merely to making the extreme of such movement as is present painless instead of painful. No power on earth will restore a full range of movement to an osteo-arthritic neck; when the osteophytes engage, the bony block is felt and further forcing is useless. The aim of treatment in such cases is then to restore pain*free* stiffness. Moreover, manipulation can be employed for extra-articular lesions, e.g. the common extensor tendon in tennis-elbow.

My definition of manipulation is simply: *passive movement with therapeutic purpose using the hands*. It is the fact that it has a definite aim that transforms moving a joint about passively into manipulation. It is not mere passive motion at a joint this way and that; it is a series of manœuvres with a defined purpose carried out with variations in technique dependent on the lesion present, the joint affected, the end-feel and the result secured when the patient is re-examined after each thrust.

PURPOSE OF MANIPULATION

The main purpose of manipulation is the correction of internal derangement. Indeed, the term is best reserved for the sequence of calculated manœuvres necessary for securing reduction in internal derangement at a joint. Primary forcing of movement in the restriction direction plays no part. In manipulation for reduction, by contrast with manipulation for breaking adhesions, the best—sometimes the only—way to restore full range to a restricted movement is to force movement in quite a different direction.

The indication is an intra-articular displacement. The essential difference between manipulation for this purpose and the other sorts of passive movement is the indirect manner of attaining a stated intention. In manipulation, an increased range of movement and diminution in pain are achieved, not by forcing movement in the direction in which it is restricted, but by a series of far more subtle manœuvres that experience has taught affords benefit in this type of disorder. The reduction of an intra-articular displacement is attempted purely on a basis of what has been found effective in similar

cases in the past. The likelihood of such reduction is, of course, enhanced if the loose fragment is given room to move; hence, manipulation with this intention is usually performed during distraction of the articulating surfaces. One passive movement—traction—is then the adjuvant to another type of passive movement.

The manœuvre that is carried out is not necessarily the one towards the direction of limitation, certainly not in early stages of attempted reduction. For example, if a patient cannot bend forwards because of lumbar pain, no effort is ever made to force flexion at the lumbar joints. The joint is blocked by internal derangement and forcing flexion is very apt to increase the degree of protrusion. The pattern of which movements are painful and which not, which are limited and which not, often helps to indicate to the experienced manipulator which manœuvre is most likely to succeed and thus determines technique. The first manœuvre to be attempted is chosen on a basis of three, sometimes conflicting, criteria: (1) The likeliest to succeed; (2) the least painful; (3) the most informative. The experienced manipulator distinguishes different types of end-feel as the joint he is treating approaches the extreme of range. Working on a basis of trial, end-feel and effect, the manipulator continues his series of manœuvres, repeating or abandoning a particular technique on a basis of result and of end-feel. If no progress is made, the attempt may well have to be abandoned. Anaesthesia is contra-indicated because the patient must be examined afresh after manœuvre; he reports any change in symptoms; the manipulator notes any change in signs. In this way the loose fragment can be watched changing (or not) its position as the manipulator proceeds, and pointers appear towards what to do next and whether to go on or stop. Moreover, as the extreme of manipulative range is reached, different sensations are imparted to the manipulator's hand that also guide him in judging his next step. For example, a stone-hard stop tells him that further forcing in that direction is useless; a soft stop encourages him to repeat the same movement more firmly. Manipulative reduction succeeds in a very few sessions, or not at all; if there is no improvement after two, it is not worth going on. No one should receive the weekly manipulation for many months on end beloved by laymen, while in fact the passage of time brings about eventual recovery.

The reduction of internal derangement may take place without full range in any direction being forced. For example, at the neck or knee, when a rotary manipulation during strong traction is begun,

a click may be felt long before the extreme of range is reached. If this click is shown by examination to have effected reduction, no more need be done. Again, in central posterior cervical protrusion, reduction is often secured by strong manual traction alone.

Passive movement for the reduction of internal derangement is the series of calculated manœuvres to which the term "manipulation" appears best suited. It is the type of passive movement that is most often required and calls for much more skill and judgement than the other types. The strength of the manœuvre varies from almost none at all to the use of a considerable, albeit controlled, thrust. It is carried out at the joint whence the symptoms originate, and consists of a sequence performed without anaesthesia, usually during traction, chosen in a succession that depends on repeated examination of the patient and on what the manipulator feels at the end of his stroke, continued—not necessarily at one session only—until all movements at the affected joint become (if possible) painless. Technique also varies with the size and position of the loose fragment, with due regard for the age, shape, tolerance and personality of the patient. Thought, care, knowledge, clinical sense and manual skill are all essential for this type of manipulation, which is by no means primarily a question of muscular power; and even less of merely forcing the joint the way it will not go.

V

Manipulation: By Whom?

Today, manipulation (except for bony displacements) is anybody's business. A patient needing a manipulation for, say, a displaced fragment of disc, is fairly unlikely to get it from his own doctor, and less probably still at any hospital he may be sent to. This situation is well known to all family doctors, if only because their patients tell them how they were cured by some lay manipulator after months of fruitless treatment within the N.H.S. Hospital consultants are far less aware of this situation; for nothing brings to their attention what happened to a patient who merely stopped coming to an out-patients' department. This is an important failure of communication; for it is not the family doctor (who recognises and deplores the hiatus) but the hospital consultant who teaches and influences medical students. Though the results of research in orthopaedic medicine are now item by item being confirmed, pressure from general practitioners has not resulted in the inclusion of this subject in the medical syllabus, nor in the creation of a centre for postgraduate tuition. Hence, only a tiny—and stationary—fraction of patients in need can ever be dealt with by the methods of diagnosis and treatment used in orthopaedic medicine. The remedy is simple—adequate grounding of medical students in what is, after all, one fifth of the whole of a family doctor's daily work.

There are five sets of people who manipulate: laymen, orthopaedic surgeons, family doctors, physiotherapists and, last as well as least, orthopaedic physicians.

LAYMEN

These consist of persons calling themselves osteopaths, chiropractors and bone-setters. However, in Britain anyone can call himself by

any of these names without ado, and start treating patients whenever he so wishes. Unlike the titles "physician" and "surgeon", which only those on the Medical Register can use, there is no restriction on the adoption of "osteopath" or "chiropractor", trained or untrained, for the simple reason that neither of these callings has achieved legal recognition. Hence, it is inevitable that the ranks of these men should contain a large number of incompetent practitioners. Even the most effective amongst them suffer from the disability inherent in lack of medical knowledge. They do not know how fully to examine the patient, nor have many of them even heard of some of the disorders that they should have in mind during such an examination. Hence, they cannot tell when to manipulate and when not, nor how to suit their technique to the lesion in suitable cases, nor what alternative treatments exist in unsuitable cases. They are often at a loss to know which part of the body to treat and it is a commonplace to find that quite the wrong region has been manipulated.

Whether or not some laymen become capable manipulators in the end is not the point at issue between these men and doctors. If that were the full extent of their ambitions and they had agreed to acceptable tuition and examinations, they would have achieved adequate status years ago. For example, the physiotherapy profession had no difficulty in securing recognition for its claims, because these were reasonable and temperately put forward. What is unacceptable is the fact that these laymen consider that they should treat by manipulation all who care to visit them, not merely those sent to them for this purpose by doctors. They are not prepared for tuition, examinations and finally to work under the supervision of medical men; they profess an independent system. Were such men to qualify first as doctors or physiotherapists, adequate competence would be assured.

The public is protected, in the case of doctors, by standards of tuition and stringent qualifying examinations. On what grounds should manipulators be excused this discipline? Manipulation is a part of Medicine to which the normal principles apply. Those who decide to give medical treatments without submitting to proper training first cannot hope for any sort of official recognition. But how is the public expected to tell the trained from the untrained? The latter form a group which cannot fail to contain a large number of get-rich-quick exponents and enthusiasts with only one idea. The National Health Service cannot recognise these self-styled individuals and employ them to treat patients in our hospitals; for no

criterion exists today by which the sincere and competent can be distinguished from the self-styled.

ORTHOPAEDIC SURGEONS

It is not so much that they cannot manipulate as that they have such a great deal else to do, most of which is more urgent and important. Fractures must be reduced at once; operation on bones and tendons cannot be delayed; union of bone is slow, and beds are occupied for long stretches at a time. To admit patients for manipulation under anaesthesia for a disc-lesion is therefore a misuse of beds, quite apart from the fact that these are better dealt with during consciousness as out-patients.

FAMILY DOCTORS

Whether they like it or not, it is upon family doctors that the duty of manipulation devolves today. A spinal intra-articular displacement exists and calls for manipulation; the most favourable moment is *now*, while the displacement is recent. Who else is so well placed as the patient's own doctor? If he has his patient's best interests at heart he is forced to make the attempt, and I know an increasing number of doctors who cope with this problem in this way. They recognise the necessity; they know that no consultant at any adjacent hospital can help the patient; it is up to themselves.

Nevertheless, the family doctor is at some disadvantage. Unless he is a fairly recent graduate of St. Thomas's Hospital, he is most unlikely to have been taught manipulation as a medical student. Different manipulations require couches of different heights, and one or two assistants are needed for some spinal work. Again, a difficult lesion may take, say, half-an-hour to treat. Since a Health Service doctor, though his manipulation may be saving the country hundreds of pounds in avoiding a long spell of invalidism, cannot charge a fee for manipulation on one of his own N.H.S. patients, there is a limit to the time and assistants that he can afford to provide for any one individual. Moreover, some doctors are too frail or too old to attempt such work themselves; others are too academically inclined.

The answer to the question: should all doctors manipulate? must, therefore, be "no"; indeed, there is probably no medical treatment

that *all* doctors should practise. They must recognise the indications and possess a general idea of how it is done, in the same way as a doctor recognises appendicitis without necessarily setting to himself to remove the appendix. The difference is that he has only to get in touch with a surgeon and the operation is performed, but who can he find to, let us say, reduce a disc-displacement? Moreover, spinal manipulation happens to be a technique required daily in ordinary general practice and it ought therefore to form part of the family doctor's armamentarium. For that reason he should receive a grounding in it during his student days.

WILSON'S REPORT

Awareness has spread of the hiatus orthopaedic medicine occupies in the medical services of the nation. Many family doctors have risen to the challenge, but as they have no access to medical students, their views cannot be communicated to them before they have graduated; by then it is largely too late.

In 1962, Wilson received answers from 92 out of 290 general practitioners to whom a questionary had been sent asking about manipulation. Here is a summary of his findings:

Do patients in your practice have manipulative treatment?	Often	15
	Occasionally	68
	Never	9
Is there a place for manipulative treatment in orthodox medicine?	Yes	75
	No	1
	Doubtful	12
	No comment	4
Are there adequate facilities in your area for such treatment under the N.H.S.?	Yes	34
	No	45
	Doubtful	13
Number manipulating personally, or with partner doing so		38
Number of these trained by:		
Medical School		3
Formal postgraduate work		5
Informal postgraduate work		18
Books		25
Other means		18
Number having difficulty in getting training		17
Do you feel there are now adequate facilities for such training?	Yes	5
	No	54

If you manipulate, is it because:	
(*a*) It is a natural part of practice?	37
(*b*) Patients could get it no other way?	11
(*c*) Other facilities overbooked or with long wait?	19
(*d*) Patients "forced" you to learn?	6
(*e*) Other reasons?	9

He states that typical comments were:

"Know only one consultant orthopaedic surgeon who ever manipulates."

"Consultants in hospital useless."

"Never knew our physical medicine consultant to manipulate anyone."

Other comments in favour of manipulation included eight statements from doctors lamenting their lack of knowledge of such procedures and asking for training to be organised:

"I should value further talks and demonstrations by experts in this field."

"I should be glad to learn where I could get further practical instruction. I feel that the present scheme whereby patients often go (on their own initiative) to an osteopath is not to their advantage in the long run, and I should do something about it."

"I do not manipulate patients myself, because I do not know how to do it, or how to get taught."

The subject of manipulative technique was raised spontaneously by many members:

"Until the subject is taught properly in Medical Schools, the osteopath will flourish."

"I should welcome a course in osteopathic techniques."

"I should like to learn more, but from whom?"

"Having sampled both from the consumer's point of view, I favour the gentler methods of the osteopath to those of the manipulative surgeon."

"Patients spend many months waiting for orthodox treatment, but often gain instant relief from visiting the osteopath."

"It is time a study was made by general practitioners of the results obtained by consultants, bonesetters and themselves. Patients have not infrequently told me of astonishing benefit from

a bonesetter's treatment, and I have not been able to shake this evidence."

There is obviously a feeling among some of these practitioners that the consultant services are not a help:

"Unfortunately, our local surgeons and physical medicine men are not prepared to try to manipulate."

"Encourage consultants in physical medicine to be realistic."

The following two remarks are aimed at the Medical Schools:

"Manipulation should be part of the students' training just as much as learning to plaster fractures."

"I feel sure it should be taught as a routine in all Medical Schools."

Finally, two comments "against":

"There are very few conditions which require manipulation in the practice of orthodox medicine, and it should only be carried out on the recommendation of an orthopaedic surgeon."

"I think manipulation without X-rays is a great mistake . . . I believe manipulation has become a dangerous fashion."

It is a sad fact that in spite of so much feeling in favour of manipulation, a doctor or a physiotherapist who wants to learn has nowhere to go. The osteopaths offer laymen a four-year course; they are also prepared to teach physiotherapists in two years and doctors in nine months. But at both the schools of osteopathy in London, pupils get embroiled in "osteopathic lesions", autonomic effects, etc. Moreover, to spend four years learning how to manipulate the spine (which I taught my students in less than a year, with equivalent results in efficacy of treatment) is a huge waste of time and money. I am sorry, therefore, that no Institute of Orthopaedic Medicine such as I advocate has been founded as, amongst other things, a centre for non-cultist teaching on the indications for and manner of manipulation.

PHYSIOTHERAPISTS

Physiotherapists have all the basic knowledge of anatomy, joint and muscle work, not to mention trained hands, that assist them to learn the theory and practice of manipulation. By now, I have

myself taught these methods to almost a thousand physiotherapists, most of them women, who have become as proficient in this part of their work as can be expected of any student—certainly expert enough to obtain good results consistently. It is a proven fact, therefore, that physiotherapists can be taught this work.

Manipulative work calls for more time and paraphernalia than a busy doctor in family practice can well afford. Today, he has no alternative but to do his own manipulations himself, whatever the difficulties, but there is no doubt in my mind that most medical men would prefer to have this measure carried out by a trained medical auxiliary. This I know; for I get enquiries from all over the country for the whereabouts of the nearest St. Thomas's trained physiotherapist. Relegation of certain treatments to competent persons other than doctors is no new departure; for example, nursing, midwifery, occupational and speech therapy, radiography and a number of laboratory tasks are properly performed by trained personnel, working under medical supervision. Where are the skilled manipulators taught by doctors and working under medical supervision? No real tuition on this subject seems obtainable in Europe. During my time at St. Thomas's I taught this subject to my physiotherapy students as a personal contribution to their knowledge of how to put patients right; my endeavour evoked no parallel at other hospitals, and received no backing from the Chartered Society of Physiotherapy.

There is no doubt in my mind that all family doctors would welcome the emergence of the manipulative physiotherapist. The addition of training in manipulation to these auxiliaries' training is long overdue and could lead to the complete replacement of the separate sorts of laymen offering different varieties of this treatment by trained personnel working within the Health Service. The family doctor would no longer be forced either to manipulate himself, perhaps hurriedly with unskilled assistance, or covertly to advise recourse to some layman. He would send the patient for manipulative physiotherapy; this would be faithfully carried out as a matter of course by an auxiliary fully trained in these methods and accustomed to working side by side with the medical profession. The arrangement has already been established in Norway, where a special register of those skilled in manipulation is available to doctors. They can send their patient to a physiotherapist who has, by attending a special course and passing an extra examination, obtained a post-graduate diploma.

ORTHOPAEDIC PHYSICIANS

There are less than a dozen in all Europe; hence their number is too small to make appreciable impact on so huge a problem. They can only write and teach and draw renewed attention to the problem and its solution, each within his small sphere of influence. Until each Orthopaedic Department insists upon an orthopaedic physician working side by side with the surgeon (as happened at St. Thomas's in my day), there exist today no orthopaedic medical posts for young doctors to train for. And the rigid structure of the N.H.S. makes the creation of new jobs—even if they can save the country's finances ten or perhaps a hundred times the outlay—extremely difficult. Whatever the country's needs, promising young men obviously cannot be expected to come forward just out of altruism to train for a medical speciality in which the Health Service offers no posts. Here lies the deadlock.

EMPTY AT THE TOP

A curious situation exists putting manipulation in an anomalous position. During my time at St. Thomas's, no other medical school offered students a grounding in such methods. Now, those doctors as do decide to practise it have to learn as best they can after qualification. They are forced to come to my unit at St. Andrew's Hospital or to go to the London College of Osteopathy, which has produced forty-eight medically qualified graduates, or to learn it out of an illustrated book.

The normal approach to medical treatment is apprenticeship under supervision; the budding surgeon starts as a dresser, then becomes house-surgeon, registrar, assistant and finally consultant. This ladder is recognised, and those who ascend to the top are accepted and respected; they were taught, made the grade, and now themselves pass their knowledge on.

The doctor who takes up manipulation is usually a good practitioner. He finds that a group of his patients, in despair after ordinary medical measures have failed and after the consultants at one or more hospitals have proved unable to help, wanders off to a lay manipulator. Sometimes cure results. A minority of doctors, finding that their patients need a certain type of treatment and that it is un-

obtainable via the Health Service, meet the challenge and decide to carry it out themselves. They do not know how to set about this worthy endeavour and must try and hope. A certain number have a natural aptitude, find the work interesting and rewarding. They therefore persevere until they become competent, with little or no guidance, while carrying on as family doctors. After a time, they become known for this work and more and more patients come to them from far and wide. In due course, they develop a part-time practice in manipulation, soon acquiring rooms in the Harley Street area. Some continue in this way; others finally shift to full-time manipulative practice. These doctors are now "specialists" in the eyes of the public, with rooms in the accepted district, plenty of patients who praise their skill, and so on. They are not so in the eyes of the medical profession; for they do not have the academic qualifications nor the hospital appointments which normal consultants all possess, and they have no opportunity to teach medical students. Naturally, if a method of treatment is seen to be practised as a speciality almost entirely by doctors who do not conform to their colleagues' idea of professional respectability, a slur falls on the method. But it is not these doctors' fault that the manipulative branch of medicine is empty at the top; it is so understaffed, and the disorders responding are so common, that today it cannot be entered modestly in the accepted way. The doctor cannot serve an apprenticeship; he can only be a specialist from the start, since *any* knowledge of this branch of medicine is so far in advance of no knowledge whatever that pressure of patients forces him right up. Who is there above him? Until my idea of an Institute of Orthopaedic Medicine comes into being, this unsatisfactory situation must persist.

VI

Manipulative Technique

The intention throughout is to do something to the affected tissue that the patient cannot do for himself. The patient can, let us say, turn his neck by using his own muscles; weight-bearing and muscle pull then combine to exert a *centrifugal* stress on the articular contents during the movement. When the same rotation movement is carried out passively during strong traction, a *centripetal* force acts on the joint and the contrary effect is exerted on the tissues within the joint. It is for this reason that exercises, or orthopaedic surgical manipulation under anaesthesia or laymen's manœuvres without traction, may have the opposite effect to that of orthopaedic medical manipulation, though to all appearances the same movement is carried out. In such cases, the orthopaedic medical manœuvre may be as strongly indicated as the surgical and lay types of manipulation are contra-indicated. This is understandable; for the surgeon wishes merely to restore the range of movement by mobilisation under anaesthesia and the osteopathic and chiropractic techniques were originally devised to shift one vertebra on another. Laymen naturally foster the idea that theirs are the valid manipulative techniques, though even osteopaths no longer regard the vertebra as displaced. By contrast, orthopaedic medicine has evolved a series of different spinal manœuvres, more soundly based on the concept of the displaced fragment of disc.

The Patient's Posture

For a number of manipulations, the joint is placed in a special position. This involves the patient, the affected part, the manipulator and his assistants adopting positions that facilitate the movement required and enable the patient to relax. When manipulation during traction is required, as is so often the case in orthopaedic medical

manipulation, the operator trains his physiotherapists to synchronise with himself. Since no two people manipulate exactly alike, this involves individuals practising as a team.

Positioning the Patient

Since manipulation is a movement of small amplitude often performed at the extreme of range, the patient's joint is usually taken passively into this position until the resistance of the tissues to further movement is felt by the operator. He is then able to add the minor thrust that constitutes the manipulation proper. Hence, in manipulating a neck at which 90° of active rotation range is present, the positioning will involve 89° of movement and the manipulation perhaps 2° more. Manipulation must not, therefore, be thought of as a huge movement involving 92° even though, in some cases, the pause between positioning and applying the extra force is not perceptible.

The Direction of the Movement

Since the vertebrae move at three joints simultaneously—the intervertebral and the two facet joints—it is best to force movement at the joint between the vertebral bodies in a manner suited to the inclination of the articular surfaces of the facet joints. This is a point well insisted upon by osteopaths. Side-flexion of the neck involves rotation towards the same side on account of the inclination of the facet joint surfaces. Hence a larger range is secured, for example, when cervical side-flexion to the left is forced if some rotation to the left is also allowed. Again, when cervical rotation is forced, the manipulator may lower his body as the extreme of range is approached so as also to obtain some side-flexion towards the same side.

Direction Indolore

Should the forcing be towards the deviation or towards correction? Maigne, probably the best-known manipulator in France and the author of the French book on osteopathic technique, has laid down the rule that all spinal manipulation must be carried out in the direction of the deformity and in the direction that has been found painless. Adherence to this rule, he states, makes it impossible to do harm by manipulation. Maigne's dicta shows how careful those who

manipulate without adequate traction have to be. Doubtless, his are excellent provisos if manipulation is to be performed in the osteopathic manner on patients regarded on osteopathic grounds as needing manipulation, but they are far from valid when orthopaedic medical methods of diagnosis and manipulation are employed. Moreover, I feel fairly sure that manipulation even with these restrictions could well do harm if a really unsuitable case were chosen for manipulation. In fact, when the lumbar spine deviates, reduction is clearly encouraged by a manipulation that stretches the painful side, giving the loose fragment room to move.

All effective treatment must carry some element of danger. Only wholly ineffective measures possess no contra-indications. But it is not usual in Medicine to assess the perils of any procedure by the results of its performance by laymen, or even by doctors using a method that militates against a good result. The proper estimate is based on suitable cases treated by trained personnel. Manipulation during traction without anaesthesia, when carried out with safeguards on which the orthopaedic physician insists, is far from being dangerous. It is usually carried out first in the direction that does not hurt, then in the direction that does.

The Type of Movement

A movement may be employed that can be carried out voluntarily by the patient's own muscles, or a movement outside the patient's active range may be required. For example, full flexion at the knee cannot be performed actively, but may well have to be forced therapeutically. Distraction of the humerus from the glenoid cavity, and antero-posterior gliding at the carpus are useful therapeutic movements that the patient cannot carry out himself.

The Type of Pressure

A sharp jerk is suited to breaking an adhesion or to shifting a small fragment of cartilage, whereas maintenance of substantial pressure is suited to stretching out a contracture.

Single or Repetitive Movement

Particularly when manipulative reduction is required, moving the joint quickly to and fro may be the best method for inducing a small fragment loose within a joint to shift its position. Moreover, in

spinal manipulation, rhythmical movement of increasing amplitude may relax the patient and enable a sudden thrust to be used at the exact moment when the manipulator feels the proper degree of tissue resistance.

More Than One Force

Some manipulations are carried out with several forces acting on the joint at once. For example, during manipulative reduction for a loose body at the knee, traction is applied, then alternate rotations are carried out during increasing extension; four separate forces in all. Again, when pressure is applied to a lumbar vertebra with the patient prone, full extension is never reached. It is a movement towards extension accompanied by a shearing force directed anteriorly. When the same manœuvre is carried out by pressure at the transverse process, to these two forces is added a third—rotation.

The Effective Movement

Benefit may result from a movement at mid-range, or towards the extreme of range or only when strong over-pressure is applied. Hence, the technique varies with the manipulator's expectation. For example, when reduction of a central cervical disc-protrusion is attempted, no effort is made to force range; strong traction with only a few degrees of rotation added is the best manœuvre. Rotation with little or no traction is the worst treatment, and almost always does harm. It is important, therefore, that patients with this particular condition should avoid osteopathy, chiropraxy or surgical manipulation under anaesthesia. These are the cases which give rise to the justified opinion that manipulation of the cervical joints is dangerous and should be eschewed. This is true of manipulation performed in these ways, but in fact the use of proper technique can often relieve this otherwise intractable and progressive condition. By contrast, a postero-lateral cervical intra-articular displacement usually shifts as the extreme of range is reached. For the ligamentous contracture at the upper two cervical joints that sets up headache in the elderly, strong stretching to beyond the apparent range is required.

The Force Employed

This varies with the lesion and the patient's sensitivity to pain. The first time a manœuvre is attempted, it is done fairly gently, to get the

feel of the joint and to judge the patient's reaction. Subsequent manipulations are carried out more strongly on a basis of: (1) What, on re-examination, the result has been; (2) what the joint felt like at the range to which it was taken last time; (3) what the manipulator feels as the joint approaches full range. At that instant, the different types of end-feel tell him what to do within the next split second. The operative hand receives sensations that determine how much further he takes the joint.

VII

Anaesthesia in Manipulation

Anaesthesia ensures muscular relaxation and freedom from pain. It is called for to help carry out any manœuvre that would in its absence afford unreasonable discomfort or to abolish such muscle spasm as would militate against success. Anaesthesia is, therefore, essential for the reduction of most fractures or dislocations, in both of which pain and muscle spasm otherwise render an attempt at reduction impracticable. Surgeons, accustomed as they are to these measures carried out under anaesthesia, have carried this habit into orthopaedic medicine, not always with the happiest results. The justification for mobilisation of the lumbar spine under anaesthesia rests on a misapprehension of the lesion present. To put a joint through its full range of movement during complete muscular relaxation restores mobility by breaking adhesions. But in backache the pain on, or limitation of, movement results not from adhesions but from a block in the joint caused by a displacement requiring reduction. Admittedly, reduction may occur during mobilisation under anaesthesia, but only by luck as opposed to by judgement, attended moreover by difficulties and dangers avoidable as long as the patient remains conscious.

There are two types of manipulation: *set* and *not set*. In the former, anaesthesia is often an advantage and in any case is never harmful: in the latter, it deprives the operator of essential information, lack of the patient's co-operation making nonsense of the whole attempt.

MANIPULATION: SET

The manipulator knows what he must do, and does it all the more easily and pleasantly for the patient's unconsciousness and relaxed state. In, let us say, the removal of the appendix or the reduction

of a fracture, the patient can take no active part in furthering the manœuvre. The same applies to a displaced fragment of meniscus at the knee: the manipulation continues until the click signalling reduction is felt. In such cases, it is easier for the manipulator and more comfortable for the patient if consciousness is abolished. When adhesions at various joints require rupture, nothing the patient can do helps the manipulator. Hence, though it is in fact often possible in cases of this sort to dispense with anaesthesia, this may be a help, is occasionally essential, and is never a hindrance; for the manipulator carries out a set series of movements without reference to the patient.

MANIPULATION: NOT SET

The manipulator does not know what technique will be required in any one case; he merely knows how to set about the work. This state of affairs exists when manipulative reduction is to be attempted at a spinal joint. Though clinical examination can often determine within small limits where a displacement lies, it has no power to establish from which part of the joint it has shifted. For example, a postero-central disc protrusion may result from a purely backward movement of a fragment lying in the mid-line or from a fragment lying to one side of the mid-line which has shifted centralwards from left or right. Hence, clinical identification of the present position of the lesion, however accurate, cannot identify in which direction the loose piece must be pushed and, by corollary, which manœuvre (if any) will restore it to its bed. Hence a number of techniques have to be tried, and the effect of each on symptoms and physical signs is repeatedly assessed on the conscious patient. What to do next, whether to go on or stop, depend on what changes are discerned after each attempt during the session. Hence, anaesthesia must be avoided; for it deprives the manipulator of all knowledge of what he is or is not achieving, and of all finesse. It is only if he can examine the conscious patient for warning signs or at least be told by him of an increase in symptoms, that the operator can even tell if he is making the protrusion larger. What technique should be tried next? This depends partly on end-feel, but largely on the effect of previous manœuvres on the degree of pain and the range of movement, e.g. of straight-leg raising, or of the joint itself tested on the conscious patient. If subjective or objective

improvement results, the same method is repeated. If not, another technique is tried. Is the patient being made worse? If so, manipulation is abandoned before appreciable harm has been done. Should manipulation cease? When examination of the conscious patient reveals that an adequate painless range has been restored to the affected joint, there is nothing left to do. If it becomes clear that manipulation is not having any effect, the endeavour is abandoned. All these vital facts are hidden from the manipulator under anaesthesia. Anaesthesia in a manipulation which is *not-set* nullifies the whole attempt, depriving it of skill, and militates strongly against a good result. Hence, if a patient who has been made worse by manipulation under anaesthesia chooses to create legal trouble for the surgeon, it would be difficult for him to maintain that it is possible to manipulate with due care for a disc-lesion without a patient's co-operation.

Spinal manipulation under anaesthesia has another disadvantage; it may necessitate a night in hospital. Since patients with backache have been estimated to form one-third of orthopaedic surgeons' practice, were they to manipulate under anaesthesia all those requiring this measure, their wards would be full of such cases to the exclusion of their proper and more important work. The waste of beds, not to say of space in the theatre and anaesthetists' time, is obvious. The overriding needs of severely injured patients have forced a situation upon orthopaedic surgeons whereby they have neither time nor beds to enable them to manipulate the many sufferers from spinal derangement who need this treatment. Consequently, the drift to laymen is inevitable. As soon as it is realised that manipulation for spinal internal derangement is best carried out without anaesthesia, it becomes feasible for the orthopaedic surgeon to delegate this work (as I do) to trained physiotherapists. Then recourse to laymen would fade away.

The displaced fragment of disc that has previously been reduced under anaesthesia is in my experience easily reduced on a second occasion without. In disc-lesions, it is fruitless to resort to anaesthesia when manipulation without has failed, since it is not the lack of relaxation that was the fault, but the fact that a protrusion irreducible by manipulation is present.

VIII

Errors in Manipulation

All effective treatments are potentially harmful. Only an entirely inert measure is incapable of causing damage. Manipulation obeys this rule; it is a genuine remedy, exerting well-defined effects. It is not very potent for harm, however, as is borne out by the infrequency of serious complaints against laymen, even the wholly untutored. They often waste clients' time and money treating cases insusceptible to manipulation, or fail to relieve a lesion in fact suited to manipulation by adopting a faulty technique or treating the wrong joint. They are certainly prepared to go on treating patients endlessly, for as long as they care to keep coming. Fifty to a hundred visits are not uncommon in chiropractice, as their own statistics show, and a contributing factor is their policy of offering a discount if the patient will pay for, say, twenty treatments in advance. Hence, they are often responsible for much delay in the initiation of correct measures. These are important disadvantages. But positive injury is uncommon, otherwise these men would be constantly in legal difficulty. However, they are as a group prone to one foolishness that gets them into recurrent trouble. They often manipulate *all* a patient's spinal joints, whereas the most cursory questioning and minimum of examination would have revealed at least which (if any) region of the vertebral column was affected. Yet it is not uncommon for patients with low back pain to be manipulated from occiput to sacrum. In consequence, some find their lumbar symptoms relieved only at the expense of being given a new pain higher up. Should the manipulator prove unable to remedy the fresh lesion, the patient is forced to turn to the medical profession for this purpose. The most elementary caution surely dictates that normal joints should not be wantonly disturbed.

THE WRONG DISORDER

Manipulation should not be carried out for negative reasons, i.e. that interference with joint function is present and the X-ray picture normal. It is called for only when positive indications are present, viz. adhesions to be broken, or a contracture to be stretched out, or a displacement to be reduced. If this rule is followed, and a proper technique used, manipulation is all but free from danger—far more so than most other effective treatment. The question is one of diagnosis.

Lesions suited to manipulation may be mimicked, for example, by the earliest manifestations of malignant disease, at a time when no erosion of bone is visible on the radiograph. However, a number of factors combine to make the doctor suspicious. The steady deterioration due to neoplasm contrasts with the long erratic course of most disc-lesions, varying as they do with exertion and posture. Neurological signs may appear before bony erosion shows, and present in a different pattern from those caused by a disc-lesion. Articular limitation of movement may be excessive for the short span of the history. Though secondary deposits in the ilium, for example, may cause pain on straight-leg raising, they limit hip flexion even more obviously. All this is clear enough to doctors, but the layman, who confines his examination to running a hand down the patient's back and sending him for radiography, is at a sad disadvantage. Hence, careful consideration of the history, proper clinical examination and postponement of all treatment in doubtful cases until the diagnosis has become clear, makes for such safety that the decision to manipulate becomes no more fallible than any other medical reasoning. On the other hand, the doctor must not be too timid when a patient who has had a cancer excised some years before develops, say, backache. This is a most difficult situation; for radiography soon after the onset of symptoms cannot be relied on to exclude metastases; yet it is a shame to let a patient continue with lumbar pain for months—meanwhile becoming daily more certain that his cancer is recurring—when all he has is a reducible low lumbar disc-lesion. Every effort must be made to look on these cases from both sides and, in such cases, the induction of epidural local anaesthesia proves an invaluable diagnostic aid. Here again, the layman is at a loss, since he is unaware of difficulties in diagnosis, cannot recognise which cases require the injection, nor can he carry it out. There are

types of arthritis that manipulation always aggravates, and in them radiography does not necessarily reveal any abnormality of the bones. At intervals I see patients with ankylosing spondylitis so advanced that one glance at the patient's back reveals the limitation of spinal movement. They may arrive with a lumbo-thoracic radiograph revealing as yet no lesion, though, of course, the radiological appearances of the sacro-iliac joints would have proved diagnostic. Yet these laymen (who claim that their sense of touch is so much more delicate than doctors') have often given them repeated treatment for the "osteopathic lesion". These types of case provide recurrent traps for the unwary lay-manipulator, who perforce relies largely on palpation and X-ray evidence.

Laymen, with little or no medical training, are not equipped to distinguish between what should and what should not be manipulated. They merely try and see; those patients who improve are satisfied; the others cease coming after some treatments. The onus of deciding that he has a manipulatable disorder is placed on the patient's shoulders. It is up to him to guess right, but he does not realise that, when frequenting a lay manipulator, the duty of diagnosis has shifted to himself. The strongly divergent views that members of the public have on these laymen stem from this situation. The patient who has decided that he needs a spinal manipulation and happens to be right swears by lay manipulators. But the patient who has guessed wrongly, and receives treatment in vain, is very apt to criticise them for lacking the diagnostic skill that, without a medical training, they cannot be expected to possess. There is much to be said, therefore, for patients being manipulated only after a medical consultation has revealed its desirability.

Laymen's real security lies in the unwitting self-selection of patients with manipulatable disorders by the passage of time. When a patient has consulted his doctor about a symptom, has had some treatment, has seen a consultant, has been further investigated and finally finds himself no better, so much time has passed that he can scarcely be suffering from progressive or serious disease. However slight the initial symptoms, important conditions advance relentlessly in the absence of treatment and finally become only too easy to identify. Since manipulation is the only effective treatment required in daily medical work which a doctor finds difficult to obtain for his patient, the group requiring manipulation sifts itself out from the general mass of suffering humanity. They end up with a bonesetter, whose safety is dependent on this situation, though he

does not realise it. There is no limit to the length of time that, without getting larger or smaller, more or less fixed, a small displaced fragment of disc can cause symptoms. Until recently, my record for a constant displacement that proved possible to reduce was twenty-three years; now, it is thirty-six. This security, however, breaks down in conditions like monarticular rheumatoid arthritis at, say, shoulder or knee. In spite of the lapse of, say, a year, the failure of routine measures of treatment and the absence of radiological evidence of disease, manipulation is the worst possible treatment, even more so if it is carried out forcibly under anaesthesia.

Much is made by the opponents of manipulation of the dangers of producing a compression palsy of the fourth sacral root by manipulation for a low lumbar disc-lesion. This is a possibility, it is true, but so far I, and the thousand physiotherapists whom I have trained, have avoided this catastrophe. Rupture of the posterior longitudinal ligament allows of massive herniation of disc substance which impinges on the fourth sacral root in the pre-ganglionic position. Hence, permanent paralysis of the bladder can ensue. We have encountered a few such cases. Some have certainly been brought about by manipulation but, to date, I am happy to say, not carried out by doctors or physiotherapists taught at St. Thomas's Hospital; they followed osteopathy (in one case after the patient had been warned by us that manipulation in her case carried this especial danger), during mobilisation under anaesthesia, and (one only) during traction; or have occurred spontaneously. So far, immediate laminectomy has proved curative, but neurosurgeons have shown that late laminectomy carries a poor prognosis.

THE WRONG STAGE

A condition may be relievable by manipulation at one phase in its evolution and not another.

In arthritis at the shoulder, for example, manipulation during the first six months is apt to make the pain worse and leads to further restriction of movement; during the second six months, it often has the reverse effect. Again, a small disc-displacement is often suited to manipulative reduction, whereas a large one is not. As soon as the protrusion becomes larger than the aperture whence it emerged, any attempt at manipulation is a waste of time.

WRONG TECHNIQUE

During the first forty years of this century, when manipulative technique was being evolved, misconceptions about the nature of the disorders present were universal.

Medical Misconception

In those early days, doctors were thinking in terms of mobilisation, i.e. putting a stiff joint through its complete range of movement under anaesthesia with the intention of restoring full mobility. Though this concept was correctly applied to the rupture of post-traumatic adhesions, it was incorrectly extended to the spinal joints, where in fact what was required was reduction. Hence, crude methods were adopted for putting the spinal joints through their full range of movement under anaesthesia that are today quite frightening to contemplate. Now the pendulum has begun to swing the other way, and many surgeons wholly avoid (in my opinion, quite rightly) any forcing of the spinal joints under anaesthesia. This enlightened attitude is by no means universal; for various surgeons' text-books on manipulative surgery continue to show the influence of the old hypothesis. Though the concept of disc-lesions as the common cause of backache (Cyriax, 1945) is now widely accepted, manipulative technique has not kept pace. If the theoretical requirement has changed from mobilisation to reduction, the manœuvres employed must also be changed to fit this new purpose.

The methods used to encourage reduction of an intra-articular displacement are quite different from those that mobilise a joint. For example, an adhesion limiting extension at a joint can be ruptured only by forcing extension. By contrast, if a displaced intra-articular loose body blocks extension, it has to be manipulated back into place without a strong extension force being applied to the joint; otherwise the thrust hurts considerably, over-stretches the ligaments, damaging the joint further. Hence, the endeavour is to reduce the displacement indirectly, i.e. without a forcing movement in the blocked direction.

The main effect of laymen's failure to realise that they were dealing with an intra-articular displacement was the neglect of traction during manipulation. Naturally, if a subluxated fragment within a joint needs to be reduced, the best way to get it to shift is to pull the

joint surfaces apart. Moreover, traction induces a negative pressure within the joint, a centripetal force thus being exerted on its contents. Traction carries the advantages of converting a manipulation that is painful and unsafe into one that is all-but painless and certainly safe. Particularly at the neck and for a loose body at the knee, manipulation must be carried out under traction. This is just what osteopaths and chiropractors do not do adequately. Hence, particularly at neck, thorax and knee, they often fail unnecessarily in cases that present no difficulty to physiotherapists trained, as all my students were, in manipulation during traction.

WRONG DIAGNOSIS

For many years patients with lumbar disc-lesions have been manipulated under the mistaken label of "sacro-iliac strain". The anachronism still survives. More lately, pain in fact due to disc-lesions has become attributed to trouble at a facet joint. Neither error matters much when a reducible disc-displacement is present, since the so-called sacro-iliac and facet manipulations put strong stress on the lumbar joints. But the misconception confuses clinical examination and thus hinders due evaluation of manipulability. If a lumbar disc-lesion is found present, certain criteria indicate whether or not manipulation is indicated. These would not apply, and would therefore not be sought, in sacro-iliac or facet trouble. Diagnosis is, therefore, important. The reverse error is also encountered. Patients with sacro-iliac arthritis causing sciatic pain are often regarded as having a lumbar disc-lesion and are apt to be treated by manipulation without avail. Moreover, limited movement at the knee caused by sprained ligament may be mistaken for internal derangement and vice versa. If this error is made, faulty choice in technique is performing the requisite manœuvres is inevitable.

WRONG DISC-LESION

The patient, his doctor and the lay manipulator whom he goes to may all have made a correct diagnosis of disc-lesion. However, many protrusions are insusceptible to reduction, did laymen but know it. These comprise:

Cervical Joints

1. Evidence of pyramidal tract involvement, e.g. a spastic gait, inco-ordination, extensor plantar response.
2. Presence of a root-palsy.
3. Primary postero-lateral protrusion, i.e. symptoms coming on in the reverse order—first paraesthetic hand, then pain in forearm and arm, finally reaching the scapula.
4. Neck movements setting up brachial pain.
5. Basilar insufficiency contra-indicates the lay manoeuvres.

Lumbar Joints

1. Menace to the fourth sacral root.
2. Hyperacute lumbago.
3. Root palsy.
4. Gross lumbar deformity with sciatic pain.
5. Root pain in a patient aged under sixty that has lasted over six months.
6. Primary postero-lateral protrusion, i.e. root pain without previous lumbar symptoms.
7. Nuclear protrusion.
8. Spinal claudication.
9. Compression phenomena.
10. Self-reducing displacement.
11. Late pregnancy.

WRONG MANIPULATION

The dangers of an operation are not usually estimated by reference to its practice by the inexpert. The efficacy of drugs is not evaluated by assessing the results when they are prescribed by herbalists. Hence, it is no valid argument against spinal manipulation to point to the harm that may ensue at laymen's hands or from the use of anaesthesia. The relevant fact would be to show how much damage results from manipulation carried out by medical men with experi-

ence of this work. In my experience, bad results are most infrequent, far less than those of other therapeutic manœuvres which patients are advised to undergo and submit to quite readily.

Still, the fact remains that the spinal joints of the people of Britain are manipulated, when they can secure this treatment at all, largely by laymen. These men are well aware of their shaky position and lack of medical knowledge. For all their confident manner and condescending attitude towards doctors, they have to be basically cautious. Hence the disadvantage consists in: eventual success after many treatments where one or two skilled sessions would have sufficed; the inability to make a diagnosis of whether manipulation is needed or not, and if so, which part to manipulate and how to vary technique to suit different lesions; endless treatments given for conditions insusceptible to manipulation. In short, the damage lay manipulators do is largely confined to waste of time, effort and money.

Some frighten the patient by alleging that he has a serious disease which can be averted only by a weekly manipulation continued endlessly. This fraud may succeed for a time but, in the end, the threat so frightens the patient that he goes to his doctor and the deceit is exposed. Any band of cultists containing many who decide to give medical treatment without becoming doctors first must contain many opportunist elements, and no-one with proper ethical standards would enter on his life's work by such a short cut. Hence, these persons are of very varied competence (to say the least of it), and some are undoubtedly unscrupulous. This is a public danger.

Lay manipulators cannot tell, and certainly do not care, whether a patient is suffering from neurosis or not. It is a commonplace to hear, when a patient describes past history, that he or she has received manipulation once or twice weekly for some years. On examination, many such patients are found to have emotional troubles without organic disease. The manipulation such patients pay for is in a way not harmful, and it can even be argued that anything that keeps a neurotic patient happy is a benefit of a sort, but many such patients have been grateful—afterwards—to have had the emotional basis of their complaint revealed to them. Psychological treatment is postponed as long as they attend for lay manipulation. Here lies another danger which cannot be avoided by men unable to make a diagnosis, who would moreover become the poorer for it if they could.

THE WRONG PATIENT

A curious situation exists when the moving parts of the body are in question; the patient's word is law. If a patient alleges that his fracture has not united or that he is anaemic, it is simple by means of an X-ray photograph or a blood test to establish fact. No such objectivity applies in lesions of the radiotranslucent moving tissues. If a patient states that he is better, he is. If he states that he is worse, this is credited too. It is, therefore, a mistake to treat patients who, however much better they are actually made, do not propose to admit it. For example, patients building up a compensation suit will certainly claim aggravation, or at least no improvement, however successful treatment proves. They attend hospital on their solicitor's advice, since he realises that their allegation of severe symptoms lacks conviction unless they are attending for regular treatment.

Similar considerations apply to highly neurotic patients who do have, say, slight backache. This is one of their main interests and subjects of conversation; naturally, they have no wish to be deprived of it. Moreover, even the gentlest manipulation compatible with having any effect may upset their emotional tone. Hence, there exists a degree of neurosis, and of slightness of the organic lesion, that precludes effective treatment. They assure the doctor that they are prepared to have manipulation, then receive it and leave the hospital quite cheerful, declaring that all their pain has ceased. When they come to think it over that evening they realise that one of their psychological props has been removed. The obvious remedy is an attack of severe pain in the back, the late result of the "brutal" measures adopted. The patient's doctor is then called out late that night, to deal with an attack of hysteria. In consequence, my clinical judgement is criticised—and rightly so. I should have realised that, though the lesion was suited to treatment, the patient was not.

If the patient is determined to have the lesion dealt with, both patient and family doctor should be warned of the likelihood of a "post-manipulative crisis", and the accompanying relative assured that it passes off without treatment.

IX

Perils of not Manipulating

All decisions on treatment are reached by weighing the dangers of action against the dangers of inaction. Since so much spinal manipulation is performed under inauspicious circumstances (i.e. either under anaesthesia, or by laymen with a mistaken concept—or no concept at all—of the lesion present) it is difficult for doctors to assess the true position. Doctors find little opportunity of noting the results of manipulation competently performed on the proper case. In consequence, their views are inevitably coloured by the types of manipulation they see going on around them. But bad results in poor circumstances do not preclude consistent good results when proper care is taken. This situation is not appreciated and medical literature abounds with warnings against spinal manipulation, with little realisation of what sort of manipulation is being criticised, laymen's and medical experts' being assessed together. The only logical attitude is to balance competent manipulation against the valid alternative; what is likely to happen if manipulation is withheld?

The avoidance of manipulation on illogical grounds has many disadvantages.

FUTURE CRIPPLEDOM

Manipulation of the neck can be dangerous when cases are not properly selected, or when performed without traction, and is potent for harm when anaesthesia is added to the lack of traction. These facts provide no argument against manipulation of the neck, but merely against manipulation done badly or in the wrong case. Unfortunately, most doctors' experience of spinal manipulation is

confined to noting the results of manipulation with improper technique. Hence, a poor opinion appears justified to those who have never seen the results of sound methods. If, however, a diagnosis of a disc-displacement at a cervical joint has been made and bonesetters' methods for attempting reduction are recognised as unsatisfactory, this should stimulate medical men to look for better techniques, not to abandon the search. This has been the policy of Orthopaedic Medicine. We have found manipulation effective in proportion as suitable patients are singled out and the correct techniques employed with proper safeguards. Not only can pain perhaps of years' standing be abolished, often lastingly, but, more important, a displacement that in future years may cause serious disease can be averted. Left where it is (as is the standard "treatment" throughout Europe, by means either of heat and traction, or by a collar) such a protrusion can lead to eventual crippledom. Neither patient nor doctor realises that failure to reduce a cervical disc-displacement during a stiff neck years before was the start of the trouble.

When pain in the neck is central or bilateral, the spinal cord is menaced, not at first, but after years of continued protrusion. Unless manipulative reduction is carried out early, the time for full success is missed. Moreover, the reduction must be maintained by renewed manipulation at whatever intervals prove necessary. Later, when pain spreads down both arms and pins and needles begin at hands and/or feet, reduction is more difficult to achieve and at times proves impossible. Moreover, the posterior longitudinal ligament has been allowed to stretch during the years of constant displacement and the reduction now becomes much less stable. If the displacement is left *in situ*, it bulges out the posterior longitudinal ligament, exerting a constant traction on it, which raises up the periosteum at the edges of the vertebral body. Bone grows out to meet its lining membrane, and central osteophytes are drawn out. These get gradually larger and compress first the dura mater, causing neckache, bilateral scapular, and central inter-scapular, pain. Then they compress the anterior spinal artery, and irreversible ischaemic degeneration of the spinal cord ensues. Such conditions as postero-lateral sclerosis result (Brain, 1948). By now, of course, it is far too late in the day to manipulate. When the patient has died of compression of the spinal cord, post-mortem studies show that at this final stage manipulation could by no stretch of the imagination have relieved the impingement on, and consequent thrombosis of,

the spinal artery. To argue from this sequence of events that pathological studies have shown manipulation of the neck to be useless is absurd. This is the criticism that the pathologically-minded level at my work, and it is based on the same fallacy as if it were argued that, because a patient had metastases all over, excision of the neoplasm at its earliest stage ought not to have been carried out. This sort of argument may save the face of those who see patients needing cervical manipulation but do not propose to carry it out, but such casuistry is unworthy of our profession.

The harm resulting from avoiding manipulation may not show for many years, but once the right moment has been missed the damage done may be irrevocable (cervical laminectomy apart). This delay between cause and effect obscures the connection, and all doctors should, therefore, be on the lookout for early postero-central displacements at a cervical intervertebral joint since, to the unwitting patient, they present at first as not more than a slight nuisance.

CONTINUED PAIN

The avoidance of eventual disablement provides one strong argument in favour of early manipulation. Relief from chronic pain, however, is scarcely less important to a patient's well-being. Why should a disc-protrusion be left to get larger or smaller as fortune dictates? Reduced at the stage of pain in the trunk only, pain ceases and the likelihood of further protrusion has been obviated as far as is humanly possible. Moreover, the correct step has been taken to stay subsequent increase in the local pain, together with the supervention of root pain. Many patients with severe root pain in the upper limb describe months or years of scapular discomfort. It is difficult to suppose that reduction early on would not have spared the patient his eventual months of severe brachial pain. The same applies to patients with lumbar pain who, left untreated, develop a sciatica which keeps them off work for many months. Admittedly, reduction at the lumbar spine avoids less certainly subsequent root-pain than is the case at the cervical spine; but at least, if this is done, no doctor can reproach himself with having neglected his duty to his patient. Then there is the elderly patient with sciatica. In young patients, sciatica seldom fails to recover spontaneously in a year, whereas after the age of sixty this becomes less likely. Elderly patients are encountered who will clearly be in pain for years or for

life unless manipulative reduction succeeds. Capsular contracture and osteophytosis combine to prevent movement between the articular surfaces. After middle age, rest in bed and traction may both prove remarkably ineffective, since neither produces enough separation of the joint surfaces to allow the displaced fragment to slip home. Hence manipulation is the only effective treatment, and the older the patient is, the more probable this becomes. But the older the patient, the more osteophytosis the radiograph discloses, the more fearful of manipulation both doctor and patient become. The consultant who, after weighing the pros and cons carefully, explains them to the patient and his doctor, setting out the chances of failure no less than of benefit and, on balance, advises manipulation, is not foolhardy—as many would maintain—he is doing his best for his patient in particularly difficult circumstances. The same applies to a medical man who, faced with what seems with reasonable certainty to be a disc-lesion in a patient who once had a cancer removed, decides to attempt manipulative reduction rather than to leave him to suffer unnecessarily, as it may turn out, for years. The sad fact is that, manipulation being so suspect within our profession, it requires courage to carry out what should be regarded as a laudable and orthodox attempt to relieve pain.

NEUROSIS

The neglect of manipulation in suitable cases of backache predisposes to neurosis. Indeed, it is a tribute to the commonsense and equable temperament of the people in this country that psychological symptoms are not more common.

The patient who strains his back lifting, perhaps at work, has no time to get worried about it if he is dealt with quickly and competently. His fragment of disc is restored to its proper position within a day or two. He returns to his job without further ado, without emotional upset. By contrast, he may be ordered to bed and stay there for a week or two without improving much. Despondent at his lack of progress and coming gradually round to the idea that, since nothing is being done for him, nothing *can* be done, he ponders on the possible outcome of his illness. He may be sent by ambulance to hospital where he is examined, X-rayed and enjoined another period of rest in bed. When he enquires about the X-ray findings the words "disc-degeneration" or "spinal arthritis" reach

his ears, even though he has no more changes than anyone else of his years, and no more than he had before his symptoms began. The patient may interpret these phrases as implying future crippledom, and he comes to doubt his ability ever to return to his previous work, and sets to thinking how he can be compensated for a permanent disability. This brings him into the orbit of the Law and the uncertain outcome of such claims soon turns concern into anxiety. The step to neurosis is further facilitated by contradictory opinions by different medico-legal experts. Since an opinion in disc-lesions can be based only on clinical criteria, without regard for radiological appearances, there is plenty of room for conflict. Doubt about diagnosis, prognosis and the natural wish of a solicitor (if any question of accident due to negligence arises) to put his client's case as cogently as possible, combine to render a perfectly healthy man with mere backache a nervous wreck. By now, severe anxiety has ensued in the self-employed; compensation neurasthenia in those who blame an incident at work. The latter event entails several years' invalidism, lasting until the suit is settled. The root of the trouble is the ubiquitous management of disc-displacement by routine recumbency. It has little to be said for it except for its simplicity as seen from the doctor's point of view. It exasperates those with work to do and anxious to get on with it, wastes their time and with that the finances of industry. It makes unnecessary invalids of many others and involves Industry, Insurance and the Law in avoidable, lengthy and expensive quarrels.

ECONOMIC DAMAGE

A patient with lumbago may well be kept in bed at home for a month; the Nation loses the work he did not do, and about £80 in sick benefit. If he is admitted to hospital, the loss is £50 a week in unnecessary in-patient recumbency. If he is given physiotherapy—i.e. heat, massage and exercises—a further loss is incurred, not only because of the cost of treatment but because in lumbago exercises tend to retard recovery. The man himself loses the difference between his sick benefit and his wages, quite apart from being left needlessly in pain. By contrast, manipulative reduction carried out during the first few days would have cost only a pound or two. The saving afforded by successful manipulation is anywhere between ten and a hundred-fold.

Similar considerations apply to a large number of other disorders within the sphere of orthopaedic medicine that keep labourers off work for months, even years, e.g. supraspinatus tendinitis, frozen shoulder, tennis-elbow—all quickly remediable. But the number of doctors and physiotherapists acquainted with the necessary remedial methods is so small that adequate treatment never reaches the majority of sufferers.

LOSS OF ESTEEM

It may be argued that if doctors and physiotherapists do not manipulate patients who require it, that is their own fault and they have no right to complain if they lose national esteem in this respect. But the real sufferer is the public. For each single patient whom a lay manipulator does help, there is a large number receiving fruitless manipulation for entirely unsuitable disorders, all on the advice of a friend who was relieved of some quite different condition causing similar symptoms. Had the patient been put right within the medical sphere, he would not have gone round extolling laymen, with the attendant evils of time and money wasted, and effective treatment postponed.

A LEGAL SPUR

There is one event which, though I should regret its taking place, would yet do so much good that it would be worth while in the long run. It is a successful action for negligence against a consultant who did not notice that a patient had a reducible disc-lesion. After all, the doctor who fails to set about manipulative reduction for many types of fracture, or to arrange for its performance by a colleague, finds himself in immediate medico-legal trouble. Why should the same reasoning not apply to a displaced fragment of disc?

The patient is examined, told he has a spinal disc-displacement and, when he enquires after the possibility of manipulative reduction, is told that this is not feasible. The next day he visits a bonesetter who effects reduction on the spot. Were such a suit to succeed, consultants would learn to be on the lookout for cases suited to manipulation. It is not that doctors are unaware of laymen's successes,

nor in general of the skill of my physiotherapy graduates. It is plain apathy that maintains an outworn conservatism. Such an event would serve to galvanise the profession into a reappraisal of traditional concepts on treatment.

X

Medico-Legal Aspect of Manipulation

Manipulative laymen often complain to their clients about their lack of recognition by the law and by the medical profession. I do not regard their dissatisfaction as soundly based.

LAYMEN'S ADVANTAGE

It is true that lay manipulators' lack of legal status prevents their obtaining dangerous drugs, signing death or N.H.S. certificates or treating a few statutory diseases. But it also carries the legal advantage —to them—of not having to exercise any great care or competence in their dealings with clients. It might well be thought that a layman, when he abrogates to himself the right to give a medical treatment, is more liable in law than a doctor if anything goes wrong. In fact, the contrary applies. The situation is that a doctor when he accepts a patient, is always tacitly understood to bring to that patient the skill and conscientious care that is universally expected from the duly-qualified medical man. This duty is less clear in the case of a lay healer or manipulator. When a bonesetter is visited, all that is taken for granted between him and his client is that some part of him will be manipulated. The layman's manifestly irregular position—giving medical treatment without being a doctor—and lack of qualification preclude any assumption that he possesses any particular level of competence, adequate ethical standards or the capacity to discriminate between those whom it is safe, and not safe, to treat. This was decided in the Courts in the case of Sones *v.* Foster, reported in "The Times" (1937). It was held that the defendant (a naturopath) could be expected to possess only the competence of the body to which he belonged. Hence, it is very

difficult to sue for damage done; for there exists no standard of knowledge established for unqualified individuals and, apart from common law duties, they cannot fall beneath a non-existent criterion. By contrast, doctors have duties implicit in their state-recognition as a profession, and behaviour that falls below can be legally punished.

Curiously enough, the osteopaths nevertheless tried to establish themselves legally, as practising an alternative system of Medicine, by an application to the House of Lords in 1935, but their answers to the medical questions put to them at the hearing brought them into a number of impossible situations. In the end, their position became untenable. Small wonder; for they denied standard tenets built up during centuries of research by doctors all over the world, without putting forward a shred of disproof, and affirmed an alternative creed without offering any evidence in its favour. They claimed to practise a complete and revolutionary alternative system of medicine, but when the Lords asked on what grounds these remarkable assertions rested, none was put forward. This ventilation was an advantage; for osteopaths were shown in their true light, not only to doctors and the public, but also to themselves. As a result, few even of the most bigoted now claim to cure *all* diseases by manipulating the spine, but grossly exaggerated attitudes on the scope of osteopathy continue.

It does not follow from the rebuff in the House of Lords that a reasonable request from a properly constituted body presenting a united front (the London College and the British School of Osteopathy were at loggerheads) would have met the same fate. Had the osteopaths put their own house in order by withdrawing from the osteopathic lesion and the panacea aspect of manipulation, establishing acceptable schools, instituting external examinations and representing their graduates as able and willing to treat by manipulation those sent to them by doctors with this request, the reproaches to them would soon have abated. Even now, recantation might help to win them approval for legal status.

STATE RECOGNITION

Were recognition granted, the public would expect the same degree of protection as is today afforded by the examining boards of the medical and physiotherapy professions. Educational standards would have to be laid down before entry. The syllabus would

require revision by authoritative medical men; teaching would need to be supervised by leading consultants, and outside examiners would have to form a panel to test those students who had completed the prescribed course of study at a school granted official approval. No such institution exists at present. Osteopaths would have to adopt the standards and ethics of medical auxiliaries. State recognition would enable doctors happily to send patients to these trained manipulative therapists.

State recognition would create welcome difficulties for those who, without preliminary tuition, wish to treat—and be paid for treating—such clients as cross their threshold. By contrast, in the long run, official recognition would prove beneficial to reputable manipulators. At present, anyone can call himself a bonesetter, chiropractor or osteopath, put up a plate and start giving treatments tomorrow. Many do start that way; for nine-tenths of all persons earning their living by manipulation do not possess even the osteopathic registration (M.R.O.). In London, only one-third of the non-medical osteopaths listed in the telephone directory publish M.R.O. after their names. Registration follows legal recognition and would, in the long run—as happened in the past to doctors and dentists—result in the virtual restriction of manipulative work to those who had been taught how to do it: an undeniable advantage. Doctors would recommend only registered manipulators; the public, no longer forced to go to laymen, would insist on treatment only from a qualified manipulator. Doctors, finding themselves in control of the availability of manipulation, would abate their concern and, in due course, prejudice would cease. This situation would redound to the public interest, since patients, now denied such treatment, would instead receive it from trained personnel via their doctor. The status of manipulation would rise, carrying with it those who practised it. Eventually, everyone would benefit from legalisation of the position. By submitting to the same discipline as other professions auxiliary to medicine, the manipulators of tomorrow would come to enjoy the same rights as other professional people, but they might well be irked by the new concept of their duties. In order to obtain the advantages of legal recognition, the leaders of the manipulating fraternities would have to adopt a disinterested attitude. This would involve their developing a readiness equal to that shown by doctors to allow of progress by admitting errors and instituting the necessary reforms. Their obduracy prevents doctors from sponsoring osteopathy.

The trouble is, however, that these laymen do too well. There are a number in London who charge more than the average family doctor gets for a private visit. This successful exploitation of the public's gullibility by self-styled cultists pains doctors who have spent seven years training before earning a penny. Moreover, all patients are grist to these laymen's mill, their lack of medical knowledge enabling them to manipulate patients whom such measures could not possibly help. If these men were to confine themselves to manipulating those sent on by doctors for this purpose, most of their income would vanish. Hence, the reorientation of lay manipulators towards an ethical position together with medical and legal recognition is an unlikely event. Though they do not admit it, they do much better outside medicine, as long as they can maintain their present monopoly. Here lies the rub; for this is exactly what I have been trying to break during the last thirty years. The Principal of the British School of Osteopathy announced in "Medical News" (1969) that my efforts to transfer the public's confidence from his members to physiotherapists had failed. He may be right, and certainly during my time at St. Thomas's Hospital, I got little encouragement from the leaders of the Chartered Society of Physiotherapy. Nevertheless, his statement may prove previous. I still advocate the quick and simple solution, viz. that the physiotherapists should take over. At St. Thomas's Hospital, the adequate training of physiotherapists in manipulation dates back almost sixty years and, were it adopted by all other training schools, skilled medical auxiliaries could be turned out in a few years in sufficient numbers to eliminate lay manipulators.

MEDICAL MANIPULATION

Difficulties crop up even when manipulation is performed by a doctor or by a physiotherapist acting under his instructions. The reason is the curious attitude taken by doctors today towards medical manipulation without anaesthesia—it is justified only if it succeeds. If an orthopaedic manipulation under anaesthesia fails to benefit a patient with, say, backache, no one thinks the less of the surgeon concerned. If taxis does not succeed in strangulated hernia, or closed reduction of a fracture is attempted but proves impossible, the surgeon is not criticised. If laminectomy for a disc-lesion makes a patient permanently worse, the surgeon suffers no loss of esteem

by his colleagues. Yet, if medical manipulation does not result at once in reduction of a displaced fragment of disc, the orthopaedic physician is apt to be looked at askance. If medical manipulation for a lumbar disc-lesion should make a patient worse, the situation is far more retrievable than after unsuccessful laminectomy; for other methods exist that can still afford relief. Nevertheless, lack of success in manipulation without anaesthesia is widely held to show that the attempt should not have been made. The lack of logic in this attitude needs to be strongly combated; it will cease only after prejudice against manipulation is replaced by a considered and unemotional view of a normal medical procedure.

Such absence of backing from his fellows puts many doctors off, and frightens some. This is particularly so in California where the legal criterion appears to be "If colleagues carrying on the same sort of practice as yourself had been faced with this patient, would they have done as you did?" Since doctors in general in California do not manipulate, no one is safe to start in so litiginous a State . . . with abiding benefit to the local chiropractors. All medical pioneers have had to face such risks and some have suffered severely from introducing methods that later gained universal acceptance, e.g. the removal of ovarian cysts. Nevertheless, the cautious doctor is apt to keep an eye open for the attitude of the courts, and the fact that a treatment, however rational, is not practised by his colleagues may well give him pause. He knows that if there is legal trouble, it will be easy to present an array of well-established medical men ready to condemn the new method, whereas it will be very difficult to find anyone to give evidence on the other side. However, it is by no means in patients' best interests that legal considerations should come between a doctor and the choice of what he believes to be the best treatment.

There is another medico-legal hazard. If a patient with a lesion of his soft moving parts maintains that some treatment has made his condition worse, objective criteria are few or absent and the tendency is to accept his word. By contrast, if a patient maintains that his fracture has not united, that his diabetes or anaemia has been aggravated, that his duodenal ulcer has been reactivated by some act or neglect, objective methods are at hand to assess the situation. However, in soft-tissue lesions, objective signs are the exception rather than the rule. If a patient cares to state that he is worse after a manipulation, he is apt to secure uncritical belief, since the allegation fits in so well with current medical opinion. While it is true that

patients can be harmed by manipulation, no less than they can by any other effective measure, in most branches of medicine there is little likelihood of legal difficulties arising as long as reasonable skill and care have been exercised. But in manipulation it is the mere fact that manipulation was employed at all that arouses prejudice, not that it was badly carried out or the disorder was unsuitable. This applies much less to manipulation under anaesthesia, which still passes for orthodox, though it is more dangerous than the methods employed by the orthopaedic physician; moreover, in spinal disorders, it is less likely to succeed.

MANIPULATION BY PHYSIOTHERAPISTS

As long as physiotherapists shelter behind treatments like heat and exercises, they are confining themselves to palliation that can scarcely do harm. But when effective measures are employed, these are potent for good but may, of course, prove damaging if administered wrongly or in an entirely unsuitable case.

Physiotherapists are protected by undertaking cases only at a doctor's request, accepting his diagnosis and instructions. He is liable in law if he orders a treatment without due care that turns out to be harmful, but the physiotherapist is liable too if she should have known that the measure was unsuitable but carried it out notwithstanding. In a case of this sort, she must let the doctor know her view; if he then insists, she is entitled to refuse and, indeed, would be lacking in her duty to her patient if she acquiesced. The same applies if it is the physiotherapist's considered opinion that the doctor's diagnosis is mistaken; she must then set out to him the medical facts that she has observed which provide the grounds for her disagreement. If, owing to her silence the correct diagnosis was missed, the physiotherapist might well be legally liable if the patient suffered as the result of an incorrect diagnosis. It follows that a physiotherapist is entitled to know the doctor's diagnosis and is not constrained to carry out his instructions. She is not a mere technician, but a skilful trained individual with the duty to use her own judgment.

These facts are particularly relevant to the manipulating physiotherapist. She may be asked to carry out manipulative reduction in a case where signs exist that such an endeavour is impossible and hazardous. Or it may be that it is only when she gets the feel of the

joint as it approaches the extreme of the possible range that her trained hand perceives the abrupt onset of muscle spasm that indicates that manipulation is contra-indicated. Alternatively, she may be asked to give traction to a patient with acute twinging lumbago; this is always disastrous. Again, the doctor may have seen a patient with root pain in the upper or lower limb one day and found no neurological weakness. By the time the patient reaches her a day or two later, this may have supervened. If so, it is her duty to inform the doctor of the change in the patient's condition so that he can review the case, now that it has become clear that neither manipulation nor traction can help any longer. Or neurological signs of a different type may have developed indicating that a diagnosis of a disc-lesion is no longer tenable. Or symptoms may be described indicating that the posterior longitudinal ligament is overstretched. All this is clear enough to the physiotherapists whom I trained, but no lay manipulator could be expected to set about his work in this way.

VASCULAR DANGERS

In the U.S.A., cases have been described since 1947 in which manipulation of the neck proved fatal owing to thrombosis of the basilar artery. In most of these cases, the manipulation was carried out by a chiropractor; in one, by the patient's wife. European authors have contributed further instances.

Thrombosis of the internal carotid artery has been described as resulting from pressure set up where the artery crosses the lateral process of the atlas. In six of a group of twenty-six such cases, rotation of the head appeared the causative factor, and at operation adhesions were found binding artery to bone.

The fact that we have not yet met with lasting trouble may be due to our techniques being different from chiropractors' or merely to the misfortune being such a rarity. There are estimated to be some 16,000 manipulators in the U.S.A. who must be regarded as likely to manipulate not less than one neck a day; indeed ten times that figure is more probable. If eleven cases have come to light in twenty-five years it works out at one in ten million manipulations. In the twenty-thousand or so neck-cases that I estimate I have treated in the last forty-four years, there have been two cases of untoward vascular symptoms following manipulation—one cerebral

(inability to write) lasting three days and the other spinal (ataxia in one leg) from which full recovery took a week. Such contingencies cannot be wholly guarded against and provide no argument against manipulation. This view coincides with that of Lord Justice Denning who stated in 1954 (Hatcher *v*. Black) that

> "It would be very wrong and indeed bad law to say that simply because a misadventure or a mishap occurred, thereby the hospital and the doctor are liable.
>
> "Indeed it would be disastrous to the community if it were so . . .
>
> "It would mean that a doctor instead of getting on with his work would forever be looking over his shoulder to see if some-one were coming up behind him with a dagger."

LEGAL ACTION FOR LAYMEN'S FEES

The law governing legal action to secure payment of fees by medically unqualified persons is contained in Section 27 of the Medical Act, 1956.

> "No person shall be entitled to recover any charge in any court of law for any medical or surgical advice or attendance, or for the performance of any operation, or for any medicine which he shall have both prescribed and supplied, unless he shall prove upon the trial that he is fully registered."

This section implies that the action can be brought only if the practitioner was fully medically qualified at the time when the services in question were rendered. The unqualified manipulator is not debarred from suing for work done short of a surgical operation—e.g. the administration of heat, exercises, massage or manipulation. But he is debarred from entering a claim for giving the advice on which the choice of treatment rested. Hence, in cases where both advice and treatment are given, he must separate the amounts and sue for the fraction arising from treatment only. In fact, lay manipulators scarcely ever sue for fees, since they do not wish for publicity for their disgruntled patients' statements.

XI

The Economics of Manipulation

The economic effect of different ways of treating disease is a subject to which little attention has so far been paid, and my endeavour to put this aspect before the Minister of Health met with no success. When it is a matter of life and death, money counts for nothing; for the relief of lethal illness and the prevention of crippledom carry benefits beyond price. But there are occasions when the economic factor should be taken into account. If, for example, a patient will have to stay an extra week in hospital because he is too anaemic to leave, the cost to the State may be £50, whereas a blood transfusion using blood costing, say, £5, may enable him to go home at once. Whichever course is adopted, the end-result to the patient is the same; the difference is in time and money. These factors deserve consideration.

Progress in medicine has been so great that many common and potentially grave disorders have ceased to prove a major financial disaster. Diabetes, pernicious anaemia, even tuberculosis itself, no longer drain the Nation's purse on anything like the former scale. Thanks to penicillin, large numbers of patients no longer spend six months off work with pneumonia followed by empyema. But large numbers are still off work with sciatica, just as they were a century ago. Indeed, it has been estimated that, each year, 28 million work-days are lost by a labour force of 20 million as the result of the so-called "rheumatic" diseases. This figure takes no account of another huge loss due to soft-tissue injuries occurring at work, at home, or during games, not included within the term "rheumatism". It may well be that the financial loss to the Nation from these two causes approaches £100 million a year. As a result of our newly-acquired control over so many grave diseases the less serious causes of disablement are thrown into ever greater prominence. Lesions of

the moving parts now constitute an increasingly important cause of absence from work, taking second place only to influenza. Since so much of invalidism from soft-tissue lesions is avoidable, more medical attention could well be devoted to them, not only on humanitarian grounds, but also to save Industry, the Insurance Companies and the Health Service from paying out large sums unnecessarily.

Let us take a simple example—a man spends three weeks off work with lumbago each year. Our figures show that 57 per cent. of early cases can be relieved by one session of manipulation. Were all such patients so treated, instead of being left to moulder in bed for indefinite periods, and every other one proved an immediate success, the profit to the Nation would be £120—£16 = £104, given a five day working week, i.e. a little over £50 per patient. This figure is based on the assumption that it takes the patient two days to receive treatment, whereas in fact it is possible to arrange for manipulation within a few hours; and it further supposes that patients not put right in one manipulation are all complete failures, which is certainly taking an unjustifiably poor view of the results of this treatment. If, then, 20,000 people a week suffer from lumbago and they are paid an average of £40 a week, the Nation is involved in a loss of £48,000,000 a year. To this sum must be added the actual cost of work not done, and then of routine physiotherapy, ambulance staff and hospital maintenance. Three hundred doctors seeing fourteen patients a day would deal with this number of cases, and they, at £10,000 a year each, would cost £3,000,000. Hence, for each £3,000,000 spent, £48,000,000 would be saved—a ratio of sixteen to one. This figure takes no account of cases of neglected lumbago that drift on to a sciatica that keeps the patient in bed for months, nor of the many other lesions of the moving parts that the orthopaedic physician can put right much more quickly than can Nature, nor of the detection of undue prolongation of disability after some genuine lesion has recovered. By coping with all this work as well, the orthopaedic physician could easily earn for the Nation at least twenty times his salary.

Did they but know it, the patients of Britain are searching for an orthopaedic physician. They cannot find one. So, after getting short shrift from the medical profession, they go off to all sorts of lay healers, sometimes with, sometimes without, success. Here lies the most expensive hiatus in the whole of Medicine today; for the commonest indication for manipulation is a small fragment of disc

lying displaced within a spinal joint. It is also the commonest organic reason for avoidable absence from work. Sooner or later, every worker faces the economic effects of a disc-lesion. So does the employer, both personally and as regards the proper running of his business by his men. Doctors adopt quite a different attitude. They are interested in patients and disease, not finance, and the varying economic effects of different methods of treatment scarcely impinge on medical thought. The doctor's concern is to get his patient well, without appreciable regard for any time-factor. Patients with disc-trouble, if put to bed for long enough, mostly recover; why then should he bother himself with active treatment, even though he suspects it secures a favourable result in less time?

INDUSTRIAL SICKNESS

Strikes are news and are widely publicised. They represent concerted voluntary acts that redound to our detriment and cause much public annoyance. Illness is not news. Everyone gets ill from time to time and sporadic sickness causes little concern or inconvenience to the population at large. Few people realise that strikes provide only one-hundredth of the time lost to Industry by disease. In 1966, 3 million man-days were lost by strikes and 300 million man-days by sickness. It is true that one-third of this is chronic invalidism—i.e. has lasted more than a year. The rate has been rising by about 1 per cent. a year ever since 1945; contrary to general belief, more among older than young employees. During the last twenty years, absences lasting less than four days have doubled. The average employee takes fourteen days off work each year; the self-employed man ten days; the rate for doctors is nine days. When it comes to spells of work lasting under seven days, the rate for employees was eleven times that for the self-employed in 1962. In 1954, the total days lost were 176 million, and in 1968, 239 million; in 1969, 300 million, of which the Secretary of State for Production stated that one-tenth was due to rheumatic diseases.

It has become apparent that as medicine has become more effective and more and more serious diseases have come under control, so has the time employees take off work increased. Tuberculosis poses little problem these days; it is influenza and bronchitis that head the list. For men, arthritis and rheumatism take second place, for women third place, in importance. Edström, analysing 62 thousand

cases, published figures in Sweden that suggest that half of all sickness attributed to arthritis and rheumatism is the result of a disc-lesion. This deduction was more than confirmed in 1969 by the Industrial Survey Unit of the Arthritis and Rheumatism Council, which reported that 60 per cent. of what was called "rheumatism" was caused by pain in the back. Not surprisingly, the Unit called for more research into lumbar troubles. This they found affected particularly dockers (highest rate), those who had to lift weights or exert their backs strongly or who were forced to adopt awkward postures. The dockers' rate was 12 per cent. per year of the registered total, with an average of two months' absence. This contrasts with the figures for ordinary people, which is 1 per cent.

In four practices, three in town and one rural, the family doctors concerned reported an almost identical figure for the incidence of back trouble. Only the label varied. In one practice, disc-lesions accounted for 46 per cent. of all back conditions; in another 54 per cent., words like strained muscle, fibrositis and lumbago being preferred.

The wages lost by dockers was assessed at £170,000 for a registered labour force of 22,000. Spinal injuries were responsible for £63,000 and numbered 756. This is only two cases a day, and a doctor would not regard himself as overworked if that were all he had to cope with. Nevertheless, if prompt treatment reduced the time off work to an average of one week, a medical man receiving £5,000 a year would save his employer £51,000—a tenfold gain. This is a measure of the advantage that would accrue to the State from the creation of enough orthopaedic physicians and physiotherapists skilled in the use of their hands. It takes no account of the other common time-consuming disorders which an orthopaedic physician could, with the help of a physiotherapist trained in precise manual methods, deal with during the rest of the day—for example, stiff shoulders, sprained knees, bursitis, tendinitis, tennis-elbow and so on, all of which at present keep men off work for far longer than would be required if skilled treatment were available.

Remarkable data were put forward at a symposium held in Glasgow in 1966, based on a study of 6½ million episodes of absence from work. The analysis showed that 5·1 per cent. of all sickness in men was due to lumbar trouble, 2·4 per cent. in women. When the patient was receiving injury-benefit, the figures were 11·4 and 6·7 per cent. Indeed, 8 per cent. of all injuries keeping people off work were lumbar. Extraordinary figures emerged for the length of time

that people remained sick with back trouble. Though only 46,000 of the 343,000 cases were labelled sciatica—which after all can last some time—the remaining 87 per cent. complained of lumbar pain only. Yet the average periods of incapacity reported in this survey were thirteen weeks in men and seventeen weeks in women under twenty-five; twenty-two and twenty-four weeks respectively after the age of forty-five. Since there must be a number of responsible people in Glasgow who suffer an attack of lumbago in the ordinary way and, after some days in bed are back at work in a week or two, these averages indicate that people there are apt to take a year off work with what my experience in London has led me to regard as a transitory disorder. If such long periods of idleness are countenanced over large parts of the country, and are at all representative of the general situation, the benefit accruing from the provision of an orthopaedic medical service far surpasses anything I had previously envisaged. It is remarkable that the main losers, the Confederation of British Industry, the National Health Service and the Insurance Companies have proved unable to abate such huge financial burdens by endowing an Institute of Orthopaedic Medicine. The only country that has seen the light is Germany, where the manner of accountancy proved the decisive factor. Hirschfeld of Bremen came over to England some ten years ago and took the methods of orthopaedic medicine (and a St. Thomas's physiotherapist) back with him. Within a year the Actuary of the Health Service there had noted the greatly enhanced speed of recovery in patients seen by him compared with the figures for previous years' invalidism. At the end of the next year, the superiority of orthopaedic medicine over traditional methods was found to be strongly maintained. As a result, a large hospital department was built for him, and a lesser premium offered to employers if they arranged that their workmen, if disabled by an orthopaedic medical condition, should attend only his department. Hirschfeld's work attracted favourable attention within a year in Germany; for the system there is based on cost per patient. Hence, the spectacular diminution in time off work, amount of sick pay and size of doctors' fees drew the Health Service's actuary's immediate attention to his work. In Britain, by contrast, no such discovery was made during my twenty-two years in our Health Service.

All doctors know of patients put right by manipulation after months off work and as many months of routine physiotherapy. Surprisingly enough, doctors and patients accept this fact with equanimity. Since the loss is economic, the feeling of urgency present

when life is endangered is absent from medical thought. Yet doctors should not ignore the time-factor; not only because some lesions pass beyond the restoration of the status quo after varying periods have elapsed, but also in order that recovery shall be ensured with a minimum of damage to the patient as a worker and an earner. In lumbago the short view taken by most medical men is that, if the patient is salaried, he gets the same money whether he is on the job or not. Hence, it makes no difference to him how many weeks it takes to recover; slowly with the passage of time or quickly because of adequate treatment. But this is not so; for the injury is not only to the Nation's purse and the patient's morale, it is also to his posterior longitudinal ligament. This suffers stretching for as long as the protrusion persists; hence, the likelihood of relapse is enhanced by leaving the displacement in situ, particularly if the patient is put into plaster and encouraged to get up and let his body-weight compress the affected lumbar joint. Similar arguments apply to athletes and to workmen who strain muscles, tendons and ligaments by over-use. Often they are told that time will bring about recovery. Of course, sometimes it does, but even so it involved months of delay, galling to the athlete and involving financial loss to those engaged in heavy work.

There is one set of individuals who flatly refuse to return to work after some minor incident or illness causing a week or two's absence. They find to their surprise that they get as much money in sickness and welfare benefit as they received before, while employed. Naturally, such a person sometimes cannot be persuaded to return to work, particularly as he can further improve on this situation by doing odd jobs clandestinely for his neighbours. It is not the duty of doctors to set themselves against the will of Parliament, and, if this is the effect of the regulations enacted, they may deplore them but must abide by them. It is no part of doctors' business to try to force a man to adopt a policy that loses him money. He can refuse to sign a sickness certificate and inform the responsible official; that is all.

Self-employed Men

Self-employed men are in a different category. They suffer immediate economic loss, together with pain and anxiety. If a tendency to

neurosis is present, this has been encouraged to appear. The sequence of events is often as follows. The patient has lain in bed, visited at weekly intervals by his doctor who has enquired after his pain, reassured him as to the gravity of his complaint, ordered him a further supply of analgesic tablets, promised to come again, and given him a certificate. If spontaneous recovery does not ensue on this regimen, the patient starts worrying about his ability to earn his living, and it soon begins to dawn on him that no treatment for his disorder appears to exist, and his doctor, when directly questioned, offers him none. He therefore deduces that his period of disablement lies beyond medical control and may thus turn out to be endless. He then begins to question the diagnosis; his friends' lumbago is a transitory affair, why is his so recalcitrant? Perhaps he has an undetected serious disease; this soon becomes, in his imagination, cancer. By now he has become a potential passenger on the Health Service for life. As a result of his protests, his doctor sends him off to hospital in an ambulance to see the orthopaedic surgeon, who has him X-rayed and sees him again a week later. He too reassures him that the radiograph shows no grave disease affecting bone to be present. Further rest in bed may be advised, or physiotherapy, or a plaster jacket; sometimes manipulation under anaesthesia or an operation is advocated.

Compare this patient's state of mind with that of the man whose displacement is reduced the same day as it appears. Compare too, the price to the patient and to the Nation of these two different approaches. I have myself seen many patients prone to recurrent bouts of lumbago who are intensely worried at the thought of, say, a month away from the office twice a year, not for themselves—for they know they get well in the end—but economically. If a director earning £12,000 a year is off work twice for a month, he has received £2,000 for nothing. When it is found that manipulation costing, say, one two-hundredth part of that sum puts him right there and then, the benefit all round is enormous. If several thousand less wealthy patients were sent to a suitable centre every day, if necessary by ambulance, the saving would still be considerable. If orthopaedic physicians and trained physiotherapists became available in every hospital throughout the country, the largest gap in avoidable invalidism would have been closed. Litigation over compensation claims would be reduced and the spectacle of fit men unable, for legal reasons, to return to work for several years would become a rarity.

TRADITIONAL CONSERVATIVE TREATMENT

Since economic considerations play so large a part in lesions of the moving parts, it is a lasting surprise to me how the traditional treatment of disc-lesions has been allowed to linger on—dating back to the days of "fibrositis". All family doctors know that methods based on a faulty pathological premise have been, in theory, superseded, but in practice continue unabated. All family doctors, but not all consultants, are aware of the recourse to lay manipulators. They deplore it but can offer no alternative. So the stream goes on. Educated patients take account of this situation; informed people often themselves patronise bonesetters, often without even bothering to go to see their own doctor first, and insist on valued employees following their example. Employers are well aware that men are off work on a large scale all over the country as a result of soft-tissue lesions, and know that the economic problem exists; so do athletes. Doctors look at the situation medically and take a philosophical attitude. The medical officers attached to large firms can scarcely bring the benefits of orthopaedic medicine to the attention of their directors, since they perforce have so little first-hand knowledge of this work. The industrialists recognise the problem but, in the absence of medical guidance, remain powerless. Here lies the stalemate.

Traditional measures are universally adopted in Britain, despite the fact that they are manifestly futile, waste endless time, use scarce and expensive personnel and equipment, and predispose to neurosis. I find it difficult to believe that even the doctors who prescribe the ordinary conservative measures have any faith in them. In my younger days, the contemporary treatment for lumbago was a belladonna plaster and salicylates—costing a few pence. In these enlightened and scientific days, equally valueless methods are employed but all expensive in time or money, or both.

Today, the usual measures are: (1) rest in bed, (2) reassurance, (3) heat and massage, (4) exercises, (5) plaster jacket, (6) corsetry.

1. **Rest in bed.** At home, this at least costs the National Health Service nothing, but it wastes the Nation's resources on a large scale. Recumbency in a hospital bed, however, is the most unnecessarily costly treatment of them all.

   The disadvantages of rest in bed for lumbago are manifold, and adversely affect the patient, the community and the doctor.

First, the patient has to suffer pain, disablement and loss of earnings for longer than is necessary; moreover, a member of his family may have to stay at home, perhaps off work, too, to look after him. Recumbency thus condemns a man to pain lasting days or weeks, during which he has to be nursed. While in bed, though in pain, he is not ill in himself. He therefore maintains his clarity of thought and time passes slowly for him. He lies there, contemplating his sorry plight and becoming increasingly impatient at the apparent absence of effective treatment. The proper attitude is exasperation, but in patients less emotionally stable, as their minds range, thoughts of incurability may begin to take root; now anxiety, sometimes leading to neurosis, is engendered. If the attack started at work, the idea of industrial compensation begins to loom. None of this chain of events would have started if brisk treatment had led to a swift recovery and return to work.

Second, there is the financial loss to the community, the salaried worker being paid by his employer for work not carried out, whereas workers are paid out of sickness benefit.

Third, there is the loss to the doctor in both esteem and time. If the patient, after some time in bed, is now treated by a lay manipulator who puts him right, the medical profession is made to look foolish. If the doctor pays him two visits the first week, and one for three weeks after that—five minutes driving there, ten minutes with him, five minutes to the next house on his round—this amounts to a hundred minutes. Examination followed by manipulation cannot take more than half that time. Hence, the very recumbency that appears to save the doctor trouble, in the end wastes his time, too.

2. **Reassurance.** This consists of taking an X-ray photograph and assuring the patient that no bone disease is present. This may help the neurotic or cancerphobic patient temporarily, but does nothing for the ordinary individual who wants to get well, not because of anxiety, but in order to return to his previous activities as soon as possible.

3. **Heat and Massage.** Superficial heat never reaches the lesion at all and is merely silly. Deep heat does reach, and in theory is harmful since it increases the traumatic oedema of the compressed structure. In practice, however, it does not seem to matter. But the

patient is receiving treatment in a room which is built, painted, lighted and swept; he occupies part of a physiotherapist's time, whose salary is about £2,000 a year, and is left to lie under a lamp which is bought, maintained, renewed and uses electric current. It has been estimated that each treatment by a physiotherapist costs the country £1, and I have encountered patients who have attended, say, three times a week for a year—all to no purpose.

4. **Exercises.** These are harmful. If the displacement is in being, exercises grind it against the sensitive tissues and cause added pain. If they are carried out after full reduction, they move the joint, maintaining mobility, and predispose to relapse. Flexion exercises are, of course, much more dangerous than extension exercises, but both are far worse than no exercises at all.

The only useful exercise is for the patient to use his sacrospinalis muscles to keep the joint motionless in extension. Inculcation of constant postural tone is highly beneficial, but is the very exercise that is least often taught.

5. **Plaster Jacket.** This is no real help, since it has to be applied loose, otherwise the patient cannot breathe after a meal. Moreover, it has to be removed in the end, leaving the detached fragment of disc as loose as it was before. A plastic jacket has none of these disadvantages, being in addition light, sanitary and permanent.

6. **Corsetry.** Corsets have a bad name with patients since they are often applied with the displacement still in being. Clearly, the orthopaedic principle is: Reduction and the maintenance of reduction. Hence the displacement should be reduced before the corset is put on.

UNSUCCESSFUL INITIATIVE

Last year I went to see the Minister of Health. I thought that he, as a business man, would be interested. I put it to him that the lack of provision within our Health Service for the non-surgical disorders of the moving parts costs the country a hundred million pounds a year. I emphasised that orthopaedic medical cases account for one-fifth of all visits to a doctor and provide the commonest reason for a

healthy individual's absence from work or games. Moreover, though apt to drag on when untreated, they largely comprise disorders that get well quickly when dealt with with a modicum of skill. These cases occupy a no-man's land bounded by orthopaedic surgery, rheumatology and neurology. Operation is seldom required; few are instances of inflammatory disease; nerves are often affected, it is true, but by pressure from without, not intrinsic defect. Who is equipped and willing to cope with the huge mass of dispirited people, penned within this triangle, and looking in vain for interest from our profession? Who can come forward to prevent their submitting their bodies to the hits and misses of all sorts of cultists? According to me, the orthopaedic physician. He is the consultant they are looking for, but they cannot put a name to their need nor demand his creation; for the title is unknown to them. Orthopaedic medicine does away with the public's—athletes' no less than workers'—uneasy dependence on various types of lay healer, to whom they turn when they realise that they get nowhere within the medical sphere. Our neglect compels them to frequent men, mostly self-styled, who hope for the best and blithely treat all comers, suitable and unsuitable cases alike.

The Minister listened with adequate marks of attention; then ushered me politely to the door. He clearly supposed that I was just another of the cranks who pester authority, each intent on giving the particular bee in his bonnet an airing. He promised to pass on my views to his medical advisers—the very situation I had hoped to by-pass; for none of them is an orthopaedic physician. I was asking nothing for myself (I am now seventy), but for steps to recognise and encourage the practice of a medical discipline of urgent value to the nation. Some months later, the same Minister listened equally attentively (and probably equally unmoved) to a speech by Sir John Wall in the course of which he stated that, were the absenteeism from back-troubles (part only of orthopaedic medical conditions) reduced by only one-tenth, the country would benefit to the tune of £20 million pounds a year. Such an economy would present no difficulty to the orthopaedic physician.

Every family doctor knows of patients in pain and disabled for months who get well after a few simple twists at the hands of a lay manipulator. He is familiar too with patients off work for many months with sciatica or a frozen shoulder who are cheerfully back in harness in a few weeks after an epidural injection or intra-articular steroids respectively. In conversation, doctor after doctor

deplores the lack of facilities for such treatments in our Service. Eleven years ago, Wilson found out by questionnaire that three-quarters of all the general practitioners in his sample were in favour of spinal manipulation, and described their quandary about getting it for their patients, not to mention on occasion for themselves.

Every medical student, the day he qualifies, knows the treatment of leprosy. But has he been taught how to examine and treat a painful back or shoulder? Manifestly not. This lack of tuition stands him in poor stead for the rest of his life, as he soon discovers on starting practice. But it is not medical students' business to ensure that they are taught about the common conditions that crop up every day. This is their teachers' duty.

Alone in orthopaedic medicine is no effort visible to prepare students for the plethora of cases that they will encounter. The reason is obvious. Since no orthopaedic physicians sit on the boards of examiners, questions on medical orthopaedics are not asked. Students realise this and orientate their studies in accordance. Consequently, as they later on discover to their dismay, their capacity to deal adequately with many simple disabilities remains limited; and they find that their seniors cannot enlighten them. The result is that thousands of people moulder at home needlessly or become fodder for the layman.

This hiatus in our Service causes concern to every doctor except hospital consultants. They cannot be expected to notice when an out-patient stops attending. It is the family doctor who learns that the reason was a bonesetter's successful manipulation. Should this event be reported to the consultant, he dismisses it with a smile and a wave of the hand, implying that there cannot then have been much the matter with that patient. He is right; there was not; but it was enough to stop him working. Since it is the hospital consultant who teaches medical students, the silence on the non-surgical aspect of orthopaedics is self-perpetuating. It is at this point where the vicious circle must be broken.

Family doctors complain to me about the lack of facilities for orthopaedic medical cases in their area. Uneconomic though it is, this dearth obtains throughout Britain. Avoidable invalidism in this type of case runs the country into huge expenses in sickness benefit, lost production and hospital treatment, whereby doctors' and physiotherapists' time is taken up to no avail. Sportsmen face loss of amenities rather than of earnings.

I know that family doctors would be happy to insist on under-

graduate grounding in medical orthopaedics, did they (or I) know to whom to do the insisting. That is why, as a last throw, I tried the short cut to the Minister, emphasising the economic rather than the humanitarian aspect. This approach has also got us nowhere.

INSTITUTE OF ORTHOPAEDIC MEDICINE

So far, the general practitioner has not been able to make his voice heard. Repeated exhortations in what I hoped were likely places have likewise proved vain. The concerted might of the Insurance Companies, of Industry and of the Health Service has completely failed to prevent the squandering of vast sums. Not many approaches remain. However, there still exists one hope, however forlorn—the creation of an Institute of Orthopaedic Medicine. It would cost very little to make a start, and would pay for itself hand over fist from the first day, as has already been proved by statistics from Germany. A trained physiotherapist, a table, two chairs, two couches and some syringes would be enough, and should save the country each week what the clinic cost each year. At last doctors would have a centre where, faced with orthopaedic medical problems in workers or athletes, they could refer patients for an expert opinion, including a medico-legal one. The load of non-surgical cases that orthopaedic surgeons are trammelled with today would be greatly lightened, and they would be released to their more important duties. Such collaboration worked very happily during my many years at St. Thomas's Hospital. Equally important would be the fact that Britain would possess a centre disseminating medical knowledge which stands in danger today of being lost and then requiring rediscovery during the rest of this century. Since this knowledge bears on conditions that afflict all members of the community at intervals throughout their lives, avoidable ignorance condemns a great many people to avoidable invalidism. As the value of the clinic became increasingly recognised, more and more budding consultants could be taken on, taught, and in due course despatched to complete every orthopaedic surgical team in the country. Patients would see an interested physician, medical students be taught, and physiotherapists be given worthwhile prescriptions to follow. Within a decade all family doctors would know how to examine the radiotranslucent moving parts, and how to treat the disorders thus

identified. But posts for orthopaedic physicians would have to be created by authority, since doctors, however strongly actuated by a wish to meet the needs of patients, will let themselves be trained only for jobs that actually exist. It is here that the deadlock has lain for the past thirty years.

Another advantage of such a centre would be the tuition that could be given to physiotherapists on the therapeutic methods of orthopaedic medicine, in particular on manipulation. This treatment would then become widely available from trained ethical personnel within our Service. In consequence the laymen who now cash in on our neglect would be eliminated, and manipulative treatment would become restricted to those likely to benefit.

I wonder if even now the Minister realises that the British doctor who wants detailed instruction on how to examine the moving parts of the body, what inferences to draw, and treatment to prescribe, has nowhere to go. Or that the doctor or physiotherapist who wants to know when, when not, and how, to manipulate is little better served.

Author's Request

Many medical men recognise this void in their education and are anxious to have it closed for future generations of students. It would be difficult for me to be regarded as an isolated eccentric if large numbers of doctors would approach the Dean of their former Medical School, who from his own experience is well aware of the hiatus in his tuition then, and his students' now. If each Dean could be urged to petition the Minister to recognise orthopaedic medicine he might be induced to take a fresh look at the problem. This is the action that I ask of those doctors who agree with my views.

XII

Osteopathy

Osteopathy and manipulation are not the same thing. Osteopathic publicity has ingeniously tried to create an equation in people's minds whereby a patient "receives osteopathy", i.e. is manipulated. This linkage makes a patient who considers that he needs manipulation turn at once to the osteopath. In fact, "osteopathy" merely denotes an unsubstantiated creed which happens to invoke manipulation as its main therapeutic weapon.

Osteopathy was begun a hundred years ago by an American, not a doctor, called Andrew Still. A divine revelation, it seems, allowed him to enunciate the hypothesis that displacement of one vertebra on another compressed the relevant spinal artery, causing local ischaemia and disease of any organ whose blood supply had thus become impaired. Later, when it was made clear to him that any spinal dislocation large enough so to block the artery would give rise to a complete paraplegia, if not instant death from rupture of aorta, he changed this "Rule of the Artery" to pressure on a nerve, disease now resulting from the cessation of vital force transmitted to an organ along the nerve-trunk. This idea has scarcely been modified since and was maintained by all the leading osteopaths at the enquiry in the House of Lords in 1935. Search in the latest edition of the Osteopathic Blue Book reveals no direct refutation of this absolutism, and only a slight oblique withdrawal. The principal of the British School of Osteopathy stated in 1960: "Osteopathy is based on the concept that musculo-skeletal abnormalities provide the most important factor in disease." In 1964 one official publication of the British Osteopathic Association entitled "Osteopathy" states on page 6 that "it is contended and emphasised that the Osteopathic lesion is a very important and dominant factor in the cause or aggravation of the many ills, disturbances and upsets to which the

body is susceptible." Later it continues: "The Osteopathic lesion is . . . therefore a principal and potent factor in the cause of disease." It would be difficult to put forward a worst-founded hypothesis; for bone disease is uncommon, muscle disease rare, and neither has the slightest bearing on the important diseases of today.

The difference between osteopathy and medical manipulation of the spine rests on the fact that osteopathy is offered as an alternative system of Medicine, in opposition to the one doctors everywhere agree. The logical outcome of this dogma is that the prevention of diphtheria requires not immunisation but manipulation of the neck, as was indeed argued by a leading osteopath at the enquiry in the House of Lords. By contrast, medical manipulation is merely a method of treatment. Its employment implies acceptance of no particular theory on the aetiology of disease; it is merely a useful way of dealing with some disorders of joints.

Osteopathic doctrine involves spinal manipulation for visceral disease. This is the tenet that brings these laymen into conflict with doctors. It is impossible for a scientific body of men to take osteopaths seriously when they cheerfully set aside a vast mass of authenticated fact and put forward an alternative theory without a shred of proof. Not only that, but they have changed their sectarian hypothesis several times without giving any reason. This naturally engenders further scepticism. Moreover, when doctors see large numbers of patients with disorders insusceptible to manipulation who have been treated by osteopaths, they get the worst impression of these men. Indeed, it can be argued that no-one has done their own calling more theoretical harm than the osteopathic fraternity.

Osteopaths' doctrine inevitably leads them wrongly to take on for treatment a high proportion of those who cross their threshold. But it is not osteopaths' many failures that doctors should study; it is their successes. In the past, medical men have thought it enough to deride osteopaths' notions and leave it at that. However, it is the cases the doctors do *not* see that matter—the vocal minority who comprise osteopaths' startling successes. These are the patients who did require spinal manipulation but had been unable to receive it via the medical profession. The public is not interested in scientists' views on whether osteopaths' notions are tenable or not; they applaud cure. And the existence of these dramatic recoveries shows that osteopaths' practice of manipulation (even when carried out with a wrong idea of what is the matter) is sometimes correct. This is the justified attitude of most people in London today. The

situation depends on doctors' neglect to single out cases requiring spinal manipulation, and then dealing with them within the medical ambit.

Doctors must not blind themselves with logic and merely reject osteopathic doctrine. If the wrong *theory* leads to correct treatment, even in only a small proportion of all cases, the *practice* must be recognised as worthwhile.

THE "OSTEOPATHIC LESION"

Dogma bars progress. Stubborn adherence to this outdated concept has proved the main obstacle to the due evolution of osteopathy. As long as the "osteopathic lesion" pervades students' teaching, their fundamental reasoning rests on a quicksand.

The "osteopathic lesion" has been defined as "the fixation of a spinal joint in a faulty position within its range of movement without irreversible change". Such fixation occurs, of course, as inspection of the back in many cases of acute lumbago will confirm; the joint is often fixed in flexion and/or lateral deviation. Movement away from the position of deformity is painful and limited; the radiograph often shows the angulation clearly. Indeed, an X-ray photograph of this phenomenon has appeared in each edition of my "Orthopaedic Medicine" since 1947. In 1967, I attended a lecture given by Stoddard, the author of the standard English text-book on osteopathic technique. He stated that the "osteopathic lesion" is of three types: It results from:

1. Adhesions leading to restricted movement at a spinal joint.
2. Ligamentous lengthening leading to a hypermobile spinal joint. (To me, elongation of a ligament does imply irreversible change, as is well-known at, for example, the lower tibio-fibular, acromio-clavicular and cruciate ligaments. I consider symptoms, caused in his view by a hypermobile spinal joint, to stem from an unstable fragment of disc within the joint, not to excessive movement of one vertebra on the other.)
3. Recurrent attacks of acute lumbar pain, following trauma. Lumbago, he averred, is an "osteopathic lesion" only if it has been precipitated by an injury. (It would thus seem that the nucleus protruded after prolonged sitting, or first apparent on waking, is not an "osteopathic lesion", even though the

spinal joint is temporarily fixed with the same visible deformity as when a fragment of the annulus shifts suddenly. Indeed, the "osteopathic lesion" must not, in Stoddard's view, be confused with displacement of a fragment of disc, since the damage is then to cartilage and thus irreversible. He admits to difficulty in telling these two entities apart, and here he has my sympathy.)

In 1973, I wrote to the School of Osteopathy in London to ask about the present status of the "osteopathic lesion". The answer was that one such lesion was traumatic arthritis at a facet joint. This certainly is a new version, but one leading to the corollary that manipulation can only do harm. I cannot believe that this was the intended conclusion.

The Medical Explanation

Unfortunately, it was medical research that finally explained the osteopathic lesion to osteopaths. No-one denied that manipulation often produced a click in the back followed by immediate cessation of symptoms and signs. Still's old hypothesis of the displaced vertebra had been shown to be false by radiography. But in 1934, Mixter and Barr proved that sciatica could be caused by a disc-lesion (i.e. a displaced piece of cartilage—a tissue invisible radiologically) and, even more to the point, lumbago (Cyriax, 1945) was shown also to be produced by displacement of a fragment of disc, causing just that fixation of the joint that the osteopaths had already noted. The nature of the tissue whose audible shift afforded relief now became clear; it was a fragment of disc, i.e. of cartilage, movement of which a straight radiograph could not demonstrate. This dependence on medical discoveries was naturally most unwelcome to osteopaths, and the more forward looking amongst them are now seeking escape from this situation by postulating that the lesion lies, not within the intervertebral joint, but in the lateral facet joints. This is a clever move, but is based on no evidence whatever. If a lumbar lesion is to be first a vertebral displacement, then subluxation of the sacro-iliac joint, then disc-protrusion and now a facet-lock, doctors would hope that some evidence would be offered to warrant these changes of front. Moreover, it is unlikely that doctors will abandon the concept of the disc-lesion in view of the hundreds of thousands of disc-protrusions found and removed by surgeons at laminectomy throughout the world.

Alleged Autonomic Effects

Osteopaths maintain that their "lesion" lastingly alters autonomic tone, and that their manipulation restores normality, thus relieving visceral disease. Were this assumption justified, it would clearly be dangerous to manipulate a healthy person's spine for fear of lasting autonomic disturbance. Moreover, the practice of osteopathy would become unnecessary, the same effect being achieved more simply by sympatho-mimetic drugs. However, it is not my experience that patients with trouble at any spinal level suffer additional illness caused by changes in vegetative tone. Even patients with long-standing displacements causing chronic backache or sciatica do not become ill in other ways. Osteopaths also credit muscle spasm with evil effects. They appear to regard the sacrospinalis muscles as in spasm during an attack of lumbago, though, if this were so, the patient would be fixed in extension not flexion. Moreover, he could never deviate away from the painful side.

The remote effects of osteopathic manipulation are considered by them as changes in vegetative tone mediated in two ways: (1) by freeing the deviated joint; (2) by relaxing muscle. Unfortunately, disorders exist in which the spinal joints are irrevocably tilted and others in which gross muscle spasm lasts for years without the supervention of any of the alleged autonomic effects. These conditions are:

Scoliosis. Gross curvature of the spine may be present at birth or come on in adolescence. The common result is marked tilting of each vertebra on the next, with a rotational deformity as well. No disease elsewhere results.

Vertebral Wedging. Fracture causes a sudden permanent deformity at two intervertebral joints: those above and below the wedged bone. Adolescent osteochondrosis causes wedging of several vertebral bodies, and senile osteoporosis may affect many vertebrae. But such tilting of the joints which, in the case of fracture, may include rupture of a supraspinous ligament, sets up no disease elsewhere.

Vertebral Caries. Tuberculosis of a spinal vertebra leads to deformity of the bone and to years of intense muscle spasm about the joint. No remote disease ensues.

Bony Ankylosis. Many patients are born with a sacralised fifth lumbar vertebra, fixed by bone to the sacrum. Arthrodesis by means of a bone graft and healed tuberculosis lead to bony fixation of one or more spinal joints. In ankylosing spondylitis, the spinal and sacro-iliac joints become fixed by ossification of the ligaments. None of these spinal diseases causes any distant effects via the autonomic nerves.

Muscle Spasm. The notion that in lumbago the sacrospinalis muscles are in spasm is obviously false. When they do go into spasm, the lumbar spine is fixed in full extension as in tetanus or strychnine poisoning, whereas the typical "every picture tells a story" posture of lumbago is flexion (see Fig. 25). Another disproof is afforded by the fact that the lumbar spine often deviates *away* from the painful side.

Autonomic Tone

The problem can also be looked at from the converse point of view.

Cervical sympathectomy is the standard operation for the relief of severe Reynaud's disease in the hands. Sympathetic tone is abolished; yet no disease ensues later. Again, for many years, lumbar sympathectomy was carried out in the attempt to relieve intermittent claudication in the leg. No disease resulted.

CONCLUSION

Severe tilting of many spinal joints, marked deformity of one vertebra with permanent tilting of the joint above and below, vertebral deformity with intense muscle spasm, ankylosis of many spinal joints, abolition of sympathetic tone—none of these conditions sets up harmful distant effects. Although, therefore, the vertebral joint can become fixed (as can any other joint containing cartilage) by internal derangement and muscle guarding may ensue, spinal lesions far more severe and more long-standing produce none of the visceral effects that osteopathic theory postulates. It is high time the propounders of this remarkable hypothesis (now held for just on a hundred years) either dropped it or put forward corroborative evidence for doctors' scrutiny.

THE "FACET SYNDROME"

These two little joints maintain stability; they do not bear weight. At the lumbar spine they prevent rotation (except sometimes at the lumbo–sacral joint) while allowing flexion, extension and side-flexion. At cervical and thoracic levels their surfaces lie obliquely and thus allow rotation as well as the other four movements. These joints have come into prominence lately, not because of any scientific discovery connecting them with backache, but by involvement in osteopaths' prestige. Disc-lesions were a medical discovery and these laymen need to be one up on doctors; they therefore revived the "facet syndrome", inculpating joints that had previously been regarded as responsible for symptoms by chiropractors. Osteopaths aver that the facet joints "bind", but neglect to exlpain how two parallel cartilaginous surfaces can suddenly become fixed: a phenomenon unknown at any other joint. Enquiry by myself from two medical men practising osteopathy who had published work on these joints elicited the response that it was pure supposition. The obvious hypothesis would of course be a small fragment displaced—within the joint; alternatively, a nipped synovial fringe. Anatomical studies have shown that small pieces of cartilage do exist within the facet joint. They have also proved that synovium contains no nerves; hence any pinching would be painless.

Much evidence exists against the facet hypothesis. Indeed two different sets of facts militate against the idea of backache resulting from facet-joint lesions. The first is that gross disorders there seldom cause backache. The second is the anatomical conflict between the physical signs found present and the existence of a lesion in that position.

Known Lesions of the Facet Joints

In many instances of the disorders detailed below, there is no backache. Strong reasons therefore exist for not ascribing lumbar symptoms to a disorder of the lateral facet joints.

Six common disorders are well-recognised, in addition to the isolated case of capsular hypertrophy described below.

(1) **Incongruence.** When a disc has become completely eroded, as often happens to elderly people, the vertebral bodies lie about

RHEUMATIC LONDON

"Every Picture Tells a Story."

Rheumatism—a very common complaint in London—is caused by uric acid poison, which the kidneys are too weak to filter out of the system.

But rheumatism is only one symptom of kidney disorder; others are:—

Pain or dull ache in the loins and back—bladder disorders—gravel—dropsical swellings — nervous headaches — giddiness — irregular heart—depression—languor—wasting away.

Doan's Backache Kidney Pills gently heal the kidneys, giving them tone and strength to withstand our trying climatic conditions. They dissolve crystallised uric acid, flush out the body's liquid impurities, and thoroughly cleanse the bladder and urinary channels. Many London men and women have been cured to STAY cured by the genuine Doan's Pills—but be sure *you* get the same kind of pills as Mr. West and Mrs. Lacey had.

London Man and Woman Cured to Stay Cured.

Mr. Geo. West, 210, Grove Street, Deptford, London, S.E., writes:—"Having had the misfortune to get wet through constantly at my work, I became a great sufferer from rheumatism and backache. I was literally doubled up with the pain. Really I thought sometimes my back would break in two. How I managed to struggle from one side of the room to the other I don't know. My whole body was racked with pain.

"I dreaded going to bed, for I could get no peace lying on my back. I had to get up two or three times every hour of the night, and I was glad when daylight came, although it meant another day of suffering for me. I could not rest in any position; I was in misery.

"I quite lost the use of my legs through the rheumatism; the pain was just as if someone was pulling the joints out of the sockets.

"I was discharged from the hospital, as they could do me no good, and I had special treatment at Bath for some time, but I got little relief.

"My friends who knew me when I was in that fearful state can hardly believe I am the same man to-day, I have altered so much since taking a thorough course of Doan's pills. I can now follow my employment regularly, and walk as well as any man, and I can help those who had to help me at the beginning of my illness.

(Signed) "G. West."

Six years after his cure, Mr. West said:—"I withdraw nothing from what I said six years ago about Doan's pills curing me of rheumatism and backache. My opinion of the pills is still as high as ever."

Mrs. C. Lacey, of 288, Lancaster Road, Notting Hill, W., says:—"It is *over four years* since Doan's backache kidney pills cured me of rheumatism and kidney and bladder disorder, and to this day I have had no return of the trouble. I was grateful for my cure years ago, and am doubly grateful now.

"As long as I live I shall never forget the suffering I endured for seven years before I used Doan's pills. The trouble started with a dragging pain in the loins; it gave me no peace, and I dreaded to stoop because of the sharp pain it brought on.

"There was rheumatism in all my joints, some of them being swollen out of shape; every movement was agony. I was worn out with suffering, and had lost all strength and energy; in the mornings my eyes were puffy and I felt dreadfully tired and weary.

"At times I used to get fearful headaches and dizzy turns. I became low-spirited and depressed, for I was unable to get permanent relief. I had treatment at a hospital, which did a little good; but I was soon as bad as ever again.

"I began to think I was beyond a cure, but I found that Doan's backache kidney pills were just the medicine for me; they soon eased the rheumatism and backache splendidly. I kept on with the pills, and in a short time they made me thoroughly well; there was no sign of the old troubles remaining. (Signed) (Mrs.) C. Lacey."

LIKE Mr. WEST AND Mrs. LACEY HAD

DOAN'S

Backache Kidney Pills

Of all dealers, 2/9 a box, six boxes 13/9 or post free from Foster-McClellan Co., 8, Wells Street, Oxford Street, London, W.

1 cm. closer together than originally. Such approximation clearly causes gross incongruence of the articulating surfaces at the facet joints, which slide down to adopt permanently the position of full extension. Yet these old people are conspicuously free from backache.

(2) **Angulation.** After a wedge-fracture of a vertebral body has united with deformity, marked tilting of the fractured bone on that above is inevitable. A much increased gap can be felt between the spinous processes and the supraspinous ligament has often ruptured. Lack of parallel between the articulating facet surfaces must supervene, but these patients seldom suffer any inconvenience.

(3) **Osteoarthrosis.** Lewin's (1966) radiological studies of people without backache showed osteo-arthrosis of the facet joints in 15 per cent. of individuals aged twenty-six to forty-five, rising to 60 per cent. above that age.

(4) **Distraction.** In posterior spondylolisthesis, the radiograph shows that the articulating surfaces of the two facets have moved apart. Again, no backache necessarily supervenes.

(5) **Spondylitic Arthritis.** Bywaters (1968) described pannus at the facet joints in spondylitis ankylopoetica, with marginal erosion of cartilage.

(6) **Adult Spondylolisthesis.** This is a disorder in which the facet joints really do "bind". Cartilaginous then bony attrition with large osteophytes can reach such a stage of degeneration that the joints become wholly disorganised. This allows the vertebra to slip forwards until the articular processes of the upper vertebra engage against the posterior aspect of the vertebral body below. This might well be regarded as painful; yet many such patients have no backache.

Conflict with Clinical Factors

The history may contain facts that exclude a facet lesion, which is not a central structure. Hence, it cannot give rise to central pain, or pain that starts centrally and then shifts to one side, or starts to one side and then becomes central. Only a fragment of cartilage loose inside

the intervertebral joint can move it this way. A cough may be stated to hurt, and the facet joint does not lie in contact with the dura mater.

Inspection may show the lumbar spine to be fixed in deviation, but this is often away from the painful side, thus excluding muscle spasm about an irritated joint. If a nipped piece of cartilage within the facet joint were responsible, mere flexion or side-flexion away from the painful side would stop the pinch at once. Few backaches disappear on full trunk-flexion. Neck-flexion stretches the dura mater; hence lumbar pain thus set up can result only from a central prominence. In cases of real doubt, epidural local anaesthesia can be induced. Since the fluid injected cannot enter the facet joint, nor block the posterior ramus (or both sacrospinalis muscles would be paralysed for the time being), relief following the induction demonstrates that the cause was pressure on the dura mater or a nerve-root.

Arthrography

Glover's arthrograms of the facet joints, displayed during a lecture in 1972, show a dumbell shadow. The oil injected within the joint flows up and down to where the joint surfaces are not in contact. Where they are in apposition, no room for the oil seems to exist. The interesting point is the large size of the upper shadow, occupying a large part of the intervertebral foramen. This sphere indicates the considerable length of ligament necessary to allow the bones to move apart when an individual bends forwards. The shadow is indented by the nerve-root which shows as a circular defect. Clearly, an effusion into the synovial joint could exert pressure on a nerve-root and set up a sciatica ceasing when the patient bent forwards. In fact, one such case has been described (Kendall, 1972). The myelographic shadow showed no disorder when the spine was straight but, on full lumbar extension, occlusion of the foramen was visible. At laminectomy the capsule of both facet joints was found hypertrophied.

CONCLUSION

The history and clinical signs are usually inconsistent with ascription of the trouble to a facet joint. Since gross lesions of the facet joints cause neither backache nor disease elsewhere, it is most unlikely

that a minor transient lesion "without irreversible change" could have any effect.

"FACET LOCKING"

Not only is this phrase a misnomer but the practice of "facet-locking" forces the osteopath to use methods of considerable complexity, less likely to succeed than the much simpler manœuvres of orthopaedic medicine, since the joints are crowded together instead of pulled apart.

Facet-locking was devised as a method of moving one joint at a time, and is based on the idea that each succeeding spinal joint reaches full range before the next starts to move. In fact, locking in the medical sense (as correctly applied to meniscal displacement at the knee), is absent. When a facet joint is forced to full range, it cannot—like any other joint—move any further. Locking is now merely a faulty description of the maintenance of a joint at its extreme position. When the facet joints are thus fixed, any further strain, so osteopathic theory goes, falls only on the joint it is proposed to treat. This incorrectly assumes that several adjacent joints can be jammed, leaving the next joint free. Having positioned the joints to their satisfaction, they then apply distant leverage. If the cause of spinal trouble were stiff joints, this method would possess considerable theoretical justification. Unfortunately, this is not so, as has been proved by myelography, discography and at laminectomy. A recent protrusion may be found at quite a mobile joint adjacent to one where the disc has atrophied completely but symptomlessly, and virtually no movement exists.

It is obvious that the best way to unlock a joint containing a displacement is to pull the articular surfaces apart as far as possible, thus giving the loose fragment room to move. Osteopaths' pride in having invented "facet-locking", i.e. crowding the joints together, thus prevents them from using traction—the most important adjuvant to spinal manipulation, especially at cervico-thoracic levels. This technical disadvantage stems from their theoretical stance, which forces them to go out of their way to make things difficult for themselves. In consequence they have unnecessary failures or require too many sessions of treatment. No wonder that osteopathic text-books contain all sorts of warnings restricting their work in a way that dpes not apply to orthopaedic medical methods.

OSTEOPATHIC LOCALISATION

Palpation of the spinal joints for restricted movement at each separate level is ascertained by mobility tests. At the lumbar spine, the test is carried out by laying the patient on his side and flexing both hips to 90°. By moving the thighs a little to and fro, the lumbar spine can be alternatively slightly flexed and extended, and the palpating finger on each spinous process in turn can feel each lumbar vertebra move. Lumbar side-flexion at each joint can also be tested seriatim in the same position. These tests are perfectly reasonable, but they are based on the idea that if restricted mobility is discovered, this is the level at which the patient's trouble lies. There would thus be nothing unreasonable in a spinal lesion at, say, the first or second lumbar level being held to cause sciatica. For that matter, a patient with lumbar pain, in whom restricted movement at a cervical joint had been found, might well receive treatment to his painless neck (sometimes with unfortunate results).

These findings appear objective to lay manipulators but are very difficult to demonstrate to others. In England, the repeated invitation to osteopaths made, particularly by Brewerton, for a trial merely involving two osteopaths working in separate rooms declaring their findings on the same patient, have so far been consistently refused. An even simpler test would be to take fifty normal people, of whom say ten had sacralisation fixing the fifth lumbar vertebra to the sacrum, and ask an osteopath to identify them.

In 1973, I attended a congress where five expert osteopathically-trained physiotherapists gave their opinion on the lesion at a doctor's painful neck. No two opinions were alike; they varied between the third cervical and the second thoracic levels, and there was no agreement on whether the rotation deformity was to the left or to the right.

I have always been very doubtful about the alleged sensitivity of osteopaths' palpation. At regular intervals, I see patients with chronic ankylosing spondylitis causing visible restriction of lumbar spinal movements. Many of these have had manipulation from osteopaths, who did not perceive that the limitation of movement was too general and too severe for any "osteopathic lesion". Hence, medical men have good reason to question the accuracy and the validity of these palpatory findings. Moreover, the restricted

mobility, the displacement and the muscle-spasm that these men feel do not have to be painful, nor to provoke the patient's symptoms, nor to exist at a relevant level, to lead to treatment at that joint. Since nearly all elderly patients have limited movement at their spinal joints, this customary stiffness enables spinal manipulation always to be recommended; it is also put forward as preventing the development of degenerative disease. As the public regards the spine as the main nerve-centre controlling processes all over the body, drawing no distinction between the spinal cord with its nerves and the vertebral column—merely a series of bones and joints—the argument receives much credence. This reliance on palpation makes it quite possible for the layman to maintain that he has completed his task when palpation "informs" him that full mobility has been restored to all the joints of the spine. This attitude enables him with apparent sincerity to claim success while that patient remains in as much pain as ever. In my view, all manipulators would do far better to discover at which joint movement reproduces the patient's symptoms, to have regard to what is and is not anatomically possible, and to leave alone structures which are causing the patient no trouble.

OSTEOPATHIC TECHNIQUE

Osteopaths use two entirely different sets of movements which they describe as "articulation" and "manipulation". By "articulation", they mean rhythmic movements within the painless range repeated smoothly for several minutes. They are pleasant, are performed by distant leverage, and involve chiefly circumduction or gliding movements. By "manipulation", they mean taking the joint as far as is possible until the tissue-tension informs them that the extreme of ordinary range has been reached, and then applying overpressure. They use leverage: e.g. rotation of thorax on pelvis, placing their fingers on a spinous process imagining that such digital pressure can localise the movement to the very joint selected. They go to great trouble to fix the spine in the suitable position, to lock the facets above and below the joint to be manipulated and, in general, are quite gentle. Some of the techniques are difficult to learn. All this is quite admirable and very impressive as a technical achievement. However, the question must arise whether their diagnostic criterion (palpable stiffness) enables them to identify the level of the lesion

that is causing the trouble, let alone whether the patient's symptoms arise from the spine at all. Even if they do, many disc-displacements are irreducible and the discovery of a spinal lesion must be followed by an assessment of whether or not there is any hope of shifting it by manipulation. None of this can be done by palpation and radiography.

Osteopaths allege that their techniques are "specific" i.e. affect one joint only. Since their palpatory efforts at diagnosis often lead them to decide on the wrong level, it is fortunate for them that the specificity is much less than they suppose. It is not uncommon for a patient, whose lesion has been carefully identified by a layman as lying at the first, second or third thoracic level, to develop a cervical root-palsy a week or two later. He has mistaken the tender spot within the area of extra-segmental reference for the actual lesion. There must be many other cases in which the same erroneous localisation is made, but in which the manipulation directed at the wrong joint is eventually successful. There is no doubt therefore in my mind that laymen's endeavour to treat one joint only is, luckily for them, impracticable.

COMPARISON OF TECHNIQUES

In patients with recurrent identical attacks of disc-displacement, on a number of occasions comparisons have been possible between treatment by St. Thomas's methods and by lay-manipulation. At the neck, I am confident that our methods are the better, one or two treatments sufficing in cases that had previously required up to, say, ten visits or even had proved entirely refractory to osteopathy or chiropraxy. Moreover, manipulation is agreed amongst laymen to be unsuited to acute torticollis; given the methods they use, I agree. But it can be treated with immediate improvement our way. Moreover, for central disc-protrusion, I regard both osteopathy and chiropraxy (and manipulation under anaesthesia) as strongly contra-indicated, the absence of really strong traction and the forcing of considerable movement both rendering manipulation dangerous. Reduction is so simple at the thoracic joints that I doubt if there is an appreciable difference, but the fact that we always manipulate this part of the spine during traction has prevented the occasional case of damage to the spinal cord that results from other techniques. At the lumbar spine we have the advantage of being able to benefit

by manipulation almost every case of acute lumbago, whereas osteopaths, using different methods, have learnt not to and often are obliged to recommend rest in bed.

Comment

It is not the elegance or alleged specificity of some manœuvre that matters, it is its therapeutic effectiveness. Crowding the facets together has no virtue in itself; indeed it diminishes the likelihood of success. Traction certainly is helpful in that respect. Methods evolved a hundred years ago for shifting a vertebra—now no longer regarded by osteopaths as displaced—should be superceded. Lay manipulators are invited to take stock of their methods and consider reappraisal.

THE VIRTUES OF OSTEOPATHY

Readers will have noted that there is much to criticise in osteopathic *theory*. However, the public cares nothing for theory, and osteopathic intention is at least to manipulate those spinal joints that need manipulation. Osteopathy, in this type of case, has more to recommend it than the inaction that so many patients they see have suffered from. In Britain, until 1916, when Mennell first tried to put manipulation on the map by introducing it at a teaching hospital, the osteopaths and chiropractors were virtually the only people who kept the idea of spinal manipulation alive. After that year, he and later myself conducted a long struggle (which still goes on) to get this measure accepted. Now the osteopaths unwittingly worked against us, antagonising medical men by the doctrine of an "osteopathic lesion", a near-panacea and an alternative system of Medicine. Had it not been for this insistence, prejudice against spinal manipulation would have abated years ago, especially once the acceptance of disc-lesions served to explain the therapeutic mechanism. We must, however, give them credit as all but the only advocates during the early years of this century.

Osteopaths do cure some of their clients. One of my registrars, who had completed the nine-months' course at the London College of Osteopathy, took over a deceased osteopath's practice for a short time; he put the proportion at one in ten. The repute that the general public accords them (Noel-Baker, 1963) shows how pleased people

are when, after perhaps months of physiotherapy under the best auspices, they are put right by a few simple manœuvres. It is useless for doctors to deride a method when a patient knows that it was just this way that a neighbour was put right a short time ago. It serves only to show him that doctors have a blind spot about spinal manipulation. If doctors want to take action to eliminate manipulating laymen, they must accept manipulation of the spine as a useful treatment, and then use better techniques with a more informed selection of patients. This presents no difficulty.

Many busy and intelligent people recognise, but wonder at, doctors' prejudice against spinal manipulation. Anxious to get well and return to work, many individuals bypass their doctors and go straight to an osteopath when they suffer trouble in neck or back. They even pay for a valued employee to go too. Often these clients are correct in deciding that spinal manipulation is what they need. Such clients are these laymen's best advertisement.

Osteopaths benefit the Nation by helping to keep people at work in a variety of disorders which the National Health Service is not geared at all to treat. For the time being, until this gap in medical work can be closed, the osteopaths are useful citizens; for it is clearly better that the hiatus should be filled by such laymen than no one at all. Until physiotherapists learn to take over, they continue to provide a useful service. For that fraction of their work that was effective in past times, we must give them their due.

XIII

Chiropractice, Naprapathy and Bonesetting

Chiropractice was founded by Palmer in 1895 after he had cured a patient of deafness by manipulating his neck. It seems that his knowledge of anatomy did not lead him to realise that the relevant nerve was wholly intracranial and could not be affected by anything done to a cervical vertebra. The idea of chiropractice was then, and is now, to put the vertebra back into place. Curiously enough, this brings them closer to Still's original idea of a displaced vertebra than today's osteopaths, whose intention has been altered to restoration of mobility at a stiff spinal joint.

During the enquiry into lay manipulation at the House of Lords in 1925, chiropractice was modestly described as the "science of palpating and adjusting the articulations of the human spinal column by hand only". This is a perfectly acceptable statement, for "adjusting an articulation" by hand can only mean manipulating a joint. The word "adjust" presupposes a displacement. Since a fragment of disc often becomes subluxated within a spinal joint—as indeed is apt to happen at any joint containing cartilage—this description is well in line with recognised pathological events. But chiropractors do not now stop at that. The official statement of the International Chiropractors' Association declares that it "is based on the premise that disease or abnormal function is caused by interference with nerve transmission and expression, due to pressure strain or tension on the spinal cord or the spinal nerves as the result of bony segments of the vertebral column deviating from their normal juxtaposition". Unfortunately, in this definition they have expanded the theory to include the cure of all disease. Since every tissue has nerves, so runs their argument, and all nerves emerge primarily from the spine, to treat the joints of the spinal column provides a panacea. They do not

take into consideration that the cranial nerves, e.g. the vagus, do not issue from the spine at all. They also forget that the intervertebral discs, the very tissues that their manipulations (in my view) do affect, are devoid of nerves. They also wrongly equate treating the bones and joints of the vertebral column with treating the nerves. The bones merely provide a framework within which the spinal cord lies, with foramina of exit for the nerve-roots. Treating the bones has nothing to do with treating adjacent nerves, any more than treating the skull is the same as treating the brain. They share osteopaths' view that their manipulations alter autonomic tone beneficially and lastingly.

CHIROPRACTICE AS A PANACEA

This is the most objectionable part of chiropractic dogma.

One chart that they use shows a human figure with arrows pointing to the neck, where the diseases "caused by vertebrae in the spinal cord slipping slightly and causing nerve pressure" include headache, epilepsy, insomnia, dizziness, emotional disturbance, sore throat, bursitis and thyroid trouble. At the upper thoracic spine, asthma, "difficult breathing and other lung troubles" may result. Lesions at mid-thoracic levels are alleged to cause enlargement of the spleen, stomach and liver troubles. Lower thoracic displacements set up disturbance in the upper bowel, gall-bladder trouble and shingles. At the lumbo-thoracic level, kidney disease, arthritis and skin disease result, it appears. In the lumbar region, sacro-iliac slip, constipation and rectal disease are held to ensue. Finally, "slippage of one or both pelvic bones sets up", it seems, "sciatica, many bladder and reproductive organ disturbances". All this headed: "Have you been introduced to Modern Chiropractice?" One earnestly hopes not. I have in my possession a book published in 1952 by a chiropractor called Garcia in London, which includes typhoid fever and tuberculosis as indications for chiropractice. Neither disease is common in Britain and one wonders whether he really encountered these diseases often enough to form a sound opinion on the effectiveness of his adjustments. Each thoracic vertebra was credited with associations; the second being manipulated for heart disease, the third for lung troubles, the fourth for disorders of the liver, and so on. Chiropractors' manipulations are more obviously exact than osteopaths'; for they use strong pressure

at one particular point, applying a direct manual thrust on the vertebra they hold to be at fault, again as a result of palpation. They make a speciality of manipulating the occiput, atlas and axis, and there exists an extreme sect among them which regards manipulation of the upper two joints of the neck as enough for all purposes, even sciatica.

STATISTICS ON CHIROPRACTICE

Various tables listing diseases have appeared, many under the name of the Parker Chiropractic Research Foundation. One is reproduced in Smith's book (1969). The figures were based on an analysis of a quarter of a million cases and some specimen figures are given below of the number of manipulative sessions necessary to effect cure: Acne 28. Angina 31. Appendicitis 22. Arthritis 49. Diabetes 51. Epilepsy 76. Haemorrhoids 51. Hyperpiesis 32. Jaundice 84. Obesity 47. Parkinsonism 58. Pneumonia 29. Renal disease 43. Rheumatic fever 52. Ulcer 46.

Figures are set out relating to the proportion of all patients offering themselves to those accepted for treatment. These are largely in the 80 to 90 per cent. range. The lowest is "paralysis" of whom only 74 per cent. were accepted; the next lowest is goitre at 82 per cent. The highest figure was 98 per cent. for headache, sacro-iliac disorders, neuritis and general back disorders. Neuralgia and spinal curvature were included at 97 per cent., with rheumatism and indigestion at 96 per cent.

The percentage of cures ("well, or much improved") varied from nausea 100 per cent., via pleurisy 95 per cent. to allergy, anaemia, menstrual, kidney and liver disorders, all in the eighties, to tension, high and low blood pressure, menopausal disorders and rheumatism (all in the seventies), to the lowest figure of 69 per cent. for paralysis.

The highest percentage for those made worse by chiropractice was for kidney disorders (4·8 per cent.); general weakness was next at 4·3; next was spinal curvature at 2·8 per cent. This is surprising; for scoliosis is the result of bony deformity and no sort of manipulation has any effect for better or worse. Migraine (2·4 per cent.), general tension (2·2 per cent.), paralysis (2·1 per cent.) and bronchitis (2·0 per cent.) were next. In many disorders, 0 per cent. of patients reported aggravation, amongst whom were cases of backache, bursitis, gall-bladder and liver disease.

Figures more or less identical with these were published as a broadsheet printed to resemble a newspaper and sent round to householders in South Australia in 1970; I have them in my possession now.

Strohmeyer (1960) described 40 cases of paraplegia brought to his neurosurgical hospital in Bremen in one year; of these, 28 resulted from chiropractic manipulation. This is not an argument against chiropractice as a manual method, but a strong indictment of the clinical grounds on which these practitioners select their cases, at least in Germany. I doubt if manipulation carried out in the osteopathic manner by distant leverage would have been so damaging as their strong direct thrust.

THE DISADVANTAGES OF CHIROPRACTICE

As things are today I regard osteopaths as performing a useful function, which will need to be continued until doctors and trained physiotherapists are available in sufficient numbers to take over. Until all those patients who need spinal manipulation receive it through or from their doctor, osteopaths are worth retaining for the useful fraction of their work.

Chiropractors are far more commercial and, as the lists they publish show, are entirely carefree in their choice of patients and diseases. They batten much more obviously on their clients. They get a patient who is wavering on the telephone to come by assuring him that the first consultation is free . . . . but he soon finds that the first manipulative treatment is not. They often assert that, say, twenty or thirty sessions will be required and attempt to get a large fee at once by explaining that the total sum is reduced for those who pay for the entire sequence in advance. They have been known to tell patients with pins and needles that "creeping paralysis" is in the offing, which can be kept at bay only by a weekly treatment continued indefinitely. They also use the word "yet" very cunningly. If the patient has, say, a bad shoulder, the chiropractor may examine the normal shoulder and remark that "there is no trouble on that side . . . *yet*". In conversation, Le Riche called it to me: "The Yet disease."

Unscrupulous methods of this sort for getting clients to come for repeated treatment have been reported as forming part of official chiropractic policy and of the tuition offered at some of the chiropractic schools in the U.S.A.

I have also found chiropractic technique inferior to osteopathic. It is quite a frequent occurrence to find that one manipulation of the orthopaedic medical sort will relieve fully a patient who has had endless—over fifty to a hundred—chiropractic manipulations. This is more seldom so with osteopathy. All in all, it is my view that the disadvantages of chiropractice outweigh the advantages. In Canada, a great tribute to the effectiveness of spinal manipulation by physiotherapists was paid by the chiropractors in 1974. They presented a petition to the Minister of Health in Ontario, complaining of encroachment, praying that physiotherapists should be prohibited from manipulating the spine. One wonders if this plea was activated by comcern for their patients or for their own livelihood.

NAPRAPATHY

According to my uncle, R. J. Cyriax (1912), one of the six schools of chiropractice in the U.S.A. "tried to disown its parentage by changing its name to 'naprapathy' ". Information that he derived from the Oakley-Smith College in Chicago, formed in 1908, revealed that the naprapathic lesion was shortened ligaments ("ligatights") which pulled "the bones too close together", bringing a pinching pressure to bear on the nerves and bloodvessels. He noted that headache, deafness, gallstones and an enlarged liver were alleged to result from such ligamentous contracture.

The sect has a topical interest; for there is a school of Naprapathy in Stockholm today.

BONESETTING

This craft started centuries ago and continues now in the country districts of Britain. Already in 1676, Wiseman was deploring bone-setters' activities. The laymen who call themselves bone-setters are largely individuals who have an inborn flair for manipulation, or come from a family that has practised it for generations.

The bone-setter does not set bones in the meaning of today—that is, reduce dislocations or fractures—but manipulates, alleging that he adjusts minor bony displacements only. He regards the click as a fragment of cartilage shifts, or the snap as an adhesion parts, as

evidence that "the bone has been put back". This is not so, of course, as an X-ray photograph soon shows.

Bone-setters do not profess any cult; they have no theories on disease; they merely manipulate to the best of their ability those who come to visit them. There is a certain rough honesty here, even if their idea of what occurs is mistaken. I regard their infectious belief in their own powers as quite sincere.

XIV

Teaching Manipulation

It is a sad fact that in Britain there is no centre which a doctor or a physiotherapist who wants to learn manipulation can attend. The osteopaths offer laymen a four-year course; they are also prepared to teach physiotherapists in two years and doctors in nine months. But at both the schools of osteopathy in London, pupils get embroiled in osteopathic lesions, autonomic effects, etc. Moreover, to spend four years learning how to manipulate the spine (which I teach my students in a few months, with equivalent therapeutic results) is a huge waste of time and money. I am sorry therefore that no Institute of Orthopaedic Medicine has been founded as a centre for amongst other things, non-cultist teaching on the indications for, and manner of, manipulation.

SHOULD MANIPULATION BE TAUGHT?

The answer can only be "yes". All medical students are grounded as a matter of course in the simpler techniques that are appropriate to everyday medical practice. There is only one exception: manipulation. Since a day does not pass without the family doctor seeing at least one patient who needs a simple manipulation, most often for an early disc-displacement, it is obvious that this is one of the methods which every doctor needs to know. Yet, today, students are taught nothing of these methods; for they are very seldom applicable to the cases that require admission to the wards, where the bulk of tuition is carried out. Out-patient manipulation is seldom performed at a teaching hospital. Indeed, the only time when a student is likely to hear about manipulation is when a patient with severe sciatica, on whom it has failed, is admitted to hospital. He then hears

the method derided, but derided unjustly; for in nearly all these cases strong contra-indications to manipulation would have been discovered had the manipulating layman known, in the first place, how to examine the patient and, in the second, understood the implications of the signs that would then have been elicited.

WHO SHOULD BE TAUGHT?

Doctors and Medical Students

Obviously, not all doctors wish to manipulate, any more than all of them want to aspirate a pleural effusion or remove an appendix. But they have all, while undergraduates, seen aspiration and abdominal surgery carried out and thus possess no prejudices based on ignorance of these procedures. As regards manipulation, the doctor should have learnt that: (*a*) it is a proper medical treatment; (*b*) what the indications for and against are; (*c*) how to set about getting it done if he does not wish to do it himself. Medical students, in short, should be shown manipulation in action (as I used to do), and have it explained to them when and when not it is called for. For those who want more knowledge, there should then be house-physician posts and registrarships. Clearly, all doctors should know at least the indications for manipulation, and some (certainly one on the staff of every teaching hospital) should know a great deal.

Doctors' natural prejudice against an unknown method, is best avioded by demonstrations. A patient with lumbago should be shown to the students, the physical signs pointed out and a session of manipulation given there and then, so that they can see how the signs regress during reduction. They can then be in no doubt about manipulation and will have no prejudice against it in their graduate years. Until this policy is followed at all teaching hospitals, our neglect will continue to provide endless cases for lay manipulators. Yet it is clearly undesirable that patients should be driven to find some laymen as best they can, at their own expense, at a time when the State has taken over the provision of all necessary medical care. Moreover, less than no guarantee exists that the manipulator once unearthed has any competence whatever.

The Royal Commission in 1935 estimated that there were between two and three thousand lay manipulators in Britain. Recognition of the disc-lesion has improved their theoretical position and their

numbers must have increased. There are three hundred names on the osteopathic register, so the seeker's chances of running into a manipulator with any sort of training may be as low as one in ten. This sorry situation is well known to all family doctors, but the entire resources of Great Britain appear powerless to alter it.

Everyone knows that family doctors may give patients an unofficial tip to try a lay manipulator. They have no option today, but they do not then indicate to him where treatment should be concentrated. This is a pity; for these laymen look for limited spinal movement and muscle guarding, and thus may well manipulate the wrong spinal joint. Doctors know what is and what is not anatomically possible and naturally look for what movements bring on or exacerbate patients' pain, drawing deductions from these signs. This is a different approach, leading medical men to the right spot. It would thus be far better, when this approach is employed, for the doctor to inform the layman, even if only by word of mouth, where the lesion lies. Having worked all his life outside the medical sphere, the layman may not care to be told where the patient's disorder is situated, but it is in the patient's interest that the information should be passed on. By contrast, this is exactly what the physiotherapist is accustomed to and expects.

If some grounding, however sketchy, were given to medical students, there would eventually be enough adequate manipulators to go round. It forms part of laymen's propaganda that it is dangerous to teach a little manipulation to doctors. I disagree; is it, for example, dangerous to teach them a little appendicectomy or a smattering of reduction of a fracture? Spinal manipulation, even carried out imperfectly, does good to a reasonable number of patients. After all, it is always open to the doctor to sent his resistant cases to an expert. Spinal manipulation poorly performed on a conscious patient rarely does any particular harm; it merely fails to cure a relievable pain. If this were not so, the hundreds of blithe manipulators—the majority—who have never had any organised tuition would have landed themselves in trouble long ago.

Giving students a grounding in manipulation would have another advantage: the proper use of such trained manipulators as do exist. Once doctors realise that it is a rational treatment, they will countenance, even encourage, its performance. Recent physiotherapy graduates of mine write me sad letters telling me that their new department contains strong young men, disabled by bad backs, actually diagnosed as caused by a displacement, anxious to return to

work, who have been attending hospital for months of heat and exercises . . . and when she asks the doctor-in-charge for permission to manipulate, he refuses. Bare favourable mention of manipulation for a displaced fragment of disc during his student days would have avoided so absurd a situation.

Physiotherapists. This subject is dealt with in chapter XV.

WHO SHOULD TEACH MANIPULATION?

Only those who practise manipulation should teach it. Clearly, medical men who employ this measure with discrimination and skill are the best placed to give useful tuition. There should be one such at every teaching hospital. His course of say six lecture-demonstrations a year should include not only manipulative reduction at neck and lower back, but also the induction of epidural local anaesthesia and the injection of a steroid suspension into joints and tendons. During my days at St. Thomas's Hospital, this is what was done, and there was also a teaching clinic once a week all the year round. The fact that most medical students became friendly with physiotherapy students played quite a big part in the education of the former in clinical examination and the virtues of manipulation! The result was that our young doctors went out into the world, not knowing much about how to manipulate, it is true, but without prejudice against it. They knew it could be done; they had seen it done; they had in their lecture notes a series of indications and contra-indications to which they could refer. Asking a physiotherapist to carry out manipulative reduction at a spinal joint appeared to them perfectly reasonable. Reason, not emotion, prevailed.

An important point in teaching medical manipulation is that it cannot usefully be taught as just a series of manoeuvres. This is the main fault, as I see it, of all the books on osteopathy which have appeared recently. They merely set out techniques. Far more important is a description of the clinical examination that makes for a clear diagnosis and indicates whether manipulation is required or not and, if not, what alternative measure should be employed. Moreover, any book on manipulation should give equal emphasis to contra-indications as to indications. No such osteopathic book exists. The examination is just as important when progress is assessed during treatment. The osteopath, concerned as he is with moving those spinal joints at which he perceives movement to be limited

until he is satisfied that a proper range has been restored, has little need to consider clinical signs nor even the effect of his treatment on the patient's symptoms. Orthopaedic medicine on the other hand demands a clear view of the whole clinical picture; first one manoeuvre, then a further examination to establish the result, then another manoeuvre, and so on. The manipulator is thus guided towards an effective technique. The necessity for this sequence depends on the fact that examination may show an articular displacement to exist, but cannot indicate whether it has protruded from left or right or centre—in other words, in which direction it needs to be pushed back.

Osteopaths should certainly not be allowed to teach their theories to medical students, since their ideas on pathology and on the effects of manipulation and its indications are not suited to those who: (*a*) have medical examinations to pass; (*b*) have not yet acquired enough basic knowledge to enable them to evaluate dogmatic statements of dubious accuracy. In particular, laymen's habit of manipulating spinal joints at a level whence the symptoms present could not possibly originate, and for autonomic effects, would confuse any medical student hopelessly. So it would physiotherapy students.

Osteopaths are obviously welcome to put forward their theories on the causation of disease during their courses for medical men. In general, doctors are not often able to swallow their hypotheses but may rightly become interested in their techniques.

WHAT METHODS SHOULD BE TAUGHT?

Osteopaths are of course welcome to spend four years teaching their manœuvres—devised originally for shifting a vertebrae—to those who join them. Such a long period of study makes no appeal to doctors and physiotherapists, for whom the methods of orthopaedic medicine are the most suitable. They are simple, safe and quickly learned. As far as the spine is concerned they have a different intention—to reduce a small displaced fragment of disc. The technique is therefore different. This pathological concept has enabled the construction of a system of clinical examination, based on the factual foundation of applied anatomy. This system indicates at once if manipulation is called for and what form it shall take; alternatively when it is useless or likely to prove harmful. Safeguards are observed during the session that warn of any tendency to untoward effects. The clinical

reassessment that follows each manoeuvre allows progress to be followed from minute to minute. End-feel enables the manipulator to decide what to do next, when to go on, when to stop.

These methods rest on the fact that normal joints move freely, whereas the blocked joint does not. If therefore the relevant part of the vertebrael column is moved passively as far as it will comfortably go, the manipulative thrust that follows must fall on the blocked joint. The manipulation cannot fail to be what osteopaths call "specific". They, by contrast, go to great trouble to discern which joint is the stiffest and are then at great pains to manipulate at that level only. Since the stiff joint is often not the one the patient's symptoms stem from, this leads to much waste of effort and unnecessary failure.

I should strongly suggest, therefore, that all doctors and physiotherapists should start by learning my methods. That will not take much of their time. Later, if they wish for a more eclectic repertoire they can then devote many months to developing expertise in oscillatory techniques, osteopathy and chiropractice. But learning something simple, safe and effective before passing on to less direct and more difficult methods seems to me only good sense. There is nothing theoretical about this view which is based on my experience in teaching a thousand physiotherapy students.

SUITABILITY OF OSTEOPATHS FOR THE N.H.S.

In my view, they are unsuitable. Before we can employ manipulative personnel in our hospitals, some guarantee of general education and competence would have to be put forward. Whom is the Health Service to accept? Who can speak for these laymen, so many of whom are self-styled? What diploma do they hold and who granted it? Was the examination conducted by external examiners and what medical men sat on the board? What official medical body supervises the school where budding osteopaths are taught? Can such a body countenance the inclusion of theories in autonomic effects that run counter to the whole of medicine? Is it realistic to suppose that a body of men indoctrinated against doctors' views on disease will adopt the physiotherapists' ethic overnight? What would be the medico-legal position? The outcry if the Ministry of Health accepted all and sundry to treat patients within the Service would stifle such a project at birth.

These facts bring us back to my original proposition: manipulation, under medical control, by trained physiotherapists. Any would-be osteopath would do far better to become a physiotherapy student at a school where manipulation was taught. He would learn much else besides manipulation, and would receive a recognised diploma and State-registration after only three years.

This would raise the status of manipulation. Today, anyone can call himself an osteopath, a chiropractor or a bonesetter without a day's tuition. Indeed, the "Daily Telegraph" (30.6.60) reported the case of a Mrs. de la Warr, D. O., who stated in court that she had obtained a diploma in osteopathy by attending a small school in London once or twice a week for two years. No qualifying examination was held. In 1962, a man describing himself as an osteopath offered "a degree course" in osteopathy for physiotherapists for a payment of 130 guineas. His dupes clearly did not realise that they were entitled to adopt the title without bothering with the course or the fee. Once the public was made aware that (*a*) physiotherapists had State recognition, and (*b*) physiotherapists manipulated—albeit differently—at least as effectively as laymen, this sort of humbug would come to an end.

The more ambitious would-be osteopath, given enough preliminary schooling, should follow the ordinary medical studies and qualify as a doctor. Thereupon he could develop his interest, just as other doctors do in other directions. A surgeon who removes the tonsils still has to learn how a baby is born and how to prescribe a drug; why not the budding manipulator? He has then acquired the knowledge which enables him to examine patients and decide what the lesion present is, and how to treat it, both by—and not by—manipulation. That this is perfectly feasible is evidenced by the fact that there exist no less than forty-eight graduates of the London College practising the osteopathic type of manipulation.

The availability of manipulation—and, with it, lay manipulators' attitude towards doctors—would be radically changed if all the physiotherapists in Britain knew how to manipulate. They would then have to do better than the manipulating physiotherapists in order to go on making a living. This would bring before them the question of diagnosis before manipulation and they might come to realise that just palpating the lumbar spine and looking at an X-ray photograph was not enough. Once diagnosis came to the fore in osteopaths' minds, they would lean towards the medical curriculum, in the endeavour to arrive at a proper selection of cases.

XV

Manipulation by Physiotherapists

This is the obvious solution, as almost every doctor and practicing physiotherapist agrees. The Association of Superintendant Physiotherapists sent a request to this effect to the Chartered Society's Council in 1973. It is the leaders of the profession who are inexplicably hesitant, in spite of Dr. Mennell's and my own experience dating back to 1916.

The orthopaedic physician's approach is easy to teach to students; for it is straight-forward and possesses an explicable basis. Moreover, at her first attempt a student often secures an immediate success. Our methods were thought out on a basis of the reduction of a small fragment of disc. They have no autonomic effects and can thus be safely used on normal people who are suffering purely from a spinal displacement (not that I believe that laymen's manœuvres really affect autonomic tone permanently). These methods are easy to learn and there is considerable irony in the fact that my simple methods are at least as effective as the more elaborate manœuvres used by laymen. Theirs, they insist, take many years to learn; they should know. Mine, when taught to physiotherapy students, take only a few months. Our intention is to render painless such movement as the joint can perform; painless limitation is left alone. Only those joints are manipulated from which symptoms are arising; for example, in sciatica, the lowest two lumber joints are treated, not the neck or the thorax. Treatment is continued until, if possible, the patient has lost all his symptoms; in other words, in orthopaedic medicine, it is the patient who decides when he is well. In my experience, manipulation succeeds in a few sessions or not at all; one to four sessions suffice. If relief has not been secured by then, alternative measures come to the fore. Once reduction has been achieved, stabilising measures intended to diminish the range of

movement at the affected spinal joint are instituted in the hope of preventing recurrence. This is the exact opposite of the restoration of full range that the osteopaths try to secure. We do not treat visceral disease by manipulation, only those cases of anterior thoracic or abdominal symptoms due to root pain which has been mistaken for visceral disease.

It is easy to see how doctors may disagree on the value of, and indications for, manipulation, when they see only the results of laymen's treatment in suitable and unsuitable cases alike, carried out with methods and intentions that conflict.

Manipulative work calls for more time and paraphernalia than a busy doctor in family practice can well afford. Today, many have no alternative but to do their own manipulations themselves, whatever the difficulties, but it is clear from the enquiries that I get from all over the country that most medical men would far prefer this work carried out by a properly trained medical auxiliary. There is nothing new in this; for example, nursing, midwifery, occupational and speech therapy, radiography and a number of laboratory tasks are properly performed by trained personnel, none of them doctors. Where are the skilled manipulators taught by doctors and working under medical supervision? Even now, undergraduate tuition is lacking at most of our physiotheraphy schools and such postgraduate courses as exist can cope with only a small fraction of the demand.

There is then no doubt in my mind that family doctors would welcome the emergence of the manipulating physiotherapist. After all, patients needing this treatment are already sent to them as a matter of course, not, it is unfortunately true, for manipulation, but for a series of futile measures that in the case of the spine cannot be dignified by the word "treatment", e.g. heat, massage, exercises. Incorporation of this subject within her undergraduate education would soon lead the family doctor to send the patient for manipulative physiotherapy; this would be faithfully carried out as a matter of course by an auxiliary fully trained in these methods and accustomed to working within the medical profession. The arrangement has already been established in Norway, where a special register of those skilled in such techniques is available to doctors. They can send their patient to a physiotherapist who has, by attending a special course and passing an extra examination, obtained a postgraduate diploma.

I do not include physiotherapists within the term "lay manipulator". It is true that they are not doctors; but no-one regards a

nurse as a layman. The reason is the same for each profession. Both are taught in hospitals by consultants; both subscribe to the same concepts of disease as medical men; both work as students and as graduates with and for doctors. Their syllabus and their examinations conform with standards approved by medical men. Everyone holds both professions to be within the medical sphere. Indeed, no hospital can be properly run without them. None of this applies to lay manipulators who conform in no way to the standards and ethics of medical auxiliaries but set themselves up as alternatives to the medical profession.

In 1938, I started tuition in manipulation for all my physiotherapy students. This was no novelty, since this teaching had also been given by Mennell, my predecessor at St. Thomas's Hospital since 1916, who was also for many years Chairman of Council of the Chartered Society of Physiotherapy. Yet he proved no more successful than myself in getting manipulation taught at all schools. It is my experience that physiotherapists are excellently suited to carrying out the manipulative work that the doctor prescribes, and in the last 35 years I have grounded a thousand in this work. No trail of disasters and crippledom has resulted. They have a practical bent; they are used to working with medical men; they have the anatomical knowledge; their general education and ethics are acceptable; most of them have aptitude and liking for the quick relief afforded by manipulative work. At St. Thomas's they learnt how to carry out the preliminary examination; they also learnt the other methods of treatment that are applicable to cases of locomotor disorders not amenable to manipulation. They have time and patience; they pass examinations held by external examiners under the highest auspices; they become State-registered. What better could anyone ask? Set against the massive lack of knowledge and dubious ethics of the average lay manipulator, the answer is clearer still.

OSCILLATORY TECHNIQUES

These were first recommended by Récamier who employed "percussion cadencée" for acute torticollis in 1838. Manual vibrations were extensively employed by Kellgren, a Swedish physiotherapist working in London at the turn of the century. Maitland of Adelaide. describes manual oscillations in his book, first published in 1964. His method involves a series of alternate antero-posterior pressures and releases given to the affected joint as the patient lies prone. In the

neck and lumbar spine, lateral oscillations can also be employed First, each spinal joint is tested in turn in order to ascertain where pain is provoked or resistance encountered; treatment is concentrated at this level. The manipulator places both thumbs on the tip of the appropriate spinous process and applies his oscillations at the rate of about two a second. Movement is generated by alternately flexing and extending both elbows synchronously, so that a series of little thrusts is delivered to the bone.

These mobilising techniques clearly provide the physiotherapist with a useful addition to those of orthopaedic medicine and, better still, with an introduction to them. She gains confidence from using gentle manœuvres and, if the case responds well—albeit in longer time—need seek no further. They cannot be expected to be as effective in considerable displacements. Then strenuous manipulation during traction must be employed; as soon as she realises that stronger measures are required, she does not hesitate to use them. Ending with such measures is very different from having to plunge straight into effective manœuvres in a case where the physiotherapist is uncertain of her skill or of the exact nature of the lesion, or of the doctor's backing.

FAVOURABLE VIEWS

I am not alone in appreciating the value of manipulation by physiotherapists. My views have been confirmed by experience in Norway, Germany, New Zealand and Australia. Twenty years ago, we took on a Norwegian physiotherapist at St. Thomas's and taught him our methods. He went home and spent a year teaching a group of physiotherapists who were subsequently examined by myself. Those who passed were put on to an register of manipulative physiotherapists, which doctors consult when they need such treatment for a patient. Miss J. Hickling, my senior physiotherapist, lectured all over New Zealand in 1952 and manipulation by physiotherapists is standard practice there. Miss Ganne, a St. Thomas's graduate who is now Vice-Principal of the School of Physiotherapy in Adelaide, teaches the preliminary examination and manipulation to her students as a matter of course. Dr. Peter Hirschfeld came to St. Thomas's some ten years ago and took back with him Miss Longton, my staff physiotherapist at that time. Within a year, the actuary attached to the Health Service of Bremen noted that patients referred to them recovered much more quickly than those treated in the

traditional way. After three years, the Service built him a hospital and put him and Miss Langton in charge of a department of orthopaedic medicine, offering a reduced insurance premium to all employers who guaranteed that, if their workman were injured, they would be sent there.

Sir Walter Mercer, Emeritus Professor of Orthopaedic Surgery, University of Edinburgh, writes in "The Practitioner" (1959): "The physiotherapist has all the basic knowledge of anatomy and joint and muscle work, and the trained hand necessary to enable him or her to learn manipulation, and has always preserved a strictly ethical standard. It is therefore only a question of adding a little more to the curriculum for competence in this matter to be assured."

Clearly then, I am not alone in finding manipulation suited to physiotherapists, provided that proper tuition is given both on identification of the suitable case and the technique required. They became as proficient in this part of their work as could be expected of any student—certainly expert enough to obtain consistent good results. It is a proven fact, therefore, that physiotherapists can be taught this work and are well able to carry it out. Oddly enough, my advocacy (Cyriax, 1950) of traction by physiotherapists for the reduction of nuclear lumbar protrusions has been universally recognised, whereas that of manipulation for cartilaginous displacements is still largely ignored. Yet one is as logical as the other.

Large numbers of physiotherapists skilled in manipulation are required today. Our hospitals are full of patients lingering on in pain and off work for lack of a physiotherapist there able to manipulate. In consequence, patients are fobbed off with heat, massage and exercises, at great cost to the community, which pays for the Sickness Benefit as well as the useless hospital treatment. This brings doctors' and physiotherapists' work into disrepute, and gives laymen a series of gratuitous advertisements. The situation calls loudly for reversal.

ADVERSE OPINIONS

What the critics of manipulation do not realise is that deprecation of manipulation in general, or its performance by physiotherapists in particular, has the contrary effect to that intended. Such opposition does nothing to diminish recourse to manipulation; it serves merely to perpetuate its performance by laymen outside medical control.

Indeed, these laymen's present prosperity depends largely on doctors refusing to ask for the reduction of their patients' disc lesions by physiotherapists. Surely, even the most hardened critic of manipulation must regard manipulation by trained physiotherapists as one better than the present stream to largely self-styled laymen.

It is hardly surprising that my advocacy of manipulation by physiotherapists is greatly resented by osteopaths, who see their livelihood threatened. At first they were understandably worried, but recent events have reassured them. It is a curious paradox that so far they have every reason to be grateful not only to the leaders of the Chartered Society of Physiotherapy but also to myself. My endeavours have had exactly the contrary effect to that intended. In lectures, articles and books my advocacy of manipulation has not been without effect. Many doctors have accepted this challenge and manipulate in suitable cases themselves, with excellent results. Others, following my suggested alternative, have asked the physiotherapist to carry out this treatment. But many physiotherapists have not yet been trained for such work. Their default has forced the doctor who has come to realise that manipulation represents the proper treatment to advise recourse to a lay manipulator. My efforts to dispel the obscurity clouding spinal manipulation and to give it a rational explanation and a good name has, alas, in so far as it has convinced doctors, increased the number of osteopaths' and chiropractors' clients. Hence these laymen are reaping an ever-larger harvest from my endeavours to render them superfluous. Unawares, the Chartered Society of Physiotherapy has held lay manipulators in the hollow of its hand for the last twenty years. During my thirty-five years at St. Thomas's, their policy of withholding tuition on manipulation from their students served only to maintain the prosperity of lay manipulators at the expense of graduates of their own Society. Immediate reversal of this policy might still swing the public round to the physiotherapists' side, though every year of further delay makes such a change of attitude more difficult. At least one teacher conversant with the methods of orthopaedic medicine would be required at each of the forty schools in Britain and the formation of a group of examiners is equally urgent. We must all hope that the Society will rise to the occasion and not let themselves, by default or procrastination, be ousted by laymen from a most rewarding part of their proper work. This is no idle warning; it has already happened in other countries.

XVI

Doctors' Dilemma

It is evident that provision of facilities for diagnosis and treatment within the sphere of orthopaedic medicine is called for urgently, since disorders of this category provide the commonest cause of unnecessary absence from work. As long as this neglect persists—and at the rate of the last thirty years, it would seem indefinitely—so long will lay manipulators remain an unfortunate necessity. But manipulation, without a proper clinical examination first, leads to so many abuses and such waste of time, money and effort that every endeavour should be made to put an end to the call for these men. The question therefore arises of replacing these laymen by pyhsio-therapists trained (as all my students were) in the methods of orthopaedic medicine. The alternative would be to set up a centre where would-be osteopaths could be taught to be ethical manipulative therapists.

ALTERNATIVE PROJECTS

The medical profession will have to make its up mind in the end to whom it wishes to delegate manipulation. Delegation there will have to be, since for many years to come there will exist nothing like enough doctors skilled in this work to go round. Clearly the present situation of two overlapping sets of semi-trained personnel has no advantage.

Do we want an enthusiastic group, eager to carry out this type of work but with, until now, faulty pathological concepts, exaggerated claims and inadequate medical guidance? Osteopathic schools work under disabling conditions. Quite apart from the lack of

teachers of professorial rank, they try to deal with anatomy without cadavers, diseases without hospital beds or postmortem facilities, operations without the possibility of students watching them. None of these restrictions exists in the case of physiotherapy students.

Or do we prefer an orthodox body, whose leaders for thirty years remained lukewarm, to say the least, about my advocacy of manipulation by physiotherapists, but whose schools are provided with everything to be desired in the way of educated students, tuition, clinical material and eminent medical backing? If we opt for this solution, no more need be done than to extend the tuition, that was given from 1916 onwards at St. Thomas's, to every physiotherapy school in Britain. Official insistence at the highest level may well prove necessary, but no real difficulties exist that cannot be overcome by the exercise of goodwill.

Osteopaths

If we choose the osteopaths, great changes will be necessary. Osteopaths would have to drop the notion of practising an alternative system of Medicine, to forget about autonomic tone and curing visceral disease, and hold themselves out as capable manipulators—as some of them are—ready thus to treat patients sent to them with this request by doctors. They would have to withdraw from the "osteopathic lesion" as the important factor in the development of disease, and agree that fixation of a spinal joint has a local effect only. Such reorientation of their thought and restriction of their sphere would not suit their leaders, who naturally enjoy the public's acceptance of their aura of mysticism. New tuition in keeping with the tenets of normal Medicine would have to be instituted, as has in fact already happened to osteopathy in the U.S.A. (Over there, it is the chiropractors who have taken over the panacea aspect of manipulation.) They would need to seek medical guidance and supervision, to arrange for joint lectures in anatomy and physiology at teaching hospitals and accept outside medically-qualified examiners of suitable standing. They would also be expected to conform to the ethics of the professions ancillary to Medicine. In due course, reproach against osteopaths would cease and official acceptance and State registration would follow. Doctors wishing for manipulative treatment for thier patients would merely consult the Register.

Recognition presupposes proper training of suitably educated students, followed by adequate examinations. This is a great draw-

back to those who, without any preliminary training, wish to treat—and be paid for treating—patients. They would be kept out. By contrast, recognition would prove beneficial to the status of reputable manipulators. Registration would follow and would, in the long run—as happened in the past to doctors and dentists—result in the virtual restriction of manipulative work to those who had been taught how to do it: an undeniable advantage. Doctors would recommend only registered manipulators; the public, no longer forced to go to laymen, would insist on treatment only from a qualified manipulator. Doctors, finding themselves in control of the availability of manipulation, would drop their concern and, in due course, prejudice would cease. This situation would redound to the public interest, since patients, now denied such treatment, would instead receive it from trained personnel via their doctor. The status of manipulation would rise, carrying with it those who practised it. Everyone would benefit from regularisation of the position. By submitting to the same discipline as other professions auxiliary to medicine, the manipulators of tomorrow would come to enjoy the same benefits as other professional people.

Financial Consideration

Osteopaths' first objection to this policy would be financial. Though these laymen often complain to their clients that doctors are too conservative to recognise them, they would be the first to complain if they were recognised. If today's osteopaths were offered employment within the Health Service at a physiotherapist's salary, they would regard the suggestion as derisory. They do far better on their own. But for the existence of the School at St. Thomas's over the past 57 years, the osteopaths would have enjoyed a monopoly in manipulators and now, when doctors are beginning to recognise the value of manipulation, they would have had it all their own way. Doctors would be applying to them cap in hand. Lately, however, they have become increasingly aware of the danger to them of my policy of manipulation by physiotherapists. It is true that the principal of their School proudly announced in 1969 that my efforts to transfer public confidence in manipulation from osteopaths to physiotherapists had failed. Time will yet show, and it may well be that osteopaths today are in a more pliable mood than at any previous time this century. The present may well, therefore, be a good moment for an attempt to bring sense and order into the provision of manual

treatment for those who need it. If all physiotherapy students were taught the clinical and manual aspect of orthopeadic medicine, osteopaths' survival would be in jeopardy. They would have to ask themselves two vital questions that have not cropped up before: (1) Is osteopathic diagnosis enough? Does it follow that, because palpatory findings at the spinal joints reveal stiffness, here lies the cause of the disease present? (2) Are the techniques of osteopathy necessarily the most effective methods of spinal manipulation? This they take for granted, whereas measures invented a hundred years ago for shifting a displaced vertebra may well be less efficient than measures elaborated during the last thirty years for shifting a subluxated fragment of disc. It is not elegance but effectiveness that should govern choice of technique. Doctors, even experienced graduates of the London College, who have tried out both osteopathy and my techniques are by no means unanimously in favour of the former. Hence, this may well be the moment when the financial pressures that osteopaths can see looming will encourage dispassionate evaluation of their policies and beliefs.

Physiotherapists

The continued prosperity of lay manipulators depends on the avoidance of a few simple manœuvres by doctors and physiotherapists. Laymen have understandably cashed in on this hiatus, with the result that many people sidestep their doctor and go straight to an osteopath, and the physiotherapist is being ousted from a legitimate field. This point was cogently made in a letter published in 1971. The President of the Chartered Physiotherapists in Australia stated that in "the course of six years chiropractic has been recognised for Workmen's Compensation and Friendly Societies' rebate and chiropractors' sickness certificates are now accepted by Insurance Companies. It is becoming increasingly obvious that, unless the tide is turned in the near future, manipulation will cease to be the province of the physiotherapist." I could not agree with him more; indeed, he voices the view that I set out before each school of physiotherapy that I lectured at in Australia in 1970. His (and my) proferred solution is undergraduate tuition, and his warning has become amply justified by events since.

Advantages of Physiotherapists

As students, physiotherapists are taught by doctors, work with doctors; mutual regard is established. In consequence, the advantages of manipulation by physiotherapists are overwhelming (Cyriax, 1949, 1970). I have myself taught one thousand in my time, and have found them adept, adequate, interested and successful. Were this tuition extended at all schools, the patient would no longer lie at the mercy of any individual claiming to be a manipulator, whether he had had any training or not. The doctor prescribing treatment would know that it would be faithfully performed by a trained medical auxiliary.

Physiotherapists manipulating would bring further benefits to doctors. The number of journeys he would need to make would, in some common conditions, be greatly diminished. For example, by asking a physiotherapist to go round to a patient's house and manipulate for lumbago, one home visit instead of six from the doctor might well suffice. Again, if a patient were off work for only a few days instead of several weeks, not only would it spare him unnecessary pain, but also Sickness Benefit a great deal of money. This is made only too clear by the astonishing statistics from Glasgow (1967). Finally, the tendency to regard disc-lesions as a good opportunity for prolonged invalidism, compensation claims, neurasthenia and lawsuits would scarcely arise. Brisk and effective treatment would not allow time for the introspection which allows these complications to burgeon.

It can be argued that an occasional difficult case in a strong heavy man might prove beyond a girl's capabilities. This is true, but it would also be beyond a small, old or frail doctor or osteopath. Moreover, there are male physiotherapists, to whom the profession would become economically practicable if they all became trained manipulators able, in eventual private practice, at least to equal the earnings of untrained laymen. Those who aver that manipulation, especially spinal, is dangerous on account of the "hypermobile segment"—a cautionary concept whereby osteopaths seek to frighten physiotherapists—and those who maintain that it takes many years to learn (as do the osteopaths—four years)—should ponder the fact that the majority of lay manipulators in Britain have never had any tuition at all, and yet have amassed many satisfied clients and very rarely figure in actions for damages. If such cheerful

people can manipulate safely, we need scarcely worry about the trained physiotherapist.

Curricular Limitation

The more is the pity, therefore, that in Britain in 1973 the Chartered Society of Physiotherapy issued its revised curriculum in which manipulation was explicitly excluded, mere mobilisation being required. The wording runs: ". . . mobilisation techniques of all joints. It is expected that students should only take these to the point where the movement can be controlled/prevented by the patient." The Society appears oblivious of the fact that it is in the very countries where physiotherapists' tuition is restricted to mobilisation that a degree of State recognition has recently been accorded to chiropractors—Australia, Denmark and Medicare in the U.S.A. It would appear that the public prefers manipulation to mobilisation. Over here, the Society's timorous policy has naturally given an ill-deserved stimulus to osteopaths and chiropractors, conferring as it does permanent inferiority on physiotherapists in dealing with the common spinal disorders. It also makes osteopaths able credibly to claim that they have the only school in Britain teaching manipulation. They tried repeatedly to get this idea over during my time at St. Thomas's, but gave up after they found it equally publicly rebutted each time. But who will contest their assertion now? I sincerely hope that all those who have the welfare of physiotherapists at heart will prevail on the Society to widen the scope of the syllabus to include manipulation. My offer, made in 1970 on my retirement from St. Thomas's Hospital, to hold a series of week-end courses, introducing the subject to all such final-year physiotherapy students as cared to come, has not been welcomed by the Education Committee, though individual students who come on their own initiative regard them as furthering their clinical prowess and manual skill.

The Society must also set about assembling without delay a panel of examiners able to assess candidates' manipulative skill. I took part in such an examination at a course in the Canary Islands in 1973, and though we—Brodin, Cyriax, Frisch and Stoddard—all ourselves employ different methods, we had no difficulty in agreeing who was a competent manipulator and who not.

Bibliography

I. ANCIENT MEDICINE

(*Abû'L Qâsim.*) *F. A. Paneth.* Ueber die echte Schrift Alberts des Grossen "De Alchimia". Jahrbuch 1955, Max-Planck-Gesellsch., pp. 141–59. — His "reposition"-manoeuvres are illustrated in the following manuscripts: Codex 3599 Bibliothèque Mazarine, Paris Codex e Museo 19 in the Bodleian Library, Oxford (both reproduced by *Sudhoff*). — Ms. Huntingdoniensis No. 156 and Ms. Marsh No. 54, Oxford.

(*Apollonius.*) *Schöne, Hermann.* Apollonius von Kitium. Illustrierter Kommentar zu der hippokratischen Schrift Peri Arthron. Leipzig, Teubner, 1896. — *Dietz, Friedrich R.* Scholia in Hippocratem et Galenum. Bd. I. Königsberg 1834 (pp. 1–50). — *Huard, Pierre, & Grmek, M. D.* Mille ans de chirurgie en Occident: Ve–XVe siècles. Paris, Roger Dacosta, 1966 (p. 159 and plate against p. 16).

Avicenna. Liber Canonis . . . Basel 1556. — *Reuben Levy.* Avicenna, his Life and Times. Med. History 1: 249, 1957. — *Otto L. Bettmann.* A Pictorial History of Medicine. Springfield, Ch. T. Thomas, 1956 (p. 59).

Brockbank, W., & Griffiths, D. L. Orthopaedic Surgery in the Sixteenth and Seventeenth Centuries. J. Bone & Joint Surg. 30B: 556, 1948. (See also *Vidius.*)

Galenus. Opera, Vol. IV, Venice 1625. — De locis affectis, Libre I, Chapt. 6. —— Om sjukdomarnas lokalisation. Transl. into Swedish by Acke Renander. Stockholm 1960 (pp. 152–5).

Garrison, Fielding H. An Introduction to the History of Medicine. 4th edit. Philadelphia and London, Saunders, 1929 (pp. 100, 116–17, 125, etc.).

(*Hippokrates.*) Hippocrates, with an English Translation by Dr. E. T. Withington. Vol. III. London, Heinemann, 1944 (pp. 279–307, 373 et seq., 401 et seq., 441–2, 453 et seq.). — The Genuine Works of Hippocrates. Transl. by Fr. Adams. Vols. I–II. London 1849. — *Sawelli Lurje.* Studien ueber Chirurgie der Hippokratiker. Dorpat 1890.

Huard, Pierre, & Grmek, M. D. See Apollonius.

Kendall, P. Hume. A History of Traction. Physiotherapy 41: 177, 1955.

Lewek, Werner L. Die Bank des Hippokrates (c). Janus 40: 21, 1936.

Ligeros, Kleanthes A. How Ancient Healing Governs Modern Therapeutics. New York and London, Putnam, 1937.

MacKinney, L. Medical Illustrations in Mediaeval Manuscripts. London 1965. (= Historical Monograph Series, No. 5, Wellcome Historical Medical Library.)

Olivieri, A. Codices Græci Bonomiensis. Studi Ital. di filol. class. Vol. III, p. 455. (Quot. Schöne.)

Paré, Ambroise. Opera. Liber XV, Cap. XVI, pp. 440–1. Paris 1582. (Also translated into English.)

Schöne, Hermann. See Apollonius.

Scultetus, Johannis (= Johann Schultes). Armamentarium chirurgicum. Lugduni Batavorum (Leyden) 1693, Tab. XXV (II) p. 60, and Tab. XXII (IV) p. 54.

Sudhoff, Karl. Beiträge zur Geschichte der Chirurgie im Mittelalter. Theil I, pp. 4–7 and 64, Tafel XIII, Fig. 7–8. Theil II, pp. 67 and 134. Leipzig 1914–18.

Toth, Andras, Zur Geschichte der Traktionske-Landlung (History of Traction Treatment). Münch. med. Wschr. 112: 479–86, 1970.

Valentin, Bruno. Geschichte der Orthopädie. Stuttgart, Thieme, 1961 (pp. 5–18, 60–1, 75–6, 158–66).

Vidius Vidio. Chirurgia è Graeca in Latinum conversa. Paris 1544 (p. 519). — Ars medicinalis, Vol. III, Venice 1611. — Opera omnia, Frankfurt 1668. — *Conrad Gesner,* De chirurgia scriptores optimi, Zürich 1555. — Collections de chirurgiens grecs, edit. by *Henri Omont*, Paris N.D. (1907). — *Brockbank, William.* The Man who was Vidius. Ann. Royal Coll. Surg. 19: 269, 1956. — *Brockbank, William.* Three Manuscript Precursors of Vidius's Chirurgia. Med. Hist. 2: 191, 1958.

II. FOLK MEDICINE

(For Scandinavian folkloristic literature see Bibliography in Schiötz, 1958).

(*Bernardino di Siena.*) *Zachariae, Theodor.* Abergläubische Meinungen und Gebräuche des Mittelalters in den Predigten Bernardinos von Siena. Z. schr. Volkskunde 22: 113, 1912 (especially p. 126).

Biederman, F. See V Chiropractic. Albert Cramer.

Black, William G. Folk-medicine. London 1883 (p. 137).

Bruce, Ian. The Nun of Lebanon. London, Collins, 1951 (p. 219).

Buckingham, J. S. Travels in Assyria. 2nd edit. London 1830 (Vol. I, pp. 187–191).

Campbell, John G. Witchcraft and Second Sight in the Highlands of Scotland. Glasgow 1902 (p. 100).

(*Cook, James.*) The Journals of James Cook . . . 3. The Voyage 1776–1780. Vol. I, London 1967, pp. 214–15. (= Hakluyt Society, Extra Series, No. 36.) (A journalistic transcription in "National Geographic" Sept. 1971.)

Country Folklore. Northumberland. 1904. London: Nutt. 48

Cramer, Albert. See V Chiropractic.

——. Curious Parallelism of Customs. Notes and Queries, June 20, 1857.

Ellekilde, Hans. Danmarks Folkeminder 28: 106, 1923.

Estlander, J. A. Finska Läk. sällsk. Handl. 14: No. 3, 1872.

Garnett, L. J. The Women of Turkey and their Folklore. Vol. II. London 1891. (On Kurdistan p. 142.)

Granone, F. (Healers and Surgical Mediums in the Philippines). Minerva Med. 63: 2935–55, 1972.

Gregor, Walter. Notes on the Folklore of the North-east of Scotland. London 1881 (pp. 45–6).

Handy, E. S. C., Pukiri, M. K. & Livermore, K. Outline of Hawaiian Physical Therapeutics. Bull. 126, B. P. Bishop Museum, Honolulu 1934 (p. 13).

Henderson, W. Notes on the Folklore of the Northern Counties of England and the Borders. 2nd edit. London 1879 (p. 155).

Horder, Lord. Fifty Years of Medicine. London 1953.

Hovorka, O. von, & Kronfeld, A. Vergleichende Volksmedizin. Bd. II, Stuttgart 1909.

Hunt, Robert. Popular Romances of the West of England (Cornwall). Second Series. London 1865 (p. 212). — A new edition was published 1881.

Illi, F. W. H. (1956). See V Chiropractic.

Kaindl, R. F. Quot. Hovorka & Kornfeld.

Kuzela, Z. Originalmitteilungen über die rutenische und polnische Volksmedizin. Lemberg 1906–7.

Lane, Edward W. An Account of the Manners and Customs of the Modern Egyptians. London 1836.

Larsen, Arnold. Ugeskrift f. Læger 15: 65, 1887.

Leland, Ch. G. Etruscian Romain Remains in Popular Tradition. London 1892 (p. 280).

Liebrecht, Felix. Des Gervasius von Tilbury Otia imperialia. Hannover 1856 (pp. 254 and 434).

Little, E. Graham. Brit. Med. J. 1925 II, 815 (Kipling's "Kim").

Lloyd, L(lewellyn.) Peasant Life in Sweden. London 1870 (p. 148).

Lunde, Peder. Kynnehuset. Christiania (Oslo) 1924 (p. 87).

M'Graith, J. Med. Times & Gaz. 1880 II, 266.

Macgowan, D. J. On the Movement Cure in China. China Inspectorate General of Customs: Medical Reports No. 29, 1884/85 (pp. 42–52).

Mah, K. L. Maker of the Heavenly Hosts. Doctors Only (Benger Lab. Ltd.) 1: No. 6 (Oct.) 1959.

(*Marcellus.*) *Grimm, J.* Ueber Marcellus Burdigalensis. 1849 (pp. 20 and 67).

Mau, C. Verhandl. Dtsch. Orthop. Gesellschaft 80: 59, 1951.

O'Brien, Frederick. Atolls of the Sun. 1922 (pp. 333–4).

O'Suilleabhain, S. O. (1942). Handbook of Irish Folklore. Dublin: Folklore of Ireland Society.

Pontén, Joh. Läke-Bok. Wexjö (Sweden) 1841 (pp. 97–8). A new edition Ekesjö 1851 (p. 208).

Reichborn-Kjennerud, Ingvald. Vår gamle trolldomsmedisin. Bd. IV. Oslo 1944 (pp. 126–30).

Scott, G. R. The Story of Baths and Bathing. London 1939 (pp. 115–18).

Stanhope, Lady. See Ian Bruce.

Steinbeck, John. Quot. Cramer (see V Chiropractic).

(*Thackeray, W. M.*) Notes of a Journey . . . to Grand Cairo. By M. A. Titmarch (pseud.). London 1846 (p. 119).

Tillhagen, C.-H. Folklig läkekonst. Stockholm, LT, 1958 (pp. 225–8).

(*Urquhart, David.*) Manual of the Turkish Bath . . . From Writings of Mr. Urquhart. Edited by *Sir John Fife*, M.D., London, Churchill, 1865 (pp. 27, 72–3, 189).

Wilke, Georg. Die Heilkunde in der europäischen Vorzeit, Leipzig 1936 (p. 281).

Wolff, H.-D. Vorformen chiropraktischer Behandlung. Zschr. f. diagn. u. therap. Sondermeth. 4: 305, 1955.

Wuttke, Ad. Der deutsche Aberglaube der Gegenwart. 2. Ausg. Berlin 1869 (No. 522).

III. BONESETTERS

Barker, Sir Herbert. Leaves from my Life. London, Hutchinson, N. D. (1928).

——. Bone-setting and the Profession. English Review Nov. 1909.— Viz.: Professor Whitehead's vindication on Herbert Barker. Ibid. June 1911.

——. Lancet Sept. 12, 1925, and 1936 II, 252.

——. Manipulative Surgery. Sir Herbert Barker's Demonstration. Brit. Med. J. 1936 II, 233 (Editorial) and 255.

——. Sir Herbert Barker's Methods Filmed. Feature article "Times" July 27, 1939 (re: Leading article, Ibid. Febr. 26, 1937).

——. Obituary. "Times" July 22, 1950.

Bennett, George M. The Art of the Bone-setter. A Testimony and a Vindication. London, T. Murby, N.D. (1884).

Bone-setting. Editorial, Lancet 1871 I, 451.

Bone-setters. Chamber's Journal 1878, pp. 711–13. Referring also to an article "a short time ago" (July 1878) on Dr. *Smiles's* biography of *George Moore*, with an account of a bonesetter in London.

Chapman, Eddie. I Killed to Live. London, Cassell, 1957. (Read in a Norwegian translation, "Drep eller dö", Oslo N.D. (1960); on manipulation of the back pp. 13–15).

Cheselden, Wm. Anatomy of the Human Body. 6th edit., London, Wm. Bowyer, 1741 (pp. 27–38).

Dal Cin, Regina. See Regina.

"*Dorin*". Science or Miracle. Bone-setting in Puttur (India). Illustr. Weekly of India Nov. 8, 1959, pp. 16–18.

Fox, R. Dacre. On Bone-setting (so-called). Lancet 1882 II, 843.

Gerling, R. Sofortige Schmerzstillung durch Handgriffe. Berlin, Wilh. Möller, N.D. (1898). At least five later editions.

Haggard, Howard W. See V, Chiropractic.

Hazard, T. R. Recollections of Olden Times. Newport (U.S.A.), J. P. Sanborn, 1878. (Quot. Joy p. 426.)

Homola, S. See V, Chiropractic.

Hood, Wharton. On the so-called "Bone-setting", its Nature and Results. Lancet 1871 I, 336–8, 372–4, 441–3, 499–501, 631. Also published in book-form:

——. On Bone-setting (so-called) and its Relation to the Treatment of Joints Crippled by Injury. London, Macmillan, 1871.

——. The Treatment of Injuries by Friction and Movement, London, Macmillan, 1902.

Hooker, Worthington. Lessons from the History of Medical Delusions. Fiske Fund Prize Dissertation of the Rhode Island Med. Soc. New York, Baker & Scribner, 1850. (Quot. Joy.)

Hutton, Richard. Obituary. Lancet 1871 I, 63; re: Letters to the Editor. Ibid. pp. 593 and 631. (See also Wharton Hood and Robert Joy.)

Jackson, J. M. "The Bone-setter's Mystery": An Explanation. Boston (England), J. M. Newcomb, 1882. (A 6d. pamphlet).

(*Jones, Sir Robert.*) The Life of Sir Robert Jones. By Frederick Watson. Baltimore 1934. (See also VII, General.)

Joy, Robert T. The Natural Bonesetters . . ., an Early Phase of Orthopedics. Bull. Hist. Med. 28: 416, 1954.

Keith, Sir Arthur. Ancient and Modern Bone-setting. Med. Press & Circ. 106: 482, 1918.

——. Menders of the Maimed. London, Frowde, 1919 (Chapt. 20). Reprinted Philadelphia, Lippincott, 1952.

Le Vay, David. British Bone-setters. Hist. Med. Quart. 3: No. 2, 1971.

(*Mapp, Mrs. Sarah*.) London Mag. 5: 457 and 520, 1736. — Gentlemen's Mag. Oct. 1736. — *J. Cauldfield*. Portraits, Memoirs . . . IV, London 1819 (p. 70). — *C. J. S. Thompson*. The Quacks of Old London. London, Brentano, 1928 (pp. 299–306). — *H. W. Haggard* (see V, Chiropractic), pp. 316–17 and illustr. against p. 50. — *Ronald Pearson*. A Pioneer Bone-setter, Mrs. Sarah Mapp. Practitioner 195: 696, 1965. — *E. J. Trimmer*. Quack Contributors to Orthodox Medicine. Image (Roche) 1965, No. 13, p. 9.

Marlin, Ths. On Bone-setting. Lancet 1932 I, 60.

Marsh, Howard. See VI.

Moulton, Thomas (friar of the Order of St. Augustine). This is the Myrrour or Glasse of Helth Necessary . . . that Wil Kepe their Bodye from the Syckenesse of the Pestilence . . . London, R. Wyer, N.D. (1539(?). — New editions 1545(?), 1546(?), 1550(?); see "A Catalogue of Printed Books in the Wellcome Historical Medical Library. I: Books Printed Before 1641", London 1962.

Moulton, (Thomas). The Compleat Bone-setter, wherein the Method of Curing Broken Bones and Strains and Dislocated Joynts . . . is Fully Demonstrated . . . Written Originally by Friar *Moulton*. Now Revised, Englished, and Enlarged by *R. Turner*. London 1656. — A second edition: The Compleat Bone-setter. Enlarged . . . London, Tho. Rooks, 1665 (for a photograph of the title page see Joy p. 417). This book does not deal with bonesetting as it is understood today, i.e. manipulation of the joints.

Paget, Sir James. Cases that Bone-setters Cure. Brit. Med. J. 1867 I, 1. With some corrections and additions reprinted in:

——. Clinical Lectures and Essays. Edited by Howard Marsh. London 1875 (pp. 84–100). — Second edition London 1879 (pp. 87–103).

Penny, W. J. On Bone-setting. Brit. Med. J. 1888 I, 1102.

"*Pertinax*". Brit. Med. J. 1963 II, 743. Re: Letters to the Editor. Ibid. pp. 889 and 1229.

Phélippeaux. Etude pratique sur les frictions et le massage, ou Guide du médecin masseur. Paris 1870. (An attack on "les rebouteux, rhabilleurs et panseurs"—"these pirates in medicine".) Quot. *C. Curman* (see VI, Mezger).

(*Regina dal Cin.*) *A. Joannides*. Lancet 1871, 734 (short summary). — *J. Nicolaysen*. Norsk Mag. f. Lægevidensk. 3: 38, 1873.

Robertson, George. The Bonesetter and his "Professional Brother". Practitioner 113: 442, 1924.

Romer, Frank. See VI.

Rorie, David. The Scottish Bone-setter. Caledonian Med. J. 5: 2, 1902.

Taylor, John M. Remarks on Mechanotherapy, Massage, Bonesetting and Osteopathy. New York Med. J. 78: 1170, 1903.

(*Thomas, Evan*; Father of Hugh Owen T.) The Life of Sir Robert Jones. By Frederick Watson. Baltimore 1934 (p. 47). See also *Le Vay*.

(*Thomas, Hugh Owen.*) Hugh Owen Thomas, a Personal Study. By *Frederick Watson*. London, H. Milford, 1934 (Chapt. 1). — The Life of Hugh Owen Thomas. By *David le Vay*. Edinburgh, Livingstone, 1956.

Torbet, John. On Diseases Simulating Acute, Inflammatory Attacks. Edinb. Med. & Surg. J. 44: 374, 1835.

Wiseman, Richard. Severall Chirurgicall Treatises. London 1676 (p. 478).

IV. OSTEOPATHY

A. Medical Precursors of the Osteopathic (and Chiropractic) Concept

Blundell, John W. F. Medicina Mechanica, or the Theory and Practice of Active and Passive Exercises and Manipulation. London, Churchill, 1852. (Nothing on the treatment of *back* disorders.)

Brown, Ths. On Irritation of the Spinal Nerves. Glasgow Med. J. 1828, No. 11, p. 131.

Parrish, Isaac. Remarks on Spinal Irritation. J. Med. Sc. 10: 293, 1832.

Player, Richard P. On Irritation of the Spinal Nerves. Quart. J. Science 12: 428, 1822. (Reprinted London Med. & Phys. J. 47: 301, 1822.)

——. On the Morbid Influence of the Spinal Nerves. Ibid. 14: 296, 1823.

Riadore, J. Evans. A Treatise on Irritation of the Spinal Nerves as the Source of . . . Functional and Organical Derangements of the Principal Organs of the Body. London, Churchill, 1842.

Roth, M. The Prevention and Cure of Many Chronic Diseases by Movements. London 1851. — The Movement Cure. London 1856.

Teale, Ths. Pridgin. A Treatise on Neuralgic Diseases, Dependent upon Irritation of the Spinal Marrow and Ganglia of the Sympathetic Nerve. London, S. Highley, 1829. — Another edition Philadelphia, Carey & Hart, 1830. — A new edition Woodstock (Vermont), N. Haskell, 1834.

B. Osteopathy

Osteopathic textbooks.

Journal of the American Osteopathic Association.

Am. Med. Ass. Report of a Committee for the Study of Relations between Osteopathy and Medicine. JAMA 152: 734, 1953 II. — Ibid. 158: 736, 1955 II.

Am. Med. Ass. Policy in Regard to Osteopathy. J. Louisiana State Med. J. 121: 30, 1969.

Am. Med. Ass. Medical Licensure Statistics.

Batchelor, J. S., & Cohen, S. M. Osteopathy. A Visit to the London College. Lancet 1948 II, 1021. (And) Leading article p. 1007. *Discussion* 1949 I, 41, 82–3, 126, 166–7, 240–1.

Booth, E. R. History of Osteopathy. Cincinnati, Caxton Press, 1924.

Braatöy, Trygve. Pasienten og legen. Oslo 1952 (p. 51).

Chesterton, Mrs. Cecil (Ada Elizabeth). This Thy Body. An Experience in Osteopathy. Foreword by Viscount Elibank. London N.D. (1936).

Churchill, Randolph. News of the World Aug. 7, 1960.

Cyriax, James. Osteopathy and Manipulation. London, Lockwood, 1949.

Cyriax, Richard J. Mechanotherapy in America. (I) The Osteopathic Colleges of the United States of America. Svenska gymn. i in- och utlandet 6: 230, 1910.

Dally, P. See V, Chiropractic.

Examination of the Doctrines and Methods of Osteopathy and Chiropractic. Brit. Med. J. 1924 I, 693.

Fishbein, Morris. The Medical Follies. New York, Boni & Liveright, 1925 (pp. 44–72). — Fads and Quackery in Healing. New York, Blue Ribbon Books, 1832 (pp. 76–97).

Haggard, Howard W. See V, Chiropractic.

Hill, Charles & Clegg, H. A. What is Osteopathy? London, Dent, 1937.

Hoad, J. M., Wilbur, V. C., & Spencer, G. B. (editors). Osteopathic Medicine. New York, McGraw-Hill, 1969. 786 pp. On pp. 6–12: *George W. Northup.* The Development of Osteopathic Medicine (on Still, etc.).

Home Study Course in Osteopathy, Massage and Manual Therapeutics. 4th edit. New York, Sydney Flower, N.D. Copyright 1902 by The Psychic Research Co., Chicago.

Keesecker, Raymond P. The Osteopathic Movement in Medicine. A Source Document. Chicago, Am. Osteopathic Ass., 1957.

Lavezzari, R. Une nouvelle méthode clinique et thérapeutique, l'Ostéopathie. Paris 1954.

Laycock, Byron E. Manual of Joint Manipulation. Des Moines, Still College of Osteopathy, 1953.

Little, E. Graham. Registration of Osteopaths. Brit. Med. J. 1925 II, 815.

MacDonald, George, & Hargrave-Wilson, W. The Osteopathic Lesion. London, Heinemann, 1935. — Viz. Lancet 1924 I, 1316.

MacDonald, Norman J. Osteopathy in its Medico-legal Aspects. Lancet 1924 I, 1316.

McKeon, L. C. Floyd. Osteopathy and Chiropractic Explained. London, Butterworth, 1927.

Masset, A, La médecine ostéopathique. Revue Rhum. 17: 273, 1950.

Mellor, Ethel. Manipulation as a Curative Factor. Osteopathy and Medicine. London, Methuen, 1931. (With an extensive bibliography.)

Mercer, Sir Walter. Osteopathy: The Present Position. Practitioner 182: 198, 1959.

Murray, Geoffrey. Fringe Medicine. Spectator Oct. 28, 1960, 644. Discussion: Brit. Med. J. 1960 II, 1299 and 1525–6.

Osteopaths Bill, The. A Report of the Proceedings before a Select Committee of the House of Lords 1935. Brit. Med. J. (Offprint of several articles in Brit. Med. J. March 9–July 27, 1935.)

Reed, Louis. The Healing Cults. A Study of Sectarian Medical Practice, Chicago, Univ. of Chic. Press, 1932.

Roques, K. R. von. Osteopathie und Chiropraktik. Medizinische 9: 291, 1952.

Sodeman, Wm. A. et al. Osteopathy and Medicine. (Congress on Medical Education.) JAMA 209: 85–96, 1969.

Still, Andrew T. Autobiography — with a History of the Discovery and Development of the Science of Osteopathy. Revised edition. Kirksville, Publ. by the Author, 1908.

Still, Andrew T. Osteopathy, Research and Practice. Kirksville 1910.

Stoddard, Alan. Manual of Osteopathic Technique. London, Hutchinson, 1969. — A German edition: Stuttgart, Hippokrates, 1969.

Streeter, Wilfred A. The New Healing. Second edit. London, Methuen, 1932.

Taylor, John M. See III, Bone-setters.

Thierry-Mieg, J. L'ostéopathie. Vie médicale, Avril 1951.

Waring, Sir Holburt J. See V, Chiropractic.

Wilde, Henry. Der osteopathische und chiropraktische Heilkultus in den Vereinigten Staaten von Amerika. Dtsch. med. W. schr. 80: 1056, 1955 II.

V. CHIROPRACTIC

(*U.S.A.*) Independent Practitioners Study. A report of Dec. 28, 1968, by U.S. Department of Health, Education and Welfare (HEW) to the Congress. — Viz. JAMA (Editorial) 208: 352, 1969.

(*U.S.A.*) Independent Practitioners Medicine. (A publication from the same Department, containing the "Study's" introduction, and the complete text as regards chiropractic.)

(*Denmark—Official.*) Indenrigsdepartementets Betænkning No. 560, 1970. Ugeskrift for Læger 132: 603–8, 1970. (From the Home Department.)

(*Norway.*) Kiropraktik. Forslag til lov om kiropraktorers rettigheter og plikter. Tidsskrift f. Den norske Lægefor. 1971, 2352–8. (A declaration from the Norwegian medical association at the request from the Ministry of Health.)

* * *

Anderson, Dewey. The Present Day Doctor of Chiropractic. Washington, Public Affairs Instit., 1956.

Albertini, A. von et al. Gutachten über die Chiropraktik. Zürich, Orell Füssli, 1937.

Ballantine, H. T. jr. Will the Delivery of Health Care be Improved by the Use of Chiropractic Services? New Engl. J. Med. 286: 237–42, 1972.

Bates, D. G. Public Seems Ripe for a little Heresy in Treatment. But can it be Controlled? Can. Med. Ass. J. 108: 647 passim, 1973. — See also Ibid. 108: 792 passim, 1973.

Biedermann, F. Grundsätzliches zur Chiropraktik vom ärztlichen Standpunkt aus. 2nd edit. Ulm, K. F. Haug, 1954.

Bryla, R. On Chiropractors. Phys. Ther. 53: 905, 1973. — Comment: Ibid. 53: 1217–8, 1973.

Buch, H.-J. Ueber Entwicklung und heutige Bedeutung der Chiropraktik. Z.schr. aerztl. Fortbildung 61: 1001, 1967.

Casterline, R. L. Unscientific Cultism: "Dangerous to Your Health". JAMA 219: 1009–10, 1972.

Chiropractic. New Engl. J. Med. 285: 1382–3, 1971.

Chiropractic. (Letter.) Phys. Ther. 53: 1217–8, 1973.

Chiropractic News — The National Health Newspaper. 1st edit. (August 1970). Printed for "Headache and Backache Chiropractic Clinics", Bankstown, Australia. Director: R. C. Roman, D.C. (Broadsheet.)

Chiropractisk Journal. Vols. I–, 1936–. (The Swedish chiropractic journal.)

Chiropractors. S. Afric. Med. J. 45: 161–2, 1971.

Cramer, Albert. Lehrbuch der Chiropraktik der Wirbelsäule. Ulm/Donau, K. F. Haug, 1955.

Cyriax, James. Spinal Manipulation and Chiropractic. Can. Med. Ass. J. 107: 485, 1972.

——. Registration of Chiropractors. Med. J. Austr. 1973 I, 1165.

Cyriax, Richard J. Mechano-therapy in America. II Chiropractic. Svenska gymn. i in- och utlandet, N.S. 2: 117, 1912. — III Naprapathy. Ibid. p. 171.

Dally, Ph. Chiropractors, Ostéopathes, Naturopathes, etc. . . . Presse méd. 42: 1509, 1934 II.

Dickmann, August, M., & Zimmer, G. A. Chiropraktik. Fürth/Bay., A. Dickmann, 1951. (Reviewed Münch. med. Wschr. 95: 617, 1953.)

An Examination of the Doctrines and Methods of Osteopathy and Chiropractic. (Editorial.) Brit. Med. J. 1924 I, 963.

Dintenfass, J. The Administration of Chiropractic in the New York City Medicaid Program. Med. Care 11: 40–51, Febr. 1973. — Comments: Ibid. 11: 436–40, 1973. — Ibid. 11: 441–8, 1973.

Doyle, Kathleen C. Science vs. Chiropractic. New York, Public Affairs Comm. Inc., Pamphlet No. 191, 1953.

Fishbein, Morris. Fads and Quackery in Healing. New York, Blue Ribbon Books, 1932. (On Dr. Abram's "spondylo-therapy" = rapid percussion or hammering, chiropractic, etc.)

Forster, A. L. Die wissenschaftlichen Grundlagen der Chiropraktik. (Translated from the English.) Dresden, Verlag für Volksheilkunde, 1935.

Garsia, Willoughby. The Original "Chiropractic" Spinal Manipulation. London, The True Health Publishing Co., N.D. (1952).

Haggard, Howard W. Devils, Drugs and Doctors. The Story of the Science of Healing. New York & London, Heinemann, 1929.

Holder, A. R. Physician's Records and the Chiropractor. JAMA 224: 1071–2, 1973.

Homola, Samuel. Bonesetting, Chiropractic and Cultism. Panama City (Florida), Critique Books, 1963.

Illi, Fred. W. Die Wahrheit über die Chiropraktik. Bern, Verlag Schweiz. Chiroprakt., 1938. — Kurze Einführung in das Wesen der neuzeitlichen Chiropraktik. Genf 1956. — The Vertebral Column, Life-line of the Body. Chicago. Nat. Coll. of Chir., 1951.

In the Wisdom of Congress. JAMA 211: 1002–3, 1970.

Janse, J., Houser, R. H., & Wells, B. F. Chiropractic Principles and Technic. Chicago, Nat. Coll. of Chir., 1947. (Later editions are published.)

Kiropraktisk Tidsskrift. Copenhagen. (The Danish chiropractic journal, in its 33rd year of issue in 1957.)

Langner, Henri. Médecine et chiropratique. Berne, Assoc. des Chiropratiens Suisses. Berne 1947. (Offprint from the chiropractic journal "Atlas".)

Lodispoto, A. (365 Days of "Heretical Medicine".) Minerva Med. 63: 789–94, 1972 (On the history of chiropractic and acupuncture.)

McKenzie, R. A. Chiropractic Treatment. New Zealand Med. J. 75: 119, 1972.

Maisel, Albert O. Can Chiropractic Cure? Reprinted from "Hygeia" (AMA) 1946. 4th printing 1953.

Nostrums and Quackery. Articles . . . Reprinted from the JAMA. Chicago, Press of AMA, N.D. (ca. 1912). (On the Am. Coll. of Mechano-Therapy pp. 480–6, etc.)

Oger, Jean. La chiropraxie est une forme de l'exercice illégal de l'art de guerir. Arch. Belges Méd. Soc. 22: 147, 1964.

Palmer, Daniel D. The Chiropractor's Adjuster. Portland 1910.

Palmer, B. J. Text Book on the Palmer Technique of Chiropractic. Davenport (Iowa) 1920 (= 1st edit.).

Palmer School of Chiropractic. Announcement. Davenport (1957).

Patchen, Georg H. Den nye fysikalske behandling. Kristiania (= Oslo) 1922. (Translated from an American edition.)

Peper, Werner. Technik der Chiropraktik. 5. Auflage. Ulm/Donau, K. Haug, 1958.

Quackery Persists. JAMA 221: 914, 1972.

Reader, W. L. Chiropractic Practice. New Zealand Med. J. 74: 346, 1971.

Reed, Louis S. The Healing Cults. A Study of Sectarian Medical Practice, Chicago, Univ. of Chic. Press, 1932.

Roques, K. R. von. See IV, Osteopathy.

Rukser, Dieter. Das heisse Eisen Chiropraktik. Rhein. Aerzteblatt 1960, 152 (No. 3).

Singleton-Ward, Richard. My Two Hands Talk. London, Chr. Johnson, N.D. (1957). With a foreword by a Harley Street doctor, under the pseudonym "Marcin Shawn".

Smith, Ralph Lee. At Your Own Risk. The Case Against Chiropractic. New York, Trident Press, 1969.

Stalvey, Richard M. What's New in Chiropractic? New York State J. of Med. 57: 49, 1957.

Turner, Chittenden. The Rise of Chiropractic. Los Angeles, Powell Publ. Co., 1931.

Waring, Sir Holburt J. Osteopathy, Chiropractic, and Medicine. Brit. Med. J. 1925 II, 679. — *Discussion* Ibid. 701–2, 708–9, 767, 815–8, 867–9, 921–2.

Weiant, C. W., & Goldschmidt, S. Medicine and Chiropractic. Third edition. New York (no publisher) 1959. (Printed for the authors?)

Wilbur, R. S. What the Health-care Consumer Should Know about Chiropractic. JAMA 215: 1307–09, 1971.

Wörner. Das sogenannte Nervoskop in der aerztlichen Diagnostik der Wirbelsäulendynamik. Arch. f. physik. Therapie 9: 158, 1957.

VI. EARLY MEDICAL LITERATURE ON MANIPULATION (UP TO 1920)

Adams, Wm. On the Selection of Cases for Forcible Movements in the Treatment of Stiff Joints, and the Method of Procedure. (With discussion.) Brit. Med. J. 1882 II, 666.

Arnold, John P. Some of the Principles of Manual Therapy. Its Application by the Physician. New York Med. J. & Philad. Med. J. 1905, 941.

Atkinson, Jim. Quot. Palmer (see V, Chiropractic).

Bonnet, A. Traité de thérapeutique des maladies articulaires. Paris 1853 (pp. 639–43).

Bryce, Alex. Remarks on Mechano-therapy in Disease: With Special Reference to Osteopathy. Brit. Med. J. 1910 II, 581.

Buck, A. H. A Case Illustrating the Use of Gymnastic Treatment. Brit. Med. J. 1882 II, 1147.

Corner, E. M. Transact. Clin. Soc. London 40: 10, 1907.

Cruveilhier. Du point dorsal et de sa valeur thérapeutique. Bull gén. thérap. méd. et chir. 12: 388, 1837.

(*Cyriax, Edgar F.*). Le docteur Edgar F. Cyriax. (Par) *R. Delval.* L'Encycl. contemp. 1910, 144.

Cyriax, E. F. & R. J. Mechano-therapeutics and Disease. BMJ 1910, 1564. (Viz. *A. A. Philip,* Ibid. p. 1824).

Cyriax, Edgar F. Practitioner 102: 314, 1919. (See also Ibid. 1918, p. 346.)

——. Journ. de chir. 15: 457, 1919. (Translated into English in "Collected Papers" p. 194.)

——. Collected Papers on Mechano-therapeutics. London, Bale & Danielsson, 1924.

——. Bibliographia gymnastica medica. Wörishofen, Published for the Author(?), 1909. 162 pp. (A valuable bibliography on Physical Medicine.)

Cyriax, Edgar F. & Kellgren-Cyriax, A. The Mechano-Therapeutics of Muscular Torticollis. New York Med. J. 95: 1031, 1922.

Cyriax, Richard J. See IV, Osteopathy, and V, Chiropractic.

Dalechamps, Jaques. Chirurgie françoice. Lyon 1573 (p. 851).

Dally, E. Manipulations thérapeutique. Dict. encycl. des sciences méd. Tome IV, 1871 (especially pp. 586–91).

Ehrlich. (Manipulation of the atlas.) Quoted in 1842 by *Riadore* (p. 82) without reference. (See IV, Osteopathy.)

Fox, R. Dacre. See III, Bonesetters.

Frétin, Paul. Traitement mécanique de la nevralgie sciatique. Bull. gén. thérap. méd. 138: 273, 1899 (especially pp. 283–86).

Georgii, Augustus. Kinetic Jottings: Miscellaneous Extracts from Medical Literature, Ancient and Modern, Illustrating the Effects of Mechanical Agencies in the Treatment of Disease. London, Renshaw, 1880. (See especially pp. 32–4, 174–81.)

Harrison, E. (1821) Observations respecting the Nature and Origin of the common Species of Disorder of the Spine. (London med. phys.) 45, 107.

Hood, Wharton. See III, Bonesetters.

Jones, Rir Robert. See III, Bonesetters.

Lannelongue. Comtes rendu de l'Acad. des Sciences 139: 495, 1904.

Lieutaud. Précis de la médecine pratique. 2e édit., Paris 1761 (p. 524). — 4e édit., 1776, Tome III (p. 6).

Luzenberger, August von. Eigene Erfahrungen über die Nägelischen Handgriffe. Z. bl. physik. Ther. u. Unfallheilk. 1904/05, 172.

Marsh, Howard. On Manipulation; or the Use of Forcible Movements as a Means of Surgical Treatment. St. Barth. Hosp. Rep. 14: 205, 1878.

——. On Bone-setting. Brit. Med. J. 1882 II, 663.

——. Cases Treated by Manipulation. Nineteenth Cent. 1884 II, 662.

——. Clinical Essays and Lectures. London 1902 (pp. 127–55).

Martin ainé & Martin jeune. Du lumbago et de quelques autre affections. Compte-rendu des trav. de la Soc. de Méd. de Lyon 1837, 138–42.

(*Mezger, Johann.*) (1) *C. von Mosengeil.* Arch. klin. Chir. 19: 428 and 551, 1870. — (2) *C. J. Rossander.* Hygiea 34: 218, 1872. — (3) *C. Curman.* Hygiea 1872, No. 9 (= Förhandl. Sv. Läkarsällsk. 1872, 188). — (4) *L. Faye.* Norsk Mag. Lægevidensk. 2: 599, 1872. — (5) *P. Winge.* Ibid. 2: 605, 1872. — (6) *J. Nicolaysen.* Ibid. 3: 40, 1873. — (7) *G. Berghman & U. Helleday.* Nord. Med. Arkiv 5: No. 7, 1873. — (8) *G. Norström.* Traité théorique et pratique du massage. (Méthode de Mezger en particulier.) Paris 1884. — (9) *L. Strecker.* Das Geheimnis der alten Massage . . . nach Dr. Mezger. Winke über Handgriffe. Darmstadt 1889. — (10) *J. Hafström.* Om massage efter Mezgers metod. Helsingborg (Sweden) 1909. — (11) *W. Haberling.* Med. Life 39: No. 4, N.S. No. 139, 1932. — (12) *Bruno Valentin.* Arch. orthop. u. Unfall-Chir. 57: 318, 1965. (And) Geschichte der Orthopädie, Stuttgart 1961 (p. 60).

Naegeli, Otto. Therapie von Neuralgien und Neurosen durch Handgriffe. Basel & Leipzig, Sallmann, 1894. — New and revised editions 1899 and 1906: Behandlung und Heilung von Nervenleiden und Nerven-Schmerzen durch Handgriffe. — Reprinted: Ulm/Donau, Karl F. Haug, 1954.

——. Ueber mechanische Behandlung der Angina (!) und der subjektiven Ohrgeräusche. Monatschr. prakt. Wasserheilk. 5: 121, 1898.

(——). *O. Ammann*. Ueber Therapie von Neuralgien und Neurosen durch Handgriffe nach Dr. Otto Naegeli. Münch. med. Wschr. 41: 687, 1894.

(——): See Luzenberger.

Nélaton, P. A. Élements de pathologie chirurgicale. 2e édit. Tome III. Paris 1874 (pp. 404 and 428).

Nothnagel. Handbuch . . . 1897. (Quot. Zukschwerdt et al.)

Paget, Sir James. See III, Bonesetters.

Penny, W. J. See III, Bonesetters.

Rankin, J. T. Manual Therapy, Rationale and some Indications. Southern Calif. Pract. 22: 361, 1907.

Recamier. Extension, massage et percussion cadencée dans le traitement des contractures musculaires. Revue méd. franç. 1838 I, 74.

Romer, Frank & Creasy, L. E. Bonesetting and the Treatment of Painful Joints. London, Nisbet, 1911. — Revised edition by *Romer* only: Modern Bonesetting for the Medical Profession. London, Heinemann, 1915.

Seguin. Torticollis . . . gueri par l'extension, le massage et la percussion cadencée. Revue méd. franç. 1838 II, 75.

Schile. Vier Fälle einseitiger Halswirbelgelenkluxation. Dtsch. med. W.schr. 30: 100, 1904.

Schlegel, E. Erschütterungsschläge, ein neues Hilfsmittel der mechanischen Therapie. Allg. med. Central-Zeitung 54: 625, 1885.

Schreiber, J. Erfahrungen über Mechanotherapie. Wiener med. Presse 25: 593 and 661, 1884.

Thomas, Hugh Owen. See III, Bonesetters.

Torbet, John. See III, Bonesetters.

Walton, G. L. (Reducing Dislocation of Cervical Vertebrae.) J. Nerv. & Mental Dis. 14: 141, 1889. (Reprinted Boston Med. & Surg. J. March 21, 1889). — Viz. Ibid. 18: 609, 1893.

——. Internat. Clin. 1892, Second Series II, p. 207.

VII. GENERAL (AFTER 1920)

The only existing medical journal on manipulative medicine is the German "*Manuelle Medizin*", in its 12th year of issue in 1974. Publisher: Verlag für Medizin Dr. Ewald Fischer, Blumenthalstrasse 38–40, 6900 Heidelberg 1, W. Germany.

A most valuable series is the German "*Die Wirbelsäule in Forschung und Praxis*" (The Spine in Research and Practice). Publisher: Hippokrates Verlag, Stuttgart. Vol. I published 1956.

Books

Armstrong, J. R. Lumbar Disc Lesions. Edinburgh, Livingstone, 1970. 1st edit. 1952.

Bankart, A. S. Blundell. Manipulative Surgery. London, Constable, 1932.

Bourdillon, J. F. Spinal Manipulation 2nd Edit., London, William Heinemann, New York, Appleton-Century-Crofts, 1973.

Broch, O. J. Lege eller kvaksalver? Oslo 1952.

Brodin, H., Bang, J., Bechgaard, P., Kaltenborn, F., & Schiötz, E. H. Manipulation av ryggraden. Stockholm, Scand. Univ. Books, 1972.

Burrows, H. Jackson, & Coltart, W. D. Treatment by Manipulation. 2nd edit., revised. London, Eyre & Spottiswoode, 1951. (First published 1939.)

Cyriax, James. Textbook of Orthopaedic Medicine. Vol. I, 5th edit. London, Baillière, Tindall, 1970. Vol. II, 8th edit. 1973.

Fisher, A. G. Timbrell. Treatment by Manipulation in General and Consulting Practice. 5th edit. London, Lewis, 1948.

Geiger, Th., & Gross, D. Chirotherapie und manuelle Therapie. Stuttgart, Hippokrates-Verlag, 1967.

Hopewell-Ash, E. L. Manipulative Methods in the Treatment of Functional Disease. London, Bale, 1935. (Not "manipulation" in the ordinary sense of the word.)

Kaltenborn, F. M. Manuelle Therapie der Extremitetengelenke. Technik spezieller Untersuchungsverfahren, Mobilisationen und Manipulationen. 2. Auflage. (Oslo, Printed for the Author, 1973.) — An English translation: Manual Therapy for the Extremity Joints. Oslo, Olaf Norli, 1974.

Lewin, Philip. The Back and its Disk Lesions. Philadelphia, Lea & Febiger, 1955.

Licht, Sidney (edit.). Massage, Manipulation and Traction. New Haven (Conn.), Eliz. Licht, 1960. (Vol. V in the series "Physical Med. Libr.".)

Maigne, Robert. Les manipulations vertébrales. Paris, Expansion Scientifique Franç, 1961. (Also translated into German and English.)

——. Douleurs d'origine vertébrale et traitements par manipulations. Paris, Expansion Scientifique Franç, 1968.

Maitland, G. D. Vertebral Manipulation. 2nd edit. London, Butterworth, 1968.

——. Peripheral Manipulation. London, Butterworth, 1970.

Marlin, Ths. Manipulative Treatment for the Medical Profession. London, Arnold, 1934.

Mennell, James. The Science and Art of Joint Manipulation. Vols. I–II. London, Churchill, 1949–52.

Mennell, J. M. Back Pain. Diagnosis and Treatment Using Manipulative Techniques. Boston, Little, Brown & Co., 1960.

Niboyet, J. E. H. La pratique de la médecine manuelle. Paris, Maisonneuve, 1968.

Paris, Stanley, V. The Spinal Lesion. Christchurch (N.Z.), Peryer, 1967.

Stoddard, Alan. See IV, Osteopathy.

Strohal, Richard. Manuelle Therapie bei Wirbelsäulenerkrankungen. München, Urban & Schwarzenberg, 1973.

Troisier, O. Lésions des disques intervertébraux. Paris, Masson, 1962.

Wiles, Philip. Essentials of Orthopaedics. London, Churchill, 1956.

Wolff, H.-D. Manuelle Medizin und ihre wissenschaftlichen Grundlagen. Heidelberg, Verlag für Physik. Med., 1970.

Articles

Alvik, Ivar. Manipulasjon. (Editorial.) Nordisk Medicin 73: 134, 1965.

Badgley, C. E. J. Bone & Joint Surg. 23: 481, 1941.

Bäker, A. Z. bl. Chir. 78: 28, 1953. (See also VIII, Complications.)

Bankart, S. S. Blundell. Manipulative Surgery in General Practice. Lancet 1932 II, 840. — Ibid. 1937 II, 595.

——. The Use and Abuse of Manipulative Surgery. Brit. Med. J. 1936 II, 416.

Barbor, R. C. Rationale of Manipulation of Joints. Arch. Phys. Med. 43: 615, 1962. — Also: Lancet 1954 I, 437. — Brit. Med. J. 1955 I, 412.

——. Treatment for Chronic Low Back Pain. Comptes rendus IV. Congr. Internat. Méd. Physique (Paris 1964). Internat. Congr. Series No. 107, Excerpta Medica Foundation, Amsterdam 1966.

Beauchamp, Guy. Manipulation. In *H. Warren Crowe,* Rheumatism, London, John Dale, 1939 (Section IV).

——. Manipulation of the Cervical Spine. Rheumatism 21: 72, 1965.

Bechgaard, Poul. Late post-traumatic Headache and Manipulation. Brit. Med. J. 1966 I, 1419.

Bendit, J. L. Brit. Med. J. 1925 II, 767.

Blaikie, E. S. JAMA 85: 1356, 1925 II.

Bourdillon, J. F. Manipulative Methods in Orthopedics. Brit. Med. J. 1955 I, 720.

Brewerton, D. A. The Conservative Treatment of the Painful Neck. Proceed. Royal Soc. Med. (Section of Phys. Med.) 57: 163, 1964. (Mentioning "a multicentre trial at present conducting by Brit. Ass. Phys. Med.".)

Bristow, W. R, Manipulative Surgery. Lancet 1936 II, 252. — Ibid. 1937 I, 546, 595 and 659.

Bristow, W. R., & Elmslie, R. C. Remarks on Manipulative Treatment. Lancet 1926 I, 218.

British Orthopaedic Association. Panel Discussion on "Low Back Pain". Brit. Med. J. 1954 II, 1349. — *Discussion*: Ibid. p. 1488. — Ibid. 1955 I, 105, 163, 167, 288–90, 348–9, 412–3, 419, 479–80, 540–1, 605–6, 669–70, 728, 790, 910–11, 970, 1032–3, 1095, 1478.

Campbell, R. Repositionsmanöver bei Lumbago traumatica. Z.schr. Unfallheilk. 48: 128, 1955.

Charnley, John. Brit. Med. J. 1955 I, 163 and (especially) 344.

Chrisman, O. D., Mittnacht, A., Snook, G. A. A Study of the Results Following Rotatory Manipulation in the Lumbar Intervertebral-Disc Syndrome. J. Bone & Joint Surg. 46A: 517, 1964.

Clement, J. Que pouvons-nous attendre des manipulations et des tractions vertébrale. Scalpel 109: 523 and 549, 1956.

Coplans, C. W. Lumbar Disc Herniation. The Effect of Torque on its Causation and Conservative Treatment. S. Afric. Med. J. 25: 884, 1951.

Coste, F., & Galmiche, P. Traitement des lombalgies et lombo-sciatiques micro-traumatiques par les manipulations. Rev. Rhum. 15: 341, 1948. — Also: Bull. et Mém. Soc. méd. Hôp. Paris 1948, 657.

Coyer, A. B., & Curwen, J. H. M. Low Back Pain treated by Manipulation. Brit. Med. J. 1955 I, 705.

Cox, H. H. Surg., Gynec. & Obstet. 45: 637, 1927.

Craig, J. G. The Place of Manipulation in the Relief of Low Back Pain. New Zealand Med. J. 53: 428, 1954.

Crisp, E. J. Lancet 1945 II, 422.

Crisp, E. J., Kersley, G. D. & Kinnimouth, D. A. (Discussion on Manipulation at the Annual Meeting of the Brit. Ass. of Phys. Med.) Annals Phys. Med. 1: 134, 1952.

Cyriax, Edgar. Letter to the Editor. Brit. Med. J. 1925 II, 868. (See also VI, Early Medical Literature).

Cyriax, James. Lumbago. Lancet 1945 II, 427.

——. Physiotherapy 1947, 102.

——. Brit. Med. J. 1948 I, 362. — Ibid. 1948 II, 251.

——. Treatment of Lumbar Disc Lesions. Brit. Med. J. 1950 II, 1434.

——. Spinal Disk Lesions. An Assessment after Twenty-one Years. Brit. Med. J. 1955 I, 140. — *Discussion*: Ibid. 288–90, 348–9, 412–13, 479–80, 540–1, 605–6, 669–70, 790, 970.

——. Lumbar Disc Lesions. S. African Med. J. 32: 1, 1958.

——. The Pros and Cons of Manipulation. Lancet 1964 I, 571.

——. Manipulations by Physiotherapists. New Zealand J. Physiotherapy 3: 8, 1969.

——. Personal View. Brit. Med. J. 1972 IV, 292.

Dandy, W. E. Loose Cartilage from Intervertebral Disk Simulating Tumor of the Spinal Cord. Arch. Surg. 19: 660, 1929.

Debeuckelaere, M. Vertebrale manipulaties. Opvattingen der Duitse School. Belg. Tijdschr. Reum. & Fys. Geneeskunde 22: 100, 1967.

Deporter, A. E. Etat irritatif du joint vertébral et manipulations vertébrales. J. Belge Rhum. & Med. Phys. 24: 129, 1969.

Douthwaite, A. H. Lancet 1936 II, 326.

Douthwaite, A. H., & Wesson, A. S. (Discussion on Manipulation in Rheumatic Disorders.) Proceed. Royal Soc. Med. 32: 273, 1938/39.

Ducroquet, R. Tours de reins, lombalgies, scolioses, sciatiques. Réductions orthopédiques. Arch. hosp. 10: 729, 1938.

Eastwood, N. B. Bonesetting in General Practice. Practitioner 172: 313, 1954.

——. Six Manipulations Suitable for Use in General Practice. J. Coll. Gen. Practit. 7: 144, 1964.

Ebbetts, John. Spinal Manipulation in General Practice. Practitioner 192: 260, 1964.

Evans, W. Brit. Med. J. 1959 II, 249.

Ewer, E. G. Manipulation of the Spine. J. Bone & Joint Surg. 35A: 347, 1953.

Figar, Š., Krausova, L., & Lewit, K. Plethysmographische Untersuchungen bei manueller Behandlung vertebragener Störungen. Acta neurovegetativa 29: 618, 1967.

Fisher, A. G. Timbrell. Principles of Treatment by Manipulation. Lancet 1925 II, 529. — Ibid. 1937 II, 595.

——. Manipulation in Lumbar Intervertebral Disc Lesions. Practitioner 187: 319, 1961.

——. Diagnosis and Treatment of Lumbar Intervertebral Disc Lesions. Ibid. 193: 642, 1966.

Fisk, J. W. Manipulation in General Practice. New Zealand Med. J. 74: 172–5, Sept. 1971.

Fredette, J. W. Manipulative Surgery. Arch. Phys. Ther. 1943, 93.

Galmiche, P. Le lumbago aigu. Rev. Praticien 5: 1893, 1955 II.

Glover, J. R. A Clinical Trial of Rotational Manipulation of the Spine in Back Cases Occurring in a Factory. Proceed. Royal Soc. Med. 59: 847, 1966.

Gray, F. J. The Lumbar Disc Syndrome . . . Traction . . . and Manipulation. Med. J. Australia 1963 II, 441.

——. Combination of Traction and Manipulation for the Lumbar Disc Syndrome. Ibid. 1967 I, 958.

Gutmann, G. Die manuelle Wirbelsäulentherapie als Niemandsland in der Heilkunde. Aerztl. Praxis 15: 2328, 1963.

——. Die Chirotherapie. Hippokrates 34: 685, 1963.

——. Wirbelsäule in Forschung u. Praxis No. 15, pp. 83–102.

Hadley, A. L. JAMA 140: 473, 1949 II.

Haggart, G. E. J. Bone & Joint Surg. 20: 851, 1938.

Hammond, M. J., & Maitland, G. D. Teaching Manipulation to Undergraduate and Postgraduate Students. New Zealand J. Physiother. 3: 4, 1969.

Harley, C. A Method of Diagnosing and Treating Acute Low Back Pain in General Practice. J. Coll. Gen. Practit. 9: 17, 1965.

Harris, R. J., & Macnab, I. J. Bone & Joint Surg. 36B: 304, 1954.

Hauberg, G. Kontraindikationen der manuellen Therapie der Wirbelsäule. Hippokrates 38: 230, 1967.

Henderson, R. S. Brit. Med. J. 1952 II, 597.

Heyman, C. H. Manipulation of Joints. J. Bone & Joint Surg. 12: 23, 1930.

Hickling, Jennifer. Lumbar Disc Lesions: The Physiotherapist's Part. Physiotherapy 50: 304, 1964.

Hirschfeld, P. Die konservative Behandlung des lumbalen Bandscheibenvorfalls nach der Methode Cyriax. Dtsch. med. Wschr. 87: 299, 1962.

Hirschkoff, S. Manipulations articulaires des membres. Modes d'action. Rhumatologie 20: 411, 1968.

Hohndorf, H. (Urgent need for repositioning in accidental cervical spinal cord injuries.) Zentralbl. Chir. 96: 257–64, 1971.

Holck, M. & al. (Treatment of Prolapsus Nuclei Pulposi by Conservative Reduction.) Chir. narz. ruchu i ortop. Polska 33: 729, 1968. (In Polish.)

Jones, Sir Robert. Manipulation as a Therapeutic Measure. Proceed. Royal Soc. Med. 25: 1405, 1932 II.

Jostes, F. A. A Manipulative Treatment without Anaesthesia. J. Bone & Joint Surg. 20: 990, 1938.

——. Manipulation of the Spine. In "Medical Physics", edited by Otto Glasser, Chicago, The Year Book Publ., 1944, p. 696.

——. Place of Manipulative Procedures in the Overall Treatment Rationale for Painful Back Conditions. Arch. Phys. Ther. 1944, 716.

Junghanns, H. Die patho-physiologischen Grundlagen für die manuelle Wirbelsäulentherapie. Proceed. IV. Internat. Congr. Phys. Med. Amsterdam, Excerpta Medica, 1966.

Kaltenborn, F. (On the so-called osteopathic examination and manipulative technique.) Nordisk Med. 69: 565, 1966. (In Norwegian.)

Kaltenborn, F. & Lindahl, O. (On the reproduction of movements of single vertebrae by examination.) Läkartidn. 66: 962, 1969. (In Swedish.) — *Discussion*: Ibid. pp. 1726–30.

Keegan, J. Jay. Diagnosis of Herniation of Lumbar Intervertebral Disks. JAMA 126: 868, 1944. — J. Bone & Joint Surg. 35A: 589, 1953.

Kemal, M. M. Ischias-Skoliose und Ischias. (Redressement.) Inaugural-Diss. Bruchsal, J. Kruse, 1931.

Kestler, O. JAMA 172: 2039, 1960.

Key, J. A. Surgery 17: 294, 1945 I.

Kuppers, J. Les manipulations vertébrales. Sujet d'actualité. Scalpel 117: 815, 1964.

Le Corre, F., & Maigne, R. L'entorse des dernières côtes; son traitement par manipulation. Comptes rendus IV. Congr. Internat. de Méd. Phys. (Paris 1964). Internat. Congr. Ser. No. 107, Excerpta Medica Found., Amsterdam 1966 (p. 173).

Leca, A. F. P. Le traitement des lombalgies et des lombo-sciatiques par les manipulations vertébrales. Thèse No. 307, Fac. de Méd. de Paris 1950.

Leemann, R. A. Die Behandlung radikulärer Syndrome (Ischias, —) mittels Adjustierung in Narkose. Helvetica Chir. Acta 24: 395, 1957.

——. Vertebragene Schmerzsyndrome und die Möglichkeit ihrer chiropraktischen Behandlung. Schweiz. med. Wschr. 87: 1289, 1957.

Leprince, A. La Côte d'Azur Medicale, Nov. 1930.

Lescure, Roger J. Etude critique d'un traitement par manipulations dans les algies d'origine rachidienne. Thèse No. 458, Fac. de Méd. de Paris, 1951.

——. Réponses à quelques questions concernant les tractions et manipulations des syndromes cervicaux. Méd. et Hyg. (Genève) 17: 761, 1959.

Lescure, R. J., & Renoult, Cl. Manipulations articulaires à longue échéance en rééducation. Comptes rendus IV. Congr. de Méd. Phys. (Paris 1964). Internat. Congr. Ser. No. 107, Excerpta Medica Found., Amsterdam 1966.

Lescure, R., & Thierry-Mieg, J. Manipulations des arthroses vertébrales . . . Contemp. Rheum. 1956, 323.

Lescure, R., Trepsat, P., Waghemacker, R. Sur les possibilités des traitement par manipulations dans la thérapeutique des rhumatismes. Rhumatologie 2: 71, 1953.

Le Vay, David, see III, Bonesetters.

Lièvre, J. A. A propos des traitement des lombalgies et des sciatiques par manipulations vertébrales. Presse méd. 22: 651, 1955. (See also VIII, Complications.)

Lièvre, J. A., Attali, P., & Leca, A. Le traitement des lombalgies et des sciatiques par manipulations. Ibid. 59: 850, 1951 I.

Logan, E. Counter-torque Suspension. Physiotherapy 44: 71, 1958.

Lovell-Smith, J. B. Manipulation and Radicular Syndromes. New Zealand Med. J. 62: 316, 1963.

Luckner, H. Zur konservativen Behandlung des hinteren Bandscheibenprolapses. Med. Klin. 43: 698, 1948.

McKee, G. K. Traction—Manipulation . . . in the Treatment of Disc Lesions of the Lumbar Spine. Lancet 472, 1956 I.

McKenzie, R. A. Manual Correction of Sciatic Scoliosis. New Zealand Med. J. 76: 194–9, Sept. 1972.

Macsay, Denys. Les principes, les techniques et les résultats de la vertébrothérapie. Rev. Rhum. 15: 344, 1948.

Maigne, Robert. Manipulations vertébrale et manipulateurs. Sem. Hôp. Paris 29: 1944, 1953.

——. Une méthode rationelle d'application des manipulations vertébrales. Rhumatologie 16: 455, 1964.

——. Une doctrine pour les traitements par manipulations . . . Ann. Méd. Phys. 8: No. 1, 1965.

——. Le choix des manipulations dans le traitement des sciatiques. Rev. Rhum. 32: 366, 1965.

——. The Concept of Painlessness and Opposite Motion in Spinal Manipulation. Am. J. Phys. Med. 44: 55, 1965.

Maitland, G. D. Low Back Pain and Allied Symptoms and Treatment Results. Med. J. Australia 1957 II, 852.

——. Lumbar Manipulation: Does it Do Harm? Ibid. 1961, 545 (Sept.).

——. Manipulation—Mobilisation. Physiotherapy 1966, 382 (Nov.).

——. Selection and Assessment of Patients for Spinal Manipulation. New Zealand J. Physiotherapy 3: No. 14, 1968.

Marlin, Ths. Lancet 402, 1932 II.

Mathews, J. A., & Yates, D. A. H. Reduction of Lumbar Disc Prolapse by Manipulation. Brit. Med. J. 696, 1969 III. — Viz.: Ann. Phys. Med. 9: 275, 1968.

Mennell, James. Role of Manipulation in Therapeutics. Lancet 400, 1932 II.

Mennell, John. Manipulation of Stiff Joints. Arch. Phys. Med. 685, 1947.

——. "Joint Play". Proceed. II. Internat. Congr. Manip. Med. Heidelberg, Verlag f. physik. Med., 1970.

Mensor, Merrill C. Non-operative Treatment, including Manipulation, for Lumbar Intervertebral Disc Syndrome. J. Bone & Joint Surg. 37A: 925, 1955. — Ibid. 47A: 1073, 1965.

Mercer, Sir Walter, see IV, Osteopathy.

Meriel, P. A propos de la chiropraxie. Toulouse Medicale 45 (I): 13, 1944.

Miltner, L. J., & Lowendorf, C. S. Low Back Pain. A Study of 525 Cases . . . J. Bone & Joint Surg. 13: 16, 1931. (Describing manipulation ad modum Sir Robert Jones.)

Mostini, M. G. Les manipulations vertébrales en rhumatologie. Ann. Méd. Physique 1960 III, 3, p. 219.

Newton, D. R. L. The Scope of Manipulative Treatment. J. Coll. Gen. Pract. Suppl. No. 3 to Vol. VI, 1963, pp. 16–20 and 26–9. (Report of a Symposium on Arthritis in General Practice.)

Oger, J., Brumagne, J., & Margaux, J. La vertébrothérapie. Scalpel 117: 527, 1964.

Paris, Stanley. The Theory and Technique of Specific Spinal Manipulation. New Zealand Med. J. 62: 320, 1963.

——. Manipulation Newsletter. New Zealand J. Physiotherapy Nov. 1967 (p. 35). — Ibid. May 1968 (p. 29). — Ibid. May 1969 (p. 26).

Paris, Stanley V. Gross Spinal Movements and their Restriction as the Basis of Joint Manipulation. Progr. Phys. Ther. 1: 208–13, 1970.

Parsons, W. B., & Cumming, J. D. A. Manipulation in Back Pain. Canad. Med. Ass. J. 79: 103, 1958. (Editorial comments p. 125). — Ibid. 77: 7, 1957.

Pearce, J., & Moll, J. H. Conservative Treatment of Natural History of Acute Lumbar Disc Lesions. J. Neur., Neurosurg., Psych. 30: 13, 1967.

Pitkin, H. C. Sacrarthrogenetic Telalgia. V: A Plan of Treatment. J. Bone & Joint Surg. 19: 169, 1937.

Pringle, Brian. An Approach to Intervertebral Disc Lesions. (With discussion.) Transact. Ass. Industr. Med. Officers 5: 127, 1956.

Proceedings of the Congresses of the International Federation of Manual Medicine.

Proceedings IV. Internat. Congr. of Physical Medicine (Paris). Symposium "Manipulative Medicine" Sept. 8, 1964. Internat. Congr. Ser. No. 107, Exerpta Medica Foundation. Amsterdam 1966.

(Proceedings.) Verhandl. Dtsch. Orthop. Gesellschaft. 43. Kongress Sept. 1955. III. Hauptthema: Aktuelle Probleme der Wirbelsäulenpathologie. Beilageheft, Z. schr. Orthop. Bd. 87, 1956.

(Proceedings.) Symposium Manipulative Treatment, Australian Med. Ass., Victorian Branch. Med. J. Australia 1967 I, 1274–80, 1195–6 and II, 88 and 136.

Ravault, P., & Vignon, G. Les manipulations vertébrales dans le traitement des lombagos et des sciatiques, et des névralgies cervico-brachiales. Lyon médicale 183: 193 (No. 39), 1950.

Rich, W. G. Three Cases of Subluxations in the Cervical Region. Med. J. Australia 1964 I, 524. — Ibid. 1969 I, 313.

Robertson, A. M. Manipulation in General and Industrial Practice. Practitioner 193: 647, 1964. — Ibid. 200: 396, 1968.

Rudd, J. L. Manipulative Therapy (Passive Stretchings) for Neck or Back Strain in Aged Patients. J. Am. Geriatric Soc. 11: 1113, 1963.

Rudd, J. L., & Margolin, R. J. Rapid Rehabilitation of Back Cases. 1949 Yearbook Phys. Med. & Rehab. Chicago, Year Book Publishers, 1950 (p. 237).

Schiötz, Eiler H. Manipulasjonsbehandling av columna under medisinsk-historisk synsvinkel. Tidsskrift f. Den norske lægeforening 78: 359–72, 429–38, 946–50, 1003–21, 1958. — *Discussion*: Nordisk Medicin 60: 1399–1406, 1958.

Sèze, S. de. (a) Les accidents de la détérioration structurale du disque. Semaine des Hôp. de Paris 31: 2267, 1955 (No. 39). — (b) Les attitudes antalgique dans la sciatique disco-radiculaire commune. Ibid. p. 2291. — (c) Les manipulations vertébrales. Ibid. p. 2314.

Sèze, S. de, Robin, J., & Levernieux, J. Vertébrotherapie par manipulations et vertébrotherapie par tractions. Rev. Rhum. 15: 337, 1948.

Sèze, S. de, & Thierry-Mieg, J. Les manipulations vertébrales. Rev. Rhum. 22: 633, 1955. — See also: Encyclopédie médico-chirurgicale 3—1956 (25.966 B[10]).

Slabok, F. (Manipulation therapy as a part of therapy of lumbosacralgias.) Acta chir. orthop. Cechoslov. 35: 427, 1968. (In Czechoslovakian.)

Slavik, J. (Pitkin's maneuvre in backache.) Ibid. 35: 425, 1969.

Smart, M. Manipulation. Arch. Phys. Med. 1946, 730.

Smyth, E. H. J. Manipulation of Acute Backache in the Home. Manuelle Med. 7: 138, 1969.

Sommer, M. Therapie pseudo-pektanginöser Beschwerden. Aerztl. Praxis 11: 587, 1959.

——. Ein Beitrag zur Behandlung des traumatischen Schiefhalses. Hippokrates 34: 820, 1963.

Sones, M. Management of Backache . . . Manipulative Therapy. Med. Clin. N. America July 1943, 1071.

Stoddard, Alan. Manipulative Procedures in the Treatment of Intervertebral Disc Lesions. Brit. J. Phys. Med. 1951, 101. (Reprinted in Physiotherapy April 1953.)

——. Manipulation. An Explanation of Osteopathic Technique. Brit. J. Phys. Med. July 1952.

Swezey, R. L., & Silverman, T. R. Radiographic Demonstration of Induced Vertebral Facet Displacements. Arch. Phys. Med. & Rehab. 52: 244–9, 1971.

Terrier, J. C. Die reversiblen funktionsmechanischen Störungen der Wirbelsäule und ihre manipulative Behandlung. Z. schr. Unfallmedizin 1959, 133.

——. Les bases de la thérapeutique manipulative de la colonne vertébrale. Méd. et Hyg. (Genève) 1959, 390 (No. 436).

——. Die Grundlagen der manipulativen Behandlung der vertebralen Diskopathien. Schweiz. med. Wschr. 1960, 419 (No. 15).

——. Chiropraktik in der Sicht des Arztes. Schweiz. Aerztezeitung 1961, 355 (No. 21).

Thierry-Mieg, J. Techniques des manipulations vertébrales utilisées dans le traitement des sciatiques par hernie discale. Indications, contre-indications et accidents. Semaine thérap. 42: 376, 1966.

Travell, J. & W. Therapy of Low Back Pain by Manipulation. Arch. Phys. Med. 1946, 537.

Troisier, O. Sur quelques indications des manipulations vertébrale. Gaz. méd. France 72: 987, 1965.

Uibe, P. Unbeabsichtigte Wirkung chiropraktischer Massnahmen. Dtsch. Gesundheitswesen (DDR) 13: 1226, 1958.

Vater, W. Die Reposition in Narkose bei lumbalen Bandscheibenvorfällen. Beiträge Orthop. & Traum. 13: 77, 1966.

Veselský, J. et al. (Experiences with lumbo-sacral manipulation therapy in an industrial polyclinic.) Acta chir. orthop. Cechoslov. 35: 421, 1968. (In Czechoslovakian.)

Watson-Jones, Sir Reginald et al. Discussion on the Present Position of Manipulative Treatment. Proceed. Royal Soc. Med. 50: 137, 1957.

Waugh, W. G. Brit. Med. J. 412, 1955 I. (Quotation from professor Thomson's lectures.)

Weiser, H. I. Early Manipulative Treatment of Acute Back Pain. Comptes rendus IV. Congr. Internat. de Méd. Phys. (Paris 1964). Internat. Congr. Ser. No. 107. Excerpta Medica Found. Amsterdam 1966.

Went, H., & Walter, R. Erfahrungen mit chiropraktischer Behandlung. Z. bl. Chir. 82: 955, 1957 I.

——. Zum Wirkungsmechanismus der Chiropraktik. Arch. Orthop. u. Unfallheilk. 49: 480, 1958.

Wilson, D. G. Results of Manipulation in General Practice. Proceed. Royal Soc. Med. 60: 971, 1967.

——. Manipulative Treatment in General Practice. Lancet 1962, 1013 (May 12). — *Discussion*: Ibid. 1071, 1127–8, 1189–90, 1243, 1305.

Wilson, R. N., & Wilson, S. Low Backache in Industry. A Review of 1163 Cases. Brit. Med. J. 649, 1955 II.

Winter, Eric de, & Renault, Cl. Manipulations lombo-pelviennes. Partie I–V. Vie Méd. 42: M.T_3, 1961 (pp. 115–126). — Ibid. 44: M.T_4, 1963 (pp. 117–136). — Ibid. 44: M.T_7, 1963 (pp. 59–78). — Ibid. 44: M.T_8, 1963 (pp. 81–94).

——. Pour une étude rationelle des thérapeutiques manuelles. Revue méd. Tours 5: 181, 1964.

Wolff, H.-D. (edit.). Hinweise zur derzeitigen Situation und zur weiteren Entwicklung der manuellen Medizin, insbesondere der Chirotherapie, in der Bundesrepublik Deutschland, vorgelegt im Februar 1972 von der Deutschen Gesellschaft für Manuelle Medizin e. V. Suppl. to "Manuelle Medizin" 1972. 8 pp. (On the present state of manipulative therapy in Germany.)

Ziegler, E. Fünf Jahre chiropraktische Tätigkeit als Landarzt. Münch. med. Wschr. 95: 948, 1953.

——. Differentialdiagnostische Erwägungen und klinische Erfahrungen in einer chiropraktisch orientierten Landpraxis. Zschr. Allgemeinmedizin 45: 510, 1969.

VIII. COMPLICATIONS

Bäker, A. Zur Redressionsbehandlung der Wirbelsäule. Medizinische 1: 318 (No. 10), 1954.

Ballantine, H. Thomas. (A Case of Paraplegia after Chiropractic Treatment.) AMA-News Nov. 4, 1968.

Bang, Jens. (Paraplegia following chiropractic manipulation in a case of sciatica.) Case report from Denmark, First Internat. Congr. Man. Ther., Baden (Switzerland) May 1958. Not published.

Barr, J. S. "Sciatica" Caused by Intervertebral Disk Lesions. A Report of Forty Cases of Rupture of the Intervertebral Disc Occurring in the Low Lumbar Spine and Causing Pressure on the Cauda Equina. J. Bone & Joint Surg. 19: 323, 1937.

Bénassy, J. & Wolinetz, E. Quadriplégie après manœuvre de chiropraxie. Revue du Rhum. 24: 555, 1957.

Blaine, Edw. S. Manipulative (Chiropractic) Dislocations of the Atlas. JAMA 85: 1356, 1925.

Boudin, G., Barbizet, J., Pépin, B., & Fouet, P. Syndrome grave du tronc cérébral après manipulations cervicales. Bull. et Mém. de la Soc. Méd. des Hôp. de Paris 73: 562, 1957.

Boudin, G., & Barbizet, J. Les accidents nerveux des manipulations du rachis cervical. Revue du Practicien 19: 2235, 1958 II.

Cambier, J. Complications neurologiques des manipulations vertébrales. Presse méd. 382, 1963.

Chiropractor Found Guilty of Second Degree Murder (treating a cancer patient). AMA-News Dec. 12, 1967.

Coste, F., Galmiche, P., Brion, S., Chabot, J., Chaouat, Y., & Illoux, G. Deux cas de mal de Pott révélés par tractions ou manipulations. Revue Rhum. 20: 710, 1953. (See also Ibid. 15: 341, 1948.)

Dandy, Walter E. Loose Cartilage from Intervertebral Disk Simulating Tumor of the Spinal Cord. Arch. Surg. 19: 660, 1929. (Case report p. 665.)

Death Resulting from Chiropractic Treatment for Headache. JAMA 103: 1260, 1934. Ibid. 109: 233, 1937.

De Kleyn, A. & Nieuwenhuyse, P. Schwindelanfälle und Nystagmus bei einer bestimmten Stellung des Kopfes. Acta Oto-laryng. 2: 155, 1927.

Deshayes, P., & Geffroy, Y. Un cas de paralysie plexique supérieure, accident d'une manipulation vertébrale. Revue Rhum. 29: 3137, 1962.

Fisher, E. D. Report of a Case of Ruptured Disk Following Chiropractic Manipulation. Kentucky Med. J. 41: 14, 1943.

Ford, Frank R., & Clark, David. Thrombosis of the Basilar Artery with Softenings in the Cerebellum and Brain Stem due to Manipulation of the Neck. Bull. Johns Hopkins Hosp. 98: 37, 1956.

(Fracture of the Spine after Chiropractic Treatment.) Lancet 1931 II, 150.

Giraud, G. A propos des risques cardio-vasculaires auxquels sont exposés les sujets soumis à une compression cervical profonde (manipulations . . .) . . . Arch. des maladies du cœur 60: 893, 1967.

Goldthwait, Joel E. The Lumbo-sacral Articulation. An Explanation of Many Cases of "Lumbago", "Sciatica" and Paraplegia. Boston Med. & Surg. J. 164: 365, 1911.

Green, David, & Joynt, R. J. Vascular Accidents to the Brain Stem Associated with Neck Manipulation. JAMA 170: 522, 1959.

Hipp, E. Gefahren der chiropraktischen und osteopathischen Behandlung. Mediz. Klinik 56: 1022, 1961 I.

Hooper, J. Low Back Pain. Paraparesis after Treatment of Low Back Pain by Physical Methods. Med. J. Austr. 549–51, 1973 I.

Jennett, W. Bryan. A Study of 25 Cases of Compression of the Cauda Equina by Prolapsed Intervertebral Discs. (Case 2 caused by manipulation.) J. of Neur., Neurosurg. & Psych. 19: 109, 1956.

Kissel, P., & Tridon, P. Gaz. méd. de France 67 II: 1789, 1960.

Knudsen, V. Cauda equina syndrom ved lumbal discusprolaps. Nordisk Medicin 74: 898, 1965.

Kuhlendahl, H., & Hensell, V. Der mediane Massenprolaps der Lendenwirbelsäule mit Kaudakompression. Dtsch. med. Wschr. 78 I: 332, 1953.

Kuhlendahl, H. et al. Nil nocere! Schäden bei "Wirbelsäulen-Reposition" in Narkose. Münch. med. Wschr. 100: 1738, 1958.

Kunkle, Charles, Muller, John C., & Odom, Guy L. Traumatic Brain-stem Thrombosis: Report of a Case and Analysis of the Mechanism of Injury. Ann. Intern. Med. 36: 1329, 1952.

Lescure, Roger J. Incidents, accidents, contre-indications des manipulations de la colonne vertébrale. Méd. et Hyg. (Genève) 12: 456, 1954.

Levernieux, J. Revue du Practicien 2725, (Oct.) 1962.

Lièvre, J.-A. Paraplégie due aux manœuvres d'un ostéopathe. Revue Rhum. 20: 707, 1953.

Lindemann, K., & Rossak, K. Anzeige und Gegenanzeige der Reposition bei Lumbago-Ischias-Syndrom und ihre Komplikationen. Z. schr. Orthop. 91: 335, 1959.

Livingston, M. C. Spinal Manipulation Causing Injury. A Three Year Study. Clin. Orthop. 81: 82–6, Nov.–Dec. 1971 (Adverse effects of chiropractic).

Lorenz, R. & Vogelsang, H. G. Thrombose der Arteria vertabralis nach chiropraktischen manipulationen an der Halsuirbelsäule (von einem Chirurgen ausgeführt). Dtsch. med. Wschr. 97=34–43, 1972—Discussion (K. Lewit) Ibid. 784–5.

Malpractice: Cerebral Hemorrhage Attributed to Chiropractic Adjustment. JAMA 105: 1714, 1935. Ibid. 109: 233, 1937.

Masson, M., & Cambier, J. Insuffisance circulatoire vertébro-basilaire. Presse méd. 70: 1992, 1962.

Mixter, W. J., & Barr, J. S. New England J. Med. 211: 210, 1934. (Case 15.)

Nick, J., Contamin, F., Nicolle, M. H., Des Lauriers, A., & Ziegler, G. Incidents et accidents neurologiques dus aux manipulations cervicales (à propos de trois observations). Bull. et Mém. de la Soc. méd. des Hôp. de Paris 118: 435, 1967 I.

Oger, J., Brumagne, J., & Margaux, J. Les accidents des manipulations vertébrales. J. Belge de Méd. physique 19: 56, 1964.

Pennybacker, J. E. Die chirurgische Behandlung der Ischias. Dtsch. Z. schr. Chir. 267: 463, 1951.

Poppen, J. L. The Herniated Intervertebral Disk. New England J. Med. 232: 211, 1945.

Pribek, R. A. Brain Stem Vasular Accident Following Neck Manipulation. Wisc. Med. J. 62=141, 1963.

Pratt-Thomas, H. R., & Berger, K. E. Cerebellar and Spinal Injuries after Chiropractic Manipulation. JAMA 133: 600, 1947.

Rageot, E. Les accidents et incidents des manipulations vertébrales. Comptes rendus IV. Congr. Internat. de Méd. Physique (Paris 1964). Internat. Congr. Series No. 107, Excerpta Medica Foundation, Amsterdam 1966.

Richard, Joseph. Disk Rupture with Cauda Equina Syndrome after Chiropractic Adjustment. New York J. Med. 67: 2496, 1967 II.

Rivoire, M. M. Lyon Méd. 208: 339, 1962.

Schulze, A. J. Ueber die Fehlanwendung chiropraktischer Behandlungsmassnahmen. Mediz. Welt No. 45, 1962 (pp. 2379–80 and 2399).

Schwarz, G. A., Geiger, J. K., & Spano, A. V. Posterior Inferior Cerebellar Artery Syndrome of Wallenberg after Chiropractic Manipulation. Arch. internat. Med. 97: 352, 1956.

Secher, Ole. Ekstensionsbehandling kontra kiropraktik. Ugeskrift for Læger 131: 1122, 1969.

Serre, H., & Simon, L. Dangers des manipulations vertébrales. Revue du Rhum. 35: 445, 1968.

Shepard, R. H. Diagnosis and Prognosis of Cauda Equina Syndrome Produced by Protrusion of Lumbar Disk. Brit. Med. J. 1959 II, 1434.

Smith, Roger A., & Estridge, N. Neurologic Complications of Head and Neck Manipulations. JAMA 182: 528, 1962.

Tatlow, W. F. T. & Banner, H. G. Syndrome of Vertebral Artery Compression. *Neurology* 7=331, 1957.

Thibodeau, A. A. Bull. New England Med. Center 11: 34, 1949.

Tomlinson, K. M. Purpura Following Manipulation of the Spine. Brit. Med. J. 1955 I, 1260.

Wilson, J. N et al. Manipulation of the Herniated Intervertebral Disc. Am. J. Surg. 83: 173, 1952.

Witt. (Ein Fall von Mb. Basedow als Folge einer manuellen Behandlung der Halswirbelsäule.) Verhandl. Dtsch. Orthop. Gesellschaft 1955, 254.

References to Part 2

Brain, W. R. (1948). Cervical Spondylosis. Proc-roy. Soc. Med. 41,509.
Bywaters, B. G. L. (1968). Case of ankylosing Spondylitis. Brit. med. J. 1,412.
Edgar, M. A. & Nundy, S. (1966). Innervation of spinal dura mater. Neurol. Neurosurg. Psychiat. 19, 530.
Edström, C. (1944). Rheumatism as public Health Problem in Sweden. Uppsala Läk. Fören. 49, 303.
Glasgow Symposium (1966). J. Coll. med. Pract. 13, supp. 1.
Glover, J. R. (1972). Lecture to Brit. Ass. Manip. Med.
Hackett, G. S. (1958). Ligament and Tendon Relaxation. Springfield: Thomas.
Kendall, B. E. (1972). Radiological Investigation of Pain referred to lower Limb. Brit. J. Hosp. Med. 7, 500.
Lewin, T. (1964). Osteoarthritis in lumbar synovial Joints. Actta. orthop. Scand. Supp. 73.
Lewis, T. (1942). Pain. New York: MacMillan.
Noel-Baker, P. (1963). Letter in "Times", 5th Feb.
O'Connell, (1956). Cervical Spondylosis. Proc. Roy. Soc. Med. 49, 202.

KU-319-408

GREEK POTTERY
AN INTRODUCTION

Brian A. Sparkes

NOTTINGHAM UNIVERSITY LIBRARY

Manchester University Press
Manchester and New York
Distributed exclusively in the USA and Canada by St. Martin's Press

Copyright © Brian A. Sparkes 1991

Published by Manchester University Press
Oxford Road, Manchester M13 9PL, England
and Room 400, 175 Fifth Avenue, New York, NY 10010, USA

Distributed exclusively in the USA and Canada by St. Martin's Press, Inc.,
175 Fifth Avenue, New York, NY 10010, USA

A catalogue record for this book is available from the British Library

Library of Congress cataloging in publication data

Sparkes, Brian A.
Greek pottery: an introduction / Brian A. Sparkes.
p. cm.
Includes bibliographical references and index.
ISBN 0-7190-2236-3 (cloth). – ISBN 0-7190-2936-8 (paper)
1. Pottery, Greek. I. Title.
NK3840.S65 1991
666′.3938—dc20 91-17266

ISBN 0 7190 2236 3 *hardback*
0 7190 2936 8 *paperback*

Typeset in Hong Kong by Best-set Typesetter Ltd
Printed in Great Britain
by Biddles Ltd, Guildford and King's Lynn

CONTENTS

ILLUSTRATIONS

Athens, British School at Athens, Stamped Amphora Handle Collection H72. Magnification × 49. Fragment of granite/gneiss and muscovite mica visible.

III Dating

1. Attic Geometric cremation grave of a woman, found in the Athenian Agora. ca. 850 B.C. (adapted from Smithson 1968, pl. 18).

2. Some of the contents of the grave of one of the Corcyrean ambassadors to Athens, found in the Athenian Kerameikos cemetery. ca. 433 B.C.

3. Detail of the Parthenon frieze (West XIII, 25) (Alison Frantz photograph).

4. Attic red-figure pelike, from Nola. ca. 430–420 B.C. Ht. 17 cm. Berlin, Staatliche Museen F 2357. Painted in the manner of the Washing Painter (Beazley 1963, 1134, no. 8). (Photo: Isolde Luckert).

5. Attic red-figure kylix, from Caere. ca. 480 B.C. Diam. of bowl 32.8 cm. Oxford, Ashmolean Museum 1911.615. Painted by the Painter of the Oxford Brygos (Beazley 1963, 399, below).

6. Attic red-figure hydria. ca. 465 B.C. Ht. 36.6 cm; diam. 29 cm. Würzburg, Martin von Wagner Museum ZA 20 (on loan from Takuhiko Fujita, Tokyo). Painted by one the Earlier Mannerists (the Agrigento or the Leningrad Painter).

7. Attic Panathenaic prize amphora, from Caere. 336–335 B.C. (Pythodelos archon). Ht. 83 cm. London, British Museum B 607. The Nikomachos series (Beazley 1956, 415, no. 4).

8. 'Hadra' hydria, from Hadra, Alexandria. 19 May 213 B.C. (Year 9, Hyperberetaios 30, Pharmeuthi 7; Timasitheos (sōn) of Dionysios of Rhodes, an Ambassador; by Theodotos, agent). Ht. 43.6 cm. New York, Metropolitan Museum 90.9.29 (purchase, 1890).

9. Rhodian transport amphorae and Rhodian stamped amphora handles. Third century B.C. Athens, Agora Museum SS 7581 and 7582, and SS 7584 (all from deposit B 13:7).

IV Shapes

1. Protocorinthian lekythos with vase name scratched retrograde in Cumaean (?) script, from a tomb at Cumae. ca. 675–650 B.C. Ht. 5.5 cm. London, British Museum GR 1885.6–13.7.

2. Protocorinthian (?) aryballos with name of pottery Pyrrhos painted retrograde in Euboean script. ca. 650 B.C. Ht. 5 cm. Boston, Museum of Fine Arts 98.900 (H.L. Pierce Fund). (Courtesy Museum of Fine Arts, Boston.)

3. Boeotian Geometric pyxis. ca. 700 B.C. Ht. 15 cm. Athens, National

Museum 11795.

4. Silver and black mugs, the silver from Dalboki, Bulgaria. ca. 400 B.C. Ht. 9.4 and 10 cm. Oxford, Ashmolean Museum 1948.104 and 1874.409.

5. Cretan relief pithos-amphora, from Arkhanes (?). ca. 675 B.C. Ht. 156 cm, diam. 87 cm. Paris, Louvre CA 4523.

6. Cooking pots and braziers used in Athens, from the Athenian Agora. Mid fifth to mid fourth century. Max. diam. ca. 23 cm. Athens, Agora Museum P 21948 on P 21958 and P 14655 on P 16521.

7. Public pots used in Athens, from the Athenian Agora: water clock (capacity 6400 cc), drinking cup, liquid measure (capacity 270 cc), and dry measure (capacity 1820 cc). Fifth and fourth centuries B.C. Athens, Agora Museum P 2084, P 5117 (diam. 13.7 cm), P 13429 (ht. 13.3 cm), P3559 (ht. 13.2 cm).

8. Attic red-figure kylix, from Vulci. ca. 500 B.C. Ht. of frieze 6.8 cm. London, British Museum E37. Painted and signed by Epiktetos (Beazley 1963, 72, no. 17).

9. Rhodian perfume pot in the shape of a swallow. ca. 600 B.C. Ht. 6.5 cm. London, British Museum GR 1860.4–4.32.

10. Drawn outlines of pots

- (a) amphorae (neck- and belly-)
- (b) alabastra, aryballoi and askos
- (c) chous and chytra
- (d) hydriai (shoulder and kalpis)
- (e) kados and kantharos
- (f) kraters (column and volute)
- (g) kraters (calyx and bell)
- (h) kylikes (lip and type B)
- (i) lebes and lekane
- (j) lekythoi (early, tall and squat)
- (k) lekanis, lydion and mug
- (l) oinochoai (trefoil and beaked) and olpe
- (m) pelike, psykter and pyxis
- (n) skyphos (Corinthian and Attic types)
- (o) stamnos, stemless and stemmed dish

V Decoration

1. Attic black-figure fragmentary amphora, Type A. ca. 540 B.C. Philadelphia, University Museum 4873. Painted by Exekias (Beazley 1956, 145, no. 16).

2. Attic white-ground fragmentary lekythos. ca. 440 B.C. London, British Museum GR 1907.7–10.10. Painted by the Bosanquet Painter (Beazley 1963, 1227, no. 10).

3. Sicilian polychrome fragmentary squat lekythos. ca. 350–325 B.C.

Ht. 13.2 cm. Malibu, The J. Paul Getty Museum 86.AE.399 (Bareiss Collection). The Lentini Group (attributed by von Bothmer).

4. Italian black plate with stamping and added colour ('Teano'). ca. 350–300 B.C. Diam. 26.2 cm. Baltimore, Walters Art Gallery 48.108.

5. Attic black stemless cup. ca. 450–440 B.C. Diam. 18 cm. London, British Museum GR 1864.10–7.1591 (Fikellura grave 39bis).

6. Apulian red-figure volute-krater. ca. 380–370 B.C. Ht. 68.8 cm. London, British Museum F 283. Painted by the Iliupersis Painter (Trendall and Cambitoglou 1978, 193, no. 7).

7. Attic hemispherical ('Megarian') bowl. ca. 200 B.C. Diam. 13.4 cm. Athens, Agora Museum P 590.

8. 'Exekias made and painted me' – a painted inscription on an Attic black-figure neck-amphora. ca. 550 B.C. Berlin, Staatliche Museen F 1720. Painted by Exekias (Beazley 1956, 143, no. 1).

9. Attic red-figure kylix. ca. 490 B.C. Diam. of bowl 22.5 cm. Basel, Antiken Museum BS 439. Painted by Onesimos (Beazley 1963, 323, no. 56).

10. Attic red-figure kylix. ca. 480 B.C. Diam of bowl 24.3 cm. Schwerin, Museum 725 (1307). Painted by Onesimos (Beazley 1963, 325, no. 73).

11. Corinthian black-figure kylix. ca. 580 B.C. Diam. of bowl 20.3 cm. Basel, Antiken Museum BS 1404. Painted by the Cavalcade Painter.

12. Attic red-figure kylix. ca. 490 B.C. Est. diam. of bowl 31.6 cm. Malibu, The J. Paul Getty Museum 86.AE.286 (Bareiss Collection). Painted by the Brygos Painter (Beazley 1971, 367, no. 1 bis addendum to Beazley 1963, 369).

VI Out of the shop

1. Graffito on underside of Attic skyphos. Sixth century B.C. Diam. 0.7 cm. Athens, Agora Museum P 17824 (Lang 1976, B 1).

2. Ostraka consisting of fragments of the wall of an Attic red-figure calyx-krater found in the Athenian Kerameikos, naming Megakles, son of Hippokrates. Early fifth century B.C. Athens, Kerameikos 4118. Painted by the Kleophrades Painter (Knigge 1970, pl. 1).

3. Graffito on underside of Attic red-figure pelike (from Johnston 1978, 222, Ill. 1). Late fifth century B.C. Ht. 37 cm. Naples, Museo Nazionale 1511600. Painted by the Nikias Painter.

4. Attic red-figure kylix. Ca. 500 B.C. Diam. of bowl 18.5 cm. Baltimore, Johns Hopkins University. Painted by Phintias (Beazley 1963, 25, no. 14).

LIST OF ABBREVIATIONS

AA	*Archäologischer Anzeiger*
AAA	*Athens Annals of Archaeology*
ABSA	*Annual of the British School at Athens*
ADelt	*Arkhaiologikon Deltion*
AJA	*American Journal of Archaeology*
AK	*Antike Kunst*
AM	*Athenische Mitteilungen*
Anat. Stud.	*Anatolian Studies*
AR	*Archaeological Reports*
Arch. News	*Archaeological News*
Arch. Class.	*Archeologia Classica*
AW	*Antike Welt*
BABesch.	*Bulletin Antieke Beschaving*
BAR	*British Archaeological Reports*
BCH	*Bulletin de Correspondance Hellénique*
BICS	*Bulletin of the Institute of Classical Studies*
CQ	*Classical Quarterly*
CR	*Classical Review*
CRAI	*Comptes Rendus de l'Académie des Inscriptions et Belles-Lettres*
EAA	*Enciclopedia dell'Arte Antica*
Expedition	*Expedition, Bulletin of the University Museum of the University Philadelphia*
Getty MJ	*The J. Paul Getty Museum Journal*
Greek Vases	*Greek Vases in the J. Paul Getty Museum* I-IV, *Occasional Papers on Antiquities* 1, 3, 2, 5 (1983, 1985, 1986, 1989)
GRBS	*Greek, Roman and Byzantine Studies*

JBM	*Jahrbuch Berliner Museum*
JDAI	*Jahrbuch des Deutschen Archäologischen Instituts*
JHS	*Journal of Hellenic Studies*
JOAI	*Jahreshefte des Oesterreichischen Archäologischen Institutes*
MJBK	*Münchner Jahrbuch der Bildenden Kunst*
MMAB	*Metropolitan Museum of Art Bulletin*
MMJ	*Metropolitan Museum Journal*
NC	*Numismatic Chronicle*
OJA	*Oxford Journal of Archaeology*
PBA	*Proceedings of the British Academy*
PBSR	*Papers of the British School at Rome*
PCPS	*Proceedings of the Cambridge Philological Society*
Phil. Trans. R. Soc. Lond.	*Philological Transactions of the Royal Society London*
RA	*Revue Archéologique*
RM	*Römische Mitteilungen*
ZPE	*Zeitschrift für Papyrologie und Epigraphik*

PREFACE

This book arose out of a half-hour lecture given in two successive one-day conferences for teachers, organised jointly by The Joint Association of Classical Teachers and the British Museum Education Service and held in the British Museum some years ago. It is not a history of Greek pottery nor is it a study of Greek painting, nor again a picture book – all those are catered for elsewhere. I have organised it in a way that highlights various aspects and approaches, and it is hoped that it will prove useful to students of Classical Greek civilisation. I am grateful to the Manchester University Press for agreeing to publish it.

The museums named in the list of illustrations were very generous in furnishing photographs and in giving permission for the reproduction of material in their care. Mr Alan Burn, Head of the Cartographic Unit at the University of Southampton, had the figures specially drawn for this book; my thanks to him.

Financial assistance towards publication was very kindly provided by The Joint Association of Classical Teachers and the University of Southampton.

I have been fairly liberal with bibliographical references, not that I imagine that readers will have access to all the publications, rather that the references provide the evidence on which statements in the text are based and can be followed up in university or specialist libraries by the more industrious student. A word of warning: the references to Beazley 1956, 1963 and 1971, and to Carpenter 1989, are to lists of illustrations, not to the illustrations themselves.

The book is dedicated to my wife who has provided inspiration and support from start to finish.

I

INTRODUCTION

Archaeologists in general and students of ceramics in particular largely live in an ancient world of their own creation. (Casson 1938, 464)

To understand the important rôle clay and pottery played in the lives of the ancient Greeks, one need only consider the many and various objects in use today that are the equivalent of those earlier products, e.g. buckets, saucepans, light bulbs, clocks, jewel boxes, perfume sprays, wine bottles, tankards, toys, feeding bottles, roof tiles, beehives. Some today are still fashioned from clay, many are not, especially the finer wares which are now usually made of glass, china or plastic. There was a vast range of pottery production in antiquity, from heavy-duty storage jars and cooking ware to elegant wine cups and miniature perfume pots. Most social needs could be answered by the potter, and his rôle in the community was central and busy. There were few areas of life in which the potter failed to assist – anything that needed a container would usually find a ready answer at the potter's shop: water, wine, oil, honey, grain, brine, vinegar, fish, olives, etc.

For the Greeks, whether in Greece itself or in the other areas of the Mediterranean and beyond, where they settled, clay was usually readily available; it was a fundamental natural resource. When fired, it was porous, so if unglazed, it kept the contents cool by allowing evaporation; it was to a large extent waterproof, especially if glazed. It was malleable and thus could be formed into a great variety of shapes. Fashion ensured constant changes in shapes and details of shapes (foot, handles, lip, etc.) and in the decoration, whilst the differences in the geological base from which clays were dug led to differences in the fabric and finish. Hence the products are susceptible to study stylistically, chronologically and geographically.

The chapters that follow look at Greek pottery from a number of viewpoints and try to present a broad picture that gives some notion of their variety and importance. This is not a history of Greek vase-painting, though painted pottery has the largest part to play. The interest and high quality of Greek figured vases have tended to concentrate attention on those in particular, and often it has been the drawings on the vases that

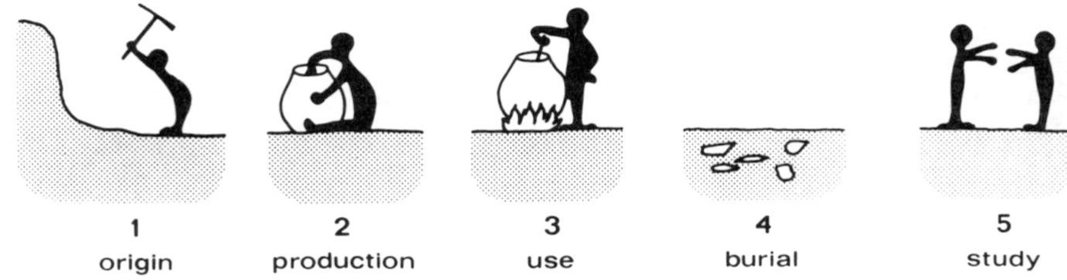

I.1 Stages in the history of a vase

have been made the focal point of Greek vase studies. This is natural, but such an approach tends to unbalance the study (as doubtless is the case here) and runs the risk of placing the vases in the category of art objects, to the exclusion of other considerations.

Greek pottery can be studied from many points of view (Fig. I.1): technique, period, place of production, function, shape, decoration, distribution, etc. The five chapters that follow deal with

(a) the techniques of forming, painting and firing with some attempt to sketch the organisation of potteries;

(b) the means used nowadays to date pottery, both relatively and absolutely;

(c) the shapes the potters created for the various needs of life and death, with a discussion of the names of potters and of shapes;

(d) the decoration that was applied to the shapes, whether incised, relief or painted, with a consideration of the different motifs, geometric, floral and figured, the last leading to a discussion of painters and subject matter;

(e) the later life of pottery: how much it cost, where, why and how it travelled, etc.

The types of evidence on which a study of this sort is based are:

(a) the pots themselves. They can be investigated singly for the techniques of making, shape and decoration, and for their petrological and chemical composition; they can be compared with others which share similarities in shape and so forth; and they can be studied in the contexts in which they were found, to help date them relatively or absolutely, to understand their function, and to see how far from their place of origin they may have been moved.

(b) the equipment of production. This can be the kiln evidence, workshop finds, trial pieces, etc.

(c) the references to pots and pottery production in written sources. There are some references in ancient authors and a few inscriptions that provide information, but the yield is not great. It has often been pointed

out that pottery, being a private, not a 'state' concern, is almost invisible in the literary record.

(d) the illustrations on painted pottery. A few show potters and painters at work; these are mainly to be found on Corinthian and Attic products and provide vital clues on technique and organisation.[1] Much more common are figured scenes with the pots in everyday use, and these are an unrivalled source of evidence.

(e) ethnography. Throughout antiquity the environment did not change: the summers were hot and dry, the winters cold and wet; the soil was mainly stony, the vegetation sparse. These conditions still obtain, and there has been much recent study of those potters in the eastern Mediterranean who continue to produce pottery by traditional methods. These may help towards creating a more vivid picture of ancient production.[2]

Ancient Greek pottery had a long development and a remarkable continuity; survival is abundant, and the areas of production are widespread, though evidence is not evenly balanced in time or place. The potters were businessmen, pot-making their livelihood. Their work was also a craft; some of them were high quality craftsmen, others, both in forming shapes and adding decoration, were poor at their job. The distinction does not tell us who were the better businessmen, that is a question of markets served and pots sold. The figured wares that carry complex and allusive stories argue a clientele that is literate and urban; such material is not a hallmark of the rural communities.

Study of the subject is constantly changing with new material and new approaches. The following paragraphs indicate the whereabouts of the actual material and some of the principal published sources of it.

Museums. The big national collections were mainly built up in the nineteenth century and contain material that was excavated in the manner of the time or that had been gathered into private collections earlier. The vases are therefore mainly isolated pieces, and the treasure aspect of them is hard to eradicate, though many museums now adopt a more didactic rôle (Figs. I.2 and 3). Some local museums in Greece, and in other countries where Greeks settled or with which they traded, house material excavated nearby and kept in the contexts in which they were found. There are also private collections, some open to the public, and these tend to contain pieces that have been acquired individually for their instrinsic art-historical interest. Catalogues of museum holdings are published from time to time, also annual bulletins of new, or studies of old, acquisitions.[3]

Exhibitions. On occasion material within a museum or borrowed from elsewhere is put on show in a special display which concentrates on e.g. a site, a centenary, a subject, an artist. A catalogue is usually produced to mark the exhibition and presents an up-to-date account of work in that

I.2 A vase gallery of the Berlin Museum ca. A.D. 1900

I.3 A modern museum display of Greek pottery, Bern

I.4 Pottery from a well in the Athenian Agora

particular field. So whereas an exhibition is temporary, the catalogue furnishes a permanent record of it.[4]

New finds. Excavations in territories bordering on the Mediterranean, and indeed in such areas as south Russia and the inland parts of European and Middle Eastern countries, and now increasingly in underwater contexts, reveal the presence of Greek pottery, often in abundance (Fig. I.4). The material may be whole (e.g. often in graves) or badly fragmented (e.g. on a town site); the condition usually depends on the type of site. Occasionally, a brief account of the finds is published within the year (e.g. in such publications as the annual *Archaeological Reports* of the Hellenic Society and the British School at Athens, or the annual *Chroniques* of the *Bulletin de Correspondance Hellénique*; for Greece there is the *Arkhaiologiki Ephemeris* and the *Arkhaiologikon Deltion*; and for Italy, *Notizie degli Scavi and Studi Etruschi* provide a similar service). With important, planned excavations, later, more detailed and definitive reports are published, either in archaeological periodicals, in single volumes, or in continuing series such as those of the American excavations in Athens and Corinth or the French at Delphi and Delos.[5]

Sale catalogues. Not all new material comes from controlled excavations. The art market, wherever based, whether Switzerland, London or New York, feeds the demands made by some museums and private collectors for new material. This material may be the contents of a private collection formed earlier that is being sold, or may consist of objects that have been illegally excavated and smuggled out of the country of discovery.[6]

Publications. As pottery can be studied from many different aspects, the range of publications is vast. Also, quite naturally, the publications serve different needs: to inform and interest scholar, student or lay person, archaeologist, historian or art-lover.

There is an international barrage of academic journals (such as *The Journal of Hellenic Studies*, *The American Journal of Archaeology*, *Revue Archéologique*, *Antike Kunst*, *Jahrbuch des Deutschen Archäologischen Instituts*) that contain articles of specific character. In these it is the expert speaking to his colleagues.[7] Other journals provide studies that are aimed at the beginner, but in most cases a general background knowledge of the subject is needed. As far as books are concerned, here too there is great variety, from the detailed monograph on a very specialised subject (e.g. a vase shape, imagery, religious use) to general histories of greater or lesser bulk and of varying emphasis (art, myth, trade). Keeping track of the work being published is an ever present task for the scholar and student; occasionally a resumé of recent work is published, with annotated bibliographies.[8]

Students are well served with histories of Greek vase-painting, in whole or part, and in some volumes the photographs are of high quality, whereas in others the emphasis is on the text, and the illustrations need supplementing from other picture books. Naturally, painted pottery bulks large in books concerned with Greek art, as indeed it does in those dealing with religion, social life, economics, etc.[9]

A special word may be said about the volumes in the *Corpus Vasorum Antiquorum* series, begun in 1923. They now comprise nearly 250 fascicules from 24 countries, and present vases from Bronze Age Cretan and Cypriot to Italiot black and relief painted, with a concentration on Attic black- and red-figured pottery. Not all are of usable quality, especially the earlier ones which tended to illustrate vases at a small scale and in poor photographs, but the more recent fascicules are of a high standard.[10]

Less attention has been paid in general publications to Greek coarse wares. Of the heavy-duty wares, the transport jars (amphorae), because of their usefulness in establishing trade relations, have been quite extensively studied and published.[11]

Congresses. Another way in which the study of pottery is advanced and promulgated is through the gathering of scholars to speak and discuss research work centring on chosen themes. The proceedings of these

congresses often provide the most up-to-date thinking on topics of interest.[12]

II
MAKING

'To make pottery': commonly said instead of 'to work hard' *The Souda* (tenth century A.D.)

The potteries

The areas of the Mediterranean and beyond in which the Greeks lived in antiquity were rich in clays: the Greek mainland, the islands, Asia Minor, Sicily and south Italy. However, not all clay deposits are equally suitable for the making of pottery or of any other clay object, as the geological make-up of the different regions varies and provides their own particular compositions of clay (Fig. II.1). For this reason, as well as for reasons of historical development, some areas were better able than others not only to produce pottery for local use but also to supply pots for others, whether as containers or as objects of value in themselves. Naturally, there were many pottery producers who had no outlets beyond a limited local area, and indeed no incentive to make more than they could sell in the immediate neighbourhood.[1]

The clays that prove useful in pottery production are those which are known as secondary or sedimentary clays: they are rocks which have been weathered and moved by erosion, and contain organic or mineral impurities such as iron, sand, stones and vegetable matter. The primary or residual clays which have not moved and are uncontaminated by foreign matter, are of less use. The fact that the composition of clays differs from region to region helps in tracking to its place of origin the pottery found scattered over the Greek world and beyond. Often the differences between the clay body of pots can be seen with the naked eye; one of the most easily discernible differences is that between the clay of Corinthian fine wares which is relatively pure and fires to a greenish yellow colour, and the less pure clay found in and around Athens which is rich in micas, feldspars and quartz, and fires to a strong red colour. But in many instances the eye is not enough, and there are differences that can be better or only understood by the use of such modern scientific techniques as optical emission spectroscopy and the thin sections of petrographic analysis (see pp. 26–7). Such analysis has shown, for instance, that some of the clay that was

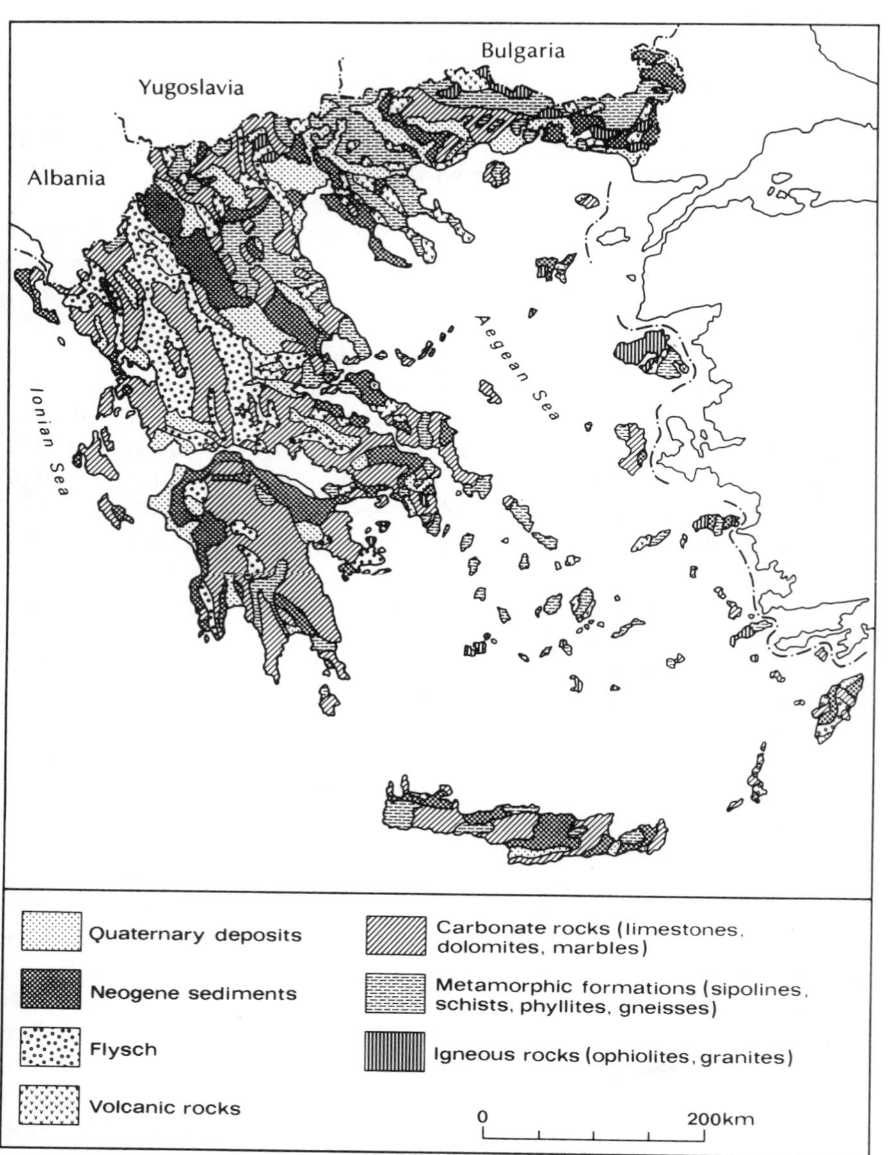
Bulgaria
Yugoslavia
Albania
Aegean Sea
Ionian Sea
Quaternary deposits
Neogene sediments
Flysch
Volcanic rocks
Carbonate rocks (limestones, dolomites, marbles)
Metamorphic formations (sipolines, schists, phyllites, gneisses)
Igneous rocks (ophiolites, granites)
0
200km

II.1 Geological map of Greece

worked near the Athenian Agora was brought in from Cape Kolias 15 km away.

The qualities which all clays share to a greater or lesser degree and which they must have if potters are to make use of them, are (a) pliability which renders the material malleable while it is being worked; (b) porosity which enables the moisture to evaporate in the drying and firing process; and (c) vitreousness which leads to hardening in the firing. Some clays are more suitable for the making of fine wares, whilst others, having a higher resistence to thermal shock, are more satisfactory for the production of cooking wares, such as the clay from the island of Aegina on the Saronic Gulf.

Greek pottery was produced in vast quantities and in many different places, but comparatively little is known of the layout of workshops and the establishments where pottery was made. Kilns have been excavated, and these give evidence for one aspect of the work involved in a pottery, but the wider picture is still relatively indistinct. Ethnological studies of modern workshop practices have suggested some methods of organisation that might have existed in classical Greek times.[2] Certainly, an effective method of work, once created, would be retained, as experimentation was likely to prove too costly. Family businesses must have been common. Plato (*Republic* 467A) has Socrates ask: 'Haven't you noticed how, in a craft like the potter's, children serve a long apprenticeship, watching how things are done, before they take a hand in the work themselves?' Sons (and maybe daughters) would follow their parents and gain experience from practical apprenticeship. Amongst the few names of potters and painters that have survived, there are some which show such relationships between father and son and other members of a family (see pp. 67, 112).

Not all production units would have worked the whole year round; the smaller, household-based industries in which the women of the family were likely to have played a major rôle in pottery production alongside the men, would have been carried on in the spring and summer, filling the gaps in the store of domestic crockery by mending the old and making new. A look at the agricultural and religious calendars shows that gaps in the farmer's year and dates for annual festivals would encourage seasonal working in the potteries. Nor would all potters have necessarily remained in one place to carry out their work; itinerant potters who served the needs of different villages by coming with their pack animal and their load of pots and/or wet clay and working among the local people, have been known in modern Greece and in other parts of the Mediterranean in recent times, and such 'strolling' potters are likely to have been in business in antiquity.[3] Some of these peripatetic concerns would also be unlikely to use a wheel; they would either use a turntable which, needing less force, might have been turned by the women, or would build up the pots on a fixed base, as has

been customary in areas of Greece and Cyprus until recently. Like wheels, kilns also were not indispensable items of equipment, as pots could (and can) be fired in surface bonfires.

Even the larger establishments have left little trace, but once again comparisons with modern traditional practices can be made. Potters may have been in business on their own, with a few assistants (perhaps members of their own family), and would seek to earn their livelihood from the making and selling of their own products. At the other end of the scale would be the groups of workshops situated in towns where wealth was concentrated, demand was high and work might continue all the year round, and where a wide variety of specialised wares would be produced, serving both local and distant demands. It is these workshops that we know best today, mainly from the study of their varied output, but it is doubtful if we should think in terms of really large businesses. Even for Athens, the most plentiful production centre of fine pottery in ancient Greece, one recent estimate suggests that the total number of people working in the potters' shops at any one time in fifth century B.C. is unlikely to have exceeded five hundred.[4] This is very much an estimated figure: for less well known centres and for the smaller outfits there is too little evidence even to hazard a guess. The potter's status is likely to have been low; some were immigrant workers, some slaves. Conditions would have been harsh, and punishment severe.

In the larger congregations of potteries work seems to have been carried out close together in a particular district, producing a social bond and intense rivalry. Athens and Corinth both had their 'potters' quarter' where it would seem that the greater proportion of the craftsmen carried out their work in fairly small individual workshops.[5] At Corinth it is suggested that the shops which were located on the fringes of the settlement, as near to the clay and fuel sources and the farmlands as to the centre of the town, were nucleated workshops with workers in separate establishments, whereas at Athens the shops were near the Agora and may have been manufactories (with the workers in one building) rather than nucleated arrangements. It has been shown that at Athens one painter might work for six different potters, and one potter serve as many as ten different painters, and this argues a more extended unit.

If we are to imagine what a potter's establishment looked like, we must envisage (Fig. II.2) an open yard with room for mounds of clay that have been brought in from the nearby clay pits, a good supply of water, and a generous store of wood needed for the firings. To one side of the yard would be the shed in which the potter's wheel, etc. was housed, and not far away would be the kiln itself, decked with small religious offerings to ensure a successful firing. Some area of the yard might be used for the building up of larger pots by hand in sections, and room would be needed

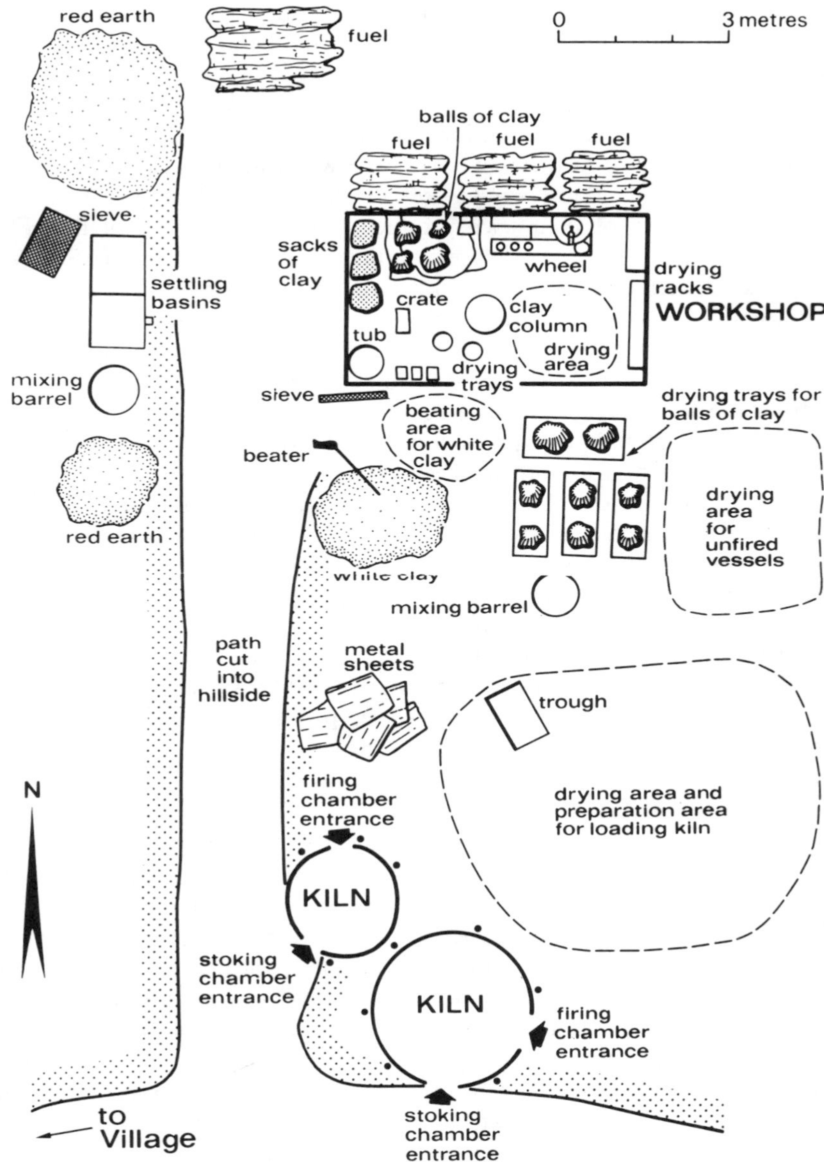

II.2 Plan of modern potter's traditional workshop in Crete

for the drying-out of the pots after they have been formed and before the firing.

The crude clays were first dug by open extraction from the clay pits and along with other materials were transferred to the potter's yard by pack animal. It is usually necessary to remove unwanted elements such as pebbles and roots, and the clay is mixed with water to form a slurry from which the impurities can be washed away. For the fine wares it is the purer clays that are wanted, whereas for the coarse, heavy-duty containers and for the larger architectural figures of terracotta, temper in the form of sand and crushed rock would have been added to give the finished article the required strength. The clay is then dried out in the yard and cut in squares, and left to weather for some months, being added to the older clays to form the mixture that the potter needs.

Let us now consider the three major stages in the making of a pot: forming, decorating and firing.

Forming

Within the potter's workroom, which may have been a fairly dark, enclosed building, the business of throwing the pots took place. The equipment in the shed would have varied. Not all pots were made on the wheel; indeed, we have already seen that some were made freehand, maybe with the help of a low-level turntable, which could be square and made of stone or wood, and was a slower process than the wheel, or maybe built up in the yard itself if they were big jars like the 'Ali Baba' pithoi that were formed in coils or slabs.[6] Some pots were made with a paddle and anvil, the paddle being struck against the emerging shape of the pot, the anvil held inside to provide a surface to receive the blows.[7] This process produced a thinness that was required for some of the shapes of cooking pots to enable them to be set on the fire and be heated without cracking. Some of the more elegant shapes were made in moulds, e.g. the perfume bottles formed in the shape of birds (Fig. IV.9), animals and humans, and vases in the shape of human and animal heads that were used as drinking cups; also mould-made were the very popular hemispherical bowls with relief decoration that are the major fine wares of the Hellenistic period (Fig. V.7) and are best known later from the shapes and patterns encountered in Roman red wares (see pp. 26, 110).

However, much the most important method was that which depended on the fast wheel. This demanded more constant, physical effort, and was most likely man's work. More standardised and livelier shapes were produced by this technique, and en masse, so not merely for one household. The invention of the fast wheel was certainly a fundamental advance in method.

II.3 Making a cup on an Attic black-figure kylix, ca. 550 B.C.

Our evidence for making wheel-thrown pottery in Classical Greece derives mainly from the pots themselves or from illustrations of potters at work that decorate some Corinthian, Attic (Fig. II.3) and Boeotian vases.[8] Virtually no written evidence on the subject has survived, and what there is is slight and unhelpful. However, the picture that we can recreate is fairly full and consistent. The potter sat on a low stool, or squatted on his heels, with his knees almost at the level of the wheel itself which was set quite close to the ground. A spindle was fitted into a socket in a pit below the floor. The

wheel itself, which acted both as throwing plate and fly wheel, was most likely made of wood and seems to have been on average between half a metre and a metre wide.[9] There was no kick wheel which the potter could work with his foot; instead the potter had an assistant, a wheel-boy, who sat opposite him on a low block or cushion and spun the wheel with both hands, while the potter guided the clay from the heel of his hands to his fingers in a counterclockwise motion. Naturally there were times when the potter needed to stand at the wheel, e.g. to put his hand down into a deep jar, and times when he would spin the wheel himself, e.g. to gauge the evenness of a vase as he moved the wheel slowly.

At his side the potter needed to have ready the tools of his trade: plenty of water in a bowl to keep the clay malleable, his shaping and measuring implements, e.g. knives, scrapers, etc. of wood, metal or bone, callipers for measuring a section, a sponge for smoothing the surface of the pot, string for removing the pot from the wheel, and drying racks and trays. But his chief tools were his sure hands and quick fingers.

The process of throwing the pot was very similar to that adopted now:[10] kneading and working the clay to remove the bubbles and to give a smooth consistency, centring the lump of clay on the wheel, forming the hollow and drawing up the sides into a cylindrical shape (Fig. II.4). Some vases were made in one piece and needed only a sponge for smoothing the surface and a string for drawing under the pot to remove it from the rotating wheel. It would be few vases, however, that could be formed in one process; many were made in sections – neck, body, stem – and later luted together with wet clay slip. An expert potter would be able to produce a series of vases of the same shape with almost identical proportions without complicated and repeated measurements.[11] His eye and a stick, maybe a rule or callipers, would be sufficient tools, together with the experience he had acquired over the years. A potter's brains were in his hands.

When a pot is taken from the wheel, it is heavy with water and must be set aside to dry. The pots must be left until they are in a leather-hard condition, and during this time they will shrink slightly through evaporation. At this stage as at others later, accidents are likely to happen. Some of the potter's daily batch of pots may sag or crack, or the joining of the sections may prove unstable. Failures at this stage can be scrapped and the clay re-used; more serious problems occur during the processes of decorating and firing, by which time the damage cannot be so easily rectified.

Next day when the pots have dried out, they need attention again. The potter places his leather-hard pot upside down on the wheel and turns it, i.e. he shaves off the unwanted clay with a sharp knife and smooths and polishes the surface to make it ready to be placed directly in the kiln, or to

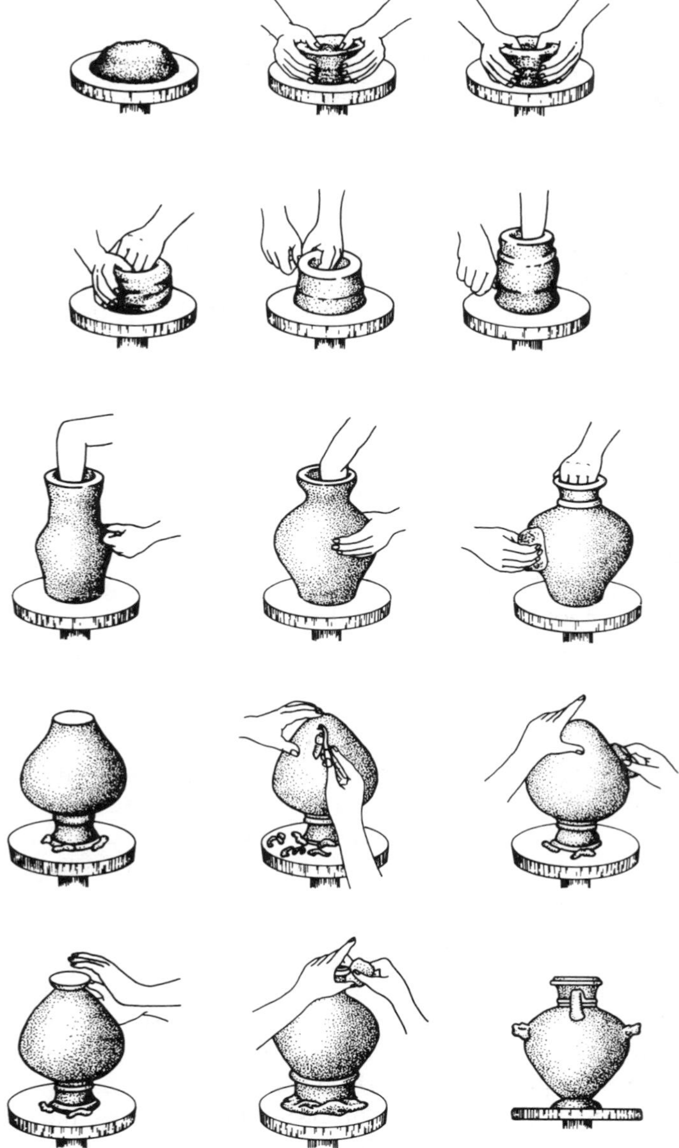

II.4 Making a hydria

receive the paint. Many pots will now need to have attachments added to them: handles, a foot, or even an appliqué in floral, animal or human form. After assembling the pot in this way, the potter turns it again. The pots are now set aside for the kiln or for decoration to be added.

Decorating

It was few pots that did not need or receive the application of decoration of some kind. Some large containers, as the transport amphorae (Fig. III.9), might receive a painted covering inside to seal the surface and render the clay less permeable, though even then it was not totally impervious to seepage. Many others were mainly left plain both inside and out but carried a small amount of decoration – stripes, wavy lines, circles; others were furnished with a complete covering of paint outside and in, which fired black – these were the cheaper forms of fine ware. The more costly products were elaborately painted with geometric, floral, animal and human compositions.

Instead of, or as well as, being painted, pots were decorated in other ways. The pithoi were often furnished with relief decoration; this could be in the form of raised strips that had patterns incised on them, or bands of figured decoration that were impressed on the wet surface with a roller (Fig. IV.5). On fine wares incised and impressed decoration was also covered with black gloss. Relief decoration is also found in conjunction with paint, and some pots have elaborate attachments added in the shape of snakes, animal and human heads, and floral details.

As for the nature of the paint used, recent practical investigations have shown that the paint is a special preparation that has as its basic ingredient the same clay as the vase.[12] To produce the 'gloss', the painters used the finer, more settled clay which had a more compact consistency than that from which the pot itself was formed. They added to it a deflocculating agent that hastened the separation process and ensured that the fine particles were suspended in the liquid. The agent used to activate the clay in this way could be rain water, potash (wood ash soaked in water) or iron-bearing sand.

When being applied, the liquid clay is deep red in colour and may not have been very different from the colour of the vase itself. Through evaporation the liquid has a creamy consistency. In some wares the surface was polished before and after the painting was done; this 'burnishing' was done with a pebble, a piece of bone or a wooden tool. Also a weak solution of clay might be washed over the whole surface of the pot as a base coat to enhance the colour.

The ways in which the clay solution was applied depended on the final appearance required. For the inside of a 'closed' pot which could not be

reached by hand, a rough swilling of the liquid might suffice. For the outside, a slapdash way of applying the paint was to pour it over the pot; another easy way was dipping, and the finger marks round the feet of many vases indicate that the potter or his assistant had plunged the pot into a bowl of liquid gloss. For more careful, but still quick painting, the vase could be set back on the wheel, perhaps on a small block, and the gloss applied with a brush as the wheel was rotated. This method could also be used for adding horizontal lines, and also for those parts of the more elaborately decorated vases that needed covering above and below the zones and panels (Fig. II.3).

For the actual painted decoration of the vases, more detailed and painstaking work was needed. Where extra special care was being taken, a preliminary mapping out of the composition might be done, and for some of the figured work a preliminary sketch with a stick of charcoal or lead was made, which guided the painter when he came to apply the gloss. This preliminary sketch was not always adhered to, and where a furrow had been made with the stick, the original sketch is sometimes visible.[13] Brushes were the most common tool for the application of the gloss. Sometimes for

II.5 A potter's shop in Athens on an Attic red-figure bell-krater, ca. 430 B.C.

concentric patterns a number of brushes were fastened together to produce an evenly executed set of circles or semicircles, applied either freehand or with compasses.[14] When using the brush the painter would sometimes sit with the vase resting lightly on his thighs (Fig. II.5) or with it standing on the motionless wheel (Fig. II.3). The angle at which some tondos were set inside kylikes would suggest that some cups were set on a table and rested on their rim and handle while being painted. It was with a brush alone that the floral and geometric patterns were created, and in some periods and places the figure work also depended on nothing more than a brush.

The techniques that have attracted the most attention and that were some of the most elaborate in antiquity are the black-figure and red-figure techniques of Corinth, Athens and elsewhere. It is on pottery decorated in these ways that ornamentation rose to an art (e.g. Figs. V.9, 10, 12). Black-figure, which was first produced in Corinth ca. 700 B.C. and was then borrowed and used more extensively in Athens from ca. 630 B.C. onwards, enhanced the old technique of the brush with the addition of engraved lines and added colours (red and white) to enliven the compositions. The engraving must have been done with a sharp pointed instrument after the gloss had dried, and if we are to imagine what other objects the painter needed to have at his elbow, we should add paint pots for the gloss and for the added colours, his brushes, sticks, compasses and sponges (Fig. II.5).

The techniques of silhouette, outline and black-figure painting (e.g. Figs. II.3; III.1, 7; V.1), as the names suggest, produced figures and designs done in black gloss with the background left in the colour of the clay or slightly heightened by the application of a wash. The technique of red-figure (e.g. Figs. II.5, 6; III.4, 5, 6; IV.8; V.9, 10, 12; VI.4), which was invented in Athens ca. 530 B.C., reversed the colours: the figures were left in the background red, and the background to them was filled in with the gloss which fired black. The red-figure technique was mainly practised in Athens, but it was borrowed by some other centres, by Athens' neighbour, Boeotia, by Corinth, and most spectacularly in Sicily and south Italy, areas to which potters and painters can be shown to have emigrated from Athens in the second half of the fifth century.

As work in red-figure embraces most other methods, it is worth spending a little time seeing how much care might be taken with Attic red-figure vases to produce the elaborate compositions that represent the high mark of Greek painted pottery. First, a preliminary sketch was made, and this was followed by the lining-out of the figures with a broad band of paint, what is now usually called the 'eighth-of-an-inch' stripe (Figs. II.6 and 9). These painted lines would stand as the outside edge of the intended shape to produce the contour of the figures. Then the figures themselves would be filled in with the details of anatomy and clothing needed and with the

addition of washes of brown dilute for the less important details. The pattern and background would then be filled in, these perhaps being left to assistants or apprentices. When the paint had dried, added colours might be applied: white (usually for women's skin), red (for blood, for the lettering, etc.) and in some cases added clay with a covering of gilt (for wreaths, golden ornaments, etc.).

From the above resumé there has been omitted an important and controversial technique. Many Attic red-figure vases show painted lines that are raised from the surface of the vase, relief lines that emphasise the contours of the figures or inner details of anatomy and clothing. They catch the light and can be felt with the fingers. Instances of this technique are found on some black-figure vases where it was used on minor details; however, it was the red-figure painters who realised its effectiveness to the full. The implement which formed the relief lines must have held a good amount of gloss and was able to dispense it evenly for some distance. Much discussion has centred round the nature of this tool, and recent suggestions have attracted a good deal of interest. One suggestion is that a bag was attached to a quill head which enabled the solution to be squeezed out almost indefinitely without the quill being lifted from the surface of the vase, like a syringe. In a second suggestion a more basic implement has been postulated: a brush with a single hard bristle or a few flexible hairs loaded with gloss. Practical demonstrations with these tools have shown that they work, but many scholars still champion such tools as the quill or reed pen with a conical point and a thin brush inserted into the hollow to restrict the flow, or a metal tube pressed flat at one end and cut on the diagonal with the gloss filling the tube.[15]

Apart from the use of the gloss which fires black or red in reaction to the firing conditions, other techniques were employed, though none was so popular. The white which was used as a supplementary colour in black- and red-figure was on occasion used as a background slip for silhouette and outline figures. Another of the rarer techniques involved covering the surface of the vase completely in gloss and then adding different colours (such as white and red) over the gloss in the form of figures or floral designs. Polychrome was a rare technique in the use both of ceramic colours and of colours applied after firing. There are also some instances where by the application of different strengths of gloss the painter was able to produce both black and coral red at one firing. For all these, see Chapter V.

The success or failure of the painting would only appear after the vases had been fired, but, although some of the failures would be caused by mistakes in the kiln, others had already been made once the pot had been painted, and even a totally successful firing could do nothing to retrieve the mistakes. Some of the commonest mistakes in painting stem from such causes as the failure to mix the correct consistency of paint, the use of two

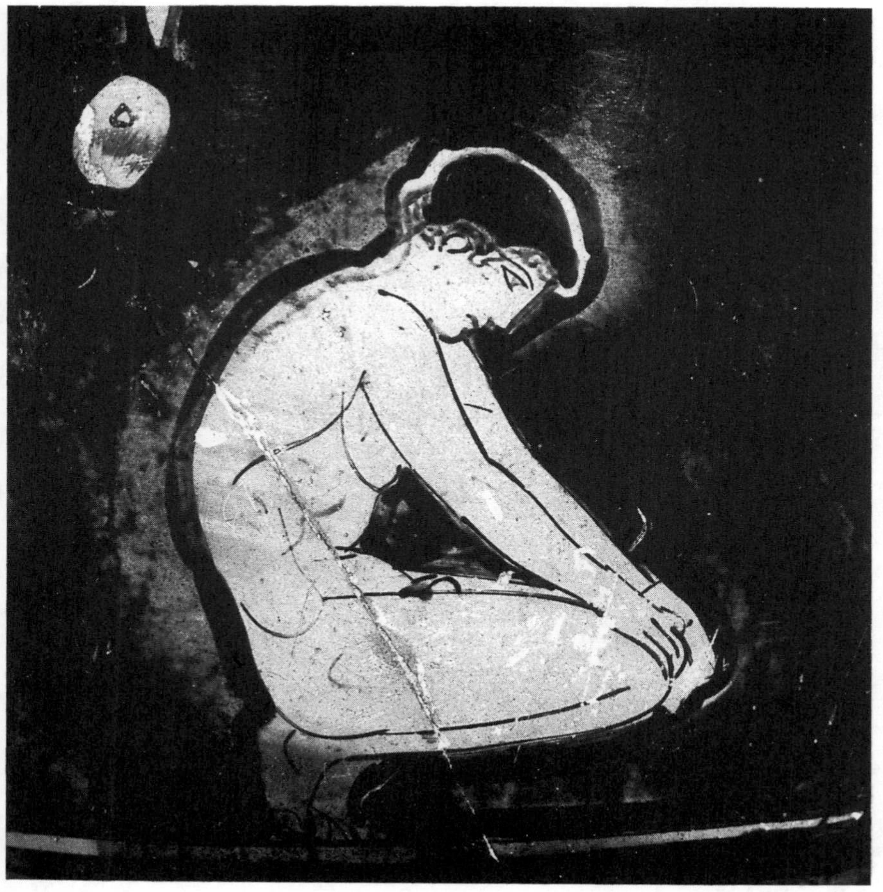

II.6 Glaze failure on an Attic mug, ca. 430–420 B.C.

different batches of paint (e.g. one for the background, one for the contours) that were affected in different ways in the kiln (Fig. II.6); less frequently we can see that a painter attempted to cover over a design he decided to change but failed to apply the gloss thickly enough to prevent the earlier drawing showing through the gloss once fired.[16]

Once the paint was dry, the pots were ready for the incisions and then for the kiln.

Firing

The firing of a batch of pottery – turning unbaked clay into terracotta – was, and still is, a tricky business. After all the previous stages in the

making of the pots – digging the clay, preparing it, forming it into useful shapes and decorating it – it was the final stage that was the most important, and it was the work at the kiln to control the heat that was crucial. A Greek poem, most likely composed in Athens in the sixth century B.C., gives a lively picture of the firing.[17] The poet has been asked for a song and expects to be paid:

> If you pay me, potters, I will sing:
> come here, Athena, and hold your hand over the kiln.
> May the cups and bowls all turn out a good black,
> may they be well fired, and fetch the price asked . . .
> But if you turn shameless and deceitful,
> then will I summon the ravagers of kilns . . .
> Stamp on the stoking tunnel and chambers, and may the whole kiln
> be thrown into confusion, while the potters cry aloud.
> As a horse's jaw grinds, so may the kiln grind
> to powder all the pots within it . . .
> And if anyone bends over to look into the spy-hole, may his whole face
> be scorched, so that all may learn to deal justly.

So care had to be taken in building the kiln, in storing the pottery in it for each firing and in arranging the firing itself from the heating to the cooling and the opening. Such troubles as those listed above would also apply to firing without a kiln, such as the surface bonfires when the pots were covered with wood, charcoal, twigs, etc. Indeed, all firings had an unpredictable outcome.

Kilns were built outside in the yard. Some examples of kilns survive in

II.7 Kiln on Corintbian votive plaque, sixth century B.C.

fragmentary form from ancient Greece, and there are a number of painted representations of firings taking place that help in recreating their appearance (Fig. II.7).[18] The kilns, partly sunk in the ground to support the structure, to preserve the heat and to give easier access to the stoking and firing chambers, were made of mud and clay with the inclusion of stones and perhaps old fragments of pottery; they were usually in a round plan, though some were square.[19] By modern standards those found are small, some under 2 metres in diameter (modern traditional sizes range from 2 to 3 metres); there is no knowing to what size they may have been built in some of the larger establishments. All are of the cylindrical, updraught type with an arched stoking tunnel projecting from the side just below ground level, leading to the firing chamber which was furnished with a pierced floor above (Fig. II.8). Directly above this was the stacking chamber which had a dome-shaped roof with a vent at the top and a chimney; old pieces of broken pottery which would be lying around the yard could be used for the chimney. The permanent structures of actual ancient kilns are preserved only a little way above ground level, and the projecting edge is smooth; this suggests that the domed covering may not have been permanent. The painted illustrations of kilns (e.g. Fig. II.7) all seem to agree on the basic shape with domed top and chimney, and they also show a door to one side, perhaps for loading the pots into the firing chamber. The door may have had a spy-hole incorporated into it or set to one side of it. A lucky mascot would usually have been hung on the outside of the kiln, to ward off the

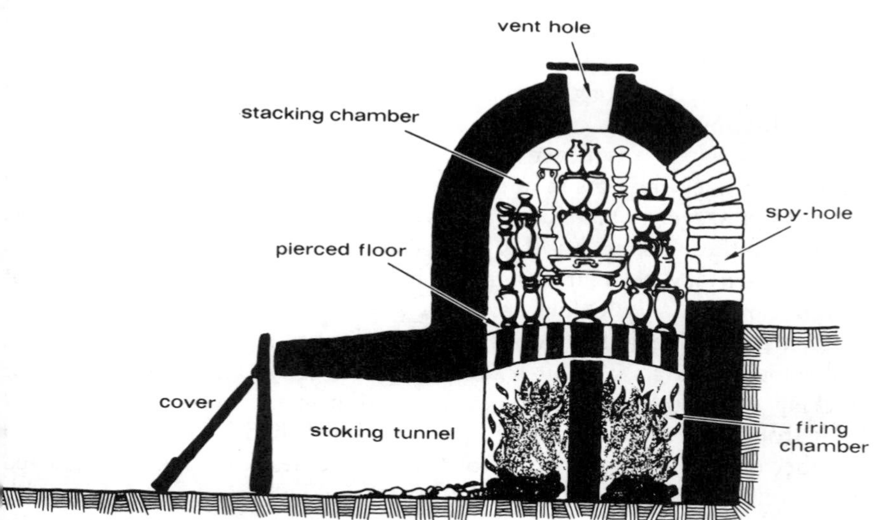

II.8 Modern reconstruction of ancient kiln

II.9 Unfinished Attic red-figure fragment used as test piece, ca. 460 B.C.

sorts of accidents to which the poet above referred. The dome, if a temporary structure, may have been made of plastered clay and brushwood that could easily be renewed for the next firing, and it is possible that the loading and stacking of the pots could have taken place before the dome was built above them.

As Greek gloss was never sticky either before or during firing, it was possible to stack the pots in and on one another. Hence there was no need for rings or saggers. Some illustrations give the impression that no care was taken with the stacking, but this may be artistic licence to enable the shapes to be drawn and seen. It is hard to believe that special pieces were not placed carefully in the kiln for such a precarious operation. However, accidents were inevitable. Some of the pots were squashed out of shape, and some of the glaze failures can be seen to derive from the methods of stacking where the different types of reaction in the firing had been held back from those vases and parts of vases which had been closely packed together or stacked inside one another, and the desired black has fired red or brown.[20] When the kiln was full, the firing chamber was closed, with only the spy-hole to gauge the colour of the flame and thus the temperature, and to enable the test pieces (Fig. II.9) to be withdrawn.[21]

The fuel for the kiln was wood, of various sorts, rarely good timber, more likely material unusable elsewhere, such as thorn bushes, olive prunings or the discard from olive pulping. It is unlikely that potters made extensive inroads into the tree-cover in antiquity.

To produce the contrast of black paint on a red ground, the firing was carried out in one process which involved three stages; the kiln was not cooled down and unloaded during this time. The whole cycle took some hours; indeed, if one includes the cooling down period at the end, the firing lasted a few days. The heat was gradually raised to about 800 degrees centigrade, and with the vent at the top open to allow oxygen to enter, the pottery was baked to a pinkish buff colour, the gloss becoming a brownish red. This is the first stage, in which the vases are baked in smokeless conditions. In the second, reducing stage, the vent was closed, as was the entrance to the stoking tunnel. Thus the air in the kiln was starved of oxygen. Water was also introduced into the stoking tunnel in the form of wet leaves, green wood, or damp sawdust or shavings. The chemical reaction that took place turned the porous body of the vase a greyish black, and the denser gloss became a sintered black which was able to resist oxidisation in the next stage. The temperature was now at its highest, about 950 degrees centigrade. In the third stage, which resembled the first, the temperature was allowed to drop a little, to about 900, with the vent and stoking tunnel open and the wet leaves, etc. raked out, so there was now only dry fuel and air once more in the kiln. This was the most crucial stage, and it was only by careful balance of temperature and atmosphere that the clay was made to revert to the reddish colour of the first stage and the paint to remain the black colour created in the second stage. In successful firings the gloss was well attached to the surface of the pot and densely compacted. It was by this three-stage process – oxidising, reducing, oxidising – that Greek black-gloss pottery was produced.

The kiln had to be allowed a day or so to cool before it could be opened and the results of the firing seen. Besides the mistakes that may have arisen from the actual painting and stacking, the firing process brought many others in its train. Pots may explode, shapes may warp and fuse in the fire. The colour of the clay and gloss will vary with the effect of the different stages: too little water will produce a poor black colour and texture, the black gloss may become reddish brown through being left too long in the heat or not being heated sufficiently high in the second stage or too high in the third stage. Stacking might shield parts of some pots from the correct atmosphere, and tell-tale marks will appear on the surfaces.[22] A perfect firing produced a sheen on the burnished clay and a bloom on the gloss through sintering; light was reflected from the surface, and the appearance of a more costly metal was imitated.

The kiln would be used again; cracks would be replastered and the dome

rebuilt. Most pots would be ready for use or sale; some would return to the workshop for the addition of further decoration or finishing. The frequency of the firings would obviously depend on the nature of the operation: every few days for a large establishment, once a week or month when working on a small scale or on one's own, seasonally if replenishing the family stock.

The three-stage firing was used for centuries by the Greeks; it seems to have been in operation already in the early second millennium B.C. However, in the Hellenistic period, when the black-on-red decoration of Greek pottery had ceased, and potters had turned to producing mould-made wares which were covered all over with gloss, a red gloss, fired under oxidising conditions only, was adopted in some areas. More importantly, when the Romans began to produce red-gloss table-wares (Arretine and others) based on the Hellenistic relief-mould vases, the potters also used oxidising firings, and the Roman red wares took over completely from the Greek black. The materials were the same, it was the processes of firing that produced the different colours.

Scientific approaches

In distinguishing the different clays and glosses of the various local pottery-producing centres, the eye is often not enough, and pottery is increasingly subjected to scientific analysis in order to investigate the make-up of the vases. Petrographic and chemical analyses enable pottery to be traced back to its clay source and to be grouped with others that share the same elements. Petrographic study seeks to find the origin of the raw materials that comprise a particular clay. By means of thin sections of pottery the mineral inclusions and rock fragments are identified under a polarising microscope (Fig. II.10) and may then be traced back to the geological area from which they originated (Fig. II.1). This method does not work well with fine wares which provide too few distinctive clues; it is used mainly on the coarse and semi-coarse material of such containers as transport amphorae. By contrast, chemical study treats pottery as pottery and seeks to determine the chemical composition of clays by distinguishing the different elements in their make-up. Nine elements are considered to be suggestive of similarities and differences in major groups, and charts are drawn in the form of dendrograms to express these relationships. The methods here include neutron activation analysis (NAA), optical emission spectroscopy (OES) and atomic absorption spectrophotometry (AAS). The study of glosses is also assisted by scientific testing.[23]

The methods proceed from the better known fabrics which may already have been fixed by non-scientific means (find spot, typology, style of decoration, stamps) to the less well known which are hard to place by sight

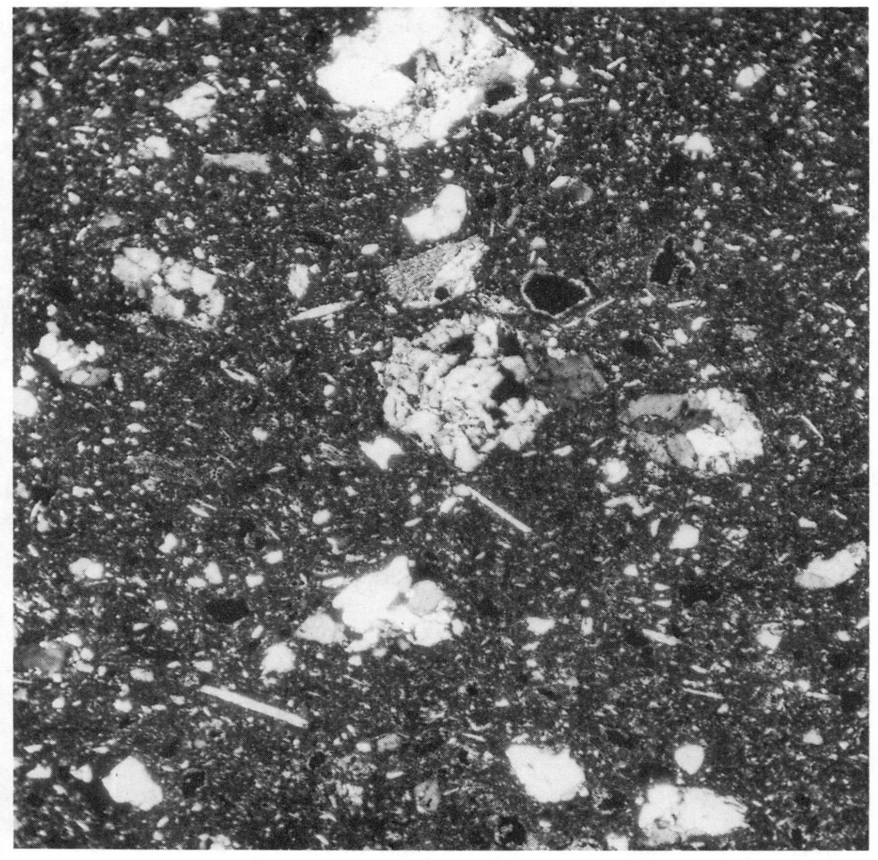

II.10 Thin section of Parian transport amphora

alone. The science is exact, but the results are still open to individual interpretation and hedged about by probabilities. Problems arise about how representative a sample might be, what effect on the raw clay the processing has had, etc. However, as more work is carried out by these methods, so more information is available for comparison, and a 'clay map' of the areas concerned is gradually being created. Thus new and independent approaches to the study of pottery production join the more traditional avenues of investigation and help to refine understanding of the subject.

III
DATING

Scratch is a position from which one can never start. (Lancaster 1947, 9)

Most museum labels in Greek galleries and books illustrating Greek pottery furnish dates for the material they present. For prehistoric periods a sequence date, e.g. Mycenaean III A 1, may be given in preference to, or as well as, a date expressed in the chronological terms we apply today. But for the Greek material of the first millennium B.C. a date in accordance with our present system is usually attempted. Sometimes such dates will be fairly precise, most will be qualified with 'about' or 'circa', or spread into a decade, a quarter century or more. How are such dates arrived at? How trustworthy are they? Why is it possible to be more precise for some pieces than for others?

Relative dates

There is of course in one sense no need to apply our form of dates to Greek pottery at all, even when such absolute dates can be calculated. The chronological relationship of one vase or group of vases to another can be devised on the basis of changes that the vases themselves underwent in shape, decoration or technique, or on the basis of association in an archaeological context, and in this way the history and development of pottery can be charted.

Most Greek vases were made to suit specific purposes, and this usually meant that their shapes persisted with small but perceptible alterations over the years. These changes could affect the contour of the body (broader or narrower, taller or shorter) or details such as the set and angle of the handles or the profile of the foot. Sometimes a shape produced in one area was borrowed by potters working elsewhere, and thus further changes were made and may now be traced. It is rare for the direction of development, whether chronological or geographical, to be misunderstood, as it is not usual for a student to be dependent on this type of evidence alone, but the time gap between pieces, whether produced in the same place or further

afield, is often difficult to assess, as it is unwise to assume a steady, uniform rate of development. Some shapes were enhanced by decoration, and so it is possible to add a second avenue of relative study. The decoration – whether geometric, floral or figured – can be placed in a stylistic progression, and thus another complementary sequence may be constructed. As with shapes, so with decoration, borrowing took place, and so the grid of connections can be extended in this way too. Naturally some of the figured decoration can be studied for its subject matter (see pp. 117–22), and this furnishes another possible avenue of approach to dating. In most centres that produced decorated pottery, the hand of individual craftsmen (sometimes even of the potters, more usually of painters) can now be recognised, and this in itself enables tentative conclusions to be drawn about the chronological span and order of a painter's career. In a few instances, the relationships of families in the pottery business (e.g. father, son, grandson) enable relative dates to be assigned to their work (see pp. 67, 122). In Attic pottery of the sixth and fifth centuries B.C. the precision of the study of vase-painters' work has enabled a grouping of shops, careers and borrowings to be traced so that in conjunction with other types of chronological evidence, a tight system of relative dating for pottery has been devised. The techniques used for the making and decorating of pottery may also be studied to give chronological clues, but these usually have less importance than shape or decoration. In all these approaches to relative dating there is inevitably a tendency to apply logic and consistency. But potters and painters individually worked at different rates of development, many were conservative and traditional in their work, a few more innovative. Also, some periods were more forward-looking than others, and thus change in general varied from time to time; this also applies to the different areas in which pottery was made. So chronology based solely on the relation of vase shapes, decoration and technique is likely to be both overprecise and imprecise at the same time.

A complementary opportunity to apply relative dating is provided by excavated contexts or stratified levels where pottery may be found in bulk, and conclusions about contemporaneity can be attempted. Such contexts may be habitation areas (public and private), shrines, wells, cisterns, pits and graves. The undisturbed embrace of a grave furnishes perhaps the simplest aggregation (Fig. III.1). As some of the vases were made for funerary purposes, they are often found whole and in good condition, and, as the dead were provided with a variety of offerings, the assemblage usually contains vases of different shapes and decoration and maybe of different techniques and origins. Here precision is again a problem, as it is often difficult to know what length of use non-funerary vases may have had before being consigned to the ground: heirlooms and precious possessions, whether larger vases or imported pieces, perhaps treated with more than

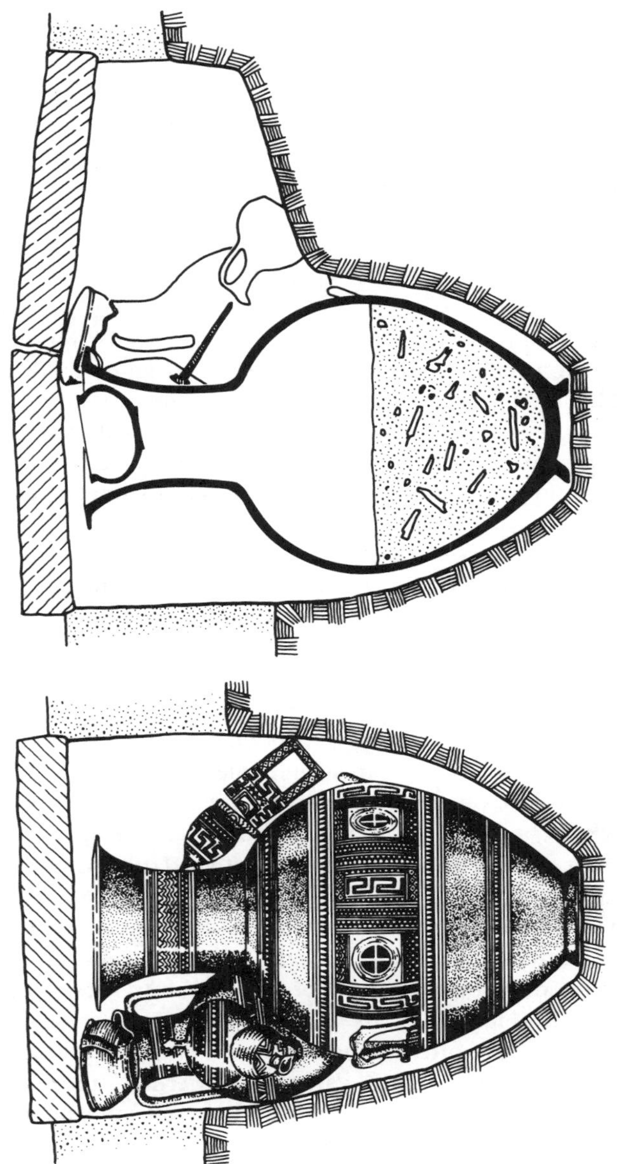

III.1 Attic Geometric cremation grave, ca. 850 B.C.

usual care, might be a generation or more older than the rest of the assemblages.[1] This problem of age is more serious when the discoveries are made in contexts of use, as the material is likely to have had a more varied active life. Shrines in which offerings were made generation after generation may furnish material going far back in time before the moment of destruction or abandonment, just as houses and public buildings will provide pottery that reflects the use of many years.

So a grid of relative dates can be established here and there, but what is needed is 'the measuring rod of absolute historical dates that may be applied to points in the relative sequence'.[2]

Absolute dates

No Greek vase of itself provides its own absolute date. However, there are various ways of arriving at absolute dates, and some of these cross one another, merge with relative dates and supply more secure fixed points by so doing. All absolute dates must be reached by a combination of different types of evidence: documentary, literary, archaeological. For much of their history the Greeks had no overall system of dating; individual states and kingdoms had their own local ways of marking the years such as annual officials or eras, and it is rare for our evidence to link these local dating systems together.[3] Thucydides, writing in the fifth century and wishing to fix the start of the Peloponnesian War (431 B.C.), shows how complex such punctiliousness could be (2.2):

> The thirty years' truce which was entered into after the reconquest of Euboea lasted for fourteen years. In the fifteenth year, the forty-eighth year of Chrysis' priesthood at Argos, the year when Aenesias was ephor at Sparta, and two months before the end of the archonship of Pythodorus at Athens, six months after the battle of Potidaea, just at the beginning of spring, a Theban force . . . made an armed entry into Plataea.

Let us therefore consider some of the ways that have been adopted for combining historical dates and pottery. As Greek pottery did not make news and the association of datable historical events and vases is as a consequence accidental, assistance from the one to the other is usually tangential. But it is from such accidental associations that one can begin to sort out the relationships of pottery and specific dates and to gauge the chronological span from one batch of pottery to another. As the value of the dates that different associations provide varies, the following pages do not move in an orderly chronological progression from Geometric (to 700 B.C.) through Archaic (to 480 B.C.) and Classical (to 323 B.C.) to Hellenistic, but are arranged by categories of association: contexts, parallels with other, more easily datable works of art, subject matter,

inscriptions, etc. The examples given are heavily selected and are chosen to give an indication of the variety of contacts; some are not as important or as fixed as others. Many relate to Athens for which, as it was the most literate state, we have most detailed historical evidence.

Contexts

In excavations pottery is found in various types of site: settlement, sanctuary, cemetery. As we have seen, vases and fragments of vases can be dated in relation to one another. However, for some finds an external date is available, as the site or the building with which the pottery is connected, may be linked with a date or dates known from written sources. Literary and documentary evidence gives dates for foundations and destructions of settlements and shrines, and it is also possible to link certain graves with known historical events. It is rarely a straightforward procedure, nor do the results or even the premises always command agreement.

What follows is a selection of such items, beginning with the more easily intelligible category of graves.

Datable graves

There are a number of graves, mainly communal, which can be linked to historical events recorded in written sources. We know the dates of many battles that the Greeks fought against one another and against foreign powers. After some of the most famous campaigns communal graves (*polyandria*) were dug either at the site of the battle itself or back in the home town of the dead; some other graves can be associated with less prestigious battles or events. As it was the custom to bury the dead with grave goods that included pottery, material is available for study, and in such cases it is not the actual importance of the event but the fact that it is dated that makes it of interest to students of pottery.

(a) Perhaps the best known communal grave is that which the Athenians erected on the plain of Marathon to house the remains of those who died in the battle against the Persians in 490 B.C.[4] Herodotus (6.117) tells us that 192 Athenians died in the battle, and Thucydides (2.34.5) and Pausanias (1.29.4 and 1.32.3) give more circumstantial information. The mound with its brick platform and underlying graves has been only partially excavated, and there has been much controversy about the finds. However, orthodox opinion is that what has been found there represents the offerings made to the dead a little time after the battle. The material consists for the most part of Attic black-figure; one fragment of an Attic red-figure cup was found, and some vases that stylistically differ from the main finds are earlier or non-Attic. Altogether the ensemble is limited in the assistance it

III.2 Some of the contents from the grave of the Corcyrean ambassadors in Athens, ca. 433 B.C.

affords. More recently a second tomb furnished with contemporary material has been excavated about a mile west of the Athenian mound.[5] This has been identified as the tomb of the Plataeans, Boeotians and slaves that Pausanias mentions (1.32.3); they fell in the same battle. However, the connection of the tomb with the same historical event is not sure.

(b) A recent excavation in the main cemetery of ancient Athens, the Kerameikos ('Dipylon') cemetery to the north-west of the town, has furnished a small group of datable material.[6] An inscribed grave marker records the identity of the two men buried beneath: 'Here the earth received in burial Thersandros and Simylos, two men dear to their native Corcyra; they came as ambassadors and accidentally died, and the sons of the Athenians gave them public funeral honours.' It has been plausibly

suggested that the occasion of the embassy was that which took place in 433 B.C. on the eve of the Peloponnesian War and is described by Thucydides (1.31–54). Beneath the marker, to left and right, were two graves; one was empty, the other contained offerings which included a white-ground lekythos, black vases of various common shapes, a few household wares and a strigil (Fig. III.2). All the vases are useful in affording evidence of the stages in development reached by 433 B.C.

(c) A better known set of burials, but one which does not provide such a simple group of material, is the Rheneia Purification Pit.[7] Once again our chief contemporary source is Thucydides. In summarising what happened in the winter of 426/425 B.C. he refers to Athenian activity on Delos (3.104, cf. 1.8):

> The Athenians, no doubt because of some oracle, carried out ceremonies of purification on Delos.... The whole island was purified in the following way. All the tombs of those who had died on Delos were dug up, and it was proclaimed that in future no deaths or births were to be allowed in the island; those who were about to die or give birth were to be carried across to Rheneia.

The French excavators of Delos discovered a pit 20 m square within a paved enclosure 500 m square, and bones and funeral offerings beneath. As this was a haphazard collection of offerings, the material was mixed in date, some vases dating as early as Geometric. It is naturally the latest material that is important for dating, and the pit contained many Attic red-figure and black vases that provide a terminus ante quem for other material of similar type elsewhere. The equation of this excavated pit with that mentioned by Thucydides is not in doubt.

(d) During the first decade of the Peloponnesian War ('The Archidamian War') the Athenians under Hippokrates invaded north-east Boeotia, and in 424 B.C. a battle was fought at Delium (Thucydides 4.93–101); this was the first pitched battle of the war and in it, according to Plato (*Symposium* 221A–B, etc.), Socrates and Alcibiades both took part. The men of the nearby village of Thespiai fought on the Boeotian side and suffered heavy losses (Thucydides 4.96). When the battle was over and the Athenians had been defeated, the Thespian dead were conveyed back home and there furnished with a public burial.[8] The tumulus and enclosure (32 m × 13 m), with the remains of a large pedestal which carried a reclining lion in marble over 3 m long, were found in a cemetery to the east of Thespiai. Remains of the bones and the funeral pyre were unearthed together with a large number of offerings. There was a very small amount of Attic pottery, a little Euboean and Corinthian, and an enormous deposit of Boeotian including red-figure lekythoi which closely copy Attic, and much black and floral ware in a wide variety of shapes. There were also terracotta figurines and offerings in other materials. Much of the casualty list inscribed on

stone has also survived. The ensemble is of vital importance for the dating of Boeotian pottery.

(e) Some years ago the German excavators of the Kerameikos cemetery of Athens uncovered, on the south-west side of the main road (*dromos*) that runs through the ancient area known as the 'state burial ground', an 11 m long, walled rectangle that carried on it the names of the dead inscribed on a cornice block.[9] The monument stands over the grave of the Lacedaimonians who fell in 403 B.C. when, a year after defeating the Athenians in the long Peloponnesian War, troops had come to assist against the democratic insurgents in the Piraeus. Remains of thirteen bodies were found in three chambers, and the fragmentary inscriptions, from right to left, in Laconian lettering, give the start of the word La[kedaimonioi] and name three of the Spartan military leaders (*polemarchoi*): Chairon, Thibrakos [*sic*] and M[—. Two of the names are the very ones that the historian Xenophon gives (*Hellenica* 2.4.33): 'In this fighting [in the Piraeus] the colonels Chairon and Thibrachos [*sic*] were killed; also Lacrates, a winner at Olympia, and other Spartans who now lie buried in the Kerameikos outside the gates of Athens.' Unfortunately, the ceramic material found in association with the monument is very fragmentary.

(f) In the same cemetery as the graves of the Corcyrean ambassadors and the Spartan warriors, but away from the public area, is the famous relief marker of young Dexileos who fell as a cavalry officer in the fighting before Corinth in 394 B.C., as the base of his monument relates. The plot did not contain his remains, as he was buried with the other cavalrymen in the area of the state burial ground. However, his family acquired the corner plot at the time of Dexileos' death, and the red-figure vases which were discovered in that family grave and may have been deposited at the time of Dexileos' death, have been used to give some indication of the stage of development reached in Attic vase-painting at that time.[10] All five vases are oinochoai, and one of them carries the subject of the Tyrantslayers (see pp. 47–8).

This small selection of datable graves perhaps gives some idea of the helpfulness and the limitations of such evidence.

Foundation, destruction and reoccupation

It is more difficult to derive absolute dates from the foundation and destruction evidence of sites, even when seemingly helpful information is provided by written evidence.

The endemic nature of ancient warfare means that many settlements were destroyed and sacked, and then either abandoned or reoccupied, and these events are the sort that we find mentioned, not always dependably or clearly, in the writings of ancient historians. It is natural that in the present-day ruins of such sites, objects of daily use, particularly pottery, will be lodged. One of the hurdles to be overcome concerns the externally

datable destruction levels, as these cannot always be easily isolated. Also the type of site excavated will affect our attitudes to the material. If the site is part of a settlement and thus likely to provide pottery that was in use at the time of the destruction, the length of the period during which the pottery had been in use has to be considered. If the site is a sanctuary, then older material is likely to be encountered, the offerings of generations of the faithful. Also, destruction does not always mean total abandonment; survivors may return and make their living again on the same site. This means that pottery is used and thrown away once more, and hence the destruction level is not always clear-cut. Another difficulty is the inevitably less precise excavation and study made by earlier excavators. This is particularly unfortunate, as their investigations were guided by their reading of ancient literature, and so they were often led to those very sites that were externally datable. Even today, with more precise methods, excavators do not clear a complete site, and so the evidence on which to base general conclusions is only partial.

There follows a small selection of the more important sites at which the foundation or destruction is dated by external evidence and which scholars have felt to be of assistance in establishing a chronology for pottery. In many instances the amount of material found on which study can be carried out has been small, and the condition in which the vases were found – worn, smashed, burnt – has often been unhelpful. Some assistance in the earlier periods for the dating of Geometric pottery might be expected to come from Greek pottery found on non-Greek sites, the history of which is sometimes chronicled by non-Greek documentary evidence, but the danger of circularity in argument has recently been stressed. There is still room for discussion.[11]

(a) *Hama(th) on the Orontes, north Syria.*[12] A neo-Hittite site destroyed by the Assyrians under Sargon II. The date of the destruction is provided by Assyrian sources. Greek imports are few and fragmentary, the latest being Late Geometric. The usual date given is 720 B.C., but two points make the connection between date and pottery uncertain: the site was not deserted but colonised with more than six thousand Assyrians, and the destruction level may not have contained the latest fragments of pottery now known.

(b) *Aziris, Cyrenaica (Libya) (modern Wadi el Chalig).*[13] This was briefly occupied by the Therans on their way to the more long-lasting colony of Cyrene. Information comes from Herodotus (4.157.3; 4.169.1) and Eusebius who may give the foundation date of Cyrene as 632 B.C. (*Chron.* 96b). There was said to have been a six-year occupation of Aziris. Remains found included Protocorinthian pottery and East Greek bowls and banded cups.

(c) *Daphnae (Tell Defenneh), Egypt.*[14] A Greek-manned frontier post on the eastern border of Egypt, Daphnae was dismantled by the Persians when

they invaded in 525 B.C. (Herodotus 2.30). Doubts have been expressed about the identity of the ancient with the modern site, but orthodox opinion makes them one and the same. Greek pottery included Attic, Rhodian, Clazomenian, Fikellura, as well as situlae which may have been made by Greeks near the site, and a fragmentary Chian transport amphora sealed with a cartouche of the Egyptian pharaoh Amasis (568–526 B.C.)

(d) *Athens.*[15] The Persian occupation and destruction of Athens in 480/479 is well attested (Herodotus 8.52–4; 9.3–13), and much of the dating of Attic Archaic sculpture and architecture is dependent on recognising the material of the 'Perserschutt', especially on the Acropolis. The Attic black-figure and red-figure pottery found on the rock has also been put to use, but even now there is still much uncertainty about its help for the purposes of dating.

(e) *Motya, Sicily.*[16] Dionysius of Syracuse was responsible for the siege and sack of this Phoenician–Punic island site off the west coast of Sicily in 397 B.C. (Diodorus 14.47–53). The site was never rebuilt, though life on the island continued. The material connected with the sack includes Attic red-figure and black pottery.

(f) *Olynthus, Chalcidice, northern Greece.*[17] This Greek settlement on the Chalcidic peninsula was destroyed by Philip II of Macedon in 348 B.C. (Diodorus 16.53–4). A great amount of Attic red-figure and black as well as local pottery was excavated from the destroyed houses on the site. Part of the site was reoccupied until ca. 316 B.C.

(g) *Koroni, Attica.*[18] This site has been identified as one of the hastily built and short-lived fortified camps used by Ptolemaic forces in the Chremonidean War of 265–261 B.C. (Pausanias 1.1.1; 1.2.3; 3.6.4–6). The material includes black vases, cooking ware and transport amphorae.

(h) *Corinth.*[19] The Greek city was destroyed by the Romans under Mummius in 146 B.C. (Pausanias 7.16). It lay waste for a century and was refounded by Julius Caesar in 46 B.C. There is abundant ceramic material from the destruction level.

There are many other sites for which the foundation and/or destruction dates provided by written testimony have been thought to help the absolute dating of pottery, e.g. Old Smyrna, Tarsus, Massalia (Marseilles). None are without their problems.[20] Destruction levels, though complicated by the factors mentioned above, are definable within limits; foundations of settlements, particularly the early ones, are less substantial and more difficult to pinpoint. The first arrival of a group of people to a site was generally on a small scale, both in terms of numbers and in the nature of the structures they erected. That initial presence was soon overlaid and obliterated by the generations that lived after them on the same site. Hence, once again a potentially simple phenomenon is rendered complex when

studied closely, none more so than the settlements that the Greeks established in the West.

The Greek migration to the West, to south Italy and Sicily, that took place mainly in the eighth and seventh centuries B.C., has naturally engaged the attention of students of Greek pottery.[21] The reason that the sites in those areas have had a particular interest for chronological purposes is that the literary evidence for the foundations is reasonably full, and in particular the historian Thucydides devotes three paragraphs (6.3–5) to the phenomenon and gives a brief account of the Sicilian foundations. His general trustworthiness has predisposed scholars to pay close attention to his statements and, with the help of later evidence, to try to extract fairly exact dates. The sources of Thucydides' information are not known and need not be all equally reliable; however, what he says has been made to yield relative and absolute dates, and, armed with these, excavators have faced the masses of material that have been unearthed from these sites, particularly the imported pottery of Corinth, and have suggested absolute dates for the different wares. Study of the excavated evidence has led some to assume that Thucydides was correct in his relative dates; others have thrown doubt on the connection. The attempt to match the two sets of evidence has once more invited a charge of circularity in argument.

Although there is early material not connected with the establishment of colonies, no Greek colony in the West has produced pottery earlier than Late Geometric I (currently dated 750–725 B.C.). Pithecusa[22] and Cumae[23] off the bay of Naples have produced ceramic material that goes back to Late Geometric I and II, and the four Sicilian colonies (Naxos, Syracuse, Leontini, Megara Hyblaea) that Thucydides says were established first seem also to provide Late Geometric I as the earliest material.[24] Other sites with similar pottery are Sybaris[25] and Taras.[26]

There is still much uncertainty surrounding the dating of Geometric pottery, and the Western colonies are symptomatic of the difficulties for which radical and far-reaching new solutions are being proposed.

As with sites, so with individual buildings that are datable from written sources, the material found in them might be expected to receive outside assistance to help with the absolute dating. But once again the clear-cut evidence is hard to find.

Stylistic comparisons with other works

Let us now move from accidental context dates and look at a different avenue of approach. One method of trying to date figured vases is by comparing them stylistically with figures in other media, particularly sculpture, for which external dates are sometimes available. This procedure mainly involves architectural sculpture (metopes, friezes, pediments,

akroteria), as it is often the building carrying the sculpture that is dated, either by literary or documentary, particularly inscriptional, evidence. Relief sculpture and free-standing statuary are less useful, but there are possible parallels. Comparisons of this sort are at best approximate and subjective, and all depend for their validity on the assumption of parallel development in the different media. There are good reasons for thinking that this is a valid assumption, indeed much of our interpretation of Greek art is based on such an assumption, but it is doubtful how closely the analogy can be argued. Related problems concern the primacy of sculpture vis-à-vis painting, the speed of influence, both within a single community and from one community to another, and the fragmentary nature of the evidence at our disposal, especially the total loss of free painting. In most cases where comparisons are being made, it is the general style of the media that forms the connection; in fewer instances the subject matter may be relevant, and more rarely close copying of sculptural or other figures in vase-painting can be studied. It is also possible to compare vase shapes with similar shapes in materials other than terracotta, e.g. metal (gold, silver, bronze), glass, stone.

Besides comparison of figures, objects within the figured scenes can be compared: illustrated vase shapes, furniture, etc., with actual or carved pieces, and also the decoration in and around the painted scenes that may resemble the decoration found in carved ornament and such.

Architectural sculpture

There first follow some examples of works of architectural sculpture that have been considered useful chronological pegs on which to hang the work of vase-painters. All have their difficulties, and some recent studies have called in doubt the generally accepted bases of traditional theories.

(a) *The temple of Artemis at Ephesos.*[27] Herodotus, writing his history in the later fifth century B.C., has this to say of Croesus, the king of Lydia, whose reign ended in 546 B.C. (1.92): 'There are many other offerings of Croesus in Hellas besides those mentioned. In Thebes in Boeotia there is a golden tripod which he dedicated to Apollo Ismenios, and at Ephesos there are golden oxen and the greater part of the pillars.' Fragments of the vast sixth-century Ionic temple of Artemis have been unearthed, and on the column base of one of the drums King Croesus' name has been thought to be recoverable. If this is so, then Herodotus' 'pillars' come to mind. An unusual feature of some of the drums is that they carry life-size carved figures, and hence such details as splaying garment folds are compared with similar treatment found on vase-paintings.

As can be judged, the connection is not a tight one. It is not even certain that Herodotus is speaking of sculptured pillars; the two previous objects mentioned are of gold. Also, the fragmentary inscription can be made to

give a reading that eliminates both 'King' and 'Croesus'. Given that it could be the temple drums that he means, it is not easy to assess the length of time that the building of such a colossal temple would have taken. Pliny (*HN* 36.14) says it was 120 years in construction, and Macrobius (*Sat.* 5.22.5) mentions the dedication of an Artemis temple at Ephesus ca. 430 B.C. – the final completion date?

(b) *The Siphnian treasury, Delphi.*[28] Herodotus mentions another building that is preserved today. Though it is in a better state of preservation, in this instance the interpretation of his words is even less easy to unravel. At Delphi, as at other sanctuaries, the Greeks built a number of treasuries: small one-room structures, like simple temples, that contained costly offerings from various city-states. That erected by the people of the island of Siphnos was one of the most elaborate, and Herodotus mentions its construction (3.17.8): 'The Siphnians were at this time very prosperous and the richest of the islanders, as they had gold and silver mines on the island. So rich were they that from the tenth part of the revenues a treasury was dedicated at Delphi, equal to the most wealthy.' The occasion to which Herodotus refers by 'at this time' was when the Spartans were attacking Polycrates of Samos and when Samian opponents of the tyrant sailed from Samos, attacked Siphnos and sacked it. He links that episode with the invasion of Egypt by the Persian king Cambyses (3.39), which we date to 525 B.C. The gaps in time between various episodes are not securely given by Herodotus, but it is usually assumed that the treasury had not been long erected when the attack took place, hence in conventional dating it is placed ca. 530 B.C. If this date is secure, then it is extremely important, as the treasury has high-quality friezes with scenes which include the Trojan War and the Battle of the Gods against the Giants as well as ambitious compositions with three-quarter views and elaborate treatment of clothing. The nearest work in vase-painting is that done by the earliest red-figure vase-painters in Athens – indeed stylistic connections between some parts of the friezes and the work of the Andokides Painter are particularly close. It is on such connections that the dating of the beginning of Attic red-figure is partly based. Recently a suggestion has been made that the Siphnian treasury is dated too early, with obvious consequences for the history of vase-painting as well as of sculpture.[29]

(c) *The Apollo temple, Delphi.*[30] Also at Delphi, the temple of Apollo was rebuilt in the late sixth century B.C., and Herodotus once more (5.62) gives us some information. He connects the building with an historical occasion: the exile of the family of the Alcmaeonidae from Athens during the rule of the sons of Peisistratus there. The exiled family were ready to lavish their generosity on the Delphian sanctuary by providing the temple with an east front of marble in place of the usual tufa. Excavations have unearthed a set of marble and a set of tufa pedimental figures at the east and west ends respectively, thus drawing attention to that detail of

Herodotus' account. The exile of the Alcmaeonidae came to an end with the Spartan expulsion of Hippias from Athens in 510 B.C. The style of the figures from the temple has been felt to be sufficiently close to the work of Attic vase-painters of what is now termed the 'Pioneer Group' to establish a chronological connection for the late sixth century.

(d) *The Athenian treasury, Delphi.*[31] Yet again at Delphi, an instructive example of the difficulties of dating centres on the treasury of the Athenians. Pausanias (10.11.4) connects the occasion for the erection of the building with the Athenian success at the battle of Marathon: 'from the spoils of the landing of Datis at Marathon'. If this is correct, then the sculptural decoration – Herakles and Theseus – would date after 490 B.C. Modern scholars are divided on the question of date, and some dissociate the treasury from any connection with Marathon (there is an inscription near the building which mentions Marathon, and it is suggested that this was the basis for Pausanias' (erroneous) assumption) and date the building and its sculptures ten or more years earlier, i.e. to the late sixth century. This lack of agreement highlights the present uncertainty in the dating of sculpture, and hence the problems of drawing any conclusions about figure decoration on vases from comparison with it.

(e) *The Apollo temple, Eretria.*[32] In their first expedition against the Greeks the Persians destroyed the temple of Apollo at Eretria before moving over the channel to Marathon later in 490 B.C. (Herodotus 6.101). Fragments of figures from the pediment of a temple have come to light and are usually connected with the Archaic temple that the Persians destroyed, thus dating prior to 490 B.C. and affording comparisons with vase-painting. However, an upper date for the temple is not known, and indeed the Archaic dating of the material has been challenged, and the figures have now been linked by some with the rebuilding of the temple after the Persians had left.[33]

(f) *The Zeus temple, Olympia.*[34] The building of the temple of Zeus at Olympia can be dated within the second quarter of the fifth century, roughly 470–456 B.C. According to Pausanias (5.10.2), the building was financed from the booty 'when Elis and the local people who joined the rebellion captured Pisa', in 471 B.C. On the apex of the east pediment Pausanias saw the dedication of a shield by the Spartans for their victory at Tanagra (5.10.4), in 457 B.C. Thus the temple must have been all but complete at that time and certainly the metopes must have been in position, and the pedimental figures are likely to have been in place by that year. The inscription on the apex which Pausanias quotes for his evidence is still partly preserved. The sculptural decoration gives parallels for Athenian vase-painting of the 'severe' period, i.e. Early Classical, and helps to anchor the style in the second quarter of the fifth century. Comparisons of drapery and composition are particularly close.

(g) *The Parthenon, Athens.*[35] The Parthenon is securely dated by the

public inscriptions that record the building programme of Periclean Athens. It was begun in 447/446 B.C. and the cult statue of Athena Parthenos was dedicated in 438/437. The metopes (and perhaps the frieze) are likely to have been finished by that year, as the roof needed to be in place, and it is then that work on the pedimental figures is first recorded. The accounts were closed in 432 B.C. Comparisons in general and in particular have been made between Attic vase-paintings and figures from the temple – not only in style, but also in subject matter and individual figures. In one or two cases the architectural figures were copied or adapted by vase-painters (Figs. III.3–4), as were the figure and details of the Athena Parthenos statue (see p. 44).

After 400 B.C. there is little opportunity for comparison, as the vase-paintings are less amenable to testing and the fairly uniform thread of development seems to have become more complex.

Free-standing and relief sculpture

Apart from architectural sculpture, there are individual free-standing and relief sculptures that afford some stylistic help in dating as they themselves can be dated fairly closely. Of original free-standing sculpture that can be linked to absolute dates, the following have been considered some of the most useful:

(a) *Kallimachos' Victory, Athens.*[36] This was set up for Kallimachos on the Athenian Acropolis, a little after 490 B.C. It is too badly preserved to render more than marginal help, but the stacked folds of the skirt, the bent knee, the backward set of the wings can be compared with those found on vase-painting.

(b) *Agorakritos' Nemesis, Rhamnous.*[37] This is also a ruin. The statue and base were made for the temple of Nemesis ('Retribution') at Rhamnous in northern Attica by Agorakritos, a pupil of Pheidias (Pausanias, 1.33.2–3, says it was by Pheidias himself). A date around 430 B.C. seems to follow from the connection of the architecture of the temple with that of the Hephaisteion in Athens and the Poseidon temple at Sounion. The drapery provides parallels with details of the clothing seen on painted pottery.

(c) *Paionios' Victory, Olympia.*[38] This was set up at Olympia soon after 421 B.C., the sculptor being Paionios of Mende. Pausanias (5.26.1) saw it, and part of the inscription connecting it with Paionios still survives. The billowing dress and cloak provide parallels for Attic vase-painting.

Copies of free-standing statues obviously offer less reliable evidence. For style, they are almost useless; for subject matter, see pp. 43–4. The Tyrantslayers of 477/476 B.C.[39] show the looser drapery folds that one associates with the end of the late Archaic phase and the beginning of the early Classical. Late copies of such works as Myron's Discobolos and

Athena & Marsyas, Pheidias' Athena Parthenos, etc. provide negligible assistance, even when a precise date for the originals can be assigned.[40]

Non-architectural reliefs may be closely dated when the carved block forms the crowning member of an inscription which can itself be dated historically. The best known is Dexileos' funerary relief in the Kerameikos at Athens, dated to 394 B.C.[41] Recently, the supporting plinth of the acanthus-crowned column surmounted by three dancing caryatids at Delphi has been shown to carry an inscription that refers the occasion of its erection to the victory of Athens and her allies over Sparta at Alyzeia (Akarnania) in 375 B.C.[42] There is also a series of reliefs, of which the earliest extant is dated to 430/429 B.C. and which continue into the third century B.C., that crown inscriptions recording or documenting treaties, gifts, agreements, etc.[43] The reliefs are slight works of art but add their small contribution by their securely fixed dates.

Influences from works of art

There are some instances of vase-painters being so influenced by works of art that they set down on their vases slightly adapted versions of the original works. The best examples are to be seen in the relationship between Attic red-figure vase-paintings and sculpture. We know that vase-painters had an alert interest in sculpture and would on occasion represent a sculptor at work or show a statue within a composition (e.g. the Athena statue in the sack of Troy). So we should not be surprised if certain figures, whether shown as statues or as characters in a composition, closely resemble sculptured works. We cannot of course be certain in every case that the immediate source is sculpture; missing wall-paintings, which may themselves have influenced sculpture, loom tantalisingly in the background, but the following seem fairly sure. Where a sculpture can be accurately dated, it provides a useful *terminus post quem* for the vase-painting that is derived from it. Sometimes the gap between the two may not have been large, but for some, the interval between original and adaptation is so wide that the connection is useless for dating purposes.

(a) *Angelitos' Athena.*[44] A case has been made for a connection between a standing statue of Athena on a column, erected on the Athenian Acropolis ca. 480 B.C., and two Attic red-figure vases which show a very similar figure of Athena, one on a column, both dated on present chronology ca. 470–460 B.C.

(b) *The Tyrantslayers.*[45] Only copies exist of this group, but the stance and meaning of the pair make the influence on vase-paintings beyond doubt (see pp. 47–8).

(c) *Athena and Marsyas.*[46] The group made by Myron of which we have marble copies dates to the middle of the fifth century. A later fifth century Attic red-figure chous seems based upon it.

III.3 Detail of Parthenon frieze with horse and rider, ca. 440 B.C.

(d) *The Parthenon sculptures.*[47] The effect of the Parthenon sculptures, both those architectural sculptures on the outside of the building and the Parthenos herself and her decorated accoutrements, was strong. The Helen and Menelaus pair of metopes from the north side of the building is recalled on an Attic red-figure oinochoe. The cows of the south frieze seem to have inspired a number of artists, and some of the human figures are alluded to as well, particularly a young knight from the west frieze (Figs. III.3–4). The pediments, especially the west with the strife of Athena and Poseidon, can be seen reflected in works of the late fifth and fourth centuries; the central figures of the east pediment have recently been recognised on a late fifth century Attic bell-krater. The late fifth century also sees adaptations of the gold and ivory figure of the Parthenos herself, and much interest was shown by vase-painters in the subject matter and arrangement of the figures that decorated the shield and other surfaces (see p. 42).

(e) *Olympian Zeus.*[48] Pheidias' other gold and ivory statue did not arouse so much interest as the Parthenos, but it has recently been argued

III.4 Attic red-figure pelike with horse and rider, ca. 430–420 B.C.

that his throne was adapted by one Attic vase-painter of the late fifth century in a composition that was a mélange of sculptural types.

Patterns

Besides the connections made between figures in sculpture and vase-painting, comparisons have been noted between the patterns that were used to decorate buildings, outside and in (whether carved, painted or mosaic), and those which formed the surround to many of the scenes on vases. Once again the dated buildings – treasuries, temples, tombs – afford a few fixed points. The complexity of the connections may be illustrated by reference to vase-painting and fourth century pebble mosaics. Pausias was a painter who worked in Sicyon in the second quarter of the fourth century B.C.; he was noted for his flower paintings. None of his own work survives, but his influence has been traced in pebble mosaics (e.g. from sites in Macedonia such as Pella and Aegae (Vergina), from Olynthus, and from Sicyon itself). The most outstanding elements of these designs are the female heads surrounded by flowers and tendrils, and the three-dimensional effect of

spiralling bell-like flowers with curling stems and scroll-like leaves. Such complicated effects are to be seen also on vases, particularly on Apulian volute-kraters and amphorae. Influence between artistic media would be difficult to deny, but the closeness of the connection is hard to establish and so the usefulness for dating purposes is impaired.[49]

History, myth and subject matter

Many of the more elaborate examples of Greek pottery carry figured compositions, and the subject matter of the scenes can sometimes be linked to historical persons or events and to literary works. Although the establishment of such connections has its pitfalls, attempts have been felt to be worthwhile, and some results can be obtained that may then be associated with others that have been reached by a different route to produce a satisfactory, if not totally precise, conclusion.

Historical figures

There are some rare instances where the compositions consist of or include historical figures.[50] It would be rash to assume that the paintings must be contemporary with the living characters or even follow closely on their deaths – indeed this is palpably not so in a number of instances, as with the Attic red-figure amphora depicting Croesus (see below) – but none the less chronological clues may be derived from some compositions. Needless to say, the figures are in no real sense portraits. Here is a selection of the more important examples.

(a) *Arkesilas.*[51] One of the best known vases that presents a named historical character is the Laconian black-figure cup with an elaborate scene on the interior of wool- or silphium-weighing in the presence of a seated figure with a sceptre, who is inscribed Arkesilas. He is to be identified with one of the kings of Cyrene, the Greek settlement in north Africa. There were four kings of that name, and this means that a choice must be made between them; thus the precise dating has to depend on other criteria. The fact that it has been said that the cup 'supports rather than establishes the chronology [of Laconian vase-painting]'[52] shows its unreliability. On present chronology it is King Arkesilas II, who reigned in the 560s B.C., who is thought to be depicted. The style of the painting is individual enough to enable other Laconian cups to be attributed to the same painter, and the shape of the cup can be linked with a similar shape produced in Athens (the 'Siana' cup) to suggest contemporary production, and other work by the Arkesilas Painter has been found in context with them.[53] Total certainty is not possible, and the fact that Arkesilas I ruled a little before and Arkesilas III in the 530s and 520s, offers other closely adjacent, though less likely, candidates.

(b) *Anakreon.*[54] The poet Anakreon was born at Teos in Ionia and after spending some time at the court of Polycrates of Samos, moved to Athens around 520 B.C. and died there in the 480s. Some early red-figure vases depict and name Anakreon, and a good number more present a similar composition to these scenes but without the name. Two of the named, and many of the unnamed, scenes depict a revel with men dressed in Ionian (Lydian) dress, with head-scarf or turban; some men wear earrings and/or soft leather boots, some carry a lyre and others a parasol. The three vases that bear the name of Anakreon are early in the series, and although individual items of dress are found earlier, the combination of items seems to belong to the late sixth century and to harmonise with Anakreon's arrival in Athens. The general assumption is that Anakreon's 'foreign' dress and ways were stressed by painters as a subject soon after his arrival.

(c) *Croesus.*[55] Croesus, king of Lydia in Asia Minor, was deposed in 546 B.C. by Cyrus of Persia. He had had contacts with the Greeks of the coast of Asia Minor and had given gifts to Delphi and elsewhere (see pp. 39–40). He soon became a semi-mythical figure for them, and Herodotus' account of his death (1.86–92) is well known. One Attic vase-painter, Myson, depicted the king on his funeral pyre on a red-figure amphora. It cannot be a contemporary painting nor one painted immediately after the event. On present chronology it belongs around the year 500 B.C., and a recent suggestion connects the choice of such a theme at this time with the revolt of the Ionian Greeks of Asia Minor from the Persians in 499 B.C.[56] As the other side of the amphora shows Theseus carrying off the Amazon queen Antiope, a Greek carrying off an Easterner, both sides may make allusion to the revolt that burned Croesus' old capital at Sardis and the Athenian assistance rendered to the Ionians against a foreign power. Such an interpretation might back up an already established chronology but would not be strong enough to create it.

(d) *The Tyrantslayers.*[57] In a similar way representations of Harmodios and Aristogeiton on Attic vases may have reference to events contemporary with the vase-paintings, not with the event that made the two famous. The Tyrantslayers received early recognition for their killing of the tyrant Hipparchus in 514 B.C. They were voted a bronze group of themselves, made by Antenor before the Persian sack of Athens, and when this group was taken to Persia at the time of the invasion of 480 B.C., another set was made in 477/476 B.C. (the archonship of Adeimantos, according to the Parian Marble). It is this latter group that is well known from later Roman copies in marble. However, there are also four vases which show the assassination in a composition adapted from this group, and on present chronology they should date between 475 and 460 B.C. They may be seen therefore as statements about Athenian democracy and its success against another tyrant who tried to dominate Athens. The heroes are also depicted

III.5 Attic red-figure kylix with Persians fighting Greeks, ca. 480 B.C.

on Attic vases of the later fifth and early fourth centuries. The choice of the pair as shield devices of Athena on black-figure Panathenaic prize amphorae, dated on other grounds to near the close of the fifth century, has been thought to reflect the newly regained democracy in 403 B.C. and thus date to that year or the next.[58] A red-figure chous which also depicts Harmodios and Aristogeiton in the same sculptural pose was found in the grave plot that adjoins the monument of Dexileos who died in 394 B.C. (see pp. 35, 43), and a reference to his defence of Athenian democracy may be likely.[59]

(c) *The Persians.*[60] After the Persians had come and gone in the early fifth century, painters of Attic vases depicted them in combat with their victorious Greek opponents (Fig. III.5). It is natural to assume that such scenes belong to the post-war years, whether post-490 or post-479 B.C., and thus a *terminus post quem* is provided. The popularity of such combats is to be found among painters of the generation after the invasion, 480–450 B.C., but one or two may date 490–480 B.C.

(f) *Pronomos.*[61] The famous Attic red-figure volute-krater in Naples with a dramatic company depicted across the front of the body presents actors, chorusmen dressed as satyrs, musicians and the poet, with Dionysos shown among his followers. Some of the figures are named, including

Demetrios the poet, Charinos the lyre-player and in the central place below, Pronomos the pipe-player after whom the vase receives its modern sobriquet of the Pronomos Vase. There was a Pronomos who taught Alcibiades to play the pipes and was said to have been no ordinary teacher; a Pronomos is also mentioned in Aristophanes' *Ecclesiazousae* (v. 102) of 392 B.C., and this may be same person. If the figure on the krater is to be equated with this historical character, a date in the late fifth or early fourth century would fit, but no precision is possible.

(g) *Alexander.*[62] There are some vases painted in Apulia in the red-figure technique that depict battles between Greeks and Persians. A leading figure on the Greek side may be Alexander himself, and the fact that he is shown with a beard when Alexander was clean-shaven is explained on the assumption that his appearance may not have been known in south Italy: his fame had preceded precise knowledge of his appearance. A date around 330 B.C. has been proposed.

Myths and heroes

Greek vase-painters only occasionally made overt references to contemporary events or historical characters, and the few just selected are unusual in this respect. Along with sculptors, vase-painters used mythological stories as paradigms of more recent events: their struggles with foreign foes were mirrored in such battles as the Greeks against the Trojans or the Amazons. It has therefore been suspected that reflections of historical events might be discovered in vase-paintings through the popularity of a particular myth or hero. In this way a rough *terminus post quem* might be suggested for the vases which carry such scenes. An approach of this kind has its obvious dangers and depends to a large extent on the ingenuity of students of the subject and on the existence of some chronological scheme that is already accepted: its validity is not autonomous. A simple example of this approach concerns the myth of Boreas, the North Wind, carrying off the Attic princess Oreithyia.[63] The episode only starts in Attic vase-painting after the Persian Wars, and its appearance has been connected with the wreck of the Persian fleet at Artemisium when Boreas was successfully beseeched and showed his favour to the Athenians. Recently the figures of Herakles and Theseus in Attic vase-painting have been studied for the light they might throw on the politics of Athens in the late sixth and early fifth centuries B.C., but this is a much more complex problem. Herakles has been seen as a figure used by the tyrant Peisistratus and his sons, and Theseus a little later as the hero of the developing democracy at Athens, as his range of stories is enlarged by novel episodes in the later sixth century, and he is promoted as a rival to Herakles. The return of Theseus' bones from Skyros to Athens by Cimon in 475 B.C., and the establishment in Athens of a sanctuary for him with

wall-paintings (now lost) showing stages of his career, heighten the popularity of the figure towards the mid century, and vase paintings of that time have in turn been seen to offer reflections of those lost wall-paintings.[64]

Literary subjects

This last point introduces a further approach to dating that has been felt to have validity: the reflection of literary subjects and stories in vase-painting. Much has been made of the influence of literary works on vase-painting, though less so now than in the past, when it would seem that vase-paintings were almost seen as 'book illustrations' and judged by their relation to literary models. Now the interdependence of the two is considered more cautiously.[65] It has been well said that '"Illustrations" in vase painting are not, of course, straight transcriptions from poem or stage to the vase surface. They necessarily contaminate the literary images with stock motifs forming the artistic repertory of the period, because the artist had to move inside the framework of his trade and could not go free to create new compositions direct from a literary experience.'[66] So we must not expect close correspondence between word and picture, and this opens the door to speculation.

The two main points of contact have always been felt to be with the early epics, including the *Iliad* and the *Odyssey*, and with Athenian drama, especially tragedy.

As far as dating is concerned, the Homeric poems, and indeed the early epics in general, are themselves so difficult to place that there is great danger of circularity of argument. Also, the appearance of mythological stories in vase-painting at the end of the eighth-century or in the early seventh century, although often connected with literary works that are thought to have been emerging at this time, might instead be the response of the artists to the widespread oral stories, now that the technique and range of vase-painting were becoming more extensive. It has been pointed out that the very early scenes that might be linked to myths are rarely linked to the *Homeric* epics, and as two general propositions from which to start, it has been suggested that 'Homer probably never saw an Attic Geometric vase in his life' and that 'no Attic Geometric artist had ever read or heard recited a single line of Homer'.[67]

Much work has been done on the possible effects of Athenian drama on vase-painters. Many plays, both lost and extant, are firmly dated to the year of production, and the appearance of the same subject matter on vases, perhaps with tell-tale signs of a theatrical flavour (e.g. types of dress, background, masks), can sometimes be linked to datable plays.[68] It is of course a temptation to work from those plays that are extant and assume that *they* provide the particular influence, even though tragic themes were

III.6 Attic red-figure hydria with chorus of satyrs, ca. 465 B.C.

repeated over and over again, and not only in drama. Let us take four examples, from tragedy, satyr-play and comedy.

(a) The tragedy of Agamemnon and Orestes' revenge is best known from the surviving trilogy of the *Oresteia* by Aeschylus produced in Athens in 458 B.C., and the appearance on an Attic red-figure calyx-krater of the murder of Agamemnon and the murder of Aegisthus seemed so close a parallel that influence from the trilogy to the vase-paintings initially appeared likely, especially as the connection of both murders on one art work is not known earlier than this example.[69] Current opinion, however, denies the connection, as conventional chronology for vase-painting places the calyx-krater earlier than 458 B.C., so in this promising instance chronology is not assisted.

(b) A more recently published case of a possible connection is perhaps more acceptable. Again the play is by Aeschylus, this time a lost satyr-play called *Sphinx* which was produced as the final play accompanying the Theban trilogy of which the third play, *Seven Against Thebes*, still survives. The date of 467 B.C. is certain, as a papyrus lists the plays and gives the archon for the year. The satyr-play burlesques the episode of the riddle set by the Sphinx to Oedipus and includes a chorus of satyrs. An Attic

red-figure hydria (Fig. III.6) carries a scene of a sphinx seated on a rock posing her riddle to satyrs elegantly seated in elaborate and uncharacteristic clothing, with diadems on their heads and holding sceptres.[70] Conventional chronology places the hydria in the 460s, and to find satyrs in such an unlikely setting argues influence from a specific source, of which the satyr-play *Sphinx* is the likeliest.

(c) A second example involving a satyr-play shows how the dramatic productions initiated in Athens might be thought to influence painters elsewhere. Euripides wrote a satyr-play entitled *Cyclops*, variously dated in the last quarter of the fifth century. A red-figure calyx-krater, painted by an artist in Lucania, southern Italy, shows Odysseus preparing to blind the Cyclops with the help of satyrs.[71] Again, the unusual context for the satyrs argues for the influence of a satyr-play, and Euripides' play has been accepted by some scholars as the catalyst.

(d) More recently, an Attic (?) red-figure calyx-krater with a pair of masked birds either side of a pipe-player has been thought to derive its inspiration either from Aristophanes' *Birds* (414 B.C.) or from the fighting cocks in the original production of his *Clouds* (423 B.C.).[72]

Close correspondence is not common, and although there are many theatre-based illustrations, particularly in south Italian vase-painting, they give little help with close dating, as they may draw their inspiration from earlier plays which were perhaps enjoying a revival, and in south Italian theatre no external dates exist to help in placing the performances.

Inscriptions

Many vases carry writing on them for one purpose or another. The letters may be painted in gloss, scratched or stamped and may be applied before or after firing; some, more rarely, may be written in ink. Thus the writers may be the painters of the pots, the potters or the shop-owners, merchants, purchasers or passers-by who have picked up a piece of broken pottery in the street to scratch a message or impugn a rival (see pp. 124–5).

The study of letter forms is now advanced,[73] and as the shapes into which the letters were formed altered fairly rapidly over the years, it is possible to date those shapes with some precision. The existence of local scripts in different parts of the Greek world means that in many cases the letter forms can not only give a clue for dating but also help in locating the origin of the letterer. So even when the subject matter is itself of little or no assistance, the inscription can none the less be placed in a series which itself has firmly fixed points. As standardisation of writing spread in the fifth century, this useful approach is reduced in importance.

The type of inscription on a vase – painted, scratched, stamped or written in ink – will affect the usefulness of the dating. Any inscription o

stamp added before firing must date from the same time as the pot which carries it; scratched or painted letters added afterwards must be judged by other criteria and can give only a *terminus ante quem* for the pot or fragment.

Here are some examples of the ways in which inscriptions added before firing have been thought useful for dating pottery (for graffiti, see pp. 124–5):

(a) *'Kalos' names.*[74] For about a century (ca. 550–450 B.C.) it was a popular conceit for painters of Attic black-figure and red-figure pottery to add the names of Athenian aristocrats to the background of some of their figured scenes, with the addition of the predicative adjective 'kalos' = '(is) handsome'. About two hundred names are known from this source, and some of them are synonymous with names of Athenians known from other sources: Miltiades, Leagros, etc. For dating purposes, much reliance has been placed on the possible connections with known historical characters: some say that too much has been made of these connections.[75] Problems certainly stand in the way of precision here: the age-span to which the word 'kalos' may have been applicable, the lack of precision in the literary and documentary evidence on which the dating is to depend, the repetition of names in families (usually each alternate generation) – all such matters make for uncertainty. Nevertheless, although there is still much room for argument about the names, they may provide a possible support for other evidence.

(b) *'Signatures'.*[76] The name of the man who 'made' or painted a vase is sometimes to be found written on the vase itself (see pp. 65–8, and 110–12). The incidence of such 'signatures' and thus the reason for them is uncertain: pride, personal habit, fashion? The occurrence of a 'signature' on more than one vase, its combination with different names of colleagues, and the rarer but welcome appearance of patronymics can yield useful evidence for work over a period of time. Such 'signatures' are not of themselves likely to provide absolute dates but may give assistance when combined with other evidence. There are one or two Attic painters whose names can be connected with families of artists whose work we know from other media, especially sculpture (e.g. Euthymides, the son of Polias),[77] and a more firm date may be available that way.

(c) *Panathenaic prize amphorae.*[78] Here we have a much more precise means of dating, though with a restricted body of evidence. The archonship of Hippocleides (566/565 B.C.) seems to have been the first year of what was to be a regular festival at Athens, the Panathenaia, held every four years. With this date has been connected the provision of black-figure prize amphorae of oil which carry on one side a picture of an armed Athena and on the other an illustration of the event for which the prize was won. Also, on the side with Athena, an inscription was added before firing which

indicated that it was an official prize from those games: 'ton Athenether athlon' = 'one of the prizes from Athens'. The well known 'Burgon amphora in the British Museum, with Athena and a chariot race, is one o the earliest inscribed Panathenaic prize amphorae that survive; as early is a fragmentary amphora from the Athenian Kerameikos cemetery which also carries a potter's name: Hyperides, son of Androgenes.[79] It cannot be known for sure that the Burgon amphora and the Kerameikos fragment date from the first year of the competition, but even if a little leeway is allowed, there is a fairly firm chronological anchor near the beginning o the series.

The production of Panathenaic prize amphorae continued as long as the Panathenaic festival was held; the technique of black-figure was retained but the appearance of the figures followed the taste of the times and the style of individual painters. At the beginning of the fourth century the traditional Athena and race were still being painted, together with the inscription, but soon afterwards, perhaps as early as 392/391 B.C. the name of the annual archon who gave his name to the year (*archon eponymos*), one of whose tasks was to see to the collection of the oil tha was to go into the amphorae, was added to the right of the Athena (Fig III.7). Twenty-six names, in whole or in part, are known, and some of the archons can be dated from other evidence. This enables the fourth-century series of Panathenaic prize amphorae to be arranged in order, based on a combination of chronological and stylistic evidence, and the series run from 392/391 B.C. (?) to 312/311 B.C. Thus the changes in the shape o the amphorae and in the painting can be closely observed.[80] In the late fourth century, names of other officials began to be added or substituted *athlothetai* = 'commissioners of the games'; *tamiai* = 'treasurers of the military funds'; *agonothetai* = 'commissioners of the contests', and thu the dating can in some cases be continued, though in fact not many can b dated precisely.[81] However, the traditional nature of the Panathenaic priz amphorae, their retention of black-figure as their technique and thei circumscribed subject matter make them less widespead in their usefulnes than one could have hoped.

(d) *'Hadra' hydriai.*[82] A late series of water-jars (hydriai) was produced in Greek Alexandria (with white ground) and in Crete (with clay ground). The majority have been found in the urban cemetery of Hadra, east o Alexandria, from which their modern name derives; others come from th Eastern cemeteries of Chatby and Ibrahimieh and from the Western cemeteries. The vases were used as ash urns for distinguished foreigner who had died when in Alexandria. The shape is an old Greek one that has been in existence for centuries, but some of the clay-ground 'Hadra' hydria carry datable inscriptions. Besides the modest decoration painted before firing (dots, palmettes, rosettes, fish, etc.), they also carry inscription

III.7 Attic Panathenaic prize amphora, 336–335 B.C.

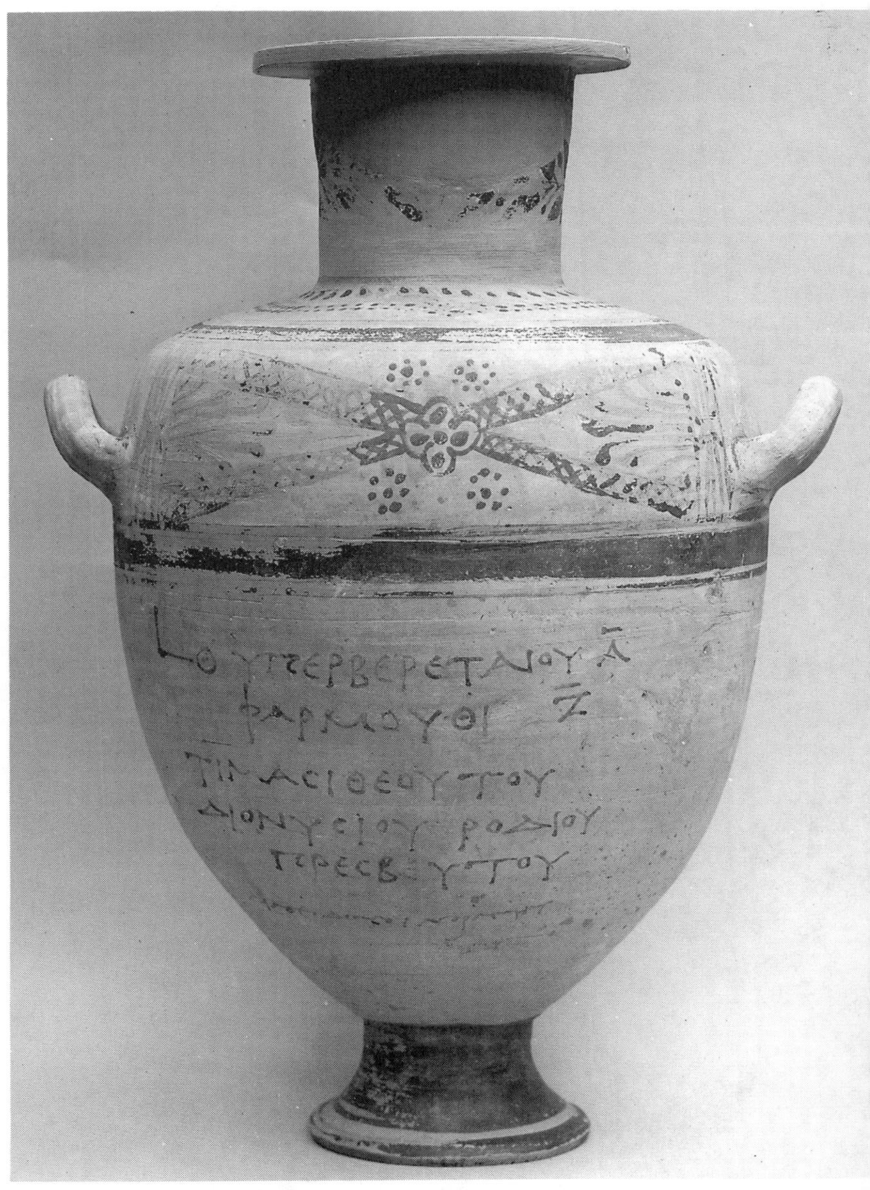

III.8 'Hadra' hydria from Hadra, Alexandria, dated 19 May 213 B.C.

added after firing, either in ink or incised. The information given usually includes the name of the dead man, the father's name, city or country of origin, and on some the date of death or burial is included, expressed by reference to the year of the reigning Ptolemy, together with the month of the Macedonian and/or Egyptian calendar, sometimes also the day (Fig. III.8). The name of the Ptolemy is sometimes omitted and has to be deduced. The name of the official who made the burial arrangements was also on occasion included in the inscription. A tight series has now been fixed from 271 to 209 B.C. and once again, as with the Panathenaic prize amphorae, development of shape and decoration within circumscribed limits can be plotted. Some of the hydriai have been found together with other tomb material, and thus there is help in dating vases of other shapes and decoration. However, as with the Panathenaics, the information won is once more restricted.

(e) *Ostraka.*[83] There are two meanings that we attach to this word: one refers to the voting sherds for the banishment of prominent citizens of Athens in the fifth century B.C., the other to fragments of pottery carrying letters written in ink; it is the first meaning of the word that is of interest here. Broken fragments of pottery, fine or coarse, were used as voting 'papers' when agreement had been reached in a particular year that a ballot for ostracism should be held. The procedure is confined to the fifth century B.C. in Athens, roughly 488/487–417 or 415 B.C. Many names are preserved on the sherds, including some prominent politicians such as Themistokles, Kimon, Megakles (Fig. VI.2), Perikles. We do not know all the occasions on which such a ballot was carried out, only some of those in which a famous figure was a candidate. It is obviously incorrect to assume, as used to be done, that every ostrakon that we have comes from the year(s) in which the named politician was exiled or is known to have been ballotted. Citizens might vote for the exile of any citizen in any year of ostracism; only the death or present exile of the person concerned is likely to have reduced the citizens' choice. This being so, once again the usefulness of the sherds is limited, particularly as the shape of the fragments is only likely to afford diagnostic help occasionally. Sometimes the name is inscribed on a fragment of figured pottery (Fig. VI.2), and hence the decoration must antedate the occasion of the voting, if that can be fixed. As with 'kalos' names, the repetition of family names may cause confusion.

(f) *Stamping.* Some of the large transport amphorae which were used as commercial containers for the transport of wine and other commodities and for their storage carry stamps on the tops of the two tall vertical handles.[84] Rhodian and Knidian stamps may carry two names, one of the manufacturer and one that indicates the official in whose term of office the wine was 'bottled' (Fig. III.9). This is also true of some jars from Sinope

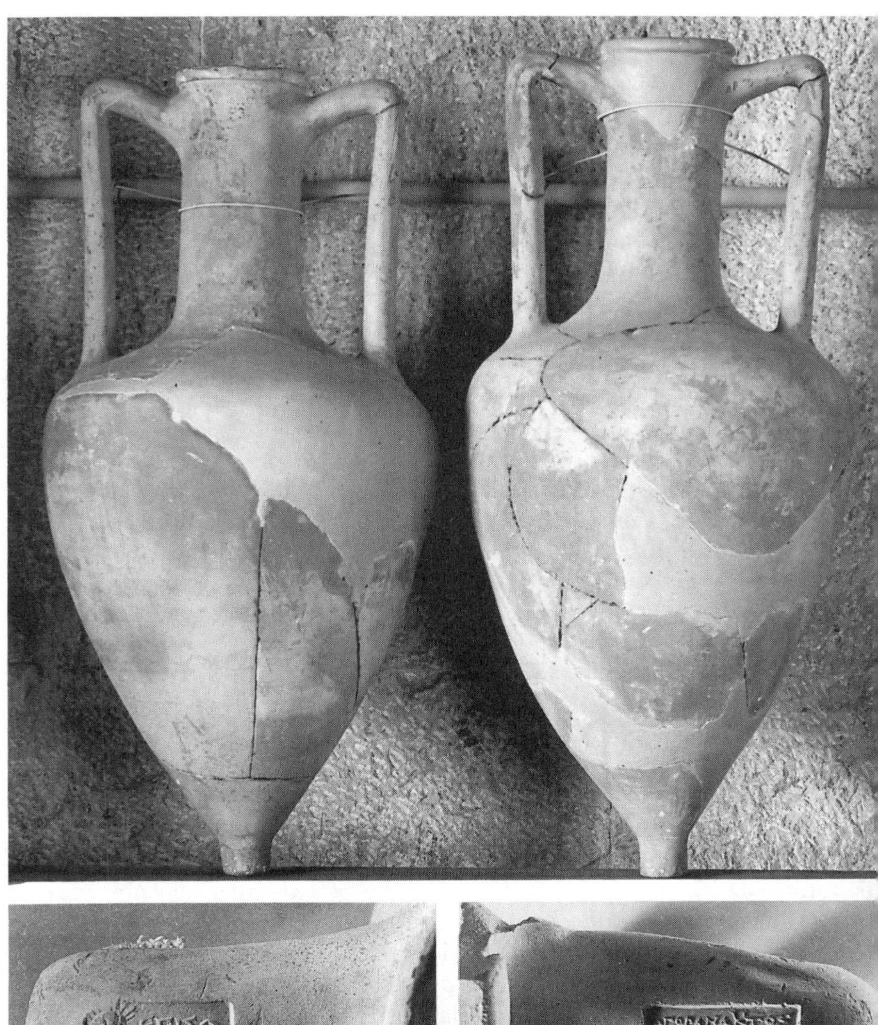

III.9 Rhodian transport amphorae and stamped handles, third century B.C.

and Thasos. The usefulness of these names is vitiated by the dearth of external dates for the officials named.

Some Chian wine jars have coins stamped on the handles in the wet clay, and the use of coins for decoration or marking is also to be seen in the centre of a class of black cups that go by the name of 'Arethusa cups', as the tondo is taken from Syracusan silver tetradrachms (398–380 B.C.) carrying the head of the local nymph. The coins of Heraclea are used on pottery in the same way. Once again the usefulness is somewhat restricted as the coins are not always easy to date, and are free objects that could be used any time after their date of minting.[85]

Scientific dating[86]

The use of scientific techniques for the dating of Greek pottery of the first millennium B.C. is still less precise than results reached by other methods. Thermoluminescence (TL), which relates to the firing of the clay and is the principal method of measuring absolute dates in relation to the age of pottery, has its uses in investigating forgeries (such as Tanagra terracotta statuettes) but is too imprecise to be of assistance in making the sort of chronological distinctions on which students of classical pottery have come to depend.

IV
SHAPES

It is, indeed, by an odd inversion of propriety that the word 'vase', with its modern connotation of ornamental un-usefulness, has attached itself to Greek pottery, and that as a result of antiquarian habit we can hardly think of this pottery outside a museum. (Lane 1971, 8)

Distinguishing functions

Most Greek pottery was shaped to serve a function or a variety of functions: for domestic tasks, for ceremonial, for leisure and pleasure. One shape might be used in a number of different contexts, and conversely some functions were served by more than one shape. In this chapter we shall be concerned with shapes and the functions that they were created to perform, and with the individuals who fashioned them.

Naturally, there are variations in the basic shapes in different areas of the Greek world: no two regions shaped a jug or a cup in precisely the same way. These variations are one of the ways that help us to assign to different sources the material found and to observe the influence of one area upon another. Similarly, shapes of pottery varied through time: they developed in certain ways, either radically or in details, and from time to time new shapes were introduced. Here again, the study of shape-changes enables a framework of relative chronology and influence to be erected. Fine wares changed more frequently and obviously than coarse wares; with the latter it is the much more recent social changes that have altered the long-standing, traditional shapes.

Clay was readily available, cheap and malleable, hence it was the basic material for containers, and potters adhered to traditional shapes, unless persuaded that a change was an advantage – easier to form, more saleable, answering new needs.

How are we able to distinguish functions? Apart from the broad distinction of fabrics – such as coarse versus fine – which will indicate whether the objects were mainly used e.g. in the kitchen, garden or workshop, or in the dining room, for the sanctuary or at the grave side, there are five main ways in which the use can be determined.

(a) The shape of the object itself often declares its purpose, either in general or in particular. An open shape, e.g. a large bowl or cup, might suggest easy access for hands or implements, for ladling, for mixing

dipping, drinking, whereas a closed shape with small mouth is likely to suggest sealing with wax or a stopper, or storage. One vertical handle and a spout or a shaped lip indicates pouring, two handles (vertical or horizontal) suggest carrying. A three-handled jar (hydria) – with one vertical and two horizontal handles – enabled the empty jar to be carried by the one vertical handle, the jar when full of water to be lifted to the head by the two horizontal handles. A small toe, on which no vase could stand, such as is found on transport amphorae, suggests storage in the earth or fixing in a stand, ease of lifting to pour out the contents (a sort of third handle) and neat stacking. A rolled rim was formed to enable a waxed or oiled cloth to be tied across the mouth to protect the contents, or for the attachment of a wooden cover or clay lid. Inner containers, whether large as in some storage amphorae or small as in some oil flasks, argue the need to keep the contents cool or perhaps contents too precious and expensive to fill the complete container.

(b) A second help towards understanding the function is the find spot: grave (Fig. III.1), sanctuary, house, etc. A straightforward example is the well, at the bottom of which broken or holed clay buckets with wide mouths, two handles and unpainted surface, declare their use readily.

(c) Much fine pottery carries figured scenes, and the illustrations shown provide valuable clues to the uses of a whole range of shapes. Naturally one must not assume that all vases depicted are painted fine ware, though occasionally some are decorated to indicate this, nor indeed must one assume that all the containers illustrated were of clay, though some are shown broken; many must be meant for metal, wood, stone, etc. However, even with this constraint, shapes may betray their purpose, no matter what their material.

The division often made between scenes of mythology and scenes of everyday life is a false one, especially when considered from the point of view of the pots illustrated, and the objects in the hands of legendary heroes rarely differ from those held by revellers and athletes. The contexts – symposium, libation at an altar, sports ground, well or fountain – reveal the functions of the vases held or set down: for example, the lekythoi shown on the steps of tombs on Attic white-ground lekythoi; the pots handled in fountain scenes; the varied jars, jugs and cups in use at drinking parties; oil bottles at athletic scenes or in scenes with women at home. Some of the mythological scenes provide help: the storage jar (pithos) in the tale of Herakles, Cerberus and Eurystheus; the drinking cup in the story of Odysseus and the Cyclops.

(d) Occasionally the lettering on a vase will assist in understanding its function. Some cups have mottoes written on them that urge the user to drink. More rarely, illustrated vases carry their names painted by their side ('hydria' by the side of a water pot; 'lebes' by a bowl on a tripod).[1]

(e) Greek literature also provides another source of evidence from which we can derive information on use. Almost unconsciously, writers on contemporary themes (Aristophanes the comic playwright; the orators of fourth century Athens) give help in understanding the objects in everyday use. However, the very fact that the words were living for them means that generally their usage is allusive. Later writers and those deliberately attempting to define old words in lexica have little more idea than we do but may be helpful in different ways. In any case, no language uses such words precisely, and our own 'saucer', 'pot', 'dish', 'bowl' etc. defy accurate visual description.[2]

The last item brings us to the difficult problem of the present bewildering names of vase-shapes that we find in modern studies of Greek pottery.

The game of the names

As Greek vases have been seriously studied since the eighteenth century and by scholars educated to an understanding of Greek and Latin literature, it has been inevitable that their knowledge of names for containers in ancient Greek and Latin literature and lexica should have been put to use in seeking to establish a nomenclature for the vases found and studied.[3] The vases then studied were mainly fine, decorated pottery, not coarse and plain wares, and so this established a bias from the start. The present chaotic system of vase names is the result of an historical accident, compounded by alterations and additions made during more recent study; however, the system, now international, would be impossible to jettison entirely. Students of both literature and ceramics suffer from the consequences, as readers of literature cannot look to the vase-shape terminology for a correct image of the word they have encountered nor can students of Greek vases necessarily derive from literature a correct idea of the name and uses of the vase they are studying, as it was named generations ago on a system that had no firm reasoning behind it. False images are raised on both sides.

Literary references to shapes need not always refer to fine wares nor even to objects made of clay. Also, the genres of literature had their own field of words, and tone and level of speech (vulgar, poetic, rhetorical) varied. Dialect and period also need to be considered. Some of the established names for shapes seem to 'work' correctly, some are partially right, some are totally wrong ('askos' was the word for a wine-skin but is conventionally used to designate a small oil-container; 'dinos', which has now been used of a form of mixing-bowl, was actually a word for cup). Also, study of Greek usage suggests that words were used generically, not specifically, and we are in innocence and error if we expect to find a one-to-one correspondence between literary references and a particular shape of vase.

Names of shapes are often encountered in inscriptional sources. Stone inscriptions such as temple inventories and the Attic stelai that listed the sale by the Athenian state of goods belonging to those accused of damaging the Herms in Athens and of profaning the Eleusinian Mysteries in 415 B.C., provide words by themselves and occasionally (by a more detailed description) supply a closer approximation to a specific shape.[4] Inscriptions on the pots may bring us nearer to naming the shape carrying the word, but the information won is still limited.[5] We have seen how occasionally a pot in a scene is given a name by the side of it; sometimes a painted inscription names the pot on which it is painted (e.g. 'kados' on an Attic black-figure amphora).[6] More commonly, the name appears in a graffito, scratched after the pot had been fired, declaring the ownership of the vase, e.g. 'I am the [cup] of [personal name], a pleasant drink'.[7] Some graffiti appear as trademarks under the foot, where they are usually abbreviated and are part of a batch list (see pp. 126–9). Here follow a few examples of such painted and incised vase-names; some provide added information on Greek social life.

(a) *Drinking cups*: the usual words painted before firing or scratched after it are 'kylix' and 'poterion'. To mark one's own drinking cup was perhaps a necessary precaution for a party, and laying claim to portable crockery was not uncommon. 'Kylix' is found (before firing) on a late seventh-century Chiot chalice ('Nikesermos made this kylix')[8] and (after firing) retrograde on a Rhodian subgeometric skyphos of ca. 700 B.C. ('I am the kylix of Korakos' – the conceit of the speaking pot is found early in ceramics)[9] and on an Attic cup-skyphos of ca. 400 B.C. ('Kephisophon's kylix. If anyone breaks it, he will pay a drachma, as it was a gift from Xenylos')[10] 'Poterion' is found (before firing) on a mid sixth-century Attic Siana cup ('I am the lovely poterion')[11] and (after firing) retrograde on a late eighth-century Rhodian Geometric skyphos from Ischia ('Of Nestor am I, a poterion pleasant to drink from. Whoever drinks from this poterion, a desire for Aphrodite of the beautiful crown will seize straightaway').[12] 'Kotylos' or 'kotylon' is found on a Boeotian mid. fifth-century black kantharos ('Mogea(s) gives a kotylos as a gift to his wife Eucharis, the daughter of Eutretiphantos, that she may drink her fill').[13]

(b) *Oil bottles*: the commonest word found is 'lekythos'. Again these were objects that were carried around and thus might need marking as a personal possession. 'Lekythos' is found (before firing) on an Attic early fifty-century red-figure aryballos ('Douris made. Asopodoros' lekythos')[14] and (after firing) retrograde on a Protocorinthian mid-seventh-century pointed aryballos (Fig. IV.1) ('I am Tataie's lekythos. Whoever steals me will go blind').[15] 'Olpe' is found (before firing) on a Corinthian early sixth-century black-figure round aryballos ('Polyterpos. Pyrrhias leading the chorus. The olpe is his very own').[16]

IV.1 Protocortinthian lekythos with graffito, ca. 675–650 B.C. (reproduced a approximately three times actual size)

(c) *Storage jars*: although we use the word 'amphora' as the general term for a shape with two vertical handles, the shape is designated by the word 'kados' painted on an Attic black-figure amphora of the late sixth century ('the kados is fine').[17] The same word 'kados' is incised on an unpainted coarse-ware bucket of the late fifth century ('I am a kados').[18]

As can be seen, we are likely to be confused if we expect any systematic ancient nomenclature. So modern names such as plate, bowl, mug tend to be adopted for new shapes being studied, with explanatory descriptions to subdivide them; sometimes a made-up name, such as one-handler, refers to the distinctive appearance of a type; occasionally, new names are invented to distinguish a shape, e.g. 'bolsal' for a shallow straight-sided drinking-cup, named from two Attic red-figure examples, one in Bol (ogna), one in Sal (onica).[19]

It would be more helpful if a systematic terminology could be devised, as for types of pottery more recently discovered or those belonging to a preliterate age, but this is unlikely.

Potters

For most of the period under study, pottery was largely formed by hands, and therefore it is natural to think in personal terms. It was mainly an anonymous craft, though study of details of shape, where enough are available and their idiosyncrasy is detectable (feet, handles, lip, contour), can lead to an understanding of an individual potter's work. So names have been invented to distinguish individuals, such as the Club-foot Potter and the Canoe Potter.[20] However, some vases carry painted (and scratched) inscriptions that indicate the men who 'made' them. These are painted in black on a clay background, or in purple on a black background where the painting is in red-figure; occasionally black was used on a black background, with a reserved outline round the lettering, or again inscriptions were incised on the black gloss, whether on black-figure or red-figure pottery. The inscription could be set on any part of the vase: body, neck, rim, foot, handle. A study of the handwriting reveals that the writer could be a 'letterer' charged with the task, not necessarily the man who 'made' the vase;[21] in some cases the letterer may be the painter who will thus finish off the work he has done, but this should not be presumed. So 'signature' is a dangerous word to use here. Letterers can't always spell correctly or consistently, but this may not mean that they do not know how to spell their own name.

There is only one instance where the verb used means 'potted', and this is on an Attic black-figure stemmed dish of the early fifth century, where the painted inscription says 'Oikopheles potted me and painted' ('ekerameusen eme Oikopheles kai egraphsen');[22] all other vases with this type of

inscription carry the more general word 'made' ('epoiesen'). This causes difficulty, as the general word 'made' may refer to the *actual* maker who threw the vase, but it could refer to the *proprietor* of the pottery shop within which the vase was made. There is scholarly disagreement here, and the solution is not simple.[23]

A 'maker's' name is first met ca. 700 B.C., i.e. not very long after the introduction of the alphabet to Greece and quite soon after its earliest use on pottery. The earliest known to us is to be found on a krater fragment from Pithecusa, Ischia ('—inos made me'), and it is written in a local script of Euboean style (the Greek settlers at Pithecusa were from Euboea).[24] Best known and clearest of the early makers' inscriptions is the Aristonothos inscription on a krater found at Caere in Etruria; it was made in Italy in the second quarter of the seventh century B.C. and shows a sea fight on one side and Odysseus and the Cyclops on the other.[25] Again the script is thought to be (colonial?) Euboean, though other suggestions have been made (Argive, Cumaean, Sicilian). There are very few 'maker's' inscriptions in the seventh century, but the habit seems to have been widespread, other examples coming from e.g. Smyrna, Chios and Ithaca.[26] One in Euboean script gives the father's name as well (Fig. IV.2): 'Pyrrhos, son of Agasileos, made me'.[27] It is the letterer's home town that is betrayed by the script, and this need be neither that of the potter nor that of the painter. The practice becomes more common in the sixth and fifth centuries, mainly in Athens;[28] another centre that has provided makers' names in that period is Boeotia, e.g. Teisias 'the Athenian' (scratched), Theodoros.[29] Most 'makers' (whether potters or proprietors) are nameless to us, and it is difficult to explain why a few should be commemorated in the way they are. There seems to be no consistency, no intelligible pattern. Some of the best quality

IV.2 Protocorinthian(?) aryballos with painted name of potter, ca. 650 B.C.

pieces carry no names of the makers, whilst some of the worst (e.g. that of Oikopheles, above) advertise the 'maker', so it is hard to believe that names were always added for quality of workmanship (see below for another solution, pp. 71, 149, n. 38).

Whether we accept the name of the man who 'made' the vase as the potter or the owner of the shop, there are certain consequences that flow from the names.

The names themselves tell us details about the men. Aristonothos (see p. 66), meaning 'Best bastard', suggests a nickname; Pyrrhos (Fig. IV.2) (see p. 66) may mean 'Redhead', another nickname, though his father's name, Agasileos, is straightforward. With names on Attic pottery, some inscriptions show that some 'makers' were also painters, e.g. Nearchos, Exekias (Fig. V.8), Euphronios (first as painter, then as 'maker'), Douris, Myson; some appear with the name of the painter, working in the same shop, e.g. Ergotimos the 'maker' and Kleitias the painter; Python the 'maker' and Douris the painter; Hieron the 'maker' and Makron the painter. Some names may reveal the origin of the men, e.g. Sikanos, from Sicily; Brygos, from Phrygia; Thrax, from Thrace; Syriskos, from Syria; some of these may be slaves, as also Epiktetos meaning 'Newly acquired'. Some add their ethnic origin, e.g. Teisias the Athenian, working in Boeotia (see above), Xenophantes the Athenian and Nikias, son of Hermokles, of Anaphlystos (a district of Attica). Amasis, a name shared with an Egyptian Pharaoh, has caused interest and discussion. Some, like Pyrrhos (see above), advertise their family connections: in Attic black-figure there are Tleson and Ergoteles, sons of Nearchos, the sons 'makers', the father both a 'maker' and a painter, and Ergotimos had a son Eucheiros and a grandson, both 'makers'; in Attic red-figure Kleophrades, who was the son of the 'maker' Amasis, was himself a 'maker'. Very occasionally, two are given as makers of one cup.[30]

It is interesting that we also have a 'maker's' name on a very early Panathenaic prize amphora, again with the father's name given (Hypereides, son of Androgenes).[31] As this public commission is likely to have been much sought after, it is remarkable that there are few instances with the 'maker's' name painted on them. A fourth-century instance of names added on Panathenaic prize amphorae has a bearing on the question of whether 'makers' were potters or proprietors. Some Panathenaic prize amphorae carry the names of Bakchios and Kittos, with the word 'made' (epoiesen) following them. One Bakchios amphora is dated by the archon name (Hippo[damosl]) to 375/374 B.C., the Kittos amphora to a decade later, perhaps to the year of the archon Polyzelos (367/366 B.C.).[32] A tombstone of ca. 330 B.C. found near Athens records in a verse inscription the name of a Bakchios, son of Amphis[——.[33] The accompanying set of verses tells us what trade he had followed: 'Of those who blend earth,

water, fire into one by art, Bakchios was judged by all Hellas first, for natural gifts; and in every contest appointed by the city he won the crown.' Towards the end of the fourth century an inscription set up in Ephesos records employment and political honours awarded to a Bakchios and a Kittos:[34] 'The council and people have agreed that Kittos and Bakchios, sons of Bakchios, Athenians, since they have undertaken to make the black pottery for the city, and the hydria for the goddess, at the price fixed by law, shall be citizens of Ephesos as long as they remain in the city . . . ' The likeliest explanation would seem to suggest that the earlier Bakchios and Kittos were brothers, and that the sons of Bakchios, themselves named Bakchios and Kittos, followed their father and uncle in the pottery business and moved from Athens to Ephesos for work, perhaps after the death of the first Bakchios.[35] On this evidence, it would look as though these 'makers' did actually fashion the clay with their own hands, and that their work was highly esteemed.

That the word 'made' was also used by metalworkers on their shapes is known from the fact that some black relief phialai made in Cales (south Italy), the mould of which was taken directly from a metal, most likely silver, phiale, have the word 'epoiei' transferred along with the design (see below).[36]

Other materials

Before considering the variety of shapes in clay, it may be helpful to speak generally of the materials available that were fashioned into the shapes of containers to hold liquids and/or solids and used for storing, pouring, transporting, cooking, eating and drinking. As clay is such a malleable and virtually indestructible substance, other materials can be seen reflected in the ceramic vases, both in shape and in details of shape, even when the original objects have had no chance of survival.

Such a basic material as animal skin, so useful for clothing, could also be cut and sewn to act as a container: if large, as a wine-skin (askos); if small, as a purse which may be reflected in the small aryballoi that were hung from the wrists of athletes. Dried gourds make excellent containers, and the swollen shape may have given rise to certain clay forms such as the phormiskos. Reeds woven into baskets, large and small, provide the prototype for certain round clay boxes (pyxides) in which the plaited designs on the walls and the radial designs on the bottom are imitated in paint (Fig. IV.3); the actual raised form of the interwoven strands is occasionally to be found where the clay appears to have been pressed against a basket, and sometimes the long rope handles are closely imitated (Fig. IV.3). Wood must have served many purposes, perhaps mainly as platters, bowls and boxes, and the few remaining pieces that have survived

IV.3 Boeotian Geometric pyxis, ca. 700 B.C.

show us the beading and other decoration that we find on some clay vases; the knobs of clay lids also seem to imitate the shapes of turned wooden knobs. Occasionally, vases were moulded into the shape of nuts, shells, etc.[37]

Leather, reeds, wood, etc. are materials that need use no other processes than cutting, stitching, plaiting and carving. Though skill was needed in their making, they were technically uncomplicated and inexpensive products. Clay, similarly cheap, needed more complex production methods. Costlier materials needing even more advanced skills lie, as it were, at the other end of the spectrum. Stone (alabaster), horn (ivory, etc.) and metals (gold, silver, bronze) are less easily accessible materials than clay, and all have left their mark on the appearance of pottery. The Egyptian alabastron, a long narrow perfume pot, originally made of alabaster (hence the name), is copied in clay in East Greece and is later adopted in Athens; the surface of the clay alabastron is later covered with a white slip in imitation of the stone surface.[38] The rhyton, a horn-shaped drinking vessel, takes its shape from natural horn. Glass too, though more rarely, may have had influence.

With metals, the connection is much more complex and, it would appear, more all-pervading. Comparatively few metal vases have survived, their value was in the material of which they were made, and they could easily be melted down. What have survived would seem to suggest that many clay vases owed their inspiration, both in particular and in general, to metal originals (Fig. IV.4): the sharp edges, the acute angles, the thin walls, the precise articulation. It is also true of details such as imitation rivets, studs, discs, and of decoration such as ribbing, incising and

IV.4 Silver and black mugs from Dalboki, Bulgaria, ca. 400 B.C.

stamping. In some instances, impressed and applied reliefs can be seen to have been taken directly from metal originals, sometimes with the word 'made' transferred to the clay as well (see above p. 68). A recent theory would extend the influence of metal beyond the areas mentioned above and connect all the various colours of Greek pottery with metal and other original materials (see Chapter V). On this theory all such influence was from the more expensive materials to the clay, with important consequences for our understanding of both shapes and decoration, and in a wider context, of the social standing of the potters and their clients, and of the value and purpose of pottery.[39]

Besides the influence from other materials, Greek pottery borrowed and adapted shapes from traditions outside their own area. The Egyptian alabastron has been mentioned above; other such borrowings are the rhyton, a drinking horn with a hole in the base that owes its origin to Persia; the phiale, a drinking and offering dish also from Persia; the lydion, a small perfume container, that originated as the name suggests in Lydia (Asia Minor).[40] Nor was the influence always from East to West. Trade with the Etruscans found the bucchero amphora of their potting traditions copied by the Athenian potter Nikosthenes, given black-figure decoration and exported back to Etruria; the kyathos, a one-handled dipper, is also an example of a similar transference.[41]

Shapes and functions

There is no single, straightforward way in which to treat the different shapes in Greek pottery. There is overlap of function, variation in place and time, etc. A simple distinction to make, but one which immediately cuts across the morphology, is a division into varieties of ceramic material.

(a) There are the heavy-duty shapes. The best known perhaps are the big commercial transport amphorae (jars for storing, sealing and conveying wine, oil, fish, etc.) with long body, narrow neck, two vertical handles and small toe (Fig. III.9). The 'Ali Baba' pithoi, which were rarely moved once in position and could last for years, were also used for the storage of commodities such as oil and dry goods (Fig. IV.5). Other heavy-duty containers were big tubs, mortars for grinding and shallow basins on stands (louteria). Some of these were mould-made.[42]

(b) There are also the less well known coarse wares made with paddle and anvil (see p. 13) which were used in kitchen contexts: kettles (chytrai), two- or one-handled; buckets (kadoi) with two vertical handles at the neck to which a rope could be attached for letting down a well; water-jars (hydriai) with one vertical and two horizontal handles; jugs with a single handle for pouring; frying-pans, casseroles, gridirons, ovens (Fig. IV.6). The shapes are not so well articulated as those of the fine wares,

IV.5 Cretan relief-pithos amphora, ca. 675 B.C.

IV.6 Cooking pots and braziers from Athens, fifth and fourth centuries B.C.

perhaps because of the method of production or the absence of metal influence. Nor do the shapes change so rapidly and might be expected to last longer provided they didn't break or spring a leak.[43]

(c) Household wares were made by the same methods as fine wares but were left mainly in the colour of the clay, with perhaps a stripe or two across the body. Gloss was often applied to the foot, handles and rim, and the interior given a waterproof coating. The commonest shapes were open bowls (lekanai) with two horizontal handles, like kraters; lidded bins for storage; small narrow-necked jars for keeping food from going bad (eggs, olives); jugs and water-jars.[44]

(d) The range of wheel-made fine wares makes any all-embracing statement difficult. The distinction between them and the household wares is basically in the greater range and sophistication of the shapes, the amount of gloss and decoration they carry (black, patterns, figures), and the contexts in which they were used.

Occasions and contexts

Let us look at some of the most obvious occasions and contexts in which pottery was used, to get some idea of the range and variety of demands that the potters had to face.[45] We'll start with men and their life: politics, athletics, work, relaxation.

In the public life of the polis men needed the potter. In Athens, there were objects of clay specifically produced with public affairs in mind (Fig.

IV.7 Public pots used in Athens, fifth and fourth centuries B.C.

IV.7): liquid and dry measures, water-clocks for measuring the length of the speeches in court, two-part voting tickets. Most were undecorated, and some would carry the ligature ΔΕ, an abbreviation of *demosion* to indicate that this was an officially recognised object. Often pottery needed for public life was the same sort as for other purposes, e.g. hydriai or kadoi used in everyday life as water-jars and buckets doubled as voting-urns, and the klepsydra or water-clock was adapted from the ordinary household bowl.[46]

In athletics, whether at practice or after an actual race, the men and boys needed their personal oil bottle by whatever name we may now choose to call it and whatever its precise shape might be, hanging from the wrist when not in use, or easily grasped in the hand when shaking out some of the contents.[47] Prizes were awarded at games meetings, and these too might be made of clay. We know that tripods and cauldrons (lebetes) of bronze were offered in earlier times, but there is enough evidence from Athens to show that clay containers were common. Apart from the evidence of

amphorae and hydriai, the fullest material is the black-figure Panathenaic prize amphorae for the Great Panathenaea (see pp. 53–4). The city gave the commission for these on some basis that we do not comprehend ('one of the prizes from Athens' is painted on them), and the oil they contained came from the sacred olive groves of Attica. This must have been a lucrative commission for a workshop to win, as over 1400 would be needed every four years (cf. Bakchios and Kittos, pp. 67–8).[48]

What a soldier took to war apart from his weapons and his armour would have been small. Travellers would also have travelled light. A mug for drinking and a flask for carrying water (pilgrim flask) may have been all they needed.[49]

For the various trades and industries, clay vessels would have been vital: if a shoemaker, a bowl for softening leather in water; if a blacksmith, a jug for water; if an oil-seller, a container for oil and a funnel to direct the oil into the narrow neck of an alabastron or lekythos; if a wine-seller, amphorae, jugs and cups for tasting. Out of town, men had to collect and tread grapes; they needed a trough for the grapes, a bowl for the squeezed-out juice and a pithos for the storing of the juice. In big wine industries, the transport amphora was vital, and thousands have been discovered. If bees were kept, then the hive might be of pot. Storage jars would also be needed for keeping meat, olives, etc.[50] This is not the territory for elegant fine wares.

An area of male society that we know well is that of the festive symposium or drinking party, and the komos or revel. A great range of pottery was needed for drinking sessions. First, the wine itself had to be stored in large, coarse amphorae that would need to be broached – sometimes they were taken along by members of the party themselves. Access to water was needed for diluting the wine (two-fifths wine, three-fifths water), and there was no tap on hand. At the party itself (Fig. IV.8), deep, open mixing bowls of various shapes stood by the couches of the drinkers as they reclined: fine-ware amphorae with wide mouths, kraters of various types, lebetes on stands, stamnoi, pelikai. For the sophisticated party, a wine-cooler (psykter) might have been provided, to sit in the mixing-bowl.

To decant the wine from the mixing-bowl to the cup, a jug or ladle was on hand. The jug was one-handled, could have a trefoil mouth, and there were various shapes and sizes; ladles (kyathoi) or dippers served the same purpose but had longer handles. But it was in the variety of drinking cups that the ingenuity of the potters was most apparent. Many were large, to receive diluted wine, and many two-handled and shallow; it is doubtful how helpful such a shape was to the drinkers as they reclined. When not in use, they were hung from the wall. Some were taller and deeper, with one handle or two. Different pottery-producing centres issued their own

IV.8 A symposium in full swing on an Attic kylix, ca. 500 B.C.

versions: Chiot chalices, Laconian lakainai, Boeotian kantharoi, etc., anc there were less popular varieties: mastoi (shaped like breasts), rhyta (shaped like a horn or an animal head), moulded tankards, phialai and sc forth. Later in the Hellenistic period the handleless hemispherical bowl (the so-called 'Megarian' bowl) became the most popular drinking cup.[51]

Other objects to help the festivities were needed – besides wooder platters for the food, perhaps stemmed plates of clay for fruit, plates fo fish, clay lamps to light the rooms in the evening; and also for those whc had taken too much to drink, a sick basin and/or chamber pot or jug (cf Fig. IV.8) were provided to afford much needed relief. The chamber po may have been something of a refinement, as the easiest move to make, if a move was going to be made at all, was outside.[52]

What of the women? Their rôle centred on the house, the food and th children. The house needed storage containers for the grain, for water olives, oil, wine. There would be a bucket for drawing water from the wel in the courtyard and a three-handled water-jar to take to the fountai nearby. Much time would be devoted to the cooking, and the kitche equipment consisted of such items as kettles, frying-pans, ovens (Fig. IV.6) gridirons – all made by the potter.[53] When not attending to the meals, th mistress of the household spent time with the children and the weaving. Fo the former, the potter's shop provided clay dolls and toys, baby feeders anc potty chairs, and perhaps dice for the older children; for the weaving, ther were clay loom weights, spindle whorls and a clay carding cover for th

IV.9 Rhodian perfume pot in the shape of a swallow, ca. 600 B.C.

thigh over which to draw the unspun wool.[54] Clay lamps too were needed for lighting. When there was time for the woman to attend to herself and her appearance, the potter provided various lidded containers (lekanides) for trinkets and also boxes (pyxides) for such cosmetics as powder, rouge, pomade for the hair. She also had small bottles in which scent and perfume were kept; these (such as alabastra and the various shapes of lekythos) had narrow necks and stoppable mouths, the latter sometimes having a drip ring at the neck. Other containers were lydia, amphoriskoi, 'askoi', gutti and unguentaria.[55] Some of these containers declare their contents by painted inscriptions: a lekythos in Athens carries the word HIPINON painted on the top of its mouth: iris perfume.[56] Some perfume vases were shaped in the form of heads, legs, birds (Fig. IV.9), etc. The exaleiptron, because of its size, must have contained scented water, to be used on special occasions such as weddings and visits to the tomb.[57]

There were also special occasions in the life of the household that demanded special pottery, occasions such as marriages, births, funerals and times when, in public or private, the family took part in religious festivals. For the marriage, there was a special range of shapes that were peculiar to weddings: especially the loutrophoros in Athens, a tall ungainly shape that provided water for the bridal bath, and the lebes gamikos, with either attached stand or short foot, in which ceremonial water was kept. On such an occasion, presents were brought for the bride, again furnished by the potter: lekythoi, amphoriskoi, epinetra, pyxides, on many of which the scenes of brides and home life link the object with a wedding.[58]

Potters must also have answered a brisk, not to say urgent, demand for

vases at the time of deaths, funerals and after. There was the laying out of the body at home, the burial, whether inhumation or cremation (with primary or secondary burial), and then the later visits to the graveside to pay respects. The graveside ritual at the time of burial demanded vases of perfumed oil, and then maybe these, certainly similar, vases were laid in the grave with the body (Fig. III.1), not all new but some certainly purchased for the occasion (e.g. clay eggs, phormiskoi, and in Attica, white ground lekythoi, and loutrophoroi and lebetes gamikoi for those who died unmarried). Sometimes the need for a coffin was expressed, small and plain, or in some parts of the Greek world, large and elaborate such as the sarcophagi from Clazomenae; if the bodies were cremated, ash urns of various shapes (amphora, hydria, lebes) were needed, sometimes bronze, more often clay. At certain stages of history, the grave location was marked by a clay vase as a grave monument, the best known being the Late Geometric amphorae and kraters, but others are not uncommon. Later visitors brought offerings to place on the steps of the tomb: lekythoi, alabastra, oinochoai, with perhaps some objects of marble (pyxides, plemochoai).[59]

Religious occasions were an important element in Greek life, and once again the potter was in demand to provide the necessary physical expressions of their religious needs. There were specific days during the year when ritual worship of one deity or another demanded particular objects. Again, it is Athens and Attica that provide the best evidence: stamnoi for the Lenaea, choes and chytrai for the Anthesteria, krateriskoi for Artemis, broken amphorae for Adonis. Throughout the year also, there were libations with jug and dish (oinochoe and phiale) at altars to the gods or for prayers at departure and return, and incense offered in the thurible (thymiaterion). Often the quality of production was poor: the ritual objects were usually decayed versions e.g. votives, miniatures, of those shapes that had a proper life. By contrast, vases offered to a deity in a sanctuary were often of high quality (e.g. those from the Athenian Acropolis), and for some the vases offered were bespoke with the name of the deity and/or the dedicator on them.[60]

So one can see that there was no area of Greek life where the potter did not furnish the necessary materials.

Aesthetics of shape

Attention has been concentrated on the function of vases – they had a job to do, and their basic form was dictated by that function. However, this still left scope for variation within the individual shapes, both locally and chronologically, and for the particular preferences of individual potters. The Greeks thought of their pots in human terms – handles were 'ears',

bases were 'feet', and we have continued this tradition by speaking of lip, neck, shoulder, body. 'In the hands of the potters, the vase is like a body being formed.'[61]

Modern aesthetic appreciation of vase-shapes must always be carried out with the practical purpose of the shape in mind: the object had to pour, stand, carry etc., but it cannot be denied that rhythm, formal balance, proportion, symmetry are factors that came into play. The visual attraction of the Greek shapes often depends on their tectonic and linear precision and proportion, and their similarity to sculptured figures has often been remarked upon. Attempts, not always accepted, have been made to connect the effect of the shapes with their relation to geometric figures, but even if agreed, this is likely to have been instinctive on the part of the potter, learnt by practical experience, not from mathematical theory.

Some shapes are obviously stereometric in their basic shape: the small spherical aryballos, the lebes and the hemispherical mould-made bowl, but many shapes are usually more complex. It has been suggested that, apart from such basic forms as those just mentioned, one might think in terms of the flexible/elastic shape where the form of the vase counterfeits the weight of the contents, i.e. such shapes as the pelike or the phormiskos in which the widest circumference is low down on the body of the vase, or in terms of the architectonic in which the structure of the form, e.g. the volute-krater (e.g. Fig. V.6), is built on architectural principles. 'The volute-krater is the vase-shape which has more of the temple in it than any other: not only do the handle-volutes recall the Ionic capital, but the designer of the upper part must have been thinking of epistyle, frieze and cornice, and the contrast of the ornamental architrave and plain shaft and capital may also have been at the back of his mind.'[62] There are also those shapes in which there is a flowing contour, more akin to classical sculpture.

Greek fine wares tend to be very disciplined in their exact shaping, precise contours, firm articulation. Certainly the effect of metal is felt in the fourth and fifth centuries (ribbing, sharp edges, plastic attachments). With the best examples, the decoration is planned to offset the shape, not to distract attention from it.[63] Kitchen ware does not so easily lend itself to this sort of treatment as fine wares. The shapes tend to be slacker, with less attention paid to refinements of feet, handles and lip. These were working shapes above all else.

Alphabetical list of vase names

The names included here are a selection of those most commonly in use today. The preponderance of them are Attic fine wares, though a few kitchen-ware names have been included. Not all are illustrated (Fig. 10.a–o). The scale is 1:7.

Alabastron (pl. Alabastra)	Based on alabaster prototype. Small vase for perfume or oil. Broad, flat mouth, narrow neck, thin bag-shaped body, sometimes with lugs, usually footless. Used for women's toilet and for cult. Contents extracted with dipstick.
Amis (pl. Amides)	A name used to signify a portable urinal. A Greek inscription indicates that one version was a wide-mouthed jug.
Amphora (pl. Amphorae)	Meaning 'carry on both sides'. Made in all fabrics. Two vertical handles, wide body, narrower neck. Some have broad foot, others a small toe. Some have lids. Size varies. For liquids and solids. The main types are: (a) Transport amphora – a large coarse-ware shape with long body, small toe and narrow mouth that can be stoppered. (b) Neck-amphora – many varieties in fine ware, all sharing an offset neck. Specially named variants are e.g. Nikosthenic, Nolan, Panathenaic, pointed. (c) Belly-amphora – body and neck in continuous curve. Forms of handles, mouths and feet differ. (d) Bail-amphora – handle reaches over the mouth. Used for storing and carrying wine, oil and other commodities, for serving wine at table, as an ash urn for the dead.
Amphoriskos (pl. Amphoriskoi)	Small version of the amphora, based on the pointed variant of neck-amphora or transport amphora. Some carry stamped designs. Used for perfumed oil.
Aryballos (pl. Aryballoi)	Conventional name for an ovoid or ball-shaped oil pot (with one or two handles). Footed or footless. Used by athletes. Some are in the shape of a head, animal or bird.
Askos (pl. Askoi)	Meaning 'wine-skin'. Conventionally (and erroneously) used for a small, flat vase, with narrow sloping spout and handle arching over body.
Bolsal	Invented name (Bol (ogna) – Sal (onica)) to designate a broad, shallow cup with short vertical sides and two horizontal handles below plain rim.

Bottle	A vase with a narrow neck, flaring lip, rounded body, and shallow foot. There is no handle.
Bowl	Word used to designate a plain, open shape without handles.
Chalice	Cup with conical foot, deep wall and horizontal handles at base of wall.
Chous (pl. Choes)	From verb 'to pour'. Broad-bodied jug, with low handle and trefoil mouth. Used in Anthesteria festival and as a measure fixed for participants in drinking bout (3.28 litres). Also small choes were used for children's day, when 3-year-olds received them.
Chytra (pl. Chytrai)	Footless cooking pot, with one or two small handles fixed at rim. Set on stand. Some versions have a lid.
Cup	General term for a two-handled container for drinking. See Kylix, Skyphos.
Dinos (pl. Dinoi)	Means 'drinking cup' but now wrongly used to designate the same shape as 'Lebes' (q.v.).
Epichysis (pl. Epichysides)	Literally 'a pouring on'. Used for a one-handled jug with long, narrow neck and reel-shaped body. Mainly south Italian.
Epinetron (pl. Epinetra) or Onos (pl. Onoi)	Long semi-circular cover for the knee and thigh, over which wool was drawn to remove dirt.
Eschara	Coarse-ware cooker.
Exaleiptron (pl. Exaleiptra)	From word 'to anoint'. Vase, usually lidded, on low or high foot (sometimes tripod-shaped). Broad, flat body. No handles. Deep mouth inside so that the liquid contents can be shaken without spilling. Used for perfumed oil in women's rooms or in grave cult. Other names which have been applied to it are Plemochoe and Kothon (see below).
Feeder	Small footed container with flat top and spout at side, for providing drinks to small children or invalids.
Fish-plate	Plate with low foot, overhanging rim, small depression in centre of floor (for sauce?). When figured, it is usually decorated with fish.

Guttus (pl. Gutti)	From Latin 'gutta' = 'a drop'. Latin name for a narrow-necked dipper. Conventionally applied to an oil pot with low body, ring handle, relief medallion and trumpet-shaped mouth at side. Some have a vertical mouth.
Hydria (pl. Hydriai)	From 'hydor' = 'water'. A water-pot for the fountain, with capacious oval body and two horizontal handles and one vertical handle. Manufactured in bronze and in coarse and fine wares. See also Kalpis.
Kados (pl. Kadoi)	A coarse-ware bucket for the well with two small vertical handles at sides and wide mouth.
Kalathos (pl. Kalathoi)	Means 'basket' for wool, etc. The shape in clay usually refers to a handleless conical vessel, quite small.
Kalpis (pl. Kalpides)	Conventional name for a shape of fine-ware Hydria (see above), with single contour from neck to foot.
Kantharos (pl. Kantharoi)	From the word for 'beetle'. Now used conventionally for a drinking cup with two vertical, usually high swung handles. The shape, most likely of metal originally, is often shown in the hands of Dionysos. There are various different forms.
Kernos (pl. Kernoi)	A cult vase, with large bowl on foot, small bowls attached to the rim.
Kothon (pl. Kothones)	Used of various different shapes. Some equate it (wrongly) with the shape noted above under Exaleiptron, others use it of a deep one-handled drinking cup, sometimes ribbed, carried by soldiers and travellers. It is also applied to the pilgrim flask shape.
Kotyle (pl. Kotylai)	Used as an alternative to Skyphos (see below) to designate a deep cup with two horizontal handles. No offset lip.
Krater (pl. Krateres)	From a word meaning 'mix'. A large, open bowl for mixing wine and water. There are four main types that carry modern distinctive names: (a) Column-krater from the shape of the columnar handles. (Ancient name 'Corinthian'.) (b) Volute-krater from the volutes that curl over the rim. (Ancient

	name 'Laconian'.) The most elaborate type. (c) Calyx-krater from the shape of the body, perhaps invented by Exekias. Handles set low on body. (d) Bell-krater from the shape of the body. Other names derived from krater are 'krateriskos' to designate a small version, and 'kotyle-krater' for an early, seventh-century shape.
Kyathos (pl. Kyathoi)	Used to indicate a deep ladle with cup-shaped container and long handle.
Kylix (pl. Kylikes)	Large wine cup with shallow bowl, two horizontal handles and high stem above foot. Many types: Komast, Band Lip, Siana, A, B, etc.
agynos (pl. Lagynoi)	Wine jug with low, bulging body, flat shoulder, tall neck and long vertical handle.
akaina (pl. Lakainai)	Ancient description equates the name with a Laconian drinking cup, with deep body and two horizontal handles set near the base.
amp	Classical lamps have small flat bodies, a round opening above and a spout with a hole for the wick. Some are provided with handles.
ebes (pl. Lebetes)	A mixing bowl with spherical body which sits on a stand. No handles, no foot. Often incorrectly called a 'dinos' (see above).
ebes Gamikos (pl. ebetes Gamikoi)	A lebes for weddings. Shape as lebes but with two high vertical handles at shoulder, a lid, a marked neck and an attached stand or foot. Used for the bridal bath.
ekane (pl. Lekanai)	A large household-ware basin or bowl, with two horizontal handles. Used in the preparation of food and for many other purposes.
ekanis (pl. Lekanides)	Shallow lidded bowl with ring foot and two horizontal handles, for trinkets. Often given as a wedding gift.
ekythos (pl. Lekythoi)	A general word used to denote an oil bottle. Now conventionally used for tall and squat shape with a foot, a single vertical handle, narrow neck and small mouth. Sometimes the basic form is fashioned into fancy shapes such as an acorn or an almond, or into a

	human figure; some carry appliqué designs.
Lopas (pl. Lopades)	A shallow lidded cooking-pot, rather like a flattened version of the lidded Chytra (see above).
Louterion (pl. Louteria)	From a word meaning 'wash'. Used to denote a bowl with two handles and a spout.
Loutrophoros (pl. Loutrophoroi)	From 'carrying to the bath' for ritual cleansing. A tall version of the neck-amphora with two very long vertical handles. A slightly different version imitates the hydria with two horizontal and one vertical handle ('loutrophoros-hydria'). Scenes relate to weddings and funerals.
Lydion (pl. Lydia)	Named from the area of Lydia in Asia Minor. A fat, handleless perfume pot with outturned flat lip. For the Lydian *bakkaris* perfume.
Mastos (pl. Mastoi)	From the word 'mastos' = 'breast'. A shape of cup resembling a woman's breast. Usuall furnished with one vertical and one horizontal handle, sometimes provided with a foot instead of a nipple.
Mortar	A grinding bowl of household or heavy-dut ware. Sometimes made of stone.
Mug	Used to designate a deep, one-handled drinking cup. See Kothon.
Nestoris (pl. Nestorides)	A wide-mouthed jar with two horizontal high-swung handles from shoulder to lip. South Italian, derived from a native, non-Greek shape.
Oinochoe (pl. Oinochoai)	Meaning 'wine-pourer'. The wine jug was fashioned in many varieties (conical, concave, convex) but was usually furnished with a single vertical handle. The mouth could be round, trefoil or beak-shaped.
Olpe (pl. Olpai)	A Greek word for 'jug', conventionally usec of a slender shape of jug with no separate neck and usually a low handle.
One-handler	A modern name to denote a shallow bowl with one horizontal handle attached just below a broad rim.

Onos (pl. Onoi)	See Epinetron.
Patera (pl. Paterai)	A Latin word for 'dish', sometimes used to designate a dish like the Phiale (see below).
Pelike (pl. Pelikai)	A conventional name for a type of amphora that has a wide mouth and the maximum width low down on the body, producing a pear-shaped outline.
Perirrhanterion (pl. Perirrhanteria)	From 'sprinkling around'. A type of font: a shallow bowl on a high stem. Mostly of stone, some of clay.
Phiale (pl. Phialai)	The shape, derived from eastern prototypes, is often found in metal. It is a flat, handleless libation bowl, sometimes with offset rim. In the centre of the floor is a raised navel (omphalos) which enables the finger to be inserted beneath when tipping the bowl. Clay phialai could be used at symposia.
Phormiskos (pl. Phormiskoi)	From a Greek word for 'basket'. A bag- or gourd-shaped flask with narrow neck which is sometimes pierced. Used as a sprinkler in ritual.
Pinax (pl. Pinakes)	A Greek word for 'Plate'. Usually now applied to a flat rectangular slab that was decorated and hung on tombs or in sanctuaries.
Pithos (pl. Pithoi)	Large, heavy-duty storage jars (Ali Baba jars) for grain, etc.; used also for interments. Sometimes decorated with relief designs. Smaller versions go by the name of Pitharion (pl. Pitharia).
Plastic vases	These are vases which have relief figures applied to the wall or are themselves in the shape of a figure: head, face, acorn, mussel shell, lobster claw. See also Rhyton.
Plate	Not a common shape in clay, more likely to have been made of wood. Figured plates seem to have been made for religious dedication; black are more common.
Plemochoe (pl. Plemochoai)	From 'full-pouring'. See Exaleiptron and Kothon.
Psykter (pl. Psykteres)	From a word for 'cooling'. Used now to denote an Attic shape with broad, hollow stem, bulging, mushroom-shaped body, and

	broad mouth. Sometimes furnished with lid and pierced tubes for cord. The psykter was filled with snow or cold water and set to float in a krater full of wine.
Pyxis (pl. Pyxides)	A round lidded box, of various shapes and sizes, for cosmetics, powder or jewellery. Some were put in tombs. The term 'skyphoid-pyxis' is used to designate a shap that became a Sicilian speciality with ovoid body and lid, and two horizontal handles.
Rhyton (pl. Rhyta)	From a word for 'flow'. A drinking cup originally made of horn, hence the shape. The idea was borrowed from Persia. Used t denote a one-handled cup that has the bowl fashioned into the shape of an animal's hea (sheep, donkey, etc.) or occasionally a more complex creation (pygmy and crane, negro and crocodile, mounted Amazon, camel an driver).
Salt Cellar	A conventional name to designate a small open bowl.
Situla (pl. Situlae)	From the Latin word meaning 'bucket'. A deep bowl for wine, mainly south Italian. The swung handle(s) suggest a derivation from metal.
Skyphos (pl. Skyphoi)	A deep cup with two horizontal handles at the rim (sometimes one horizontal and one vertical). See also Kotyle. Hybrid names such as 'cup-skyphoi' indicate hybrid forms
Stamnos (pl. Stamnoi)	Conventionally (and wrongly) used to designate a storing and mixing bowl with two small horizontal handles attached to a compact, bulbous body, a short neck and a lid.
Stemless (Cup)	A modern name to indicate a shape like a Kylix (see above) but with a ring foot, not a stem.
Stemmed Dish	Handleless bowl on stem. Most small, som large.
Stemmed Plate	Shallow plate on stem, often with overhanging rim and central dip like the Fish Plate (see above).

Strainer — Perforated bowl for straining wine or in larger form for use in cooking.

Thymiaterion (pl. Thymiateria) — from a word meaning 'fume'. A censer or thurible for the house, tomb or sanctuary. A small bowl, sometimes on a tall stem. The lid is often perforated to let out the scent.

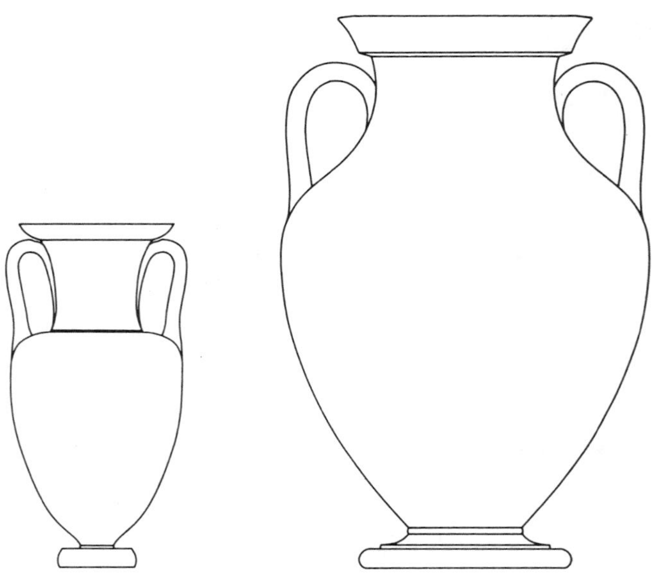

IV.10 Drawn outlines of pots
(*a*) amphorae (neck- and belly-)

(*b*) alabastra, aryballoi and askos

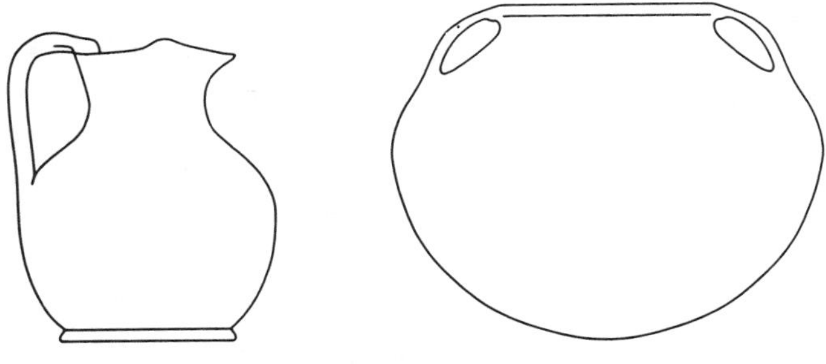

(*c*) chous and chytra

(*d*) hydriai (shoulder and kalpis)

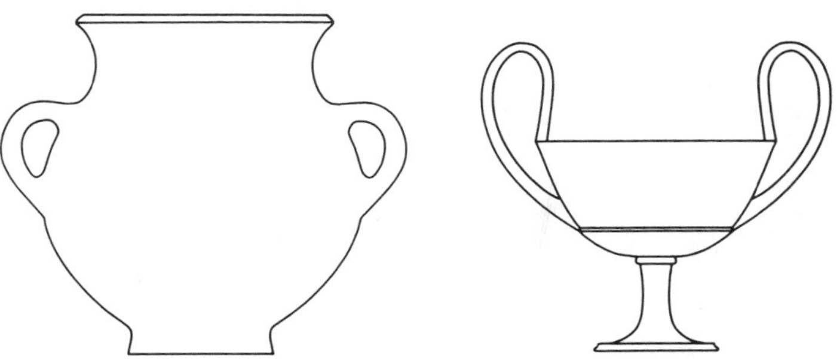

(*e*) kados and kantharos

(*f*) kraters (column and volute)

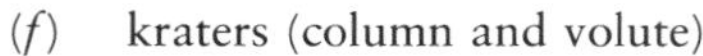

(*g*) kraters (calyx and bell)

(*h*) kylikes (lip and type B)

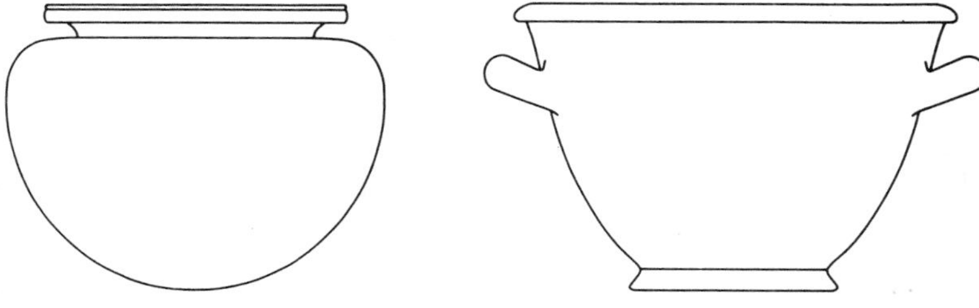

(*i*) lebes and lekane

(*j*) lekythoi (early, tall and squat)

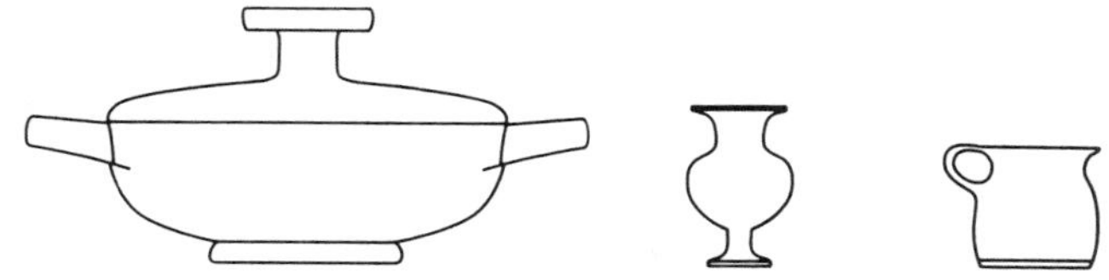

(*k*) lekanis, lydion and mug

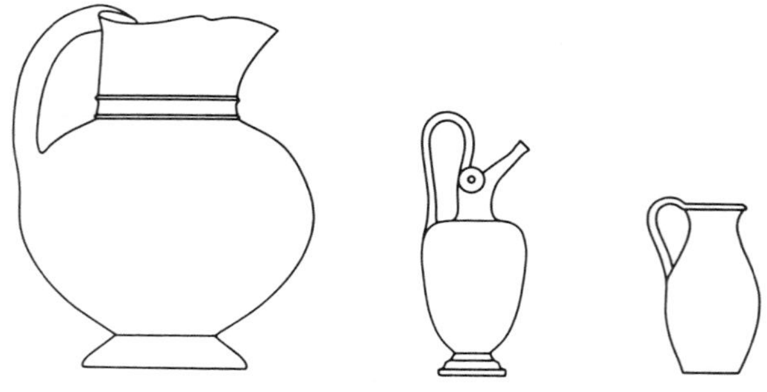

(*l*) oinochoai (trefoil and beaked) and olpe

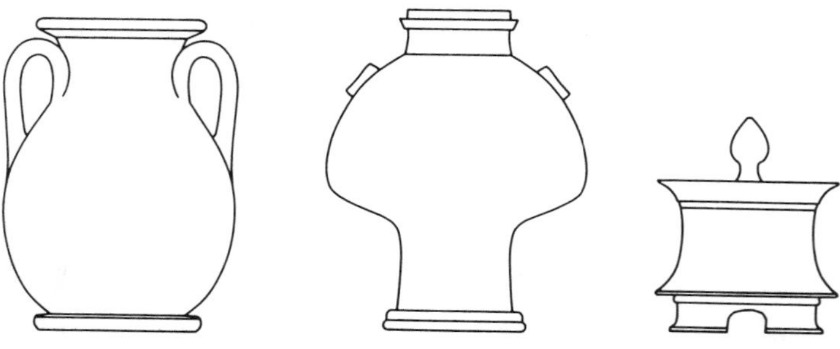

(*m*) pelike, psykter and pyxis

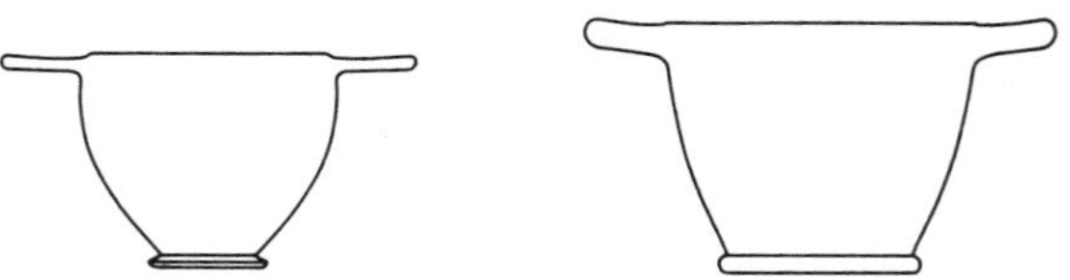

(*n*) skyphos (Corinthian and Attic types)

(*o*) stamnos, stemless and stemmed dish

V
DECORATION

Greek painted vases, looked at with detachment, are a very curious phenomenon. (Robertson 1951, 151)

The study of Greek vases has concentrated on, indeed has been felt to be synonymous with, painted pottery with elaborate figured scenes. It is this painting that has attracted the interest of professionals and laymen alike, and the fascination of it cannot be denied. However, it needs to be seen in perspective. The vast majority of Greek pottery was plain or only slightly daubed, and the figured fine wares represent only a small percentage of the total output. Decoration was not indispensable for the function of a vase, though it was obviously felt to be an attractive addition to it. It would be a mistake to imagine the Greeks using figure-decorated pottery in any and every task in their lives; in fact, such pottery was an urban phenomenon, rural areas made do with plainer products.

There were basically two ways in which the shape of a vase was enhanced with decoration – (a) by raising, puncturing, incising or stamping the surface and (b) by adding paint to the surface. These techniques were used both separately and together. Occasionally three-dimensional additions were applied (florals, heads, figures) or the vase was shaped in the form of a head or figure, human or animal (cf. Fig. IV.9).

The kitchen wares were usually left, as one would expect, undecorated, as they were for domestic chores only.[1] Similarly, the transport amphorae rarely carried decoration, either incised or painted, except for the control stamps. Some unpainted heavy-duty shapes (such as pithoi that were made in the Cyclades, Rhodes, Boeotia and Laconia) were decorated with various patterns that were produced by incision (combing), stamps (geometric, floral or figured designs) and by raised reliefs which carried simple designs or complex arrangements of mythological stories and mythical beasts, e.g. Fig. IV.5. Some freehand shapes, similarly unpainted, carried incised and impressed patterns.[2]

Monochrome

Application of a coat of paint to a surface could be functional: applied internally to delay seepage of the contents, applied externally to provide a

smooth surface for the touch. The functional can, however, soon become decorative, and bands and stripes may be placed in such a way that they emphasise and articulate a shape and enhance an otherwise plain surface. Monochrome painting, without any help from other colours or from incision, was widespread in time and space, and for many potters this was the only way in which they chose to enhance their pots: a single flourish might distinguish hand or shop. The colour was mainly brown or black, depending on the composition of the gloss applied and on the firing. The outstanding examples of this use of one colour are to be found in the Geometric period (ca. 900–700 B.C.): it is the designs on the pottery that have given this historical period its name (e.g. Fig. III.1). During this time the plainer monochrome patterning that had preceded it (Protogeometric: ca. 1050–900 B.C.) was elaborated and made more various.[3] The compass-drawn circles and semicircles of Protogeometric were extended by more complex designs of tongues, triangles, cross-hatching, meander and other Geometric shapes; some of these were most likely derived from basketry and textiles. Eventually fauna appeared: animals (goats, deer, horses, birds) and by the mid eighth century figures and narrative scenes, mainly funerary (laying out of the dead, laments, processions), suitable for the funerary purposes for which many of the vases were made.

The figures, conceptually treated, were mainly in silhouette, with a little outline that helped to isolate and highlight inner details, presented in a diagnostic view that harmonised with the pattern set all around. The designs, both patterns and figures, were well fitted to the shape on which they were placed, and in the more careful pieces there is an admirable discipline and economy of line. Athenian potters and painters led the way, and their work was copied, adapted and handed on by craftsmen in Corinth, Euboea, Argos, Boeotia (Fig. IV.3), the Cyclades, Asia Minor and the Greek West. The regional styles of all these areas have been distinguished, and it is in the ambitious compositions of the eighth century that the individuality of painters becomes particularly marked.

Monochrome decoration did not die with the end of Geometric. If a 'progressive' history of vase-painting were being traced, then it would be usual to move directly from monochrome to chart the rise of the black-figure technique (see below), etc., as though the break was complete. However, monochrome painting continued and is to be found in many areas, even in those where some craftsmen had begun to add other colours and make surface incisions to enhance the drawing. It takes a less important rôle in many centres, but many types of simple pottery still carried quasi-functional bands, small floral designs and indeed sometimes figured scenes in monochrome, for which perhaps lack of initiative and contact is to be stressed as much as lack of ability. Simple decoration was far commoner than the more elaborate.

Black-figure

Towards the end of the Geometric period (late eighth century), when the patient application of the patterns was becoming less careful, monochrome painting began to be enhanced in two main ways: by the addition of colour and by incision. Colour was sometimes used without incision: for instance, lines and areas of colour (usually red/purple, yellow/white) were added to island and East Greek designs, where in mainland wares incision would now generally be expected as well. However, colour is often found together with incision, and from the late eighth century onwards this combination of black/brown gloss silhouette, of incision made through the paint for inner structure, and of added colours (white, yellow, purple) is what characterises the 'progressive' development of vase-painting and which affects other less advanced centres to a large or small extent (casual incision, etc.). Thus the flat monochrome figures and patterns began to be enlivened, and this seems to have started tentatively around 700 B.C. on small vases such as containers for perfumed oil in Corinth, where there were imports of eastern metal work and ivory in which the technique of incising played a large part. Corinth, being an important centre, imported goods from the Near East (via Syria), and it was the influence of these, and maybe of immigrant craftsmen, on Corinthian work that drew these techniques to the fore. It was certainly not the importation of foreign pottery that brought this about, as there is little sign that such decoration was characteristic of Near Eastern pottery, nor was that pottery of any interest to the Corinthians.[4] Incision was used from now on to mark inner junctures and outlines whether of bodies, legs, heads or of floral patterns. The colours came to be used to heighten details, such as purple for cloaks, nipples, etc., white for women's skin.

In the seventh century, the subject matter of vase-painting was enlarged in some centres by the increasing prominence given to mythological scenes (such as Herakles, Perseus, Odysseus, etc.), and also by the introduction of animals and monsters not seen previously in Geometric painting (lions, sphinxes, chimaera) and of genre scenes such as hare hunts. Animal friezes became a very popular way of covering the pot surface and were relatively more frequent than figured scenes. Some of these new images were borrowed as a result of the more extensive connections with the Near East, as also were the technique and the new floral elements in chains or single blossoms (palmette bushes, the tree of life, lotus, etc.). After centuries of controlled lines, whether straight or circular, the seventh century saw more natural, if unbotanical, curves; Geometric patterning had given way to controlled floral designs.

The black-figure technique continued at Corinth into the sixth century (Fig. V.11) and was adopted and adapted by other centres: Laconia,

Boeotia and so forth.[5] Some borrowed directly from Corinthian ideas, others took their inspiration from the one centre that improved on the Corinthian technique: Athens. The gloss the Athenian workshops produced became shinier, it adhered better to the clay, and the contrast between the orange and the black was more definite than the Corinthian pale yellow clay and the creamy brown gloss. Gradually, the quality of Athenian work improved until in the sixth century Corinth was lagging behind and even tried to ape the orange clay colour of Attic pottery by adding an orange/red slip of its own. More importantly, Athens further enlarged the repertoire of subjects, with more emphasis on humans; the floral designs began to take a subsidiary rôle.[6]

Athens' adoption of the black-figure technique was not sudden. For a while in the seventh century the outline technique was popular there and elsewhere with a heavy use of white and less dependence on incision, but eventually it gave way to the clearer silhouette figures enlivened by colour and incision. Indeed, outline never had more than a subsidiary role to play in the history of vase-painting; it was more important in panel-painting. During the sixth century Athenian black-figure was for the most part sharp and precise (e.g. Fig. V.1). It continued in the fifth century but was less important and less competent then; indeed it ceased to attract good painters. It was retained for the special commission of the Panathenaic prize amphorae (Fig. III.7) which continued into Roman times (see pp. 53–4), and is also found for a generation or so on the small, cheap funerary lekythoi. Outside Attica, it is found in Boeotia in the late fifth and fourth centuries when it is used on the idiosyncratic Cabeiric vases at the sanctuary near Thebes.[7]

Red-figure

A reverse technique that left the figures and patterns in the background colour of the clay (sometimes improved with a dilute wash and polishing), and filled in the surrounding areas with black, is now known as red-figure.[8] Whereas black-figure had set silhouette figures in an open space against the light, with red-figure the effect was like a spotlight isolating figures against a black background (e.g. Figs. II.5; III.6; IV.8; V.9–10, 12; VI.4). It was invented in Athens, perhaps ca. 530 B.C., and a number of reasons have been given for this reversal of the old scheme. Some scholars see the change already heralded in black-figure in the work of the Amasis Painter, others look elsewhere beyond vase-painting. Painted bas-relief sculpture in which the background colour is usually blue has been thought by some to have had a strong influence, and as usual, panel-painting has also been considered to have been an influence. More recently, a controversial theory has suggested that both black- and red-figure owe their appearance to their

V.1 Attic black-figure amphora, ca. 540 B.C. Archer grazing horse.

mitation of the silver and gold of metal vases, and that red-figure mirrors he changeover of metals.[9] It is impossible to name the inventor(s) of the new technique with any certainty. Possible contenders are thought to be the Andokides Painter, Psiax and Nikosthenes.[10] There are vases on which both techniques are used ('bilinguals'), but close study of them shows that hey are not to be considered intermediate stepping stones from the one echnique to the other. Some completely red-figure vases antedate them, and the 'bilinguals' may have been display pieces, for customers who had come to the shops to place an order. The reversed figures, with their inner narkings now indicated in gloss paint, make a strong and bold effect

against the black background, their musculature is shown to advantage with the flexible brush, and their clothing has gained substance and depth. Variations in the slip enabled gradations of tone to appear: with a thin slip there are light brown or golden lines, with a thicker slip a relief line was created with a special pen (see p. 20).

Development in drawing moves from what was initially a reversed black-figure picture through an experimental period when the potentialities of the new technique gradually began to be realised (the so-called Pioneers), to the Late Archaic generation of painters (ca. 500–480 B.C.), who used the technique to its fullest and best, not only in composing the scenes to fit the space available, but also in maintaining the nature of vase decoration (e.g. Figs. V.9–10, 12). Strong and simple forms unite with the floral patterns to fit the available area. Later this balance was lost and under the influence of panel-painting[11] with its freedom of space and illusion of reality, the vase painters, hampered by their blank, black wall, tried ideas that did not fit their ceramic medium, e.g. lack of groundline, foreshortening, etc., until by the end of the fifth century we are faced with sketchy figures with broken lines, shading and perspective, three-quarter views and overlapping elements. In earlier red-figure the added colours are used sparingly; later, clay relief lines enhanced with gilding became a feature, and in the fourth century the so-called 'Kerch' vases (named from the find-spot of many in south Russia) have a wide variety of colours: white, yellow, gold, blue, green.[12]

Other centres borrowed the red-figure technique that the Athenians had pioneered. In Greece itself the borrowing was only slight, and the products were mainly popular on a local basis; Boeotia (mid fifth century onwards) and Corinth (425–350 B.C.) were poor imitators.[13] The most important influence was exerted amongst the Greeks of Sicily and south Italy, and we know that Attic vase-painters emigrated there, to such places as Thurii, Metapontum and Tarentum, to set up shops in the second half of the fifth century.[14] Attic ideas were transferred and developed further away, and the results are sometimes ornate in the extreme (Fig. V.6). Also, there was red-figure produced in the fifth and fourth centuries in Etruria and Latium, where other modifications were made.[15] There were few centres that were producing red-figure after 300 B.C.

White-figure and white-ground

We have referred to white as an added colour for black-figure (women's skin, etc.) and for red-figure, though used to a lesser extent there, and it is also found as a minor element in decoration in other periods and places, sometimes directly on the clay, more usually added on the top of the black paint. It was also used in other ways: for whole figures and as a background slip, or priming coat, to receive the designs.

The less important and more restricted technique is that of 'white-figure' painted on a black background (conventionally known as 'Six technique' from the scholar, Jan Six, who studied it).[16] Here the figures, male and female, skin and clothes, were applied in white over black, and then the inner details were either incised through the white to reveal the black beneath or added in red; some outlines were also incised. It seems to have been one of the experimental techniques that were tried in Athens at the same time as the introduction of red-figure, and the names usually connected with its invention or at least its initial use are Nikosthenes and Psiax. It was never more than a side-line, and, though other black-figure painters continued the tradition, the quality deteriorated during the fifth century, and Athenian painters abandoned the technique before the mid-century. It was confined to a few special shapes such as the phiale and the lekythos. More important and widespread was the technique of covering the clay colour with a (yellowish) white slip. The practice became quite common from the middle of the eighth century and was used to cover rather poor quality, coarse and dark clays, giving a clearer surface for decoration. In the seventh and sixth centuries it is to be seen on a number of fabrics such as Laconian and East Greek, and particularly on vases made on the island of Chios where groups of dedicatory vases (chalices, kantharoi) also carry customers' inscriptions painted on the surface.[17]

In the early years Athenian painters adopted the technique less than others, perhaps they had less call to do so, but after the middle of the sixth century 'white-ground' gains in popularity there.[18] Painters painted black silhouette figures on a white ground, as a subspecies of black-figure. This then gave way to black outline figures on white. During the fifth century experiments and refinements were made by the red-figure painters, or perhaps it is more likely the potters who had the larger say. The second quarter of the fifth century saw the black relief lines diluted into lines of golden brown, with other colours added (two shades of red and a second 'whiter' white for the female figures), then in the third quarter, areas of matt colours (red, yellow, brown) were popular. Finally in the late fifth century, pale matt contour lines were applied over the white with much extra colour: greens, blues, mauves, together with a gold effect and shading, producing a much more polychrome appearance with a softening of the lines and less precise contours. The technique died out in the early fourth century. As the white slip did not adhere closely to the clay during the firing, vases decorated in this way were not suitable for everyday usage, and we find the technique confined to special purpose shapes: there were 'white-ground' cups in the second quarter of the fifth century which are thought to have been special orders (for dedications or gifts), but apart from a few other shapes (oinochoai, kraters) the main output from the mid fifth century was in funerary lekythoi which were consigned directly to the tomb (Fig. V.2). The influence of panel-painting has been seen to lie behind

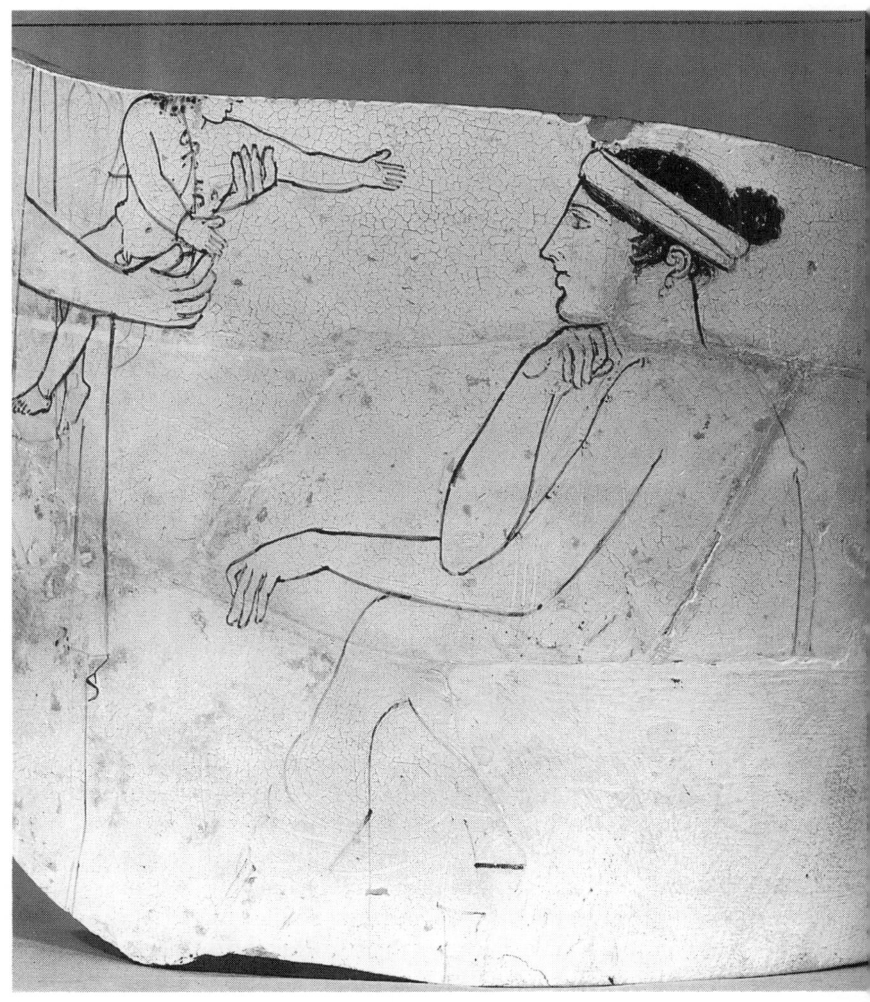

V.2 Attic white-ground lekythos, ca. 440 B.C. Mother and child.

this technique, though the funerary iconography was a deliberat restriction of subject.

Later some other centres of vase production made use of a (yellowish white slip for covering the surface. Two types from the Hellenistic perio are the so-called 'Hadra' hydriai (see pp. 54–7), mainly made and foun in Egypt, and the lagynoi, some of which were most likely made i Pergamum. Both carry decoration in brown or black applied on top of th white.[19]

Polychrome

In some areas and periods vase-painters used an unusually wide variety of colours on their pottery, sometimes directly on the clay, sometimes on the black gloss or on the white slip (see above pp. 98–100), sometimes on the already fired clay. Such an approach, however, is never common and fairly isolated, and the motives for doing so are thought by some to derive from influences outside the workshops of the vase-painters, such as panel-painting. This connection can on occasion be seen in the choice of colours: brown with black outline for males, white with red outline for females – these are the conventions known to apply to panel-painting, etc.[20]

There are a number of instances of polychromy on vases in the seventh century. From early seventh-century Knossos on Crete a group of cremation pithoi have matt red and indigo on a white slip, and some have received a second coat over the ordinary painting, after firing. Later in the century there are the examples from Corinth, of which the Chigi olpe in the Macmillan Group (680–650 B.C.) is the best known, and later still some Protoattic (seventh-century Athenian) with red, yellow, brown and blue. Some other centres in the archaic period show an interest in varied colouring, such as Argos, Chios, Melos, Thasos; and in the sixth century there are the Caeretan hydriai from Etruria. Some seventh- and sixth-century polychrome was also applied over the black, found in Corinth and the areas influenced from there, in Chios and on the so-called 'Vroulian' cups from the island of Rhodes.[21]

In the fifth century a group of small vases made in Athens, the St Valentin group, was decorated with a more varied palette than usual. There is also a very strange group of late fifth-century coarse-ware jugs from the Athenian Agora that carry scenes of comic caricature applied directly to the unglazed surface of the pots in red outline, filled with such colours as pink, white, blue and green; the reason for this decoration and for its use on coarse pottery has never been satisfactorily explained. We have already seen that the white-ground lekythoi can display a wide variety of colours. Also Attic, but with adaptations produced elsewhere, is a series of vases, such as lekythoi and oinochoai, that carry relief scenes applied to their walls enhanced by polychromy; the major period of production is the fourth century.[22] Also in the fourth century the south Italian and Sicilian red-figure painters show a propensity for lavish colours (red, yellow, white) that match their more elaborately ornate compositions (Figs. V.3 & 6).[23]

In the Hellenistic period there is polychromy on some 'Hadra' vases, mostly made and found in Alexandria, and here the colours have been added on a white ground after firing. The practice of adding colours after firing is also to be seen in Sicily and south Italy. Some of the most outstanding are those from Canosa in Apulia and from Centuripe in Sicily. The colours are varied: blue, pink, white, red, yellow, black with some

V.3 Sicilian polychrome squat lekythos, ca. 350–325 B.C. Piping satyr.

gilding. Such vases were never made for use in everyday life and must have had funerary or religious significance. With the end of red-figure decoration it is not surprising that potters and painters turned to white-over-black (see pp. 104–6) and to colours added after firing, to enliven the appearance of their products.[24]

Coral red

Brief mention may be made here of a rare and difficult technique that wa developed during the century from 550–450 B.C. as a background to Atti

lack-figure and as a subsidiary element in red-figure. The process used imed to produce two colours of background gloss: the standard black nd, beside and around it and applied after it, a brilliant coral red. The red loss, perhaps of a different composition from the gloss that fired black, lid not adhere well and has tended to flake. The red was used to enhance ome plain black shapes: cups, aryballoi, pyxides; or it served in subsidiary reas on figured shapes: a zone round the tondo inside cups, on the outside f cups below the figures or on the lip; occasionally it was carefully applied ound the edges of black-figure designs, as on the famous cup by Exekias vith Dionysos sailing on a coral-red sea. The technique may indeed have een invented by Exekias, at least it is first found on the cup mentioned. As vith white-ground, the planning is more likely to have been the potter's han the painter's. Such a difficult process that would need special firing onditions cannot have been practised in more than a few workshops. Most shapes so treated are small, though one volute-krater combines a ed-figured rim with a coral-red neck and body. The ingenious and delicate ieces that issued from the workshop of the potter Sotades in the middle of he fifth century, are the most startling in that some combine black, coral ed and white; they are also the last.[25]

Black gloss

t is usual to equate Greek fine wares with the figured vases that are ertainly the most distinctive products of the Greek workshops. But these ame workshops also produced less expensive wares, often in the same hapes but with no figured work on the surface, merely a covering of black. uch plain decoration can be found before the sixth century but it was in he sixth century that black-gloss pottery emerged as a distinctive line.[26]

A main early producer of black-gloss pottery was Athens. Other centres vere issuing black vases (with a little decoration) as early, but in numbers and variety of output, in quality of potting and firing, in the added decoration and in distribution, no other centre approached Athens. This dominance lasted until ca. 400 B.C. when the other, mainly south Italian, workshops which had copied and adapted Attic red-figure ware began to turn out black-gloss pots as well, once again mainly using Attic pieces as prototypes. Although black continues to be made in the Greek areas of the eastern Mediterranean until about 100 B.C., it is eventually superseded by red wares such as 'Pergamene'. In the Western Greek areas the production of black is strong and continues for a generation or so longer, and is then replaced by the red wares such as Arretine.

Attic craftsmen who painted the black pottery were usually careful with the actual painting and reserving of such areas as the handle-panels and undersides, quite often creating on the latter a variety of circles, wide and

narrow, executed with great precision and sometimes associated with moulded undersides. The fact that the gloss was added as the vase turned on the wheel gave it an even spread. Less good work was dipped and consequently gives an altogether more lackadaisical impression. The shapes that were painted black were often closely similar to those decorated in the black- and red-figure techniques, and this all-black work was undoubtedly mainly produced in the same workshops. The tendency was to avoid the more delicate and sophisticated shapes and to concentrate on the sturdier and simpler forms. As time went on, there was a change in the appearance of the gloss. After control over the firing process had enabled a deep, rich black to be produced, Attic potters, in the late sixth and for most of the fifth century, issued shapes that were covered with a brilliant blue-black gloss. From the second half of the fifth century onwards the black became more metallic in appearance, more silvery in effect. Certainly, the effect of metalwork was making itself more felt, and this can be seen also in the thinness of the walls, as well as in the ribbing, incising and stamping that became features of the black ware at this time (see below, pp. 106–7).

The black pottery produced in other centres is for the most part distinguishable from Attic in clay colour, gloss and shapes. Sometimes Attic shapes were borrowed and adapted more or less closely, otherwise local ideas asserted themselves. On the Greek mainland there were centres of black in Corinth, Boeotia, the West Peloponnese, Laconia – in fact the distribution of such workshops is likely to have been very widespread, and the islands and coastal areas of Asia Minor produced their own variations. Apulia, Campania and Etruria (both Greek residents and natives) were some of the Italian centres of production.

Many shapes were simply covered with a black gloss which was sometimes enlivened by the addition of a purple line or two and by those areas that were left in the colour of the clay. Some however had decoration to enhance the effect of the black: colour added on top of the black ((a) below), designs incised or stamped into the still damp clay before the application of the gloss (b), relief either added separately to the vase before the painting (c) or created in a vase mould (d).

(a) We have met the use of colour painted on the top of the black in connection with 'white figure' and polychrome (see pp. 98–9, 101–2). The use of white to enhance the plain black vases, sometimes with thin trails of added clay topped with gilding, is mainly found from the fourth century onwards and may be said to be the late companion and successor to red-figure. The ware goes under the name of West Slope from the examples found in the slopes of the Acropolis at Athens. The decoration consists of yellow and white flora (wreaths, festoons, myrtle, ivy, etc.) and objects (ribbons, musical instruments), and on occasion there are inscriptions. The period of production seems to stretch from the third century onwards; the ware wa

nade in Athens and in other centres. More important is the Gnathia echnique (named from the site in Apulia where examples have been ound), that was a popular line in south Italian workshops. It was issued by number of centres (mainly in Apulia, but also in Campania, Latium, truria and Sicily) and had a vogue for about a century (ca. 360–250 .C.). Initially the colours applied were orange, brown, pink and green, hen the main emphasis narrowed to white, yellow and red. The designs night consist of single figures or heads (e.g. Eros or Victory) or maybe igured scenes, but more often the choice was limited to objects and florals n complex patterns. The shapes decorated in the Gnathia technique were nainly small, and ribbing was occasionally a feature. Some workshops

.4 Italian black plate with stamping and added colour ('Teano'), ca. 350–300 .C.

combined the added colour(s) with incised motifs, stamping and rouletting (Fig. V.4).[27]

(b) Besides the paint applied over the black, incision, stamping and rouletting were important methods of decoration. These were applied before the gloss was added and are to be distinguished from the incision that accompanies the black- and red-figure painting.

The technique of incision on the black, no doubt borrowed from metal designs, is first found on Attic vases of the middle of the fifth century B.C. The early designs covered the interior of stemless cups and consist of rosettes, radiating lines and arcs – a laborious procedure that produces some excellent results when carefully carried through. The technique seems to have been initiated in workshops that produced red-figure cups, as some of the earliest examples share the decoration with red-figure scenes on the outside.

The use of incised patterns by themselves is short-lived, as it was obviously a time-consuming and expensive process. Results could be achieved more quickly by the use of stamps, and the history of incising and stamping is one of decline for the former and rise for the latter. Once again it is found first on shapes alongside red-figure scenes, towards the end of

V.5 Attic black stemless cup with stamping, ca. 450–440 B.C.

he fifth century, and there is evidence that it was also used with white-ground. The stamps or poinçons, which could presumably have been made of clay, metal, bone or such, must have been small with a single design at he end: ivy, palmette (e.g. Fig. V.5), lotus, rosette, circle, ovule, but occasionally there were larger examples that carried figures or parts of figures (heads, limbs, wings, columns) and may indicate a wider and more elaborate usage than the main body of our present evidence suggests.[28]

The range of shapes that carry stamped decoration widens: as well as open shapes which carry the designs on the interior wall (e.g. stemless cups e.g. Fig. V.5), phialai, bolsals), stamped designs are also found on the outside of closed shapes (e.g. lekythoi, amphoriskoi, mugs). The more usual exterior decoration was ribbing, another influence from metal. This could run horizontally (on phialai, mugs, etc.) but the more popular version is the vertical which is either scored or moulded, wide or narrow, sometimes mixed with and edged by stamping. The shapes so treated are small mugs, oinochoai and various shapes of cups and kantharoi, and the massive ourth-century calyx-kraters, amphorae and hydriai.

The incising and stamping techniques are found in other centres, not only in Greece but also, more importantly, in the West, in different areas of taly. The individual stamping continues, though not always, as in Attic, ollowing the circular shape of the cup floor. It is sometimes found in conjunction with overpainting (see pp. 105–6 and Fig. V.4) and can become very elaborate. It is in the Western factories that we find numerous nstances of human figures (e.g. Herakles), animals (e.g. a dolphin) and objects (e.g. a club) that have been pressed in the wet clay, perhaps with stamps but maybe using signet rings or cut gemstones. A special category consists of those designs which were impressed with coins, either directly or rom an intermediate mould, the best known of which are those late fourth-century cups, some silvered, that carry the head of Arethusa from a ate fifth-century Syracusan decadrachm signed by Euainetos.[29]

(c) A further method of adding decoration to a pot was by the application of clay fashioned into figured or floral shapes. A vase could usually function without these appliqué designs: they were ornamental additions, some with symbolic meaning. The appliqués were made eparately and then attached to the vase with wet clay. Such attachments were popular in all types of pottery and in many different areas, e.g. snakes were set along the rims and handles of seventh-century Attic funerary vases, heads were fixed to top and bottom of handles, leaves served as humb rests, animal paws and knuckle-bones as feet. Early production was by hand (like fashioning terracotta figurines, e.g. the horse handles on Geometric pyxides and the mourning women on amphora rims); later the plaques were made in moulds which allowed for easy repetition. When applied to black gloss pottery, the reliefs might themselves be highly coloured or be varnished with the same gloss as the background. Mention

V.6 Apulian red-figure volute krater, ca. 380–370 B.C. Funerary scene.

has already been made of the Attic oinochoai and lekythoi that have polychrome appliqué figures (see p. 101), some others have figures covered with a white slip. In Hellenistic Cretan pottery there was a vogue for attached plaques (sometimes with added colour), and the so-called 'Plakettenvasen', which carry applied medallions with scenes from myth or religion that are covered with black gloss, may have been made there or in Alexandria. Appliqué designs are found fitted to horizontal tops of small askoi, made in Athens and South Italy, where a face or figured scene may be set. Mention might also be made of the placing of round plaques in the volutes of south Italian (Apulian) volute-kraters – mascaroon handles (Fig. V.6).[30]

(d) Mould-made vases were not uncommon, examples of them being found in many periods of Greek vase production and decorated in various techniques. Perfume pots from the seventh century onwards were shaped as

V.7 Attic 'Megarian' bowl, ca. 200 B.C.

heads, legs, birds (Fig. IV.9), etc., and drinking cups and jugs took on the appearance of human heads, sphinxes, etc. The rhyta which had the lower half of their container in the shape of an animal head were quite a popular line. All these are usually enhanced with painted details to express the elements of the shape and/or have red-figured painting added. The head vases were treated in the same way, with lifelike faces topped by a vase-neck that carries figured decoration.[31]

The use of the mould for shaping vases increased in popularity in the Hellenistic period, and the moulds were usually elaborated with decorative designs. Some of the most ornate are the flat, open phialai that were based on metal originals; their whole shape and decoration were transferred from the silver prototype and the surface of the clay covered with a gloss that fired a silvery black in imitation of the metal effect. More popular were the so-called 'Megarian' bowls which were made in many different centres from the late third century onwards. They too derived their inspiration from metal originals which in the early years of production most likely provided the actual prototypes, as with the phialai. The shape was made in a hemispherical mould with the plain rim attached later. The whole was covered with gloss. The wall of the mould was shaped into different designs: ribs, floral patterns, individual figures (Herakles, Pan, Erotes, goats, birds, e.g. Fig. V.7), myth and genre scenes.[32]

The 'Megarian' bowls were fired to produce a gloss that was black, with a metallic sheen imitating the metal originals on which they were based. Sometimes the firing accidentally produced a red, brown or mottled effect, and this is to be observed on other Hellenistic pottery shapes. Eventually with influences from traditions outside the Greek orbit, red became the colour consciously aimed at, and the way forward to the red-gloss pottery of the Roman world was open.

Having surveyed some of the different ways in which Greek pottery was decorated, let us now turn to some specific topics that have been uppermost in the study of the Greek vase-painting. These topics have usually been chosen for investigation because of the quality of the work, its bulk, its intrinsic interest, and the light it throws on various aspects of Greek life and imagination.

Inscriptions

We spoke of lettering in the chapter on shapes, when concerned with the word 'epoiesen', whether indicating the potter or the owner of a shop (pp. 65–6). We shall now speak of painters' names and of inscriptions in general.[33]

The work 'epoiesen' = 'made' may have initially covered both th

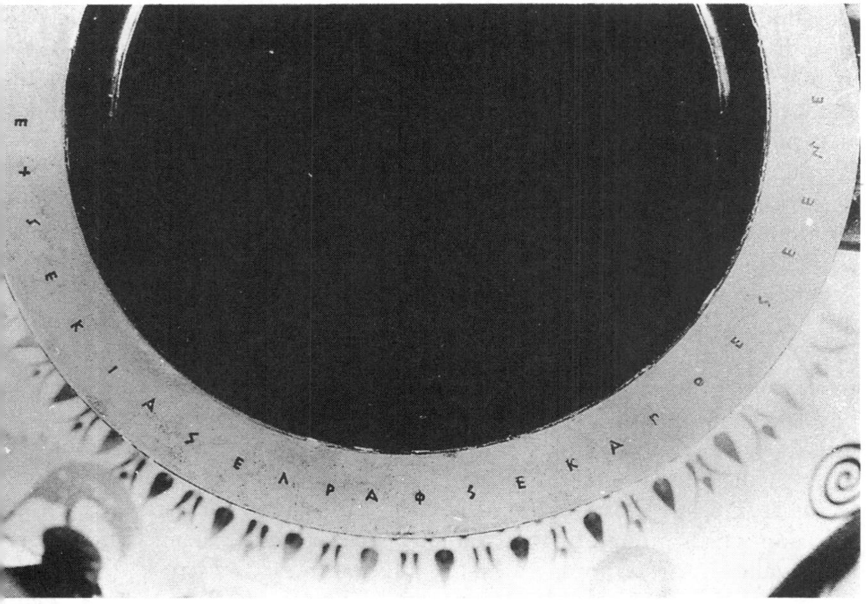

.8 A painted inscription on an Attic neck-amphora: 'Exekias made and painted ne', ca. 550 B.C.

otting and the painting; certainly the work 'egrapsen' = 'painted' is found ater and less frequently, the earliest being a Naxian fragment of ca. 620 .C. where the name of the painter is unfortunately missing.[34] In the sixth entury the convention is more common and is found on Corinthian ottery (e.g. Timonidas, etc., ca. 580 B.C.) and Attic (Sophilos, Exekias, ig. V.8, etc.); in the late sixth and fifth century the evidence comes wholly rom Attic black-figure and red-figure.[35] Some names are followed by both made' and 'painted' (e.g. Fig. V.8). Names of painters are rare elsewhere, ut are found on Paestan pottery (Asteas and Python) and on a 'Hadra' ase made in Crete (Pylon).[36] In the main the names, set on different parts f the vase, were painted in black, purple or added white, or incised. The ames may be the autographs of painters who may also have added the otter's names where these occur, or it may have been that some literate ssociate wrote for both painter and potter.[37]

The names of painters are not essential for knowledge of the style of a nan's work, but they may provide helpful ancillary information. The sorts f help they can give are: origin (Lydos = 'Lydian'; Sikelos = 'Sicilian'; kythes = 'Skythian'), status (Lydos ho doulos = 'the slave'; Epiktetos = newly acquired'), nicknames (Smikros and Makron = 'Little' and 'Large';

Onesimos = 'Useful'); identity with the 'maker' (Exekias, Fig. V.8, Nearchos, Myson, Douris, Euphronios), relation by blood (Timonidas, son of Bias; Tleson and Ergoteles, sons of Nearchos, the father both a potter and a painter, the sons only potters); workshop connections between potter and painter (Ergotimos and Kleitias; Hieron and Makron) (see also Chapter IV pp. 66–7). There has been no satisfactory theory yet proposed to explain the appearance of names on vases: it seems to have been a random choice with no necessary relation to the quality of the painting (see also Chapter IV pp. 65–8).[38]

Other lettering found on pottery, some of it adding to the effect of the decoration, some spoiling a good design, can be presented in brief form (for graffiti added after firing, see Chapter VI pp. 124–5). Letterers may have started to write on pottery as soon as the alphabet was being used by Greeks; some of the earliest inscriptions were written retrograde, as with inscriptions on stone and metal. Captions sometimes make reference to what is illustrated, e.g. characters (usually mythological), objects ('lyre', 'cauldron', 'seat', 'spring'), the scene itself ('the games for Patroklos').[39] On occasion words uttered by the characters are set beside them (' "Look, here is a swallow", "Yes, by Herakles, spring has come" "Here it is" ').[40] The painter may wish to send greetings to the user ('hail and drink well'). Names are added to indicate either the owner ('Asopodoros' lekythos', therefore a bespoke piece), or of a deity (also then bespoke, as on Chios chalices of the early sixth century, some of which have the name of the dedicator as well).[41] Sometimes a painter makes a comment about a colleague or rival ('as never Euphronios').[42] A rare use of lettering is to be found on some Attic red-figure vases which show papyrus rolls with a small sample of the text, always an extract from verse, fitted into the space available.[43] The appearance of 'kalos' names which mention specific individuals (e.g. 'Leagros kalos' = 'Leagros is handsome') has been mentioned in the chapter on Dating (p. 53); they are in the main an Athenian peculiarity and stretch from the mid sixth century to the later fifth.[44] Also mentioned under Dating (pp. 53–5) were the Panathenaic prize amphorae. These had begun before the mid sixth century with the inscription 'one of the prizes from Athens' and in the fourth century had begun to carry the names of Athenian archons as well.[45]

Some inscriptions were never intended to mean anything, either they simply filled a space or they were poor copying by an illiterate in the workshop. General questions of literacy are raised by these instances and by the numerous mis-spellings that abound. Accuracy seems to have been a hit-and-miss affair, dependent on pronunciation. Not all centres of production added inscriptions: most literate was Athens; others were Corinth, Chios, Laconia, Boeotia, Etruria, south Italy.[46]

The actual lettering (dialectal spelling, shapes of letters) helps to pi

down the origin of the letterers, e.g. the lettering on the mid-sixth-century pottery that we now know as 'Chalcidian', for which the find-spots would indicate an origin in south Italy, possibly Rhegium, is connected with that of Chalcis in Euboea and suggests that the ware was made by emigrés from Chalcis. Some letterers have a fairer hand than others, and individual enough to be recognised.[47] It is also possible to speak of periods of handwriting: in Attic work the late seventh and early sixth centuries have been characterised as 'subrustic', one thinks of Sophilos; the letterers of the mid sixth century were careful and neat, such as Kleitias and the cup painters of his time and going down to Exekias (Fig. V.8); later in the sixth century the lettering became swifter, more frequent and less epigraphic.[48]

Painters and names

A painter's name is not essential to an understanding of his work, provided that his style is distinctive enough to be individually recognisable. The ancient names of painters, as we have seen, are useful for the incidental assistance they might give, but it is study of the actual handiwork of the artist that reveals his identity: details such as ears, ankles and shoulder blades, drapery, and overall conception and composition (Figs. V.9 & 10). Such an approach is linked to the name of Morelli who applied the method to Renaissance painting. However, it was the scholar Sir John Beazley who carried out the fundamental research on the same lines in the study of Greek vases. 'The essence of the Morellian method is careful scrutiny of details, especially those which an artist reproduces so regularly that they can be considered as characteristic of his hand as his handwriting.' Nor is the approach limited to figures only. 'Furthermore, subtleties of shape offer additional information, as does subsidiary pattern-work, which can be abstract, floral, or figural. The shapes of vases and their patterns are reliable guides to attribution; their connoisseurship, therefore, combines Morellian analysis of draughtsmanship with observations of potter-work and pattern-work.'[49] This century much research has been devoted to the differentiation of painters and groups, and not only in those times and techniques in which ancient names are known, nor has the research been confined to painting of quality. Although much vase-painting is still unattributed to individual hands, our present understanding of the history of Greek vase-painting, its workshops, the interconnections between painters and potters, etc. has been enormously enlarged by this type of investigation.[50]

This identification of painters has meant that in the various centres of production (Corinth, Athens, Boeotia, Laconia, south Italy, etc.), an overall view of the ceramic industry is available at different periods of time. Specific connections between centres in techniques, shapes, styles and

V.9 Attic red-figure kylix by Onesimos, ca. 490 B.C. Warrior.

subjects, recognised from general stylistic similarities, are also possible to plot more closely, e.g. Athens, Boeotia and Corinth in the sixth century; also in the sixth century East Greece and the West to which artists emigrated in the face of the Persian advance; Corinth and Athens in the fifth (the Suessula Painter of the late fifth century did most of his work in Athens, but his hand has been recognised in work on Corinthian clay technique and shape); Attica and south Italy also in the fifth century (examples of painters moving from Athens to south Italy and from Sicily to Campania).[51]

The plethora of modern names given to painters whose ancient names are unknown, but whose work has been recognised from their individual styles of drawing and painting, can look, and indeed can be, confusing. Listed below are some of the main types of name that are used:[52]

(a) The painter is given his modern name from the potter whose work he has decorated and whose name is known, e.g. the Amasis Painter, the Brygos Painter, the Kleophrades Painter, where Amasis, Brygos and Kleophrades are known names of potters. The decoration of many

V.10 Attic red-figure kylix by Onesimos, ca. 480 B.C. Youth.

ɔmetimes all, of their vases can be shown by stylistic study to have been ainted by one individual artist.

(b) The painter is named from a subject: the Nausikaa Painter, the isyphus Painter, the Darius Painter.

(c) The painter is named from a 'kalos' name, such as the Antiphon ainter, the Kleophon Painter.

(d) The name may be taken from a find-spot of one or more of the ases: the Dipylon Painter, the Eretria Painter, the Agrigento Painter.

(e) The present whereabouts (museum or private collection) of one or ıore vases by a painter may give the name: the Berlin Painter, the Ionolulu Painter.

(f) The shape of one of the vases an artist decorated may provide a ame: the Dinos Painter, and sometimes (e) and (f) may be combined as in ıe Painter of the Berlin Dinos to isolate another painter.

(g) Sometimes a memorable nickname has been thought to be ppropriate: the Affecter, the Worst Painter, Elbows Out.

Attribution of vase decoration to painters, most of whom have had to be iven invented names like those above, has been the main thrust of research

in this century, particularly in the sphere of Attic vase-painting. Th method of careful scrutiny of every line a painter drew, of h compositional preferences, of his choice of subject, of his whole approac to the task, of the development of his style during his career (Figs. V.9 & 10), of the connection between workshops where he plied his craft – a these facets have been patiently constructed into a synthesis of livin communities of craftsmen. However, both the method and particularly th continuing emphasis being placed on it in present-day research hav recently been called into question. The method has its difficulties: ho characteristic must a painter's style be, to be his own? how tightly must w set the parameters? how far can a painter's talent be allowed to deca before he becomes another painter with a different sobriquet? These a vital problems for any connoisseur but do not affect the central core of th attributions. It may be however that too much emphasis is being placed o connoisseurship at the expense of other avenues of research, as the return are now smaller than they used to be.[53]

Patterns

In the general history of Greek vase-painting, decorative pattern yielded i position of primacy to figured composition. On Protogeometric and earlie Geometric pottery, pattern was all – concentric circles and semicircle meander, triangles, lozenge, all placed to enhance the effect of the shape (Fig. III.1). In later Geometric, when figured designs had begun to appea the patterns started to retreat to the edges of the composition, belov above, at the sides, on the neck. In the early stages the figures themselve were drawn as an animated pattern, and one of the most momentou developments in the history of vase-painting was the gradual emergence o the figures from their decorative chrysalis. By the seventh century th patterns had become freer under influences that came from the arts o non-Greek areas rather than from a direct observation of nature itself, an the severe precision of geometric designs gave way to forms based o artistic flora: palmettes, lotus, spiralling tendrils, rosettes, pomegranate and different leaves, buds and petals. In some fabrics these were fine drawn and precisely placed, in others they were slapdash and ungainly, a if released from constraint without a guiding hand. Concentration on th finest examples of the craft should not disguise the fact that much of th work was poorly executed.

Floral patterns in Greek vase decoration were never entirely natural.[54] I some centres, painters presented a more luscious and freer treatment of th flora (e.g. on Caeretan hydriai),[55] often in areas that were themselves i East Greece or influenced from it. But usually the designs, though based o natural shapes at whatever remove, were unbotanical in their final forn

irmly controlled and conceptualised. With black- and red-figure of the sixth and fifth centuries the floral element was, as it were, tamed, was arely intrusive, and served to enhance both the shape and the figured composition, often providing a link between the two. The development in he variety and association of floral shapes can be traced in some detail. The rise and fall of the popular rosette design at Corinth is well known, rom the detailed and painstaking treatment in the seventh century down to he scratched blob of the sixth. The palmette also shows many ransformations: broad, narrow, angular, slanting, single or double, alternating with the lotus, circumscribed by tendrils, etc. The base rays derive from the leaves round the stalks of plants. Time, tradition, personal preference and ability dictated the appearance and popularity of individual patterns.[56] Some floral elements such as ivy, vine and laurel seem not to have excited the designer to any great extent, and indeed by their very hape lent themselves less to elaboration. Even in the fifth century, some geometric patterns, e.g. meander, saltire square and St. Andrew's cross, were combined in various ways to provide the base line for the figures or to act as the surround of a cup tondo (Figs. V.10 & 12). Occasionally and usually for humorous reasons, some of the figures took notice of the floral pattern by swinging on it or handling it in some way.

In the fourth century the floral patterns became more elaborate, and on ome of the south Italian vases, particularly Apulian, the flora burgeoned at he expense of the figures, in fancy, and in some cases extremely intricate, designs (Fig. V.6).

Compositions and subjects

t is natural that the figured scenes on Greek pottery should have attracted great interest. In the development of the drawing, one sees artists coming to grips with the fundamental problems of creating scenes on a two-dimensional surface. The fact that the surface was usually curving and its outline dictated by the form of the vase meant that to succeed in their ffect, compositions had to be shaped to fit the space available. The decoration veers away and approaches as the object is turned in the hands. A vase is not a canvas, and the modern drawings that flatten out the designs do less than justice to the original. The vase-painters were first decorating a curved surface; only later did they conceive themselves as reating a window on a world that lay behind.

For the figured scenes the characters are set, as it were, on a narrow edge (Fig. V.11) or later arranged on different levels (Fig. V.6). The silhouette stands out boldly from the curving wall; where outline was used, the effect was thinner and more insubstantial, and the figures appear to be blown across the receding surface. Most compositions were enclosed in a

tall, narrow space that allowed room for only a few figures, or in a broa low space that reduced the height of the figures but made room for a large cast. On the interiors of cups the difficult circular space was treated in variety of ways: as a porthole on a passing scene, with a horizontal line t act as the floor for the figures, or with no verticals or horizontals indicate and the figures carefully composed to fit the circular frame (Figs. V.9, 10, 12 There is little setting or background, and the figures are generally containe within their own space, with little hint of spatial depth in the Archai period but in the fifth century, under the influence of panel-painting, give more corporeality. Black-figure painting gives the effect of figures sh against the light; red-figure compositions seem to be bathed in their ow spotlights (see earlier p. 96).[57]

Narrative compositions were introduced into Greek vase decoration i the eighth century B.C. and from that time onwards played an increasin rôle in the decoration of the fine wares of many pottery-producing centre. From scenes of death, mourning and funerals which enhanced some of th funerary vases of the eighth century, the range of subjects increased. Figur decorated pottery was popular, both at home and abroad, and continue so for over four hundred years. As with the funerary scenes on Lat Geometric pottery, later one finds certain subjects related to shap fountain scenes on the water-pots of later Attic black-figure, Panathenai events on the amphorae that were prizes in the games, and the continue choice of funerary subjects (e.g. laying out of the dead, mourning, visit t the grave, Charon, Sleep and Death) for vases destined for the grave. Bu for many scenes the reason for the choice is not so apparent. The gre number of vases that carry figured decoration argues that they must hav had mass appeal, it was popular culture, even though it is still difficult t say for whom precisely they were intended.

Although the division of subject matter between myth and real life oversimple, it is none the less helpful. The real-life scenes centred on suc fundamental aspects of life as fighting and hunting, seafaring, athletic music and dancing, theatre, home life (weddings, children, educatio spinning and weaving, the fetching of water), religious occasions, wor partygoing and lovemaking, death and the life beyond. Most of the scen are based on life in the city, and many of them reflect the life of the upp classes. The Attic vases that carry scenes of the symposium or komos, som with overt expressions of drunkenness, brawling and sex, may have bee ordered especially for parties, just as those with weddings (whether real o mythological), children and home life may have been made as weddin presents for a specific occasion.[58]

The other major category of subject matter is that which relates to myt The stories of the gods and heroes bulk large in the literature of ancie Greece, and this interest is also reflected in vase-paintings.[59] The ma

ppeal of the stories means that the majority are presented in a traightforward way, often with the names (for those who could read) and ttributes of the characters included, to make the meaning plain (Zeus and is thunderbolt, Herakles and his club and lion skin). Subjects attracted an conography whereby the same incident was presented with the figures and ubsidiary elements fixed in a stock arrangement. This meant that an xcerpt could be recognised and related to the full story; it also means that cholars can now connect even small fragments of larger compositions with pecific myths. Some vases show myths that are not preserved in literature r show them centuries earlier than their preserved literary versions. Jaturally, new iconographic arrangements were invented with changes in roupings: tradition absorbed innovation. It is also natural that over the our centuries and more during which illustrations of these stories were roduced, specific myths and incidents from myth should vary in opularity and in the ways in which they were understood, presented and nterpreted. For instance, we have a scene of Orestes leading Aegisthus to is death on a seventh century Protoattic krater, no similar scene for the ext 150 years and then a surge of interest from the late sixth century for ne next fifty years. Is this to be set down to the vagaries of survival or is nere some deeper explanation?[60]

Scenes on vases of the Archaic period were usually presented in a traightforward manner, and the emphasis was on action. Painters, nowing the development of the story they were drawing, tended to ombine successive episodes into one single (synoptic) composition,[61] e.g. scene depicting Odysseus and his companions blinding the Cyclops might how the limbs of an already dead companion that the giant has started to at, the cup that caused the giant's drunkenness, and the stake being thrust nto his eye. As one moves into the fifth century, especially in Athens, it can e seen that some artists were capable of deepening the meaning of a story, .g. Ajax who in most earlier versions of his suicide was shown dead on his word (Corinthian: Fig. V.11) is later shown planting it in the ground (as n Exekias' amphora)[62] or discovered by Tecmessa (Attic: Fig. V.12), thus nvolving the emotions of another in what had earlier been represented as an olated act. The fifth-century artists tended to dramatise the episodes from nyth, but some of the serious and majestic stories of the sixth century such s the Judgement of Paris were trivialised and made hollow, and by the late fth century myth was valued more for the spectacle it afforded than for ne story it embodied – the figures pose and the narrative wilts.[63]

Myths on vases may give us a clearer understanding of the popular ersions of myths than the literary versions that we know through epic, rama and such. Certainly, no treatment of Greek mythology can be onsidered complete that does not take into account the preferences shown y the vase painters and their customers. Whether the stories are well

V.11 Corinthian black-figure kylix, ca. 580 B.C. Ajax dead.

known from the extant literature or not, the evidence from vases can act as a control, corrective and supplement to the literary sources. Many of the major figures and stories from mythology are known to us only from later reworkings in literature or from lexica and summaries of the Roman period; an account based on a conflation of these various versions is going to differ strongly from an account built up solely of early literary sources in combination with the evidence of vase paintings and of the other artistic media such as sculpture, bronze reliefs, etc.[64]

It is inevitable that in seeking to understand a myth as shown on a vase painting, recourse should be had to the literary versions, and these may be seen to harmonise or differ. However, the intelligence of a vase-painter may need to be questioned when we are presented with an aberration that is hard to accept – often the name of one of the participants in an episode may differ from what we might expect or may be applied to the wrong character. It is good to be reminded 'that vase-painters were neither theologians nor philosophers – not literary critics nor art historians – but that they were artisans who surely intended the imagery of their pictures (when they thought about it at all) to be accessible to potential buyers'.[65] None the less, a high level of 'mythological literacy' was often demanded by the choice of subject. It would be foolish to treat the vase-painters as unfailing sources of true wisdom. Indeed, the present trend in the study of myth would deny the validity of a view that sought to sift the true from the false. A given myth, it is claimed, is made up of all its variants; the narrative sequence and content of the episodes is largely irrelevant; it is

V.12 Attic red-figure kylix, ca. 490 B.C. Ajax dead, with Tecmessa.

he structure of the myth that is important. The essential elements in the Cyclops story are the barbaric cannibalism of the giant and the blinding hat is his retribution, with his drunkenness as an enabling element between he two; other elements are all equally acceptable, provided that the essential structure of the myth is preserved. The Structuralist school has provided some exciting new views on the subjects of vase-paintings, and not only in the field of myth – sacrifice, hunting, animals have been 'decoded' in terms of the anthropological themes they embody.[66] 'No figurative system is created as the simple illustration of a story, oral or written, nor as the straight photographic reproduction of reality. Imagery is a construction, not a tracing; it is a work of culture, the creation of a language, which, like any other language, introduces an essential element of choice.'[67]

The word 'iconology' is coming to the fore as a contrast to 'iconograph with which students of vase-painting have been concerned for some year 'Iconography' represents the positive, objective, descriptive, specifi approach, arguing a conscious, intellectual rationale behind the choice o images. 'Iconology' stands for the general, interpretative, symboli approach, seeking for unconscious attitudes and 'irrational' content. As on can see, the former accords with the classicist's credo; the latter takes u into the world of the anthropologist.

Influences

Borrowing and influence naturally occurred within the world of the vase painters themselves, and we have had cause to mention the ways in whic the younger men learned their craft from their more experienced colleague on the bench and how ideas and craftsmen moved from one centre t another (Corinth to Athens, Boeotia and Laconia, East Greece to Attica Athens to the West). But vase-painters did not live in a cultural vacuum and it is natural that their paintings, both in technique and in choice o subject matter, should have been influenced by what was happening aroun them. We have already seen that, for their subject matter, the life of the cit in all its facets became a general source of interest and inspiration. It ma be possible, however, to recognise other influences at work. Some scholar have felt that there was a close connection between literature and th subjects on vase-paintings,[68] so much so that direct influence has bee thought discernible, i.e. that the recitation of a particular epic[69] or th performance of a play may have inspired the painter to interpret the stor he has just heard and seen (cf. Fig. III.6). Certainly there would be no tex available; all literature was oral. Some such influence may be possible t detect in certain instances, but an all-pervading literary influence has fewe adherents today than earlier, now that it is felt that stories told i childhood and passing in general circulation are more likely to lie at th basis. We have seen earlier (see pp. 50–2) that the direct inspiration o the theatre may be traced in Athens, and the immense popularity of th stage in south Italy and Sicily accounts for scores of vase paintings tha present theatrical scenes.[70] Other literary connections do not always carr conviction. History in terms of specific figures and events has been seen t have had its effect, and in a more general way the choice of Persia combats can be seen to derive its source from the Persian Wars of the earl fifth century (Fig. III.5, p. 48). Politics and the use of mythologica figures in vase-paintings to make allusions to contemporary political view have had a vogue recently in the study of Attic vase-painting of the lat sixth and earlier fifth centuries.[71]

Influences from other arts may also be seen at work. These influence

may concern techniques and choice of decoration. As we have seen, ncision itself seems to have come from the observation of goods metalwork and ivory) imported from the East in the eighth century, along vith patterns and subjects (see below). The influence of 'free' painting also an sometimes be detected in polychrome decoration (brown with a black outline for men, white with a red outline for women),[72] and mention has lready been made of the possible influence of the colours on marble relief culpture on the appearance of red-figure in Athens (see pp. 96–7).

Patterns and subject matter can also be seen to derive on occasion from other artistic media. Textile and basketwork may have provided some basic patterns, and at times a close similarity can be seen between architectural decoration and vase-painting. As far as subject matter is concerned, culpture and 'free' painting can be seen to have inspired (if that is the orrect word) vase-painters to adapt their compositions. This is most learly observed in Athens after the erection of the Parthenon (see e.g. Figs. II.3–4, pp. 41–2), but also individual figures were introduced into vase-paintings either as statues or as actual figures within a scene (see pp. 4–5). In view of the patchy evidence, in the survival both of sculpture nd of vase-paintings, this practice may have been more common than we ealise.[73] The almost complete absence of 'free' painting on panels in the ixth and fifth centuries makes agreed statements about the source of nfluence on vases more than usually difficult. Pausanias' famous lescriptions of Polygnotan panel-paintings in Athens (1.17–18) and particularly Delphi (10.25–31) can be related to certain novelties in Attic ase-painting of the mid fifth century and to the popularity of themes that Pausanias details in his descriptions (Amazons, Theseus, etc.).[74]

A different type of influence on subject matter may have been exerted by narket forces. Not all subjects would have appealed to all customers, and ertain subjects would have been more acceptable at home than away, and ice versa. It has been noted that subjects with Persian connections were avoured in Persian areas, that Aeneas was popular in the West, and that Amazonomachies and the story of Arimaspians fighting griffins in the orth-east were popular in the Greek cities on the north of the Black Sea in he fourth century.[75] It is debatable to what extent such instances of local references can be ascribed to deliberate demand.

VI

OUT OF THE SHOP

Whatever the amount of pottery produced, its appearance on the market will have had but a limited impact – no shares rose or fell, no banks failed or prospered as a result. (Burford 1972, 60)

This chapter looks at various aspects of Greek (mainly painted) pottery once it was finished and ready for sale. There are more questions than answers.

Before considering 'trade' in pottery, we'll look at some evidence on the pots themselves for their daily use. Many vases give signs of a useful life everyday wear and tear: rubbed rims, mending with lead rivets, even patching with fragments of other vases.[1] Even when irretrievably broken, a vase could be put to secondary uses: as a door knocker, as a stopper, as a counter in a game, as 'scrap paper' on which to scratch a message, practise the alphabet, etc. (see below).

Graffiti and dipinti

The propensity of owners and others to scratch words on pots wa widespread, whether the pot was whole or broken. Many of these graffit spoil the effect created by the decorators of fine wares; the need to scratch the message must in many cases have been paramount, or the purpose malign. Here follow some of the more usual types of graffito added to whole pots while still in use (for 'trademarks', usually set out of the way under the foot, see below pp. 126–9).

(a) It was not unusual for an owner to mark a pot with his own name (in the possessive case, 'of . . . '). Small, portable objects were easily lost o stolen, and so it was perhaps prudent to establish one's claim (se p. 63), e.g. an Attic black mug found at Olympia carries the simpl statement 'I belong to Pheidias'. Or maybe the object was engraved fo someone else, as the Attic black-figure kylix found at Taranto, which carries the message, scratched under the foot in Western Greek letter forms 'I am the prize of Melosa. She beat the girls at carding.' Sometime abbreviations or monograms of individuals are incised, and the Athenian community (demos) marked some of its public property with the ligatur (joined letters) ΔΕ for 'demosion' = 'public' (cf. Fig. IV.7).[2]

(b) On occasion the inscriber named the pot itself (see Fig. IV.1 and pp. 53–5 where a good selection is given).

(c) A message might be incised without the name of the owner or the hape, as the Attic Dipylon jug of the later eighth century, which seems to ıave been given as a prize in a dancing competition held perhaps at a lrinking party, and written when the party was well under way: ‘Whoever lances most saucily, will receive me . . . [the rest is unintelligible and almost llegible]’. Other messages may be toasts, invocations or insults, sometimes ıaming sexual proclivities.[3]

(d) Some inscriptions were added when the pot was about to be ledicated in a sanctuary. Thus we may learn the name of the deity vorshipped; sometimes the dedicator also added his own name. Famous ıames are found but do not necessarily belong to the figures who made hem famous, e.g. the name of Herodotus has been found scratched on two ledications at Naukratis, but neither should be linked to the historian.[4] The words *hieros* = ‘sacred possession of’ and *anetheke(n)* = ‘dedicated’ ıre often added. Even broken vases were sometimes dedicated.

(e) for capacity, for home use when measuring or for taking to the narket to fill.

(f) tare, i.e. weight when empty.[5]

When vases were broken, the fragments might furnish small surfaces for cribbled notes:

(g) for practising the alphabet;[6]

(h) for messages such as expressions of love, errands or instructions, e.g. Put the saw under the threshold of the garden gate’ (Fig. VI.1);[7]

(i) for accounts and lists of names or objects, e.g. the complex list of ıames on a fourth-century Attic black plate that seems to refer to the mployment of slaves in Athenian potteries;[8]

(j) for voting ballots in a case of ostracism at Athens (see p. 57). This s now perhaps the best known use to which vase fragments were put. The sherds usually carried the name of the man being voted for ostracism, ıis father’s name and the name of his deme (district) (Fig. VI.2).[9]

Epigraphers can assist in elucidating graffiti by fixing the approximate late on the basis of the letter forms, and pinpointing the origin of the etterer by the spelling, the dialect and the letter forms, e.g. the graffito on f) above is written in the Megarian script, so we must assume that a man rom Megara was seeking to borrow, or asking for the return of, a saw rom a neighbour in Athens where the sherd was found. Similarity of ettering on ostraka sometimes shows that the voting sherds had been repared beforehand for distribution to those citizens who could not write.

Painted letters that were added in red after firing (dipinti), easily became vorn and are thus less common now than graffiti. They seem to have been ısed mainly in commercial transactions, by or for the ultimate purchaser.[10]

VI.1 Graffito on underside of Attic skyphos, sixth century B.C.

Trademarks[11]

There is a specific category of marks that concerns commercial transactions in pottery. These marks were scratched (graffiti) or more rarely painted (dipinti), usually under the feet of decorated pottery. They would not have been visible during ordinary use, and it is generally agreed that they were marks made by the potters or dealers, some before, but the majority shortly after, firing. The study and interpretation of the marks is a complex business, and words like 'inscrutable', 'cryptic', 'intractable' and 'uninspiring' have been used in reference to them. All dealers like to cloak their transactions in secrecy, so the present ambiguity of the marks would no doubt delight the original parties concerned.

The marks, mainly to be found on Attic pottery in the late sixth and the fifth centuries, usually vary from single letters and non-alphabetic signs to

---

VI.2 *opposite* Ostraka with Megakles, son of Hippokrates, marked for ostracism, early fifth century B.C.

ΗΙΠΠΟΚΡΑΤΟΣ

ΗΙΠΟΚΡΑ

two-letter abbreviations and monograms or ligatures; more rarely as many as five lines of text were scratched. In the main, the substance of the graffit relates to one or more of the following:

(a) numerals that note the number of pots in a batch. For numbers the letters of the alphabet were earlier used to denote the digits, later they were acrophonic (e.g. delta for 'deka' = 10).

(b) vase-names, abbreviated (Σ or ΣTA for 'stamnos' or 'stamnion') o in full ('krateres', 'lakythia', 'oxides', 'oxybapha'), some referring to the vase carrying the graffito, others giving a list of names that includes smalle vases that travelled in the same consignment as the large, inscribed vase The 'trademark' names present some that are well known but also show that in some instances present nomenclature is misapplied or applied to strictly (stamnos/stamnion refers to amphorae and pelikai), or they are little known or unknown names that may be special to the trade.

(c) prices (see below).

Occasionally other information is added, e.g. 'p(oi)' for 'poikiloi/ai' = 'decorated', 'mik' for 'mikra' = 'small', 'en' for 'enthemata' = 'contents (of a batch, not of a vase).[12] There seems to have been no unified system not surprisingly given the nature of Greek society and trading, and o merchants' varied jargon.

Some graffiti seem to have been added before the pots were fired, by th personnel in the potter's shop, so presumably ordered on sight (or even earlier) by the trader, but the marks were more usually added after th firing. The largest amount of evidence derives from Attic pottery (som from Corinthian and East Greek), and where the graffito is in the dialect o the originating centre, one must assume that the marks were added a source. It is also possible that the Attic vases that carry graffiti in Ioni script, were marked in Athens by Ionian merchants; where a graffito on a Attic vase is in Doric and the vase in question is found in e.g. Doric speaking Sicily, the marks would most likely have been added at the end o the route[13] Certainly no graffiti were added in transit whilst the potter was stored on shipboard.

The majority of vases inscribed with trademarks have been found awa from the place of manufacture. Some small shapes of Attic pottery hav been found in Greece, but the big shapes (e.g. kraters and hydriai) tha carry the marks went to Etruria (the largest number have been found a Vulci) and Campania, with some to Sicily (especially Gela).

Here is an example (Fig. VI.3) of one of the longer texts with a explanation and expansion of the substance.[14] The vase is an Attic red figure pelike by the Nikias Painter, dating to the late fifth century, and wa found in a tomb in Naples. The letters are in Ionic script. The listed batc was a mixed one, with table ware and oil containers.

There is a mark on the left side which runs across the foot and was mad

VI.3 Trademark on underside of Attic red-figure pelike, late fifth century B.C.

after the lettering – it has been interpreted as an indication that the transaction had been completed and the batch was ready to leave port. The lettering will thus have been added in Athens where the order was made up.

Line 1 stamnoi 3, price 3 drachmas 3 obols [i.e. 7 obols per stamnos]
one stamnos is the 'pelike' carrying the graffito.
'TI' is short for 'time' = 'price'.
⊦ is the sign for a drachma, – for an obol (6 obols = 1 drachma).

Line 2 oxides 11, 1½ obols.
the shape of an oxis is uncertain, maybe a small bowl.
Δ for 'deka' = 'ten'. Ↄ = ½ (?).

Line 3 lekythia small 50, 3 obols.
small oil pots were very cheaply made.
'MIK' is short for 'mikra' = 'small', lekythia is already a diminutive.

Line 4 lekythoi guaranteed 6, price 3 obols.
these oil pots were larger.
Π for 'pente' = 'five'. The two dots are punctuation.
'MIK' (line 3) and 'DIK' (line 4) may be a popular jingle. 'DIK' may mean 'honest', 'guaranteed', i.e. capacity matches appearance.

Line 5 oxybapha 13, 1 obol.
oxybapha, like oxides, may be small bowls, 80 for a drachma.

Prices[15]

It is not easy to speak of vase prices with any confidence. Evidence for prices of any goods is lamentably thin, and the evidence for vases is beset with many difficulties. Once again, only Athens provides any usable information, much of it won from the trademark graffiti, and it is patchily

bunched in time, mainly in the fifth and fourth centuries. In general, for prices to make any sense, the cost of living needs to be known. In late fifth-century Athens a mason could earn a drachma a day, as could a sailor; a juror received up to 3 obols (half a drachma) for a day's work.[16] All these were jobs paid by the state. We also know the price of some articles at that time: a ladder cost 2–8 drachmas, wheat 2–4 drachmas a bushel, olives 1½ drachmas a bushel, a shield 20 drachmas, a cloak 20 drachmas.

As for the evidence concerned with pottery, that from trademarks under the feet of vases is complex and difficult to interpret. Questions abound. Who was charging the quoted price: the potter or the merchant? Was the sum an asking price or an agreed figure? What was the charge for: the pot itself or the pot including contents (where there were any)? How many pots would a potter expect or be able to make in a day?[17] How do the prices scratched on the pots relate to the amount asked at the far end of a trade route? What profit could be expected for the potter or for the merchant? Sometimes a pot price is given in a graffito on the body of a vase, e.g. Kephisophon's 'kylix' quoted on p. 63 where the charge for breaking it is given as a drachma. To what extent this is a true figure and to what extent inflated to recompense the man for the loss of a cup that was a gift, is not known. Literary references to pot prices are rare, the best known is that in Aristophanes' *Frogs* v. 1236 (produced in 405 B.C.): 'you will get it [a lekythion – cf. p. 63] for an obol, and it's very fine and good.' Again, as with Kephisophon's kylix, the precise interpretation is hard to disentangle.[18] Another major source for prices is the inscription recording the sale by the state, of goods belonging to the men convicted of damaging the Herm statues in Athens and of profaning the Eleusinian Mysteries in 415 B.C.; here it must be remembered that the goods were second-hand, e.g. the Panathenaic amphorae fetched between 2 and 4 obols each at the sale.[19]

The following is a selected list of those shapes and prices that seem generally agreed to be correct (6 obols = 1 drachma). Quotation marks indicate those names that are found in the batch list, not the names of the actual shape.

early fifth century	belly amphora	5–7 obols	decorated
	hydria	7 obols	decorated
	lekythos	⅔ obol	decorated
mid fifth century	hydria	12–18 obols	decorated
	column-krater	10 obols	decorated
	bell-krater	9 obols	black
	lekythos	6 obols	decorated
	'lekythis'	1/12 obol	–
late fifth century	neck-amphora	6 obols	decorated

pelike (see above)	7 obols	decorated
bell-krater	3–4½ obols	decorated
'lekythos'	½ obol	–
'lekythion'	¾ obol	–
skyphos	½ obol	decorated
bolsal	½ obol	black

Size, difficulty of potting, presence of decoration, complexity of decoration, etc. no doubt affected the prices, though it is interesting to note that there have been differences of opinion on some of these matters. One may contrast the statement 'Utility, then, must have been the main factor in determining ancient prices for pottery, and we should be mistaken if we thought that the usual painted decoration of vases was prized very highly'[20] with 'a considerable premium was put on the painted decoration'.[21]

Distribution

In any study of goods traded, pottery must be seen in the context of all commodities. The subject is complex, because the nature of the operation was diverse, and the evidence is faulty and tilted to certain places and periods. Ideas change rapidly with new evidence and new perspectives.[22]

The important cargoes consisted above all of grain, and of metals such as iron, copper, lead, silver, of timber[23] and stone,[24] with worked objects in various materials, including coin; live cargoes, such as slaves and horses, should also be noted. Certain important commodities needed clay containers, above all wine, which would be carried in the plain large transport amphorae (roughly 60–80 cm. high, 30 cm in diameter, with a capacity of 23 litres) (Fig. III.9).[25] This was the standard carrier, shaped for ease of stacking, and was used also for other liquids such as oil[26] and for such foodstuffs as olives and fish. Research on the amphorae (shapes, stamps, petrological and chemical make-up) has enabled many local varieties to be distinguished: Chiot, Thasian, Rhodian, etc., and they provide an incomparable source of evidence for trade routes. It is the transport amphorae above all other pottery shapes and fabrics that assist towards an understanding of economic history. The shipwrecks[27] that have been found up and down the Mediterranean show the ubiquity of the amphorae, but they also show that cargoes were generally mixed, and alongside the amphorae and other goods that have survived, there lie the fine wares that were not traded for their contents but for themselves, for whatever reason – personal use, prestige and status, dedication in a sanctuary, deposition in a tomb – in this last instance one thinks particularly of Etruscan tombs in which some of the best quality Attic painted pottery was placed. It is perhaps too extreme to suggest that fine wares were stowed aboard as space fillers and might make the merchant a

bare profit on the side. Both weight and volume are important to an seagoing merchant or shipowner, and the care with which the fine ware would have to be packed aboard would suggest that they were profitabl enough to pay the man back for the trouble expended on them.[28]

Pottery, whether for itself or as a container, was made to be sold, bu there is little hard evidence on the different aspects of selling – where th sales took place, how and by whom the transactions were made, etc. Ther was doubtless much variety: a potter in business in a small way might tak his products round by donkey to local villages or set up his stall in th market square of the nearest town. We read of a 'pot-market' in ancien Athens,[29] the word used (*hai chytraï*) suggesting that it may have been fo the sale of coarse wares; smaller towns would not perhaps have neede such a precise point of sale. Some potters might venture in a caique fron island to island, perhaps taking a selection of pots for sale and receivin orders for the next visit. Travel by sea could be dangerous, though easie than the slow overland routes, but for both methods, large consignments o pottery would need very careful packing.

Some Attic vase scenes show selling in progress. Some indicate clearl

VI.4 Buying pottery in an Athenian shop, ca. 500 B.C.

that it is the contents that are being sold (oil, perfume, wine), others may be pictures of customers buying pottery in the shop (Fig. VI.4).[30]

The big concerns are likely to have had customers come to their workshop, either individuals buying in small quantities for home use, a projected party, a family funeral or a dedication, or traders who would sell to customers further away. The traders either came themselves and ordered goods on sight, already made or in the process of being shaped and painted, or may have sent along an order for a particularly popular line, whether plain or decorated, to be picked up later by slaves, or taken down to an agreed point by some of the pottery personnel. It is doubtful how much buying of pottery was carried on at the quayside; the trademarks (see pp. 126–9), especially the batch notations for party sets, table ware or mixed, seem to suggest that the order was made up at the shop.

In those cases where the pots were made as containers, the orders would presumably be delivered to the local vineyards, oil presses, etc. for filling before being sent for dispatch or distribution. Many of these would be heavy-duty pieces, but special commissions might be in fine ware such as the Attic black-figure Panathenaic amphorae (see pp. 53–5), made every four years as containers for the prize oil and handed out in large numbers to the winners at the festival, who no doubt took both pride and pleasure in the prize and in the contents.[31]

Merchants are rarely named, and their names and origins are only detected in part and with difficulty from such evidence as the trademarks.[32] We know of a Sakon, a Simon (most likely an Athenian), Achenatos (perhaps a Sicilian) and then such partial names as Archi-, Mnesi-, Smi-, Ar-, Me-. The best-known name is that of Sostratos of Aegina.[33] He is mentioned by Herodotus (Book 4, ch. 152): 'The Samian merchants, on their return home [from Tartessos], made a greater profit on their cargo than any Greeks of whom we have precise knowledge, with the exception of Sostratos of Aegina, the son of Laodamas – with him, nobody can compare.' Recently an inscribed stone anchor-stock was found just outside the sanctuary of Hera at Gravisca, the port for Tarquinia, the Etruscan city in southern Etruria. It carries the words, in Aeginetan script of ca. 500 B.C.: 'I am of Aeginetan Apollo; Sostratos, son of [ ], made'. Either this is the very same man mentioned by Herodotus or a member of his family. Further evidence to link the name to one and the same man comes from the trademark SO on almost a hundred Attic vases of the later sixth century, some tied indirectly with graffiti in Aeginetan script. The principle of Occam's razor might reduce all three sets of evidence to one man, but Sostratos did not make his fortune simply from selling pottery. He came to Athens to buy pottery that would accompany his more profitable cargo and would have exchanged his load for some commodity such as Etruscan metal, which he would carry on to another port of call or bring back as his

return cargo. Sostratos is good evidence for merchants in the century, no matter what their place of origin, moving from port to port, carrying and trading in goods of various states and cities. Some merchants may have owned more than one ship, some only one; many would have owned none at all and hired a ship in whole or part. The long-distance merchants (*emporoi*) who took Corinthian pottery to southern Italy and Sicily in such quantities or to Naucratis in Egypt, and those who took Attic black- and red-figure to all corners of the known world, were not assisting the states of Corinth and Athens; whether they were Eretrians, Aeginetans, Ionians or Phoenicians, their profit was for themselves, the shipowners, the moneylenders or maybe even the potters.

Much fine pottery never strayed far from its place of manufacture and the majority is to be found in its home town or in neighbouring areas. Protoattic and Boeotian are rarely found beyond their own local boundaries, nor is Corinthian red-figure. South Italian and Sicilian wares, having developed out of imported Attic pottery, were themselves mainly restricted in their distribution to their own regions. It would seem that some pottery-making centres had special connections at some distance away, e.g. Chios with Naukratis.[34] Long-distance movement is the exception, and Athens is unique in the spread and quantity of her exported vases, though even some particular shapes of her pottery were not exported, especially funerary vases.[35]

In the matter of long-distance movement the best known examples are perhaps the pendent semicircle skyphoi which mark the spread of Euboean influence both East and West,[36] and the numerous vases that went from Corinth to the West in the late eighth and seventh centuries (and which have always been central to any study of Greek settlement in south Italy and Sicily).[37] By the late seventh century, Athenian vases are found in Corinthian Western markets; the earliest Attic vase yet found in the West, ca. 600 B.C., is a fragment (most likely of an amphora) by the Nessos Painter from Caere, in Etruria.[38] During the sixth century, pottery from Athens is found as far away as Etruria, France and Spain in the West, deep into Asia Minor, round the Black Sea, and in Egypt and Africa. The work of the painter Kleitias (575–550 B.C.) has been found in an Etruscan tomb, in Egypt and in Gordion, the capital of Phrygia in Asia Minor.[39] The earliest example of Attic pottery in south Russia is a vase by the Painter of Acropolis 606, from Theodosia (ca. 550 B.C.).[40] It is also in the sixth century that Athenian potters and painters begin to produce work that was specifically directed at foreign markets; the best known example is Nikosthenes who provided for the needs of the Etruscans by imitating and elaborating on their own pottery and also using East Greek features which were accepted by his Etruscan customers.[41] The Persian expansion in the sixth century saw East Greek potters and painters leaving their homeland

on the coast of Asia Minor and transferring their skills to the West, e.g. the potters and painters of Caeretan hydriai in Etruria.[42]

In the fifth century markets changed. After the battle of Cyme in 474 B.C. Etruscan imports of Attic pottery are fewer, whereas the north Italian centres such as Felsina and Spina at the head of the Adriatic route rise in importance after the Archaic period. It was still possible for an enterprising potter to find varied outlets for his wares. The work of Sotades and the Sotades Painter has been found at Vulci and Capua, on Cyprus, in Egypt, and in the Black Sea region and Persia. The potter and painter of the piece found in Egypt (at Memphis) furnished a scene of Greeks versus Orientals on a vase in the shape of a camel with Persian mahoot; it doubtless found an eager purchaser.[43] Though pottery would have travelled alongside basic commodities and would not have dictated trade routes, destination cannot have been altogether pot-luck. Some Attic black-figure pottery was deposited in Celtic tombs, the best known being that at Vix in central France.[44] Another example is that from Klein-Aspergle (near Ludwigsburg, Wirtemberg) where the Attic cups, both red-figure and black, were decorated with thin gold attachments of Celtic design that enhanced the appearance of the ware in a manner to suit the family of the deceased.[45] More recently, Attic black and patterned pieces have been discovered in the tomb of Philip II of Macedon, at Ageae (Vergina).[46]

It is difficult to calculate the effects of the Peloponnesian War on the distribution of pottery, both within Greece itself and beyond. As there was no state control of such dealings, potteries doubtless continued to seek the outlets they could find. The decline of Athenian imports into Corinth has been linked to the development of a local red-figure at the time.[47] The Sicilian expedition of 415 B.C. has been blamed for the fall in imports to the Greeks on the island and in southern Italy, and has been seen to lead to an increased output of the local businesses which provided for the home markets.[48] Athens' main export areas in the fourth century lie to the east (the Greek islands and Cyprus), to the south (Egypt and North Africa) and to the Black Sea area.[49]

NOTES

I Introduction

1. Ziomecki 1975, 88–98.

2. See Jones 1986, ch. 12 on present-day traditional potteries, with Table 12. for a list of fifty. See now Blitzer 1990.

3. For some notes on the more important museums, see Cook 1972, 360–4.

4. For exhibitions, see e.g. Mayo 1982 (on south Italian pottery), von Bothme 1985 (on the Amasis Painter); Aellen, Cambitoglou and Chamay 1986 (on th Darius Painter); Spivey 1988 (on the Micali Painter).

5. E.g. *The Athenian Agora, Results of Excavations conducted by the America School of Classical Studies at Athens* (Princeton, 1953–); *Corinth, Results of th Excavations conducted by the American School of Classical Studies at Athen* (Princeton, 1932–); *Fouilles de Delphes, École française d'Athènes* (Paris, 1902–) *Délos, Exploration archéologique de Délos faite par l'École française d'Athène* (Paris, 1909–).

6. For salerooms and catalogues, see e.g. Sotheby's, Christie's and Ede's Münzen und Medaillen in Basel. For the case against trade in antiquities, see Meye 1977; Greenfield 1989; Cleere 1989.

7. Some of the periodicals are quoted in the notes to the following chapters; they provide the source for statements made in the text.

8. The most important listing of publications in the field of Classical archaeology is to be found in the annual *L'Année philologique* which contains information on publications on all aspects of classical studies. Also useful is the biennial bulletin on pottery that is published in *Revue des Études Grecques*.

9. Best-known general treatments of Greek pottery are Arias, Hirmer and Shefton 1962; Lane 1971; Cook 1972; Simon and Hirmer 1981; Williams 1985 See also Sparkes 1991. Scheibler 1983, which looks at all aspects of the pottery industry, is to be translated into English (see review by Johnston 1985b).

10. For a thread through the *CVA* labyrinth, see Carpenter 1984. Mention migh also be made here of Beazley's volumes 1956, 1963, 1971 and the addend Carpenter 1989. They have no illustrations and list with publication references the Attic black-figure and red-figure vase-painters that Beazley distinguished. This work of connoisseurship and taxonomy is now under the aegis of the Beazley Archive in the Ashmolean Museum, Oxford.

11. E.g. Empereur and Garlan 1986; Peacock and William 1986, esp. ch. 2.

12. For congresses, see e.g. Lissarrague and Thelamon 1983 (Rouen); Moon 1983 (Wisconsin); Brijder 1984 (Amsterdam); True 1987 (Malibu); Christiansen and Melander 1988 (Copenhagen).

II Making

1. For aspects of pottery production, see Noble 1966 (rev. ed. 1988); Shepard 1968; Jones 1986; Rice 1987; Arafat and Morgan 1989. See also Birmingham 1974 and Brijder 1984, Cuomo di Caprio 1985.

2. Recent studies which concentrate on or make use of evidence for modern traditional potteries are Hampe and Winter 1962 and 1965; Peacock 1982; Arnold 1985; Jones 1986. See also Blitzer's chapter on traditional pottery production at Kentri, Crete in Betancourt 1984, 143–57. See now Blitzer 1990.

3. For the transport of clay in small and large quantities, see Benson 1985, Jones 1986, 53 and ch. 12; Boardman 1986, 252–3; Gill 1987a, 82–3.

4. Cook 1959; Johnston 1979, 50–1; Snodgrass 1980a, 126–9.

5. For Corinth and its potteries, see Roebuck 1972, 116–25; Stillwell and Benson 1984; Benson 1984; Salmon 1984, ch. 7. See also Pemberton 1970, 265–70; Amyx and Lawrence 1975. For Athens, see Scheibler 1983, 107–8 with nn. 63–7; Jones 1984, 23–5. For both Corinth and Athens, see Arafat and Morgan 1989, esp. 311–29.

6. For modern pithos making, see Hampe and Winter 1962 and Jones 1986, 853ff. For freehand pottery, see Kourou 1987 and 1988.

7. See Sparkes and Talcott 1970, 34–6. For cooking-pot clays, see Jones 1984, 29.

8. For ancient illustrations of vases being made, see Richter 1923, 64–79 (for the written evidence, see 87–105; Cuomo di Caprio 1985, part 3); Beazley 1944 (now in Kurtz 1989), 87–103; Metzler 1969; Ziomecki 1975, 88–98; Arafat and Morgan 1989, 316–19. One picture shows a woman at work as a painter, see Kehrberg 1982.

9. Strong and Brown 1976, 75–6. Clay wheels have a small diameter and may have had a wooden frame attached to the outer rim. For Minoan potters' wheels, see now Evely 1988.

10. A detailed series of photographs showing the stages in making a modern version of an Attic black-figure kylix is included in Noble 1966 (rev. ed. 1988) figs. 1–72.

11. Hambidge 1920 and Caskey 1922 have not been superseded for their collection of detailed and accurate line-drawings of Greek pottery.

12. There has been much discussion on the nature of the paint used, see Noble 1966 (rev. ed. 1988), 31–47; Winter 1978.

13. On the preliminary sketch, see Corbett 1965; de Puma 1968. It seems to have been first used in the seventh century.

14. For multiple brushes, see Boardman 1960; and against, Eiteljorg 1980. Some have detected the use of templates for patterns, see Hemelrijk 1984, 88–9, 96–7, 105–8, 112–15.

15. For different suggestions, see Noble 1966 (rev. ed. 1988), 56–68; Seiterl 1976; Winter 1978, 57–8.

16. For mistakes in painting, see Farnsworth 1959.

17. The author of the poem is not known. For interpretations, see Cook 194 and 1951; Noble 1966 (rev. ed. 1988), 102–13 (by M.J. Milne).

18. For illustrations of firing, see the Penteskouphia plaques: Richter 1923, figs 72–80 and Cuomo di Caprio 1984, 72–82; Arafat and Morgan 1989, 317–19.

19. For kilns, see Cook 1961; Winter 1978; Peacock 1982, 67–83 (Roman); Scheibler 1983, 107–10 and 204, nn. 63–9; Cook 1984a; Jones 1986, 832–3, esp Table 10.2; Arafat and Morgan 1989, 321–5.

20. For failures in stacking, see Farnsworth 1959.

21. For test pieces, see Beazley 1944 (now in Kurtz 1989) 121, n. 1; Farnswort 1960; Noble 1966 (rev. ed. 1988), 74.

22. For failures in firing, see Farnsworth 1959.

23. See Jones 1986 for all these aspects. For a recent statement of th petrographic method, see Williams 1990. The Munsell code is often used t establish a colour or shade.

III Dating

Ideas about chronology are always in a state of flux, particularly for the Archai period and earlier. What is presented here is in the main the orthodo understanding, with some references to recent challenges, mainly centred on th Late Archaic/Early Classical periods. For a review of the recent controversy ove chronology spearheaded by E.D. Francis and M. Vickers, see Cook 1989 which list the relevant articles.

1. The best known example is the so-called Brygos Tomb at Capua, see Beazle 1945; Williams 1985, 45–8. See also Vickers and Bazama 1971 for an example c a tomb in Cyrenaica, and Corbett 1960, 60 for other comments on the dangers c laying too much stress on the evidence of isolated tomb-groups. For dating i relation to potters' and painters' families, see Boardman 1988a.

2. Lane 1971, 20.

3. For ancient chronology, see Bengtson 1970, 27–35; Samuel 1972, 57–138 Bickermann 1980, 62–91; Crawford and Whitehead 1983, 618–22.

4. Marathon: Kurtz and Boardman 1971, 108–12, 121, 247; Francis 1990, 134 n. 82. Koumanoudes 1978 argues against the identity of the mound as that c Marathon.

5. Themelis 1977, 226–44, 297–8; Snodgrass 1983a, 166.

6. Athens, Kerameikos, the tomb of the ambassadors from Çorcyra: Knigg 1972a, 584–605; 1972b, 258–65; 1976, pls. 112–13.

7. Rheneia, Purification Pit: Dugas 1952; Cook 1955, 267–9; Kurtz an Boardman 1971, 189 and 198; Zaphiropoulou 1973; Bruneau and Ducat 1983, 2 and 268.

8. Thespian polyandrion: Kurtz and Boardman 1971, 248; Schilardi 1977.

9. Athens, Kerameikos, the tomb of the Lacedaimonians: Ohly 1965, 314–22 Kurtz and Boardman 1971, 108–12, 121, esp. 110; Willemsen 1977.

10. Athens, Kerameikos, the Dexileos monument: Vermeule 1970; Kurtz and oardman 1971, 108; Burn 1987, 7–8, 87–8.

11. For an attempt to sort out the early dates, see Cook 1969. For a recent etailed study of the chronology of Corinthian pottery on which the early dating inges, see Amyx 1988, 397–434. The following notes give references to recent eactions to Cook's timetable, and Snodgrass 1987, 57 points to 'the danger of xpecting the evidence of excavation to speak to us in the same clear language as aat of an historical event' and questions the connections that have previously been aken as fundamental. I have adhered to more traditional approaches.

12. Hama(th): Coldstream 1968, 311–13; Hawkins 1982, 415–17; Braun 982, 9; Francis and Vickers 1985, 131–6.

13. Aziris: Boardman 1966; 1980, 153–5.

14. Daphnae: Cook 1954, 57–60; Austin 1970, 20; Braun 1982, 44 ('Daphnae annot fail to be identical with Tell Defenneh, excavated in 1880'); Francis and ickers 1985, 137–8.

15. Athens: the evidence is very complex. See Vickers 1985b, 22–33; Francis nd Vickers 1988; Francis 1990, 109–11. The relief figures on the statue bases uilt into the Themistoklean Wall in 479 B.C. are close in appearance to the figures f the Pioneer Group of Attic vase-painters, see Robertson 1987, 15.

16. Motya: Coldstream 1964, 105–12, 118–22; Isserlin and du Plat Taylor 974.

17. Olynthus: Gude 1933 (for the sources); Robinson et al. 1929–52; Scichilone 963.

18. Koroni: McCredie 1966; Grace 1974.

19. Corinth: Edwards 1975, 189–91.

20. See e.g., Francis and Vickers 1985, 137 (Old Smyrna); Boardman 1965 Tarsus); Graham 1982, 140–1 (Massalia).

21. There is a vast bibliography on the Western colonies, see Coldstream 1968, 22–7 and recently Graham 1982, 83–195 and 480–7, with the review by Burn 983, 251–2. For the pre-colonial Greek presence, see Ridgway 1984, Part I, Vhitehouse and Wilkins 1985, and for a recent general survey, Cordano 1986. On hucydides and the Sicilian chapters, see Gomme, Andrewes and Dover 1970, 98–210 (Dover).

22. Pithecusa: Coldstream 1968, 316–17; Kurtz and Boardman 1971, 307; ook 1972, 263; Graham 1982, 97–103; Ridgway 1984, Part II, and 1988a & b, 55–61.

23. Cumae: Graham 1982, 97–103; Ridgway 1988b, 655–61.

24. Sicilian colonies: Graham 1982, 103–4 (Naxos), 105–6 (Syracuse), 104–5 eontini), 106–8 (Megara Hyblaea). For Megara Hyblaea, see also Boardman 980, 174–7. See more generally Snodgrass 1987, 51–64.

25. Sybaris: Boardman 1980, 178–9; Graham 1982, 109–10.

26. Taras: Kurtz and Boardman 1971, 308–9; Graham 1982, 112–13.

27. Ephesos, Artemis temple: Robertson 1975, 83–4 (sixth-century temple), 07–8 (fourth-century temple); Ridgway 1977, 9; Boardman 1978a, 160–1; 1980, 9–100; Bammer 1982, 72 and 1984. For a new theory on the date, see Vickers 985b, 9–22 (with bibliography).

28. Delphi, Siphnian treasury: Picard and de la Coste-Messelière 1928, 57–171;

Robertson 1975, 152–9; Moore 1977; Ridgway 1977, 8–9; Boardman 1978 158–9; Watrous 1982, 159–72; Moore 1985; Hurwit 1985, 295–301; Daux ar Hansen 1987; Stewart 1990, 128–9. For the close connection with the Andokid Painter, see von Bothmer 1966.

29. Francis and Vickers 1983, 54–67; a reply, Boardman 1984b, 162–. Vickers 1985a, 9–12 (n. 36 casts doubt on the identity of the building); anoth reply, Amandry 1988, 593–609.

30. Delphi, the Apollo temple: Picard and de la Coste-Messelière 1931, 15–7 Robertson 1975, 161–2; Boardman 1978a, 155–6; Amandry 1988, 609; Stewa 1990, 86–9.

31. Delphi, the Athenian treasury: de la Coste-Messelière 1957, esp. 259– (Appendix 2, Chronology); Robertson 1975, 167–70; Ridgway 1977, 236– Boardman 1978a, 159–60; Boardman 1982, 3–165; Stewart 1990, 131–. Francis 1990, 44–5, 100–4.

32. Eretria, the Apollo temple: von Bothmer 1957, 124–6; Robertson 197 163–4; Touloupa 1986, 143–51; Boardman 1988d, nos. 120–1; Stewart 199 137.

33. Francis and Vickers 1983, 49–54; replies, Boardman 1984b, 161–2 ar Amandry 1988, 602. See now Francis 1990, 8–16, 24–5.

34. Olympia, the Zeus temple: Ashmole, Yalouris and Frantz 1967, 6– Ashmole 1972, 1–89; Robertson 1975, 271–91; Boardman 1985, 33–50; Stewar 1990, 142–6.

35. Athens, the Parthenon: the bibliography is large, see Robertson 1975, 292 316; Robertson and Frantz 1975; Brommer 1963, 1967, 1977, 1979; Cook 1984 Boardman and Finn 1985; Boardman 1985, 96–145; Stewart 1990, 150–60. F the accounts, see Burford 1963; Lewis 1981, 436–51; cf. Meiggs and Lewis 19 (rev. ed. 1989) no. 59.

36. Kallimachos' Victory (Athens, Acropolis 690): Raubitschek 1949, 18ff., n 13; Shefton 1950, 140–64; Harrison 1971, 5–24; Robertson 1975, 644–5, n. and pl. 56a; Boardman 1978a, 86–7; Hurwit 1985, 324; Stewart 1990, 131–2.

37. Agorakritos' Nemesis at Rhamnous: Despinis 1970; 1971; Ridgway 198 171–3; Boardman 1985, 147, 207; Stewart 1990, 269–70. The base: Petrak 1981, 227–53; 1986.

38. Paionios' Victory at Olympia: Robertson 1975, 287–8; Ridgway 198 108–11; Boardman 1985, 176; Stewart 1990, 89–92.

39. Tyrantslayers at Athens: Shefton 1960; Ridgway 1970, 79–83; Brunnsåk 1971; Taylor 1981; Boardman 1985, 24–5; Landwehr 1985, 27–47; Boardm 1988d, no. 141; Stewart 1990, 135–6 and 251–2. See also n. 57.

40. (a) Myron's Discobolos: Ridgway 1970, 84–86; Robertson 1975, 34 Boardman 1985, 80, 148–9. (b) Myron's Athena & Marsyas: Ridgway 197 85–6; Robertson 1975, 341–3; Weis 1979; Daltrop 1980; Boardman 1985, 8 Stewart 1990, 147. (c) Pheidias' Athena Parthenos: Schuchhardt 1963, 31–5 Leipen 1971; Robertson 1975, 311–16; Ridgway 1981, 161–7; Boardman 198 110–12; Stewart 1990, 157–8.

41. Dexileos' grave monument: Robertson 1975, 369; and see n. 10 above.

42. Dancing caryatid monument: Vatin 1983. The inscription also nam Praxiteles as the sculptor.

43. Record reliefs: Robertson 1975, pl. 123a (409/408 B.C.), 373 and 684, n. 32 ›artial list); Fuchs 1979, figs. 608 (409/408 B.C.), 619 (375/374 B.C.), 624 347/346 B.C.), 626 (295/294 B.C). See also Meiggs and Lewis 1969 (rev. ed. 1989) os. 84 and 94.

44. Angelitos' Athena (Athens Acropolis 140): Raubitschek 1939–40, 28–36; aubitschek 1949, 26ff., no. 22; Ridgway 1970, 29–31; Brouskari 1974, 129–30; obertson 1975, 179; Boardman 1978a, 87 and 1988d, no. 136. The two vases are n Attic red-figure neck-amphora by the Alkimachos Painter, London BM 1928.1–7.57 (Beazley 1963, 529, no. 12; Carpenter 1989, 254) and an Attic red-figure inochoe from the Group of Berlin 2415, New York, MM 08.258.25 (Beazley 963, 776, no. 3; Carpenter 1989, 288).

45. See nn. 39 and 57.

46. See n. 40 and Boardman 1956, 18–20. The vase is an Attic red-figure chous, erlin F 2418 (Robertson 1975, pl. 113b; Boardman 1985, fig. 64).

47. The treatment of the connections between the Parthenon sculptures and ase-painting is extensive. See especially Brommer 1967, 182–3; 1977, 154–5; hefton 1982; Schwab 1986; Arafat 1990, 166–72. The vase that has been onnected with the Helen and Menelaus metopes (North 24–5) is an Attic red-gure oinochoe, Vatican 16535 (Beazley 1963, 1173, below; Carpenter 1989, 329) nd that with the young knight (West 25) is an Attic red-figure pelike in the manner f the Washing Painter, Berlin F 2357 (Beazley 1963, 1134, no. 8). For the West ediment and vases, see Metzger 1951, 324–6, and for the East pediment and ases, see Harrison 1967, 30, 39–40 and Shefton 1982. For the Parthenos and ase-painting, see Leipen 1971. Arafat and Morgan 1989, 324 suggest that the birth f Athena in vase-painting was killed off by the pedimental treatment of the arthenon.

48. Zeus at Olympia: Shefton 1982, for the throne.

49. Pausias: Pliny *HN* 35.123–7 (Overbeck 1760). Pebble mosaics: Robertson 965; 1967; 1975, 485–91; Williams and Fisher 1976, 114, n. 13; Robertson 981a, 172–6; Salzmann 1982. For the vases, see Trendall and Cambitoglou 1978, 89–90; Trendall 1989, 80.

50. For historical characters and scenes, see Hölscher 1973, 30–31.

51. Arkesilas by the Arkesilas Painter, Paris, Cab. Méd. 189 (4899): Chamoux 953, 258–63; Arias, Hirmer and Shefton 1962, pls. 74 and XXIV; Stibbe 1972, 15ff., 195ff., pl. 61, 2, no. 194; Hölscher 1973, 30; Hooker 1980, 86f.; Simon nd Hirmer 1981, pl. XV; Boardman 1984a, no. 372. On silphium, see Chamoux 985. On the cup Schaus 1983, 88–9 interprets 'Onexo' as 'Enoxo', wife of rkesilas II.

52. Shefton 1954, 308.

53. Lane 1933–4, 161–2; Boardman 1974, 195.

54. Anakreon: Caskey and Beazley 1954, 55–61 on no. 99; Kurtz and oardman 1986, 65–70.

55. Croesus by Myson, Paris, Louvre G 197: Beazley 1963, 238, no. 1; Beazley 971, 349; Arias, Hirmer and Shefton 1962, pl. 131; Hölscher 1973, 30–1; oardman 1975a, fig. 171, and 1988d, no. 230; Carpenter 1989, 201. The date of e fall of Sardis: Andrewes 1982, 401–2.

56. Boardman 1982, 15–16. See also Francis 1990, 71–2.

57. For the Tyrantslayers, see n. 39 and Beazley 1948, 26–8; Hölscher 197 85–8; Robertson 1975, 185–6; Prag 1985, 102–3.

58. The Panathenaic prize amphorae are London BM B 605, and Hildeshein Pelizaus Museum 1253 and 1254 (Beazley 1956, 411, nos. 4 and 412, nos. 2 and Carpenter 1989, 107).

59. Boston MFA 98.836: Vermeule 1970, 103–7, fig. 7; Brunnsåker 1971, p 24, 7; Thompson and Wycherley 1972, 155–8.

60. The Persians: Bovon 1963; Hölscher 1973, 38–49; Hölscher 1974; Barre and Vickers 1978, 17–24 and pls. 1–2; Pinney 1984, 181–3; Williams 1986 (n. 1 gives a full bibliography of Persians on vases); Boardman 1988d, no. 236. See als Kahil 1972.

61. Pronomos: Duris 76F29 (= Athenaeus 4.184D). The Pronomos krate Naples 3240: Beazley 1963, 1336, no. 1; Arias, Hirmer and Shefton 1962, pl 218–19; Trendall and Webster 1971, 28, no. II, 1; Simon and Hirmer 1981, pl 228–9; Simon 1982a, pl. 9; Carpenter 1989, 365.

62. Alexander: Naples 3256 and 3220; Hölscher 1973, 174–80; Giuliani 197 Trendall and Cambitoglou 1982, 18/40 and 18/47 and 484–5; Trendall 1989, 1 and 89.

63. Boreas and Oreithyia: Kaempf-Dimitriadou 1979, 105ff., nos. 340–39 Brommer 1980, 11–16; Simon and Hirmer 1981, pls. 178–9; Robertson 198 14–15; Boardman 1988d, no. 231. Cf. Aegina, Arafat 1990, 77–88, etc.

64. Herakles: Boardman 1972; 1975b; 1978c; 1989b; Williams 1980, 144, 25; Boardman 1982; Shapiro 1983. Theseus: Sourvinou-Inwood 1971; Barro 1972; Sourvinou-Inwood 1979; Boardman 1982; Francis and Vickers 1983, 49 54; Francis 1990, 49–51 and passim. For recent comments on this trend, s Osborne 1983–4 and Cook 1987a.

65. For the Geometric and Archaic periods, see Carter 1972; Snodgrass 197 1980a, 183–94; 1980b; 1982; 1987, ch. 5. See also more generally March 1987.

66. Vermeule 1966, 6.

67. Boardman 1983, 29.

68. Trendall and Webster 1971.

69. Boston MFA 63.1246, by the Dokimasia Painter: Beazley 1963, 165 Vermeule 1966; Davies 1969; Boardman 1975a, fig. 224; Prag 1985, 102– Carpenter 1989, 234.

70. Tokyo, Fujita: Simon 1982a, pl. 7, 1–2; 1982b, 141–2, pl. 37a–l Boardman 1988d, no. 200. See also Sutton 1980, 28–9.

71. London BM 1947.7–14.8: Trendall 1967, 27, no. 85, pl. 8, 1; Trendall an Webster 1971, II.11; Sutton 1980, 95–133 (424 B.C.); Seaford 1982; 1984, 49–5 (ca. 408 B.C.); Vickers 1987, 187–97; Trendall 1989, 19–20.

72. Malibu, The J. Paul Getty Museum 82.AE.63: Green 1985, 95–8, 111–1 Taplin 1987, 93–6.

73. Jeffery 1961 (2nd. ed. 1990) 63–5; Woodhead 1981; Millar 1983, 9 Immerwahr 1990.

74. 'Kalos' names: Richter 1958, 43–5, 65, 93, 117; Beazley 1956, 664–7 1963, 1559–1616; 1971, 317–19, 505–8; Carpenter 1989, 147–8 and 388–9 Kleine 1973, 78–93. New names: Carpenter 1989, 391–9.

75. Francis and Vickers 1981, 97–136.

76. 'Signatures': Payne 1931, 158–69; Beazley 1956 and 1963 passim and 553–8; 1971, 523; Lorber 1979; Amyx 1988. New names appear from time to ime, see Frel 1973 and pp. 145, n. 28, 149, n. 38.

77. Polias: Boardman 1956, 20–24.

78. Panathenaic prize amphorae: Beazley 1951 (rev. ed. 1986) ch. 8; 1956, 03–17; Frel 1973; Boardman 1974, ch. 7; Brandt 1978; Rhodes 1981, 671 and ommentary on 49.3 and 60; Andrewes 1982, 410–11; Moore & Philippides 1986, 2–17; Carpenter 1989, 105–9.

79. The Burgon amphora, London BM B 130: Beazley 1956, 89, no. 1; Corbett 960, 52–8; Boardman 1974, fig. 296; Boardman 1988d, no. 204; Carpenter 989, 24. Athens, Kerameikos: Frel 1973, 7, fig. 4 and 11, fig. 7.

80. Frel 1973, 18–19; Eschbach 1986.

81. Edwards 1957; Frel l973, 29–30 (Sarapion, agonothetes, 98–97 B.C.).

82. 'Hadra' hydriai: Guerrini 1964; Cook 1966; 1968–9; Fraser 1972, I 138ff.; I 104ff. with nn. 248–9; Callaghan 1980; Callaghan 1984; Cook 1984b; allaghan and Jones 1985, Enklaar 1985 and 1986; Jones 1986, 734–77.

83. Ostraka: Vanderpool 1970; Lewis 1974; Francis and Vickers 1981, 100–1; Iarvey 1984, 72; Francis and Vickers 1988, 144–5. See now Lang 1990.

84. Transport amphorae: Grace 1979; Empereur and Garlan 1986. For a prime xample of the use to which stamped amphora handles can be put for dating urposes, see Grace 1985 on the Middle Stoa in the Athenian Agora.

85. Impressed cups; Lévêque and Morel 1980, 91; Morel 1981, 46–50. See hapter V n. 29.

86. Scientific dating: Jones 1986, ch. 10.

IV Shapes

1. The best-known example of a vase name denoting an object in a scene is the ıydria' on the François vase, Florence 4209: Beazley 1956, 76, no. 1; Carpenter 989, 21. For 'lebes', see Athens, Acropolis 590: Graef and Langlotz 1925, pl. 27a.

2. See Sparkes 1975.

3. Still basic is Richter and Milne 1935, with older bibliography cited. See also ow Kanowski 1984. Most general books on Greek pottery have a section on ames; those books that deal with one shape sometimes go into the question of the riginal name(s) for the shape, e.g. Haspels 1936, 127–8 (on the lekythos) and hilippaki 1967, xvii-xxii (on the stamnos).

4. Stone inscriptions: Amyx 1958 on the vase names on the Attic Stelai; for ıventories, see Lewis 1986.

5. Vase names on vase inscriptions: Sparkes and Talcott 1970, 4–9; Lazzarini 973–4; Johnston 1979, 32–3. This evidence tends to show how wide a usage a ame could have. The names used in trademark graffiti present a slightly different erminology, see pp. 126–9.

6. For kados, see nn. 17–18 below.

7. For scratched names, see n. 5 above and nn. 8–18 below.

8. Chiot chalice, Chios, from Chios: Jeffery 1961 (new ed. 1990), pl. 65, 42e;

Boardman 1967, pls. 97, 614; Lazzarini 1973–4, pl. 66, 3 and p. 346; Lemc 1986, 234, fig. 1.

9. Rhodian skyphos, Copenhagen NM 10151: Jeffery 1961 (new ed. 1990), p 67, 1; Lazzarini 1973–4, pl. 66, 1 and p. 346; Boardman 1984a, no. 379b.

10. Attic cup-skyphos, lost: Vanderpool 1967; Lazzarini 1973–4, pl. 70, 2 an p. 351.

11. Attic Siana cup, Paris, Louvre F 66, from Etruria: Lazzarini 1973–4, pl. 6: 1 and p. 343.

12. Rhodian Late Geometric skyphos, Ischia, from Ischia: Jeffery 1961 (new ec 1990) pl. 47, 1; Coldstream 1968, 277; Meiggs and Lewis 1969 (rev. ed. 1989), no 1; Lazzarini 1973–4, pl. 64, 1 and p. 342; Boardman 1980, 167, fig. 20: Boardman and Hammond 1982, 100, fig. 16; Millar 1983, 93–4; Boardma 1984a, no. 378; Ridgway 1988a, 105, n. 2 (for bibliography).

13. Boeotian black kantharos, Paris, Louvre, MNC 370 (L 198), from Thespia Jeffery 1961 (new ed. 1990), pl. 9, 18; Lazzarini 1973–4. pl. 73, 1 and p. 357.

14. Attic red-figure aryballos, Athens NM 15375, from Athens: Richter an Milne 1935, fig. 106; Beazley 1963, 447, no. 274; Lazzarini 1973–4, pl. 74, 2 an p. 360; Carpenter 1989, 241.

15. Protocorinthian pointed aryballos, London BM A 1054, from Cumae: Jeffe 1961 (new ed. 1990) pl. 47, 3; Lazzarini 1973–4, pl. 73, 2 and p. 360; Lorbe 1979, no. 9.

16. Corinthian aryballos, Corinth Museum C-54-1, from Corinth: Roebuc 1955; Boegehold 1965 (he proposes ⟨m⟩olpa = 'dance' and thus removes th connection with the shape); Lazzarini 1973–4, pl. 74, 1 and p. 362; Lorber 197 no. 39; Amyx 1988, 560, no. 17.

17. Attic black-figure amphora, once on the market: Sparkes and Talcott 197 7; Lazzarini 1973–4, pl. 75, 1, 3 and p. 364; Sparkes 1975, 127, n. 27.

18. Athens, Kerameikos 7357, from the Athenian Kerameikos: Sparkes 1975, p 12b; Knigge 1976, pl. 95, 1 and p. 192.

19. Beazley 1940–5, 18–19, n. 2.

20. The study of potters on the basis of direct comparison of shapes ha increased recently. A pioneering work is Bloesch 1940 on Attic kylikes and 1951 o amphorae. For more recent studies of individual shapes (mainly Attic), see Diel 1964 (hydriai); Philippaki 1967 (Attic stamnoi); Rudolph 1971 (Attic squa lekythoi); Callipolitis-Feytmans 1974 (Attic plates); Becker 1977 (Attic pelikai Borell 1978 (Geometric cups); Schneider-Hermann 1980 (south Italian nestorides Brijder 1983 (Attic sixth-century kylikes); Neeft 1987 (Protocorinthian aryballoi McPhee and Trendall 1987 and 1990 (fish plates); Stibbe 1989 (Laconian mixing bowls); Kearsley 1989 (skyphoi). There are also many articles that deal wit particular shapes, some of which are mentioned in the following notes.

21. Immerwahr 1984a and 1990.

22. Oxford, Ashmolean Museum 189: Beazley 1956, 349 bottom; Beazley 197 159–60.

23. For the problem of 'epoiesen' (= 'made'), see Beazley 1944 (now in Kur 1989), 107–15 and more recently Cook 1971; Robertson 1972; Eisman 197 Vickers 1985c, esp. 126, n. 175; Robertson 1985, 21–2; Arafat and Morgan 198 319–21.

24. Krater fr., Ischia, from Ischia: Buchner 1971, 67; Jeffery 1977, 64; oardman 1980, 167, fig. 184; Boardman, Edwards, Hammond & Sollberger 1982, 29, fig. 106, 2.

25. Krater, Rome, Conservatori: Arias, Hirmer and Shefton 1962, pls. 14–15; oardman 1980, 193, fig. 227; Simon and Hirmer 1981, pls. 18–19; Boardman 984a, no. 367.

26. From Smyrna: Boardman 1984a, no. 380; from Chios: see n. 8 above; from thaca: Lorber 1979, no. 7, Amyx 1988, 683.

27. Protocorinthian aryballos, Boston MFA 98.900: Jeffery 1961 (new ed. 990), pl. 6, 22; Lorber 1979, no. 10.

28. For Athens the information is full. See Beazley 1944 (now in Kurtz 1989), 956, 1963 and 1971. For new names, see Carpenter 1989, 400–6.

29. Boeotian names: Raubitschek 1966; Sparkes 1967, 122–3 (on Teisias the thenian); Maffre 1975, 415–25; Kilinski 1982, 272.

30. For the Attic evidence, see Beazley 1956, 1963 and 1971, and Carpenter 989. See also Boardman 1974 and 1975a. For Xenophantos, see Beazley 1963, 407; 1971, 488. For Nikias, see Beazley 1963, 1333, no. 1; 1971, 480 and arpenter 1989, 365. For Amasis, see von Bothmer 1981a and 1985, 37–9 and oardman 1987b. For Kleophrades, see von Bothmer 1981a and 1985, 230–1; oardman 1988d, no. 172. For the two makers of one kylix (Glaukytes and rchicles, and Anakles and Nikosthenes), see Beazley 1944 (now in Kurtz 1989), 08–9, and for the Nearchos and Ergotimos families, see Boardman 1988a.

31. Frel 1973, fig. 4.

32. Bakchios: Beazley 1956, 413, nos. 1 and 2; 1986, pl. 99, 6; Carpenter 1989, 07; Kittos: Beazley 1951, pl. 46, 4 and 47, 1; 1956, 413; 1986, pl. 100, 3–4; arpenter 1989, 107.

33. Athens EM 161: Kern 1913, pl. 27, 5; Kirchner 1940, 6320; Peek 1955, 97.

34. Keil 1913, 232 and 239; Preuner 1920, 70–1; Engelmann 1980, no. 1420.

35. Beazley 1943, 456–7; 1951, 97; Robertson 1985, 21–2.

36. Richter 1941, 388; Vickers 1985c, 127, n. 177.

37. For the phormiskos, see Touchefeu-Meynier 1972; for reeded baskets, see rann 1962, 14–15 and 62; for wood, see Rieth 1940; Brann 1962, 14; Boardman 987a, 289–90. Nuts and shells: Beazley 1940–5; Greifenhagen 1982.

38. Alabastron: Beazley 1938, 4; Boardman 1980, 142–3 and 152–3; oardman 1984a, no. 301; Vickers 1985c, 112, n. 34; Robertson 1985, 23.

39. The relationship between clay and metal vases has recently become a subject or lively discussion. See especially the work of Vickers 1983; 1984; 1985c; 1986, 37–51; Vickers, Impey and Allan 1986, pls. 1–30; Gill 1986a, 9–30, and 1988a; ill and Vickers 1989 and 1990. For contrary views, see Robertson 1985, 20–3; ook 1987b; Boardman 1987a.

40. Persian rhyton: Hoffmann 1962, 1967 and 1989; phiale: von Bothmer 1962; oardman 1968; Freyer-Schauenburg 1986; Boardman 1987a, 289; lydion: oardman 1980, 99, figs. 114–16; 1984a, no. 300. See also Boardman 1967, 69ff. and Shefton 1989.

41. Jackson 1976, 38; Rasmussen 1979, 68ff., 110–16, and 1985; Kurtz and oardman 1986, 35–7.

42. Transport amphorae: Grace 1979; Empereur and Garlan 1986; cf. Peaco and Williams 1986. Pithoi, etc.: Courby 1922, 40–108; Schäfer 1957; Sparkes ar Talcott 1970, 36–7. Cf. Weinberg 1954.

43. Coarse wares: Amyx 1958; Sparkes 1962 and 1965; Sparkes and Talco 1970, 33–6; Riley 1979; Scheffer 1981; Jones 1986, 724–7.

44. Household wares: Sparkes and Talcott 1970, 34.

45. Many books on Greek pottery are concerned with or have a section c shapes and list the functions under each name, e.g. Richter and Milne 1935; Nob 1966 (rev. ed. 1988), 11–28; Cook 1972, ch. 8; Boardman 1974, 1975a ar 1989a; Schiering 1983, 139–59; Kanowski 1984. In this chapter functions a dealt with first, followed by a partial list of modern and conventional names wi some outline drawings. For a small book on usage, see Sparkes and Talcott 19 and cf. Thompson 1971. For an attempt to formalise the study of shapes, s Gardin 1976.

46. Public pots: Lang 1960; Lang and Crosby 1964, 1–68; Thompson ar Wycherley 1972, 44–5, 55; Lang 1976, 51–2. For the hydria as voting urn, s von Bothmer 1974, 15.

47. For the aryballos, see Beazley 1927–8 and Haspels 1927–8.

48. Panathenaics: Beazley 1951 (rev. ed. 1986), ch. 8; Frel 1973; Boardma 1974, ch. 7. For the total, see Johnston 1987a. A warning has recently been give against using the surviving inscribed Panathenaics to gauge the total output f other vases, see Arafat and Morgan 1989, 326–7. The vases without an inscriptic were not given as prizes; they were replicas. The shape was borrowed for red-figu painting in Attic and south Italian potteries.

49. Traveller's mug: Mallwitz and Schiering 1964, 169–82; pilgrim flas Mingazzini 1967.

50. Metalworkers and shoemakers: Ziomecki 1975; oil-sellers: Boardma 1976b; vintage: Sparkes 1976; bee-keeping: Jones, Graham and Sackett 197 397–414 with Appendix I (by Geroulanos) and II (by Jones). On rural finds, s now Snodgrass 1990.

51. Most books on Greek pottery show examples of drinking cups, bowls ar jugs, and the scenes with the objects in use were very popular subjects for va decoration. See now particularly Vickers 1978 and Lissarrague 1987. As is to expected at a party, some cups were meant to amuse the guests with trick stems th leak and rattle, with sexual organs in place of feet and with bowls in the shape breasts. The figured scenes also show the nature of the entertainment; s Lissarrague 1987, 49–59. For symposia in a wider context, see Murray 1990. F moulded cups, see Richter 1967, Kahil 1972 and Guy 1981. For 'Megarian' bow see pp. 109–10.

52. For fish-plates, see McPhee and Trendall 1987 and 1990. Two small usef books on lamps: Perlzweig 1963 and Bailey 1963. For chamber pots, see Spark and Talcott 1970, 8, 65 and 231; Sparkes 1975, 128; Knauer 1985.

53. Kitchen pots: Sparkes 1962 and 1965; Sparkes and Talcott 1970, 187–23 Sparkes 1981; Scheffer 1981. See also Morris 1985 and Grandjean 1985.

54. For dolls and such, see Thompson 1971; for spinning and weaving, Jenki 1986. For an Attic black-figure cup given as a prize for wool-working, see Mil 1945.

55. Oil and perfume containers: Haspels 1936; Hellström 1965, 23–8; Boardman 1976b; for the residue in pots found today, see Jones 1986, 839–47. For moulded perfume-pots, see Higgins 1959; Trumpf-Lyritzaki 1969; Amyx 1988, 512–33. For unguentaria, see Anderson-Stojanovic 1987.

56. Athens NM 12271: Haspels 1936, 124–30. Other names inscribed on vases are for nard and cinnamon.

57. Exaleiptron: Scheibler 1964 and 1968.

58. Weddings: Fink 1974; Roberts 1978.

59. Funerals and funerary vases: Kurtz and Boardman 1971; Vermeule 1979; Kurtz 1984; Garland 1985. Clay sarcophagi: Cook 1981. On the change from metal to clay offerings, see Hoffmann 1988, 151–3.

60. Festivals: Parke 1977; Simon 1983. Anthesteria: van Hoorn 1951; Artemis festival: Kahil 1977; Adonis festival: Weill 1966; Servais-Soyez 1981. Vases from the Athenian Acropolis: Graef and Langlotz 1925 and 1933.

61. Bron and Lissarrague 1984, 8 and see all their chapter I; Lissarrague 1987, 56.

62. Beazley 1974, 6.

63. Aesthetics: Sichtermann 1963; Lane 1971; Schiering 1983.

V Decoration

1. For the rare addition of decoration, see n. 22 below.

2. Decorated pithoi: Courby 1922, 33–114; Schäfer 1957; Ervin 1963; Caskey 1976. Cf. Weinberg 1954. For some with polychrome paint, see n. 21. For freehand pots, see Kourou 1987 and 1988.

3. Protogeometric and Geometric: Desborough 1952; Coldstream 1968; Schweitzer 1971; Murray 1975. For early Boeotian see Ruckert 1976.

4. Protocorinthian and Corinthian (seventh and sixth centuries): Payne 1931 and 1933; Amyx 1988. For incision on bronzes, see Boardman 1980, 69–71.

5. Black-figure (non-Attic): Lane 1933–34, Stibbe 1972, Pipili 1987 (Laconian); Sparkes 1967 (Boeotian); Boardman 1952, von Bothmer 1969, Ure 1973 (Euboean); Beazley 1947, Spivey 1987, Martelli 1987 (Etruscan).

6. Protoattic (= seventh-century Athenian): Cook 1934–5; Morris 1984 (she suggests that the island of Aegina was a production centre); Osborne 1989. Black-figure (Attic): Beazley 1928 (now in Kurtz 1989), 1951 (rev. ed. 1986), 1956; Boardman 1974; Moore & Philippides 1986; Carpenter 1989, 1–148. Corinthian orange-ground: Amyx 1988, 387–95.

7. Cabeiric: Wolters and Bruns 1940; Sparkes 1967, 125–7; Braun and Haevernick 1981, 1–74.

8. Red-figure (Attic): the bibliography is immense. Richter 1958; Beazley 1963 and 1971; Boardman 1975a and 1989a; Carpenter 1989, 149–390. Beazley's lectures on some red-figure painters are now in Kurtz 1989.

9. For panel-painting, see n. 11 below. New theory: Vickers 1985c; Cook 1987b; Boardman 1987a, 286–8.

10. For inventors, see e.g. von Bothmer 1966, 205 (the Andokides Painter); Williams 1985, 36–7 (Nikosthenes and Psiax). Psiax worked in black-figure, red-figure, white-ground, Six techniques and coral red.

11. Panel-painters: Rumpf 1934, 1947, 1951; Robertson 1959, 121–35; 197 240–70; Schaus 1988; Stansbury-O'Donnell 1989.

12. For a recent appreciation of late fifth century vase-painting, see Burn 198 Kerch vases: Schefold 1930; Boardman 1989a, 190–4.

13. Boeotian red-figure: Lullies 1940; Ure 1958; Sparkes 1967, 123– Corinthian red-figure: Herbert 1977; McPhee 1983. Laconian red-figure: McPh 1986. Red-figure made in Chalcidice: McPhee 1981.

14. Sicilian and South Italian red-figure: Trendall 1967; Trendall ar Cambitoglou 1978 and 1982; Mayo 1982; Trendall 1987 and 1989. Emigratio MacDonald 1981.

15. Etruscan and other red-figure: Beazley 1947; del Chiaro 1974; Marte 1987.

16. Attic white-figure: Haspels 1936, 106–7, 153–6; Haspels 1969; Boardma 1974, 64, 178, 188; Kurtz 1975, 116–17. Etruscan: Beazley 1947, 178–9, 195, c xii; Trendall 1987, 364.

17. Early white-ground: Coldstream 1968, 168, etc.; Williams 1982, 24, n. 2 Boardman 1986 (some Chiot possibly made at Naukratis).

18. White-ground (Attic): Beazley 1938 (now in Kurtz 1989); Mertens 197 Kurtz 1975; Mertens 1977; Wehgartner 1983; Boardman 1989a, ch. 4. Invento of Attic white-ground have been suggested: von Bothmer 1966, 207 and Merte 1974, 91 (the Andokides Painter); Williams 1982, 25–7 and 1985, 34– (Nikosthenes); Wehgartner 1983 (Nikosthenes). Nikosthenes' two signed oinocho are considered to be the very earliest Attic white-ground. White-ground cup Mertens 1974; Burn 1985.

19. 'Hadra' hydriai: see Chapter III, n. 82. Lagynoi: Leroux 1913.

20. Payne 1931, 100; Beazley 1951 (rev. ed. 1986) 19; Robertson 1959, 5 Williams 1983a, 33; Schaus 1988. Examples of early non-vase painting are e.g. t Thermon metopes of the seventh century: Payne 1925–6; the Isthmia wa paintings of the seventh century: Broneer 1971, 33–4, pls. A–C; the wooden Pit plaques of the sixth century: Boardman 1984a, no. 323; the wooden Saqqa plaque, ca. 500 B.C.: Boardman 1984a, no. 299; Lycian tomb paintings, ca. 5 B.C.: Mellink 1973.

21. Polychrome: Payne 1927–8 (Cretan pithoi); Payne 1933, 18–21, 94–7 ar Amyx 1988, 539–40 (Protocorinthian and Corinthian); Boardman 1968 (Chiot Hemelrijk 1984, 65 (Caeretan). General: Boardman 1986, 252; Schaus 198 107–8.

22. St Valentin: Howard and Johnson 1954. Coarse ware: Crosby 1955. Relie Zervoudaki 1968.

23. The Lentini Group (Sicilian): Trendall 1967, 583–92; 1989, 235–8.

24. 'Hadra' hydriai: see Chapter III, n. 82. The Lipari Group: Bernabò Brea ar Cavalier 1986; Trendall 1989, 239–42. Canosa: Williams 1985, 69. Centurip Wintermeyer 1975.

25. Coral red: Farnsworth and Wisely 1958; Winter 1968; Sparkes and Talco 1970, 19–20; Cohen 1970–1. The intentional red should not be confused with t accidental and random red which many vases fire. The Exekias cup is Muni 2044: Beazley 1956, 146, no. 21; Carpenter 1989, 41. The early fifth-centu volute-krater is in the J. Paul Getty Museum in Malibu, 84.AE. 974: Walsh 198

170, no. 24; Noble 1988, colour plate VII. For Sotades and the technique, see Burn 1985, 100–2.

26. Black gloss: Sparkes and Talcott 1970, 9–31, 47–186, 236–336 (Attic); Morel 1980 and 1981 ('Campanian'). For a good recent catalogue of the rich variety of black, see Hayes 1984.

27. Attic fourth century: Köpcke 1964. West Slope: Thompson 1934 (new ed. 1987) 438–47; Rotroff 1991. Gnathia: Forti 1965; Green 1976; Morel 1980, 89–91. Etruscan: Pianu 1982.

28. Attic red-figure cups with incision and with stamping: Ure 1936 and 1944. An example of a white-ground oinochoe with stamping is London BM D 14: Beazley 1963, 1213, no. 2; Carpenter 1989, 347. Figured stamps: Sparkes 1968.

29. Non-Attic incising and stamping: Morel 1980; 1981, 46–50; Hayes 1984, 87 (Herakles); Jentel 1968, 19ff.; Morel 1980, 91 and Boardman 1987a, 284 (Arethusa heads). Fourth-century kraters, etc.: Köpcke 1964. Silvering on south Italian black: Boardman 1987a, 284–5.

30. Appliqué: Courby 1922, 123ff; Köpcke 1964; Zervoudaki 1968; Trumpf-Lyritzaki 1969. Plakettenvasen: Thompson 1934 (new ed. 1987), 423–6; Andreassi 1979; Hayes 1984, 89; Dohrn 1985. Askoi and gutti: Jentel 1976.

31. Moulded vases: Higgins 1959; Tuchelt 1962 and Ducat 1966 (plastic); Hoffmann 1962, 1967 and 1989, Guy 1981 (rhyta); Beazley 1929 and Biers 1983 (head vases). See also Kahil 1972 and Chapter IV p. 76.

32. Phialai: Richter 1941 and Boardman 1987a, 284–5. 'Megarian' bowls: Courby 1922, 227–447; Hausmann 1959; Rotroff 1982 (new chronology).

33. For a useful resumé on inscriptions, see Cook 1972, ch. 10. On Corinthian vase inscriptions, see Amyx 1988, 547–615 and for Attic, Immerwahr 1990. For graffiti, see Chapter VI.

34. Naxian fragment: Daux 1961, 851, fig. 3.

35. Corinthian: Lorber 1979, 109–10; Amyx 1988, 201, 255–6. Attic: Beazley 1956 and Boardman 1974 (black-figure) and Beazley 1963 and Boardman 1975a and 1989a (red-figure). See also Carpenter 1989.

36. Paestan: Trendall 1987, chs. v and vii. The Lasimos signature on an Apulian volute-krater in the Louvre (K 66) is a modern addition, see Trendall and Cambitoglou 1982, 913. Hadra: Berlin inv. 3767: Guerrini 1964, 10ff., pl. 1 A 1; Cook 1968–9, 127ff.; Callaghan 1984, 791.

37. Letterers: Immerwahr 1984 and 1990. Occasionally the letters of an inscription are reserved with the black adjusted around them, see Robertson 1981b, 23–4 and Vickers 1985c, 118, n. 98.

38. For the names, see Beazley 1956 and 1963; Boardman 1974 and 1975a; Carpenter 1989, 400–6. For Timonidas, see Amyx 1988, 563–4. For Lydos the slave (not the same as the more famous Lydos), see Canciani 1978. Vickers 1985c, 126–8, has recently advanced the unorthodox view that the 'egrapsen' man was the designer of a presumed metal original from which the pottery vase was copied, and the 'epoiesen' man was the original silversmith.

39. E.g. the François vase (Florence 4209: Beazley 1956, 76, no. 1; Carpenter 1989, 21) has words for 'seat', 'spring' and 'cauldron'. The Sophilos lebes (Athens NM 15499: Beazley 1956, 39, no. 16; Carpenter 1989, 10) has 'games for Patroklos'.

40. Leningrad inv. 615: Beazley 1963, 1594, no. 48; Carpenter 1989, 389.

41. Asopodoros' lekythos is Athens NM 15375: Beazley 1963, 447, no. 274; Carpenter 1989, 241. Chiot vases: Cook and Woodhead 1952; Boardman 1967, 243–5; Williams 1983b; Lemos 1986; Boardman 1986.

42. Munich 2307: Beazley 1963, 26, no. 1; Carpenter 1989, 155–6. This inscription, which was once seen as a challenge from the painter Euthymides to a rival's skill in painting, is now being understood to refer to the dancers on the vase, and it is these that Euphronios is said to be incapable of emulating. See Arafat and Morgan 1989, 320.

43. Papyrus rolls: Immerwahr 1964, 1973 and 1990; March 1987, 61.

44. Kalos names: see Chapter III, nn. 74–5.

45. Panathenaics: see Chapter III, nn. 78–81.

46. Literacy, nonsense and poor spelling: Vickers 1985c, 127. Non-Attic centres: Corinth: Lorber 1979, Amyx 1988, 547–615; Laconia: Stibbe 1972. For a foreigner writing on a Laconian cup, see Schaus 1979 who suggests that the Naukratis Painter (if he was the letterer of his own paintings) may have been from Cyrene and gone to work in Sparta. For literacy, see Havelock 1982 and 1986; Gentili 1988; Harris 1989.

47. Immerwahr 1984 and 1990.

48. Beazley and Payne 1929, 266–7.

49. Kurtz 1985a, 237–8. See also Kurtz 1983 and von Bothmer 1987. The Beazley Archive in the Ashmolean Museum, Oxford keeps track of new publications of Beazley's attributions and of new attributions by means of computer.

50. Mention might be made here of books that have been devoted to individual painters. In the 1930s a series *Bilder Griechischer Vasen* dealt with such painters as Exekias, the Berlin Painter, the Pan Painter, the Lewis Painter. Recently a new series, *Kerameus*, has begun on a much larger scale and includes the Affecter (Mommsen 1975), the Swing Painter (Böhr 1982), the Antimenes Painter (Burow 1989), the Shuvalov Painter (Lezzi-Hafter 1982), the Eretria Painter (Lezzi-Hafter 1988) and the Phiale Painter (Oakley 1990). There are also *Kerameus* volumes on Clazomenian Sarcophagi (Cook 1981) and the Caeretan Hydriai (Hemelrijk 1984). See also Bakir 1981 on Sophilos, Tiverios 1976 on Lydos, Karouzou 1956 and von Bothmer 1985 on the Amasis Painter, Burn 1987 on the Meidias Painter, Schmid 1960 on the Apulian Darius Painter.

51. Athens and Corinth: Herbert 1977, 48, Amyx 1988, 679–81; East Greece and the West: e.g. Boardman 1980, 202–6; Corinth, Athens and Boeotia: Kleinbauer 1964, Sparkes 1967, 119–20, Amyx 1988, 678–82; Athens, south Italy and Sicily: MacDonald 1981, Trendall 1989, 17–18, 29, 158, 233.

52. For examples of modern names, see Beazley 1956 and 1963; Amyx 1988; Trendall 1989; Carpenter 1989.

53. For a critique of the present state, see Hoffmann 1979 and 1988; Vickers 1985c, 126–8; for a defence, see Robertson 1976; 1985.

54. See Jacobsthal 1927. For a basic general book of wide range, see Petrie 193 and for a simple book of Greek ornament, see Connell 1968.

55. Hemelrijk 1984, 88–115.

56. For an attempt to provide a systematic code for organising pattern, see ;ardin 1978. See also Salomé 1980.

57. Tondo compositions: van der Grinten 1966. See also von Bothmer 1972b new ed. 1987) 3; Hurwit 1977.

58. Everyday life: see Chapter IV, nn. 45–60 for various aspects, and for the use which can be made of vase-paintings for other aspects, see e.g. Snodgrass 1964 arms and armour); Morrison and Williams 1968 and Morrison and Coates 1986 oared ships); Anderson 1961 (horsemanship); Harris 1964 and 1972 and waddling 1980 (athletics and sports); Beck 1975 (education); Williams 1983c women); Garland 1990 (daily life); Dover 1978 (homosexuality); Thompson 1984.

59. For the definitive lexicon of mythological compositions, see Kahil 1981–. For series of well illustrated books of myth, see Schefold 1966; 1978; 1981; Schefold nd Jung 1988. Also helpful are the lists of mythological stories in art in Brommer 971–6; 1973; 1980; and Brommer's monographs on Herakles (1953 and 1984), 'heseus (1982) and Odysseus (1983). There are useful treatments and bibliographies in Boardman 1974; 1975a; 1989a. A popular book is Henle 1973 and ee now Carpenter 1991.

60. Orestes: Prag 1985.

61. Synoptic treatment: Snodgrass 1982; 1987, ch. 5.

62. Boulogne 558: Beazley 1956, 145, no. 18; 1971, 60; Carpenter 1989, 40.

63. Burn 1987, 67.

64. For a recent treatment of myths using vase-painting to elucidate texts, see Iarch 1987 and see also Carpenter 1991.

65. Carpenter 1986, xvi.

66. For structuralist/anthropological treatments of vase-painting, see Hoffmann 977 and 1979; Bérard 1983; Lissarrague and Thelamon 1983; Bérard 1984; Ioffmann 1985–6; Lissarrague 1987; Hoffmann 1988.

67. Bérard 1984, 5.

68. Literature: Stewart 1983; March 1987. For the Kleophrades Painter's loseness to literature, see Boardman 1976a.

69. Epic: Johansen 1967; Kannicht 1982; Cook 1983.

70. Theatre: Trendall and Webster 1971.

71. Persians: see Chapter III, n. 60. Politics: Boardman 1978b; 1984c; 1989b; rancis 1990; anti: Cook 1987a; Arafat and Morgan 1989, 331–2. The example of egina: Arafat 1990, 77–89; Boreas: Chapter III, n. 63.

72. Schaus 1988.

73. Arafat 1990, 166–72.

74. See now Stansbury-O'Donnell 1989.

75. Persians: de Vries 1977, 546–8; Aeneas: Galinsky 1969; Arimaspians: Ietzger 1951, 327–32.

VI Out of the shop

'his chapter looks mainly at figured wares and hence is only a partial icture. The wider picture of ceramics and trade needs much more space.

1. Nogara 1951; Noble 1966 (new ed. 1988) 207 and fig. 254; von Bothm 1972a, 9–11.

2. Lang 1976, 23–51. Pheidias' mug, found at Olympia: Mallwitz and Schierin 1964, 169–82; Heilmeyer 1981, 447–8. Melosa's cup, New York, Metropolita Museum 44. 11. 1: Milne 1945; Jeffery 1961 (new ed. 1990), pl. 53, 1; Coo 1987c, fig. 54. Public pots: Lang 1976, 51–2. For a booklet on graffiti, see Lan 1974.

3. Dipylon jug, Athens NM inv. 192, from the Athenian Kerameikos: Simon an Hirmer 1981, pl. 11, below. Insults: Lang 1976, 11–15; Vermeule 1984, 302.

4. Gill 1986b.

5. Tare: Lang 1976, 64–8.

6. Abecedaria: Lang 1976, 6–7; Boardman 1984a, nos. 376–7 (Jeffery).

7. Messages and lists: Lang 1976, 8–11. Athens, Agora P 17824: Lang 197 fig. 18; Lang 1976, 8, B1, pl. 2. Names on sherds: Lang 1976, 16–21.

8. Johnston 1985a; cf. the 'shopping list', Athens, Agora P 10810: Sparkes an Talcott 1958, fig. 23; Lang 1974, fig. 49; Lang 1976, 10, B12, pl. 2.

9. For ostraka, see Chapter III, n. 83. The words 'ostrakon/ostraka' are also use to denote pottery fragments that have lists, accounts, etc. written in ink on the surface; they are mainly found in Egypt and are Hellenistic in date.

10. Dipinti: Lang 1976, passim; Johnston 1979, 48.

11. Trademarks: Amyx 1958; Johnston 1974; and especially Johnston 1979.

12. Beazley 1967, 143 (poi); Johnston 1978, 224–5 (en).

13. Johnston 1973; 1978.

14. Naples 151600: Johnston 1978. It is also published in Scheibler 1983, 14 figs. 128–9.

15. See n. 11 for bibliography; cf. also Pritchett 1953 and 1956; Lang 1976.

16. Markle 1985, 293–7. See now Vickers 1990.

17. Johnston 1978, 223, n. 9 quotes modern potters who see 'no difficulty i thinking in terms of a production (from clay to fired vessels) of at least a hundre small glazed bowls a day'.

18. The possible double-entendre in the scene makes the reference difficult t interpret closely, see Anderson 1981.

19. Amyx 1958, 178–86.

20. Amyx 1958, 279.

21. Johnston 1974, 149; cf. Boardman 1988b, 30.

22. Glotz 1926; Hopper 1979; Boardman 1980, 16–18 and passim; Garnse Hopkins and Whittaker 1983.

23. Timber: Meiggs 1982, ch. 12.

24. Stone: Snodgrass 1983b.

25. Transport amphorae: Grace 1979; Koehler 1979; 1981; 1986; Garlan 198 Empereur and Garlan 1986; Whitbread 1986a and b; Peacock and Williams 198 Trademarks are scratched on amphorae but do not connect with those found c fine wares; they may have served the same purpose.

26. Attic/Chalcidian SOS amphorae for oil: Johnston and Jones 1978; Jon 1986, 706–12. cf. Boardman 1976b and Valavanis 1986.

27. For a useful brief listing of those ships carrying mixed cargoes, see G

987a, 83–5; 1987b, 123–4; 1988c, 178–9; 1988d, 4–6. See generally hrockmorton 1987.

28. Recent polemic: Boardman 1988b; Gill 1988a and b; Boardman 1988c; Gill 988c and d; McGrail 1989. For pottery and economics, see also Vallet and Villard 963; Morel 1983; Scheffer 1988; Hannestad 1988; Arafat and Morgan 1989, 36–41. Some fine wares that could be sealed may have carried contents: perfume aryballoi and lekythoi, olives and figs in amphorae and pelikai. Coarse wares ere also traded, see de Paepe 1979; Riley 1984; Arafat and Morgan 1989, 336, ho point out that coarse wares were imported for immediate, practical reasons – ey were better at their job than locally produced pots.

29. Wycherley 1957, nos. 656, 684; Thompson and Wycherley 1972, 170–3.

30. See Webster 1972, 61, 67, 99–101, 248. Oil- and perfume-sellers: Beazley 956, 393, no. 16; 396, nos. 22 & 25; Beazley 1963, 185, no. 30; 285, nos. 1–2; 96, no. 1; 604, no. 51; 1154, no. 38bis; Haspels 1936, 209, no. 81; Florence inv. 2732; Tarquinia RC 1663; Vatican 413. Wine-sellers: Beazley 1956, 299, no. 20; eazley 1963, 445, nos. 252; 1162, nos. 17 & 18; Altenburg 189; Athens Acr. 681 .; Athens Agora P 10408. Pottery-sellers and buyers: Beazley 1963, 24, no. 14; 56, no. 1; 540, no. 4; Beazley 1971, 216 (?).

31. Panathenaics have been found in graves, sanctuaries and domestic contexts. or Panathenaics, see Chapter IV nn. 78–81.

32. Johnston 1974; 1979, 49.

33. Sostratos: Harvey 1976; Boardman 1980, 206; Snodgrass 1980a, 138; 1illar 1983, 95–6; Johnston 1987b, 134.

34. Chios-Naukratis: Boardman and Vaphopoulou-Richardson 1986.

35. For the Athenian pottery trade, see Boardman 1979, with charts showing the roportions of black-figure and red-figure, and proportions of red-figure shapes, om selected sites. See now Perreault 1986 (for export to the Near East) and Rosati 989 for computer analysis on the distribution of Attic pottery. White-ground kythoi found outside Attica indicate where Athenians were living and dying: see urtz 1975, 59, 141–3; Boardman 1980, 229; Williams 1982.

36. Kearsley 1989.

37. See Roebuck 1972; Salmon 1984, 103–16; Benson 1985; Amyx 1988, 94–484; Arafat and Morgan 1989, 337–9. Those states known in literature as ading states but with no recognisable local pottery production (e.g. Aegina and 1iletus) cannot yet be traced in the archaeological record.

38. Nessos Painter: Beazley 1956, 5, no. 3; Carpenter 1989, 2.

39. Kleitias: Beazley 1956, 76, no. 1 (from Chiusi, 'The François Vase'); 78, no. 3 (from Gordion); 78, no. 14 (from Naukratis); von Bothmer 1981b (from uxor).

40. The Painter of Acropolis 606: Beazley 1956, 81, no. 7 (from Theodosia).

41. Nikosthenes: Rasmussen 1985; cf. also the earlier Tyrrhenian ovoid neck-mphorae. See Williams 1982, 26 for Nikosthenes' use of East Greek features. cf. hapter V, n. 75 for subject matter in vase decoration that was tailored to suit the references of particular customers.

42. Caeretan: Hemelrijk 1984.

43. The Sotades workshop: Beazley 1963, 764, no. 9 (from Paphos, Cyprus);

772, no. θ (from Meroe, Nubia) and Carpenter 1989, 287; Beazley 1963, 768, n 31 and 773, middle (Susa) and Carpenter 1989, 287; Beazley 1963, 765 no. 1 (Kerch); 767, no. 21 (Babylon); Beazley 1971, 416, iota (Egypt) and Carpent 1989, 287; and see Kahil 1972.

44. Vix: Beazley 1956, 20, no. 14, and 1971, 86; Joffroy 1979, pls. 56–8, X pp. 74–5, 137–9; Collis 1984, 97, fig. 24d.

45. Klein-Aspergle: Jacobsthal and Langsdorff 1929, pls. 33 & 34c; Beazl 1963, 831, no. 25, and 1971, 422; Collis 1984, 125, fig. 34j–k; Kimmig 1988.

46. Vergina: Andronikos 1984, 156, figs. 121–2.

47. Corinth: MacDonald 1982; Arafat and Morgan 1989, 338–9.

48. South Italy: Trendall 1989, ch. 1. Gnathia (see pp. 105–6) is exceptional i that it wins orders in the eastern Mediterranean and beyond, and has been found i north Africa, Egypt, the Greek islands, Cyprus and the Black Sea region. See Gree 1979.

49. See Shefton 1982 and Boardman 1989a, 235–6.

BIBLIOGRAPHY

Adriani 1983 & 1984, *Alessandria e il mondo ellenistico-romano: studi in onore di Achille Adriani*, Rome, 1983 & 1984.

Aellen, Cambitoglou & Chamay 1986, Aellen, C., Cambitoglou, A. & Chamay, ., *Le Peintre de Darius et son milieu*, Geneva, 1986.

Amandry 1988, Amandry, P., 'A propos de monuments de Delphes', *BCH* 112 (1988) 591–610.

Amyx 1958, Amyx, D.A., 'The Attic Stelai III: vases and other containers', *Hesperia* 27 (1958) 163–307.

Amyx 1988, Amyx, D.A., *Corinthian Vase-Painting of the Archaic Period*, Berkeley and Los Angeles, 1988.

Amyx & Lawrence 1975, Amyx, D.A. & Lawrence, P., *Archaic Corinthian Pottery & the Anaploga Well, Corinth VII.II*, Princeton, 1975.

Anderson 1961, Anderson, J.K., *Ancient Greek Horsemanship*, Berkeley & Los Angeles, 1961.

Anderson 1981, Anderson, G., 'ΛΗΚΥΘΙΟΝ and ΑΥΤΟΛΗΚΥΘΟΣ', *JHS* 101 (1981) 130–2.

Anderson-Stojanovic 1987, Anderson-Stojanovic, V.R., 'The chronology and function of ceramic unguentaria', *AJA* 91 (1987) 105–22.

Andreassi 1979, Andreassi, G., 'Una idria inedita con relievi e la fabbrica delle 'Plakettenvasen"', in Trendall 1979, 21–9.

Andrewes 1982, Andrewes, A., 'The tyranny of Pisistratus' in Boardman & Hammond 1982, 392–416.

Andronikos 1984, Andronikos, M., *Vergina*, Athens, 1984.

Arafat 1990, Arafat, K., *Classical Zeus*, Oxford, 1990.

Arafat & Morgan 1989, Arafat, K. & Morgan, C., 'Pots and Potters in Athens and Corinth: a review', *OJA* 8 (1989) 311–46.

Arias, Hirmer & Shefton 1962, Arias, P.E., Hirmer, M. & Shefton, B.B., *A History of Greek Vase Painting*, London, 1962.

Arnold 1985, Arnold, D.E., *Ceramic Theory and Cultural Process*, Cambridge 1985.

Ashmole 1972, Ashmole, B., *Architect and Sculptor in Classical Greece*, London, 1972.

Ashmole, Yalouris & Frantz 1967, Ashmole, B., Yalouris, N. & Frantz, A *Olympia, the Sculptures of the Temple of Zeus*, London, 1967.

Austin 1970, Austin, M.M., *Greece and Egypt in the Archaic Age*, *PCP* Supplement 2 (1970).

Bailey 1963, Bailey, D.M., *Greek and Roman Pottery Lamps*, London, 1963.

Bakir 1981, Bakir, G., *Sophilos, ein Beitrag zu seinem Stil*, Mainz, 1981.

Bammer 1982, Bammer, A., 'Forschungen im Artemision von Ephesos von 197 bis 1981', *Anat. Stud.* 32 (1982) 61–87.

Bammer 1984, Bammer, A., *Das Heiligtum der Artemis von Ephesos*, Gra: 1984.

Barker, Lloyd & Reynolds 1985, Barker, G., Lloyd, J. & Reynolds, J., *Cyrenaic in Antiquity*, *BAR International Series* 236 (1985).

Barrett & Vickers 1978, Barrett, A.A. & Vickers, M., 'The Oxford Brygos cu reconsidered', *JHS* 98 (1978) 17–24.

Barron 1972, Barron. J.P., 'New light on old walls: the murals of the Theseion *JHS* 92 (1972) 20–45.

Beazley 1927–8, Beazley, J.D., 'Aryballos', *ABSA* 29 (1927–8), 187–215.

Beazley 1928, Beazley, J.D., 'Attic Black-figure: a sketch', *PBA* 14 (1928) 217 63.

Beazley 1929, Beazley, J.D., 'Charinos', *JHS* 49 (1929) 38–78.

Beazley 1938, Beazley, J.D., *Attic White Lekythoi*, Oxford, 1938.

Beazley 1940–5, Beazley, J.D., 'Miniature Panathenaics', *ABSA* 41 (1940–5 10–21.

Beazley 1943, Beazley, J.D., 'Panathenaica', *AJA* 47 (1943) 441–65.

Beazley 1944, Beazley, J.D., 'Potter and painter in Ancient Athens', *PBA* 3 (1944) 87–125.

Beazley 1945, Beazley, J.D., 'The Brygos tomb at Capua', *AJA* 49 (1945) 153–8

Beazley 1947, Beazley, J.D., *Etruscan Vase-Painting*, Oxford, 1947.

Beazley 1948, Beazley, J.D., 'Death of Hipparchos', *JHS* 68 (1948) 26–8.

Beazley 1951, Beazley, J.D., *The Development of Attic Black-figure*, Berkeley an Los Angeles, 1951 (rev. ed. by D. von Bothmer & Mary Moore, 1986).

Beazley 1956, Beazley, J.D., *Attic Black-Figure Vase-Painters*, Oxford, 1956.

Beazley 1963, Beazley, J.D., *Attic Red-Figure Vase-Painters*, Oxford, 1963.

Beazley 1967, Beazley, J.D., 'An oinochoe in Basle', *AK* 10 (1967) 142–3.

Beazley 1971, Beazley, J.D., *Paralipomena*, Oxford, 1971.

Beazley 1974, Beazley, J.D., *The Berlin Painter*, Mainz, 1974.

Beazley 1986, see Beazley 1951.

Beazley & Payne 1929, Beazley, J.D. & Payne, H.G.G., 'Attic black-figure fragments from Naukratis', *JHS* 49 (1929) 253–72.

Beck 1975, Beck, F.A.G., *Album of Greek Education*, Sydney, 1975.

Becker 1977, Becker, R.M., *Formen Attischer Peliken von der Pionier-Grupp zum Beginn der Frühklassik*, Tübingen, 1977.

Bengtson 1970, Bengtson, H., *An Introduction to Ancient History*, Los Angele & London, 1970.

Benson 1984, Benson, J.L., 'Where were the Corinthian workshops no represented in the Kerameikos of Corinth (750–400 B.C.)?' in Brijder 1984, 98 101.

:orinthian pottery' in *Greek Vases II*, 17–20.

Bérard 1983, Bérard, C., 'Iconographie – Iconologie – Iconologique', *Etudes de* *.ettres* 1983, Pt. 4, 5–37.

Bérard 1984, Bérard, C. et al., *La Cité des Images, Religion et Société en Grèce* *ntique*, Fernard Nathan – L.E.P., 1984 (English ed. *A City of Images, Iconography* *nd Society in Ancient Greece*, trans. D. Lyons, Princeton, 1989).

Bernabò Brea & Cavalier 1986, Bernabò Brea, L. & Cavalier, M., *Le ceramica* *olicroma liparese di età ellenistica*, Rome, 1986.

Betancourt 1984, Betancourt, P.P., *Eastern Cretan White-on-Dark Ware*, ennsylvania, 1984.

Betts, Hooker & Green 1988, Betts, J.H., Hooker, J.T. & Green, J.R., *Studies in* *Ionour of T.B.L. Webster II*, Bristol, 1988.

Bickermann 1980, Bickermann, E.J., *Chronology of the Ancient World*, London, 980.

Biers 1983, Biers, W.R., 'Some thoughts on the origins of the Attic head vase' in Aoon 1983, 119–26.

Birmingham 1974, Birmingham, J., *Domestic Pottery in Greece and Turkey*, ydney,1974.

Blitzer 1984, Blitzer, H., 'Traditional pottery production in Kentri, Crete: vorkshops, materials, techniques and trade' in Betancourt 1984, 143–57.

Blitzer 1990, Blitzer, H., 'Storage jar production and trade in the traditional Aediterranean', *Hesperia* 59 (1990) 675–711.

Bloesch 1940, Bloesch, H., *Formen Attischer Schalen*, Bern, 1940.

Bloesch 1951, Bloesch, H., 'Stout and Slender in the Late Archaic Period', *JHS* 71 1951) 29–39.

Boardman 1952, Boardman, J., 'Pottery from Eretria', *ABSA* 47 (1952) 1–48.

Boardman 1956, Boardman, J., 'Some Attic fragments: pot, plaque and lithyramb', *JHS* 76 (1956) 18–25.

Boardman 1960, Boardman, J., 'The multiple brush', *Antiquity* 34 (1960) 85–9.

Boardman 1965, Boardman, J., 'Tarsus, Al Mina and Greek chronology', *JHS* 85 1965) 5–15.

Boardman 1966, Boardman, J., 'Evidence for the dating of Greek settlements in :yrenaica', *ABSA* 61 (1966) 150–2.

Boardman 1967, Boardman, J., *Excavations in Chios 1952–1955: Greek* *:mporio*, *ABSA* Supplementary Vol. 6 (1967).

Boardman 1968, Boardman, J., 'A Chian phiale mesomphalos from Marion', *:eport of the Department of Ancient Cyprus* 1968, 12–15.

Boardman 1972, Boardman, J., 'Herakles, Peisistratos and sons', *RA* 1972, 7–72.

Boardman 1974, Boardman, J., *Athenian Black Figure Vases*, London, 1974.

Boardman 1975a, Boardman, J., *Athenian Red Figure Vases, the Archaic Period*, .ondon, 1975.

Boardman 1975b, Boardman, J., 'Herakles, Peisistratos and Eleusis', *JHS* 95 1975) 1–12.

Boardman 1976a, Boardman, J., 'The Kleophrades Painter at Troy', *AK* 19 1976) 3–18.

Boardman 1976b, Boardman, J., 'The olive in the Mediterranean: its culture and ıse', *Phil. Trans. R. Soc. Lond.* 275 (1976) 187–96.

Boardman 1978a, Boardman, J., *Greek Sculpture, the Archaic Period*, Londo 1978.

Boardman 1978b, Boardman, J., 'Exekias', *AJA* 82 (1978) 11–25.

Boardman 1978c, Boardman, J., 'Herakles, Delphi and Kleisthenes of Sikyor *RA* 1978, 227–34.

Boardman 1979, Boardman, J., 'The Athenian Pottery Trade', *Expedition* 197 33–40.

Boardman 1980, Boardman, J., *Greeks Overseas* (3rd ed.), London, 1980.

Boardman 1982, Boardman, J., 'Herakles, Theseus and Amazons' in Kurtz Sparkes 1982, 1–28.

Boardman 1983, Boardman, J., 'Symbol and story in Geometric art' in Moc 1983, 15–36.

Boardman 1984a, Boardman, J. (ed.), *The Cambridge Ancient History, Plates Volume III*, Cambridge, 1984.

Boardman 1984b, Boardman, J., 'Signa tabulae priscae artis', *JHS* 104 (198 161–3.

Boardman 1984c, Boardman, J., 'Image and politics in sixth century Athens' Brijder 1984, 239–47.

Boardman 1985, Boardman, J., *Greek Sculpture, the Classical Period*, Londo 1985.

Boardman 1986, Boardman, J., 'Archaic Chian pottery in Naukratis' Boardman & Vaphopoulou-Richardson 1986, 251–8.

Boardman 1987a, Boardman, J., 'Silver is white', *RA* 1987, 279–95.

Boardman 1987b, Boardman, J., 'Amasis: the implications of his name' in Tr 1987, 141–52.

Boardman 1988a, Boardman, J., 'Dates and doubts', *AA* 1988, 423–5.

Boardman 1988b, Boardman, J., 'Trade in Greek decorated pottery', *OJA* (1988) 27–33.

Boardman 1988c, Boardman, J., 'The Trade Figures', *OJA* 7 (1988) 371–3.

Boardman 1988d, Boardman, J. (ed.), *The Cambridge Ancient History, Plates Vol. IV*, Cambridge, 1988.

Boardman 1989a, Boardman, J., *Athenian Red Figure Vases: the Classic Period*, London, 1989.

Boardman 1989b, Boardman, J., 'Herakles, Peisistratos and the Unconvinced' *JHS* 109 (1989) 108–9.

Boardman, Edwards, Hammond & Sollberger 1982, Boardman, J., Edward I.E.S., Hammond, N.G.L. & Sollberger, E., *The Cambridge Ancient History III.* (2nd ed.), Cambridge, 1982.

Boardman & Finn 1985, Boardman, J. & Finn, D., *The Parthenon and Sculptures*, London, 1985.

Boardman & Hammond 1982, Boardman, J. & Hammond, N.G.L., *Th Cambridge Ancient History III.3* (2nd ed.), Cambridge, 1982.

Boardman, Hammond, Lewis & Ostwald 1988, Boardman, J., Hammon N.G.L., Lewis, D.M. & Ostwald, M., *The Cambridge Ancient History IV* (2nd ed. Cambridge, 1988.

Boardman & Vaphopoulou-Richardson 1986, Boardman, J. & Vaphopoulo Richardson, C.E., *Chios, A Conference at the Homereion in Chios*, Oxford, 198

Boegehold 1965, Boegehold, A.L., 'An archaic Corinthian inscription', *AJA* 69 (1965) 259–62.

Böhr 1982, Böhr, E., *Der Schaukelmaler*, Kerameus 4, Mainz, 1982.

Borell 1978, Borell, B., *Attisch Geometrische Schalen, Eine spät-geometrische Keramikgattung und ihre Beziehungen zum Orient*, Mainz, 1978.

von Bothmer 1957, von Bothmer, D., *Amazons in Greek Art*, Oxford, 1957.

von Bothmer 1962, von Bothmer, D., 'A gold libation bowl', *MMAB* 21 (1962) 154–66.

von Bothmer 1966, von Bothmer, D., 'Andokides the potter and the Andokides Painter', *MMAB* 25 (1966) 201–12.

von Bothmer 1969, von Bothmer, D., 'Euboean Black-figure in New York', *MMJ* 2 (1969) 27–44.

von Bothmer 1972a, von Bothmer, D., 'The ancient repairs' in Moore & von Bothmer 1972, 9–11.

von Bothmer 1972b, von Bothmer, D., *Greek Vase Painting: an Introduction*, New York, 1972 (new ed. 1987).

von Bothmer 1974, von Bothmer, D., 'Two bronze hydriai in Malibu', *Getty MJ* 1 (1974) 15–22.

von Bothmer 1981a, von Bothmer, D., '῎Αμασις, ᾿Αμάσιδος', *GettyMJ* 9 (1981) 1–4.

von Bothmer 1981b, von Bothmer, D., 'A new Kleitian fragment from Egypt', *AK* 24 (1981) 66–7.

von Bothmer 1985, von Bothmer, D., *The Amasis Painter and his World*, Malibu & London, 1985.

von Bothmer 1987, von Bothmer, D., 'Greek Vase-Painting: two hundred years of connoisseurship' in True 1987, 184–204.

Bovon 1963, Bovon, A., 'La représentation des guerriers perses et la notion de barbare dans la 1re moitié de Ve siècle', *BCH* 87 (1963) 579–602.

Brandt 1978, Brandt, J.R., 'Archaeologica Panathenaica I: Panathenaic prize amphorae from the sixth century B.C.', *Acta ad archaeologiam et artium historiam pertinentia, Institutum Romanum Norvegiae et Oslo, Universitëtsforl* 8 (1978) 1–23.

Brann 1962, Brann, E.T.H., *Late Geometric and Protoattic Pottery, the Athenian Agora VIII*, Princeton, 1962.

Braun 1982, Braun, T.F.R.G., 'The Greeks in Egypt' in Boardman & Hammond 1982, 32–56.

Braun & Haevernick 1981, Braun, K. & Haevernick. Th. E., *Bemalte Keramik und Glas aus dem Kabirenheiligtum bei Theben, Das Heiligtum bei Theben IV*, Berlin, 1981.

Brijder 1983, Brijder, H.A.G., *Siana Cups I and Komast Cups, Allard Pierson Series 4*, Amsterdam, 1983.

Brijder 1984, Brijder, H.A.G. (ed.), *Ancient Greek and Related Pottery, Proceedings of the International Vase Symposium in Amsterdam, 12–15 April 1984, Allard Pierson Series 5*, Amsterdam, 1984.

Brijder, Drukker & Neeft 1986, Brijder, H.A.G., Drukker, A.A. & Neeft, C.W., *Enthousiasmos: essays on Greek and related pottery presented to J.M. Hemelrijk*, Amsterdam, 1986.

Brommer 1953, Brommer, F., *Herakles, die zwölf Taten des Helden in antik Kunst und Literatur*, Münster-Köln, 1953 (4th ed. 1979, Eng. ed. 1980).

Brommer 1963, Brommer, F., *Die Skulpturen der Parthenon-Giebel*, Mair 1963.

Brommer 1967, Brommer, F., *Die Metopen des Parthenon*, Mainz, 1967.

Brommer 1971–6, Brommer, F., *Denkmälerlisten zur griechischen Heldensa I-IV*, Marburg, 1971–6.

Brommer 1973, Brommer, F., *Vasenlisten zur griechischen Heldensage* (3rd ed Marburg, 1973.

Brommer 1977, Brommer, F., *Der Parthenonfries*, Mainz, 1977.

Brommer 1979, Brommer, F., *The Sculptures of the Parthenon*, Londc 1979.

Brommer 1980, Brommer F., *Göttersagen in Vasenlisten*, Marburg, 1980.

Brommer 1982, Brommer, F., *Theseus, die Taten des griechischen Helden in a antiken Kunst und Literatur*, Darmstadt, 1982.

Brommer 1983, Brommer, F., *Odysseus, die Taten und Leiden des Helden antiker Kunst und Literatur*, Darmstadt, 1983.

Brommer 1984, Brommer, F., *Herakles II, die unkanonischen Taten des Held* Darmstadt, 1984.

Bron & Lissarrague 1984, Bron, C. & Lissarrague, F., 'Le vase à voir' in Béra 1984, 7–17.

Broneer 1971, Broneer, O., *Temple of Poseidon, Isthmia I*, Princeton, 1971.

Brouskari 1974, Brouskari, M.S., *The Acropolis Museum: a descripti catalogue*, Athens, 1974.

Bruneau & Ducat 1983, Bruneau, P. & Ducat, J., *Guide de Délos* (2nd ed Paris, 1983.

Brunnsåker 1971, Brunnsåker, S., *The Tyrantslayers of Kritios and Nesiotes* (2 ed.), Stockholm, 1971.

Buchner 1971, Buchner, G., 'Recent work at Pithekoussai (Ischia) 1965–71', *A 1970–1*, 63–7.

Burford 1963, Burford, A., 'The builders of the Parthenon' in *Parthenos a Parthenon, Supplement to Greece and Rome* 10 (1963), 23–35.

Burford 1972, Burford, A., *Craftsmen in Greek and Roman Society*, Londc 1972.

Burn 1983, Burn, A.R., 'CAH III', *CR* 33 (1983) 249–55.

Burn 1985, Burn, L., 'Honey pots: three white-ground cups by the Sotad Painter', *AK* 28 (1985) 93–105.

Burn 1987, Burn, L., *The Meidias Painter*, Oxford, 1987.

Burow 1989, Burow, J., *Der Antimenesmaler*, Kerameus 7, Mainz, 1989.

Callaghan 1980, Callaghan, P.J., 'The trefoil style and second-century Had vases', *ABSA* 75 (1980) 33–47.

Callaghan 1984, Callaghan, P.J., 'Knossian artists and Ptolemaic Alexandria' Adriani 1983 & 1984, 789–94.

Callaghan & Jones 1985, Callaghan, P.J. & Jones, R.E., 'Hadra hydriae a central Crete: a fabric analysis', *ABSA* 80 (1985) 1–17.

Callipolitis-Feytmans 1974, Callipolitis-Feytmans, D., *Les Plats attiques à figur noires*, Paris, 1974.

Cameron & Kuhrt 1983, Cameron, A. & Kuhrt, A., *Images of Women in* *ntiquity*, London, 1983.

Canciani 1978, Canciani, F., 'Lydos, der Sklave', *AK* 21 (1978) 17–22.

Carpenter 1984, Carpenter, T.H., *Summary Guide to* CVA, Oxford, 1984.

Carpenter 1986, Carpenter, T.H., *Dionysian Imagery in Archaic Greek Art*, xford, 1986.

Carpenter 1989, Carpenter, T.H., *Beazley Addenda* (2nd ed.), Oxford, 1989.

Carpenter 1991, Carpenter, T.H., *Art and Myth in Ancient Greece*, London, 991.

Carter 1972, Carter, J., 'The beginnings of narrative art in the Greek Geometric eriod', *ABSA* 67 (1972) 25–58.

Cartledge & Harvey 1985, Cartledge, P. & Harvey, F.D., *Crux, essays presented* *G.E.M. de Ste. Croix on his 75th birthday*, Exeter, 1985.

Caskey 1922, Caskey, L.D., *Geometry of Greek Vases*, Boston, 1922.

Caskey 1976, Caskey, M.E., 'Notes on relief pithoi of the Tenian-Boeotian roup', *AJA* 80 (1976) 19–41.

Caskey & Beazley 1954, Caskey, L.D. & Beazley, J.D., *Attic Vase-Paintings in* *e Museum of Fine Arts, Boston, II*, Oxford, 1954.

Casson 1938, Casson, S., 'The modern pottery trade in the Aegean', *Antiquity* 12 938) 464–73.

Chamoux 1953, Chamoux, F., *Cyrène sous la monarchie des Battiades*, Paris, 953.

Chamoux 1985, Chamoux, F., 'Du silphion' in Barker, Lloyd & Reynolds 1985, 65–72.

del Chiaro 1974, del Chiaro, M.A., *Etruscan Red-figured Vase-painting at Caere*, erkeley, 1974.

Christiansen and Melander 1988, Christiansen, J. and Melander, T., *Ancient* *reek and Related Pottery, Proceedings of the 3rd Symposium, Copenhagen* *ugust 31-September 4 1987*, Copenhagen, 1988.

Cleere 1989, Cleere, H. (ed.), *Archaeological Heritage Management in the Modern* *orld*, London, 1989.

Cohen 1970–1, Cohen, B., 'Observations on coral-red', *Marsyas* 15 (1970–1) –12.

Coldstream 1964, Coldstream, J.N., 'Motya, a Phoenician–Punic site near arsala, Sicily', *The Annual of the Leeds University Oriental Society* 4 (1962–3) 4–131.

Coldstream 1968, Coldstream, J.N., *Greek Geometric Pottery*, London, 1968.

Collis 1984, Collis, J., *The European Iron Age*, London, 1984.

Connell 1968, Connell, P., *Greek Ornament*, London, 1968.

Cook 1934–5, Cook, J.M., 'Protoattic pottery', *ABSA* 35 (1934–5) 165–219.

Cook 1948, Cook, R.M., 'Notes on the Homeric epigram to the potters', *CR* 62 948) 55–7.

Cook 1951, Cook, R.M., 'The Homeric epigram to the potters', *CR* 1 (1951) 9.

Cook 1954, Cook, R.M., *Corpus Vasorum Antiquorum Great Britain, London,* *ritish Museum 8 (13)*, London, 1954.

Cook 1955, Cook, R.M., 'Thucydides as Archaeologist', *ABSA* 50 (1955) 266–0.

Cook 1959, Cook, R.M., 'Die Bedeutung der bemalten Keramik für de griechischen Handel', *JDAI* 74 (1959) 114–23.

Cook 1961, Cook, R.M., 'The "double stoking tunnel" of Greek kilns', *ABSA* 5 (1961) 64–7.

Cook 1966, Cook, B.F., 'Inscribed Hadra vases', *Metropolitan Museum of A Papers 12*, New York, 1966.

Cook 1968–9, Cook, B.F., 'A dated Hadra vase in the Brooklyn Museum', *Th Brooklyn Museum Annual* 10 (1968–9) 114–38.

Cook 1969, Cook, R.M., 'A note on the absolute chronology of eighth an seventh centuries B.C.', *ABSA* 64 (1969) 13–15.

Cook 1971, Cook, R.M., '"Epoiesen" on Greek vases', *JHS* 91 (197 137–8.

Cook 1972, Cook, R.M., *Greek Painted Pottery* (2nd ed.), London, 1972.

Cook 1981, Cook, R.M., *Clazomenian Sarcophagi*, Kerameus 3, Mainz, 1981.

Cook 1983, Cook, R.M., 'Art and epic in archaic Greece', *BABesch.* 58 (198 1–10.

Cook 1984a, Cook, R.M., 'The Calke Wood kiln' in Brijder 1984, 63–6.

Cook 1984b, Cook, B.F., 'Some groups of Hadra vases' in Adriani 1983 an 1984, 795–803.

Cook 1984c, Cook, B.F., *The Elgin Marbles*, London, 1984.

Cook 1987a, Cook, R.M., 'Pots and Pisistratan propaganda', *JHS* 107 (198 167–9.

Cook 1987b, Cook, R.M., 'Artful crafts: a commentary', *JHS* 107 (1987) 169 71.

Cook 1987c, Cook, B.F., *Greek Inscriptions*, London, 1987.

Cook 1989, Cook, R.M., 'The Francis–Vickers chronology', *JHS* 109 (198 164–70.

Cook & Woodhead 1952, Cook, R.M. & Woodhead, A.G., 'Painted inscriptio on Chiot pottery', *ABSA* 47 (1952) 159–70.

Corbett 1960, Corbett, P.E., 'The Burgon and Blacas Tombs', *JHS* 80 (196 52–8.

Corbett 1965, Corbett, P.E., 'Preliminary sketch in Greek vase-painting', *JHS* 8 (1965) 16–28.

Cordano 1986, Cordano, F., *Antiche Fondazioni Greche. Sicilia e Ital Meridionale*, Palermo, 1986.

de la Coste-Messelière 1957, de la Coste-Messelière, P., *Sculpture du Trésor d Athéniens, Fouilles de Delphes IV. iv*, Paris, 1957.

Courbin 1963, Courbin, P. (ed.), *Etudes archéologiques*, Paris, 1963.

Courby 1922, Courby, F., *Les Vases grecs à reliefs*, Paris, 1922.

Crawford 1983, Crawford, M. (ed.), *Sources for Ancient History*, Cambridg 1983.

Crawford & Whitehead 1983, Crawford, M. & Whitehead, D., *Archaic a Classical Greece*, Cambridge, 1983.

Crosby 1955, Crosby, M., 'Five comic scenes from Athens', *Hesperia* 24 (195 76–84.

Cuomo di Caprio 1984, Cuomo di Caprio, N., 'Pottery kilns on pinakes fro Corinth' in Brijder 1984, 72–82.

Cuomo di Caprio 1985, Cuomo di Caprio, N., *La ceramica in archeologia*, ome, 1985.

Daltrop 1980, Daltrop, G., *Il Gruppo Mironiano di Atena e Marsia nei Musei aticani*, Rome, 1980.

Daux 1961, Daux, G., 'Chronique des Fouilles 1960', *BCH* 85 (1961) 601–954.

Daux & Hansen 1987, Daux, G. & Hansen, E., *Le Trésor de Siphnos, Fouilles de elphes II*, Paris, 1987.

Davies 1969, Davies, M.I., 'The Oresteia before Aischylos', *BCH* 93 (1969) 4–60.

Desborough 1952, Desborough, V.R. d'A., *Protogeometric Pottery*, Oxford, 52.

Despinis 1970, Despinis, G., 'Discovery of the scattered fragments and congnition of the type of Agorakritos' statue of Nemesis', *AAA* 3 (1970) 407– .

Despinis 1971, Despinis, G.I., Συμβολὴ στὴ μελέτη του ἔργου τοῦ γορακρίτου, Athens, 1971.

Diehl 1964, Diehl, E., *Die Hydria: Formgeschichte und Werwendung im Kult des ltertums*, Mainz, 1964.

Dohrn 1985, Dohrn, T., 'Schwarzgefirnsste Plakettenvasen', *RM* 92 (1985) 77– 06.

Dover 1978, Dover, K.J., *Greek Homosexuality*, London, 1978.

Ducat 1966, Ducat, J., *Les Vases plastiques rhodiens archaiques en terre cuite*, ris, 1966.

Dugas 1952, Dugas, C., *Les Vases attiques à figures rouges. Dèlos XXI*, Paris, 952.

Edwards 1957, Edwards, G.R., 'Panathenaics of Hellenistic and Roman times', *esperia* 26 (1957) 320–49 & 383.

Edwards 1975, Edwards, G.R., *Corinthian Hellenistic Pottery, Corinth VII.iii*, inceton, 1975.

Eisman 1974, Eisman, M.M., 'A further note on ΕΠΟΙΕΣΕΝ signatures', *JHS* 94 974) 172.

Eiteljorg 1980, Eiteljorg, H., 'The fast wheel, the multiple brush compass and thens as home of the Protogeometric style', *AJA* 84 (1980) 445–52.

Empereur & Garlan 1986, Empereur, J.-Y. & Garlan, Y., *Recherches sur les nphores grecques, Athens Colloquium 1984, BCH* Supplément XIII, Paris, 1986.

Engelmann 1980, Engelmann, H., *Die Inschriften von Ephesos* IV, Bonn, 1980.

Enklaar 1985, Enklaar, A.H., 'Chronologie et peintres de hydries de Hadra', *ABesch*. 60 (1985) 106–51.

Enklaar 1986, Enklaar, A.H., 'Les hydries de Hadra II: formes et ateliers', *ABesch*. 61 (1986) 41–65.

Ervin 1963, Ervin, M., 'A relief pithos from Mykonos', *ADelt* 18 (1963) 37–75.

Eschbach 1986, Eschbach, N., *Statuen auf Panathenäischen Preisamphoren des 4 s v. Chr.*, Mainz, 1986.

Evely 1988, Evely, D., 'The potters' wheel in Minoan Crete', *ABSA* 83 (1988) –126.

Farnsworth 1959, Farnsworth, M., 'Types of Greek glaze failure', *Archaeology* (1959) 242–50.

Farnsworth 1960, Farnsworth, M., 'Draw pieces as aids to correct firing', *AJA* 6 (1960) 72–5.

Farnsworth & Wisely 1958, Farnsworth, M. & Wisely, H., 'Fifth centu intentional red glaze', *AJA* 62 (1958) 165–73.

Fink 1974, Fink, F.F., *Hochzeitsszenen auf attischen schwarzfigurigen u rotfigurigen Vasen*, Diss., Vienna, 1974.

Forti 1965, Forti, L., *La ceramica di Gnathia*, Naples, 1965.

Francis 1990, Francis, E.D., *Image and Idea in fifth century Greece: art a literature after the Persian Wars*, London, 1990.

Francis & Vickers 1981, Francis, E.D. & Vickers, M., 'Leagros kalos', *PCPS* 2((1981) 97–136.

Francis & Vickers 1983, Francis, E.D. & Vickers, M., 'Signa priscae artis: Eretr and Siphnos', *JHS* 103 (1983) 49–67.

Francis & Vickers 1985, Francis, E.D. & Vickers, M.J., 'Greek Geometric potte at Hama and its implications for Near Eastern chronology', *Levant* 17 (198 131–8.

Francis & Vickers 1988, Francis, E.D. & Vickers, M.J., 'The Agora revisite Athenian chronology c. 500–450 B.C.', *ABSA* 83 (1988) 143–67.

Fraser 1972, Fraser, P.M., *Ptolemaic Alexandria*, Oxford, 1972.

Frel 1973, Frel, J., *Panathenaic Prize Amphoras*, Athens, 1973.

Freyer-Schauenburg 1986, Freyer-Schauenburg, B., 'Eine attisch rotfigurige Phia in Kiel' in Schauenburg 1986, 115–20.

Fuchs 1979, Fuchs, W., *Die Skulptur der Griechen* (2nd ed.), Munich, 1979.

Galinsky 1969, Galinsky, G.K., *Aeneas, Sicily and Rome*, Princeton, 1969.

Gardin 1976, Gardin, J.C., *Code pour l'analyse des formes de poteries*, Par 1976.

Gardin 1978, Gardin, J.C., *Code pour l'analyse des ornaments*, Paris, 1978.

Garlan 1983, Garlan, Y., 'Le commerce des amphores grecques' in Garnsey a Whittaker 1983, 37–44.

Garland 1985, Garland, R., *The Greek Way of Death*, London, 1985.

Garland 1990, Garland, R., *The Greek Way of Life*, London, 1990.

Garnsey, Hopkins & Whittaker 1983, Garnsey, P.D., Hopkins, K. & Whittak C.R., *Trade in the Ancient Economy*, London, 1983.

Garnsey & Whittaker 1983, Garnsey, P.D. & Whittaker, C.R., *Trade a Famine in Classical Antiquity* (Cambridge Philological Society Suppl. Vol. 8 Cambridge, 1983.

Gentili 1988, Gentili, B., *Poetry and its Public in Ancient Greece*, Baltimo 1988.

Gill 1986a, Gill, D.W.J., 'Classical Greek fictile imitations of precious met vases' in Vickers 1986, 9–30.

Gill 1986b, Gill, D.W.J., 'Two Herodotean dedications from Naukratis', *JHS* 1 (1986) 184–7.

Gill 1987a, Gill, D.W.J., 'Metru. menece: an Etruscan painted inscription on mid 5th century B.C. red-figure cup from Populonia', *Antiquity* 61 (1987) 82–7.

Gill 1987b, Gill, D.W.J., 'An Attic lamp in Reggio: the largest batch notati outside Athens', *OJA* 6 (1987) 121–5.

Gill 1988a, Gill, D.W.J., 'Expressions of wealth: Greek art and society', *ntiquity* 62 (1988) 735–43.

Gill 1988b, Gill, D.W.J., 'Trade in Greek decorated pottery: some corrections', *JA* 7 (1988) 369–70.

Gill 1988c, Gill, D.W.J., 'The distribution of Greek vases and long distance trade' Christiansen and Melander 1988, 175–85.

Gill 1988d, Gill, D.W.J., 'Silver anchors and cargoes of oil: some observations on hoenician trade in the western Mediterranean', *PBSR* 43 (1988) 1–12.

Gill & Vickers 1989, Gill, D.W.J. & Vickers, M., 'Pots and kettles', *RA* 1989, 79–303.

Gill & Vickers 1990, Gill, D.W.J. & Vickers, M., 'Reflected glory: pottery and recious metal', *JDAI* 105 (1990) 1–30.

Giuliani 1977, Giuliani, L., 'Alexander in Ruvo, Eretria und Sidon', *AK* 20 1977) 26–42.

Glotz 1926, Glotz, G., *Ancient Greece at Work*, London, 1926.

Gomme, Andrewes & Dover 1970, Gomme, A.W., Andrewes, A. & Dover, K.J., *istorical Commentary on Thucydides, Vol. IV*, Oxford, 1970.

Grace 1974, Grace, V.R., 'Revisions in early Hellenistic chronology', *AM* 89 1974) 193–203.

Grace 1979, Grace, V.R., *Amphoras and the Ancient Wine Trade*, Princeton, 979 (rev. ed.).

Grace 1985, Grace, V.R., 'The Middle Stoa dated by amphora stamps', *Hesperia* 4 (1985) 1–53.

Graef & Langlotz 1925, Graef, B. & Langlotz, E., *Die Antiken Vasen von der kropolis zu Athen I*, Berlin, 1925.

Graef & Langlotz 1933, Graef, B. & Langlotz, E., *Die Antiken Vasen von der kropolis zu Athen II & III*, Berlin, 1933.

Graham 1982, Graham, A.J., 'The colonial expansion of Greece' and 'The Vestern Greeks' in Boardman & Hammond 1982, 83–175.

Grandjean 1985, Grandjean, Y., 'Tuyères ou supports?', *BCH* 109 (1985) 265–9.

Green 1976, Green, J.R., *Gnathia Pottery in the Akademisches Kunstmuseum onn*, Mainz, 1976.

Green 1979, Green, J.R., 'Ears of corn and other offerings' in Trendall 1979, 1–90.

Green 1985, Green, J.R., 'A representation of the *Birds* of Aristophanes', *Greek ases* II (1985) 95–118.

Greenfield 1989, Greenfield, J., *The Return of Cultural Treasures*, Cambridge, 989.

Greifenhagen 1982, Greifenhagen, A., 'Eichellekythen', *RA* 1982, 151–62.

van der Grinten 1966, van der Grinten, E.F., *On the Composition of the Medallions in the Interior of Greek Black- and Red-figured Kylixes*, Amsterdam, 966.

Gude 1933, Gude, M., *A History of Olynthus*, Baltimore, 1933.

Guerrini 1964, Guerrini, L., *Vasi di Hadra: tentativo di sistemazione cronologica una classe ceramica*, Rome, 1964.

Guy 1981, Guy, R., 'A ram's head rhyton signed by Charinos', *Arts in Virgin* 21 (1981) 2–15.

Hambidge 1920, Hambidge, J., *Dynamic Symmetry: the Greek Vase*, Ne Haven, 1920.

Hampe & Winter 1962, Hampe, R. & Winter, A., *Bei Töpfern und Töpferinn in Kreta, Messenien und Zypern*, Mainz, 1962.

Hampe & Winter 1965, Hampe, R. & Winter, A., *Bei Töpfern und Zieglern südItalien, Sizilien und Griechenland*, Mainz, 1965.

Hannestad 1988, Hannestad, L., 'The Athenian potter and the home market' Christiansen and Melander 1988, 222–30.

Harris 1964, Harris, H.A., *Greek Athletes and Athletics*, London, 1964.

Harris 1972, Harris, H.A., *Sport in Greece and Rome*, London, 1972.

Harris 1989, Harris, W.V., *Ancient Literacy*, Harvard, 1989.

Harrison 1967, Harrison, E.B., 'Athena and Athens in the east pediment of th Parthenon', *AJA* 71 (1967) 27–58.

Harrison 1971, Harrison, E.B., 'The Victory of Kallimachos', *GRBS* 12 (197 5–24.

Harvey 1976, Harvey, F.D., 'Sostratos of Aegina', *La Parola del Passato* 3 (1976) 206–14.

Harvey 1984, Harvey, F.D., 'The Conspiracy of Agasias and Aeschines', *Klio* 6 (1984) 58–73.

Haspels 1927–8, Haspels, C.H.E., 'How the aryballos was suspended', *ABSA* 2 (1927–8) 216–23.

Haspels 1936, Haspels, C.H.E., *Attic Black-figure Lekythoi*, Paris, 1936.

Haspels 1969, Haspels, C.H.E., 'A lekythos in Six's technique' *Muse* 3 (196 24–8.

Hausmann 1959, Hausmann, U., *Hellenistische Reliefbecher*, Kohlhamme 1959.

Havelock 1982, Havelock, E.A., *The Literate Revolution in Greece and i Cultural Consequences*, Princeton, 1982.

Havelock 1986, Havelock, E.A., *The Muse Learns to Write*, Yale, 1986.

Hawkins 1982, Hawkins, J.D., 'The Neo-Hittite States in Syria and Anatolia' i Boardman, Edwards, Hammond & Sollberger 1982, 372–441.

Hayes 1984, Hayes, J.W., *Greek and Italian Black Gloss Wares and Relate Wares in the Royal Ontario Museum*, Toronto, 1984.

Heilmeyer 1981, Heilmeyer, W.-D., 'Antike Werkstättenfunde in Griechenland AA 1981, 440–53.

Hellström 1965, Hellström, P., *Labraunda, Swedish Excavations and Research II, ii Pottery of Classical and Later Date, Terracotta Lamps and Glass*, Lund, 196

Hemelrijk 1984, Hemelrijk, J.M., *Caeretan Hydriae*, Kerameus 5, Mainz, 1984

Henle 1973, Henle, J., *Greek Myths, A Vase Painter's Notebook*, Bloomingto 1973.

Herbert 1977, Herbert, S., *The Red-figured Pottery, Corinth VII. iv*, Princeto 1977.

Higgins 1959, Higgins, R.A., *Catalogue of the Terracottas in the Department Greek and Roman Antiquities, British Museum, Vol. II, Plastic Vases*, Londo 1959.

Hölscher 1973, Hölscher, T., *Griechische Historienbilder des 5. und 4. 'ahrhunderts v. Chr.*, Würzburg, 1973.

Hölscher 1974, Hölscher, T., 'Ein Kelchkrater mit Perserkampf', *AK* 17 (1974) '8–85.

Hoffmann 1962, Hoffmann, H., *Attic Red-figured Rhyta*, Mainz, 1962.

Hoffmann 1967, Hoffmann, H., *Tarentine Rhyta*, Mainz, 1967.

Hoffmann 1977, Hoffmann, H., *Sexual and Asexual Pursuit: a structuralist ɪpproach to Greek vase painting*, RAI Occasional Papers no. 34, 1977.

Hoffmann 1979, Hoffmann, H., 'In the wake of Beazley' *Hephaistos* 1 (1979) ;1–70.

Hoffmann 1985–6, Hoffmann, H., 'Iconography and iconology', *Hephaistos* '–8 (1985–6) 61–6.

Hoffmann 1988, Hoffmann, H., 'Why did the Greeks need imagery? An nthropological approach to the study of Greek vase painting', *Hephaistos* 9 (1988) 43–62.

Hoffmann 1989, Hoffmann, H., 'Rhyta and Kantharoi in Greek ritual', *Greek 'ases* IV (1989) 131–66.

Hooker 1980, Hooker, J.T., *The Ancient Spartans*, London, 1980.

van Hoorn 1951, van Hoorn, G., *Choes and Anthesteria*, Leiden, 1951.

Hopper 1979, Hopper, R.J., *Trade and Industry in Classical Greece*, London, 979.

Howard & Johnson 1954, Howard, S. & Johnson, F.P., 'The Saint-Valentin 'ases', *AJA* 58 (1954) 191–207.

Hurwit 1977, Hurwit, J., 'Image and frame in Greek art', *AJA* 81 (1977) 1–30.

Hurwit 1985, Hurwit, J., *The Art and Culture of Early Greece, 1100–480 B.C.*, :haca, 1985.

Immerwahr 1964, Immerwahr, H.R., 'Book rolls on Attic vases' in Ullman 1964.

Immerwahr 1973, Immerwahr, H.R., 'More book rolls on Attic vases', *AK* 16 1973) 143–7.

Immerwahr 1984, Immerwahr, H.R., 'The Signatures of Pamphaios', *AJA* 88 1984) 341–52.

Immerwahr 1990, Immerwahr, H.R., *The Attic Script*, Oxford, 1990.

Isserlin & du Plat Taylor 1974, Isserlin, B.J.J. & du Plat Taylor, J., *Motya I*, eiden, 1974.

Jackson 1976, Jackson, D.A., *East Greek Influence on Attic Vases*, Society for the romotion of Hellenic Studies, Supplementary Paper no. XIII, London, 1976.

Jacobsthal 1927, Jacobsthal, P., *Ornamente griechischer Vasen*, Berlin, 1927.

Jacobsthal & Langsdorff 1929, Jacobsthal, P. & Langsdorff, A., *Die ronzeschnabelkannen*, Berlin, 1929.

Jeffery 1961, Jeffery, L.H., *The Local Scripts of Archaic Greece*, Oxford, 1961 nd ed. 1990).

Jeffery 1977, Jeffery, L.H., *Archaic Greece*, London, 1977.

Jenkins 1986, Jenkins, I., *Greek and Roman Life*, London, 1986.

Jentel 1968, Jentel, M.-O., *Corpus Vasorum Antiquorum, France, Paris, Louvre, 5 (23)*, Paris, 1968.

Jentel 1976, Jentel, M.-O., *Les Gutti et les askoi à reliefs étrusques et apuliens*, eiden, 1976.

Joffroy 1979, Joffroy, R., *Vix et ses trésors*, Paris, 1979.

Johansen 1967, Johansen, K.F., *The Iliad in Early Greek Art*, Copenhagen, 196

Johnston 1973, Johnston, A.W., 'A graffito from Vassallaggi', *ZPE* 12 (197 265–9.

Johnston 1974, Johnston, A.W., 'Trademarks on Greek vases', *Greece and Ron* 21 (1974) 138–52.

Johnston 1978, Johnston, A.W., 'Lists of contents: Attic vases', *AJA* 82 (197 222–6.

Johnston 1979, Johnston, A.W., *Trademarks on Greek Vases*, Warminster, 197

Johnston 1985a, Johnston, A.W., 'A fourth century graffito from th Kerameikos', *AM* 100 (1985) 293–307.

Johnston 1985b, Johnston, A.W., review of Scheibler 1983, *AJA* 89 (198 181–3.

Johnston 1987a, Johnston, A.W., 'IG II 2 2311 and the number of Panathena amphorae', *ABSA* 82 (1987) 125–9.

Johnston 1987b, Johnston, A.W., 'Amasis and the vase trade' in True 198 125–40.

Johnston & Jones 1978, Johnston, A.W. & Jones, R.E., 'The "SOS" amphora *ABSA* 73 (1978) 103–41.

Jones 1984, Jones, R.E., 'Greek potters' clays' in Brijder 1984, 21–30.

Jones 1986, Jones, R.E., *Greek and Cypriot Pottery, a Review of Scientif Studies*, Athens, 1986.

Jones & Catling 1986, Jones, R.E. & Catling, H.W., *Science in Archaeolog* (Fitch Occasional Papers 2), Athens, 1986.

Jones, Graham & Sackett 1973, Jones, J.E., Graham, A.J. & Sackett, L.H., 'A Attic country house below the cave of Pan at Vari', *ABSA* 68 (1973) 355–452.

Kaempf-Dimitriadou 1979, Kaempf-Dimitriadou, S., *Die Liebe der Götter in de attischen Kunst des 5. Jahrhunderts v. Chr.*, Bern, 1979.

Kahil 1972, Kahil, L., 'Un nouveau vase plastique du potier Sotadès, au Muse du Louvre', *RA* 1972, 271–84.

Kahil 1977, Kahil, L., 'L'Artémis de Brauron: rites et mystère', *AK* 20 (197 86–98.

Kahil 1981–, Kahil, L., *Lexicon Iconographicum Mythologiae Classicae I* Zürich and Munich, 1981–.

Kannicht 1982, Kannicht, R., 'Poetry and art: Homer and the monumen afresh', *Classical Antiquity* 1 (1982) 70–86.

Kanowski 1984, Kanowski, M.G., *Containers of Classical Greece*, St. Luci 1984.

Karouzou 1956, Karouzou, S., *The Amasis Painter*, Oxford, 1956.

Kearsley 1989, Kearsley, R., *The Pendent Semi-circle Skyphos*, *BICS*, Suppleme 44, 1989.

Kehrberg 1982, Kehrberg, I., 'The Potter-painter's wife', *Hephaistos* 4 (198 25–35.

Keil 1913, Keil, J., 'Ephesische Bürgerrechts- und Proxeniendekrete ausde vierten und dritten Jahrhundert v. Chr.', *JOAI* 16 (1913) 231–44.

Kern 1913, Kern, O., *Inscriptiones Graecae, Tabulae in usum scholarum*, Bon 1913.

Kilinski 1982, Kilinski, K., 'Theodoros: a new Boeotian potter', *AJA* 86 (1982) 272.

Kimmig 1988, Kimmig, W., *Das Kleinaspergle. Studien zu einem Füstengrabhügel der frühen Latènezeit bei Stuttgart*, Stuttgart, 1988.

Kirchner 1940, Kirchner, J. (ed.), *Inscriptiones Graecae, II-III, Inscriptiones Atticae Euclidis anno posteriores*, ed. minor, Part 3, Berlin, 1940.

Kleinbauer 1964, Kleinbauer, E., 'The Dionysios Painter and the "Corintho-Attic" problem', *AJA* 68 (1964) 355–70.

Kleine 1973, Kleine, J., *Untersuchungen zur Chronologie der attischen Kunst von Peisistratos bis Themistokles*, Tübingen, 1973.

Knauer 1985, Knauer, E.R., 'οὐ γὰρ ἦν ἀμίς: a chous by the Oionokles Painter', *Greek Vases* II (1985) 91–100.

Knigge 1970, Knigge, U., 'Neue Scherben von Gefässen des Kleophrades-Malers', *AM* 85 (1970) 1–22.

Knigge 1972a, Knigge, U., 'Untersuchungen bei den Gesandtenstelen im Kerameikos zu Athen', *AA* 1972, 584–629.

Knigge 1972b, Knigge, U., 'Die Gesandtenstelen im Kerameikos', *AAA* 5 (1972) 258–65.

Knigge 1976, Knigge, U., *Der Südhügel, Kerameikos, Ergebnisse der Ausgrabungen IX*, Berlin, 1976.

Koehler 1979, Koehler, C.G., 'Transport amphoras as evidence for trade', *Arch. News* 8 (1979) 54–61.

Koehler 1981, Koehler, C.G., 'Corinthian developments in the study of trade in the fifth century B.C.', *Hesperia* 50 (1981) 449–58.

Koehler 1986, Koehler, C.G., 'Handling of Greek transport amphoras' in Empereur and Garlan 1986, 49–67.

Köpcke 1964, Köpcke, G., 'Golddekorierte attische schwarzfirniskeramik des vierten Jahrhunderts v. Chr.', *AM* 79 (1964) 22–84.

Koumanoudes 1978, Koumanoudes, P., 'A Marathon', *AAA* 11 (1978) 232–44.

Kourou 1987, Kourou, N., 'A propos de quelques ateliers de céramique fine, non tournée du type "Argien Monochrome"', *BCH* 111 (1987) 31–53.

Kourou 1988, Kourou, N., 'Handmade pottery and trade: the case of the "Argive monochrome" ware' in Christiansen and Melander 1988, 314–24.

Kurtz 1975, Kurtz, D.C., *Athenian White Lekythoi: Patterns and Painters*, Oxford, 1975.

Kurtz 1983, Kurtz, D.C., 'Gorgos' cup: an essay in connoisseurship' *JHS* 103 (1983) 68-86.

Kurtz 1984, Kurtz, D.C., 'Vases for the dead, an Attic selection 750–400 B.C.' in Brijder 1984, 314–28.

Kurtz 1985a, Kurtz, D.C., 'Beazley and the connoisseurship of Greek vases', *Greek Vases* II (1985) 237–50.

Kurtz 1985b, Kurtz, D., *Beazley and Oxford*, Oxford, 1985.

Kurtz 1989, Kurtz, D.C. (ed.), *Greek Vases, Lectures by J.D. Beazley*, Oxford, 1989.

Kurtz & Boardman 1971, Kurtz, D.C. & Boardman, J., *Greek Burial Customs*, London, 1971.

Kurtz & Boardman 1986, Kurtz, D.C. & Boardman, J., 'Booners', *Greek Vase* III (1986) 35–70.

Kyrieleis 1986, Kyrieleis, H. (ed.), *Archaische und Klassische Griechische Plastik*, Mainz, 1986.

Lancaster 1947, Lancaster, O., *Classical Landscape with Figures*, London, 1947.

Landwehr 1985, Landwehr, C., *Die antiken Gipsabgüsse aus Baiae*, Berlin, 1985.

Lane 1933–4, Lane, E.A., 'Laconian Vase-Painting', *ABSA* 34 (1933–4) 99–189.

Lane 1971, Lane, A., *Greek Pottery*, London, 1971 (3rd ed.).

Lang 1960, Lang, M., *The Athenian Citizen*, Princeton, 1960.

Lang 1974, Lang, M., *Graffiti in the Athenian Agora*, Princeton, 1974.

Lang 1976, Lang, M., *Graffiti and Dipinti, The Athenian Agora XXI*, Princeton, 1976.

Lang 1990, Lang, M.L., *Ostraka, The Athenian Agora XXV*, Princeton, 1990.

Lang & Crosby 1964, Lang, M. & Crosby, M., *Weights, Measures and Tokens The Athenian Agora X*, Princeton, 1964.

Lazzarini 1973–4, Lazzarini, M.L., 'I nomi dei vasi greci nelle iscrizioni dei vasi stessi', *Arch. Class.* 25–6 (1973–4) 341–75.

Leipen 1971, Leipen, N., *Athena Parthenos: a reconstruction*, Toronto, 1971.

Lemos 1986, Lemos, A.A., 'Archaic Chian Pottery in Chios' in Boardman & Vaphopoulou-Richardson 1986, 233–49.

Leroux 1913, Leroux, G., *Lagynos, recherches sur la céramique et l'art ornemental hellénistiques*, Paris, 1913.

Lévêque & Morel 1980, Lévêque, P. & Morel, J.-P. (ed.), *Céramiques hellénistiques et romaines*, Paris, 1980.

Lewis 1974, Lewis, D.M., 'The Kerameikos Ostraka', *ZPE* 14 (1974) 1–4.

Lewis 1981, Lewis, D.M., *Inscriptiones Graecae I*(3rd ed.), Berlin, 1981.

Lewis 1986, Lewis, D.M., 'Temple Inventories in Ancient Greece' in Vickers 1986, 71–81.

Lezzi-Hafter 1982, Lezzi-Hafter, A., *Der Schuwalowmaler. Ein Kannenwerkstatt der Parthenonzeit*, Kerameus 2, Mainz, 1982.

Lezzi-Hafter 1988, Lezzi-Hafter, A., *Der Eretria-maler, Werke und Weggefährten*, Kerameus 6, Mainz, 1988.

Lissarrague 1987, Lissarrague, F., *Un Flot d'images: une esthétique du banquet grec*, Paris, 1987. (Eng. ed. *The Aesthetics of the Greek Banquet, Images of Wine and Ritual*, trans. Andrew Szegedy-Maszak, Princeton, 1990)

Lissarrague & Thelamon 1983, Lissarrague, F. & Thelamon, F., *Image et céramique grecque, actes du colloque de Rouen, 25–26 novembre, 1982*, Rouen 1983.

Lloyd 1979, Lloyd, J. (ed.), *Excavations at Sidi Khebrish, Bengahzi (Berenice) II* Supplement to *Libya Antiqua*, 1979.

Lorber 1979, Lorber, F., *Inschriften auf korinthischen Vasen*, Berlin, 1979.

Lullies 1940, Lullies, R., 'Zur boiotischen rotfigurigen Vasenmalerei', *AM* 65 (1940) 1–27.

McCredie 1966, McCredie, J.J., *Fortified Military Camps in Attica, Hesperia* Supplement XI, 1966.

MacDonald 1981, MacDonald, B.R., 'The emigration of potters from Athens in

e late fifth century B.C. and its effect on the Attic pottery industry', *AJA* 85 981) 159–68.

MacDonald 1982, MacDonald, B.R., 'The import of Attic pottery to Corinth and e question of trade during the Peloponnesian War', *JHS* 102 (1982) 113–23.

McGrail 1989, McGrail, S., 'The shipment of traded goods and of ballast in ntiquity', *OJA* 8 (1989) 353–8.

McPhee 1981, McPhee, I., 'Some red-figure vase-painters of the Chalcidice', *BSA* 76 (1981) 297–308.

McPhee 1983, McPhee, I., 'Local red figure from Corinth 1973–80', *Hesperia* 52 983) 137–53.

McPhee 1986, McPhee, I., 'Laconian red-figure from the British excavations in parta', *ABSA* 81 (1986) 153–64.

McPhee & Trendall 1987, McPhee, I. & Trendall, A.D., *Greek Red-figured ish-plates*, Basel, 1987.

McPhee & Trendall 1990, McPhee, I. & Trendall, A.D., 'Addenda to *Greek ed-figured Fish-plates*', *AK* 33 (1990) 31–51.

Maffre 1975, Maffre J.J., 'Collection Paul Canellopoulos: Vases Béotiens', *BCH* 9 (1975) 409–520.

Mallwitz & Schiering 1964, Mallwitz, A. & Schiering, W., *Die Werkstatt des heidias in Olympia (Olympische Forschungen V)*, Berlin, 1964.

March 1987, March, J.R., *The Creative Poet*, *BICS*, Supplement 49, London, 987.

Markle 1985, Markle, M.M., 'Jury pay and assembly pay at Athens' in Cartledge nd Harvey 1985, 265–97.

Martelli 1987, Martelli, M., *Le ceramica degli Etruschi: la pittura vascolare*, ovara, 1987.

Mayo 1982, Mayo, M.E., *The Art of South Italy: Vases from Magna Graecia*, ichmond, Virginia, 1982.

Meiggs 1982, Meiggs, R., *Trees and Timber in the ancient Mediterranean World*, xford, 1982.

Meiggs & Lewis 1969, Meiggs, R. & Lewis, D., *A Selection of Greek Historical nscriptions to the End of the Fifth Century B.C.*, Oxford, 1969 (rev. ed. 1989).

Mellink 1973, Mellink, M., 'Excavations at Karatas-Semayük and Elmali, 1972', *JA* 77 (1973) 293–303.

Mertens 1974, Mertens, J.R., 'Attic white-ground cups: a special class of vases', *MJ* 9 (1974) 91–108.

Mertens 1977, Mertens, J., *Attic White-ground – its development on shapes other an lekythoi*, Diss., New York, 1977.

Metzger 1951, Metzger, H., *Les Représentations dans la céramique attique du Ve siècle*, Paris, 1951.

Metzler 1969, Metzler, D., 'Eine attische Kleinmeisterschale mit Töpferszenen in arlsruhe', *AA* 1969, 138–52.

Meyer 1977, Meyer, K.E., *The Plundered Past, the traffic in art treasures*, armondsworth, rev. ed. 1977.

Millar 1983, Millar, F., 'Epigraphy' in Crawford 1983, 80–136.

Milne 1945, Milne, M.J., 'A prize for wool-working', *AJA* 49 (1945) 528–33.

Mingazzini 1967, Mingazzini, P., 'Qual'era la forma del vaso chiamato dai grec kothon?', *AA* 1967, 344–66.

Mommsen 1975, Mommsen, H., *Der Affekter*, Kerameus 1, Mainz, 1975.

Moon 1983, Moon, W.G. (ed.), *Ancient Greek Art & Iconography*, Madison Wisconsin, 1983.

Moore 1977, Moore, M.B., 'The gigantomachy of the Siphnian Treasury reconstruction of the three lacunae', *BCH Supplement* IV (1977) 305–35.

Moore 1985, Moore, M.B., 'The west frieze of the Siphnian Treasury: a new reconstruction', *BCH* 109 (1985)131–56.

Moore & von Bothmer 1972, Moore, M.B. & von Bothmer, D., 'A neck amphora in the collection of Walter Bareiss', *AJA* 76 (1972) 1–11.

Moore & Philippides 1986, Moore, M.B. & Philippides, M.Z.P., *Attic Black figured Pottery*, *The Athenian Agora XXIII*, Princeton, 1986.

Morel 1980, Morel, J.P., 'La céramique campanienne: acquis et problèmes' in Lévêque & Morel 1980.

Morel 1981, Morel, J.P., *Céramique campanienne: les formes*, Rome, 1981.

Morel 1983, Morel, J.P., 'La céramique comme indice du commerce antiqu (réalités et interprétations)' in Garnsey & Whittaker 1983, 66–74.

Morris 1984, Morris, S.P., *The Black and White Style*, New Haven & London 1984.

Morris 1985, Morris, S.P., 'ΛΑΣΑΝΑ: a contribution to the ancient Greek kitchen', *Hesperia* 54 (1985) 393–409.

Morrison & Coates 1986, Morrison, J.S. & Coates, J.F., *The Athenian Trireme* Cambridge, 1986.

Morrison & Williams 1968, Morrison, J.S. & Williams, R.T., *Greek Oared Ship 900–322 B.C.*, Cambridge, 1968.

Murray 1975, Murray, R.L., *The Protogeometric Style: the First Greek Style* Göteborg, 1975.

Murray 1990, Murray, O. (ed.), *Sympotica, a symposium on the* Symposion Oxford, 1990.

Murray and Price 1990, Murray, O. and Price, S. (eds.), *The Greek City: from Homer to Alexander*, Oxford, 1990.

Neeft 1987, Neeft, C.W., *Protocorinthian Subgeometric Aryballoi*, Amsterdam 1987.

Noble 1966, Noble, J.V., *The Techniques of Painted Attic Pottery*, London, 196 (rev. ed. 1988).

Noble 1988, see Noble 1966.

Nogara 1951, Nogara, B., 'Un frammento de Douris nel Museo Gregoriano Etrusco', *JHS* 71 (1951) 129-32.

Oakley 1990, Oakley, J.H., *The Phiale Painter*, Kerameus 8, Mainz, 1990.

Ohly 1965, Ohly D., 'Kerameikos-Grabung Tätigkeitsbericht 1956-61', *AA* 196 277–376.

Olin & Franklin 1980, Olin, J.S. & Franklin, A.D. (edd.), *Archaeologic Ceramics*, Washington, 1980.

Osborne 1983–4, Osborne, R., 'The myth of propaganda and the propaganda of myth', *Hephaistos* 5–6 (1983–4) 61–70.

Osborne 1989, Osborne, R., 'A crisis in archaeological history. The sevent

:entury in Attica', *ABSA* 84 (1989) 297–322.

Overbeck 1959, Overbeck, J.A. *Die antiken Schriftquellen zur Geschichte der ›ildende Künste bei den Griechen*, Hildersheim, 1959.

de Paepe, de Paepe, P., 'A petrological study of coarse wares from Thorikos, S.E. Attica (Greece)' in *Miscellanea Graeca 2, Technological Studies*, Gent, 1979, 61–88.

Parke 1977, Parke, H.W., *Festivals of the Athenians*, London, 1977.

Payne 1925–6, Payne, H.G.G., 'On the Thermon metopes', *ABSA* 27 (1925–6) 124–32.

Payne 1927–8, Payne, H.G.G., 'Early Greek vases from Knossos', *ABSA* 29 1927–8) 224–98.

Payne 1931, Payne, H.G.G., *Necrocorinthia*, Oxford, 1931.

Payne 1933, Payne, H.G.G., *Protokorinthische Vasenmalerei*, Berlin, 1933.

Peacock 1982, Peacock, D.P.S., *Pottery in the Roman World: an ethno-archaeological approach*, London, 1982.

Peacock & Williams 1986, Peacock, D.P.S. & Williams, D.F., *Amphorae and the Roman Economy: an introductory guide*, London, 1986.

Peek 1955, Peek, W., *Griechische Vers-Inschriften I Grab-Epigramme*, Berlin, .955.

Pemberton 1970, Pemberton, E.G., 'The Vrysoula Classical Deposit from Ancient Corinth', *Hesperia* 39 (1970) 265–307.

Perlzweig 1963, Perlzweig, J., *Lamps from the Athenian Agora*, Princeton, 1963.

Perreault 1986, Perreault, J.Y., 'Les importations attiques au Proche-Orient du VIe au milieu du Ve', *BCH* 110 (1986)145–75.

Petrakos 1981, Petrakos, B., 'La base de la Némésis d'Agoracrite', *BCH* 105 1981) 227–53.

Petrakos 1986, Petrakos, B., 'Προβλήματα της βάσης του αγάλματος της Νεμέσεως' in Kyrieleis 1986, II 89–107.

Petrie 1930, Petrie, F., *Decorative Patterns of the Ancient World*, London, 1930.

Philippaki 1967, Philippaki, B.,*The Attic Stamnos*, Oxford, 1967.

Pianu 1982, Pianu, G., *Ceramiche Etrusche sovradipinte (Tarquinia)*, Rome 982.

Picard & de la Coste-Messelière 1928, Picard, C. & de la Coste-Messelière, P., *Les Trésors 'ioniques', Fouilles de Delphes IV. II*, Paris, 1928.

Picard & de la Coste-Messelière 1931, Picard, C. & de la Coste-Messelière, P., *Sculptures des temples, Fouilles de Delphes IV.III*, Paris, 1931.

Pinney 1984, Pinney, G.F., 'For the heroes are at hand', *JHS* 104 (1984) 181–3.

Pipili 1987, Pipili, M., *Laconian Iconography of the Sixth Century*, Oxford, 987.

Prag 1985, Prag, A.J.N.W., *The Oresteia: Iconographic and Narrative Tradition*, Warminster, 1985.

Preuner 1920, Preuner, E., 'Archäologisch-Epigraphisches', *JDAI* 35 (1920) 59–2.

Pritchett 1953 & 1956, Pritchett, W.K., 'The Attic Stelai Parts I and II', *Hesperia* 2 (1953) 225–311 and 25 (1956) 178–328.

de Puma 1968, de Puma, R.D., 'Preliminary sketches on some fragments by Makron in Philadelphia and Bryn Mawr', *AJA* 72 (1968) 152–4.

Rasmussen 1979, Rasmussen, T.B., *Bucchero Pottery from Southern Etruri* Cambridge, 1979.

Rasmussen 1985, Rasmussen, T., 'Etruscan shapes in Attic pottery', *AK* 2 (1985) 33–9.

Raubitschek 1939–40, Raubitschek, A.E., 'Early Attic votive monuments', *ABS* 40 (1939–40) 28–36.

Raubitschek 1949, Raubitschek, A.E., *Dedications from the Athenian Akropoli* Cambridge, Mass., 1949.

Raubitschek 1966, Raubitschek, I.K., 'Early Boeotian potters', *Hesperia* 3 (1966) 154–65.

Rhodes 1981, Rhodes, P.J., *A Commentary on the Aristotelian* Athenaio Politeia, Oxford, 1981.

Rice 1984, Rice, P. (ed.), *Pots and Potters: Current Approaches in Ceram Archaeology*, Los Angeles, University of California Press, 1984.

Rice 1987, Rice, P.M., *Pottery Analysis: a source book*, Chicago, 1987.

Richter 1923, Richter, G.M.A., *The Craft of the Athenian Potter*, New Have 1923.

Richter 1941, Richter, G.M.A., 'A Greek silver phiale in the Metropolita Museum', *AJA* 45 (1941) 363–89.

Richter 1958, Richter, G.M.A., *Attic Red-figured Vases: a survey*, New Have 1958 (2nd ed.).

Richter 1967, Richter, I., *Das Kopfgefäss. Zur Typologie einer Gafässform*, Diss Cologne, 1967.

Richter & Milne 1935, Richter, G.M.A. & Milne, M.J., *Shapes and Names Athenian Vases*, New York, 1935.

Ridgway 1970, Ridgway, B.S., *The Severe Style in Greek Sculpture*, Princeto 1970.

Ridgway 1977, Ridgway, B.S., *The Archaic Style in Greek Sculpture*, Princeto 1977.

Ridgway 1981, Ridgway, B.S., *Fifth-Century Styles in Greek Sculpture*, Princeton 1981.

Ridgway 1984, Ridgway, D., *L'Alba della Magna Grecia*, Milan, 1984.

Ridgway 1988a, Ridgway, D., 'The Pithekoussai shipwreck' in Betts, Hooker an Green 1988, 97–107.

Ridgway 1988b, Ridgway, D., 'Italy from the Bronze Age to the Iron Age' an 'The Etruscans' in Boardman, Hammond, Lewis & Ostwald 1988, 623–33 an 634–75.

Rieth 1940, Rieth, A., 'Die Entwicklung der Drechseltechnik', *AA* 1940, 616–3

Riley 1979, Riley, J., 'The Pottery' in Lloyd 1979, 91–467.

Riley 1984, Riley, J., 'Pottery analysis and the reconstruction of ancient exchan systems' in van de Leeuw and Pritchard 1984, 55–78.

Roberts 1978, Roberts, S.R., *The Attic Pyxis*, Chicago, 1978.

Robertson 1951, Robertson, M., 'The place of vase-painting in Greek art', *ABS* 46 (1951) 151–9.

Robertson 1959, Robertson, M., *Greek Painting*, Geneva, 1959.

Robertson 1965, Robertson, M., 'Greek mosaics', *JHS* 85 (1965) 72–89.

Robertson 1967, Robertson, M., 'Greek mosaics: a postscript', *JHS* 87 (196 133–6.

Robertson 1972, Robertson, M., '"Epoiesen" on Greek vases: other onsiderations', *JHS* 92 (1972) 180–3.

Robertson 1975, Robertson, M., *A History of Greek Art*, Cambridge, 1975.

Robertson 1976, Robertson, M., 'Beazley and after', *MJBK* 27 (1976) 29–46.

Robertson 1981a, Robertson, M., *A Shorter History of Greek Art*, Cambridge, 981.

Robertson 1981b, Robertson, M., 'Euphronios at the Getty', *Getty MJ* 9 (1981) 3–34.

Robertson 1985, Robertson, M., 'Beazley and Attic vase painting' in Kurtz 985b, 19–30.

Robertson 1987, Robertson, M., 'The state of Attic vase-painting in the mid-sixth entury' in True 1987, 13–28.

Robertson & Frantz 1975, Robertson, M & Frantz, A., *The Parthenon Frieze*, ondon, 1975.

Robinson et al. 1929–52, Robinson, D.M. et el., *Excavations at Olynthus I-XIV*, altimore, 1929–52.

Roebuck 1955, Roebuck, M.C. & C.A., 'A prize aryballos', *Hesperia* 24 (1955) 58–63.

Roebuck 1972, Roebuck, C., 'Some aspects of urbanization in Corinth', *Hesperia* 1 (1972) 96–127.

Rosati 1989, Rosati, R. (ed.), *La ceramica attica nel Mediterraneo. Analisi omputerizzata della diffusione. Le fasi iniziali (630–560 B.C.)*, Bologna, 989.

Rotroff 1982, Rotroff, S., *Hellenistic Pottery: Athenian imported and moldmade owls. The Athenian Agora XXII*, Princeton, 1982.

Rotroff 1991, Rotroff, S., 'Attic West Slope Vase Painting', *Hesperia* 60 (1991) 9–102.

Ruckert 1976, Ruckert, A., *Frühe Keramik Böiotiens* (10 Beiheft *AK*, 1976).

Rudolph 1971, Rudolph, W.W., *Die Bauchlekythos: ein Beitrag zur ormgeschichte der attischen Keramik des 5. Jahrhunderts v. Chr.*, Diss. Göttingen, loomington, 1971

Rumpf 1934, Rumpf, A., 'Diligentissime mulieres pinxit', *JDAI* 49 (1934) –23.

Rumpf 1947, Rumpf, A., 'Classical and post-Classical Greek painting', *JHS* 67 1947) 10–21.

Rumpf 1951, Rumpf, A., 'Parrhasios'. *AJA* 55 (1951) 1–12.

Salmon 1984, Salmon, J.B., *Wealthy Corinth: a history of the city to 338 B.C.*, xford, 1984

Salomé 1980, Salomé, M.-R., *Code pour l'analyse des représentations figurées sur s vases grecs*, Paris, 1980.

Salzmann 1982, Salzmann, D., *Untersuchungen zu den antiken Kieselmosaiken*, erlin, 1982.

Samuel 1972, Samuel, A.E., *Greek and Roman Chronology*, Munich, 1972.

Schäfer 1957, Schäfer, J., *Studien zu den griechischen Relief-pithoi des 8.-6. ahrhunderts v. Chr. aus Kreta, Rhodos, Tenos und Boiotien*, Kallmünz, 1957.

Schauenburg 1986, Böhr, E. & Martini, W. (edd.), *Studien zur Mythologie und asenmalerei. Konrad Schauenburg zum 65. Geburtstag am 16 April 1986*, Mainz, 986.

Schaus 1979, Schaus, G.P., 'A foreign vase painter in Sparta', *AJA* 83 (1979) 102–6.

Schaus 1983, Schaus, G.P., 'Two notes on Laconian vases', *AJA* 87 (1983) 85–9.

Schaus 1988, Schaus, G.P., 'The beginning of Greek polychrome painting', *JHS* 108 (1988) 107–17.

Scheffer 1981, Scheffer, C., *Acquarossa II, Part I: Cooking and Cooking Stands in Italy 1400–400 B.C.*, Stockholm, 1981.

Scheffer 1988, Scheffer, C., 'Workshop and trade patterns in Athenian black figure', in Christiansen & Melander 1988, 536–46.

Schefold 1930, Schefold, K., *Kertscher Vasen*, Berlin, 1930.

Schefold 1966, Schefold, K., *Myth and Legend in Early Greek Art*, London, 1966.

Schefold 1978, Schefold, K., *Götter- und Heldensagen der Griechen in der spätarchaischen Kunst*, Munich, 1978.

Schefold 1981, Schefold, K., *Die Göttersage in der klassischen und hellenistischen Kunst*, Munich, 1981.

Schefold & Jung 1988, Schefold, K. & Jung, F., *Die Urkönige, Perseus, Bellerophon, Herakles und Theseus in der klassischen und hellenistischen Kunst*, Munich, 1988.

Scheibler 1964, Scheibler, I., 'Exaleiptra', *JDAI* 79 (1964) 72–108.

Scheibler 1968, Scheibler, I., 'Exaleiptra: addenda', *AA* 1968, 389–97.

Scheibler 1983, Scheibler, I., *Griechische Töpferkunst*, Munich, 1983.

Schiering 1983, Schiering, W., *Die griechische Tongefässe: Gestalt, Bestimmung und Formenwandel* (2nd ed.), Berlin 1983.

Schilardi 1977, Schilardi, D.U., *The Thespian Polyandrion (424 B.C.): The Excavations and Finds from the Thespian State Burial*, PhD Princeton, Ann Arbor, 1979.

Schmidt 1960, Schmidt, M., *Der Dareiosmaler und sein Umkreis*, Münster, 1960.

Schneider-Hermann 1980, Schneider-Hermann, G., *Red-figured Lucanian and Apulian Nestorides and their Ancestors*, Amsterdam, 1980.

Schuchhardt 1963, Schuchhardt, W.-H., 'Athena Parthenos', *Antike Plastik* I, 31–53, Berlin, 1963.

Schwab 1986, Schwab, K.A., 'A Parthenonian centaur', *Greek Vases* II, 89–94.

Schweitzer 1971, Schweitzer, B., *Greek Geometric Art*, London, 1971.

Scichilone 1963, Scichilone, G., 'Olinto', *EAA* V (1963) 661–7.

Seaford 1982, Seaford, R.A.S., 'The date of Euripides' *Cyclops*', *JHS* 102 (1982) 161–72.

Seaford 1984, Seaford, R., *Euripides* Cyclops, Oxford, 1984.

Seiterle 1976, Seiterle, G., 'Die Zeichentechnik in der rotfigurigen Vasenmalerei', *AW* 7 (1976) 2–10.

Servais-Soyez 1981, Servais-Soyez, B., 'Adonis' in Kahil 1981, 222–29.

Shapiro 1983, Shapiro, H.A., 'Painting, politics and genealogy: Peisistratos and the Neleids' in Moon 1983, 87–96.

Shefton 1950, Shefton, B.B., 'The dedication of Callimachos (*IG* 1/2 609)', *ABSA* 45 (1950) 140–64.

Shefton 1954, Shefton, B.B., 'Three Laconian vase painters', *ABSA* 49 (1954) 299–310.

Shefton 1960, Shefton, B.B., 'Some iconographic remarks on the Tyrannicides' *AJA* 64 (1960) 173–9.

Shefton 1982, Shefton, B.B., 'The krater from Baksy' in Kurtz & Sparkes 1982, 149–81.

Shefton 1989, Shefton, B.B., 'East Greek influences in sixth century Attic vase-painting and some Laconian traits', *Greek Vases* IV (1989) 41–72.

Shepard 1968, Shepard, A.O., *Ceramics for the Archaeologist*, Washington, 1968.

Sichtermann 1963, Sichtermann, H., *Die griechischen Vasen: Gestalt, Sinn und Kunstwerk*, Berlin, 1963.

Simon 1982a, Simon, E., *The Ancient Theatre*, London, 1982.

Simon 1982b, Simon, E., 'Satyr-plays on vases in the time of Aeschylus' in Kurtz & Sparkes 1982, 123–48.

Simon 1983, Simon, E., *The Festivals of Attica*, Madison, Wisconsin, 1983.

Simon & Hirmer 1981, Simon, E. & Hirmer, M. & M., *Die griechischen Vasen*, Munich, 1981 (2nd ed.).

Smithson 1968, Smithson, E.L., 'The tomb of a rich Athenian lady, ca. 850 B.C.', *Hesperia* 37 (1968) 77–116.

Snodgrass 1964, Snodgrass, A.M., *Arms and Armour of the Greeks*, London, 1964.

Snodgrass 1979, Snodgrass, A.M., 'Poet and painter in eighth century Greece', *PCPS* 205 (1979) 118–30.

Snodgrass 1980a, Snodgrass, A., *Archaic Greece, the age of experiment*, London, 1980.

Snodgrass 1980b, Snodgrass, A.M., 'Towards an interpretation of the Geometric figure-scenes', *AM* 95 (1980) 51–8.

Snodgrass 1982, Snodgrass, A.M., *Narration and Illusion in Archaic Greek Art*, London, 1982.

Snodgrass 1983a, Snodgrass, A., 'Archaeology' in Crawford 1983, 137–84.

Snodgrass 1983b, Snodgrass, A.M., 'Heavy freight in archaic Greece' in Garnsey, Hopkins & Whittaker 1983, 16–26.

Snodgrass 1987, Snodgrass, A., *An Archaeology of Greece*, Berkeley and Los Angeles, 1987.

Snodgrass 1990, Snodgrass, A., 'Survey archaeology and the rural landscape of the Greek city' in Murray and Price 1990, 113–26.

Sourvinou-Inwood 1971, Sourvinou-Inwood, C., 'Theseus lifting the rock and a cup near the Pithos Painter', *JHS* 91 (1971) 94–109.

Sourvinou-Inwood 1979, Sourvinou-Inwood, C., *Theseus as Son and Stepson*, *BICS*, Supplement 40, London, 1979.

Sparkes 1962, Sparkes, B.A., 'The Greek kitchen', *JHS* 82 (1962) 121–37.

Sparkes 1965, Sparkes, B.A., 'The Greek kitchen: addenda', *JHS* 85 (1965) 162–3.

Sparkes 1967, Sparkes, B.A., 'The taste of a Boeotian pig', *JHS* 87 (1967) 116–30.

Sparkes 1968, Sparkes, B.A., 'Black Perseus', *AK* 11 (1968) 3–15.

Sparkes 1975, Sparkes, B.A., 'Illustrating Aristophanes', *JHS* 95 (1975) 122–35.

Sparkes 1976, Sparkes, B.A., 'Treading the grapes', *BABesch.* 51 (1976) 47–64.

Sparkes 1981, Sparkes, B.A., 'Not cooking, but baking', *Greece and Rome* 28 (1981) 172–8.

Sparkes 1991, Sparkes, B.A., *Greek Art. Greece and Rome, New Surveys in the Classics no.* 22, Oxford, 1991.

Sparkes & Talcott 1958, Sparkes, B.A. & Talcott, L., *Pots and Pans of Classical Athens*, Princeton, 1958.

Sparkes & Talcott 1970, Sparkes, B.A. & Talcott, L., *Black and Plain Pottery of the 6th, 5th & 4th centuries B.C., The Athenian Agora XII*, Princeton, 1970.

Spivey 1987, Spivey, N.J., *The Micali Painter and his Followers*, Oxford, 1987.

Spivey 1988, Spivey, N., *Un artista etrusco e il suo mondo: II pittore di Micali*, Rome, 1988.

Stansbury-O'Donnell 1989, Stansbury-O'Donnell, M.D., 'Polygnotos' *Iliupersis*: a new reconstruction', *AJA* 93 (1989) 203–15.

Stewart 1983, Stewart, A., 'Stesichoros and the François vase' in Moon 1983, 53–74.

Stewart 1990, Stewart, A.F., *Greek Sculpture: an exploration*, Yale, 1990.

Stibbe 1972, Stibbe, C.M., *Lakonische Vasenmaler des sechsten Jahrhunderts v. Chr.*, Amsterdam, 1972.

Stibbe 1989, Stibbe, C.M., *Laconian Mixing Bowls*, Amsterdam, 1989.

Stillwell & Benson 1984, Stillwell, A.N. & Benson, J.L., *The Potters' Quarter, The Pottery, Corinth XV.III*, Princeton, 1984.

Strong & Brown 1976, Strong, D. & Brown, D. (edd.), *Roman Crafts*, London, 1976.

Sutton 1980, Sutton, D., *The Greek Satyr Play*, Meisenheim am Glan, 1980.

Swaddling 1980, Swaddling, J., *The Ancient Olympic Games*, London, 1980.

Taplin 1987, Taplin, O., 'Phallology, *Phlyakes*, Iconography and Aristophanes', *PCPS* 213, n.s. 33 (1987) 92–104.

Taylor 1981, Taylor, M.W., *The Tyrant Slayers, the heroic image in fifth century B.C. Athenian art and politics*, New York, 1981.

Themelis 1977, Themelis, P., 'Μαραθών: τὰ πρόσφατα ἀρχαιολογικὰ εὑρήματα σὲ σχέση μὲ τὴ μάχη', *ADelt* 29 (1974) A (1977) 226–44.

Thompson 1934, Thompson, H.A., 'Two centuries of Hellenistic pottery', *Hesperia* 3 (1934) 311–480 (reissued in H.A. Thompson and D.B. Thompson, *Hellenistic Pottery and Terracottas*, with preface by S.I. Rotroff, Princeton, 1987).

Thompson 1971, Thompson, D.B., *An Ancient Shopping Center: The Athenian Agora*, Princeton, 1971.

Thompson 1984, Thompson, H.A., 'The Athenian Vase-Painters and their Neighbors', in Rice 1984, 7–19.

Thompson & Wycherley 1972, Thompson, H.A. & Wycherley, R.E., *The Agora of Athens, The Athenian Agora XIV*, Princeton, 1972.

Throckmorton 1987, Throckmorton, P. (ed.), *History from the Sea: Shipwrecks & Archaeology*, London, 1987.

Tiverios 1976, Tiverios, M., 'Ο Λύδος καὶ τὸ ἔργο του, Athens, 1976.

Touchefeu-Meynier 1972, Touchefeu-Meynier, O., 'Un nouveau "phormiskos" à figures noires', *RA* 1972, 93–102.

Touloupa 1986, Touloupa, E., 'Die Giebelskulpturen des Apollon Daphnephoros-tempels in Eretria' in Kyrieleis 1986, I, 143–51.

Trendall 1967, Trendall, A.D., *The Red-figured Vases of Lucania, Campania and Sicily*, Oxford, 1967.

Trendall 1979, Cambitoglou, A. (ed.), *Studies in Honour of A.D. Trendall*, Sydney, 1979.

Trendall 1987, Trendall, A.D., *The Red-figured Vases of Paestum*, The British School at Rome, 1987.

Trendall 1989, Trendall, A.D., *Red-figure Vases of Southern Italy and Sicily*, London, 1989.

Trendall & Cambitoglou 1978 & 1982, Trendall, A.D. & Cambitoglou, A., *The Red-figured Vases of Apulia*, Oxford, 1978 & 1982.

Trendall & Webster 1971, Trendall, A.D. & Webster, T.B.L., *Illustrations of Greek Drama*, London, 1971.

True 1987, True, M. (ed.), *Papers on the Amasis Painter and his World*, Malibu, 1987.

Trumpf-Lyritzaki 1969, Trumpf-Lyritzaki, M., *Griechische Figurenvasen des reichen Stils und der späten Klassik*, Bonn, 1969.

Tuchelt 1962, Tuchelt, K., *Tiergefässe in Kopf- und Protomen-gestalt*, Berlin, 1962.

Ullman 1964, *Classical, Mediaeval and Renaissance Studies in Honour of Berhold Louis Ullman*, ed. Charles Henderson, Jr., Vol. I, Rome, 1964.

Ure 1936, Ure, A.D., 'Red figure cups with incised and stamped decoration I', *JHS* 56 (1936) 205–15.

Ure 1944, Ure, A.D., 'Red figure cups with incised and stamped decoration II', *JHS* 64 (1944) 67–77.

Ure 1958, Ure, A.D., 'The Argos Painter and the Painter of the Dancing Pan', *AJA* 62 (1958) 389–95.

Ure 1973, Ure, A.D., 'Observations on Euboean black-figure', *ABSA* 68 (1973) 25–31.

Valavanis 1986, Valavanis, P., 'Les amphores panathénaiques et le commerce athénien de l'huile' in Empereur & Garlan 1986, 453–60.

Vallet & Villard 1963, Vallet, G. & Villard, F., 'Céramique grecque et histoire économique' in Courbin 1963, 205–17.

Van de Leeuw & Pritchard 1984, van de Leeuw, S.E. and Pritchard, A.C., *The Many Dimensions of Pottery, Ceramics in Archaeology and Anthropology*, Amsterdam, 1984.

Vanderpool 1967, Vanderpool, E., 'Kephisophon's kylix', *Hesperia* 36 (1967) 187–9.

Vanderpool 1970, Vanderpool, E., *Ostracism at Athens*, Cincinnati, 1970.

Vatin 1983, Vatin, C., 'Les danseuses de Delphes', *CRAI* 1983, 26–40.

Vermeule 1966, Vermeule, E., 'The Boston Oresteia krater', *AJA* 70 (1966) 1–22.

Vermeule 1970, Vermeule, E., 'Five vases from the grave precinct of Dexileos', *JDAI* 85 (1970) 94–111.

Vermeule 1979, Vermeule, E., *Aspects of Death in Early Greek Art and Poetry*, Berkeley and Los Angeles, 1979.

Vermeule 1984, Vermeule, E., 'Tyres the lecher', in *Studies presented to Sterling Dow on his eightieth birthday*, Durham, North Carolina, 1984, 301–4.

Vickers 1978, Vickers, M., *Greek Symposia*, London, 1978.

Vickers 1983, Vickers, M., 'Les vases peints: image ou mirage' in Lissarrague and Thelamon 1983, 29–42.

Vickers 1984, Vickers, M., 'The influence of exotic materials on Attic white ground pottery' in Brijder 1984, 88–97.

Vickers 1985a, Vickers, M., 'Persepolis, Vitruvius and the Erechtheum Caryatids: the iconography of Medism and servitude', *RA* 1985, 3–28.

Vickers 1985b, Vickers, M., 'Early Greek coinage, a reassessment', *NC* 14 (1985) 1–44.

Vickers 1985c, Vickers, M., 'Artful crafts: the influence of metalwork on Athenian painted pottery', *JHS* 105 (1985) 108–28.

Vickers 1986, Vickers, M. (ed.), *Pots and Pans, Precious Metals and Ceramics in the Muslim, Chinese and Graeco-Roman Worlds* (Oxford Studies in Islamic Art), Oxford, 1986.

Vickers 1987, Vickers, M., 'Alcibiades on stage: *Philoctetes* & *Cyclops*', *Historia* 36 (1987) 171–97.

Vickers 1990, Vickers, M., 'Golden Greece: relative values, minae, and temple inventories', *AJA* 94 (1990) 613–24.

Vickers & Bazama 1971, Vickers, M. & Bazama, A., 'A fifth century B.C. tomb in Cyrenaica', *Libya Antiqua* 8 (1971) 69–85.

Vickers, Impey & Allen 1986, Vickers, M., Impey, O. & Allen, J., *From Silver to Ceramic*, Oxford, 1986.

de Vries 1977, de Vries, K., 'Attic pottery in the Achaemenid Empire', *AJA* 8 (1977) 544–8.

Walsh 1985, Walsh, J., 'Acquisitions 1984', *GettyMJ* 13 (1985) 161–258.

Watrous 1982, Watrous, L.V., 'The sculptural program of the Siphnian Treasury at Delphi', *AJA* 86 (1982) 159–72.

Webster 1972, Webster, T.B.L., *Potter and Patron in Classical Athens*, London, 1972.

Wehgartner 1983, Wehgartner, I., *Attisch Weissgrundige Keramik*, Mainz, 1983

Weill 1966, Weill, N., 'Adoniazousai ou les femmes sur le toit', *BCH* 90 (1966) 664–98.

Weinberg 1954, Weinberg, S., 'Corinthian relief ware: pre-hellenistic period', *Hesperia* 23 (1954) 109–37.

Weis 1979, Weis, H.A., 'The "Marsyas" of Myron: old problems and new evidence', *AJA* 83 (1979) 214–19.

Whitbread 1986a, Whitbread, I., 'The application of ceramic petrology to the study of ancient Greek amphorae' in Empereur and Garlan 1986, 95–101.

Whitbread 1986b, Whitbread, I.K., 'A microscopic view of Greek transport amphorae' in Jones and Catling 1986, 49–52.

Whitehouse & Wilkins 1985, Whitehouse, R. & Wilkins, J., 'Magna Graecia before the Greeks: towards a reconciliation of the evidence', *BAR* International Series 245 (1985) 89–109.

Willemsen 1977, Willemsen, F., 'Zu den Lakedämoniergräbern im Kerameikos', *AM* 92 (1977) 117–57.

Williams 1980, Williams, D., 'Ajax, Odysseus and the arms of Achilles', *AK* 23 (1980) 137–45.

Williams 1982, Williams, D., 'An oinochoe in the British Museum and the Brygos Painter's work on a white ground', *JBM* 24 (1982) 17–40.

Williams 1983a, Williams, D., 'Sophilos in the British Museum' in *Greek Vases* 1 (1983) 9–34.

Williams 1983b, Williams, D., 'Aegina, Aphaia-Tempel, V: the pottery from Chios', *AA* 1983, 155–86.

Williams 1983c, Williams, D., 'Women on Athenian vases: problems of interpretation' in Cameron & Kuhrt 1983, 92–106.

Williams 1985, Williams, D., *Greek Vases*, London, 1985.

Williams 1986, Williams, D., 'A cup by the Antiphon Painter and the battle of Marathon' in Schauenburg 1986, 75–81.

Williams 1990, Williams, D.F., 'The study of ancient ceramics: contribution of the petrographic method' in *Scienze in Archeologia*, edd. T. Mannoni & A. Molinari, Florence, 1990.

Williams & Fisher 1976, Williams, C.K. & Fisher, T.E., 'Corinth 1975: Forum Southwest', *Hesperia* 45 (1976) 99–162.

Winter 1968, Winter, A., 'Beabsichtigtes Rot (Intentional Red)', *AM* 83 (1968) 315–22.

Winter 1978, Winter, A., *Die Antike Glanztonkeramik, praktische Versuche*, Mainz, 1978.

Wintermeyer 1975, Wintermeyer, U., 'Die polychrome Reliefkeramik aus Centuripe', *JDAI* 90 (1975) 136–241.

Wolters & Bruns 1940, Wolters, P. & Bruns, G., *Das Kabirenheiligtum I*, Berlin, 1940.

Woodhead 1981, Woodhead, A.G., *The Study of Greek Inscriptions*, Cambridge, 1981 (2nd ed.).

Wycherley 1957, Wycherley, R.E., *Literary and Epigraphical Testimonia, The Athenian Agora III*, Princeton, 1957.

Zaphiropoulou 1973, Zaphiropoulou, P., 'Vases et autres objets de marbre de Rhenée', *BCH* Supplement I (1973) 601–36.

Zervoudaki 1968, Zervoudaki, E.A., 'Attische Polychrome Reliefkeramik des späten 5. und des 4. Jahrhunderts v. Chr.', *AM* 83 (1968) 1–88.

Ziomecki 1975, Ziomecki, J., *Les Représentations d'artisans sur les vases antiques*, Warsaw, 1975.

INDEX

Not all references to individual shapes, painters' names or mythological characters have been included in this index. For an alphabetical list of the major shapes, see pp. 79–92.

Ancient references

NOTTINGHAM UNIVERSITY LIBRARY

SUBMARINE INSIGNIA
& SUBMARINE SERVICES OF THE WORLD

Lieutenant-Commander W M Thornton
MBE RD* RNR (Rtd)

with the collaboration of
Capitán de Navio Gustavo Conde, Argentine Navy

LEO COOPER
London

First published in 1997 by
Leo Cooper
190 Shaftesbury Avenue, London WC2H 8JL
an imprint of
Pen & Sword Books Ltd,
47 Church Street, Barnsley, South Yorkshire S70 2AS

© Lieutenant-Commander W. M. Thornton, 1997

A CIP catalogue record for this book is available from the British Library

ISBN 0 85052 536 5

Printed in Singapore by Kyodo Printing Co (Singapore) Pte Ltd

CONTENTS

Foreword

In this book an attempt has been made to depict all the insignia that have been worn and are being worn by qualified submariners world-wide. No doubt readers will come across insignia that do not appear but these will, for the most part, be variation in manufacture, size and material. This reference should therefore, at the very least, serve to identify the country of origin and give relevant background information. New insignia will be produced as new submarine forces are formed. Hopefully these will be included in a revised volume to follow at some later date.

Various insignia have been produced, the authenticity of which, at this stage, cannot be verified. These are shown for information, and in some cases, assumptions made.

As an additional aid to identification, unofficial designs, if actually worn, are included. Some of these were the fore-runners of authorized insignia that were to follow.

Where actual examples of the insignia are not available, or where the illustrations are not suitable for reproduction, the author has prepared drawings for identification purposes. Note that the illustrations are not to scale.

Abbreviations Used In The Text

SS	Conventionally powered(diesel/electric) submarine
SSC	Conventionally powered (diesel/electric) small coastal submarine
SSK	Conventionally powered (diesel/electric) submarine with anti-submarine warfare capability
SSB	Conventionally powered (diesel/electric) ballistic missile submarine
SSG	Conventionally powered (diesel/electric) cruise missile submarine
SSN	Nuclear powered hunter-killer attack submarine
SSBN	Nuclear powered ballistic missile submarine
SSGN	Nuclear powered cruise missile submarine
SDV	Swimmer delivery vehicle
	(The above refer only to post-1945 construction)
SLBM	Submarine launched ballistic missile
SSM	Surface to surface missile
USM	Underwater to surface missile
A/S	Anti-submarine
ASW	Anti-submarine warfare
ICBM	Intrecontinental ballistic missile
NM	Nautical miles

Soviet Submarine Classification

NATO terminology is used in the text for most Soviet or ex-Soviet submarine classes.

SS	*Quebec*	SSB	*Golf*
	Whiskey	SSG	*Juliet*
	Romeo	SSBN	*Hotel*
	Zulu		*Yankee*
	Foxtrot		*Delta*
SSK	*Tango*		*Typhoon*
	Kilo	SSGN	*Echo*
SSN	*November*		*Charlie*
	Victor		*Papa*
	Alpha		*Oscar*
	Sierra		
	Mike		

Explanation Of Early Submarine Types

Early submarine types were usually known after their inventors, some of these were:

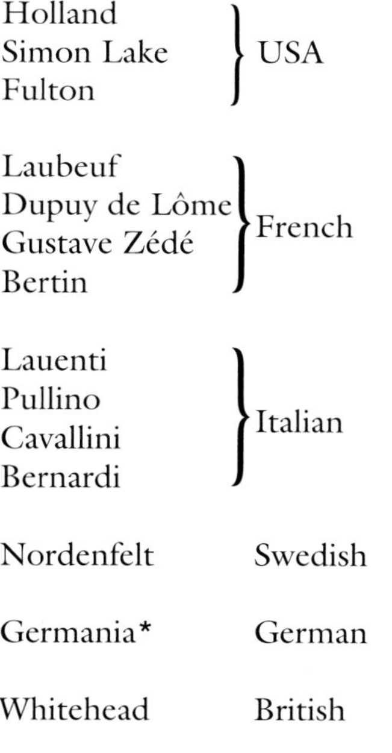

Holland Simon Lake Fulton	USA
Laubeuf Dupuy de Lôme Gustave Zédé Bertin	French
Lauenti Pullino Cavallini Bernardi	Italian
Nordenfelt	Swedish
Germania*	German
Whitehead	British

* This is named after the shipyard.

Note that early submarines were termed submarine torpedo boats, consequently they are always referred to as boats, rather than ships.

ALBANIA

SUBMARINE SERVICE

The Albanian submarine branch was formed in 1960 with the transfer of two *Whiskey* Class submarines (SS) from the USSR. When in 1961, after the split with Albania, the Soviet Union attempted to withdraw from its bases two further *Whiskey* Class submarines, then in Albanian ports, these were seized, thus doubling the Albanian submarine strength.

One submarine was deleted in 1976 and shortly thereafter another one relegated to harbour service. The remaining boats, which are the only significant vessels in the navy, are assumed to be operational.

SUBMARINE INSIGNIA

Very little information is available from Albania. In line with their Chinese Communist patrons, all ranks and insignia, apart from the red star cap badge, were abolished about 1966 and an universal Chairman-Mao style uniform adopted. Later, following the Chinese lead, the Navy changed to a more traditional uniform based almost entirely on the Chinese style.

After the collapse of Communism in March, 1992, more conventional uniforms and insignia of rank were introduced. A submarine badge made its appearance about early 1993. It consisted of the image of a conventional submarine measuring 92mm x 18mm facing the wearer's right. It was crudely embroidered in light grey thread on a dark blue background which usually followed the profile of the submarine. Further details are, at this stage, unavailable.

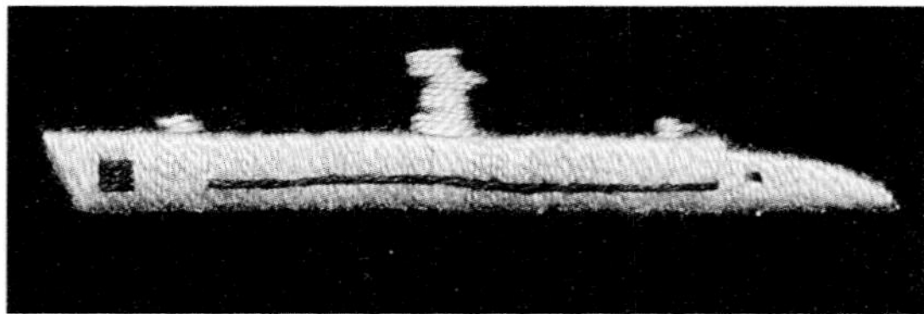

Albanian submarine insignia introduced early 1993.

ALGERIA

SUBMARINE SERVICE

The Algerian Submarine Force was formed in January, 1982, with the delivery of a Soviet *Romeo* Class submarine (SS). A second submarine of the same class was delivered the following year. Both boats were on loan for a five year period and were subsequently returned to the Soviet Union. In 1987 a *Kilo* Class submarine (SSK) was purchased from the Soviet Union and was followed by a second one in 1988. These two modern submarines are likely to constitute the Algerian submarine force for the foreseeable future.

SUBMARINE INSIGNIA

In 1992 official sources indicated that no formal insignia was authorized. Since then various unsubstantiated reports have rumoured that a submarine badge has been 'seen' but no details have emerged.

ARGENTINA

SUBMARINE SERVICE

Though experiments with a small electric powered vessel were reported in 1906/7, it was not until 1927 that Argentina ordered its first submarines. The new vessels, three in number, with a surface displacement of 775 tons, were purchased from Italy, and were based on the Italian Navy's *Mameli* Class. Named *Salta, Sante Fé* and *Santiago del Estero* after Argentine provinces, these became traditional names for Argentinian submarines. They served for nearly three decades; the *Salta,* the last to be withdrawn, served until 1960.

In the same year as *Salta* was decommissioned the United States transferred two wartime-built *Balao* class submarines (SS), of 1,816 tons surface displacement, to Argentina. They became the *Sante Fé* and *Santiago del Estero*. Eleven years later both were replaced by two modernised *Balao* Class submarines (*Guppy 1A* and *Guppy 11).* The names adopted were the same as the names of the two submarines that they had replaced. The *Sante Fé* was later to gain notoriety when she became the first war loss in the Falklands conflict. She was disabled off South Georgia on the 26 April, 1982, by missiles fired from a Lynx helicopter from

HMS *Brilliant*, and was subsequently beached to become a total loss.

In the late 1960s two 209 class — 1200 type submarines (SSK) of 980 tons surface displacement were ordered from West Germany. They were built in sections at Kiel and shipped to Argentina for assembly. Both were commissioned in 1974 and were named *Salta* and *San Luis*. Plans for an additional two type 209s were dropped in favour of a further order from West Germany of six of the more advanced TR 1700 type (SSK) displacing 2,116 tons surfaced. The first two of this class, the *Sante Cruz* and the *Santa Juan*, were constructed in West Germany and sailed for Argentina in 1984 and 1985 respectively. The remaining vessels, the first two of which have been named *Santiago del Estero* and *Sante Fé*, are being constructed in Argentina with West German help. It is likely that the class will be reduced to a total of five boats. At the time of writing Argentina has in commission two type TR 1700 Class and two type 209 *Salta* Class.

Submarine Insignia

The original submarine badge, proposed by Presidential Decree on 16 December, 1933, was based on the design of the Italian-built *Mameli* Class submarines. It faced the wearer's right as did all subsequent badges.

It came in three grades, one for officers, one for senior ratings and one for junior ratings. The officer's insignia, which was of gilt metal, bore an enamel oval device centrally located below the conning tower. This consisted of three equally spaced horizontal segments of light blue, white and light blue with a gilt sunburst in the centre of the white segment. The senior rating's insignia was similar but made of brass with an anchor within the oval. Junior ratings wore a cloth badge on the sleeve. The ovals were surrounded by a representation of a rope. Both the metal badges had horizontal pin fastenings and measured 75mm x 20mm.

In 1945 the officer's badge was modified by replacing the central oval with the national coat-of-arms in full colour enamel. In 1969 the senior ratings badge was similarly modified but was now made in silver. At the same time it was authorized for all ranks below commissioned officer.

A small version of the submarine badge 37mm long can be worn on mess kit or worn at sea as a beret badge. The submarine insignia is also produced in yellow or white embroidery on navy blue cloth for wear on the sea service jacket. Gold or silver embroidery versions are also produced, probably for private purchase.

The submarine insignia was originally worn on the left breast below the pocket on the blue uniform or above the pocket on the khaki and

white uniforms. Foreign submarine qualification badges are permitted to be worn below the Argentine insignia by personnel who have successfully completed submarine courses in other countries. From 1970 officers were authorized to wear the submarine insignia on the right breast.

Two new qualification badges were introduced about 1993/4. The first is the Submarine Support Badge and is worn only by commissioned ranks who serve ashore but who are attached to the submarine service. Originally restricted to medical officers specializing in underwater medicine (they formerly wore the standard officer's badge) it now includes naval engineering constructors and architects. The badge is the same design and size as that for sea-going officers but the central device is all gilt and not in coloured enamel.

The second and most individual of Argentinan submarine badges came with the appointment of Senior Chief Petty Officer of the Submarine Force. Based at Submarine Headquarters this senior rating wears a special badge depicting the rating's type submarine badge but on a blue enamel field within a gilt 'roped' frame measuring 45mm x 29mm overall.

The cap tallies of ratings serving in submarines bear the name of the submarine prefixed by the letters 'ARS' (*Armada de la Republica Argentina*) or in the case of the submarine school the words 'A. R. A. ESC. DE SUBMARINOS'.

Argentine submarine qualification insignia first pattern.
Top: officers 1933 to 1945.
Bottom: senior ratings 1933 to 1969.

Argentine submarine qualification insignia second pattern.
Top: officers 1945.
Bottom: senior ratings 1969.

Argentine submarine support badge 1993/94.

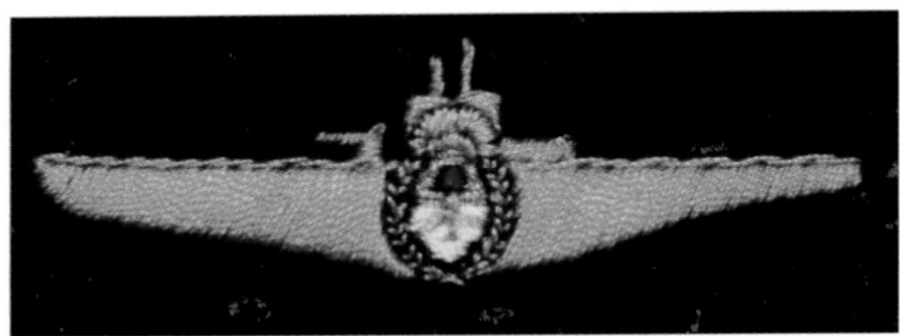

Officer's cloth submarine insignia worn on sea service jacket. A similar insignia in white embroidery is worn by ratings.

Miniature insignia worn by submarine officers on mess dress and berets. It is also found on tie slides.

AUSTRALIA

SUBMARINE SERVICE

The Australian Submarine service commenced with the launching by Vickers of the Submarine AE1 on 22 May, 1913, followed by the launching of AE2 on 18 June, 1913. Both were of the British E Class and had a surface displacement of 725 tons.

The two small submarines made the 13,000-mile voyage from Barrow to Sydney under their own power shortly before the commencement of World War I.

AEI disappeared on 14 September, 1914, off New Britain while in support of operations in New Guinea. AE2 sailed with the second AIF to the Mediterranean on the last day of 1914.

On 25 April, 1915, she forced her way through the Dardanelles and five days later crippled a Turkish cruiser with torpedoes. Shortly after the attack AE2 lost control due to damage caused by currents and was forced to surface. Attacked by an enemy destroyer, she was compelled to scuttle herself and her company became prisoners of war. The loss of the two submarines constituted the only RAN losses of World War I.

In 1919 all six boats of the RN J Class were transferred to the RAN. These vessels had a surface displacement of 1,210 tons and were completed between 1915 and 1917. Their service in the RAN was short- lived; none were kept in commission for more than three years.

In 1924 it was decided to order two new submarines from Britain to replace the obsolete J Class. HMAS *Oxley* was launched in June, 1926, and HMAS *Otway* in October of the same year. Both were of the 1,475 tons surface displacement O Class. They arrived in Australian waters in 1929 just before the Great Depression of Australia. When Depression came, both submarines fell victims of the economic situation and were transferred to the RN in April, 1931.

In 1943 a Dutch submarine, K-9, manned by the RN with a section of RAN volunteers, was commissioned into the RAN but was paid off within nine months. No further submarines were to serve in the RAN until after World War II.

From 1956 to 1969 the RN based its 4th Submarine Squadron (comprising three to four submarines) at Sydney to assist the RAN in anti-submarine warfare training.

The reinstatement of the Australian submarine service was heralded in January, 1963, when the Minster of the Navy announced that four

Oberon Class submarines (SS) were to be built for the RAN: HMA submarines *Onslow*, *Otway*, *Ovens* and *Oxley* were subsequently launched between 1965 and 1968 and commissioned between 1967 and 1969. Two further boats HMA Submarines *Orion* and *Otama* were launched in 1974 and 1975 and commissioned in 1977 and 1978.

Known as the *Otway* Class these six submarines comprised the 1st RAN submarine squadron. They have a surface displacement of 2,186 tons. Six were modernized by Vickers at Cockatoo Island between 1977 and 1985, and were fitted with USM upgrading them to SSK. *Oxley*, *Otway* and *Ovens* were deleted in 1992, 1994 and 1995 respectively.

On 18 May, 1987, the Australian Defence Minister announced that the replacements for the *Otway* Class would be the Type 471 Swedish submarine (SSK) designed by Kockums Marine. To be known as the *Collins* Class they are to have a surface displacement of 3,051 tons and will be constructed in Australia. The first of the class HMAS *Collins* was commissioned in January, 1995. The remainder, HMA submarines *Farncomb*, *Waller*, *Dechaineux*, *Sheean* and *Rankin*, should all be in service by 1999.

Submarine Insignia

The Australian submarine insignia was authorized by Australian Navy Order 411/64 promulgated on 25 July, 1966. It was officially described as a 'gold plated gilding metal brooch depicting two dolphins, nose to nose supporting a crown' and is the same for both officers and ratings. The first issues were made on 17 December, 1966. It is produced in two sizes; the dimension of the standard size is 72mm x 21mm and the miniature, for wear on mess dress, measures 51mm x 16mm. Both types are secured to the uniform by clutch fasteners. Gold wire embroidered versions are produced for private purchase. The insignia is worn on the left breast above medal ribbons. On 19 August, 1987, a similar yellow embroidered badge on dark cloth was authorized by Australian Submarine Temporary Memorandum (ASSTM 50/87), to be worn on working jackets by all qualified personnel.

For officers the qualification requirement is six months' sea-service after completion of training. For ratings it is granted after training and passing a submarine sea test normally held after sixteen weeks' service in a submarine.

Junior ratings wear cap ribbons bearing the submarine's name prefixed by the letters HMAS in exactly the same manner as for surface ships and establishments.

Australian submarine qualification badges worn by all ranks from 1966. Top: insignia normally worn. Centre: miniature insignia for wear on mess dress. Bottom: cloth variation worn on working rig.

AUSTRIA-HUNGARY

SUBMARINE SERVICE

The Austro-Hungarian Navy formed its submarine arm in 1908. In that year four boats were ordered, two American Lake type designated U1 and U2 and two Improved Holland type from Vickers Ltd designated U3 and U4. The following year two further boats designated U5 and U6 were ordered from Krupps Germania yard at Kiel. All six were delivered in 1910.

At the outbreak of the World War I Austria-Hungary had the aforementioned six submarines plus five building at Krupps. The new class was to be designated U7 to U11, but with the intervention of the war they were incorporated into the German Navy.

Five classes of submarines, totalling fourteen boats, were added to the Navy during the war. Most were Austro-Hungarian built, but some were acquired from Germany. The boats built in wartime were all designated by roman numerals as follows: XV completed 1914, XVII and XI completed 1915, XXI and XXII completed in 1916, XXVII, XXIX and XXXII also completed in 1916 and XL, XII, XLII and XVLII completed

SUBMARINE INSIGNIA

Though Bulgaria had no operational submarines before 1959 a silver-plated submarine badge was said to have been worn between 1940 and 1944. It took the form of a submarine (U-Boat profile) facing to the wearer's right and measured 72mm x 22mm. It can only have been unofficial and if worn would probably have been for volunteers serving with the German Navy.

Bulgaria played only a small part in World War II, allowing Germany to occupy her territory on the promise of new lands from her neighbours. She never declared war on the USSR, though she did declare war on Great Britain and the United States of America. After the Soviet occupation she threw in her lot with the Allies.

The official Bulgarian submarine insignia was introduced in August, 1984, being the thirtieth anniversary of the foundation of the Submarine Division (primarily formed to embrace trainee submariners in the USSR). The device is made of brass with coloured enamelled details. It is shield-shaped with the upper part bearing the War Ensign and the lower part being plain light blue. A submarine, in gold, bearing a central red star facing the wearer's left is located in the middle. The shield measures 30mm x 39mm and the submarine overlaps being 38mm long.

The insignia is worn on the right breast by all qualified ranks on duty and in the reserve.

A similar badge but lacking the red star on the War Ensign and with dark blue on the lower segment is available for presentation to friends and guests. It is not worn on uniform.

In common with all Bulgarian insignia the red star was dropped in 1992. The present submarine insignia, therefore, lacks the red star on the War Ensign and on the submarine's hull.

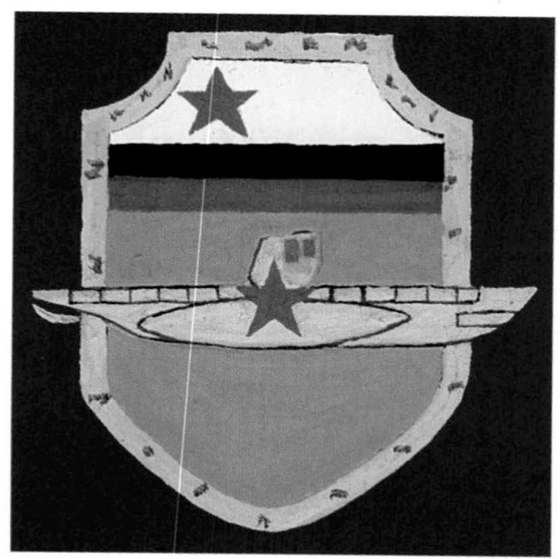

Bulgarian submarine insignia introduced in 1984. The red stars on the War Ensign and on the submarine's hull were removed in 1992.

Bulgarian submarine insignia, probably unofficial, said to have been worn between 1940 and 1944.

Unofficial Bulgarian submarine insignia for friends and guests. The red star was removed in 1992.

CANADA

SUBMARINE SERVICE

Canada's first submarines were two Holland type boats, CC1 and CC2. They were built in Seattle for Chile but purchased by Canada in 1914 just before the outbreak of World War I. They were small boats of about 310 tons surface displacement and were used for coastal patrols. Both were disposed of in 1920.

In 1919 the United Kingdom Government presented Canada with two H Class submarines, H14 and H15, which were re-designated CH14 and CH15. However, due to financial restraints, both were deleted in 1922.

It was not until well after World War II that the submarine branch was re-established. In 1961 the US *Balao* Class submarine USS *Burrfish* was purchased and renamed HMCS *Grilse*. Her function was to act as a training target for anti-submarine warfare, a role previously undertaken by Royal Navy submarines on loan to Canada. She remained in service until 1969, being replaced by the US *Tench* Class submarine USS *Argonaut*.

Renamed HMCS *Rainbow*, she continued in service until 1974. The post-war ex-USN submarines were all classified SS.

In the meantime three *Oberon* Class submarines had been ordered from British Yards in order to carry on the task of anti-submarine warfare training. The first, HMCS *Ojibwa*, entered service in 1965, the second, HMCS *Onodaga*, entered service in 1967 and the third, HMCS *Okanagan*, entered service in 1968. These three 'O' boats constitute the present strength of the Canadian Navy's submarine arm. The *Oberons* were originally classified SS, later upgraded to SSK.

The need to protect Canada's Arctic coastline led to tenders abroad for four submarines and possibly eight or twelve, probably nuclear powered, as they would be required to carry out under-ice patrols. Selection was scheduled for 1990 and completion dates were projected as 1995 to 1999. British or French designs were most likely to be accepted. This programme was cancelled in April, 1989, on economic grounds. In the same year the British submarine *Olympus* was acquired for static harbour training and in 1992 *Osiris* was acquired for spare-part cannibalization.

Submarine Insignia

With the reforming of the submarine branch of the RCN in 1961 a cloth badge depicting a single diving dolphin was authorized for qualified submariners. For officers it was produced in gold bullion on a navy blue backing. This was also worn by ratings on their number one uniforms. For working dress, ratings wore the same badge red on dark blue and for tropical uniform dark blue on white.

The badge measured 40mm high x 21mm wide. It was worn on the left sleeve immediately above rank devices in the case of officers and chief petty officers and 3in above the cuff in the case of petty officers and other ratings. Variations of size have appeared and an unofficial gilt badge was produced.

With the unification of the Canadian Forces the insignia was altered for all ranks to yellow rayon on dark green. This style was worn from 1968 to 1972. Metal versions have appeared but these are quite unofficial.

In April, 1972, the Queen approved the new Canadian Forces submarine badge. It was officially described as 'a crimson garnet wreath of laurel between two swimming dolphins in gold, above the wreath a crown, within the centre of the wreath a gold coloured maple leaf'. The device measured 82mm long x 33mm high and was of cloth material. In July, 1970, the badge was produced in metal 70mm long x 30mm high. It was secured to the uniform by two clutch fasteners. These new badges

were worn in cloth or wire embroidery above the left breast pocket of the CF green service dress and in metal above the left breast pocket of the CF green or white short-sleeved shirt. Miniature devices were available for mess dress.

With the reintroduction of the traditional dark blue (actually black) naval uniforms, in May, 1986, the device in cloth or bullion has reverted to the left cuff, the metal badge being confined to shirts and working dress. The design has remained unaltered, though in the case of the cloth insignia the backing has been changed from dark green to the new uniform colour.

The only cap ribbons worn for submarine service bore the submarine's name. They were 'HMCS RAINBOW', 'HMCS OJIBWA', 'HMCS ONONDAGA' and 'HMCS OKANAGAN'. No cap tally was produced for HMCS *Grilse,* nor were any produced with 'HMC SUBMARINES' (in the RN manner).With the adoption of the CF green uniforms cap tallies became obsolete and have not been reintroduced for the new naval type uniforms (which began to be issued in 1985). In this uniform all members of the naval service wear peaked caps.

The Royal Canadian Sea Cadets had a submarine orientated badge, acquired after successfully completing a basic course in a naval establishment. Like all RCSC badges it was embroidered silvery white on navy blue cloth. It took the form of two dolphins nose-to-nose above which was a maple leaf and below a short scroll bearing the word 'CADET'. The backing cloth was contoured. It was intended for wear on the left breast. This badge was replaced by a sleeve device depicting an O Class submarine (facing left) below a maple leaf, again white on navy blue.

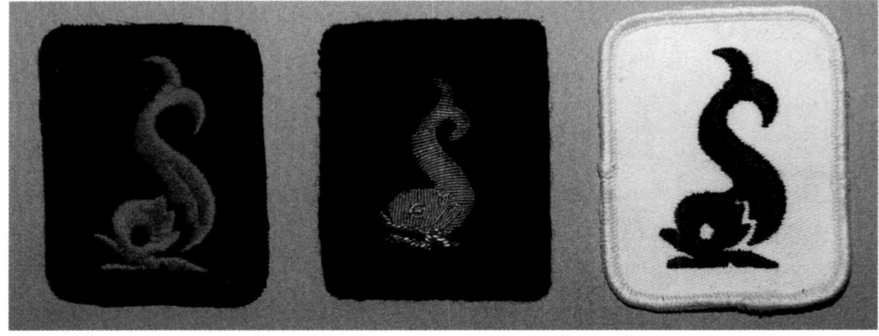

Canadian submarine qualification insignia 1961 to 1968. Left to right, ratings on No 2 and 3 uniforms, officers for normal wear and ratings for No 1 uniform, ratings tropical uniforms. Royal Canadian Navy.

Canadian submarine qualification insignia, Maritime Command, Canadian Forces (N). All ranks 1968 to 1971, deep yellow on dark green backing.

Canadian submarine qualification insignia, Maritime Command, Canadian Forces (N). All ranks 1972 to 1986, dark green backing.

Canadian submarine qualification insignia, Maritime Command, Canadian Forces (N). All ranks from May 1986, for new 'traditional' uniforms with black backing.

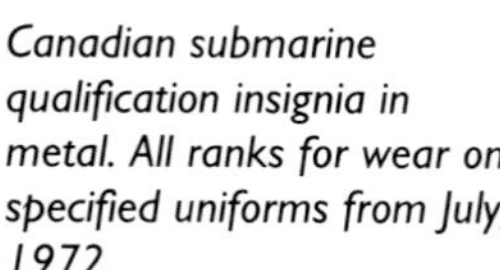

Canadian submarine qualification insignia in metal. All ranks for wear on specified uniforms from July, 1972.

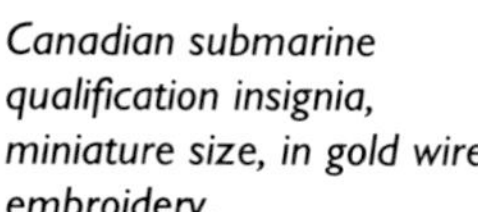

Canadian submarine qualification insignia, miniature size, in gold wire embroidery.

Canadian submarine qualification insignia, probably produced unofficially, for wear by ex-submariners or for wear on dress uniforms of other services.

Royal Canadian Sea Cadet, submarine dolphin badge. First type.

Royal Canadian Sea Cadets, submarine branch badge worn on the sleeve. Second type.

Chile

Submarine Service

The first Chilean submarines were built between 1915 and 1917. These were six Holland type boats constructed in the USA. Designated H1 to H6 they were originally intended for delivery to Great Britain but were interned in the USA on the outbreak of World War I. When the USA entered the war in 1917 they were released, but Great Britain ceded them to Chile in part payment for Chilean warships building in UK yards in 1914 and appropriated by the Royal Navy. They had a surface displacement of 355 tons and were later re-named *Gualcolda, Tegualda, Rucumilla, Guale, Quidora* and *Fresia* (names of heroines who fought the Spanish invaders). Four were broken up just after the war and the remainder, amazingly, not until between 1955 and 1956.

In 1928 and 1929 three Vickers Armstrong submarines of the O Class were purchased, newly constructed, and named after the Naval heroes *Capitan O'Brien, Capitan Thomson* and *Almirante Simpson*. They had a surface displacement of 1,540 tons. In 1958 all three were discarded.

In 1959 two ex-USN *Balao* Class submarines (SS) were scheduled to replace the O Boats but they were not finally transferred until 1961. They became *Simpson* (ex-USS *Spot*) and *Thomson* (ex-USS *Springer).*

Two British *Oberon* Class submarines (SS) were then ordered and both were delivered in 1976 and were given the names of *O'Brien* and *Hyatt*. On their being commissioned, the *Balao* Class *Thomson* was paid off and used for spares. *Simpson* was similarly paid off in 1975, but re-activated in 1977, only to be finally disposed of about three years later.

Two new 209 Class (type 1300) patrol submarines (SSK) were ordered from West Germany in 1980 and arrived in Chile in 1984. Of 1,260 tons surface displacement they are armed with eight 21in torpedo tubes.

The present submarine force consists of the two 209 Class and two *Oberon* Class. A further two 209s are contemplated.

Submarine Insignia

On 20 July, 1918, coinciding with the arrival of the first H Class submarine, officers and ratings commenced to wear on their left breast the first submarine insignia. This device depicted a Holland type submarine facing its wearer's right and measured 60mm long. Various minor variations existed. Unofficial at first, it became authorized on 5 August, 1927,

and was to be gilt for officers and aluminium for ratings. In 1929, a year after O Class submarines were purchased, a new badge in the style of this class appeared, this time facing its wearer's left. Ship's companies wore the different designs in accordance with which class they served. In 1955 the O Class design was universally adopted because it 'looked more modern'. Known in the Chilean Navy as the *Piocha,* the insignia depicts the O Class submarine with jumping stays and measures 67mm by 14.5mm. It comes in one size only and is worn by all ranks on the left breast above medal ribbons. It is fixed with lugs, pins or clutch fasteners. In 1963 a new die replaced the former one which had been lost. This resulted in some minor variations. In 1971 a new badge appeared without jumping stays but proved unpopular. These were said to have been manufactured in the United Kingdom during a visit to Portsmouth by the O Boats.

The Uniform Regulations of 25 August, 1987, reintroduced the previous design in gilt for all ranks; at the same time a frosted silver insignia of the same design was authorized for certain non-sea-going personnel attached to the submarine service. These included technicians, suppliers and medical personnel.

A special beret insignia is worn by submariners. It is officially described as 'an elliptical diadem with national heraldic flowers which surround the silhouette of an O Class submarine 38mm long. The diadem dimensions are, main axis 55mm, minor axis 40mm. Diadem and submarine (which are separate) are in gold colour'. The wreath is surmounted by a naval crown.

Chilean Navy submarine service beret badge.

Chilean submarine insignia first authorized 5 August, 1927.

Chilean submarine qualification insignia from 1955, all ranks. From top to bottom:

Insignia without jumping stays 1971 to 1987.

Insignia with jumping stays 1955 to 1971 and from 1987.

Frosted silver insignia for associated personnel from 1987.

Miniature.

People's Republic of China

Submarine Service

China first included submarines in its Navy in 1954. By the end of the 1970s the Chinese submarine fleet was the world's third largest.

Between 1954 and 1957 the Soviet Union transferred to China fourteen small coastal vessels of prewar design. Most of these were deleted by 1963. These were followed by the transfer of six Soviet *Whiskey* Class (SS) and the assembling in Chinese shipyards of a further fifteen from Soviet components. At about the same time four Soviet *Romeo* Class (SS) were also supplied to China. The *Romeo* Class proved popular with

the Chinese and they commenced to produce them in Chinese yards at the rate of six per year. Of a slightly larger design, designated the Chinese *Romeo* Class, the first of these was launched in 1962.

In 1962 China produced her first ballistic missile firing submarine (SSB). Based on the Soviet *Golf* Class, it was conventionally powered and was fitted with two vertical missile launching tubes (the Soviet version had three tubes).

Between 1971 and 1981 a new class of submarines appeared. The *Ming* Class (SS) were Chinese-designed, but were heavily influenced by the *Romeo* Class.

The first Chinese nuclear powered submarines were the *Han* Class (SSN) of 5,550 tons submerged displacement, armed with six 21in torpedo tubes. A class of five, they were launched between 1971 and 1990. This class was followed by the much larger *Xia* Class Type 092 (SSBN) of 8,000 tones dived displacement. These are armed with Css-N3 SLBM, with a range of 1,460 NM, and six 21in torpedo tubes. The first of this class was launched in 1981 and the second in 1982, though one may have been lost in an accident. A new type of SSBN (Type 093) with a longer range missile is being developed. A class of four is envisaged to be launched by the year 2000. Four *Kilo* Class SSNs were ordered from Russia in 1993. The first arrived in China early in 1995 and a second followed in September the same year. Production of a new class of SSNs was commenced in late 1994 with Russian aid. This class is due to be launched between 1998 and 2001.

At the time of writing (1996) the Chinese submarine fleet consists of one SSBN (*Xia*), one SSB (*Golf*), two SSN (*Kilo*), five SSN (*Han*), one SSG (modified *Romeo*), ten SS (*Ming*) and thirty (plus thirty-five in reserve) SS (*Romeo*).

SUBMARINE INSIGNIA

The People's Liberation Army, of which the Navy is a component part, abolished all ranks and insignia on 1 June, 1965. At the same time the various branches of the PLA adopted a universal olive-drab uniform of austere appearance. Several years later the Naval and Air branches gradually incorporated more distinctive designs for their uniforms.

On 21 May, 1984, it was announced that new uniforms would be introduced and that proposals would be made to reintroduce ranks and rank insignia. The new uniforms for all three traditional services appeared in mid-1985 and the new rank insignia along with branch badges were authorized on 1 October, 1988.

By April, 1990, a submarine badge had made an appearance though

its authenticity has, as yet, not been confirmed by official sources. It is said to be awarded to submarine commanders for superior performance. (The term 'commander', before rank titles was reintroduced, referred to all commissioned officers, so it is possible that other officers may qualify.) It is made of a dull gold-coloured metal and consists of the starboard bow view of a submarine within a wreath on the base of which is a tablet bearing the inscription 'HGTZH'. The whole is surmounted by a star, the centre of which encircles the Chinese inscription '8,1' (commemorating the date of the formation of the People's Liberation Army, 1 August, 1928). Representations of waves spread out from either side of the centre device.

The badge measures 60mm x 24mm and on the reverse are four Chinese characters, below which is the English inscription 'PPR Navy'. The insignia is normally fixed by two clutch fasteners, though other fixings are possible. It is presented in a box displaying two rows of Chinese characters.

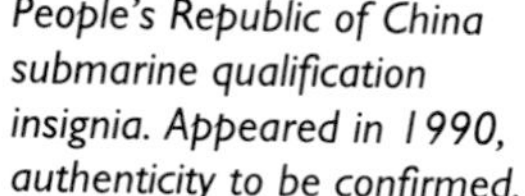

People's Republic of China submarine qualification insignia. Appeared in 1990, authenticity to be confirmed.

Colombia

Submarine Service

The first Colombian submarines entered service in 1972. These were two midget SX-506 type submarines purchased in sections in Italy and transported to Colombia for assembly. Named *Intrepido* and *Indomable* they are of 58 tons surface displacement, 75.4 ft long and can carry eight attack swimmers with two tons of explosives as well as two SDVs (Swimmer Delivery Vehicles).

These were followed in 1975 by two 209 (type 1200) (SS) West German-built patrol submarines of 1,000 tons surface displacement and named *Pijao* and *Tayrona*. These four boats constitute the submarine force at the time of writing.

SUBMARINE INSIGNIA

The Colombian submarine badge, which is the same for all personnel, was instituted in 1973. It is made of metal with clutch fastenings and measures 70mm x 25mm. A cloth version is stamped on working overalls. The insignia is worn on all uniforms and is generally positioned on the left-hand-side breast pocket.

The insignia, which is coloured gold, depicts a 209 (type 1200) submarine in the centre of which is the Colombian Navy coat-of-arms in coloured enamel. Either side of the coat-of-arms is an inward-facing dolphin. A miniature version, 42mm x 14mm, also exists.

About 1991 a silver variation of the full-size badge appeared and was said to be for ratings. This has not been verified and it is quite possible that, like Spain and Chile, the insignia is for shore-based supporting personnel.

About the same date a new version of the standard insignia also put in an appearance. The two dolphins are replaced by two sharks which are situated entirely below the submarine, whereas the standard badge has their heads midway up the hull, also the naval coat-of-arms is replaced by the national coat-of-arms. It is possible that this may be a third variation

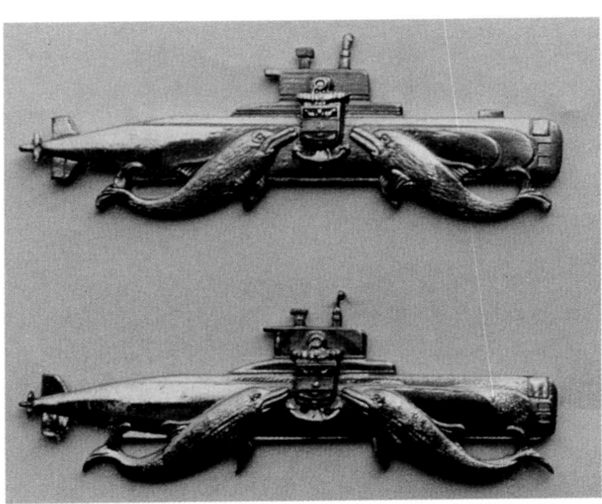

Colombian submarine qualification insignia, authorized 1973, showing slight variations in manufacture.

of the Amphibious Commando badge, the sharks being traditionally used on insignia by that unit. The first badge worn by the Amphibious Commandos depicted a gold or silver submarine below which were two sharks; behind the submarine was a parachute canopy. The second pattern showed a commando knife in place of the submarine with a full parachute overlaid by the navy coat-of-arms in the middle.

CROATIA

SUBMARINE SERVICE

The submarine service commenced about 1991 with the capture of the Yugoslav midget *Una* Class submarine 914. On incorporation into the Croatian Navy she was renamed *Soca*. Built in 1985 she displaced 86 tons surfaced. She can carry mines or six combat swimmers plus four swimmer delivery vehicles (SDV). In Croatian hands she was lengthened by twelve feet to incorporate a diesel engine. The construction of a 120 ton midget submarine to be armed with torpedo tubes and carrying SDVs is under consideration. There are also, in service, two former Yugoslav *Mala* Class SDVs.

SUBMARINE INSIGNIA

With such a small submarine force it is unlikely that any specialist insignia exists, though there may be an associated combat swimmers badge.

CUBA

SUBMARINE SERVICE

The Soviet Union transferred a *Foxtrot* Class submarine (SS) to Cuba in February, 1979. In May of the same year a Soviet *Whiskey* Class submarine (SS) was also transferred to Cuba. It became non-operational in 1987 and became a charging station and training facility.

A second *Foxtrot* was transferred to Cuba in January, 1980, and was followed by a third in February, 1984. These submarines are thought to be non-operational.

SUBMARINE INSIGNIA

It is unlikely that special submarine qualification badges exist at present.

DENMARK

SUBMARINE SERVICE

The submarine service was established in 1909 and the first Danish submarines were the eight boats of the *Havmanden* Class. These were Whitehead-built Holland type of Austrian design of which the first three were constructed in Italy in 1911 and the remainder in Denmark from 1911 to 1913. They had a surface displacement of 162 tons and were armed with two torpedo tubes. At the same time one Fiat *San Giorgio* type also entered service. This was a smaller boat of 105 tons surface displacement.

From 1912 to 1915 five *Aegir* (*Neptun*) Class Hay-Whitehead Holland type were constructed in Copenhagen. These boats had a surface displacement of 185 tons and were armed with three 18in torpedo tubes and one 1 pdr gun. They were followed in 1915/18 by three *Bellona* Class *Navy* type submarines of 301 tons surface displacement and armed with four torpedo tubes.

The *Daphne* Class of two boats was completed in 1925 and 1926. These had a surface displacement of 300 tons and were armed with six torpedo tubes and a 14 pdr AA gun.

By 1931 the service consisted of two *Daphne* Class, three *Bellona* Class, two *Aegir* Class and three *Havmanden* Class submarines. This was the force that was in being when Denmark was invaded by Germany in 1940. As a result of the invasion the Danish submarine service ceased to exist, all its boats being either scuttled or captured. After World War II the submarine branch was reconstituted with the transfer to Denmark of three ex-Royal Navy V Class submarines. They became UI (ex-Polish *Dzik*, ex-HMS/M P52), U2 (ex-HMS/M *Vulpine*) and U3 (ex-HMS/M *Morse*, ex-HMS/M *Vortex*) and remained in service until 1957, 1958 and 1968.

Between 1958 and 1964 four new submarines designated the *Delfinen* Class (SS) were constructed in Copenhagen. They had a surface displacement of 600 tons and were armed with four torpedo tubes. These were joined between 1968 and 1969 by two *Narhvalen* Class submarines (SSK) of the West German improved 205 Type built in Denmark under licence. They have a surface displacement of 370 tons and are armed with eight 21in torpedo tubes.

In 1987 Denmark purchased three German-built Type 207 *Kobben* Class submarines (SSK) from Norway. Modernization, including lengthening, commenced the same year.

By 1990 the *Delfinen* Class had been withdrawn from service leaving only the two *Narhvalen* Class and the three *Tumleren* Class (ex-*Kobben*) in service.

Submarine Insignia

The first distinctive submarine badge actually worn was an unofficial one designed in 1972 by Lieutenant-Commander P. B. Soerensen. This came after a period of general discontentment in the submarine service, mainly over pay and career prospects. During this period repeated requests for a special insignia were turned down. The general idea was to keep the uniform free from the multiplicity of insignia worn by some other navies.

This unauthorized insignia was manufactured in gold and red embroidery on dark blue cloth. It consisted of a fouled encircled anchor surmounted by a crown and with a dolphin on each side. It measured 84mm by 41mm and was worn sewn onto the right breast. Sixty badges were made and were worn, as a protest, by all officers in the submarine squadron. The Naval Command reacted quickly and an official badge was authorized in less than a year.

At the same time as this unofficial embroidered badge an unofficial home-made metal badge was quite popular among submarine crews. It was made in quantity by submarine engineering personnel and showed a *Delfinen* Class submarine cut from an aluminium ring. This ring is the component left behind when a submarine signal is fired through an ejector. It was then mounted on the back part of a navy button and worn on the working rig.

The official insignia was approved by the Chief of the Navy on 12 October, 1973, and was authorized for wear from 25 April, 1974. The insignia is made in gold thread embroidery on dark blue fabric. It shows a fouled anchor under a crown with a leaping dolphin on either side. The dimensions are 50mm wide by 50mm high. There is only one grade and size and the same insignia is worn by both officers and ratings.

The insignia is worn by personnel attached to the Submarine Squadron who have passed their submarine training and have served in submarines for five months. Personnel with at least three years' service in submarines are entitled to wear the insignia in perpetuity.

The insignia is worn sewn onto the right side of the uniform in such a way that a horizontal line through the centre of the device would be level with the top of the breast pocket.

A gilt metal badge was produced at the beginning of 1989 measuring 47mm x 44mm with a brooch fastening. The original design was not popular mainly due to the shape of the dolphins. A second more pleasing

version was produced in August, 1989, and, though still not official, it is universally worn on shirts and sweaters.

A cloth insignia can be worn on the upper right arm of the sweater. It consists of a disc 87mm in diameter with the Danish word for Submarine at the top and the abbreviation for Squadron at the bottom. The central device is the crest of the Submarine Squadron. The cap ribbons of ratings serving in submarines bear the word 'UNDERVANDSBÅD' meaning submarine.

Danish unofficial submarine qualification insignia worn by officers 1972-3.

Danish official submarine qualification insignia, all ranks, authorized 25 April, 1974.

Danish submarine identification badge worn on the right sleeve of the sweater.

Danish submarine qualification insignia in metal.
Left: first type (January, 1989) with dolphins' fins above anchor flukes.
Right: second type (August, 1989) with dolphins' fins touching anchor flukes.

ECUADOR

SUBMARINE SERVICE

The Submarine Branch of the Ecuadorian Navy was established in 1974 with the commissioning of the West German-built type 209 patrol submarine (SSK) *Shyri*. A second type 209, the *Huancavilca*, was commissioned in 1987. They have a surface displacement of 980 tons and are armed with eight 21in torpedo tubes. These two boats constitute the present Ecuadorian Navy Submarine Squadron.

SUBMARINE INSIGNIA

The submarine insignia was authorized in June, 1974. It is the same for all rank grades. The insignia is manufactured in metal and consists of a type 209 submarine with a central device, in silver of an eagle encircled by a rope all superimposed on a wreath. It faces the wearer's left. Early badges were of bronze metal and lacked a schnorkel on the sail. Stars may be added to the ballast tank to the right of the eagle device. One silver star represents one patrol of forty-five days duration and one gold star replaces three silver stars. The insignia comes in two sizes. The standard device measures 70mm x 20mm and the smaller one, for wear on mess dress, is about half the size. Fixings consist of brooch, clutch and screw fastenings and the insignia is worn on the right-hand pocket of jackets and shirts.

Qualification for the badge consists of successfully completing the basic submarine course, of one and a half years, within Ecuador or elsewhere.

Ecuadorian submarine qualification insignia with one patrol star.

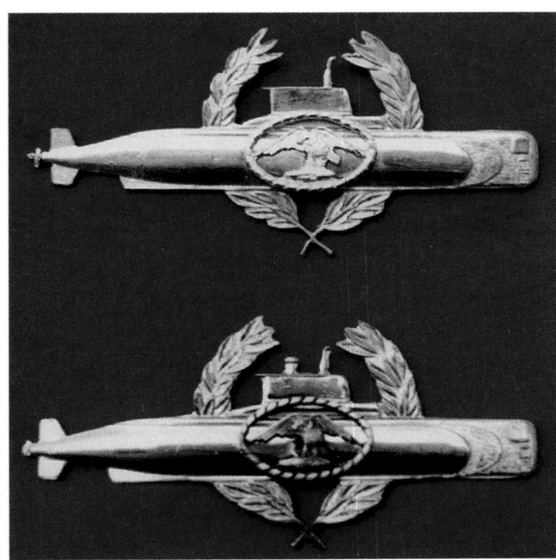

Ecuadorian submarine qualification insignia. Top first type 1974 with periscope only, bottom second type with 'snort' added 1980.

EGYPT

SUBMARINE SERVICE

The Egyptian Navy first included submarines in its order-of-battle in 1957. Between that year and 1969 the Soviet Union transferred nine *Whiskey* class submarines (SS) and three MV class small coastal submarines (SS) to Egypt. The latter only remained in service for a short period.

Eight Soviet *Romeo* Class submarines (SS) were transferred between 1966 and 1969, during which time two of the *Whiskeys* were returned to the USSR.

By the mid-1970s the submarine flotilla consisted of six *Romeos* and six *Whiskeys*. The mid-1980s saw the deletion of two of the *Romeos* but these were replaced by four Chinese-built *Romeos*. The remaining *Whiskeys* were also subsequently deleted. In 1994 approval was given for the USA to fund the construction, in Germany, of two Type 209 Class submarines (SSK) to be fitted with US equipment. These are not likely to enter service much before the end of the century.

The present (1996) submarine force consists of two ex-Soviet *Romeos* and four ex-Chinese *Romeos*. There are also several Italian-designed two-man SDVs.

SUBMARINE INSIGNIA

Little information is available on the Egyptian submarine insignia. Most likely it was authorized in the early 1960s. The badge comes in two sizes, 83mm x 24mm for submarine commanders and a smaller version 55mm x 16mm for submarine officers. They are variously described as being manufactured in gold plate, gilt or bronze metal but most appear to be stamped in brass. The insignia comprises a submarine, facing to the wearer's left, with the national Falcon device in the centre. They are fixed to the uniform with brooch fasteners. The original design varied from the present one in that the conning tower was less streamlined and it was said that they were hand-stamped in the Egyptian Naval Dockyard.

Two other badges, that cannot be verified, are said to exist. One for senior ratings similar to the officer's badge but mounted on a brass ring approximately 50mm in diameter, and one for ratings, possibly in silver or white metal, measuring 45mm x 12mm but without the ring.

A further design exists. This depicts a simple submarine facing the wearer's left. The hull is ornamented by a series of six ovals, then three Arabic characters followed by a further three ovals. It measures 81mm x 20mm (though this can vary) and is made in gold plate, polished brass or casting metal. The quality varies considerably. It is also produced mounted on a 52mm diameter brass ring. Some of these are made in Egyptian bazaars and others are made by an Egyptian company in Canada who claimed that they would gain official approval in 1989. Egyptian Naval Authorities are adamant that these are bogus and certainly unofficial.

Egyptian submarine qualification insignia for commanding officers and other officers.

Examples (right) of bogus Egyptian submarine insignia.

ESTONIA

SUBMARINE SERVICE

Estonia's submarine service was short-lived. Two submarine minelayers were constructed in Great Britain for Estonia and entered service as the *Kalev* and *Lembit* in 1937. They had a surface displacement of 620 tons and were armed with four 21in torpedo tubes and a single 4in AA gun. The mine-laying capacity consisted of twenty mines. Both boats were seized by the Soviet Union on 17 June, 1940, and were incorporated into the Soviet Navy.

SUBMARINE INSIGNIA

It is unlikely that any special submarine insignia ever existed.

FINLAND

SUBMARINE SERVICE

Finland's first submarine was a Holland Class ex-Russian boat, the AG16. It had been scuttled by its Russian crew on 3 April, 1918, at Hango, then raised by Finland in 1924. It was never repaired and was eventually broken up in 1929.

In the years 1926 and 1927 three submarines were laid down in Finnish shipyards. These were commissioned between 1924 and 1931 as the *Vetehinen*, *Vesihiisi* and *Ikuturso*. They had a surface displacement of 493 tons and were armed with four 21in torpedo tubes, one 76mm gun and one 20mm machine gun.

A fourth submarine, the *Saukko*, was laid down in 1929 and commissioned in 1931. A tiny boat, she displaced just 90 tons and was armed with two 18in torpedo tubes and a 13mm gun.

In 1933 a fifth submarine was launched. She was funded by the German Government to carry out trials and to act as a prototype at a time when such activity was prohibited by the Versailles Treaty. In 1934 she was taken over by the Finnish Navy and named *Vesikko*. She had a surface displacement of 250 tons and was armed with three 21in torpedo tubes.

All five submarines survived the Winter War and the Continuation War (World War II) and were credited with sinking at least four Soviet submarines. At the end of the war they were disarmed by the Allied Supervisory Committee.

The Treaty of Paris in 1947 prohibited Finland from having submarines. All but the *Vesikko* were sold to Belgium in 1953 for scrap.

The *Vesikko* was preserved in the hope that the Navy would be allowed to keep one submarine for A/S training purposes. This was not allowed. In 1959 she was transferred to the Military Museum of Finland at Helsinki and opened to the public in 1973.

Submarine Insignia

It is unlikely that any special submarine insignia ever existed.

France

Submarine Service

France was the first country to adopt the submarine as a vessel of war. The honour of being the world's first offensive submarine went to the *Gymnôte*, a boat of 30 tons displacement armed with two torpedos carried in slings. She was launched in 1888 and a year later she was followed by the *Gustave Zédé*. This second submarine was considerably larger, displacing 270 tons, and was armed with one torpedo tube. The *Morse*, of 146 tons displacement, followed in 1899. All three were extremely successful. Numerous similar boats followed.

Seventeen classes were constructed before World War I. At the commencement of hostilities France had ninety-two submarines. At the war's end sixty-two submarines remained in service. After peace was declared, forty-six ex-German U-Boats were ceded to France of which ten were incorporated into the French Navy.

Between the wars, as an economical alternative to battleships and for mercantile warfare, France built up a sizable submarine fleet. Among these vessels was, perhaps, the world's most famous submarine, the *Surcouf*. Classed as a submarine cruiser, she displaced 2,880 tons and was armed with two 8in guns, eight 21.7in torpedo tubes, four 15.7in torpedo tubes, two 37mm AA guns and two 13.2mm AA guns. In addition she carried a sea-plane, only the fifth submarine in the world to do so. She was designed for extended operations against trade and could cruise unreplenished for ninety days. A boarding launch was carried and there was a compartment sufficiently large to hold forty prisoners-of-war.

At the outbreak of World War II France had just under one hundred

submarines in service. However, by the Fall of France the great majority were either sunk, scuttled or interned. Fifteen submarines escaped to join the Fighting French, including the *Surcouf*. Five were eventually lost, one of which was the *Surcouf*, lost in a collision in 1942. A further two were scrapped before the war's end. The Free French Flotilla was augmented by the transfer of three ex-Royal Navy U/V Class submarines and one ex-Italian boat.

The reconstituted French Navy started its peacetime service with thirty-six submarines, the majority of which had spent the war years interned. This number was increased by the acquisition of five ex-German U-Boats.

Post-war submarine construction commenced with the 1,320 ton *Narval* Class (SS) of six vessels and the smaller 400 ton *Aretuse* Class (SS) of four vessels, all of which were launched between 1957 and 1960. These were followed by the highly successful *Daphne* Class (SSK) of 860 tons surface displacement. Ten of this class were constructed for the French Navy of which the *Eurydice* was lost and *Sirene* was sunk but later recovered and returned to service. Further boats were built for export.

In 1964 a conventionally powered experimental submarine of 3,000 tons, the *Gymnôte*, was launched. She was armed with two missile launching tubes and her role was to carry out trials for the firing of ICBMs for France's future deterrent force.

The first nuclear propelled submarine was *Redoutable*, the name-ship of her class (SSBN). She had a surface displacement of 8,080 tons and carried sixteen ballistic missiles plus four 21in torpedo tubes. Five sister submarines were added between 1973 and 1985. The lead ship was paid off in December, 1991, and the class was re-named *L'Inflexible*.

Perhaps the last conventionally powered French submarines, the four 1,200 ton *Agosta* Class (SSK), entered service between 1977 and 1978. Equally successful to the *Daphne* Class, they also led to foreign orders.

France's first nuclear-powered hunter-killer submarine (SSN) made its appearance in 1979 with the launching of the 2,385 ton displacement *Rubis*, the name-ship of its class. She commissioned in February, 1983, and five further vessels commissioned between 1984 and 1993. Boats of the *Rubis* Class are armed with four 21in torpedo tubes and are capable of firing missiles.

A follow-on class of three, possibly four, SSBNs to the *L'Inflexible* Class are the *Le Triomphant* Class. The name-ship will be commissioned in September, 1996, and the remainder should be in service by 2005. These large submarines will have a surface displacement of 12,640 tons and will be armed with sixteen SLBM of an advanced nature. At the time

of writing (1996) the French Submarine Force consists of five *L'Inflexible* Class (SSBN) '*Le Force de Dissuasion*', six *Rubis* Class (SSN), four *Agosta* Class (SSK) and three *Daphne* Class (SSK).

SUBMARINE INSIGNIA

Before the approval of a special submarine qualification badge for all ranks, submarine service ratings, from the early 1930s, wore a distinctive cloth branch badge on their upper left sleeve. The device consisted of crossed torpedoes with six bolts of lightning radiating outwards. It was worn in gold, yellow or red on blue, depending on rank, and measured 70mm wide.

On 24 December, 1946, a metal badge for all qualified submarine personnel was created. This depicted a gold-coloured *Narval* class submarine in its original configuration with a stepped sail (conning tower) facing its wearer's left. This was superimposed on a white metal compass rose in the form of a ring with an upright white metal sword with a gold hilt (behind the submarine) in the centre. It measured 55m x 48mm and was secured by clutch fasteners. A cloth version in red or yellow embroidery was phased out in the mid-1950s. (On 16 August, 1961, this badge was redesigned as a superior grade insignia intended primarily for officers and certain senior ratings with special qualifications.) At the same time a second badge, designated as an elementary grade insignia, was authorized mainly for junior ratings and later for certain other categories pending qualification for the superior insignia. Its design consisted of the same gold-coloured submarine, but mounted on a smaller diameter compass rose and bearing the cardinal points only. This also lacked the vertical sword. It measured 55mm x 30mm. This was phased out in 1967. From 1961 to 1967 the superior grade insignia was restricted to officers who had been in command for two years and other officers with four years of submarine service.

The system was changed with the implementation of three grades on 16 December, 1974. The new badges are much like their two predecessors but the sail (conning tower) of the submarine is streamlined. The lowest grade is issued to officers who hold a certificate of general knowledge in submarines and to ratings with an elementary submarine certificate. It is similar in design to the original superior badge but lacks the vertical sword and is known as 'without swords'. The next grade is issued to officers who are qualified in submarine navigation, or as seamen or engineer watch officers of a nuclear submarine or who hold a superior submarine certificate. For ratings it is granted to those who hold a submarine certificate of the higher grade. The design is almost identical to

the previous superior badge. It is known as 'with one sword'. The highest grade is worn by commanding officers and former commanding officers only. It is known as 'with two swords criss-crossed'. All three badges measure 55mm x 48mm and have clutch fastenings.

The submarine badges are worn on uniform in one size only, though a smaller version, 19mm x 16mm is available for wear on civilian clothes. The insignia can be worn throughout the recipient's service but it can be withdrawn for disciplinary reasons.

A new version (its authenticity has yet to be verified) was introduced about 1989. This bears the 1974 submarine design mounted on a simple

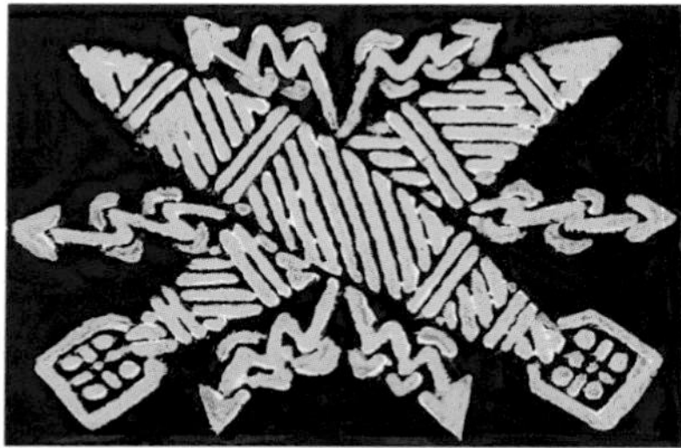

French submarine crew branch badge pre-1946. Gold wire embroidery optional for senior ratings otherwise yellow embroidery. Not worn by officers.

French submarine crew branch badge pre-1946. Red embroidery for junior ratings. These badges were replaced in 1946 by the new metal insignia, though junior ratings at first wore the new design in red embroidery on cloth.

French submarine qualification insignia 1946 to 1974.
Top: elementary qualification.
Bottom: superior qualification.

silver-coloured ring 25mm in diameter. This may be for shore based support personnel.

The official description of how insignia is to be worn is as follows, 'worn on the right-hand side of the chest on all dress uniforms where decorative ribbons are allowed. The insignia is placed in the middle of the chest pocket on all white and khaki jackets and shirts, and above the pleat on the chest of the blue jacket'.

Sailors serving in submarines wear on their cap tallies the words 'SOUS-MARIN' followed by the submarine's name.

French submarine qualification insignia 'without swords' 1974.

French submarine qualification insignia 'with one sword' 1974.

French submarine qualification insignia 'with two swords' 1974.

French submarine insignia about 1990, possibly shore support, elementary, or maybe unofficial.

GERMANY: EMPIRE

SUBMARINE SERVICE

Uncertain as to the value of the submarine as a tool of war, Germany was a late starter in this field. Using the knowledge gained by other nations her first boats, when they did appear, were right up-to-date. The first boat, the U-1, was launched on 30 August 1905 (though two experimental boats had been launched in 1890 but were never actively employed).

U-1 was very successful and was roughly equivalent to the British D Class. She had a displacement of 197 tons and was armed with one bow torpedo tube and three 17.7in torpedoes were carried. A further twenty-nine boats in five classes were completed so that Germany commenced World War I with thirty submarines in service of which twenty were operational. These, unlike the Royal Navy's submarines, were all in home waters based at Kiel, Wilhelmshaven and Heligoland.

Being a military power, Germany initially did not appreciate the value of the submarine. It was not until stalemate on the Western Front that submarine warfare was stepped up. Once the U-boat's value was appreciated the U-boat arm was given priority. It was a very efficient organization and its personnel were well trained. Their average diving time was a remarkable twenty-seven seconds. By 1917 seventy-two submarines had been constructed.

Wartime construction was based on nine main classes including: ocean going, coastal, mine-laying and merchant types. By the war's end 345 had been built. Some mounted 5.9in guns and U-12 made history on 1 January, 1915, when she operated a small aircraft from her foredeck.

German submarines sank nearly 12 million tons of Allied shipping in World War I but lost 178 U-boats and 5,364 out of the 13,000 officers and men in the U-boat arm. After the armistice the U-boat arm was either interned or scuttled. Two hundred and three boats surrendered; all, with the exception of ten ex-French boats, were scrapped between 1922 and 1923.

SUBMARINE INSIGNIA

On 1 February, 1918, by order of the Kaiser, submariners of the Imperial German Navy were authorized to wear a distinctive insignia. It was manufactured in heavy gold-coloured metal 48mm x 46mm. The design consisted of a U-boat facing the wearer's left completely surrounded by a wreath. The official description stated that the composition of the up-

per half of the wreath was to be of laurel leaves and the lower half was to be of oak leaves. However, only laurel leaves actually appear on the badge. The leaves of the wreath were bound together by a representation of a ribbon. The entire device was surmounted by an Imperial Crown. On the reverse was a substantial vertical hinged securing pin and hook and the name of the manufacturer, Zeither-Berlin, was inscribed on the back of the submarine.

The same design was worn by all ranks on the lower part of the left breast. Unlike the submarine insignia of most other countries which were for professional qualifications, the German insignia was regarded more as a reward for war service. An unofficial miniature (34mm x 29mm) appeared some years after World War I.

U-boat crews were distinguished by their cap ribbons which bore the words 'UNTERSEEBOOT' or 'U-BOOT' in conjunction with the number of their flotilla, half flotilla, base or function. All tallies were in capital letters during World War I, changed to lower case in World War II.

German Submarine War Badge 1918.

Germany: 1918-45

Submarine Service

The Treaty of Versailles forbade Germany from having submarines. However, in order to gain experience for the future, the German Government financed the construction of two submarines in the Netherlands for the Turkish Navy. Later this method was again used to supply five submarines to Finland, one to Spain and a further one to Turkey. When the Treaty was finally abrogated, the U-boat arm was one of the first units to be re-established.

The first post-war submarines, three in number, were commissioned in 1936. They displaced 862 tons, mounted two 5.9in guns and carried six 19.7in torpedo tubes. These were quickly followed by five more classes totalling fifty-eight boats.

At the commencement of war in 1939 Germany had fifty-seven U-boats in commission. A massive production programme then began. It consisted of five main types: cruiser, ocean-going, sea-going, coastal and mine-laying submarines. In all 1,074 submarines were completed. Perhaps the two most potent developments were the schnorkel (originally a Dutch invention) and the acoustic homing torpedo (Gnat).

Germany's U-boat arm very nearly changed the course of the war. As a measure of its success, at the peak of the Battle of the Atlantic, in June, 1943, it sank nearly 650,000 tons of Allied shipping. The total tonnage destroyed during the war amounted to 14.5 million tons.

At the end of the war, of the 1,162 U-boats in operational service, it is generally accepted that 784 were lost, 157 surrendered and 221 were scuttled. Of the 39,000 U-boat officers and men only 7,000 survived. Germany was again without a submarine fleet.

(As there is a vast literary coverage of the Kriegsmarine U-boat arm — probably more than any other similar force — this section has been deliberately abbreviated and only the salient details have been mentioned.)

SUBMARINE INSIGNIA 1939-45

Following the Kaiser's example Hitler authorized a submarine war badge (*U-Boot Kriegsabzeichen*) on 13 October, 1939. Like its predecessor it was more of an award than a qualification. It was awarded to submariners after two sorties against the enemy. However, an immediate award could be made to individuals who won a bravery decoration, were wounded or who had been involved in a particularly successful mission. The insignia, which was manufactured in heavy-gold coloured metal, showed a submarine facing the wearer's right surmounted by an eagle and swastika. Behind the eagle's wings and surrounding the submarine was a laurel wreath tied together at the base by a crossed ribbon. The badge measured 48mm x 39mm.

The insignia was produced in various standards of quality and with minor differences in design. The insignias made early in the war were of a very fine quality but the workmanship of later models, some of which were made in France, could not compare. The early badges displayed the manufacturer's name on the reverse (Schwerin und Sohn, Berlin) and were secured by a broad vertical hinged pin and hook. The later models

showed the manufacturer's initials only, eg FO (for Frederich Orth), and had a narrow pin and hook fastener. Later patterns made in France had horizontal pins. There was also a cloth version, gilt wire on silk for officers and gold cloth on felt for ratings.

A special insignia was presented to particularly successful U-Boat commanders who had first to be holders of the Knight's Cross of the Iron Cross with oak leaves. It was of the same standard design but was manufactured in silver and had nine diamonds inset on the swastika.

Grossadmiral Karl Dönitz was presented with a unique insignia produced in gold with twenty-one diamonds on the swastika and a further twelve on the wreath.

On 26 July, 1957, the submarine war badge was de-nazified by the removal of the eagle and swastika. It also appears in miniature with a black Maltese Cross in place of the eagle and swastika. This style was worn by submarine old comrades organizations. Like other de-nazified insignia it was, in 1957, miniaturized in silver and worn on uniforms attached to a small black ribbon 30mm wide and worn in conjunction with medal ribbons.

U-Boat crew could also be distinguished by their cap ribbons which bore the words, in gothic lettering, 'Unterseebootsflottille' followed by the flotilla name. Unofficial badges were often worn on the sides of caps by individual U-Boat crews. There were numerous designs such as sharks, weapons and flowers. They were not allowed to be worn ashore. U-Boat Captains were distinguished at sea by wearing white cap covers.

To bring awards to U-Boat crews in line with awards available to the Army and Air Force, submarine combat clasps (*U-Boat Frontspange*) were introduced in 1944. The insignia was created in bronze metal on 15 May and in silver metal on the 24 November. Later in the war a gilt or gold badge was authorized but it is unlikely that it was ever awarded.

The U-Boat combat clasp depicted a central device similar to the submarine war badge, the only differences being that the wings of the eagle followed the curvature of the wreath and the crossed ribbon at the base was replaced by crossed swords. On either side was a spray of six oak leaves. The reverse had a large horizontal hinged pin and hook fastener and bore the manufacturer's mark and the name of the designer, 'PEEKHAUS'. For exceptional U-Boat Commanders the badge was awarded with diamonds. It measured 74mm x 24mm. The U-Boat combat clasps were awarded for continuous service in action, gallantry and tenacious conduct on active service. The various grades indicated ascending achievements. On 26 July, 1957, the insignia was de-nazified by the removal of the eagle and swastika. This altered device measured 77mm

x 24mm and like the submarine war badge was miniaturized and worn on a black ribbon 30mm wide.

Though not primarily a submarine award, the combat badge for small fighting units (*Kampfabzeichen der Kleinkampfmittel*, otherwise 'K' men or frogmen) is included because the insignia was also awarded to crews of miniature submarines. The award was created on 30 November, 1944, and came in seven classes, the first four of which were cloth and the remainder in metal (though cloth versions of these were also produced). The four cloth insignias were of yellow or gold embroidery on a navy blue disc 80mm in diameter. The basic design consisted of a leaping swordfish (or sawfish) behind which was a circle of rope knotted at the top. The first (or basic) class displayed the swordfish and rope only and was awarded for two months' service in which a mission was planned and achieved good results. The second class displayed a single sword on a forty-five degree angle pointed to the wearer's right behind the basic design. It was awarded for one combat action. The third class displayed two crossed swords behind the basic device and was awarded for two combat actions. The fourth class displayed three swords behind the basic device and was awarded for three or four combat actions.

The three senior awards in metal consisted of a leaping swordfish superimposed on a loosely coiled and knotted rope, measuring 70mm x 22mm and secured by a horizontal pin and hook on the reverse. The bronze or fifth class was awarded for five or six combat actions. The silver or sixth class was awarded for seven, eight or nine combat actions and the gold or seventh class was awarded for ten or more combat actions. Little evidence exists as to whether these badges were ever actually worn in wartime, though, as they contained no nazi emblems, they were reintroduced by the Bundesmarine as commemorative awards in 1957.

Though not a submarine qualification badge, a bronze insignia was presented to dockyard employees working on U-Boats. It depicted a U-Boat facing the wearer's right with a cogged wheel encircling its middle section and surmounted by the German Eagle and swastika. It measured 33mm x 23mm and was fixed to clothing by a 49mm stick pin. Its German name was *Werftleistungsabzeichen*.

There are several types of U-Boat old comrade badges dating from about 1957. Most depict miniature, de-nazified versions of the U-Boat War Badge or U-Boat Combat Clasp in gold, silver or bronze. Numerous other unofficial badges connected with the U-Boat service abound. Most are connected with specific units. An insignia resembling an oval breast badge was said to have been worn by recruits on completion of their training and awaiting assignment to a U-Boat. This was of course

quite unofficial. It consisted of a diving submarine below the inscription '*frontreif*' ('ripe for the front') surrounded by a German Eagle and swastika. It was secured by a vertical flat brooch pin and clasp and was made in either brass or grey metal.

German Submarine War Service Badge 1939-45.

German Submarine War Service Badges 1939-45, de-Nazified 1957. (50mm x 37mm).

German Submarine War Service Badge 1939-45, de-Nazified for Submarine Old Comrades Association.

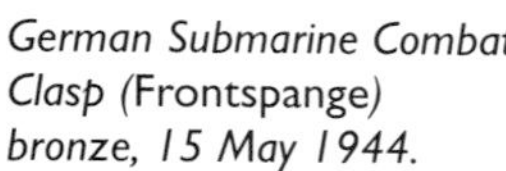

German Submarine Combat Clasp (Frontspange) *bronze, 15 May 1944.*

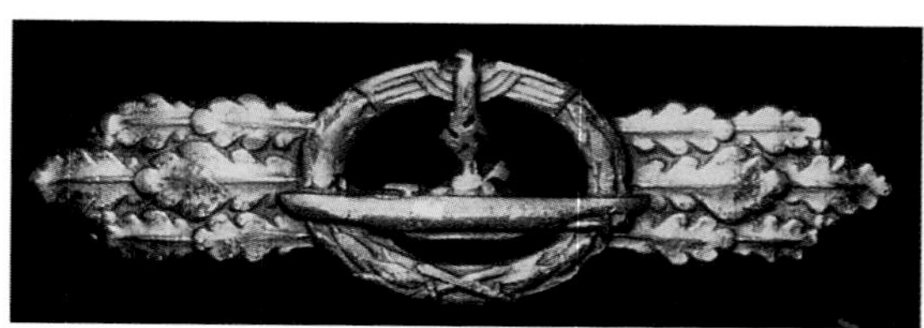

German Submarine Combat Clasp (Frontspange) silver, 24 November 1944.

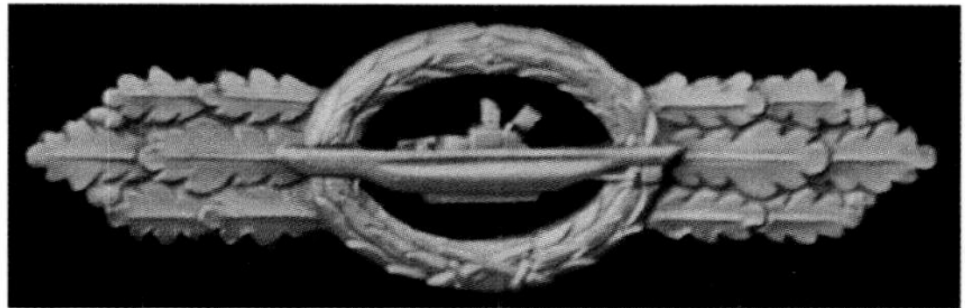

*German Submarine Combat Clasp (*Frontspange*), 1944-5, de-Nazified 1957.*

*German Small Fighting Units (*Kampfabzeichen der Kleinkampfmittel*) insignia 1944. In yellow embroidery on black cloth for junior grades. Left: 1st grade, right: 2nd grade.*

*German Small Fighting Units (*Kampfabzeichen der Kleinkampfmittel*) insignia 1944. Left: 3rd grade, right: 4th grade.*

*German Small Fighting Units (*Kampfabzeichen der Kleinkampfmittel*) insignia 1944. In metal for three senior grades. 5th grade bronze, 6th grade silver, 7th grade gold.*

German lapel badge for civilian dockyard employees working on U-Boats, 1944-5.

GERMANY: FEDERAL REPUBLIC

SUBMARINE SERVICE

After gaining full independence in 1955 West Germany was allowed to build up a naval force. The first submarines entered Bundesmarine service in 1956. There were three re-built former wartime U-Boats, two of the XXIII Type and one of the XXI Type. They were followed by two classes of small coastal submarines, eleven 419 ton Type 205 (SS) from 1961 to 1969 and eighteen 450 ton Type 206 (SSK) from 1973 to 1975.

A further class of four vessels designated the Type 212 (SSK) is projected to enter service by 2003. These boats will have a surface displacement of 1,320 tons and will be armed with six 21in torpedo tubes. They will also have a minelaying capacity.

At the time of writing (1996) the German submarine force numbers six Type 206 and twelve Type 206A (modified Type 206). These are supported by two type 205, relegated for trails and target duties.

SUBMARINE INSIGNIA

The first appearance of a submarine badge was about 1965. This was the Submarine Specialist Qualification, awarded to ratings on completion of training at the Basic Submarine Training School (Gesubtng), Neustadt. Made of cloth, it depicted, on a disc of 50mm diameter, an embroidered submarine of basic design facing the wearer's right above two rows of waves. It was worn on the left sleeve just above the cuff and was manufactured in red on blue and red on white (gold and yellow versions on blue and white were worn by senior ratings). This insignia which first appeared in the 1968 Dress Regulations became obsolete in 1982. From 1972 to 1982 it was worn by ratings who did not qualify for the later breast insignia described below.

In June, 1972, a new submarine qualification badge was authorized. The first dress regulations illustrating this badge appeared on 16 March, 1982, some ten years later. It was to be awarded to all ranks after six months' service on board a submarine plus successfully completing submarine training. The insignia was manufactured in cloth and showed a submarine design facing the wearer's left, behind which was a simple oak leaf wreath. The device was to be worn on the right upper breast. It was manufactured in deep yellow on dark blue, but officers, at their own discretion, could wear it in gold wire embroidery. For other types of uniform it also came in yellow on olive drab and yellow or gold on white. The standard measurement was 78mm x 33mm but some were produced in widths of 80, 83 and 84mm. By mid-1988 it was generally felt that these badges were too big so they were all reduced to 64mm x 28mm.

A gold-coloured metal version of the cloth badge appeared some time before 1984. It was quite unofficial but was universally worn on shirts. It depicted a more stylized submarine resembling the 206 Class and on the back it bore the inscription 'NAVY-YACHT-SERVICE 04421/203090'. It was fixed to the shirt by horizontal brooch type pin and it measured 59mm x 35mm. A miniature was also produced measuring 30mm x 24mm on a vertical stick pin. In 1990 this unofficial metal insignia was upgraded to a more detailed design. The backs either bore the inscription 'DEUMER Ludenscheid' or were plain. This model measured 63mm x 35mm but several hand-made variations appeared, mostly measuring 77mm x 35mm. Occasionally these badges are worn on leather thongs incorporating a button hole for suspension of the insignia from buttons on certain types of uniforms.

In mid-1987 an official gold-coloured metal badge was authorized for wear on shirts and sweaters. It consisted of a submarine of the same design as the earlier cloth insignia but embossed on a curved and contoured pebbled plate measuring 75mm x 25mm. Two clutch fasteners were provided for fixing the insignia to clothing. It was awarded for six months' service on board a submarine, a somewhat lesser qualification than that stated for the cloth badge. It has not proved popular and many submariners continue to wear the unofficial versions.

Cap ribbons further distinguish submarine ratings by the inclusion of the word 'UNTERSEEBOOT'. This has now largely lapsed as, since 1974, the lowest submarine rank is Petty Officer.

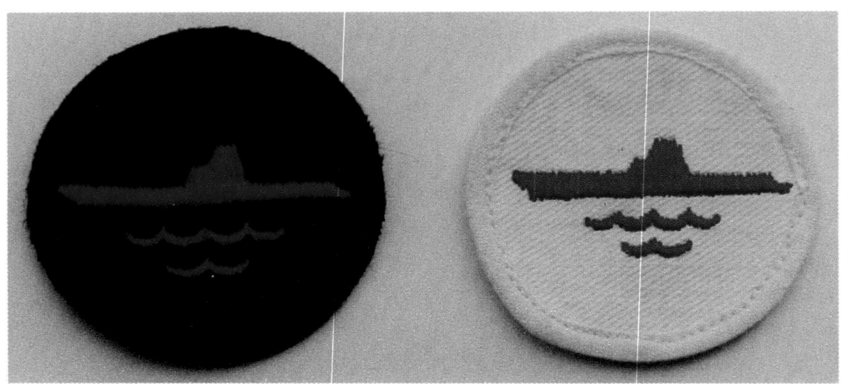

German first post-war submarine badge, about 1965 to 1972. Specialist qualification awarded to ratings on completion of training at the Basic Submarine School (Gesubtng) Neustadt. It was worn on the left sleeve just above the cuff.

German submarine qualification insignia, yellow on dark blue, worn in winter by all ranks after six months on board a submarine plus successful completion of submarine training. Worn from June ,1972. (80mm).

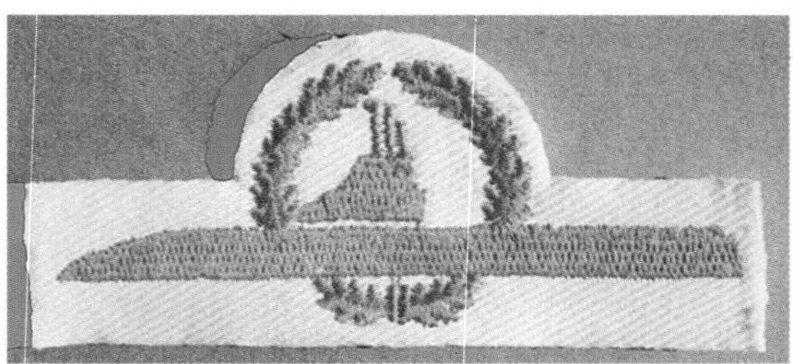

German submarine qualification insignia, as above but yellow on white. (84mm).

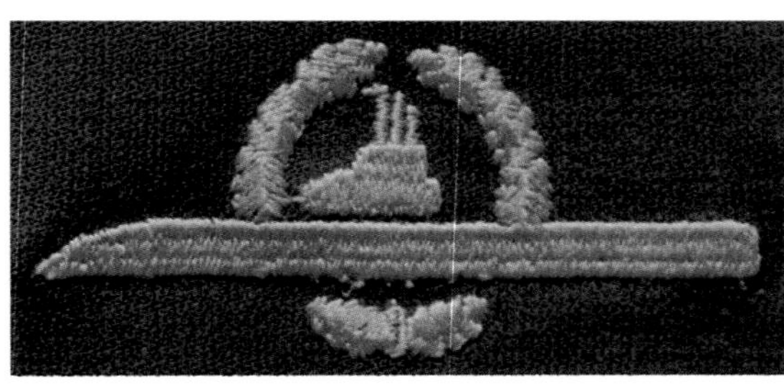

German submarine qualification insignia, as previous example but yellow on olive drab for working uniform. (84mm).

German submarine qualification insignia embroidered in gold wire. Worn by officers and warrant officers at their discretion. Various sizes.

German official metal submarine qualification insignia produced mid-1987. Though the only official metal submarine badge it is seldom worn. Most personnel favour the unofficial styles.

German unofficial metal submarine qualification insignia, first design 1984. Depicts a Type 206 submarine. Inscription on reverse is 'Navy-Yacht-Service 04421/203090'.

German unofficial metal submarine qualification insignia, second design 1990. Depicts a Type 206 submarine as before, but has more detail. Inscription on reverse is 'DEUMER Ludenscheid' or left plain.

Greece

Submarine Service

Greece first showed interest in submarines when in 1886 she purchased a Nordenfelt I, the first type to be armed with a torpedo. Used for experimental purposes, it is doubtful if she every entered active Naval service. The first submarines to join the fleet were two French-built Laubeuf type, the *Delphin* and the *Xiphias*. Completed in 1911 and 1912 they displaced 295 tons and were armed with five torpedo tubes. Both were seized by the French in December, 1916, and incorporated into the French Navy, only to be returned in 1917.

The next submarines to enter Greek service were two Schneider Laubeuf type, again French-built. They displaced 576 tons and were armed with four 21in torpedo tubes, one 4in gun and one 3 pdr AA gun. Named *Katsonis* and *Papmicolis* they were commissioned in 1927. Within a year four more submarines were completed in France for the Greek Navy. They were designated the *Glavkos* Class and named *Nereus*, *Proteus*, *Triton* and *Glavkos*. They displaced 700 tons and were armed with eight 21in torpedo tubes, one 4in gun and a 3 pdr AA gun. Three of these boats were later to be lost in World War II.

During the invasion of Greece in 1940 five submarines escaped to serve under Allied operational control. Between 1943 and 1946 the Royal Navy loaned six submarines to the Greek Navy, one P Class and five U/V Class. All were returned by 1956. In addition to these one Italian submarine was taken over in 1943 and continued in service until 1954.

The United States loaned the post-war Greek Navy two ex-*Gato* Class submarines (SS) in 1957. One was returned in 1967 and the other returned in 1972. In addition an ex-*Balao* Class (SS) was loaned in 1965 and purchased in 1976.

The first modern submarines, purposely built for Greece, were four 209 Class (type 1100) (SSK) constructed in West Germany. They displaced 1,100 tons and were armed with eight 21in torpedo tubes. They entered service between 1971 and 1973 as the *Glavkos* Class. These were followed by the acquisition of two more ex-USN submarines, a *Guppy* IIA (SS) in 1972 and a *Guppy* III (SS) in 1973. West Germany supplied a further four submarines of the 209 Class (type 1200) (SSK) between 1979 and 1980. Similar in most respects to the previously delivered 209s, they were incorporated into the same class. Both *Guppies* were deleted in 1993.

At the time of writing (1996) the submarine arm consists of eight *Glavros* Class type 209 Class (SSK).

SUBMARINE INSIGNIA

The Greek submarine insignia was first authorized in 1916. The badge in current use is made of gold coloured metal, for officers and petty officers, and measures 65mm x 10mm. For junior ratings it is made in silver-coloured metal and measures 45mm x 10mm. The design is the same for all ranks and consists of a British Type U/V Class submarine facing the wearer's right. Both types can be fixed to clothing by clutch or screw fasteners. An embroidered gold wire insignia is available to officers and petty officers at their own discretion as is a miniature badge for mess dress.

The insignia is worn on the upper part of the left breast above decorations. In order to qualify personnel must successfully complete the submarine school course. For Officers the course lasts five months, for senior Petty Officers three to five months and for junior ratings two to three months.

Until 1970 submarine badges were hand-made by Naval technicians. Because of this slight variation occurred in their manufacture. They are now produced commercially being cast/pressed and follow a uniform pattern.

About 1957 an unofficial design appeared in the shape of foreshortened *Gato* Class (ex-US) submarine. It was made of highly polished flat .032in thick brass, faced its' wearer's right and was fixed by two clutch fasteners. Its dimensions were 60mm x 22mm. There is also an unofficial velcro-backed cloth badge.

Sailors serving in submarines wear a cap tally prefixed with the letters 'Y/B', meaning submarine, followed by the boat's name eg 'Y/B Τπιτον' (submarine Triton). By 1988 few junior ratings were employed in submarines; the smaller silver badge has therefore been withdrawn

from issue and the submarine cap tallies are seldom seen.

The Greek Royal Navy Campaign Cross (ribbon equal widths of blue, white, blue) was instituted on 22 December, 1943, and awarded for at least six months' active and meritorious service at sea during World War II. It was awarded for those serving in submarines for more than a year and taking part in at least three patrols. On service dress when only ribbons were worn an additional black ribbon 37mm wide was worn. On this, in the form of metal clasps, were fixed miniature submarines, gold for officers, silver for petty officers and bronze for junior ratings.

Greek submarine qualification insignia. Top: in gold-coloured metal (65mm) for officers and senior ratings. Bottom in silver-coloured metal (44mm) for junior ratings. Design based on original hand-made badges (1916) but from 1970 professionally manufactured.

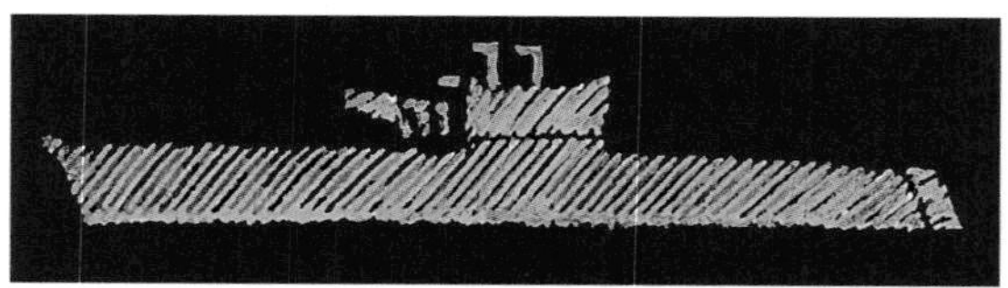

Greek submarine qualification insignia in gold wire embroidery for officers.

Devices worn on the Greek Royal Navy Campaign Cross 1943 for six months' active or meritorious service at sea World War II. Gold for officers, silver for senior ratings and bronze for junior ratings.

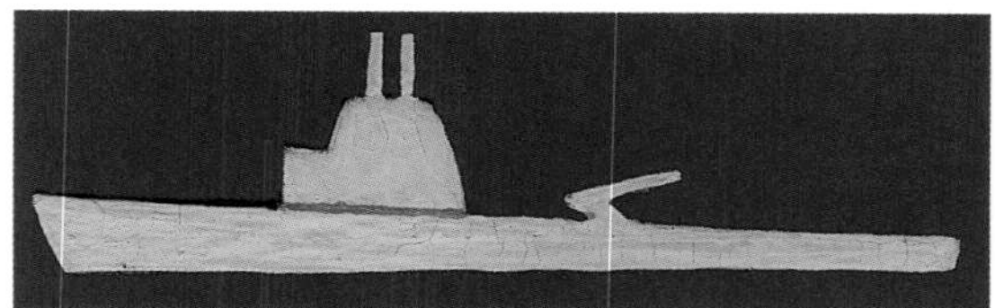

Greek unofficial submarine insignia worn from about 1957 to 1972 in Gato Class submarines on loan from the United States.

INDIA

SUBMARINE SERVICE

India took delivery of its first submarines between 1968 and 1969 with the arrival of three newly constructed Soviet *Foxtrots* (SS). Five more followed between 1970 and 1975.

In 1986 six 209 Class (type 1500) submarines (SSK) were ordered from West Germany. Two were completed under licence in Bombay, then the remainder were cancelled in favour of six larger 2000 types. However, these too were later cancelled and construction reverted to the type 1500 of which a final total of four were constructed. Also in 1986 the Soviet Union delivered the first of eight *Kilo* Class attack submarines (SSK) with an option for a further two.

On 3 February, 1988, India joined the 'nuclear club' by leasing from the Soviet Union a *Charlie* I Class SSGN. She was intended to be the lead-boat of a class of from four to six units but she was returned to the Soviet Union in January, 1991, and the whole scheme was abandoned.

There are presently eight *Kilo* Class (SSK), four 209 Type 1500 *Shishumar* Class (SSK) and six *Foxtrot* (SS) in the Indian Navy. In addition there are up to twelve Italian-built two-man SDVs for commando operations.

SUBMARINE INSIGNIA

The Indian submarine insignia was authorized on 8 December, 1967. In appearance it closely resembles that of the United States Navy. The design consists of the state arms, the Pillar of Asoka, with an inward-facing dolphin on either side, all resting on a surf-like base. The badge is made in gold plated metal, measures 71mm x 24mm and has a lug and pin fastening on the reverse. A plastic version is also reported to exist. This is probably reserved for wear on working rig only.

The same device is worn by all ranks and is worn above the pocket on the left-hand breast. There is no official miniature size insignia. Unofficial badges exist in silver metal and in gold bullion embroidery, the latter bearing an anchor, sometimes enclosed in a wreath, below the national emblem and lacking the surf-like base.

Indian submarine qualification insignia, 8 December, 1967.

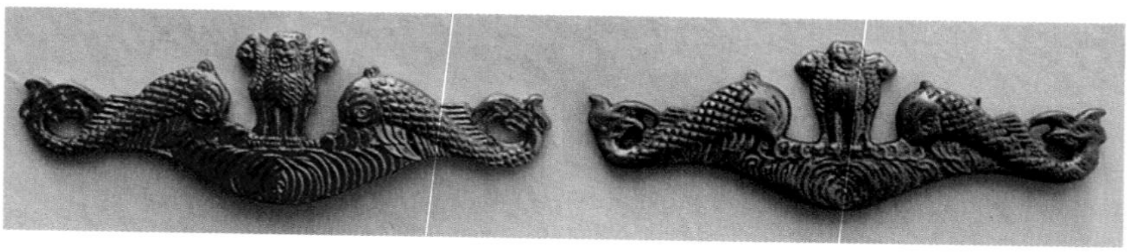

Indian submarine qualification insignia in light gilt casting and in heavy dull brass casting.

Indonesia

Submarine Service

Poland supplied Indonesia with its first submarines with the sale, in 1959, of three ex-Soviet *Whiskey* Class (SS). A further four arrived from the USSR in 1962 and eventually fourteen units were acquired. By 1970 only six were operational; of the remainder, six were in reserve and two were being cannibalized for spares. All but three had been disposed of by 1975 and the last one went out of service in the early eighties.

In 1981 two 209 Class (Type 1300) (SSK) were delivered from West Germany. Named the *Cakra* and the *Nanggala,* they are the initial units of a submarine force to eventually number four. It is envisaged that the other two will be similar to the 209s but of larger dimensions. In 1996 the submarine force still comprised only these two boats.

Submarine Insignia

According to official sources two designs of submarine qualification badges have been authorized. The first type appeared in 1959 when the Submarine Force was first formed. It consisted of a joined two piece, gold-coloured, stamped metal badge. This depicted a diving shark surrounded by a circular wreath; overlaid on this was a *Whiskey* Class submarine, on waves, facing the wearer's left. Badges were shipyard-made and varied considerably in detail.

In 1975 the design was changed to the port bow view of a submarine

flanked either side by sharks all resting on a representation of waves. It was crudely made of bronze metal and variations in detail frequently occurred. Dimensions could also vary; the following sizes have been noted: 85mm x 24mm, 79mm x 21mm and 78mm x 18mm, plus miniatures measuring 45mm x 13mm and 43mm x 11mm. Fixings could be brooch pins or clutch fasteners. This insignia was also produced in gold embroidered thread on black cloth. For various types of other uniforms other types of cloth badges were also worn. These could be embroidered yellow on black or embroidered yellow edged in brown all on a dark olive rectangle with an inner yellow border. This latter insignia measured 105mm x 37mm overall. No doubt other colour combinations existed. This basic design remains in use today. Again there is considerable variations in details of insignia.

A third type of device can also be found. This may have been an earlier prototype or an unofficial version of the present badge. It is made of bronze metal and depicts a *Whiskey* Class submarine facing the wearer's left with diving sharks either side of the central hull section. It measures 82mm x 35mm.

The same design of qualification badge is awarded to all grades of personnel after successfully completing the one-year Submarine Course. It is worn above the left breast pocket.

Indonesian submarine qualification insignia, original type 1959.

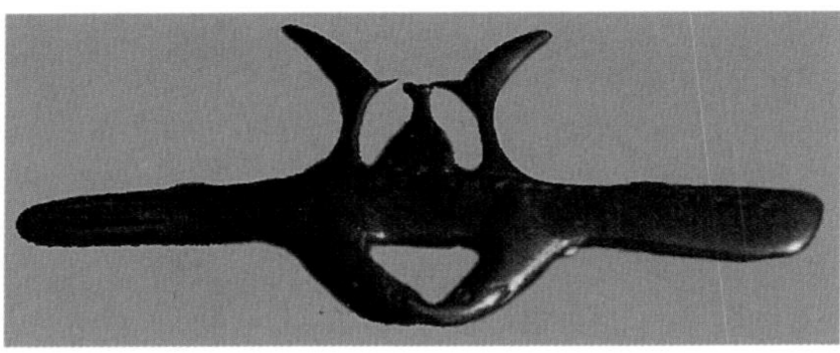

Early Indonesian submarine insignia, dates unknown, possibly a prototype. Design consists of a Whiskey Class submarine and two diving sharks (or dolphins?).

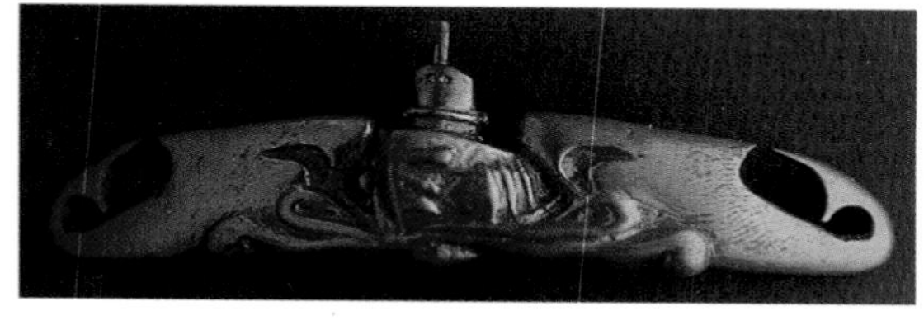

Indonesian submarine qualification insignia 1975.

Indonesian submarine qualification insignia 1975, full size and miniature, showing variations in shark's fins and wave formation.

Cloth versions of Indonesian submarine qualification insignia.

Iran

Submarine Service

In 1976 the Shah's Government ordered nine submarines, three from the United States of America and six from West Germany. The American submarines, which had formerly served in the US Navy, were of the *Tang* Class (SS). Originating from 1951, they were to be named *Kousseh* (SS101), *Nahang* (SS102) and *Dolfin* (SS103). The submarines from West Germany were to be of the new construction 209 Class (Type 1400).

Imperial Iranian Submarine *Kousseh*, with personnel trained in the

US Navy, was commissioned on 19 December, 1978. Shortly afterwards the Shah was overthrown and the boat, still in US waters, was returned to the United States. The other two were then redirected to Turkey. The West Germany order was suspended and eventually cancelled.

In 1987 the new Islamic Republic constructed a miniature submarine based on a combined Germany/Japanese design. This was followed a year later by one of North Korean design. Reports in 1990 and 1991 suggested that two more submarines had been launched. Since then various reports indicate that more midget submarines have been obtained from the former Yugoslavia and it is estimated that these, plus locally made midgets, now number nine.

A Russian *Kilo* Class (SSK) arrived at Bandar Abbas on 13 November, 1992, and was commissioned as *Tareq* (Morning Star) ten days later. A second *Kilo* joined the fleet in 1993. A third is expected to join shortly, with the possibility of a fourth joining at a later date.

SUBMARINE INSIGNIA

The American shipyard that refitted IIS *Kousseh* in 1978 produced insignia closely resembling the unofficial USN SSN badge but incorporating the Shah's crown. The design was of a bow-on view of a modern 'tear drop' submarine with the Imperial Crown above, the central device flanked by dolphins supported on waves. These badges were manufactured in gold plate for officers and in silver plate for ratings. They were fixed by clutch fasteners and measured 75mm x 25mm. Miniatures in both colours were also made. The shipyard presented the badges to the ship's company of IIS *Kousseh* and they were worn, for a short period, on the left upper breast. The commissioning book for the *Kousseh* also showed the same badge on its front cover. When the Monarchy ceased all the badges and commissioning books were ordered to be destroyed. Whether or not this took place is debatable as a fair number of these badges are still available to collectors. It is quite likely that more were manufactured for this purpose. It is clear that they were never an official Iranian issue.

Late in 1992, following the purchase of three *Kilo* Class submarines from Russia, Iranian submariners began to wear insignia in gold and silver. The design was that of a *Kilo* Class submarine facing its wearer's left. Dominating the central part of the badge are the State Arms, which take the form of a religious symbol within a cogged wheel, at the bottom of which are the flukes on an anchor. The basic colour follows that of the rest of the badge, being gold-coloured for officers and silver-coloured for ratings. The religious symbol is normally enamelled in red, though some have been noted in blue on a white central disc. This motif extends over both the sail and hull. Some are manufactured in Russia and these

are normally solid brass or white metal, though some white metal examples are in pressed metal. Some of the Russian-made officer's badges have the red religious symbol outlined in blue enamel. The Russian-made badges have screw fixings. Locally made badges are not nearly so well made, they are produced in stamped or pressed metal and have a small, flimsy, brooch fastener. The insignia measures 64mm x 23mm and is believed to be worn on the right breast.

Imperial Iranian submarine qualification insignia, gold for officers and silver for ratings. Though worn, these were quite unofficial having been produced by the American shipyard that had prepared submarines prior to transferring them to the Iranian flag (1978).

Iranian Islamic Republic submarine qualification insignia about 1990. In brass for officers and in white metal for ratings.

ISRAEL

SUBMARINE SERVICE

The Israeli submarine service began in 1958 with the purchase of two ex-Royal Navy S Class submarines. They were named *Rahav* (ex-HMS

Sanguine) and *Anin* (ex-HMS *Springer*); both remained in service until the early seventies. A further three submarines were purchased from Great Britain between 1967 and 1968. These were of the T Class and were given the names *Leviathan* (ex-HMS *Turpin*), *Dolphin* (ex-HMS *Truncheon*) and *Dakar* (ex-HMS *Totem*). The *Dakar* was subsequently lost in the Mediterranean on 25 January, 1968.

Three IKL Vickers Type 206 (later redesignated Type 540) patrol submarines (SSK) were ordered in 1972 to replace the S and T classes. The *Gal*, *Tanin*, and *Rahav*, displacing 420 tons and armed with eight 21in torpedo tubes plus Sub-Harpoon, were all commissioned in 1977.

Two, possibly three, 1,550 ton submarines designated *Dolphin* Class (SSK) (similar to the German 212 Class but improved) have been ordered from Germany. The projected completion date is 1999.

Submarine Insignia

On the formation of the Israeli submarine arm (in 1958) an insignia was authorized for qualified submarine crews. The original design was of an S Class submarine facing the wearer's right, over which was a centralized motif of a dagger, anchor and laurel wreath spray. It was stamped in light silver-coloured metal, measured 80mm x 36mm, and it had a single screw fixing. A smaller size (not miniature) was also produced measuring 66mm x 29mm and had two clutch fasteners. Shortly afterwards a senior grade insignia was produced. This was the same as the basic badge but was surmounted by the Star of David. The insignia was worn on the left breast above medal ribbons.

In the mid to late 1970s the insignia was altered so that the submarine resembled the more streamlined 540 Class. The central motif remained the same. The insignia came in two grades and two sizes, though the miniature version was unofficial. The basic design was the same as the previous badge apart from the hull form. It measured 75mm x 37mm. The back fixing could be either a single screw and circular nut or two clutch fasteners. The miniature, measuring 40mm x 17mm, had a brooch fixing. There were three versions of it: with the lower part of the anchor voided, non-voided, and made of heavier, more solid metal, probably privately purchases. At the same time a senior insignia was also authorised (termed The Veteran's Badge); it was the same as the standard badges but a laurel wreath arched over the sail and was joined at the top by the Star of David. It measures 75mm x 36mm and again is produced voided and non-voided. In 1992 the basic submarine badge was also made to include the Star of David. Some badges are mounted on a coloured plastic profiled background, mid-blue for war service and red for combat service (other than war service).

Israeli submarine qualification insignia, all ranks 1958.

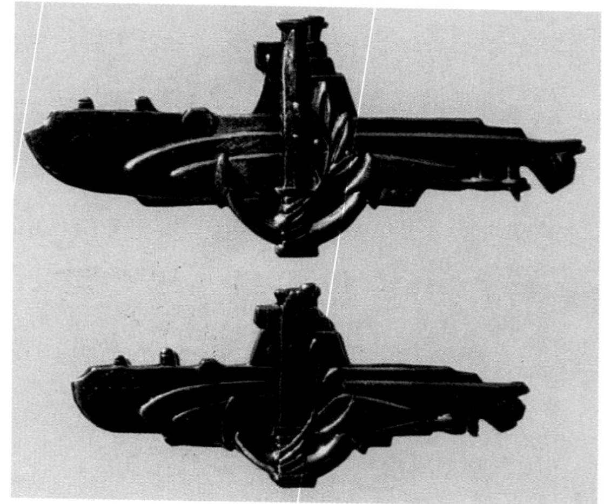

Israeli submarine qualification insignia, all ranks 1958 (80mm x 65mm).

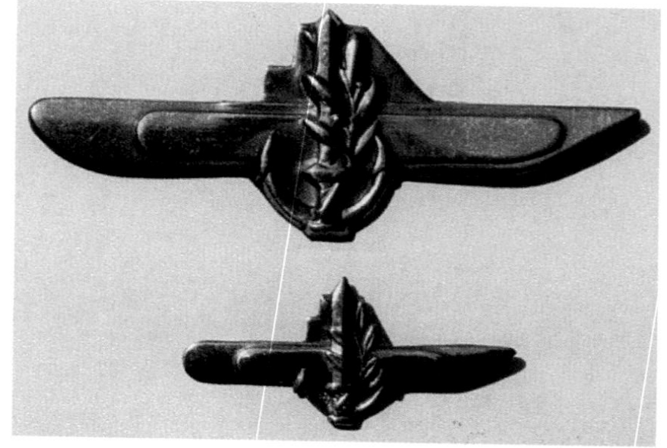

Israeli submarine qualification insignia, second pattern, late 1970s. Full size and miniature, non-voided.

Israeli submarine qualification insignia for veteran, second pattern, voided, late 1970s.

Israeli submarine qualification insignia, with blue plastic profiled backing for combat in war.

Israeli submarine qualification insignia for veteran, full size and miniature non-voided. Late seventies.

Israeli submarine qualification insignia, second pattern, late 1970s, voided, for veterans.

Israeli submarine qualification insignia with Star of David 1992.

ITALY

ROYAL ITALIAN NAVY SUBMARINE SERVICE

The first Italian submarine was the Pullino-designed *Delfino* which entered service in 1895. She displaced 95 tons and was armed with a single torpedo.

Between 1903 and 1905 five Laurenti-designed boats designated the *Glauco* Class were added to the fleet. They displaced 150 tons and were armed with two torpedo tubes. These were followed by five classes of submarines displacing between 180 and 250 tons. Totalling fourteen units, all were armed with two torpedo tubes.

When Italy entered World War I she had twenty submarines in service and eight building. War construction added eight new classes. At the conclusion of hostilities the submarine arm consisted of eleven ocean-going submarines, thirty-five coastal submarines (including seven Canadian-built H Class) and three mine-laying submarines, one of which was ex-Austro-Hungarian. In addition there were thirty-one older boats that were paid off within the year. Ten ex-German U-Boats were ceded to Italy after the Armistice.

Between the wars Italy concentrated on the production of large cruising submarines for the protection of its overseas empire. These ocean-going boats were also seen as a cheap alternative to battleships. Among them was the *Ettore Fieramosca*. Built in 1929, she was, at the time, the world's largest submarine. Designed to carry a sea plane, she was never delivered. When the Empire collapsed these large submarines were found to be unsuitable for Mediterranean deployment. A crash programme was, therefore, commenced to produce smaller types.

Some twelve classes were laid down between the wars. Most of these classes had only two to four units. Nevertheless, it gave Italy the largest submarine fleet of the day.

Production fell off during World War II and only three classes totalling about nineteen submarines were completed. Italy failed to appreciate the strategic value of the submarine on mercantile warfare. Though technically the Italian submarines were probably the world's best, they were not effectively used.

A field in which the Italians did excel was in the use of midget submarines and human torpedoes. Wartime production of these included twenty-six midget submarines (first developed in 1935-6) and over eighty SLCs (*silvro a lento corsa*, or slow course) torpedoes. These were two-man torpedoes or chariots.

After the defeat of Italy thirteen of her submarines came under Allied operational control. At the war's end the Italian Navy mustered sixty-eight submarines including five midgets. Shortly thereafter the submarine branch ceased to exist.

The branch was reactivated in 1954 with the transfer of two ex-USN *Gato* Class submarines. Between 1952 and 1955 five ex-wartime submarines were either completed or reconditioned and entered service. The first Italian-built post-war submarines were the four units of the *Toti* Class (originally SS, later upgraded to SSK) constructed between 1968 and 1969. They were hunter-killer boats of 460 tons armed with four 21in torpedo tubes. Between 1979 and 1982 four more Italian-built submarines entered service. These were of the highly successful *Sauro* Class (Type 1081) (SSK) of 1,456 tons armed with six 21in torpedo tubes. A further four improved *Sauro*s capable of firing the Harpoon missile were commissioned between 1988 and 1994. A possible further order for two larger Type 212 *Sauro* Class units is under consideration.

The present submarine force (1996) consists of four improved *Sauro* Class (SSK), four *Sauro* Class (Type 1081) (SSK) and two *Toti One* (Type 1075)(SSK). The future is uncertain as the projected number of units is to be cut from ten to eight.

ROYAL ITALIAN NAVY SUBMARINE INSIGNIA

Many and varied have been the insignia relating to the Italian Submarine Service. The first device was worn between 1915 and 1918 by junior ratings only. It was regarded as a trade badge and was worn on the left sleeve above rank and branch badges. The insignia was manufactured in silvered metal and depicted a leaping dolphin, facing the wearer's left, encircled by a broad band with a voided background. The top of the band bore the inscription '*Sommergibili*'. The letters were normally painted in dark blue and more rarely in pale blue or black. The entire device was surmounted by the Royal Crown. It measured 45mm (diam-

eter) x 65mm (diameter plus crown) though these dimensions could vary slightly. It was held in position by two fastenings on the back locked by a pin or brooch.

On 16 January, 1918, the device was changed so that the dolphin faced in the other direction (towards the wearer's right) and the Royal Crown was removed.

Officers and chief petty officers were authorized to wear a Submarine Duty Badge on 25 September, 1924. This consisted of a small gilt device worn on the left breast 10mm above, or in place of, medal ribbons. It was similar in design to the original junior rating's trade badge of 1915 but measured 15mm (diameter) x 20mm (diameter plus crown), though this too could vary slightly, some measuring as much as 17mm in diameter. This device could only be worn during the period of assignment to submarines.

On 11 November, 1941, a larger insignia was instituted for officers and chief petty officers. Designated the Submarine Honour Badge, it was similar in design to the Duty Badge, but 25mm (diameter) x 37mm (diameter plus crown) and the lower part of the circular band was in the form of a semi-laurel wreath. It was originally awarded for three war patrols, but later, if this qualification was lacking, it could be awarded for five years' service in submarines. The Honour Badge was made retroactive to include World War I and the Spanish Civil War and it could be worn for life.

During World War II junior ratings wore a special cloth insignia on the left breast of the grey-green working rig. It consisted of a black disc approximately 65mm in diameter on which was a leaping dolphin in yellow, facing the wearer's left.

Italian submariners who were based at Bordeaux and operated in the Atlantic from 1941 to 1943 were granted a special insignia. For officers, warrant officers and senior petty officers the gilt Duty and Honour badges had a red enamelled capital letter 'A' superimposed on the dolphin and the junior rating's silver badge had a 12mm high blue enamelled capital letter 'A' similarly positioned. The letter 'A' also appeared centrally or below or above the dolphin and the crown could vary in detail.

On 11 December, 1943, a series of nine special war service badges were authorized for various elements of the Royal Italian Navy. For the submarine service it was designated the *Distintivo D'Honore Per Lunga Navigazione in Guerra*. The design consisted of a flattened diamond shape with curved sides surmounted by a royal crown. In the centre was a shark facing the wearer's left below which was a torpedo, both superimposed on an anchor. The background was voided. It was awarded in

bronze for 18 months embarkation in a submarine or 1,000 hours at sea with at least one engagement with the enemy, in silver for 30 months or 3,000 hours with three engagements and in gold for 48 months or 5,000 hours with six engagements. The insignia was allowed to be worn after the war. Its dimensions were 49mm x 47mm. Its original shape was oval.

In common with surface ships, many wartime submarines had individual badges. These were later manufactured in metal as lapel badges to be worn on civilian clothes. These usually took the form of a voided circular band bearing the submarine's name and, across the centre of and extending beyond the edges, a submarine. The whole was surmounted by a royal crown.

Cap ribbons worn by junior ratings in peacetime indicated the name of the submarine prefixed by SMG. In wartime only the word 'SOMMERGIBILI' was worn. In common with other Italian cap tallies a star appeared at each end of the lettering. The same system remained after the republic was declared in 1946.

A special device was worn by Italian personnel serving in submarines on loan to Nationalist Spain during the Spanish Civil War. It took the form of an *Archimede* Class submarine, facing the wearer's right, bearing a Royal Crown in the centre (mid-way between the hull and conning tower). Behind the submarine was the insignia of the Spanish (Foreign) Legion. The insignia was worn on the left breast and was in gilt metal for officers, warrant officers and senior petty officers and in silver metal for junior ratings. Two *Archimede* Class submarines, the *Archimede* and *Galilei* and two *Perla* Class submarines the *Onice* and *Iride,* were transferred to Spain in 1936 and 1937 and re-named *General Sanjuro*, *General Mola*, *Avillar Tablada* and *Gonzalaz Lopez.* All were returned to Italy after the Nationalist victory.

(left) Italian officer's, warrant officer's and senior rating's Submarine Duty Badge authorized 1924. 15mm x 20mm.

(right) Italian officer's, warrant officer's and senior rating's Submarine Honour Badge authorized 1941. 25mm x 37mm.

(left) Italian junior rating's trade badge 1915-20.

Italian junior rating's sleeve badge authorized in 1920 and still worn.

(right) Italian junior rating's wartime submarine patch worn on the left breast of the grey-green working rig.

Italian Royal Navy Submarine Service Special War Service Badge in Silver. Authorized 1943.

(right) Italian Submarine Duty Badge, Atlantic, worn by officers, warrant officers and senior ratings 1941-3. Submarine Honour badge similar. Personnel based at Bordeaux. 15mm x 20mm

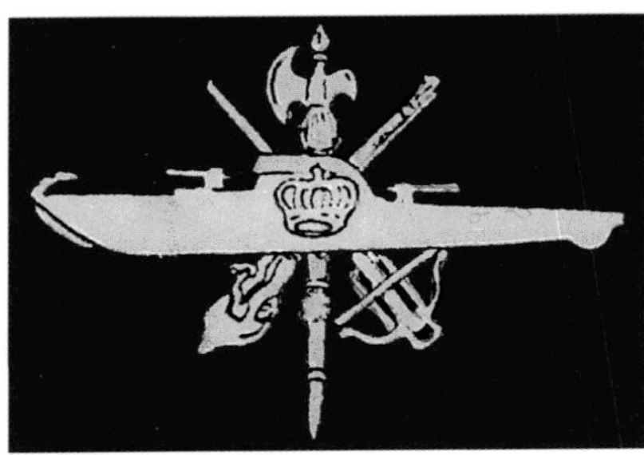

Submarine insignia worn by officers, warrant officers and senior petty officers serving in submarines on loan to Nationalist Spain during the Spanish Civil War. Junior ratings' insignia was the same but in silver.

Italian junior rating's submarine qualification badge, Atlantic, worn by personnel based at Bordeaux 1941-3.

ITALIAN SOCIALIST REPUBLIC SUBMARINE SERVICE

SEPTEMBER 1943 TO MAY 1945 (*REPUBBLICA SOCIALE ITALIANA* — RSI)

It is difficult to ascertain the exact number of submarines that served in the RSI Navy — there cannot have been many. A Fascist Honour Badge was authorized for the Battle of the Atlantic; whether this was to be worn retroactively or worn by personnel actively engaged, is open to speculation. At the time of the Italian Armistice (9 September, 1943) three Italian submarines were seized by the Germans at their Bordeaux base. It is possible that one or more of these continued to serve under Fascist colours. At the same time thirteen others were captured by the Germans in Italian ports and two were captured by the Japanese. These figures do not include submarines captured while still under construction. Though possible, it is unlikely that any of these served with the RSI. What is known is that ten CB Class four-man midget submarines, captured by the Germans, were transferred to the RSI Navy. They mainly operated in the Adriatic. One was used for spares, seven more were sunk or otherwise destroyed and two were captured by the Allies.

ITALIAN SOCIALIST REPUBLIC SUBMARINE INSIGNIA

RSI Navy personnel continued to wear the former insignia of the Royal Navy but with the royal crown removed. The ratings' silver badge also appeared in bronze.

On 27 May, 1944, the Navy of the RSI authorized the wearing of the

nine special war service badges previously authorized by the Royal Italian Navy. The design was the same but without the royal crown. The qualifications for the awards were the same as before.

An Honour Badge was introduced on 27 May, 1944, for submarine crews who took part in the Battle of the Atlantic. It bore a bow view of a submarine, above which was a horizontal *fasces* in the centre of which was a disc bearing a Swastika. A wide oval border carried the inscription '*Atlantico Fedelta 8 Settembre 1943*'. The badge was made of silver metal with the background of a blue sky.

A special badge was also produced for subaqua assault swimmers that was not specifically a submarine badge, but allied to it. It depicted an arm thrust up from the sea grasping a harpoon. It was surrounded by combined wreath and scroll bearing the inscription '*Mezzi de Assalto*'. At the top there was an anchor in the centre of which was a disc bearing the letter 'Xª' (10th Flotilla). It was made in greyish metal.

Towards the end of the war an Atlantic Division Combat sleeve badge was created. It took the form of a frosted silver metal shield 48mm x 79mm depicting a dolphin swimming around a short Roman sword below which was inscribed '*Divisione Atlantica*'. The device had five small holes to enable it to be sewn to the uniform. It was intended for Italian naval personnel (of the RSI) serving at the Atlantic bases of Germany and France from which Italian submarines operated and who stayed behind to combat the advancing Allied troops.

Numerous other special badges were created to commemorate various combat units. Most took the form of a submarine on waves surrounded by a combined wreath and scroll. Many included the letter 'Xª' in the design. (See the illustration of the Barbarigo Battalion.)

The elite SCIRE Submarine Battalion from 1943 to 1945 wore a gold device resembling the silver rating's badge but with the letter 'Xª' (10th) centrally located just above the dorsal fin of the dolphin. The wording on the outer band was '*Btg Sommergibili SCIRE*'.

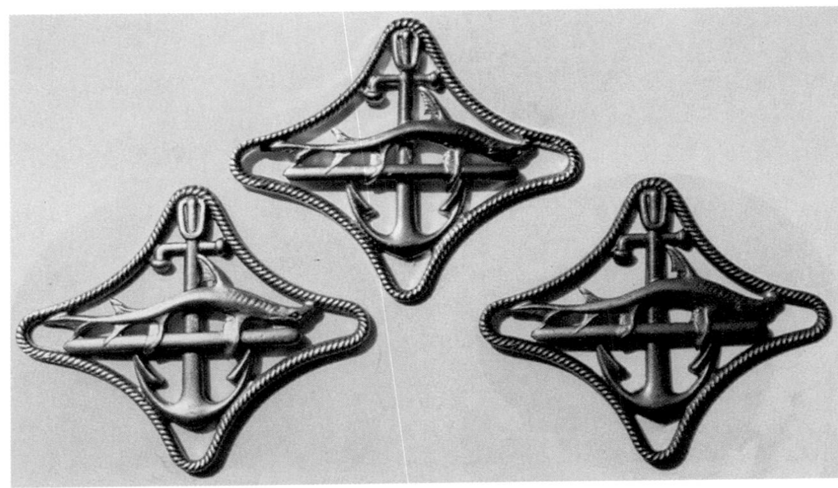

Italian Submarine Service Special War Badge (Distintivo D'Honore Per Lunga Navigazione In Guerra) gold, silver and bronze, authorized in 1944. (Frogman's badge is similar but shark replaced by a frogman astride a 'human torpedo'). Italian Socialist Republic.

Italian Socialist Republic Distinction of Honour for the Barbarigo Battalion, Nettuna Front. Scroll at the top bears the inscription 'FRONTE DI NETTUNO'.

(right) Italian Socialist Republic sleeve insignia for service in the Atlantic Division.

Republic of Italy Submarine Insignia

Since the Republic was declared in 1946, submarine insignia has remained in much the same design as in the former Royal Navy but without the crown.

Since 1948 the Italian submarine qualification insignia comes in three sizes. Officers and senior ratings wear the design of 1924 and 1941 without the crown and junior ratings the same design as for 1920 (this comes in chrome or frosted silver). Officers and senior ratings wear the Duty Badge measuring 15mm in diameter and the Honour Badge measuring 25mm in diameter. The junior ratings' sleeve badge is 45mm in diameter. Two unofficial badges exist. One, an Honour Badge 55mm in diameter, is said to be worn by some senior officers (but this is not confirmed), and the other a standard-size Honour Badge surmounted by a mural crown* is worn as a beret badge only.

In 1990 the Duty and Honour badges had a naval crown** added, making them look very much like the beret badge but smaller.

An unidentified badge has recently appeared, being of the same design and materials as the rating's badge of 1920 but of the size now worn by officers. This may be a commemorative badge.

---

* Mural Crown — a three-turreted castle.

** Naval Crown — similar to the mural crown but with an anchor superimposed on the central turret and with representations of the prow of a Roman galley below the two other turrets and extending either side of the base.

Italian Republic officer's, warrant officer's and senior rating's Submarine Duty Badge 1948-90, then Naval Crown added. 15mm diameter.

(above, right) Italian Republic officer's, warrant officer's and senior rating's Submarine Honour Badge 1948-90, then Naval Crown added. 25mm diameter.

Italian Republic admiral's large (unofficial) Submarine Honour Badge (55mm diameter).

Italian Republic submarine service insignia for junior ratings, 1948, in chrome and frosted silver. 45mm diameter.

Italian Republic submarine qualification insignia with naval crown, authorized in 1990 for officers, warrant officers and senior ratings, (25mm x 33mm and 17mm x 21mm).

Italian Republic submarine beret badge, with mural crown. 24 x 35mm.

JAPAN

SUBMARINE SERVICE

Early Japanese submarines were based on British, German and French designs. The submarine arm commenced in 1904 with the purchase from Great Britain of five elementary Holland type boats. Numbered 1 to 5, they had a submerged displacement of 120 tons, were 65ft long and were armed with a single 18in torpedo tube. The next vessels were built in Japan two years later and were numbered 6 and 7. These were of 180 tons, 100ft long and armed with three 18in torpedo tubes. Numbers 8 and 9, British built, were added in 1907 and 1908. Displacing 320 tons, they were similar to the British C Class. Of the same type, numbers 10 to 15 were constructed in Japan. France built numbers 16 and 17 just before World War I. All seventeen were serving in the Imperial Japanese Navy at the onset of war.

War construction amounted to less than twelve additions. Like the rest of the Japanese Navy, after mopping up Germany's few possessions in the Pacific and Far East, they spent the remainder of World War I on patrol duties in the Pacific. At the end of hostilities Japan was allocated six ex-German ocean-going and two ex-German mine-laying submarines. They were used for experimental purposes only and were not commissioned into the fleet.

In order to counter American Naval supremacy in the Pacific between the wars Japan commenced a large submarine construction programme. For the most part these new vessels were large ocean-going cruising boats capable of long endurance at sea, a necessity in the vast expanses of the Pacific. They also featured deep-diving capabilities and many were fitted with a catapult and sea-plane and 5.5in guns.

Japan entered the war in 1941 with fifty-six front line submarines and some seventeen older craft used for training and ancillary purposes. Well over sixty-five were building or on order. War construction added sixty-seven large, medium and coastal submarines. Among them were a number of specialist types: supply submarines which could carry cargo, landing craft and amphibious tanks, ocean-going submarines which could carry midget submarines and human torpedoes, command submarines with special telecommunication facilities and tanker submarines for refuelling sea-planes and flying boats. The I 400 Class, when completed in 1944, were, at 5,223 tons, the world's largest underwater vessels. They carried three bombing air-craft and had a range of 30,000 nautical miles at 14 knots. They shipped dummy funnels to disguise themselves when 'steam-

ing' on the surface and had an endurance of ninety days. In addition, two classes of unarmed supply submarines were built by the Army and well over two hundred midget submarines were built by the Navy. These midget craft displaced between 46 and 60 tons, were normally armed with two 18in torpedoes and had a complement of two to five men.

The value of the submarine in mercantile warfare was ignored to Japan's cost. The submarine force was, for the most part, used as scouts for the fleet and for attacking enemy fleet formations. Their failure to utilize the submarine as a commerce raider was reflected by the poor results achieved. Just over two hundred Allied vessels were sunk throughout the war. Little heed was paid to anti-submarine warfare and as a result the Japanese submarines suffered grievously at the hands of the USN A/S escorts.

As a last desperate measure hundreds of one-man and two-man suicide craft (human torpedoes) styled *Kaiten* were constructed. They displaced between 8 and 18 tons and carried a 3,428lb warhead. They came too late and achieved little tangible results.

Some one hundred and twenty-five Japanese submarines were lost during the conflict. Fifty-eight, including six ex-German and two ex-Italian boats, were surrendered. All were subsequently broken up by the Allied Powers.

Following Japan's defeat her armed forces were disintegrated and the nation was demilitarized. In 1954 the Japanese Maritime Self Defence Force was formed, a navy in everything but name.

The first submarine of this new force was an ex-USN *Gato* Class (SS) the *Kuroshio* (ex-USS *Mingo*), commissioned into the JMSDF in 1955 and deleted in 1966. All further submarines to enter the service were Japanese designed and built.

The first of these 'all Japanese' submarines was a one-ship prototype Class the *Oyashio* (SS). She was launched in 1959 and displaced 1,100 tons. Her weapon fit was four 19.7in torpedo tubes. She continued in service until 1976. *Oyashio* was followed by the four-ship *Hayashio/Natsushio* Class (SS) of 750 tons displacement and armed with three 21in torpedo tubes. They were launched between 1961 and 1962 and were finally deleted by 1987. The five *Ooshio* Class (SS) of 1,600 tons armed with eight 21in torpedo tubes were launched between 1964 and 1968 and continued in service until 1968. These were followed by the six-ship *Uzushio* Class (SS) of 1,850 tons displacement and armed with six 21in torpedo tubes. They were launched between 1970 and 1975. Three were paid off by 1991. Two later classes are the ten ship *Yuushio* Class (SSK) of 2,200 tons displacement armed with six 21in torpedo

tubes launched between 1979 and 1988 and the seven *Harushio* Class (SSK) launched between 1989 and 1995. These 2,450 ton displacement submarines are armed with six 21in torpedo tubes which are also capable of launching Sub Harpoon SSM.

The first unit of an improved *Harushio* Class of 2,500 tons displacement was laid down in 1993 and will enter service in 1998. It is anticipated that others will follow on in twelve month intervals.

The submarine force at the time of writing (1996) comprises one improved *Harushio* Class (SSK), six *Harushio* Class (SSK), ten *Yuushio* Class (SSK) and two *Uzuhio* Class (S) used for training.

SUBMARINE INSIGNIA

From 1932 petty officers and junior ratings who had completed the course in the Submarine Training School were entitled to wear a special insignia. This consisted of a rudimentary representation of a submarine in silver facing its wearer's right. It was superimposed on a 38mm diameter nut-brown (some were orange-brown) cherry blossom by means of a bolt the head of which was peined over the centre of the reverse of the blossom (on reproductions this head was either stuck on, or missing altogether). The cherry blossom flower was fairly thick and the blossom segments in section were convex. The insignia was fixed to the uniform by means of a horizontal flat hinged pin secured by a single hook and was worn on the right side of the uniform jacket approximately mid-way between collar and skirt. Unofficial sources indicate the existence of a similar device for officers but with a gold submarine. This is thought to be unlikely. On security grounds the insignia ceased to be worn in 1940 and was abolished altogether in 1942. Few originals survived as they were required to be returned to stores in 1942 and most were melted down for other purposes.

There were also various other symbols associated with the submarine. One of these was an arm or head band made in white linen, printed with orange and black stripes top and bottom. In the centre was a ship's screw within a circle and with Japanese characters for *Gaku-To* on either side. This stood for 'Youth who learn at university'. It was worn by ex-students who volunteered to serve in small submarines, including human torpedoes. It was said to contain 'the soul of the owner'.

In June, 1961, after the formation of the Japanese Maritime Self Defence Force, a submarine qualification badge was authorized. This insignia is the same design for both officers and ratings, though in the case of officers it is gold and in the case of ratings it is silver. The insignia, manufactured in metal of the appropriate colour, comprises a central motif of

a cherry blossom on the shank of an anchor; inward-facing dolphins are on each side. Anchor, cherry blossoms and dolphins rest on symbolic waves. The device closely resembles the submarine badge of the US Navy. It is produced in two sizes, 70mm x 22mm and 60mm x 21mm. Both brooch and clutch fastening can be used for securing the insignia which is worn by all ranks on the left upper breast.

Japanese Imperial Navy insignia for completion of training at The Naval Submarine School, 1932-45.

Japanese Imperial Navy unofficial device worn by suicide crews in miniature submarines in 1945.

JMSDF submarine qualification insignia, in gold, for officers.
Top: 70mm in gilded gold.
Bottom: 61mm in standard gold. Authorized June, 1961.

JMSDF submarine qualification insignia in silver for ratings.
Top: 70mm in standard silver.
Bottom: 61mm in frosted silver.
Authorized June, 1961.

Democratic People's Republic of Korea (North Korea)

Submarine Service

The submarine service was formed in late 1959 with the acquisition from the Soviet Union of two *Whiskey* Class submarines (SS). This number was increased to four by the end of the decade. By 1991 all four had been reduced to a training role.

In 1973 two Chinese-built *Romeo* Class submarines (SS) were added to the underwater fleet followed by a further two in 1974 and three more in 1975. These were followed by similar boats built in North Korea of which one was lost off the East coast of Korea in 1985. By 1993 only two of the original Chinese-built boats remained in service but the North Korean-built boats numbered twenty-four.

In addition to conventional submarines, some ten coastal submarines have been built since 1988. Reported to be of Yugoslav design, some have been built and are termed the *Sang-o* Class. They displace 76 tons surfaced and can carry limpet mines and or combat swimmers. Over fifty-five submarines (SDV) have also been locally constructed since 1974. Their function is to land small clandestine commando units behind enemy lines.

Between 1993 and 1994 thirty old Russian submarines were delivered to North Korea for 'scrapping'. These consisted of F, GII, R and W Classes (SS).

The present submarine force consists of between twenty-two and twenty-four *Romeo* Class (SS), ten small coastal submarines (SSC) and fifty midget submarines (SDV).

SUBMARINE INSIGNIA

No information is available on submarine insignia. It is unlikely that any exist.

REPUBLIC OF KOREA (SOUTH KOREA)

SUBMARINE SERVICE

Three KSS-1 *Tolgorae* Class and eight *Cosmos* Class (Italian designed) midget submarines have been constructed with the first entering service in 1983. The former are armed with two 406mm torpedo tubes and the latter with two 533mm torpedo tubes. Both displace 150 tons surfaced, but the *Cosmos* are primarily SDVs.

In 1987 three 209 (Type 1200) submarines (SSK) were ordered from West Germany. To be known as *Chang Bogo* Class, the first was constructed in Germany and entered service in 1993. The other two were constructed in the ROK and were commissioned in 1994 and 1995. 1989 and 1993 saw the ordering of two further batches of three, all to be built in the ROK. All should be in service by 1999.

SUBMARINE INSIGNIA

Submarine qualification badges were authorized on 17 September, 1992, gold for officers and silver for ratings. The design is similar to the USN insignia and shows a bow-on view of a submarine either side of which are inward-facing dolphins supported either side of the submarine on four upward and outward sloping stylized waves. The prow of the submarine bares the ROK National symbol, the *Yin Yang* disc, below which appears the bottom portion of an anchor.

These badges are also embroidered in gold and silver on dark cloth and dimensions are 62mm x 23mm and a miniature version also exists. The device is worn on the left upper breast, by means of two clutch fasteners. Qualifications required are a seven-month specialist course, employment in submarines or an appointment as a Submarine Squadron Staff Officer.

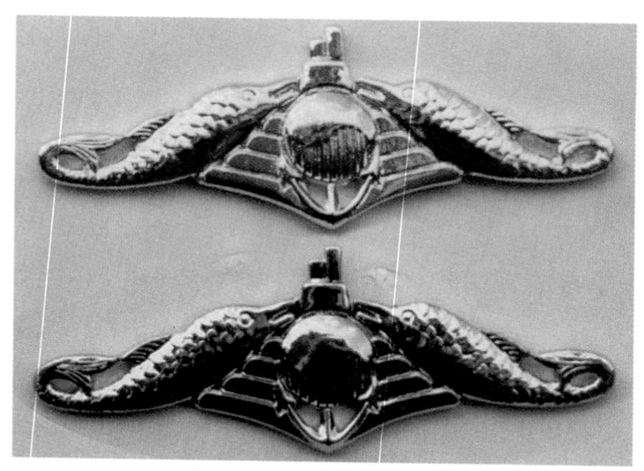

Republic of Korea submarine qualification insignia, gold for officers and silver for ratings. Authorized 17 September, 1992.

LATVIA

SUBMARINE SERVICE

In the early 1920s two coastal submarines were ordered from France. Named *Ronis* and *Spidola* they entered service in 1926. Armed with six 17.7in torpedo tubes and eight guns they displaced 390 tons and were 180.5ft long.

Difficulties in maintenance and lack of qualified personnel led to the vessels being laid up. When war came both were unserviceable. They were seized by Soviet Forces in June, 1940.

SUBMARINE INSIGNIA

It is unlikely that any specialist insignia ever existed. However, cap ribbons bore the submarine's name or indicated that the wearer was serving in the Submarine Division.

LIBYA

SUBMARINE SERVICE

The submarine service was formed in 1976 with the acquisition of the first of six Soviet *Foxtrot* Class (SS) the last of which entered service in 1983. One was subsequently deleted in 1992 and another was lost in 1993.

Two Yugoslav R2 *Mala* Class miniature free-flood submarines, similar to the British wartime torpedo-shaped Chariots, were delivered in 1977. These were followed by two more in 1981 and a further two in 1982, with others possibly to follow.

SUBMARINE INSIGNIA

Little information is known about any specialist submarine insignia. A cloth badge is said to have been authorized about 1990. This depicts a simple submarine design, facing the wearer's right embroidered in gold wire on a black contoured backing. It measures 71mm x 22mm and is fixed to the uniform with either a pin-back or a screw-on device. A metal version was produced in about 1994 which more closely resembles a *Foxtrot* Class submarine.

Libyan submarine qualification insignia gold wire embroidery on black cloth.

Libyan submarine qualification insignia in brass, in the style of a Foxtrot *Class submarine.*

MALAYSIA

SUBMARINE SERVICE

In late 1988 the Malaysian Government ordered an ex-Royal Navy *Oberon* Class submarine from Great Britain, but it was never delivered.

In the spring of 1991 the Royal Malaysian Navy ordered four submarines from Sweden, two reconditioned ex-Swedish Navy *Draken* Class dating from the 1960s, one to be used for sea training and the other for alongside training, and two of the latest A19 Type boats. In 1992 the programme was postponed. A 1994 report suggested that a possible six ex-UK *Oberon* Class submarines might be purchased and that some personnel had already been trained. This purchase is now unlikely to materialize, though there is a strong move to acquire submarines in the near future. Malaysian Naval personnel are presently (1996) receiving submarine training in Australia, India and Pakistan.

SUBMARINE INSIGNIA

Malaysian naval officers have been trained in Germany, the United Kingdom, Sweden, Australia, Pakistan and India. It is possible that some may have qualified for submarine insignia for those countries. To date no information is available regarding the existence of similar Malaysian insignia. In 1994 it was rumoured that 'trained personnel' were wearing Australian dolphins.

NETHERLANDS

SUBMARINE SERVICE

The world's first submarine was built by a Dutchman, Cornelius Drebbel, in 1620. The first submarine to enter Dutch naval service was simply designed Boat No1. It displaced 120 tons and was armed with one torpedo tube. It entered service in 1905. Between 1910 and 1912 a further nine boats in three classes were added to the Navy. They had a surface displacement of between 131 and 380 tons and were armed with two torpedo tubes.

As the need for larger long-range submarines arose in order to protect the Netherlands Overseas colonies, submarines were identified by either K (*Kolonien*) for colonial service or O (*Onderzeeboot*) for home service before their numerals. The K-boats were of at least 500 tons

displacement as opposed to the smaller O-boats which were deployed in or near the North Sea. This system remained until 1937 when submarine areas of operation become interchangeable and the K and O prefixes were dropped.

Eleven classes consisting of both categories were added to the Navy between 1913 and 1920. These included an ex-British H Class interned in 1916 and subsequently purchased and an ex-German minelaying type purchased in 1917.

By 1931 there were twenty-two submarines in service and nine building. Of those building the 021 class, commenced in 1937 and ready for service just before the war, were the world's first submarines to incorporate a telescopic breathing tube so that the submarine could cruise at periscope depth under diesel power. The Germans later developed this, from examples found in Rotterdam in 1943, into what became famous as the schnorkel.

When war commenced there were thirty submarines in Dutch service. Six were captured in Dutch ports and four were to be sunk or scuttled due to enemy action. After Japan's entry into the war a further six were sunk or scuttled due to action with Japanese Forces. In all, fourteen Dutch submarines escaped to the Allies either to survive the war or to be scrapped in Allied yards as of no further use. Four British submarines (HMS/Ms *Sturgeon*, *Talent*, *Tarn* and P47) were transferred to the Dutch flag during the war.

The first post-war submarines to join the Netherlands submarine service were two ex-USN *Walrus* Class (ex-USS *Icefish* and ex-US *Hawksbill* later restyled *Balao* Class) (SS). They were transferred on loan for a five-year period commencing in 1953. These were followed by four Dutch-built submarines of the *Potvis* Class (SS), later subdivided into two classes of two submarines each (known as the *Potvis/Zeehond* Class). They had a surface displacement of 1,200 tons and were armed with eight 21in torpedo tubes. All entered service between 1961 and 1966.

The *Zwaardvis* Class (SSK) of two submarines was completed in 1972. Of 2,350 tons surface displacement, they are armed with six 21in torpedo tubes.

The latest class, an improved *Zwaardvis* design, is the *Walrus* Class (SSK). They have a surface displacement of 2,450 tons and are armed with four 21in torpedo tubes and Harpoon missiles. By early 1994 all four were in commission and constitute the present submarine force.

Both *Zwaardvis* Class were put up for sale in 1993 and will be available by 1996. The remaining *Potvis/Zeehond* Class have been relegated to other duties or disposed of.

SUBMARINE INSIGNIA

The Dutch submarine badge was authorized on 24 February, 1965, though it was not worn until the early 1970s. The wearing of the insignia is not compulsory.

The design comprises two outward-facing dolphins, with tails crossed, supporting the bow view of a modern Royal Netherlands Navy submarine. It is made in gilt metal measuring 62mm x 22mm and is fixed either by a hinged pin or by clutch fastenings. An unofficial gold bullion variation also exists. There is also an unofficial miniature in metal. It measures 25mm long and it has a brooch fastening.

The same device is worn by all ranks serving in submarines or in the submarine service. It is worn on the left breast below medal ribbons if worn.

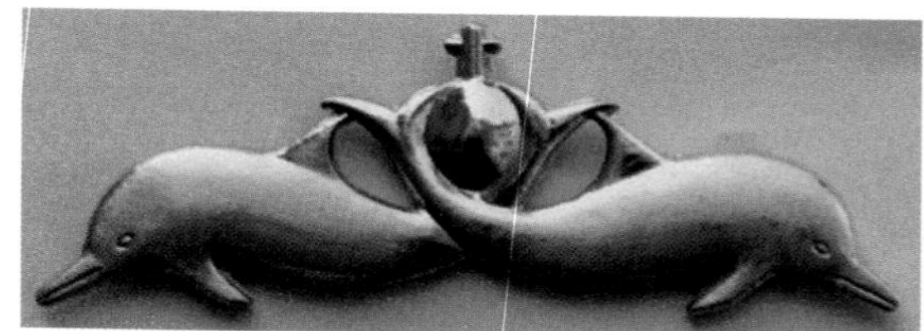

Netherlands submarine qualification insignia for all ranks, 24 February, 1965.

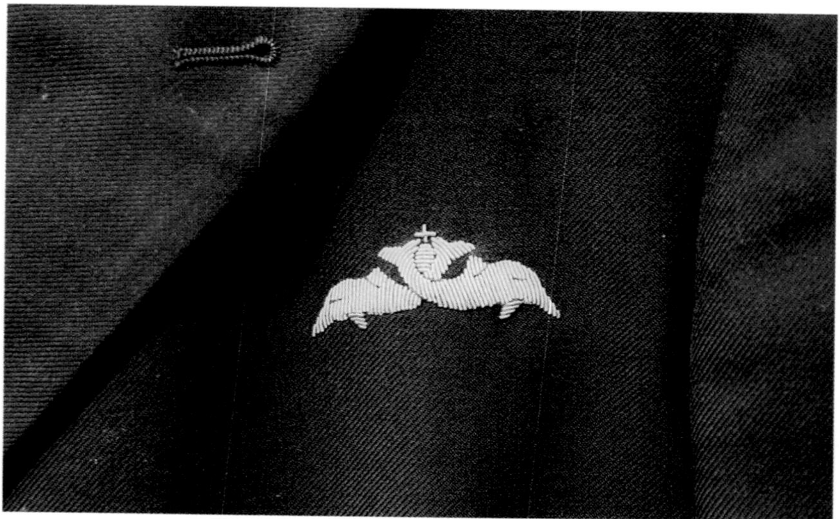

Netherlands submarine qualification insignia embroidered on uniform in gold wire.

NORWAY

SUBMARINE SERVICE

Norway formed its submarine service in 1908 with the acquisition from Germany of a small submarine of the Krupp Germania Type. This boat entered service in 1909 as the *Kobben* but was shortly redesignated A1.

A further four, slightly larger, boats were ordered from Germany to be designated A2, A3, A4 and A5. The first three were delivered in 1913. However, A5 was appropriated by Germany on the outbreak of war in 1914.

In the mid to late 1920s Norway constructed six submarines of the Holland Type, designated B1 to B6. It was with this class of 413 tons surface displacement with four torpedo tubes that Norway entered the war in 1940, the previous A Class having been decommissioned by 1931.

All the B boats fell into German hands with the exception of B1 which was scuttled in Ofotfjord to escape falling into enemy hands. She was raised after the Second Battle of Narvik and escaped to join the free Norwegian Forces in Britain.

The Royal Navy transferred five U Class submarines to the Norwegian ensign between 1943 and 1944. All survived the war to serve in the post-war Norwegian Navy, the last being broken up in 1965.

Three German VII C Type U-boats were ceded to Norway at the end of the hostilities, the last one being taken out of service in 1964.

In the early 1960s a new class of fifteen submarines was ordered from West Germany. In order to train crews for these new boats, West Germany loaned a similar type, the U3, to Norway for a period of two years. She was temporarily re-named *Kobben* while serving under the Norwegian colours.

These new vessels, designated the 207 (or *Kobben*) Class, are small coastal attack submarines (SSK). They are driven by diesel and electric engines with a surface displacement of 370 to 435 tons and are armed with eight 21in torpedo tubes. One was cancelled and the remainder all entered service by 1967. Two were sold to Denmark in 1986 and a third in 1989. One was scrapped in 1989 following an accident. Six were modernized and lengthened by 1989 but apart from these the remainder will gradually be phased out of service.

A new class designated *Ula* Type P6071 (ex-210) (SSK) was contracted in 1982; also German-built, they have a surface displacement of 1,040 tons and are armed with eight 21in torpedo tubes. The six boats of this class all commissioned between 1989 and 1992. They, with the

six modernized *Kobben* (Type 207) SSKs form the present (1996) Norwegian submarine force.

Norwegian submarine qualification insignia for officers with twelve months service in submarines, full size and miniature (1958). A more stylizes embroidered insignia has recently emerged to conform more closely with the metal badges.

Norwegian submarine qualification insignia in metal. Top for officer's shirts and bottom for officers with less than 12 month's service and for ratings, all uniforms (1958).

Norwegian Submarine Service cloth badge for wear on sweaters by all ranks. As the submarine faces the other way, it indicates that the badge is worn on the left sleeve.

SUBMARINE INSIGNIA

It was in 1958 that the Royal Norwegian Navy adopted its present style submarine badge. Before that time no specialist insignia was worn. It consists of a royal crown with submarine below, facing the wearer's right. Either side are two inward-facing sea creatures.

The design of the badge is the same for all ranks. For officers who have completed twelve months' service it is embroidered on the dark blue service uniform in gold bullion wire and is available in gold-plated silver with a pin back for wear on khaki or tropical uniforms. Officers who have not qualified for the gold wire badge and all ratings wear a bronze metal badge with a pin fastening. This is awarded after completing the submarine course and having satisfactorily served on board a submarine for six months. The badge is available in two sizes. The standard uniform item measures 60mm x 20mm and an embroidered miniature measuring 40mm x 15mm is available for mess dress.

The submarine insignia is worn on the right-hand side of the chest level with the arm pit. Officers wear the miniature badge on the lapel of the mess dress. A circular cloth badge 98mm in diameter is worn by all personnel on the sleeve of the sweater.

Ratings, dressed as seamen, in the submarine service wear a distinctive cap ribbon bearing the inscription 'KNM UNDERVANNSBAT' (KNM = Kongelige Norske Marine, ie Royal Norwegian Navy Submarine).

PAKISTAN

SUBMARINE SERVICE

The Pakistan Navy began its submarine arm in 1964 with the loan of a submarine from the United States. This was the *Tench* Class (SS) USS *Diablo* renamed *Ghazi* (Defender of the Faith). In 1970 three French *Daphne* Class submarines (SSK) were commissioned. This number was made up to four in 1975 with the acquisition of the Portuguese submarine *Cachalote*, which replaced the *Ghazi*.

During 1972-3 six SX 404 Class midget submarines (SDV) were purchased from Italy. Displacing 40 tons, their main function was to transport up to twelve commando special forces on clandestine raids. One was lost in an accident in 1976, some were discarded in 1982-3 and all were out of service by 1990. They were replaced by three larger midget submarines (SSC) of 110 tons dived displacement. These were the Italian-made SX 756 Type (MG110 Class), armed with two 21in torpedo

tubes and can carry eight combat swimmers and explosives plus two SDVs. Italy has also provided Pakistan with a number of two-man chariots.

Originally intended for South Africa, two French *Agosta* Class submarines (SSK) were purchased in 1978. In 1984/5 they were fitted with US Sub-Harpoon anti-ship missiles. In September, 1994, it was announced that three more of this class have been ordered. The first and probably the second are to be built in France and the last in Pakistan.

In 1996 the submarine force stood at two *Hashmat* (*Agosta* Class) SSK, four *Hangor* (*Daphne* Class) SSK and three MG110 (SX 56 Type) SSC.

SUBMARINE INSIGNIA

The submarine insignia was designed in June, 1964. It was manufactured in metal and measures 66mm x 29mm (though this can vary slightly). It is normally secured to the uniform by a hinged brooch pin and hook. For officers it is gilt metal and for ratings silvered or chromed. Ratings on promotion to officer continue to wear the silver badge until they requalify.

The device consists of a submarine facing the wearer's right; around the centre of the submarine is a wreath closed at the top with a star and crescent. The insignia is worn on the left breast above medal ribbons if any.

A miniature, 54mm x 22mm, exists and cloth versions of the full sized insignia are produced, red on blue and blue on white, details on both being picked out in white.

Combat swimmers (Special Service Group) wear a very similar badge. It is similar to the submariners' badge but has an upright dagger in the centre. The grip starts just below the wreath and the blade just touches the crescent. A cloth variation also exists.

Pakistan submarine qualification insignia in gilt for officers and chrome for ratings. Authorized June, 1964.

PERU

SUBMARINE SERVICE

During the War of the Pacific with Chile in 1879-83 a submersible craft designed by Fredrico Blume was built at the port of Pita. It made several test dives but had to be scuttled to prevent it from falling into enemy hands.

The first true submarines to be commissioned were the French-built Laubeuf Types *Ferre* and *Palacios.* Purchased in 1911, they displaced 300 tons and were armed with one bow torpedo tube. During the period of World War I they became inactive, due to the unavailability of batteries, and were eventually scrapped in 1919.

At the instigation of the US Naval Missions in 1920, four R Class submarines were built in the United States. They were given the designations of R1 to R4 and served until well into the sixties. They displaced 576 tons and were armed with four 21in torpedo tubes and a 3in gun.

Between 1952 and 1957 four US-built submarines based on the *Mackerel* Class (SS) were purchased to form the *Tiburnon* Class (later renamed the *Abtao* Class); one was deleted in 1990. Two more US-built boats were purchased in 1974. These were of the *Guppy* 1A Class (SS) ex-USS *Sea Poacher* and ex-USS *Atule.* They were deleted in 1992 and 1993.

During 1969 two 209 (Type 1200) submarines (SSK) were ordered from West Germany. These were followed by four more of the same class in 1976-7. All were commissioned between 1975 and 1980.

The present force consists of six 209 Class and two *Abtao* Class.

SUBMARINE INSIGNIA

The submarine speciality badge, authorized 8 June, 1949, is produced in metal 73mm x 23mm and is secured to the uniform by a hinged brooch pin and hook. It is produced in gilt for officers and in silver for ratings. Miniatures of both types also exist.

The design consists of an R Class submarine facing the wearer's left. Centrally located towards the bottom of the hull is an enamel shield bearing the national arms in full colour, either side of which is an inward-facing dolphin. Early badges depicted the dolphins and shield just below the submarine's hull; later styles showed them partially on the submarine's hull. The insignia is worn on the left breast above medal ribbons. Originally ratings wore a similar cloth embroidered badge on the left sleeve just below the shoulder seam.

An updated version with a modern submarine is said to exist.

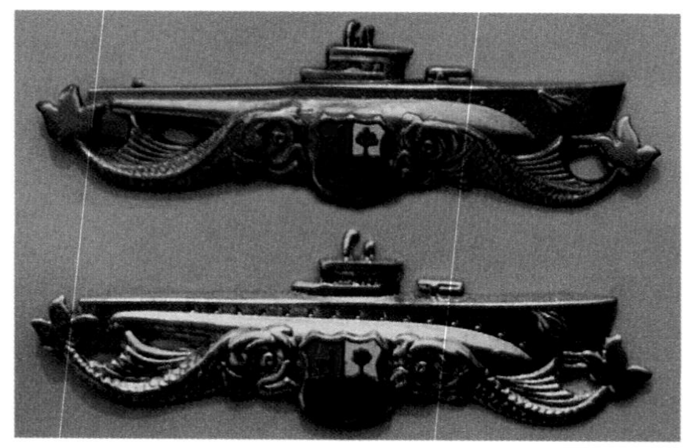

Peruvian submarine qualification insignia for officers in gilt and for ratings in silver. Authorized 8 June, 1949.

Poland

Submarine Service

The first submarines to sail under the Polish flag were three 980 ton French-built boats which entered service in 1931. These were given the names *Rys*, *Zbik* and *Wilk*. Intended for Baltic service, they had a relatively small radius of action but a substantial torpedo armament and mine-laying capacity.

Just before World War II Poland took delivery of two Dutch-built submarines. These were given the names *Sep* and *Orzel*. Of 1,110 tons their armament and mine-laying capacity was double that of their predecessors.

At the outbreak of war *Sep*, *Rys* and *Zbik* sailed to Sweden and internment. However, *Orzel* and *Wilk* escaped to serve under Allied command. Thus the entire submarine force escaped falling into the hands of the enemy. *Orzel* was lost in 1940 but *Wilk* survived the war.

Three Allied submarines were transferred to the Free Polish Navy; the British U Class submarines P52 and *Urchin* were renamed *Dzik* and *Sokol* and the American PSSI (ex-British S25) was renamed *Jastrzab*. *Dzik* and *Sokol* survived the war but *Jastrzab* was lost in 1942, having struck a mine.

After the war *Dzik* was transferred to Denmark and *Sokol* was returned to Britain. *Rys*, *Wilk* and *Zbik* continued to serve until 1957 and the last of the wartime boats, *Sep*, went out of service in 1971.

With the restructuring of the post-war Polish Navy, six ex-Soviet MV Class submarines (SSC) were acquired between 1956 and 1957. These

were replaced by five ex-Soviet *Whiskey* Class (SS), four of which were transferred to Poland between 1962 and 1965 and the fifth some time later. By 1989 all had been withdrawn from service. They were replaced by two former Soviet *Foxtrots* (SS) in 1987-8.

In 1986 the Soviet Union transferred a *Kilo* Class submarine (SSK) to Poland. The *Kilo* (SS) and the two *Foxtrots* (SS) constitute the present (1996) Polish submarine arm.

SUBMARINE INSIGNIA

The Polish submarine insignia was authorized in 1964 by Ministry of National Defence Order number 9.

The device is made of lightweight stamped metal secured by a single clutch fastener or a screwed lug. It consists of a conventional submarine facing the wearer's left. Centralized over the hull and conning tower is the Polish eagle below which appear the arms and flukes of an anchor.

The insignia is worn in three colours, gold for commanding and ex-commanding officers, silver for other officers and bronze for ratings. It comes in one size only measuring 70mm x 23mm and all ranks wear the device on the right breast. There can be some variation in detail and quality and the rating's badge is sometimes produced in dull bronze-like very thin metal.

Like the Soviet Navy the Polish Navy produces a number of ship

Polish submarine qualification insignia, in gold-coloured metal for commanding officers, in silver-coloured metal for other officers and in bronze for ratings, (about 1964).

commemorative badges for wear on the right breast. As an example, the first *Kilo* in service had such a badge. This took the form of a wreath on the base of which was a scroll bearing the inscription '*Pierwsza Zatoga* 1986' (First Crew 1986) surmounted by the Polish eagle on a shield and all in silver. Within the wreath from top to bottom was a white sky, a black *Kilo* Class submarine and a red 'sea' which bore the inscription '*Orp Orzel* III' (Polish Republic Ship *Orzel*). The badge which was enamelled measured 30mm x 42mm and had a screw back.

Portugal

Submarine Service

Portugal's submarine history goes back to 1913 when the 245 ton *Espadarte* of the Italian Laurenti type was commissioned. Three more submarines of Italian construction followed in 1916/17. Known as the *Foca* Class (*Foca*, *Golfinho* and *Hidra*) they displaced 260 tons and were armed with two 18in torpedo tubes, similar to the *Espadarte*.

In the early 1930s Italy supplied a further two submarines designated the *Delfim* Class (*Delfim* and *Espadarte*). Considerably larger than their predecessors they displaced 770 tons and were armed with six 21in torpedo tubes. Both remained in service until well into the mid-1940s.

In 1948 three ex-British S Class (HMS/Ms *Spearhead*, *Saga* and *Spur*) were purchased. They were renamed *Neptuno*, *Nautilo* and *Narval* and served until 1967, 1969 and 1979 respectively. This class was followed by the purchase of four French *Daphne* Class submarines (SSK) between 1967 and 1969. One of these, the *Cachalote*, was, sold to Pakistan in 1975.

The present force consists of the three *Daphne* Class submarines *Albacora*, *Barracude* and *Delfim*.

Submarine Insignia

The first submarine insignia was authorized in 1915. It was originally intended for officers only but it was later extended to all ranks. The badge depicted the Navy's first submarine *Espadarte*. It faced the wearer's right and measured 52mm x 31mm. Worn on the right sleeve 50mm below the elbow, it was embroidered in gold for officers and senior ratings and in red on blue or blue on white for junior ratings.

In 1920 the design was altered to feature a *Delfim* Class submarine. This time it faced the wearer's left and measured 91mm x 22mm. Above the conning tower was placed a detached disc displaying the national

arms in full colour. At this stage the badge was repositioned for officers and senior ratings to the right side of the upper chest. Junior ratings continued to wear the insignia on the sleeve.

In 1936 the national arms device was removed from the badges worn by senior and junior ratings.

In the mid-1950s a more modern badge appeared for officers and senior ratings. It was made in gilded stamped brass and took the form of a British 'A' Class submarine facing its wearer's left. The official version bore the National Arms in the centre, whereas the one for senior ratings was plain. It measured 63mm x 22mm and was fixed to the uniform by a long brooch fastener. Its authenticity cannot be verified — but it was worn well into the 1960s.

The present more modern hull form design was adopted in 1960 with the national arms device worn by officers surrounded by a wreath. Senior and junior ratings continued to wear it without the national arms device.

In 1961 the national arms device worn by officers was lowered to cover the central part of the submarine. At the same time polished brass badges became available for officers and senior ratings for wear on white uniforms. Junior ratings continued to wear the cloth sleeve badge, red on blue, and blue on white.

The insignia is worn by all qualified submariners and the present badge measures 65mm x 25mm. The metal version has a hinged brooch pin and hook fastener. There is no miniature badge; officers wear the full size badge on mess dress. Both officers and senior ratings can wear a gold embroidered badge on service uniform at their option. Some badges produced later show a slightly more modernized version of the submarine.

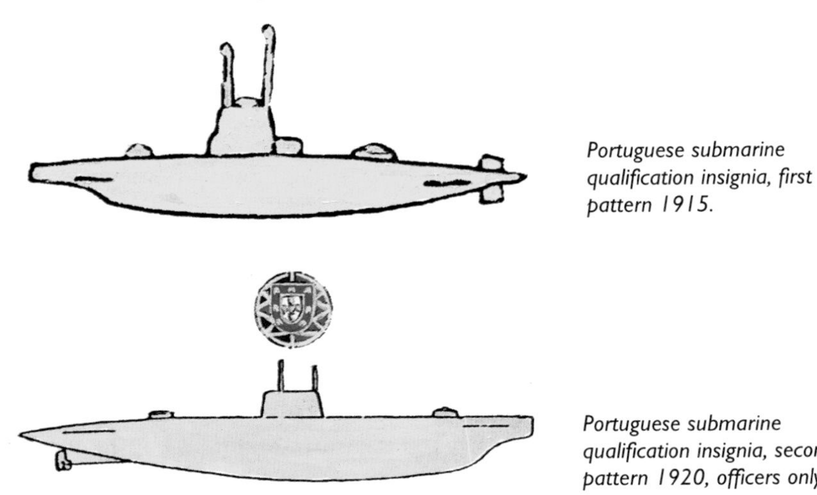

Portuguese submarine qualification insignia, first pattern 1915.

Portuguese submarine qualification insignia, second pattern 1920, officers only.

Portuguese submarine qualification insignia, 1936 pattern for career petty officers.

Portuguese submarine qualification insignia, third pattern for officers 1960.

Portuguese submarine qualification insignia variation about. 1956 to 1960, for career petty officers. Officers badge is the same but with the National Arms in the centre.

Portuguese submarine qualification insignia for officers 1961.

Portuguese submarine qualification insignia for career petty officers 1961.

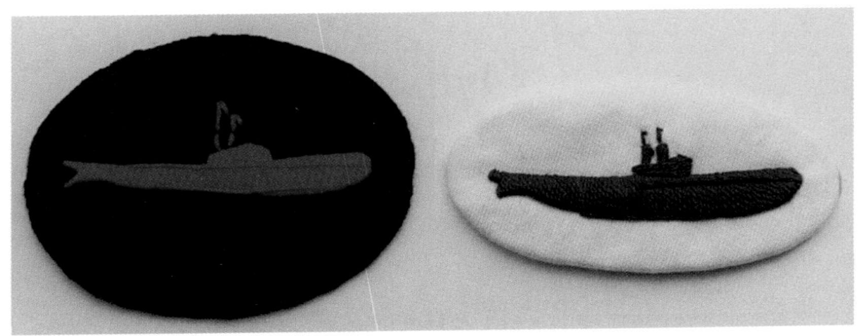

Portuguese submarine qualification insignia for wear on the sleeve by junior ratings. Embroidered in blue on white cloth for summer or red on dark blue cloth for winter.

ROMANIA

SUBMARINE SERVICE

Romania's first submarine was ordered from Italy in 1927, completed in 1931 and entered service in 1936. Named *Delfinul*, she had a surface displacement of 650 tons and was armed with six 21in torpedo tubes plus one 4in gun.

The next submarine to enter service was the *Marsuinul*. She was built in Romania to a German design. Slightly smaller than her predecessor, she displaced 620 tons and was armed with six 21in torpedo tubes plus a 4in gun and a 37mm gun. She was laid down in 1938 and completed in 1942.

Similar to the *Marsuinul*, the *Rechinul* was also built in Romania to a German design. A mine-laying submarine, she displaced 585 tons and was armed with four 21in torpedo tubes and had capacity for forty mines. She also entered service in 1942.

Five Italian midget submarines of the CB class CB1, 2, 3, 4 and 6 were transferred to Romania in September, 1943; all were subsequently scuttled in August, 1944.

Delfinul remained in service until 1957. *Marsuinul* and *Rechinul* were deleted in 1967, though all had been withdrawn from active service in 1961. Romania was then to be without a submarine arm for nineteen years.

In December, 1986, the Soviet Union transferred a *Kilo* Class submarine (SSK) to the Romanian flag. It is anticipated that a number of others of the same class will follow, though this depends entirely on funds being made available which at present seems unlikely.

SUBMARINE INSIGNIA

As far as can be ascertained Romania originally had no specialist submarine qualification badge. However, a series of war badges were created on 17 June, 1943. There were seven categories, one of which was for submarines. It was awarded for forty days' active service at sea but immediate awards could be made for actual combat or for being wounded.

The insignia, which was in metal, was very similar in design to the Italian submarine service badge. It consisted of a leaping dolphin (said to allude to the first Romanian submarine of that name) surrounded by a broad band of which the bottom part was in the form of a wreath. The word 'Svbmarine' was inscribed at the top of the band. The device was surmounted by the Royal Crown. It was worn in gilt by officers, silver for petty officers and a dull white metal for junior ratings.

After the Monarchy was overthrown (December, 1947) a new insignia made its appearance. It was quite different in design from the insignia worn by other countries. It was manufactured in metal and was in the shape of an eagle (facing the wearer's left) above two crossed swords. On the eagle's chest was an enamelled shield in red, on which was a double white cross atop three blue hills. The insignia was worn on the left side of the jacket, fixed by a screw fastening, and was gold for officers, silver for petty officers and a grey metal for junior ratings. It was said to measure 20mm x 13mm. Unusual in appearance for a submarine badge, especially as the central device closely resembles the national arms of Slovakia (the Apostolic Cross and representation of the Tatra Mountains). This may allude to some former connection between the two states or the design may 'just have been borrowed'. Nevertheless the details here came directly from the Romanian Naval Authorities. It is possible that the insignia may have been specifically authorized for service in miniature submarines which had a dual role for torpedo attack and for carriers of combat swimmers (frogmen). Further speculation on its authenticity cannot be ruled out. With the demise of the submarine service in 1967 the insignia ceased to be awarded. Official information received in 1993 stated that no special insignia exists for submariners.

A small white metal anodized aluminium badge appeared about 1994. It depicts a black *Kilo* Class submarine with an open-topped white metal wreath around the central part of the hull and sail, in the centre of which

is the numeral '55' in red. At the base of the wreath are the national colours, blue, yellow and red, the whole being picked out in white metal. It measures 49mm x 28mm and has a very flimsy pin and hook fixing at the back.

Because of its metal and fixing it is unlikely to be a uniform item for submarine qualification and more likely to be a commemorative badge of some kind. Specialist insignia for a one-submarine fleet would be of a low priority.

Romanian War Badge created 1943 in gold for officers, silver for senior ratings and dull white metal for junior ratings. Lapsed with fall of monarchy in 1947.

(above) Romanian submarine insignia about 1994 probably a commemorative badge for wear on civilian clothes.

Romanian submarine service insignia, post-war to about 1961.

Russia: Monarchy

Russian Submarine Service

Experiments were carried out with a German-built submarine in the Baltic as early as 1854. In 1866 a submarine was built by an engineer named Alexandrovsky. It proved to be a failure as were some fifty four-man, hand-propelled, mine-laying submersibles that followed in 1878. Most were either cancelled or converted into mooring buoys.

The first Czarist submarine to actually enter service was the *Petr Kochka* completed at Kronstadt in 1902. She was built in sections so that she could be transported by rail to Port Arthur. Her displacement was a mere 20 tons but she could carry two small torpedoes. A second submarine, the *Delphin*, foundered at Kronstadt but was raised and used for training. Both boats were out of service before World War I commenced.

Between 1904 and 1905 a few small experimental submarines were deployed at Port Arthur and Vladivostok but failed to achieve any results against the Japanese. Several boats were then purchased from America, Germany and Italy. Just before World War I the *Tigr* class was laid down. These were the first Russian-designed submarines.

On the outbreak of war in 1914 Russia had thirty-seven submarines and nineteen under construction. Of the active boats fourteen were in the Baltic, eleven in the Black Sea and twelve were in the Siberian Flotilla based at Vladivostok. Pre-war boats were mostly Holland and American Lake types of between 150 and 200 tons and armed with two to four torpedo tubes. Among these was the world's first mine-laying submarine, the *Krab*. The majority were underpowered and poorly constructed, requiring constant repairs.

Six more classes were built during the war, including eighteen US-manufactured H Class assembled in Russian yards (of which three survived to serve in World War II). Altogether fifty-eight submarines served under the Russian flag during World War I; of these seven were discarded and eight were lost before October, 1917. Of the remainder twenty-four were lost during the Civil War, including four that escaped to Bizerta on the collapse of the White Cause. Thirteen were scuttled by the British to prevent them falling into Bolshevik hands. Shortly after the Civil War three submarines in the Baltic fleet and four in the Caspian Flotilla were deleted. The Czarist fleet had ceased to exist.

The performance of the Russian submarine fleet during World War I was not spectacular, though a few minor successes were achieved against German and neutral Swedish merchant ships in the Baltic. Its record in

the Black Sea was much better, with Turkish transports being the main targets. At no time did it pose a serious threat to the German Navy.

RUSSIAN SUBMARINE INSIGNIA

The submarine distinguishing badge was an insignia only available to officers who had graduated from the Navy Department Submarine Course. It was authorized on 26 January, 1909, and was manufactured in silver metal measuring 43mm x 45mm. The design consisted of a fouled anchor over which, and facing to the wearer's left, was a submarine. Anchor and submarine were surrounded by the links of an anchor chain.

Imperial Russian insignia for Officers Submarine Class, Navy Department, 1909-17.

USSR & POST-COMMUNIST RUSSIA

SOVIET SUBMARINE SERVICE

After the Revolution the Russian Navy was re-styled the Red Fleet. Few submarines remained from Czarist days and most of those that did were unserviceable. Only ten were left in the Baltic, five in the Black Sea and one in the Arctic.

It was not until 1928 that the first class of new submarines was laid down. This was the D Class of six vessels based on Italian design. These were followed by the L Class of twenty-five mine-laying submarines based on British design. The SHCH Class, originally of four boats but many more were to follow, made their first appearance in 1930.

It was evident that by now the Soviet Union was intent on making her submarine force the spearhead of her Navy. Between 1927 and 1939 twenty classes (and sub-classes) consisting of 281 submarines were laid down. In 1939, at the commencement of the Winter War with Finland, one hundred and eighty-five had been completed. This made it the world's largest submarine force. Despite having fifty-five submarines in the Baltic only six small merchant ships were sunk, of which two were neutral. Against this the Red Fleet lost six of its submarines.

In 1941, when Hitler attacked the Soviet Union, the Red Fleet had 218 submarines in commission and many more were in various stages of construction. Ninety-one were laid down during the war. However, only fifty-two of these were completed before the war ended. Of those that remained, most were destroyed on their slipway or abandoned. Twenty-two other submarines, including five pocket submarines, were acquired from abroad. Great Britain and America transferred five each and the Soviet seized two from Estonia, two from Latvia and eight from Romania.

The Stalin purges of 1937-8 decimated the officer corps, resulting in a lack of expertise to develop submarine tactics. This lack of expert leadership, despite much evidence of courage, accounted in some part for the poor performance of the Red Fleet submarines during World War II. Soviet figures at the end of the war claimed that their submarines had sunk a total of 417 enemy vessels. Allied estimates made the figure 136. Although 173 Soviet submarines survived the war at least 108 were lost.

In 1948 Stalin announced the first post-war building programme. It called for the construction of 1,200 submarines to be built at the rate of seventy-eight per year. This figure was later raised to one hundred per year. With the advent of nuclear propulsion a large proportion of this vast programme was cancelled. Five classes totalling 388 diesel/electric submarines were completed. These were the coastal submarines of the *Quebec* Class, the medium range submarines of the *Whiskey* and *Romeo* Classes and the long-range submarines of the *Zulu* and *Foxtrot* Classes (all SS).* Construction of submarines then split into three groups: attack submarines (SS), cruise missile submarines (SSG) and ballistic missile submarines (SSB).

The next generation of conventional attack submarines (SSK) were the eighteen boats of the *Tango* Class in 1973, followed in 1979 by the

*Note: NATO designators are used for class names with the exception of the *Severodvinsk* Class.

first of thirteen *Kilo* Class. Nuclear-powered attack submarines (SSN) made their appearance between 1959 and 1963 with the twelve vessels of the *November* Class. With a displacement of 4,200 tons and armed with eight 21in torpedo tubes, their primary task was to attack enemy surface shipping. The *Victor* Class (I, II, III) of forty-four SSNs followed between 1967 and 1978. Armed with six 21in torpedo tubes (and the IIIs were capable of firing the SS-N-15 anti-submarine missiles through their tubes) they were the first of the hunter-killers (anti-submarine submarines).

The revolutionary *Alpha* Class (SSN), initially of six boats, first appeared in 1970. They were the world's first submarines to be constructed from titanium, which not only returns a low magnetic signature, but also its great strength enables the submarines to dive to a depth of more than 3,000ft, twice that of Western submarines. Their high speed also enabled them to out-run all current Western A/S torpedoes. Two *Sierra* and one *Mike* Class (SSNs) entered service in 1983-4 armed with torpedoes and SS-N-21 (land attack) missiles and two *Sierra* IIs (SSN) commissioned in 1990-3. The *Akula* Class first appeared in 1984-5. Of advanced design, they have a dived tonnage of 8,000 tons and are armed with six 21in torpedo tubes and the SS-N-21 missile. This missile system can be fired through the torpedo tubes. A number of older ballistic missile submarines had also been converted to the attack role. The lead ship of a new class, the dual purpose SSN/SSGN *Severodvinsk* Class of three and possibly four more is due to enter service in 1998.

In the early 1950s experiments were carried out with submarine-mounted cruise missiles, a type of weapon that remains a Soviet monopoly. The first submarines to be so mounted were the *Whiskey* Class (SSG). In 1956 one boat was fitted with a single SS-N-3 (range 12 NM). In 1959 a further five were fitted with two SS-N-3A (range 250 NM). These elderly versions required the submarine to fire its missiles on the surface. In 1961 six *Whiskeys* were converted to carry four SS-N-3 which were enclosed within the control tower. The first purpose-built cruise (or guided) missile submarines (SSG) were the sixteen *Juliet* Class boats. They entered between 1961 and 1968. They had a displacement of 3,000 tons and were armed with four SS-N-3A missiles and six torpedo tubes.

All further cruise missile submarines were to be nuclear-propelled (SSGN). The first of these were the *Echo* Class. Five mark Is with six SS-N-3 and twenty-nine mark IIs with eight SS-N-3 were built. Like all Soviet SSGNs they were also armed with torpedo tubes. Then came the *Charlie* Is and IIs between 1967 and 1980. The eleven Is had eight SS-N-7 (range 35NM) and the six IIs had eight SS-N-9 (range 60 NM).

One *Papa* Class entered service in 1971 armed with ten SS-N-9. The latest submarines of this type are the *Oscar* Class I and II (SSGN) of which five had been built, the first entering service in 1980. Huge vessels of 12,500 and 13,400 tons (dived) they mount twenty-four SS-N-19 (range 295 NM). They also are armed with new large 22.6in torpedoes. A number of older Y Class SSBNs have been converted to a SSGN role.

Ballistic missiles were first fitted into submarines in 1958. Selected for this purpose were ten conventional submarines of the ZV Class. Each was fitted with two vertical launch tubes for SS-N-4 (range 300 NM) in the sail. The purpose-built *Golf* Class (SSB) followed between 1958 and 1962. Twenty-three altogether, the mark IIIs had six SS-N-8 (range 4,260 NM) and the single mark V had one SS-N-20 (range 4,540 NM). There were five groups in all but various submarines within the class were re-graded. Like all Soviet SSBNs, they were also armed with torpedoes.

Future vessels of this type were all nuclear-powered (SSBN). The first of these were the *Hotel* Class of eight. They were originally armed with six SS-N-4s. They were later upgraded to SS-N-5 and finally to SS-N-8. Next came the *Yankee* Class. Thirty-four were built between 1967 and 1974, of which thirteen were later converted to SSNs. Their missile armament consisted of sixteen SS-N-6 (range 1,300 NM later upgraded to 1,640 NM). This relatively short range made it necessary for them to transit great distances in order to arrive 'on station'. The *Deltas* (I, II, III, IV) that followed in 1972/84 all had long-range missiles which meant that they could remain in the relatively safe waters off their own coastline. The eighteen mark Is had twelve SS-N-8. The four mark IIs had sixteen SS-N-8, the fourteen mark IIIs had sixteen SS-N-18 (range 3,550 NM) and the four mark IVs had sixteen SS-N-23 (range 4,540 NM). Large boats, they displace between 8,300 and 11,000 tons.

The latest SSBNs to come into service are the *Typhoon* Class. Estimated to have a displacement of between 25,000 and 30,000 tons, they are the largest submarines ever built. Their missile armament consists of twenty SS-N-20 (range 4,540 NM). The first of a planned class of six entered service in 1983.

The Soviet Navy ceased to exist on the 1 January, 1992. On that date the Soviet Union was split into fifteen independent republics and assumed the name of the Commonwealth of Independent States. The armed forces were shared out, but the vast bulk of the former Red Fleet went to Russia. As far as is known this included all submarines.

The Russian submarine fleet as of 1996 consists of thirty-nine SSBNs,

eighteen SSGNs, one SSG, fifty-two SSNs, forty-two SSKs and fifteen auxiliaries. Numerous older submarines have transferred to other navies, been laid up or have been scrapped.

Despite Russia's economic situation and the hugely rising costs in the construction and maintenance of keeping ships operational, Russia is continuing to build submarines at a yearly rate of one SSBN, one or two SSNs and two or three SSKs. It is estimated that by the end of the century there will be nearly sixty more submarines in service than those at present. The world should take note!

SUBMARINE INSIGNIA

Accurate information on the Soviet/Russian submarine insignia is extremely difficult to obtain. The reader is therefore warned that the following details have been based on the best available information, but lacks official Soviet sanction.

The first submarine badge was authorized in 1942 and was styled the badge for 'Submarine Commander'. This has been interpreted as the badge for commanding officers of submarines. This may be an over-simplification as between 1918 and 1943 all Soviet officers were collectively referred to as Commanders. Photographic evidence exists of officers who appear too junior to be in command wearing the badge. It is therefore still not clear who is entitled to wear it. It is awarded for meritorious service and achievement.

Originally the badge was manufactured in grey oxidised metal (perhaps due to wartime restrictions) but later models were made in bright silver. It depicts a conventional submarine with two deck guns facing the wearer's left. In the centre of the hull there is a red enamel star. It measures 68mm x 22mm and it has a screw fastening on the back. The securing nut is round and bears, in the Cyrillic alphabet, the inscription 'Forward to Victory, Moscow'. The badge comes in one size only and it is worn on the right breast. Recipients may continue to wear the insignia throughout their service careers. It is regarded in much the same light as a medal and it is awarded with due ceremony. Illustrations that appeared about 1965 show a slightly different design, the main difference being that the submarine has no deck guns. Little has been seen of this variation since that time.

In the early 1990s a gold version of the insignia appeared. This is said to be worn by highly ranking officers though illustrations show Admirals wearing the silver badge. The Soviet Navy has always had a gold and silver ranking system, denoting line or service; thus the colour may relate to a specific appointment. Otherwise gold-coloured badges should be

treated with suspicion. A miniature, possibly unofficial, measuring 38mm x 13mm appeared about 1992.

Graduates of the Submarine Academy wear the usual diamond-shaped academy badge 45mm high. It has a red star with the Soviet coat-of-arms in its centre, below which, on a small plate, are the Cyrillic letters for 'VVMU' denoting the Submarine Service Naval Academy Plavania.

A series of seven proficiency badges known as Best Soldier (Sailor) Badges were instituted on 21 May, 1942. They were all the same basic design, being shield shape with oak leaves on either side. The top portions bore a white circlet, bearing a Cyrillic inscription, surrounding a hammer and sickle on a red field. At the base of the shield was an emblem denoting the speciality. In the case of the submarine service this was a small gold submarine. The badges measured 34mm x 38mm and were worn on the right breast. This series of insignia eventually totalled twenty-three specialities but only the one remained specifically for submariners. On 1 April, 1967, these badges were replaced by three new ones, one each for the Army, Navy and Air Force; thus submarine ratings lost their only distinctive emblem.

Officers and ratings can also qualify for Long Cruise Badges. These are made of coloured enamel metal badges and take various forms. The 1961 Long Cruise pattern depicts a submarine above an inscribed base and semi-wreath, above which is a Naval Ensign. The one for 1976 is shaped rather like a shield. It displays a Soviet Naval Ensign at the top, a nuclear submarine with a representation of a globe over an inscription in the centre and an anchor over waves at the bottom. These badges are worn on the right breast. As long cruises became more common such badges became less prolific.

Numerous submarine-related badges also exist. These are for commemorative events or anniversaries or are for long and special service. Most are not intended for wear on uniform; those that are usually (but not always) have a screw fixing on the back.

No changes in submarine insignia has occurred since the collapse of communism. It is assumed that the existing insignia will continue to be worn, though other types may be added.

Soviet Union, submarine qualification insignia for commanding officers.

Unofficial in gold.

Soviet Union, ratings submarine proficiency badge 1942-57.

Soviet Union Submarine Long Cruise Badge 1961.

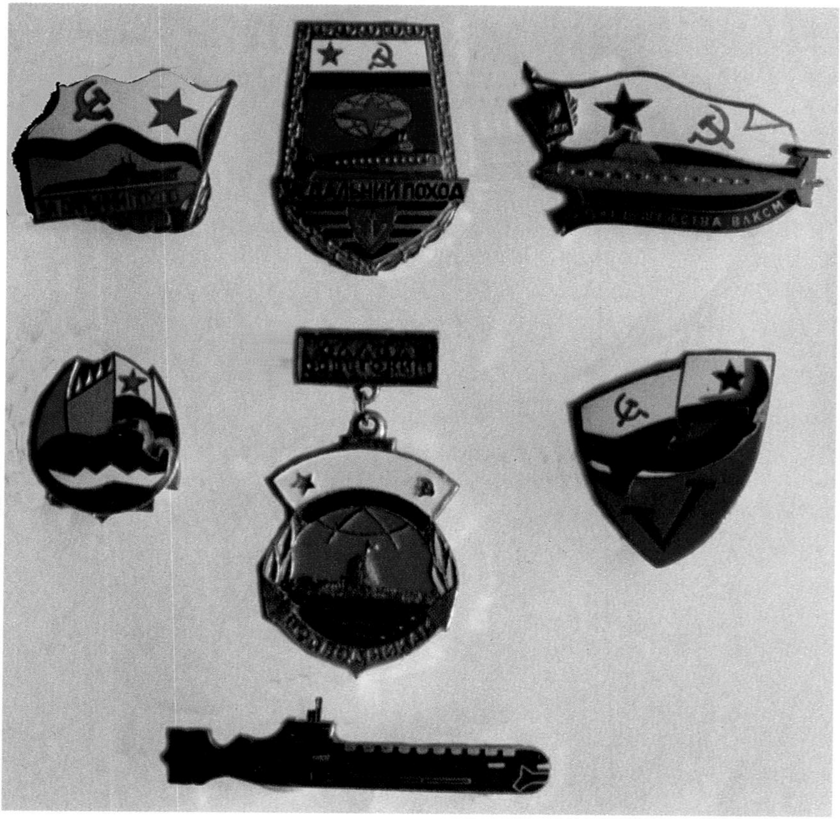

Soviet Union, selection of commemorative and similar insignia not meant for wear on uniforms.

Soviet Union Submarine Long Cruise Badge 1976.

Saudi Arabia

Submarine Service

Persistent rumours have indicated that Saudi Arabia has been considering the purchase of patrol submarines (SSK). Saudi naval officers have received training in the navies of France and Pakistan, which points to the French *Agosta* Class as being front-runners. The acquiring of such submarines is, however, a low priority. It is more likely that smaller submarines, probably suited for commando infiltration (SDV), will enter service first.

Submarine Insignia

Thought to be quite unofficial, a small number of badges were contracted for about 1981 to a United States insignia manufacturer who sub-contracted the order to a small company that did casting work. The casting company reportedly went out of business in 1983 and efforts to track down the moulds proved unsuccessful.

The insignia depicted a central motif of unfouled anchor about which were crossed scimitars and above that a palm tree and crossed flags, all surmounted by a royal crown. Either side were inward-facing dolphins similar in design to those depicted on USN submarine badges. Between the crown and the dolphin's heads, on each side, were three bolts of lightning.

The badges were made in heavy metal casting with clutchback fasteners. The finish was in bright gold but with a silver anchor. It measured 75mm x 43mm and there was a miniature version. It is likely that these badges were intended for the crews of midget submarines and SDVs who would also be combat swimmers.

Saudi Arabian submarine insignia, probably for SDV crews and may be unofficial.

SINGAPORE

SUBMARINE SERVICE

Singapore purchased the 28-year-old Swedish submarine *Sjöbjörnen* of the *Sjöormen* Class (SSK) in October, 1995. She is expected to be delivered in the second half of 1997. She is more than twice the size of the projected German Type 206 Class which are thought to be front-runners for the new submarine service. This submarine will be used as a training ship to provide personnel for from two to four smaller submarines to follow. Her large size will provide accommodation for trainees and space for fitting trial equipment for tropical conditions. The new submarines are not expected to be ordered before 1998/9.

SUBMARINE INSIGNIA

No details are presently available.

SOUTH AFRICA

SUBMARINE SERVICE

Only three submarines have served in the South African Navy. They are the French-built *Daphne* Class, *Maria Van Riebeeck*, *Emily Hobhouse* and *Johanna Van Der Merwe*. The first was commissioned in 1970 and the other two in 1971.

Two French *Agosta* Class were ordered in 1975. A subsequent United Nations ban on the sale of armaments to South Africa resulted in them being sold, instead, to Pakistan.

The three submarines in service have all been modernized to enable them to continue in service until 2005.

SUBMARINE INSIGNIA

On the formation of the submarine arm, a submarine service badge was authorized. It took the form of a simplistic representation of a modern submarine in gilt metal facing the wearer's left. The device measured 65mm x 16mm and was the same for all ranks. It was first presented on 16 January, 1970.

In 1974 the design was changed. This followed the introduction

into the Navy of four specialist badges for all sea-going personnel. The categories were 'independent ships', 'strike craft', 'mine counter measures' and 'submarines'. All were produced in metal and were of a similar basic design.

The submarine badge depicts a *Daphne* Class submarine in gold colour facing the wearer's left. Behind the submarine is an upright trident and wreath in silver colour. The device is worn on the right mid-breast and is secured by a pair of clutch fasteners. The dimensions are 58mm x 40mm.

The qualifications required are:

1 be medically fit for submarine service,
2 successfully complete submarine course part I,
3 be up-to-date with submarine escape training,
4 have served in a submarine at sea for at least forty-five days,
5 complete applicable qualifying task book,
6 be recommended by commanding officers as being competent and suitable to fill a post on board commensurate with rank and
7 display the required ability, sense of responsibility and submarine awareness.

The insignia may be worn throughout the recipient's service. A miniature version is said to exist but this may not be official. A printed cloth version is available for the all-weather working uniform.

South African submarine qualification insignia, all ranks.
Top: 1970-4.
Bottom: from 1974.

SPAIN

SUBMARINE SERVICE

The Spanish submarine service began in 1915 with the ordering from the United States of a 488 ton submarine of the Holland type. She was named *Isaac Peral* and was armed with four torpedo tubes and a 3in QF gun. Three more submarines were laid down in 1917 in Italian yards and were delivered between 1916 and 1920. Much smaller than their predecessor, they displaced 260 tons and had an armament of two 18in torpedo tubes and a 3 pdr gun.

Between 1923 and 1925 six more submarines were constructed in Italy. They formed the C Class, displaced 915 tons and were fitted with six 21in torpedo tubes and one 4.7in gun. Two were sunk during the Spanish Civil War, though one was subsequently raised and refitted. During the Civil War four Italian submarines served with the Spanish Nationalist Forces. For details see the section on Italy.

The D Class, Spanish-built, consisting of three submarines, entered service between 1941 and 1943. They displaced 1,050 tons and were armed with six 21in torpedo tubes, a 4.7in gun and two machine guns. The German U 573 which had been interned in Spain in 1942 was purchased in 1943 and was renamed G7.

In 1959, after most of the earlier boats had been paid off, the United States transferred the *Balao* Class submarine (SS) USS *Kraken* to Spain.

In 1957 and 1958 Spain added two classes of midget submarines to her Navy. The first class of two boats, designated the *Foca* Class, displaced 16 tons, were armed with two 21in torpedo tubes and had a crew of three. Both were deleted in 1971. The second class, also of two boats, designated the *Tiburnon* Class, displaced 78 tons and had a similar armament and were manned by a crew of five. Both were disposed of in 1977.

By 1971 the remaining D Class and the ex-German U-boat had been broken up. The United States transferred four more submarines between 1971 and 1974. These were the USS *Ronquil*, *Picuda*, *Bang* and *Jallao* of the *Guppy* IIA Class (SS).

More modern purpose-built submarines were built in Spain between 1968 and 1974. Designated the S60 *Delfin* Class they were based on the French *Daphne* Class and were built under licence. Four more French-designed submarines were constructed in Spain between 1977 and 1984. These were of the French *Agosta* Class and were given the Spanish designation of S70 *Galerna* Class.

The present (1996) Spanish Submarine Arm consists of these last two

classes. The next generation of submarines which have been designated S80 *Scorpene* Class are being developed in conjunction with France. Of about 2,000 tons displacement, construction is scheduled to commence in 1999.

SUBMARINE INSIGNIA

The Spanish Navy first authorized a submarine qualification badge on 5 September, 1919. It depicted a stylized version of a Holland type submarine with a single deck gun. It faced the wearer's left and was surmounted by a Royal Crown. It was manufactured in both gold wire embroidery and in gold-coloured metal. The metal version had a brooch fixing and was intended for wear on the white uniform. A red enamel oval was situated in the centre of the hull and below the conning tower for all personnel serving in or having served in submarines. For cadets at the Submarine School and for personnel who had completed their training but had not been assigned to submarines, the oval was in blue enamel. In the case of the metal badge the crown was detached; consequently many survive without the crown.

Admiralty order dated 30 March, 1934, further defined the insignia and gave its dimensions as 85mm wide, though slightly narrower examples may be found. No mention was made regarding the Royal Crown. Despite the fact that King Alfonso XIII was forced to leave the country in April, 1931, and a republic was proclaimed, the King refused to abdicate. It was not until 1941 that he renounced his rights in favour of his son Don Juan. This may explain why the crown may have been retained.

New orders on 1 October, 1934, dropped the mention of the blue oval, but as it was again mentioned in later orders this is not thought to be significant, though at this stage reports suggest that the same design but with a mural crown had the coloured stone replaced by a gold-coloured anchor on a red oval background. This was said to have been worn from 1931 to 1939.

During The Spanish Civil War (18 July, 1936 to 29 March, 1939) submarine personnel on the Nationalist side began to change the badge to a different one, also with a crown, but depicting a *Cavallini* Class submarine with two deck guns. This measured 66mm x 22mm and much later an unofficial miniature was produced measuring 34mm x 12mm. On 10 June, 1939, the crown was replaced by a coronet as shown on the then Spanish coat-of-arms. This was prescribed by Generalissimo Franco in a letter to the Under-Secretary of the Admiralty on 27 May, 1938.

The regulations were again altered on 10 January, 1941; these orders

elaborated on the wearing of the submarine insignia by ratings. For seamen the badge without the coronet but including a red disc (rather than the previous oval shape) was to be embroidered on a rectangular piece of dark blue cloth measuring 67mm x 34mm. This insignia was to be worn 148mm below the shoulder seam on the right upper arm. For petty officers the same badge but with the coronet was to be sewn on the right breast, the only one to be worn there. This badge was of a different design being somewhat similar to the submarine used on the 1919 insignia but with upswept bows.

Admiralty Order of 14 January, 1957, reiterated previous regulations, but stated that the badge depicting the red disc could continue to be worn by those who had left the submarine service because of age or injury.

Admiralty Order dated 28 December, 1962, stated that any badge differing from the regulations would be exchanged by the Submarine School. This may explain the proliferation of insignia showing variations in design.

The next significant change came on 30 July, 1975, when all qualified personnel were to wear the badge with a red translucent circular stone imbedded in the centre of the hull. Cadets were to wear a similar stone in green and personnel associated with the submarine service but not actually serving at sea, but with a minimum of two years service, were to wear the stone in black. These associated personnel included maintenance engineers, supply personnel, chaplains and medical personnel, plus various smaller categories serving ashore.

The regulations of 25 October, 1978, reintroduced the Royal Crown (King Juan Carlos acceded to the throne on 22 November, 1975). It gave the dimensions of the new badge as 65mm x 22mm. Flag officers, officers, petty officers and re-enlisted leading seamen (*cabos primeros*) were to wear the insignia on the right breast and junior ratings were to wear it on the right upper sleeve. The metal badge had a brooch fixing. An unofficial miniature measuring 34mm x 14mm was later produced. Finally the Admiralty Order dated 29 July, 1986, altered the design of the insignia reverting to the original style of 1919 but with the following changes: the Royal Crown now included red cushions (in the metal version it was attached to the periscopes), the overall dimensions were reduced to 70mm x 30mm (though some variations measure 68mm x 30mm), and the translucent stones retain their circular shape. In future these stones were to be red for officers and green for ratings, the black stone for associated personnel was done away with altogether, leaving only the submarine device. The metal version was fixed to the uniform

with three clutch fasteners. There is no official miniature but doubtless an unofficial one will appear.

Junior ratings in the submarine service can further be distinguished by the name or number of their submarine on their cap ribbon. Those attached to the Submarine School bear the inscription 'SUB-MARINOS'.

Spanish submarine qualification insignia 1919-38.

Spanish submarine qualification insignia 1919-38 (crown missing).

Spanish submarine qualification insignia for officers and senior ratings 1941-78. Red stone for submarine officers and black stone for associated officers. During most of this period junior ratings wore the same insignia as submarine officers but without the coronet.

Spanish submarine qualification insignia worn by petty officers 1941-78, original version.

Spanish submarine qualification insignia worn by junior ratings on right sleeve 1941-78, original version.

Spanish submarine qualification insignia first pattern, monarchy, (stone missing) 1978-86, and second pattern, monarchy, with red stone for officers, from 1986.

Spanish submarine qualification insignia 1978-86 with red stone for officers and black stone for attached personnel (doctors, supply officers and chaplains, etc). This design also appears with a slightly smaller crown and a cable cutter on the bow.

Spanish submarine qualification insignia from 1986 in gold wire embroidery.

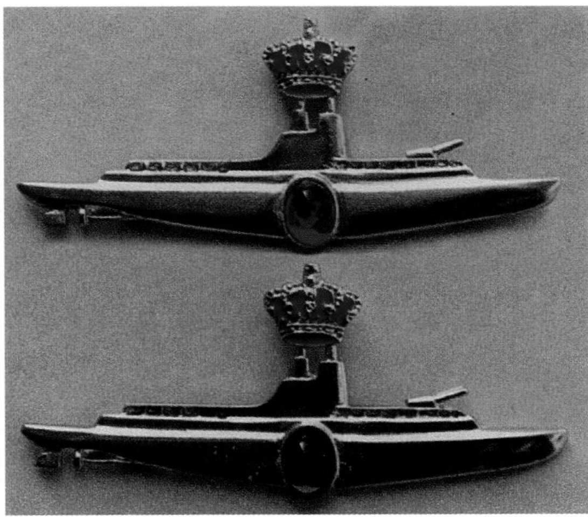

Spanish submarine qualification insignia, second pattern, for monarchy, with red stone for officers and green stone for junior ratings, from 1986.

SWEDEN

SUBMARINE SERVICE

Traditionally Sweden has built her own warships, and submarines, for the main part, were no exception. The first submersible came into service in 1904. Named *Hajen,* it was based on the Holland type, displaced 107 tons and was fitted with one 18in torpedo tube. She was followed by the Laurenti type *Hvalen* in 1909. Slightly larger, she displaced 180 tons and had double the armament. She was the sole exception to tradition, being Italian-built. Between 1910 and 1911 a class of five, numbered 3 to 7 (instead of being named) were constructed. Their displacement and armament was the same as their Italian-built predecessor.

During World War I three classes, consisting of seven submarines,

were completed (*Tumlaren*, *Delfinen* and *Abboren* Classes). Some of these remained in service until the mid-1970s. The *Haljen* Class of 300 tons, three in number, followed in 1920. Between 1920 and 1923 four more submarines designated the *Bavern* Class were constructed. They displaced 500 tons and were armed with four 20.8in torpedo tubes, one 6 pdr gun and one machine gun. One of this class, the *Valen*, was fitted out as a mine-layer.

The *Draken* Class of three boats entered service between 1924 and 1929. They displaced 700 tons and were armed with four 21in torpedo tubes and a 3in gun. The *Ulven* of this class was sunk by a mine in 1943. The three submarines of the *Delfinen* Class, constructed between 1934 and 1935 were of 540 tons and were armed with four 21in torpedo tubes, a single 57mm AA gun and were fitted as mine-layers.

Laid down just before World War II the *Sjölejonet* Class of nine vessels was completed during that war. They were of 580 tons and were fitted with six 21in torpedo tubes, two 40mm AA guns and two machine guns. They were the first fully Swedish designed submarines. War construction produced nine coastal submarines of the U Class. Numbered U1 to U9 they displaced 367 tons and were armed with four 21in torpedo tubes and a 20mm AA gun.

Post-war development began in 1964 with the launching of the first submarine of the six *Hajen* Class. These vessels were 790 tons displacement and mounted four 21in torpedo tubes and one 20mm AA gun. The former British X Class midget submarine HMS *Stickleback* was purchased in 1968 and remained in service until the early 1970s. The six-vessel *Draken* Class (Type A II) (SS) of 835 tons with four 21in torpedo tubes were launched between 1960 and 1961.

The first 'tear drop' submarines were launched between 1967 and 1968. Designated the *Sjöormen* Class (Type A 12) (SSK), they displace 1,125 tons and are armed with four 21in and two 15.75in torpedo tubes. Returning to a more conventional appearance, the *Nacken* Class (Type A 14) (SSK) were launched in 1978-9. This class of three units of 1,015 tons surface displacement is armed with six 21in torpedo tubes and two 15.75in torpedo tubes, plus a minelaying capability. In 1978 an underwater rescue vehicle was launched and in 1985 two Yugoslav Chariot Type swimmer vehicles were purchased designated R1 and R2. R1 was deleted in 1990. A midget submarine, *Spiggen II*, displacing 14 tons dived, was launched in 1990.

The *Vastergötland* (Type A 17) Class (SSK) was constructed between 1983 and 1988. The class numbers four boats displacing 1,070 tons and armed with six 21in and three 15.75in torpedo tubes. They also have the

capacity to carry twenty-two mines. A new class designated *Gotland* (Type A19) (SSK) is to be commissioned between 1996 and 1997. They will displace 1,240 tons and will eventually replace the *Sjöormen* Class.

Swedish submarine design, by Kockums of Malmo, has reached a high level which has led to a high export trade.

The submarine force at spring 1996 consisted of four *Vastergötland* Class (SSK), three *Nacken* Class (SSK), four *Sjöormen* Class (SSK) and one midget (*Spiggen II*) used as ASW training target.

SUBMARINE INSIGNIA

The first Swedish submarine badge appeared in 1956. It was quite unofficial but, despite the threat of arrest by the military police, it was worn with much pride by most submariners. The badge was made in gold-coloured metal measuring 66mm x 22mm and it had a brooch fixing. The design was of a Neptune's trident, behind which was the sail (or conning tower) of an on-coming partially submerged submarine flanked by two waves.

In January, 1978, the Swedish Navy authorized an official insignia. It is the same for all ranks and is embroidered in gold on dark blue cloth. The design depicts a trident within a shield surmounted by a Royal Crown. Guarding the central motif on either side is an outward-facing shark (alluding to Sweden's first submarine *Hajen,* named after the Swedish for shark). The device, including background, measures 82mm x 30mm.

In 1986 a gold-coloured metal version was authorized for wear on shirts and sweaters. It was sponsored by the Swedish submarine yard Kockums after being initially vetoed by the Swedish Naval Command. It received their consent on condition that it would not be made available to the general public. It measures 73mm x 23mm and can have clutch or screw fastenings. Each badge is numbered on the reverse. Submariners are issued with one each. Replacements can only be obtained by producing genuine evidence that the original has been lost.

The submarine insignia is worn on the right side of the uniform above the breast pocket by all qualified personnel. The qualifications for wear are: for officers to complete six months' service in a submarine after graduating from the qualifying course, for conscripts to have completed their military service with sufficient grades to be part of a wartime submarine crew. Swedish Naval conscripts serve 10 to 17½ months, then return at six-year intervals for 18 to 40 days refresher periods until the age of 47.

Swedish sailors serving in submarines wear the name of their vessel on the cap ribbon. Branch badges are surmounted by the letter U.

Swedish unofficial submarine qualification insignia made in 1956 and worn until the 1960s.

Swedish official submarine insignia in gold wire embroidery 1978, all ranks.

Swedish submarine qualification insignia in metal, all ranks 1986.

Syria

Submarine Service

Three elderly ex-Soviet *Romeo* Class submarines (SS) were transferred to the Syrian flag in 1986. A year earlier an even older *Whiskey* Class submarine (SS) was acquired. It was relegated to harbour service and provided battery-charging facilities for the three *Romeo* Class units. Two *Romeos* were deleted in 1993-4 leaving only one in service.

Two R1 and two R2 *Mala* Class SDVs were acquired from Yugoslavia in the early 1980s. Their present status is unknown.

Submarine Insignia

Official sources (as of 26 April, 1989) confirm that no specialist submarine insignia exists.

TAIWAN

SUBMARINE SERVICE

The first submarines to serve in what is termed the 'Republic of China Navy' were two ex-American *Tench* Class (SS) modernized under the *Guppy* II programme. These are *Haih Shih* (ex-USS *Cutlass*) and *Haih Pao* (Ex-USS *Tusk*). Launched in 1944/5, both were transferred to Taiwan in 1973.

In 1984 a German-built midget research submarine was accepted into service. Forming the *Hai Lung* Class (SSK), *Hai Lung* and *Hai Hu* were built in the Netherlands. Both were laid down in 1982, launched in 1986 and commissioned in 1987/8. They are improved versions of the Dutch *Zwaardvis* Class, displace 1,870 tons and are armed with four 21in torpedo tubes. All these submarines remain in service today (1996). Plans to acquire new submarines have been thwarted because of protests from mainland China.

SUBMARINE INSIGNIA

The submarine insignia qualification badge was authorized on 10 January, 1977. It is the same design for all ranks. However, officers wear the device in gold, senior ratings wear it in silver and junior ratings wear it in grey metal. It comes in one size only and measures 70mm x 20mm. It is secured by a pair of clutch fasteners on the reverse.

The pattern consists of the national emblem in silver and blue enamel over a bow view of a modern 'tear drop' submarine flanked by dolphins. It bears a close resemblance to the submarine insignia of the US Navy.

The two dolphins on either side of the central motif symbolize the submarine fleet's responsibility of safeguarding the nation's territorial waters. The cross-shaped command tower (sail) represents the four codes of the submarine fleet: loyalty and boldness, absolute obedience, enthusiasm and initiative, and alertness and calmness.

The device is worn in the centre of the upper left pocket, above medal ribbons, if they are worn. There is also an unofficial miniature badge measuring 38mm x 11mm with two clutch fasteners.

For officers and petty officers the qualifications for wear are to have graduated from a submarine qualification course either at home or abroad and then to have been assigned to a submarine. Junior ratings have a less stringent requirement.

Taiwan (Republic of China) submarine qualification insignia. Gold for officers and silver for senior ratings.

THAILAND

SUBMARINE SERVICE

Thailand's first submarines were four Japanese-built boats acquired between 1936 and 1937. They displaced 370 tons and were armed with five 21in torpedo tubes and one machine gun. Named *Majchanu*, *Plaichumpol*, *Sinsamut* and *Wirun,* they served until 1961 and were then decommissioned.

Since then the Royal Thai Navy has had no submarines. Plans to purchase submarines from Sweden and China in the late eighties were dropped due to financial restrictions.

At the beginning of 1995 the Thai Cabinet approved funds for the acquisition of three advanced submarines. These are likely to be built in Sweden, Germany or the Netherlands, though Russia and France have also shown an interest. A decision is likely to be made in the near future.

SUBMARINE INSIGNIA

There is some controversy concerning Thai submarine insignia. According to official sources no official submarine qualification device ever existed. An unofficial badge was, however, allowed to be worn by regular submarine officers and ratings on special occasions.

The insignia was the same for all ranks and was worn pinned to the right breast. It was manufactured in alloy and enamel and depicted a blue submarine, facing the wearer's left, surrounded by a 'Victory' wreath with seven white blossoms (*chaiya-pruek*). A small anchor was linked to the lower part of the submarine's bow. It was locally manufactured and was said to be worn between about 1937 and 1961.

Another badge often mistaken for a submarine badge is that of the combat swimmer. It consists of a central shield bearing the national colours red, white, blue, white and red, behind is a silver fouled anchor. Leaping sharks in silver on a gold representation of waves face the central motif on either side. These come in several sizes and variations and are also produced in cloth. The design is similar in nature to many other countries' submarine insignia and is included here to avoid confusion.

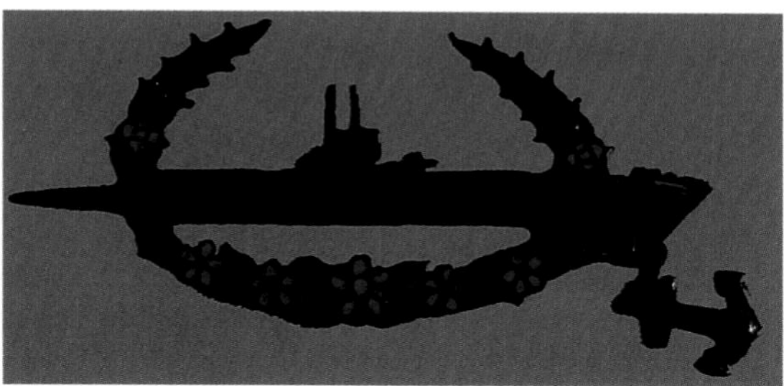

Unofficial submarine qualification insignia about 1937.

Thai combat swimmers insignia. Frequently mistaken for submarine insignia.

TURKEY

SUBMARINE SERVICE

During World War I the Turks, with German help, unsuccessfully attempted to refit two derelict Nordenfeldt submarines of 1889 vintage. It was not until 1928 that the first submarines actually entered service. These were the Dutch-built *Birinc Inônü* and the *Ikinci Inônö*. They displaced 506 tons and were armed with six 17.7in torpedo tubes and one 37mm gun. They were followed in 1931 by the Italian-built *Dumlupinar* of 830 tons and the submarine mine-layer *Sakarya* of 950 tons. Between 1935 and 1937 Germany built three submarines for Turkey. Named *Saldiray*, *Yildiray* and *Gür*, the first two displaced 934 tons and the third 760 tons.

It was not until the late 1940s that further submarines were added.

During that period and the early 1950s the United States transferred eight *Balao* Class (SS) to Turkey, and Great Britain transferred three P Class (SS). In the next few years various further *Balao* Class were exchanged for more modern variants. The most serving at any one time was ten.

In the early 1970s the *Balao*s were replaced by two ex-US *Guppy III*s (SS), seven ex-US *Guppy IIA*s (SS) and one *Guppy IA* (SS). These were further supplemented by two ex-*Tang* Class (SS) in 1980-3 for a five-year loan period.

A class of six new submarines entered service between 1975 and 1988. These are of the West Germany 209 Class (Type 1200). Known in Turkey as the *Atilay* Class (SSK), the first three were built in Kiel and the second three in Gölcük (Turkey). A further four are planned. These will be Type 1400 of the same class (SSK).

At the time of writing there are seventeen submarines in commission and three older submarines being used as shore accommodation hulks and power generating plants.

SUBMARINE INSIGNIA

On 24 September, 1926, the Turkish Navy announced that a submarine insignia would be authorized. This specialist badge came into being in 1928. For officers the device was manufactured in stainless cast brass and measured 56mm x 52mm. It consisted of a thick gold-coloured wreath of oak leaves on the right (representing war) and olive leaves on the left (representing peace). The wreath was tied together at the bottom with a ribbon and closed at the top with a star and crescent. Overlaid on the wreath was a representation of a submarine in black enamel outlined in silver and facing the wearer's left. This design, with slight modification, remains today. It is worn at the intersection of a centre line drawn from the left upper pocket and a line from the second button from the top of the jacket. There is also a miniature variation for use on mess dress. The miniature measures 18mm x 18mm and is of solid manufacture, whereas the standard device is voided within the wreath.

Career petty officers and conscripts, in the same year, were authorized to wear a solid brass oval device. This consisted of a similar wreath, ribbon and star and crescent to the officers badge but in the centre there was a submarine facing the wearer's right, behind which was a rising sun and above this were the letters 'TC'.

In 1935 the device ceased to be worn by junior ratings who were then authorized to wear a cloth insignia depicting a submarine facing either left or right. This device remains in use to this day and is normally

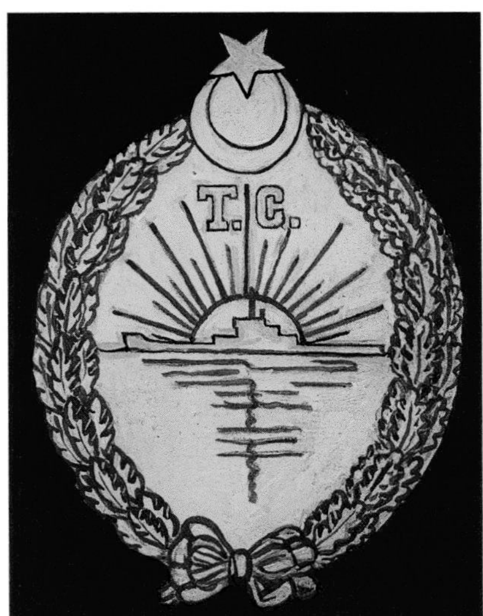

Turkish submarine qualification insignia for petty officers and conscripts 1928-31.

Turkish submarine qualification insignia worn by petty officers 1956-9.

Turkish submarine qualification insignia for petty officers 1959-64.

Turkish submarine qualification insignia. Large for officers and small for petty officers. Worn from 1977 (though officers wore a similar design from 1926).

Turkish submarine qualification insignia for petty officers 1964-77. This same badge was produced, probably erroneously, with the submarine facing in the opposite direction.

worn on the left sleeve below other specialist and rank insignia. For professional ratings the device is manufactured in yellow on blue or white (depending on the uniform) and for conscripts, red on blue or white.

In 1956 career petty officers were granted a metal badge depicting a submarine facing the wearer's right, behind which was an oval rope device with a simple bow and a star and crescent at the top. In 1959 the device was altered so that the submarine faced the wearer's left and the bow became more elaborate.

The device was again altered in 1964 with the bow changing design slightly and the rope behind the submarine becoming more circular. It measures 55mm x 50mm and had a vertical brooch fastening. These early metal badges were rather crudely cast. A gold wire embroidered version also appeared. The wreath was slightly different, being more 'leafy' in appearance, with two buds at the base. It measured 52mm x 65mm.

In 1977 career petty officers were granted the right to wear the same insignia as that worn by officers, but to measure 26mm x 25mm. These new badges were much more fashionable and, in line with those worn by officers, were well made.

Dimensions and details of all insignia can vary considerably. Similar to the submarine badge is Frogman/Charioteer Badge. The submarine is replaced by a two-man chariot (torpedo-like craft with two frogmen sitting astride) in black or black edged in gold, facing the wearer's right.

Turkish submarine qualification insignia for junior ratings in cloth. Normally worn on right sleeve (in this case coxswain and electrician).

UKRAINE

The new Ukranian Navy seeks to acquire some former Soviet submarines, but no details of them or of any specific insignia are currently (1996) available.

UNITED KINGDOM

SUBMARINE SERVICE

The Royal Navy's submarine arm was born against a background of resentment and criticism. Most senior officers considered the submarine to be 'underhand and damned un-English'. Thus the Royal Navy reluctantly entered the submarine era rather later than did most other modern Navies. Originally submarines were termed 'submarine torpedo boats', hence they are usually referred to as 'boats'.

The first submarine to be launched was HM *Submarine No. 1* in October, 1901. She was a Holland VI boat, built under licence by Vickers Sons and Maxim. Her displacement was 120 tons and she was armed with a single torpedo tube. Four near sisters were constructed shortly afterwards. Boat *No. 1* was lost in 1913 while on tow to the breakers. Eventually raised in 1982, she is now preserved outside the submarine museum at HMS *Dolphin*, Gosport.

Having once started in the submarine field, construction began in earnest. By the start of World War I the Royal Navy possessed eighty-two submarines with twenty-two building. They were deployed world-wide with flotillas based in the Mediterranean, Gibraltar and China, plus nine flotillas in home waters.

After the original Hollands the first class to be constructed was the A Class of thirteen submarines built in 1904. They displaced between 120 and 200 tons and mounted two bow torpedo tubes. The B Class, of eleven 285 ton boats, followed in 1904-6 and the C Class of thirty-eight larger boats followed in 1906-10. The D Class of 1908-11, displacing 550 tons and armed with three torpedo tubes, were the first British submarines to mount a deck gun and be equipped with W/T. They were also the first to use diesel fuel rather than petrol.

The E Class of fifty-five boats were completed between 1913 and 1917. This type displaced 660 tons and six were the first British submarines to be fitted for mine-laying. War construction produced 118 boats in eleven main classes. Of note were the highly successful US-designed

H Class of which thirty were built during the war (followed by fourteen between 1918 and 1920). The first ten were built at Vickers in Montreal and the next eight were built at the Fore River Yard in the USA. Eight of these US-Built boats were impounded until America's entry into the war. Britain then transferred six to Chile in payment for Chilean ships building in British Yards and taken over by the Royal Navy. The remainder, referred to as the H21 type, were British-built. Some continued in service to be operational during World War II.

In 1916 the first steam-powered submarine, HMS *Swordfish*, was completed. She was followed by the notorious steam-powered fleet submarines of the K Class. Designed to accompany the battle fleet, their steam turbines gave them a surface speed of 24 knots. Originally flush-decked, bulbous clipper bows were later added to improve sea-worthiness. Each had two funnels which had to be lowered before submerging. Five of the class of seventeen were lost in accidents; thereafter steam propulsion was abandoned in submarines.

In April ,1916, E22 flew off two small sea-planes from a ramp fitted on the stern, the first British submarine to launch an aircraft.

The L Class of 1917-18, a development of the E Class, was perhaps the most effective war-built design. A number survived to participate in World War II. The M Class of 1918 were designed as submarine monitors and mounted a 12in gun. It had to be loaded on the surface but could be fired when all but the muzzle was submerged. After the war M2 had its 21in gun replaced by a hangar and aircraft.

At the conclusion of World War I 105 U-Boats were surrendered to the Royal Navy. At least three later flew the White Ensign.

With minor exceptions, Royal Navy submarines did not receive names until 1926. Up to that time they simply bore a number prefixed by the class letter. Shortly after the outbreak of war in 1939 the numbering system was restored, only to revert to naming in 1943.

Submarine production slackened after World War I. Experiments were made in the 1920s with submarine cruisers. The X-1 launched in 1923 was the largest submarine ever built for the Royal Navy until the nuclear-powered submarines of the 1960s. She displaced 3,050 tons and was armed with four 5.2in guns in two turrets, four machine guns and six 21in torpedo tubes. She was the only post-war submarine to be scrapped before 1939.

As war clouds gathered, submarine production once again picked up. By 1939 peacetime construction had added another nine classes to the fleet. When war commenced there were sixty-five submarines in service, of which thirteen were veterans of World War I building programmes.

War construction resulted in the production of 182 submarines; in addition seventeen were acquired from abroad. Of this last category: nine were ex-US, four were ex-Turkish, three were ex-Italian and one was ex-German. War construction was in three main classes: S, T and U. The later A Class was designed for use in the Pacific War, but hostilities ended before any entered service. Thirty-one midget submarines and numerous two-man chariots and a few one-man submarines designated Welmans had also been constructed. At the end of the war some one hundred and twelve enemy submarines, including midget craft, were surrendered to the Royal Navy. Eighty-five British submarines had been lost.

Post-war construction saw the completion of the A Class of fourteen and the launching of the *Explorer* Class of two unarmed experimental high-speed hydrogen-peroxide-powered submarines. At the same time four midget submarines (X Craft) were built, one of which was transferred to Sweden in 1958. By the 1960s both the experimental boats and the X Craft had been deleted.

The first post-war class of conventional patrol submarines (SS) were the eight boats of the *Porpoise* Class, followed by the launching between 1957 and 1964 of the similar *Oberon* Class (SS later SSK), of thirteen boats.

Britain's first nuclear-powered submarine was HMS *Dreadnought*, launched in 1960 and powered by a US reactor. She was a nuclear attack submarine (SSN), otherwise known as a hunter-killer (anti-submarine submarine). She displaced 3,500 tons and was armed with six 21in torpedo tubes. Her active life continued until 1986.

The first all-British nuclear attack submarines were the five vessels of the *Valiant/Churchill* Class (SSN). Launched in 1966-7, they displaced 4,000 tons and were armed with six 21in torpedo tubes, which could also launch Sub-Harpoon missiles. By 1994 all had been paid off.

The *Resolution* Class of four SSBNs, launched 1964-5, became Britain's Strategic Nuclear Deterrent Force when they came into service in the late sixties. They displaced 7,600 tons and were armed with sixteen Polaris A3 missiles and six 21in torpedo tubes.

The *Swiftsure* Class SSNs were launched between 1971 and 1979. There were five in the class, which displaced 4,000 tons, and were armed with five 21in torpedo tubes, which could also launch Sub-Harpoon missiles. The *Trafalgar* Class SSNs followed in the 1980s. Slightly larger than the *Swiftsures*, they displaced 4,200 tons but had a similar armament. The initial class totalled seven boats. A second batch of five will be constructed to replace the *Swiftsures*.

Returning to conventionally powered submarines (SSK), the *Up-*

holder Class (Type 2400) was ordered. Proposed as a class of ten, the first, HMS *Upholder*, was launched in 1986 and commissioned a year later. Three others followed, then further production was cancelled. These submarines displaced 2,400 tons (dived) and were given an armament of six 21in torpedo tubes which could also launch Sub-Harpoon SSM.

To update the United Kingdom's Strategic Nuclear Deterrent Force, a new generation of four SSBNs was initiated. Designated the *Vanguard* Class (SSBN), they are Britain's biggest ever submarines. They have a dived displacement of 16,000 tons and are armed with sixteen Trident D5 SLBMs, plus four 21in torpedo tubes. The first of the class was laid down in 1986 and commissioned in 1993, the second commissioned in 1995; the rest should follow into service by 1999.

Following the political upheavals in Eastern Europe in the early 1990s and the resultant proposed defence cuts, reductions were made. HMS *Revenge* (SSBN) was deleted in 1992 and her sister *Resolution* was deleted in 1994; the remainder of the class will be phased out and be replaced by the *Vanguard* Class. All four of the *Upholder* Class were paid off by June, 1994, the last conventionally powered submarines to serve in the Royal Navy.

At the time of writing (1996) the Royal Navy submarine fleet, consists of two *Vanguard* Class (SSBN), seven *Trafalgar* Class (SSNs) and five *Swiftsure* Class (SSNs).

Submarine Insignia

The first submarine distinguishing badge was a sub-speciality insignia for ratings only and made a brief appearance between 1958 and 1964. Irreverently referred to as the 'pregnant sausage' or 'sausage on a stick'. It proved unpopular and few were actually worn. It depicted a Holland type submarine facing its wearer's front (or to the left when observed) and was embroidered in gold on blue cloth, red on blue cloth and blue on white cloth. The dimensions were 70mm x 35mm. The dress regulations of the period stated it was to be worn on the right sleeve, by chief petty officers 1¼in above the centre button and by all other ratings 1½in above the cuff. Some official sources state that the insignia were never issued. This is true; they were never issued, but as their wear was optional naval stores did have them in stock and they were available for private purchase. This may explain why so few were actually worn.

Some sources claim that unofficial submarine badges were worn in World War I. This is entirely unfounded and quite misleading.

Inspired by the submarine badge of the Royal Australian Navy, submariners of the Royal Navy were authorized to wear a similar insignia, the first being awarded at Ceremonial Divisions on 15 July, 1971. Nicknamed the 'Kissing Kippers', it consists of a fouled anchor above which is a St Edward's Crown. Either side of this device is an inward-facing dolphin. It measures 60mm x 21mm and has two clutch fasteners on the back. It differs from its RAN counterpart in three aspects: it is smaller, the dolphins are scaled (RAN example is smooth) and the RAN badge does not include the fouled anchor.

Unofficial versions exist in gold wire, cloth and in metal miniature. The miniature measures 45mm x 15mm, universally worn on mess kit, and an even smaller novelty type, sometimes worn on the tie, measures 19mm x 7mm. All ranks and ratings wear the same insignia which is worn on the left breast above the medal ribbons.

For officers the requirements for qualification are to successfully complete parts 1, 2, and 3 of the submarine qualification course. Part 3 includes two to six weeks at sea in a submarine depending on the branch. The total period is about six months. Requirements for ratings are similar.

Junior ratings can further be distinguished by their cap tallies. Originally they bore the submarine name prefixed by 'HMS' or the number prefixed by 'HM SUBMARINE'. This was later altered to the inscription 'HM SUBMARINE' on its own and later still to 'HM SUBMARINES.', the full stop being dropped in the early 1950s.

Some branch badges common to the surface fleet, but with specialist submarine sub-qualifications, have the letters 'SM' added below.

United Kingdom submarine branch sub-speciality badge, worn by ratings on the right lower sleeve 1958-64. Supplied in cloth embroidered gold on navy blue, red on navy blue and blue on white.

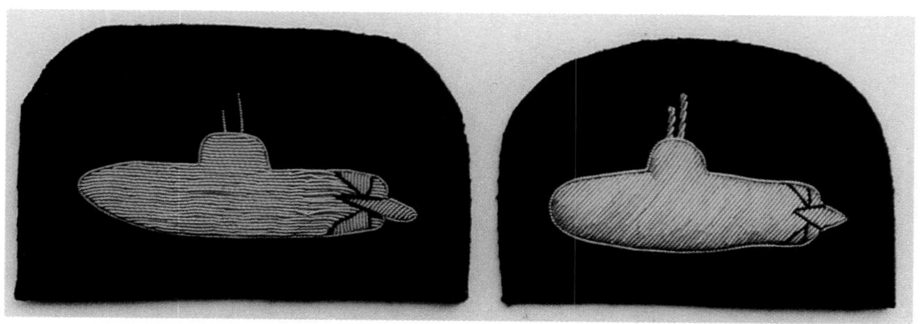

Left: official design in gold wire embroidery; right: unofficial design, probably produced for collectors well after insignia was deleted.

United Kingdom submarine qualification insignia all ranks, 15 July, 1971. In three sizes, 60mm, 45mm and 19mm.

United Kingdom, unofficial cloth badges.

United Kingdom, unofficial cloth badge.

UNITED STATES OF AMERICA

SUBMARINE SERVICE

The first United States underwater vessel was the *Turtle*, a one-man submersible propelled by a hand crank. Built in 1776, it was the first submersible to attack an enemy when it attempted to destroy Lord Howe's flagship in New York harbour. A similar vessel was built in 1801 for experimental purposes. In 1863 the Confederate Army built five rudimentary submarines. The CSS *H. L. Hunley* was the first submarine ever to destroy an enemy. Her sister the *David* destroyed a Union frigate the following year. The weapon used was a spar torpedo. Unfortunately, *David* herself was blown up in the ensuing explosion. A submarine named the *Plunger* was constructed for the Navy in 1896 but was never accepted into service.

The first submarine to actually form a part of the United States Navy was the *Holland* type SS1 in 1898. She displaced seventy-five tons, had a complement of five and was armed with an 8in dynamite gun and one 18in torpedo tube. The A Class of seven boats followed between 1901 and 1903. Four were Lake types and three were Holland types but their military characteristics were the same. They displaced 107 tons and were armed with a single 18in torpedo tube. The B and C Classes totalling eight boats were commissioned between 1906 and 1909. Slightly larger than previous boats they were armed with two 18in torpedo tubes. The forty-one boats of the D, E, F, G, H, K and L Classes built between 1909 and 1917 were all progressively larger and mounted four 18in tor-

pedo tubes. The single M Class submarine constructed in 1915 included a 3in deck gun in its armament.

The United States entered World War I with fifty-seven submarines in service and fourteen nearing completion. War construction added over one hundred more in four classes (N, O, R, S) of which at least fifty-five were completed after the Armistice. Six U-Boats were ceded to America on the cessation of hostilities.

Between the wars the United States concentrated on the construction of 125 large ocean-going submarines designed to cruise the Pacific. Their displacement ranged from 900 to 2,000 tons, and some were armed with 6in guns.

At the outbreak of the Pacific War in 1941 the United States Navy had 112 submarines in commission and sixty-five building or on order. War construction consisted of three classes, *Gato*, *Tench* and *Balao*. All were very similar, displacing 1,525 tons and armed with ten 21in torpedo tubes, one 5in gun and one 40mm AA gun. The United States Pacific submarine force proved a formidable weapon, accounting for 1,125 Japanese merchant ships and numerous warships of all categories.

On the conclusion of the war the war-built submarines were either modernized, converted to specialist roles or transferred to friendly navies. In the 1950s a few experimental classes were built. The first post-war attack submarines, the six boats of the *Tang* Class (SS), entered service in 1951-2. They were high-speed vessels of 1,615 tons armed with eight 21in torpedo tubes. (Three improved 'tear drop' *Tang*s were later completed in 1959.) Then followed three *Barbacuda*, three *Barbel* and one *Darter* Class submarines (SS).

The world's first nuclear powered submarine, the *Nautilus*, was commissioned in 1954. It also had the distinction of being the first submarine to sail under the North Pole. A nuclear attack submarine (SSN), she displaced 3,200 tons and was armed with six 21in torpedo tubes. A near sister, the *Seawolf*, was commissioned shortly afterwards.

In 1958 two experimental nuclear submarines, the *Grayback* and *Growler*, were commissioned. They were originally armed with the Regulus guided missile but were later converted into amphibious support vehicles. At this stage it was decided that all future submarines in the United States Navy should be nuclear-powered.

The first class of SSN was designated the *Skate* Class. Improved *Nautilus/Seawolf* boats, they were completed in 1958. The *Triton*, commissioned in 1959, was a large (5,900 tons standard) nuclear-powered Radar Picket Submarine (SSR(N)). She was later converted to an SSN.

The five-boat *Skipjack* Class was commissioned in 1959 to 1961. They were the first SSNs to adopt the 'tear drop' profile. They were followed by the single *Tullibee* and the thirteen-boat *Permit* Class (SSN) between 1960 and 1968. The latter boats displaced 3,750 tons standard and were armed with four 21in torpedo tubes and equipped to launch Subroc A/S torpedoes. Similarly armed, the 4,460 ton standard displacement *Sturgeon* Class (SSN) were commissioned between 1967 and 1975. A class of thirty-seven, twelve had been withdrawn by 1995 due to defence cuts. Two single-class ships *Narwhal* and *Glenard P. Lipscombe* (SSNs), were commissioned in 1969 and 1974. The *Los Angeles* Class of fifty-five large SSNs started to enter service in 1976, with the last due to be commissioned late in 1996. They have a standard displacement of 6,927 tons and are armed with torpedoes, nuclear land-attack missiles and mines.

The West's first ballistic missile submarines were the five *George Washington* Class (SSBN) which entered service in 1959/61. They displaced 5,900 tons standard and were armed with sixteen Polaris A3 missiles and four 21in torpedo tubes. They were followed by the five *Ethan Allen* (SSBN) in 1961-3, also armed with sixteen Polaris A3 missiles. The *Benjamin Franklin/Lafayette/James Madison* Classes (SSBN) were next to come into service in 1963-7. The twenty-nine submarines in these classes displaced 6,650 tons and were armed with sixteen Poseidon C3 or Trident missiles. Like all United States submarines they were also armed with torpedo tubes. All were out of service by 1995.

The *Ohio* Class (SSBN) came into service in 1979 and the total of eighteen should be in commission by 1997. Huge ships of 16,600 tons surface displacement, they are, nevertheless, about half the size of their Russian counterparts the *Typhoon* Class. The *Ohio*s were armed with twenty-four Trident missiles and four 21in torpedo tubes. This class is now the sole representative of the US Navy's strategic missile submarine fleet.

At the time of writing (1996) the United States Navy has a submarine force of fifteen SSBNs and eighty-five SSNs. Some older submarines have been converted to other roles such as platforms for special operations.

SUBMARINE INSIGNIA

Captain Ernest J. King (later Fleet Admiral) in 1923 suggested that it would be appropriate for submariners to have a distinguishing badge. Thus prompted, the Naval Authorities authorized a distinctive insignia on 24 March, 1924. It was intended for wear only while the individual

was actually serving in submarines.

The device displayed two dolphins on waves, with a bow view of a submarine between them. The dolphins symbolized the mythical benevolence of Poseidon (Neptune) towards ships and mariners. The device was made in gold-plated metal for warrant and commissioned officers and originally had a pin fastening. Later examples were secured by clutch fasteners. The badge came in two sizes: 70mm x 20mm and 39mm x 11mm. (A miniature version measured 15mm x 5mm.) It was worn on the left breast above medal ribbons.

Enlisted men wore the same design but in cloth. For various styles of uniform it was manufactured in silver embroidery on blue, white embroidery on blue, blue embroidery on white and blue embroidery on light khaki. At this stage there was no miniature. It was worn mid-way between the wrist and elbow of the right sleeve. In 1941 permission was given for the insignia to be worn throughout the recipient's service career. New regulations in 1943 permitted enlisted men who were promoted to warrant or commissioned rank to wear the enlisted men's insignia on the left breast until they qualified as submarine officers.

In mid-1947 the enlisted men's embroidered insignia was moved from the right sleeve and repositioned to the left breast the same as for officers. On 21 September, 1950, officers were permitted to wear gold embroidered badges as well as metal. At the same time enlisted men had their insignia changed to silver plate metal, though the embroidered pattern could still be worn. Enlisted men were also granted a metal miniature in the same style as that for officers.

In the mid-1980s a printed black on light blue denim cloth 'iron-on' insignia was made available for wear on the blue working rig shirt. In 1989 this was replaced by cloth embroidered 'iron-on' badges measuring 91mm x 32mm. There are two types, in yellow for officers and light grey for enlisted men. Both are outlined in black. In 1992 a solid black embroidered cloth badge was produced for combat uniforms.

On 26 March, 1943, a new insignia was authorized. This was the Combat Patrol badge. It was issued to submariners who completed one or more patrols in which at least one enemy vessel was sunk or a special mission successfully accomplished. The device, which was made in dull grey metal, depicted a *Flying Fish* Class submarine, facing the wearer's right, below which were waves and a scroll. It measured 56mm x 13mm and had clutch or pin fastening. A miniature version was also produced. Up to three ⅛in stars could be worn on the scroll; more could be worn on either side. A gold star was added after the second patrol and each subsequent patrol. A silver star equalled five gold stars. The device was

worn on the left breast below medal ribbons. It was only awarded for service in World War II. At least two variations of this badge exists.

21 May, 1943, saw the authorization of a special submarine badge for medical officers. On 11 August, 1952, it was reduced slightly in size. The design is the same as for other officers but the submarine motif is replaced by an oval device on which is a silver acorn over a gold oak leaf. It measures 70mm x 17mm and it too has a miniature version. The original version was two-piece.

On 13 July, 1950, officers assigned to submarine engineering duties were also granted a special device. Again it is the same as for other officers but the central device was then altered to a gold disc, within which was the letter 'E.' This was altered on 11 August, 1952, to a silver three-bladed ship's screw surrounded by a silver border. It measured 73mm x 17mm and also had a miniature version.

Submarine supply officers were awarded a distinctive insignia on 9 February, 1964. This too resembled the line officer's badge but the central device now took the shape of three oak leaves and acorns in gilt plate similar to the device worn on the cuff. It measured 70mm x 22mm and, like the other badges, there was also a miniature version. The Supply Corps, Medical and Engineering miniatures all measure 40mm x 10mm.

The Deterrent Patrol Badge was authorized on 28 January, 1969. It is awarded to crews in SSBNs who complete one or more three-month patrols. The device is made in dull white metal and depicts a *Lafayette* Class SSBN facing the wearer's right. In the centre there is a vertical ballistic missile supporting a nuclear symbol below which is a scroll. Up to six ⅛in stars can be fixed to the scroll. One gold star (after the initial patrol) for each patrol and one silver star for five patrols. It measures 57mm x 22mm and the miniature measures 38mm x 14mm. It has clutch fastenings and is worn on the left breast below medal ribbons.

The crews of Deep Submergence Rescue Vehicles (DSRV) were authorized to wear a special device on 6 April, 1981. It depicts a DSRV behind which is an upright trident flanked by two diving dolphins. The insignia is made in gold plate for officers and silver plate for enlisted men and is secured by clutch fasteners. It measures 36mm x 21mm. In 1971 a similar solid design with a bottom scroll bearing three stars was produced but never adopted.

A number of unofficial badges also exist. Perhaps the most famous is the 'Diesel Boats Forever' badge. This was a 'lament' for the phasing out of diesel/electric submarines in the USN. It originated with EMCS (SS) Doug Smith of the USS *Barbel* and a group of his shipmates during a cruise in the Western Pacific in 1967. One from this group, Leon

Siguerito, had been a commercial artist before he joined the Navy. Siguerito drew five sample sketches of a new pin. These were taken to the 'Thieves Alley' section of Yokosuka where the designs were discussed with Japanese craftsman. They decided on the design of a *Tang* Class submarine hull and two mermaids along with the letters 'DBF'. They had one thousand of these pins made up at $1.00 each. When they returned to Pearl Harbor the word of these pins soon got around and they were soon sold out, apparently at cost. They were evidently worn on navy bases and on leave. In 1968 the drawing was sent to the Navy Department for official approval which was never given. It seems likely that some commanders were lenient about this, pending word from the Navy. It is thought to have been worn by the crew of USS *Tigrone* in 1971. It is now sometimes seen on the chests of diesel boat veterans at annual reunions. The badge was made in gilt for officers and dull grey metal for enlisted men. They measured 66mm x 25mm and were secured with clutch fasteners. Many restrikes have been made.

Another unofficial badge takes the form of a normal submarine badge but with a bow view of a tear drop submarine in the centre. It is said to be worn by SSN crews.

The Maryland Naval Militia, which was formed in 1774 and disbanded in 1975, had a submarine badge (but no submarines) apparently for former submariners. It took the form of a normal submarine badge but the central device was replaced by the state seal.

A so-called Deep Water or Wave badge also exists. Several years ago US submariners on the Pacific Coast considered themselves to be 'Deep Water' sailors (compared to the Atlantic Coast submariners) due to the very deep regions of the Pacific Ocean. This boast was picked up by a militaria manufacturer who produced the 'Deep Water' or 'Deep Sea' dolphins. Entirely unofficial, though it may have been tolerated for wear by some individual submarine commanders, it is very similar to the official insignia but the waves are deeper and more calm and the dolphins are more animated.

As will appear evident, there is a multiplicity of design and material of USN badges, plus numerous unofficial versions. Every mode of dress seems to have been catered for.

US submarine qualification insignia in gold for line officers, 70mm and 39mm, 1924.

US submarine qualification insignia in cloth for enlisted men 1924-47. White on blue, silver embroidery on blue, blue on light khaki, and blue on white.

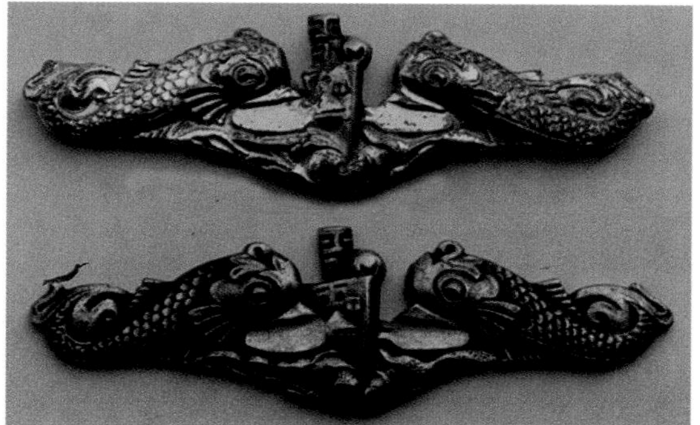

US submarine qualification insignia in silver for enlisted men, 70mm and 39mm, 1947. Bright silver and silver substitute.

US submarine qualification insignia for medical officers, authorized 1943.

US submarine qualification insignia for officers assigned to engineering duties. The original badge, authorized on 13 July, 1950, contained the letter 'E' within the circlet. This was altered to a three, bladed screw on 11 August, 1952.

US submarine qualification insignia for supply officers, authorized 1964.

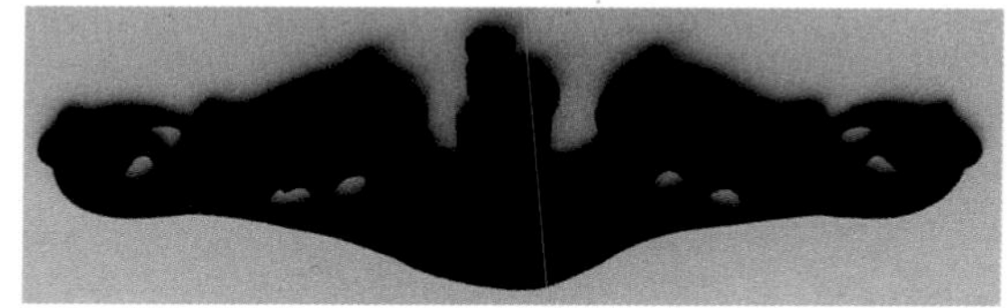

US submarine qualification insignia, subdued in black metal, about the late 1970s.

US submarine qualification insignia, 'iron-on', for enlisted men's working shirts, mid-1980s.

US embroidered cloth 'iron-on' badges about 1989 for working uniforms. Officers and enlisted men.

US submarine qualification insignia for officers, embroidered in yellow thread on dark blue cloth for wind-breaker jackets.

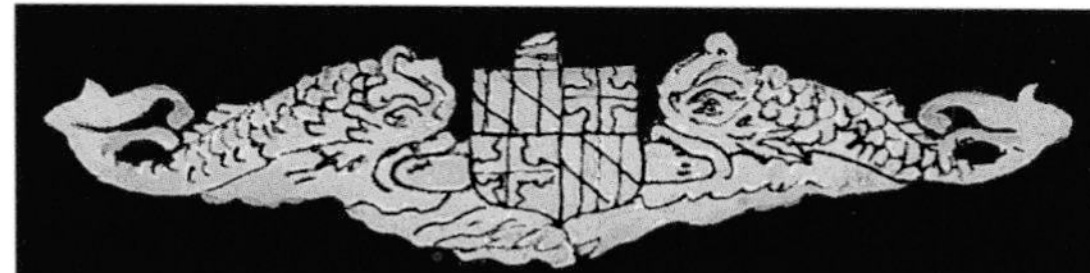

US Maryland Naval Militia insignia (obsolete).

US Deep Submergence Rescue Vehicle Badge, gold for officers and silver for enlisted men, 1981.

US Combat Patrol Badge, World War II, authorized 1943, with three gold patrol stars.

US Deterrent Patrol Badge authorized 1969, 58mm and 38mm, with one silver patrol star.

US unofficial 'Deep Water' submarine insignia.

US unofficial nuclear submarine qualification insignia.

US novelty submarine badge 'Diesel Boats Forever', gold for officers and silver for enlisted men. Stars were added for patrols. Produced in 1971 to lament the demise of conventional submarines in the US Navy.

VENEZUELA

SUBMARINE SERVICE

Venezuela entered the submarine field in 1960 with the purchase from the United States of the *Balao* Class (SS) USS *Tilefish*. She was renamed *Carite* and served until 1977.

In 1972 and 1973 two American *Guppy II* Class (SS) the USS *Cubera* and the USS *Grenadier* were purchased and re-named *Tiburon* and *Picua*. *Tiburon* was deleted in the early 1980s and *Picua* was relegated to harbour training in 1990.

New submarines were purchased from West Germany in 1972 and were commissioned in 1976-7. They are of the 109 Class (1300 type) (SSK) and are named *Sabalo* and *Caribe*. There are plans for two more of this class.

SUBMARINE INSIGNIA

The submarine qualification badge was authorized in 1960. It is worn in gold-plated metal for officers and silver-plated metal for ratings. The design is of a bow view of a modern submarine below which is a coloured enamel shield bearing the national arms. This is flanked either side by an inward-facing dolphin. Submarine and dolphins are supported by a representation of waves. Qualified commanding officers wear an arch of seven stars over the submarine. The standard insignia measures 71mm x 22mm (though slightly larger variations exist). They are fixed to the uniforms with clutch fasteners and worn over the left breast pocket. Honorary submarine officers, which include shore-based support staff, wear the insignia on the right breast.

Venezuelan submarine qualification insignia. Top: commanding officers. Bottom: other officers.

Qualifications are to have attended the Submarine School and to have six months on-board service. This was extended to one year in 1989.

Venezuelan unofficial sleeve patch for non-uniform wear, Submarine Picua.

YUGOSLAVIA

SUBMARINE SERVICE

The first Yugoslav submarines were the British-built *Hrabri* and *Nebojsa* launched in 1927. They displaced 975 tons and were armed with six 21in torpedo tubes and two 4in guns. They were followed into service by the French-built *Smeli* and *Osvetnik* in 1928-9. These were 639 ton boats armed with 19.7in torpedo tubes, one 4in gun, and one 1 pdr AA gun and one machine gun.

Hrabri, *Osvetnik* and *Smeli* were captured by the Italians in April 1941. *Nebojsa* escaped to join Allied Naval Forces. After the war it was reported that three ex-Italian CB Class pocket submarines had been captured by Yugoslavia. *Nebojsa* was renamed *Tara* and finally deleted in 1958. She was replaced by the ex-Italian submarine *Tritone*, renamed *Sava*.

A new class of Yugoslav-built patrol submarine was constructed between 1958 and 1960 this was the *Sutjeska* Class (SS) of two boats, the *Sutjeska* and the *Neretva*. They displaced 820 tons and were armed with six 21in torpedo tubes. They were followed by three boats of the *Heroj* Class (SS): the *Heroj*, *Junak* and *Uskok*. The first was launched in 1968. They displace 1,068 tons and are armed with six 21in torpedo tubes.

In the early 1970s a class of two-man submarines began trials. Designated the R2 *Mala* Class, they displace 1.4 tons and are swimmer delivery vehicles (SDV). They are fitted to carry two 50kg mines. A number of smaller swimmer delivery vehicles or 'wet chariots', designated R1, also became operational. These are operated by a single crewman. Five *Una* Class midget submarines have also been built. The first entered service in 1985. They have a displacement of 90 tons and can carry six mines or six swimmer delivery vehicles and have a crew of four or five. Three names have been reported: *Una*, *Zeta* and *Socha*.

The latest patrol submarines were commissioned in 1978 and 1981. These are the *Sava* Class (SS) *Sava* and *Drava*. They displace 770 tons and are armed with six 21in torpedo tubes and carry twenty mines.

In 1996 the submarine force consisted of two *Sava* Class and three *Heroj* Class patrol submarines and five *Una* Class midget submarines. There are also an unspecified number of *Mala* Class swimmer delivery vehicles. Some of these craft may have become victims of the civil war.

SUBMARINE INSIGNIA

From 1918 to 1929 the country was known as the Kingdom of Serbs, Croats and Slovenes. A metal two-piece submarine badge was authorized about 1927 depicting a silver-coloured submarine facing its wearer's left. This was fixed to a gold-coloured fouled anchor above which was a similarly coloured crown and below an escutcheon bearing the symbols of the three states. The flukes of the anchor and the crown on the left side were joined by a laurel wreath and on the right by an oak wreath, (both in gold colouring and with the submarine protruding both sides). The insignia measured 90mm x 72mm and was secured to the uniform by means of two broad blades north and south.

After 1929 a new insignia appeared. It consisted of a gold-metal-coloured laurel wreath at the top of which was a gold crown inlaid with red. A separate piece of silver metal in the form of an *Osvethik* (*Ojventnik*) Class submarine was placed over the central part and protruded either side. The submarine faced its wearer's left and on the back of both sections was the inscription '*Griesbachiknaus Zagreb*'. It was fixed to the uniform by two long vertical prong-like pins with pigtail loops at the top to provide spring. They were fixed to the bottom of the badge by simple hooks. The insignia measured 49mm x 44mm.

Kingdom of Serbs, Croats and Slovenes, submarine qualification insignia about 1927-9.

Kingdom of Yugoslavia, submarine qualification insignia, after 1929.

Yugoslavia: People's Republic (Now the Federation of Serbia and Montenegro)

Submarine Insignia

The first submarine badge was authorized in 1960 and was worn by all sailors, career petty officers and officers as a recognition of submarine service. The design was of a submarine facing the wearer's left on a squat diamond-shaped background, the bottom of which had waves and at the top was a red enamelled star. Behind the diamond were crossed fouled anchors. The insignia was made in white metal and had a single screw fastener. It measures 55mm x 40mm.

In 1970 a new design was authorized for career petty officers and

officers. Sailors continued to wear the original design. This new insignia consists of a laurel wreath with a red enamel star at the top and a relief silhouette of a submarine passing through the middle towards the wearer's left. Within the wreath the top part is void and the bottom is filled in with a blue and silver sea and a yellow rising sun, in the centre of which is a small black and silver stockless anchor. The reverse is smooth with a screw fastener and registration number. It measures 46mm x 38mm and is worn in the middle of the left side of the breast.

The badge is worn in silver by active officers and career petty officers after completing qualification courses and being assigned to serve in a submarine. After five years' service the badge becomes his personal property and can be worn throughout his service career. Officers and career petty officers are awarded the badge in gold after ten years' service. This badge has been produced with gold and silver wreaths.

With the demise of communism it is likely that, eventually, the red stars may be replaced by a new device.

Yugoslavian submarine qualification insignia for officers and career petty officers 1960-70 and for junior ratings from 1960 to the present.

Yugoslavian submarine qualification insignia, officers and career petty officers (silver hull) from 1970 to the present. Gold-hulled submarines are worn after ten years' service.

Acknowledgements

So much help has been given by so many people that I felt it would be better to divide them into two categories, those who contributed information of a general nature and those who contributed details concerning a particular country. The former are: AB UC S/M Keith Howe, Royal Australian Navy; Commander T. L. Nissen, Royal Danish Navy; William J. Crosby; Captain A. G. Soderlund, South African Navy; Surgeon Lieutenant-Commander Mark Smith, Royal Navy; Captain Viktor Toyka, German Navy and C. G. Vowls, Royal Naval Association.

The one exception to all these contributors is my old friend Captain Gustavo Conde of the Argentine Navy. He too was writing a book on submarine insignia and was actively researching the subject when he discovered that I was already well advanced on the same theme. Unselfishly he passed all his notes onto me; consequently this book represents our combined effort.

My appreciation also goes to Nigel Thomas for assisting with translations and to my wife 'Peggie' who typed most of the original manuscript, and to my daughter Jayne for the final print-out.

Those who have contributed details concerning individual countries are listed below. To all I extend my heartfelt gratitude.

Argentina: Captain Gustavo Conde, Argentine Navy.

Australia: Lieutenant-Commander B. W. Evans, Royal Australian Navy, Australian Submarine Liaison Officer Gosport 1986-7; AB UC S/M Keith Howe; Royal Australian Navy; J. H. Straczek, Senior Historical and Archives Officer for Director of Public Information — Navy.

Austria-Hungary: Dr Franz Kaindl, Director Military Museum Vienna.

Brazil: Captain Oscar Moreira Da Silva, Brazilian Navy, Brazilian Naval Commission Europe 1986.

Bulgaria: Colonel N. A. King, British Defence Attaché Sofia 1990.

Canada: Colonel J. G. Boulet, Director of Information Services, Department of National Defence, Ottawa, 1981; Lieutenant-Colonel L. D. Dent, Director of Information Services, Department of National Defence, Ottawa, 1986; Ms Marilyn Smith, Curator, Maritime Museum, Halifax.

Chile: Captain T. Lelaand, Royal Navy, British Defence Attaché, Santiago 1987-9.

Colombia: Ricardo Samper, Chargé d'Affaires Colombian Embassy, London 1987.

Denmark: Captain P. Kirketerp-Møller, Royal Danish Navy, Commander Danish Submarine Squadron 1988; Commander T. L. Nissen Royal Danish Navy, late captain of submarine HDMS *Narhvalen*; Colonel F. Tingleff, Royal Danish Air Force, Defence Attaché, London 1987.

Ecuador: Group Captain W. M. Watkins, Royal Air Force Defence Attaché, Quito 1988-9; Sergeant R. J. Fleming, PA to Defence Attaché, Quito 1987.

Egypt: Commanding Officer of the Egyptian Submarine Brigade; Captain J. M. Stock, Royal Navy, British Naval Attaché ,Cairo 1988. Commander Michael Maddox Royal Navy, British Naval Attaché, Cairo 1990.

Finland: Tom C. Bergroth, Finnish National Committee for Genealogy and Heraldry.

France: Vice-Admiral Doniol, French Navy, Major-General of the Navy 1987; Rear Admiral Bergot, French Navy, Assistant Chief of Staff, Operations 1987; Squadron-Leader J. Chambers, Royal Air Force, Office of the Naval Attaché, Paris 1987.

Germany: Captain Viktor Toyka, German Navy, Dr Med F. Hermann, Colonel German Army Medical Corps (Retired).

Greece: Commander D. I. Ladopoulos, Hellenic Navy, General Staff, Athens 1989; Captain C. L. MacGregor, Royal Navy, Naval and Air Attaché, Athens 1987.

India: Lieutenant-Commander N. S. Rawat, Indian Navy, Office of the High Commission for India, London 1987; Lieutenant-Commander A. V. Shiggaon, Indian Navy, Office of the High Commission for India, London 1988-9.

Indonesia: Colonel Syam Soemanagara, Indonesian Defence Attaché, London 1990; Colonel Wartono Soedarman, Commanding Officer Submarine Unit, East Fleet 1990; Warrant Officer K. Tomlinson, RAOC Office of the British Defence Attaché, Jakarta 1987.

Israel: Brigadier Y. Even, Israeli Defence Force, Defence Attaché, London 1987.

Italy: Captain Franco D'Agostino, Italian Navy, Naval Attaché, Bonn 1988, Captain G. Rondonotti, Italian Navy, Defence Attaché, London 1987; Captain Francesco Ricci, Italian Navy; Captain U. Cuzzola, Italian Navy, Naval Attaché, London 1989; Captain A. Serveri, Italian Navy, Director Naval Historical Branch; Franco Scandaluzzi, Milan.

Japan: Captain Isamu Kyoda, Japanese Maritime Self Defence Force, Defence Attaché, London 1986-9.

Netherlands: Commander A. Veentjer, Royal Netherlands Navy, Assistant Naval and Air Attaché, London 1986; Edgar Van Engeland, Netherlands.

Norway: Captain T. Nikolaisen, Royal Norwegian Navy, Defence Attaché, London 1986; Commander J. Osthus, Royal Norwegian Navy, Staff Officer to Commander Training Submarines, 1986; Commander Bjarne Tingvoll, Royal Norwegian Navy, Staff Officer to Commander Training Submarines, 1987.

Pakistan: Commander J. D. St J. Ainslie, Royal Navy, British Naval Adviser, Islamabad 1990.

Poland: Lieutenant-Colonel R. C. Eyres, 7th Gurkha Rifles, British Defence Attaché, Warsaw, 1988-9; Lieutenant-Commander R. B. Turner, Royal Navy, Assistant British Naval Attaché, Moscow and Warsaw, 1987-8; K. Barbarski, Polish Institute, London.

Portugal: Captain J. M. T. P. Germano, Portuguese Navy, Naval Attaché, London 1987-9.

Romania: Lieutenant-Colonel Peter Crocker, British Defence Attaché, Bucharest 1990; Lieutenant-Colonel Nicolaescu Gheorghe, Head of (Romanian) Foreign Liaison Section; Captain Cioenaru, Romanian Navy, 1990.

Russia/USSR: Captain J. E. Dykes Royal Navy, Defence Attaché, Moscow 1987; Commander R. B. Turner Royal Navy, Assistant Naval Attaché, Moscow and Warsaw 1988; Michael Clarke, London; Major M. Moss, TD* Intelligence Corps, London.

Saudi Arabia: Lee R. Lacey.

South Africa: Commander R. D. Stephen, South African Navy, Office of the Chief of Staff South African Defence Force, 1987-9.

Spain: Captain José Luis Carranza, Spanish Navy, Defence Attaché, London 1986; Captain P. A. Voute, Royal Navy, Services Attaché, Madrid 1988; Captain Alejandro J. Cuerdo, Spanish Navy, Defence Attaché, London 1989; Major R. D. Peters, Assistant British Defence Attaché, Madrid 1991; Captain José M. Pascual, Spanish Navy, Defence Attaché, London 1992; Lieutenant Commander J. M. Trevino, Spanish Navy.

Sweden: Captain S. Swedlund, Royal Swedish Navy, Naval Attaché, London 1987; Peter Von Busch, Director Marinmuseum, Sweden. Hans Ellerström, Sweden.

Syria: Major-General M.S. Akel, Director of Army Supply Bureau, 1989.

Taiwan: Hoh-Tu Lui, Director General, Far East Trade Office, The Hague 1987; Lieutenant-General Wang Jo-Yu, Republic of China Army, Deputy Chief of Staff for Personnel, Taiwan 1987-9.

Thailand: Rear Admiral Prida Karasuddhi, Royal Thai Navy, Director of Naval Operations, 1989; Wing-Commander H. W. Hughes, Royal Air Force, Naval and Air Attaché, Bangkok 1988.

Turkey: Commander B. Jones, Royal Navy, British Naval Attaché, Ankara 1987-8; Captain Orhan Aydin, Turkish Navy, Naval Attaché, London 1989.

USA: Harold D. Langley, Curator, Naval History Division of the Armed Forces, National Museum of American History, Smithsonian Institute, Washington DC 1988; Charles R. Steitz, USA.

Venezuela: Captain C. R. Pack, Royal Navy, British Defence Attaché, Caracas 1987; Captain Rafael I. González-Molero, Venezuelan Navy, Commander Submarine Squadron, 1987.

Yugoslavia: Colonel E. J. Everett-Heath, British Defence Attaché, Belgrade 1987; Wing-Commander M. B. M. Canavan, Royal Air Force, Naval and Air Attaché, Belgrade 1990; Colonel Slavko Jovic, Yugoslav Army, Foreign Liaison Section, Federal Secretariat for National Defence, Belgrade 1988.

Acknowledgements are due to the following for supplying illustrations:
Commander Danish Submarine Squadron: page 36 (top).
Commander T. L. Nissen: page 36 (centre left).
Marine Nationale: page 45 (top and lower left).
K. Howe: pages 61 (top), 63 (top).
Portuguese Navy: page 98.
Royal Thai Navy: page 126 (top).

Bibliography

To the author's knowledge, no other book has been published commercially on the subject of submarine insignia. The following list, therefore comprises books that are of interest for those wishing to read more on the subject of submarines generally.

Botting, Douglas, *The U-Boats* (Time-Life Books, 1979)

Compton-Hall, Richard, *Submarine Boats* (Conway Press Ltd, 1983)

Gunston, Bill, *Submarines in Colour* (Blandford Press Colour Series, 1976)

Jane's Fighting Ships (Jane's Information Group Ltd, published annually).

Navies of the Second World War (series) (MacDonald & Co [Publishers] Ltd, 1965-91)

Showell, J. P. Mallmann, *U-Boats under the Swastika* (MacDonald and Jane's, 1977)

Warship series (Ian Allan, 1968)

Watts, Anthony J., *Allied Submarines and Axis Submarines* (MacDonald and Jane's, 1977)

Contents

PART ONE

THE HISTORY OF MANIPULATION

PART TWO

MANIPULATION: PRESENT DAY

First published in 1975

Part One translated and summarised from
four articles entitled "Manipulasjons-behandling av columna
under medisinsk-historisk synsvinkel"
published in 1958 in the
journal of the Norwegian medical association
(reviewed in the British Medical Journal 1960 I, p. 1562)
with the addition of newly discovered material.

© E. Schiötz and J. Cyriax 1975

Dr. Schiötz was awarded the Lederle Award in 1958 *for his valuable historical research*

ISBN 0 433 07010 2

MADE AND PRINTED IN GREAT BRITAIN
BY CHAPEL RIVER PRESS
ANDOVER, HANTS

KU-319-971

THE BRITISH SCHOOL OF OSTEOPATHY
1-4 SUFFOLK ST., LONDON SW1Y 4HG
TEL: 01-930 9254-8

MANIPULATION PAST and PRESENT

WITH AN EXTENSIVE BIBLIOGRAPHY

EILER H. SCHIÖTZ, M.D.

Consultant in Industrial Medicine.
Former Librarian at the Medical Faculty of the University of Oslo

JAMES CYRIAX,
M.D.(Cantab.), M.R.C.P.(London)

former Orthopaedic Physician,
St. Thomas's Hospital, London.
Visiting Professor in Orthopaedic Medicine
Rochester University Medical Centre (New York)

WILLIAM HEINEMANN MEDICAL BOOKS LTD
LONDON

Contents

Illustrations

Acknowledgments

I am indebted to numerous persons for their assistance during the time span when I was occupied with this project. My first thanks goes to Jonathan Brown, who acted as my adviser while I worked on the dissertation from which this book derives. He pointed to the need for a study of Rubens and Spain in his publications on Spanish art and in 1987 encouraged me to conduct such a study. His ground-breaking work on the history of art in Spain has been a constant source of inspiration, and his personal support during my years as a graduate student and thereafter have made this publication possible. I am immensely grateful to him.

The idea to undertake a study of Rubens and Spain was first suggested to me by Arnout Balis, from the Rubenianum in Antwerp. For his initial encouragement and for his assistance I am very thankful. Professor Haverkamp-Begemann, from the Institute of Fine Arts, also gave decisive support to the project at an early date, and has been a source of wise counsel and criticism for much of its duration.

In Madrid, where I conducted much of my research, Matías Díaz Padrón, of the Prado Museum, was kind enough to discuss his work with me. His own studies of Rubens' work in Spain have provided the foundation for parts of my research, and for that I am also indebted to him. At the Prado I was also aided by a number of curators and staff members. I want especially to thank Carmen Garrido, from the Gabinete Técnico; the curators Trinidad de Antonio, Mercedes Orihuela, and Jesús Urrea; the conservator Alberto Recchiutto, and also Rocío Arnáez, who made me feel at home in the library of the museum. Fernando Bouza, from the Universidad Complutense de Madrid, was as generous with me as he is with so many other students in sharing his archival findings.

Like many students who have come to the United States from abroad, I never cease to be amazed by the wealth of holdings and the user-friendly nature of the libraries of American universities. I have profited from a number of these libraries, which I wish to acknowledge. While still a student at the Institute of Fine Arts, I worked on the final stages of my dissertation at the Art History and Classics Library of the University of California at Berkeley. Anne Gilbert and Oliver Heyer made my work there both possible and pleasurable. I carried out most of the work of transforming my dissertation into a publishable manuscript while teaching in the Department of Visual Arts at the University of California, San Diego. I am thankful to the staff of the libraries there, especially those in the Art and Architecture section and Special Collections. The finishing touches and last-minute revisions to this manuscript took place while I was teaching in the Department of Art History and Archeology at Columbia University. I wish to thank the staff at Avery Library, especially Paula Gabbard and Kitty Chibnik.

I have greatly profited from consulting a series of inventories of Spanish seventeenth-century collections that Marcus Burke and Peter Cherry will have published under the auspices of The Getty Provenance Index just as this book goes to press. I am very grateful to both authors and to the Provenance Index for allowing me to consult this work before its publication. Maria Gilbert, from the Provenance Index, assisted me in the consultation of the inventories and was kind enough also to provide help when I needed to consult other materials from the library at the Getty Center. Sarah Schroth provided me with a copy of her unpublished dissertation on the collecting of the duke of Lerma that was of great assistance in preparing the first chapter of this book. Cocó Alcalá also allowed me to consult an unpublished research paper on the collecting activities of the admirals of Castile that was very helpful to me.

Some of the ideas and information presented here were tested in various conferences in which I participated. I especially wish to thank Peter Sutton for inviting me to speak in the symposium "The Age of Rubens" held at the Museum of Fine Arts, Boston, in 1993; the organizers who invited me to participate in the sessions "Trading Images in the Art of the Netherlands and Spain, 1400–1700" at the College Art Association annual meeting in 1994; and "Portraiture and the Politics of Identity in the Seventeenth-Century" at the Second Annual Meeting of the Group of Early Modern Cultural Studies, also in 1994; Christopher Brown and Jonathan Brown, who included me among the participants in the course entitled "Artistic Relations between Spain and the Netherlands in the Sixteenth- and Seventeenth-Centuries," held at the *Cursos de Verano de la Universidad Complutense, San Lorenzo de El Escorial*, in 1995; and, finally, Tom Glen, who invited me to Montreal in 1997 to speak at McGill University on my research on Rubens and Spain. I am also indebted to a number of colleagues and friends who shared with me their knowledge on different subjects and made helpful suggestions on specific points. I wish to thank Marcus Burke, Barbara Folsom, Alisa Luxenburg, Donald Posner, Elaine Stainton, and the anonymous readers for Cambridge University Press, who forced me to look hard again at aspects of the book that I had prematurely considered finished. I also wish to thank Christopher Brown, Fernando Checa, and Jeffrey Muller for their help in finding some of the photographs that are used as illustrations.

Part of the research that I conducted for my doctoral dissertation was funded by two grants from the Kress Foundation and by a Dean's Dissertation Fellowship from the Graduate School of Arts and Science, New York University, for which I am very grateful. My postdoctoral research has been funded by senior fellowships (Andrew W. Mellon Fellowship and Theodore Rousseau Fellowship) awarded by The Metropolitan Museum of Art through its Department of European Paintings. I wish to thank Walter Liedtke for his support in gaining this fellowship. Part of the cost of reproducing the figures included in this book was paid with funds provided by the Faculty Research Allowance Program of the Department of Art History and Archeology, Columbia University.

My greatest debt of gratitude is for the support that I have always received from my family. My father, José Vergara, has been an intellectual model throughout my life. I am deeply saddened by the fact that his untimely death has precluded his seeing the end of my research on Rubens and his Spanish patrons, and regret that I am left to imagine the sight of him, the most avid reader I have known, with this book in his hands. To my mother, Julia Sharp, and my brothers, José and Agustín, I owe much of what I am. I am very glad that this book gives me an opportunity to express my gratitude to them. Finally, my wife, Viviana Waisman, has borne more than her share of the burden during the time this project has lasted. More than anyone else, she is responsible for the fact that this ceased to be a project and became a book. I am extremely grateful to her for her patience, her support, and her love – and also for her help in making this text read like English rather than Spanglish.

Introduction

For nearly four hundred years, Peter Paul Rubens (1577–1640) has held the attention of art enthusiasts, critics, and historians. The reasons for this critical success can be found, not only in the painter's artistic powers, but also in the identification of his succulent images with the era in which he lived and in his artistic and political involvement with some of the leading courts of seventeenth-century Europe.

Rubens was heir to the artistic traditions of classical antiquity and Renaissance Italy, as well as to those of the Netherlands. He treated a wide variety of subjects, from religious paintings embodying the spirit of contemporary Catholicism to sophisticated landscapes, which he endowed with a poetic immediacy. He painted for the Church, for the aristocracy, and for wealthy patrons from the merchant classes. He was also a painter of the world of the court, for which he produced eloquent portraits and other works charged with overt ideological content, as well as mythologies and hunts, often populated by exuberant nudes.

Rubens was an extremely prolific artist who directed one of the largest workshops of his time. In addition to his full-scale paintings, he was also the author of vivacious sketches and drawings, and he designed sets of splendid tapestries and numerous other images that were made into prints and widely circulated.

In addition to his artistic occupations, Rubens was a man of great learning. His extensive correspondence includes exchanges with some of the leading men of letters and statesmen of Europe. He was an important collector of paintings and other objects such as classical statues, ancient gems, and figures carved in ivory, and he also took on the role of diplomat, acting in this capacity in important missions on behalf of the rulers of his homeland, the Spanish Netherlands.

Rubens enjoyed great success during his lifetime. He lived like an aristocrat in an Italianate palace that he built for himself in Antwerp. He was a true cosmopolite who traveled extensively. He spent his childhood in Germany (the first year in Siegen, where he was born, and then ten years in Cologne). Subsequently he spent most of his life in Antwerp, the largest city of the southern Netherlands. He also resided in Italy from 1600 to 1608, and he made extended visits to the courts of Spain, France, and England.

Rubens' herculean capacities and artistic merits justify the scholarly attention that he has received. Many aspects of his art have been carefully and fruitfully studied, from his stylistic evolution to his working methods; from his collecting and his correspondence to the different subjects that he treated in his paintings; from his relationship with Italy and Italian art to specific projects involving paintings, tapestries, or prints. However, some aspects of Rubens' work remain that are in need of study. This book concentrates on one of these: Rubens' Spanish patronage.

The absence of an adequate study of this topic may seem surprising.[1] To anybody who has visited the Prado Museum, which houses the remains of the Spanish royal collections, the importance of the presence in Spain of works by Rubens seems self-evident. According to my own count, there were at least 172 original paintings by the artist in Spain during the seventeenth century, the period covered in this study. Some of these works were in the country only a short time, but most remained for an extended period, many permanently. An important series of twenty tapestries designed by Rubens could also be seen in Madrid after 1628. In addition, there were at least 134 other paintings attributed to Rubens in seventeenth-century Spain. Many of these were probably not autograph originals, but some no doubt were. The Spanish royal collection also included as many as fifty-four paintings by other Flemish artists after designs by Rubens.[2]

Rubens painted so often for Spanish patrons, and the number of paintings sent from his workshop in Flanders to Spain was so large, that nearly all extensive studies of the artist's career have had to concern themselves with Spain in one form or another. Even when this has been done, however, the artist's Spanish patronage has been treated tangentially, as an incidental aspect of the discussion. This book will focus primarily on Rubens' Spanish patronage.

In my view, the best way to move beyond the sporadic attention generally given to Rubens' relationship with Spain is to go back to the basics, to gather together all the fragmented pieces of information that we have on this topic and with them create a coherent historical account. Thus, the first chapter of this book discusses Rubens' first visit to Spain, which provided the occasion for his first direct contact with Spanish patrons. Chapter 2 deals with the gradual development of Rubens' ties with Spanish patrons between 1603 and 1628, when the artist visited Spain for a second time. This second visit is covered in Chapter 3. Here the most important paintings that Rubens made during his stay in Madrid are carefully studied, as are the effects the Spanish context had upon the artist's work.

As Rubens' relationship with the Spanish milieu developed, one figure of special significance gradually emerged, that of King Philip IV, who occupied the Spanish throne from 1621 to 1665. The king would eventually own the largest collection of Rubens' paintings of his time, and his patronage was so important to Rubens' work that he is the coprotagonist of a large part of this book. Chapter 4 deals with the last decade of Rubens' life, from 1630 to 1640, when Philip IV was the artist's most avid – and sometimes impatient – client, ordering a succession of extensive series of paintings.

It is because of the importance of Philip IV as Rubens' patron that this book deals with the period beyond the death of the artist. Chapter 5 studies the numerous purchases of paintings by Rubens made by the king before the end of his reign in 1665. It also deals with the collecting of Rubens' works by the king's son and heir, Charles II, and by other collectors through the end of the century.

As can be seen from this synopsis, this study has a double focus. The book centers primarily on Rubens and his paintings – the artist's production for Spain and Spanish patrons, and his visits to that country. Overlapping with this principal theme is a second one. The presence of Rubens and his works in Spain reached such magnitude that I discuss not only the artist but also the artistic milieu of Spain, including Spanish patronage and the reception of Rubens' paintings in that country.

I should point out here that I have not addressed – at least not in a comprehensive manner – an issue that might be considered in a study of Rubens and Spain: the influence of the Flemish master on Spanish painters and his contribution to the development of the artistic taste of that country.[3] Although those approaching this book from the viewpoint of the history of Spanish art might have profited from such a study, for those whose interest lies in the career of the artist an adequate treatment of this issue would have been cumbersome and excessive. In the end, the decision not to treat Rubens' influence on Spanish painting has been motivated by one overriding factor: the need to clarify one aspect of the artist's career that has remained muddled by the very fact that it is always studied in conjunction with others. In view of this, I have thought it most beneficial to consider the presence of Rubens and of his paintings in Spain as a self-contained topic.

The importance of Rubens' paintings for Spain can be measured in ways other than their influence on local painters. While working on this book I have come to a conclusion concerning Rubens' role in the cultural – as opposed to the specifically artistic – history of Spain: the magnitude of Rubens' presence and reputation in Spain suggests that we consider the Flemish master, not only as a foreign element in Spanish culture, but also as an integral component of that culture. The significance of his presence in seventeenth-century Spain is defined by several factors: first, the large number of his paintings existing in that country; second, the fact that most of these paintings were collected by the king and members of his circle, figures whose position at the apex of society caused their taste to be widely imitated; and third, the esteem in which those paintings were held, as evidenced both by their prominent display by their owners – as will be seen throughout this book – and by the writers of the most important Spanish texts about the arts of the period.

The division of the history of art into national schools has accustomed us to identifying nations with the images created by local artists. This nationalistic interpretation of art, which existed in Rubens' own lifetime,[4] can be explained to some extent as serving practical purposes, reflecting timely needs in the history of a community to assert differences rather than similarities. However, the fact that this nationalistic view has a sociological logic and a historical pedigree does not mean that it offers the most accurate view of the past. The division of the history of culture and of art into national schools often has the effect of forcing historical realities into narrow, prefixed categories. Most readers will agree that we have learned to identify seventeenth-century Spain with the paintings made by Spanish artists. This has resulted in an excessive disassociation between Rubens and the culture of that country. A statement by an illustrious Spaniard exemplifies this position. Speaking to his friend the Mexican artist and writer Marius de Zayas, Picasso once said: "Velázquez left us an idea of the people of his epoch. Undoubtedly they were different from the way he painted them, but we cannot conceive a Philip IV in any other way than the one Velázquez painted. Rubens also made a portrait of the same king and in Rubens' portrait he seems to be quite another person. We believe in the one painted by Velázquez, for he convinces us by his right of might."[5] Picasso was probably sincere in his belief that the superiority of Velázquez's representation of Philip IV over Rubens' stems from its "right of might" – which may be interpreted as referring to its pictorial power. Nevertheless, it is safe to assume that this statement is imbued with the subconscious consequences of the nationalistic view of art history that I have described: Velázquez better represents the Spanish past simply because he is a Spaniard.

There is some basis for the widespread association of seventeenth-century Spain exclusively with local artists such as Velázquez, and not with Rubens, because local artists share a common historical experience with the people in their community. Continuing with the comparison made by Picasso, Velázquez was a native of Seville and a longtime resident at the Spanish court in Madrid. His paintings can thus claim to express a certain Spanish experience made up of the memory of events that he shared with his compatriots. But it is important to remember that there were more pictures designed and painted by Rubens than by Velázquez in the Spanish court. The success of Rubens' paintings in the highest circles of Spanish patronage in the seventeenth century indicates that they were an essential part of the visual culture of the dominant group in Spanish society at the time. They provided images that affected contemporaries in the fabrication of their mental worlds. The pictures that will be studied in this book should therefore be seen as part of the cultural identity of seventeenth-century Spain.

Finally, a few words should be said on the method that I have followed in this study. As is shown by the outline of the chapters contained in this book presented above, this is an attempt to reconstruct a historical case through the presentation of data in the form of a narrative account. As has been mentioned, the relationship of Rubens with his Spanish patrons has never been treated historically as a whole – at least not fully and recently enough. The immediate need was thus to make this historical case available. The expositive clarity of a narrative account suggested its selection as a method.

There is much debate in the fields of the humanities and the social sciences about the validity of narrative reconstructions, which can be naive as a result of their sense of realism and may also be seen as politically biased because they irremediably favor and legitimate the viewpoint from which they are taken.[6] Although this has led some to discard conventional ways of recounting the past, a more fertile response is to acknowledge that there is no single correct way to write history. The fact that knowledge is always partial and relative – that the exact same events are likely to be seen differently by different people – demands a multiplicity of methods. What matters in order to achieve the goal of increasing historical consciousness is not so much the selection of one method over another, but rather that research be carried out in a spirit of skeptical rationalism.

CHAPTER ONE

The First Visit to Spain, 1603–1604

Ambitious for a Little Flattery

By his very birth in 1577 into a Flemish family, Rubens' life was linked to Spain. When Rubens settled in Antwerp in 1589 with his mother and siblings he moved to the largest and most prosperous city of the Spanish Netherlands. That territory had fallen under Hapsburg rule by right of descent from the dukes of Burgundy in 1506 and shortly afterward was incorporated into the domains of the Spanish Hapsburgs. Throughout Rubens' life, the southern Netherlands remained the Spanish monarchy's stronghold in the north of Europe, and the territory was ruled by members of the Spanish royal family. Following the governorships of Alexander Farnese and the archduke Ernst of Austria, another nephew – and brother law-of Philip II of Spain, the archduke Albert, arrived in Brussels as governor-general in 1596. Two years later, in 1598, Albert married his cousin the infanta Isabella Clara Eugenia, daughter of Philip II. The Netherlands were the dowry Isabella brought to the marriage, and thus the archdukes, as Albert and Isabella would be called, ruled as joint sovereign princes, with the stipulation that the territory would revert to the Spanish Crown if they had no children, as occurred after the death of Albert in 1621. The infanta continued to rule as governor until her death in 1633, and from then until after Rubens died in 1640 the post was occupied by the cardinal-infante Ferdinand, brother of King Philip IV.[1]

As a youth in Antwerp, and in nearby Brussels, Rubens must have become familiar with some aspects of Spanish culture and patronage. He probably met members of the Spanish colony and the Spanish administration, for whom local artists sometimes worked – including his teacher, Otto Van Veen, and also his friend the portrait painter Frans Pourbus the Younger.[2] However, no specific projects executed by the young Rubens for Spanish patrons are documented before his first visit to Spain in 1603–1604, and given the painter's young age and his still developing professional status, there probably were none. It was during his Spanish sojourn that Rubens had his first direct interaction with Spanish patrons and, equally important for the painter's development, with the works of art existing in Spanish collections.

Rubens' Activities in Spain

7

The First Visit to Spain, 1603–1604

The circumstances of Rubens' first visit to Spain are known to us through the correspondence of the painter with other persons who were involved in his mission to the Spanish court. After completing his apprenticeship in Antwerp and becoming a member of the local Guild of Saint Luke in 1598, Rubens decided to continue his artistic education in Italy. He traveled there on May 9, 1600, and soon entered the service of Vincenzo Gonzaga, duke of Mantua. Rubens' visit to Spain came about three years later, when he was selected to form part of an embassy from the ducal court of Mantua to the court of King Philip III in Valladolid.[3]

Rubens left Mantua on March 5, 1603, charged with delivering to the Mantuan representative in Valladolid a series of gifts for the king and other courtiers, including a group of paintings intended for the king's favorite, Francisco Gómez de Sandoval y Rojas, first duke of Lerma (1552–1625). The gift included close to forty paintings, among them a *St. Jerome* by Quentin Massys, an unspecified portrait of the duke of Mantua, seventeen copies after Raphael believed to be by Pietro Facchetti, and copies after Titian and others.[4] This is the first of several instances in this book where one sees that Rubens' art, and to some extent also himself, were used as commodities in a form of economic transaction typical of the period, namely the exchange of gifts among Europe's dignitaries. In this case, Rubens was chosen to assist in the delivery of the paintings, and to contribute to the gift by adding paintings of his own if the occasion demanded.[5] After embarking from Livorno on April 2, the painter first set foot on Spanish soil in the port of Alicante, where he had arrived by April 22. From there he traveled nearly four hundred miles across the Castilian plateau to Valladolid, where he arrived on May 13.

Immediately after his arrival, Rubens set to work repairing the pictures in the shipment, which had been damaged on the arduous trip. The deterioration of the paintings was first believed to be very severe but later turned out to be somewhat less so. Nonetheless, Rubens' restoration work must have been extensive, as a large number of paintings were repaired. Iberti, the Mantuan representative in Valladolid, informs us that all the paintings were restored with the exception of a *St. John* and a small *Madonna*, which were thought to be beyond repair – as it turned out, at least the *St. John* was also mended.[6] Rubens also added to the gift a painting by his own hand, a *Democritus and Heraclitus*, his first documented painting in Spain. According to the correspondence, this was painted in Valladolid sometime between June 14 and July 6 and was intended to make up for two of the damaged paintings that Rubens had brought to Spain for the duke of Lerma.[7] After delivering the gift to the king and his favorite, Rubens began to work on a commission he had received from the duke of Mantua to paint a series of portraits of ladies of the Spanish court.[8] Little is known about the results of this commission. The artist was not pleased with the job, and although the documents say that he worked on the portraits,[9] he tried to keep the project to a minimum. In his correspondence he refers to it as a humble occupation,[10] and he avoided going to France, where he had been instructed to travel in order to complete the commission.[11] The fact that no trace of these portraits exists suggests that he must have painted only a few.[12]

The only documented commission that Rubens received from the Spanish court is an *Equestrian Portrait of the Duke of Lerma* on which he began to work in September of 1603. This is the most important work that emerged from the Spanish visit, and more will be said about it later. As far as is known, Rubens did not paint a portrait of the king at this point, apparently not yet having attained a status that warranted a royal sitting.[13]

During the years he had spent in Italy, Rubens had carefully studied antique sculpture and Renaissance works by artists such as Michelangelo, Raphael, Leonardo, and Titian, and his visit to Spain offered him the chance to continue his studies. As we shall see, Rubens visited the royal collections and was impressed by the amount and quality of the paintings he saw there. But the only unequivocal evidence of Rubens' study of other artists at this time is a sheet that includes figures drawn by him after a painting of the *Martyrdom of Saint James* by Fernández de Navarrete "El Mudo," several drawings by Leonardo, and other, unidentified sources.[14] Navarrete's painting hung in El Escorial (where it remains today), and Rubens must have copied it there. Aside from the merits of the painting itself, Rubens' interest in this picture reflects the esteem in which this painter was held in the Spanish court, and it is an indication of the status the Spanish artist had gained since his early death in 1579.[15] The drawings after Leonardo were probably copied from the collection of drawings by the great Florentine artist that the sculptor Pompeo Leoni had brought to Spain at the end of the sixteenth century.[16] Rubens must have met Pompeo Leoni in Spain, either in Madrid, where the sculptor was based and where he is documented in the summer of 1603, or in Valladolid, where he also worked regularly.[17] It was natural for the Italianized Rubens to seek out Italian company in Spain. Leoni's link with his father, the great sculptor Leone Leoni, and his privileged position at the court, certainly would have incited Rubens' curiosity.

Mention should be made here of an additional work by Rubens that he is believed to have brought to Spain during this trip, but that may actually never have existed. In 1607 and thereafter, the inventories of the Spanish royal collection list a *Portrait of the Duke of Mantua* attributed to Rubens.[18] This portrait has been linked in the literature with a painting referred to in the correspondence between the Mantuan embassy in Valladolid and the court in Mantua.[19] However, the correspondence shows that the only picture mentioned is a portrait by Frans Pourbus the Younger, who also worked for the duke.[20] We are thus left with the royal inventories as the only source to mention Rubens' portrait of the duke. There are, however, reasons to believe that the attribution may be incorrect. The painting first listed in the royal collection in 1607 as by Rubens is probably identical to an anonymous portrait of the duke of Mantua that belonged to the duke of Lerma in 1603, and that is probably the portrait by Pourbus mentioned above.[21] It is likely that this painting is the same one that later appears in the royal collection, where it presumably entered as a gift or sale from Lerma. It is easy to imagine that when the portrait was first inventoried in 1607 in the royal collection it was attributed to Rubens, the person in charge of its delivery, instead of Pourbus. The initial mistake was probably perpetuated in later inventories, which were often based on previous listings and not on observation of the actual collection.[22]

During the months Rubens was in Spain, he had a chance to tour the royal collections in the monastic and palatial complex of El Escorial and elsewhere. He wrote about this visit in a letter to Mantua dated May 24, 1603, where he expressed the great impression made on him by the array of Italian masterpieces but also noted his lack of interest in the modern paintings owned by the king. In the letter he refers to the "many splendid works of Titian, of Raphael and others, which have astonished me, both by their quality and quantity, in the King's palace, in the Escorial, and elsewhere. But as for the moderns, there is nothing of any worth."[23]

Rubens' mention of Raphael is surprising, given the small presence of works by the painter from Urbino in Spain at this time. The *Madonna of the Rose* (Madrid, Prado) was probably in El Escorial when Rubens visited there and must be one of the pictures that he had a chance to view. A small number of additional works by Raphael, all of them unidentified, are documented in Spain in the early seventeenth century and may also account for the statement made by Rubens.[24] The mention of Titian is especially interesting, given the number of works by this painter the Spanish monarchs had assembled in the sixteenth century.[25] In El Escorial, Rubens must have seen the *Trinity* (Madrid, Prado) and the late *Martyrdom of Saint Lawrence* (El Escorial; Fig. 41), among other pictures, and in and around Madrid he could have contemplated several portraits of Spanish monarchs (among them the famous *Charles V at the Battle of Mühlberg* and the *Philip II in Armor*, both in the Prado; Figs. 31 and 37); the mythologies known as the *poesie*; the so-called *Pardo Venus* (Paris, Louvre), as well as many others. Titian's style did not have the long-lasting impact on Rubens at this point that it would have in later years, especially after his second visit to Spain. Even though some authors believe that he carefully studied Titian's works at this time by making copies after some of them, this is not certain.[26] What Rubens' reference to Titian in the letter mentioned above does show is that the Venetian master made an impression on him at this time. Titian's influence has been detected in some of Rubens' post-Spanish works, especially in his use of color.[27] This is not yet the close artistic relationship that would emerge after Rubens' second Spanish trip, but it is an anticipation of things to come.

The fact that Rubens' correspondence does not mention one painter who was active in Spain at the time is worth noting. El Greco lived in Toledo until his death in 1614. Two of his works (the *Adoration of the Name of Jesus* and the *Martyrdom of Saint Maurice*) could be seen in El Escorial at the time of Rubens' trip to Spain. Also, one of El Greco's most important series of paintings had been recently installed in the College of Doña María de Aragón in Madrid, very close to the Alcázar (as the royal palace was known), one of the sites where Rubens presumably viewed the royal collection.[28] Perhaps the work of this idiosyncratic genius baffled Rubens as much as it did other contemporary critics. Francisco Pacheco, for example, commended El Greco for his erudition and his struggles in support of the professional status of painters, but was puzzled by the lack of drawing in his works and by the primacy given in them to color.[29]

In another passage of the letter of May 24, 1603, quoted above, Rubens wrote about his opinions of the painters then active at the Spanish court in Valladolid.[30] He stated that he associated little with the local court artists, whose work he described with great contempt, saying of them: "the incredible incompetence and carelessness of the painters here, whose style (and this is very important) is totally different from mine." This often quoted opinion, which is sometimes used to legitimize criticism of the painters of the court of Philip III, may have been expressed with excessive haste. The painters present at the court at the time included the Florentine Bartolomé Carducho (originally Bartolommeo Carducci), who was one of the most influential figures at court in artistic matters, and who probably met Rubens when he inspected the paintings included in the gift from Mantua.[31] Also there was Bartolomé's younger brother Vicente Carducho, nearly an exact contemporary of Rubens; and the aging portrait specialist Juan Pantoja de la Cruz; in addition to other lesser-known artists. The Carduchos and some of the other painters were certainly competent, if less than great.[32] Rubens' letter shows that he disapproved of the style of the painters in Valladolid. Given Rubens' interests during his first Italian years, and the strong naturalism prevalent in Spanish painting at the time, this may indicate that he thought the work of the local artists was too far removed from the classical ideal. But Rubens' critique of these artists, made when he had spent only ten busy days in Valladolid, can also be seen as a reflection of his state of mind. A late bloomer who was still trying to accelerate his career, he appears to have been annoyed by these artists, whom he regarded as inferior, perhaps because, as the painter of a lesser prince, he could be seen as having less status than they did.[33]

The *Portrait of the Duke of Lerma* and the *Heraclitus and Democritus*

The most important painting made by Rubens in his visit to Spain is the *Equestrian Portrait of the Duke of Lerma*.[34] It is also the only painting documented in the correspondence from this trip that can be identified with certainty with an extant work; it is now in the Prado (Fig. 1). Only a few of Rubens' other early paintings match this work in ambition and grandeur. Among them are the panels of the *Ecstasy of St. Helena* (Grasse, Chapel of the Municipal Hospital), the *Mocking of Christ* (Grasse, Chapel of the Municipal Hospital) and the *Raising of the Cross* (now lost), which formed the altarpiece for the church of Santa Croce in Gerusalemme in Rome of 1602; the large *Entombment* now in the Borghese Gallery in Rome; and some of the early mythologies that Rubens painted in his first Italian years, such as the *Assembly of the Olympians* (Prague, Castle), and the *Hercules and Omphale* (Paris, Louvre). In these scenes, Rubens had tested his artistic abilities by creating large and complex compositions for important patrons. In comparison with these paintings, the *Equestrian Portrait of the Duke of Lerma* offers a glimpse of a more evolved stage in Rubens' development as an artist. In the earlier images, the powerful anatomies of the figures are mitigated by their delicate facial features and sensitive expressions and gestures, as can be seen, for example, in the *Entombment* from the Borghese Gallery (Fig. 2). The poses of these and other figures from Rubens' early Italian pictures are reminiscent of the aesthetics of mannerism in their emphasis on grace and artistry. In these early works, light is used in a discontinuous way that adds both drama and confusion to the images. Although the movement of the figures and the painter's concentration on marginal areas of the compositions result in scenes that are somewhat disjointed, they are nevertheless successful because of their emotional intensity.

In the portrait of the duke of Lerma, significant changes have taken place in the artist's style. As in his earlier work, the forms are robust, but here the gestures are consonant with the powerful anatomies of the horse and rider. The light is still unrealistically dramatic, but it is used to enhance the horse and the mounted figure and does not distract the viewer's attention from them. The sinuous grouping of trees behind and above the sitter are reminiscent of the intricacy of the background elements in the earlier paintings, but now they too are less distracting. The result is a more unified composition, where every element is directed at exalting the splendor of the sitter and the viewer's contemplation of him. As in the works from his first years in Italy, in this portrait Rubens makes abundant use of specific elements taken from other sources and artists. Among the numerous sources, direct or indirect, that have been cited for this painting are: a description in Pliny the Elder's *Natural History* of a painting by Apelles showing Antigonos, king of Macedonia, advancing with his horse; a series of anonymous Flemish paintings of emperors on horseback in Lerma's collection; prints of equestrian Roman emperors by Collaert and Jan van der Straet (or Stradanus); and Titian's *Charles V at Mühlberg*, which was in the Spanish royal collection.[35] But these – or other similar influences that can be cited, such as Hans Burgkmair's print of *Saint George*[36] – are now more successfully transformed into a personal idiom than the classical quotations in his earlier paintings.

The innovations evident in the portrait of Lerma do not represent the beginning of an entirely new phase of Rubens' career, because in the following years the artist would occasionally return to elements of his earlier style. Perhaps this phase of his artistic evolution is best characterized as one of trial and error. However, the Lerma portrait does exhibit for the first time many features that Rubens would develop more fully in the future. The forceful presentation of the horse and rider, and the subordination of all parts of the image to a central theme, which are absent in earlier paintings, can be seen again in *The Gonzaga Adoring the Trinity*, painted shortly after Rubens' return from Spain to Mantua. The same boldness of conception and execution characterizes pictures such as the *Portrait of Marchesa Brigida Spinola Doria* in the National Gallery of Art in Washington, D.C., the *Saint George Slaying the Dragon* (Fig. 68) from the Prado, and other works that Rubens executed in the years immediately preceding his return from Italy to Flanders in 1608. Another aspect of Rubens' art that would become increasingly important later in his career is the ideological conviction that he instilled in the images he made for Europe's governing class. In the *Equestrian Portrait of the Duke of Lerma*, Rubens underscored the political stature of the sitter by using as a source for his design the images of past emperors and rulers mentioned above.

The exact circumstances that led to the creation of *Equestrian Portrait of the Duke of Lerma* are not fully documented, leaving this matter open to speculation. One obvious possibility is that Lerma personally commissioned the portrait. This is supported by one interpretation of the painting, which suggests that Rubens' equestrian portrait should be seen as part of a campaign by Lerma to call attention to his descent from a family of warriors who had served the Spanish Crown for centuries, a campaign that also included the commissioning of commemorative fres-

FIGURE 1

Facing page
Rubens, *Equestrian Portrait of the Duke of Lerma*. Madrid, Museo del Prado.

FIGURE 2

Rubens, *Entombment of Christ.* Rome, Galleria Borghese.

coes and oil paintings from Bartolomé and Vicente Carducho for the duke's quarters in the royal palace in Valladolid.[37]

The theory that the commission came from the sitter is certainly plausible, but it is not certain. All we know from the documentation is that in July of 1603 the duke of Lerma asked Rubens to paint him a picture of his own invention ("di suo capriccio").[38] The next document that can be related to this work is a letter of September 15 of the same year, in which Rubens excitedly refers to a "great equestrian portrait" of the duke that he is to paint.[39] The fact that what had originated as an unspecified commission from Lerma had now become a monumental equestrian portrait may indicate that the subject matter of this work was decided, at least in part, by the painter. If this is the case, it is a measure of the ambition with which Rubens approached his stay at the Spanish court.

Whatever the origin of the painting, the importance of the Spanish court, and also of the sitter, help to explain the unprecedented splendor of the equestrian portrait of Lerma. The court of Philip III was among the most important in Europe at the time, and, as the favorite of the Spanish king, the duke of Lerma was one of the most powerful men of the period. The king and his minister were also important collectors and patrons of the arts who ruled over a court known at the time for its pageantry and lavish festivities. The royal and ducal households in and around Valladolid were richly decorated with canvases and fresco paintings inscribed in gilded moldings, and they also housed natural wonders and numerous other objects typical of the taste of collectors of the day. Even though he was not the equal of his father, Philip II, who had been one of the greatest collectors of the sixteenth century, Philip III clearly had inherited his high standards and was well aware of the importance of creating for himself an image of splendor.[40]

As the protagonist and recipient of what may be considered Rubens' most important painting to date, the duke of Lerma needs some further explaining. From 1598 to his downfall in 1618, Lerma was the first true favorite, or *valido*, to serve the Spanish king, a powerful political figure typical of the early seventeenth century in Europe. He was also the most important art patron and collector of his generation in Spain and one of the most avid collectors – in terms of the number of paintings purchased – in all of Europe.[41] During Rubens' visit to Valladolid in 1603–1604, Lerma's collection of paintings was in the midst of a period of rapid growth. An inventory of the duke's quarters in the royal palace in Valladolid taken in September of 1603 (the same time when Rubens was working on Lerma's equestrian portrait) listed 488 paintings, including copies of the works of many leading Italian painters whose originals were extremely difficult to acquire (such as Titian and Raphael); many Netherlandish works (some attributed to Bosch); and works by Sánchez Coello, Ribalta, and other important Spanish painters.[42] The collection continued to grow in the following years, so that by 1606 it included close to 1,500 paintings, and the quality of the works would gradually became more selective: by 1606 Lerma owned originals by Titian, Veronese, the Bassani, and Mor, among others, and it should also be remembered that he owned Giambologna's monumental marble group *Samson Slaying a Philistine* (London, Victoria and Albert Museum), which he had received as a gift from Ferdinando de' Medici in 1601.

In a letter cited earlier in this chapter, Rubens wrote to Mantua about Lerma's "knowledge of fine things" and his "particular pleasure and practice" of seeing the great works that had been assembled in the royal collection.[43] Lerma's power and position at the court also impressed Rubens, perhaps even more than his interest in the arts. In a letter to a friend written in 1626, the painter remembered an incident that had taken place during his visit to Spain more than two decades earlier:

> The king, in granting audience to an Italian gentleman, referred him to the Duke of Lerma (with whom an audience was extremely difficult). "But if I had been able to have an audience with the Duke," replied the gentleman, "I should not have come to Your Majesty."[44]

The importance of the Spanish court, and Lerma's position within it, must have made Rubens feel that the opportunity to portray the duke was a unique occasion to display his talents. The resulting equestrian portrait shows that the painter responded brilliantly with a work that was a magnificent debut to his relationship with Spain's rulers and patrons.

Aside from the portrait of Lerma, the only other work made by Rubens in Spain that has been tentatively identified with an extant picture is the *Democritus and Heraclitus*, which is probably identical to a painting in a private collection in Princeton, New Jersey. (Fig. 3).[45] This picture can be considered as something of a statement by the young Rubens as it was made on his own initiative in substitution for two religious images, a *St. John in the Wilderness* and a painting of the Virgin that were judged to have been damaged beyond repair upon their arrival in Valladolid.[46] The idea of replacing religious paintings with a work that uses classical and Renaissance sources suggests that Rubens wished to present himself as a learned artist, and perhaps also that he was taking a stance vis-à-vis the naturalism favored by local artists. Also, the theme of the two philosophers who react to the fortunes of the world, one by crying and the other by laughing, was used by contemporary Spanish writers. It may be that Rubens was responding to this stimulus with his painting.[47] The *Democritus and Heraclitus* is an awkward picture. The fine features of Democritus, on the left, contrast with the strenuous pose of Heraclitus, and with the massive musculature of his neck and arm. The intensity of the gazes of the two figures, however, makes this a strangely engaging work. As Michael Jaffé has suggested, Rubens' eagerness to please his patrons with this painting appears to have been successful, as it was painted before the equestrian portrait of Lerma and therefore may have prompted the duke to award him that commission.[48]

The paintings produced by Rubens in Spain are ambitious works that, together with his correspondence, reveal a determined artistic personality. In a letter written from Valladolid to Mantua, Rubens denied being "ambitioso di un poco di fumo" ("ambitious for a little flattery").[49] But his opinions about the artists of the Spanish court, the general tone of his correspondence, and the paintings that he executed during his stay in Spain appear to contradict this denial. Rubens seems to have been a determinedly ambitious artist, somewhat impatient with his status, to the point of complaining about delivering a gift to the Spanish court that did not include a single painting by his own hand.[50] Clearly, Rubens had high hopes for his first Spanish sojourn. Seen in the light of these hopes, his 1603–1604 visit to the Spanish court can be considered a success. One sign of this was Lerma's desire to have Rubens remain in Spain and work for the king, as was reported by Iberti in a letter to the duke of Mantua.[51] Also revealing is the praise accorded Rubens' paintings, the *Heraclitus and Democritus* being referred

FIGURE 3

Rubens, *Democritus and Heraclitus*. Princeton, New Jersey, The Barbara Piasecka Johnson Collection Foundation.

to as *bueno* (or "good") in the 1607 inventory of the collection of the duke of Lerma, and the portrait of the duke receiving praise both during its execution and after its completion.[52]

But the Spanish trip also reveals a less familiar side of Rubens that is characteristic of the early part of his career. He emerges at this period as an artist who has not yet achieved the status that he will attain later and who is bound by the constraints common to his profession. The only specifically painterly instruction that Rubens received from Vincenzo I Gonzaga on his trip to Spain was to paint portraits of women from the court. (It is worth noting that Rubens' activity during his years in Mantua was remembered shortly after his death as mainly that of a portrait painter. In 1642, the critic and art historian Giovanni Baglione wrote that, when in Mantua, Rubens "made various works, and in particular he painted some very beautiful portraits.") As we have seen, Rubens considered this a humble occupation for a painter, reflecting a prejudice of his time.[53] At another juncture, his Mantuan patrons suggested that he paint "cose boscareccie," or woodland scenes, again associating him with a comparatively lesser genre.[54]

Rubens' success at the Spanish court did not have any significant impact upon local painters at the time. In addition, his visit to the court does not seem to have found a place among the memorable events in Rubens' relation with Spain. It is not mentioned by the two most important sources on seventeenth-century painting in Spain, the *Arte de la Pintura* by Francisco Pacheco, and the *Lives of the Eminent Spanish*

Painters and Sculptors by Acisclo Antonio Palomino, also a writer as well as a painter.[55] Both authors deal extensively with Rubens' second Spanish visit and treat the Fleming as a major figure of the Spanish artistic scene. Their omission of Rubens' first visit to Spain is thus highly significant and demonstrates that it had been forgotten – in the case of Pacheco, only four decades after it had taken place.

The exact date of Rubens' departure from the Iberian peninsula is not known, but it probably took place in the first months of 1604.[56] When he returned to the Spanish court in the summer of 1628 his status had greatly improved. To a large degree this was due to the increasing flow of his paintings into Spain in the intervening years.

CHAPTER TWO

A Growing Presence, 1604–1628

Almost a decade elapsed between Rubens' departure from Spain in 1604 and the next arrival of his works there. In the interim he had returned from Italy to Antwerp, where he soon established himself as one of the leading painters in the Spanish Netherlands. In a context of prosperity prompted by the Twelve Year Truce signed between Spain and the United Provinces on April 9, 1609, Rubens soon attained great success, set up a large workshop, and his fame spread throughout Europe.

Don Rodrigo Calderón and the Early Collecting of Rubens in Spain

The first painting by Rubens to enter Spain after the trip of 1603–1604 did so as a consequence not only of the artist's growing reputation but also of the political ties that bound Spain and the Netherlands. In the spring of 1612, Don Rodrigo Calderón (ca. 1576–1621), one of the leading courtiers of Philip III and a close associate of the duke of Lerma, left Spain and traveled as ambassador extraordinary in France and the Spanish Netherlands, where he was received with lavish receptions and gifts.[1] It was thought in Spain that Calderón had run into trouble at the court and had been dispatched on his mission as a means of separating him from the capital, but this may have been a rumor intended to protect his true mission, which was to attempt to turn the truce signed in 1609 into a permanent peace between Spain and the United Provinces.[2] In Antwerp, as elsewhere, Calderón was courteously met, and on September 2, 1612, he was presented with a monumental painting of the *Adoration of the Magi* by Rubens as a gift from the city council. The painting had been commissioned by the city in late 1608 or early 1609, on the occasion of the negotiations that led to the announcement of the Twelve Year Truce, and was originally significantly smaller than it is today.[3] Calderón was a native of Antwerp, a fact that may have contributed to the idea of presenting him with a gift. However, the main intention behind the offering was to gain the favor of this powerful favorite of the duke of Lerma, as the correspondence shows. The letter from the city magistrates that accompanied the painting states:

[The magistrates], imploring . . . that you take this city under your protection . . . with the hope that it will be assisted by the Holy Catholic King of Spain, through the hand of your Lordship, have decided to present to Your Lordship the painting of "The Magi," which is the best and rarest gift that they own. [The Magistrates] beg you to do them the favor of accepting the painting, in the memory of this city, not considering its value, but the good will in which it is presented.[4]

Calderón accepted the painting on the same day it was offered to him, promising to shed his favor whenever possible on the magistrates and the city of Antwerp.[5] Shortly afterward, the *Adoration* was shipped by sea to Spain, where it arrived at the beginning of 1613. It remained in Calderón's collection, either in Madrid or in Valladolid, until after he was arrested and publicly executed in 1621, following his fall from power. In September of 1623 the painting was either purchased or confiscated by Philip IV, the new king of Spain. It thus became one of the first works by Rubens to be acquired by the man who would later become his most important patron.[6]

As we shall see in the next chapter, Rubens made important changes in the *Adoration of the Magi* when he encountered the painting in the royal collection during his second visit to Spain in 1628–1629 (Fig. 38). Even though the later additions and repaintings have concealed much of the original surface of this picture, it must have been an imposing painting from the start. The importance of the commission from the city of Antwerp, from which this work originated, guarantees that Rubens gave it his best effort. Indeed, some portions of the picture, such as the two muscular porters in the foreground, are prime examples of Rubens' powerful style in the years immediately following his return to Flanders from Italy.

Rodrigo Calderón was also involved in the acquisition of the next set of paintings by Rubens to enter Spain. In 1614, the courtier, who in that year had become count of Oliva and would soon also become marquis of Siete Iglesias, received from Flanders a series of paintings of Christ and the twelve apostles by Rubens.[7] The circumstances under which this *Apostolado* series entered Calderón's collection can be tentatively reconstructed from the documents of his indictment after his arrest in 1619.[8] It appears that the *Apostolado* belonged first to Charles de Croy, fourth duke of Aarschot, and later to his brother-in-law Charles, Count of Arenberg, two of the highest-ranking aristocrats in the Netherlands.[9] Arenberg gave the paintings to Calderón, probably in return for a favor, as the text of the accusation against Calderón at the time of his arrest and trial suggests: "recognizing the great hand that the said marquis [Calderón] had in business, [Arenberg] used him in order to receive help in his dealings, and in order for him to do this as well as possible, and have him indebted, he sent to him some large paintings in the past year of 1614; they were a Christ with the twelve Apostles, . . . by Rubens."[10] A letter written from Philip III to the archduke Albert of Austria on March 31, 1613, may explain why Calderón had received this gift; the king wrote to Brussels that he had received notice from Calderón of his dealings with Arenberg and granted Arenberg the substantial annual pension of 2,000 ducats.[11] Calderón did not keep the *Apostolado* series for long; it is probably identical to an *Apostolado* group that belonged to the duke of Lerma in 1618, and is now in the Prado Museum (Fig. 4).[12]

The paintings in the series, of which the *Saint Paul* is a good example, are characterized by the powerful anatomies of the figures and the brilliant coloring that define Rubens' art during this period. In these works, as in the *Adoration of the Magi*, Rubens has given form to the longing of the period for heroic Christian saints by creating a pictorial language of monumental proportions, based on the models of classical antiquity and Renaissance Italy. Nothing comparable had been seen in Spain since the decoration of El Escorial in the 1590s by Pellegrino Tibaldi and others.[13] Since then, painting in Spain had evolved toward naturalism, gradually leaving behind the grand manner favored in El Escorial. Rubens' *Adoration* and *Apostolado* were an exception to this trend. Even though these works had no apparent impact on local artists, they made a strong impression on local collectors, judging from the acquisition of the *Adoration* by King Philip IV after Calderón's fall and by the enthusiasm with which Spanish patrons turned to Rubens in later years. This taste for Rubens was activated, one may speculate, not only by his virtuosity, but also by the power of the vision he brought to life in his paintings. The novelties present in Rubens' paintings were easy for local art enthusiasts to accept due to the international nature of collecting in Spain. Patronage of foreign artists had been a common practice in the Spanish court for over a century and had shaped the taste of local patrons, who could encourage a specific style in the work of local painters and at the same time embrace a number of other styles coming into the country from artistic centers abroad.

Not long after the arrival in Spain of the *Apostolado*, Calderón received two more paintings by Rubens, a pair of portraits of the joint rulers of the Spanish Netherlands, the archdukes Albert of Austria and infanta Isabella Clara Eugenia. The portraits of the archdukes were sent to Calderón in Spain by Albert before October 13, 1615, as shown by a record of payments made by the archduke to Rubens on that date.[14] It is not known if the paintings were purchased by Calderón through the archduke Albert or if they were a gift from him.

These portraits are probably identical to two paintings, now in the Prado (Figs. 5 and 6), which were first inventoried in the Alcázar in

Madrid in 1636: they are the only pair of portraits of Albert and Isabella attributed to Rubens recorded in seventeenth-century Spain.[15] In these paintings, the sitters are shown seated on armchairs set against red curtains and placed on a balustraded terrace. The archdukes are dressed in dark costumes fitted with regalia and other adornments. The large ruff collars, similar to the one worn by the duke of Lerma in his equestrian portrait, were the fashion in Spain and its area of influence in the late sixteenth and early seventeenth centuries, and they show how large such collars had grown in spite of efforts to keep them more modest.[16] Although the portraits are formal, they are less iconic and emblematic and more vivid in the characterization of the sitters than contemporary Spanish portraiture. These qualities must have appeared as novelties to local viewers.

The large landscape vistas in the backgrounds of the portraits were another relative novelty for a Spanish audience, who were more accustomed to indoor portraits. Even though the paintings are attributed to Rubens alone in the Spanish inventories, the backgrounds are generally thought to have been painted by Jan Brueghel the Elder (1568–1625), Rubens' friend and frequent collaborator, who was one of Isabella's favorite painters. The attribution to Rubens of the figures has also been questioned. Indeed, the rather disjointed compositions of the two portraits, the frozen appearance of the figures, and the stiffness of the costume and hands in the portrait of the infanta justify an attribution to Rubens' studio. The head of the archduke, on the other hand, is so full of vitality that it must have been painted by Rubens himself. The awkwardness in the compositions can be ascribed to an unsuccessful blending of the different hands that executed the paintings: those of Rubens, of Jan Brueghel the Elder, and of a member of Rubens' studio.

An unusual aspect of these portraits in Rubens' oeuvre is the prominence assigned to the palaces in the background, the castle of Tervuren in the portrait of the archduke and the castle of Mariemont in the portrait of Isabella. Together with the landscapes in which they are set, the buildings occupy approximately half of each scene. This must reflect the love of the archdukes for these particular places, and probably also a desire on the part of these two rulers of foreign origin to be identified with their Netherlandish territories. At the time these works were painted, it was already a common practice for portraits to include in the background small depictions of sites or events, usually a city or a battle, related to the figure portrayed in the foreground. Rubens himself painted distant views and events in the background of many of his equestrian portraits. What is different here is the importance assigned to the background views of the two palaces. The fact that similar backgrounds never receive such prominent treatment again in Rubens' work suggests that the archdukes themselves had determined the large

FIGURE 4

Rubens, *St. Paul.* Madrid, Museo del Prado.

role the palaces would play in the paintings, a role with which Rubens apparently was not pleased.

There may be an echo of the presence of buildings in Rubens' portraits of Albert and Isabella in a painting by Diego Velázquez. This can be seen as an example of the way in which Rubens' work acted as a vehicle for the incorporation of foreign elements into the pictorial vernacular in Spain. As royal painter to King Philip IV, Velázquez was well acquainted with the portraits of the archdukes, which entered the royal collection in the 1620s, after the death of Rodrigo Calderón. As is the case with Rubens' portraits, Velázquez's painting of the *Riding*

Lesson of Baltasar Carlos (Fig. 7) combines in a single image portraits of Spain's leaders – the king and queen in the balcony in the background; the count-duke of Olivares, who was the favorite of the king, in the middle ground; and prince Baltasar Carlos on the horse in the foreground – with a large background image of a building, in this case probably the palace of the Buen Retiro.[17] Even though there are important differences between this painting and Rubens' portraits – the impression of verisimilitude is increased in Velázquez's work by the figures' involvement in other activities – the unusually prominent place ascribed to the royal dwellings by both artists is an important and noteworthy similarity. Of course, Velázquez could have thought of inserting the image of the Buen Retiro palace into his painting on his own. There were good reasons for him to do this, as the count-duke of Olivares, for whom the *Riding Lesson* was probably painted, would have been pleased by the prominence of the palace that he had personally sponsored.[18] Yet, considering how well he must have known them, even if Velázquez did not use Rubens' portraits as actual prototypes, they may well have lived for a moment in his imagination when he designed his painting, encouraging and confirming the appropriateness of his own design.

In addition to the aforementioned paintings that Calderón brought to Spain, he may also have commissioned a portrait of himself from Rubens, or more likely from his workshop.[19] An equestrian portrait of

FIGURE 5

Rubens and Jan Brueghel, *Portrait of Albert, Archduke of Austria*. Madrid, Museo del Prado.

the Spanish aristocrat attributed to Rubens is recorded in a private collection in Madrid in 1651 and 1687 and can be tentatively identified with a painting now in the English royal collection at Windsor Castle (Fig. 8). The painting shows a rider on a silver-gray horse pacing forward toward the viewer. In the background, the city of Antwerp can be identified by the towers of its cathedral. The rider wears a ruff collar and armor, and his left arm is adorned with a red officer's scarf, red being the distinguishing color of the soldiers of the Hapsburgs.[20] An insignia hanging over the sitter's chest may be an emblem of the noble order of Santiago, to which Calderón belonged. This painting is generally dated to circa 1610–1615 on the basis of style; if indeed it is the portrait of Calderón, it could have been painted during his visit to Antwerp in 1612.

The equestrian portrait at Windsor belongs to a known type created by Rubens and repeated by the master himself and by his followers on a number of occasions.[21] The identification of this painting with the portrait of Calderón recorded in the inventories in Spain is likely but not certain, and the attribution to Rubens is questionable; it is probably a product of the workshop. What is important, however, is that the similarities between the description of the portrait of Calderón and a known type of equestrian portrait created by Rubens, and repeated often in his studio, demonstrates that a portrait of Calderón was indeed painted by Rubens or by some artist in his circle. This suggests that

FIGURE 6

Rubens and Jan Brueghel, *Portrait of Isabella, Infanta of Spain*. Madrid, Museo del Prado.

FIGURE 7

Velázquez, *Riding Lesson of Baltasar Carlos*. By kind permission of His Grace the Duke of Westminster OBE TD DL.

Calderón not only received paintings by the Flemish master as gifts from other patrons, but that he also commissioned one such painting himself.

Calderón's role in bringing these paintings to Spain deserves further comment because he emerges as the most important among early Spanish collectors of Rubens; by 1615, seventeen paintings by or attributed to the Fleming had at least passed through his hands, and possibly remained in his collection for some time. Calderón must have met Rubens in Valladolid in 1603, where the courtier had acted as intermediary between the Mantuan embassy and the Spanish court, and where he received from the Mantuan envoys a gift of twenty-four paintings of emperors and empresses, probably copied after Titian.[22] Given his interest in the arts, he probably also met the painter when he visited Antwerp in 1612, the time when he received the *Adoration of the Magi* from the city magistrates, and when he must have posed for his equestrian portrait. Unfortunately, the exact role that Calderón played in the acquisition of the paintings by Rubens cannot be fully established at

FIGURE 8

Rubens' workshop, *Portrait of a Knight (Don Rodrigo Calderón?)*. The Royal Collection. © 1997 Her Majesty Queen Elizabeth II.

present, but it appears that many of them were not directly purchased by him. The equestrian portrait now at Windsor may have been a personal commission, but in the case of the *Adoration of the Magi*, Calderón was a passive player, merely receiving the painting as a gift. His exact role in the matter of the *Apostolado* and the portraits of Albert and Isabella is unclear, but again he appears to have done nothing more than receive the paintings. What appears to have happened with these pictures is an instance of the practice, common among the courts of Europe, of bestowing important gifts on visiting dignitaries. Thus, the arrival of these paintings in Spain is not a consequence of a decision made by Calderón, but of Spain's political power, which made granting gifts to Spanish dignitaries desirable in many European courts.

Another figure who should be mentioned here is Fray Iñigo de Brizuela y Arteaga. He was the confessor of archduke Albert from 1596 to 1621 and participated in some of the important political events of the time taking place in the Spanish Netherlands.[23] After his return to Spain in 1621, he became president of the consejo de Flandes (the Council of the Netherlands) until his death in 1629. Brizuela owned a *Virgin and Child* attributed to Rubens at the time of his death, which he must have brought back from Flanders in 1621, and which may be identical to a painting now in the convent of San Esteban, in Salamanca.[24] The exact manner in which Brizuela attained the painting is unknown. However, this work offers an example of a Spanish official acquiring a painting by Rubens (or his shop) while serving in Flanders.

Brizuela should be seen as a small-scale version of figures like Calderón or the marquis of Leganés (whom I shall discuss later), officers of the Spanish administration in the Netherlands who became acquainted with the art of Rubens through their political posts. The case of Fray Iñigo de Brizuela is also interesting in that it shows that some of these men could assist Rubens in his dealings with the Crown after their return to Madrid. As we shall see later in this chapter, in his capacity as president of the Council of the Netherlands, Brizuela submitted to King Philip IV a petition of nobility in favor of Rubens in 1624.

Early Acquisitions of Rubens Paintings for the Spanish Court

On March 31, 1621, when he was only sixteen years old, Philip IV was crowned king of Spain. The new monarch eventually became one of the great art collectors and patrons of his time, and one of Rubens' most important supporters, but it would still take some time before he applied his considerable savvy as a collector to the Flemish master. As we have seen, the first painting by Rubens the king purchased was probably the *Adoration of the Magi*, which entered his collection in 1623. This acquisition was an early sign of the king's interest in painting and his intention to enlarge the royal holdings. It should not be seen, however, as the beginning of a deliberate effort by Philip IV to collect works by Rubens, but rather as an isolated event resulting from the availability of the picture.

The king's role in the acquisition of the first group of paintings associated with Rubens for the royal residence was actually a minor one. In the early months of 1623, Philip's first wife, Isabella of Bourbon, commissioned from Flanders a group of over twenty-five paintings. They were intended to decorate the *torre nueva* or New Tower, one of the queen's rooms in the Alcázar, the royal palace in Madrid.[25] With the exception of the *Apostolado*, this commission included the largest number of paintings attributed to Rubens yet to enter Spain on a single occasion: six pictures in the group were attributed to the master when they were first inventoried in 1636. The six paintings are: *Ceres and Pan* (Madrid, Prado; now attributed to Rubens and Frans Snyders);[26] *Diana and Nymphs Setting Out for the Hunt* (Madrid, Prado, now attributed to Rubens and Snyders; Fig. 9);[27] *Vertumnus and Pomona* (whereabouts unknown, presumably lost; assigned to Rubens and Snyders in the inventory);[28] a tall and narrow canvas of a *Garland of Flowers and Fruits* (Madrid, Prado; assigned to Rubens and Snyders in the inventory, but possibly painted by Snyders alone);[29] and an *Allegory of Sight and Smell* and an *Allegory of Touch, Hearing and Taste*, which formed a pair and were attributed to Rubens and Jan Brueghel (both in Madrid, Prado; Figs. 10–11). These last two paintings are primarily the work of Jan Brueghel, to which other artists such as Gerard Seghers and Frans Francken the Younger may have contributed by executing the reproductions of paintings that hang in the background of the scenes.[30]

Nothing is known about the queen as a collector other than the information found in the 1636 inventory of the Alcázar and the document of payment for these paintings, where she is shown to be responsible for ordering the shipment of the pictures to Madrid. Isabella (1602–1644), daughter of King Henry IV of France and Maria de' Medici, married Philip IV of Spain in October of 1615, when she was twelve years old and her husband only ten. For many years her life at court was circumspect due to court protocol. Later in her life, her involvement in Spanish politics would show that she had a strong personality.[31] The commission from Flanders shows that she indeed took matters into her own hands when decorating her quarters in the Alcázar.

Even though Philip IV did not initiate the commission for the queen's quarters, he did intervene with respect to this group of paintings at a later date, sometime before 1636. The royal inventory of that year informs us that the king ordered these paintings reinstalled in his dining room in the summer apartments.[32] It is hard to know what to make of this transfer of paintings from the queen's to the king's quarters. It may have resulted from minor redecoration and construction that took place in the queen's quarters in 1629, but it is unclear whether these activities affected the New Tower.[33] Another possible factor in the transferal of the paintings may have been the nudity of many of the figures, which makes them mildly erotic. The queen was uncomfortable with this type of painting – a reaction that may have been exacerbated by the notorious infidelities of her husband.[34] The scholar and collector Cassiano dal Pozzo, who was in Madrid in 1626 in the retinue of Cardinal Franceso Barberini, quoted a local courtier who said that every time the queen entered the king's summer apartments, where many of the erotic mythologies by Titian that belonged to the royal collection were installed, she ordered that the scenes with nudes be covered before her arrival.[35] The king, in contrast, greatly favored such paintings and collected them in great numbers later in his life.

The importance of this early commission by Queen Isabella of Bourbon to the history of the presence of Rubens in Spain is underscored by the fact that the largest number of attributed paintings in the group was ascribed to Rubens, perhaps indicating a special interest in that artist. In the inventory of 1636, six of the paintings are attributed to the master (five of them in collaboration), one to Snyders, and the rest unattributed. Even though there are mistakes in the attributions, all the paintings assigned to Rubens bear some relationship to him, either as originals or as workshop pieces. In spite of the importance of this commission, the interest the Spanish court had in the Flemish master at this time should not be exaggerated. The paintings by Rubens are part of a larger ensemble, and there is no reason to believe that his authorship was a requirement of the commission. The group includes, aside from the paintings by Rubens, genre scenes, wedding scenes, landscapes with figures, views of the palace and gardens of Brussels, a series of scenes of the *la vida del hombre* ("the life of men"), and a battle painting, most of them unattributed.[36] The variety of the paintings suggests that they were not executed on commission, but rather that they were rounded up in order to satisfy a petition from the queen. Considering Rubens' status in Flanders, it was natural that the largest number possible of his paintings would be included in the group. Also, there is a high percentage of erroneous attributions among these pictures in the 1636 royal inventory, which probably reflects the attributions given the paintings at the time of their arrival in Madrid in 1623. The participation of Rubens in two of the paintings, the *Allegory of Sight and Smell* and the *Allegory of Touch, Hearing and Sight*, is at most secondary to that of Jan Brueghel, and it is also uncertain in two other paintings, the *Ceres and Pan* and the *Garland of Flowers and Fruits*. Of the two remaining paintings, the *Diana* is an autograph work, probably with studio collaboration, and the *Vertumnus and Pomona* is not known.[37] The errors in attribution suggest that Rubens' work was still not well known in Spain at this point.

Precisely because Rubens' art was still not well known in Madrid, the paintings that arrived for the queen must have helped form an impression of the artist and his work at this early stage in his relationship with the Spanish Crown. Compared to the paintings by Rubens that were already in Spain at the time of the arrival of this group, which consisted primarily of religious scenes and portraits, the paintings for Queen Isabella presented some novelties. Among the pictures attributed to Rubens were one decorative garland, three mythological scenes, and two allegorical scenes, which associated Rubens with a considerably

FIGURE 9

Rubens and Snyders, *Diana and Nymphs Setting Out for the Hunt*. Madrid, Museo del Prado.

broader range of subject matter than had been previously possible at the Spanish court. The mythological paintings, with their large, fleshy representations of ancient deities and creatures, placed Rubens in the grand tradition of Italian Renaissance painting. This was a category of the highest artistic prestige, sanctioned by the fame of the great Italian masters of the sixteenth century – so well represented in Madrid by Titian – and it boded well for Rubens' future reputation in Madrid to become a part of it.

The two paintings *Allegory of Sight and Smell* and *Allegory of Touch, Hearing and Sight*, on the other hand, presented Rubens in a more Flemish, and also more novel, guise. Even though it is hard to find any trace of his hand in these two large canvases, they were attributed to him in the royal collection, as mentioned above. They also have strong connections with the master, both in the presence of seven small copies of his works in the *Allegory of Sight and Smell* and in the conspicuously Rubensian pedigree of the figures in both paintings.[38] As a result of these two scenes, Rubens could be associated in Madrid with a recently created and specifically Flemish genre, the painting of picture galleries (also known as *kunstkamers*, or paintings of art cabinets).[39] The Flemish nature of this genre may not have been well established at this point, given the fact that these two works are probably the first paintings of picture galleries to arrive in Madrid. But the link of the two allegorical paintings with the Netherlands is enhanced by the presence in the *Allegory of Sight and Smell* of typically Flemish genres such as landscape paintings, the garland with a Virgin and Child reproduced in the lower left corner, or the scene of dead game and fowl that appears in the upper right corner.[40]

The image of the palace of Mariemont that can be seen in the background of the *Allegory of Touch, Hearing and Taste* must have also helped to define Rubens' origin and identity for his Spanish viewers. Mariemont was one of the palaces of the archdukes Albert and Isabella. It could be recognized in Madrid because it had already appeared in the background of the *Portrait of the Infanta Isabella*, one of the pendant portraits of the archdukes that had arrived in Spain via Rodrigo Calderón. The association with the sovereign princes of the Spanish Netherlands is reinforced by the reproduction of a double portrait that Rubens painted of them at the lower right of the *Sight and Smell*. The references to Albert, who had died in 1621, and to his wife, Isabella, must have acted in Madrid as a reminder of Rubens' strong link with the archdukes, his most important protectors and patrons.

In January 19, 1625, a large canvas depicting *Achilles Discovered among the Daughters of Lycomedes* (Madrid, Prado; Fig. 12) was in the *Salón*

FIGURE 10

Jan Brueghel and others, *Allegory of Sight and Smell*. Madrid, Museo del Prado.

Nuevo or New Room of the Alcázar, one of the main ceremonial rooms of the royal palace in Madrid. This painting, according to Rubens' own description, had been painted by his best pupil – undoubtedly Van Dyck – and then extensively retouched by Rubens himself.[41] The painting may have entered Spain as early as 1618, but the exact date and the way this occurred is not known. It is first documented in a letter of April 1618, when Rubens attempted to sell it to the English ambassador and art dealer Sir Dudley Carleton. Pushing for the sale, the artist stressed the beauty of the female figures in the scene by stating that it was "full of many very beautiful girls" ("pieno de molte fanciulle bellissime").[42] This must be an allusion to the sensuality of the painting, defined by the exposed breasts of the two female figures on the left side of the sumptuous scene. The same feature may have played a role in the entry of the *Achilles* into the royal collection; throughout his life Philip IV greatly favored the erotic component of Rubens' vision of classical antiquity, and this may be seen as an early example of that pattern of collecting. The location of this painting in an important hall of the palace, the New Room, is a measure of its success at the Spanish court and indicates the rise of Rubens' reputation in Spain.[43] The mistaken attribution of the painting exclusively to Rubens, with no mention of Van Dyck, may be another sign of his growing reputation. Cassiano dal Pozzo refers to the painting as a work by Rubens, which must be a reflection of the standing of the picture at the court. Also, the scene is

FIGURE 11

Jan Brueghel and others, *Allegory of Touch, Hearing, and Taste*. Madrid, Museo del Prado.

attributed to Rubens alone again in the royal inventories of 1686 and 1700.[44]

The painting of *Achilles* is a feast of powerful forms, demonstrative gestures, and rich and seductive colors that shows Van Dyck at his most Rubensian moment. In his early career, when he worked in Rubens' studio from approximately 1615 to 1620, Van Dyck often tried to paint as much like his master as possible.[45] This must have been especially true when a painting was to be sold by Rubens himself, as is the case here, which explains the confusion in the court in Madrid about the attribution.

Because Madrid at the time considered this to be a painting by Rubens, and given the important location where it was exhibited in the Alcázar, we can assume that it played a significant role in defining Rubens' reputation there in the early years of the reign of Philip IV. The imposing presence of the figures, the sculptural pose of Achilles (disguised as a woman) with a raised sword, and the antique architectural setting make it the most spectacular scene of classical antiquity associated with Rubens that had reached Spain. As he had done earlier in religious paintings and in portraits, Rubens, the presumed author of the painting, again demonstrated to his Spanish patrons his ability to create a grand vision of a classical theme.

In late 1624 or early 1625, Rubens set to work on a sketch for a portrait of Gaspar de Guzmán, count-duke of Olivares (1587–1645), who was favorite minister, or *valido*, of King Philip IV. This sketch was intended to serve as a prototype for an engraving by Paul Pontius.[46] Even though this may not have been an official project, in hindsight it was an important undertaking: it was Rubens' first direct involvement with the court in Madrid since the *Equestrian Portrait of the Duke of Lerma* of 1603, and it also provided his first contact with Velázquez, as some paintings by the Spanish artist were used as models.[47] In the first stage of the development of the scene, Rubens painted a sketch of a portrait of Olivares surrounded by allegorical representations (Fig. 13). As has been noted in the literature, the image of the count-duke in this preparatory sketch is similar to a portrait by, or after, Velázquez now in the Museo de Arte, São Paolo; Rubens must have used a version of that portrait as a source for his sketch.[48] The portrait of Olivares in this first design for the print was soon replaced by a new one, which appears in the final engraving (Fig. 14). The face in the second version of the sketch is similar to a portrait of the count-duke that Velázquez painted in 1625 (New York, The Hispanic Society of America; Fig. 15). Given the fact that the print shows the sitter dressed in armor, another prototype may also have been used – a lost portrait of Olivares in armor that was painted by Velázquez probably in late 1625.[49] There is a drawing by Velázquez (Fig. 16) that may also have assisted Rubens in his design for the print. Even though it shows Olivares facing the viewer frontally, and not slightly turned to one side as he appears in the print by Pontius, the Spanish minister is dressed in armor and is surrounded by an oval frame of the type often used in prints.[50]

The inscription on the printed portrait of Olivares reads: "Ex Archetypo Velasquez-P. P. Rubenius ornavit et Dedicavit L. M.-Paul. Pontius sculp." confirming that the final image was based on an image by Velázquez, with the framing allegories designed by Rubens. Once finished, the print was sent to Madrid, where it arrived before August 8, 1626. On that date, Olivares acknowledged its receipt in a warm and personal letter to the painter; he expressed condolences for the death of Isabella Brandt, Rubens' first wife, and told the painter about losses in his own family.[51]

Olivares had a keen sense of the importance of creating an image of leadership, and his use of painters and other artists to fabricate the image of the monarchy was at the forefront of his era.[52] One can

FIGURE 12

Van Dyck and Rubens, *Achilles Discovered among the Daughters of Lycomedes*. Madrid, Museo del Prado.

FIGURE 13

Rubens, *Don Gaspar de Guzmán, Count-Duke of Olivares*. Oil sketch. Brussels, Musées Royaux des Beaux Arts (Copyright A. C. L., Brussels).

FIGURE 14

Facing page

Paulus Pontius, *Don Gaspar de Guzmán, Count-Duke of Olivares*. Engraving. The Metropolitan Museum of Art, Gift of Junius S. Morgan, 1923 (23.106.57).

imagine the minister being pleased (as indeed his correspondence shows that he was) by the symphony of allegorical elements that surround his likeness, all unified in praise of the guidance that he provided to Hesperus, the six-pointed star that symbolizes Spain.

The exact origin of this print is not documented. The facts that Olivares was the sitter and the prototype was by Velázquez, whose early career at the court was promoted by Olivares, suggest that it was ordered by the count-duke. But Olivares' letter to Rubens upon reception of the engraving indicates that this may not have been the case. The

HESPERE, QVIS CÆLO LVCET FELICIOR IGNIS?
PHILIPPI IV. MVNIFICENTIA.
Bætis OLIVIFERÆ debet cui serta CORONÆ,
Palladiâ clarus non semel arte Comes:
Sic gerit os, magno sic pectora fida Monarchæ
Sæcula cui nullum prisca dedêre parem.
Elucet vultu Probitas, frontique serenæ
Pondus adest: mixtâ stat Grauitate Lepor.
Clauso nec vnius Prudentia finibus Orbis,
Publica quâ Regnis vindice nata Salus.
O Superi, longos fœcunda virescat in annos,
Augustosque beet mitis OLIVA Lares,
Quæ partis latè Terrâque Marique triumphis
Pacificas toto spargat in Orbe comas.

FIGURE 15

Velázquez, *Count-Duke of Olivares*. New York, The Hispanic Society of America.

Spanish nobleman wrote to the painter: "I appreciate the love that you have for me. A good sign of it is the portrait that you have ordered printed."[53] This indicates that the print may have been a project originated by Rubens himself. It is easy to see why the painter would have done this. By looking for clients in high places Rubens could further his career as an artist. He may also have been motivated by his increasing interest in diplomatic affairs. Shortly before the date of the print of Olivares, Rubens had become involved in a series of negotiations intended to prolong the Twelve Year Truce between Spain and the United Provinces, which had expired on April 9, 1621.[54] Rubens, acting as an agent of the infanta Isabella (who had become sole governor of the Spanish Netherlands after the death of her husband on July 13, 1621) established contacts with Jan Brandt, a cousin of his wife who resided in Holland and represented the Dutch.[55] The negotiations to prolong the truce were unsuccessful from early on and came to a defi-

FIGURE 16

Velázquez, *Count-Duke of Olivares*. Drawing. Ecole des Beaux-Arts, Paris.

nite end on April 23, 1625, with the death of the stadholder Maurice of Nassau, who the rulers of the Spanish Netherlands had earlier selected as the most viable representative of the United Provinces. Soon after the collapse of this affair, Rubens was engaged in a new set of negotiations, this time an attempt to bring about a peace between Spain and England that would eventually lead to the painter's second visit to the Spanish court.

Rubens certainly made use of his position as an artist in order to advance the treaty between Spain and England. In 1626 and 1627, he negotiated the sale of his collection of paintings and antiques with emissaries of the duke of Buckingham, the favorite of King Charles I of England.[56] An early biography of the painter, purportedly written by his nephew Philip Rubens, suggests that the cause of the sale was political, because Rubens was asked by the archduchess Isabella to "cherish and nourish the benevolent favor of the Duke of Buckingham," undoubtedly to further the discussions of peace between Spain and England in which Rubens was then engaged.[57] The print of Olivares, if originated by the painter, could be a similar case of Rubens making use of his artistic talent and reputation in order to secure the favor of another of the leading political figures of the time.

The print of Olivares is the only occasion when Rubens designed a portrait of the Spanish favorite. Given the fact that Olivares had ample opportunity to commission works from the Flemish painter in the following years (during Rubens' trip to Spain in 1628–1629, or during the next decade), the question arises as to why he chose not to do so.

One possible answer to this question is that Rubens' portraits did not correspond to Olivares' taste, at least not when they included his own image. A problem with this assumption is that the known images of the Spanish minister commissioned by himself do not conform to a single artistic idiom. The two portraits by Velázquez in São Paolo and in the Hispanic Society of America (Fig. 15), mentioned above, are markedly different from Rubens' style of portraiture in the directness with which they represent the sitter. Other known representations of Olivares, such as Velázquez' *Riding Lesson* (Fig. 7) and his *Equestrian Portrait of the Count Duke of Olivares* (Madrid, Prado), are more elaborate emblems of the ruler, even if they do not reach the rhetorical level characteristic of Rubens. Another painting that includes a portrait of Olivares is the *Recapture of Bahía*, painted by Juan Bautista Maino for the Buen Retiro palace in 1634–1635.[58] In this picture, Olivares, King Philip IV, and the goddess Minerva all stand over the allegorical figures of Heresy, Discord, and Treachery. The language of allegory is more overt – and closer to Rubens – in this work than in the cases mentioned above, which is proof of the range of Olivares' taste when considering the representation of his own image.

A better explanation for the fact that Olivares never commissioned a portrait from Rubens after the engraving of 1624–1625 may be his limited taste for the art of painting. Even though the count-duke could promote painting as a means of propaganda in the service of the king and occasionally of himself, he is conspicuously absent from the roll of important collectors of paintings in the Spanish court. The reason for this is that, on a personal level, the count-duke of Olivares was more interested in books than in paintings. He was a learned man who frequented writers and humanists and amassed a fabulous collection of books and manuscripts.[59] Although the print designed by Rubens may be a representative portrait for a man with such interests – the base on which the portrait rests is inscribed with a poem by the Antwerp humanist and friend of Rubens Jan Gaspar Gevaerts, and the allegories that flank the bust portrait seem appropriate for a man drawn to the conceptual wit of poetic images and literary conceits – it does not seem to have changed Olivares' preference for the written over the visual language.

Rubens' growing reputation in Spain in the mid-1620s can be inferred from a little-known commission from Seville of 1624. In a letter of April 21 of that year, the *racionero* (or prebend) Diego Vidal de Liendo wrote from Seville to the canon Don Gregorio Sarmiento in Antwerp asking him to purchase a series of paintings, among them a "Veronica by the famous painter Peter Paul Rubens, by his own hand, for a person who understands the art of painting, who wishes to have it as an original among other paintings by famous masters." The painting was to be paid for by Diego Vidal and sent to Seville.[60] There is no other record of this work, and it is unknown whether it was ever executed. Diego Vidal the Younger was *racionero* of the cathedral of Seville from 1602 until his death in 1648.[61] He is also known to have been an amateur painter and to have personally known Murillo, and he owned one painting attributed to Titian, another to Bosch, and an engraving by Dürer (but nothing by Rubens). From the letter reproduced above, it appears that the *Veronica* was destined for a third person, a collector, which indicates that the *racionero* was acting as an agent. It is unclear if the author of the letter was asking to purchase a Veronica that he already knew about or if he hoped to have it painted specifically for the occasion. Either way, this document is relevant as proof of the spread of interest in Rubens to Seville at this early date, and of the high status enjoyed by the painter. We do not know, however, if anything came of the commission, or if it ever reached Rubens.

The printed portrait of Olivares and possibly the equestrian portrait of Calderón are the only scenes by Rubens that appear to have been painted specifically for Spanish patrons between the artist's first visit to Spain of 1603–1604 and the middle years of the decade of 1620. During the same period, Rubens was directly involved in the sale of a painting to Spain in only one additional case, the *Achilles*, if at all. In only one commission, the group including six scenes by Rubens ordered by the queen in 1623, were paintings sent to Spain as a result of a request from that country. Thus, we can conclude that the link between Rubens and Spain had not been firmly established at that point. In other words, there was no serious effort to collect works by Rubens, and the painter was not focusing special attention on Spanish clients. However, it is also apparent that the appreciation for Rubens was gradually gaining strength; whereas it was almost nonexistent in the second decade of the century, the arrival on the Spanish throne of Philip IV in 1621 seems to have initiated a new phase in the relationship, as witnessed by the queen's commission and the print of Olivares.

In the two intervening years between August of 1626, when Olivares received his engraved portrait, and the arrival of Rubens in Madrid in the summer of 1628, the painter was busy with two projects destined for Spain. One was the design of a series of tapestries of the Eucharist that were to decorate the convent of the Descalzas Reales in Madrid. The second is a lesser-known set of eight paintings for the Alcázar that the painter brought to Madrid when he visited there in 1628. Both projects represent an important step in Rubens' relationship with Spain. The Eucharist tapestries definitely, and the group of eight paintings probably, were commissioned specifically to be sent to Madrid, and both were installed in very prominent locations in the Spanish capital. All together, the two commissions included a large number of scenes, many of which were of the highest artistic quality. In short, they were the most important artistic projects Rubens had undertaken for Spanish clients up to the time of his second visit to Spain.

The Eucharist Series and the Patronage of the Infanta Isabella

The history of the Eucharist Series is well known and will be only briefly summarized here.[62] The series was commissioned for the convent of the Descalzas Reales in Madrid in 1625 or 1626 by the infanta Isabella Clara Eugenia. The series consisted of twenty tapestries executed after the designs by Rubens (Fig. 17). They depict scenes exalting the Eucharist and were intended to decorate the chapel of the convent during Eucharist feasts and other special occasions. The infanta paid Rubens the very high price of 30,000 florins (in addition to "some pearls") for his designs for the tapestries, and she also paid close to 100,000 florins for the actual tapestries.[63] The finished set was shipped to Madrid on July 19, 1628, and must have arrived there during the month of August, barely a few weeks before Rubens himself entered the city on his second visit to Spain. In addition to the tapestries themselves, other works were produced during the preliminary stages of their design and execution. By the last quarter of the century, eight *modelli* (Fig. 18) and six cartoons for the series had made their way to Spain.[64]

The convent of the Descalzas had been a favorite retreat for members of the royal family in Spain since its foundation in 1556. Isabella had spent long periods of time in the Descalzas before her departure for the Netherlands in 1599. During these periods she became familiar with the combination of gravity and luxury that resulted from the frequent donations of works of art to the convent by members of the royal family who professed there.[65] As a consequence of these gifts, the convent of the Descalzas became a showcase for art and a reflection of the collecting taste of the Hapsburg family. Isabella's commission of the series from Rubens fits well into this context; when the tapestries arrived at the convent in the summer of 1628, they would have seemed, not an oddity, but part of a well-established pattern of collecting. The subject of the triumph of the Eucharist reflects another Hapsburg tradition, the devotion to and defense of the Eucharist. There is an important Spanish component in this tradition, best represented in the kneeling figures of the royal family at El Escorial by Pompeo Leoni (which Rubens had seen on his first trip to Spain and had used as a source for his painting of *The Gonzaga Adoring the Trinity* when he returned to Mantua), but it is part of an international Hapsburg imagery and is not defined exclu-

FIGURE 17

J. Raes, J. Fobert, and H. Vervoert, after Rubens, *The Defenders of the Eucharist.* Tapestry. Patrimonio Nacional. Madrid, Convent of the Descalzas Reales.

sively by the Spanish branch of the family. In the Eucharist project, the general subject matter must have been chosen by the infanta, who probably left the specifics of each scene to Rubens. His designs are drawn from his own knowledge of this particular Hapsburg tradition.[66]

The sheer size of the tapestries in this series – the larger scenes measure nearly five meters in height – and the spectacular figures and actions taking place in them, provided the Spanish capital with one of its most sumptuous sets of images, and must have endowed the religious ceremonies at the Descalzas with considerable magnificence. Unfortunately, we have no direct references of the specific occasions when the tapestries could be publicly viewed in Madrid. However, the convent of the Descalzas was frequently used for special religious events and was one of the primary retreats for the royal family and its entourage when they were out of the Alcázar. Even if the tapestries were only hung on special occasions, they must have been well known, given the importance of the setting. Indeed, the Eucharist series enjoyed considerable fame in Spain; the insistence with which Philip IV asked for the cartoons from Brussels in the late 1640s,[67] the arrival in Spain of some of the *modelli*, and the abundant copies recorded in the second half of the century are best explained if the existence of these tapestries was well publicized. The numerous prints after scenes in the series that circulated in Spain and were copied by local painters are witness to the same popularity. It is also noteworthy that this success was not limited to Spain; Bellori dedicated extensive passages to this series of tapestries in his *Vite* of 1672.[68]

The commissioning of the tapestries for the Descalzas Reales exemplifies the instrumental role that the infanta Isabella played in making Rubens and his work known in Spain. One of the scenes in the series, *The Defenders of the Eucharist* (Fig. 17), served as a reminder of this role for those who could view it, as one of the figures included in the image, Saint Clare, is rendered with the features of the infanta. Isabella's links to her homeland and family remained strong throughout her life; the person at the head of the Spanish monarchy after 1621, King Philip IV, was her nephew. Together with her husband, Albert of Austria – who also had strong ties to Spain, where he had spent an important part of his youth – Isabella had been Rubens' main patron since the time of the painter's return from Italy to Flanders in 1608.[69] In September of 1609, the archdukes had named Rubens their court painter, allowing him to

FIGURE 18

Rubens, *The Triumph of the Church. Modello* for a tapestry from the Eucharist series. Madrid, Museo del Prado.

remain at his home in Antwerp rather than reside at the court in Brussels.

After the death of the archduke in 1621, Rubens became one of Isabella's closest confidants. The relationship between the painter and the infanta involved political affairs more often than artistic ones. However, as Isabella's court painter, Rubens also worked on some of her artistic projects. In the early 1620s he probably continued to supply paintings for the decoration of the archduchess's palaces, as he had done in the previous decade.[70] In 1625, he painted a portrait of Isabella dressed in the habit of a poor Clare, which was to serve as her official image. He also designed a version of this portrait that was engraved by Paul Pontius (Fig. 19).[71] Isabella continued her patronage of Rubens until her death in 1633. Among other works, she asked him to paint a series of portraits of members of the Spanish royal family in 1628, and circa 1630–1632 she commissioned from him the monumental *St. Ildefonso Triptych* for the church of Sint Jacob op de Coudenberg in Brussels.[72]

Of all Rubens' artistic projects for the infanta, none was as large or as opulent as the Eucharist series. The gratitude that Isabella felt toward the convent where she had often stayed in her youth must have reinforced other factors to bring about this commission around the years 1625–1626. One contributing factor may have been the close contact between the painter and the infanta that resulted from Rubens acting as her diplomatic agent in the early 1620s. Another may have been the growing presence of Rubens' works in European courts, most notably in Paris, where from 1622 to 1625 the artist had worked on a large cycle of paintings commemorating the life of Isabella's friend, the French queen Maria de' Medici. This may have made Isabella feel that Madrid, too, should be able to boast an important series by her court painter.

The Eight Paintings for the New Room

The second commission for Spain undertaken by Rubens immediately preceding his 1628 visit to Madrid was a group of eight paintings destined for the Alcázar. These scenes almost certainly arrived in Madrid with Rubens himself, and any impact they may have had on creating an awareness of Rubens' art in the Spanish capital can only have happened after the summer of 1628. Within the master's oeuvre, however, they belong to the previous years, and for that reason they will be discussed here.

This set of eight paintings is documented by Pacheco, who writes in his *Arte de la Pintura*: "[Rubens] brought to the Majesty of our Catholic king Philip IV eight paintings of different subjects and sizes, which are installed in the new room, among other famous pictures."[73] The eight paintings were not gifts by the painter, as has often been assumed in the literature, but rather were commissioned for the king, either personally or through the infanta, who handled the payments. In a letter written upon Rubens' arrival in Madrid, Averardo Medici, the Tuscan ambassador, informed his correspondent that the artist had arrived in the court with eight of his paintings, which had been ordered for the king.[74] On December 22, 1629, the council of finance in the Netherlands asked the infanta about a debt to Rubens of 7,500 pounds for paintings that he "made or had made by order of Your Highness for the service of His Majesty, and sent to Spain during the past year."[75] The infanta answered that the price had been previously arranged and should be paid, and that the paintings had been finished and were in Spain.[76] On September 22, 1630, the king wrote to Isabella that Rubens was owed money for some paintings that he had delivered to Madrid.[77] Rubens actually seems to have been paid on March 18, 1630,[78] but the king was unaware of that, or perhaps payment had not yet reached the painter.

The commission included the following works: *Reconciliation of Jacob and Esau; Gaius Mucius Scaevola before Porsenna; Samson Breaking the Jaws of a Lion; David Strangling a Bear; Satyr Squeezing Grapes; Nymphs Filling the Horn of Plenty; Calydonian Boar Hunt*; and *Diana and Nymphs Hunting Deer*.[79] Of these eight scenes, only three have been identified with extant works, all of them high-quality, autograph paintings by Rubens: the *Reconciliation of Jacob and Esau* is in Schleissheim (Staatsgalerie, on deposit from Munich, Alte Pinakothek; Fig. 20),[80] the *Samson Breaking the Jaws of a Lion* is in a private collection in Madrid (Fig. 21),[81] and the *Nymphs Filling the Horn of Plenty* is in the Prado Museum (Fig. 22).[82] One other painting, the *Satyr Squeezing Grapes*, may be a workshop piece in the Gemäldegalerie, Dresden (Fig. 23).[83] The rest of the paintings have either been lost or are unidentified; we can form some idea of their appearance through prints, copies, and sketches.[84]

The group of eight paintings brought by Rubens to Madrid is more coherent in structure and thematic content than is often assumed and therefore must have been devised according to a predetermined plan.[85] The eight paintings are organized in four pairs, which are complementary in size and subject matter, as the royal inventories show.[86] In addition, these paintings have a certain degree of thematic unity; as Orso has shown, they should be interpreted as symbolic references to the virtues of the Spanish rulers.[87] The paintings of *Jacob and Esau* and *Gaius Mucius Scaevola* are symbols of reconciliation and courage. The former, a story taken from Genesis (33:1–16), shows the moment of the peaceful reconciliation between Jacob, the third of the great Hebrew patriarchs, and his twin brother, Esau. The latter represents an ancient

FIGURE 19

Paulus Pontius, after Rubens, *Infanta Isabella Dressed in the Habit of a Poor Clare*. Engraving. Vitoria, Instituto Ephialte.

story of the Roman Gaius Mucius, who demonstrated his courage to his captor, the Etruscan king Porsenna, by holding his arm in the flames of a fire. The paintings of David, the shepherd boy who would become king of Israel, and of Samson, the Old Testament hero of supernatural strength, represent the struggle between virtuous men and dangerous animals. The *Satyr Squeezing Grapes* and the *Three Nymphs Filling the Horn of Plenty* are interpreted by Orso as references to abundance, which results from good government. The first of these scenes includes one adult and two young satyrs, mythic creatures with goatlike features often used by Rubens as personifications of sexual excess. The tigress and satyrs were part of the retinue of Bacchus, god of wine, who was commonly associated with licentiousness. The presence in the scene of two generations of satyrs and of felines may be intended to underscore the theme of the painting: the fertility that results from licentious behavior.[88] The picture of the *Three Nymphs*, now in the Prado, is one of the most sensuous and beautiful scenes painted by Rubens for Philip IV. In this case, the reference to abundance seems to be expressed in more frankly sexual terms, as the cornucopia placed between the legs of

FIGURE 20

Rubens, *Reconciliation of Jacob and Esau.* Schleissheim, Staatsgalerie, on deposit from Munich, Alte Pinakothek.

one of the figures appears to represent the male member. The sexual symbolism of this cornucopia underscores its use as a symbol of abundance.[89]

The subject matter of the two remaining paintings in the group that we are dealing with, the *Calydonian Boar Hunt* and *Diana and Nymphs Hunting Deer*, is harder to explain in the context of the decoration of the New Room. As Orso has suggested, they may refer to the hunt as an ideal activity for princes, because it provided them with a chance to train and to display their valor in times of peace.[90] The devotion of Philip IV to the chase may have also played a role in their inclusion in the group.

In 1636, the eight paintings in this commission were inventoried in the New Room, where they probably hung from the time of their installation in the summer of 1629.[91] The New Room was the main focus of the decoration of the Alcázar in the first years following the

FIGURE 21

Rubens, *Samson Breaking the Jaws of a Lion*. Madrid, private collection.

accession to the throne of Philip IV in 1621.[92] At that time, the king ordered some of the most important paintings in the royal collection transferred there from other locations. The *Achilles Discovered among the Daughters of Lycomedes* painted by Van Dyck and retouched by Rubens was also installed in the New Room in the 1620s, as seen earlier, and Rubens' *Adoration of the Magi* was probably also placed in the same location when the king acquired it after the fall of Rodrigo Calderón.[93] As early as 1625, and increasingly thereafter, new works of art were commissioned for this prominent chamber in the Alcázar. In 1625, Velázquez painted his now lost *Equestrian Portrait of Philip IV* for the New Room, and in early 1627 a competition was called between the king's painters to paint another scene for the same location (the competition was won by Velázquez with a picture of the *Expulsion of the Moriscos*, which has also been lost). Sometime between 1626 and 1628, Philip IV commissioned his first paintings from Italy, also for this room, including works by Domenichino, Orazio Gentileschi and his daughter Artemisia, among others.[94] Throughout this process, the New Room grew into a Hall of Princely Virtue, intended to display the achievements and honor of the Hapsburg rulers, represented through the history paintings, mythologies, biblical scenes, and portraits that were assembled there. In view of the nature of the New Room and the process of decoration it was undergoing, it is safe to assume that the

FIGURE 23

Workshop of Rubens, *Satyr Squeezing Grapes*. Dresden, Gemäldegalerie Alte Meister.

eight pictures were commissioned from Rubens specifically for that location.[95]

The exact manner in which the commission was devised and developed is unclear. As we have seen, the infanta Isabella handled the payments for it. In the early and mid-1620s, just prior to this project, Rubens was working for Isabella both as her diplomatic agent and as an artist for the design of the Eucharist series. This suggests that she may have played some role in the origin of the paintings for the New Room, perhaps by indicating to Madrid the suitability of the painter for the project. When Isabella was consulted about the amount of money owed to Rubens for these pictures, she answered that the price had been agreed upon before they were painted.[96] This indicates that some of the specifications for the commission must have been set beforehand, such as the number of paintings to be executed, their dimensions, and possibly also the themes to be depicted. Some of these instructions, especially those concerning the dimensions of the canvases, had to come from Madrid, as that was the intended destination for the paintings.

FIGURE 22

Facing page

Rubens and Snyders, *Nymphs Filling the Horn of Plenty*. Madrid, Museo del Prado.

It is not known who in the Spanish capital may have specified these requirements to Rubens, but some names may be suggested. The first and most obvious is the king himself, for whom the paintings were destined. As mentioned above, in the years 1626–1628 he commissioned several paintings from Italy to decorate the New Room.[97] It is likely that Rubens' commission was part of the same decoration campaign and therefore that it originated with the king. At this early stage in his reign, Philip IV may well have made decisions regarding the decoration of the New Room with his trusted favorite, the count-duke of Olivares. Olivares was firmly in command of the affairs of the Spanish court during the second half of the 1620s. He saw it as part of his duty to groom the young king in the appreciation of the arts and was well aware of the value of patronage of the arts as a means to add splendor to the monarchy. In the 1630s he was responsible for the decoration of the Buen Retiro, the new summer palace that was built for the king in the outskirts of Madrid, and some evidence suggests that he was also involved in the decoration of the New Room in the Alcázar.[98] The contest mentioned above between the painters of the court to produce a large composition for this room was decided in 1627 by two judges who were members of Olivares' circle: the Italian nobleman Giovanni Battista Crescenzi and the painter Juan Bautista Maino. Furthermore, the program of the decoration of the chamber was most forcefully and clearly expressed during the years when Olivares was in power. Considering these facts, it seems probable that Olivares played some role at the Spanish end of the commission from Rubens of paintings for the New Room.

The possibility that one of Olivares' protégés, the painter Velázquez, may have been involved in some capacity in this commission should also be mentioned. In his biography of the Sevillian painter, his father-in-law, Pacheco, stated that Rubens and Velázquez had corresponded sometime before 1628.[99] Pacheco may have been referring to an earlier project, the engraving of the count-duke of Olivares by Paul Pontius that was designed by Rubens using a model provided by Velázquez. But the possibility, suggested by some authors, that the correspondence between the two painters concerned the paintings for the New Room cannot be discarded.[100] Later in his career Velázquez played an active role in the decoration of the Alcázar and the hanging of the royal collection of paintings. The commission for the New Room may have provided an early opportunity for some training in palace decoration.[101]

Exactly when the project originated is not known. It may have been initiated as soon as 1625 or in the following two or three years, when the decoration of the New Room was under way. If the commission was awarded before early July of 1628, it was not at first intended that Rubens should deliver the paintings to Spain, because the idea of calling him to Madrid was only proposed then. Perhaps the commission was actually prompted by the decision to bring the painter to the Spanish court. If so, the group of paintings had to be created hastily, probably in less than two months, between July 4, 1628, when Rubens was summoned to Madrid, and the end of August, when he embarked on the trip.[102] Even though this seems too short a time for the artist to have produced eight paintings of sufficient quality for the king of Spain, it was not impossible for him to have done so. We know that Rubens used assistants, as is indicated by a report from the council of finance mentioned above, where the paintings are referred to as "faict et faict faire" by the master.[103] He may also have used some paintings in his studio that were already finished, complementing them with new works. The two mythological hunting scenes may be a case in point; this would explain the lack of consonance of their subject matter with the rest of the paintings in the group. Likewise, the paintings of *Jacob and Esau* and *Gaius Mucius Scaevola before Porsenna* are based on a drawing now in Berlin executed by Rubens circa 1617–1619, which suggests that they might have been painted before they were intended for the New Room.[104]

The commission of eight paintings for the New Room was an important milestone in the relationship between the painter and the Spanish court. This is the first commission received by Rubens that was specifically intended for Philip IV, and probably ordered by him. It is also the first of several large groups of paintings that Rubens painted for the Spanish king. Why did such an important commission emerge at this point? Keeping in mind that it is not likely that a single cause can explain the origin of this project, some suggestions can be put forth.

The first is precedent. The paintings by Rubens already in Spain when the project was developed may have created a taste for the master's art. Perhaps also, as in the case of the infanta Isabella and the tapestries for the Descalzas Reales, Rubens' growing reputation and the knowledge of some of his recently created ensembles had reached Spain by the time of this commission. As early as 1611, the Flemish master was directing a workshop so successful that he could say: "From all sides applications reach me. Some young men remain here for several years with other masters, awaiting a vacancy in my studio."[105] By 1620 Rubens' fame allowed him to count among his clients many prominent citizens of the Spanish Netherlands, and some from beyond. In the following years his reputation grew even more. In 1620–1621 he prepared the thirty-nine scenes for the decoration of the new Jesuit Church in Antwerp, and around the same time he was discussing the decoration of the new Banqueting Hall in Whitehall Palace for Charles I of England, which was later postponed.[106] From 1622 to 1625, Rubens worked on the series of *The Life of Maria de' Medici* for the Luxembourg Palace in Paris.[107] Given the intensity of the diplomatic relations between the French and Spanish courts at this time, and the fact that the

French queen, Anne of Austria, was the sister of Philip IV, and that Philip's wife, Isabella, was the sister of the French king Louis XIII, Philip must have known of this series.[108] By 1627 Rubens had painted another important work for another prominent European courtier: the monumental equestrian portrait of the duke of Buckingham.[109] News of some of these events may have ignited a sense of competition in Madrid, making the king and his entourage feel that Rubens' work should be better represented in the Spanish capital. This in turn may have prompted the commission for the New Room.

Rubens himself may have been a factor in originating this commission. His artistic endeavors were sometimes linked with his diplomatic activities.[110] An example of this was mentioned earlier: in 1626 and 1627 Rubens used his artistic profession to gain access to Buckingham. He may have done the same with the king of Spain. The commission for the New Room in the Alcázar dates from a time when Rubens was acting as an agent of the Spanish Crown working toward a peace with England. Although we do not know that he had any part in initiating the project, he may have, and if he did his action would have strengthened his ties with the Spanish court, with potential benefits for him in both artistic and nonartistic matters.

Rubens' Social Merits

In the seventeenth century and thereafter, accounts of Rubens' position in the history of art in Spain make it clear that his reputation and exemplary role resulted not only from his art but also from his social standing; he was honored by kings and noblemen, and he attained noble status himself.[111] The first extraordinary privileges received by Rubens from the Spanish administration date to the 1620s. On September 30, 1623, the infanta Isabella issued an order granting Rubens a monthly pension of ten *escudos*; the stipend resulted from Rubens' merit and from the services he had provided to the king of Spain, and it was intended to allow him to continue providing them.[112] In all likelihood, he was being rewarded for acting as an agent of the infanta in the attempt to prolong the Twelve Year Truce after it expired in 1621; his engagement in this affair is documented in two letters, one of them dated September 30, 1623, the day he received the pension.[113]

Two aspects of the infanta's order on behalf of Rubens are worth emphasizing. First, the document demonstrates that the favor conferred upon the painter resulted from his proximity to the infanta Isabella and from his service to the king. Rubens' service to the Spanish monarchy and his relationship with persons in high places would be mentioned frequently by those who reported on his career and his success in seventeenth-century Spain. Second, as Gachard noticed long ago, the stipend ordered by the infanta was not to be paid from the local coffer (as was the case with the salary assigned to him when he entered the service of the archdukes in 1609), but rather from funds of the Spanish army in Flanders.[114] This documents the first instance of Rubens' extra-artistic activities on behalf of the Spanish monarchy.

Rubens' correspondence relating to this and other instances when he was involved in political events shows that he had a genuine interest in these matters, stemming from a profound love for his homeland. But there were also personal gains to be made by an involvement in politics in the service of the infanta and the Spanish king, as the pension that he received in September of 1623 shows. Four months later a request was presented to the king on behalf of the painter, this time asking for his ennoblement. Coming as it did at the time of his participation in discussions with the United Provinces, we must assume that this second request resulted, at least in part, from the same events that prompted the pension.

On January 29, 1624, the petition asking for Rubens' ennoblement was presented to King Philip IV by Don Iñigo de Brizuela, bishop of Segovia and president of the council of Netherlands in Madrid.[115] According to Brizuela, whose letter to the king shows that he took a personal interest in the matter and that he supported the petition, Rubens based his claims on the services that he and his family had provided to the Spanish Netherlands and the Spanish Crown; on his dexterity in painting and his learnedness; on his fame, which had spread throughout the courts of Europe; and finally on his wealth. The petition succeeded, and the king ennobled Rubens on June 5, 1624.

There are several interesting aspects to this petition. The person who endorsed the request, Fray Iñigo de Brizuela, almost certainly knew Rubens. He had returned from Flanders to Spain in 1621 with a painting attributed to Rubens, as seen earlier in this chapter, and was confessor to the archduke Albert, a high post at a time when Rubens was court painter. Also, like Rubens, Brizuela had taken part in the attempts of the court in Brussels to extend the twelve-year truce, [116] which further suggests a link between the petition for Rubens' noble status and those negotiations.

The petition for ennoblement opens by referring to Rubens' position as court painter to the infanta Isabella, and shows how important the link between the artist and the regent was for Philip IV. The mention of the infanta, and Brizuela's involvement in the petition, demonstrate the importance of the Flemish–Spanish connection in establishing Rubens' artistic position in Spain. As a citizen of the Spanish Netherlands active in affairs of diplomacy and politics, Rubens met with officials of the Spanish administration, who were often Spaniards. As we have seen before and will see again, he came out of these meetings having made contacts with figures who later became patrons and clients, and who played an important role in introducing his art into Spain.

Rubens' quest for ennoblement has been explained as testimony to his desire to improve the status of his profession.[117] This is probably true, but less specific reasons also need to be considered. The desire to become a member of the nobility was a natural aspiration of the time, especially for someone with the wealth, reputation, and connections that Rubens had earned. The painter would have agreed with an anonymous contemporary from Spain, who stated that, "according to the customs of this century, [nobility] is not only convenient, it is necessary."[118]

In spite of the importance of the achievement, Rubens' newly gained status must be put into perspective. Even though he was now a nobleman, he remained at the lower end of this privileged group. In the seventeenth century, those who received letters of nobility in reward for services to the Crown – known in Flanders as *noblesse de concession* and in Spain as *nobleza de privilegio* – formed the lower ranks of the class, below those who had inherited their status. The frequent distinction made at the time between the inherited nobility and the other nobles resulted from the growing numbers of the latter, who were often no wealthier than the middle classes. "Men take the view that persons ennobled by letters or dignities are not as estimable as nobles by lineage," wrote the Frenchman Charles Loyseau in 1610.[119]

Rubens' social standing also remained compromised by his profession as an artist. A confrontation that took place in 1633 between Rubens and one of the leading Flemish aristocrats, Philip Charles d'Arenberg, duke of Aarschot, illustrates this. The duke, rebuking Rubens for not showing him the proper respect at a time when they were both involved in negotiations with the United Provinces, wrote to the painter: "I should be very glad that you should learn for the future how persons in your position should write to those of my rank" – and this came after Rubens had been knighted by both Charles I and Philip IV.[120] Also telling is a statement made by Philip IV three years after he had granted Rubens his noble privileges. When it was suggested to him in 1627 that the artist would represent Spain in a round of diplomatic negotiations, the king saw it as a "great discredit" due to Rubens' occupation as a painter, an apprehension that was shared even by Rubens' closest patron, the infanta Isabella.[121]

Regardless of how others felt, receiving letters of nobility from the king was an important step for Rubens and a sign of his growing links with Spain during the decade of 1620. Both as a result of his paintings that had arrived in Spain, and of his rise in social status, by the time of his second visit to the Spanish court in 1628–1629, Rubens had already begun to carve out the preeminent position that he still occupies in the history of art in Spain.

CHAPTER THREE

Rubens' Second Visit to Spain, 1628–1629

His Majesty Knows Him and His Good Qualities

When Rubens visited Spain for the second time, in 1628, he had already established an important clientele in several European nations and had undertaken major commissions. Among the works he had completed in the last decade were the decoration of the Jesuit Church in Antwerp, the cycle of the *Life of Maria de' Medici* for the Luxembourg Palace in Paris, and the twelve tapestries depicting *The Life of the Emperor Constantine*, in addition to numerous monumental altarpieces and important portraits.[1] In the 1620s, as we saw in the previous chapter, Rubens had also become increasingly well known in Spain. The events that took place during his second stay in Madrid would further enhance his status.

The circumstances that led to Rubens' second Spanish visit and his activities during his nearly eight-month stay in Spain are recorded in the painter's own correspondence, and also through facts provided by Francisco Pacheco. Pacheco must have received much of his information from his son-in-law, Velázquez, who had recently become the main painter in the Spanish court.[2] Rubens' close ties to the infanta Isabella, whom he served as a personal adviser, and his English connections, caused him to become involved at least as early as 1627 in a series of political negotiations between Spain and England. Rubens' English contacts included Sir Dudley Carleton, who acted as English ambassador in The Hague and whom the painter had met in 1618 to negotiate an exchange of ancient sculptures for paintings. He was also acquainted with the duke of Buckingham, whom he had met in Paris in 1625 and to whom he had sold a large group of antiques and some paintings and jewels; and with the painter Balthasar Gerbier, a Zeelander by birth, who was in the household of the duke of Buckingham and acted as an agent for the duke at this time.[3]

Rubens served the infanta first as an intermediary and later as the main agent in the secret diplomatic efforts to achieve a peace treaty between England and Spain that were led by Isabella and the marquis Ambrogio Spinola, her principal minister and adviser.[4] Rubens' profession posed a problem for his official selection as a representative of Spain in these negotiations. As was seen at the end of the last chapter, in the summer of 1627 King Philip IV wrote to the infanta expressing his concern about the "great discredit" that the selection of a painter for this important mission would signify for the monarchy.[5] It may be said as a disclaimer for the king that he had not met Rubens and had no reason to believe that he was anything more than a talented painter – scant credentials for such high dealings. The infanta justified the painter's involvement by alluding to the early stage of the discussions and assured the king that, if the negotiations progressed, "direction will naturally be entrusted to persons of the highest rank."[6]

The prejudice expressed in these statements is a reflection of the rigid social structure of the time. However, it should not hide the fact that it was precisely Rubens' profession that led him to become involved in this round of diplomatic conversations in the first place: he had made his English connections as a consequence of his artistic dealings, and the fact that he was a painter had provided convenient anonymity in the early stages of the negotiations.

By the summer of 1628, Rubens had become so deeply involved in the discussions between Spain and England that his presence in Madrid was deemed necessary by Philip IV. On July 4 the council of state decided to summon the painter from Flanders, and on August 13 the infanta notified the king from Brussels that Rubens would leave for the Spanish capital shortly.[7] On August 28, 1628, Rubens was still in Antwerp dealing with issues relating to the estate of his deceased first wife, Isabella Brandt, but on September 1 it was reported that he had departed for Spain,[8] passing through France in great haste. By September 15 he had arrived in Madrid, where the secret nature of his visit had become known, as was reported by the papal nuncio and the ambassadors of Venice and Tuscany to their courts.[9]

Rubens' diplomatic activity in Madrid began with a meeting of the council of state on September 28, 1628, where he notified the council members of his negotiations and a decision was made to continue diplomatic discussions with England. The negotiations advanced slowly, in part because of news of the assassination of Buckingham, which had occurred in August. As a consequence of these circumstances, Rubens' mission in Spain was prolonged. When the discussions regained momentum in the early spring of 1629, Rubens was chosen to represent the Spanish position at the English court and to prepare the terrain for a permanent Spanish ambassador who would arrive in London to sign the treaty. On April 27, 1629, Philip IV wrote to the infanta of his decision to send the painter to London.[10] On that same day, the king appointed Rubens as secretary to the privy council of the Netherlands, an important post within the bureaucracy of the monarchy that provided the painter with a more official status with which to undertake his mission. This post, which Rubens' son Albert had the right to inherit, was worth 1,000 ducats each year. It was regarded as important enough by Gevaerts to be mentioned in the epitaph for Rubens that he wrote after the painter's death.[11]

On April 29, after receiving a ring worth 2,000 ducats from the king, which was delivered by the count-duke of Olivares, Rubens left Madrid with gifts for the infanta consisting of a rosary of calaba-tree wood studded with gold and diamonds; two pairs of *Guantes de ambar*, (gloves treated with ambergris, a substance formed in the intestine of the sperm whale that was highly esteemed for its scent); with two small boxes containing "piedras antiguas" (perhaps antique gems or cameos); and with a group of twelve paintings (and possibly also some additional works painted on copper plates). These were presumably some of the pictures that Rubens himself had painted in Madrid.[12] On his return trip from Spain, Rubens passed through Paris, arrived in Brussels on May 13, and was off to England by the end of the month to continue his mission, which he would later remember as having "succeeded most favorably."[13]

As has long been recognized, the reasons for Rubens' visit to the Spanish court in 1628 were political, not artistic; his correspondence reveals that he remained informed about the diplomatic issues that had brought him to Madrid. However, from the information provided by Pacheco, we can deduce that Rubens the artist was also very active in Madrid. As we have seen, he was preceded in Spain by the tapestries of the Eucharist series he had designed for the convent of the Descalzas Reales, and he himself arrived with eight paintings for the king, which would be installed in the New Room in the royal palace. Immediately following his arrival, and after reporting to Philip IV and Olivares, Rubens again turned to his profession, painting extensively.

While in Madrid, Rubens stayed in a suite of rooms in the Alcázar, where he was visited almost daily by the king, as documented by the painter's correspondence. On December 2, 1638, Rubens wrote to his friend Nicolas-Claude Peiresc: "[The king] takes an extreme delight in painting, and in my opinion this prince is endowed with excellent qualities. I know him already by personal contact, for since I have rooms in the palace, he comes to see me almost every day." Some weeks later, on December 29, he wrote to Jan Gevaerts: "The king alone arouses my sympathy. He is endowed by nature with all the gifts of body and spirit, for in my daily intercourse with him I have learned to know him thoroughly."[14] Rubens' studio was probably located in the northern wing of the royal palace. An *Equestrian Portrait of Philip IV*, which Rubens painted in Madrid and will be studied later, included a landscape background that corresponds with the view visible from the northern rooms of the Alcázar.[15] It seems plausible that the landscape Rubens included in the portrait was the one he could see while he was at work. The presence of this landscape in the portrait of the king also supports the possibility that Rubens shared his studio with Velázquez;

the Spanish artist is believed to have had his shop in a room located in the northern part of the Alcázar that was known as the Gallery of the North Wind.[16]

Rubens' artistic output during his visit to the court of Philip IV is carefully detailed by Pacheco, who mentions the following works: an indeterminate number of half-length portraits of the king, queen, and the infantes; five portraits of the king (one on horseback); a portrait of an infanta from the Descalzas and copies of it; "five or six" portraits of private citizens; copies of all the paintings by Titian in the royal collection (he specifically mentions twelve paintings and says that there are "others"); and copies of paintings (presumably by Titian) from other collections. He partially repainted his own *Adoration of the Magi*, Pacheco continues, and painted an *Immaculate Conception* for the marquis of Leganés, and a *St. John the Evangelist* for Don Jaime de Cárdenas.[17] Given this extensive list, one can only agree with Pacheco when he expresses his astonishment at Rubens' productivity. After the gradual increase in the number of his works in Spanish collections during the three preceding decades, the Flemish master was now about to become a major artistic force in Spain.

Portraits of the Royal Family

According to Pacheco, Rubens' first artistic enterprise after his arrival in Spain was to satisfy the wishes of the infanta Isabella, who had asked him to paint portraits of the royal family and have them sent to her in Brussels.[18] Rubens must have painted replicas after these copies upon his return to Antwerp, as versions of them are recorded in his collection. They may have been displayed for view in a portrait gallery in Rubens' house in Antwerp, thus proclaiming the painter's allegiance to the Hapsburg monarchy. They also must have served as models for commissions of official portraits.[19]

The portraits of the royal family consisted of images of the king, of "queens," and, according to Pacheco, of the "infantes," a term that encompasses all the sons and daughters of a king except for the heir to the throne; therefore, in this case it could include the infantes Carlos and Ferdinand and the infanta Doña María. This last person, the king's sister María, is probably not referred to by the term "infante" but rather by the plural use of the word "queens" in the sources; she was betrothed to Ferdinand, king of Hungary (the future Emperor Ferdinand III), in June of 1626, and was often referred to as queen of Hungary in the Spanish court after that date.[20] All the portraits that Rubens painted of the royal family were probably painted in a half-length format.[21]

Most of Rubens' efforts in this group of portraits were focused on depicting the king, of whom he painted four portraits to deliver to Flanders (in addition to the equestrian portrait that was to stay in Spain, which will be discussed later in this chapter). Before his trip to Spain, Rubens had painted the king in one of the scenes for the Eucharist series, the *Secular Hierarchy in Adoration*, presumably from portraits available to him in Flanders.[22] The trip to Madrid was the first and only occasion when the artist and the king met personally, and therefore the only time when Rubens painted the king from life.

The identification of these portraits of the king is complicated by the existence of various written references and extant versions; an attempt to sort them out can be made, but many uncertainties inevitably remain.[23] Leaving the equestrian portrait momentarily aside, two types of portraits of the king can be identified with certainty among those executed by Rubens during his visit. One of them shows the sovereign in a half-length format, with sword and dagger (Fig. 24); in the other, he is seen in bust-length wearing a brocaded costume (Fig. 25). Both of these portrait types are known through various versions (some of which may be original) and prints.[24] Both portraits were executed as one of a pair; their companions are portraits of Queen Isabella of Bourbon. Two very similar types of portraits of the queen are recorded through prints and copies as pendants to portraits of Philip IV. One shows the queen in half-length facing to the left against a red curtain. Her right hand rests on a table and holds a fan; her left hand holds a handkerchief (Fig. 26 shows an engraving by Paulus Pontius after Rubens' original).[25] The second type is almost identical to the first, except for some details in the costume; it shows the queen in a bust portrait wearing a pearl-embroidered dress.[26] Pacheco states that Rubens painted the queen, but unfortunately he does not specify the number of these portraits. Taking this into account, it is possible that only one of the queen's portraits was painted in Madrid, and that the other was painted after the Madrid prototype upon Rubens' return to Antwerp.

The two additional portraits of the king described by Pacheco are probably reflected in two portraits of Philip IV listed in the painter's own collection after his death.[27] One is described as depicting the king wearing a hat (no extant versions of it are known).[28] The other is probably a half-length portrait of the king dressed in armor that is reproduced in a painting by Cornelis de Bailleur presumably showing Rubens' collection; the portrait of the king in armor appears on the floor, near a set of brushes and a palette (Fig. 27).[29] The king's appearance resembles that in the other portraits of this period, especially the "half-length with sword and dagger" type. Because the armored portrait of the king is shown in a room that has been identified as a free variation on the interior of Rubens' residence in Antwerp,[30] and knowing that Rubens owned two portraits of Philip IV, it is possible that the portrait included in de Bailleur's picture is one of those two portraits.

In addition to these painted portraits, there is also a problematic and beautiful drawing by Rubens that shows either Philip IV or his brother

FIGURE 24

?Rubens, *Portrait of Philip IV (half-length with sword and dagger).* Munich, Alte Pinakothek.

the infante Don Carlos, and must have been executed in Madrid (Fig. 28).[31] Drawn primarily in black and reddish-brown, the figure stands at an angle, but looks directly at the viewer. The identification of this portrait with either Philip IV or Don Carlos is based on the similarity of the facial features of the figure portrayed to those of both the king and his brother as they are known through other contemporary paintings, especially those by Velázquez (Figs. 29–30).[32] The portrait drawing is executed with all the vigor and finesse that characterize Rubens' draftsmanship. Even though the engaging gaze of the sitter and the placement of the hands demonstrate that this is a posed portrait, it is not directly related to any known representation of the king or of the infante. The drawing could be related to an unknown portrait, or it could be a study that was never developed into a painting. The similarity of this drawing to Velázquez's work is intriguing. Indeed, as Huemer has noticed, the pose of the figure, the positioning of the head, and the facial expression are closer to Velázquez's portraits than to those painted by Rubens himself of the royal family during the years 1628–1629.[33] Perhaps the Flemish artist was preparing to paint a portrait for the Spanish court, and he was adapting his work to the style of portrai-

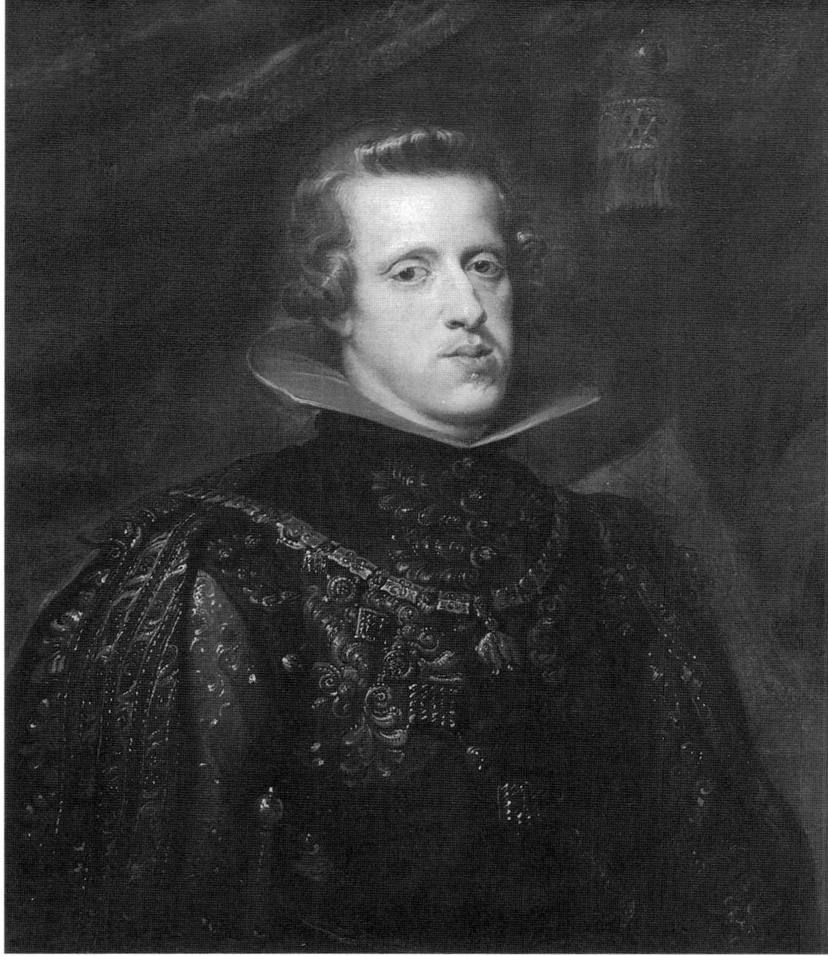

FIGURE 25

?Rubens, *Portrait of Philip IV (bust in brocaded costume)*. Carnegie Museum of Art, Pittsburgh, Collection of Howard A. Noble.

ture preferred by the Spanish royal family. Another possibility is that the drawing was executed soon after Rubens' arrival in Madrid as a way for him to become acquainted with one of the figures that he was to portray through the paintings of Velázquez.

As mentioned earlier, the portraits of the king and queen painted by Rubens in Spain were intended to be taken to Flanders for the infanta Isabella; their stay in Spain was therefore short-lived and their role in the history of art in Spain minimal. It may be surprising in light of the taste of the Spanish court for Rubens' work that none of these portraits, or replicas of them, found their way into the royal collection.[34] The best explanation for this is that it was never intended for Rubens to interfere with the work of the local portrait painters, including Velázquez. According to Pacheco, in 1623 Olivares granted Velázquez the privilege of being the only painter who was allowed to paint portraits

FIGURE 26

Paulus Pontius, after Rubens, *Portrait of Isabella of Bourbon, Queen of Spain, in Half-Length, against a Red Curtain*. Engraving. Madrid, Biblioteca Nacional.

of the king.[35] This may be no more than a repetition of a well-known convention that established the recipient of such a favor as part of a long tradition: it had begun with Apelles and Alexander the Great, and had a more recent and relevant antecedent in the promise made by Charles V in 1533 to Titian that he alone would be allowed to paint his image. However, the fact that throughout the reign of Philip IV most of his portraits were actually painted by Velázquez does indicate that there may have been some real meaning behind Olivares' promise. If that is the case, the portraits painted by Rubens in Madrid were probably not seen as infringing upon the rights of the local painter because they were to be taken to Flanders.[36]

Rubens' portraits of Philip IV have not become the canonical images of the king that his portraits by Velázquez are. There is an important reason for this: it was Velázquez's images, not Rubens', that remained in Spain, where they were used to decorate the royal palaces. But on account of their representational quality alone the portraits by the Flemish painter should not be dismissed: they are vivid personal studies of the monarch and as such, provide an important supplement to Velázquez's better-known images of Philip IV.[37]

FIGURE 27

Attributed to Cornelis de Bailleur, *Gallery of Rubens*. Florence, Galleria Palatina. Art Resource, N.Y.

As was mentioned above, during his stay in Madrid, Rubens also painted portraits of the king's sister, María, and the infantes Carlos and Ferdinand. The portrait of María may be identical with a picture now in a private collection in Switzerland, which had been part of Rubens' collection.[38] The portrait of the infante Ferdinand may be a picture where the sitter appears dressed as a cardinal. This is known in two versions, one in Munich, Alte Pinakothek; the other in Althorp, England, collection of Earl Spencer.[40]

Another portrait made by Rubens at the time of his stay in Madrid that may also have been destined for the infanta Isabella is the work described by Pacheco as an "infanta from the Descalzas, in more than half-length."[41] This painting is probably a portrait of Sor Ana Dorotea, the illegitimate daughter of Rudolf II.[42] The origin of the commission is not documented, but the sitter's relation to the Descalzas suggests that it was commissioned by the infanta Isabella with the intention that Rubens deliver it to her in Flanders. Ana Dorotea had entered the convent of the Descalzas in Madrid in 1623 and was seventeen years old in 1628, when she took her religious vows, an occasion that may have motivated the commission. After mentioning this original portrait, Pacheco goes on to say that, while in Madrid, Rubens made "copies" of it. Thus, two or more replicas were painted by the artist, presumably in response to commissions by local patrons.[43]

The Equestrian Portraits of Philip IV and Philip II

The most important portrait painted by Rubens during his stay in Madrid is a monumental and elaborate equestrian likeness of Philip IV.

FIGURE 28

Rubens, *Portrait of Philip IV*. Drawing. Bayonne, Musée Bonnat.

FIGURE 29

Velázquez, *Philip IV*. Madrid, Museo del Prado.

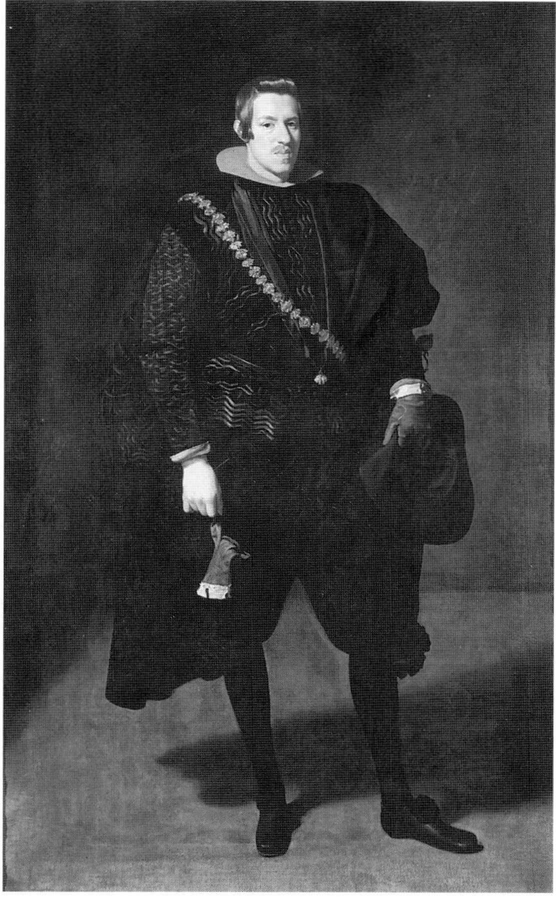

FIGURE 30

Velázquez, *Infante Don Carlos*. Madrid, Museo del Prado.

This undertaking was different from the other royal portraits: it was commissioned by the king and was destined to remain in Madrid, hung in the most prominent chamber in the Alcázar at the time, the New Room.

The king's decision to commission a portrait may have been precipitated by the images of the royal family painted by Rubens for the infanta Isabella. In addition, the high prestige of equestrian representations since classical antiquity naturally made an equestrian portrait desirable. Several models that were available in Spain must have encouraged the king's desire to own a similar representation of himself. The first was Titian's *Charles V at the Battle of Mühlberg* (Fig. 31), a painting with special significance in Spain because of the importance of the king portrayed, and one that had already caught the attention of Philip IV. Shortly after he inherited the crown, the young king had this equestrian portrait transferred from the Pardo palace, a royal residence near Madrid, to the more central Alcázar, where it was prominently installed in

FIGURE 31

Titian, *Charles V at the Battle of Mühlberg.* Madrid, Museo del Prado.

FIGURE 32

Facing page

Copy after Rubens, *Equestrian Portrait of Philip IV.* Florence, Uffizi. Alinari/Art Resource, N.Y.

1624.[44] A second model was a monumental bronze equestrian statue of Philip III, originally commissioned from Giambologna and executed primarily by Pietro Tacca, which had arrived in Madrid in October of 1616 as a gift from Ferdinando I de' Medici to its honoree.[45] The unveiling in January 1617 of this statue in the Casa de Campo, a rural palace close to the Alcázar, must have stood out as one of the important events in the artistic life of the court. A painting by Rubens himself may have also inspired the king. Philip IV owned Rubens' *Equestrian Portrait of the Duke of Lerma* (Fig. 1), which had entered the royal collection when it was sold by Lerma to Philip III in 1606. The painting had remained in Valladolid, presumably because the duke of Lerma had fallen into disgrace, but Philip IV must have been familiar with the impressive picture.

Philip IV's desire to be represented in a monumental equestrian

portrait was first satisfied by his young court painter Velázquez, who in 1625 painted the king "in armor on horseback shown from life."[46] This portrait, which is now lost, was installed in the New Room in the Alcázar. At the time of Rubens' visit to Madrid in 1628, the king decided to replace the portrait by Velázquez with one by the Flemish

FIGURE 33

Rubens, *Reconciliation of Maria de' Medici and Her Son on the Fifteenth of December 1621.* Paris, Louvre. Giraudon/Art Resource, N.Y.

painter. As was the case with the paintings executed by Rubens for the New Room immediately preceding his voyage, the king may have been encouraged by news of Rubens' work as a political propagandist for Maria de' Medici in his paintings for the Luxembourg Palace, or by the equestrian portrait that he painted of the duke of Buckingham after meeting the English minister in Paris in 1625. And the presence in his collection of the *Equestrian Portrait of the Duke of Lerma* offered proof of the talent of the Flemish master for this type of image.

Rubens' work on the king's equestrian portrait began in early October, approximately one month after his arrival at the Spanish court.[47] On October 10, the painter was given materials from the palace armory and stables as models for his work on the painting. According to the playwright Lope de Vega, the portrait was completed two weeks later. On December 2, Rubens wrote to his friends Peiresc and the French humanist Pierre Dupuy that he had finished the picture.[48] The portrait was installed in the New Room, where it remained until its loss to fire in 1734. It is now known through a contemporary copy in the Uffizi (Fig. 32). This copy includes some changes: the white plumes of the king's hat in the original have been transformed into red plumes, and the face of the king has been changed so that he appears older. Also,

FIGURE 34

Justus Tiel, *Education of Prince Philip*. Madrid, Museo del Prado.

FIGURE 35

Michele Parrasio, *Allegory of the Birth of the Infante Ferdinand*. Madrid, Museo del Prado.

the abrupt manner in which the painting in Florence ends on the left side suggests that the original composition may have extended farther in that direction.[49]

Rubens' *Equestrian Portrait of Philip IV* is a grand emblem of the leader of the Catholic forces in their fight against heresy. It shows a portrait of the king dressed as a military commander, sitting on a horse that he holds in a difficult pose reminiscent of the exercise known as the *levade*, and surrounded by the personifications of Divine Justice, Faith, and other allegorical figures. In the background is a landscape which, as mentioned earlier, shows a view of the Manzanares river as seen from the northern section of the Alcázar. Rubens painted a small independent panel of this view in preparation for the background, and a drawing for the allegorical figure of Faith is also known.[50]

Upon completion, Rubens' painting was installed facing Titian's *Charles V at the Battle of Mühlberg*, where the equestrian portrait of the king by Velázquez had previously hung. As has been suggested, the importance of this setting, the magnificence of the composition, and the size of the portrait indicate that it must have been commissioned with its final location in mind. This further suggests that from its inception the painting was meant to replace Velázquez's picture, as well as to complement Titian's celebrated painting of Charles V.[51]

The *Equestrian Portrait of Philip IV* is a milestone in the history of the presence of Rubens in Spain. The displacement of the Velázquez painting, the hanging of the portrait as a counterpart to Titian's *Charles V*, and the pairing of Rubens with Titian that is implicit in this hanging, all indicate that with this work Rubens had reached a preeminent position in the art world of Spain. Titian was an important painter in that country because of his relationship with Charles V, Philip II, and other Hapsburg rulers.[52] These rulers had become emblematic of Spain's golden past in the early years of the reign of Philip IV, and Titian, as their painter, was associated with that same period. Philip IV, like many of his ancestors, was greatly interested in the arts and was certainly aware of the time-honored tradition of artistic patronage in his family. Indeed, he would eventually become the greatest collector among them. When he selected Rubens to paint this equestrian portrait, he was proclaiming himself the heir to his great-grandfather Charles V, and Rubens as the heir to Titian.

In fact, there is evidence that the idea of comparing Rubens with Titian was current at the Spanish court at the time. Lope de Vega had already called attention to the pairing of the two artists and to the parallelism between kings and painters in the poem "Al cuadro y retrato de su Magestad que hizo Pedro Pablo de Rubens, pintor excelentísimo" written shortly after the completion of the equestrian portrait by Rubens. In that poem the Flemish artist is referred to as "el nuevo Ticiano" ("the new Titian").[53] And Rubens also must have realized that he had become Titian's heir as the favorite painter of the Hapsburg ruler. This explains his unprecedented desire to emulate Titian from this point onward, which is expressed in his intense study of the Venetian's work during his stay in Madrid, and also in the frequent incorporation into his own works of specific elements taken from Titian's paintings. More on the relations between these two artists will be said later.

In spite of similarities between the equestrian portraits of Charles V and Philip IV, Rubens' work differs from its model in one important aspect: it is an overt allegorical representation of the monarch. The *Charles V at the Battle of Mühlberg* is a commemorative portrait, and as such it includes subtle allusions to the ideal of kingship that the emperor embodied, and to the actual battle he had led against the unified Protestant forces on April 24, 1547. The symbolism, however, is not overt.[54] In contrast, Rubens' image includes several allegorical representations. In the lower right of the canvas a Native-American boy holds a helmet, signifying the material wealth that was provided to the Spanish monarchy by the Americas. This figure is one of a surprisingly small number of representations of American Indians, or any other references to the Americas, that can be found in Spanish paintings in the early modern period – an indication of the marginal place which the conquest and colonization of America occupied in the minds of the art-collecting elites.[55]

Above the boy with the helmet are two putti supporting the world globe. To the left are the two most prominent allegorical figures in the painting, a personification of True Faith, who holds a cross in one hand and the garlands of victory in the other, and an allegory of Divine Justice, who prepares to throw her thunderbolts in the direction of a snake – representing heresy – that appears in the lower left corner. The figure of Divine Justice is reminiscent of another painted by Rubens between 1623 and 1625, a thunderbolt-bearing woman who appears in the painting *Reconciliation of Maria de' Medici and Her Son on the Fifteenth of December 1621* (Fig. 33), one of the scenes in the cycle of the *Life of Maria de' Medici*.[56] The reusing of this figure in an otherwise unrelated painting is characteristic of Rubens' working method.

In the sixteenth and seventeenth centuries, portraits of the Spanish royal family did not usually include overt allegories.[57] There are, however, some important exceptions to this rule that must have facilitated the acceptance by the king of Rubens' allegorical likeness. One precedent was the work of a little-known Flemish artist employed by King Philip II, Justus Tiel. He is the author of the painting *Education of Prince Philip* (Madrid, Prado; Fig. 34), which shows the future Philip III as a boy, dressed in armor. Behind him stands the figure of Time, who fends Cupid off from the prince while guiding a female figure of Justice toward him. Two earlier examples of allegorical portraiture came from Italy. Titian had painted an allegorical portrait of Philip II offering his son Ferdinand to the heavens. This was sent to Spain in 1575, and in the seventeenth century it was hung by Philip IV in the New Room in the Alcázar.[58] Also in 1575, the Venetian painter Michele Parrasio sent to Philip II the painting *Allegory of the birth of the Infante Ferdinand* (Fig. 35; Madrid, Prado), an astrological allegory showing the queen and the newborn prince receiving gifts from the Provinces.[59]

These three paintings by Tiel, Titian, and Parrasio reveal an intriguing aspect of portraiture in Hapsburg Spain: generally speaking, foreign artists painted portraits of the royal family employing more overt allegorical representations than their Spanish counterparts.[60] The reasons for this may have to do with the image of the monarchy favored by the Spanish Hapsburgs, who considered their own effigies as the best symbols of kingship and used few outward symbols of their power, such as crown or scepter. The fact that local painters closest to the court generally did not embellish their portraits with allegorical representations suggests that they were responding to the wishes of the monarchs themselves, who apparently preferred simplicity is this area. But even if they had their preferences, the taste of the Spanish Hapsburgs, like their monarchy, was not homogeneous, as is shown by the examples of Rubens and other artists mentioned above. The allegorical nature of the *Equestrian Portrait of Philip IV* was not an exception in the Spanish court, but rather one of a number of allegorical portraits executed, for the most part, by non-Spanish artists.

There is another aspect of the *Equestrian Portrait of Philip IV* that is of interest here because of the repercussion it had in Spain. As Susan Koslow has noticed, foam is frequently seen emanating from the mouths of horses painted by Rubens.[61] Koslow connects this feature to an account by the Roman scholar Pliny the Elder about the ancient painters Protogenes and Nealkes. The former, annoyed by his inability to paint the froth that he saw on the lips of animals in a convincing fashion, threw a sponge at a picture of a dog, an action which resulted in the desired image. Nealkes, similarly, achieved the effect he was striving for by throwing a sponge at a painting of a horse. Rubens appears to have been the first modern painter to paint foam around the mouths of horses. Given Pliny's great popularity among artists during the early-modern period, and how well Rubens knew his *Natural History*, it seems likely that he was indeed inspired by this legend.[62] As Koslow shows, the Flemish master included foam around a horse's mouth as early as the *Portrait of Giancarlo Doria* (Florence, Palazzo Vecchio) of 1606. Another early example is the *Saint George Slaying the Dragon* (Madrid, Prado; Fig. 68), of approximately the same date; and the foam appears frequently in horses in Rubens' paintings from then on.

The copy in the Uffizi from which we know the portrait of Philip IV shows abundant foam around the mouth of the animal on which the king sits. Rubens would repeat this feature during his stay in Madrid: it can be seen in the horse that he added to the painting of the *Adoration of the Magi* (Fig. 38), and again in the *Equestrian Portrait of Philip II* (Fig. 36).[63]

The detail of the froth that Rubens added to the pictorial image of horses appears to have been noticed by Velázquez. At least five of his known depictions of equines, all of them dating from the mid-1630s, include conspicuous speckles of white paint around the muzzles of the animals, representing the frothy liquid that emerges from their mouths.[64] The decision by the Spanish painter to emulate his elder peer in this small detail is a revealing example of the artistic dialogue that was stimulated by Rubens' presence in Madrid. Prompted, perhaps, by the example of Rubens' careful study of the art of Titian, Velázquez focused on and learned from the art of the Flemish master. By incorporating the detail of the foam into his own pictures, Velázquez was adopting from Rubens qualities that we still associate with the art of the Fleming: the erudite use of ancient sources and lifelike animation. The ancient source for the detail of the foam in Rubens' paintings must have been recognized by Velázquez, as this was a time when images were meant to be interpreted by their viewers and Pliny was a familiar source – Velázquez owned two copies in Italian and one in Latin of his *Natural History*.[65] As for the quality of lifelike animation, "the foam on the horses' muzzles testifies to animate existence, to breath itself," as Koslow has eloquently explained; it is a detail, she adds, that brings the horses to life. Rubens' ability to infuse his scenes with a spirited sense of life, as if actual blood were throbbing beneath the flesh of his painted creatures, is among the most salient and also the most novel qualities of his painting. The same qualities of learnedness and lifelike animation, incorporated in and adapted to his own artistic idiom, were to become defining features of Velázquez's art as well.

During his visit to the court in Madrid in 1628–1629, Rubens may have painted a second equestrian portrait of a Spanish Hapsburg ruler, the *Equestrian Portrait of Philip II*, mentioned above (Madrid, Prado; Fig. 36). The origin of this work is not known. Although it is not recorded in the royal collection until 1686, it seems likely that it was painted during Rubens' Spanish visit of 1628–1629.[66] The painting combines features of two other portraits the Flemish master painted in the Spanish court at that time, the *Equestrian Portrait of Philip IV* and a copy after Titian's famous portrait of Philip II in armor. The figure of Philip II in Rubens' equestrian portrait is a close copy of Titian's likeness, including the glittering reflection on the metal of the king's identical breastplate.

One possible explanation for the origin of this painting is that Rubens' work on the *Equestrian Portrait of Philip IV* and his copy after Titian's portrait of *Philip II in Armor* (Fig. 37) prompted King Philip

FIGURE 36

Rubens, *Equestrian Portrait of Philip II*. Madrid, Museo del Prado.

IV to order the equestrian likeness of Philip II.[67] Much like his father, Charles V, Philip II was exalted during the reign of his grandson Philip IV as a legendary figure of the country's past, due to the power and respect commanded at home and abroad by the Spanish monarchy under his rule. Philip IV had embraced the example of his grandfather's rulership as a model to follow from the first years of his mandate, hoping to distance himself from the reign of his father, Philip III, who was considered corrupt and weak.[68] In addition, the fact that an equestrian portrait of Philip II did not yet exist must have made it seem appropriate to complement the portraits of Charles V (by Titian) and

FIGURE 37

Titian, *Philip II in Armor*. Madrid, Museo del Prado.

Philip IV (by Rubens) with a similar portrait of Philip II, who, like his father, is presented as a new Caesar and a Christian knight.

Given how little we know about the origin of the *Equestrian Portrait of Philip II*, another possibility can be considered: that it was commissioned by Rubens' main patroness, the infanta Isabella Clara Eugenia. Isabella, as we have seen, was the daughter of Philip II and had been very close to her father, especially in the last years of his life. She may have seen in Rubens' trip to Madrid an opportunity to own a monumental portrait of her late father based on the portraits in the Spanish royal collection. The belated appearance of this picture in the Spanish inventories suggests that it may have been taken to Flanders by Rubens when he departed Madrid, only to be returned to the Spanish capital later in the century. Of course, another possibility is that the portrait was painted not in Spain but in Flanders.[69] Even if this were the case, Rubens' stay at the Spanish court clearly had an effect on the *Equestrian Portrait of Philip II*, as evidenced by its similarities with the copy after Titian and the equestrian portrait of Philip IV discussed above.

There is a tendency to see the posthumous portrait of Philip II as representing a figure from another era. However, for much of Rubens' life, Philip II, who died in September 1598, was in fact the artist's contemporary. In that same year Rubens reached twenty-one years of age, became a master, and took his first pupil. His view of the deceased king must have been similar to that of his older brother Philip Rubens, who was prompted by the king's death to write a funeral oration in his honor.[70] When Rubens painted Philip II's portrait, presumably in 1628–1629, he must have thought of the Spanish king as a part of the recent past.

At first sight, the *Equestrian Portrait of Philip II* (Fig. 36) appears conventional, due mainly to the stiff pose of the rider and the excessively small size of the horse. The stiffness of the sitter can be explained by the need to incorporate the portrait of the deceased king taken from Titian into an entirely different composition. The apparent smallness of the horse is partly a result of the enlargement of the canvas, which was extended in its upper and lower sections at an unknown date.[71] Within the painting's original dimensions, the horse must have appeared more monumental than it does today. Other areas of the painting offer a mixture of energy and beauty that is characteristic of Rubens' work. Particularly noteworthy is the allegorical figure of Victory, per-

FIGURE 38

Rubens, *Adoration of the Magi*. Madrid, Museo del Prado.

FIGURE 39

Rubens, *Adoration of the Magi*. Sketch. Groningen, Collection Groninger Museum. Photo John Stoel.

FIGURE 40

Follower of Rubens, *The Adoration of the Magi*. London, private collection.

sonified by a powerful woman who hovers over the horse and rider while delicately crowning the king with a laurel wreath.

The *Adoration of the Magi*

Like the equestrian portrait of Philip IV (and probably the portrait of Philip II), another of the artistic endeavors that occupied Rubens in Madrid was also associated with royal patronage. The *Adoration of the Magi*, which Rubens painted for the city hall in Antwerp in 1609, had arrived in Spain via Rodrigo Calderón and had been in the Alcázar since 1623. Sometime during his eight-month stay at the court – it is uncertain exactly when – Rubens made substantial changes in this image.[72]

The exact circumstances under which his repainting and enlargement of the *Adoration* took place are not known. As the king owned the painting, he may have encouraged the painter to make the changes, and he certainly had to approve them. The dimensions of paintings were occasionally altered in the Spanish royal collection when rooms were redesigned or redecorated and parts of the collection were reinstalled. Events such as these may have occasioned the enlargement of the *Adoration*. On the other hand, the decision to rework the canvas may have originated with the painter himself. During Rubens' stay in Madrid, the painting was installed in a section of the Alcázar known as the king's summer apartments.[73] This part of the palace must have been unoccupied during most of Rubens' visit to Spain, which took place between mid-September, when the scorching summer heat of Madrid begins to abate, and the end of April, still a cool time in the Spanish capital.[74] As we shall see later in this chapter, during this period Rubens spent time in the presumably unoccupied summer apartments studying Titian's *poesie*.[75] This was a private matter, Rubens undertaking the study of the Venetian master for his own pleasure and benefit, and it raises the possibility that the enlargement of the *Adoration* may have also originated privately, with the painter proposing the change to the king.

However the idea to rework the *Adoration* emerged, the scene was significantly expanded at this time by the addition of portions of canvas to the upper and right sides of the painting, thus reaching its present dimensions of 346 cm in height and 438 cm in width (Fig. 38). Rubens added several new figures to the composition as well as repainting many others from the original scene. A comparison with the sketch made by the painter in preparation for the original painting, and with a replica presumably made in Rubens' studio shortly after the completion of the original version of the *Adoration* (Figs. 39 and 40), reveals the changes that were made in the composition.[76] Observing the image from left to right, one of the first changes that can be noted is also one of the most significant. At the far left, the base and lower part of the shaft of a monumental fluted column has been added to the bare wall of the barn where the Adoration takes place. This added column has the effect of ennobling the setting by associating it with the classical world. More importantly, by placing the column on the same vertical axis as the Virgin and infant Christ, Rubens must have also intended to emphasize the role played in the painting by these two figures.[77] This aspect of the enlargement of the canvas serves to emphasize the counterreformatory interpretation that Rubens had given to the theme of the Adoration from the outset. The very selection of the theme of the picture may have been motivated in part as an answer to the condemnation of the cult of the Magi by Luther and Calvin.[78] Also, as the replica of the original painting shows (Fig. 40), Rubens depicted the *Adoration* as a ritual similar to the celebration of the Mass.[79] This is made clear by the liturgical aspect suggested by the long scarf or stole that is placed under the infant Christ; by the appearance of grapevines in the canopy in the upper-left section of the image, a symbol of the Eucharistic wine; and by the sacramental symbolism of placing the naked Christ on an altar-like block.

When he reworked the canvas in Madrid, Rubens further emphasized the counterreformatory content of the image. The new prominence given to the figure of the Virgin by the addition of the column is a forceful answer to the Protestant aversion to Mary. Also, because of the traditional use in art of columns as metaphors for the church,[80] the alignment of the column on the same axis as Mary implies an association between her and the church, a belief characteristic of the culture of the Counter-Reformation.

The morning light that shines, in the Prado painting, in the area close to the column, bathing its shaft and base, also carries a symbolic meaning: it is a reference to the dawn of a new age that resulted from the Incarnation of Christ.[81] The conception of the theme of the *Adoration* as a mass is also clarified in the enlarged painting by the addition of bunches of grapes to the grapevines in the canopy to the right of the column and a sheaf of wheat on the altarlike block where Christ sits, a traditional reference to the miraculous transformation of the bread into the body of Christ that takes place during the mass.[82]

The presence of a donkey in the right section of the enlarged canvas is yet another means used by Rubens to add emphasis to the counter-reformatory message expounded in the *Adoration*. The manner in which the animal is painted, with its eyes covered and looking away from the central scene, is probably a reference to the refusal by some to see the light represented by the Incarnation. Also significant is the addition of the two angels on the top of the scene, one of whom looks out directly at the viewer. As messengers of God and guides to the Magi, they serve the purpose of emphasizing the presence of the divine in the scene of the Adoration-mass taking place below.

The painter has also eliminated some of the figures that once stood to the right of the Virgin in the original composition, thus compensating for the addition of other figures in the new portions of canvas. Two black youths carrying lamps and three other figures have disappeared from the background group that stood close to the wall of the barn, opening this area of the picture to the faint light of an early morning sky. Some traces of the changes that were made in this part of the painting are visible to the naked eye: the shape of one of the lamps can be seen under the overpainting in the area above the right shoulder of a soldier who wears a helmet and looks toward his left. Immediately to the left of this area stands a bearded figure who now carries a lance and appears to stare into a void that was previously occupied by other figures with whom he was engaged in dialogue. The figure of a black boy who blows on a bowl containing burning coals in this area of the composition should also be mentioned. This figure was not altered by Rubens when he repainted the scene. It is interesting because it is a pictorial interpretation of Pliny the Elder's description of a work by the painter Antiphilos of a boy blowing on fire that reflected on his face.[83] Like other uses of the same ancient source, this figure must have contributed to the status of Rubens as a learned painter to his Spanish viewers.

In the central portion of the *Adoration* two angels, as we have seen, have been added at the top, and slight changes have been made in the positioning of some of the torches. These are painted with thick, heavy brushwork reminiscent of the style of Titian in works such as the late *Martyrdom of Saint Lawrence* (Fig. 41), at the time located in the old chapel in El Escorial where Rubens must have seen it.[84] It is actually possible that Rubens was inspired by Titian's altarpiece, as is suggested by the existence of other more striking similarities between the two works. The general scheme of the enlarged *Adoration* is marked by a strong directional thrust from upper right to lower left, which is also found in Titian's scene. The addition by Rubens of the two angels at the top of the picture is also reminiscent of Titian's picture. Also, in both works a figure mounted on a white horse and wearing a crimson coat adorned with a golden band – representing a heavy chain in Titian's painting, a strap in Rubens' – closes the composition at the right end of the canvas.

Other changes made by Rubens on the right side of the *Adoration* are also extensive, and they serve further to illustrate his working method. The figure standing behind the Magus with a red robe at the center of the painting and in the act of covering the Magus' head, has lost his beard and looks younger than in the original scene. In the first version of the painting, immediately above this figure two men were busy unloading large bags from a camel. In the enlarged canvas, the camel carrying the load and another standing next to it have been moved slightly upward, beyond the limits of the original canvas, and the porters have been removed. The space they formerly occupied now opens onto the background, its darkness broken by two lit torches. A newly added figure rides a camel and holds a long torch high above the animated scene. With only slight changes, the figures that were unloading the camel in the earlier version reappear in the revised painting in the upper right quadrant of the canvas, now unloading heavy sacks from a newly added and larger camel whose head looks down toward the center of the composition. Thus the reutilization of elements that Rubens so often practiced can be seen here within a single painting, from the earlier version to the later.

As mentioned above, a donkey has been added above the horse that stares out from the painting, and the plumage and hat worn by the horseman have been subdued in the repainted image into a dark headpiece. Judging from the known replica of the painting, a black man stood behind the muscular porter at the right end of the original composition. Now that figure is gone, and the viewer can see beyond the foreground in the expanded composition.

To the right, in the added portion of canvas, Rubens has painted a horse, and behind him, a figure representing a young dismounted rider or a groom. The contrapposto pose of the youth and the powerful, sweeping curve formed by the neck of the horse are among the most exquisite features of the enlarged canvas, a prime example of Rubens' skill in handling masses of form. The horse and the figure behind it appear somewhat detached from the scene of the *Adoration* and are reminiscent of Venetian painting in the elegance of their design and the depth of their hues.

The group composed of the horse and groom had been painted by Rubens in almost identical fashion on at least two previous occasions,[85] and horses very similar to the one in the *Adoration* – with its neck bent downward and one of its front legs bent upward to allow the animal to rub its knee or stroke at its bit – can also be seen in other works by Rubens.[86] This type of horse has many forerunners from antiquity onward, in painting as well as in prints and sculpture, and Rubens' repeated use of the motif – with or without the accompanying groom – is a revealing example of his art-historical awareness.[87]

In the case of the horse and groom in the *Adoration*, Rubens may have been influenced by a painting he saw in Spain in deciding to repeat the design he had used in earlier works. As Michael Jaffé has shown, the group formed by the horse and dismounted figure in Rubens' *Adoration* is similar to a group of horse and page that appears at the center of an *Adoration of the Magi* by Titian.[88] Two identical versions of Titian's composition were present in Spain in 1628–1629 (Fig. 42), one of them in the old church in El Escorial, the same chapel where Rubens must have studied Titian's *Martyrdom of Saint Lawrence*.[89] In Titian's

FIGURE 41

Titian, *Martyrdom of Saint Lawrence*. Patrimonio Nacional. San Lorenzo de El Escorial, Iglesia Vieja.

images, the raised leg of the horse, the design of the neck, and the placement of the page behind the animal, with his hand on the front of the saddle, are very similar to the figures in Rubens' painting.

Let us return, then, to the additions to the *Adoration* painted by Rubens. Immediately above and behind the horse and dismounted rider we find one of the most striking features of the enlarged painting: as has long been noted, Rubens introduced here a portrait of himself astride a white horse, looking toward the central scene of the Adoration. He appears to be in the act of moving away from the scene, turning his head as he rides by to look at the Adoration, as if by adding this air of passerby casualness to his presence he was compensating for the immodesty of including himself in the holy event. The identification of the self-portrait, which is universally accepted, is based on the attributes worn by the painter (chain and sword), and on the similarity to other known portraits of Rubens, such as the one made by Van Dyck that was engraved by Pontius for the collection of portraits known as the *Iconography* (Fig. 43).[90] As in Van Dyck's print, in the *Adoration* Rubens has combed his hair forward to conceal his baldness, and he appears to be younger than fifty-one years, his age at the time.[91]

The repainted version of the *Adoration of the Magi* has a very different character than the original image, judging from the sketch and the known replica of the first version. The area added to the right of the composition has accentuated the diagonal line that funnels the energy from the right side of the painting to a point of convergence in the lower left, formed by Mary, the infant Christ, and the kneeling Magus. As a result, the stability of the original scene has been broken. The rectangular design that organized the composition and echoed the form of the canvas has been replaced by a triangular structure that infuses tension and energy into the painting. The emptying out of some areas of the original image also helps to create a more dynamic composition. By removing the three black youths carrying the lamps on the left, Rubens has added depth to the picture. The artist made a similar change on the right side of the painting, by leaving out the groom standing in the dark area behind the two muscular porters.

FIGURE 42

Titian, *Adoration of the Magi*. Madrid, Museo del Prado.

FIGURE 43

Paulus Pontius, after Van Dyck, *Rubens*. Engraving, from *Iconography*.

Another interesting change has occurred in the painting as a result of the addition of the figures on the right. In the original composition, the focal area at the left formed by the figures of the infant Christ, Joseph, Mary, and the kneeling king was enveloped by the larger semicircle formed by the rest of the figures. In the final version of the painting, the self-portrait of Rubens, the dismounted horseman, and the other elements added to the right of the scene act as an additional row of spectators that fans out from the axis at the opposite end of the canvas. Even though the figures in the added portion of the painting can appear somewhat disconnected from the focal event, they also serve, by contrast, to emphasize the intimacy and warmth of the central area of the composition.

The history of the *Adoration of the Magi*, in addition to its quality and its sheer size, makes it one of Rubens' most important and interesting works. The repainting of the composition twenty years after its original conception provides a fascinating example of the artist's revising his earlier ideas, and an unusually direct view of his creative imagination at work. Students of this painting have paid much attention to different aspects of the work, generally concentrating on the development of the commission and on the revisions of the original composition that were made in Madrid. In spite of all that is known about the painting, two issues need some further explaining. The first is the influence that Titian's art exerted on Rubens when he repainted the *Adoration*. The second is the presence of the painter's self-portrait in the picture.

As explained above, there are some features of the enlarged *Adoration of the Magi* (the design of the mounted figure on the right side of the composition, the group below formed by a horse and a dismounted rider, the overall compositional structure) that in all likelihood were inspired by works of Titian. Rubens' interest in Titian during his Spanish visit has been mentioned already in connection to the *Equestrian Portrait of Philip IV* (Fig. 32), and will be discussed again in connection to the copies he made after the Venetian master. What is important to note here is that the use of elements taken from Titian in the *Adoration* is not an isolated event. Rather, it is part of an extensive focus on the Venetian painter. This focus was inspired, at least in part, by the tradition of patronage and the artistic culture that Rubens found in the Spanish court and by the exalted position which that culture assigned to Titian.

One of the most puzzling features of the *Adoration of the Magi* is Rubens' addition of his own portrait at the right of the enlarged canvas. This aspect of the painting has been treated only in summary fashion by the literature and will be studied more extensively here. In his self-portrait, Rubens appears elegantly dressed, and he displays a sword and a chain as signs of distinction: they are intended to underscore his links to rulers and kings, and perhaps also his noble status.[92] During Rubens' lifetime, the right to carry a sword was associated by custom with the nobility, and laws were enacted so that this custom was not subverted.[93] The sword that Rubens displays in the *Adoration* may therefore be a reference to the noble rank that Philip IV granted him in 1624.[94] The privilege of carrying arms apparently could also be conferred upon an individual who was not a member of the nobility as a special honor, judging from a statement in Pacheco's biography of Rubens. According to Pacheco, shortly after the painter returned to Flanders from Italy late in 1608, and having painted two portraits of the archduke Albert of Austria and the infanta Isabella, "the infanta, in the presence of her husband, fitted a sword around his waist, and she put a very rich golden chain around his neck."[95] The sword that Rubens wears in the *Adoration* may allude to this event.

The golden chain plays a role similar to that of the sword in Rubens' self-portrait; such chains had been associated since antiquity with gifts received by select individuals from their social superiors, generally princes, in recognition of services rendered. In the sixteenth century they were an emblem of status coveted by artists. In Rubens' time, a chain was generally recognized as a symbol of high honor (even though it could also symbolize servitude).[96] By 1628, Rubens had received three golden chains: one from the duke of Mantua in his early years in Italy; one from the archdukes Albert and Isabella when he became their official court painter in 1609; and one from King Christian IV of Denmark in 1620. The artist would receive still one more in 1639, from Charles I of England. If Rubens intended to refer to one specific chain on this occasion, it must have been the chain he had received from the archdukes in 1609, as that would have served as a reminder of the important role played by the infanta in promoting his visit to Madrid as a diplomat in the service of the Spanish monarchy.

The primary interest of Rubens' self-portrait in the *Adoration*, however, is as a statement about the painter's identity, the importance of which is underscored by its exceptional nature within Rubens' oeuvre. There are several self-portraits where the artist appears either alone or in the company of his family or others.[97] In these images, though, Rubens and the other figures pose as themselves, as sitters in a portrait. The *Adoration of the Magi* is the only occasion upon which Rubens placed his portrait in a painting depicting an event at which he could not have been present. Critics occasionally recognize Rubens' features in various other paintings such as the *Garden of Love* in the Prado (Fig. 77), where he and his wife are sometimes identified as the couple on the left edge of the scene.[98] The essential difference between the *Adoration* and all other paintings is that this is the only case where Rubens has portrayed himself in a manner that is specific and distinctive enough to remove all doubts that it is he.

The presence of a painter's image within a narrative, what has been termed the "participant self-portrait," is an artistic genre that flourished during the Renaissance as part of the growing cult of the personality of the artist.[99] This type of self-representation could take on different meanings. In many cases painters would insert their image into a composition primarily as a way of signing the work (a famous case in point is Dürer's *Adoration of the Trinity* of 1511, where the painter stands below a celestial gathering holding a plaque inscribed with his name and the date of the work). Occasionally, the thematic context of the paintings suggests that painters were using their portraits to express a more personal concern. Among the best-known examples of this usage are Michelangelo's portrayal of himself in the flayed skin carried by Saint Bartholomew in the *Last Judgment* and Caravaggio's equally pathological inclusion of his portrait as the severed head of the giant in the *David and Goliath* (Rome, Borghese Gallery), to cite two painters who were especially dear to Rubens. In both these cases, the artists associated the subject they were painting with their own concerns and used the scenes to make a statement of the most personal nature.

Although Rubens' self-portrait in the *Adoration* lacks the pathos of those by Michelangelo and Caravaggio, it is similar in that the portrait is emphatically inserted into the narrative, making one feel that this is more than a mere reference to a tradition or a form of signature; rather, it is a painting that takes on an autobiographical character. The fact that Rubens' inclusion of himself in this painting is unique in his oeuvre further suggests that he may have attached a specific and personal meaning to his presence in it, and calls out for an interpretation. What motivated the painter to incorporate his self-portrait into this particular scene? How should we interpret Rubens' presence in the *Adoration of the Magi*?

Because of the lack of information available, not to mention the very nature of interpreting self-portraits, any answers that can be provided must be speculative. Frances Daugherty, the only scholar who has seriously considered this problem, has made some perceptive suggestions.[100] She proposes three reasons for the inclusion of Rubens' likeness in the enlarged painting: that the king requested the portrait be included along with the other additions; that it was a device used to place a believable participant in the scene; and, finally, that Rubens may have intended his image in the *Adoration* to be a statement of commitment to the Catholic cause at a time when he was being considered for a diplomatic mission to England. These possibilities can be neither confirmed nor dismissed; they may all be true, and there may be other motivating factors as well. Daugherty's last suggestion, the idea that the inclusion of the painter's portrait may have had some connection to his current mission in Spain, is the most intriguing in the context of this study. A closer look at the Spanish setting in which the enlargement of the painting took place will broaden this interpretation.

The original version of the *Adoration of the Magi* was painted in the context of the negotiations between Spain and the United Provinces that led to the Twelve Year Truce. Because of the date of the commission and the intended destination of the painting – the room where the signing of the treaty took place in April of 1609 – the *Adoration* is generally believed to allude to the truce negotiations. Frans Baudouin has made the plausible suggestion that the theme of the arrival of the three Magi to visit the newly born Christ was selected by Rubens to symbolize the arrival of the delegates in Antwerp, the Magi and their gifts representing the emissaries who negotiated the truce that would bring peace and prosperity to the city.[101]

Rubens' presence in Madrid in 1628–1629, the time when he repainted the *Adoration*, resulted from a similar set of diplomatic conversations in which the painter himself was very involved. As was discussed earlier, after being selected by the infanta to represent the Spanish side in the negotiations with England, Rubens had been called to Madrid by the king in the summer of 1628. When Rubens began to repaint the *Adoration* in Madrid, the similarities between the current negotiations and those which had led to the Twelve Year Truce two decades earlier must have become apparent to him. If in the original painting he had alluded to the arrival of the ambassadors who were negotiating a peace for his country in 1609 in Antwerp, Rubens now would have seen himself in a similar diplomatic role. If this scenario is correct, then what Rubens did upon repainting the *Adoration* was to include his image among the emissaries. In so doing he was updating the symbolic reference made in the painting from the truce negotiations of the first decade of the century to those between Spain and England, in which he was personally involved.

It is here that the emphasis on the counterreformatory aspect of the *Adoration* mentioned earlier comes into play. By stressing the religious points made in the painting, Rubens was underscoring his conformity with a monarchy that acted in the theater of European politics as the secular defender of the Catholic faith. This may have served to strengthen his own position as a diplomat in the service of Philip IV.

Another possible meaning – which need not exclude the interpretation presented above – may be attached to Rubens' portrait in the Prado's *Adoration of the Magi*. The clue to this second interpretation is the fact that the painting in which the artist inserted his own likeness belonged to the king of Spain, Philip IV. Even though Rubens' presence in the painting is rather unassuming among so many other figures, the inclusion of his portrait must have been approved by the king, because the painting belonged to the royal collection and was displayed in the Alcázar. The importance of the king's acceptance of Rubens' presence in the work is underscored by its uniqueness; there were very few paintings in the Spanish royal collection that included the artist's self-portrait.[102] And the *Adoration* was certainly the only picture owned by the king at the time that included a painter who was alive and present at the court.

Even though there is no documentary proof that the king recognized Rubens in the mounted figure at the right edge of the *Adoration*, it is difficult to imagine that he could have missed it. Rubens stated in a letter he wrote from Madrid that he met with the king daily.[103] Even if there is some exaggeration in this statement, it must be a reflection of frequent visits by the king to the painter's studio. Certainly in some of these meetings Rubens and Philip IV discussed the changes in the *Adoration*. Also, to imagine that Rubens could have added his self-portrait to a painting owned by the king without prior consent is to imagine a situation that seems scarcely possible, given the etiquette that ruled the relationship between a patron and an artist at the time.

Assuming, then, that Philip IV approved of it, the inclusion of Rubens in the *Adoration* can be interpreted as a form of association between the painter and the king, and as such it is a demonstration by Rubens of his status. One of the arguments used by painters to elevate the social position of their profession – an issue that had occupied them since the sixteenth century – was their proximity to kings and princes. There can be no doubt that Rubens was aware of the exceptional nature of such relationships, as it was part of the cultural baggage of the time. In 1625, for example, he alluded to the distance that separated painters from princes when writing to his friend Valavez that the prince of Wales: "asked for my portrait with such insistence that I found it impossible to refuse him. Though to me it did not seem fitting to send my portrait to a prince of such rank."[104] That three years after this letter Rubens included his self-portrait in a painting owned by Philip IV reinforces the importance of this inclusion.

There are reasons why the issue of the status of the artist may have had a very personal relevance for Rubens at this time. As seen earlier in this chapter, Rubens' profession had posed a problem for his official selection as a representative of Spain in the diplomatic dealings that ended with his sojourn in Madrid.[105] The presence of Rubens' self-portrait within the *Adoration* suggests that he used this occasion to respond to the prejudice against his profession. By painting his portrait in the guise of a nobleman in a painting that belonged to the king, Rubens may have intended to make a statement about his own personal standing, and also about that of his profession. As is shown by the correspondence, Rubens' personal relationship with the Spanish king matured during his stay in Madrid to the point where such a statement was possible.

The professional concerns of his Spanish contemporaries at this time may have provided another reason for Rubens to make a comment about his status, or that of painters in general. After decades of debate, the plea of Spanish painters to raise the social standing of their activity peaked in 1626. In that year a group of artists in Madrid had their paintings taxed as manufactured goods, thus denying their higher status as works of art. This led them to increase their demands that their profession be accorded a higher status.[106] The issue of the nobility of the art of painting remained very much alive at the time of Rubens' visit to Madrid in 1628–1629. We do not know if Rubens was aware of the concerns of his Spanish peers. One may imagine a cursory interest, of the kind demonstrated by the painter during his first visit to Spain in 1603–1604, when he expressed his distaste for the painters active in Valladolid. If so, Rubens may have been induced to place himself in the *Adoration* in response to their concerns. By including his ennobled likeness in the scene and with the king's permission, he may have intended to show that he belonged to a higher status than his Spanish contemporaries, and that he was above the problems of common painters. Or he may have intended to support the local artists by legitimizing their social aspirations through his own example.

All attempts to understand Rubens' intentions in including his likeness in the *Adoration of the Magi* must also contend with the fact that the painter's portrait was apparently not widely recognized by his contemporaries, with the probable exception of the king. One would think that other members of the court who saw this painting would have identified the painter, given Rubens' fame and his presence in Madrid. Yet there is no reference to the self-portrait in the *Adoration* until the second half of the eighteenth century.[107] None of the descriptions of the painting in the royal inventories mentions the self-portrait. Equally surprising is the fact that neither Pacheco, Carducho, nor Palomino, the three most important sources for the arts of Spain during the period, appear to have known of it. Carducho must have met Rubens personally in Madrid, and Pacheco and Palomino should have heard from their sources (which in the case of Pacheco included Velázquez) of the inclusion of the portrait, if it was publicly known.

It is unlikely that these writers knew about the self-portrait but did not think it significant enough to mention in their treatises. It may be that the presence of the painter was not widely recognized – perhaps because Rubens appears younger in his self-portrait than he was at the time. A more likely explanation is that the *Adoration of the Magi* was a little-known painting, for it was installed, as previously stated, in the king's summer apartments. Even though some persons could occasionally see the paintings in this part of the Alcázar,[108] the summer apartments were primarily a private section of the palace. The *Adoration* may therefore have been a private work for the king, and the self-portrait intended as a private message for Philip IV.

In light of the preceding discussion, it is possible that Philip IV asked for the additions to the *Adoration of the Magi*, and he certainly had to approve them. Of the works painted by Rubens during his seven-month stay at the court only one was unquestionably commissioned by the king: the *Equestrian Portrait of Philip IV*. It seems likely that he also commissioned the equestrian portrait of his grandfather, Philip II, but this is not certain. The fact that the king commissioned so few paintings is surprising when one considers that he was an avid collector, and on occasion, as Rubens would later discover, an impatient one. There is no question that Philip IV greatly favored Rubens during his stay in Madrid, as demonstrated by his frequent visits to Rubens' studio in the Alcázar and by the importance of the commission of his own equestrian portrait. One explanation for this apparent contradiction is probably the fact that the king's collecting activities, though well under way, were still not at the level they would reach in the next decade. Also important is the relative freedom Philip IV appears to have granted his favorite painters. Velázquez is known for the sparseness of his production; the king was ready to do without him for long periods of time, as his two extended stays in Italy demonstrate.[109] Rubens appears to have enjoyed the same freedom, which allowed him to paint for other patrons, and also extensively for himself, while he was in Madrid.

Work for Other Patrons

Among the other art patrons who commissioned works from Rubens during his 1628–1629 visit to Spain the most noteworthy is Don Diego Mexía, marquis of Leganés. He is important not so much for his patronage of Rubens at this time as for the magnitude that his collection of Rubens' paintings would reach in the following decades. Born circa 1585, Leganés was a first cousin of the count-duke of Olivares, the favorite of Philip IV. Don Diego Mexía, who received the Leganés title in 1627, rose through the ranks of the nobility in the 1620s and served in important positions in the court and the military. Many of these posts were in the Spanish Netherlands. He served in the army of Flanders from 1600 onward, and in the archducal court in Brussels at an early age. He is recorded in the Netherlands at the end of the second decade of the century, and again in the early 1620s, in 1626, and from February 1627 to March 1628, when he returned to Spain. In Madrid he was president of the Council of the Netherlands, and he was sent to Flanders again in February 1630 as general of the cavalry and deputy to the commander of the army. After an interim back at the court in Madrid, he is recorded again as having been in Flanders in 1634–1635. While in the Netherlands, Leganés had opportunity to become familiar with Flemish painting and to meet Rubens, who remained one of his favorite artists.[110]

Leganés was one of the earliest private collectors of Rubens in seventeenth-century Spain. Only Rodrigo Calderón owned a significant number of paintings by Rubens before Leganés. But there is an important difference between the two: Calderón received most of his paintings by Rubens as gifts, whereas Leganés, as we shall see, commissioned at least one painting directly from Rubens and probably purchased many of the others personally.

Leganés had known Rubens since 1627, and possibly earlier. The marquis resided in Brussels from September 1627 until March of the following year as a special envoy of the king. It is probable that Rubens painted his portrait at that time, and in a letter dated January 1628, he referred to Leganés as one of the greatest connoisseurs of painting in the world.[111] At some point during his stays in Flanders, the marquis must have purchased and brought to Spain a *Garland of Fruits and Flowers with Virgin and Child* by Rubens and Jan Brueghel, which is recorded in the Leganés collection in Madrid in 1630. This was a typically Flemish type of scene that would become increasingly popular in Spain.[112] When Rubens was in Madrid, he renewed his contacts with

Leganés. The Spaniard commissioned from him an *Immaculate Conception* (Fig. 44; Madrid, Prado), presumably with the intention of giving it as a gift to the king, in whose collection it hung in 1636.

The Leganés *Immaculate Conception* reveals a joyful and lighthearted vision of a religious subject quite different from the more austere images being produced in Spain at the time.[113] The unusually thin application of the paint in this canvas, which barely conceals the ground underneath, suggests that Rubens spent less time on it than other works he is known to have painted in Madrid. He may have been pressed for time, or it could be that Leganés was paying comparatively little for the painting.[114]

Another work by Rubens that Leganés probably acquired during the painter's visit to Spain is a half-length or bust portrait of Philip IV. This picture, which has not been identified, is first listed in the Leganés collection in 1630 and must have been painted in Spain in 1628–1629. It could be a study by Rubens in preparation for the large *Equestrian Portrait of Philip IV*, as the king is described as wearing the same items of dress in both pictures: a suit of armor adorned with a red sash, and a hat with a white feather.[115] The low price of the Leganés painting in a later inventory also suggests that this is a study rather than a finished work; in 1655 it was appraised at 440 reales, in comparison to the 1,100 reales at which another half-length portrait by Rubens (of Ambrogio Spinola) was valued in the same inventory.[116]

According to Pacheco, another member of the local aristocracy, Jaime de Cárdenas (? – 1652), marquis of Belmonte de Campos, commissioned Rubens to paint a life-size *Saint John the Evangelist*, which has also not been identified.[117] The marquis of Belmonte de Campos, who would later become duke of Maqueda and Nájera, was a relative of the count-duke of Olivares and part of his circle in the 1620s. He became a gentleman of the king's chamber (*gentilhombre de la cámara del rey*) in July of 1621, and a member of the Order of Alcántara in December of 1622. He must have played an active role during the visit of the Prince of Wales to Madrid in 1623, as he made a gift of four horses to the prince upon his departure. In spite of some troubled times in 1630, when he was expelled from court, Cárdenas went on to become lord high steward (*mayordomo mayor*) to the queen in 1647.[118] The commission from Rubens of a painting of Saint John is the only known mention of his involvement with the arts.

The paintings that Rubens executed for Don Jaime de Cárdenas and for Leganés reveal a certain penetration into the local market that goes beyond the occasions provided the artist by the infanta's commissions or by works executed for the king. The "five or six" portraits of unidentified "private persons" that Pacheco credits Rubens with painting while in Madrid are also presumably the result of local commissions.[119] None of these portraits have been identified, but several sitters can be sug-

FIGURE 44

Rubens, *Immaculate Conception*. Madrid, Museo del Prado.

gested on the basis of their proven interest in the art of Rubens. Leganés and Jaime de Cárdenas commissioned paintings from Rubens, as we have seen, so they are obvious candidates. Another possible sitter is Ambrogio Spinola (1569–1630), commander-in-chief of the army of the Spanish Netherlands under Albert and Isabella, who had left Brussels for Madrid in January of 1628 and was thus in Spain at the same time as Rubens.[120] Rubens painted several portraits of Spinola after a single prototype between 1625 and 1628, and may have done so again in

Madrid. A portrait of Spinola outfitted with the ceremonial dress of the Order of the Golden Fleece has been identified as having been painted in Spain.[121] However, the features of Spinola in this portrait repeat the earlier likenesses of him painted by Rubens in Flanders, which suggests that it may have been produced in the artist's studio in Antwerp. A different portrait of Spinola attributed to Rubens is recorded in the collection of the marquis of Leganés in 1642, which raises the possibility that it was painted in Spain.[122] Leganés married Spinola's elder daughter, Policena Spinola, in March of 1628, which may have prompted him to commission a portrait of his father-in-law. It is uncertain, however, that he did so while Rubens was in Madrid. The painting in the Leganés collection was not recorded there at the time when the collection was inventoried in 1630, as it should have had it been painted in 1628 or 1629. It may have been commissioned later, or may have entered the Leganés collection through other means, perhaps as a result of inheritance after Spinola's death in 1630.[123]

Other possible candidates for the portraits mentioned by Pacheco are members of the higher ranks of the nobility or other figures involved in the artistic life at court during Rubens' stay in Madrid (but probably not someone of the rank of Olivares or the familiarity of Velázquez, whom Pacheco would have mentioned by name). Chief among them is Giovanni Battista Crescenzi, a Roman nobleman and artist who had been in Madrid since 1617, and who by the time of Rubens' visit was an important artistic figure at court.[124] The painter and Dominican friar Juan Bautista Maino was Rubens' contemporary (he was born ca. 1578).[125] The son of a Milanese father and a Portuguese mother, Maino was in Italy in the early years of the century (at the same time Rubens resided there), where he came into contact with figures such as Annibale Carracci and Guido Reni, and where he was influenced by Caravaggio. After 1618 he took up residence at the court in Madrid, where he taught drawing to Prince Philip, the future Philip IV, and played a very important role in the artistic affairs of the court during the 1620s and 1630s. Maino's cosmopolitan culture and his proximity to the highest circles of the court must have made him a target of Rubens' interest. He is therefore another candidate who may have sat for the Flemish painter.

Other private patrons whom Rubens could have met and portrayed are individuals who were present at the court and with whom Rubens shared some of his time in Spain as a result of their participation in the same endeavors. Among them are two foreign representatives who were in Madrid for the same negotiations that had brought Rubens there: Endymion Porter, an English painter and agent of the duke of Buckingham, and the abbot Scaglia, who arrived in Madrid in January of 1629 as ambassador of Savoy.[126]

A suggestion that has been made regarding an additional project that Rubens may have worked on while in Madrid is as difficult to confirm as the identity of some of his Spanish patrons. According to Julius Held, Rubens may have painted a sketch of the *Incarnation as Fulfillment of All the Prophecies* for the Benedictine convent of San Plácido while he was in Spain, presumably in preparation for a larger altarpiece never actually painted.[127] This suggestion is based on the likelihood that this sketch by Rubens was used as a model in 1668 by Claudio Coello, one of the leading painters in the later part of the century in Madrid, when he painted the large altarpiece for the church of San Plácido. The person responsible for a commission from Rubens would have been Jerónimo de Villanueva, one of the most powerful figures in the government of Spain at the time of Rubens' visit and founder of the convent of San Plácido in 1623.[128] If correct, the suggestion by Held adds a new project, and a new patron, to Rubens' activity during his Spanish sojourn. However, the early history of the sketch is not known, and the evidence for the San Plácido project remains uncertain.

Rubens' Paintings for His Own Collection and His Study of Titian

We know from Pacheco that all of the remaining paintings Rubens executed in Madrid were painted by the artist for his own collection. One of them is a landscape view of El Escorial, probably an oil sketch, which Rubens referred to on one occasion as "a design of mine done upon the spot."[129] This painting, now lost, remained in Rubens' possession and appears to have enjoyed some fame, judging from the copies made after it (Fig. 45), and by the recommendation made to King Charles I of England by the painter Edward Norgate that he purchase one of the copies that he had seen in Rubens' studio. The description of the painting written by Rubens in the letter that accompanied the copy delivered to Charles I offers a rare chance to share the painter's memory of the occasion:

> The mountain . . . is very high and steep, and very difficult to climb and descend, so that we had the clouds far below us, while the sky above remained very clear and serene. There is, at the summit, a great wooden cross, which is easily seen from Madrid, and nearby a little church dedicated to St. John, which could not be represented in the picture, for it was behind our backs; in it lives a hermit who is seen here with his mule. I need scarcely to say that below is the superb building of St. Lawrence in Escorial, with the village and its avenues of trees, the Fresneda and its two ponds, and the road to Madrid appearing above, near the horizon. The mountain covered with clouds is called La Sierra Tocada, because it almost always has a kind of veil around its top. There is a tower and a house on one side; I do not remember their names particularly, but I know the King used to go hunting there occasionally. The mountain at the extreme left is La Sierra y Puerto de Buitrago. . . .

In a postscript Rubens adds: "I forgot to say that at the summit we found large deer (*forze venayson*), as you see in the picture."[130]

In his description of the site and in his rendering of it, as far as can be judged from the extant copies, Rubens allowed himself some poetic license. The spot from which Rubens viewed El Escorial – proudly marked today on trail maps of the area as *monumento a Rubens* – indeed rises "very high and steep" above the town below, but it is unlikely that the wooden cross could be seen from Madrid, which is nearly sixty kilometers away. The copies that are known of the lost original also exaggerate the proximity of El Escorial to the mountains rising to its north and south – the left and right sides in the paintings.[131]

The letter in which Rubens describes the view of El Escorial indicates that he was accompanied during his climb to the mountain. As we know from Pacheco that Velázquez joined Rubens in a visit to El Escorial, it is plausible and tempting to see the letter as referring to the young Spanish painter.[132]

The rest of the pictures Rubens painted for his own keeping while he was in Spain were copies of originals by Titian. We have it from Pacheco that he copied numerous paintings by the Venetian master in the royal collection. The belief that Rubens kept them for himself derives from the inventory of his collection made after his death, where there is a section entitled "paintings made by Rubens in Spain, Italy and other places, after Titian and other famous masters." This is followed by sections described as "pictures made by the said sr Peter Paul Rubens after Titian" and, later, "These twenty-one portraits were made after Titian."[133] By supplementing these two sources with our knowledge of the paintings by Titian in Spain at the time of Rubens' visit, an attempt can be made to identify the copies painted by the Fleming after Titian during his second Spanish visit.[134]

After stating that Rubens copied "all the things by Titian that the king has," Pacheco goes on to cite twelve specific paintings by Titian copied by Rubens in Madrid:[135] two "baths," which must be *Diana and Acteon* and *Diana and Callisto*; a *Venus and Adonis*; the *Rape of Europa*; a scene of Venus and Cupid; the *Adam and Eve*; the *Portrait of Philip von Hesse, Landgrave*; the *Portrait of Johann Friedrich, Elector of Saxony*; the *Portrait of the Duke of Alba*; the *Portrait of Francisco de los Cobos*; a *Portrait of a Venetian Dux*; and a portrait of Philip II, which is almost certainly the famous *Philip II in Armor* in the Prado.[136]

Of these paintings, the following copies by Rubens are known today: the copy of Titian's *Diana and Callisto* is in Lancashire, Knowsley, Collection of the earl of Derby; the *Rape of Europa* is in the Prado; the "scene of Venus and Cupid" is in the Museo Thyssen-Bornemisza in Madrid; the *Adam and Eve* is in the Prado (Fig. 46); and the copy of the portrait *Philip II in Armor* is in Chatsworth, in the collection of the duke of Devonshire. The whereabouts of the other copies by Rubens are not known; they are presumably lost.

A drawing in a private collection in the Getty Museum in Los Angeles that includes figures from the first three paintings cited above is the only working drawing by Rubens that survives from this set of copies, but more must have existed.[137]

The statement that Rubens painted all the Titians in the royal collection is best read as a rhetorical phrase and should not be taken literally, but it suggests that additional copies can be identified. Aside from the twelve paintings listed by subject matter, Pacheco informs us that Rubens also copied "other things" by Titian and "many paintings outside of those owned by the king," presumably also referring to works by Titian. Indeed, and judging from the recorded copies by Rubens, mainly in his own collection, we can be certain that the number of Titians copied by Rubens in Spain was indeed extensive.

One of the copies Pacheco does not identify by title is probably a *Venus and Cupid with an Organist*.[138] The original by Titian hung in the summer apartments in the Alcázar, the same location as other paintings copied by Rubens, and the painting of "Venus and Cupid on a Bed," a copy probably after that composition, appears in Rubens' collection among the copies after Titian. There is also a group of portraits listed as copies of Titian in Rubens' collection for which the prototypes were in Spain, indicating that they must have been copied there. These

FIGURE 45

P. Verhulst, copy after Rubens, *A View of El Escorial*. Longford Castle, Collection of the Earl of Radnor.

portraits are: *Portrait of Alfonso d'Este, Duke of Ferrara,*[139] *Portrait of the Dwarf Estanislao,*[140] a portrait of a Venetian Courtesan,[141] *Portrait of Charles V with Drawn Sword* (Fig. 47),[142] *Portrait of Charles V with Baton* (Fig. 48),[143] *Portrait of the Empress Isabella,*[144] *Double Portrait of Charles V and the Empress Isabella.*[145] A *Bust Portrait of Charles V Wearing a Helmet* was probably painted in Spain after Titian's large *Charles V on Horseback.*[146]

There is a problem with the dating of this group of portraits. It is not certain that they were all copied from Titian during Rubens' second visit to Spain, because the prototypes existed there during both of the painter's visits. The four portraits of Charles V and his wife and the portrait of the Venetian courtesan are sometimes dated to the first Spanish visit in 1603–1604, fundamentally on the basis of style.[147] This argument can be misleading when dealing with faithful copies of past masters, because Rubens may have attempted to imitate the style of his model rather than to paint in a manner of his own at a given date.

Another clue that has been used to date these paintings to 1603–1604 is also inconclusive. An anonymous engraving attributed to Lucas Vorsterman exists that shows a portrait of Charles V in which the head is taken from Titian's *Charles V with Baton* and the body and background from *Portrait of Charles V with Drawn Sword.*[148] This engraving, inscribed "E Titiani Prototypo P. P. Rubens excud. Cum Privilegiis," has been dated before February 24, 1620, because after that date the "Cum Privilegiis" would have been replaced by a more lengthy inscription alluding to the foreign privileges obtained in 1620.[149] It follows that this print must have been executed before that date and therefore that its source, Rubens' copy, was executed before his second trip to Spain in 1628–1629. However, the inscription "Cum Privilegiis" can be found on prints of a later date that were not made under Rubens' initiative: Vorsterman is known to have used the formula "Cum Privilegiis" liberally, and Dutch engravers also frequently used it.[150] Titian's fame as a portrait painter, which dates back to the painter's own lifetime, is justification enough for Rubens to have desired to paint copies of these portraits on either of his visits to Spain. However, there are reasons to favor a date on the second trip. The first of these is the documented interest of Rubens during the 1628–1629 visit in making copies after Titian. Also, it makes more sense for Rubens to have painted for his own collection at this point, when the copies could be shipped back to Antwerp with the painter, rather than in his earlier years, when he would have had to return with them to Mantua or have them shipped.

Other portraits that Rubens copied from Titian (as documented by the list of his own collection) may have been painted in Spain or in another location. A *Portrait of Francesco Sforza, Duke of Milan* was painted either in Spain or in Antwerp, where there was an original by

FIGURE 46

Rubens, copy after Titian, *Adam and Eve*. Madrid, Museo del Prado.

Titian.[151] Another portrait after Titian is described in Rubens' collection as showing a man with a dog.[152] This is most likely a copy after Titian's *Portrait of Federigo Gonzaga*, and could have been copied either from the Leganés collection in Madrid or from the ducal collection in Mantua. In addition, there are paintings in Rubens' collection that he copied from Titian and for which the prototypes are either unknown or have an unknown provenance;[153] some of these paintings could also have been executed in Spain, given the extensive number of paintings by Titian in the Spanish royal collection.

If all the copies mentioned above were executed in Madrid in 1628–1629, we must add ten paintings and the Escorial landscape to the twelve specifically mentioned by Pacheco, but the possibility that this number may need to be significantly reduced (if many of the copies after Titian were executed in 1603), or slightly enlarged, should be kept in mind.[154]

Rubens' study of Titian during his second visit to Spain is a rare and fascinating case of an encounter of one great master with another.[155] As Julius Held has pointed out, Rubens focused his study of Titian on two types of paintings: mythological scenes (especially Titian's paintings for Philip II known as the *poesie*)[156] and portraits. Only the copy of Titian's painting of *Adam and Eve* falls outside of these two categories. The monumental nudes and sensuous appeal of this religious painting had earlier induced the Spanish kings to separate it from most of the other religious images in their possession and hang it in a section of the Alcázar largely dedicated to mythological works.[157] It must have been the display of this painting in its secular context that prompted Rubens to copy it along with the portraits and mythological paintings.

It is hard to know exactly why Rubens focused on Titian's mythologies and portraits, but there may have been a practical reason. While in Madrid, the Flemish painter resided in the Alcázar, as we have learned from his correspondence with Peiresc.[158] He could only have had adequate time and facilities to paint the copies when he was in that palace, where Titian's mythological paintings and portraits were most abundant. The religious paintings of Titian were displayed primarily in El Escorial, where Rubens must have seen them but might have had more limited time for copying.

The exquisite sensuousness of Titian's mythologies, their warm and rich color, the abstract qualities of their execution, and their ability to create the impression of a live presence are the reasons for which these paintings are admired today, and also are surely among the reasons Rubens dedicated part of his time in Madrid to their study. The translation of ancient sources – mainly Ovid – undertaken by Titian, and his unleashing of the erotic potential of the themes he represented, must have also appealed to Rubens' interests and taste. Certainly his concentration on Titian's mythological paintings had an important effect on Rubens' own art. As Held has pointed out, the vivid reenactment of ancient myths that characterizes Titian's mythologies and Rubens' copies after them would emerge again in Rubens' late mythologies, many of them painted for Philip IV.[159]

When copying the portraits by Titian, Rubens concentrated primarily on those of well-known and distinguished subjects. His interest in these portraits derives from the exemplary role assigned to them at the time. Titian's portraits of European rulers had come to be seen as ideal representations of nobility in the age of the Counter-Reformation, especially in the lands governed by the Hapsburgs, who had been his greatest patrons. Titian had managed to endow his sitters with an admired "heroic majesty," as it was described by Ludovico Dolce,[160]

FIGURE 47

Rubens, copy after Titian, *Portrait of Charles V with Drawn Sword*. Yorkshire, Collection of Lord Mountgarret.

FIGURE 48

Rubens, copy after Titian, *Portrait of Charles V with Baton*. Detmold, Collection of Wilfred Goepel.

and his fame as a portrait painter long outlived him, as is shown by Palomino, who in the early eighteenth century wrote: "there was no man of standing or person placed in a position of honor in his day who did not ask to have a painting or portrait from his [Titian's] hand, because he was such an outstanding artist in this field."[161] The extensive number and prominent display of Titian's portraits in the collection of Philip IV underscored their status as models at the time of Rubens' stay in the Spanish court. Fueled by the reputation of the Venetian in Madrid, Rubens' interest in the portraits probably originated in a concern with developing his own style of portraiture and adapting it to an ideal of nobility that had been so successfully expressed by Titian.

One aspect of Rubens' relationship with Titian during his stay in Madrid that could benefit from further attention is the Spanish context in which he encountered the art of the Venetian master. Throughout his career Rubens was a careful student of the masters of the past. Given Titian's reputation in the seventeenth century and Rubens' proven interest in studying and purchasing his paintings before 1628, there is nothing surprising in the interest he took in Titian's mythologies and portraits during his stay in Spain. Nevertheless, his concentration on the art of the Venetian at this time is an extraordinary event. Rubens' apparently exclusive focus on works by Titian, ignoring works by other painters, is unprecedented in his career.[162]

Also unique is the impact the study of Titian had on Rubens' own work during the last decade of his life; Titian's art became the defining factor in his stylistic evolution at this point, probably more so than any other single influence at any other time.

Rubens' intense and productive scrutiny of Titian during his Spanish visit is thus clearly exceptional. Julius Held has explained this phenomenon as a result of Rubens' own stylistic evolution, which made the Flemish painter especially open to Titian's colorism at a time when he was transforming his own art in the same direction, and also as a consequence of Rubens' finding an affinity with Titian's understanding of the nature of painting.[163] These arguments should be supplemented by a third element: the fact that Rubens' encounter with the art of Titian at this point took place in Spain. The most important consequence of this, and the most often noted, is the size and superior quality of the collection of Titians in the Spanish royal residences, which provided Rubens with a unique opportunity to study the art of the Venetian master. Titian's high reputation in Spain is another important factor in explaining Rubens' copies. Titian had been the favorite painter of the Spanish royal family from the time of Charles V and continued to hold the same status under Philip IV.[164] The unparalleled esteem for his art close to the time of Rubens' visit to the court is recorded by Vicente Carducho in his *Diálogos de la Pintura* published in 1633, where the painter and writer states that, among all the paintings in the royal collection in Madrid, "the most esteemed by all were always the paintings by Titian."[165]

There is a third, more specific and provocative reason why Rubens studied Titian with such intensity at this time. As we have seen, during his stay at the Spanish court, Rubens was commissioned to paint an equestrian portrait of the king as a pendant to Titian's *Charles V at the Battle of Mühlberg*. This commission effectively placed Rubens in the role of Titian's heir, with all the expectations associated with that position. Seeing himself as the seventeenth-century version of Titian, he had special reason to focus on the paintings of his predecessor. Even if Rubens saw these events in a less lofty manner, the mechanics of having to execute an equestrian portrait that was to hang alongside a recognized masterpiece by Titian would have forced the painter to study the Venetian's works closely. This, in turn, might have reignited his interest in this great master and prompted further studies and copies.[166]

Based on the information presented in this chapter, we can attempt to estimate the number of paintings made by Rubens during his second visit to Spain. He painted at least nine portraits of the royal family (ten, if he painted two portraits of the queen); three (or more) portraits of the unidentified infanta from the Descalzas; two religious works for Leganés and Cárdenas; five (or six) portraits of unidentified sitters; two landscapes; at least twelve and possibly up to twenty-three copies after Titian; possibly an equestrian portrait of Philip II; and an extensive enlargement of a previous work, the *Adoration of the Magi*. The total amounts to at least thirty-three plus the enlargement (counting only twelve copies after Titian, and not including the Philip II on horseback), but the count is more likely closer to forty-four paintings. Of these, probably only eleven, in addition to the enlargement, remained in Spain: they are the equestrian portrait of Philip IV and possibly the one of Philip II if it was painted at this time, two of the portraits of the infanta from the Descalzas, the two religious paintings, and possibly the five or six unidentified portraits.

In addition to the paintings executed by Rubens in Spain, other paintings that he had produced in Flanders arrived in Madrid during or very close to the time of his visit. These are: the *Garland of Fruits and Flowers with Virgin and Child* brought to Spain by Leganés, the eight paintings brought by Rubens from Flanders that were discussed in the previous chapter, and the twenty tapestries designed for the Descalzas Reales, also noted earlier. These paintings raise the already significant number of works by Rubens that entered and remained in Spain between 1628 and the painter's departure in the spring of 1629.

Rubens, Velázquez, and Crescenzi

During the nearly eight months Rubens was in Madrid he met two of the most important figures in the artistic life of the court, the painter Diego Velázquez and the Roman noble and artist Giovanni Battista Crescenzi.

The possibility that Rubens and Velázquez may have shared a studio during this time has been mentioned. More secure evidence of contacts between the two is provided by an oft-quoted passage by Pacheco: "[Rubens] communicated little with painters. He only established a friendship with my son-in-law (with whom he had earlier corresponded), and he greatly favored his works for their modesty, and together they went to see the Escorial."[167]

The most important effect that Rubens' presence in Madrid appears to have had on Velázquez was cultural rather than more specifically artistic. Rubens was an example of the highest status artists could reach: he was a highly successful painter, and also a courtier. Personal contact with the worldly Fleming must have contributed to shaping Velázquez's own social and professional ambitions. As was suggested early on by Palomino, Rubens probably also played a role in encouraging Velázquez to visit Italy, which the Spaniard did from August 1629 until early 1631.[168] While he was in Spain, Rubens thought of embarking on a visit to Italy, a thought he may have shared with Velázquez.[169] He may also have made the Spanish painter (and his royal employer) realize that he needed to develop important aspects of his art, most notably history painting, regarded at the time as the noblest of pictorial genres.[170] This was best studied in Italy in direct contact with the great art of the past.

We have little evidence of the opinions that the two artists held of each other's paintings. If we can trust Pacheco, Rubens appreciated Velázquez's art for its "modesty." This enigmatic comment seems appropriate in view of the differences between the restricted palette and cerebral compositions of Velázquez's work, especially in the 1620s, and Rubens' effusive pictorial language. However, given Pacheco's championing of Velázquez, this comment may well reflect the opinion of the writer rather than that of Rubens. In a letter he wrote to Jan Gaspar Gevaerts from Madrid on December 29, 1628, Rubens stated: "The King alone arouses my sympathy."[171] The omission of Velázquez's name is worth noting. Rubens' statement cannot be taken literally, but it suggests that the impression made on Rubens by the Spanish painter, if it had been highly favorable, might have been mentioned.

Given Rubens' twenty-two-year seniority over Velázquez, and the difference in professional maturity between the two painters at this time, an artistic influence of Velázquez on Rubens could hardly be expected. The exact degree to which Rubens' paintings influenced the art of the Spaniard at this time is difficult to evaluate.[172] Velázquez, as we can see from his paintings, had sufficient artistic personality and maturity to retain his own idiom even in the presence of Rubens. In other words, he was too advanced in his career for his style to develop as had that of Van Dyck and the other Flemish artists who learned Rubens' artistic language at an early age. Velázquez's painting of the *Feast of Bacchus* (Fig. 49) was probably executed during Rubens' stay in Madrid and serves to illustrate the differences, and also some similarities, between the two artists.[173] The style of Velázquez's painting remains emphatically naturalistic, and far from the flamboyance and idealism of the Flemish master. On the other hand, the selection of a mythological theme, which is unusual in the career of Velázquez up to this point, may have been encouraged in part by Rubens' presence and by his study of Titian's mythologies.[174] The compositional arrangement of the *Feast of Bacchus* may also owe something to Rubens. Velázquez appears to have made some changes in his composition as he worked on the scene that are similar to the ones made by Rubens in his *Adoration of the Magi*, as they were explained earlier in this chapter. The two dark figures in the lower-left and upper-right corners of the *Feast of Bacchus* were probably added by Velázquez at a late stage in the making of the painting.[175] These figures have the effect of altering the compositional personality of the work, adding to the preexisting rectangular

FIGURE 49

Velázquez, *Feast of Bacchus*. Madrid, Museo del Prado.

structure a diagonal emphasis, both on the surface of the canvas and also in depth. When one considers the similarities of these changes and their effects in comparison with those Rubens made in the *Adoration*, it does not seem too farfetched to suggest that it was Rubens' work which inspired the alterations made by Velázquez in his own picture.

Another instance when Velázquez drew inspiration from Rubens' work is the case, studied above, of the foam painted on the mouths of horses by both artists. This particular instance of mimetic practice is of some importance, as explained earlier. The detail of the froth that Rubens rendered dripping from the mouths of the horses in his paintings added to the vigor so characteristic of his work. The fact that this element had originated in a text by Pliny the Elder must have contributed to Rubens' image as a learned artist – an image Pacheco documents when he cites Rubens' knowledge of *letras* ("letters") among the reasons that gained him honor.[176] Velázquez recognized the significance of the small detail of the foam. By incorporating it into his own paintings, he added the same qualities of animation and erudition to his pictorial language.

Another issue that demands attention is the possible influence that Rubens's technique had on Velázquez during the former's stay in Madrid. It is true, as has recently been pointed out by Frances Huemer, that the stylistic development of Rubens and Velázquez followed similar paths throughout their careers.[177] Both of them evolved from a youthful style marked by the plasticity and chiaroscuro that had been made fashionable by the influence of Caravaggio, to a more Venetian manner defined by the use of brighter colors and less emphasis on the contours of figures and objects, with a greater freedom in the application of the paint. Even though the similarities between the two artists are problematic (the early Rubens, for example, is different from the young Velázquez in his taste for stronger colors; and the techniques of both artists can vary according to subject matter or other circumstances), the idea of a similar evolution is, broadly speaking, valid. It may be that during his stay in Madrid Rubens gave some advice on these matters, or had some influence over his younger colleague, as Huemer suggests. But it is important to remember that the presence of Rubens in Madrid did not cause an immediate inflection in the development of Velázquez's art. After Rubens left Spain, Velázquez spent nearly a year in Italy. During this experimental period, his technique underwent some changes – his paint became thinner and more translucent – but his application of the paint remains rather controlled in his Italian works, with color and brushstrokes often clearly defining the contours of the forms depicted.[178] The change in Velázquez's technique is more marked at a later date, in his paintings of the 1630s and thereafter.[179] The intervening Italian trip makes the influence of Rubens' direct contact with the Spaniard in 1628–1629 difficult to evaluate. It should also be kept in mind that Rubens' paintings continued to arrive in Spain long after his visit to Madrid, as the following chapters of this book will show. If Rubens had an effect on the evolution of Velázquez's technique – and this, as we have seen, is not certain – it could have resulted from the presence in Madrid of Rubens' paintings, but not necessarily of Rubens himself.

The second mention of an artistic acquaintance made by Rubens in Madrid is included in a text by the writer and court musician Lázaro Díaz del Valle, who wrote his *Epílogo y Nomenclatura de Angunos Artífices* between 1656 and 1659.[180] According to this source, during his stay at the Spanish court Rubens had a chance to meet the Roman nobleman and artist Giovanni Battista Crescenzi.[181] Crescenzi (1577–1635), a contemporary of Rubens, had arrived at the Spanish court in 1617 and remained there until his death.[182] By the time of Rubens' arrival in Madrid, Crescenzi had been made marquis de la Torre, a member of the Order of Santiago, and had become one of the most important artistic figures at the court. He produced architectural designs for the king, collected paintings, and sponsored one of the most talented young artists in Madrid, Antonio de Pereda. Rubens may have already met Crescenzi in the first years of the century in Rome, where both moved in the same circles.[183] In 1628–1629, Crescenzi's status at the Spanish court and his aristocratic origin must have awakened Rubens' interest. Also, Crescenzi's collection in Madrid included paintings by Elsheimer, the painter of whom Rubens had once said: "in my opinion he had no equal in small figures, in landscapes, and in many other subjects." Rubens' taste for the German painter must have motivated him to visit Crescenzi's pictures while he was in Spain.[184]

A Reputation Established

Rubens' second visit to the Spanish court appears in retrospect to be a cornerstone of his ties to Spain. This is in part due to the actual presence of the artist on Spanish soil and to his personal contact with Philip IV, who would soon become his greatest patron, and with Velázquez – all of which factors provide irresistible fuel to the historical imagination. Moreover, Rubens' visit to Madrid was of great importance to the formation of his exemplary role in the history of art in Spain.

As we have seen, during his tenure at the Spanish court, Rubens received the most important commission proposed by the king, the large *Equestrian Portrait of Philip IV* for the New Room, and he also undertook some other important projects for the monarch, such as the additions to the *Adoration of the Magi*. The equestrian portrait, in effect, cast Rubens in the role of Titian's heir. As a result of his association with so famous a figure, Rubens was endowed with an aura of timeless respectability and was immediately regarded as a historical figure of prominence.

The commission of the equestrian portrait, and the consequent association with Titian, both stemmed from the personal favor of Philip IV. Rubens himself referred proudly to his association with the king when he wrote in his correspondence from Madrid that Philip IV visited him personally every day. Further evidence of the same personal favor can be found at a somewhat later date, in April 1631, when Philip IV wrote to the infanta Isabella concerning Rubens' possible trip to London for a second time to continue negotiations with England: "Rubens [the king wrote] is highly regarded at the Court of England and very capable of negotiating all sorts of affairs. . . . In such matters one needs ministers of proven intelligence, with whom one is satisfied."[185] By that time, however, Rubens was tiring of his involvement in politics and was not inclined to accept the mission.[186] What is of interest here is the very favorable opinion expressed by the king, which undoubtedly was based on the meeting of the two men in Madrid.

The crucial importance of the personal favor bestowed by Philip IV on Rubens is also reflected in the written sources. Palomino, who best summarizes the history of the arts in seventeenth-century Spain, repeatedly insists on the high position and honors earned by Rubens outside of his profession as a painter and writes about the "great esteem" in which the ministers at the court and the king held Rubens, "for his person and his talent."[187] Closer to the time of Rubens' visit, Pacheco, who has guided us through much of this chapter, uses his short biography of the Flemish painter as an example of the exalted social position that can be reached by painters. He refers extensively to the favor shown to Rubens by kings, princes, and other high-ranking figures as proof of his elevated position, although he ends by concluding, no doubt correctly, that Rubens' fame ultimately derived from his talent as a painter.[188]

The personal favor of the king, established during the painter's visit to Spain, also played an important role in one of the highest honors that Rubens would ever receive. On August 20, 1631, two years and four months after his departure from Madrid, Rubens received from Philip IV a Spanish knighthood, the title of *caballero*.[189] This title added distinction to the noble status the artist had enjoyed since 1624, but without elevating him above the level of the plain nobles.

The petition for the knighthood, dated July 16, 1631, reveals the factors that contributed most to Rubens' rise in Spain. It was issued by the Council of the Netherlands and was addressed to the king by the infanta Isabella:

Peter Paul Rubens, secretary of Your Majesty's privy council of the Netherlands, states that he has served Your Majesty in the affairs that Your

Majesty and his ministers know, and with all fidelity and satisfaction. And wishing to continue this service with added luster and authority, he begs Your Majesty to honor him with the title of *caballero*.

Her Serene Highness the Infanta writes to Your Majesty recommending this request, noting the services of the nominee, and begging Your Majesty to grant him the honor he [she?] requests. Your Majesty knows him and his good qualities, and knows how rare he is in his profession. In consideration of this and for his services in important matters, and as he has served as Your Majesty's secretary, this will not have the consequence of encouraging others of his profession to seek a similar favor. The Emperor Charles V made Titian a Knight of Santiago. And thus it seems wise for Your Majesty to honor the nominee with the title of *caballero* he pretends to.[190]

First, this text shows that Rubens' request was justified by the fact that it was backed by the infanta Isabella. This indicates the importance of her support in the honor awarded to the painter by her nephew, the king of Spain, and serves as a reminder that Rubens' trip to Spain was encouraged by Isabella. Second, the document reminds the king of his personal acquaintance with the painter, indicating that the visit of Rubens to Madrid was important because it allowed him personally to display and prove his "good qualities," which made him a rarity among painters. Third, the petition repeatedly states that Rubens should be knighted as a consequence of his service to the king, and despite his profession as a painter, thus demonstrating the importance of proximity to the king for Rubens' claim to a higher status. Finally, the text alludes to the example of the knighthood granted by Charles V to Titian, cited as a precedent. This reveals the importance of Rubens' claim to Titian's inheritance within the tradition of the patronage of the Spanish Hapsburgs.

Two additional aspects of this petition are worth noting. One is the fact that two of the reasons mentioned in support of the petition, the patronage of Isabella and service to the Spanish monarchy, echo the reasons alluded to for the first privileges that were granted to Rubens by the Spanish Crown in 1623 and 1624, thus underscoring the continuity of Rubens' services to the Crown. The petition also shows that, in spite of his extensive participation in the diplomatic affairs of Spain and the positive impression caused during his visit to Madrid, Rubens' profession as a painter remained a problem that had to be addressed. As has been noted,[191] the infanta assures Philip IV in the text of the petition that the example of Rubens' knighthood will not serve to encourage other painters to seek similar honors, because it is Rubens' services to the Crown, not his profession, that justify his being honored.

After the visit of 1628–1629, Rubens never returned to Spain. Gradually, he also ceased his diplomatic duties on behalf of Philip IV. Two new conflicts would still require his diplomatic skills, but only briefly, between 1631 and 1633.[192] One was the struggle between the exiled

Marie de' Medici and her son the duke of Orleans, on one side, and Cardinal Richelieu and Louis XIII, on the other, the painter siding with his former patroness in the belief that her cause represented an opportunity to undermine Richelieu's France, Spain's greatest enemy.[193] The second was an attempt initiated by the infanta to negotiate a new peace treaty with the United Provinces. On these, as on previous occasions, Rubens represented the infanta, and through her the Spanish Crown. However, with the death of Isabella in December of 1633, Rubens' diplomatic activities finally came to an end, allowing the tired artist to return full-time to his "beloved profession" of painting.[194]

The relationship between Rubens and the Spanish court in the remaining years of the painter's life was to be primarily artistic. The fame and favor he had earned during his visit had established Rubens' reputation in the eyes of the Spanish king. This newly gained status would find its fruition in the large number of paintings produced by Rubens and his studio that entered Spain in the 1630s.

CHAPTER FOUR

The King's Chosen Painter, 1630–1640

Few mentions of Rubens' paintings are recorded in Spain in the years immediately following his departure from Madrid. This may seem at odds with the recognition gained by the painter during the 1628–1629 visit to the Spanish court, but it can be explained by events affecting the lives of his Spanish patrons and by his own professional preoccupations at the time. By 1636, when circumstances were right, the foundation laid in earlier years allowed for a large number of works by Rubens to arrive in Spain.[1]

The First half of the Decade: A Slow Beginning

The first painting by Rubens to enter Spain after the painter's departure was probably *Wolf and Fox Hunt* (New York, Metropolitan Museum of Art, Fig. 50). This work was executed at an earlier date. It was originally probably intended for the archduke Albert, but was eventually sold in the marketplace, where it was purchased in 1617 by a leading Flemish aristocrat, Philippe Charles d'Arenberg, duke of Aarschot.[2] The arrival of this painting in the Iberian Peninsula was an indirect consequence of Spain's political position in Europe, and it follows a pattern previously observed in the cases of the duke of Lerma and Calderón. On November 16, 1633, the duke of Aarschot left Flanders for Madrid, where he was to act as a representative of the States General of Flanders, which was then involved in negotiations with the Dutch.[3] After writing in a letter from Madrid of December 27, 1633, that he was staying with the marquis of Leganés "as in paradise,"[4] Aarschot was arrested on April 15, 1634, for his participation in a rebellion of Flemish nobles against Spanish rule in the Netherlands that had taken place in 1632. First he was imprisoned, and in December he was placed under house arrest in Madrid, where he died on December 17, 1640 – ironically, at a time when his case was being favorably reviewed. In the Spanish capital, Aarschot furnished his residence with an important collection of Flemish paintings, which included this *Wolf and Fox Hunt*, his only painting by Rubens.[5] Even though the picture is first recorded in Madrid in

1641, it is safe to assume that Aarschot had brought it from Flanders before this date, perhaps as early as the time of his arrival in Spain, as he had owned it since 1617. After the duke's death, the painting was purchased by the marquis of Leganés, who was then in the process of forming his important collection of paintings by Rubens.

The *Wolf and Fox Hunt* occupies an important place in Rubens' oeuvre as the first monumental hunting scene the artist created. Although the work had been painted some years before its arrival in Madrid in the 1630s, the subject of the *Wolf and Fox Hunt* was a novelty to Spanish eyes, because it was the first pure hunting scene by the master to enter Spain. Apparently, the painting caused a sensation, as hunting scenes were soon among the king's most favored and copiously collected themes by Rubens.

The duke of Aarschot and Rubens had become bitter rivals in the years that preceded the former's travel to Spain. On one famous occasion, Aarschot reprimanded Rubens for not showing him the respect he believed he was due as a high-ranking nobleman.[6] In view of this, Aarschot's decision to bring the *Wolf and Fox Hunt* from Brussels to Madrid seems surprising.[7] It may be that "what the picture signified outweighed all other considerations," as Susan Koslow has suggested in her study of the painting. According to the same author, the particular manner in which Rubens represented the hunt in this picture (the protagonist is a nobleman of distinction, as indicated by the golden spur he wears, who makes use of his right to hunt with a pack of hounds and a hunting horn) alluded to the privileges of the high nobility in the Netherlands, and also to their role as loyal defenders of the state. By hanging this painting in his residence-prison in Madrid, Aarschot may have hoped to benefit from associating with the political message of loyalty to the Hapsburg rulers depicted in it.[8]

There is another explanation of why Aarschot brought the *Wolf and Fox Hunt* to Madrid in spite of his hostility toward its author: the reputation enjoyed by Rubens in the Spanish court. As we saw in the last chapter, Rubens' visit to Spain in 1628–1629 had resulted in the painter's reaching an exalted status there. The king's extensive collecting of his works during the 1630s further enhanced the prestige associated with owning them, and the king's taste was soon imitated by a handful of Spain's elite collectors. In this context, the presence in Aarschot's residence of Rubens' monumental picture must have been read as a sign of extraordinary distinction.

As in other collections, the number of works by Rubens owned by the royal family increased very slowly in the first half of the decade of the 1630s. The Alcázar, the main repository of the royal paintings, was inventoried in 1636. At that time it included only one painting by Rubens of which there is no earlier notice, a *Devotion of Rudolf I* (Madrid, Prado; Fig. 51).[9] In the inventory, the scene is attributed to

Rubens alone. The powerful modeling of the figures and the rhythmic disposition of their forms on the large canvas, subtly accentuated by the mirroring poses of the dismounted hunters, are indeed characteristic of the master's style. The landscape setting, on the other hand, lacks the vivacity of Rubens' brush and is often attributed to Jan Wildens.

The painting must have entered Spain shortly before 1636, because the Alcázar inventory of that year is the first existing record of it.[10] The fact that the scene depicts Rudolf I (1273–1313), the Hapsburg count who was the first of his family to become Holy Roman Emperor, may indicate that it was commissioned for, or by, a member of the Hapsburg family. The importance of the landscape, and the humorous, genre-like treatment of the subject matter, underscored by the unstable mount of the sacristan and the urinating dog, exhibit the more Flemish side of Rubens' art. This suggests that the painting was made for a local audience – possibly for the archdukes.

However this may be, after its arrival in Spain the dynastic content certainly elicited appreciation. The dynastic reference is linked with the devotion of the Hapsburgs to the Sacrament of the Eucharist. The scene shows Rudolf of Hapsburg guiding a horse that he has given to a priest who is bringing the Eucharist to a dying peasant. This gesture demonstrated the piety of the future Rudolf I and gained divine favor for him and his successors. The devotion of Philip IV (and his immediate ancestors and successors) to the Eucharist must have been an

FIGURE 50

Rubens and assistants, *Wolf and Fox Hunt*. New York, The Metropolitan Museum of Art, John Stewart Kennedy Fund, 1910.

additional reason for the king to favor this work. The painting was installed in the king's bedroom in the summer apartments of the Alcázar, together with other works that referred to the long line of Hapsburg rulers.[11] Given Philip IV's fixation on his genealogy, and on his role as defender of the faith and the holy sacraments, it was fitting that the *Devotion of Rudolf I* hung in his room when he died on September 17, 1665, as was noted in a convoluted epitaph written in Latin for the occasion:

By chance, but not by chance, have the ministers laid out the royal bedchamber beneath this picture, which reports the origin of the glory and the grandeur of the grandfathers of the prince, [glory and grandeur] that will have their promised end not on earth, as long as the constant sacrifice in Heaven endures, as long as the nuptials of the Immaculate Lamb endure. So [by hanging this picture here] it befitted the everlasting empire of the Austrias to be marked out. Philip, who, with Rudolf, by an equal (if not identical) reverence, venerated the admirable sacrament of the Catholic Faith while he lived.[12]

An omission in this epitaph is worth noting: even though considerable attention is devoted to the painting of Rudolf I, the name of its author is never mentioned.[13] The extensive collecting of Rubens' work documented throughout this study indicates that his paintings could be regarded as a commodity whose value derived from his authorship. However, the omission of the painter's name in the epitaph for Philip IV is important as a reminder of the purely representational value of Rubens' art; it shows that his paintings were displayed and appreciated, not only for what his "signature" meant in material terms, but also for their symbolic power.

It is sometimes difficult to be precise about dates when attempting to establish a pattern for the arrival in Spain of paintings by Rubens. This is the case with a set of five exquisite scenes painted by Jan Brueghel and Rubens in 1617–1618 depicting the senses, which are now in the Prado (Figs. 52–56). The paintings in the series show some of the palaces of the archdukes Albert and Isabella, and also objects that are known to have been part of their collection, indicating that it was probably the archdukes themselves who commissioned the pictures.[14] Albert and Isabella must have given the paintings as a gift to Wolfgang-Wilhelm von Zweibrücken, Count Palatine and duke of Neuburg, a famous convert to Catholicism in 1614, who is the first recorded owner of these works. According to the earliest record of these paintings, which is the inventory of the Alcázar of 1636, the duke of Neuburg gave them as a gift to the cardinal-infante Ferdinand, brother of Philip IV. Ferdinand, the inventory continues, gave the set to the duke of Medina de las Torres, who in turn gave them to the king.[15] The gift from Neuburg to the cardinal-infante could have occurred during the former's visit to Spain from October 1624 to March 1625. However, if the paintings were brought to Spain at this time, it is hard to explain why they were given to the king's younger brother, and not to the king himself. A more likely occasion when the five senses might have entered the collection of the cardinal-infante Ferdinand is October 1634, when Neuburg met Ferdinand, who was on his way to Brussels from the battle of Nördlingen, and presented him with some unspecified gifts.[16]

Precisely when the paintings were given to Medina de las Torres by the cardinal-infante, and the reasons for the gift, are also unclear, as are the circumstances under which Medina de las Torres in turn gave the paintings to the king. Ramiro Pérez de Guzmán was made first duke of Medina de las Torres in August 1626. He later became one of the leading figures of the reign of Philip IV. Medina de las Torres played an important role in the collecting activities of the king, assisting him in the decoration of the Buen Retiro palace in the 1630s and presenting him with paintings by the Bassani, Correggio, Raphael, Titian, and Veronese, in addition to the series under discussion here. Medina de las Torres is also known as a collector in his own right.[17] It is not known when he gave the paintings of the senses to the king.

FIGURE 51

Rubens and Wildens, *Devotion of Rudolf I.* Madrid, Museo del Prado.

FIGURE 52

Jan Brueghel and Rubens, *Allegory of Sight*. Madrid, Museo del Prado.

FIGURE 53

Jan Brueghel and Rubens, *Allegory of Hearing*. Madrid, Museo del Prado.

FIGURE 54

Jan Brueghel and Rubens, *Allegory of Touch*. Madrid, Museo del Prado.

FIGURE 55

Jan Brueghel and Rubens, *Allegory of Smell*. Madrid, Museo del Prado.

Medina de las Torres appears to have been born around 1612, though there is some confusion surrounding this date.[18] Given his probable age, it seems likely that the paintings were transferred to the royal collection in the early 1630s, close to the time when they are first inventoried in 1636. If so, then the five senses should be counted among the handful of pictures by Rubens that entered the royal collection immediately before the king's flurry of collecting works by the Flemish master in 1636–1640.

We now consider these exquisite images to be primarily the work of Jan Brueghel, with Rubens' role limited to the execution of the small figures.[19] However, the first record of their presence in Spain, the 1636 royal inventory, stresses the participation of Rubens by dividing the labor of the two artists in the following terms: "Five paintings . . . of the five senses, the figures by the hand of Rubens, and the landscapes, fruits, flowers, hunting items, musical instruments and armor by the hand of Brugul [*sic*]."[20] If one considers the appearance of the five paintings, this description of the participation of Rubens and Brueghel emphasizes the role of the former by listing his name first, reflecting Rubens' reputation in the court of Philip IV at the time the inventory was compiled. This bias is underscored by the fact that some of the paintings in the set bear the signature of Jan Brueghel and none are signed by Rubens.

The five allegories of the senses were kept by the king in a reading room in the northern section of the Alcázar. This was not the main library of the palace, but rather a more private chamber located in a

FIGURE 56

Jan Brueghel and Rubens, *Allegory of Taste*. Madrid, Museo del Prado.

part of the building occupied during the summer months, where the king withdrew from his daily chores to read by a window overlooking a garden.[21] At the time, the room was decorated with two bookshelves made of ebony and bronze, and from its walls hung numerous small paintings, some of them attributed to Patinir, Dürer, and Titian. The king's placing of the five panels attributed to Rubens in this room reveals that he considered them precious pictures, well suited for intimate contemplation. The pleasure derived from them was enhanced by the gemlike quality of the execution. The curtains that appear to be suspended above three of the scenes (the allegories of sight, hearing, and touch) add to the impression that the viewer is contemplating rare treasures indeed. In one of the paintings, the *Allegory of Sight* (Fig. 52), the illusionistic curtain reveals a view that is probably similar to the one that could often be seen in front of the panels inside the Alcázar: the allegorical personification appears as Philip IV must have done, absorbed in the contemplation of wondrous objects in the mist of lavishly decorated rooms that open onto a landscape.

One aspect of these paintings must have contributed to defining Rubens' status in the mind of the king. The senses were traditionally interpreted as instruments of knowledge or of sin. In this particular case, an important additional component of their meaning is a glorification of painting and collecting.[22] Four of the five panels (all except the *Allegory of Smell*) include reproductions of numerous paintings that hang in richly decorated palatial settings. As some of the works reproduced are paintings by Rubens – especially in the *Allegory of Sight* – the love of art and of collecting these images invoke is specifically associated with the Flemish master. At the time when they were executed, these paintings reflected Rubens' status in his hometown of Antwerp. When viewed in Madrid years later, they must have made Philip IV feel proud of the paintings by Rubens that he already owned and incited him to acquire new ones.

Rubens and the Palace of the Buen Retiro

Because of extensive plans to decorate the royal residences in Madrid in the 1630s, these were very active years in the growth of the royal collection.[23] The first surge of collecting during this period came about in 1633, as the new summer palace, the Buen Retiro, was almost completed and thus ready to be decorated.[24] Between that year and 1640, enormous effort, time, and money were poured into this project, which was directed chiefly by the count-duke of Olivares and inspired by the king's taste for paintings. In a concerted effort, many of Spain's diplomats managed to acquire for the Retiro works by some of the most important contemporary painters, including Claude, Lanfranco, and Poussin in addition to many works commissioned from Flanders and

Spain.[25] For this study, the most interesting feature of the decoration of the Buen Retiro is the limited involvement of Rubens; his name only appears in connection with this project on two occasions.[26]

Rubens is first mentioned in relation to the new summer palace as part of a plan to commission an equestrian likeness of King Philip IV. On May 2, 1634, Olivares notified the Florentine envoy in Madrid that the king wished to be portrayed in an equestrian image by a Florentine artist. This project was described by the minister as a "medal or portrait on a horse, in bronze, in agreement with portraits by Peter Paul Rubens and with the design of the one which stands in the Casa de Campo."[27] (The last phrase refers to the equestrian bronze statue of Philip III by Pietro Tacca that had arrived in Madrid earlier in the century.) This letter indicates that some undetermined portrait or portraits of the king by Rubens were at least considered as models in the early stages of this commission, which would eventually materialize into a monumental equestrian statue of Philip IV, also designed and executed by Tacca (Madrid, Plaza de Oriente).[28]

Apparently, original paintings by Rubens were never actually used as models. On September 22, the Florentine envoy notified his court from Madrid that the portrait of the king to be used as a model by the sculptor was not yet finished, and that it would be dispatched to Florence with the drawings for the armor and costume of the king as soon as it was delivered by Olivares.[29] This correspondence appears to rule out Rubens as the author of the image that was used as the model, at least for the figure of the king, as we learn that the model was under way, presumably in Madrid, in 1634, long after Rubens had left the Spanish court.

It may be that the idea of using paintings by Rubens was discarded after the initial phases, or that from the beginning the images being considered as models were copies after paintings by Rubens that were in Spain, rather than originals.[30] Whatever the case, when the statue was completed and installed in the Queen's Garden in the Buen Retiro in October of 1642, it was closer to the work of other artists than to that of Rubens.[31] In light of this, the fact that paintings by Rubens were looked upon as models at an earlier stage may seem of little consequence. This occurrence, however, is highly significant; the fact that in 1634 the Flemish master was Olivares' first choice as the artist who should portray the king is unmistakable proof of the special status Rubens enjoyed in Madrid at that time.

In addition to the possible involvement of Rubens with the equestrian statue, there is only one other painting by him that may have been commissioned for the Buen Retiro, a large *Judgment of Paris* (Fig. 57), and this only in 1638, when the main phase of the decoration of the palace was over.[32] The *Judgment of Paris* was commissioned by the king, whose brother the cardinal-infante Ferdinand, by then governor of the

Spanish Netherlands, acted as his intermediary.[33] The completion of othe painting was delayed until February 27, 1639. The first notice of this work in Spain dates to 1653, when it hung in the Buen Retiro Palace, its splendid nudes prudently concealed behind a curtain. This suggests that it was originally commissioned for that location.[34]

In light of the importance of the commissions received by Rubens during his second visit to Spain in 1628–1629, his limited involvement in the Buen Retiro, the main decorative project of the Spanish Crown in the mid-1630s, is surprising. This may be partly explained by the nature of the project. The decoration of the principal room of the Buen Retiro, the Hall of Realms, represents the most carefully thought-out artistic program of the reign of Philip IV. It is also the most sophisticated campaign during his reign of what we now term political propaganda, exercised through the art of painting. A program that needed to be so carefully planned would seem to require a painter who could be close at hand to direct the decoration and supply images for it. The ready availability of Velázquez for this task is a sufficient reason to explain the exclusion of Rubens from it. The local talent of the Andalusian painter represented a more realistic, and no less fortunate, choice over Rubens.[35]

The fact that no individual paintings by Rubens were commissioned for the decoration of other rooms in the Buen Retiro is more difficult to explain, especially in light of the selection of many works by other leading European painters. The project for the equestrian statue of the king discussed above, and the more uncertain commission of the *Judgment of Paris* for the Retiro, demonstrate that Rubens was in the minds of those in charge of planning and carrying through the decoration of

FIGURE 57

Rubens, *Judgment of Paris*. Madrid, Museo del Prado.

the building. This suggests that his lack of participation was not the result of a predetermined exclusion from the project. A more likely explanation may be found in other factors. The infanta Isabella died in December 1633, and her successor as governor of the Spanish Netherlands, the cardinal-infante Ferdinand, did not arrive in Brussels until November of the following year. Because Rubens' contacts with the Spanish Crown had mostly been channeled through the regent in Brussels, this vacuum of power at the point when the Retiro was being planned may have made Rubens' participation difficult.[36] The amount of work in which Rubens was involved during the early and mid-1630s, when the decoration of the palace was taking shape, must also have had some effect. After his departure from Madrid in April of 1629, the painter was occupied with his diplomatic mission to England. There he received the commission from Charles I to paint a series of paintings for the ceiling of the New Banqueting Hall at Whitehall Palace. He finished this series in August 1634 and dispatched it, after further retouching, in October of 1635.[37] In the latter part of 1634, Rubens received a commission from the magistrates of Antwerp to design the decorations that were intended to celebrate the entry of the cardinal-infante Ferdinand into the city, a project that occupied him into the following year. The extent to which this project kept Rubens busy is best explained in a letter he wrote to Peiresc on December 18, 1634: "Today I am so overburdened with the preparations for the triumphal entry of the Cardinal Infante (which takes place at the end of this month), that I have time neither to live nor to write."[38] During the same period, Rubens also worked on numerous individual commissions for various clients. This extensive activity may well have limited his availability for work destined for the Buen Retiro.

The Torre de la Parada

The reasons for Rubens' absence from the decoration of the Buen Retiro appear to have subsided when the next major artistic project was undertaken at the Spanish court, the decoration of a hunting lodge near Madrid known as the Torre de la Parada.[39] The paintings in this commission are the first that Rubens is certain to have executed for Spain in the 1630s. The Torre de la Parada is also the largest project undertaken by Rubens for the Spanish king (or any other patron in Spain) throughout his career, and it marks the beginning of his heaviest involvement with the Spanish Crown.

The facts surrounding this commission are well known and need to be restated only briefly. Philip IV personally directed the project to the extent that the distance between Madrid and Flanders allowed. The king had a most distinguished agent in Brussels to handle the instructions he sent from Spain: his brother the cardinal-infante Ferdinand.[40]

Ferdinand had had earlier contacts with Rubens. When the painter was in Madrid in 1628–1629, he had painted the infante's portrait along with those of other members of the royal family. In November of 1634 the cardinal-infante had assumed the post of governor of the Spanish Netherlands, and nearly two years later, on June 13, 1636, he confirmed Rubens in his position as court painter and thus continued the support that the infanta Isabella had granted the artist before her death.[41] As a result of the enthusiasm King Philip IV had developed for Rubens' art by this time, the cardinal-infante had fewer opportunities than his predecessor to enlist the painter's services for himself. In the limited time during which he governed the Netherlands before his premature death at the age of thirty-nine on November 9, 1641, Ferdinand's interaction with Rubens was chiefly as the king's agent to ensure the completion of some of Rubens' most important projects for Spain.[42]

The first mention of Rubens' involvement in the Torre de la Parada project dates to November 20, 1636, when the cardinal-infante wrote to Philip IV that the painter had received word of the commission and had begun work on some of the scenes. Rubens proposed dividing the work in two lots, one to be designed by himself and executed by himself and other artists, and the other half to be assigned to a painter referred to as "Esneyre," probably Frans Snyders.[43] In January 1638 the paintings entrusted to Rubens were finished but not yet dry. A couple of months later, on March 11, they were sent from Antwerp to Madrid, where they had arrived by May 1. They were installed in the Torre shortly after that date. The king appears to have asked for some new paintings to make up for some unspecified problems that he found in the original shipment, and these new pictures were probably painted by Rubens. They are probably part of a group that was delivered to Spain on February 27, 1639.[44] By then, the decoration of the Torre was probably complete.

Rubens began his work on the commission by producing sketches for all the scenes that were assigned to him. These sketches were painted in full-scale both by Rubens himself and by other artists. Although the sketches had found their way to Spain by the eighteenth century, they were probably not intended to be sent to the king, for they are not mentioned in the correspondence pertaining to this commission.[45]

The total number of paintings included in the project is uncertain. The earliest inventory of the Torre de la Parada, which dates to 1701–1703, lists sixty-three mythological works by Rubens and his assistants. This number must be very close to the original installation in the Torre during the reign of Philip IV, but it is possible that minor variations occurred before the date of the inventory.

The paintings for the Torre illustrate Ovidian fables and other mythological themes, in addition to two paintings of the ancient philosophers Democritus and Heraclitus. The final series apparently followed no unified program; rather, it was an informal arrangement of related paintings, most of them depicting the loves of gods and goddesses.[46]

Fourteen surviving paintings have been identified as works by Rubens himself, and more may have existed originally. The rest were painted by pupils, assistants, and independent painters who were available for the commission.[47] When the decoration of the Torre was completed, the paintings designed by Rubens joined other works also painted for the same location. These works included fifty hunting and animal scenes presumably by Snayers, Snyders, and Paul de Vos, in addition to pictures by Velázquez, Vicente Carducho, views of royal residences, and other works.[48]

Philip IV took an unprecedented interest in this project. It seems that he personally initiated the commission from Rubens in a memorandum or *memoria original* that is mentioned in a letter from Ferdinand to the king.[49] Because this document is lost, we cannot be sure what instructions were given from Madrid, and what was left for the painter to decide. However, knowing the intended destination of the paintings, the king must have sent at least approximate instructions about the dimensions and number of canvases to be painted. He also certainly gave some instructions on the subject matter, but we have no indication of how specific these were. The correspondence of this commission shows that instructions of Philip IV could sometimes be modified by suggestions from Rubens, even though the final decisions had to be approved by the king. For example, on December 6, 1636, Ferdinand wrote to the king: "I gave him [Rubens] license to change something in this way: in four small ones, where they have asked for fables with few figures, Rubens would like to alter this. I have told him not to change anything until Your Majesty learns what Rubens intends, and orders what should be done."[50] On the other hand, it was left to Rubens to select the artists who were to take part in the execution of the series.[51]

The king may also have been aided by Velázquez in designing the decoration of the Torre. As we saw above, the Spanish painter was probably active in this role in the Buen Retiro, and his supervision is documented in some of the king's decorating projects in the Alcázar and the Escorial at a later date.[52]

The correspondence between Philip IV and the cardinal-infante Ferdinand shows that the Torre de la Parada was a personal project of the king, in contrast to the public and carefully planned Buen Retiro, which had been largely directed by Olivares.[53] In decorating the Torre, the king was concentrating on personal retreat where he could enjoy two of his favorite pastimes, art and hunting.

The private nature of the hunting lodge does not mean that the paintings that hung there were isolated and did not augment knowledge of Rubens' art in Madrid. On at least two occasions in the seventeenth century, important visitors were taken to view the lodge. In October of

1638, Francesco d'Este, duke of Modena, who was in Madrid on a state visit (and was portrayed by Velázquez at the time), was given a tour of the hunting lodge; and years later, in 1677, Count Harrach, the ambassador from Vienna, made the same visit.[54] Surely others must have seen the paintings as well, either because of their own artistic interests, or because they were shown to them by the king or a member of his court. The facts that Bellori referred to this decorative series in 1672, and De Piles did so again in 1681, are further proof that knowledge of Rubens' work at the Torre de la Parada was widespread.[55] Furthermore, at least seventeen copies after paintings in the Torre were made by the court painter Juan Bautista Martínez del Mazo for the royal collection, possibly before 1656.[56] This made the images designed by Rubens available to yet more viewers.

An unusual aspect of the Torre de la Parada commission is the use of painters from outside Rubens' workshop. Even though the extensive use of painters from both inside and outside the shop is not unique, what is unusual, as Alpers has noted, is that the paintings in this set are signed by their authors and are not retouched by Rubens.[57] This has led Alpers to note the mediocre quality of many of the finished paintings and to suggest that it might have been this mediocrity that prompted Rubens to ask other artists to sign their works, in order to distance himself from them. Although it is true that many of the works by Rubens' assistants for the Torre are not paintings of the first rank, the low quality of the group as a whole has been exaggerated. After all, at least fourteen of the paintings executed for the Torre were works painted by Rubens himself; they are all worthy of his talent, and some of them are memorable indeed. The *Ganymede*, for example, renders the rape of the young Trojan shepherd with great intensity (Fig. 58). The drama of the action is emphasized by the contrast between the centrifugality of the youth's limbs and the paralyzing clamp in which he is held by the claws and head of the eagle – Jupiter. The quiver and arrows resemble a phallus that penetrates the young hero, an allusion to the love that Ganymede's beauty aroused in the god. The *Saturn* is equally impressive in rendering the powerful will and ferocity of the god as he devours one of his own children (Fig. 59). Other paintings, such as the *Battle of the Lapiths and the Centaurs* and the *Rape of Proserpina*, manage to recreate with poignancy scenes of overwhelming chaos.[58] In the *Mercury and Argus* (Fig. 60), the artist has stilled the action in order to express the awesome quietness of the moment when Mercury, sword lifted, prepares to strike the sleeping, multi-eyed Argus. The landscape setting in this painting, recently cleaned in the Prado, emerges from the background with startling freshness, exposing beautiful passages of painting.

The impression made by the paintings executed by Rubens for the Torre de la Parada should not be minimized. When the series was first

FIGURE 58

Rubens, *Ganymede*. Madrid, Museo del Prado.

installed in 1639, and even thereafter, few places could match it as an ensemble of original works by Rubens.[59] Indeed, the fact that the Flemish master received important commissions from Philip IV after this one, and that the king ordered Martínez del Mazo to paint copies after many of the scenes, indicates that he held the paintings for the Torre de la Parada in high regard.

Given the few paintings Rubens had produced for the Spanish monarch since the time of his visit to Madrid in 1628–1629, his selection for this commission late in the next decade calls for an explanation. By 1636, when the decoration of the Torre de la Parada was under way,

FIGURE 59

Rubens, *Saturn*. Madrid, Museo del Prado.

FIGURE 60

Rubens, *Mercury and Argus*. Madrid, Museo del Prado.

Rubens had established his reputation in Spain, primarily as a result of his last visit to the court. He had also proven his ability to design large ensembles of allegorical paintings, both abroad, especially in his work for Maria de' Medici and Charles I of England, and in Spain, with his designs for the tapestries of the Eucharist series, which were housed in the convent of the Descalzas Reales in Madrid. No other painter as readily available to the Spanish king as Rubens had comparable credentials for executing a project of the nature of the Torre de la Parada, with its classicizing and allegorical subject matter. The tapestries of the Eucharist series, with their full supply of antique imagery and allegorical personifications, provide the clearest precedent in Spain for the paintings of the Torre de la Parada. It is easy to imagine that an ardent collector such as Philip IV, viewing the tapestries of the Descalzas, must have longed for the time when he could own a large ensemble of similar images created by Rubens.

The size of the commission also made Rubens the best candidate. In purely practical terms, he was the painter best suited for the project because of the organization and size of his workshop and his ability to rally a large number of painters around a single project.

The link that had been established between Rubens and Titian at the Spanish court may also have contributed to the selection of Rubens for the Torre de la Parada project. As explained earlier, during his visit to Madrid in 1628–1629 the Flemish painter had taken on the role of heir to Titian, chiefly as a result of the commission for the *Equestrian Portrait of Philip IV*. During the same visit, Rubens had also carefully studied Titian's mythological paintings. They were the most famous mythological allegories to be seen in Spain, and for that reason they must have been in the mind of the king when he envisioned the Torre project.[60] Philip IV must have considered Titian's *poesie* a precedent for the project he was now planning for his hunting lodge, and the link that had earlier been established between Rubens and Titian may have contributed to his selection of the Flemish painter.

The Last Commissions from the King

Two commissions of paintings for the Alcázar followed the series for the Torre de la Parada. One of these consisted of eighteen scenes ordered in 1639 for the *bóveda de palacio* (the vaulted rooms of the palace), part of the king's summer quarters; the other included four paintings commissioned for the New Room in the same year. The primary source of information for these commissions is the correspondence between the courts in Brussels and Madrid. This evidence is often confusing because it includes references to more than one commission at a time. Nevertheless, it provides sufficient data for a tentative reconstruction of events.

A letter of June 22, 1639, from Ferdinand to the king provides the first mention of a commission for eighteen paintings from Rubens for the *bóveda de palacio*.[61] One month later, on July 22, the artist had completed all the sketches. His intention was to execute the figures and the landscapes himself in the final works, while Snyders would paint the necessary animals.[62] By September 25 of the same year, work on this commission was delayed due to Rubens' preoccupation with another group of paintings for the king: the four scenes commissioned for the New Room (which will be discussed later).[63] Further delays were caused by an attack of gout that struck the painter in the last months of his life. On January 10, 1640, eight of the paintings in the *bóveda* commission were finally completed and ready for shipment to Spain.[64] The remaining scenes were well advanced by April 5, 1640, and were finished and delivered to Brussels by Rubens on May 20, 1640.[65] Some of the paintings were then sent to Spain, whereas others were held until they could be shipped with the other four pictures Rubens was painting for the king. By late March of 1641 the entire set of eighteen canvases had arrived in the Spanish court.[66]

The identification of these eighteen paintings is problematic because their subjects are not mentioned in the correspondence. By combining the information in the inventories of the Spanish royal collection and information on existing and recorded paintings by or after Rubens, Arnout Balis has reconstructed the commission to the extent possible.

The set can be divided into at least two different groups according to subject matter and dimensions. The two groups appear to have been executed somewhat independently of one another, as one of them was ready for shipment to Spain before the other. One consists of eight large canvases, each measuring approximately 125 × 300 cm, and includes pure hunting scenes and mythological scenes in which hunting played some part. Only one of these eight paintings, a *Diana and Nymphs Hunting Fallow Deer*, is described by subject in the royal inventories. Based on the evidence provided by related sketches, copies, and tapestries, the other seven paintings can be tentatively identified as: *Calydonian Boar Hunt*, *Diana and Nymphs Attacked by Satyrs*, *Death of Actaeon*, *Death of Adonis*, *Death of Silvia's Stag*, a *Bull Hunt*, and a *Bear Hunt*.[67] Of these eight paintings only the *Diana and Nymphs Attacked by Satyrs* and the *Bear Hunt* can be identified with certainty with extant paintings: the first is in the Prado (Fig. 61); the second is preserved in fragment in the North Carolina Museum of Art in Raleigh.[68] The *Death of Silvia's Stag* and the *Bull Hunt* have been tentatively identified with two paintings in the Museo Arqueológico Provincial in Gerona, Spain; however, this identification is less certain.[69] The rest of the paintings in the series are not recorded after the seventeenth century.[70]

The remaining ten paintings in the *bóveda* commission were smaller in size (approximately 42 × 84 cm). They have been identified by Balis as: *Hercules Slaying the Centaur*, *Hercules and the Cretan Bull*, *Hercules and the Lion of Nemea*, *Hercules and the Erymantian Boar*, *Cyparissus Embracing the Stag* (none of these paintings survives), and three unspecified scenes of Hercules or fables.[71] There are also two additional scenes that were somewhat larger than the rest. The identity of these scenes is uncertain. They are probably either a *Hercules Strangling the Lion* and *Hercules Slaying the Dragon* (the former is lost; the second now in the Prado, Fig. 76); or a pair described as *Hercules* and *Diana*, which cannot be identified with any known paintings.[72]

Even though the eighteen paintings in this group resulted from a single commission, the different sizes, and to a lesser extent subject matters, suggest that they did not form a self-contained series. This reflects the collecting style of Philip IV who, generally speaking, was guided more by his taste for a certain artist or style of painting than by an interest in any strict thematic content. The king did not require clearly defined cycles of paintings, but rather appears to have favored groups loosely arranged around a common subject, thus allowing artists a certain freedom when working on projects for him.

As in the Torre de la Parada series, Philip IV appears to have taken a personal interest in this commission. This is revealed in the correspondence and by the fact that his brother, the cardinal-infante Ferdinand, personally handled the commission, as he had done for the hunting lodge.

The exact degree to which the details of the commission were specified from Madrid is not known. In all probability, the location of the paintings in the *bóveda* of the Alcázar was decided by the king. The dimensions of the paintings must also have been specified from the Spanish court. Some indication of the subject matter was also certainly given by the king, but the variety of the themes depicted suggests that Rubens was allowed some leeway in this area.

It has been suggested that the *bóveda* commission may have issued from an event that had taken place in the Spanish court. The heir to the throne, the king's nine-year-old son, Prince Baltasar Carlos, had managed to kill both a boar and a bull on the hunting grounds of the Pardo palace near Madrid on January 26, 1638.[73] Although this event is not necessary to explain the origin of this commission, because similar projects existed with no relation to any specific occurrence,[74] the young prince's feat was commemorated in a text illustrated by an engraving showing the same motifs outlined in this set of paintings. This suggests that the paintings may have been ordered on the same occasion. If so, Rubens would certainly have received notice of the affair being commemorated, and thus it is probable that specific instructions were given from Madrid.

As Rubens had done in the paintings for the Torre, he personally executed the sketches for all the *bóveda* scenes, as the correspondence reveals. The documents also indicate that his participation in the final paintings was more extensive than in the series for the Torre de la Parada; he appears to have executed the figures and landscapes in every painting, only leaving the animals to Snyders. This degree of personal participation by Rubens must have been required by the king because of the importance of the intended destination of the paintings. And the relatively small size of this commission, in comparison to the Torre de la Parada, allowed a higher degree of personal involvement by the master.

The great number of paintings by Rubens and his shop arriving in Madrid at this time makes it easy to overlook the quality of the pictures. In the case of the *bóveda* commission, most of the paintings in the series have been lost, making an artistic evaluation difficult. The available clues indicate that although the paintings may have been of variable quality, some were true masterpieces and should serve as a reminder of the remarkable quality of the paintings by Rubens entering the Spanish royal collection throughout the seventeenth century. All that can be identified in this series are: one surviving painting (*Diana and Nymphs Attacked by Satyrs*); a portion of another (*Bear Hunt*); two tentative identifications of paintings that are certain to have been part of this series (the *Death of Silvia's Stag* and the *Bull Hunt*); and one extant painting that may have been (*Hercules Slaying the Dragon*). Although these works do not provide enough evidence to make a final evaluation of the group, this information is sufficient to warrant some general comments.

The quality of the works was probably uneven; the pieces in which the number of figures was larger required more personal participation by Rubens, as he was committed to painting the figures and landscapes, and thus may have been higher in quality. The paintings in which animals figured more prominently (such as the *Bear Hunt*) probably had less intervention by the master. One of the paintings for the *bóveda de palacio*, the *Diana and Nymphs Attacked by Satyrs* (Fig. 61), deserves to be singled out for praise. The rhythmically organized sequence of figures gives the scene a melodic quality. The elaborate richness of the flesh tones in the naked female figures, and the liveliness and immediacy of their expressions, also contribute to the beauty of this extraordinary painting. The known sketches and copies of other paintings that formed part of this group suggest that the quality of this picture was shared by the others. The harmony achieved in the *Diana and Nymphs Attacked by Satyrs* by the interlocking of the figures, for example, can be seen in many of the other sketches for this series.[75] If the *Diana* is representative of the quality of the entire group, then it is no surprise that the cardinal-infante Ferdinand could write to his brother, after the paintings had been received in Madrid: "I am pleased that the paintings have been to Your Majesty's liking."[76]

In 1639, probably during the summer months, Philip IV commissioned four paintings from Rubens for the New Room in the Alcázar. As we have seen, this was one of the most important chambers in the palace for the display of paintings, and it was already well supplied with works by Rubens. The New Room exhibited the *Achilles Discovered among the Daughters of Lycomedes*, painted by Van Dyck and retouched by Rubens; most or all of the eight paintings brought by Rubens to Spain in 1628; and the *Equestrian Portrait of Philip IV*, painted by the artist during his stay at the Spanish court in 1628 and 1629.[77] Painted after the works for the Torre de la Parada and the *bóvedas* of the Alcázar, the four paintings for the New Room are the third and last major commission that Rubens painted for Philip IV in the 1630s, and the last commission he received from the king before his death.

The four pictures are first documented on September 25, 1639, when Rubens appears to have recently begun working on them.[78] This commission, too, was handled in Brussels by the cardinal-infante; it consisted of two large canvases depicting the *Abduction of the Sabine Women* and the *Reconciliation of the Romans and the Sabines* (both now lost), and two smaller paintings of *Perseus and Andromeda* (Madrid, Prado; Fig. 62) and *Hercules and Antaeus* (possibly a painting in New York, Central Picture Galleries).[79] Rubens' worsening health caused delays in the execution of the paintings,[80] and by the time of his death on May 30, 1640, the four canvases remained in his studio in varying degrees of completion. One large canvas was almost finished; another of the same size was barely sketched; and the other two paintings, which were smaller, were very far advanced.[81] Subsequently, the cardinal-infante embarked upon a search for painters who could finish the commission. After an unsuccessful attempt to hire Van Dyck,[82] two artists were contracted in the fall of 1640. Jacob Jordaens agreed to finish the two smaller pictures, and by November 10 an unidentified painter was at work on at least one of the large canvases.[83] Judging from a letter written by the cardinal-infante, three of the four paintings were in Spain by June of 1641[84] and must have been installed in the New Room close to that date. The last picture remained in Flanders, still unfinished, on July 20, 1641, when the cardinal-infante Ferdinand wrote to Madrid that he did not believe it would be finished by the end of August.[85] The date of its final delivery to Spain remains unknown.

Although they were commissioned together, these four paintings do not form a unified group. They are divided into two pairs by both their dimensions and their subjects. The paintings of the *Sabine Women* and the *Romans and Sabines* were larger, and they were inventoried as a pair throughout the century. The other two scenes hung in the same room, but separately from the first pair. Also, the four paintings did not hang alone but shared a room with many other pictures.[86] Furthermore, as

Orso has shown, the meaning of the four paintings is best understood in the context of the whole installation of the room, which was dedicated to glorifying the virtues and feats of the Hapsburg kings. The two paintings dealing with the Sabine women and the Sabines and Romans referred to compassion and reconciliation.[87] The scene of Perseus rescuing Andromeda can be read as a reference to the rescue of the Catholic religion, or alternatively of Spain, by a Christian knight (an allusion to the king of Spain). The scene of Hercules may represent the triumph over evil of the virtuous Greek hero, from whom the Spanish kings claimed descent.[88] The hanging of these four paintings in the midst of numerous other works with a common theme indicates that they should be considered, not as an independent group, but as part of the program of the New Room.

Because these paintings were commissioned to be integrated into the existing decoration of the New Room, their subject matters and dimensions must have been carefully specified from Madrid.[89]

The importance of the New Room in the Alcázar indicates that this was an ambitious project in the mind of the king. What we know of the final paintings suggests that Rubens responded accordingly. The two large canvases of the Sabines and Romans and the Sabine women are lost. From what can be discerned from the sketches on which they were probably based, they were complex and dynamic compositions, but full artistic appraisal cannot be made without knowledge of the originals.[90] *Hercules and Antaeus* is either lost or can be identified with a painting that shows little or no trace of Rubens' hand, and therefore was probably executed mostly after the master's death. The *Perseus and Andromeda* (Fig. 62) is the only one of the four paintings in this group that has been identified with an extant painting largely by Rubens. In spite of obvious intervention by Jordaens, there are important sections of the

FIGURE 61

Rubens and Snyders, *Diana and Nymphs Attacked by Satyrs.* Madrid, Museo del Prado.

composition which demonstrate Rubens' best efforts. Especially noteworthy are the rich texture and layering of the flesh of Andromeda, which makes this work a paradigmatic example of Rubens' late style.

One last aspect of the two commissions for the Alcázar of 1639 that should be mentioned is the fact that they have much in common with the paintings for the Torre de la Parada. All three were personal projects of the king. There are also similarities in the subjects of the three sets of paintings, all of which include mythologies and images of Hercules. The paintings for the Torre had arrived in Madrid in May 1638, approximately one year before the commissions for the Alcázar are first documented. These dates, and the common features of the three groups, suggest that arrival in Madrid of the paintings for the Torre de la Parada led the king to commission the later paintings.

Private Collectors

Apart from the king, two other patrons collected paintings by Rubens in the late 1630s: one was a prominent Spanish aristocrat whom we have already encountered, the marquis of Leganés; the other was Jan Van Vucht, a citizen of the Spanish Netherlands who lived in Madrid.

The marquis of Leganés was Rubens' most important Spanish patron after the king. As mentioned in the previous chapter, by 1629 Leganés already owned three paintings by the Flemish master.[91] In later years, he added an enormous number of works to his collection. By 1642 more than one thousand new paintings were inventoried in his possession, among them twenty new paintings attributed to Rubens.[92]

Little is known about Leganés' collecting of Rubens' work in the 1630s or when he acquired the paintings recorded in 1642. The *Wolf and Fox Hunt* (Fig. 50), first owned by the duke of Aarschot and mentioned earlier, is the only painting by Rubens with a documented entry date into Leganés' collection. This painting was acquired by the marquis from the Flemish aristocrat between 1640 and 1642, and therefore falls outside the scope of this chapter.[93] We can assume that some of the newly inventoried paintings were acquired during the 1630s, given that Leganés resided in Flanders at different points during that decade. However, we do not know this for certain, nor can we identify which ones they might be. Thus, Leganés' role in bringing Rubens' work to Spain in the decade of the 1630s remains obscure.

The single independent commission executed by Rubens for a patron in Spain recorded in the 1630s involves Jan Van Vucht, a rich merchant from Brabant who was the agent in Madrid for the famous Plantin Press, which at this time was directed by Rubens' longtime friend Balthasar Moretus.[94] From Madrid, Van Vucht attempted to purchase paintings by Rubens on two occasions. During the summer and fall of 1630, not long after the painter's departure from the Spanish capital,

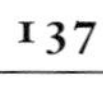

FIGURE 62

Rubens and Jordaens, *Perseus and Andromeda*. Madrid, Museo del Prado.

Van Vucht made his first attempt; but apparently nothing came of it.[95] On an uncertain date in 1638 or 1639, the Flemish merchant embarked on a more successful artistic project when he commissioned from Rubens a large canvas of the *Martyrdom of Saint Andrew* (Fig. 63), which was shipped to Madrid shortly thereafter.[96] In April of 1639, Van Vucht willed the *Saint Andrew* to the hospital of San Andrés de los Flamencos, a hostel for Flemings in Madrid, to which the painting still belongs today.[97]

Van Vucht's two attempts to purchase paintings by Rubens came at a time when the painter's name must have sounded with special force in Madrid. The first, as we have seen, took place in 1630, shortly after Rubens' second visit to Spain. The *Saint Andrew* was commissioned in the last years of the 1630s, coinciding with the royal commissions for the Alcázar and the Torre de la Parada. The fame that Rubens had acquired in Madrid no doubt persuaded Van Vucht to import a painting by his famous compatriot.

The details of the *Saint Andrew* commission remain uncertain. The painting's purchase must have been facilitated by the connections between Van Vucht and Moretus, and the latter's friendship with Rubens. The exact date of its installation in the church is not known, nor is it clear how available the painting was to local artists. This is of some importance, because it is precisely this type of scene that would have been most influential in Spain, given the predominance of religious commissions in the country. Indeed, there is evidence that this image did have an impact on local artistic circles. The painting was used as a model by several important artists at a later date.[98] Also, its atmospheric effects, dynamic composition, and theatrical gestures have much in common with the style that would become pervasive after mid-century in Spanish painting, which suggests that this painting may indeed have had some influence on that development.

Two additional aspects of the commission for the *Martyrdom of Saint Andrew* should be noted. The manner in which the painting arrived in Madrid is unusual, because it is the only documented painting that entered Spain in the late 1630s that was not a purchase by the king or the marquis of Leganés, a member of the king's close circle. The nationality of Van Vucht is also noteworthy; the *Saint Andrew* is one of very few paintings by Rubens to enter Spain through Flemish hands, not only at this time, but throughout the seventeenth century. (The only other cases are the *Wolf and Fox Hunt*, which arrived in Spain with the duke of Aarschot, and possibly the five paintings of the senses painted by Jan Brueghel and Rubens, which may have been brought by the duke of Neuburg to the cardinal-infante Ferdinand in 1624.)

One final episode pertaining to Rubens' art in Spain took place in the late 1630s. In 1638, the first documented print after the master was engraved in that country. It shows Rubens' *Martyrdom of Saint Lawrence* and is based on a preexisting Flemish print. The maker of the Spanish print is Pedro Rodríguez; its publisher was Cornelius de Beer.[99] The number of prints after Rubens' work to enter Spain was massive, especially after mid-century. These works played an important role in the diffusion of the master's art. The market for prints in Spain – especially quality prints – was controlled to a large extent by Flemish painters and

FIGURE 63

Rubens, *Martyrdom of Saint Andrew*. Madrid, Fundación Carlos de Amberes, Church of the Hospital of San Andrés de los Flamencos.

publishers, and thus the prints after Rubens most commonly used were of Flemish origin. The engraving by Rodríguez may actually be the only print after Rubens by a Spanish artist in the seventeenth century. Not until the reproduction by Manuel Salvador Carmona of the *Daughter of Rubens* in 1762 was another made.[100] The engraving by Pedro Rodríguez is therefore a rare and important event.

This print also provides a glimpse into future developments in the presence of Rubens' art in Spain. As the decade of the 1630s came to an end, and with it Rubens' life, there was a gradual shift in the type of works associated with the Flemish master that could be found in Spain. Together with the many original paintings that continued to arrive in the country, an increasing number of improbable attributions, copies, and prints began to crop up in local collections, reflecting Rubens' growing popularity, and also the inability of collectors outside of the highest social circles to acquire originals by the master.

The period between the Torre commission in 1636 and the painter's death in 1640 saw the arrival in Spain of more paintings by Rubens than any other period of similar duration. In the early years of the decade, a *Wolf and Fox Hunt*, and possibly a *Devotion of Rudolf I* and five paintings of the senses, arrived in Madrid. After 1636, as we have seen, Rubens designed and directed the execution of eighty-seven paintings in the three commissions for the king. Other scenes of hunts and mythologies for the royal collection may also have entered Spain at this date, as did the *Judgment of Paris* for the Buen Retiro, which was commissioned in 1638. The *Martyrdom of Saint Andrew* also came to Madrid in the last years of the decade, and some of the paintings owned by Leganés in 1642 may have entered Spain during the 1630s. This places the total number of paintings designed by Rubens that arrived in Madrid in the 1630s at over one hundred, of which probably nearly fifty were personally executed by the master to some degree. Such an increase in the number of works by Rubens cannot have gone unnoticed in the artistic circles of the Spanish capital. Indeed, scholars generally agree that Rubens' style began to exert a significant impact upon Spanish painters beginning in the following decade.[101]

The large commissions carried out by Rubens for the king during the 1630s may have had a negative impact on local artists. Traditionally, Spanish patrons commissioned certain types of scenes, such as mythologies and paintings incorporating nudes, from foreign painters. This niche was filled by Rubens during the 1630s, and his presence probably had the effect of continuing to hold back the development of local talent in these areas.[102]

The paintings executed for Spanish patrons by Rubens in the late 1630s represent a very large percentage of his total production for the period.[103] As we have seen throughout this chapter, the majority of these paintings were commissioned by Philip IV. Several factors explain the favor the king showed toward the art of Rubens during this time. One may be the organization of Rubens' workshop, which enabled the master to execute large commissions as few others could have done. Clearly, the king also esteemed Rubens' work highly and found the Flemish master's style and interpretation of subject matter particularly to his liking. Rubens' heroic representation of Christian and antique themes had already gained favor at the court in earlier years. The grandeur of the earlier images is also present in the late commissions, especially the scenes destined for the ceremonial rooms in the Alcázar, which were intended to add splendor to the royal residence and consequently to augment the glory of the Spanish Crown. There is also a more personal side to the king's preference for Rubens. As we have seen, many of the paintings by Rubens that arrived in Spain in the late 1630s were commissioned for the *bóveda de palacio*, which was part of the king's private summer apartments in the Alcázar, and also for the recreational palace of the Torre de la Parada. The fact that Philip IV decorated these relatively private dwellings with so many paintings designed by Rubens indicates that his taste for his art was to a large extent personal, that he took delight in Rubens' paintings.

One aspect of Rubens' paintings that probably had some bearing on the king's preference was their erotic content. This eroticism is evident in many of the scenes for the Torre de la Parada and the Alcázar, and also in the *Judgment of Paris* presumably commissioned for the Buen Retiro palace, and it was probably also apparent in some of the paintings ordered by the king in the late 1630s that are now lost. In the 1620s, Philip IV had shown a liking for similar scenes, as was manifested by the purchase of the painting *Achilles Discovered among the Daughters of Lycomedes* (Fig. 12). Some other paintings by the Fleming that arrived in Madrid in the 1620s and 1630s, such as the *Diana and Nymphs Setting Out for the Hunt* (Fig. 9), purchased in 1623 by the queen but later transferred to the king's apartments, or the *Nymphs Filling the Horn of Plenty* (Fig. 22), brought by Rubens to Spain in 1628, may have encouraged that taste; and the same is true of the copies after Titian painted by Rubens in Madrid in 1628.

We can be sure that the erotic charge of these images did not go unnoticed. A measure of the sensitivity of the time to the eroticism of paintings like the ones we are concerned with here can be gained by looking into the reaction caused several decades earlier by similar paintings by Titian. After the Venetian master finished his painting of *Venus and Adonis* (now in the Prado) for Philip II in 1554, the Spanish ambassador in Venice wrote to Madrid that it was "a thing of great esteem, in which Titian has put much effort, but it is excessively lascivious."[104] Over a half-century later, by the time Philip IV occupied the throne, many warnings against images including naked figures, especially female, had been advanced, as the king was certainly aware.[105] In at least one of the paintings by Rubens mentioned above, the *Judgment of Paris*, the nudity of the goddesses had been cause for concern. When the painting was finished and ready to be shipped to Spain, the cardinal-infante Ferdinand wrote to his brother the king from Brussels in the following terms:

Judging from what all the painters say, without doubt this is the best painting that Rubens has done; it only has one fault which it has not been possible to get him to amend. And this is that the three goddesses are excessively naked, but he says it is necessary to see the valor [*valentía*] of the painting. The Venus that is in the middle is a portrait very similar to his own wife, without doubt it is among the best of what is here now.[106]

These qualms did not stop the king from ordering the painting sent to Madrid, even though he did consider it prudent to cover the canvas with a curtain once it was installed in the Buen Retiro. (Probably in the eighteenth century, the central female figures in the *Judgment of Paris* were partially covered by painted draperies that augmented the size of the original cloths painted by Rubens. Recent restoration has made these additions clearly evident to the naked eye.)

The problems that viewing undraped female figures like those depicted by Rubens could entail is made explicit by a statement of the Spanish humanist Juan Luis Vives (1492–1540). Writing nearly one century before the events here narrated, he states that there are parts of the human body which "nature and honesty demand remain covered," so much so, he continues (citing Pliny's *Historia Naturalis*), that "the bodies of men fallen into the sea float face up, while those of women float face down. Therefore nature takes care of their honesty. . . ."[107] In a social milieu that continued to view the naked female body with similar prudery, the discomfort caused by Rubens' paintings in the eyes of some onlookers is easy to understand.

This is not the place to expound further on the history of the reception of erotic images in Spain. Of interest in the context of our study is the fact that the content of the paintings by Rubens commissioned by Philip IV indicates that the king had no problem with such images. On the contrary, it seems clear that the erotic component often present in Rubens' paintings contributed to the sovereign's enthusiasm for them, and to his extensive commissions from the artist in the 1630s.

The patronage that Rubens received from Philip IV in the late 1630s, not only demonstrated the king's preference for his art, it may also have had some influence on the painter's work. Most obviously this occurs in the selection of subject matter. Considering how much time Rubens devoted in the last years of his life to commissions from Philip IV, the subjects that were selected by the king, or at least in collaboration between the artist and his royal patron, formed an important part of the painter's total output. Even if there is no reason to believe that Rubens' taste for classical narratives would have been any different without the patronage of Philip IV (much of the artist's production for other patrons consists of similar scenes), it does seem likely that in this area the king's patronage reinforced the artist's natural vocation.

A second area where the patronage of the king may have affected Rubens' art is in the development of his late style. It is generally recognized that the evolution of this style resulted in part from the influence of the works by Titian that Rubens had viewed in the Spanish royal collection during his 1628–1629 visit. The commissions of the late 1630s were intended for the owner of those very works by Titian, and in many cases were also meant to hang in the same palace with them and dealt with related subject matters.[108] This almost certainly reinforced certain stylistic traits that Rubens shared with Titian, such as the broken application of colors, broad and unblended brushwork, the tactile appeal and elaborate layering of flesh tones, as well as the unifying effect of the atmosphere.

As the events narrated in this chapter show, the relationship between Rubens and Philip IV that had developed in previous years grew into an almost ideal painter–patron partnership in the late 1630s. During this period, no other painter, Spanish or foreigner, executed as many works for the king as Rubens. At the time of the artist's death on May 30, 1640, more of his paintings were owned by the Spanish king than by any other single patron, and many of them had arrived in Spain only shortly before, as a result of the collecting efforts of the previous years. Even though he did not hold an official position as a painter at the Spanish court, these numbers indicate that in the late 1630s, Rubens could be considered the king's favorite painter.

Only Velázquez could be said to share this acclaim at the time. In the 1630s, he had consolidated his place at the court, and was in the midst of the most productive period of his career.[109] The positions held by Rubens and Velázquez at the Spanish court in the 1630s complemented each other. The Fleming supplied mythologies and hunting scenes from Flanders, while the Spaniard was occupied mainly with court portraiture and with assisting in the decoration of the royal residences. Thus, it appears that at this time there was a division of labor between the two leading painters of the Spanish monarchy. There was no stated distribution of roles, and they were probably not decided a priori. The situation emerged gradually, as the artistic taste of the king developed, adapting to the art of both the mature Rubens and the young Velázquez, and at the same time influencing their careers.

CHAPTER FIVE

A Continued Presence: The Collecting of Rubens in Spain from 1640 to 1700

Final Acquisitions by Philip IV: The Sale of Rubens' Collection and Purchases from Other Sources

The years following Rubens' death in 1640 were difficult times for Philip IV. In 1640, Catalonia and Portugal attempted to secede from the monarchy, the latter successfully. On January 17, 1643, Olivares was exiled from the court, ending his twenty-two years at the helm of Spain's government. On October 5, 1644, Queen Isabella died, leaving her by then loving husband in profound despair: "I find Myself in the most intense condition of sorrow that could ever be . . . God's aid must be infinite if ever I am to recover from this loss," he wrote to his spiritual adviser, Sor María de Agreda, little over a month after the queen's death.[1] In 1646 the king received a further blow when prince Baltasar Carlos, the much heralded heir to the throne, died suddenly just days before his seventeenth birthday.[2] The mental state into which this new tragedy threw the king can be measured again by a letter to Sor María de Agreda: "This latest loss, coming in the middle of so many other woes, has transfixed my heart. I don't know whether what is happening to me is real or only a nightmare."[3] Throughout these travails the king's passion for art collecting and his taste for Rubens remained steadfast, suggesting that in this area he found some respite from his struggles with government and with fate.

Since the time of Rubens' visit to Spain in 1628, King Philip IV had known the painter personally, had used his services in important diplomatic affairs, and had avidly collected his works. There was no significant break in the exportation of Rubens' paintings into Spain immediately following the artist's death, as Philip IV continued to purchase his works until the end of his reign in 1665.

However, the death of the artist did bring some inevitable changes, the most immediate and apparent being the abrupt termination of direct commissions to Rubens from the king. The consequences of this change can be grasped when we consider the large number of works Rubens painted in the last years of his life for the Spanish monarch. Even though aesthetic enjoyment and the identification of collecting with wealth and power were important driving forces behind the collecting activities of the king – as is suggested by the sheer number of paintings he owned – he also commissioned works of art with the specific intention of using them as political propaganda. As has been seen in the previous chapters, pictures such as the *Equestrian Portrait of Philip IV* were intended to extol the king and his monarchy and were hung in the most important rooms of the Alcázar. It was this aspect of Rubens' art that would be most affected by his death: though his paintings could still be purchased in the market, he was no longer there to create images specifically intended to express the values and aspirations of the Spanish Hapsburgs.

On June 10, 1640, the cardinal-infante Ferdinand sent notice to Madrid of Rubens' recent death.[4] The king's response to this news is not known, but the cardinal-infante expressed his own regret at the interruption of the ongoing royal commissions. As things turned out, however, the death of Rubens was followed almost immediately by the sale of his extensive collection, and the king bought important paintings in that sale.

The main source of information about the purchases made by the king of Spain from Rubens' collection is the account of the sales from the painter's estate submitted by his heirs to the city of Antwerp in 1645.[5] The correspondence between Ferdinand and Philip IV, the list of paintings owned by Rubens that were put up for sale after the painter's death (known as the *Specification*), and the provenance of a number of paintings sold on that occasion also add to our knowledge of this event.

The exact date or dates of the Spanish purchases are uncertain. The inventory of Rubens' possessions and the initiation of their sale were carried out in great haste.[6] At an unknown date, presumably in the summer of 1640, the king of Spain indicated to his brother, the cardinal-infante Ferdinand, that he was interested in purchasing paintings from the estate. On September 23, 1640, in response to the king's wishes, the cardinal-infante sent him a memorandum of the available paintings from Rubens' collection, a list that has been lost.[7] Sometime between 1640 and 1645 – possibly between March and May of 1642, when the large public sale of Rubens' collection occurred – the king purchased thirty-two paintings from the artist's estate.[8] The memorandum sent by the cardinal-infante to the king indicates that Philip IV participated in the selection of the paintings, though it is uncertain to what extent. His personal intervention in the commissions to Rubens of the late 1630s suggests that he was probably closely involved in the purchases again at this time. The aforementioned letter from Ferdinand to the king of September 23, 1640, shows that until his death in 1641 the cardinal-infante was the king's main agent in dealing with this purchase. The details of the transaction were actually handled by Don Francisco de Rojas, who was *guardajoyas* (keeper of precious objects) and *ayuda de cámara* (valet) to the cardinal-infante.[9] Rojas was aided by the painter Gaspar de Crayer and apparently to a lesser degree, presumably in the evaluation of the pictures, by Jan Wildens, Frans Snyders, and the lesser-known painter, print publisher, and dealer Jacob Moermans.[10]

Of the thirty-two paintings purchased by the Spanish king, fifteen were works by Rubens and the rest by other artists.[11] Those by Rubens are: *Diana and Actaeon* (whereabouts unknown, presumably lost);[12] *Diana and Callisto* (Lancashire, Knowsley, Collection of the earl of Derby);[13] *Venus and Adonis* (whereabouts unknown, presumably lost);[14] *Rape of Europa* (Madrid, Prado);[15] a *Venus and Cupid Lying on a Bed* (whereabouts unknown, presumably lost);[16] *Worship of Venus* (Stockholm, Nationalmuseum, Fig. 64);[17] *Bacchanal of the Andrians* (Stockholm, Nationalmuseum, Fig. 65);[18] *Nymphs and Satyrs* (Madrid, Prado, Fig. 66);[19] *Virgin with Saint George and Other Saints in a Landscape* (whereabouts unknown, presumably lost);[20] *Swiss Troops with Peasants;*[21] *Dance of Italian Peasants* (Madrid, Prado, Fig. 67);[22] *Supper at Emmaus* (Madrid, Prado);[23] *Saint George Slaying the Dragon* (Madrid, Prado, Fig. 68);[24] a *Deer Hunt* by an anonymous artist, retouched and with figures by Rubens (whereabouts unknown, presumably lost),[25] and *Three Nymphs with the Horn of Plenty* (whereabouts unknown, presumably lost).[26] Also among the purchases was a *Landscape with Psyche and Jupiter* by Paul Bril (Madrid, Prado), a painting that is often believed to show some work by Rubens in the small figures but was never associated with him in the seventeenth century.[27]

In addition to these works are several pictures by Rubens, listed separately in the account of the sales from his collection, that were also transferred to Spanish hands. A painting that can be identified with the *Equestrian Portrait of Ferdinand, Cardinal-Infante of Spain* in the Prado (Fig. 69), was sold to a Michiel de Olivares.[28] This buyer has not been identified, but he probably acted on behalf of the king, for whom he purchased other paintings from Rubens' collection.[29] The probability that this portrait was acquired for the king is also supported by the fact that after it was sold from Rubens' collection it is first recorded in the 1666 inventory of the Spanish royal collection.[30] Given that Ferdinand died in 1641, it is possible that he had commissioned this portrait but had not paid for it by the time of his own death, after which it was purchased by his brother the king. It is also possible, as has been suggested, that this painting was originally commissioned by the king, who was now simply paying for his picture.[31]

A small painting of the *Virgin and Child Adored by Saints* is documented as a gift from Rubens' heirs to Francisco de Rojas for his services in facilitating the sale to the king.[32] This was described in the *Specification* as being similar to Rubens' altarpiece of the *Madonna and Child Adored by Saints* for the church of the Augustinian fathers in Antwerp, and was probably a *ricordo* painted by the master after the finished altarpiece.[33] It was taken to Spain by its owner shortly afterward and is probably identical to a small painting on copper now in the Prado (Fig. 70).[34]

Rojas also received a copy of an unidentified scene by a certain Jan Baptista – possibly Jan-Baptist Borrekens, one of the painters who participated in the Torre de la Parada – presumably for the same reason as the previous painting.[35] In view of the circumstances, it seems probable that this was a copy after a picture by Rubens. Francisco de Rojas is not known as a collector, but he was an important courtier who had previously been in contact with Rubens. In 1639 he was in charge of paying Rubens and Snyders for some of the works they had painted for Philip IV.[36] He later went on to occupy several important posts at the court in Madrid, where he was valet, or *ayuda de cámara*, to Prince Baltasar Carlos before 1646, and later to the king in 1648. In 1652 he was considered for the post of *aposentador mayor de palacio* (first keeper of the palace), which in the end was given to Velázquez, and in 1660 he was appointed to that same post following the death of the Spanish painter.[37]

The account of the sales from Rubens' estate does not tell the complete story of the purchases for Spain from the painter's collection. In addition to the thirty-two documented purchases, there are four other paintings by the artist, listed in his own collection after his death, which later in the century appeared in the royal collection in Spain. The paintings are: *The Three Graces* (Madrid, Prado, Fig. 71);[38] the *Adam and Eve* copied after Titian (Madrid, Prado, Fig. 46);[39] *Pythagoras Forbids the Eating of Animals and Beans* (London, Buckingham Palace, Fig. 72);[40] and *Landscape with the Calydonian Boar Hunt* (Madrid, Prado, Fig. 73).[41] The *Adam and Eve* is first recorded in Spain when it was in the Prado palace, near Madrid, in 1674. The other three paintings are first inventoried in the royal collection in the Alcázar in 1666. These four could have been early purchases made for the king from Rubens' estate for which no documentation survives – a fact that would not be surprising, because only a small percentage of the sales of paintings from Rubens' collection after his death are recorded.[42] They could also have been purchased by other buyers present at the sale and then resold to the king, or exchanged for other pictures. It is also possible that at least some of them were acquired at a later date, as individual items and from different collections.[43]

The paintings mentioned above add up to a total of twenty-one paintings by Rubens (or twenty-two if the *Landscape with Psyche and*

FIGURE 64

Rubens, copy after Titian, *Worship of Venus*. Stockholm, Nationalmuseum.

FIGURE 65

Rubens, copy after Titian, *Bacchanal of the Andrians*. Stockholm, Nationalmuseum.

Jupiter by Paul Bril is included in the count).[44] However, it is uncertain whether all of them actually entered Spain. Four of the scenes documented in the sales as Spanish acquisitions are never recorded in the country: *Diana and Actaeon*, *Swiss Troops with Peasants*, *Deer Hunt*, and *Three Nymphs with the Horn of Plenty*. Three other paintings – *Venus and Cupid Lying on a Bed*, *Venus and Adonis*, and *Diana and Callisto* – can only be identified very tentatively with items included in Spanish royal inventories.[45] These paintings may have been resold immediately after their purchase or exchanged for other paintings – perhaps some of the undocumented pictures that entered Spain which are listed above. The presence of numerous buyers from all over Europe at the sale of Rubens' collection provides the context for this possibility. The fact that two of the paintings that cannot be safely identified in Spain, the *Diana and Callisto* and *Diana and Actaeon*, are possibly identical to two paintings recorded in England in 1649 shortly after they were bought by the Spanish king favors this possibility.[46]

Philip IV is the largest documented purchaser from Rubens' collection and the main buyer of paintings by the master's hand. The signifi-

FIGURE 66

Rubens, *Nymphs and Satyrs*. Madrid, Museo del Prado.

cance of these facts is uncertain, as there are documents for the sale of only a small number of the paintings included in the *Specification*, and other important but undisclosed purchasers could have existed. Nevertheless, the numbers are impressive. They show that Philip IV found in the sale of Rubens' collection a way to continue amassing paintings by the Flemish artist, and that his enthusiasm for Rubens' art survived the death of the painter.

To some extent, the nature of the king's purchases must have been defined by availability. However, an overview of the paintings acquired indicates that matters of taste and personal choice still played an important role. Philip IV bought a relatively small number of paintings by Rubens compared to the nearly 150 works by the master that were for sale. Among them, however, were many of the best works available.

Another factor that appears to have shaped the king's choice of purchases from Rubens' estate is the content of his own collection. A case in point are the copies after Titian: eight of the paintings the king bought were copies by Rubens after works by the Venetian artist. Five or six had been copied by Rubens during his visit to Madrid in 1628–1629.[47] The number of paintings by both Titian and Rubens in the Spanish royal collection apparently made these copies desirable. The fact that some of them had been painted in Spain may have reinforced this desire, as the connection that had been established in the court in

FIGURE 67

Rubens, *Dance of Italian Peasants*. Madrid, Museo del Prado.

FIGURE 68

Rubens, *Saint George Slaying the Dragon*. Madrid, Museo del Prado.

Madrid between Rubens and Titian may also have done. The fact that four of Rubens' copies after Titian (*Diana and Callisto*, *Diana and Actaeon*, *Worship of Venus*, and *Bacchanal of the Andrians*) were the most expensive purchases made by the king – or anyone else – from the estate of the Flemish artist demonstrates that the connection with Titian indeed was an added incentive.[48] It should be kept in mind, however, that Rubens' collection also included many copies after Titian that the king did not purchase. This indicates that the link with Titian was only one of several aspects considered by the king when making his selection of pictures.[49]

Some other paintings purchased from Rubens' estate are closely related to works already in the Spanish royal collection. The voluptuous female nudes that appear in the splendid painting of *Three Graces* (Fig. 71), for example, can be seen as a continuation of the king's taste for Rubens' erotic mythological scenes, and the same can be said about the

Nymphs and Satyrs (Fig. 66). The *Pythagoras Forbids the Eating of Animals and Beans* (Fig. 72) includes another voluptuous display of nymphs and satyrs on the right side of the composition. Below these figures is a large heap of fruits and vegetables painted by Snyders, who was also

FIGURE 70

Rubens, *Virgin and Child Adored by Saints*. Madrid, Museo del Prado.

extensively represented in the royal collection by this time, both as an independent artist and as a collaborator of Rubens.[50] The *Three Nymphs with the Horn of Plenty* (now lost) depicted the same subject of one of the eight paintings brought by Rubens to Spain in 1628–1629. Another canvas that was probably bought from Rubens' heirs, the *Landscape with the Calydonian Boar Hunt* (Fig. 73), now in the Prado, repeats a theme already represented in Madrid by two paintings by Rubens; one of them the artist had brought to Spain in 1628–1629; the other was commissioned for the *bóvedas del verano* (the vaulted rooms for summer use) in the Alcázar in 1639 (Fig. 74).[51] These three paintings of the Calydonian boar hunt share not only their subject matter but also some figures and other elements: Meleager and the wounded Calydonian boar, for example, are repeated in almost identical fashion in all three scenes. This offered Spanish viewers the opportunity to observe Rubens' practice of

FIGURE 69

Facing page
Rubens, *Equestrian Portrait of Ferdinand, Cardinal-Infante of Spain*. Madrid, Museo del Prado.

FIGURE 71

Rubens, *The Three Graces*. Madrid, Museo del Prado.

repeating identical figures in different compositions. The recurrence of figures in these three paintings is a telling symbol of the magnitude that Philip IV's collection of works by Rubens had reached by the time of the artist's death.

Even though mythological scenes and portraits formed the bulk of the king's purchases, some important religious works and genre scenes were also acquired by Philip IV on this occasion. He bought three religious paintings and two pictures that were thought to be genre scenes but one of which, a *Dance of Italian Peasants*, turned out to be a representation of a mythological subject. Especially noteworthy among the religious scenes is the *Saint George Slaying the Dragon* (Fig. 68). Probably painted circa 1606–1608, at the end of Rubens' stay in Italy, this picture was one of the earliest of his own works that the master kept in his collection.[52] In spite of the bold conception of the scene and its vigorous composition, this painting apparently did not find great favor in Spain. Where the picture was installed immediately after its purchase is not known. By 1674 it hung in the Pardo palace, a secondary location in comparison to the Alcázar, and was attributed to an unnamed student of Rubens. This suggests that it was not among the favorite paintings of King Charles II, who had succeeded his father, Philip IV, in 1665. We cannot be sure if the same status was given to the painting during the reign of Philip IV, but this may well be the case, as there is no indication that the painting was in a different location than the Pardo during his lifetime. Perhaps the tight framing of the composition, with its mannerist overtones, was not to the king's liking; another painting of similar style that had been in the royal collection, the *Equestrian Portrait of the Duke of Lerma*, was given away by Philip IV in 1632.

The story of the reception in Spain of one of the presumed genre scenes, the *Dance of Italian Peasants* (Fig. 67), is also interesting, for it suggests that the meaning attached to his paintings by Rubens could occasionally elude their later owners.[53] At first sight, this delightful scene of dance in a landscape appears to be indebted to the tradition of Peter Bruegel's paintings of Flemish peasant celebrations. However, as has often been noted, upon close scrutiny an antique component of the picture becomes apparent. Two of the dancers wear wreaths on their

FIGURE 72

Rubens, *Pythagoras Forbids the Eating of Animals and Beans.* The Royal Collection. © 1997 Her Majesty Queen Elizabeth II.

heads and outfits that identify them as Bacchus and a satyr. The figure in the tree holds a flute, a traditional Bacchic instrument. These three figures indicate that this painting was not conceived by Rubens as pure genre, but rather as an arcadian scene in the tradition of pastoral poetry and landscape painting. The two mythological figures, the spontaneous nature of the event, and the licentiousness suggested by the partial undress of some of the female figures and by the struggle of two of the men to kiss their dancing partners, make this plain.[54] The title by which the painting is now known, *Dance of Italian Peasants*, comes from the documents of Rubens' collection and must be a reference to the mythological, Italianate content of the painting. However, when this picture was inventoried after its arrival in Spain it was described as a *baile de villanos flamencos* ("dance of Flemish villagers").[55] If this description can be taken to express how the painting was interpreted in Spain, then the mythological allusions were lost when the panel was transferred to Madrid – and this in spite of the presence in the Spanish royal collection of famous pictures with related themes, such as Titian's *Bacchanals* and Velázquez's *Feast of Bacchus*.

The *Equestrian Portrait of Ferdinand, Cardinal-Infante of Spain* (Fig. 69) is the only portrait included among the purchases from Rubens' collection that were sent to Spain. As mentioned above, rather than a painting executed by Rubens for his own keeping, this may have been an earlier commission that had remained in the painter's studio waiting

FIGURE 73

Rubens, *Landscape with the Calydonian Boar Hunt*. Madrid, Museo del Prado.

FIGURE 74

Rubens, *Calydonian Boar Hunt*. Jersey, Collection of Lady Cook.

for payment before being delivered. The painting shows the cardinal-infante dressed in armor and adorned with the red sash of the Hapsburg army.[56] He sits on a gray horse, which he holds in a position reminiscent of the *Equestrian Portrait of Philip IV* painted by Rubens during his second visit to Spain (Fig. 32). In the background is a battle scene the inscription at the lower edge of the painting describes as the battle of Nördlingen, Ferdinand's victory over the German and Swedish Protestant forces, which took place on September 6, 1634. Above the prince appear two splendid allegorical representations, an eagle and a Winged Victory, who descend upon the scene. These two figures are identified by the text included in the painting; the thunderbolt that Victory carries in her right hand signifies Divine Vengeance, and the eagle is the imperial eagle, which represents the union of the armies of the Spanish and Austrian Hapsburgs that led to victory. In addition to the specific portrayal of the battle of Nördlingen, the painter incorporated a dynastic reference, as was common in Hapsburg portraits, by composing the piece in a way that reminds the viewer of his own equestrian portrait of Philip IV, and also of the earlier *Portrait of Charles V at Mühlberg* by Titian (Fig. 31). The dynastic allusion is further reinforced by mention of the cardinal-infante's forebears in the inscription.

The large size of the canvas, the allegorical figures, and the inscription all indicate that this was an official portrait. As mentioned earlier, the commission must have originated either with the cardinal-infante or with his brother the king. The picture must have been ordered either circa 1634, shortly after the date of the battle celebrated in the portrait, or closer to the date of Rubens' death in 1640, which would explain the presence of the painting in his studio at that time.

The *Equestrian Portrait of Ferdinand, Cardinal-Infante of Spain* was Rubens' fourth equestrian portrait of a Spanish statesman, the others being the likenesses of the duke of Lerma, Philip II, and Philip IV.[57]

The arrival of this portrait in Spain in the early 1640s signified, for Spanish audiences, the end of Rubens' role as an image maker for Spanish leaders.

After his purchases from Rubens' collection in the 1640s, Philip IV continued to acquire works by the Flemish painter until his own death in 1665. There are twenty-four paintings attributed to Rubens that are first documented in the royal collection in Spain at the time of the king's death. The main source of evidence for the identification of these paintings is the inventory of the Alcázar, the king's palace in Madrid, compiled in 1666.[58] The paintings attributed to Rubens in this inventory are: *Dido and Aeneas* (Frankfurt, Städelsches Kunstinstitut);[59] *Diana and Callisto* (Madrid, Prado, Fig. 75);[60] *Hercules Strangling the Lion* (whereabouts unknown);[61] *Hercules Slaying the Dragon* (Madrid, Prado, Fig. 76); [62] *Hercules* (whereabouts unknown);[63] *Diana* (whereabouts unknown);[64] *Alexander's Lion Hunt* (whereabouts unknown);[65] *Calydonian Boar Hunt* (whereabouts unknown);[66] two scenes of the Judgment of Paris (both in Madrid, Prado);[67] *Goddesses and Nymphs after the Bath* (Madrid, Prado; now attributed to Jordaens);[68] *Flora* (Madrid, Prado; school of Rubens);[69] *Garden of Love* (Madrid, Prado, Fig. 77);[70] *The Recognition of Philipoemen* (Madrid, Prado, Fig. 78);[71] *Holy Family With Saint Anne* (Madrid, Prado, Fig. 79);[72] *Beheading of Saint John the Baptist* (whereabouts unknown);[73] *Moses with the Brazen Serpent* (Madrid, Prado;

FIGURE 75

Rubens, *Diana and Callisto*. Madrid, Museo del Prado.

now recognized as a work by Van Dyck);[74] *Portrait of an Old Man* (which should probably be identified as a *Portrait of an Old Man with Gray Hair, Dressed in Black*; whereabouts unknown);[75] *Portrait of Anne of Austria, Queen of France* (Madrid, Prado);[76] *Garland of Fruit* (whereabouts unknown; this painting is inventoried anonymously in the royal collection in 1666 but attributed to Rubens in 1700);[77] *Garland of Fruit with Children* (whereabouts unknown);[78] *Cages and Hares* (whereabouts unknown);[79] and *Kitchen Scene* (whereabouts unknown).[80] A *Portrait of Maria de' Medici* (Madrid, Prado) is first recorded in Spain in 1686 but may have entered the royal collection at an earlier date, together with the *Portrait of Anne of Austria, Queen of France*, mentioned above.[81] In addition, two scenes attributed to Van Dyck in the 1666 inventory of the Alcázar, a *Mercury* and a *Saturn*, both unidentified, are attributed to Rubens in 1686 and are described as copies, presumably after his paintings, in 1700, raising the possibility that they are his works.[82]

Probably also in this period, six of the twenty cartoons painted in Rubens' workshop in preparation for the tapestries of the Eucharist series arrived in the royal collection. In 1648, and again in 1649, Philip IV requested their delivery to Madrid, but he met with some resistance in Brussels, where they were kept rolled up in one of the galleries in the palace. The king finally managed to have at least six scenes sent to him.[83]

Except for the *Holy Family with Saint Anne*, which was in El Escorial,

FIGURE 76

Rubens, *Hercules Slaying the Dragon*. Madrid, Museo del Prado.

FIGURE 77

Rubens, *Garden of Love*. Madrid, Museo del Prado.

and the cartoons for the Eucharist series, whose location immediately after their arrival in Spain is not known, the rest of the paintings mentioned above were in the Alcázar at the time of the king's death.

In order to establish the final number of Rubens' paintings acquired by the king between 1640 and 1665, excluding the purchases from the artist's collection, additional factors need to be considered. First, there is a possibility that some of the paintings first recorded in the royal collection in this period were among the purchases made by the king from Rubens before 1640.[84] Second, the 1666 inventory of the royal collection includes mistakes in the attributions of at least three, and possibly up to seven, paintings assigned to Rubens. The *Flora* has been identified with a picture painted in Rubens' workshop, but not by Rubens, and the *Garland of Fruit with Children*, judging from the title, may also be a workshop piece. The *Garland of Fruit*, and the scene of *Cages and Hares*, based on the descriptions in the inventories, are also probably not paintings by Rubens, but rather by painters such as Frans Snyders, Jan Fyt, or Peter Boel, and the same may be true of the *Kitchen Scene*, even though this is less certain, given the vagueness of the title. The *Goddesses and Nymphs after the Bath* that was attributed to Rubens is actually a painting by Jordaens, and the *Moses and the Brazen Serpent* is a work by Van Dyck. This last painting has a false signature ("P. P. Rubens F.ct.") on the lower part of the canvas. This signature may be responsible for the attribution to Rubens in the royal inventories. The false signature must have been added prior to the sale of the picture to Spain, presumably to increase its price or the chances for its sale.[85] This suggests that the painting was sold to the king by a dealer.

FIGURE 78

Rubens and Snyders, *The Recognition of Philipoemen*. Madrid, Museo del Prado.

FIGURE 79

Rubens, *Holy Family with Saint Anne*. Madrid, Museo del Prado.

Considering all the evidence, and excluding the purchases from the painter's collection, the number of paintings by Rubens that entered the royal collection between 1640 and 1665 must be placed at a maximum of twenty-one, plus at least eight workshop pieces (the six or more cartoons for the Eucharist, the *Flora*, and *Garland of Fruits with Children*), and a minimum of close to fifteen (if we exclude the three paintings of Hercules and one of Diana mentioned earlier, and the two pictures of *Mercury* and *Saturn*, attributed to Van Dyck in one of the inventories).

There is little information on how all these paintings entered Spain. Most of them are first recorded there when they appear in the royal inventories, which suggests that the king acquired most of the pictures outside the country. There is no record of a large sale of Rubens paintings to Philip IV between 1640 and 1665, other than the sale of the artist's estate. The king must have purchased many of the works by Rubens mentioned above in various sales that took place in different parts of Europe, in which he was often an eager participant.[86] A documented example of the king's collecting in this way took place between 1650 and 1655, when Philip IV was among the most active buyers in the sales that followed the English Civil War.[87] One of the paintings by Rubens that entered the royal collection at this time, the *Portrait of an Old Man with Gray Hair, Dressed in Black*, was bought at such a sale by a Spanish nobleman, the count of Fuensaldaña, and sent to Spain shortly thereafter. Later, at an uncertain date, it entered the royal collection. We do not know if it was purchased in London specifically for the king, if it was later given to the king as a gift, or if it was appropriated for the Crown.[88]

In 1659 two pictures attributed to Rubens were sent to the king from Flanders as gifts from Don Juan José de Austria, the king's illegitimate son, who had been governor of the Spanish Netherlands from 1656 until that year.[89] These two paintings were described as "a portrait of the queen of France by Rubens" and "a portrait of the same queen dressed in mourning by Rubens."[90] They may be identical with two works mentioned earlier, the *Portrait of Anne of Austria, Queen of France* and the *Portrait of Maria de' Medici*, both now in the Prado.[91]

Another painting, the *Goddesses and Nymphs after the Bath*, believed to be by Rubens at the time and now recognized as a work of Jordaens, also belonged to a private collector before it entered the collection of the king. It is listed in 1647 in Madrid among the belongings of Juan Alfonso Enríquez de Cabrera, ninth admiral of Castile.[92] Possibly some of the other paintings by Rubens that entered the royal collection during this period were also gifts.

The history of the cartoons for the Eucharist tapestries shows that, in his efforts to increase his collection of paintings, the king attempted to bring to Madrid paintings associated with Rubens over which he believed he had ownership rights. The Eucharist cartoons had remained in Brussels, in the collection of the king's aunt, the infanta Isabella, after the completion of the tapestries. In the late 1640s Philip IV thought that the cartoons had been painted by Rubens himself and evidently believed that he could order them sent to Spain without payment.

Philip IV's acquisitions of works by Rubens after 1640 made the royal collection a more representative sample of his art, as the paintings that arrived in Madrid during this period included pieces from different phases of his development. For example, one of the two scenes of the *Judgment of Paris* (Fig. 80), first recorded in the Alcázar in 1666, is one of the few examples of Rubens' Italian years to be found in Spain. The compact and stylized anatomies of the figures in this painting differ markedly from those in most other paintings by Rubens that could be viewed in the king's palaces. The other *Judgment of Paris* (Fig. 57) is a painting from Rubens' last years discussed in Chapter 4. It was installed in the Buen Retiro palace in 1653, for which location it was probably specifically commissioned. Another contrast to the late works that were more common in the Spanish royal collection was provided by the arrival at the court of *The Recognition of Philipoemen* (Fig. 78). This is one of only a handful of paintings from Rubens' first Antwerp years that entered the royal collection in the seventeenth century.

Some of the paintings being studied here are very important works and were regarded as such in seventeenth-century Spain. The *Garden of Love* (Fig. 77) was hung by the king in his own bedroom and has to be considered a major addition to the royal collection on the basis of quality alone. The harmonious blending of the amorous theme with the warm hues and fluent forms in which it is represented made this one of the most captivating works by the Flemish master that could be seen in the country at that time. The *Holy Family with Saint Anne* (Fig. 79) is also a painting of the highest quality, endowed with Rubens' characteristic psychological immediacy and composed with extraordinary fluidity. The location of this painting demonstrates that it was very highly regarded; it hung in the prominent Chapter Room of the Prior in El Escorial, alongside masterpieces by Raphael, Titian, and others, including the *Immaculate Conception* that Rubens had painted during his stay in Spain in 1628–1629.[93]

Another painting that is noteworthy for its quality, and also for its historical importance within Rubens' oeuvre, is the *Recognition of Philipoemen*, mentioned above. Painted circa 1609–1610, this is one of the earliest and most important examples of the collaboration between Rubens and Snyders. In the scene, the three figures of the Achaean general Philipoemen and his two hosts, represented in the act of discovering the general's true identity, are all characterized with exceptional power. These three figures, painted by Rubens, combine beautifully with the sweeping forms of the game birds and other foodstuffs painted by Snyders after a design provided by a rough sketch by Rubens. With this work, Rubens and Snyders made an important contribution to still-life painting: they endowed the still-life elements in the scene with an unprecedented combination of size, energy, and grandeur.[94]

The *Diana and Callisto* (Fig. 75), a late work, is a perfect complement to many of the erotic mythological paintings by Rubens that Philip IV had commissioned in the late 1630s and still hung in the Alcázar in the 1660s. This is one of Rubens' most heartfelt and sensuous paintings.[95] The chaste Diana, to the left of the scene, appears to regret the punishment she is imposing on Callisto, one of her companions who has been seduced and violated by Jupiter, and who is now expelled from the goddess's retinue. Rather than the cruel indifference of the goddess and her nymphs that one finds in the most famous depiction of this theme, the *Diana and Callisto* by Titian (which Rubens had copied in the Spanish royal collection), here we find a scene of compassion and shame. As Julius Held has elegantly explained, this is one of Rubens' most personal and telling transformations of the art of the Venetian master.[96] Rubens had not only copied Titian's painting of the same subject in Madrid, but very early in his career had also drawn some figures from it, probably after a reproduction in an engraving by Cornelis Cort.[97] His version of the *Diana and Callisto* is his own invention, but some elements in the painting are derived from Titian. As pointed out by Held, the black servant who attends Diana is inspired by the goddess's attendant in Titian's *Diana and Actaeon*, the companion piece of the *Diana and Callisto*.[98] The fountain that appears behind Callisto and her attending nymphs is sculpted in the form of a satyr – a personification of lust – with water pouring from his horns and mouth. Although this fountain is different from the one in Titian's painting of the same subject, it was probably also inspired by that one. As in Titian's painting, the water spouting forth from the satyr's head represents the discharge that culminates the act of love and thus serves as a reminder of Jupiter's rape of Callisto, which has brought about her punishment.[99]

The *Diana and Callisto* was a magnificent addition to the Spanish royal collection and serves as an example of the importance of Philip IV's purchases from Rubens' estate after the artist's death. The painting is first inventoried in the Alcázar in 1666, which is also the first mention of any kind about this work, in Spain or elsewhere. At that time it hung in the *Galería del Cierzo* or Gallery of the North Wind, a large room located in the northern section of the main floor of the palace. Velázquez had his studio in the room from the 1620s to 1646, and later, in 1652, he was placed in charge of redecorating it.[100] It was probably at that time that the *Diana and Callisto* was installed there, where, according to the 1666 inventory of the Alcázar, it hung with fifty-eight other

FIGURE 80

Rubens, *Judgment of Paris*. Madrid, Museo del Prado.

pictures. These included works by Antonis Mor, Jan Brueghel, El Greco, Tintoretto, and Rubens himself,[101] and also some of the most spectacular mythologies painted in the seventeenth century: Annibale Carracci's *Venus and Adonis*, Guido Reni's *Hipomenes and Atalanta*, and the more subdued *Feast of Bacchus* by Velázquez, all of them now in the Prado. In the company of these illustrious paintings, the *Diana and Callisto* must have made the Gallery of the North Wind one of the most arresting rooms in the Alcázar.

The events narrated in the preceding pages prove that Philip IV remained an avid collector of Rubens' art even after the death of the painter in 1640. Additional evidence of the king's enduring enthusiasm for Rubens' paintings is provided by the commissioning from the painter Martínez del Mazo of over twenty-five copies of original works by the Flemish master in the royal collection. These were mainly copies after the pictures for the Torre de la Parada, but they also included copies after other mythological and historical paintings by Rubens in the Alcázar.[102] Martínez del Mazo (or Mazo, as he is often referred to) was Velázquez's son-in-law and his successor as court painter, a post that he held from 1661 to his death in 1667.[103] He was an important portraitist for the court and is also noted as a painter of landscapes and of copies of works by Titian and Rubens. It is not known exactly when he made his copies after Rubens, but he most likely did so in the period under consideration here, between 1640 and 1665. Mazo's first independent works of some significance probably date to the late 1630s, and more important documented works are known from the mid-1640s onwards. In 1647–1648, he restored some paintings in the Octagonal Room in the Alcázar, among them possibly some by Rubens. Perhaps this occasion prompted the commissions to paint copies of Rubens.[104] In 1655, at least two small copies after Rubens are listed in Mazo's collection, which indicates that the larger copies painted for the Alcázar may also have already been executed by that date.[105]

The Enthusiasm of Philip IV for Rubens' Paintings

When Philip IV died on September 17, 1665, the remaining half of the unique partnership between Rubens and his foremost patron came to an end. Given the king's paramount importance for the collecting of Rubens' work in Spain, we should summarize here the reasons for Philip's enthusiasm for the art of the Flemish master.

Seventeenth-century viewers, among them Philip IV, must have appreciated Rubens' works for the same qualities that we admire in them today: they are *bellísimas pinturas* ("very beautiful paintings"), as Pacheco described a set of Rubens' pictures destined for another patron.[106] Indeed, the richness of Rubens' glazes and the luminosity of his colors, the immediacy and excitement with which his figures are characterized, and the enraptured rhythm of his compositions must have been reasons enough to captivate the king. Philip IV, after all, had been brought up among the superlative paintings assembled by his ancestors, which had trained his eye to appreciate the visual riches of the art of painting.

The tradition of patronage that existed within the king's family is important in another respect. The international scope of the Spanish monarchy had given its kings the sophistication to look beyond the frontiers of their Iberian kingdoms for artistic talent. From the fifteenth century on, the Netherlands and Italy provided many of the most important works of art that could be seen in Spain. By the second half of the sixteenth century, painters from the Netherlands shared with Italian artists the favor of Philip II.[107] This king amassed an extraordinary collection of works by Titian, and called to Spain Netherlandish artists such as Antonis Mor, who played an important role as a creator of the image of the Spanish monarchy, and Anton Van den Wyngaerde (or Antonio de las Viñas, as he was known to Spaniards), who drew for the king a large number of detailed topographical views of Spanish cities before dying in Madrid in 1571.[108] In the seventeenth century, Rubens was an heir to both the Northern and the Italian traditions. In view of the styles traditionally favored by the Spanish monarchs, his paintings offered a combination that Philip IV was especially well equipped to understand.

Another important reason for Philip's taste for Rubens' art has already been pointed out in this study: the erotic content of many of the

Flemish master's paintings. In this area, as in others, Rubens was a perfect match for his royal patron. The frank sexuality and erotic feeling that are basic ingredients of Rubens' art were ideally suited to satisfy the taste for erotic painting that had developed during the Renaissance. Philip IV's penchant for women, evident in his numerous extramarital affairs, further explains his taste for pictures depicting women that appear "meant to be enjoyed."[109] Even though the reception in Spain of Rubens' erotic images cannot be given the extensive treatment it deserves here, one element that may explain the king's liking for them can be briefly noted: these images correspond closely with the ideal of feminine beauty that existed in Spain at the time. Numerous texts from the seventeenth century demonstrate the preference for young women with blonde hair (often referred to as golden), very fair skin (pearl or snowlike), and red lips and cheeks (like roses or rubies), a physical type identical to that painted by Rubens – and conspicuously different from that of most Spanish women.[110] Also relevant to understanding Rubens' role as a supplier of images of sensuous women is the fact that there were vehement complaints against this type of painting on the part of the most conservative moralists of the time, who laid the blame not as much on the owners of such works as on their authors.[111] This may help explain why it was easier for Rubens than for his Spanish contemporaries to supply the king with this type of picture.

Rubens was an immensely versatile artist, and the king acquired works of his that are neither erotic nor mythological, including important religious paintings and portraits. This suggests that Rubens' broad range of subject matter was another reason for Philip IV's favor.

Still other explanations for the king's enthusiasm for the Fleming's work should be sought in the culture of the time. The persuasive and demonstrative nature of Rubens' paintings was well suited to serve an era that believed very keenly in the importance of appearances. The ability of his compositions to overwhelm and compel the beholder was well attuned to a concept of rulership that had reacted to the confusion and instability of the recent past by attempting to inspire assurance and awe. Also, in many of his works Rubens created a synthesis between Christianity and classical culture that embodies the ideals of Counter-Reformation Europe. The fact that Philip IV considered himself the political and military defender of Catholicism must have reinforced his affinity for the paintings by the Flemish master.[112]

Many of the components that explain Philip IV's taste for Rubens were not unique to the Spanish king, as is shown by the success of the artist in other European courts. But Philip's close connection to the Spanish Netherlands, combined with the lasting power and wealth of his monarchy, put him in a privileged position to turn his penchant for Rubens' paintings into actual purchases.

The taste of Philip IV for Rubens' work was also influential in Spain, given the exemplary role played by the king in the society of the time. The collecting of the king had the effect of setting the nobility on a scramble for works of art, and his preference for Rubens made the Fleming one of the most sought-after artists. After Philip's death, his son and successor, Charles II, assumed his father's activities as a collector, and his taste for Rubens, until the end of the century.

Royal Acquisitions during the Reign of Charles II, 1665–1700

Charles II, the last Spanish Hapsburg king, inherited the crown in 1665 and reigned until his death in 1700. When the new king arrived on the throne he was only four years old. During the first years of his reign, royal power was held by the king's mother, Queen Mariana, and such successive favorites and ministers as Don Juan José de Austria and the duke of Medinaceli. The patronage of painting continued, with the leading court painters of the last years of Philip IV carrying on their activities and occupying their positions into the new reign. When Charles II reached adulthood, he took personal control of artistic matters and managed to maintain the high standards of patronage established by his ancestors. The king supported numerous local artists by appointing them to court positions and spent large sums in decorating his palaces and other buildings.[113]

Concerning Rubens, one of the important actions taken by the king was his effort to keep his second wife, Mariana of Neuburg, from sending an excessive number of paintings from the royal collection to her brother, Johan Wilhelm, Elector Palatine, who was an avid collector.[114] For example, in 1694, the queen sent away several paintings, including works by Velázquez and Luca Giordano, and at least two pictures by Rubens, one of them a sketch, the other apparently a finished painting.[115] However, Charles II managed to restrain his wife when she attempted to export Rubens' large *Adoration of the Magi*, the painting Rubens had reworked and enlarged during his stay in the Spanish court in 1628–1629. In a letter of November 22, 1696, the queen's confessor, Father Gabriel de la Chiusa, wrote to Johan Wilhelm about this incident: "When the queen asked her husband [for the *Adoration*], to give it as a gift for her brother, putting all her interest in the petition, the king denied it, alleging that it was not merely hung, but rather that it formed part of the decoration of the chamber, and was therefore part of the patrimony of the crown."[116]

The contents of the royal collection during the reign of Charles II are known primarily through two inventories: the inventory of the Alcázar of 1686, and the inventory of the entire collection compiled between 1700 and 1703, following the death of the king in 1700.[117] A measure of the size and quality of the collection owned by the king can be gained from a document included in the 1686 inventory of the Alcázar, the main royal palace in Madrid where the bulk of the king's collection was deposited. According to this summary, in that year the Alcázar was home to a total of 1,547 paintings, including numerous works attributed to major masters. The inventory proudly concludes that the collection in the Alcázar alone, even without counting the paintings in other royal palaces, was "larger than that owned by any Monarch or Prince, as confessed even by foreigners."[118]

To a large extent, the inventories of 1686 and 1700 reflect the artistic patronage and collecting activities of Philip IV, not of Charles II, who had simply inherited most of the collection from his father. The last Spanish Hapsburg was less occupied with collecting than Philip IV, which resulted in a reduction in purchases of paintings. His merit would consist primarily in keeping the collection he inherited largely intact. Charles did, however, manage to acquire some new paintings, including works by Rubens. Seventeen new works by the Flemish master are recorded in the inventories of the royal collection during his reign. Only four of them are first recorded in Spain at this time. They are a *Diana Hunting*, which is listed in the 1686 inventory of the Alcázar;[119] a "large canvas" described as *Abundance* that is recorded in the inventories of the Pardo palace near Madrid in 1674 and in 1700–1703;[120] and two small panels showing a *Calvary* and a *Flagellation of Christ*, which are first recorded in the royal collection in 1700–1703, the former in the Casa de Campo, a country house situated near the Alcázar, and the latter in the Alcázar itself.[121] Nothing is known about the origin of these pictures, nor about the time or manner in which they arrived in Spain.

Of the remaining thirteen pictures, eleven were already in Spain prior to their entry into the collection of Charles II; they were added to the royal collection circa 1689–1691 from the collection of Gaspar de Haro, apparently as payment for a past debt.[122] These paintings are a *Virgin and Child Adored by Saints* (Madrid, Prado, Fig. 70), which is the same picture that Francisco de Rojas received from Rubens' heirs after the painter's death; an *Infant Jesus with the Infant Saint John* (Madrid, Prado);[123] a *Landscape with the Rest on the Flight to Egypt and Several Saints* (Madrid, Prado),[124] and eight of the original *modelli* executed by Rubens in preparation for the tapestries of the Eucharist series.[125] The two remaining scenes are a *Mercury* and a *Saturn*, two works of uncertain status that were mentioned earlier in this chapter. Both were attributed to Van Dyck when they were first recorded after the death of Philip IV; in the 1686 inventory of the Alcázar they were attributed to Rubens; and when they were again inventoried after the death of Charles II, they were described as copies, presumably after (not by) Rubens.

The group of pictures by Rubens that Charles II acquired for the royal collection was significantly less important than those which had entered the collection under Philip IV. One reason for this may be the reduced opportunities for purchases after Rubens' death in 1640 and the dispersal of many of his paintings immediately after that date. But it also appears that Charles II focused much of his artistic patronage on the support of contemporary painters, and consequently that Rubens' paintings lost some of the favored treatment they had received under the previous king. We can conclude that, after 1665, the Spanish king no longer played a fundamental role in promoting Rubens' work in Spain.

Paintings by Rubens in Aristocratic Collections: The Marquis of Leganés

As we have seen in previous chapters, private collecting of Rubens' works in Spain had only timidly emerged prior to the painter's death in 1640. After that date, members of the Spanish aristocracy became more interested in acquiring works by the Flemish master to the point where they play a fundamental role in defining Rubens' presence in their country.[126] To the extent it is known, the chronology of the private collections that include works by Rubens suggests that Philip IV's massive commissions from him in the late 1630s, and his purchases of works by the artist between 1640 and 1665, were the sparks that ignited the interest of other collectors of Rubens. In the following pages I shall review nearly all the private collections where paintings by Rubens are recorded in the period here under consideration. The large size and the extraordinary quality of some of these collections – those of the marquis of Leganés, the admirals of Castile, and the Haro family – demand that we pay close attention to all the works by Rubens there recorded.

The most important Spanish collector of Rubens in seventeenth-century Spain aside from Philip IV was Don Diego Mexía, marquis of Leganés, whose early collecting activities have been traced in previous chapters. Leganés' activities as Rubens' patron are first recorded in 1628, when he commissioned from the painter an *Immaculate Conception* (Fig. 44). When the Leganés collection was first inventoried in 1630, it included two additional works attributed to Rubens: a *Garland of Fruits and Flowers with Virgin and Child*, which the marquis probably purchased in Flanders at an earlier date, and a portrait of Philip IV, possibly a study by Rubens made in Madrid in 1628–1629 to use as a model for an equestrian portrait of the king.[127] The collecting activities of Leganés increased dramatically in the following years, as is shown by the inventories of the collection compiled in 1642 and 1655.

In 1642, the Leganés collection numbered over a thousand pieces. Nineteen of these pictures (including the two works from the 1630 inventory) were attributed to Rubens.[128] Eight of these paintings are almost certainly authentic works by the master (if works designed and finished by Rubens but executed with studio participation are considered). These eight paintings are: *Garland of Fruits and Flowers with Virgin and Child* (Madrid, Prado; painted with Jan Brueghel);[129] *Vision of Saint Hubert* (Madrid, Prado; in collaboration with Jan Brueghel; Fig. 81);[130] *Portrait of Ambrogio Spinola* (of uncertain identification);[131] *Diana and Nymphs Setting Out for the Hunt, with Satyrs* (Malibu, California, The J. Paul Getty Museum);[132] *Annunciation* (Collection Gaston Dulière, Brussels, on loan to Rubenshuis, Antwerp; Fig. 82); [133] *Saint Dominic* (Dublin, National Gallery of Ireland);[134] *Saint Francis of Assisi* (Dublin, National Gallery of Ireland); *Portrait of Charlotte-Marguerite de Montmorency, Princess of Condé* (Pittsburgh, Pennsylvania, The Frick Art Museum).[135]

The other eleven attributions are less certain as the paintings have not been identified with any extant works. The eleven paintings are:[136] *Virgin and Child with Two Angels; Virgin and Child; Portrait of Philip IV with a Feathered Hat* (this is one of the works already owned by Leganés in 1630); two landscapes with animals (the subject of these two scenes makes the attributions to Rubens unlikely); *Penitent Saint Gerome; Saint Magdalene Repentant;*[137] *Holy Family; Holy Family with Saint John;*[138] *Daniel in the Lions' Den;*[139] and *Portrait of Isabella Clara Eugenia, Infanta of Spain, in the Habit of a Poor Clare.*[140]

The 1642 Leganés inventory also included an anonymous painting described as an *Infant Jesus and Infant St. John with Two Angels, Playing with a Lamb*. This was assigned to Rubens in the 1655 inventory of the collection (discussed below), which suggests that it is an original work.[141] Another painting listed anonymously in the 1642 inventory is a *Wolf and Fox Hunt*, which has been identified with a painting by Rubens in The Metropolitan Museum of Art, New York (Fig. 68).[142] We can conclude that, in 1642, Leganés owned as many as twenty-one paintings by Rubens, and no less than nine.[143]

The exact date and manner in which Leganés acquired these paintings is not known. The marquis was active as a patron in Flanders in the early 1630s[144] and may have bought some of the paintings in the open market at that time. The only painting by Rubens for which the entry into the Leganés collection is documented is the *Wolf and Fox Hunt*, which the marquis purchased in Madrid from the collection of the duke of Aarschot in or shortly before 1641. This, and the heterogeneous assortment of paintings Leganés owned, suggests that he took advantage of every opportunity to buy works by Rubens, and that many of the paintings must have entered his collection as a result of such opportunistic purchases. The seemingly accidental nature of the group is best exemplified by the nine paintings owned by the marquis in 1642, where the attributions to Rubens are almost certain. Two of these paintings were done in collaboration with Jan Brueghel (the *Garland of Fruits and Flowers with Virgin and Child* and the *Vision of Saint Hubert*); five are paintings executed with different degrees of assistance from the workshop (*Diana and Nymphs Setting Out for the Hunt, with Satyrs*, *The Annunciation*, *Wolf and Fox Hunt*, *Saint Francis of Assisi*, and *Saint Dominic*). The other two paintings are portraits; one of them, the *Portrait of Ambrogio Spinola*, may have originated as a commission, as Leganés was married to Spinola's daughter.

The marquis may also have commissioned some paintings directly from Rubens before the painter's death, given the previous ties between the two. Other possible means for the entry of Rubens' paintings into the Leganés collection can be tentatively suggested. Leganés is known to have received some paintings as gifts from the king.[145] Although none of the recorded gifts are known to have been by Rubens, this nevertheless raises the possibility that the same occurred with works by the Fleming. Another possibility is suggested by an order given by Leganés that copies be made for his own collection from paintings in the royal collection.[146] These were copies of pictures that Leganés had previously donated to the king's Buen Retiro palace and probably did not involve copies from Rubens, but it is possible that copies of Rubens were made at another time. If so, some of the paintings attributed to Rubens in the Leganés collection could be copies rather than originals.

Leganés' position at court also made him the recipient of gifts from abroad intended to win his political support. On one occasion, the States General in Brussels commissioned a set of pictures for Leganés on the recommendation of the duke of Aarschot, who was Leganés' guest in Madrid in late 1633 and early 1634.[147] Even though this gift

FIGURE 81

Rubens and Jan Brueghel, *Vision of Saint Hubert*. Madrid, Museo del Prado.

FIGURE 82

Rubens, *Annunciation.* Rubenshuis, Antwerp. Scala/Art Resource, N.Y.

did not include paintings by Rubens, it is indicative of one way in which Flemish pictures arrived in the collection of the marquis of Leganés.

The 1642 Leganés inventory shows that the marquis had a preference for Venetian and Flemish artists, as did the king. This suggests that the royal collection may have been a model for Leganés, and thus that the marquis' interest in Rubens may have peaked only after Philip IV's commissions from the painter in the late 1630s. On the other hand, considering Leganés' connections to the Spanish Netherlands, his taste for Rubens may have predated, or at least run parallel to, the royal commissions. Thus, he may have had some influence on the king's taste and his collecting activities at an early date.

Leganés continued to enlarge his extensive collection of paintings after 1642. There is no record of when or how he acquired additional art works during those years, but when his paintings were inventoried for a final time after his death in 1655, he owned over two hundred pictures acquired after 1642.[148] Among the new acquisitions were twelve paintings attributed to Rubens: *Four Boys Playing with Doves, and a Basket of Fruit*; two paintings of the labors of Hercules; *Abduction of the Sabine Women; Bacchus;*[149] *Four Women and an Angel, Five Boys, and Fruits; Seven Women and Angels; Three Woman, and Two Children, and Flowers; Holy Family with Saints;*[150] *Holy Family with Saints, and Other Figures;*[151] *Portrait of Leonor de Guzmán,*[152] and *Portrait of an Unknown Sitter with a Red Hat, Holding a Glass and a Bag, and Laughing.*[153] The 1655 Leganés inventory also includes a portrait of the archduke Albert listed as a copy after Rubens and an unattributed copy after Rubens' *The Death of Seneca*, now in Munich.[154] It is also worth noting that in the same inventory the painter Quentin Massys is referred to as Rubens' teacher, as if that incorrect reference to Rubens would increase the status of Massys.[155]

The twelve paintings attributed to Rubens listed above, when added to the previous twenty-one, make a total of thirty-three paintings by or attributed to Rubens in Leganés' collection at the time of his death. Unfortunately, the 1655 inventory presents even more uncertainties than the 1642 list. None of the twelve paintings attributed to the Flemish master has been identified, and therefore the attributions cannot be confirmed.

In spite of the many unresolved issues in the study of the Leganés collection, some conclusions can be drawn. Leganés probably owned more paintings attributed to Rubens than any other aristocratic collector in Spain – with the possible exception of Gaspar de Haro. Even though many of the attributions cannot be verified, there are enough autograph works to assure that this was the most important collection aside from the king's, and some of the uncertain attributions are likely to have been autograph works as well. The subjects of the paintings are also significant. Many of the Rubens pictures owned by Leganés are of religious subjects. This preponderance differs markedly from the contents of the king's collection, which includes very few religious scenes painted by Rubens. This difference indicates that Leganés did not associate Rubens with classical subject matter as much as the king did, and that the marquis followed his own taste when collecting. As we shall see in the following pages and in the appendix, most of the other important collectors of Rubens in seventeenth-century Spain shared with Leganés this preference for Rubens' religious paintings.

The whereabouts of the Leganés collection – and therefore of the Rubens paintings that were in it – after the 1655 inventory is not documented. It is generally believed that the collection remained largely intact in the possession of Leganés heirs until the nineteenth century.[156]

The Admirals of Castile

The next important collector of paintings documented in Spain worthy of mention is Juan Alfonso Enríquez de Cabrera (1597–1647), ninth admiral of Castile and duke of Medina de Rioseco. Enríquez de Cabrera was one of the most prominent courtiers of the reign of Philip IV; he was *gentilhombre de cámara* (gentleman to the king's chamber) and *mayordomo mayor* (lord high steward) to the king, viceroy of Sicily in 1641, and of Naples from 1644 to 1646. Like many of the elite aristocrats of the time of Philip IV, Enríquez de Cabrera devoted a considerable amount of money and effort to collecting works of art.

The admiral of Castile had owned a painting by Rubens as early as 1632. In that year Philip IV gave him the *Equestrian Portrait of the Duke of Lerma* (Fig. 1) as a gift, perhaps because the admiral was married to a granddaughter of the duke of Lerma, Doña Luisa de Sandoval y Padilla. Another reason for the gift may be found in the attempt by the monarch to secure support for his military endeavors. In spite of his official posts, Enríquez de Cabrera had a turbulent relationship with Philip IV. In 1626 he was exiled from the court following a quarrel with the count-duke of Olivares. He returned to Madrid in 1629, where he remained until he ran into trouble again in 1634 for refusing to comply with a request to contribute men to the royal army. The gift of Rubens' equestrian portrait of Lerma may have been part of another attempt by the king to gain greater contributions from the admiral of Castile.[157]

When the admiral's collection was inventoried at the time of his death in 1647, it included nearly 1,400 paintings, in addition to tapestries and sculptures. [158] Five of the paintings were attributed to Rubens. One was the *Equestrian Portrait of the Duke of Lerma*. There were also a *Susanna*,[159] a *Martyrdom of Saint Lawrence*,[160] and a *Venus, Mars, and Cupid*,[161] all of them as yet unidentified. The fifth painting attributed to Rubens was the *Goddesses and Nymphs after the Bath*, which is now recognized as a work by Jordaens, not Rubens, as was mentioned earlier. The inventory also describes an empty frame that had been used for a *Venus and Adonis* by Rubens that was no longer in the collection, thus suggesting that the admiral had previously owned this painting.[162]

How the ninth admiral acquired these paintings is uncertain. The greater part of the collection, which contained primarily Italian pictures, was probably acquired by him during his posts as viceroy in Sicily and Naples.[163] This raises the possibility that some of the paintings by Rubens were purchased in Italy. However, Enríquez de Cabrera also bought some of his pictures in Spain, where he was already known as a collector in the 1630s. In 1638 the English ambassador in Madrid, Sir Arthur Hopton, mentioned in a letter that the admiral of Castile was among the most distinguished collectors in the Spanish capital. The admiral's interest in painting is also mentioned in the treatise *Diálogos de la Pintura* by Vicente Carducho, published in Madrid in 1633.[164] It is therefore possible that some of his works by Rubens were acquired in Spain in the decade of the 1630s.

The attributions in the inventory of the Juan Alfonso Enríquez de Cabrera appear excessively optimistic in view of the large numbers of works assigned to painters such as Leonardo or Raphael. However, the *Equestrian Portrait of the Duke of Lerma* is an original and important painting by Rubens, and the others (except for the painting by Jordaens) cannot be dismissed. The prices assigned to the Rubens paintings are among the highest in the inventory: the *Susanna* was valued at 1,800 *reales*; the *St. Lawrence* at 4,400; the *Venus, Mars, and Cupid* at 3,000; and the portrait of Lerma at 5,500. This demonstrates that the paintings were highly regarded and suggests that they may have been originals.[165]

More important for a study of Rubens than the collecting activities of the ninth admiral of Castile were those of his son, Juan Gaspar Enríquez de Cabrera (1625–1691), tenth admiral of Castile. Juan Gaspar was one of the leading aristocrats of his time and is one of the most important collectors of the latter part of the century in Spain. Among other important posts, he was member of the council of state after 1669, was made *caballerizo mayor*, or Master of the Horse, in 1683, and was one of the favorite courtiers of the queen mother Mariana of Austria. In spite of his political prominence, the tenth admiral appears to have been more interested in the social life of the court than in politics, and was a lover of both literature and art. Like his father before him, Juan Gaspar took to collecting. Also like his father, and like most contemporary collectors, the admiral's interest in painting was modeled upon the collecting activities of Philip IV and thus included a taste for Rubens.[166]

The tenth admiral kept his paintings in a residence in Madrid known as the "casa del Jardín del Prado de San Jerónimo," where they were organized according to subject matter and artist. The contents of the collection are known through an inventory drawn in 1691. Together with rooms dedicated to mythological painting, religious painting, landscapes, and other subjects, and to artists such as Raphael, Bassano, Tintoretto, Ribera, and others, the collection included a "Pieza de Rubens" ("Rubens Room") containing twenty-one paintings. The paintings are unattributed in the inventory, but the name of the room implies at least some connection to Rubens. Indeed, the detailed descriptions in this inventory reveal that of the twenty-one paintings in the "Rubens Room" eight coincide in their descriptions with well-known paintings by the Flemish master.[167] These eight paintings are: an *Andromeda Bound to the Rock*, which is described in a way that is identical to the painting of the same subject in Berlin-Dahlem, Gemäldegalerie; a *Landscape with the Castle Steen* and a *Triumph of Caesar*, both of which coincide with pictures in the National Gallery in London (Figs. 84–85); a *Venus Trying to Restrain Mars*, which coincides with a painting in Potsdam, Neues Palais; a *Rainbow Landscape* similar to a picture in the Wallace Collection (Fig. 86); an *Infant St. John and the Infant Christ with Angels*, coinciding with the picture in the Kunsthistorisches Museum in Vienna; *A Switzer, His Mistress, and a Satyr*, coinciding with a painting in Genoa, Palazzo Bianco; and a *Venus, Mars, and Cupid*, coinciding with a scene now in London, Dulwich College Picture Gallery. In addition to these pictures, the "Rubens Room" included ten portraits, two paintings of philosophers, and a mythological scene with Neptune.

It is uncertain when and how Enríquez de Cabrera acquired the paintings in the "Rubens Room." One of the pictures in the collection, *Venus, Mars, and Cupid*, was probably inherited by the tenth admiral from his father, and another, the *Scene with Neptune*, is previously recorded in another collection, that of Gaspar de Haro. The admiral must have acquired it from him. Similarly, the rest of the paintings must have also been purchased by the tenth admiral, possibly in the 1670s, when he was active in the art market and when his political power and wealth were at their peak.

One surprising fact emerges from the list of paintings in the tenth admiral's "Rubens Room." Five of the paintings listed above (*Andromeda Bound to the Rock; Landscape with the Castle Steen; Rainbow Landscape; The Triumph of Caesar*; and *A Switzer, His Mistress, and a Satyr*) are identical to paintings listed in Rubens' collection after his death in 1640. It is not impossible that the paintings owned by the admiral are actually the same pieces that were in the painter's collection rather than copies. The strongest evidence in support of this identification stems from the painting *The Triumph of Caesar*. The list of Rubens' collection includes a copy by the painter himself after Mantegna's *Triumph of Julius Caesar*; the copy is divided into three canvases, pasted on panels. The painting of the same subject matter in the collection of the admiral in 1691 has the same unusual support and could therefore be one of the three canvases from the painter's estate.[168] A painting of the same subject by Rubens in the National Gallery in London (Fig. 85) shares the unusual support with the pieces in the collections of the artist and of the admiral of Castile and may therefore be the same item.[169]

It should be noted that, even if the provenance from Rubens' collection is correct, the admiral was only fifteen years old when Rubens died, which would indicate that the paintings were probably not purchased directly from the painter's estate.

Luis and Gaspar de Haro

Another important aristocratic family of art collectors is that of Luis de Haro and his son Gaspar. Luis de Haro, sixth marquis of Carpio (1598–1661), was a nephew of the count-duke of Olivares and a lifelong acquaintance of Philip IV. Even though he never reached the level of power enjoyed by his uncle, Haro was the most trusted minister of Philip IV during the years when the king took personal charge of his reign, from 1643. Following the example of the king, Haro managed to amass an extraordinary group of paintings, as is demonstrated by what remains of the inventory of his collection of 1661.[170] In regard to Rubens, Luis de Haro's role is not as significant as that played by his son Gaspar in later years, but it is not negligible. In the first half of the 1650s, he purchased three paintings by the Fleming, or at least attributed to him, from the various sales in London following the English Civil War. One of these is described as a "Virgin with Saint Margaret and Saint George in a landscape," and is probably identical to a *Landscape with the Rest on the Flight to Egypt and Several Saints* in the Prado Museum.[171] The second was a *Nativity*, which has not been identified.[172] The third was a picture described as "the abundance by Rubens with many figures of his family." This was acquired for Luis de Haro in London between 1651 and 1654.[173] The description of this picture probably corresponds to the famous *Peace and War* in the National Gallery, London (Fig. 83), which was painted by Rubens for Charles I while the painter was in London negotiating a peace between the Spanish and English Crowns in 1629–1630.[174] The reference to the figure of Abundance in the description is justified by the prominent presence in the picture of a cornucopia with fruits; of a satyr, a personification of sexual fecundity; and of a woman who nourishes a child with milk from her breast. The mention of figures from Rubens' family can also be explained. Three of the children that appear in the right-hand side of the *Peace and War* – a young girl who looks out from the scene, a girl in profile to the far right, and the figure of Hymen holding a torch in his right hand – are borrowed from a portrait painted by Rubens of the family of Sir Balthasar Gerbier.[175] The conspicuous portrait-like appearance of some of these figures in the *Peace and War*, and the knowledge that they represented actual children portrayed by Rubens, appears to have caused their mistaken identification with the painter's own family.

The dimensions of the canvas in the Haro Collection are also similar to those of the London *Peace and War*.[176] It appears, therefore, that

FIGURE 83

Rubens, *Peace and War*. London, National Gallery.

Haro managed to purchase Rubens' original *Peace and War* after it was sold from the collection of Charles I of England.

More important than Luis de Haro for the history of the collecting of Rubens' art in Spain was his son Gaspar, one of the great collectors of the seventeenth century.[177] Gaspar de Haro (1629–1687) was marquis of Heliche and later became seventh marquis of Carpio. Even before he inherited his father's paintings, Gaspar had already begun to collect on his own. The first inventory of his collection dates to 1651. At the time, he was only twenty-two years old, but he already owned over three hundred pictures. This was a remarkable feat for such a young man, and it demonstrates the importance of collecting art in the Spain of Philip IV.[178]

Seven of the paintings owned by Gaspar de Haro in 1651 were attributed to Rubens: *Landscape with the Temptation of Saint Anthony; Virgin and Child Adored by Saints; Lamentation of Christ, with Saint John, the Magdalene, and an Old Woman; Scene with Neptune; Portrait of a Pilgrim*; a *Portrait of a Doctor*, and an *Equestrian Portrait of Don Rodrigo Calderón*.

One of these paintings, the *Virgin and Child Adored by Saints*, appears to be identical to the small painting mentioned earlier that Francisco de Rojas had received from Rubens' family for his assistance with the sale of the painter's collection (Fig. 70); it must have been purchased by Haro from Rojas. The *Lamentation of Christ, with Saint John, the Magdalene, and an Old Woman* is probably identical to an *Entombment* attributed to Rubens that belongs to the J. Paul Getty Museum.[179] The equestrian portrait of Calderón is the same picture that was mentioned in Chapter 2 (Fig. 8). None of the other paintings can be reconciled with extant or recorded works, which suggests that some of the attributions are incorrect. It is worth noting in this context that, after the death of Gaspar de Haro in 1687, when his paintings were put up for sale, questions were raised about the authenticity of some of the works in the collection. A letter written from Naples to Haro's widow about the collection of paintings stated that some unspecified local experts: "believe that his excellency was tricked, and that there are a number of copies that were taken for originals."[180] This opinion must refer to the paintings present in the collection of Gaspar de Haro in Naples, where he was viceroy, but it also casts doubts on the attributions of the works in the collection as a whole. Also, in 1674, the imperial ambassador, Count Harrach, wrote about a visit to a sale of paintings from the collection of Gaspar de Haro: "There was almost nothing on sale except pictures, and most of them only copies, if from good originals."[181] It should be kept in mind, however, that Gaspar de Haro owned important original paintings in 1651, most notably Velázquez's *Rokeby Venus* (London, National Gallery), so it is imprudent to dismiss the attributions of paintings in his collection entirely.

In addition to the pictures attributed to Rubens, the 1651 inventory of the collection of Gaspar de Haro also included seven paintings listed as copies after the master.[182] One of these is especially noteworthy; it reproduces the *Portrait of Philip IV, on Horseback* that Rubens had painted in Madrid in 1628. The equestrian portrait of the monarch was the most demonstrative display extant of the bond between the king and Rubens. By ordering a copy of the portrait, Gaspar de Haro incorporated the association between painter and king into his own collection. With this painting hanging in his palace, the status associated with owning other works by Rubens, the king's painter, must have become immediately apparent to anyone visiting the collection.

As is evident from the next inventory of the collection, Don Gaspar's activities as a collector continued to increase after 1651. The portion of the collection that was kept in Madrid was inventoried in 1687, following Haro's death in Naples.[183] This inventory, which lists over 1,200 works, included sixteen paintings attributed to Rubens. Two of them, a *Virgin and Child Adored by Saints*, and an *Equestrian Portrait of Rodrigo Calderón*, were already owned by Gaspar de Haro in 1651.[184] Three other paintings, a *Landscape with the Rest in the Flight to Egypt and Several Saints*, an *Abundance*, and a *Nativity*, were inherited from his father, Luis de Haro, who had died in 1661. The 1687 inventory also included the following items attributed to Rubens: *Virgin with Christ the Child Asleep, Saint Joseph, and Saint Anne;*[185] *Infant Jesus with the Infant Saint John;*[186] *Christ on the Cross;*[187] *Landscape with the Dream of Jacob;*[188] a *Scene with a Queen Being Poisoned;*[189] *Charity;*[190] *Bathsheba Seated by the Fountain;*[191] A *Portrait of a Man from Moscow, with a Gold Chain and a Golden Key,*

FIGURE 84

Rubens, *Landscape with the Castle Steen*. London, National Gallery.

FIGURE 85

Rubens, copy after Mantegna, *Triumph of Caesar*. London, National Gallery.

FIGURE 86

Rubens, *Rainbow Landscape*. London, The Wallace Collection.

Dressed in Blue, with a Golden Cape Lined in Fur, and a Cap on his Head;[192] a *Portrait of the Cardinal-Infante Ferdinand;*[193] *Triumph of Peace;*[194] and *Voyage of the Prince from Barcelona to Genoa.*[195]

The collection of Gaspar de Haro was inventoried again in the following years as part of the process of its dispersal. The records of this period show that Haro also owned eight of the original *modelli* executed by Rubens in preparation for the Eucharist tapestries (which he later used as payment to Charles II, as seen above)[196] and nineteen drawings attributed to Rubens that he purchased from Flanders.[197] As we have seen earlier, he may also have owned the six cartoons executed in Rubens' workshop for the tapestries of the Eucharist series that were sent from Brussels to Philip IV earlier in the century. There is mention of a final work attributed to Rubens owned by Gaspar de Haro. This is an unidentified *Virgin and Child*, which Haro dispatched from Rome to Naples in 1682 or 1683.[198]

The chronology of Gaspar de Haro's collecting activities and the source for many of his works by Rubens are not well known. It appears that most of the purchases made after the 1651 inventory date from well after that year, probably from the 1670s and 1680s. In 1674, Haro sold part of his collection, probably copies, which suggests that he was refining his holdings. In 1676 he left for Rome, where he was to serve as ambassador to the Holy See. During his successive posts in Italy, and until his death in 1687, he was very active as an art patron and collector.[199]

Except for the works that he inherited from his father and the Eucharist cartoons, which probably arrived in the Haro collection from the royal collection, the source of the other paintings is undocumented. The fact that Don Gaspar purchased nineteen drawings in Flanders and had them shipped to Spain suggests that he may have also purchased other paintings there, or in other locations, presumably through agents.

The attributions of many of the paintings assigned to Rubens in this collection are also problematic. The *modelli* for the Eucharist series (and the workshop cartoons, if indeed they were owned by Gaspar de Haro), of course, are well-known and important works by Rubens. Of the other paintings incorporated into the collection after 1651, at least one, the *Infant Jesus with the Infant Saint John*, is known today. It is one of the paintings that King Charles II received from the Haro collection circa 1689–1691 and is now in the Prado. None of the other paintings listed in the collection can be identified with certainty with an extant or recorded work, and their attributions therefore cannot be confirmed.

Don Juan José de Austria

Juan José de Austria (1629–1679) is less important as a collector of Rubens than the figures who have been discussed above. Nevertheless, his proximity to the king and the little attention his paintings by Rubens have received make him an interesting figure. Don Juan José was recognized by Philip IV as his illegitimate son in 1642 and was therefore half-brother to Charles II, thus enjoying a distinguished position at court, although he had no claim to the throne. During the last fifteen years of his life, Don Juan José became one of the leading military and political figures of the monarchy. Among the many positions he held was the governorship of the Spanish Netherlands, where he served between May 1656 and April 1659.[200] The main source of information on his artistic patronage is the inventory of his collection compiled after his death.[201] The pictures were appraised by two of the leading painters in Spain, Francisco Rizi and Juan Carreño de Miranda, on March 15, 1680. Although the collection was willed to King Charles II, none of the paintings attributed to Rubens in the documents were ever recorded in later inventories of the royal collection.

The inventory of Juan José's property includes four paintings attributed to Rubens: a large scene described as a *Bodegón* (a term that probably refers to either a still life or a kitchen scene);[202] a *Bacchus* painted on panel;[203] a small panel described as a *Head* (probably a sketch);[204] and a panel of the *Reconciliation of Jacob and Esau*.[205] The group also included a large painting "which shows the tigers" listed as a copy after Rubens.[206] None of these paintings have been identified. It is worth noting that the copy after Rubens showing "the tigers" was less expensive than three of the originals, but more valuable than the small panel showing a head. Evidently, the size, and presumably also the subject matter of a painting, could compensate for the fact that it was a copy.

In spite of the difficulty of identifying these paintings, there are reasons to take the attributions to Rubens seriously. Most of the pictures in the inventory are not attributed, suggesting that there were specific reasons for those attributions which are given. The artists in charge of the appraisals, Rizi and Carreño, were well acquainted with Rubens' work. Both painters had developed their own art under the influence of the Flemish master, and as royal painters they were able to study his paintings carefully.[207] Further, the positions held by Juan José de Austria in the Netherlands, and the fact that he was a member of the royal family, also suggest that if he owned paintings attributed to Rubens the attributions have a good chance of being correct.

The origin of one of the paintings by Rubens in Don Juan José's collection, the *Bacchus*, is of some interest. This work is probably identical to a painting Juan José sent to Madrid when he was governor-general of the Spanish Netherlands as a gift for the king.[208] Although, for reasons that are not known, this painting remained in Don Juan José's own possession instead of entering the royal collection, its history shows that at least one of his Rubens paintings was purchased in Flanders during his tenure as governor. Spanish officials who served in Flanders played an important role throughout the entire century in bringing paintings by Rubens to Spain. As noted in previous chapters, paintings by the master arrived in Spain under the auspices of Rodrigo Calderón and the marquis of Leganés, among others, and the Spanish origin of the infanta Isabella was also an important factor in making Rubens a familiar artist in Spain. Don Juan José de Austria can be seen as a continuation of this phenomenon in the later part of the century.

Other Collectors

In addition to the collections that have been discussed, there are many other paintings attributed to Rubens recorded in Spain in the period 1640–1700. As a detailed account of all these works would be too tedious, an overview can offer some interesting conclusions.[209] The collectors who will be mentioned below are less important from a quantitative standpoint than those previously studied. Most of these figures were associated in some capacity with the court of King Philip IV and thus offer additional proof of the interest in Rubens that existed in the circles closest to the Crown. In some cases, the lives of these collectors continued into the reign of Charles II, carrying the taste for the art of the Flemish master through the end of the century.

Don Fernando de Borja y Aragón was a member of an important aristocratic family who held various positions at the court and in the government before his death in 1665. In the early years of the seventeenth century he served as gentleman-in-waiting to the chamber of Prince Philip, the future Philip IV. He later served as *sumiller de corps*, or groom of the stole, a position that made him the closest servant of the prince Baltasar Carlos.[210] A recently discovered inventory shows that Borja was interested in art collecting, and that he owned, among other paintings, two small works, perhaps sketches, which were attributed to Rubens: a *Descent from the Cross* and a *Saint Peter with two Angels*.[211]

Another figure who belonged to court circles in the years of the transition between the reigns of Philip IV and Charles II was Blasco de Loyola, a member of the council of state between 1660 and 1669. Loyola's collection, which is documented in Madrid in January of 1670, included a *Judgment of Solomon* attributed to Rubens.[212] From his official post, Loyola often dealt with matters relating to the government of the Spanish Netherlands,[213] which suggests a possible origin for his picture.

Diego de la Torre probably also acquired works by Rubens as a result of his connections to the Netherlands. De la Torre was secretary of state in Madrid from 1671 to 1674 and is presumably the same person who is documented in Flanders as serving in the Spanish administration as early as 1635, and is again documented there in 1641, and in 1652.[214]

De la Torre owned a *Judith* attributed to Rubens when his collection was appraised on January 9, 1674.[215]

It was not only the aristocracy and high officers of the court who followed the king's example and set their sights on Rubens' work. Andrés Guillón, a cook for Philip IV and Don Juan José de Austria, owned a small panel of "Our Lady with the Child in Her Arms" in 1657 that is listed in his inventory as having "come from Rubens."[216] Another interesting case is that of the painter Felipe Diricksen (1590–1679), who owned three *borrones* or sketches attributed to Rubens when his collection was inventoried after his death: *Holy Trinity*, *Baptism of Christ*, and *Adoration of the Magi*. He also owned a portrait of Philip IV copied after Rubens.[217] Diricksen was the son of Rodrigo Diricksen, a painter of Flemish origin, and grandson of the more famous Anton van den Wyngaerde, who painted topographical views for Philip II in the sixteenth century.[218] Felipe Diricksen's artistic activity, which spans from circa 1620 through the end of his life, often brought him in contact with the court. The Flemish background and his court connections provide an explanation for his ownership of three paintings attributed to Rubens.

The records of copies and prints made after Rubens' works offer similar evidence of the growing circle of people in Spain who wished to own his work in the second half of the seventeenth century. It appears from these records that Rubens' paintings, for the most part, went to members of the highest circles of the court and of society. To others were left copies and prints. But even these most often were owned by members of the upper classes.

Among the collectors who owned copies after Rubens during the last years of the reign of Philip IV is the lawyer Diego de Altamirano, who became famous for successfully defending the count of Oñate against a suit by the king in 1631. Altamirano's collection included a copy after Rubens when it was inventoried in 1642.[219] Five more copies are recorded in the collection of the otherwise unknown Constanza Pardo in 1655,[220] and documents also mention the remittance to the city of Málaga in 1663 of four small copies painted by Willem van Herp after hunting scenes by Rubens.[221]

In fact, between 1665 and 1700 copies after Rubens appear so often in Spanish inventories that they are almost impossible to count.[222] The most significant of these, because of the identity of their owner, are three copies that belonged to Claudio Coello, one of the most important painters active during the reign of Charles II. Although the author of the copies is not named in the inventory, it was presumably Coello himself. They were copies after eight of Rubens' original *modelli* for the Eucharist series, and three additional scenes after Rubens described in his collection as "some children from the Bacchic scene"; "two heads"; and "a sketch of the *Adoration of the Magi*."[223] These eleven copies were kept in Claudio Coello's collection along with eight copies after Titian, and smaller numbers of copies after Veronese, Bassano, Giordano, Velázquez, and Van Dyck, among others.

The period under consideration in this chapter also witnessed a growing presence in Spanish collections of prints based on Rubens' designs. In Spain, prints were commonly used for devotional purposes and to publicize especially noteworthy events. These images were often locally produced and did not demand high artistic quality. Better prints could be purchased by more demanding collectors. They could be hung in houses in place of more expensive paintings, or they could be used as models by artists. These works, where quality was more of a prerequisite, were frequently of foreign origin, often from Flanders. The records show that prints after Rubens were an especially valuable commodity. A contract signed in Madrid in 1655 between local store owners and two Flemish merchants who lived in the capital can serve as a representative example. In this contract the Spaniards state that they will sell a large number of prints of various subjects; the only two artists whose names are mentioned are Rubens and Van Dyck.[224] There are numerous other references to prints after works by Rubens in Spain in the last decades of the century, and undoubtedly more will be found.

Tapestries also contributed to the spread of Rubens' reputation in Spain, as is shown by a literary piece dating from the middle of the seventeenth century. The writer Baltasar Gracián wrote, in a section of his allegorical novel, *El Criticon*: "Look – he said to them – what a happy sight of tapestries. How can they be compared even to the richest and most embroidered hangings of the famous duke of Medina de las Torres? Or to the finest tapestries from Flanders, even if they were designed by Rubens?"[225]

The most famous tapestries designed by Rubens that were sent from the Spanish Netherlands to Madrid were mentioned in an earlier chapter. They are the twenty tapestries of the Eucharist series commissioned for the Descalzas Reales in Madrid in 1625 or 1626 by the infanta Isabella Clara Eugenia. Several other sets of tapestries after designs by Rubens are recorded in Spain between 1640 and 1700, the period covered in this chapter. Two of the leading collectors of Rubens' works who were studied above, Juan Alfonso Enríquez de Cabrera and Luis de Haro, owned tapestries after Rubens' designs; the former's were famous enough to be mentioned in a letter from the Florentine ambassador in Madrid to his court in Florence.[226] In other cases, tapestries are recorded in lesser-known collections, or in collections not otherwise known to have contained works by the Flemish master, offering additional proof of the widening circle of Rubens' presence in Spain in the second half of the century. Isabel de Zúñiga y Fonseca, marchioness of Tarazona, owned a set of tapestries of the Triumph of Alexander when her goods were inventoried in Madrid in 1648.[227] Tapestries of the history of Decius Mus designed by Rubens were willed in 1657 by María Tofiño de Vallejo to her husband, Pedro de Arce, an important art collector who was a member of the court of Philip IV (Velázquez painted his famous *Fable of Arachne* for Arce).[228] And in 1658, Jerónimo de la Torre, a counsellor to the same king who was also secretary of state for Flanders, owned a set of five tapestries with the story of Alexander the Great, presumably by Rubens.[229] Finally, a number of Spanish noblemen who served in the Netherlands – among them Don Benavides Carrillo y Toledo, marquis of Frómista y Caracena, the count of Peñaranda, and the count of Fuensaldaña – also purchased sets of tapestries based on designs by Rubens, and may have taken them back to Spain upon their return.[230]

During the seventeenth century, tapestries were considerably more expensive than paintings.[231] From an artistic standpoint, however, pictures could be considered more valuable, at least in the mind of Rubens. In a letter to a client written on June 1, 1618, the painter stated: "One evaluates pictures differently from tapestries. The latter are purchased by measure, while the former are valued according to their excellence, their subject, and number of figures."[232] As a result of the presence in Spain of tapestries after Rubens' designs, the Flemish master could be associated in that country, not only with the artistry exerted in painting, but also with the high material worth of tapestries.

The numerous works of art, copies, and prints referred to in this chapter witness that the fame enjoyed by Rubens in Spain was extended through the end of the seventeenth century. Palomino, one of the authors who has guided us throughout this study, provides further proof of Rubens' lasting reputation. As mentioned in the introduction to this book, in 1724 Palomino published the biographies of 226 artists – which he entitled *El Párnaso español pintoresco y laureado* – as part of his larger treatise on painting, *Museo pictórico y escala óptica*. This text was actually written at least one decade before its publication and is generally believed to reflect the attitudes about art prevalent in the last years of seventeenth-century Spain.[233] Palomino included Rubens among the nearly two dozen foreign artists whose biographies merited inclusion in a book dedicated to Spanish painting. More telling than his inclusion is a quote from the concluding paragraph of the biography of Rubens, which demonstrates that the Flemish master enjoyed a special status among his peers:

Among the moderns, Peter Paul Rubens is the artist who has given greatest luster to the brush by his person, nobility, virtue, literary accomplishments, expertise in languages, appointments, high offices, favors, and extraordinary honors received from princes and royal persons, all these endowments accompanied by great modesty and a pleasing manner. . . . And in the end, loaded with riches and honors, he lived more like a great prince than like a great painter. . . .[234]

The treatment that Rubens receives from Palomino indicates that, more than a half-century after his death, time had played into his favor: rather than fading into the past, by the end of the seventeenth century Rubens had secured himself a place in the pantheon of Spanish art.

With the evidence presented in this chapter we have completed the survey of Rubens' Spanish patronage during the seventeenth century, which has served to chart the arrival and the reception of Rubens' works in Spain. In the early years of the century, the power and influence of the Spanish monarchy facilitated the contact between the painter and a Spanish audience: it enabled Rubens to visit the court in Valladolid as part of an embassy from Mantua, and it was the reason why many Spanish officials served in the Spanish Netherlands, where they became acquainted with Rubens' art and began to collect it. Once Rubens' paintings came to be known by Philip IV, the king developed a strong liking for them. The king's influence over the society he ruled soon inspired others to imitate his taste, and thus to acquire paintings by the Flemish master in increasing numbers. By the time of Rubens' death in 1640, and for the remainder of the century, owning his works had become a sign of distinction in Spain.

The result of the extensive collecting of Rubens' works in Spain during the seventeenth century was that no other contemporary painter, Spanish or foreign, had as many paintings in court circles as did Rubens – and few artists were as well represented anywhere in the country.[235] As was stated in the introduction to this book, Rubens' great success in Spain suggests that he should be incorporated into the history of art of that nation more assertively than he has been hitherto. This is one of the challenges that lie ahead for those studying Rubens' presence in Spain – or, for that matter, the presence of any work of art in a foreign environment. We need to see Rubens' images, not only as adornments on the walls of local palaces or as commodities in the trade of power and prestige, but also as objects that had an effect on the mental worlds of their audiences, giving form to their desires and aspirations. In his work *El gran teatro del mundo*, Calderón de la Barca (1600–1681) explains the capacity of the art of painting to give material form to one's fantasies: "pintadas todas mis glorias son imaginadas" ("when painted, all my glories are imagined").[236] The evidence presented in this study shows that Rubens was among those artists better able to give form to the "imagined glories" of contemporary Spaniards. We thus need to overlay the images that he created onto our existing view of seventeenth-century Spain, allowing them to contribute to shaping our understanding of the period.

Appendix 1

The following is a translation of the biography of Rubens included in the treatise by Francisco Pacheco, *Arte de la Pintura*. It is taken from the edition of the treatise by B. Bassegoda i Hugás (Pacheco, ed., 1991, pp. 193–202); translation by the author.[1] Pacheco's book was finished by January of 1638 and was published posthumously in 1649. The section that includes Rubens' biography was written after 1630, as is indicated by the passage where the author refers to "the past year of 1630."[2]

Another [painter] worthy of being remembered (even though it is those of his nation who are in charge of his praise, since he belongs to the most excellent amongst them) is Peter Paul Rubens, born to much nobility and abundance in the famous city of Antwerp. His father was a person of important origin, and secretary of a great prince of Flanders. He had a brother named Felipo Rubenis, very learned in human letters, who was titled the second Lipsio for his excellency, and whose books demonstrate his studies, and he died Secretary of the city of Antwerp. Peter Paul Rubens, being an outstanding student of Octavio Venio, skillful [*valiente*] Flemish painter, went to Italy in his youth, where he stayed for more than twelve years, and after returning very improved to his country he built a grand home in which he now lives. Their Highnesses the archduke Albert and the infanta Doña Isabel, his wife, always esteemed him greatly, because having done two famous portraits of them sitting in chairs shortly after his arrival, the infanta, in the presence of her husband, fitted a sword around his waist, and she put a very rich golden chain around his neck, calling him the honor of his homeland. The archduke was godfather to a son of his, who lives today, and he was named Albert after him, and often he came to see him to his houses when he was in Antwerp. Some years ago he went from Flanders to Paris, where he enriched the new palace built by the queen mother with the most beautiful paintings by his hand. He made many and very excellent paintings for the king of England and the emperor of Germany. Later, when the duke of Buckingham came to France to negotiate the marriage of the king of England (by whom he was most favored) with the sister of the king of France (which occurred in the year

1625), he communicated closely with him (due to his great capacity and learning), discussing the peace between England and Spain on behalf of his king. This caused his visit to Spain, on order from Her Highness the infanta Doña Isabel, by whom (as has been said) he was very esteemed, and who called on him, and sent him by post from the court in Brussels to that of Spain, where he arrived by the month of August of 1628. He brought to the Majesty of our Catholic King Philip IV eight paintings of different subjects and sizes, which are installed in the new room, among other famous pictures. In the nine months that he spent in Madrid, without missing the important business for which he had come, and being ill some days with gout, he painted many things, as we shall see (such is his dexterity and his ease). First of all, he portrayed the kings and infantes in half-length, to take to Flanders; he made of His Majesty five portraits, and among them one on horseback with other figures, of great value. He painted a portrait of the infanta from the Descalzas in more than half-length, and made copies after them: of private persons he painted five or six portraits: he copied all the things by Titian that the king has, which are the two baths, the Europa, the Adonis and Venus, the Venus and Cupid, the Adam and Eve, and other things: and of portraits, the one of the Lansgrave, the one of the duke of Alba, the one of Cobos, a Venetian dux, and many more paintings outside of those owned by the king: he copied the portrait of Philip II full-length, in armor. He modified some things in the painting of the Adoration of the Magi by his hand, which is in the palace: he painted an image of the Conception of two *varas* for D. Diego Megía (who was a great admirer of his); and to D. Jaime de Cárdenas, brother of the duke of Maqueda, a Saint John the Evangelist, of life size. It is incredible that he painted so much in such little time, and with so many occupations. He communicated little with painters. He only established a friendship with my son-in-law (with whom he had earlier corresponded), and he greatly favored his works for their modesty, and together they went to see the Escorial.

Finally, during the time when he was at the court, His Majesty and the most important ministers highly esteemed his person and his talent. And His Majesty awarded him with the position of Secretary of the Privy Council in the court in Brussels, for life, and with the future succession in that post for his son Albert, which is worth one thousand ducats each year.

Having finished the business when he bade farewell to His Majesty, the count duke gave him a ring worth two thousand ducats on behalf of the king. He left by post on April 26 of the following year of 1629, and went straight to Brussels to see the infanta; and from there to England, where, having finished the peace, King Charles I, honoring his person and his known nobility, esteeming his diligence, his talent and knowledge and eminence in painting, knighted him for a third time. And he returned to Antwerp, being approximately fifty years of age, and with a fortune of one hundred thousand ducats, he married for a second time in the past year of 1630.

It is clear from this discourse, which is as honorable as it is truthful (as much as this is possible), that over all the talents of this famous painter, that which makes him grand, which gives him reputation, and inclines kings and great princes to elevate to emulation such an illustrious subject, is the greatness, beauty, and abundance of his talent, which shines in his paintings; and it is his own hand that enriches him, worthy, and in fairness, of so many honors.

Appendix 2

This is an order from the infanta Isabella Clara Eugenia, dated September 30, 1623, granting Rubens a monthly pension of ten *escudos*. This transcription is taken from Gachard, 1877, Appendix 1, pp. 265–266 (see also in Rooses-Ruelens, 3: 248–249).

Don Gaspar Ruiz de Pereda, of the order of Santiago, of the council of war of the king, my lord, in these states, and inspector general of this his felicitous army, and Luis Casuso Maeda, its auditor, you should know that considering the merits of Peter Paul Rubens and what he has served His Majesty, so that he can continue to do so more comfortably, we have decided to assign to him, as we do in this order, ten *escudos* as monthly allowance in the castle of Antwerp, without obligation to present himself to the reviews. We therefore order and command that you deliver and confirm them in your books, so that he will enjoy them from this day onward: such is our will, and they should be paid in the same manner as the others that we entertain in the same castle. Dated in Brussels, on September 30, 1620.

A postscript reads:

Your Highness assigns Peter Paul Rubens a monthly allowance of ten *escudos* in the castle at Antwerp, without obligation to show up at the reviews.

Original Text

Don Gaspar Ruiz de Pereda, del hábito de S. Tiago, del consejo de guerra del rey, mi señor, en estos Estados y veedor general deste su felicissimo exército, y Luis Casuso Maeda, contador dél, saved que teniendo consideración á las buenas partes de Pedro Paulo Rubens y á lo que ha servido á Su Magestad, para que pueda continuarlo con mas comodidad, hemos tenido por bien de señalarle, como por tenor de la presente le señalamos, diez escudos de entreteniemiento al mes en el castillo de Anveres, sin obligacion de presentarse á las muestras. Por tanto os ordenamos y mandamos se los asenteis y hagais buenos en los libros de vuestros officios, para que goze dellos desde el dia de la data desta en adelante: que tal es nuestra voluntad, y que se libren y paguen segun y como á los demás entretenidos en el dho castillo. Datta en Brusselas á treinta de setiembre de mill y seiscientos y veinte años. Postscript:

V. A. señala á Pedro Paulo Rubens diez escudos de entretenimiento al mes en el castillo de Anveres, sin obligación de presentarse á las muestras.

Appendix 3

Text of a petition asking for Rubens' ennoblement that was presented to King Philip IV by Don Iñigo de Brizuela, bishop of Segovia and president of the council of Flanders in Madrid. This document is dated Madrid, January 29, 1624, is signed by the bishop, and is followed by the king's resolution: *Como parece* ("as it appears"). The beginning of this document refers to a *memorial* or petition written by Rubens that is not known. Rubens must have addressed his petition to Brizuela, who then acted as his intermediary with the king. The original document is transcribed in Gachard, 1877, pp. 266–267, and in Rooses-Ruelens, 3: 266.

Sir, Peter Paul Rubens, painter to the infanta Isabella, states in his memorandum that he descends from honest parents, that they have always been loyal vassals of the Crown of Your Majesty and served in important occupations: his father, a doctor in laws, alderman of the city of Antwerp; Philip Rubens, his brother, Secretary of the city. The petitioner has studied painting since his childhood, visiting many lands in order to gain in ability. And due to the great experience and practice that he has, the archduke Albert made him his painter with a salary of two hundred *escudos* a year. He begs Your Majesty to grant him letters of nobility without paying fees, given the fact that he is a servant of the house of Her Highness.

The petitioner, Peter Paul Rubens, is very rare in his art and very esteemed in all of Europe, and it is true that many European princes have tried to have him leave Antwerp with great promises of honors and money. And adding to this that he is the son of honest parents who are loyal vassals of Your Majesty, and that the petitioner, in addition to the excellence and beauty of his painting, has other qualities in letters, and knowledge of history and languages, and has always conducted himself splendidly, having abundant means for it. And therefore it seems that Your Majesty could make him the grace and honor of nobility that he solicits, and exempt him from the payment of fees.

Original Text

Señor, Pedro Pablo Rubens, pintor de la señora infanta doña Isabel, refiere en su memorial que desciende de parientes honrrados, que siempre han sido muy fieles vasallos de la corona de V. Md y servido en oficios príncipales: su padre, doctor en leyes, esclavin de la ciudad de Anveres; Phelipe Rubens, su hermano, secretario della; y el suplicante se ha aplicado desde su niñez á la pintura, frecuentando muchas tierras para habilitarse mas; y por la grande experiencia y plática que tiene, el señor archiduque Alberto le recibió por su pintor con doscientos escudos de sueldo al año. Suplica á V. Md se sirva de concederle letras de nobleza sin pagar finanzas atento á que es criado doméstico de S.A.

El suplicante Pedro Pablo Rubens es muy raro en son arte y muy estimado en toda Europa; y cierto que muchos príncipes della le han procurado sacar de Anveres con grandes promesas de honrra y dinero, y juntándose á esto ser hijo de padres honrrados y fieles vasallos de S.Md, y que el suplicante, además de la excelencia y primor de la pintura, tiene otras buenas calidades de letras y noticia de historias y lenguas, y se ha tratado siempre muy lucidamente, teniendo mucho caudal para ello. Y assí parece podria V.Md servirse de hacerle la merced y honrra que pretende de nobleza, y dispensar en la paga de finanzas.

Notes

Abbreviations

AHN Archivo Histórico Nacional
AHPM Archivo Histórico de Protocolos, Madrid
APM Archivo del Palacio Real, Madrid

Introduction

1. The only attempt to date to provide a complete history of the relationship between Rubens and Spain is Vosters, 1990. Vosters provides much erudition and interesting information, especially in the area of the relationship between Rubens' paintings and Spanish literature of the time. In the end, however, his book is far from comprehensive – many of the catalogues that it includes are incomplete – and it does not live up to the standards of modern art history – the disorderly organization of the book makes it difficult to read or to use as a reference. The basic, if partial, studies of Rubens and Spain are Cruzada Villaamil, 1874; the catalogue of the Flemish paintings in the Prado Museum published by Matías Díaz Padrón in 1975 (*Museo del Prado. Catálogo de Pinturas. Escuela Flamenca Siglo XVII*, 2 vols.), and the catalogue of the exhibition *Pedro Pablo Rubens 1577–1640* by the same author (Díaz Parón, 1977). The book by Díaz Padrón, *El Siglo de Rubens en el Museo del Prado*, published in 1995, amounts to a revised edition of the 1975 Prado catalogue cited above, with the important addition of large, high-quality, color illustrations. Throughout this work I will use the 1995 publication as the basic work of reference for paintings in the Prado.
2. The numbers cited in this passage derive from my doctoral dissertation, "The Presence of Rubens in Spain," Institute of Fine Arts, New York University, 2 vols., 1994 (cited throughout this study as Vergara, 1994), from which this book derives. The second volume of that dissertation consists of a catalogue of all the paintings by or attributed to Rubens that were in Spain during the seventeenth century (totaling 451 entries). This book includes references to many but not all the paintings in that volume. The twenty tapestries designed by Rubens belong to the series of the *Triumph of the Eucharist*, discussed in Chapter 2. The fifty-four scenes painted after designs supplied by Rubens were destined for the hunting lodge known as the Torre de la Parada, which is studied in Chapter 4.

   Throughout this study I will use the term "Flemish art" as it has come to be used in modern art history, that is, as referring to all the arts of what is now Belgium (Flanders, of course, is only one of several regions in the Spanish Netherlands, together with Brabant the one with the wealthiest artistic tradition). The term "Flanders" was already being used in the seventeenth century to refer to the entire Spanish Netherlands. For example, the council of the Spanish monarchy that was in charge of the affairs of the Netherlands was known in Madrid as the Consejo de Flandes, and King Philip IV spoke of the Payses Bajos de Flandes when referring to his territories in the Netherlands (e.g., letter written by the king in De Maeyer, 1955, doc. no. 262, pp. 414–415).

3. For the influence of Rubens in Spain, see the general comments in Brown, 1990, pp. 228–231; and Pérez Sánchez, 1992, pp. 70–71, and passim. For comments on specific cases of the influence of Rubens on Spanish painters, see Brown, 1964, p. 243; Gállego, 1977, pp. 118ff.; Pérez Sánchez, 1977, pp. 86ff.; Mallory, 1982, pp. 92–104; Freedberg, 1989, pp. 195–196; and Vosters, 1990, pp. 335ff.
4. For the issue of nationalism in the treatises of the Baroque period in Spain, see Gross, 1984. For the issue of nationalism as a constitutive element of the discipline of art history, see Podro, 1982 (especially the introduction); Minor, 1994; and Moxey, 1994, pp. 67–70. For the case of Spain, see also Lafuente Ferrari, 1951. A nationalistic viewpoint is present in the two most important early sources of Rubens' relationship with Spain. One is the treatise *Arte de la Pintura* by Francisco Pacheco, which was begun ca. 1600 and was finished by 1638 (it was published in 1649, five years after the artist's death). Pacheco begins his account of Rubens' life by stating: "Another [painter] worthy of being remembered (even though it is those of his nation who are in charge of his praise) is Peter Paul Rubens" (see Appendix 1). The second source is the *Lives of the Eminent Spanish Painters and Sculptors* by Acisclo Antonio Palomino, which was published in 1724 as the third part of a larger treatise entitled *Museo pictórico y escala óptica*. The *Lives* were probably completed by 1715 and are based on information compiled during the last years of the seventeenth century. Palomino's lengthy subtitle reads: "the lives of the eminent Spanish painters and sculptors who have adorned the nation with their glorious works, and of those illustrious foreigners who have come together in these realms and enriched them with their works" (Palomino, ed., 1987, p. 3). In spite of the nationalism of the authors, it is noteworthy that they both include Rubens (and other non-Spanish artists) in their texts. This integration of key foreign figures to the history of art in Spain is an approach that gradually lost momentum as the field of art history developed there and only very recently is being recovered (for the best example of this corrective trend, see Brown, 1991, pp. 1–8).
5. "Picasso Speaks," *The Arts*, New York, May 1923, pp. 315–326 (reprinted in Alfred Barr, *Picasso* [New York 1946], pp. 270–271).
6. For thoughtful treatments of the issues affecting the historical profession today, see Appleby, Hunt, and Jacob, 1994; and the collection of essays in Roth, 1994.

Chapter One: The First Visit to Spain, 1603–1604

1. For the history of the Spanish government of the Netherlands, see Pirenne, 1911; Alcalá Zamora, 1975; Parker, 1977; Parker, 1979; and Israel, 1982.
2. Van Veen was made court painter by the governors of the Spanish Netherlands in 1599, and he had worked for King Philip II of Spain designing images that were made into prints by the Flemish reproductive engraver Pedro Perret (see López Serrano, 1963; and Müller Hofstede, 1975). Pourbus the Younger worked for the governors in Brussels before leaving for Italy in 1600 (see Gerson and Ter Kuile, 1960, pp. 55–56). One reason for the presence of a Spanish colony in Antwerp was the importance of the local publishing industry, with which Rubens would develop close ties (for this issue, see *Cristobal Plantino. Un Siglo de Intercambios Culturales entre Amberes y Madrid* [Madrid: Fundación Carlos de Amberes, 1995]). For Rubens' early years, see Glück, 1933; Müller Hofstede, 1962; Regteren Altena, 1972; Belkin, 1978; and Held, 1983.
3. The best overviews of this visit are Baschet, 1866; Cruzada Villaamil, 1874, pp. 55–96; Jaffé, 1977, pp. 67–69; and Vosters, 1990, pp. 11–49. The correspon-

dence pertaining to this first visit is published in Rooses-Ruelens, vol. 1, pp. 79–230. Earlier contacts between Rubens and the Spanish court are not known, but during his stay in Spain, Rubens commented that his reputation was "not unknown here" ("la mia fama non sconosciuta qui"; Rooses-Ruelens, 1: 145; unless otherwise stated, translations are by the author). As Díaz Padrón suggests (in Díaz Padrón, 1995, p. 1076) the commission that Rubens received from the archduke Albert of Austria for an altarpiece for the church of Santa Croce in Gerusalemme in Rome in 1602 may have been known in Spain, given the close contacts between Albert and the Spanish court. Rubens' reputation, however, could not have been very great at this point in his career. For Rubens's Italian years and his service at the Mantuan court, see Müller Hofstede in Exhibition, Cologne, 1977, pp. 13–354; Jaffé, 1977; Exhibition, London, 1982; and Huemer, 1996.

4. For the paintings included in this gift, see Rooses-Ruelens, 1:139–140, and Schroth, 1990, pp. 25, 28–29, 132–133. For the copies after Raphael, see Exhibition, Madrid, 1985. For an important study of the practice of state gifts between Italian courts and the Spanish court at this time, see Goldberg, 1996, which includes documents pertinent to Rubens' visit to Spain (p. 111, n. 37). See also Jardine, 1996, pp. 418–424, for a more general assessment of the importance of giving works of art as gifts in early modern Europe.
5. That Rubens was more than a mere carrier of paintings can be gleaned from the correspondence between the court in Mantua and the Mantuan embassy in Valladolid: in a letter to Annibale Iberti, his representative in Valladolid, the duke of Mantua wrote: "Peter Paul Rubens, who, according to our wish, should be presented with the gifts as a person who has been sent from here" (for the original letter, see Rooses-Ruelens, 1:80). A letter from Rubens to Chieppio, the secretary of state at the court in Mantua, refers to work he is undertaking for the duke of Mantua, stating: "I shall not interrupt the work unless I am summoned by some whim of the King or the Duke of Lerma" (Rooses-Ruelens, 1:181; translation from Magurn, 1955, p. 36). In another letter between the same correspondents, Rubens writes that Iberti "has had the disposal of me and my work, to satisfy the taste and demand of the Duke of Lerma, and the honor of His Highness" (Rooses-Ruelens, 1:211; translation from Magurn, 1955, pp. 36–37).
6. For reports on the damaged paintings, see Rooses-Ruelens, 1:139, 142–146, 151, 165. For the repairing of the *St. John*, see Schroth, 1990, pp. 132–133.
7. See Rooses-Ruelens, 1:154–155, 165, 170.
8. This commission is documented in a letter from the duke of Mantua to Chieppio dated March 5, 1603 (Rooses-Ruelens, 1: 81), and in a letter from Iberti to Chieppio of July 31, 1603 (Rooses-Ruelens, 1:198).
9. Rooses-Ruelens, 1:198.
10. Ibid., p. 226.
11. See Magurn, 1955, pp. 36–37, for Rubens' orders to go to France.
12. The only known painting by Rubens that can be even tentatively identified with this commission is a *Portrait of Isabella of Valois* (London, collection of Mrs. M. Q. Morris), third wife of King Philip II, which Rubens copied from a portrait by the Cremonese artist Sofonisba Anguissola in the Pardo Palace (for this painting, see Müller Hofstede, 1965, pp. 116–120, 149, n. 121. For the prototype by Sofonisba Anguissola, now lost, see Kusche, 1989, p. 398). It should be noted that there is a possibility that Rubens copied the painting by Anguissola, not in 1603–1604, but rather during his second visit to the Spanish court in 1628–1629; the location of the original portrait at that date is not known, but variations after it were available in Madrid at the time (for these versions, see Exhibition, Madrid, 1990, especially cat. no. 6).
13. There is a *Portrait of Philip III* engraved by Pieter de Jode II after designs by

Rubens (it includes the inscription *P. P. Rubens pinxit*), which is sometimes believed to reflect an original painted by Rubens in his visit to Valladolid. However, there is no evidence of such a portrait in the inventories or the correspondence, and thus its existence cannot be considered certain (for the print, see Huemer, 1977, no. 29, fig. 85).

14. For this drawing (whereabouts unknown, previously in the collection of Dr. Victor S. Bloch), see Jaffé, 1966(I), 1:66 and 2:218 (illustration in vol. 1, Fig. XXV).
15. For Navarrete, who worked in the service of Philip II, see Brown, 1991, pp. 58–60, and Mulcahy, in Exhibition, Logroño, 1995, pp. 141–178. For the location of the painting in El Escorial, see Sigüenza, 1602, pp. 238–239, and Ximenez, 1764, p. 72.
16. As suggested by Jaffé 1966(I), 2:218. For Pompeo Leoni's Leonardo manuscripts, including Rubens' knowledge of them, see Clark, 1968, 1:ixff.; Roberts, 1992; and Sánchez Esteban, 1995.
17. For Pompeo Leoni in Spain, see Martí y Monsó, 1898–1901, pp. 247–286, and Exhibition, Madrid, Prado, 1994 (see especially the essay by M. Estella: "Los Leoni, escultores entre Italia y España," pp. 29–62). Rubens' viewing of Leoni's collection is often placed in Milan. However, as Jaffé has suggested, the combination of drawings after Navarrete and Leonardo on the same sheet indicates that Rubens saw Leoni's manuscripts in Spain in 1603 (Jaffé, 1966(I), 2:218).
18. See inventory of the Palace of La Ribera, Valladolid, 1607, in Florit, 1906, p. 154 ("A Portrait of Peter Paul Rubens, one *vara* and one fourth, with gilded pine trimmings"; similar descriptions are repeated in the later inventories); 1621 inventory of the royal palace in Valladolid in Cruzada Villaamil, 1874, p. 337; and 1635 inventory of the Palace of La Ribera, in Cruzada Villaamil, 1874, p. 337.
19. See Jaffé, 1977, p. 68.
20. The portrait of the duke of Mantua listed in the inventories has been linked with a portrait mentioned in a letter dated July 18, 1603, written by the Mantuan representative at the Spanish court, to the duke of Mantua (see this letter in Rooses-Ruelens, 1:170–171); the relevant section of the original Italian letter reads:

> [The duke of Lerma] Gionse nell'ultimo al ritratto di V.A. come anco vi fissò gli occhi nel entrar in camera, e dopo haverlo mirato e rimirato considerando minutamente ogni parte, osservò e comendò la vivacità degli occhi, la maesta e serenità delle facia e la proportione de tutto, e da quella effigie disse che ben si conosceva la grandezza dell'animo di V.A. di cui l'havrebbe giudicato fra mille per la relatione particolare che ha delle qualità dell'A.V. L'occasione di darlo fra l'altre pitture fu che nel ragionamento del giorno antecedente parlando dell 'età, del valor et altre parti di V.A. mi domandò se il Pittore mandato da lei havrebbe saputo cavarne uno di memoria, che desiderava in estremo haverlo ancor che fosse bisogno scriverne in Italia, onde vedendo io questo desiderio e l'occasione a proposito gli offersi quello che si degnò mandarmi V.A. come cossa mia, parendome bene non mostrarne affettatione. Di che mi ringratio assai e più d'una volta, se ben confesso a V.A. che non restarei contento d'essermi privato di gioia a me tanto cara et venutami dalla benigna mano di V.A. se non anteponesse il suo servitio ad ogni mio gusto e non credessi d'esserne ricompensato presto con un altro, et quel che sarà a me di maggior contento con la S[ma] presenza di V.A.

According to the reading of this document included in Jaffé, 1977, p. 68, a portrait by Pourbus was viewed by Lerma in Valladolid, prompting Lerma to ask Iberti if Rubens could paint another portrait of the same sitter, or if one by him could be sent from Mantua. As a result of Lerma's request, Iberti produced a portrait of the duke by Rubens that had been sent for his own keeping; this would be the portrait by Rubens listed in the inventories. In my view, however, the letter in question refers to only one portrait of the duke of Mantua, a portrait painted by Pourbus (as demonstrated by the correspondence; see Rooses-Ruelens, 1:85–87, 185), not Rubens (for a more extensive explanation of this matter, see Vergara, 1994, vol. 2, no. B38).

21. "A Portrait of the duke of Mantua one *vara* in height four hundred *reales*" (inventory of the ducal quarters of the Royal Palace in Valladolid, dated in September 1603; transcribed in Schroth, 1990, pp. 161–162).
22. Reference should also be made at this point to another painting that has been identified in the literature as a work by Rubens that was commissioned during this first trip to Spain (see Morán Turina and Portús Pérez, 1997, p. 80) but that may also not have existed. This is a scene first described in the 1606 inventory of the royal collection in Valladolid as a still life with a woman dressed in yellow and many other figures, attributed to a "*Pablo flamenco*" ("Un Lienço grande al Olio de un bodegon que en el medio tiene una figura de mujer vestida de amarillo con otras muchas figuras de mano de Pablo flamenco en marco con molduras doradas"; APM, Caja 10977/5; this inventory reference was first noted in Morán 1989, p. 174; for references to the same painting in later inventories, see Cruzada Villaamil, 1874, 328; Martí y Monsó, 1898–1901, p. 617; and *Museo del Prado. Inventarios Reales*, 3:136, no. 1). The description of the painting and its author suggests that this was not a work by Rubens, but rather by the Antwerp artist active in Venice, Paolo Fiammingo (or Pauwels Franck; ca. 1540–1596).
23. Letter dated May 24, 1603, written to Chieppio (see in Rooses-Ruelens, 1:146; translation from Magurn, 1955, p. 33).
24. For early references to works by Raphael in Spain, see Mena Marqués, "Presencia histórica de obras de Rafael en España," in Exhibition, Madrid, 1985, pp. 11–28.
25. For the collecting of Titian in Spain, see Checa, 1994.
26. The suggestion that Rubens copied some of Titian's works in 1603–1604 is based on inconclusive stylistic evidence and on evidence provided by three paintings: *Portrait of Charles V with Drawn Sword*, a *Portrait of Charles V with Baton*, and a *Portrait of the Empress Isabella*, which also is not conclusive. In my opinion, there is no reason at present to favor a date in the first trip over the second for these paintings, or vice versa. I have chosen to deal with these works in Chapter 3, along with all the other paintings that Rubens is certain to have copied after Titian during his second Spanish trip of 1628–1629.
27. See Huemer, 1996, for the effect of Titian on Rubens' art at this time.
28. For El Greco, including the paintings mentioned, see Brown et al., 1982. The commission for the College Doña María de Aragón was completed by 1600. The identification of the paintings for the college remains an unresolved problem; the retable appears to have included an *Incarnation* (Villanueva y Geltrú, Museo Balaguer), a *Baptism of Christ* and a *Crucifixion* (both in the Prado), and an *Adoration of the Shepherds* (Bucharest, National Museum). Rubens may have also seen a less important work by El Greco, a *Saint Francis in Meditation*, which may have belonged to the duke of Lerma when Rubens was in Valladolid in 1603–1604 (for this painting, which is not known today, see Schroth, 1990, pp. 44–46).
29. See Pacheco, ed., 1933, pp. 155, 159.
30. See the letter cited in n. 23.
31. Bartolomé Carducho's inspection of the gift is documented in a letter from Iberti to the duke of Mantua of July 31, 1603 (see Rooses-Ruelens, 1:195).
32. For painting at the court of Philip III in Valladolid, see Morán Turina, 1989;

Brown, 1991, pp. 89–98; Pérez Sánchez, 1992, pp. 76–121, and Exhibition, Prado Museum, 1993–1994 (the essay by Morán Turina in this last publication is reprinted in Morán Turina and Portús Pérez, 1997, pp. 13–30).

33. A similar conclusion is reached in the essay by Morán Turina in Exhibition, Prado Museum, 1993–1994, mentioned in the previous note.
34. For this painting, see Huemer, 1977, no. 20, with further references.
35. For the reference to Pliny, see Held, "Rubens' 'Het Pelsken,' " in Lowenthal, Rosand, and Walsh, Jr., eds., 1982, p. 110 (*Natural History*, 35:96). See Huemer, 1977, pp. 22–23 (which includes further references to earlier works dealing with this issue); Vlieghe, in *La Pintura Flamenca en el Prado* (Antwerp, 1989), p. 146; and Schroth, 1990, pp. 11, 33, n. 28.
36. Hollstein, 5:74–75. In this print by the famous Augsburg artist the saint appears as a Christian knight mounted on a horse that faces the spectator diagonally. The theme of the Christian warrior, and the fact that Burgkmair worked in the circle of Maximilian I, an ancestor of the Spanish king, may have favored the use of this image by Rubens during his visit to the court of the Spanish Hapsburgs.
37. Schroth, 1990, p. 11.
38. See the letter from Iberti, secretary of the duke of Mantua in Spain, to his master in Mantua, written on July 3, 1603 (Rooses-Ruelens, 1:195).
39. Rubens to Chieppio, the ducal secretary of state; Rooses-Ruelens, 1:210–211; for an English translation, see Magurn, 1955, pp. 36–37.
40. For collecting at the court of Philip III, see the bibliography cited in n. 32.
41. For Lerma's career as an art patron and collector, see Schroth, 1990. For Lerma's political career, see Feros, 1994, and Feros, 1995.
42. For the 1603 inventory, see Schroth, 1990, pp. 26–36, 116–189.
43. See the letter cited in n. 23.
44. Letter dated October 22, 1626, from Rubens to Pierre Dupuy. Rooses-Ruelens, 3:479–481; English translation from Magurn, 1955, pp. 148–149.
45. Collection of Barbara Piasecka Johnson. See Jaffé, 1968, pp. 183–187, and Exhibition, Padua, Rome, Milan, 1990, no. 11.
46. Schroth, 1990, p. 33, first suggested that this painting shows Rubens' interest in making an impression at the Spanish court. As mentioned above, the painting of the *St. John in the Wilderness* was actually restored by Rubens, and was included in the gift to Lerma.
47. For Rubens' use of classical and Renaissance sources in this painting, see Jaffé, 1977, p. 68, and Exhibition, Padua, Rome, Milan, 1990, no. 11. For references to Democritus and Heraclitus in contemporary Spanish literature, see Vosters, 1990 (where it is first suggested that Rubens may have selected the subject of the two philosophers in response to Spanish writers), and Rico, 1991.
48. Jaffé, 1977, p. 68.
49. Letter to Chieppio of July 17, 1603; Rooses-Ruelens, 1:180–181 (English translation taken from Magurn, 1955, p. 35). Rubens made this statement in the context of complaining about the secondary status that he felt he had been assigned in the Mantuan embassy.
50. See Rubens' letter to Chieppio of May 24, 1603 (Rooses-Ruelens, 1: 145).
51. For Lerma's desire to have Rubens remain in Spain, see the letter of July 18, 1603, in Rooses-Ruelens, 1:172; Iberti writes that Lerma had asked him: "If Your Highness [the duke of Mantua] had sent Rubens to remain in the service of His Majesty, which would have pleased him very much. I answered so as not to lose this servant . . ." ("se l'haveva mandato per fermarsi al servitio di S.M. che ne havrebbe havuto piacere. Io risposi per non perder questo servitore . . .").
52. For the 1607 Lerma inventory, see Schroth, 1990, p. 262. Praise for the equestrian portrait is recorded in Rooses-Ruelens, 1:213, 222. Rubens' success in

Valladolid is also recorded in the correspondence (Rooses-Ruelens, 1:178, 187–190, 210–211).

53. For the statement from Baglione, see Baglione, 1642, fol. 362. Raffaello Soprani wrote, in his *Vite de Pittori, Scoltori, et Architetti Genovesi* . . . (Genoa, 1674), of Rubens' visit to Spain: "there [Rubens] made the portraits of Their Majesties, and other important works, which earned him great fame" (fol. 301). In this text the author is probably not documenting specific paintings, but rather voicing his own expectations of what Rubens might have painted.
54. Rooses-Ruelens, 1:139–140; the translation of "cose boscareccie" as "woodland scenes" is taken from Jaffé, 1977, p. 68.
55. For Pacheco's treatment of Rubens' second visit to the Spanish court, see Pacheco, ed., 1990, pp. 193–202 (an English translation of the section of Pacheco's text that deals with the biography of Rubens is provided in Appendix 1). For Palomino, see Palomino, ed., 1987. Palomino appears to be aware of an early trip made by Rubens to Spain, but incorrectly dates it to 1623 (Palomino, ed., 1987, p. 101).
56. Rubens is not documented in Italy until June 2, 1604 (Exhibition, Mantua, 1977, pp. 60–66, n. 42). Baschet suggests that he returned from Spain in or before April 1604 (Baschet, 1867, p. 307). Ruelens speculates that Rubens probably arrived in Italy in February of the same year, based on a Latin poem written in honor of the painter by his brother Philip, and on the probable date of a meeting between the two brothers after Peter Paul's arrival from Spain (see Rooses-Ruelens, 1:236–241). As Baschet has noted, there are indications in the correspondence that Rubens traveled to Valencia, probably at the end of 1603, which suggests that he may have left for Italy from some port in that region of Spain (Baschet, 1867, p. 307, n. 1; see also Rooses-Ruelens, 1:251–252). The statement of Ceán Bermúdez that while he was in Valencia Rubens praised the abilities of Ribalta and other local painters is not credible in light of his opinions about the painters in Valladolid mentioned earlier.

Chapter Two: A Growing Presence, 1604–1628

1. For Calderón, see Martín González, 1988, which focuses on his artistic patronage. For his journey to the Netherlands see the document cited by Martín González, 1988, pp. 269ff., n. 8, and Cabrera de Córdoba, 1857, p. 473. Volk, 1981, p. 525, n. 55, already noted the importance of Calderón as a collector of Rubens.
2. See Martín González, 1988, p. 269, for the interpretation of the trip as a maneuver to distance Calderón from the court. That this was intended as a cover-up is stated in Israel, 1982, pp. 16–17.
3. For this painting, now in the Prado (inv. no. 1638), see Rooses, *L'Oeuvre*, vol. 1 no. 157, pp. 203–207; Norris, 1963, pp. 129–136; Baudouin, 1972, pp. 50–51; Devisscher, 1992; and Díaz Padrón, 1995, 2: 864–867, no. 1638.
4. Rooses-Ruelens, 2:60.
5. Ibid.
6. The only painting associated with Rubens (but actually executed by Van Dyck and retouched by Rubens) that may have been purchased by the young king at a slightly earlier date is an *Achilles Discovered among the Daughters of Lycomedes* that will be discussed below.
7. For this *Apostolado*, see Vlieghe, 1972, nos. 6–18, pp. 34–53, which should be complemented by his entry in *La Pintura Flamenca en el Museo del Prado*, p. 154, no. 48; Díaz Padrón, 1995, 2:882–907, nos. 1646–1657; and Vergara, 1994, 2: 345–349.
8. See Martín González, 1988.

9. Aarschot's ownership is first stated in Beroqui (1930, pp. 116–117, n. 6, no source cited) and can also be inferred from the documentation of Calderón's trial, which refers to an *almoneda* sale (see Martín González, 1988, p. 288, n. 47) that could be identical with the sale of Aarschot's collection in Brussels on July 15, 1614 (see E. Van Even, "Notice"; for Aarschot as a collector of Rubens, see Magurn, 1955, pp. 55, 439, letter 22, n. 1, and Bonnafé, 1883, p. 215). Arenberg's ownership is recorded in the indictment against Calderón (Martín González, as cited above).
10. The text of the accusation (the same text referred to in the previous note), is reproduced in full in Martín González, 1988, p. 288, n. 47.
11. See Loncahy and Cuvelier, 1923, p. 399, no. 942.
12. As is suggested by Vlieghe (in *La Pintura Flamenca en el Museo del Prado*, p. 154). An *Apostolado* is documented in Lerma's collection through a letter from Rubens to Sir Dudley Carleton dated April 28, 1618, which refers to an original series of paintings of the twelve Apostles and Christ by Rubens "que ha il Ducca di Lerma" (Rooses-Ruelens, 2:135–138). As Vlieghe points out, the often held assumption that the *Apostolado* owned by the duke of Lerma was commissioned by the duke himself (and therefore that it cannot be the same series owned by Calderón) is uncertain; the aforementioned letter from Rubens to Carleton only says that the *Apostolado* belonged to Lerma in April of 1618, not that it was commissioned by him. The suggestion by Vlieghe that Lerma received the *Apostolado* after Calderón's fall from power is mistaken; Calderón's fall did not occur until late in 1618, and he was not arrested until February of 1619, after Rubens' letter of April 1618 in which the painter states that the Apostolado belongs to Lerma.
13. For the decoration of El Escorial, see Mulcahy, 1994. For the role played by the Escorial painters in the history of art in Spain, see Brown, 1991, pp. 58–67.
14. See Pinchart, 1863, p. 172 (also reproduced in De Maeyer, 1955, p. 322, doc. 109).
15. For the Prado paintings, see Díaz Padrón, 1995, 2:1076–1083, nos. 1683–1684. For an opinion contrary to the identification of the Prado paintings with the ones received by Calderón, see Vlieghe, 1987, pp. 39–43, nos. 64–65, and pp. 43–45, nos. 66 and 67. If the Prado portraits are the same ones that were owned by Calderón, they must have entered the royal collection in or shortly after 1621, when Rodrigo Calderón was put to death.
16. For the collars work in Spain at this time, see Anderson, 1969, and the essay by Carmen Bernis, in Exhibition, Madrid, 1990.
17. For Velázquez's painting, which dates to 1636, see Harris, 1976.
18. For the Buen Retiro palace, see Brown and Elliott, 1980.
19. For this painting, see Vergara, 1994, 2:279–281.
20. For the colors used by the different armies in the seventeenth century, see Parker, 1995, p. 44.
21. See Glück, 1933, pp. 28–45; and Vlieghe, 1987, pp. 35–37, Figs. 1–2, 4.
22. See Rooses-Ruelens, 1: 125–127, 137, 154, 159, 170, 171, 195.
23. For Brizuela, see *Diccionario de Historia Eclesiástica de España*, 1: 285–286. For his participation in the political events then preoccupying the court of Brussels, see Gachard, 1877, pp. 10ff.
24. For the painting owned by Brizuela, see Rodríguez G. de Ceballos, 1987, pp. 70–72, where the inventory description is transcribed ("a painting of Our Lady with Christ on Her lap, with full figures, on panel, with its frame, it was valued in sixty ducats"). The same author is responsible for the possible identification of the picture owned by Brizuela with the one now in Salamanca (which is a replica of a *Virgin and Child* painted by Rubens for the archdukes ca. 1615,

as noted by Ceballos; see Rooses, *L'Oeuvre*, 1: 255ff., no. 1890). Whether the Salamanca painting is an autograph Rubens or a workshop replica cannot be determined because of the difficulty of viewing the picture in its present location.

25. Our knowledge of this commission stems from two sources. The 1636 inventory of the Alcázar refers to paintings brought from Flanders for the queen at an unspecified date: "And these twenty-five paintings in this room [the king's dining room, in the *quarto bajo de verano*] are the ones that were brought from Flanders to our lady the queen, and they were hung in the new tower of her upper room [*torre nueva de su quarto alto*] and his Majesty the King our Lord ordered that they be put here" (the relevant section of the inventory is reproduced in Volk, 1981, Appendix 2, p. 526; this section actually includes twenty-four, not twenty-five, paintings as the inventory states). As Madrazo, 1884, pp. 109–110, first suggested, this group of paintings must be identical to a series of pictures for which payments were made on April 22, 1623, when the paintings were already in Madrid: "The duchess of Gandía, on 22 April 1623, sent a paper to the marquis of Malpica from the queen asking him to pay for some paintings that had been ordered from Flanders for her room." For the queen's rooms in the Alcázar, see Barbeito, 1992, pp. 136ff.
26. For this painting, see Díaz Padrón, 1995, 2: 1100–1101, no. 1672.
27. For this painting, see Díaz Padrón, 1995, 2: 1022–1023, no. 1727. For a transcription of all the inventories where it is listed during the seventeenth-century, see also Vergara, 1994, 2: 213, no. A9.
28. See Vergara, 1994, 2: 229, no. A20.
29. As opposed to the other five paintings in this group, which are listed in the 1636 inventory of the Alcázar among the paintings purchased for the queen in Flanders, the inventory description of the *Garland* (which in 1636 hung separately from the others) only states that at one point it had been in the Queen's Tower, where the paintings purchased for the queen in Flanders were originally installed. This does not guarantee that it is part of the paintings purchased in Flanders for the queen, but it strongly suggests that this is the case. For this painting, see Díaz Padrón, 1995, 2: 1092–1093, no. 1420; and Robels, 1989, pp. 382–383, no. 287.
30. For these paintings, see Díaz Padrón and Royo Villanueva, 1992, pp. 154–175, nos. 17–18 (in this publication the *Allegory of Touch, Hearing and Taste* is attributed to Jan Brueghel, Seghers, and Francken, and the *Allegory of Sight and Smell* to the same painters, with the additional collaboration of Hendrick van Balen and Joost de Momper; Rubens is given no part in either of the pictures). See also Díaz Padrón, 1995, 1: 236–245, nos. 1403–1404, which includes mistakes in the transcriptions of the inventories: the name of Brueghel that appears in the inventories has been changed for the name Snyders, presumably following an erroneous transcription of the 1636 Alcázar inventory available in the Prado library; the correct transcriptions are included in Vergara, 1994, 2: 452–453, nos. B22–B23.
31. For Queen Isabella, see Stradling, 1988, pp. 240–241, 337–338, and also Orso, 1990. See also the high praise of the queen made by the Jesuit Baltasar Gracián in his works *El Discreto, Agudeza y Arte e Ingenio* (see in Gracián, ed., *Obras Completas*, Madrid 1960, pp. 137, 312–313).
32. See n. 25 for the text of the inventory.
33. For the 1629 works in the palace, see Barbeito, 1992, p. 138.
34. For the love affairs of the king, see Deleito Piñuela, 1964, and Stradling, 1988, pp. 327–330. Among the probable results of the king's numerous extramarital relationships was the birth in April of 1629 to the actress María Inés Calderón (known as "la Calderona") of Don Juan José de Austria. He went on to become

an important political and military figure, as well as a collector of paintings by Rubens (see Chapter 6).

35. Cited in Wethey, 1975, 3: 81. Wethey, for reasons that are not clear, doubts the veracity of the tale told to Cassiano dal Pozzo, which corresponds with the expected public stance of a virtuous woman and queen. For the paintings that were in the summer apartments in 1626, see Volk, 1981.
36. For the identification of some of these paintings, see Volk, 1981, pp. 520–521.
37. These mistakes are only relevant here if, as I presume, the 1636 inventory of the Alcázar was compiled based on tradition and earlier information. It is significant that of all the paintings that are ascribed to Rubens in the 1636 inventory (a total of twenty-four), only the pictures mentioned above can be said with some certainty to be incorrectly attributed.
38. For the identification of the pictures reproduced these two paintings, including the seven paintings by Rubens in the *Allegory of Sight and Smell*, see Díaz Padrón and Royo-Villanova, 1992, nos. 17, 19, pp. 155–175.
39. For this genre, see Speth-Holterhoff, 1957; Filipczak, 1987, esp. pp. 125–139; Díaz Padrón and Royo-Villanova, 1992; Schwartz, 1993; Schütz, 1993; and Müller Hofstede, 1994.
40. The association that was made in Spain of Flemish artists with the genre of landscape painting can be seen in numerous texts. Cervantes, for example, refers in *La Gitanilla* (written in 1613) to "cuadros y paises de Flandes" ("paintings and landscapes of Flanders") (see in *Clásicos Castellanos*, XXVII, p. 72). Vicente Carducho writes in his *Diálogos de la Pintura* published in 1633: "[In the works of Flemish painters] there are excellent things, and in the matter of Landscapes, and extreme colors, they have priced themselves with special care, and they have done greatly . . ." (*Diálogos*, pp. 94–95). Pacheco writes in his book *Arte de la Pintura*: "the exercise of painting landscapes, to which the flemings especially, have been very inclined" (see in Sánchez Cantón, 1956, 2: 127). Paintings of animals, and of garlands of flowers combined with religious images, may have been more difficult to recognize as Flemish in Madrid in the early 1620s but would soon start flowing from Flanders into Spanish collections in significant numbers.
41. For this painting, see De Poorter, in *La Pintura Flamenca*, p. 157, no. 49; and Díaz Padrón, 1995, 2: 1086–1089, no. 1661. The assertion in Díaz Padrón, 1975, 1: 318, that this painting was brought by Rubens to Philip IV in 1628 is mistaken. For Rubens' description of his role in the execution of the work, see his letter of April 28, 1618, in Rooses-Ruelens, 2: 137 (English translation available in Magurn, 1955, pp. 60–61). The location of the painting in the New Room in January of 1625 is documented by payments made at that time for a frame (Harris, 1970, p. 372, n. 37, and Orso, 1986, pp. 46–47, n. 45).
42. See the letter cited in the previous note.
43. For the New Room at this date, see Orso, 1986, pp. 43–58.
44. For the 1686 inventory, see Bottineau, no. 70 (by this time the New Room had become known as the *Salón de los Espejos* or Hall of Mirrors; this room was not included in the 1666 inventory of the Alcázar). For the 1700 inventory, see *Museo del Prado. Inventarios Reales*, 1: 19, no. 10. The painting is unattributed in 1636, the other Spanish seventeenth-century inventory in which it appears (Orso, 1986, p. 190, no. 15).
45. For the collaboration between Rubens and the young Van Dyck, see Susan J. Barnes, in Exhibition, *Anthony Van Dyck*, Washington, D.C., 1990–1991, pp. 17–25.
46. For this print, see Harris, 1970, p. 367, and Brown, 1976. It should be noted that Gaspar de Guzmán added the title of Duke of San Lúcar la Mayor to the one of Count of Olivares that he previously held on January 5, 1625. During

the early stages of the production of this portrait he may not yet have been know as the *Conde-Duque*, or the count-duke, of Olivares (for Olivares, see Elliott, 1986).

47. As Harris has suggested (Harris, 1970, p. 367), Pacheco may have been referring to this commission when, writing about Rubens' visit to Spain of 1628–1629, he says that the Flemish painter had previously corresponded with Velázquez (see Pacheco's text in Appendix 1). See below for another, less likely occasion that Pacheco may have had in mind: a commission of paintings received by Rubens for the New Room in the Alcázar.
48. See Brown, 1976, p. 49.
49. This suggestion is made in Harris, 1970.
50. For this drawing, and the suggestion that it was used by Rubens in this project, see Brown, 1976, p. 49.
51. Rooses-Ruelens, III, pp. 453–454. This was not the first time Olivares and Rubens had corresponded. In a letter of December 1625, Rubens proudly wrote to his friend Palamède de Fabri, Sieur de Valavez, that he had been informed by Olivares of the fate of the Spanish fleet (Rooses-Ruelens, 3: 411).
52. Olivares' role as a propagandist is especially important in the palace of the Buen Retiro (see Brown and Elliott, 1980).
53. Rooses-Ruelens, 4: 453–454.
54. See Gachard, 1877, pp. 6–7, 9–37. A summary of Rubens' activity as a negotiator on this occasion can be found in Magurn, 1955, pp. 84–86.
55. Rubens' participation in these events is documented in two letters of September 30, 1623 (letter from Rubens to Pierre Pecquis, chancellor of Brabant, who was serving the archdukes in this diplomatic mission; see letter no. 55 in Magurn, 1955, pp. 94–96), and March 24, 1624 (letter from Pecquis to Rubens; see in Gachard, 1877, p. 25).
56. For the dates of the Buckingham sale, see Muller, 1989, p. 78. For the paintings included in the sale, see also Rooses-Ruelens, 4: 23–25, and Held, 1976, p. 548.
57. The complete passage from the "Life of Rubens" by Philip Rubens (taken from Lind, 1946, p. 40) reads as follows:

    > While Rubens was at Paris . . . he met there by chance the Duke of Buckingham. . . . The Duke begged Rubens to paint his portrait. He also confided to Rubens his heartfelt wish that the hatreds and wars stirred up heretofore between the King of England and the King of Spain would be lulled to rest. Rubens brought this news back to Brussels. The Infanta Isabella bade him cherish and nourish the benevolent favor of the Duke of Buckingham. Rubens did so to the best of his ability and the Duke reciprocated by sending a member of his household to Antwerp to buy at the price of one hundred thousand florins all the treasures of Rubens.

58. For this painting, see Brown and Elliott, 1980, pp. 184–192.
59. See Elliott, 1986, pp. 21–27.
60. "A Veronica by Pedro Rubens, famous painter, it should be by his own hand, and let him know that it is for a person who knows about the art of painting, and wants to have it as an original amongst other paintings by famous masters" (see in Denucé, 1934, p. 43).
61. I owe my information on Vidal de Liendo to José Antonio Ollero, of the University of Seville, who is currently working on a history of the cannons of the cathedral of Seville (I also owe thanks to professor Juan Miguel Serrera, who let me know of Ollero's research). For published material on Vidal de Liendo, see also *La Catedral de Sevilla*, pp. 413–414.
62. For this commission see De Poorter, 1978, from which the following pages largely derive.
63. For the payments, see De Poorter, 1978, vol. 2, doc. 9, p. 433 (with references to earlier publications); for the pearls the infanta gave Rubens for his work on

this project, see De Poorter, 1978, vol. 2, doc. 7, p. 432 (with references). Compare these prices to the 1,000 florins that Rubens received for three paintings for the infanta's oratory painted in or before 1621 (De Maeyer, 1955, doc. 255, no s. 25–27, 407); the 100,000 florins at which Rubens valued his entire collection of sculptures, paintings, gems, and other objects when negotiating its sale to the duke of Buckingham in 1625–1627 (see Muller, 1989, p. 78, with further references; the most expensive painting by Rubens included in this sale was an *Ascent of the Blessed* valued at 6,000 florins); or the 1,800 florins that were paid for the most expensive works by Rubens sold from his estate in the 1640s (see Muller, 1987, p. 79).

64. The eight *modelli* are first recorded in Spain in 1689 in the collection of Gaspar de Haro, marquis of Carpio, and were probably in the country at a slightly earlier date. The six cartoons were in the royal collection in Spain in 1687, and may have already been there by mid-century. For the *modelli*, see De Poorter, 1978, pp. 109–131, and Held, 1980, 1:139–166. For the cartoons, see De Poorter, 1978, 1:133–160.
65. For the patterns of collecting in the Descalzas, see Checa, 1989, pp. 21–30, which focuses on the sixteenth century. The most complete study of the paintings in the convent is Tormo, 1917–1957. The collection of the Descalzas is still not well known, and there is little information on the provenance of the paintings in the convent, which are generally believed to be gifts of nuns, mainly of the sixteenth and seventeenth centuries (the original documentation in the convent was lost in 1936 and has not been recovered).
66. For Rubens' responsibility in the iconography of the series, see De Poorter, 1978, 1:165–169.
67. See Chapter 5.
68. For the prints executed in Spain after this series, see De Poorter, 1978, 1:213–222. The earliest set of engravings was probably published between 1648 and 1652, and many sets of prints followed throughout the century. As Pérez Sánchez, 1977, pp. 89–91, has suggested, this series had more influence upon local artists than any other work by Rubens. For Bellori, see Bellori, 1672, pp. 233ff.
69. For Rubens and the infanta Isabella, see De Maeyer, 1955. For Isabella, see also Terlinden, 1943, and de Villermont, 1912.
70. For some paintings possibly executed by Rubens for the infanta at this time, see Balis, 1986, pp. 57–58; Sutton, 1994, no. 24, pp. 281–284.
71. See Vlieghe, 1987, pp. 119–123.
72. The portraits of the Spanish royal family will be discussed in Chapter 3 in this book. For the *St. Ildefonso Triptych*, see Vlieghe, 1972–1973, vol. 2, no. 117.
73. See the text by Pacheco in Appendix 1. For this set of paintings, which has only recently received significant scholarly attention, see Orso, 1993, pp. 88–90 (this book also provides the best visual reference available for this commission, as it includes reproductions of all the remaining works included in the set, together with prints, copies, and sketches related to the paintings that have been lost; see Figs. 30–38 in Orso's book); Balis, 1986, pp. 180, 183, nn. 5–8; and Orso, 1986, pp. 56–117. Balis, 1986, p. 183, n. 5, has noted that the eight paintings might not have been brought to Spain by Rubens, but might have been shipped there beforehand, in the month of July of 1628, along with the tapestries of the Eucharist. This stems from the document of the shipment of the tapestries, which also included canvases and paintings, among other things. The documents that will be referred to below, however, make this possibility unlikely.
74. "Rubens has arrived in Madrid . . . carrying eight paintings by his own hand ordered for the service of His Majesty" (reproduced in Justi, 1888, 1: 240, n. 1).
75. Rooses, 1: 129; also transcribed in Balis, 1986, p. 183, n. 7.

76. Gachard, 1877, pp. 183–184.
77. "... Rubens brought some paintings here for my service. He is owed payment for them...." (Gachard, 1877, p. 184, n. 1).
78. Finot, 1888, p. 126.
79. These paintings were identified correctly for the first time in Harris, 1970, p. 372, n. 37. For this issue see also Balis, 1986, pp. 180, 183, n. 4 (the identifications proposed in Volk, 1980, 2:176; and Vosters, 1990, pp. 117–124, are incorrect). The identification is based on the statement by Pacheco that the paintings brought by Rubens were located in the *Salón Nuevo*, or New Room, in the Alcázar, and on an analysis of the paintings that were listed in that room when it was first inventoried in 1636 (inventory reproduced in Orso, 1986, Appendix C, pp. 189–192). In addition to an *Equestrian Portrait of Philip IV* that Rubens painted in Spain, there are nine paintings in the inventory attributed to Rubens. One of them is the *Achilles Discovered among the Daughters of Lycomedes* that was in Spain before 1628. The remaining eight paintings are the ones that we are dealing with here. Not all the paintings are described in detail in the inventory of 1636. The *Calydonian Boar Hunt* and *Diana and Nymphs Hunting Deer* are the two paintings described as a "boar hunt" and a "deer hunt," as suggested by Balis, 1986, pp. 180–181. The *Nymphs Filling the Horn of Plenty* is the painting described as "Ceres with Two Nymphs," as first noted by Beroqui, 1918, no. 1664. There is some controversy surrounding the exact subject of this painting, which now belongs to the Prado (inv. no. 1664): it has also been called *Ceres and Two Nymphs*, *Ceres and Pomona*, and *Three Nymphs Filling the Horn of Plenty*. The best attempt to resolve this problem is in Held, 1980, 1:344, whose title I follow.
80. See D'Hulst-Vandenven, 1989, p. 68, no. 16.
81. For this painting, see Díaz Padrón, 1977, p. 93, no. 79, and D'Hulst-Vandenven, 1989, no. 26, pp. 96–99.
82. Díaz Padrón 1995, 2:1094–1095, no. 1664; and Held 1980, 1:344.
83. Several extant versions of this composition are known (see Held, 1988, vol. 1. no. 263, pp. 353–354, who does not mention the painting in the Alcázar); the best of them is the one in Dresden (220 × 148 cm; see in Orso, 1986, Fig. 37; not included in a recent catalogue of the museum, *Gemäldegalerie Alte Meister Dresden. Katalog der Ausgestellten Werke*, 1983).
84. For the prints, copies, and sketches through which we know the paintings of *Gaius Mucius before Porsenna*, *David Strangling a Bear*, *Calydonian Boar Hunt*, and *Diana and Nymphs Hunting Deer*, see: Held, 1980, 1: 348; D'Hulst-Vandenven, 1989, no. 35, pp. 121–122, fig. 80; Held, 1980, 1: 340–341, no. 251, 2: pl. 273; and Held, 1980, 1:324–325, no. 237, 2: pl. 274, and Balis, 1986, pp. 187, 192, nos. 12a, 13a. For the history of these paintings, in addition to the references cited, see Vergara, 1994, vol. 2, nos. A53, A99, A4, and A6; and Balis, 1986, pp. 180–181, 184, nn. 16–22.
85. For the traditional view on this matter, see Justi, 1888, 1: 240–241; Volk, 1980, 2: 176; and Balis, 1986, p. 180.
86. The inventories of the New Room of 1636 (when they were first recorded) and thereafter list six of the paintings as three pairs of pendants. One pair consists of *Samson Breaking the Jaws of a Lion* and *David Killing a Bear*. Another, of *Satyr Squeezing Grapes* and *Nymphs Filling the Horn of Plenty*. The third pair includes *Calydonian Boar Hunt* and *Nymphs Hunting Deer* (for the inventory see Orso, 1986, Appendix C, pp. 189–192). The paintings in the fourth pair, *Jacob and Esau* and *Gaius Mucius Scaevola before Porsenna*, were located in the same room throughout the century and show subjects that are known to have been seen by Rubens as complementary at an earlier date in his career (a drawing in Berlin, Staatliche Museen Preussicher Kulturbesitz, inv. no. 3241, depicts both of

these paintings on the same sheet of paper; the drawing has been dated ca. 1617–1619 in Held, 1988, 1:428–29).

87. See Orso, 1986, pp. 97–100, 102, 109–110.
88. The *Satyr Squeezing Grapes* has not received much scholarly attention, and the interpretation of its subject matter is open to question. For this painting, see Held, 1980, vol., 1 no. 263, pp. 353–354. For the use of satyrs as symbols of lust, see emblem 132 (*Luxuria*) in Cesare Ripa's *Iconologia* (ed. E. A. Maser, 1971). For an example of satyrs, grapes, and tigers appearing together in the train of Bacchus, see the *Triumph of Bacchus*, a painting designed by Rubens for the Torre de la Parada, a hunting lodge of Philip IV that will be studied in Chapter 4 of this book (see in Alpers, 1971, cat. no. 7).
89. The symbolism of the cornucopia in this painting was pointed out to me by Nicole Goude, a student in a Rubens seminar that I taught at the University of California, San Diego. Other readings of the cornucopia – it could symbolize the fruit that will issue from the womb of the female figure who holds the horn – do not necessarily exclude the interpretation presented here.
90. Orso, 1986, p. 109.
91. Ibid., p. 56.
92. For the history of the decoration of this room, see ibid., pp. 32–117. For a detailed description of the New Room, see also Barbeito, 1992, pp. 131ff.
93. Orso, 1986, p. 46.
94. Gérard, 1982, pp. 10–14.
95. This conclusion was first reached in Orso, 1993, pp. 89–90, 181, n. 117.
96. See the documentation cited in n. 76.
97. See Orso, 1986, pp. 55–56, 58–59, and Orso, 1993, pp. 87–90.
98. As first noted by Orso, 1986, pp. 112–113. For Olivares' relation to the arts in the Spanish court, see Brown and Elliott, 1980, pp. 42–44, 190–191; Brown, 1986, pp. 42–43, 89, 107; and Orso, 1993, pp. 44–45.
99. Pacheco, ed., 1991, p. 202 (see Pacheco's text in Appendix 1).
100. This suggestion is made in Cruzada Villaamil, 1874, p. 138; and after him in Balis, 1986, p. 180.
101. For Steven Orso (in Orso, 1993, p. 181, n. 122), the early stage of Velázquez's career at this point makes his participation in this project unlikely.
102. For these dates, see Chapter 3, p. 58.
103. Rooses, 1:129 (this is the same documentation cited in n. 75). This statement appears to mean that some paintings were executed by Rubens and others by other painters on his orders (as suggested by Beroqui, 1918, p. 58), but it may also be interpreted as saying that Rubens executed the paintings with some intervention by other artists (Balis, 1986, p. 183, n. 8, believes that the statement "faict et faict faire" refers to paintings done by Rubens with collaboration from painters such as Snyders or Wildens).
104. For the Berlin drawing, see Held, 1988, 1:428; it belongs to the Staatliche Museen Preussicher Kulturbesitz, inv. no. 3241 (this is the same drawing mentioned in n. 86). A recent publication by Gary Schwartz has noted that Rubens' *Jacob and Esau* and *Gaius Mucius Scaevola before Porsenna* appear reproduced in two paintings of picture galleries by the Antwerp painter Guillam van Haecht. The *Jacob* is included in the so-called *Joseph and Potiphar's Wife in a kunstkamer*; the painting of Gaius Mucius is reproduced in van Haecht's *Kunstkamer with Van Dyck's Mystic Marriage of Saint Catherine*; see Schwartz, 1996, pp. 48–52 (I am grateful to Steven Orso for bringing this article to my attention). The inclusion of Rubens' works in the picture galleries by Van Haecht may mean that Rubens' paintings were well known in Antwerp before they were sent to Madrid in the summer of 1628. If this is the case, the paintings of *Jacob and Esau* and *Gaius Mucius Scaevola before*

Porsenna were probably not painted by Rubens specifically for the Alcázar, but rather were selected from among the most notorious works that the artist had available. However, it is also possible that Rubens' two paintings were executed specifically for the Spanish court, and that they were reproduced by Van Haecht shortly after they were finished and before they were dispatched to Madrid.

105. Rubens made this statement in a letter of May 11, 1611, to the engraver and antiquarian Jacob de Bie, who was asking the painter to accept a friend of his as a student, a favor the painter had to refuse (Rooses-Ruelens, 2:35–37; English translation from Magurn, 1955, p. 55).
106. For the decoration of the Jesuit church, see J. R. Martin, 1968. For the Banqueting Hall, see Millar, 1958, p. 5.
107. See Millen and Wolf, 1989.
108. For the relations between Spain and France at this point see Devéze, 1:127–140; and Elliott, 1984. The importance of the Luxembourg palace cycle was recognized in Pacheco's text (ed. 1990, p. 195), which further suggests that it may have already been known at this time in Spain. The rivalry in the patronage of the arts that had existed between the French and Spanish courts since the sixteenth century (see Woodall, 1995, pp. 81–84) also points to a familiarity in one court of artistic events taking place in the other.
109. For the portrait, see G. Martin, 1966, pp. 613–618, and Liedtke, 1989, pp. 24–25, 260–261.
110. See Baudouin, 1977, pp. 173–207.
111. For this point of view see Pacheco, ed., 1990, pp. 193, 202; Lázaro Díaz del Valle, ed. Sánchez Cantón, *Fuentes*, 2:332 and 358–359; the text *Jurídica demostració de la noblesa de la art y professors de la pintura*, Barcelona, 1688; included in Calvo Serraler, 1981, pp. 571–577; and Palomino, ed., 1987, p. 104.
112. The infanta's order is transcribed, with an English translation, in Appendix 2. According to a document that is reproduced in Appendix 3, Rubens had earlier been awarded an annual salary of 200 *escudos* by the archduke Albert, presumably in 1609; a monthly pension of ten *escudos* was therefore a significant increase for the painter.
113. See letters cited in n. 55.
114. Gachard, 1877, pp. 6–7.
115. For this matter see Gachard, 1877, pp. 7–9, Appendix 2, pp. 266–267; Génard, 1886; and Filipczak, 1987, p. 77. The petition is transcribed in Gachard, 1877, pp. 266–267, and also in Rooses-Ruelens, 3:266. An English translation (together with the original document) is provided in Appendix 3 in this book.
116. See Gachard, 1877, pp. 10ff.
117. Filipczak, 1987, p. 74. For Rubens' social standing and social ambitions, see, in addition to Filipczak, Muller, 1989, pp. 48–63.
118. Cited in Domínguez Ortiz, 1973, p. 193. For the nobility in the Spanish Netherlands during Rubens' lifetime, see Pirenne, 1911, pp. 436ff., and Fourez, 1932.
119. Loyseau, 1994, p. 80.
120. Rooses-Ruelens, 6:34–35 (English translation taken from Magurn, 1955, p. 503). See also Koslow, 1996, p. 703. For the knighthood awarded to Rubens by Charles I in 1630, and by Philip in 1631, see Filipczak, 1987, pp. 98–99, with further references. Philip Charles d'Arenberg should not be confused with his uncle, Charles de Croy, fourth duke of Aarschot, who was mentioned earlier as an owner of the *Apostolado* series that found its way to Spain.
121. See letter from the king to his aunt the infanta, where the king refers to Rubens' selection as a representative of Spain as a "cosa de tan gran descrédito" (letter of June 15, 1627; Rooses-Ruelens, 4: p. 82–83). For the infanta's response, see Rooses-Ruelens, 4:p. 85, n. 1.

Chapter Three: Rubens' Second Visit to Spain, 1628–1629

1. For a summary of Rubens' activity from 1620 to 1628, see Baudouin, 1989, pp. 173–207.
2. For Pacheco's text, see Appendix 1. Palomino's "Life of Peter Paul Rubens" also deals extensively with this trip but takes most of his information from Pacheco (when the author adds to this source he is most often mistaken; see in Palomino, ed., 1987, pp. 101–103). R. De Piles should also be cited, because in his *Abregé de la Vie de Rubens* of 1699 he adds to the information presented by other authors. According to De Piles (pp. 398–399), during his Spanish trip Rubens was called to Portugal by the duke of Bragança, the leading aristocrat of Portugal and, after 1640, king of Portugal as John IV. The author states that Rubens embarked on the trip to Villa Viçosa, where the duke resided, but that at the last moment he was discouraged from going by Bragança. It is unclear if the text implies that the painter arrived in Portugal or not (Smith, 1831, pp. xxxvi–xxxvii, and Jaffé, 1966, 2: 595, also mentions this trip to Portugal, presumably after De Piles). De Piles traveled to Portugal with his master, Michel Amelot, who was to represent the French Crown in Lisbon after 1685 (for the biography of De Piles, see Mirot, 1924; for the Portuguese mission of Amelot and De Piles, see especially pp. 50–51). It is possible that the Portuguese contacts of De Piles could have led him to hear of an otherwise unrecorded trip by Rubens to that country earlier in the century.
3. For Rubens and Carleton, see Magurn, 1955, pp. 5, 50, 59–68, 441; for Rubens and Buckingham, see ibid., pp. 161–163; and for Rubens and Gerbier, see ibid., pp. 118, 460.
4. For a summary of Rubens' diplomatic activities leading up to his sojourn to Spain and during his stay in Madrid, see Cruzada Villaamil, 1874, pp. 131–149; Gachard, 1877, pp. 38–117, and Magurn, 1955, pp. 221–227 and 283–290. For the historical context in which Rubens' diplomatic activities took place, see Elliott, 1986, pp. 323–331, 346–358. The selection of Rubens by the infanta as the representative of the Spanish side is documented in a letter from Philip IV to Isabella (letter dated June 15, 1627; Rooses-Ruelens, 4: 83).
5. See n. 121 in chapter 2.
6. Rooses-Ruelens, 4: 85; translation from Magurn, 1955, p. 163.
7. For Rubens' summons to Madrid, see Cruzada Villaamil, 1874, pp. 134–135. For the infanta's notification of Rubens' departure, see Gachard, 1877, p. 93, n. 2.
8. For the documents showing that Rubens was in Antwerp on August 28, see Rooses, 1896, pp. 154–188; Rooses-Ruelens, 4: 456. That Rubens had left by September 1 is stated in a letter by Philippe Chifflet, chaplain to the infanta's oratory, cited in Rooses-Ruelens, 4: 456.
9. On September 15, Giovanni Battista Pamphili, papal nuncio in Madrid, notified Rome of the painter's arrival (Gachard, 1877, pp. 95–96). In view of this, and of the documents cited in the previous note, Pacheco's statement that Rubens arrived in Madrid in the month of August must be considered incorrect (see Pacheco's text in Appendix 1; this statement is often followed in the literature). That the secret nature of his visit was known is revealed by Chifflet's letter of September 1 cited in n. 8, and by the letters written from the papal nuncio; by those of the Venetian ambassador, Alvise Mocenigo, probably written at the end of September 1628, reproduced in Rooses-Ruelens, 4: 234; and by Averardo Medici, Tuscan ambassador in Madrid, dated September 25, 1628, published in Justi, 1888, 1: 240, n. 1. Rubens comments on his rush in passing through France in a letter to his friend Pierre Dupuy of December 2, 1628 (Magurn, 1955, p. 291).
10. Rooses-Ruelens, 5: 33.

11. Ibid., pp. 36–39, for Rubens' appointment by the king. This document states only that Rubens was appointed to the king's privy council, but a later document (a petition for knighthood on Rubens' behalf dated July 16, 1631; see pp. 110–111 in this chapter) refers to the council to which Rubens had been appointed secretary as the privy council of the Netherlands. For the epitaph by Gevaerts, see Lind, 1946, p. 42. It was the abbot Scaglia, ambassador of Savoy in Madrid, who suggested in a letter that Rubens' appointment was intended to enhance his status as a negotiator (Rooses-Ruelens, 5: 39–40). A letter that Rubens wrote in December of 1632 to Frederick Henry, prince of Orange, asking him to provide a passport for a trip to The Hague suggests that the painter also saw the post of secretary as a way of adding to his status. In his letter Rubens writes: "It is not necessary to insert any other title [in the passport] other than 'Secretary to the King of Spain in his Privy Council' " (Rooses-Ruelens, 6: 27; English translation from Magurn, 1955, pp. 387–388). The exact significance and obligations of the post of secretary of the privy council of the Netherlands are uncertain, because the councils (or *consejos*), the main policy-making bodies of the Spanish monarchy, are still not well studied. The number of secretaries who served in the different councils of the monarchy had grown from 39 during the reign of Philip II to 187 during the reign of Philip IV, suggesting that by the time of Rubens' appointment the post had lost some importance (this information derives from *Historia de España Menéndez Pidal*, vol. 25: *La España de Felipe IV. El Gobierno de la Monarquía, la Crisis de 1640 y el Fracaso de la Hegemonía Europea* [Madrid, 1982], pp. 117–124; and *Historia General de España y America*, vol. 8: *La Crisis de la Hegemonía Española, S. XVII* [Madrid: Ediciones Rialp, 1986], pp. 352–353).
12. The date of Rubens's departure from Madrid is documented through the dispatches sent to their courts by Alvise Mocenigo, Venetian ambassador, and by the abbot Scaglia, ambassador of Savoy (cited in Gachard, 1877, p. 117). A document dated April 27, 1629, and two documents of April 28 (all of them unpublished) granted Rubens permission to exit Spain with a series of gifts and paintings. The document of April 27 reads: "Dese pasaporte para que P[o] Pablo Rubens pueda sacar destos Reynos para flandes una docena de pinturas en lienço y laminas, dos caxetas con piedras antiguas y una Joya sortixa de diamantes sin pagar ninguno derechos, sin embargo de qualesquiera leyes y pragmáticas con las cuales dispenso para este casso" (AHN, consejos, leg. 13195). Of the two documents of April 28, the first allowed Rubens to leave Spain with a "Rosario de calambuco tachonado de diamantes y oro que va en vna caxa larga cubierta de encerado verde y [?] dos pares de Guantes de ambar," all for the infanta (AHN, Consejos Suprimidos, Libros de Paso, Libro 636, fol. 1v–2r). The second document of April 28, 1629, reads: "Nro. capp[an] Gen[l] de la Prov[a] de Gupuzcoa X[a] [?] saved que Pedro Pablos rubens ba a los nros estados de flandes y lleba vna docena de Pinturas en lienco y laminas. dos caxetas con Piedras antiguas y vna Joya, sortixa de diamantes. Por ende os mandamos le dexeis y Consintais pasar por qualquiera de essos puertos y passos libremente sin pedir ni llebar derechos ni otra cossa alguna . . ." (AHN, Consejos Suprimidos, Libros de Paso, Libro 636, 2r–2v. I owe my knowledge of these two documents to Fernando Bouza). The gift of a ring from the king (presumably the same one mentioned in the documents above) is also documented in Pacheco (see Appendix 1). The reference to the twelve paintings exported by Rubens poses some problems. As shown above, the documents refer to *una docena de pinturas en lienço y laminas*. In a Spanish dictionary of 1611 the term *lámina* is defined as "a sheet of some metal" (see Covarrubias, 1611), and the *Diccionario de Autoridades* of 1732 (p. 354) says that it can also refer to "a painting made on a copper plate." Indeed, a view of seventeenth-century sources shows that the term *lámina* was used for the copper plates from which prints were made (see, for example, Morán Turina and Portús Pérez, 1997, p. 266), whereas the term *lienzo*

was used for canvases, and *tabla* for wood panels. The statement in the documents should thus be translated as "twelve paintings on canvas and metal [probably copper] plates." The problem is how to read this without having the actual baggage to contrast it with. It could mean that Rubens carried twelve pictures, some painted on canvas and others on copper plates, or it could mean that he carried with him twelve paintings, in addition to some copper plates.

13. This quote from Rubens is taken from a letter to his friend the French humanist Nicolas-Claude Fabri de Peiresc, dated December 18, 1634 (Rooses-Ruelens, 6: 87). Rubens' arrival in Brussels is documented in a letter dated, in Brussels, May 18, 1629, written by J. J. Chifflet to Cardinal Guidi di Bagno: "This past Sunday, the 13th of this month, Rubens arrived here by post with the portraits of the king, the queens and the infantes. It is said that he will need to go to England . . ." (De Maeyer, 1955, p. 392). Gachard, 1877, p. 119, cites a different source for the same date of arrival. For an overview of the continuation of Rubens' negotiations with England, see White, 1987, pp. 221–230.
14. For the letter to Peiresc of December 2, see Magurn, 1955, pp. 292–293. For the letter to Gevaerts, see Magurn, 1955, p. 295.
15. For the identification of the landscape, see Adler, 1982, pp. 128–129. A copy of the *Equestrian Portrait of Philip IV* is reproduced in Fig. 32. (The original has been lost.)
16. For the location of Velázquez's studio, see Orso, 1986, p. 18.
17. See the text by Pacheco in Appendix 1.
18. This information comes from Pacheco, and is confirmed by a letter from Rubens to Peiresc dated December 2, 1628: "I have also done the heads of all the royal family . . . for the service of the Most Serene Infanta, my patroness" ("Ho fatto ancora le teste di tutta la famiglia Reggia . . . per servicio della sereniss^ma^ Infante mia sig^ra^ . . ."; Rooses-Ruelens, 5:10), and another letter of the same date to Pierre Dupuy: "I have also done the portraits of all this royal family, for the particular interest of the Most Serene Infanta my patroness" (Magurn, 1955, p. 291). Also, the letter from J. J. Chifflet to Cardinal Guidi di Bagno of May 18, 1629 (cited in n. 13), indicates that Rubens arrived in Brussels after his Spanish trip with "the portraits of the king, the queens and the infantes" ("les portraits du Roy, des Roynes et des Infantes").
19. See Muller, 1989, pp. 44, 61.
20. María's marriage by proxy actually took place on April 25, 1629. For references to sources of information on her life, see Harris and Elliott, 1976.
21. Our knowledge of the format of the portraits derives from the sources cited in n. 18; Rubens describes his portraits as "heads" in his letters, and Pacheco refers to them as "half-length"; in view of the extant paintings, it seems likely that the portraits were larger than head studies, and that Rubens' description as "heads" is an idiomatic use that derives from the concentration on the facial features.
22. De Poorter, 1978, 1:274–278.
23. The best study of these portraits is Huemer, 1977, pp. 68–69. My conclusions stem from the evidence presented there, from which I have greatly profited. In the end, however, some of my conclusions are different from those of this author.
24. For the "half-length with sword and dagger" type, see Huemer, 1977, pp. 156–158, no. 33, and Vergara, 1994, vol. 2, cat. no. A85. For the "bust in brocaded costume" type, see Vergara, 1994, vol. 2, cat. no. A86; and for the extant versions, see Huemer, 1977, pp. 71–72, 161–162, no. 35.
25. For this type, see Huemer, 1977, pp. 158–161, nos. 34, 34a, 34b, figs. 98, 100, 102, 104, 108–110.
26. See Huemer, 1977, pp. 162–163, no. 36, fig. 113. For both of these portraits see also Vergara, 1994, vol. 2, cat. no. A77.
27. They are numbers 123 and 115 in the *Specification* (see Muller, 1989, pp. 117–118). Huemer, 1977, pp. 68–69, identifies two different portraits with those

painted by Rubens in Madrid; they are two full-length portraits known through a painting in Genoa (Galleria Durazzo Pallavicini), and a copy in the collection of the duke of Wellington (see Huemer, 1977, figs. 105, 107; she is followed in these identifications by Vosters, 1990, p. 167). According to the author, these portraits show similarities to Velázquez's portraits of the king, which would indicate that they were painted by Rubens during his stay at the Spanish court. There is no evidence, however, that these two portraits reflect types created by Rubens or that they were painted in Madrid; they are more likely workshop variations of Rubens' original half-length types.

28. For possible identifications of this portrait with other recorded portraits of Philip IV by Rubens, see Vergara, 1994, vol. 2, cat. no. A88.
29. For this painting, now in the Galleria Palatina, Florence, see Exhibition, Florence, 1977, pp. 50–52, and Vergara, 1994, vol. 2, cat. no. A87. Huemer, 1977, p. 156, no. 33, believes that the painting known through the record in Rubens' collection is identical with the half-length portrait with sword and dagger catalogued above, but I believe the identification proposed here is more likely.
30. See Exhibition, Florence, 1977, p. 51, no. 1 (catalogue entry by D. Bodart), and Muller, 1989, p. 136, n. 2.
31. For this drawing, see Held, 1986, pp. 136–136, no. 173, and Huemer, 1977, no. 32, pp. 155–156. It is now in Bayonne, Musée Bonnat (inv. no. 1417).
32. The two paintings by Velázquez here illustrated are *Philip IV* and *Infante Don Carlos* (Prado inv. nos. 1182 and 1188). Even though Rubens' drawing is generally identified with the king, the possibility that it depicts his brother cannot be dismissed.
33. Huemer, 1977, pp. 67–68. The author is comparing Rubens' drawing exclusively to Velázquez's portraits of the king, not of his brother, but the similarities are also present in the portrait of Don Carlos by Velázquez here illustrated.
34. Two copies of the portraits of Philip IV in bust length wearing a brocaded costume, and of the portrait of Queen Isabella that is its pendant, are now in the collection of the Patrimonio Nacional (inv. nos. 1073–1074). Even though their provenance is uncertain, their present location suggests that they may have been in the Spanish royal collection since the seventeenth century. In any event, these are clearly not copies made by Rubens himself.
35. Pacheco, ed., 1990, p. 205. As Orso has noted, this must mean that he was the only painter who could paint the king from life (Orso, 1993, p. 44).
36. It should be noted here that in the fall of 1628, while Rubens was in Madrid, Velázquez may also have been at work on a group of royal portraits. On October 23, Velázquez received instructions to work on a series of portraits of the royal family (see Harris and Elliott, 1976, pp. 25–26). It is unclear if the order indicates that the portraits were already begun or not, and it is possible that Velázquez never actually executed them (see Brown, 1986, p. 290, n. 26).
37. Huemer, 1977, pp. 67–80, believes that there is a strong influence of Velázquez in Rubens' painted portraits (she cites especially two full-length portraits, which in my opinion were probably not executed in Madrid and are probably not by Rubens, and the drawing in Bayonne, which was probably never made into a finished painting). In my view, the influence of Velázquez is not a very important factor. Huemer is convincing in pointing out the similarities with Velázquez in the drawing by Rubens in Bayonne (Huemer, 1977, p. 68). However, the only painted portraits that can be identified with certainty as executed by Rubens in Madrid, the half-length portraits, are very personal and different from those by Velázquez.
38. Collection of Professor M. Ros, Zürich. See Muller, 1989, no. 114, pp. 116–117, pl. 55; and Huemer, 1977, pp. 144–146.
39. It may be reflected in a painting that is reproduced in Huemer, 1977, fig. 59 (see pp. 113–114 in that same publication).
40. See Huemer, 1977, nos. 12–13, pp. 119–120, figs. 61–62. For the three por-

traits of María, Carlos, and Ferdinand, see also Vergara, 1994, vol. 2, cat. nos. A71–A73.

41. For Pacheco's text, see Appendix 1.
42. For this painting, see Huemer, 1977, pp. 101–102, no. 1. For alternative identifications of the sitter, see also Bassegoda i Hugás, in Pacheco, ed., 1990, p. 197, n. 8.
43. For the reference to the two replicas of the original portrait, see Pacheco's text in Appendix 1. Two paintings have been identified in the literature with the three or more portraits of the infanta from the Descalzas painted by Rubens in Madrid. One is in the Wellington Collection, London, Apsley House (see Huemer, 1977, pp. 101–102, no. 1, fig. 41); the other is in the Descalzas Reales in Madrid (see Díaz Padrón-Padrón Mérida, 1989, pp. 90–93). These identifications are not certain because the works mentioned are portraits in half-length format (or less), and the portraits mentioned by Pacheco are described as "more than half-length." For suggestions on other paintings that may be identified with the works mentioned by Pacheco, see L. Burchard, in Exhibition, London, 1950 (Wildenstein and Co.), p. 45, under no. 35; Huemer, 1977, no. 23, pp. 142–144; and Vosters, 1990, p. 170, no. M11.
44. Orso, 1986, p. 44. Titian's painting is now in the Prado Museum.
45. It is now in the Plaza Mayor, in Madrid (see Liedtke, 1989, pp. 204–205).
46. For Velázquez's portrait, see Orso, 1986, pp. 49–52; and Harris, 1970. The description of the portrait cited is from Cassiano dal Pozzo, as transcribed in Harris, 1970, p. 372.
47. The most complete study of this picture is Huemer, 1977, pp. 150–154, no. 30.
48. For Lope de Vega's reference to this painting, included in his *Al Cuadro y Retrato de Su Majestad* . . . , see Ligo, 1970, pp. 352, 354, n. 35. For the letters to Peiresc and Dupuy, see Magurn, 1955, pp. 291–293.
49. Uffizi, inv. no. 792; canvas, 339 × 267 cm.
50. For the allegorical figures present in the painting and their interpretation, see Orso, 1986, p. 91, with further references; Millen and Wolf, 1989, p. 210; and Vosters, 1990, pp. 147–153. For the position of the horse and its symbolic importance, see Liedtke-Moffitt, 1981, p. 536, and Liedtke, 1989, pp. 19–20. For the landscape panel, known only through copies and an engraving, see Held, 1980, 1: 618, no. 452; and Adler, 1982, pp. 127–129, no. 37. For the drawing, now in the Albertina in Vienna, see Burchard-d'Hulst, 1963, vol. 1, pp. 243–244, no. 157; vol. 2, pl. 157.
51. E. Michel, 1899, 2:111, was first to suggest that this portrait was conceived as a pendant to Titian's painting. This idea is developed further in Ligo, 1970, pp. 348–350 (and see also Huemer, 1977, p. 153). Orso, 1986, p. 96, believes that when Rubens painted his portrait he also had another painting that hung in the room in mind: this is a *Tityus* by Titian (Madrid, Prado), which was installed next to the portrait and thus appeared to be the target for the thunderbolts wielded by Rubens' allegorical figure of Divine Justice.
52. For Titian's status in Spain from the late sixteenth century onward, see Pérez Sánchez, 1976, pp. 140–159; McKim-Smith et al., 1988, pp. 24–27; and especially Checa, 1994. Some interesting information on this issue is also included in J. Portús Pérez, "Entre el divino artista y el retratista alcahuete: El pintor en el teatro," pp. 142–143, in Morán Turina and Portús Pérez, 1997.
53. For Lope's poem, see Ligo, 1970, pp. 348–350. Other references that appear in contemporary literature are a further indication of the new status gained by Rubens in Spain as a result of this painting. The first textual references about Rubens to appear in Spain do so at this point, as comments and interpretations of this equestrian portrait in the narration *Casos prodigiosos y nueva encantada*, of

1628, by the poet and novelist Juan de Piña (ca. 1566–1643), and in a poem by Francisco López de Zárate (ca. 1580–1658), of uncertain date, in addition to the piece by Lope de Vega. For the poems by Juan de Piña and Francisco López de Zárate, see Vosters, 1990, pp. 147–165, and Ligo, 1970, p. 350.

54. See Panofsky, 1969, pp. 84–87, and Checa, 1994, pp. 39–45.
55. For the depiction of America and its inhabitants in European art, see Honour, 1975; Honour, 1976; Chiappelli, ed., 1976; and Exhibition, Antwerp, 1992.
56. For this painting, see Millen and Wolf, 1989, pp. 205–219.
57. For portraiture in the court of the Spanish Hapsburgs, see Serrera, 1990 (for the problem of allegorical portraiture, see especially pp. 40–43).
58. The *Allegorical Portrait of Philip II Offering the Infante Ferdinand* is now in the Prado (inv. no. 431); see Checa, 1994, pp. 52–56, 274, no. 55.
59. Checa, 1994, pp. 56–57, 312. This painting may have been known to Rubens at an earlier date, presumably during his first trip to Spain, as it seems to have inspired his picture of the *Birth of the Dauphin at Fontainebleau* from the Maria de' Medici cycle (see Millen and Wolf, 1989, p. 91). The two pictures share an unusual iconography, a frontal allegorical depiction of the birth of a royal heir. The early impression that the painting by Parrasio appears to have made on Rubens may have again stimulated his decision to use the language of pictorial allegory in the equestrian portrait of Philip IV.
60. For portraiture in sixteenth- and seventeenth-century Spain, see Brown, 1986, passim; Exhibition, Madrid, Prado, 1990; and Checa, 1992, pp. 100–110, 190–195. As in the paintings, the numerous allegorical printed portraits of the Spanish Hapsburgs are also more often than not the work of non-Spanish artists (at least until ca. 1650, when Pedro de Villafranca began to work on his numerous printed portraits of Philip IV). As opposed to what occurs with paintings, however, this results from the lack of sufficient quality printmakers in Spain at the time as much as from a lack of specialization in the area of allegorical portraiture (for printed portraits, see Carrete Parrondo, Checa Cremades, and Bozal, 1994, pp. 231–232, 260–268).
61. Koslow, 1996, p. 695.
62. For the legend of Protogenes and Nealkes, see *Natural History* 35:102–104. For Rubens' use of themes described by the Elder Pliny, see J. S. Held, "Rubens' 'Het Pelsken,' " in Lowenthal, Rosand, and Walsh, Jr., eds., 1982. Rubens quoted Pliny in two of his letters, which shows how well he knew his work (see in Magurn, 1955, pp. 247 and 407); and, like many of his educated contemporaries, he owned a copy of the *Natural History* (see MacRae, 1971, p. 94).
63. Both of these paintings will be discussed later in this chapter.
64. The five paintings are: the *Surrender of Breda* in the Prado; and the equestrian portraits of Margaret of Austria, Philip IV, Isabella of Bourbon, and the count-duke of Olivares – all in the Prado. The *Rearing Horse* that belongs to the Patrimonio Nacional may also include the same feature, but it is not clear from photographs. The small *Equestrian Portrait of the Count Duke of Olivares* in the Metropolitan Museum, of questionable attribution, also shows this detail. Velázquez's sketchy style makes it hard to determine whether or not the few other pictures of his that depict horses also include this element (e.g., *Riding Lesson of Baltasar Carlos*).
65. *Velázquezs; Homenaje en el tercer centenario de su muerte* (Madrid, 1960), pp. 313 (no. 416), 314b (no. 522), 314c (no 552) (for Velázquez's library, see also Sánchez Cantón, 1925). For the culture and customs of the art-viewing public in seventeenth-century Spain, see J. Portús Pérez, "Público, públicos e imágenes," in Morán Turina and Portús Pérez, 1997. The quotation from Pliny in Rubens' work was probably recognized not only by Velázquez but also by other members of the elite and cultured audience that was the Spanish court at the time.

66. For this painting, see Díaz Padrón, 1995, 2:970–973, no. 1686; and Vergara, 1994, vol. 2, no. A83. For the 1686 inventory, see Bottineau, no. 134.
67. The statement in Díaz Padrón, 1975, 1: 275–276, no. 1686 (and Díaz Padrón, 1995, 2:p. 970, no. 1686), that a petition of materials in 1628 to the royal stables and the *armería* is related both to this portrait and to the *Equestrian Portrait of Philip IV* is unsubstantiated; the language in the petition appears to refer to a portrait of a living king, who must therefore be identified with Philip IV.
68. For Philip II as a model of kingship during the reign of Philip IV, see Elliott, 1977, and Elliott, 1986, pp. 82, 91, 103, 170–171, 186–187, and 374. A proof of the exemplary role assigned to Philip II close to the time when Rubens was in Madrid is found in an anonymous manifesto of June 1629, in which Philip IV is encouraged to dismiss his favorite minister, Olivares, and initiate a more personal government after the example of his grandfather Philip II and his great-grandfather Charles V (See Novoa, 1876, pp. 74–76).
69. Jaffé, 1977, p. 34, states that this portrait is painted on a coarse canvas typically Spanish, and that the ground is also of a type used in Spain. However, current research on materials and techniques used by Rubens is insufficient to justify accepting such evidence as accurate.
70. *S. Asterii Episcopi Amaseae Homiliae, Graece et latine nunc primum editae Philippo Rubenio interprete. Eiusdem Rubenii Carmina, Orationes, et Epitolae selectiores: itemque amicorum in vitâ functum pietas* (Antwerp, 1615), pp. 179–186. For Philip Rubens, see Huemer, 1996, p. 31, from which I take this reference.
71. The canvas in the Prado shows added strips of canvas on the top and bottom of approximately 40 and 25 cm (and probably another added strip on the right side of approximately 10 cm). The 1686 inventory of the Alcázar, the first existing record of this painting, lists its dimensions as *tres varas de alto y dos y media de ancho* (see in Bottineau, no. 134). This is smaller than the actual painting by approximately 62 cm in height and 20 cm in width, and suggests that the painting was altered at a later date.
72. For the history of this painting, see the bibliography cited in Chapter 2, n. 3.
73. For the summer apartments in the Alcázar, see Volk, 1981; Orso, 1986, p. 23; and Barbeito, 1992, pp. 154–157. Commenting on the location of the painting after 1636, Daugherty (1976, p. 224), states that it was in a room called Pieza de la Aurora. This statement has no bearing on our discussion but should be corrected. The *Adoration* was indeed in the room of the Aurora (named after a fresco painted by the Bolognese painters Agostino Mitelli and Angelo Michele Colonna ca. 1658) in the 1666 inventory of the Alcázar and thereafter. But in the 1636 inventory the painting is inventoried in the king's dining room in the summer apartments (see APM, sección administrativa, leg. 768, fol. 32; transcribed in Cruzada Villaamil, 1874, p. 340, no. 2), which apparently was adjacent to the room later known as the Pieza de la Aurora (as stated in the 1666 and 1686 inventories of the Alcázar; see Bottineau, 1958, p. 294).
74. The usage of the summer apartments is documented at the end of the century in a letter of November 22, 1696, written by Father Gabriel de la Chiusa, confessor of Queen Mariana of Neuburg, to Johan Wilhelm, Elector Palatine. There it is stated that the *Adoration of the Magi* was in the king's summer apartments, "which [are] only used in the summer" (Herrero García, 1943, p. 88). This was probably also true earlier in the century.
75. A drawing by Rubens of a female nude and female heads (Los Angeles, J. Paul Getty Museum) after Titian's *Diana and Actaeon* and *Diana and Callisto* demonstrates that he had studied those originals, which were in the *bóvedas del verano*, part of the summer apartments. For Rubens' study of these paintings by Titian, see Volk, 1981, p. 526. For the location of Titian's paintings, see also Wethey, 3: nos. 9–10.
76. For the sketch (now in Groningen, Groninger Museum) and copy (London,

private collection; formerly in the collection of Christopher Norris) see Held, 1980, 1: no. 325, pp. 450–453, plate 322 and fig. 21; and Norris, 1963.

77. This emphasis may be more than simply visual, because a tradition existed of using pillars as symbols of Mary (a column could refer to the column against which Mary had stood when giving birth to Christ, according to some sources; see Panofsky, 1953, p. 277, and Blum, 1969, p. 20), and of Christ (because Christ had been tied to a column while he was scourged, columns were used as a symbol of the Passion).
78. For Protestant rejection of the theme of the Adoration of the Magi, see Trexler, 1997, p. 158, who also points out, however, that the Feast of the Magi continued to be celebrated throughout Protestant Europe after the Reformation.
79. For the association between the theme of the Adoration of the Magi and the ritual of the mass in Rubens' work, see Glen, 1977, pp. 135–142 (also pp. 91–96, 124–135 for other relevant cases of eucharistic symbolism in Rubens' work); Held, 1980, 1:455–456; and Haeger, 1997, 48–50. My interpretation of the Prado *Adoration* draws extensively from Glen, 1977, and from Haeger, 1997 (this publication concentrates on another *Adoration of the Magi* by Rubens, one he painted around 1624 for the high altar of St. Michael's Abbey, now in Antwerp, Koninklijk Museum voor Schone Kunsten. Many of the points made by Haeger regarding the meaning of this image are also valid for the Prado *Adoration*). I wish to thank Professor Thomas Glen for reminding me of the importance of the counterreformatory aspects of the *Adoration of the Magi*.
80. For an explanation of this iconographic tradition, which has its origin in the Bible, see Haeger, 1997, pp. 50–53.
81. Ibid., pp. 48, 50, 53, provides this interpretation (including textual sources) for Rubens' use of light in the *Adoration of the Magi* for the high altar of St. Michael's Abbey.
82. For the tradition of referring to the Eucharist by placing the infant Christ on a sheaf of wheat, see Nilgen, 1967, p. 314; Glen, 1977, pp. 127–128; and Lane, 1984, pp. 53–65.
83. *Natural History* 35.138. See Held, 1980, 1:451.
84. For Titian's *Martyrdom of Saint Lawrence*, see Wethey, vol. 1, no. 115, p. 140, and Checa, 1994, pp. 75–79, 255–256, no.21.
85. They are *The Consecration of Decius Mus* from his Decius Mus cycle of ca. 1617 (see Baumstark, 1983; also Held, 1980, vol. 1, cat. no. 3, vol. 2, pl. 3, for a sketch of the same image); and the sketch of *Triumphant Rome*, dated ca. 1622 (Held, 1980, vol. 1, cat. no. 51, pp. 84–85, and vol. 2, pl. 52).
86. The earliest appearance of this type of horse in Rubens' work is in a copy drawn in Italy after a painting by Elsheimer (Jaffé, 1977, p. 53, fig. 156). Its first use in an independent work appears in a sketch for one of the wings of the *Conversion of St. Bavo*, the triptych that Rubens designed in 1611–1612 for the cathedral of St. Bavo in Ghent but which was never completed in its intended form (the sketch is now in the National Gallery in London; see Held, 1980, vol. 1, cat. no. 400, pp. 547–550, vol. 2, pl. 392). For a history of this type of horse in Rubens' work, see Held, 1958, pp. 139–149.
87. It may be noted here that when Rubens painted the sketch for the altarpiece of St. Bavo mentioned in n. 86, he may have intended to echo Hubert and Jan Van Eyck's famous *Ghent Altarpiece*, which was in the same cathedral. The design of the neck of the horse and the positioning of its legs in Rubens' sketch resemble several of the horses that appear in the two lower-left panels of the painting by the Van Eycks, showing the *Soldiers of Christ* and the *Just Judges*. The position of Jan Van Eyck as a mythical forerunner of Flemish painters justifies Rubens' interest in this work.
88. Jaffé, 1977, p. 35; and Jaffé, 1989, no. 948, p. 309.
89. For Titian's *Adoration* in El Escorial, see Wethey, vol. 1, no. 3, pp. 65–66; the

other *Adoration* is a painting in the Prado, assigned to Titian and workshop (this is the picture reproduced in Fig. 42); see Wethey, vol. 1, no. 4, p. 66.

90. For the portrait from the *Iconography*, see Mauquoy-Hendrickx, 1956, pp. 223–224, no. 62. For Rubens' self-portraits and related portraits, see Müller Hofstede, 1993; Vlieghe, 1987, especially nos. 133–141, pp. 151–173; and Daugherty, 1976.

91. A small sketch showing the head of the artist that is sometimes attributed to Rubens may have been executed in Madrid, in preparation for the portrait in the addition to the *Adoration*. The sketch is in Antwerp, Koninklijk Museum voor Schone Kunsten; see Rooses, *L'Oeuvre*, 4:254–255, no. 1047; and Daugherty, 1956, pp. 321–324, no. II-2.

92. For the appearance of chain and sword in self-portraits by Rubens and their interpretation, see Filipczak, 1987, pp. 98–101.

93. For the traditional association of the sword with the nobility, and the history of the legislation on this matter, see De Ridder, 1922, and Fourez, 1932. The issue of the right to bear swords merits a brief digression, as it is a matter of some iconographic importance for portraits by Rubens, and also by other painters of the period. At the end of the sixteenth century, the distinctive marks of the appearance of a nobleman, including the right to carry a sword, were frequently subverted throughout Europe by members of the lower classes. Frequent examples of this can be found in contemporary literature (e.g., Calderón de la Barca's play *El Alcalde de Zalamea*, where Crespo, a wealthy farmer, carries a sword; see ed. J. M. Díez Borque [Madrid, 1976], p. 217) and in other documents (e.g., the diaries of the Swiss doctor Felix Platter [1536–1614], in Le Roy Ladurie, 1997, pp. 158, 310).

In 1595, King Philip II issued a decree ordering an end to the excesses in the Spanish Netherlands (Fourez, 1932, pp. 339–352), but with no specific instructions concerning the use of swords. By 1616 little had changed, and the archdukes Albert and Isabella needed to issue another similar decree ordering that those who were not members of the nobility should not make use of symbols or honors reserved for noblemen (Fourez, 1932, pp. 353–364, and De Ridder, 1922, p. 10). Even though not specifically stated, it was generally believed that among these privileges was the right to carry a sword. In 1623, an official by the name of Polchet wrote to the privy council of the Netherlands that there were so many people using swords that the problem needed to be remedied (De Ridder, 1922, p. 10). Specific legislation on this matter was not adopted until 1654, and the abuses continued well into the next century.

There were, however, some exceptions to the restrictions imposed by tradition and law. Officers of justice were allowed to carry swords, as were soldiers (Fourez, 1932, p. 191. A decree issued in Lille in 1661 in the name of Philip IV states that: "le port d'epées en est une marque d'honneur déffendüe à toutes personnes s'ils ne sont Gentil-hommes, officiers de Justice, ou de ceux qui sont de profession et ont droit de porter espée"). For the external marks of social rank and the rules governing the public behavior of the different social classes in the early seventeenth century, see also Charles Loyseau's *Traité des ordres ey simples dignités*, first published in 1610 (for the right to carry a sword, see 1994 ed., pp. 103, 121–125).

94. The documents relating to Rubens' patent of nobility of 1624 do not specifically mention a sword. However, on another similar occasion, when the painter was knighted by Charles I of England in 1630, the gift of a sword was part of the honor bestowed upon the artist (see Filipczak, 1987, pp. 98–99).

95. For Pacheco's text, see Appendix 1. Palomino offers a slightly different version of this story in his *Lives of the Eminent Spanish Painters and Sculptors*, published in 1724. He states that it was the archduke Albert, and not Isabella, who placed a sword at the painter's waist (Palomino, ed. 1987, pp. 101). None of the other

biographers of Rubens mentions this sword, which makes the veracity of Pacheco's account uncertain. Rubens had already painted himself wearing a sword around 1610 in the *Self-Portrait with his Wife Isabella* (Munich, Alte Pinakothek). The statement by Pacheco, if correct, indicates that Rubens had the right to wear a sword at that time.

96. Chapman, 1990, pp. 50–52; Filipczak, 1987, pp. 98–104; and Held, 1969, pp. 32–41.
97. Examples of these are the *Self-Portrait with Justus Lipsius, Philip Rubens and Jan Woverius* in the Galleria Pitti in Florence; the *Self-Portrait with Friends* in Cologne, Wallraf-Richartz-Museum, and the family portraits with Isabella Brandt and Elena Fourment.
98. For the issue of Rubens' possible presence in paintings by his own hand that are not portraits, see Daugherty, 1976, pp. 188ff.
99. For the history of the presence of portraits in paintings with broader narrative meanings, see Chapman, 1990, pp. 13–21. Interesting ideas on this issue are also included in Garrard, 1989, pp. 337–370.
100. Daugherty, 1976, pp. 224–225.
101. See Baudouin, 1972, pp. 50–51, who states that the magistrates arriving in Antwerp would have recognized themselves in the painting. Held, 1980, vol. 1, no. 325, p. 453, questions Baudouin's idea. Held believes that the painting was finished and installed after (not before, as Baudouin states) the negotiations, and therefore the negotiators could not have seen the painting. This does not negate the idea that the Magi could be associated with the negotiators arriving in Antwerp for the signing of the truce; if the painting was commissioned after the signing of the truce, as Held implies, it still must have been ordered to commemorate the event, in which case the identification of the Magi (and their entourage) with the emissaries suggested by Baudouin remains possible. For the meaning given to the theme of the Adoration in this painting, see also Auwera, 1994, p. 233, who suggests that the abundance of exotic wares carried by the Magi is a reference to one issue at stake in the negotiations for the truce between the United Provinces and the Spanish Netherlands: the right to trade with the East and the West Indies.

    The coexistence in the first version of the *Adoration of the Magi* of references to a specific historical event with the broader counterreformatory meaning that was explained earlier is intriguing. It appears that the theme of the Adoration allowed Rubens to link the truce – and the prosperity that was expected to result from it – to the cause of the Catholic faith.
102. To my knowledge, only three paintings in the royal collection in 1628–1629 may have included a portrait of a painter. One is Titian's *Trinity* (Madrid, Prado), which was commissioned by Charles V. The painting was in El Escorial at the time of Rubens' visit to Spain (see Wethey, 1969–1975, 1:165–167; and Checa, 1994, pp. 247–248, no. 6). It is often believed to include a portrait of Titian on the right side of the canvas, below the portrait of Philip II. It is not certain that this figure was recognized as a portrait of the painter in Spain in the sixteenth or seventeenth centuries. Two other works in El Escorial included portraits of their authors: one is Luca Cambiaso's *Glory*, the fresco that covers the choir of the church; the other is a painting of *St. Mark and St. Luke* by Navarrete, where Luke is probably a self-portrait of the painter (for these two paintings, see Mulcahy, 1994, pp. 66, 71–77, and 24, respectively).
103. Letter of December 29, 1628; as cited in note 14.
104. Magurn, 1955, pp. 101–102.
105. See Chapter 2.
106. For the debate over the social status of the artist in Spain, see Gállego, 1976; Volk, 1977; and the summary offered in Brown, 1991, pp. 94–95, 216. For the events of 1626, see Gállego, 1976, pp. 119–148.

107. The first identification of Rubens' self-portrait appears to have been made by Richard Cumberland, who visited Spain from June 1780 to April 1781; cited in J. Smith, *A Catalogue Raisonné of the Works of the Most Eminent Dutch, Flemish and French Painters*, vol. 2 (London, 1831), p. 135, no. 472. I have been unable to identify the source cited by Smith, where Cumberland is quoted as saying about the *Adoration* that "Rubens, in putting the finishing hand to it, has inserted his own portrait on horseback among the group of magi." That the portrait of Rubens is not recognized in writing until a late date was noted by Daugherty, 1976, pp. 221–222. The same author (p. 222) states that R. Cumberland does not mention the self-portrait in his *Anecdotes of the Most Eminent Painters in Spain during the Sixteenth and Seventeenth Centuries* (London, 1782).
108. The painter Carducho is known to have visited the rooms (see Carducho, ed., 1979, p. 427), and Rubens' access to the paintings that hung in them has already been mentioned.
109. In the first trip Velázquez left Madrid in August 1629 and arrived in Madrid a year and a half later (see Brown, 1986, pp. 69–79). His second trip began at the end of November 1648 and lasted two years and eight months. The king grew impatient with the length of this stay and gave instructions for a hurried return, but only after his painter had been absent for over one-and-a-half years. See Harris, 1960, pp. 109–110.
110. For Leganés and his activities as a collector, see López Navío, 1962, and Volk, 1980a. For additional biographical data, see also Loncahy and Cuvelier, 1923, passim; Cuvelier and Lefèvre, vols. 1 - 2, passim (much of the biographical information included below derives from these two sources); Elliott and de la Peña, 1981, 2:55, and Elliott, 1986, pp. 274–277, 405, 485–486.
111. For the portrait, see Vlieghe, 1987, pp. 125–127, nos. 115–115a (this portrait is not documented to have entered Spain). For the letter, see Rooses-Ruelens, 4:357.
112. For the 1630 Leganés inventory, see Volk, 1980a, pp. 266–267. That the painting was probably purchased by Leganés in Flanders, not painted by Rubens in Madrid, can be derived from its date, generally placed in 1621 or earlier (on the basis of style), and its panel support, more commonly used in Flanders than Spain at this time. For this painting, which is now in the Prado, inv. no. 1418, see also Ertz, 1979, pp. 304–305, no. 368; *La Pintura Flamenca en el Museo del Prado*, p. 131, no. 38; and Díaz Padrón, 1995, vol. 1, 290–291, no. 1418.
113. This commission is documented by Pacheco (see text in Appendix 1). For this painting, see Díaz Padrón, 1967, p. 13. For other paintings of the same theme in Spain during these years, see Stratton, 1994.
114. For the practice in the Renaissance and Baroque periods of painters adjusting their work to their pay, see Sohm, 1991, pp. 17–18. The other known paintings executed by Rubens in Madrid in 1628–1629 (admittedly on incomplete evidence, as only some of the copies after Titian and probably the *Equestrian Portrait of Philip II* can be identified with any certainty) are clearly more labored than the *Immaculate Conception*.
115. "a portrait of the king our lord Philip IV . . . in half-length, in armor, with a white feathered hat and a red sash over him, with an ebony frame engraved in waves, an original work by Pedro Rubens . . ." For the 1630 inventory, see Volk, 1980a, pp. 266, and 267, no. 40.
116. For the Leganés inventory, see López Navío, 1962, pp. 272, no. 40, and 273, n. 61. That this was probably not a finished original painted for Leganés is also supported by the fact that Pacheco would most likely have referred to it if that had been the case (as he referred to the *Immaculate Conception*). It is also possible that it is a copy by another artist after one of Rubens' original portraits of the king executed in Madrid.

117. For Pacheco's reference, see Appendix 1. There is a possibility that this is identical with a painting on panel depicting the beheading of Saint John the Baptist, listed in the Spanish royal collection throughout the seventeenth century and attributed to Rubens, that is now lost (84 × 126 cm). In 1666 it is listed in the *Galería del Mediodía* in the Alcázar: "Another of one and one half *varas* in length and one and one quarter *varas* in height, a panel of the beheading of Saint John the Baptist by Rubens valued at sixty silver ducats;" an annotation in similar hand and ink on the margin says, "it is in the *bovedas de la priora*" (APM, sección administrative, leg. 38, fol. 47v). For the 1686 inventory, where the description is almost identical, see Bottineau, no. 760. For the 1700 inventory, see *Museo del Prado. Inventarios Reales*, vol. 1 (1975), p. 59, no. 417. The difference in subject matter and the support (a picture by Rubens in Spain is more likely to have been painted on canvas) make the identification of this painting with the one painted in Madrid for Cárdenas unlikely.
118. For Jaime, or Jaime Manuel, de Cárdenas, see Gascón de Torquemada, ed., 1991, pp. 104, 116, 140, 171, 257, 313, 416.
119. See Appendix 1.
120. For Spinola, see Rodríguez Villa, 1904, and J. Lefèvre, 1947.
121. For this painting, see Vlieghe, 1987, pp. 188–189, no. 151; whereabouts unknown, presumably lost. The suggestion that this portrait was painted in Madrid comes from Jaffé, 1976, pp. 83–96.
122. In 1642: "another half-length portrait in armor of the marquis of Balbases Ambriggio Spinola by the hand of Rubens" (Volk, 1980, vol. 1, p. 267, no. 61). This may be one of three extant versions in Prague, Národní Galerie, inv. no. 09688; Brunswick, Herzog Anton Ulrich-Museum, no. 85; and Saint Louis, Missouri, City Art Museum, inv. no. 33.34.
123. As suggested by Vlieghe, 1987, p. 185.
124. A closer look at Crescenzi is offered later in this chapter.
125. For Maino, see Angulo and Pérez Sánchez, 1969, pp. 299–325; Pérez Sánchez, 1992, pp. 105–108; and Pérez Sánchez, 1997.
126. For Rubens' relationship with Porter and Scaglia, see Magurn, 1955, especially pp. 181–182, 186, 283–284, 285, 296, 474.
127. Held, 1980, 1: 442–445, no. 319. The sketch, painted on panel, 64.7 × 46.9 cm, is now in Merion, Pennsylvania, Barnes Foundation.
128. As suggested by Brown, 1986, p. 161.
129. "Un mien desein fait sur le lieu mesme" (letter to Balthasar Gerbier of March 15, 1640, in Rooses-Ruelens, 6: 257–258). Magurn, 1955, p. 412, translates the French word *desein* as "drawing." That term, however, is more likely to refer to an oil sketch, as shown by Muller, 1975, pp. 371–377. For this painting, see Adler, 1982, pp. 129–131, no. 38. It should be noted that Rubens visited El Escorial on both of his Spanish visits, and that therefore this landscape could have been painted in either 1603–1604 or 1628–1629. The sheer productivity of the painter during the second visit, and the fact that Rubens appears not to have painted oil sketches as early as 1603 (as Adler, 1982, pp. 129–131, points out) support a date in 1628–1629.
130. Rooses-Ruelens, 6: 279–280. This translation of Rubens' letter is taken from Magurn, 1955, p. 414 – except for the words *forze venayson*, which remain untranslated by Magurn, and literally mean "strength" (from the Italian *forza*) and "venison" (from the French *venaison*).
131. For the copies, see Adler, 1982, pp. 129–131, no. 38, figs. 107–110.
132. As suggested in Adler, 1982, pp. 129–131. For Pacheco's statement, see Appendix 1.
133. See Muller, 1989, pp. 102, 105, and 109 (the last sentence is written in French in the original).

134. Previous attempts have been made by Bassegoda i Hugás, in Pacheco, ed., 1990, pp. 198–201, notes 9–19, and Vosters, 1990, pp. 125–144, with results similar to those presented here. Jaffé, 1977, pp. 333–344, has suggested that Rubens' copies of Titian documented by Pacheco are probably not large finished paintings but quick studies, and that the large final paintings documented in his collection were executed in Antwerp (this idea is expressed earlier by Palomino, ed., 1987, p. 102, who cites Bellori as his source). Jaffé argues that Rubens did not have enough time in Spain to execute so many large and finished paintings. Rubens indeed appears to have left Spain with a dozen paintings (but see the problem posed by the use of the term *láminas* in the documents, in n. 12 above), not with over twenty works. However, the copies could have been dispatched to Flanders at a later date. Even though it remains inconclusive, the evidence favors an identification of the copies made by Rubens after Titian in Spain as large, finished paintings (as indicated in Held, 1982, p. 303). As seen earlier, the list of paintings owned by Rubens at the time of his death refers to his copies after past masters, not as studies, but as finished paintings (which in many cases can be identified). Also in favor of identifying the copies as large pictures is Pacheco's surprise at the large number of paintings executed by Rubens in Madrid (see Pacheco's text in Appendix 1).
135. See in the appendix. Pacheco's text seems to indicate that Rubens only copied paintings by Titian and not by other painters. The list of paintings owned by Rubens at the time of his death also indicates that most of the copies made in Madrid were after Titian (see Muller, 1989, pp. 102–110, nos. 38–78). In spite of this, the possibility that Rubens made some copies after other artists cannot be discarded.
136. For a more detailed study of these copies, see the corresponding entries in Muller, 1989, and also Vergara, 1994, vol. 2, nos. A135–137, A139–141, A145, A151, A154–A156, A158.
137. For this drawing, see Glück-Haberditzl, 1928, no. 3, and Burchard-D'Hulst, 1963, pp. 244–245, no. 158.
138. Whereabouts unknown, presumably lost (see Muller, 1989, p. 104, no. 47, and Vergara, 1994, vol. 2, no. A142).
139. The whereabouts of Rubens' copy is not known.
140. Whereabouts unknown, presumably lost.
141. Whereabouts unknown, presumably lost.
142. Yorkshire, Collection of Lord Mountgarret. For this painting, see Burchard, 1950, pp. 28–30, no. 26.
143. Detmold, Collection Wilfried Goepel (see Müller Hofstede, 1967, pp. 47ff., and Müller Hofstede, 1977, no. 86, pp. 311–313).
144. Whereabouts unknown, presumably lost. It is worth noting here that a recent publication places two copies by Rubens after Titian's portraits of Charles V and his wife, Isabella, in Spain in 1636, which would suggest that they were not taken to Antwerp by Rubens upon his departure from Madrid. Fernando Checa (in Checa, 1994, p. 137), states that the *galería del mediodia* in the Alcázar contained two copies by Rubens of Titian's portrait of Charles V with a baton and of his wife, Isabella. (The same author, in *El Real Alcázar de Madrid*, p. 400, makes the same statement, but confuses the two separate portraits of the emperor and his wife for their double portrait.) However, the 1636 inventory of the Alcázar (APM, sec. adm., leg. 768) lists in the "galeria que mira al mediodia sobre el jardin de los emperadores" two copies after Titian's portraits of Charles and Isabella, but with no attribution. This suggests that these copies were not made by Rubens but by some other painter. It may be significant that the two paintings listed in the inventory immediately follow-

ing these anonymous copies are portraits, attributed to Rubens, of the infanta Isabella and her husband, the archduke Albert of Austria.

145. Madrid, Casa de Alba.
146. Princes Gates collection, Courtauld Institute of Art, London (see Seilern, 1955, 1: 23–24, no. 13; Seilern, 1971, pp. 21–22, and Exhibition, Canberra, 1992, pp. 140–142, no. 40). For additional information on this and the other portraits mentioned above, see the corresponding entries in Muller, 1989, and Vergara, 1994, vol. 2, nos. A146–150, A153, A157.
147. See, for example, Scharf, 1935, pp. 259–260; Glück, 1937; Seilern, 1955 and 1972; Jaffé, 1989, no. 31.
148. See Müller Hofstede, 1977, no. 86.
149. For this matter, see Hymans, 1893, pp. 24–25.
150. The use of the inscriptions of Rubens' prints as proof of date is an unresolved problem. See Renger, 1974, and Ingeborg Polen, 1985.
151. The whereabouts of Rubens' copy is not known. For the listing of this item in Rubens' collection, and the possibility that the copy was painted in Madrid, see Muller, 1989, p. 107, no. 59.
152. Muller, 1989, no. 64, p. 108.
153. See Muller, 1989, Catalogue 1, nos. 40, 41, 69.
154. There were probably at least twice the number of paintings by Titian in the Spanish royal collection in 1628–1629 other than those possibly copied by Rubens (a list of paintings by Titian in the Spanish royal collection included in Checa, 1994, pp. 245–274, lists 55 original paintings, most of which were in Madrid at the time of Rubens' visit).
155. For the best study of this issue, see Held, 1982, pp. 283–339.
156. One painting in this series, the *Danaë* (Madrid, Prado), is not documented to have been copied by Rubens, which is surprising, as it hung in the summer apartments of the Alcázar along with the rest of the *poesie* copied by Rubens (for the location of Titian's paintings in Spain, see Checa, 1994, pp. 266–268, nos. 36–41). The sheer quality of another painting by Titian, the *Tarquin and Lucrecia* (Cambridge, Fitzwilliam Museum), which also hung in the same section of the palace, suggests that Rubens may have painted a copy after it that is not recorded; but the violence of the subject, which separates this painting from the others Rubens copied, may have been at odds with Rubens' interests at the time.
157. For the hanging of paintings by Titian in the Alcázar, including the *Adam and Eve* (sometimes known as the *Fall of Man*), see Checa, 1994, pp. 130–148, 252–253, no. 15.
158. See the letter cited in n. 14.
159. Held, 1982, p. 312. For Rubens' late mythologies for Philip IV, see Chapter 4 in this study.
160. Ludovico Dolce, ed., 1960, 1: 145.
161. Palomino, ed., 1987, p. 29.
162. One of the many artists whose work Rubens did not copy in Madrid is worth mentioning in this context. Antonis Mor, a fellow Netherlander, succeeded Titian as the court portrait painter of the Spanish Hapsburgs, for whom he worked from 1549 (for Mor, see Groeneveld, 1981, and Woodall, 1991). Some of his most famous portraits could be seen in the royal collection in Spain when Rubens was there. Rubens had two paintings by Mor in his own collection (Muller, 1989, p. 130, nos. 202–203), which suggests that he held him in high regard. That he did not copy any of the portraits in the royal collection during his stay at the Spanish court can serve as a measure of how he restricted his activity to the paintings by Titian.
163. Held, 1982, pp. 307–312. Muller, 1982, p. 244, similarly states that "Titian's

late work offered a confirmation and guide for the path that Rubens had already taken. . . ."

164. See Checa, 1994.
165. Carducho, ed., 1979, p. 433.
166. See Seidel, 1993, pp. 171–205, for an interesting discussion of other cases – involving Titian and Rubens as well as Jan van Eyck and Velázquez – where a symbolic link was established between painters of different periods in the context of the Spanish court. See also Rosand, 1987, for another case of Rubens "styling himself *Titianus redivivus*" (through his copies of Titian's *Worship of Venus* and *Bacchanal of the Andrians*).
167. See the text by Pacheco in Appendix 1.
168. For the suggestion that Rubens acted as an incentive for the social and professional ambitions of Velázquez, see Brown, 1986, p. 65. The connection between Rubens' visit to Madrid and Velázquez's plans to visit Italy that is made by Palomino in the early eighteenth century (ed., 1987, p. 147), is frequently repeated thereafter.
169. Rubens' plan to visit Italy in 1629 is documented in Rooses-Ruelens, 5:10–11, 148, and Magurn, 1955, pp. 291–293, 321.
170. For Velázquez's art at the time of Rubens' visit to Madrid, see Brown, 1986, chap. 2; and Orso, 1993, chap. 2.
171. Rooses-Ruelens, 5:14–17 (English translation in Magurn, 1955, p. 295).
172. Most authors agree that Rubens' artistic influence on Velázquez at this point was limited (see especially Justi, 1889, pp. 133–138; see also López Rey, 1968, pp. 49–51; Harris, 1982, p. 73; and Brown, 1986, pp. 65–66. But also see Cruzada Villaamil, 1874, p. 141; and Huemer, 1996).
173. For this painting, see Garrido Pérez, 1992, pp. 66–79, and especially Orso, 1993 (for the dates of the painting, see Orso, 1993, pp. 5–7).
174. As suggested by Orso, 1993, p. 94. It should be noted that, as Orso shows, the selection of the subject was prompted primarily by Velázquez's status as a young court painter and his need to prove himself in the genre of history painting. Rubens' presence in Spain may well have acted as an additional factor, but it is not necessary to explain the theme of Velázquez's work.
175. See the technical analysis of this painting in Garrido Pérez, 1992, pp. 66–79.
176. See Pacheco's text in Appendix 1.
177. Huemer, 1996, pp. 96, 128, 144–145, n. 26.
178. See the studies of two of Velázquez's Italian paintings, *Joseph's Bloodied Coat Presented to Jacob* and *Forge of Vulcan*, in Garrido Pérez, 1992, pp. 218–245. For Velázquez's technique, see also McKim-Smith et al., 1988; and Zahira Veliz, "Velázquez's Early Technique," in Exhibition, Edinburgh, 1996, pp. 79–84. For Velázquez's trip to Italy in 1629–1631, see Brown, 1986, pp. 69–79.
179. For Velázquez's career in the 1630s, see Brown, 1986, pp. 79–168.
180. This is a compilation of biographical data that includes short biographies of Bosch, Peter de Kempeneer (or Pedro de Campaña), and Rubens. See Sánchez Cantón, ed., *Fuentes*, 2: 323–393. For studies of the text by Díaz del Valle, see Calvo Serraller, 1981, pp. 459–463; and Hellwig, 1994.
181. Díaz del Valle states of Rubens: "he was very prized by Juan Bautista Crescenci Marques de la Torre, a member of the order of Santiago, superintendent of the royal works and brother of cardinal Crescencio, a person of great knowledge in all that regards this most noble art" (see in Sánchez Cantón, 1923–1941, 2:358; the only other early notice of this encounter is included in Palomino, ed., 1987, p. 103, who uses Díaz del Valle as a source).
182. For Crescenzi, see Brown and Elliott, 1980, pp. 44–45; Brown, 1986, pp. 60–61, 288, n. 55, with further references; Cherry, 1987, pp. 299–305; and Barbeito, 1992, p. 158.
183. As suggested by Alpers, 1971, p. 28, n. 1.

184. For the Elsheimer painting in the collection of Crescenzi and the likelihood that Rubens saw it in Madrid, see Shakeshaft, 1981, p. 551. For Rubens' opinion on Elsheimer, see his letter to Johann Faber of January 14, 1611, from which the quote is taken (in Magurn, 1955, pp. 53–54).
185. Magurn, 1955, p. 358 (see original letter in Gachard, 1877, pp. 312–316, and in Rooses-Ruelens, 5:374). The king's wish to have Rubens travel to London came in the wake of a denial to the painter of a position as interim ambassador of Spain to the English court. On December 21, 1630, the council of state in Madrid resolved that "Peter Paul Rubens would have been very appropriate for the post. . . . But because he practices a craft that in the end is base and one by hand, it would seem to present difficulties if Your Majesty were to give him the title of one of your ministers" (Cruzada Villaamil, 1874, pp. 267–268). Clearly, Rubens had made less of an impression on other members of the Spanish administration than he had on Philip IV. The insistence on the part of the king that Rubens should be part of the English negotiations in some capacity is further proof of his personal favor toward the painter.
186. As stated in a letter from the infanta to Philip IV dated June 8, 1631 (see in Gachard, 1877, pp. 198–199, and Rooses-Ruelens, 5: 375).
187. Palomino, ed., 1987, pp. 101–105.
188. See Appendix 1.
189. For the letter in which the king conceded the title to Rubens (known only in French but presumably originally written in Spanish), see Rooses-Ruelens, 5: 420–422.
190. For the petition, see Rooses-Ruelens, 5: 392 (a translation of the second paragraph of this document appears in Brown, 1978, p. 106).
191. See Brown, 1978, p. 106.
192. For an overview of Rubens' last diplomatic engagements, see Magurn, 1955, pp. 358–363, and Baudouin, 1977, pp. 231–233.
193. In addition to the bibliography cited in the previous note, see Rubens' letter to the count-duke of Olivares of August 1, 1630 (Rooses-Ruelens, 5:404–411; English translation in Magurn, 1955, pp. 374–381).
194. This quote is taken from a letter written by Rubens to Peiresc on July 18, 1634 (see in Magurn, 1955, pp. 391–396).

Chapter Four: The King's Chosen Painter, 1630–1640

1. There is no study that focuses on the presence of Rubens' art in Spain after his visit of 1628–1629. Cruzada Villaamil's landmark study of 1874 ends with Rubens' diplomatic efforts in the 1630s. The author adds a list of paintings by him recorded in Spain, which is fundamental for the study of Rubens there in later decades but is not accompanied by a narrative text. The only other study dedicated exclusively to Rubens and Spain is the idiosyncratic text by S. Vosters (1990). The author offers a useful survey of literary references to Rubens in Spain throughout the century (chaps. 5 and 6), and refers to cases of Rubens' influence on local painters, and vice versa (chap. 7). The study by Vosters, however, does not offer a comprehensive view of the presence of Rubens in Spain during this period.
2. For this painting, see Balis, 1986, pp. 95–104, no. 2; W. Liedtke, *Flemish Paintings in America*, pp. 193–196; and Koslow, 1996.
3. For Aarschot, including his involvement in the arts and his tense relations with Rubens, see *Biographie nationale Belge*, vol. 1 (1866), cols. 388–401 (L. P. Gachard); and Balis, 1986, pp. 22–25, with further references.
4. Koslow, 1995, p. 346, n. 6.
5. The inventory of Aarschot's collection in Madrid has recently been discovered by Peter Cherry, and will soon be published in Burke and Cherry, forthcoming.

Whether Aarschot brought his collection with him at an early date or this occurred closer to his death is not known.

6. This is the same occasion mentioned in Chapter 2.
7. As suggested by Balis, 1986, p. 25, and by Koslow, 1996, p. 703.
8. See Koslow, 1996, pp. 703–706.
9. For this painting, see Rooses, *L'Oeuvre*, 4:30–31; Díaz Padrón, 1995, 2:1110–1113, no. 1645; and Vergara, 1994, vol. 2 no. A132.
10. This painting is sometimes identified with one of the same subject attributed to Wildens that was in the collection of the marquis of Leganés in 1642 and 1655; see Volk, 1989a, p. 262; Devisscher, in *La Pintura Flamenca en el Museo del Prado*, p. 159, no. 50; and Díaz Padrón, 1995, p. 1110. It seems unlikely, however, that the painting included in the royal collection in 1636, and still there in 1686 and 1700, is identical with the picture listed in the Leganés collection in those years. It is also unlikely that a painting with large figures painted by Rubens would be attributed to Wildens.
11. Orso, 1993, pp. 118–122. Among the paintings in the room was Titian's *Religion Aided by Spain* and numerous portraits of four generations of Hapsburgs.
12. Translation taken from Orso, 1989, p. 123 (where the full text is reproduced). For the Latin epitaph, see pp. 122–123 in the same publication; for Rubens' painting, see also p. 76.
13. The identification of the unnamed painting mentioned in this epitaph with Rubens' *Devotion of Rudolf I* is based on the description of the work and on the fact that, after the death of Philip IV, Rubens' painting is recorded in "the room where His Majesty died" (see the 1666 inventory of the Alcázar, APM, sección administrativa, leg. 38; and also the 1686 inventory, in Bottineau, no. 618).
14. For this matter, see De Maeyer, 1955, pp. 43–44. See also Balis, 1986, pp. 138–139.
15. The 1636 inventory locates the pictures in the "Pieça donde su Mag[d] que Dios g[de] lee en el quarto bajo con bentana al Jardin de la Priora," and reads: "Cinco Pinturas en tabla con molduras de evano y Perfiles de oro pintados en que estan los cinco sentidos de mano de Rubenes las figuras Y los paises, frutas, flores, cosas de caça, instrum[tos] musicos y belicos son de mano de Brugul son los que dio al S[r] Ynfante Cardenal el duq[e] de namburg su A. al duq[e] de medina de las torres y el duq[e] a su Mag[d] son de quatro pies y m[o] de largo" (APM, sección administrativa, leg. 768).
16. This last possibility was first suggested by Beroqui, 1917, no. 1394 and was turned into a fact in *Museo del Prado. Catálogo*, 1972, p. 88, and followed in Díaz Padrón, 1975, 1: 42, and in Ertz, 1979, p. 337. For the gifts given by Neuburg to Ferdinand in 1634, see Aedo y Gallart, 1635, p. 179. For the relationship between Neuburg and the Spanish Crown, which provides the context for the gift, see Cuvelier and Lefèvre, 1930, pp. 22–53.
17. For Medina de las Torres, see Elliott, 1986, pp. 166–168, 278, and Stradling, 1976. For his relation to the arts, see Tormo, 1909, pp. 304–308; Brown-Elliott, 1980, pp. 36, 62, 117, 123, 216; Brown, 1984, pp. 145–146, and Burke, 1989, pp. 132–135.
18. For this date, see Elliott, 1986, p. 167. According to Stradling, 1976, p. 3, Medina de las Torres was born in ca. 1600.
19. Vlieghe, 1979, p. 651, attributes the small figures in these paintings to Rubens' workshop. For this series see also Díaz Padrón, 1995, 1:264–287.
20. APM, sección administrativa, leg. 768 (translation by the author; transcription available in Díaz Padrón, 1995, 2:266). The five paintings are attributed to Brueghel alone, with no mention of Rubens, in the Alcázar inventories of 1666 (see in Cruzada Villaamil, 1874, nos. 60–64, p. 380), 1686 (in Bottineau, nos. 573–577), and 1700 (in *Museo del Prado. Inventarios Reales*, vol. 1, p. 49, no. 318).
21. See Santiago Paez, in Checa, ed., 1994, pp. 332–334.

22. For the meaning of allegorical paintings of picture galleries such as these, see Schwartz, 1993, and Schwartz, 1996. See also Vinge, 1975.
23. See Brown, 1991, pp. 197–211.
24. For the Buen Retiro, see Brown and Elliott, 1980.
25. Ibid., pp. 114–140.
26. Members of Rubens' circle and workshop also worked on projects for the Buen Retiro, but without any intervention by the master. On May 1, 1638, 112 landscape paintings ("paesi e pitture boscheresce") arrived from Flanders for the Buen Retiro and the Torre de la Parada (it is uncertain how many were intended for each palace); these paintings have been connected to Rubens' workshop, but there is no specific indication that there was any kind of direction or intervention from Rubens (for these paintings, see: Alpers, 1971, pp. 50–51; Brown and Elliott, 1980, pp. 130–132; and Balis, 1986, p. 227, n. 3). Rubens' shop is also reported to have produced twelve paintings representing the months of the year for the Buen Retiro (see Brown and Elliott, 1980, pp. 131–132).
27. "Su Mag.d Dios le Guarde ha mostrado deseo de q.[e] se le haga una medalla, o effigie a Cavallo de su real persona que sea de bronze, conforme a unos retratos de Pedro Pablo Rubens, y a la traza de la q.[e] está en la Casa de Campo" (letter reproduced in Gualandi, 1844–1856, pp. 85–86).
28. The details of this commission, especially as it concerns the models used by Pietro Tacca, remain obscure. For an account of the commission, see Justi, 1908, pp. 253–274, where most of the available documentation was first published, and Brown and Elliott, 1980, pp. 111–114. The Florentine writer Filippo Baldinucci mentions two portraits of the king by Rubens, which he says he has seen in Tacca's studio as models for this commission (Baldinucci, 1681, p. 172). This source should be considered with care, as Baldinucci's account of this commission contains mistakes (see Cruzada Villaamil, 1885, p. 80, and Huemer, 1977, p. 153). Baldinucci believed that Rubens was in Madrid at the time of this commission, which was not the case. Velázquez is generally considered a more likely candidate as author of the works seen by Baldinucci in Tacca's home, and it could also be that the paintings Baldinucci saw were copies after either Velázquez or Rubens.
29. Gualandi, 1844–1856, pp. 89–90.
30. The only portrait of Philip IV by Rubens known to have been in the Royal Collection at the time is the equestrian portrait painted in 1628. It could be that a copy of this painting was sent to Florence (this cannot be the copy now in the Uffizi, as indicated by Huemer, 1977, p. 153; see ibid., p. 151, copies nos. 2 and 3, and fig. 92 for other copies that may be identified with the ones sent to Tacca in Florence).
31. Based on appearance alone, it seems that at some point Velázquez was substituted for Rubens as a model, as the statue now extant is very close to Velázquez's *Philip IV on Horseback* in the Prado of ca. 1634 (in this conclusion I follow Harris, 1982, p. 103). The head of the king in the final statue was based on a bust sculpture by Juan Martínez Montañés sent to Florence from Madrid (the sculpture on which Montañés is seen working in his portrait by Velázquez in the Prado); for this sculpture, see Orso, 1989.
32. Madrid, Prado. For this painting, see Díaz Padrón, 1995, 2: 962–963, no. 1669. The painting, now measuring 199 × 379 cm, has been cut down from its original dimensions of approximately 210 × 504 cm.
33. For the correspondence between Philip IV and his brother regarding this painting, see Rooses-Ruelens, 6: 220, 221, 226, 227, 228.
34. As suggested by Brown and Elliott, 1980, pp. 130–31.
35. For the probability that Velázquez played a supervisory role in the decoration of the Hall of Realms in the Buen Retiro, see Brown and Elliott, 1980, pp. 190–191.

36. As suggested by Brown and Elliott, 1980, p. 130.
37. For this commission, see Millar, 1958.
38. See J. R. Martin, 1972. For Rubens' letter, see Rooses-Ruelens, 6:82; English translation from Magurn, 1955, p. 393. Rubens probably began working on this project in mid-November, and the entry took place in April.
39. For this commission, see Alpers, 1971, from which the following pages largely derive. See also Held, 1980, 1: 251–255.
40. For the cardinal-infante, see Van der Essen, 1944.
41. Evers, 1943, p. 84.
42. Ferdinand commissioned at least two portraits from Rubens for his own keeping (see Vlieghe, 1987, nos. 91, 92, 94, pp. 80–82, 87; the equestrian portrait of the cardinal-infante that is now in the Prado may have been commissioned to send to Madrid, not to remain in Brussels).

    He may also have purchased some paintings from Rubens' collection for the palace in Brussels (see Chapter 5, n. 91). In spite of these isolated events, the cardinal-infante Ferdinand appears to have been a far less important patron of Rubens than both his brother, the king, and his aunt and predecessor, the infanta Isabella. For the date of Ferdinand's death, see Gascón de Torquemada, ed., 1991, p. 412.
43. Alpers identifies "Esneyre" with Pieter Snayers (Alpers, 1971, pp. 117–118). However, as Held, 1980, 1:251–252, has suggested, it is more likely that "Esneyre" should be identified as Frans Snyders, as Snayers was not known as an animal painter and the painter "Esneyre" is sometimes mentioned in different contexts where he can only be identified with Snyders. A third group of paintings consisting of at least five scenes of hunting at the Spanish court was executed by Pieter Snayers (see Alpers, 1971, pp. 122–125).
44. That paintings needed to be added after the original shipment stems from a letter of June 30, 1638 – just after the arrival of the pictures in Madrid – from the cardinal-infante to the king: "The memorial of the paintings that Your Majesty has ordered done again I have given to Rubens, who is painting them all himself to gain time . . ." ("La Memoria de las pinturas que V.M. manda se hagan nuevas, he dado yo mismo à Rubens, quien las hace todas de su mano por ganar tiempo . . ."; Rooses-Ruelens, 4:220). Alpers, 1971, p. 41, seems to believe that this letter refers to paintings by Snyders, but the content of the letter indicates otherwise. For the delivery of pictures to Madrid on February 27, 1639, see Alpers, 1971, pp. 40–41, and Balis, 1986, p. 218.
45. As noted by Alpers, 1971, p. 68. For the sketches, see Held, 1981, 1:251–301.
46. See Alpers, 1971, pp. 107–173.
47. The other painters involved in the commission are Frans Snyders, Jan Boeckhorst, Jan-Baptist Borrekens, Jan Cossiers, Jan van Eyck, Jacob Peter Gowy, Jacob Jordaens, Erasmus Quellinus, Peter Symons, Theodoor van Thulden, Cornelis de Vos, and Thomas Willeboirts (see Alpers, 1971, p. 34, and Held, 1980, 1:251–252).
48. Alpers, 1971, pp. 41–42.
49. Ibid., pp. 34–36.
50. "Dile licencia para mudar algo desta manera: que en algunos cuatro pequeños piden fabulas de pocas figuras, que querria [Rubens] trocar esto. Yo le he dicho no mude nada hasta que V.A. sepa lo que le parece á Rubens y mande lo que se ha de hacer . . ." (Rooses-Ruelens, 6:171).
51. As documented in Rooses-Ruelens, 6:171.
52. That Velázquez may have intervened in the design for the Torre is suggested in Alpers, 1971, p. 30. For Velázquez and the decoration of the royal residences, see Brown, 1986, pp. 191ff.
53. This interpretation of the Torre was first suggested by Justi, 1903, 2d ed., 1: 319, and is followed in Alpers, 1971, pp. 104–105.

54. See Alpers, 1971, pp. 27, 33, 105, with further references. Alpers, contrary to my opinion, regards the visit by only two dignitaries as proof of the isolated nature of the Torre.
55. Bellori, 1672, p. 233, and De Piles, 1681, p. 24.
56. For the copies, see the individual entries in Alpers, 1976.
57. Alpers, 1971, pp. 34–35.
58. Prado nos. 1658 and 1659 (see Alpers, 1971, nos. 37 and 53).
59. In 1639 there was no equivalent gathering of originals by Rubens anywhere in Spain; the largest group was the *Apostolado*, which had belonged to Lerma earlier in the century (its location in the 1630s is not known). The Descalzas Reales had twenty scenes designed by Rubens, but in the form of tapestries. Other private collectors had a total of fifteen or sixteen additional paintings, some of them in uncertain locations and none of them forming a group as large as the one in the Torre. The total number of Rubenses in the royal collection by that time, excluding the Torre, was thirteen paintings, not all of which hung together (these numbers are derived from the information included in this and the previous chapters).
60. For Titian's paintings, see Wethey, vol. 3, 1975, and Checa, 1994, pp. 89–126.
61. Rooses-Ruelens, 6:232. The most plausible attempt to sort out this commission is Balis, 1986, pp. 218ff., on which the following pages are based. Important research on this set of paintings has also been undertaken by Held, 1980, 1:305–306, and Alpers, 1971, pp. 39–41. For details concerning the arrangements for the actual shipment of these paintings to Spain, see also Orso, 1997.
62. Rooses-Ruelens, 6:236.
63. Ibid., p. 238; English translation available in Orso, 1986, p. 61.
64. Rooses-Ruelens, 6:247–248 (the references to different commissions included in the correspondence are sorted out in Balis, 1986, pp. 218–233).
65. Rooses-Ruelens, 6:261, 280–281, and 294.
66. Ibid., p. 316.
67. The arguments for the identification of these eight scenes are complex and involve very extensive evidence. For a detailed explanation of this matter, see Balis, 1986, pp. 218–233 (slightly different conclusions are reached in Held, 1980, vol. 1, nos. 221–227, pp. 305–312).
68. Prado, inv. no. 1665; and North Carolina Museum of Art, inv. no. 52.9.208.
69. Inv. no. 3-p and 39-p (these paintings are on loan from the Prado).
70. Some of them can be identified through copies and sketches; e.g., the *Calydonian Boar Hunt* (Fig. 74); see Balis, 1986, cat. no. 20a.
71. Balis, 1986, pp. 223–225.
72. Ibid., pp. 224–225.
73. Ibid., pp. 226–227.
74. As noted in ibid., p. 226.
75. See the sketches reproduced in Balis, 1986, figs. 110, 118, 119, 122.
76. Letter from Ferdinand dated June 2, 1641; Rooses-Ruelens, 6: 316 (that this letter refers to this commission can be derived from its date, as Balis, 1986, p. 228, n. 15, has noted).
77. Orso, 1986, pp. 70–71.
78. Rooses-Ruelens, 6:238. The best study of this commission is J. R. Martin, 1976–1978, pp. 113–118, who deals mainly with two of the four paintings. See also Orso, 1986, pp. 60–63, figs. 43–46, and Vergara, 1994, 2:231–236, nos. A21–A24.
79. The contents of this commission were first identified by Rooses in Rooses-Ruelens, 6:238.
80. As reported by the cardinal-infante to the king on May 2, 1640 (Rooses-Ruelens, 6:280).
81. This information derives from a letter from the cardinal-infante to Philip IV

dated June 10, 1640 (Rooses-Ruelens, 6:304). The large canvases measured approximately 418 × 460 cm. The small one is approximately 152 × 126 cm.

82. Rooses-Ruelens, 6:310–312.
83. Denucé, 1932, p. 83, no. 115.
84. Rooses-Ruelens, 6:316 (it is not entirely certain that this letter refers to this commission).
85. Letter from Ferdinand to the king: "The painting is very advanced, but it will not be finished by the end of August, no matter how much the painter may hurry. But I hope that it will be very good, because as he is new, he tries to gain reputation, especially since this will be together with the ones by Rubens. Your Majesty may rest assured that I will send it as soon as possible" (Rooses-Ruelens, 6:317).
86. For the location of these paintings in the context of the New Room, see Orso, 1986, pp. 74–117, and Appendix D, nos. 8–9, 12, 15. In 1686 these four scenes hung in the Hall of Mirrors along with twenty-seven other paintings.
87. Orso, 1986, pp. 96–97.
88. J. R. Martin, 1976–1978, pp. 117–118, and Orso, 1986, pp. 99–100.
89. For the installation of the New Room shortly before the time of this commission, see the 1636 inventory of the room in Orso, 1986, Appendix C, pp. 189–192.
90. For reproductions of the sketches, see Orso, 1986, figs. 45–46.
91. See Chapter 3, pp. 93–94.
92. For the 1642 inventory of the Leganés collection, see Volk, 1980a, pp. 267–268.
93. The marquis of Leganés as a collector of Rubens after 1640 will be studied in Chapter 5.
94. For Rubens and Moretus, see Judson-Van de Velde, 1978, 1:25–40.
95. For Van Vucht and his attempts to purchase a painting from Rubens, see Rooses-Ruelens, 5:294–295, 300–301, 304, 333–334, 338. These attempts are first recorded in a letter from Balthasar Moretus to Van Vucht dated June 25, 1630, and are last heard of on October 22 of the same year, when the painter and his client were still negotiating the price of a possible commission.
96. For this painting, see Vlieghe, 1972, pp. 87–88, no. 62, fig. 109. See also Díaz Padrón, 1995, 2:1068–1071.
97. The hostel and its church have been incorporated into a foundation known as the *Real Diputación San Andrés de los Flamencos, Fundación Carlos de Amberes.* The painting belongs to this foundation; it can sometimes be seen in its church in Madrid and is often on loan to the Prado.
98. For the influence of this painting on Carreño de Miranda and Francisco Rizzi, see Pérez Sánchez, 1977, pp. 105–109. For a possible influence on Murillo, see Angulo, 1981, vol. 1, p. 435, and vol. 2, no. 277.
99. See Carrete Parrondo et al., 1988, p. 227 (where the print is mistakenly dated to 1632), and p. 341, fig. 496. The print was probably executed after Lucas Vorsterman's engraving of 1621, which it reverses (for the print by Vorsterman and the original painting, see Vlieghe, 1973, nos. 126, 126b, pp. 107–109, figs. 71–72; as the print by Rodríguez reverses the print by Vorsterman, it shows the image with the same orientation as the original). Rodríguez's print is dedicated to the learned politician and collector Lorenzo Ramírez de Prado. Little is known about de Beer except that he was one of the most active publishers of prints in Madrid in the second quarter of the century and was father of the printmaker María Eugenia de Beer. Also, his name denotes a northern origin.
100. For the history of prints in seventeenth-century Spain, see Carrete Parrondo et al., 1988, pp. 203–391. See also Portús Pérez, "Uso y función de la estampa suelta en los Siglos de Oro," in Morán Turina and Portús Pérez, 1997,

pp. 257–277. For the print by Salvador Carmona, see Carrete Parrondo, 1977, p. 140.

101. For the influence of Rubens in Spain, see the references cited in Introduction, n. 3.

102. For the roles assigned to Spanish and foreign painters in Spain, see Brown, 1991, pp. 307–314 (esp. p. 311).

103. The total number of paintings executed and directed by Rubens between 1636, when the Torre de la Parada series was commissioned, and 1640, is impossible to determine due to problems of attribution and dating. Rubens was very active during these years; he painted landscapes, altarpieces, allegories, history paintings, mythologies, and portraits. M. Jaffé (1989, pp. 347–375) lists a total of 206 paintings between 1636 and 1640, of which approximately sixty-nine are sketches; Rooses (1903, pp. 571–609) is less precise in his listing but also places the number of works of this period at well over a hundred.

104. Ferrarino, 1977, p. 39.

105. For the reaction of the Counter-Reformation to naked and indecent images in art, see Freedberg, 1971.

106. "Sin duda ninguna por dho de todos los pintores es la mejor que ha hecho Rubens; solo tiene una falta que no ha sido posible que la quiera enmendar. Y es estar demasiado desnudas las tres Diosas, pero dice que es menester para que se vea la valentía de la pintura. La Venus que está de enmedio es retrato muy parecido de su misma muger que sin duda es de lo mejor de lo que ahora hay aquí" (Rooses-Ruelens, 6: 228).

107. In *De Institutione feminae christianae*, ed. Madrid, 1935 (*Instrucción de la Mujer Cristiana*), p. 67.

108. For Titian's paintings in Spain, see Checa, 1994.

109. For Velázquez's career at this time, see Brown, 1986, pp. 79–168.

Chapter Five: A Continued Presence

1. Letter written by Philip IV to Sor María on November 15, 1644; see in Seco Serrano, ed., 1958, 1:12 (cited in Stradling, 1988, p. 241, from which I take the translation). Philip IV would remarry in 1649 by wedding his niece Mariana of Austria.
2. For the political history of Spain during the 1640s, see Elliott, 1986, pp. 553–673, and Stradling, 1988, pp. 117–301 (for the king's personal losses in the 1640s, see especially pp. 240–241).
3. Seco Serrano, ed., 1958, 1:83; translation in Stradling, 1988, p. 242.
4. Rooses-Ruelens, 6:304.
5. This account was first published by Génard, 1865–1866, pp. 83–85. It is also published in Denucé, 1932, pp. 74–76, the source that will be quoted here. A detailed study of the purchases made for the king from Rubens' collection does not exist. The best studies of the sales from Rubens' collection, and of the Spanish purchases, are still Rooses, *L'Oeuvre*, 1:135, and Rooses, 1903, pp. 620–626. See also Muller, 1989, pp. 79, 92–93. For the complete contents of Rubens' collections that were put up for sale, see Muller, 1989, pp. 94–155.
6. See Muller, 1989, pp. 91–93, for an account of the process that led to the sale immediately following Rubens' death.
7. The letter from Ferdinand to Philip IV reads: ". . . the ones that Rubens has in his house are many and very good, and in order to avoid mistakes and to better guess the taste of Your Majesty, I am sending you this memorandum of all of them, so that you can notify me what should be done. There is no danger in waiting for Your Majesties' response, because they want to print this account and circulate it all around Europe, and I do not know which party will be better for

them (*no sé cual partido les mestará mejor*). I beg Your Majesty to order what should be done, and I will do it immediately" (Rooses-Ruelens, 6:310–311). The memorandum mentioned in this letter is not known. That the king had probably indicated, before the date of this letter, that he wished to make purchases from the painter's collection derives from the contents of the letter.

8. As documented in the account of Rubens' estate, which is dated in 1645 (see in Denucé, 1932, pp. 83–85; the price paid by the king for the paintings was 27,100 guilders). The account of the estate actually states that twenty-nine paintings were sold to the king but then goes on to list thirty-two items, which should therefore be considered the correct number. For the date of the public sale of Rubens' collection, see Génard, 1685–1686, p. 80. The Spanish purchases were probably not part of this sale, but may have been arranged close to that date.
9. The role played by Rojas is documented in the account of the sales presented by Rubens' heirs to the city of Antwerp, where the group of paintings sold to the king is said to have been ". . . sold to Don Francisco de Rochas, for His Majesty the King" (see in Denucé, 1932, p. 74, no. 43).
10. As documented in the account of Rubens' estate. For the assistance of De Crayer, who received a painting from Rubens' heirs in recognition for his services, see Denucé, 1932, p. 76, no. 45. For the assistance of the other painters, see Denucé, 1932, p. 74, no. 43.
11. Rooses, *L'Oeuvre*, p. 135, believes that seventeen of the paintings documented as sold to Philip IV are by Rubens (in addition to another painting, the *Adam and Eve*, which will be dealt with later); he is mistaken in assigning to Rubens a "Savior with a World in His Hands" and a "Saint Peter Martyr," which are listed as anonymous copies after Titian in the account of the sales from Rubens' estate but are probably originals by Titian, as that is how they are listed in the *Specification* (see Muller, 1989, p. 95, nos. 2–3). The paintings by artists other than Rubens purchased by the king are two works by Titian, two by Tintoretto, one by Muzziano, three by Veronese, four by Elsheimer, and three by Van Dyck, in addition to a landscape by Paul Bril that will be mentioned immediately below. It is also worth noting that the king did not purchase the two paintings by a Spanish artist owned by Rubens, two religious works by Ribera (see Muller, 1989, p. 100, nos. 27–28).
12. See Muller, 1989, p. 104, no. 44, for the presence of this painting in Rubens' collection, and for references to the document of its purchase and to tentative identifications of the painting with extant works made in the literature.
13. Ibid., p. 103, no. 43. This painting, copied after Titian, should not be confused with another of the same subject (now in the Prado) of Rubens' own invention that also entered the royal collection during the last years of the reign of Philip IV and will be studied later in this chapter.
14. Muller, 1989, p. 104, no. 45.
15. Ibid., no. 46.
16. Ibid., no. 47. The subject matter of this painting is uncertain. It is listed as a copy after Titian, and there is no known painting by Titian that shows only Venus and Cupid on a bed, as this is described in Rubens' collection. That description best fits two versions of *Venus and Cupid with an Organist* (Madrid, Prado, and Berlin-Dahlem, Staatliche Gemäldegalerie; see Wethey, vol. 3, nos. 47–48), a *Venus and Cupid with a Lute Player* (Cambridge, Fitzwilliam Museum; Wethey, vol. 3, no. 46) and a *Venus and Cupid with a Partridge* (Florence, Uffizi; Wethey, vol. 3, no. 49). Of these, only the originals in the Prado (which was in Spain when the artist visited there in 1628–1629) and Berlin (which may have been in Spain on the same date) could have been copied by the artist during his lifetime (the other originals by Titian were never seen by Rubens after 1626, when this painting was executed).
17. Muller, 1989, p. 111, no. 81. For the presence of this and the following painting

in Rubens' estate, and their purchase by Philip IV, see also J. M. Muller, 1987, pp. 75–80. For their earlier history, see Cruzada Villaamil, 1874, p. 324, and Wethey, vol. 3, p. 152.

18. Muller, 1989, p. 111, no. 82.
19. Ibid., no. 83.
20. Ibid., pp. 111–112, no. 84. The painting purchased from Rubens' collection is sometimes identified with a *Landscape with the Rest on the Flight to Egypt and Several Saints*, now in the Prado (see Díaz Padrón, 1975, vol. pp. 231–232, no. 1640), but that identification is probably incorrect (as noted by Adler, 1982, p. 145, no. 43). The Prado picture is painted on panel, not canvas like the painting in Rubens' collection. As suggested in Vergara, 1994, 2:342, the painting purchased by the king from Rubens' estate – the picture that we are dealing with here – is more likely identical with a painting that is recorded in the royal collection in Spain throughout the seventeenth century and is not heard of thereafter. It is inventoried in 1666 in the *Galería de Mediodía* of the Alcázar: "Another painting, two *varas* in length and one and one half *varas* in width, of Our Lady with Saint Joseph and Saint Margaret, by Rubens, in 150 silver ducats" (APM, sección administrativa, leg. 38, fol. 49v; it is unclear in this document which of the dimensions cited corresponds to the height and which to the width). In 1686 it is inventoried in the same location: "Another picture, two *varas* in length and one and one half *varas* in width, Our Lady with Saint Joseph, Saint George and other saints, by Rubens" (Bottineau, no. 285). In 1700, it is again inventoried in the same location with an identical description (*Museo del Prado. Inventarios Reales*, vol. 1, p. 27, no. 96).
21. Muller, 1989, p. 113, no. 90.
22. Ibid., p. 115, no. 103.
23. Ibid., p. 120, no. 138. For this painting, in addition to the references cited in Muller, 1989, see Freedberg, 1984, p. 48, no. 9.
24. Muller, 1989, p. 122, no. 155.
25. Ibid., no. 154.
26. Ibid., p. 123, no. 164.
27. Ibid., p. 100, no. 26. The painting is attributed to Bril alone in Rubens' collection. The attribution of the figures to Rubens dates to the nineteenth century (it is first published in the Prado catalogue of 1889, no. 1780). For this painting, see Díaz Padrón, 1995, vol. 1, pp. 192–193, no. 1849.
28. For the document of the sale, see Denucé, 1932, p. 72. Rooses, *L'Oeuvre*, 4:156–158, no. 930, suggested that this painting is identical with a picture listed in Rubens' collection at the time of his death in 1640 as "Un portrait du Prince Cardinal Infant, sur toile," "The picture of the Infant Cardinal" (see Muller, 1989, p. 115, no. 101). However, the existence of other portraits of Ferdinand by Rubens makes this identification uncertain (for the other portraits that could also be identified with no. 101 in the *Specification*, see Vlieghe, 1987, pp. 80–82, nos. 91–92).
29. See Denucé, 1932, pp. 83–84, no. 139.
30. See Cruzada Villaamil, 1874, pp. 367–368, no. 32 of the extant works.
31. Vlieghe, 1987, p. 84.
32. See Génard, 1865–1866, p. 86.
33. See the *Specification*, in Muller, 1989, p. 136, no. 248.
34. Prado inv. no. 1703. For the Prado painting, see Díaz Padrón, 1995, vol. 2, pp. 1018–1021, no. 1703. The known provenance of this painting goes back only to the eighteenth century. The attribution to Rubens of the Prado painting has been contested, in my opinion without reason, by Van Puyvelde, 1948, p. 82, no. 57, and Vlieghe, 1979, pp. 652–653. Rooses, *L'Oeuvre*, 1: 288, and Held, 1980, 1:522, call it a copy (presumably not by Rubens). The identification of the Prado picture with the one included in the *Specification* and given to

79. Ibid., p. 555, no. C1.
80. Ibid., p. 274, no. A61.
81. For this painting, see Huemer, 1977, pp. 147–148, no. 27; and Díaz Padrón, 1995, vol. 2, pp. 968–969, no. 1685. Both of these authors believe that this and the *Portrait of Anne of Austria* were purchased for the king from Rubens' estate, but this is not certain, as will be seen below.
82. For the 1666 inventory, see Orso, 1986, p. 202, nos. 2–3. For the 1686 inventory, see Bottineau, nos. 164–165. For the 1700 inventory, see *Museo del Prado. Inventarios Reales*, 1:21, where they are described as "Two paintings measuring two *varas* in length and half a *vara* in width, one of Mercury, the other of Saturn, by Rubens, copies, with black frames, valued in thirty *doblones* each" ("Dos Pintturas de a dos Uaras de largo y media de ancho. la Vna de Mercurio y la ottra de Saturno de mano de Rubenes Copias Con Marcos negros tasadas a treinta Doblones Cada Vna"). The wording here is unclear; it is likely to mean that the pictures are copies after Rubens, but it could be read as describing the paintings as copies painted by Rubens himself. Orso, 1986, p. 156, n. 36, refers to a *Bacchus and Nymphs* in the Alcázar that is attributed to Van Dyck in 1666 and the author states is attributed to Rubens in 1686, in which case it should be listed in this section. However, the 1686 and 1700 inventories of the Alcázar attribute the painting to Van Dyck (see in Bottineau, no. 163, and in *Museo del Prado. Inventarios Reales*, vol. 1, p. 21, no. 25), with no mention of Rubens.
83. For these cartoons, see De Poorter, 1978, 1:133–160, 2:446–449. The date of this dispatch from Brussels to Madrid is not known. The cartoons are not recorded in Spain until the early eighteenth century, when they belonged to the convent of Loeches, on the outskirts of Madrid. The scenes in these cartoons were probably *The Triumph of Faith*, *Abraham and Melchizedek*, *The Four Evangelists*, *The Defenders of the Eucharist*, *Elijah and the Angel*, and *The Gathering of the Manna* (see De Poorter, 1978, 1:158–160, who follows Ponz, 1787, 1:269–273, for the identification of the scenes, and dismisses other early sources). They are first documented in Loeches by Palomino, in his book *Lives*, published in 1724 (Palomino, ed., 1987, p. 102). In the seventeenth century, this convent had been under the patronage of Luis de Haro and his son Gaspar de Haro, who will be discussed later in this chapter. The convent's connection to the Haro family suggests that the cartoons were given as a gift by the king to one of them at some point before the death of Gaspar in 1687.
84. Four of the paintings first documented in the collection of Philip IV after his death (*Hercules Strangling the Lion*, *Hercules Slaying the Dragon*, *Hercules*, and *Diana*), were mentioned in Chapter 4, p. 132, as possible candidates to be identified with two works that were part of a commission of eighteen paintings for the *bóveda* of the Alcázar in 1639. At most, only two of these paintings may be part of that commission (sixteen other pictures have been tentatively identified as part of the *bóvedas* commission).
85. Barnes, in Exhibition, Washington, D.C., 1990–1991, pp. 117–119, no. 15, suggests that this signature may have been added to the painting in Spain, as a seventeenth-century Flemish copy does not include it. Whether the signature was added in Spain or in Flanders, this must have occurred before the entry of the picture into the royal collection because, to my knowledge, there is no case where a signature was added to a painting while it belonged to the royal collection.
86. For the king's purchases from different collections in Europe, see Brown, 1989, pp. 202–204.
87. For the Spanish purchases in the sales that followed the civil war, see Brown, 1995, pp. 59–93.

88. For Fuensaldaña's purchases in London, including this painting, see Vergara, 1989, pp. 127–129, and 130, no. 15.
89. As documented in two orders dated January 12, 1659, from Juan José de Austria to ship fourteen paintings from Brussels to Spain (see in De Maeyer, 1955, pp. 433, 435). The same shipment also included another work by Rubens, a Bacchus, but this apparently remained in the possession of Juan José de Austria, where it is documented in 1679 (the collection of Juan José de Austria will be studied below).
90. De Maeyer, 1955, p. 435. Another document of the same date that refers to the paintings to be shipped to Spain actually only lists one of the two portraits; see De Maeyer, 1955, p. 448. This may be a mistake, as the document states that it includes fourteen paintings but then only lists thirteen. It may also be that at this time only one of the portraits was shipped to Madrid; only the *Portrait of Anne of Austria* is inventoried there in 1666; the other is first documented in Madrid in 1686.
91. The Prado portraits show two different sitters, not the same one, as the paintings sent to the king were described, but this could be an error. The Prado portraits were in Rubens' collection at the time of his death in 1640 (see Muller, 1989, p. 124, nos. 166 and 167) and are generally believed to have been purchased from there for Philip IV (as stated in Díaz Padrón, 1975, 1:279; Huemer, 1977, pp. 102–104, no. 2; and Díaz Padrón, 1995, 2:980), but there is no documentation to prove this. They may also be identical to the two portraits sent to Spain from Brussels in 1659. If this is the case, they must have been purchased from the painter's collection for the palace in Brussels, presumably by the cardinal-infante Ferdinand, who was governor at the time of Rubens' death, or by one of his successors.
92. The admiral of Castile, who also owned other paintings attributed to Rubens, will be studied later in this chapter.
93. For the hanging of the Chapter Room of El Escorial, see Brown, 1986, pp. 237–238.
94. For this painting, in addition to the bibliography cited in n. 71 above, see Koslow, 1995, pp. 74–79, 89.
95. For this painting, in addition to the literature cited in n. 60 above, see Klessmann, 1994.
96. Held, 1982, p. 324. Titian's *Diana and Callisto* is in Edinburgh, National Gallery of Scotland.
97. See Burchard-d'Hulst, 1963, no. 49, and Jaffé, 1977, p. 33.
98. Held, 1982, p. 324.
99. For the use of water emerging from a fountain as a symbol of ejaculation (most often in the context of references to fertility and reproduction), see Rona Goffen, "Titian's Sacred and Profane Love: Individuality and Sexuality in a Renaissance Marriage Picture," in *Titian 500*, p. 131. The association of fountains with love is common from the Renaissance onward (and can be found often in Rubens' own work) and does not necessarily invite explicit sexual associations. In the case we are dealing with here, Rubens does seem to make a sexual reference, as suggested by the precedent provided by Titian's painting, by the subject matter of the work, and by the profuse and lustful representation of the fountain. There are many other works by Rubens and painters in his circle dealing with the issue of sexual desire where the presence of fountains can be interpreted in the same way, such as Rubens' *Susanna and the Elders*, Madrid, Real Academia de Bellas Artes de San Fernando; the *Cimon and Iphigenia*, Vienna, Kunsthistorisches Museum (in both of these paintings the fountain probably reproduces a fountain that was owned by Rubens, as noted by Held, 1980, 1:321–322, and Muller, 1989, p. 35); or Van Dyck's *Susanna and*

the Elders, Munich, Bayerische Staatsgemäldesammlungen – to cite only a few. For the association between fountains and themes of love, see Raimon van Marle, 1971, 2:429–445; and Watson, 1979, pp. 70–72. For similar associations in literature that was known to Rubens, see Goodman, 1992, p. 70.

100. For the decoration of this gallery, see Harris, 1960, p. 128, and Brown, 1986, pp. 242–243. For the location of Velázquez's studio, see Orso, 1986, p. 48.

101. For the contents of this gallery in 1666 (which in addition to the paintings mentioned also included less secure attributions to Leonardo da Vinci, Titian, Veronese, Lanfranco, Van Dyck, and others), see Orso, 1993, pp. 146–148 and 162–169 (with a transcription of the 1666 inventory of the gallery).

102. For the copies after the Torre de la Parada paintings, see the catalogue entries in Alpers, 1971. For the copies by Mazo after other paintings, see Bottineau, nos. 917–922. See also Díaz Padrón, 1995, pp. 1128–1133, 1136–1137, 1142–1143, 1152–1155, 1158–1159, and 1164–1169, with large reproductions of some of Mazo's copies. The inventories of the Alcázar include numerous paintings described as copies after Rubens by Mazo, many of which, judging from the descriptions, are probably copies after paintings by Snyders, Paul de Vos, or others, but not Rubens (e.g., Bottineau, nos. 905–911, 912–916, 934–936).

103. For Mazo, see Gaya Nuño, in *Varia Velazqueña*, 1:471–481, and Cherry, 1990.

104. See Orso, 1986, p. 156.

105. For the small copies, see Cherry, 1990, pp. 515, n. 22, 524, nos. 38, 41.

106. See Pacheco's text in Appendix 1. Pacheco's statement refers to the paintings in the Medici cycle.

107. For the arts in Spain during the fifteenth century, see Yarza, 1993. For the sixteenth century, see Checa, 1983; Marías, 1989; Brown, 1991, pp. 9–67; and Checa, 1992.

108. For Mor, see Friedländer, 1975; for Van den Wyngaerde, see Kagan, ed., 1989. For Philip II as a collector of Titian, see Checa, 1994.

109. This phrase is taken from Goodman, 1992, p. 48.

110. For examples of the ideal of beauty in Spain during Rubens' time, see Bomli, 1950. María del Carmen Simón Palmer, "La Higiene y la Medicina de la Mujer Española a traves de los libros (S. XVI a XIX)," in *Actas de las II Jornadas de Investigación Interdisciplinaria. La Mujer en la Historia de España (siglos XVI–XX)*, Madrid, 1984, ed. M. A. Durán, refers to efforts made by local women to make their hair blonder and their skin whiter, thus approximating the ideals set by contemporary taste. For some literary pieces that include descriptions conforming to these standards of beauty, see, among others, Góngora's 1582 poem "Mientras por competir con tu cabello" (in *Luis de Góngora. Poesía Selecta*, ed. A. Pérez and J. M. Micós [Madrid, 1991], p. 96); the works by Cervantes cited in Cotarelo y Valledor, 1905; María de Zayas' 1637 work "*El Prevenido Engañado*," in *Novelas Amorosas y Ejemplares* (Madrid, 1948: Real Academia Española, Biblioteca selecta de clásicos españoles); and Juan de Zabaleta's "Dia de Fiesta por la mañana" of 1654 (cited in Bomli, 1950, pp. 143–153). For a general treatment of the nude in painting in Spain, see also J. Portús, "Indecencia, mortificación y modos de ver," in Morán Turina and Portús Pérez, 1997, pp. 227–256.

111. See Portús, "Indecencia, mortificación y modos de ver," pp. 235–236.

112. For Philip IV's political ideology, see Stradling, 1988, p. 300. A useful overview of the political and cultural environment of Rubens' time can be found in Rabb, 1975.

113. For the arts under Charles II, see Brown, 1989, pp. 285–306. For the political history of the period, see Kamen, 1980, and Molas Ribalta et al., 1993.

114. For the paintings sent by the queen to her brother from Madrid, see T. Levin, 1904–1911.
115. The sketch, described as a "Boceto de Rubens," is included among a list of paintings purchased by the Elector Palatine that accompanied a letter written by Wisser, the queen's personal secretary, to Johan Wilhelm on October 16, 1694 (see in Baviera and Maura, 1927–1935, 2:254). This sketch has not been identified. The painting, also unidentified, is mentioned in three letters. A letter from Wisser to the Elector Palatine of September 3, 1694, refers to an unnamed painting by Rubens from the *cuarto del Rey* the queen had prepared for shipment to her brother: "It appears that Höffgens will leave next week, and he will take, in addition to the other paintings, a very pretty (*bonito*) one by Rubens, which the queen asked for from the king" (see in Baviera and Maura, 1927–1935, 2:239–240). On September 16, the queen wrote to her brother that she was sending through Höffgens: "three paintings by Jordaens and one by Rubens which hung in the king's room, a painting which she had not noticed earlier. When the shipment was ready and she did not imagine sending anything else, she noticed the painting, she unhung it, and she did not stop until she had gained permission from the king to give it as a gift. She hopes that this gift will show that she is a person of good taste." (This text is taken from the transcription in Baviera and Maura, 1927–1935, 2:240–241. In Herrero García, 1943, p. 83, the same letter is dated to September 10, 1694.) This is probably the same painting that the Elector Palatine refers to in a letter of October 1, 1694: "He is pleased that Hoeffgens will also bring him a pretty painting by Rubens." (Baviera and Maura, 1927–1935, 2:247.)
116. See in Herrero García, 1943, p. 88; the letter is also included in Baviera and Maura, 1927–1935, 3:92. There is a possibility that this is the same painting mentioned in the previous note, which was believed assured by the queen but may have later been retrieved by Charles II. That painting was said to be in the *cuarto del Rey*, which may refer to any of the rooms in the king's quarters, where the *Adoration* and many other paintings by Rubens hung (for the king's quarters, see Orso, 1986, pp. 17–24).
117. The 1686 Alcázar inventory is published in full in Bottineau. The 1700–1703 inventory is published in *Museo del Prado. Inventarios Reales*, 3 vols., 1975–1985.
118. For a summary of the 1686 Alcázar inventory, see Pérez Sánchez, in Checa, ed., 1994, pp. 182–187. The inventory included eight attributions to Dürer, seven to Leonardo da Vinci, three to Michelangelo, seven to Raphael, five to Correggio, seventy-six to Titian, forty-three to Tintoretto, twenty-nine to Veronese, twelve to Guido Reni, six to Luca Giordano, three to Poussin, six to Bosch, sixty-two to Rubens, nineteen to Van Dyck, thirty-eight to Jan Brueghel, eight to El Greco, forty-three to Velázquez, and thirty-six to Ribera – to mention only some of the most significant artists and numbers.
119. See Bottineau, no. 1484. For this painting, see also Vergara, 1994, vol. 2, pp. 211–212, no. A8.
120. See the 1700–1703 inventory in *Museo del Prado. Inventarios Reales*, vol. 2, no. 91, p. 140. According to a transcription of this inventory available in the library of the Prado Museum, it is a repetition of the Pardo 1674 inventory. The copy of the 1674 inventory of the Pardo that is available in the library of the museum lists this painting under no. 66. There is no other mention of this work.
121. For the *Calvary*, see the inventory in *Museo del Prado. Inventarios Reales*, vol. 2, no. 46, p. 200; for a later reference in the inventory of 1794, see Cruzada Villaamil, 1874, p. 310, no. 5. For the *Flagellation*, see the 1700–1703 inventory in *Museo del Prado. Inventarios Reales*, vol. 1, no. 24, p. 20; for later inventories where this scene is listed, see Cruzada Villaamil, 1874, pp. 310–311, no. 6, and Marqués de Saltillo, 1953, pp. 208–209.

122. For the use of the paintings as payment for debt, see Burke, 1984, 1:193–194, and 2:376.
123. In recent years this painting was attributed to Van Dyck in the Prado Museum, based on the opinion of Díaz Padrón; the painting has recently been restituted to Rubens by the same scholar; see Díaz Padrón, 1995, vol. 2, pp. 1072–1073, no. 1545.
124. For this painting, see Chap. 5, pp. 169, 178, and 180.
125. See De Poorter 1978, pp. 109–131, and Held, 1980, 1:139–166.
126. For an overview of collecting in Spain during this period, see Burke, 1984, vol. 1; Morán and Checa, 1985, pp. 283–306; Brown, 1989, pp. 197–211, and Brown, 1995, pp. 95–145. The study of collecting in Spain still presents problems. For the most part, the activities of collectors are recorded only at the times when their collections were inventoried, often after the owner's death, making it difficult to establish a definite chronology. It should be kept in mind that many paintings probably entered a collection long before they were first documented.
127. For 1630 Leganés inventory, see Volk, 1980a, pp. 266–267. This inventory shows that by that date Leganés only owned eighteen paintings.
128. For the paintings attributed to Rubens in the 1642 inventory of Leganés, see Volk, 1980, 1:267–268. The list published by Volk includes two paintings not attributed to Rubens, nos. 105 and 336. As will be seen below, the former (a *Devotion of Rudolf I*) is attributed to Wildens, not Rubens, while the later (an *Infant Jesus with the Infant Saint John and Two Angels, Playing with a Lamb*) is assigned to Rubens in a later inventory of Leganés.
129. This is the painting that was already owned by Leganés in 1630 (see Chap. 3).
130. For the Leganés inventory, see Volk, 1980a, p. 267, no. 38. For the painting, see Rooses, *L'Oeuvre*, 2:285; Vlieghe, 1979, p. 652, no. 1411; Ertz, 1979, p. 619; and Díaz Padrón, 1995, vol. 1., pp. 288–289, no. 1411.
131. It is possibly one of three extant versions in Prague, Národní Galerie, inv. no. 09688; Brunswick, Herzog Anton Ulrich-Museum, no. 85; and Saint Louis, Mo., City Art Museum, inv. no. 33.34 (see Vlieghe, 1987, pp. 183–187, nos. 147–150). For the inventory entry, see Volk, 1980a, p. 267, no. 61.
132. See Volk, 1980a, p. 267, no. 214; and, for the identification of the painting, Fredericksen, 1972, pp. 66–68, no. 83. This painting is largely a workshop product, probably finished by Rubens himself. Wildens may be the author of the landscape background and Snyders of the animals.
133. Volk, 1980a, p. 267, no. 264. For this painting, see also Goris and Held, 1947, p. 32, no. 41; Haverkamp Begemann, 1953, p. 75; and Held, 1980, vol. 1, pp. 441–442, no. 318.
134. For this and the following painting, see Volk, 1980a, p. 267, nos. 274–275. See also Vlieghe, 1972–1973, vol. 1, p. 132–133, nos. 86–87.
135. For the inventory, see Volk, 1980a, pp. 265–266, no. 326. For the painting, see also Vlieghe, 1987, pp. 74–75, no. 86.
136. Except where otherwise stated, none of the paintings listed below have been identified with any extant works, and therefore their present locations are not known. For the description of these paintings in the Leganés inventory of 1642, see Volk, 1980a, pp. 266–267, nos. 6, 7, 40, 70, 71, 223, 228, 267, 317, 325, 498.
137. There is a known, but now lost, painting by Rubens that matches the description of this work in the Leganés collection, which may be the same item (see Vlieghe, 1972–1973, vol. 2, pp. 118–120, no. 130).
138. The description of this scene in the Leganés inventory is similar to one of the types of Holy Families painted by Rubens (see Rooses, *L'Oeuvre*, vol. 1, p. 302, no. 228).
139. This is either a copy or a replica of a painting in the National Gallery in

Washington. For the Washington painting, which is larger in size and has a different provenance from the Leganés picture, see D'Hulst and Vandenven, 1989, pp. 187–192, no. 57.

140. Rubens painted a portrait of the infanta Isabella in 1625, a portrait now known through an engraving and three copies (see Vlieghe, 1987, pp. 119–123, nos. 109–112). The Leganés painting may be one of these, or a copy, or replica after them.

141. For the 1642 inventory listing, see Volk, 1980a, p. 268, no. 336. In 1655 it is described as "una pintura de bara y media de ancho y una de alto, de mano de Rubens, de nro señor con san Juan y dos angeles jugando con un cordero arrimado a una almuadilla blanca junto a un çestiillo de frutas, en tabla en . . . en 3.000 reales" ("a painting of one-and-one-half *varas* in width and one *vara* in height, by Rubens, of Our Lord with Saint John and two angels playing with a little lamb that is near a small white cushion and a small basket of flowers, on panel . . . in 3,000 *reales*"; AHPM, prot. 6267, fol. 599v; the transcription in López Navío, 1962, p. 284, no. 336, is incorrect). The description of this painting in the Leganés inventory is identical to a known work by Rubens (see Rooses, *L'Oeuvre*, vol. 1, p. 251, no. 186; vol. 5, p. 318, no. 186, and Rosenberg, 1909, p. 123).

142. This is the painting brought to Spain by the duke of Aarschot that was studied in the previous chapter.

143. A painting of the *Devotion of Rudolf I* in the 1642 Leganés inventory (see Volk, 1980a, p. 267, no. 105) is attributed to Wildens but is sometimes believed to be identical with the painting by Rubens now in the Prado that was mentioned in the previous chapter. This is unlikely, as the Prado painting is recorded in the royal collection in 1636 and thereafter.

144. See Volk, 1980a, pp. 263–264; and Koslow, 1995, pp. 346–347, n. 6.

145. See Volk, 1980a, pp. 258–259.

146. See Brown and Elliott, 1980, p. 268, n. 39.

147. Koslow, 1995, pp. 346–347. Arschot is the same figure who brought to Madrid the *Wolf and Fox Hunt* mentioned in the previous chapter.

148. The 1655 inventory of the Leganés collection is published in López Navío, 1962. His transcription includes some mistakes. The original inventory is in AHPM, leg. 6267; there are two identical inventories, one without prices, in fols. 425ff.; and one with prices, in fols. 548ff.

149. The description of this painting is identical to a Rubens painting known through versions in the Uffizi and the Hermitage (see Rooses, *L'Oeuvre*, vol. 3, pp. 60–61, no. 574, and Exhibition, Florence, 1977, p. 230, no. 98). It cannot be determined whether it is identical with one of those paintings or if it is a copy or replica of one of them.

150. The description in the inventory coincides with extant paintings by Rubens (see Liedtke, 1984, 1:140–146), but it is not known whether it can be identified with one of them, or if it is a copy or a replica after them.

151. This painting appears to repeat the painting made by Rubens for his funerary chapel, Antwerp, St. Jacobskerk (see Jaffé, 1989, p. 369, no. 1368), of which it may be a copy or a replica.

152. The item inventoried prior to this in the 1655 Leganés inventory is an unattributed portrait of the husband of Leonor de Guzmán, the count of Uceda and marquis of Loriana, Don Diego Mesia Obando. The attribution to Rubens of the portrait of the wife suggests that the portrait of the husband may also have been regarded as a Rubens.

153. Unless otherwise stated, the paintings here listed have not been identified. For the description of these paintings in the 1655 Leganés inventory, see Lopéz Navío, 1962, nos. 322, 1198–1199, 1210, 1233 1239, 1241, 1242, 1306, 1243, 448, 1237. Some of the transcriptions in López Navío include mistakes; for

the correct transcriptions, see the entries in Vergara, 1994, vol. 2, cat. nos. B28, B5–B6, B16, B2, B91, B92, B30, B80, B81, B39, B52.

154. López Navío, 1962, nos. 452 and 882.
155. Ibid., no. 33.
156. See ibid., pp. 265–266, and Volk, 1980a, p. 262, n. 35. Leganés' eldest son, Gaspar, of whom little is known, inherited the Leganés title from his father and must also have inherited the collection. During the final decades of the century the collection must have been owned by Diego Felípez de Guzmán Spinola, third marquis of Leganés and grandson of the man with whom we have been concerned here. Don Diego inherited the Leganés title in 1666 and carried it into the eighteenth century. He was a grandee of Castile and held posts as viceroy of Catalonia from 1684 to 1688 and viceroy of Milan in 1691. The Leganés collection is believed to have been inherited in the early eighteenth century by the eighth count of Altamira, who incorporated the Leganés title into his own.
157. For the gift of the portrait of Lerma to Enríquez de Cabrera, see Pescador del Hoyo, 1987, p. 151. For the history of the admiral himself, see Matías de Novoa, 1876; Elliott, 1986, p. 263; and Stradling, 1988, pp. 156, 159.
158. For the collection of the ninth admiral of Castile, see Fernández Duro, 1903, pp. 103ff., where the 1647 inventory is published. See also Burke, 1984, 1:86–92, and Morán and Checa, 1985, pp. 298–299.
159. Fernández Duro, 1903, p. 194, no. 161.
160. Ibid., p. 204, no. 415. A painting by Rubens of this subject is in Schleissheim (see Vlieghe, 1972–1973, vol. 2, pp. 107–108, no. 126). This may be a copy or replica of that scene.
161. Fernández Duro, 1903, p. 202, no. 379. This scene is probably identical to a painting in London, Dulwich College Picture Gallery (see Exhibition, Antwerp, 1977, p. 233, no. 100). It is not known if they are the same work.
162. Fernández Duro, 1903, p. 211.
163. As is suggested by Burke, 1984, 1:86–87.
164. For Hopton's letter, see Brown and Elliott, 1980, p. 115; for Carducho's mention of the admiral of Castile, see Carducho, ed., 1979, p. 417.
165. In the collection of the admiral of Castile, which included close to 1,000 paintings, prices of over 1,000 *reales* approximately are reserved for works attributed to well-known artists (see Fernández Duro, 1903, pp. 188–210). The great majority of the items inventoried are valued below that price. Paintings attributed to Titian reach 5,500 *reales*, and works by other painters such as Van Dyck and Guercino are in the 3,000 range. The two most expensive paintings in the inventory are two works by Ribera valued at 7,700 and 6,000 *reales* (these are the only paintings that are more valuable than Rubens' portrait of Lerma).
166. For the admiral of Castile as a collector, see Vergara, 1995, with further references.
167. See Vergara, 1995, pp. 35, 36–38.
168. There are, however, other paintings of the same subject and with the same support that are stylistically close to Rubens (see Wood, 1995, pp. 21–22). This does not allow for certainty in identifying the references to the painting in the collection of the admiral with the ones in Rubens' collection.
169. For the London painting, see Martin, 1970, pp. 163–170, no. 278.
170. For Luis de Haro as a collector, see Burke, 1984, 1:101–124; Brown, 1986, pp. 210–213; and Brown, 1995, pp. 69–87, 95, 134–138. The inventory of the collection of 1661 is only partially known through an incomplete and later copy (see Burke, 1984, 2:194–206, who has studied the available documents and has come to the conclusion that they can be accepted as at least a fragment of the 1661 inventory). For Haro's political career, see also Stradling, 1988, pp. 246–268.

171. Prado, inv. no. 1640. For the purchase of this painting, see Vergara, 1989, pp. 128, 130, no. 14. For the history of this painting, see also Vergara, 1994, vol. 2, cat. no. A103; and n. 20 in this chapter.

172. This painting is mentioned in the correspondence between Haro and Cárdenas of January 21, 1651 (original document in Madrid, Archivo de la Casa de Alba, caja no. 182–166), and is documented as having been purchased by Cárdenas on October 20, 1651 (Madrid, Archivo de la Casa de Alba, caja no. 182–175). For the purchase of this painting, see Burke, 1984, 2: 153. See also Vergara, 1994, vol. 2. cat. no. B64.

173. Purchased for Haro by Alonso de Cárdenas. At the time of the purchase it was described as "la paz y la abundancia," 2 1/3 × 3 1/2 *varas*, attributed to Rubens, and painted on canvas. This information is taken from Burke, 1984, 2: 162ff., and 167, no. 34; see also Brown, 1995, p. 81. The more detailed description transcribed in the text is taken from a 1687 inventory of the collection of Haro's son, Gaspar de Haro (Burke and Cherry, forthcoming; earlier included in Burke, 1984, 2: 259; the original document is in AHPM, prot. 9819, fol. 777). The *Abundance* in the collection of Luis de Haro was inherited by Luis' son Gaspar, and sold in 1695 to an unidentified Antonio Ordóñez (see Saltillo, 1953, p. 238).

174. The identification of this painting with the *Peace and War* was suggested to me by Jonathan Brown. A similar description of the *Peace and War* is recorded when it was in the Doria collection in Genoa in the eighteenth century, listed as "Family of Rubens" (see Rooses, *L'Oeuvre*, 4: 46). For the *Peace and War*, see Martin, 1970, no. 46, pp. 116–126, and also Rosenthal, 1989.

175. Washington D.C., National Gallery of Art. For this painting, see Stechow, 1973, and Huemer, 1977, pp. 95–98, 120–127.

176. The dimensions of the painting when it is first documented in the Haro collection are 2 1/3 × 3 1/3 *varas*, or approximately 196 cm high by 294 cm wide. The canvas in the National Gallery measures 203 × 298 cm.

177. For the collecting activities of Gaspar de Haro, see Pita Andrade, 1952; Burke, 1984, 1: 131–201; and Brown, 1995, pp. 138–139.

178. For the 1651 inventory, see Pita Andrade, 1952, pp. 223–236; and Burke, 1984, 2: 212–230. This inventory was probably done on the occasion of the separation of Gaspar de Haro's finances from those of his wife, doña María Antonia de la Cerda.

179. I am grateful to Maria Gilbert, from the Provenance Index, the Getty Art History Information Program, for sharing this information with me. It will be published in Burke and Cherry, forthcoming. The painting in the Getty Museum is inscribed with the number 146 in white paint on the lower right-hand corner. This number coincides with the number of this picture in the 1651 Carpio inventory. As suggested by Maria Gilbert, the discrepancies between the dimensions of the paintings in the 1651 Haro inventory (approx. 21 × 112 cm) and the canvas in the Getty (131 × 130.2 cm) may be explained as resulting from a mistake made in the transcription of the dimensions in the Haro inventory (where the height was probably meant to read one *vara* and one-fourth, and not one-fourth of one *vara*). For the Getty painting, see Rooses, *L'Oeuvre*, 2: 134, and *Getty Museum Journal*, vol. 22 (1994), p. 75, no. 24.

180. Letter written by Don Esteban Carrillo; see in Pita Andrade, 1952, p. 224.

181. See Burke, 1984, 1: 150, which includes the quote from Harrach and an explanation of the nature and circumstances of the collection of Gaspar de Haro at that point.

182. For these copies, see the inventory of the collection that will soon be published by the Getty Provenance Index, and Vergara, 1994, 1: 152, n. 67.

183. The inventory is transcribed in Burke and Cherry, forthcoming; original document in AHPM, prot. 9819 (there is a transcription in Burke, 1984, vol. 2,

doc. 4.8, pp. 251–271). The paintings were appraised by the painters Claudio Coello and José Donoso.

184. That only two of the seven paintings attributed to Rubens in 1651 remained there at this point suggests that at least some of the others may have been copies.

185. "A painting of Our Lady with the child Jesus asleep, with Saint Anne and Saint Joseph, original by Rubens, two-and-one-fourth *varas* in height and two *varas* minus one-fourth in width, with a frame, in six hundred ducats" (transcription from Burke and Cherry, forthcoming; included earlier in Burke, 1984, vol. 2, doc. 4.8, p. 252i, no. 142; the original inventory is in AHPM, prot. 9819, fol. 1016). There is no other notice of this item. The description coincides with a *Virgin with the Child Christ Asleep, Saint John, and Saint Anne* in Raleigh, North Carolina Museum of Art, of uncertain provenance (see Exhibition, Antwerp, 1977, p. 209, no. 89, and Held 1980, 1:508). According to Burchard (cited in Held, 1980, 1:507–508), the painting in Raleigh was executed for the convent of the Descalzas Reales in Madrid, but this is not certain.

186. For this painting, see the reference cited in n. 121 in this chapter.

187. "A Saint Jesus Christ crucified with a skull by the foot of the cross and the city of Jerusalem in the background, original by Rubens, with a gilt engraved frame, over one *vara* in height, and one *vara* minus one-third in width, in two thousand *reales*" (the painting is in the "room behind the Sacristy"; transcription taken from Burke and Cherry, forthcoming; earlier included in Burke, 1984, vol. 2, p. 252L, no. 208; original document in AHPM, prot. 9819, fol. 1020v).

188. "A landscape painting of Jacob's Ladder, of a *vara* (*de vara*), by Rubens, in two thousand seven hundred and fifty *reales*" (transcription from database Burke and Cherry, forthcoming; earlier included in Burke, 1984, vol. 2, p. 262, no. +1; see original in AHPM, prot. 9819, fol. 1043v).

189. "In the ceiling of this room, a canvas of a queen who is fed poison, original by Peter Paul Rubens, in three thousand *reales*" (transcription from Burke and Cherry, forthcoming; earlier included in Burke, 1984, vol. 2, p. 252r, no. 310; the original is in AHPM, prot. 9819, fol. 1029–767v).

190. "A canvas of Charity with four children and a small dog, original by Rubens, in four thousand *reales*" (transcription from Burke and Cherry, forthcoming. Earlier included in Burke, 1984, vol. 2, p. 252r, no. 311; original document in AHPM, prot. 9819, fols. 1028v and 767v). The description of the scene is similar to a painting in Pommersfelden, Graf von Schönbornsche Kunstsammlungen, *Charity* (see Rooses, *L'Oeuvre*, vol. 4, pp. 41–42, no. 822).

191. "Another canvas of bersabe [*sic*] and a woman who combs her hair, with an arm placed over a fountain, and a black child who brings to her a paper, and a dog in the bottom, original by Rubens, in four thousand *reales*" (transcription from Burke and Cherry forthcoming; earlier partially reproduced in Burke, 1984, 2:52r; original document in AHPM, prot. 9819, fol. 1029v, and 767v). The description is identical to a well-known painting by Rubens in Dresden, Gemäldegalerie (see Rooses, *L'Oeuvre*, vol. 1, pp. 149–150, no. 121).

192. "A painting of the same size as the previous one [one-and-one-half *varas* x one *vara* +] of a man from Moscow, with a Gold Chain and a Golden Key, Dressed in Blue, with a Golden Cape Lined in Fur, and a Cap on his Head also lined, original by Peter Paul Rubens, with a gilt and engraved frame, in three thousand *reales*" (transcription from database Burke and Cherry, forthcoming; earlier partially reproduced in Burke, 1984, vol. 2, p. 256, no. 383; see original in AHPM, prot. 9819, fol. 1034v).

193. "A portrait of the cardinal-infante in half-length, original by Rubens, of one

vara minus one-sixth in height, and one-sixth in width, with a black frame, in fifty ducats" (transcription from database, Burke and Cherry, forthcoming; earlier partially reproduced in Burke, 1984, 2:254; original in AHPM, prot. 9819, fol. 1032).

194. "A small painting on panel (*Vn quadritto En lamina*) of the Triumph of Peace, with two men with their hands tied behind by the spoils of war, original by Rubens, of little more than half a *vara* in height and one-and-one-sixth *varas* in width, with a gilded and engraved frame, in two thousand *reales*" (transcription from Burke and Cherry, forthcoming. Partially reproduced earlier in Burke, 1984, vol. 2, p. 258, no. 620; for the original, see AHPM, prot. 9819, fol. 1037v). The description suggests that this small panel is probably identical to a scene of *Two Captive Soldiers* in a private collection in Wedellsborg; see in Held, 1980, vol. 1, pp. 365–366, vol. 2, fig. 264.

195. "A painting for over a door (*quadro sobrepuertta*) of Neptune with some women in a chariot and horses. With ships where the Cardinal-Infante made his passage to Milan, original by Rubens, three *varas* in height and three *varas* and two-thirds in width, black frame, in sixteen thousand five hundred *reales*." (Notice the high price of the painting; transcription from database Burke and Cherry, forthcoming; earlier included in Burke, 1984, vol. 2, p. 260, no. 465; for the original document, see AHPM, prot. 9819, fol. 1040.) The scene depicted is identical to the scene of *Voyage of the Prince from Barcelona to Genoa* designed by Rubens for the *Pompa Introitus Ferdinandi* (see J. Rupert Martin, 1972, pp. 49–55, no. 3). It may be a replica of that painting rather than the original, which is more likely identified with a picture now in Dresden.

196. These *modelli* are recorded for the first time in a list of paintings sold from the estate of Gaspar de Haro between 1689 and 1691 (see De Poorter, 1978, pp. 109–131, and Held, 1980, 1:139–166). This is the first time that these *modelli* are recorded in Spain, but it is not impossible that, as occurred with other pictures, they were inherited by Gaspar de Haro from his father, Luis de Haro.

197. According to a document published in Pita Andrade, 1952, p. 229, n. 12, which states that on January 24, 1691, Don Isidro de Camargo (who was representing Doña Catalina de Haro y Guzmán in the affairs relating to the estate of her husband, Gaspar de Haro, as shown in Burke, 1984, 2: 369) paid Don Pedro de Oreytia Vergara for the remittance of "eleven drawings on paper, originals by Rubens, of the nineteen that he is documented to have sent from Flanders to Your Excellency. Their cost was one hundred twenty-six and one-half *pesos*." This apparently means that on an unspecified date Oreytia Vergara had sent nineteen drawings by Rubens from Flanders to Gaspar de Haro, and that he was now receiving payment for eleven of them.

198. The painting is described as: "A painting that represents the Virgin caressing the child Jesus, by Peter Paul Rubens, which measures half a palm, with its ebony frame, gilt borders, in 50." (See the document where this painting is cited, in the transcription from Burke and Cherry, forthcoming; included earlier in Burke, 1984, vol. 2, p. 312, no. 1037.)

199. For the chronology of Haro's collection, see Burke, 1984, 1:141–173.

200. See Cuvelier and Lefèvre, 4:541–546, 635, for letters that date the beginning and the end of Juan José de Austria's tenure in Brussels. For Juan José de Austria, see Maura Gomazo, 1954; Stradling, 1988, pp. 243, 328–330; and "The Problem of Don Juan José," in Greer, 1991. It is not certain that Don Juan José was the son of Philip IV, and many at the time believed him to be the son of the king's friend Medina de las Torres, who had shared Philip's passion for the child's mother, the actress María Inés Calderón (for this matter, see Stradling, 1988, pp. 328–330).

201. The inventory is published in Barrio Moya, 1991, pp. 335–352. The original is in AHPM, prot. 12945.
202. "Another large painting, original by Rubens, of a *Bodegón*, with its frame, 2.200 *reales*" (see in Barrio Moya, 1991, p. 337).
203. "Another painting, on panel, original by Rubens, of the god Bacchus, with its black frame, 1200 *reales*" (see in Barrio Moya, 1991, p. 338).
204. "Another small painting, on panel, of a head, original by Rubens, with its small black frame with gilt borders, 220 *reales*" (Barrio Moya, 1991, p. 341).
205. "Another painting on panel with its black frame, when Jacob found his brother Saul, original by Rubens, 1200 *reales*" (Barrio Moya, 1991, p. 341). The description of this work indicates that it may be similar to the version of the same subject that was among the eight items brought by Rubens to Spain in 1628. The fact that it is painted on panel suggests that it may have been a sketch for that painting (for the sketch, see Held, 1980, vol. 1, pp. 427–429, no. 310).
206. "One painting copy after Rubens, large, which shows the tigers, with its black frame, 880 *reales*" (Barrio Moya, 1991, p. 337).
207. For a summary of the careers of Francisco Rizi and Juan Carreño de Miranda, see Brown, 1991, pp. 231–239, 289–292.
208. As documented in De Maeyer, 1955, pp. 433–435. This painting may also be identical to an item listed in Rubens' estate (it may be number 91 in the *Specification*: "A Bacchus," "Vn Bacchus auec la tasse à la main"; see Muller, 1989, p. 113, no. 91). It may have been purchased there for the governor's palace in Brussels.
209. For records of works attributed to Rubens in Spain after 1640, in addition to those which will be mentioned below, see Vergara, 1994, vol. 2, nos. B3, B10, B25, B87, B98, B99, B100. See also García Chico, 1946, p. 393, and Burke, 1984, 2: 57.
210. For Fernando de Borja, see Alvarez Baena, 1789–1791, 2: 53–55.
211. They are described as: " "Another of a descent from the cross, small, of three quarters, with no frame, by Rubens, valued in fifty *reales*"; and "Another of the same size, of Saint Peter and two angels, by Rubens, in fifty *reales*" (transcribed in Burke and Cherry, forthcoming). I owe my knowledge of this collection to Burke and Cherry, forthcoming, where the inventory will be published.
212. "A painting of the Judgment of Solomon by Rubens in one thousand one hundred *reales*" (taken from Burke and Cherry, forthcoming).
213. See Cuvelier and Lefèvre, 4: 686, 742, 781, 781, and 5: 83.
214. See Cuvelier and Lefèvre, 3: 35, 89, 225, 437, 538, 583; 4: 315, 633–634; 5: 102, 136, 192, 194, 198; 6: 586.
215. "Another painting of Judith by Peter Paul Rubens, of seven-fourths in width and one-and-one-half *varas* in height, with its gilt and engraved frame, of a woman, it is of *mayorazgo (de una mujer es de mayorazgo)*" (transcription taken from Burke and Cherry, forthcoming).
216. See in Agulló Cobo, 1981, p. 55. The collection was appraised by the royal painter Juan Carreño de Miranda, who was in a position to make trustworthy attributions.
217. The sketches are described as: "Three paintings, *vorrones* by Rubens, of one *vara* more or less, one of the Holy Trinity = another of the Baptism of Christ = and the other, which is a bit larger, of the Adoration of the Magi" (see in Agulló Cobo, 1978, p. 61; for the copy, see Agulló Cobo, 1978, p. 62).
218. For Felipe Diricksen, see Angulo and Pérez Sánchez, 1969, pp. 338–348.
219. "A hunt, with large figures of life size, copied from one by Rubens, five *varas* in length, 2,000 *reales*" (see in Burke and Cherry, forthcoming). For the trial, see Gascón de Torquemada, ed., 1991, p. 327.
220. "Five paintings, copies after Rubens. Four are the same, all large, and the

other is much wider, almost twice as the previous ones. One shows Hercules; another Romulus and Remus; another Ganymede; another the head of Cirus, and the large one a Satyr. They are valued in twenty [*beynta*] ducats each; 1650" (taken from Burke and Cherry, forthcoming).

221. See Balis, 1986, p. 222. The document is published in Denucé, 1949, p. 275.
222. For notices of copies of paintings by Rubens in seventeenth-century Spain (where the originals are not recorded in Spain), see Agulló Cobo, 1981, pp. 89 and 217; Burke and Cherry, forthcoming (see the sections devoted to the collections of Juan de Castañeda; of Pedro de Portocarrero, count of Medellín; and of Juan de Echauz); Pérez Sánchez, 1977, pp. 86–109, and Freedberg, 1984, p. 47, n. 1.
223. For these copies by Coello, see Saltillo, 1953, pp. 200–201 (they are also cited in De Poorter, 1978, 1: 224). For Coello's collection of paintings, see Sullivan, 1986, pp. 272–275 (the copies after Rubens are listed as nos. 157–167).
224. See Agulló Cobo, 1981, p. 211. The Spanish shopkeepers state that they have received "different prints and papers (*estampas y papeles*) of Rubens and Van Dyck, and others where there is a gallery made by the said Rubens with the Twelve Emperors of the House of Austria, and three hundred pieces of Miracles of Saint Dominic; and thirteen thousand in *oauo y quarto* [?] of different saints; and another two thousand of one *folio*, one thousand of them of Our Lord Jesus, and the other one thousand of different saints = And another two thousand five hundred prints of *boutatos* vellum = And another five thousand two hundred and thirty two vellum prints by different authors and saints = And one thousand one hundred small booklets for mass [*librillos de Misterio de la Missa*] with red covers = And other different pieces, prints and papers of Rubens (*pieças, estampas y papeles de Rubens*), some fine and some ordinary, some large, some of medium size, of saints, and of landscapes; some to learn how to paint, and others different. . . ."
225. *El Criticón* (originally published in two parts in 1651 and 1653; ed. Madrid, 1960, *Baltasar Gracián. Obras Completas*, p. 854).
226. The tapestries owned by the admiral of Castile that are said in the inventories to be based on designs by Rubens are a history of "Pablo Milio," and two sets of eight tapestries described as *The History of Alexander* and *The History of Achilles* (see Fernández Duro, 1903, pp. 185–186, and Haverkamp Begemann, 1975, pp. 82ff.). For the mention of the tapestries owned by Haro, see Goldberg, 1992b, p. 106.
227. See in Burke, 1984, 2: 102.
228. For Arce as a collector, see Burke, 1984, chap. 5. These tapestries were not attributed, but the subject matter suggests that they were executed after designs by Rubens (for the tapestries, see Burke, 1984, 2: 475).
229. See Artiles Rodríguez, 1928, p. 84.
230. See Haverkamp Begemann, 1975, pp. 83–84. None of these sets are recorded in Spain, but it is probable that they were taken there when their owners returned to their country of origin.
231. Among the many documents that show this is one mentioned earlier in this chapter. The list of purchases made by the count of Fuesaldaña after the English Civil War shows that ten tapestries cost the same as 44 important paintings (by Titian and Rubens, among others). For this purchase, see the document published in Vergara, 1989. For the relative worth of paintings versus tapestries, see also the comments in Brown, 1995, pp. 228–229.
232. Letter to Sir Dudley Carleton; Magurn, 1955, pp. 67–68.
233. For Palomino's treatise, see Palomino, ed., 1987, with an introductory study by N. A. Mallory.
234. Palomino, ed., 1987, p. 104.
235. The summary of the 1686 inventory of the Alcázar shown in n. 118 offers a

good indication of the number of Rubens paintings that could be seen in the court near the end of the century, relative to other artists.

236. From *Obras Completas*, ed. A. Valbuena (Madrid, 1952), 3: 234. (I have taken this quote from Morán Turina and Portús Pérez, 1997, p. 269.)

Appendix 1

1. An earlier English translation of part of the text reproduced here appeared in Aureliano de Beruete, *Velázquez*, London, 1906), which is translated, not from the Spanish original, but from a French version.
2. Pacheco's text is one of the earliest accounts of the life of Rubens, along with Giulio Mancini's *Considerzioni sulla pittura*, ca. 1621 (ed. A Marucchi, 2 vols., Rome, 1956–1957), and Giovanni Baglione's *Le Vite de' pittori*, published in Rome in 1642.

Selected Bibliography

Adler, W. *Landscapes*, I. *Corpus Rubenianum Ludwig Burchard*, part 18. London, 1982.

Aedo y Gallart, D. *Viaje del Infante Cardenal Don Fernando de Austria, desde el 12 de Abril de 1632 . . . hasta 1634*. Antwerp, 1635.

Agulló Cobo, M. *Noticias sobre pintores madrileños de los siglos XVI y XVII*. Granada, 1978.

Más noticias sobre pintores madrileños de los siglos XVI al XVIII. Madrid, 1981.

Alcalá, L. E. *The Painting Collection of the Tenth Admiral of Castile; His House-Museum and Its Spanish Paintings*. Qualifying paper for the Master's degree, New York University, Institute of Fine Arts, 1992.

Alcalá Zamora y Queipo de Llano, J. *España, Flandes y el mar del Norte, 1618–1639*. Barcelona, 1975.

Alciati, A. *Andreae Alciati emblematum flumen abundans*. Ed. Henry Green. The Holbein Society's Facsimile Reprints. London, 1872.

Aldana Fernández, S. "Rubens en España y el programa iconográfico de la Torre de la Parada." *Archivo de Arte Valenciano* 49 (1978): 82–95.

Allende Salazar, J., and Sánchez Cantón, F. J. *Retratos del Museo del Prado*. Madrid, 1919.

Alpers, S. *The Decoration of the Torre de la Parada*. *Corpus Rubenianum Ludwig Burchard*, part 9. Brussels, 1971.

Alvarez y Baena, J. A. *Hijos ilustres de Madrid*. 4 vols. 1789–1791 (reprinted in Madrid, 1972–1973).

Anderson, R. M. "The Golilla: A Spanish Collar of the 17th Century." *Waffen und Kostümkunde* 2 (1969): 1–19 (reprinted in New York: Hispanic Society, 1969).

Angulo, D. *Murillo. Su vida, su arte, su obra*. 3 vols. Madrid, 1981.

Angulo, D., and Pérez Sánchez, A. E. *Pintura madrileña del primer tercio del siglo XVII*. Madrid, 1969.

Aparicio Fernández, C. *Obras restauradas de Thomas Willeboirts Bosschaert*. 1988.

Appleby, J.; Hunt, L.; and Jacob, M. *Telling the Truth about History*. New York and London, 1994.

Artiles Rodríguez, J. "Una rica colección artística en Madrid (siglo XVII)." *Revista de la Biblioteca, Archivo y Museo del Ayuntamiento de Madrid* 17 (1928): 83–87.

Auwera, J. "The Artistic Relationship between Abraham Janssen and Peter Paul Rubens. Some Contextual Evidence." *Studien zur niederländischen Kunst: Festschrift für Prof. Dr. Justus Müller Hofstede/ Wallraf Richartz Jahrbuch* 55 (1994): pp. 227–238.

Azcárate, J. M. "Noticias sobre Velázquez en la Corte." *Archivo Español de Arte*. 132 (1960): 357–385.

Baglione, G. *Le vite de pittori, scultori et architetti . . . .* Rome, 1642.

Baldinucci, F. *Delle Notizie de' professori del disegno . . . .* Florence, 1681.

Balis, A. *Hunting Scenes*, II. *Corpus Rubenianum Ludwig Burchard*, part 18. London, 1986.

Barbeito, J. M. *El Alcázar de Madrid*. Madrid, 1992.

Barrio Moya, J. L. "Don Juan de Austria y sus donaciones a iglesias manchegas. Nuevas aportaciones." *Cuadernos de Estudios Manchegos*. Offprint 20, n.d. (1991): 335–352.

Basan, F. *Catalogue des estampes gravées d'après P. P. Rubens*. 1767.

Baschet, A. "Pierre-Paul Rubens. Peintre de Vincent Ier de Gonzague duc de Mantoue (1600–1608). Son séjour en Italie et son premier voyage en Espagne." *Gazette des Beaux-Arts* 21 (1866): 401–452.

"Pierre Paul Rubens. Rubens revient d'Espagne á Mantoue (1604–1606)." *Gazette des Beaux-Arts* 22 (1867): 305ff.

Baudouin, F. "Altars and Altarpieces before 1620." *Rubens before 1620*. Ed. J. R. Martin. Princeton, N.J., 1972.

Pietro Paolo Rubens. New York, 1977.

Baumstark, R. "The Decius Mus Cycle of Tapestries at Valduz." *The Ringling Museum of Art Journal* (1983): 178–191.

Baviera, Principe Adalberto de, and Maura, G. *Documentos inéditos referentes a las postrimerías de la Casa de Austria en España*. 5 vols. Madrid, 1927–1935.

Belkin, K. *The Costume Book*. *Corpus Rubenianum Ludwig Burchard*, part 24. Brussels, 1978.

Bellori, G. P. *Le vite de' pittori, scultori e architetti moderni*. Rome, 1672.

Bennassar, B. *The Spanish Character: Attitudes and Mentalities from the Sixteenth to the Nineteenth Century*. Berkeley and London, 1979.

Bermejo, E. "Bartolomé Zúmbigo, arquitecto del siglo XVII." *Archivo Español de Arte* 107 (1954): 291–302.

Beroqui, P. "Adiciones y correcciones al Catálogo del Museo del Prado. III.

Escuela flamenca." *Boletín de la Sociedad Castellana de Excursiones* 171–181 (1917–1918). Offprint.

"Apuntes para la Historia del Museo del Prado." *Boletín de la Sociedad Española de Excursiones* 38 (1930): 112–127.

Tiziano en el Museo del Prado. Madrid, 1946.

Blum, S. N. *Early Netherlandish Triptychs: A Study in Patronage*. Berkeley, 1969.

Bodart, D. *Rubens e l'incisione nelle collezioni del Gabinetto Nazionale delle Stampe*. Rome, 1977.

Bomli, P. W. *La Femme dans l'Espagne du Siècle d'Or*. The Hague, 1950.

Bonnaffé, E. "Notes sur les collections des Richelieu." *Gazette des Beaux-Arts* 26 (1882): 5–112.

"Rubens et le Médaller de Ch. De Croy." *Bulletin-Rubens* 2 (1883): 212–217.

Bottineau, Y. "L'Alcázar de Madrid et l'inventaire de 1686." *Bulletin Hispanique* 58 (1956): 421–452; 60 (1958): 30–61, 145–179, 289–326, 450–483. Cited in this study as Bottineau.

L'Art de cour dans l'Espagne de Philippe V, 1700–1746. Bordeaux, 1962.

Brown, C. *The Drawings of Anthony Van Dyck*. The Pierpont Morgan Library. New York, 1991.

Brown, J. "On the Origin of Las Lanzas by Velázquez." *Zeitschrift für Kunstgeschichte* 27 (1964): 240–245.

"A Portrait Drawing by Velázquez." *Master Drawings* 14 (1976): 46–51.

Images and Ideas in Seventeenth-Century Spanish Painting. Princeton Essays on the Arts, no. 6. Princeton, N.J., 1978.

"Mecenas y coleccionistas españoles de Jusepe de Ribera." *Goya* 183 (1984): 140–150.

Velázquez. Painter and Courtier. New Haven, Conn., 1986.

The Golden Age of Painting in Spain. New Haven, Conn., 1991.

"Der Spanische Hof und die Flämische Malerei." In *Von Brueghel bis Rubens. Das goldene Jahrhundert der flämischen Malerei*. Vienna and Cologne, 1992.

Kings and Connoisseurs. Collecting Art in Seventeenth-Century Europe. The A. W. Mellon Lectures in the Fine Arts, 1994, The National Gallery of Art, Washington, D.C. Bollingen Series XXXV:43. Princeton, N.J., 1995.

Brown, J., and Elliott, J. H. *A Palace for a King: The Buen Retiro and the Court of Philip IV*. New Haven, Conn., 1980.

Brown, J., et al. *El Greco of Toledo*. Boston, 1982.

Burchard, L., and d'Hulst, R.-A. *Rubens Drawings*. 2 vols. Brussels, 1963.

Burchard, W. "The 'Garden of Love' by Rubens." *Burlington Magazine* 105 (1963): 428–432.

Burke, M. *Private Collections of Italian Art in Seventeenth-Century Spain*. 2 vols. Ph.D diss., New York University, 1984.

"Paintings by Ribera in the Collection of the Duque de Medina de las Torres." *Burlington Magazine* 131 (1989): 132–135.

Burke, M., and Cherry, P. *Documents for the History of Collecting: Spanish Inventories 1. Collecting in Madrid in the 17th and 18th Centuries*. The Getty Provenance Index. Los Angeles, 1998. (Herein cited as Burke and Cherry, forthcoming.)

Cabrera de Córdoba, L. *Relaciones de las cosas sucedidas en la Corte de España desde 1599 hasta 1614*. Madrid, 1857.

Calvo Serraller, F. *La teoría de la pintura en el Siglo de Oro*. Madrid, 1981.

Carducho, V. *Dialogos de la pintura*. Ed. Francisco Calvo Serraller. Madrid, 1979.

Carrete Parrondo, J. "Una pintura de Rubens grabada por Manuel Salvador Carmona." *Goya* 140–141 (1977): 140.

Carrete Parrondo, J.; Checa Cremades, F.; and Bozal, V. *Grabado en España (siglos XV al XVIII). Summa Artis* 31. Madrid, 1988.

Cavalli-Björkman, G., ed. *Bacchanals by Titian and Rubens. Papers Given at a Symposium in Nationalmuseum, Stockholm, March 18–19, 1987. Nationalmusei Skriftserie n.s. 10*. Stockholm, 1987.

"Rubens and Titian." *Nationalmuseum Bulletin* (Stockholm) 11 (1987): 101–113.

Ceán Bermúdez, J. A. *Diccionario histórico de los más ilustres profesores de las bellas artes en España*. 6 vols. Madrid, 1800.

Chapman, H. P. *Rembrandt's Self-Portraits. A Study in Seventeenth-Century Identity*. Princeton, N.J., 1990.

Checa, F. *Pintura y escultura del Renacimiento en España, 1450–1600*. Madrid, 1983.

"Monasterio de las Descalzas Reales: Origenes de su colección artística." *Reales Sitios* 102 (1989): 21–30.

Felipe II. Mecenas de las artes. Madrid, 1992.

Tiziano y la monarquía hispánica. Madrid, 1994.

Checa, F., ed. *El real Alcázar de Madrid. Dos siglos de arquitectura y coleccionismo en la corte de los reyes de España*. Madrid, 1994.

Cherry, P. "La intervención de Juan Bautista Crescenzi y las pinturas de Antonio de Pereda en un retablo perdido (1634)." *Archivo Español de Arte*, 239 (1987): 299–305.

"Juan Bautista Martínez del Mazo, Viudo de Francisca Velázquez (1653)." *Archivo Español de Arte* 252 (1990): 511–527.

Chiappelli, F., ed. *First Images of America: The Impact of the New World on the Old*. 2 vols. Berkeley, Los Angeles, and London, 1976.

Clark, K. *The Drawings of Leonardo da Vinci in the Collection of Her Majesty the Queen at Windsor Castle*. Revised by Carlo Pedretti. London, 1968.

Connors, J. "Borromini and the Marchese di Castel Rodrigo." *Burlington Magazine* 133 (1991): 434–440.

Cotarelo y Valledor, A. *La belleza femenina en las obras de Cervantes*. Santiago, Chile, 1905.

Covarrubias Orozco, S. *Emblemas morales*. Madrid, 1610.

Tesoro de la lengua castellana o española. Madrid, 1611 (Barcelona, 1943).

Cruzada Villaamil, G. *Rubens diplomático español*. Madrid, 1874.

Anales de la vida y de las obras de Diego de Silva y Velázquez. Madrid, 1885.

Cuvelier, J., and Lefèvre, J. *Correspondance de la cour d'Espagne sur les affaires des Pays-Bas au XVIIe siècle*. Vols. 2 (1927), 3 (1930), 4 (1933), 5 (1935), 6 (1937). Brussels.

Daugherty, F. P. *The Self-Portraits of Peter Paul Rubens: Some Problems of Iconography*. Ph.D. diss., University of North Carolina, 1976.

De Bie, C. *Het gulden cabinet vande edel vry schilder const inhoudende den lof vande vermarste schilders, architecten, beldthouwers ende plaetsnyders van dese eeuw*. Antwerp, 1661.

Deleito Piñuela, J. *El Rey se divierte*. Madrid, 1935 (3d. ed., Madrid, 1964).

La mala vida en la España de Felipe IV. Madrid, 1950 (latest ed., Madrid, 1987).

Della Pergola, J. "P. P. Rubens e il tema della Susanna al bagno." *Bulletin Musées Royaux des Beaux-Arts de Belgique* 16 (1967): 7ff.

De Maeyer, M. *Albrecht en Isabella en de Schilderkunst. Bijdrage tot de Geschiedenis van de XVIIe-eeuwse Schilderkunst in de Zuidelijke Nederlanden*. Brussels, 1955.

Denucé, J. *Kunstuitvoer in de 17e eeuw te Antwerpen de firma Forchoudt*. Antwerp, 1931.

De Antwerpsche "Konstkamers": Inventarissen van Kunstverzamelingen te Antwerpen in de 16e en 17e eeuwen. . . . Antwerp, 1932.

Brieven en Documenten Betreffend Jan Bruegel I en II. Antwerp, 1934.

Na Peter Pauwel Rubens, Documenten uit den kunsthandel te Antwerpen in de XVIIe eeuw van Matthijs Musson. Antwerp, 1949.

de Poorter, N. *The Eucharist Series*. 2 vols. *Corpus Rubenianum Ludwig Burchard*, part 2. London, 1978.

De Ridder, A. "Prérogatives nobiliaires et ambitions bourgeoises I. Le port de l'épée." *Noblesse Belge, Annuaire de 1921*. Brussels, 1922.

Devéze, M. *L'Espagne de Philippe IV (1621–1665)*. 2 vols. Paris, 1970–1971.

de Villermont, M. *Isabelle, governante des Pays-Bas*. 2 vols. Tamines-Paris, 1912.

Devisscher, H. *Peter Paul Rubens. Aanbidding der koningen*. Bloemendaal, 1992.

D'Hulst, R. A. *Jacob Jordaens*. Ithaca, N.Y. 1982.

D'Hulst, R. A., and Vandenven, M. *The Old Testament. Corpus Rubenianum Ludwig Burchard*, part 3. London, 1989.

Díaz Padrón M. "El dibujo del 'Pequeño Juicio Final' de Rubens, en la Academia de San Fernando." *Archivo Español de Arte* 145 (1964): 203–206.

"Un nuevo Rubens en el Museo del Prado: *La Inmaculada* del Marqués de Leganés." *Archivo Español de Arte* 153–156 (1967): 1–13.

"La cacería de Venados de Rubens para el ochavo del Alcázar en Méjico." *Archivo Español de Arte* 43 (1970): 131–150.

"Thomas Willeboirts Bosschaert, Pintor en Fuensaldaña. Nuevas obras Identificadas en Amberes y Estocolmo." *Archivo Español de Arte* 178 (1972): 83–102.

"Algunas fuentes para composiciones de Rubens." *Archivo Español de Arte* 189 (1975a): 126–129.

Museo del Prado. Catálogo de pinturas. Escuela flamenca siglo XVII. 2 vols. Madrid, 1975b.

Museo del Prado, Studia Rubeniana, I, Dibujos de Rubens en el Museo del Prado. Madrid, 1977a.

Pedro Pablo Rubens 1577–1640. Madrid, 1977b.

El Siglo de Rubens en el Museo del Prado. Catalogo razonado de pintura flamenca del Siglo XVII. 3 vols. Barcelona, 1995.

Díaz Padrón M., and Orihuela, M. *El Prado. Escuela flamenca del Siglo XVII*. Madrid, 1983.

Díaz Padrón M., and Padrón Mérida, A. *Fundación Carlos de Amberes 1594–1989*. Madrid, 1989.
Díaz Padrón M., and Royo Villanueva, M. *David Teniers, Jan Brueghel y los gabinetes de pinturas*. Madrid, Museo del Prado, 1992.
Diccionario de Autoridades. Madrid, 1732 (Madrid, 1963).
Diccionario de Historia Eclesiástica de España. Madrid, 1972.
Dolce, L. *Dialogo della pittura*. Ed. P. Barocchi. Bari, 1960.
Domínguez Ortiz, A. *Las clases privilegiadas en el Antiguo Régimen*. Madrid, 1973.
Eisler, C. "Rubens' Uses of the Northern Past." *Bulletin Musées Royaux des Beaux-Arts de Belgique* 16 (1967): 43ff.
Elbern, V. H. "Die Rubensteppiche des kölner Domes, ihre Geschichte und ihre Stellung im Zyklus Triumph der Eucharistie." *Kölner Domblatt* 10 (1955): 43–88.
Elliott, J. H. *El conde-duque de Olivares y la herencia de Felipe II*. Valladolid, 1977.
Richelieu and Olivares. Cambridge, 1984.
The Count-Duke of Olivares: The Statesman in an Age of Decline. New Haven, Conn., 1986.
Elliott, J. H., and de la Peña, J. F. *Memoriales y Cartas del Conde Duque de Olivares*. 2 vols. Madrid, 1981.
Ertz, K. *Jan Brueghel D. A. Die Gemälde*. Cologne, 1979.
Evers, H. G. *Rubens und sein Werk, neue Forschungen*. Brussels, 1943.
Exhibition. *Peter Paul Rubens*. London, Wildenstein, 1950 (Catalogue by L. Burchard).
Exhibition. *Flemish Art 1300–1700*. London, Royal Academy of Arts, 1953.
Exhibition. *Velázquez y lo Velázqueño*. Madrid, 1960.
Exhibition. *Rubens Diplomate*. Elewijt, Chateau Rubens, 1962.
Exhibition. *La Toison d'or. Cinq siècles d'art et d'histoire*. Bruges, 1962.
Exhibition. *Le Siècle de Rubens*. Brussels, Musées Royaux des Beaux-Arts, 1965.
Exhibition. *Paintings by Old Masters at Christ Church, Oxford*. London, 1967.
Exhibition. *Peter Paul Rubens*. Cologne, Wallraf-Richartz Museum, 1977 (Catalogue by J. Müller Hofstede).
Exhibition. *P. P. Rubens. Paintings. Oilsketches. Drawings*. Antwerp, Royal Museum of Fine Arts, 1977.
Exhibition. *Rubens a Mantova*. Mantua, 1977.
Exhibition. *Rubens e la pittura fiamminga del Seicento nelle collezioni pubbliche fiorentine*. Florence, Palazzo Pitti, 1977.
Exhibition. *Le Siècle de Rubens dans les collections publiques françaises*. Paris, Grand Palais, 1977–1978.
Exhibition. *El arte en la epoca de Calderón*. Madrid, Palacio de Velázques, 1981–1982.
Exhibition. *Splendours of the Gonzaga*. London, Victoria and Albert Museum, 1982.
Exhibition. *Rafael en España*. Madrid, Museo del Prado, 1985.
Exhibition. *Liechtenstein. The Princely Collections*. New York, Metropolitan Museum of Art, 1985–1986.
Exhibition. *El arte en las colecciones de la Casa de Alba*. Madrid, Fundación Caja de Pensiones, 1987.
Exhibition. *Rubens copista de Tiziano*. Madrid, Museo del Prado, 1987.
Exhibition. *Pietro Paolo Rubens*. Padua, Rome, and Milan, 1990.
Exhibition. *Rubens: Dédalo y el Minotauro*. La Coruña, Museo de Bellas Artes, 1990.
Exhibition. *Sánchez Coello y el retrato en la corte de Felipe II*. Madrid, Museo del Prado, 1990.
Exhibition. *Anthony Van Dyck*. Washington, D.C., National Gallery of Art, 1990–1991.
Exhibition. *America. Bride of the Sun*. Antwerp, Royal Museum of Fine Arts, 1992.
Exhibition. *Esso Presents Rubens and the Italian Renaissance*. Canberra, Australian National Gallery, 1992.

Exhibition. *Von Bruegel bis Rubens. Das goldene Jahrhundert der Flämischen Malerei.* Vienna and Cologne, 1993.

Exhibition. *Pintores del Reinado de Felipe III.* Traveling exhibition organized by the Prado Museum, 1993–1994.

Exhibition. *Los Leoni (1509–1608). Escultores del renacimiento italiano al servicio de la corte de España.* Madid, Museo del Prado, 1994.

Exhibition. *Navarrete "el Mudo," pintor de Felipe II.* Logroño, 1995.

Exhibition. *Los Cinco Sentidos y el Arte* Madrid, Museo del Prado, 1997. (This is a version, with some variations, of the catalogue for the exhibition *I cinque sensi nell'arte. Immagini del sentire*, organized by Sylvia Ferino-Pagden for the Associazione Promozione Iniziative Culturali di Cremona, Cremona, 1996.)

Exhibition. *Velázquez in Seville.* Edinburgh, National Gallery of Scotland, 1996.

Fernández Duro, C. *El último Almirante de Castilla, Don Juan Tomás Enríquez de Cabrera.* Madrid, 1903.

Feros, A. "The King's Favorite, the Duke of Lerma: Power, Wealth and Court Culture during the Reign of Philip III. Ph.D. diss., Johns Hopkins University, 1994.

"Two Souls: Monarchs and Favourites in Early Seventeenth-Century Spain." In R. L. Kagan and G. Parker, eds., *Spain, Europe and the Atlantic World. Essays in Honour of John H. Elliott*, pp. 27–47. Cambridge, 1995.

Ferrarino, L. *Lettere di artisti italiani ad Antonio Perrenot de Granvella.* Madrid, 1977.

Filipczak, Z. Z. *Picturing Art in Antwerp, 1550–1700.* Princeton, N.J., 1987.

Finot, J. "Documents relatifs à Rubens conservés aux Archives du Nord." *Rubens-Bulletijn* 3 (1888): 97–124.

Flemish Paintings in America: A Survey of Early Netherlandish and Flemish Paintings in the Public Collections of North America. Selected by G. C. Bauman and W. A. Liedtke. Antwerp, 1992.

Florit, J. M. "Inventario de los cuadros y otros objetos de arte de la quinta real llamada 'La Ribera' en Valladolid." *Boletín de la Sociedad Española de Excursiones* 14 (1906): 153–160.

Fourez, L. *Le Droit héraldique dans les Pays-Bas Catholiques.* Brussels and Louvain, 1932.

Fredericksen, B. *Catalogue of the Paintings in the J. Paul Getty Museum.* Malibu, Calif., 1972.

Freedberg, D. "Johannes Molanus on Provocative Paintings." *Journal of the Warburg and Courtauld Institutes* 34 (1971): 229–245.

The Life of Christ after the Passion Corpus Rubenianum Ludwig Burchard, part 7. New York, 1984.

Friedländer, M. J. *Early Netherlandish Painting.* Vol. 13, *Antonis Mor and His Contemporaries.* Leyden-Brussels, 1975.

Gachard, L. P. *Histoire politique et diplomatique de Pierre-Paul Rubens.* Brussels, 1877.

Gállego, J. *El pintor de artesano a artista.* Granada, 1976.

"La alegoría en Rubens." *Goya* 140–141 (1977): 118–131.

Garas, K. *The Budapest Gallery. Painting in the Museum of Fine Arts.* Budapest, 1973.

García Carraffa, A. and A. *Diccionario Heráldico y Genealógico de Apellidos Españoles y Americanos.* 86 vols. Madrid, 1957–1963.

García Chico, E. *Documentos para el estudio del arte en Castilla.* Vol. 3. Universidad de Valladolid, 1946.

Garrard, M. D. *Artemisia Gentileschi: The Image of the Female Hero in Italian Baroque Art.* Princeton, N.J., 1989.

Garrido Pérez, C. *Velázquez, técnica y evolución.* Madrid, 1992.

Gascón de Torquemada, G. *Gaçeta y nuevas de la corte de España desde el año de 1600 adelante.* Madrid, 1991.

Génard, P. "De nalatenschap van P. P. Rubens." *Antwerpsch Archievenblad.* 2 (1865–1866): 69ff.

"Les Armes de la famille Rubens." *Rubens Bulletin* 3 (1886): 68–70.
Gérard, V. "Philip IV's Early Italian Commissions." *Oxford Art Journal* 5, no. 1 (1982): 9–14.
Gerson, H., and Ter Kuile, E. H. *Art and Architecture in Belgium 1600–1800*. The Pelican History of Art. Harmondsworth, Middlesex, and Baltimore, 1960.
Glang-Süberkrüb, A. *Der Liebesgarten: Eine Untersuchung über die Bedeutung der Konfiguration für das Bildthema im Spätwerk des Peter Paul Rubens*. Bern, 1975.
Glen, T. L. *Rubens and the Counter-Reformation. Studies in His Religious Paintings between 1609 and 1620*. New York and London, 1977.
Glück, G. "Rubens' Liebesgarten." *Jahrbuch der Kunsthistorischen Sammlungen in Wien* 35 (1920): 49–98.
Rubens, Van Dyck und ihr Kreis. Vienna, 1933.
"Bildnisse aus dem Hause Habsburg." I: "Kaiserin Isabella." *Jahrbuch der Kunsthistorischen Sammlungen* in *Wien* 7 (1933): 183–210; III: "Kaiser Karl V." *Jahrbuch der Kunsthistorischen Sammlungen in Wien* 2 (1937): 165ff.
Die Landschaften von Peter Paul Rubens. Vienna, 1940.
Glück, G., and Haberditzl, F. M. *Die Handzeichnungen von Peter Paul Rubens*. Berlin, 1928.
Göbel, H. *Wandteppiche*. Leipzig, 1923–1934.
Goldberg, E. L. "Velázquez in Italy: Painters, Spies, and Low Spaniards." *Art Bulletin* 74 (1992a): 453–456.
"Spanish Taste, Medici Politics and a Lost Chapter in the History of Cigoli's 'Ecce Homo.' " *Burlington Magazine* 134 (1992b): 102–110.
"Artistic Relations between the Medici and the Spanish Courts, 1587–1621: Part I." *Burlington Magazine* 138 (1996): 105–114.
Goodman, E. *Rubens: The Garden of Love as "Conversatie à la mode."* Amsterdam and Philadelphia, 1992.
Goris, J. A., and Held, J. *Rubens in America*. New York, 1947.
Greer, M. R. *The Play of Power: Mythological Dramas of Calderón de la Barca*. Princeton, N.J., 1991.
Groeneveld, E. "Een Herziene biografie van Anthonis Mor." *Jaarboek van het Koninklijk Museum voor Schone Kunsten Antwerpen* (1981): 97–117.
Gross, S. "A Second Look: Nationalism in Art Treatises from the Golden Age in Spain." *Rutgers Art Review*, Spring 1984, pp. 8–27.
Grossmann, F. "Holbein, Flemish Paintings and Everhard Jabach." *Burlington Magazine* 93 (1951): 16–25.
Gualandi, M. *Nuova Raccolta di lettere sulla Pittura, Scultura ed Architettura scritte da' più celebri personaggi dei secoli XV a XIX*. Bologna, 1844–1856.
Guinard, P. *L'Influence flamande sur la peinture espagnole du siècle d'or*. Budapest, n.d.
Haeger, B. "Rubens' 'Adoration of the Magi' and the Program for the High Altar of St. Michael's Abbey in Antwerp." *Simiolus* 25 (1997): 45–71.
Harris, E. "La misión de Velázquez en Italia."*Archivo Español de Arte* 130–131 (1960): 109–2136.
"Cassiano dal Pozzo on Diego Velázquez." *Burlington Magazine* 112 (1970): 364–373
"Velazquez's Portrait of Prince Baltasar Carlos in the Riding School." *Burlington Magazine* 118 (1976): 266–275.
Harris, E., and Elliott, J. H. "Velázquez and the Queen of Hungary." *Burlington Magazine* 118 (1976): 24–26.
Härting, U. A. *Frans Franken der Jüngere (1581–1642). Die Gemälde mit kritischen Oeuvre Katalog*. 1989.
Haverkamp-Begemann, E. *Olieverfschetsen van Rubens*. Museum Boymans. Rotterdam, 1953.
The Achilles Series Corpus Rubenianum Ludwig Burchard, part 10. Brussels, 1975.
Held, J. "Le Roi à la Chasse." *Art Bulletin* 40 (1958): 139–149.

Rubens. Selected Drawings. 2 vols. London, 1959 (updated edition, New York, 1986).

Rembrandt's Aristotle and Other Rembrandt Studies. Princeton, N.J., 1969.

"Rubens' Sketch of Buckingham Rediscovered." *Burlington Magazine* 118 (1976): 547–551.

The Oil Sketches of Rubens. 2 vols. Princeton, N.J., 1980.

"Rubens and Titian." In D. Rosand, ed., *Titian and His World*, pp. 283–339. New York, 1982.

"Thoughts on Rubens' Beginnings." *Ringling Museum of Art Journal*, pp. 14–27. Sarasota, Fla., 1983.

Hellwig, K. "Diego Velázquez y los escritos sobre arte de Lázaro Díaz del Valle." *Archivo Español de Arte* 265 (1994): 27–41.

Hermann, H. "Rubens y el Monasterio de San Lorenzo de El Escorial." *Archivo Español de Arte y Arqueología* 27 (1933): 237–246.

Herrero García, M. *Contribución de la literatura a la historia del arte*. Madrid, 1943.

Ideas de los españoles del siglo XVII. Madrid, 1966.

Hollstein, F. W. H. *Dutch and Flemish Etchings, Engravings and Woodcuts ca. 1450–1700*. 19 vols. Amsterdam, 1949–1969.

Honour, H. *The New Golden Land. European Images of America from the Discoveries to the Present Time*. London, 1975.

The European Vision of America. Cleveland, Ohio, 1976.

Howarth, D. *Lord Arundel and His Circle*. New Haven, Conn., 1985.

Huemer, F. *Portraits*. I. *Corpus Rubenianum Ludwig Burchard*, part 19. London, 1977.

Rubens and the Roman Circle: Studies of the First Decade. New York and London, 1996.

Hulst, R.-A. d', and Vandenven, M. *The Old Testament. Corpus Rubenianum Ludwig Burchard*, part 3. London, ca. 1989.

Hymans, H. *Lucas Vorsterman 1595–1675, et son oeuvre gravé*. 1893 (reprinted Amsterdam, 1972).

Israel, J. D. *The Dutch Republic and the Hispanic World 1606–1661*. Oxford, 1982.

Jaffé, M. "Rubens' Sketching in Paint." *Art News* 52 (1953): 34–37, 64–67.

"Rubens in Italy: Rediscovered Works." *Burlington Magazine* 100 (1958): 411–422.

"The Dukes of Devonshire." In Douglas Cooper, *Great Family Collections*. New York, 1965.

"A Landscape by Rubens, and Another by Van Dyck." *Burlington Magazine* 108 (1966): 410–416.

Van Dyck's Antwerp Sketchbook. 2 vols. London, 1966a.

"Rubens." *Encyclopedia of World Art*. London, 1966b.

"Rubens in Italy. Part II." *Burlington Magazine* 110 (1968): 180–187.

"Rubens as Collector." *Journal of the Royal Society of Arts* 117 (1969): 641ff.

"Figure Drawings Attributed to Rubens, Jordaens, and Cossiers in the Hamburg Kunsthalle." *Jahrbuch der Hamburger Kunstsammlungen* 16 (1971a): 39–50.

"Rubens and Snijders: A Fruitful Partnership." *Apollo* 93 (1971b): 184–196.

"Rubens Drawings in the Warsaw University Library." *Bulletin du Musée National de Varsovie* 17 (1976): 83–96.

Rubens and Italy. Oxford, 1977.

Rubens. Catalogo completo. Milan, 1989.

Jardine, L. *Worldly Goods: A New History of the Renaissance*. New York, 1996.

Jordan, W. B. *Spanish Still Life in the Golden Age, 1600–1650*. Fort Worth, Tex., 1985.

Journal des voyages de M. de Monconys: Voyage de Espagne fait l'anée 1628. Vol. 3. Lyons, 1666.

Judson, J. R., and Van de Velde, C. *Book Illustrations and Title-Pages*. 2 vols. *Corpus Rubenianum Ludwig Burchard*, part 21. London, 1978.

Justi, C. *Diego Velázquez und sein Jahrhundert*. 2 vols. Bonn, 1888. English edition: *Diego Velázquez and His Times*. London, 1889.

"Verzeichnis der fruher in Spanien befindlichen, jezt verschollenen oder ins Ausland gekommenen Gemälde Tizians." *Jahrbuch der Koniglich Preussischen Kunstsammlungen* 10 (1889): 181–186.

"Die Reiterstatue Philipps IV von Pietro Tacca." *Miscellaneen aus drei jahrhunderten Spanischen Kunstlebens*, 2: 253–274. Berlin, 1908.

Kagan, R. L., ed. *Spanish Cities of the Golden Age: The Views of Anton van den Wyngaerde*. Berkeley, Los Angeles, and London, 1989.

Kamen, H. *Spain in the Later Seventeenth Century, 1665–1700*. London and New York, 1980.

———. *Inquisition and Society in Spain in the Sixteenth and Seventeenth Centuries*. London, 1985.

Katalog Altere Pinakothek. Munich, 1936.

Kauffman, C. M. *Catalogue of Paintings in the Wellington Museum*. London, 1982.

Kieser, E. "Tizians und Spaniens einwirkungen auf die Spateren Landschaften des Rubens." *Münchener Jahrbuch für Bildene Kunst* 8 (1931): 281–291.

Klessmann, R. "Bemerkungen zu Rubens Gemälde 'Diana und Callisto' in Madrid." *Studien zur niederländischen Kunst: Festschrift für Prof. Dr. Justus Müller Hofstede/ Wallraf Richartz Jahrbuch* 55 (1994): 85–94.

Knipping, J. B. *Iconography of the Counter-Reformation in the Netherlands. Heaven-on Earth*. Leiden, 1974.

Koslow, S. *Frans Snyders: The Noble Estate. Seventeenth-Century Still-Life and Animal Painting in the Southern Netherlands*. Antwerp, 1995.

"Law and Order in Rubens's 'Wolf and Fox Hunt.' " *Art Bulletin* 78 (1996): 680–706.

Kusche, M. "Sofonisba Anguissola en España. Retratista en la corte de Felipe II junto a Alonso Sánchez Coello y Jorge de la Rua." *Archivo Español de Arte* 248 (1989): 391ff.

"La Antigüa Galería de Retratos del Pardo: Su reconstrucción arquitectónica y el orden de colocación de los cuadros." *Archivo Español de Arte* 253 (1991): 1–28.

"La Antigüa Galería de Retratos del Pardo: Su importancia para la obra de Tiziano, Moro, Sánchez Coello y Sofonisba Anguissola y su significado para Felipe II, su fundador." *Archivo Español de Arte* 257 (1992): 1–51.

La Catedral de Sevilla. Seville, 1984.

Lafond, P. *Cartons de Rubens pour la suite de tapisseries de l'Histoire d'Achille, Réunion des Sociétés des Beaux-Arts des Départements* 26 (1902): 232–238.

Histoire d'Achille par Rubens. Les Arts anciens de Flandre 4 (1909–1910): 125–129.

Lafuente Ferrari, E. *La fundamentación y los problemas de la historia del arte*. Madrid, 1951.

Lane, B. *The Altar and the Altarpiece*. New York, 1984.

La pintura flamenca en el Prado. Antwerp, 1989.

Larsen, E. "Three Lesser-Known Works by Rubens." *Jaarboek Koninklijk Museum voor Schone Kunsten*, pp. 151–155. Antwerp, 1969.

L'opera completa di Van Dyck. 2 vols. Milan, 1980.

Lefèvre, J. *Spinola et la Belgique (1601–1627)*. Brussels, 1947.

Le Roy Ladurie, E. *The Beggar and the Professor: A Sixteenth-Century Family Saga*. Chicago and London, 1997.

Levin, T. "Beitrage zur geschichte der Kunstbest rebungen in dem Hause Pfalz Neuburg." *Jahrbucher des Dusseldorfer Geschichtsvereins* 19 (1904), 20 (1906), 23 (1911).

Liedtke, W. A. *Flemish Paintings in the Metropolitan Museum of Art*. 2 vols. New York, 1984.

Royal Horse and Rider: Painting, Sculpture and Horsemanship 1500–1800. New York, 1989.

Liedtke, W. A., and Moffitt, J. F. "Velázquez, Olivares, and the Baroque Equestrian Portrait." *Burlington Magazine* 123 (1981): 529–537.

Ligo, L. L. "Two Seventeenth-Century Poems which Link Rubens' Equestrian Portrait of Philip IV to Titian's Equestrian Portrait of Charles V." *Gazette des Beaux-Arts* 65 (1970): 345–354.

Lind, L. R., "The Latin Life of Peter Paul Rubens by His Nephew Philip, a Translation." *Art Quarterly* 9 (1946):37–44.

Logan, A.-M. "Rubens Exhibitions 1977." *Master Drawings* 16 (1978): 419–450.

Lonchay, H., and Cuvelier, J. *Correspondance de la Cour d'Espagne sur les affaires des Pays-Bas au XVIIe siècle*. Vol. 1. Brussels, 1923.

Longueville, T. *Policy and Paint, or some incidents in the lives of Dudley Carleton and Peter Paul Rubens*. London, 1913.

López, M. A. "Alonso Carbonel y la Igleisa de Loeches." *Archivo Español de Arte* 25 (1952): 167–169.

López Navío, J. "La gran colección de pinturas del Marqués de Leganés." *Analecta Calasanctiana*, pp. 259–330. Madrid, 1962.

López Rey, J. "A Head of Philip IV by Velázquez in a Rubens Allegorical Composition." *Gazette des Beaux-Arts* 53 (1959): 35–43.

Velázquez' Work and World. London, 1968.

López Serrano, M. *Catálogo de dibujos. I. Trazas de Juan de Herrera y sus seguidores para el Monasterio del Escorial*. Madrid, 1944.

"El grabador Pedro Perret." In *El Escorial*, 2:689–716. Madrid, 1963.

López Torrijos, R. *La mitología en la pintura española del Siglo de Oro*. Madrid, 1985.

Lowenthal, A. W.; Rosand, D.; and J. Walsh, Jr., eds. *Rubens and His Circle: Studies by J. S. Held*. Princeton, N.J., 1982.

Loyseau, C. *A Treatise of Orders and Plain Dignities*. Cambridge, 1994.

Lozoya, Marqués de. "Pintura venatoria en los palacios reales." *Reales Sitios* 3, no. 9 (1966): 22–25.

Lugt, F. *Musée du Louvre, Inventaire Général des Dessins des Ecoles du Nord, Ecole Flamande*. Paris, 1949.

Luna, J. J. *Claudio de Lorena y el ideal clásico de paisaje en el siglo XVII*. Madrid, 1984.

Lleó Cañal, V. "The Art Collection of the Ninth Duke of Medinaceli." *Burlington Magazine* 131 (1989): 108–116.

MacRae, S. "Rubens' Library." M.A. thesis, Columbia University, 1971.

McGrath, E. "Celebrating the Eucharist." *Art History* 4 (1981): 474–479.

" 'The Drunken Alcibiades': Rubens's Picture of Plato's Symposium." *Journal of the Warburg and Courtauld Institutes* 46 (1983): 228–235.

McKim-Smith, G., et al. *Examining Vélazquez*. New Haven, Conn., 1988.

Madrazo, P. de. *Viaje artístico de tres siglos por las colecciones de cuadros de los Reyes de España*. Barcelona, 1884.

Magurn, R. S., ed. *The Letters of P. P. Rubens*. Cambridge, 1955.

Mallory, N. A. "Rubens y Van Dyck en el arte de Murillo." *Goya* 169–171 (1982): 92–104.

Mancini, M. *Genuine Memoires of Madam Maria Manchini, Constables of Colonna, eldeste Sister to the Duches of Mazarin*. London, 1679.

Marías, F. *El largo siglo XVI*. Madrid, 1989.

Martí y Monsó, J. *Estudios histórico-artísticos relativos principalmente a Valladolid*. Valladolid-Madrid, n.d [1898–1901].

"Los Calderones y el Monasterio de Nuestra Señora de Portaceli. Documentos." *Boletín del Seminario de Arte y Arqueoloía* (Valladolid) 4 (1909–1910).

Martin, G. "Rubens and Buckingham's 'fayrie ile.' " *Burlington Magazine* 108 (1966): 613–618.

National Gallery Catalogues. The Flemish School 1600–1900. London, 1970 (reprinted 1986).

Martin, J. R. *The Ceiling Paintings for the Jesuit Church in Antwerp. Corpus Rubenianum Ludwig Burchard*, part 1. Brussels, London, and New York, 1968.

The Decorations for the Pompa Introitus Ferdinand. Corpus Rubenianum Ludwig Burchard, part 18. Brussels, London, and New York, 1972.

"Rubens's Last Mythological Paintings for Philip IV." *Gentse Bijdragen* 24 (1976–1978): 113–118.

Martínez, Jusepe. *Discursos practicables del nobilísimo arte de la pintura*. Edited by Julián Gállego. Barcelona, 1950.

Martín González, J. J. "Bienes artísticos de Don Rodrigo Calderón." *Boletín del Seminario de Arte y Arqueología* 54 (1988): 267–292.

Mauquoy-Hendrickx, M. *L'Iconographie d'Antoine Van Dyck: Catalogue Raisonné*. 2 vols. Brussels, 1956.

Maura Gomazo, G. *Vida y reinado de Carlos II*. 2 vols. Madrid, 1954.

Mencik, F. *Dokumente zur Geschichte der kunsthistorischen Sammlungen des allerhöchsten Kaiserhauses* 30 (1911–1912).

Michel, E. *Rubens: His Life, His Time, and His Work*. 2 vols. London, 1899.

Michel. J. F. M. *Histoire de la vie de P. P. Rubens*. Brussels, 1771.

Millar, O. *Rubens: The Whitehall Ceiling*. London, 1958.

"The Inventories and Valuations of the King's Goods 1649–1651." *Walpole Society Annual* 43 (1970–1972).

Millen, R. F., and Wolf, R. E. *Heroic Deeds and Mystic Figures. A New Reading of Rubens' Life of Maria de' Medici*. Princeton, N.J., 1989.

Minor, V. H. *Art History's History*. Englewood Cliffs, N.J., 1994.

Mirot, L. *Roger de Piles. Peintre, amateur, critique*. Paris, 1924.

Molas Ribalta, P., et al. *Historia de España Menéndez Pidal*. Vol. 28, *La transición del siglo XVII al XVII*. Madrid, 1993.

Morán Turina, J. M. "Felipe III y las Artes." *Anales de Historia del Arte* 1 (1989): 159–179 (reprinted in Morán Turina and Portús Pérez, 1997).

Morán Turina, J. M., and Checa Cremades, F. "Las colecciones pictóricas del Escorial y el gusto Barroco." *Goya* 179 (1984): 252–261.

El coleccionismo en España. Madrid, 1985.

Las casas del Rey. Casas de campo, cazaderos y jardines. Siglos XVI y XVII. Madrid, 1986.

Morán Turina, M., and Portús Pérez, J. *El arte de mirar. La pintura su público en la España de Velázquez*. Madrid, 1997.

Moxey, K. *The Practice of Theory. Poststructuralism, Cultural Politics, and Art History*. Ithaca and London, 1994.

Mulcahy, R. *The Decoration of the Royal Basilica of El Escorial*. Cambridge and New York, 1994.

Muller, J. M. "Oil Sketches in Rubens' Collection." *Burlington Magazine* 117 (1975): 371–377.

"Rubens's Theory and Practice of the Imitation of Art." *Art Bulletin* 64, no. 2 (1982): 229–247.

"Rubens's Cupids and Andrians. The First Documents and What They Tell Us." In G. Cavalli-Björkman, ed., *Bacchanals by Titian and Rubens. Papers given at a symposium in Nationalmuseum, Stockholm, March 18–19, 1987. Nationalmusei Skriftserie n.s. 10*, pp. 75–80. Stockholm, 1987.

Rubens: The Artist as Collector. Princeton, N.J., 1989.

Müller Hofstede, J. "Zur Antwerpener Frühzeit von P. P. Rubens." *Münchner Jahrbuch der Bildenden Kunst*. 3d ser. 13 (1962): 179–215.

"Bildnisse aus Rubens' Italienjahren." *Jahrbuch der Staatlichen Kunstsammlungen in Baden-Württemberg* 2 (1965a): 116f.

"Beitrage zum zeichnerischen Werk von Rubens." *Wallraf-Richartz-Jahrbuch* 27 (1965b): 259–356.

"Rubens und Titian: Das Bild Karl V." *Münchner Jahrbuch der Bildener Kunst* 28 (1967a): 33–96.

"Eine Kreidenstudie von Rubens für den Kreuzaufrichtungsaltar." *Pantheon* 25 (1967b): 35–43.

"Zum Werke der Otto van Veen, 1590–1600." *Bulletin Musées Royaux des Beaux-Arts de Belgique* 6 (1975): 157–159.

"Peter Paul Rubens 1577–1640. Selbstbildnis und Selbstverständnis." In *Von Bruegel bis Rubens. Das Goldene Jahrhundert der Flämischen Malerei*, pp. 103–120. Vienna and Cologne, 1993.

"Van Dyck's Authorship Excluded: The Sketchbook at Chatsworth." *Studies in the History of Art*. Vol. 46, *Van Dyck 350*. National Gallery of Art, Washington, D.C., 1994.

"Zur Theorie und Gestalt des Antwerpner Kabinettbildes um 1600." *Die Malerei Antwerpens Gattung, Meister, Wirkung: Internationales Colloquium Wien 1993*. Cologne, 1994.

Museo del Prado. Inventarios Reales. Testamentaría del Rey Carlos II, 1701–1703. 3 vols. Madrid, 1975–1985.

Museo del Prado. Inventario General de Pinturas. Vol. 1, *La Colección Real. . . .* Madrid, 1990. Vol. 2, *El Museo de la Trinidad*. Madrid, 1991.

Nilgen, U. "The Epiphany and the Eucharist: On the Interpretation of Eucharistic Motifs in Mediaeval Epiphany Scenes." *The Art Bulletin* 49 (1967): 311–316.

Norris, C. "Rubens in Retrospect." *Burlington Magazine* 93 (1951): 4–11.

Review of *La Peintre Flamande à Flandre*. *Burlington Magazine* 95 (1953): 107–108.

"Rubens' Adoration of the Kings of 1609." *Nederlands Kunshistorisch Jaarboek* 14 (1963): 129–136.

Novoa, M. de. *Historia de Felipe IV, rey de España (Colección de Documentos Inéditos para la Historia de España)*. Vol. 69. Madrid, 1876.

Obras restauradas de Thomas Willeboirts Bosschaert. Valladolid, Museo Nacional de Escultura, 1988.

Oldenbourg, R. *Klassiker der Kunst*. Vol. 5, *P. P. Rubens. Des Meisters Gemälde*. 4th ed. Stuttgart-Berlin, 1921.

Orso, S. N. *Philip IV and the Decoration of the Alcázar of Madrid*. Princeton, N.J., 1986.

"A Note on Montañés's Lost *Bust of Philip IV*." *Source: Notes in the History of Art* 8, no. 2 (1989): 21–24.

"Praising the Queen: The Decorations at the Royal Exequies for Isabella of Bourbon." *Art Bulletin* 72 (1990): 51–73.

Velázquez, Los Borrachos, and Painting at the Court of Philip IV. Cambridge and New York, 1993.

"A Note on Rubens's Last Commissions for Philip IV." *Source: Notes in the History of Art* 16, no. 3 (1997): 12–16.

Pacheco, F. *El arte de la pintura*. Edited by B. Bassegoda i Hugás. Madrid, 1990. See also the edition in F. J. Sánchez Cantón, *Fuentes literarias para la historia del arte español*. Vol. 2. Madrid, 1933.

Palomino, A. *Lives of the Eminent Spanish Painters and Sculptors*. Edited by N. Ayala Mallory. Cambridge, 1987.

Panofsky, E. *Early Netherlandish Painting*. 2 vols. Cambridge, Mass., 1953.

Problems in Titian: Mostly Iconographic. New York, 1969.

Parker, G. *The Dutch Revolt*. London, 1977.

Spain and the Netherlands, 1559–1659. London, 1979.

"The Soldier." In *Baroque Personae*, R. Villari, pp. 32–56. Chicago and London, 1995.

Pérez Sánchez, A. E. "Dos breves novedades en torno a José Antolínez." *Archivo Español de Arte* 135 (1961): 276–277.

"Un grabado de Rubens en casa de Diego Valentín Díaz." *Boletín del Seminario de Arte y Arqueología* 36 (1970): 515–516.
"Presencia de Tiziano en la España del Siglo de Oro." *Goya* 135 (1976): 140–159.
"Rubens y la pintura barroca española." *Goya* 140–141 (1977): 86–109.
Pintura barroca en España 1600–1750. Madrid, 1992.
"Sobre Juan Bautista Maino." *Archivo Español de Arte* 278 (1997): 113–125.
Pescador del Hoyo, M. del C. "De como llegó al Prado el retrato del duque de Lerma, Rubens." *Goya* 201 (1987): 148–151.
Piles, R. de. *La Vie de Rubens.* In R. de Piles, *Dissertation sur les ouvrages des plus fameux peintres.* Paris, 1681.
Abregé de la vie des peintres. Paris, 1699.
Pinchart, A. *Archives des arts, sciences et lettres.* Ghent, 1863.
Pirenne, H. *Histoire de Belgique.* Vol. 4. Brussels, 1911.
Pita Andrade, J. M. "Los cuadros de Velázquez y Mazo que poseyó el Séptimo Marqués del Carpio." *Archivo Español de Arte* 99 (1952): 223–236.
Podro, M. *The Critical Historians of Art.* New Haven, Conn., 1982.
Poglyaen-Neuwall, S. "Titian's Pictures of the Toilet of Venus and Their Copies." *Art Bulletin* 16 (1934): 258–384.
Ponz, A. *Viaje de España.* Madrid, 1947.
Popham, A. E. *The Drawings of Leonardo da Vinci.* New York, 1945.
Rabb, T. K. *The Struggle for Stability in Early Modern Europe.* New York, 1975.
Regteren Altena, I. Q. van. "Het vroegste werk van Rubens." *Medelingen van de Koninklijke Academie voor Wetenschappen, Letteren en schone Kunsten van België* 34 (1972): 3–21.
Renger, K. "Rubens dedit dedicavitque: Rubens's Beschäftigung mit deret Reproduktionsgraphik, I teil: Der Kupferstich." *Jahrbuch der Berliner Museen* 16 (1974): 122–175
Rico, F. "Los filósofos de Veláquez, o El Siglo de Oro de la pintura española," pp. 345–358. Madrid, 1991.
Robels, H. *Frans Snyders.* Munich, 1989.
Roberts, J. "Il collezionismo dei disegni di Leonardo." In *Leonardo e Venezia,* pp. 155–178. Milan, 1992.
Rodríguez G., and de Ceballos, A. *Bartolomé de Bustamante y los origines de la arquitectura jesuítica en España.* Rome, 1967.
"Una Virgen con El Niño, de Pedro Pablo Rubens, en el Convento de San Esteban de Salamanca." *Archivo Español de Arte* 237 (1987): 70–72.
Rodríguez Villa, A. *Ambrosio Spínola, primer marqués de los Balbases.* Madrid, 1904.
Etiquetas de la casa de Austria. Madrid, 1913.
Rooses, M. *L'Oeuvre de P. P. Rubens.* 5 vols. Antwerp, 1886–1892.
"Staet van den sterffhuyse von jouffrouwe Isabella Brandt." *Rubens-Bulletijn* 4 (1896): 156ff.
"La Galerie du Marquis de Léganes." *Rubens-Bulletijn* 5 (1900) (I): 164–171.
"Oeuvre de Rubens. Addenda et corrigenda." *Rubens-Bulletijn* 5 (1900) (II): 172–192.
"De schenker der Martelie van den H. Andres aan het gashuis del Vlamingen te Madrid." *Rubens-Bulletijn* 5 (1900) (III): 121–137.
Rubens. Sa vie et ses oeuvres. Paris, 1903.
Rooses, M., and Ruelens, Charles. *Correspondance de Rubens et documents épistolaires concernant sa vie et ses oeuvres.* Published, translated, and annotated by Ruelens (vol. 1), by Max Rooses and Ch. Ruelens (vols. 2–6). Antwerp, 1887–1909.
Rosand, D. "An Arc of Flame. On the Transmission of Pictorial Knowledge." In G. Cavalli-Björkman, ed., *Bacchanals by Titian and Rubens. Papers given at a symposium in Nationalmuseum, Stockholm, March 18–19, 1987. Nationalmusei Skriftserie n.s. 10,* pp. 81–92. Stockholm, 1987.

Rosenberg, A. *Klassiker der Kunst*. Vol. 5, *P. P. Rubens. Des Meisters Gemälde*. Stuttgart and Leipzig, 1906.

Rosenthal, L. "The *Parens Patriae*: Familial Imagery in Ruben's *Minerva Protects Pax from Mars*." *Art History* 12 (1989): 22–38.

Roth, M. S., ed. *Rediscovering History: Culture, Politics, and the Psyche*. Stanford, Calif., 1994.

Rowlands, J. *The Paintings of Hans Holbein the Younger. Complete Edition*. Oxford, 1985.

Ruelens, C. "La Vie de Rubens par Roger de Piles." *Rubens-Bulletijn* 2 (1883): 157–175.

Ruiz Alcón, M. T. "Otro Rubens en las Descalzas." *Goya* 56–57 (1963): 250–251.

Sainsbury, W. N. *Original Unpublished Papers Illustrating the Life of Sir Peter Paul Rubens*. London, 1859.

Salas, X. de. *Museo del Prado. Studia Rubeniana, II, Rubens y Velázquez*. Madrid, 1977.

Saltillo, Marqués de. *Mr. Fréderic Quillet, Comisario de Bellas Artes del Gobierno Intruso*. Madrid, 1933.

"Artistas madrileños (1592–1850)." *Boletín de la Sociedad Española de Excursiones* 53 (1953): 137–243.

Sánchez Cantón, F. J. *Fuentes literarias para la historia del arte español*. 5 vols. Madrid, 1923–1941.

"La librería de Velázquez." In *Homenaje ofrecido a Menéndez Pidal*, 3:379–406. Madrid, 1925.

Los retratos de los reyes de España. Barcelona, 1948.

Sánchez Esteban, N. "El legado de Pompeo Leoni: Su biblioteca y los manuscritos de Leonardo." In *Leone Leoni tra Lombardia e Spagna*, pp. 105–112. Como, 1995.

Sánchez Rivero, A., ed. *Viaje de Cosme de Médicis por España y Portugal (1668–1669)*. Madrid, 1933.

Sánchez-Mesa Martín, D. *José Risueño, escultor y pintor granadino 1665–1732*. Granada, 1972.

Sandrart, J., von. *Academie der Bau-, Bild- und Mahlerey-Künste von 1675*. Edited by A. R. Peltzer. Munich, 1925.

Santos, F. de los. *Descripción breve del Monasterio de San Lorenzo el Real del Escorial*. Partially published in F. J. Sánchez Cantón, *Fuentes literarias para la historia del arte español*, 2:225–319. Madrid, 1933.

Scharf, A. "Rubens's Portraits of Charles V and Isabella." *Burlington Magazine* 66 (1935): 259–266.

Schroth, S. *The Private Picture Collection of the Duke of Lerma*. Ph.D. diss., New York University, 1990.

Schütz, K. "Das Galeriebild als Spiegel des Antwerpener Sammlertums." *Von Bruegel bis Rubens. Das goldene Jahrhundert der Flämischen Malerei*. Vienna and Cologne, 1993.

Schwartz, G. "Lady Pictura Painting Flowers." *Tableau Fine Arts Magazine* (Summer 1993), pp. 66–81.

"Love in the Kunstkamer. Additions to the Work of Guillam van Haecht (1593–1637)." *Tableau Fine Arts Magazine* (Summer 1996), pp. 43–52.

Scribner, C. "Sacred Architecture: Rubens's Eucharist Tapestries." *Art Bulletin* 57 (1975): 519–528.

The Triumph of the Eucharist: Tapestries Designed by Rubens. Ann Arbor, Mich., 1982.

Seco Serrano, C., ed. *Cartas de la Venerable Sor María de Agreda y del Señor Rey Don Felipe IV*. Biblioteca de Autores Españoles. Vols. 108–109. Madrid, 1958.

Seidel, L. *Jan van Eyck's Arnolfini Portrait. Stories of an Icon*. Cambridge and New York, 1993.

Seilern, A. *Flemish Paintings and Drawings at 56 Princes Gate London SW7*. 2 vols. London, 1955.

Corrigenda and Addenda to the Catalogue of Paintings and Drawings at 56 Princes Gate London SW7. London, 1971.

Sentenach y Cabañas, N. *Catálogo de los quadros, esculturas, grabados, y otros objectos artísticos de la antigua casa ducal de Osuna, expuestos en el Palacio de la industria y de las artes*. 2d ed. Madrid, 1896.

La pintura en Madrid desde sus orígenes hasta el s. XIX. Madrid, 1907.

"Miscelánea. Fondos selectos del Archivo de la Academia de San Fernando. Cuadros famosos condenados al fuego." *Boletín de la Real Academia de Bellas Artes de San Fernando* (1921), pp. 46–54.

Serrera, M. "Pedro de Campaña: Obras dispersas." *Archivo Español de Arte* 62 (1989): 1–14.

Shakeshaft, P. "Elsheimer and G. B. Crescenzi." *Burlington Magazine* 123 (1981): 550–551.

Sigüenza, Padre J. *Fundación del Monasterio de El Escorial por Felipe II*. Madrid, 1986.

Smith, J. *A Catalogue Raisonné of the Works of the Most Eminent Dutch, Flemish and French Painters*. Vol. 2. London, 1831.

Sohm, P. *Pittoresco. Marco Boschini, His Critics, and Their Critiques of Painterly Brushwork in Seventeenth- and Eighteenth-Century Italy*. Cambridge, 1991.

Soprani, R. *Le vite de pittori, scoltori, et architetti genovesi*. Genoa, 1674.

Speth-Holterhoff, S. *Les Peintres flamands de cabinets d'amateurs au XVIIe siècle*. Brussels, 1957.

Steppe, J. K. "Vlaamse wandtapijten in Spanje. Recent gebeurtenissen en publicaties." *Artes Textiles* 3 (1956).

Stradling, R. A. "A Spanish Statesman of Appeasement: Medina de las Torres and Spanish Policy, 1639–1670." *Historical Journal* 19 (1976): 1–31.

Philip IV and the Government of Spain 1621–1665. Cambridge, 1988.

Stratton, S. *The Immaculate Conception in Spanish Art*. Cambridge, 1994.

Suarez Quevedo, D. "La Colección de Pinturas del Arquitecto Toledano Bartolomé Zumbigo y Salcedo (1620–1682)." *Archivo Español de Arte* 245 (1989): 91–98.

Sullivan, E. J. *Baroque Painting in Madrid: The Contribution of Claudio Coello, with a Catalogue Raisonné of His Works*. Columbia, Mo., 1986.

Sutton, P. C. *The Age of Rubens*. Boston, 1994.

Terlinden, C. *Archiduchesse Isabelle*. Brussels, 1943.

The Thyssen-Bornemisza Collection. Castagnola, 1969.

Titian 500. Edited by J. Manca, *Studies in the History of Art* 45. Center for Advanced Study in the Visual Arts. Symposium Papers 25. National Gallery of Art, Washington D.C., 1993.

Tormo, E. "Al Señor Serrano Fatigati sobre 'Escultura en Madrid,' y sobre deudos del Conde-Duque (los Felípez de Guzmán)." *Boletín de la Sociedad Española de Excursiones* 17 (1909): 291–294.

En las Descalzas reales. Estudios históricos, iconográficos y artísticos. 4 vols. Madrid, 1917–1957.

Trexler, R. C. *The Journey of the Magi: Meanings in History of a Christian Story*. Princeton, N.J., 1997.

Valdivieso, E. *La pintura en Valladolid en el siglo XVII*. Valladolid, 1971.

Van der Essen, A. *Le Cardinal-Infant et la politique européenne de l'Espagne, 1609–1641*, I, Louvain and Brussels, 1944.

Van Even, E. "Notice sur la bibliothèque de Charles de Croy, duc d'Aerschot (1614)." *Bulletin du Bibliophile Belge* 9:380–393, 436–451.

Van Gelder, J. G. "Rubens Marginalia." *Burlington Magazine* 122 (1980): 165–168.

Van Marle, R. *Ichnographie de l'art profane au moyen-âge à la Renaissance*. New York, 1971.

Van Puyvelde, L. *Les Esquisses de Rubens*. Basel, 1948.

Varia Velazqueña. 2 vols. Madrid, 1960.

Vergara, A. "The Count of Fuensaldaña and David Teniers: Their Purchases in London after the Civil War." *Burlington Magazine* 131 (1989): 127–132.

The Presence of Rubens in Spain. 2 vols. Ph.D. diss., New York University, 1994.

"Don Rodrigo Calderón y la introducción del arte de Rubens en España." *Archivo Español de Arte* 267 (1994b): 275–283.

"The Room of Rubens in the Collection of the Tenth Admiral of Castile." *Apollo* 141 (1995): 34–39.

Vergara, L. *Rubens and the Poetics of Landscape*. New Haven, Conn., 1982.

Vinge, L. *The Five Senses. Studies in a Literary Tradition*. Regiae Societatis Humanorum Literarum Lundensis, 72. Lund, 1975.

Vives, J. L. *Instrucción de la mujer cristiana*. 1953.

Vlieghe, H. *Saints*. 2 vols. *Corpus Rubenianum Ludwig Burchard*, part 8. London, 1972–1973.

"Rubens and Italy." *Burlington Magazine* 120 (1978): 471–473.

Review of M. Díaz Padrón, *Museo del Prado. Catálogo de pinturas. Escuela flamenca siglo XVII*. *Art Bulletin* 61 (1979): 651–653.

Portraits. Antwerp, Identified Sitters. Corpus Rubenianum Ludwig Burchard, part 19. London, 1987.

Volk, M. C. "New Light on a Seventeenth-Century Collector: The Marquis of Leganés." *Art Bulletin* 67 (1980a): 256–268.

"Rubens in Madrid and the Decoration of the Salón Nuevo in the Palace." *Burlington Magazine* 122 (1980b): 168–180.

"Rubens in Madrid and the Decoration of the King's Summer Apartments." *Burlington Magazine* 123 (1981): 513–529.

"On Rubens and Titian." *The Ringling Museum of Art Journal* (1983), pp. 140–153.

Voorhelm Schneevoogt, C. G. *Catalogue des estampes gravées d'aprés Rubens*. Haarlem, 1873.

Vosters, S. A. "Lope de Vega, Rubens y Marino." *Goya* 180 (1984): 321–325.

Rubens y España. Madrid, 1990.

Waagen, G. F. *Treasures of Art in Great Britain*. London, 1854. With supplementary volume *Galleries and Cabinets of Art in Great Britain*. London, 1857.

Watson, P. F. *The Garden of Love in Tuscan Art of the Early Renaissance*. Cranbury, N.J., 1979.

Wethey, H. E. *The Paintings of Titian*. 3 vols. London, 1969–1975.

White, C. *Peter Paul Rubens: Man and Artist*. New Haven, Conn., 1987.

Wood, J. " 'Damaged by Time and Rubens.' Rubens's Restorations and Retouchings." *Apollo* 142 (1995): 16–23.

Woodall, J. "An Exemplary Consort: Antonis Mor's Portrait of Mary Tudor." *Art History* 14 (1991): 192–224.

" 'His Majesty's most majestic room.' The Division of Sovereign Identity in Philip II of Spain's Lost Portrait Gallery at El Pardo." In "Image and Self-Image in Netherlandish Art 1550–1750," ed. H. Roodenburg, *Netherlands Yearbook for History of Art* 46 (1995): 53–103.

Wranke, M. *Kommentare zu Rubens*. Berlin, 1965.

Peter Paul Rubens. Leben und Werk. Cologne, 1977.

Ximenez, Fray Andres. *Descripción del Real Monasterio de San Lorenzo del Escorial*. Madrid, 1764.

Index

NOTTINGHAM UNIVERSITY LIBRARY